# ANNOTATED TEACHER'S EDITION

## HOLT

# AMERICAN CIVICS

William H. Hartley ■ William S. Vincent

**HOLT, RINEHART AND WINSTON**

A Harcourt Education Company

Orlando • **Austin** • New York • San Diego • Toronto • London

## About the Authors

**William H. Hartley**, a former classroom teacher, was Professor of Education, Emeritus, at the Towson State University, Baltimore, Maryland. He was well known to teachers of the social studies as a president of the National Council for the Social Studies. His monthly article "Sight and Sound " was for many years a highlight of *Social Education*. Dr. Hartley wrote several textbooks, a number of motion picture and filmstrip scripts, and many articles in the field of education.

**William S. Vincent**, a former teacher of junior high school social studies, was Professor of Education, Emeritus, at Teachers College, Columbia University, where he organized and directed the Citizen Education Project. Dr. Vincent wrote several books on citizenship and produced a number of educational films. He authored *Indicators of Quality*, a method of training teachers to measure the educational quality of schools and school systems.

Cover photo: [flag] ©Joseph Sohm; ChromoSohm Inc./Corbis; [crowd] AP/Photo/Ed Reinke

For acknowledgments, see page R55, which is an extension of the copyright page.

Printed in the United States of America

ISBN 0-03-038052-9

1 2 3 4 5 6 7 8 9 032 09 08 07 06 05 04

# It's All About

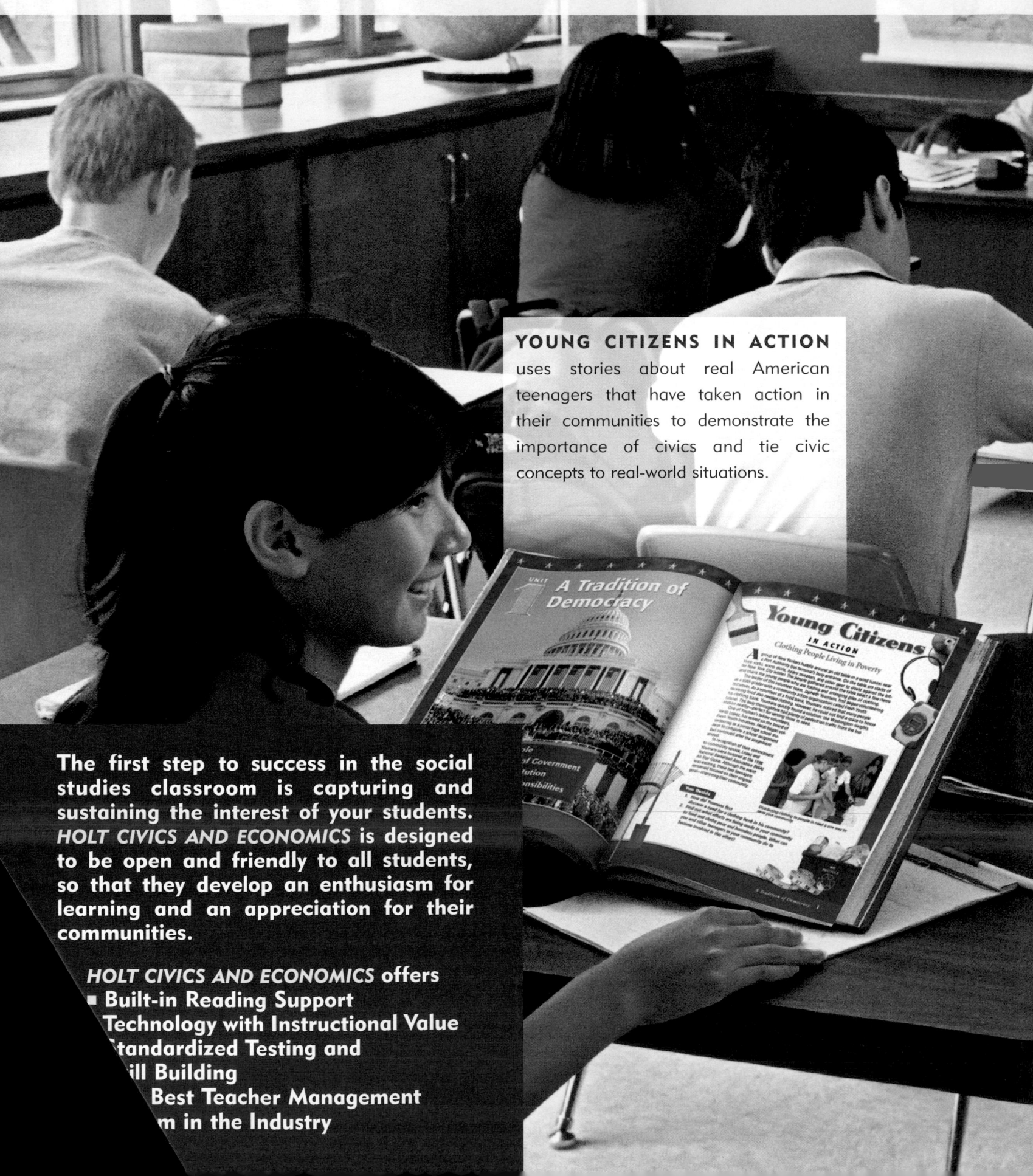

**YOUNG CITIZENS IN ACTION**
uses stories about real American
teenagers that have taken action in
their communities to demonstrate the
importance of civics and tie civic
concepts to real-world situations.

The first step to success in the social
studies classroom is capturing and
sustaining the interest of your students.
*HOLT CIVICS AND ECONOMICS* is designed
to be open and friendly to all students,
so that they develop an enthusiasm for
learning and an appreciation for their
communities.

*HOLT CIVICS AND ECONOMICS* offers
- Built-in Reading Support
- Technology with Instructional Value
- Standardized Testing and
  Skill Building
- Best Teacher Management
  System in the Industry

# RELEVANCE

**CNNfyi.com**™ is a site designed to give students in grades 6–12 access to people, places, and environments around the globe while offering "real-world" articles, career and college resources, and online activities.

## In-Text Features that Put Civics into Perspective

- Biographies
- Did You Know?
- Global Connections
- What's Your Opinion?

- Why Civics Matters
- Young Citizens in Action
- Historical Documents
- Supreme Court Cases

# Reading for

At Holt, we don't assume that students know how or have any desire to make sense of what they're reading, and we develop our programs based on that assumption. We don't just ask students questions about content, we give them strategies to get to that content. Through design, research, and the help of experts like Dr. Judith Irvin, we make sure students' reading needs are covered with our programs.

## Helping Students Make Sense of What They're Reading

**An Essay by Dr. Judith Irvin, Ph.D.**

Who in middle and high schools helps students become more successful at reading and writing informational text? When I ask this question of a school faculty, the Language Arts/English teachers point to the social studies and science teachers because they are the ones with this type of textbook. The social studies and science teachers point to the Language Arts/English teachers because they are the ones that "do" words.

I advocate teachers taking an active role in helping students learn how to use text structure and context to understand what they read. Through consistent and systematic instruction that includes modeling of effective reading behavior, teachers can assist students in becoming better readers while at the same time helping them learn more content material.

The strategies in this book are designed to assist students with getting started, maintaining focus with reading, and organizing information for later retrieval. They engage students in learning material, provide the vehicle for them to organize and reorganize concepts, and extend their understanding through writing.

When teachers combine the teaching of reading and the teaching of content together into meaningful, systematic, and corrected instruction, students can apply what they have learned to understanding increasingly more difficult and complex texts as they progress through the school years.

## READING STRATEGIES FOR THE SOCIAL STUDIES CLASSROOM

by Dr. Judith Irvin,
Ph.D. Reading Education

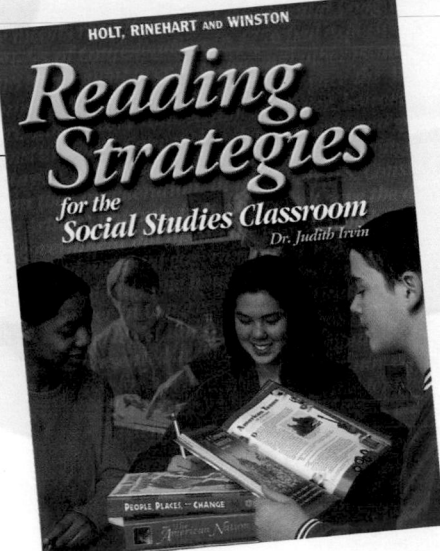

HOLT, RINEHART AND WINSTON

**Reading Strategies** for the Social Studies Classroom
Dr. Judith Irvin

## Additional Reading Support

- Main Idea Activities
- Graphic Organizer Activities
- Audio CD Program
- Guided Reading Strategies
- Vocabulary Activities

# MEANING

**SECTION 1**

## The Bill of Rights

**Read to Discover**
1. Why was the Bill of Rights added to the Constitution?
2. How does the First Amendment protect personal freedoms?
3. What other rights does the Bill of Rights guarantee?

**WHY CIVICS MATTERS**
The freedoms spelled out in the Bill of Rights are essential to our democratic system. Use CNNfyi.com or other **current events** sources to investigate a recent issue concerning the Bill of Rights. Record your findings in your journal.

**Define**
- separation of church and state
- slander
- libel
- petition
- search warrant
- grand jury
- indict
- self-incrimination
- double jeopardy
- due process of law
- eminent domain
- bail

**Identify**
- Bill of Rights

---

## Successful Readers must have:

### 1 AN ENGAGING NARRATIVE

Great care is taken in selecting and presenting content in a way that students will find motivating and engaging. Features such as **Young Citizens in Action** help students connect their own lives to those who have played a role in the development of our nation.

### 2 A FORECAST OF WHAT THEY WILL LEARN

**Read to Discover** questions give students insight into the content they will cover in the chapter to come. In features such as **What's Your Opinion?** students are encouraged to give their opinions, thus helping them develop an ownership of the material.

### 3 OPPORTUNITIES TO ACTIVATE PRIOR KNOWLEDGE

In the pre-reading feature **Build on What You Know**, students are encouraged to connect content they have covered in previous chapters or other courses to the material they will learn about in the upcoming chapter.

### 4 VOCABULARY DEFINED IN CONTEXT

Important new terms are identified at the beginning of every section and are defined in context so students will develop an understanding of the contextual meaning of all terms.

### 5 STRATEGIES FOR UNDERSTANDING WHAT THEY READ

Through the design of the text, students are led through the content using built-in reading strategies. For example, **Reading Checks** in the text are used as a comprehension tool. The checks remind students to stop and engage with what they have read, functioning as a "Tutor in the Text."

# Get Your Students

Your students love activities that get them involved with the content. That's why Holt offers active-learning resources that link directly to program content and provide a multitude of different lessons for large-group, small-group, and individual projects.

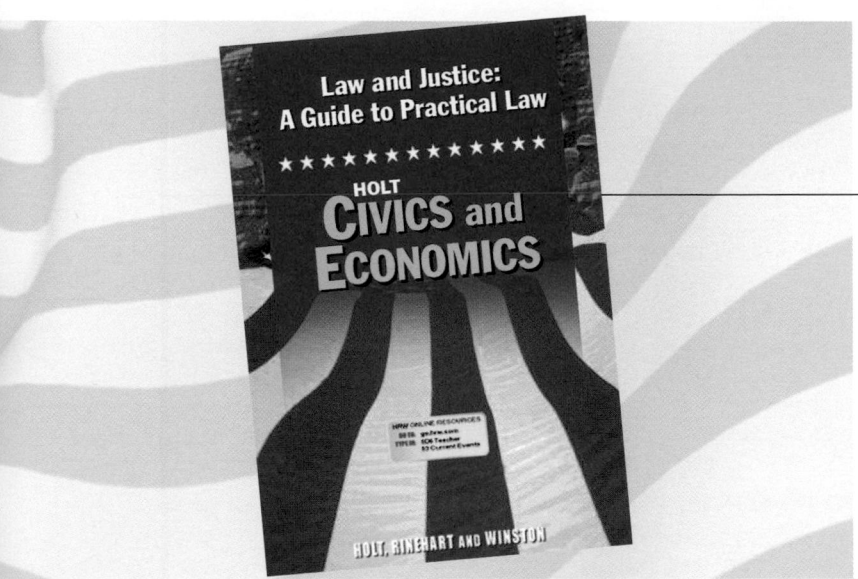

## LAW AND JUSTICE: A GUIDE TO PRACTICAL LAW

This guide provides you and your students with a resource that reinforces concepts dealing with Street Law. Readings, lesson plans, and students activities are included to help with planning and reinforcement.

## SIMULATIONS AND CASE STUDIES WITH BLOCK SCHEDULING OPTIONS

Your students will explore issues about U.S. citizenship with this resource. These creative, hands-on activities encourage students to explore their rights and roles in their community by having them analyze Supreme Court cases, having them produce a television news program about their state executive branch, and more.

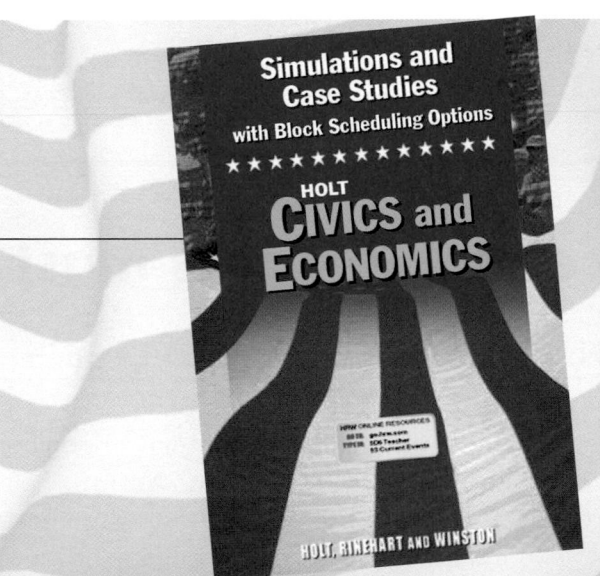

## COMMUNITY SERVICE AND PARTICIPATION HANDBOOK

This handbook offers activities for each chapter that engage your students and ask them to explore ways they can help improve their local communities through hands-on projects. The handbook also provides you with various forms and documents, such as tax forms, job applications, and voter registration materials so your students can practice real-world experiences. Project guidelines, teacher implementation information, and evaluation guidelines for student work are included.

# Involved
# in Learning

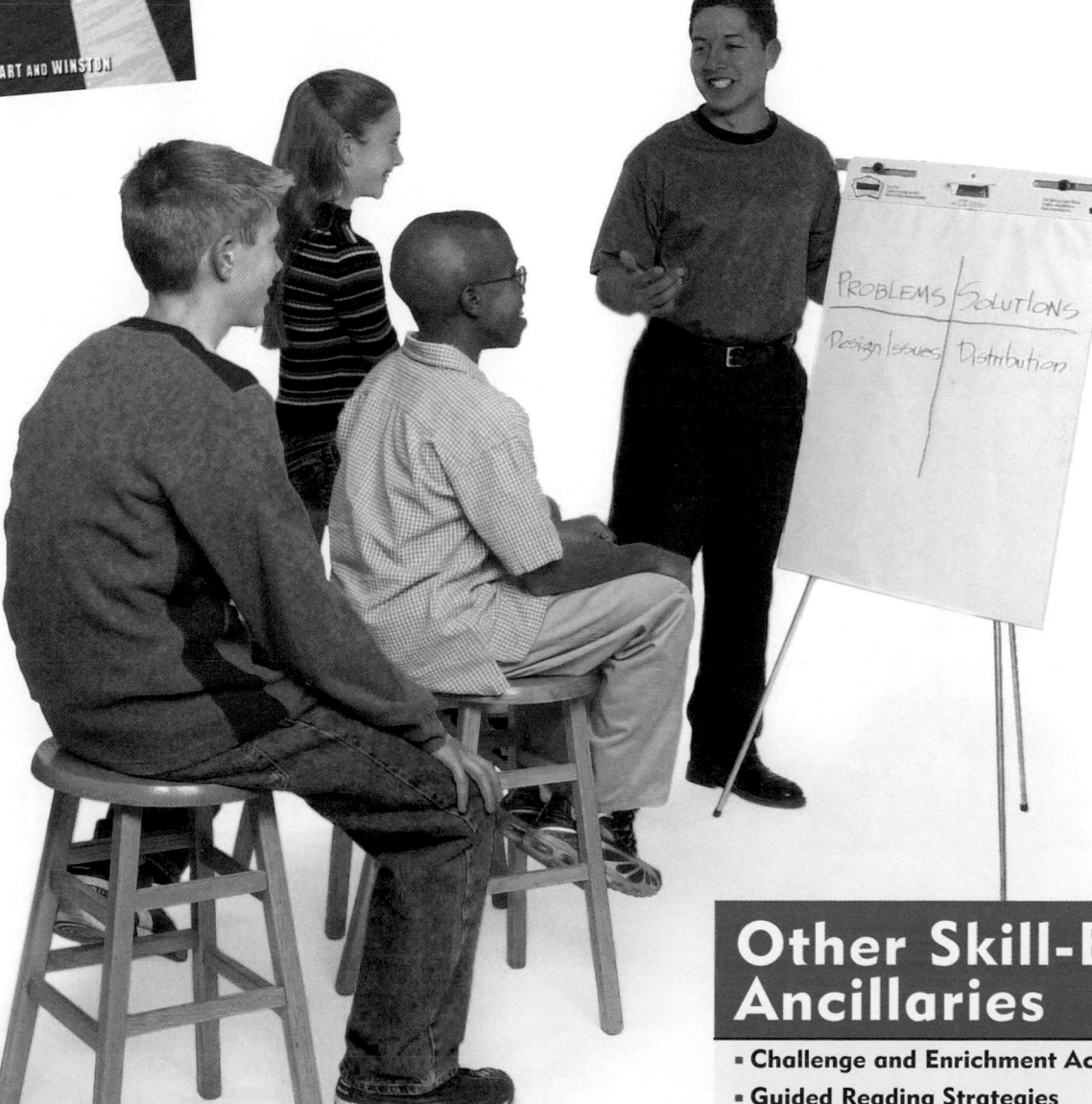

## CREATIVE TEACHING STRATEGIES

These innovative teaching strategies can be utilized at various points in your lesson. The wide range of cooperative-learning activities, including learning stations and simulations, motivate your students and help them develop critical-thinking skills.

## Other Skill-Based Ancillaries

- **Challenge and Enrichment Activities**
- **Guided Reading Strategies**
- **Law and Justice: A Guide to Practical Law**
- **Political Cartoons for Civics, Government, and Economics**
- **The Constitution: Past, Present, and Future**

# Joining Forces

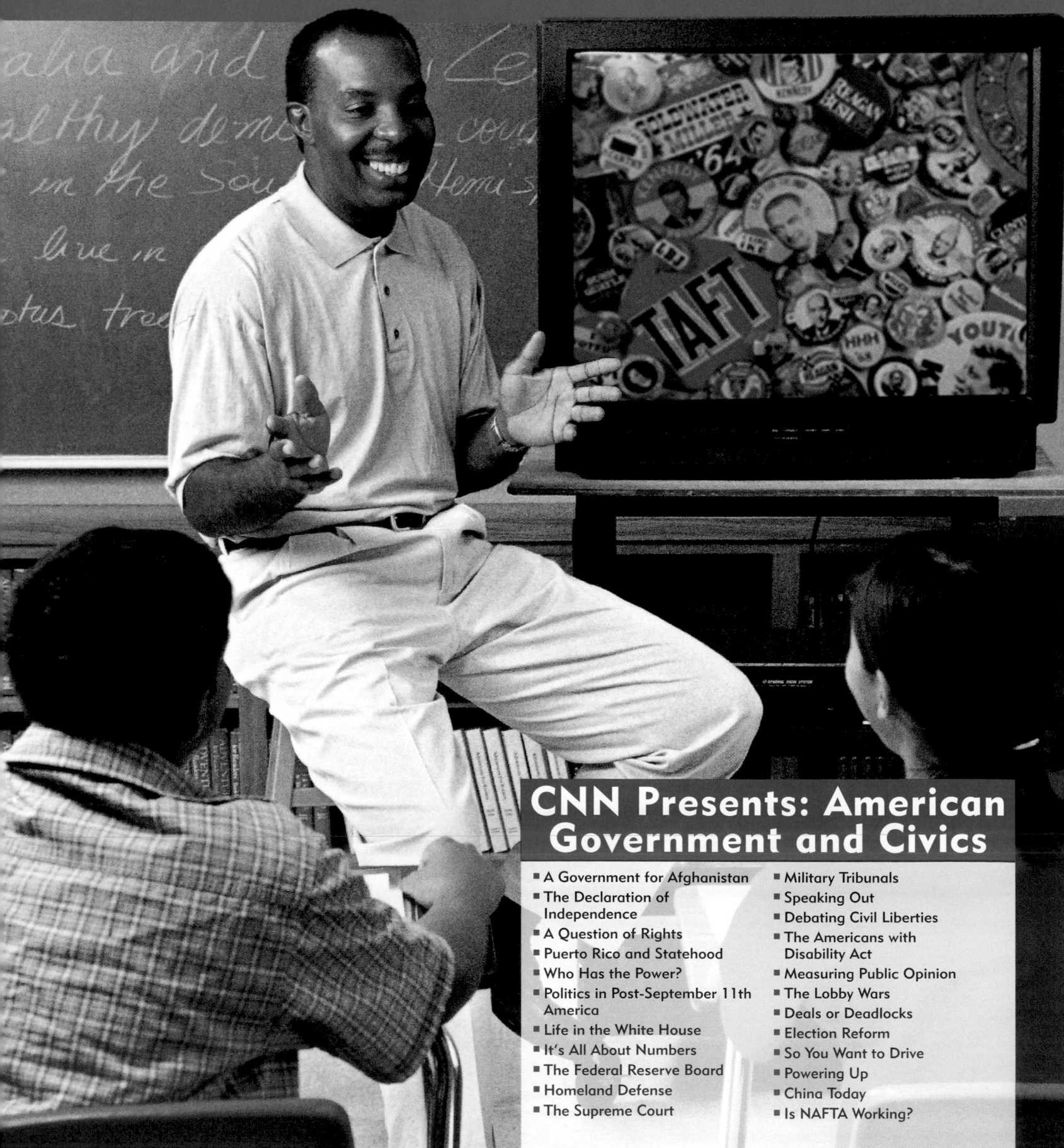

## CNN Presents: American Government and Civics

# to Enrich your Classroom

## CNNfyi.com

At **CNNfyi.com**, students will love exploring news stories written by experienced journalists as well as student bureau reporters complete with links to homework help and lesson plans.

Named "Best Online Current Events Program" by techlearning.com!

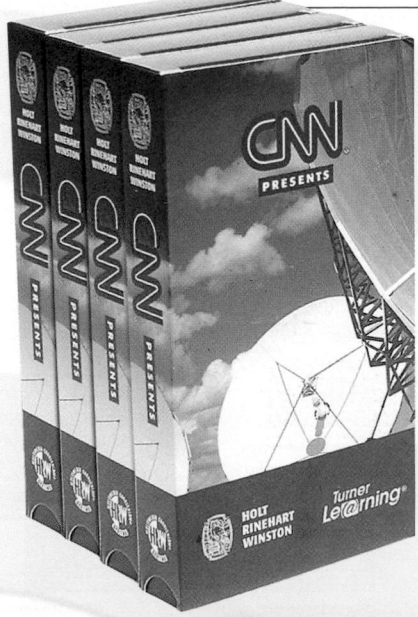

## CNN PRESENTS VIDEO LIBRARY

The **CNN PRESENTS** video collection tackles the issue of making content relevant to students head on. Real-world news stories enable students to see the connections between classroom curriculum and today's issues and events around the nation and the world.

### CNN PRESENTS...

- **American Government and Civics**
- **America: Yesterday and Today, Beginnings to 1914**
- **America: Yesterday and Today, 1850 to Present**
- **America: Yesterday and Today, Modern Times**
- **Geography: Yesterday and Today**
- **World Cultures: Yesterday and Today**
- **Economics**
- **September 11, 2001: Part 1**
- **September 11, 2001: Part 2**

**Holt is proud to team up with CNN/TURNER LEARNING to provide you and your students with exceptional current and historical news videos and online resources that add depth and relevance to your daily instruction. This information collection takes your classroom to the far corners of the globe without students ever leaving their desks!**

# Online Resources

## HOLT RESEARCHER CD-ROM: ECONOMY AND GOVERNMENT

Holt's fully searchable database, **Holt Researcher Online,** is now on the Web making it easier for you and your students to access up-to-date information about government and economics. Use it for in-class presentations or have students log on and research hundreds of interactive timelines, biographies, treaties, acts, supreme court cases, thematic maps, and more!

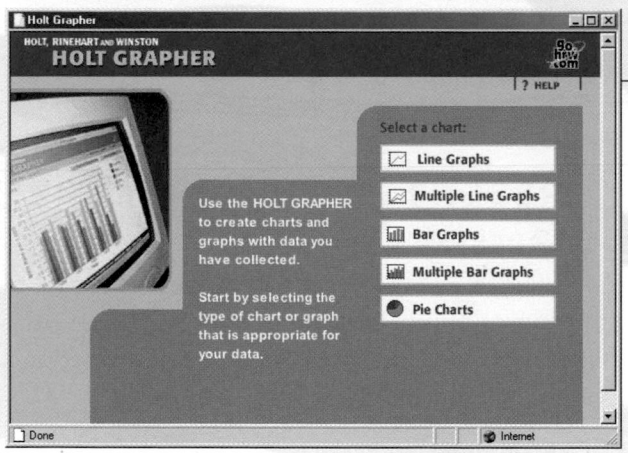

## HOLT GRAPHER

Students can access the **Holt Grapher** online and create the graph of their choice—line graphs, multiple line graphs, bar graphs, multiple bar graphs, and pie charts. Using data they have collected on their own, they can use these graphs in their research, presentations, and for a visual study tool.

## SUPREME COURT WATCH

The **Holt Civics and Economics** program includes an online resource that offers students up-to-date and comprehensive news about important Supreme Court events.

# and Technology
# for Students

## AMERICAN CIVICS CITIZENSHIP SKILLS VIDEO PROGRAM

Informative and enlightening, these eight segments include "The Roles of a Citizen," "The Critical Consumer," and "The Citizen and Local Media"; all designed to enhance how you teach citizenship skills.

## AMERICAN CIVICS AUDIO CD PROGRAM

The **Audio CD Program** provides in-depth audio section summaries and self-check activity sheets to help those students who respond to auditory learning. Available in English and Spanish.

Audio CD Program

## Multimedia Products

- **American Music Audio CD**
- **Global Skill-Builder CD-ROM**
- **Chapter Summary Audio CD Program in English and Spanish**
- **Holt Researcher CD-ROM: American History**
- **Holt Researcher CD-ROM: Economy and Government**

# Technology with

## go.hrw.com FOR TEACHERS

Throughout the *Annotated Teacher's Edition*, you'll find **Internet Connect** boxes that take you to specific chapter activities, links, current events, and more that correlate directly to the section you are teaching. Through **go.hrw.com** you'll find a wealth of teaching resources at your fingertips for fun, interactive lessons.

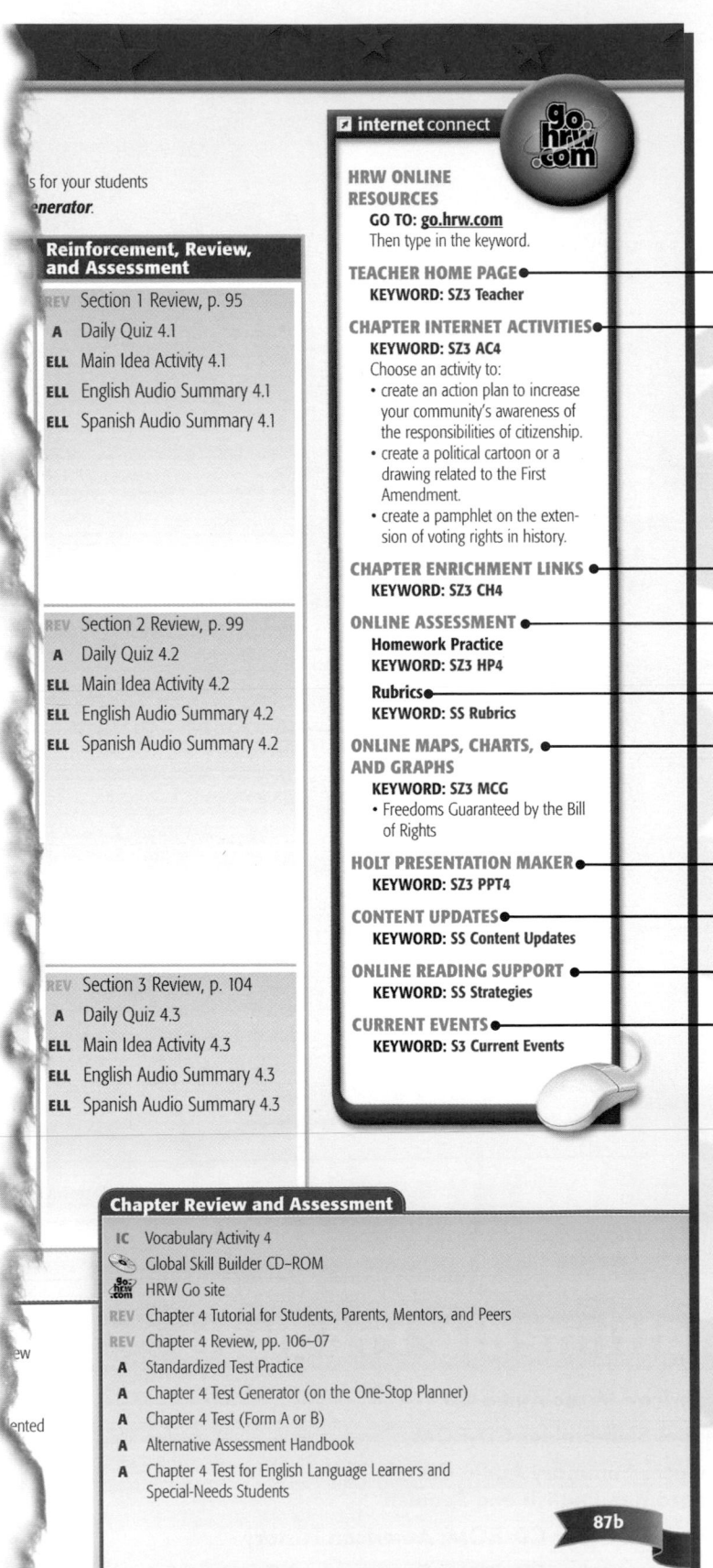

**HRW ONLINE RESOURCES**
GO TO: go.hrw.com
Then type in the keyword.

**TEACHER HOME PAGE**
KEYWORD: SZ3 Teacher

**CHAPTER INTERNET ACTIVITIES**
KEYWORD: SZ3 AC4
Choose an activity to:
• create an action plan to increase your community's awareness of the responsibilities of citizenship.
• create a political cartoon or a drawing related to the First Amendment.
• create a pamphlet on the extension of voting rights in history.

**CHAPTER ENRICHMENT LINKS**
KEYWORD: SZ3 CH4

**ONLINE ASSESSMENT**
Homework Practice
KEYWORD: SZ3 HP4

Rubrics
KEYWORD: SS Rubrics

**ONLINE MAPS, CHARTS, AND GRAPHS**
KEYWORD: SZ3 MCG
• Freedoms Guaranteed by the Bill of Rights

**HOLT PRESENTATION MAKER**
KEYWORD: SZ3 PPT4

**CONTENT UPDATES**
KEYWORD: SS Content Updates

**ONLINE READING SUPPORT**
KEYWORD: SS Strategies

**CURRENT EVENTS**
KEYWORD: S3 Current Events

**DIRECT LAUNCH TO CHAPTER ACTIVITIES**

**GUIDED ONLINE ACTIVITIES**

**LINKS FOR EVERY SECTION**

**INTERACTIVE PRACTICE AND REVIEW**

**RUBRICS FOR SUBJECTIVE GRADING**

**MAPS AND CHARTS**

**CLASSROOM LECTURE SUPPORT**

**UP-TO-DATE INFORMATION**

**PRACTICE FOR READING SUCCESS**

**WEB RESOURCES FOR CURRENT ISSUES**

---

ls for your students
*enerator.*

### Reinforcement, Review, and Assessment

REV  Section 1 Review, p. 95
A    Daily Quiz 4.1
ELL  Main Idea Activity 4.1
ELL  English Audio Summary 4.1
ELL  Spanish Audio Summary 4.1

REV  Section 2 Review, p. 99
A    Daily Quiz 4.2
ELL  Main Idea Activity 4.2
ELL  English Audio Summary 4.2
ELL  Spanish Audio Summary 4.2

REV  Section 3 Review, p. 104
A    Daily Quiz 4.3
ELL  Main Idea Activity 4.3
ELL  English Audio Summary 4.3
ELL  Spanish Audio Summary 4.3

### Chapter Review and Assessment

IC   Vocabulary Activity 4
     Global Skill Builder CD-ROM
     HRW Go site
REV  Chapter 4 Tutorial for Students, Parents, Mentors, and Peers
REV  Chapter 4 Review, pp. 106–07
A    Standardized Test Practice
A    Chapter 4 Test Generator (on the One-Stop Planner)
A    Chapter 4 Test (Form A or B)
A    Alternative Assessment Handbook
A    Chapter 4 Test for English Language Learners and Special-Needs Students

87b

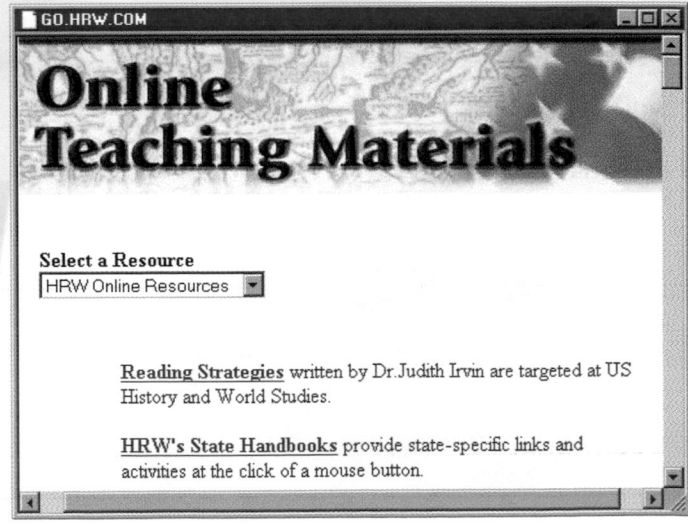

GO.HRW.COM

## Online Teaching Materials

**Select a Resource**
HRW Online Resources

**Reading Strategies** written by Dr.Judith Irvin are targeted at US History and World Studies.

**HRW's State Handbooks** provide state-specific links and activities at the click of a mouse button.

# Instructional Value

## ONLINE TEACHING SUPPORT

Teacher materials on **go.hrw.com** offer you multiple resources for keeping content current. From **American History Maps and Charts** to **State Handbooks,** we've got it all.

## CLASSROOM PRESENTATION SUPPORT

Lecture notes and animated graphic organizers help add visual support to your classroom presentations.

# Technology that

## go.hrw.com FOR STUDENTS

Your students can access interactive activities, homework help, up-to-date maps, and more when they visit **go.hrw.com** and type in the keywords they find in their text.

## CHAPTER HOME PAGE

The **Chapter Home Page** contains pre-screened enrichment links that extend content, teaching resources, and interactive activities that combine guided research with specific product-based projects. The **Home Page** also directs students to **Homework Practice Online, Holt Researcher, Holt Grapher,** and more!

## ONLINE TEMPLATES

Your students can use these interactive templates to create newspapers, travel brochures, postcards, journals, creative works, and more. The instructional design of this tool allows students to do something with the content they have learned.

## HOMEWORK PRACTICE

This helpful tool allows students to practice and review content by chapter anywhere there is a computer.

## HRW ONLINE ATLAS

This helpful online tool contains over 300 well-rendered and clearly labeled country and state maps. The clean design and easy-to-use navigational tools make accessing information simple. These maps are continually updated so you can rest assured that you and your students have the latest and most accurate geographical content available. Maps are available in English and Spanish.

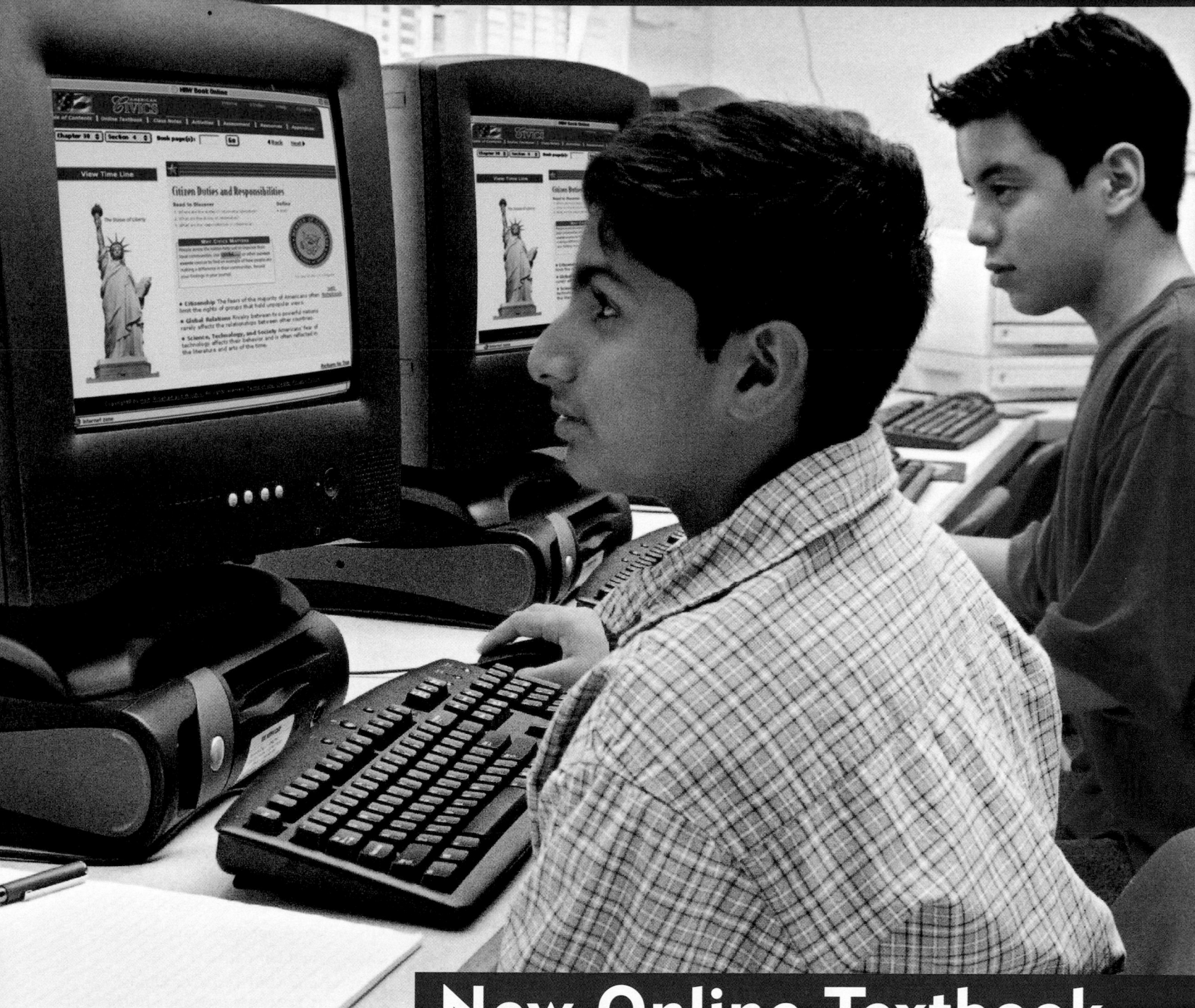

# Delivers Content

## New Online Textbook

**You'll know what to do when you see it!**
Finally, an online textbook that takes full advantage of Web technology in a way that makes sense—*HOLT CIVICS AND ECONOMICS ONLINE EDITION.*

- **Entire *Student Edition* online formatted to match printed text**
- **User-friendly navigation**
- **Hot links to interactive activities, practice, and assessment**
- **Student Notebook for online responses**

# Unique Teacher's

## In-Text Chapter Planning

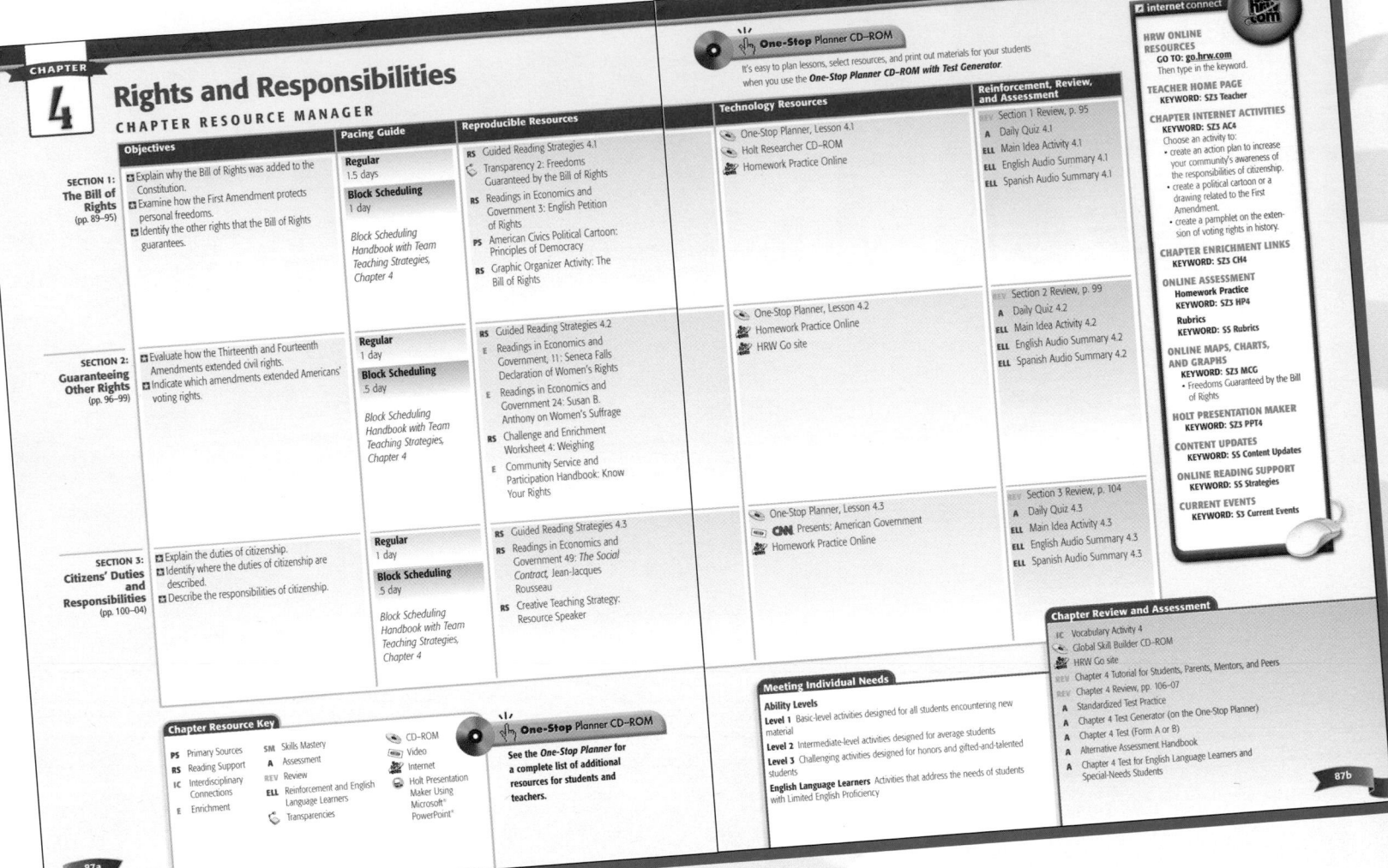

# Program Resources at Your Fingertips

## Reading Support
- Graphic Organizer Activities
- Guided Reading Strategies
- Main Idea Activities for English Language Learners and Special-Needs Students
- Reading Strategies for the Social Studies Classroom
- Vocabulary Activities

## Primary Sources
- The Constitution: Past, Present, and Future
- From the Source: Readings in Economics and Government
- Political Cartoons for Civics, Government, and Economics

## Active-Learning Support
- Block Scheduling Handbook with Team Teaching Strategies
- Challenge and Enrichment Activities
- Community Service and Participation Handbook
- Creative Teaching Strategies
- Law and Justice: A Guide to Practical Law
- Mathematics for Economics Activities
- Simulations and Case Studies with Block Scheduling Options
- Teaching Transparencies with Teacher Notes

## Review and Assessment
- Alternative Assessment Handbook
- Chapter and Unit Tests
- Chapter and Unit Tests for English Language Learners and Special-Needs Students
- Chapter Tutorials for Students, Parents, Mentors, and Peers
- Daily Quizzes
- Social Studies Skills Review
- Standardized Test Practice Handbook

# Management System

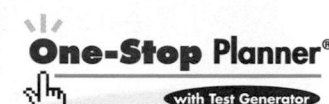

**One-Stop Planner®**
with Test Generator

## ONE-STOP PLANNER CD-ROM WITH TEST GENERATOR

Holt brings you the most user-friendly management system in the industry with the *One-Stop Planner CD-ROM with Test Generator.* Plan and manage your lessons from this single disc containing all the teaching resources for *Holt Civics and Economics,* valuable planning and assessment tools, and more.

- **Editable lesson plans**
- **Classroom Presentations**
- **ExamView® Pro test generator**
- **Previews of all teaching and video resources**
- **Easy printing feature**
- **Direct launch to go.hrw.com**

**Everything you need is on one disc!**

## BLOCK SCHEDULING HANDBOOK WITH TEAM TEACHING STRATEGIES

This is more than a pacing guide—it provides daily lesson plans that suggest practical ways to cover more than one textbook section in an extended class period and ways to make interdisciplinary connections.

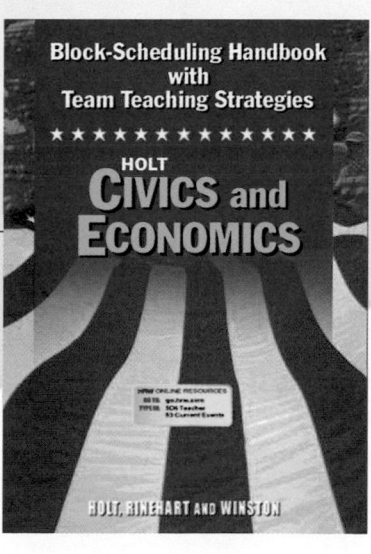

Block-Scheduling Handbook
with
Team Teaching Strategies

★★★★★★★★★★★★★

HOLT
CIVICS and
ECONOMICS

HOLT, RINEHART AND WINSTON

**M15**

# Energize

Guaranteeing Other Rights

**Voting Rights for Americans**

| Amendment | Year Ratified | Group Benefiting from Ratification |
|---|---|---|
| 13th | 1870 | African Americans |
|  |  | Citizens living in the District of Columbia |
|  | 1971 | Citizens 18 and over |

HOLT, RINEHART AND WINST

## Presentations That Benefit Learning

Classroom presentations and lecture notes can be accessed with ease when you use Holt's presentation tool found on the *One-Stop Planner*® *CD-ROM.* This resource helps you spice up your presentations and gives you ideas to build on. You'll find Microsoft® PowerPoint® presentations that include lecture notes and animated graphic organizers for each chapter and section of your text.

# Your Classroom Presentations

## SECTION 1

### OBJECTIVES

*After completing Section 1, students should be able to*

1 **Explain why the Bill of Rights was added to the Constitution.**
2 **Examine how the First Amendment protects personal freedom.**
3 **Identify the other rights that the Bill of Rights guarantees.**

### LET'S GET STARTED!

As students enter the classroom, organize the class into three or four groups. Remind students that the states ratified the Constitution only when assured that a list of the rights of the people would be added. Ask each group to create a list of 10 rights that its members believe are important. (*Students might suggest the right to free speech or religious worship, the right to vote, and so on.*) Compare lists to find the 10 rights mentioned most often. Write that final list on the chalkboard for later reference. Finally, conduct a class vote to determine whether a three-fourths majority of students would support all of the rights listed on the board. Tell students that in Section 1 they will learn more about civic rights and responsibilities and the privileges of freedom.

### TEACH OBJECTIVE 1

**LEVEL 1:** Lead a class discussion about why the Bill of Rights was added to the Constitution. (*Students should indicate that upon ratification of the Constitution, a number of states recommend that a Bill of Rights be added.*) Ask students to imagine that they live in colonial America and are members of a committee urging the inclusion of a bill of rights. Have each student create a handbill listing five reasons why a bill of rights will be an essential part of the Constitution. **ENGLISH LANGUAGE LEARNERS**

**LEVEL 1:** Discuss with students why the Bill of Rights was added to the Constitution. Then ask students about real-life situations in which various freedoms guaranteed in the Bill of Rights affect teenagers. On the chalkboard, write each of their suggestions as well as which of the first 10 amendments they correspond to. (*Students might indicate how freedom of the press affects their activities in working on the school newspaper. Students might also indicate how the freedoms of speech and of petition protect their right to have their concerns heard by their student government.*) **ENGLISH LANGUAGE LEARNERS**

**ALL LEVELS:** Copy the following graphic organizer onto the chalkboard, omitting the italicized answers. Ask students to complete the chart to list the rights that are guaranteed by the Bill of Rights. Then lead a class discussion about why the inclusion of the Bill of Rights was important. **ENGLISH LANGUAGE LEARNERS**

| The Bill of Rights | |
|---|---|
| • separation of church and state | • the inclusion of rights not specifically listed in the Constitution |
| • freedom of the press | |
| • freedom of petition | • freedom of speech |
| • no quartering of soldiers | • freedom of assembly |
| • protection for those accused | • the right to bear arms |
| | • protection from unreasonable search and seizure |

## OBJECTIVE-BASED LESSON CYCLE

With lively activities and presentation strategies such as **Let's Get Started, Building Vocabulary,** and **Graphic Organizers,** your step-by-step lesson cycle makes planning your lessons easy and productive.

### TEACH OBJECTIVE 2

**LEVEL 1:** Lead a class discussion about how the First Amendment protects personal freedoms. Then organize students into small groups. Ask each group to create a poster that illustrates the freedoms that the First Amendment guarantees. (*Students' posters should depict the freedom of religion, freedom of speech, freedom of the press, freedom of assembly, and freedom of petition.*) Display the groups' posters around the classroom. **ENGLISH LANGUAGE LEARNERS, COOPERATIVE LEARNING**

**LEVELS 2 AND 3:** Review with the class the freedoms described in the First Amendment. (*See the Level 1 lesson for the freedoms.*) Then ask students to imagine that they have been assigned to work in a foreign country that does not enjoy the same freedoms that U.S. citizens do. Ask each student to write a letter to a family member back home, describing what it is like to live without particular rights that he or she possessed prior to moving abroad. Have volunteers read their letters to the class.

**HOMEWORK** Tell each student to create a political cartoon illustrating a freedom protected by the Bill of Rights.

**LEVELS 2 AND 3:** Bring several newspapers to class and then organize the class into groups. Ask groups to study the newspapers to find national and international stories that address one of the First Amendment rights. Have groups share their findings with the class. (*Students might present a story about a country that suppresses negative accounts of government policies.*) Finally, have students explain whether our rights guaranteed by the Bill of Rights ensure a better way of life and why. **COOPERATIVE LEARNING**

### CLOSE

Have students compare the Bill of Rights to the list of 10 rights that the class created in the *Let's Get Started!* activity. Discuss the differences and have volunteers come to the chalkboard to create a chart with the 10 amendments of the Bill of Rights listed in one column and the class's 10 rights listed in a second column. Have students discuss which list best covers the most important rights of citizens.

### REVIEW AND ASSESS

Have students complete the **Section 1 Review** on page 95. Then have students complete **Daily Quiz 4.1.** As Alternative Assessment, you may want to use the handbill or essay activities in this section's lessons.

### RETEACH

Have students complete **Main Idea Activity for English Language Learners and Special-Needs Students 4.1.** Then assign each student one of the sections in this chapter. Ask students to create a study guide for the sections that they have

been assigned. After they have finished their study guides, ask volunteers to present their guides to the class. **ENGLISH LANGUAGE LEARNERS**

### EXTEND

Have students read the Ninth Amendment. Then ask each student to write an essay discussing how this amendment further establishes the flexibility of the Constitution. Students might name other basic rights and freedoms that are not specified in the Bill of Rights or the rest of the Constitution. Invite volunteers to discuss their essays with the class. **BLOCK SCHEDULING**

# Assessment for

## INTERACTIVE PRACTICE ACTIVITIES

### SECTION 1 Review

go.hrw.com
Homework Practice Online
keyword: SZ3 HP4

1. **Define** and explain:
   - separation of church and state
   - slander
   - libel
   - petition
   - search warrant
   - grand jury
   - indict
   - self-incrimination
   - double jeopardy
   - due process of law
   - eminent domain
   - bail

2. **Identify** and explain:
   - Bill of Rights

3. **Analyzing Information** Copy the web diagram below. Use the web to describe the freedoms guaranteed by the First Amendment.

First Amendment

4. **Finding the Main Idea**
   a. Why did Americans want a bill of rights added to the Constitution?
   b. List at least five rights guaranteed in the Second through Eighth Amendments.

5. **Writing and Critical Thinking**
   Supporting a Point of View Imagine that you are a state legislator ratifying the Bill of Rights. Write a brief speech explaining why the Ninth and Tenth Amendments are necessary.
   **Consider:**
   - experiences under British rule
   - the powers of government

## THE SUPERIOR TEST GENERATOR THAT REALLY WORKS!

## Chapter 4 Review

### Chapter Summary

#### Section 1

- The first 10 amendments, known as the Bill of Rights, clearly define the rights of all Americans.
- These amendments guarantee such priceless rights as the freedoms of religion, speech, the press, assembly, and petition and the right to a speedy and fair trial by a jury.
- The Ninth Amendment states that the rights listed in the Constitution are not the only rights Americans hold.
- The Tenth Amendment reserves to the state governments and to the people all powers not specifically given to the federal government by the Constitution.

#### Section 2

- Later amendments to the Constitution further expanded the civil rights of Americans.
- The Thirteenth and Fourteenth Amendments protected the rights of newly freed African Americans after the Civil War.
- Six other amendments to the Constitution expanded the voting rights of the American people.

#### Section 3

- Along with the rights and freedoms of U.S. citizenship come important duties and responsibilities.
- The duties of citizenship include obeying the law, attending school, paying taxes, protecting the country if it is threatened, and appearing in court.
- Responsibilities of citizenship include voting, staying informed, taking part in government, helping your community, and respecting and protecting others' rights.

MR. PRESIDENT WHAT WILL YOU DO FOR WOMAN SUFFRAGE

### Define and Identify

| | |
|---|---|
| 1. Bill of Rights | 6. bail |
| 2. petition | 7. civil rights |
| 3. indict | 8. suffrage |
| 4. double jeopardy | 9. poll tax |
| 5. eminent domain | 10. draft |

### Understanding Main Ideas

**Section 1** (Pages 89–95)
1. Which amendments focus on the rights of people accused of crimes? What rights do these amendments guarantee?
2. Why was the Ninth Amendment included in the Bill of Rights?

**Section 2** (Pages 96–99)
3. How did the Thirteenth and Fourteenth Amendments extend the civil rights of Americans?
4. How have voting rights been expanded through constitutional amendments?

**Section 3** (Pages 100–04)
5. What are the duties of citizenship?
6. What are the responsibilities of citizenship?

### What Did You Find Out?

1. Why was the Bill of Rights added to the U.S. Constitution?
2. How might the country be affected if citizens failed to perform their duties and responsibilities?
3. Why has the Constitution been amended over time?

### Thinking Critically

1. **Supporting a Point of View** Unlike most of the amendments contained in the Bill of Rights, the Third Amendment's "no quartering" rule has never been tested in a court of law. Because this amendment seems to be far removed from Americans' modern-day lives, should it be repealed? Why or why not?
2. **Evaluating** Which freedom in the Bill of Rights do you consider to be the most important, and why?
3. **Identifying Cause and Effect** Why did Americans want to ensure that accused persons had the right to trial by jury? What might happen to our system of justice if citizens refused to serve on juries?

## CRITICAL-THINKING REINFORCEMENT

# Every Student

## CONSISTENT STANDARDIZED TEST PREPARATION

### Building Social Studies Skills

STANDARDIZED TEST PREP ONLINE
keyword: SZ3 STP4

#### Interpreting Political Cartoons

Study the political cartoon below. Then use the information in the cartoon to help you answer the questions that follow.

LIBERTY'S CROWN

1. What do the words on the spikes of the Statue of Liberty's crown represent?
   a. the rights listed in the Declaration of Independence
   b. each of the rights guaranteed in the amendments that form the Bill of Rights
   c. rights that all Americans should have whether they are listed in the Constitution or not
   d. the rights that the cartoonist feels are some of the most treasured rights guaranteed by the Bill of Rights

2. Why do you think the artist chose the Statue of Liberty as the symbol to associate with these ideas?

#### Analyzing Primary Sources

Read the following quote from President John F. Kennedy and then answer the questions that follow.

"The right to vote in a free American election is the most powerful and precious right in the world—and it must not be denied on the grounds of race or color. It is a potent [powerful] key to achieving other rights of citizenship. For American history—both recent and past—clearly reveals that the power of the ballot has enabled those who achieve it to win other achievements as well, gain a full voice in the affairs of their state and nation, and to see their interests represented in the governmental bodies which affect their future. In a free society, those with the power to govern are necessarily responsive to those with the right to vote."

3. Which of the following statements best describes President Kennedy's point of view?
   a. The only way that people can influence their government is by writing to elected officials.
   b. You are not a citizen if you do not vote.
   c. Voting affects everyone's future.
   d. Government officials are more likely to respond to citizens if they know that citizens can vote them out of office.

4. Based on what you know about the Constitution of the United States, what amendment is President Kennedy probably referring to when he says that people of any race or color should not be denied the right to vote?

### Alternative Assessment

#### Building Your Portfolio

American Civics

**Interdisciplinary Connection to Math** Research voter participation in your community. What are the statistics on voter registration? In what elections is voter participation highest? Is participation increasing or decreasing? Create a set of graphs that illustrate the answers to these questions. Present your findings to the class in an oral report. Include some suggestions for improving voter participation in your area.

#### internet connect

**Internet Activity: go.hrw.com**
**keyword: SZ3 AC4**

Access the Internet through the HRW Go site to research the rights and responsibilities of citizenship. Then choose one of the responsibilities outlined in the chapter and create an action plan to increase your community's awareness of this responsibility. Your action plan should outline the responsibility on which you will focus and how you will increase awareness of it.

*Rights and Responsibilities* **107**

**ACCESS ONLINE RUBRICS FOR GRADING PROJECTS AND PORTFOLIO ASSIGNMENTS**

## STANDARDIZED TEST PRACTICE HANDBOOK

This resource helps your students gear up for future standardized tests. Content-specific practice exposes them to a variety of question types—like multiple choice and short answer—commonly found in today's standardized assessments.

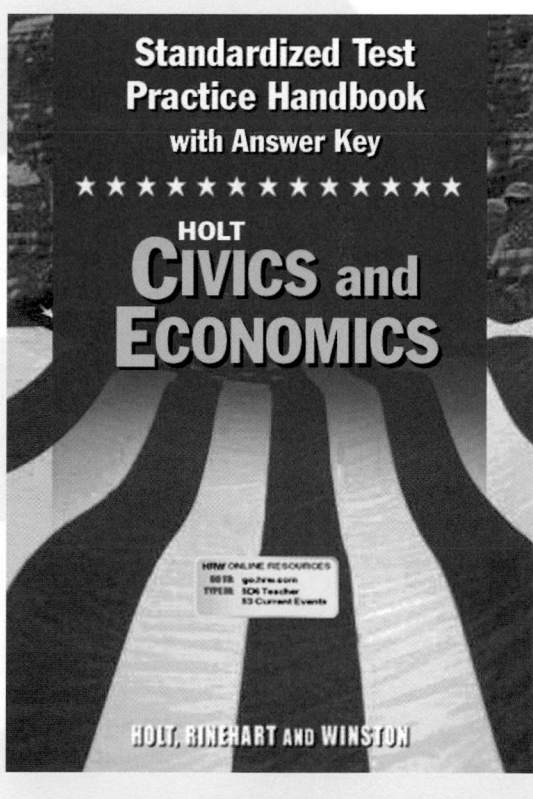

Standardized Test Practice Handbook with Answer Key
★ ★ ★ ★ ★ ★ ★ ★ ★ ★ ★ ★ ★
HOLT CIVICS and ECONOMICS

HRW ONLINE RESOURCES
GO TO: go.hrw.com
TYPE IN: SC4 Teacher
S3 Current Events

HOLT, RINEHART AND WINSTON

## Additional Print and Technology Assessment Resources

- Alternative Assessment Handbook
- Audio CD Program in English and Spanish
- Chapter and Unit Tests
- Chapter and Unit Tests for English Language Learners and Special-Needs Students
- Chapter Tutorials for Students, Parents, Mentors, and Peers
- Daily Quizzes
- Main Idea Activities for English Language Learners and Special-Needs Students
- Test Generator (located on the One-Stop Planner)

# AMERICAN CIVICS

## CONTENTS

*A group of immigrants taking the oath of citizenship*

Seals of the U.S. Senate, Department of Justice, and the President of the United States

American citizens exercising their First Amendment rights of freedom of speech and freedom of assembly

*A town hall meeting*

*Volunteers making phone calls for a political campaign*

I'm worth it! VOTE!

*Young volunteers helping their community*

A high-tech worker

*Painting of a Ford motor plant, by muralist Diego Rivera*

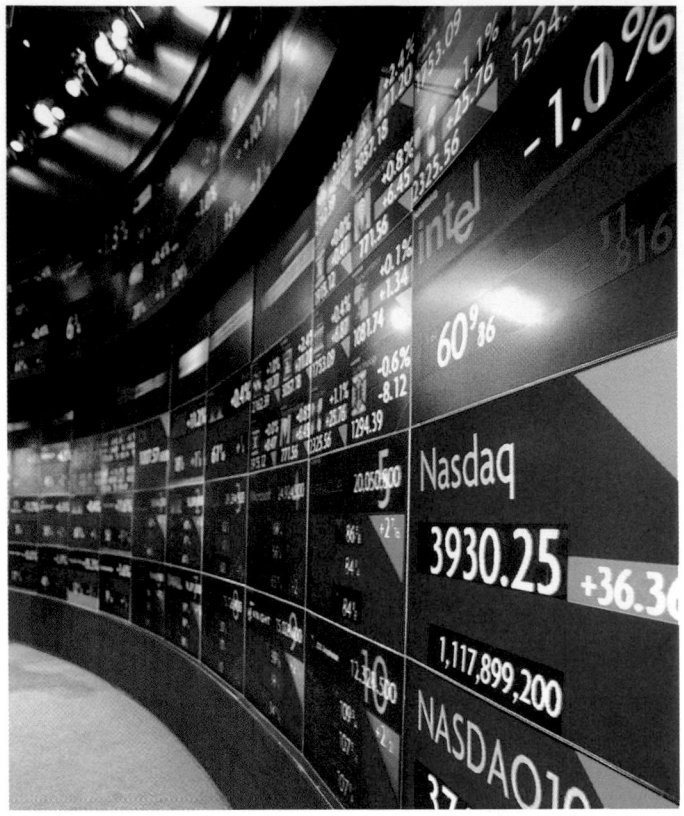
Stock quotes from the NASDAQ composite index

*Camera technician*

Director-General Jong-wook Lee of the World Health Organization (left)

*A cargo ship*

*Solar panels*

# Features

## Historical Documents

Martin Luther King Jr.

## SUPREME COURT CASE STUDY

## Young Citizens IN ACTION

## That's Interesting!

# Features, *continued*

## BIOGRAPHY

## GLOBAL CONNECTIONS

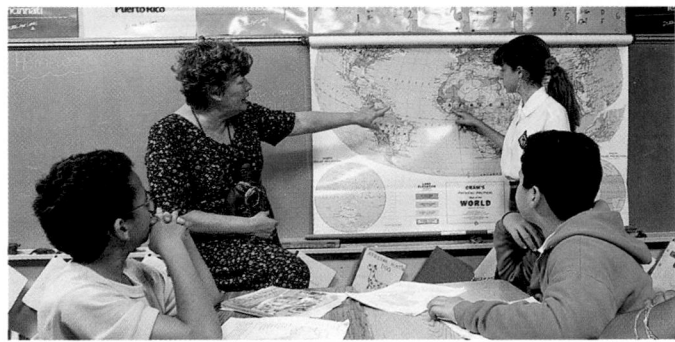

*A geography teacher with her students*

# Technology Activities

# Technology Activities, continued

## Holt Researcher

*President Richard Nixon*

# Skill-Building Activities

## Civics Lab

## Civics Skills WORKSHOP

# Skill-Building Activities, *continued*

## GRAPHS AND CHARTS

## MAPS

# How to Use Your Textbook

**Read to Discover** questions begin each section of your textbook. These questions serve as your guide as you read through the section. Keep them in mind as you explore the section's content.

**Define and Identify** terms are introduced at the beginning of each section. The terms will be defined in context.

CHAPTER ★ ★ ★ ★ ★ ★

## 5 The Legislative Branch

What's Your Opinion?

### Build on What You Know

Every year on January 3, unless otherwise specified, representatives, senators, clerks, and congressional staff take their places in the Capitol Building in Washington, D.C., for the start of a new session of Congress. They reconvene to fulfill their constitutional responsibility of making the country's laws. Congress decides issues such as how large the U.S. armed forces will be and whether federal taxes will increase. Each session lawmakers make decisions that affect not only your life, your school, and your community but also national and world affairs.

**Themes Journal** Do you **agree** or **disagree** with the following statements? Support your point of view in your journal.

- Any U.S. citizen can become a Congressmember.
- Congress would not be able to function without congressional committees.
- Congress should have the power to put federal officials on trial.

112 Chapter 5

---

SECTION 1

## The Senate and the House of Representatives

**Read to Discover**
1. How many members are in the House and Senate, respectively, and what is the term length for each position?
2. What are the qualifications and salaries for members of the House and of the Senate?
3. How does Congress deal with misconduct by its members?

**Define**
- apportioned
- gerrymandering
- term limits
- franking privilege
- immunity
- expulsion
- censure

**WHY CIVICS MATTERS**

Congress is organized to allow fair representation of all the states. Use **CNNfyi.com** or other **current events** sources to find out how your state is represented in Congress. Record your findings in your journal.

### Reading Focus

The legislative branch makes the country's laws. "Members of Congress are the human connection between the citizen and . . . government," noted one member of Congress. The framers discussed the legislative branch in Article I of the U.S. Constitution to emphasize that representatives of the people would govern the United States.

### ★ Two Houses of Congress

Congress is the lawmaking body of the federal government. The Constitution states that the Congress shall be composed of two houses—the Senate and the House of Representatives.

The leaders who drew up the U.S. Constitution in 1787 created a bicameral legislature, a lawmaking body of two houses. They did this in part to make sure that both small and large states would be fairly represented. Membership in the House of Representatives is based on state population, while each state is represented equally in the Senate. The system also allows each house to check the actions of the other. This system helps prevent Congress from passing laws in haste.

✔ **Reading Check Analyzing Information** Why does the Constitution specify a bicameral legislature?

*House members must follow strict rules of conduct while in session.*

The Legislative Branch 113

---

**Build on What You Know** bridges the material you have studied in previous chapters with the material you are about to study. As you read the Build on What You Know feature, take a few minutes to think about the topics that might apply to the chapter you are starting.

**What's Your Opinion?** allows you to express your opinion about subjects covered in the chapter. In this feature you will be asked to respond to three general statements about the chapter. You should respond based on your own knowledge and then record your responses in your journal. There are no right or wrong answers, just your informed opinion.

**Why Civics Matters** is an exciting way for you to make connections between what you are reading in your textbook and the world around you. In each section you will be invited to explore a topic that is relevant to our lives today by using **CNNfyi.com** connections.

# Use these built-in tools to read for understanding.

**Interpreting the Visual Record** features accompany many of the book's rich images. Pictures are one of the most important primary sources used to illustrate a concept. These features invite you to examine the images and to interpret their content.

**Reading Check** questions appear throughout the book to help you check your comprehension while you are reading. As you read each section, pause for a moment to consider each Reading Check. If you have trouble answering the question, go back and examine the material you just read.

---

**Interpreting the Visual Record**

**Congress** *The Senate and the House of Representatives meet together in a joint session when the president wishes to address Congress. How does this image illustrate the size and importance of the Congress?*

*The desks used in the Senate are based on a design more than 100 years old.*

### ★ Qualifications of Members

The Constitution lists the qualifications that members of Congress must meet. A representative in the House must
1. be at least 25 years old;
2. have been a U.S. citizen for at least seven years; and
3. be a legal resident of the state he or she represents. (Usually a representative lives in the district from which he or she is elected. However, the Constitution does not require this.)

The qualifications for members of the Senate differ slightly from those for members of the House. The Constitution lists the following qualifications for senators. A senator must
1. be at least 30 years old;
2. have been a U.S. citizen for at least nine years; and
3. be a legal resident of the state he or she represents.
   In addition to these qualifications, members of Congress traditionally have shared other characteristics. For example, they usually have had previous political experience, often in their state legislatures. Most members of Congress also have been active members of community and volunteer organizations.
   Many members of Congress are lawyers, businesspeople, public servants, or educators. Senators tend to be older than representatives. In 2001 the average age for representatives was 54. The average age for senators was 59. As of 1999, only 14 senators were under the age of 50.
   In the past, most members of Congress have been white men. In recent years, the number of women, African Americans, Hispanic Americans, Asian Americans, and American Indians in Congress has increased. In 2001, for example, there were 61 women in the House and 13 women in the Senate. Thirty-eight African Americans served as representatives. However, the numbers of women and ethnic minorities in Congress remain well below their percentages in the population.

✔ **Reading Check** Drawing Inferences and Conclusions Why do you think so many educators, public servants, lawyers, and businesspeople become Congressmembers?

**116** Chapter 5

---

# Use these tools to review all the information you have learned.

---

**SECTION 3 Review**

**1. Define** and explain:
- elastic clause
- implied powers
- treason
- impeachment
- ex post facto law
- bill of attainder
- writ of *habeas corpus*
- constituents

**2. Categorizing** Copy the chart below. Use it to explain the special powers of Congress and how congressional powers are limited.

| Special Powers | Limits on Powers |
|---|---|
| | |
| | |
| | |

**3. Finding the Main Idea**
a. In what five major areas does Congress have the power to make laws?
b. Why is the elastic clause useful?

**4. Writing and Critical Thinking**
**Evaluating** Imagine that you are a Congressmember who supports building a new military academy. Write a speech that explains why Congress has the power to set up this academy. Be sure to address the fact that the Constitution does not specify that Congress can do this.

**Consider:**
- Article I, Section 8 of the Constitution
- why the academy is necessary

---

**Homework Practice Online** lets you log on to the go.hrw.com Web site to complete an interactive self-check of the material covered in the section.

**Writing and Critical Thinking** activities help you to explore a section's topic in greater depth and to build your writing and thinking skills.

**Graphic Organizers** will help you review important information from the section you have read. You can use the graphic organizer as a study tool to prepare for a test or writing assignment.

**The Chapter Summary** is a brief summary of the main ideas of the chapter.

**Social Studies Skills Workshop** is a way for you to build the skills of analyzing information and to practice answering standardized-test questions.

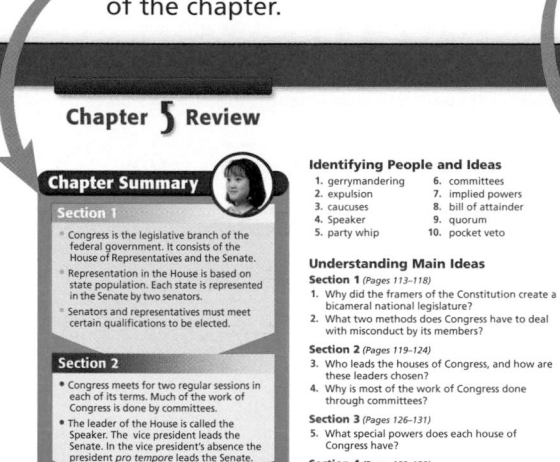

## Chapter 5 Review

### Chapter Summary

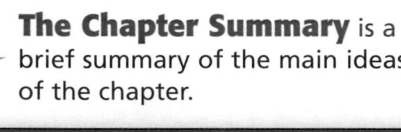

**Section 1**
* Congress is the legislative branch of the federal government. It consists of the House of Representatives and the Senate.
* Representation in the House is based on state population. Each state is represented in the Senate by two senators.
* Senators and representatives must meet certain qualifications to be elected.

**Section 2**
* Congress meets for two regular sessions in each of its terms. Much of the work of Congress is done by committees.
* The leader of the House is called the Speaker. The vice president leads the Senate. In the vice president's absence the president pro tempore leads the Senate.

**Section 3**
* The Constitution grants Congress lawmaking authority to finance government, regulate trade and industry, defend the country, enforce laws, and provide for growth.
* The elastic clause allows Congress to exercise implied powers not specifically granted to it.
* The Constitution reserves certain powers for the states and specifically forbids some powers to Congress.

**Section 4**
* Congress considers thousands of bills each year that come from U.S. citizens, organized groups, congressional committees, Congressmembers, and the president.
* The legislative process is long and involves many steps. To become a law, each bill must be passed by both houses before being signed by the president.

### Identifying People and Ideas
1. gerrymandering
2. expulsion
3. caucuses
4. Speaker
5. party whip
6. committees
7. implied powers
8. bill of attainder
9. quorum
10. pocket veto

### Understanding Main Ideas
**Section 1** (Pages 113–118)
1. Why did the framers of the Constitution create a bicameral national legislature?
2. What two methods does Congress have to deal with misconduct by its members?

**Section 2** (Pages 119–124)
3. Who leads the houses of Congress, and how are these leaders chosen?
4. Why is most of the work of Congress done in committees?

**Section 3** (Pages 126–131)
5. What special powers does each house of Congress have?

**Section 4** (Pages 132–139)
6. How do bills become laws?
7. What can the president do to a bill passed by Congress?

### What Did You Find Out?
1. What qualifications must a person meet to run for Congress?
2. How do committees affect the work of Congress?
3. Describe the impeachment process.

### Thinking Critically
1. **Drawing Inferences and Conclusions** Why do you think that the House limits debate on a bill, but the Senate does not?
2. **Supporting a Point of View** The Senate has fewer members than the House, and senators have longer terms of office than representatives. The Senate also receives more media attention than the House. Do you think these factors affect how responsive the Senate is to the needs of the people? Explain your answer.
3. **Comparing and Contrasting** What are the advantages and disadvantages to the American people of having a lengthy and complex law-making process?

140 Chapter 5

### Building Social Studies Skills

STANDARDIZED TEST PREP ONLINE keyword: SZ3 STP5

**Interpreting Tables**
Study the table on Standing Committees of Congress below. Then use the information in the table to answer the questions that follow.

#### Standing Committees of Congress

**House**
Agriculture; Appropriations; Banking and Financial Services; Budget; Commerce; Economic and Educational Opportunities; Government Reform and Oversight; House Oversight; International Relations; Judiciary; National Security; Resources; Rules; Science; Small Business; Standards of Official Conduct; Transportation and Infrastructure; Veterans' Affairs; Ways and Means

**Senate**
Agriculture, Nutrition, and Forestry; Appropriations; Armed Services; Banking, Housing and Urban Affairs; Budget; Commerce, Science, and Transportation; Energy and Natural Resources; Environment and Public Works; Finance; Foreign Relations; Governmental Affairs; Indian Affairs; Judiciary; Labor and Human Resources; Rules and Administration; Small Business; Veterans' Affairs

1. Which of the following committees exist in both the House of Representatives and the Senate?
   a. Appropriations and Government Reform and Oversight
   b. Finance and Ways and Means
   c. Small Business and Standards of Official Conduct
   d. Budget and Veterans' Affairs
2. Based on your knowledge of Congress and the names of the committees shown in the table, would you say that economic issues are or are not an important subject of congressional affairs? Explain your answer.

**Analyzing Primary Sources**
Read the following quotation from Senate Majority Leader and Democrat Tom Daschle as he calls for a vote on a special resolution. Then answer the questions that follow.

"Mr. President, as I think certainly everyone on the floor knows, but for those who may be viewing our proceedings, and should know, our caucuses have been meeting for the last hour to review the work which has been done by colleagues on both sides of the aisle in concert with the administration and with the House of Representatives. This work has been ongoing now for several days. . . . Let me say, before I do read the request, how much I appreciate, once again, the leadership of our Republican leader [the president]. . . . I commend him, and I thank all of our colleagues for their remarkable participation during this difficult week."

3. Which of the following statements best expresses Daschle's point of view?
   a. He is happy that the Senate and the president have worked together against the House of Representatives.
   b. He appreciates the cooperation that Congress, the president, and members of both political parties have shown.
   c. He appreciates how the president has led both houses of Congress.
   d. He is upset at the lack of progress that has been made during a difficult week.
4. How does this quotation demonstrate the importance of cooperation between the executive branch, political parties, and both houses of Congress during times of crisis?

### Alternative Assessment

#### Building Your Portfolio

**Interdisciplinary Connection to Government**
Choose one person who serves your state as a representative or senator in Congress. Write a profile of this person. Be sure to provide background information, such as place of birth, education, and occupation. Also provide information on the person's political experience such as offices held, length of service in Congress, political party membership, and positions on key issues.

#### internet connect
**Internet Activity: go.hrw.com**
keyword: SZ3 AC5

Access the Internet through the HRW Go site to compare and contrast the roles, requirements, and powers of both houses of Congress. Then create an illustrated diagram to present your information. Focus on issues such as term lengths, number of members, and any other information that is unique to either the House or Senate.

*The Legislative Branch* 141

**Thinking Critically** questions ask you to use the information you have learned in the chapter in greater depth. You will be asked to analyze information by using your critical thinking skills.

**Building Your Portfolio** is an exciting and creative way to demonstrate your understanding of the chapter material.

# Use these online tools to review and complete online activities.

#### internet connect
**Internet Activity: go.hrw.com**
keyword: SZ3 AC5

Access the Internet through the HRW Go site to compare and contrast the roles, requirements, and powers of both houses of Congress. Then create an illustrated diagram to present your information. Focus on issues such as term lengths, number of members, and any other information that is unique to either the House or Senate.

### Internet Connect
activities are just one part of the world of online learning experiences that awaits you on the go.hrw.com Web site. By exploring these online activities, you will take a journey through some of the richest materials available on the World Wide Web. You can then use these resources to create real-world projects, such as newspapers, brochures, reports, and even your own Web site!

Holt, Rinehart & Winston

**The Legislative Branch**

**The Legislative Branch**
Chapter Home
Senate and House of Representatives
Running for Congress
How a Bill Becomes a Law
Charts and Graphs
Chapter Enrichment Links
Homework Practice Help
Standardized Test Prep

**Student Resources**
Holt Researcher
Holt Grapher
HRW Atlas
Gazetteer
Glossary
Reading Support
Current Events
Content Updates
State Resources

**Web Resources**
CNNfyi.com
CNN Student News

**Activities**

Senate and House of Representatives
Compare and contrast the roles, requirements, and powers of both houses of Congress, and then create an illustrated diagram.

Running for Congress
Research the role of a congressperson and Congressional elections. Then imagine that you are running for Congress, and create a campaign poster, flyer, or commercial.

How a Bill Becomes a Law
Learn about the process by which a bill becomes a law. Then assume the point of view of a bill, and write a short story on your journey through Congress.

**Chapter Resources**

Chapter Enrichment Links
Learn more about the legislative branch.

Charts and Graphs
View charts and graphs for this chapter.

Homework Practice Online
Quiz yourself on what you have learned about the legislative branch.

xix

# Why Civics Matters

*Do you know what it means to live in a democracy? What are your rights and responsibilities as a citizen in a democratic country? What would a new U.S. citizen need to know about fulfilling these responsibilities? The answers to these questions can be found in the book you are about to read.*

## The Meaning of Civics

What do you think of when you hear the word *civics?* Maybe you envision government buildings. Perhaps you imagine elected officials. *Civics* is the study of the rights and duties of a citizen. Because Americans live in a democratic society, they must take part in the process of self-government. This means that as an American you are responsible for how your government functions and who your leaders are. Participation by concerned citizens is key to keeping a democracy thriving. By studying and learning civics, you become the kind of citizen your country needs—an informed citizen.

## Civics and You

Civics involves the study of many subjects. You will learn about your role in the U.S. political and economic systems. Can you list ways to participate in the U.S. political system before you are eligible to vote? Do you know what to do if you believe a certain law should be passed? The structure of the

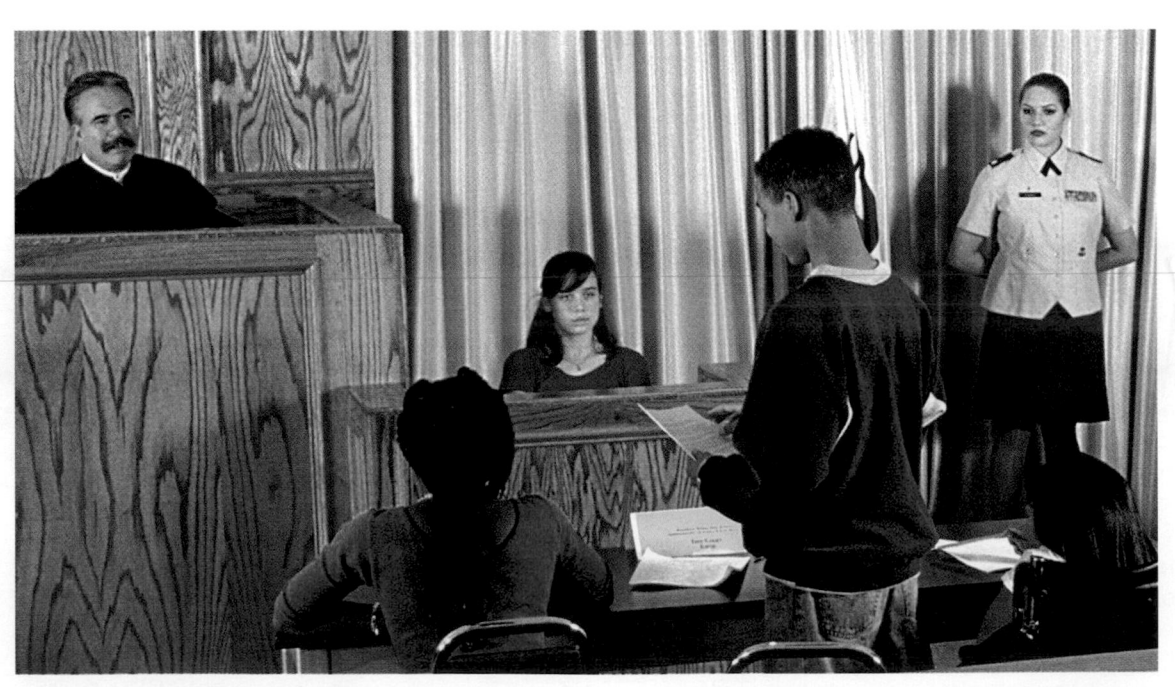

*A group of students learns about government by holding a mock trial.*

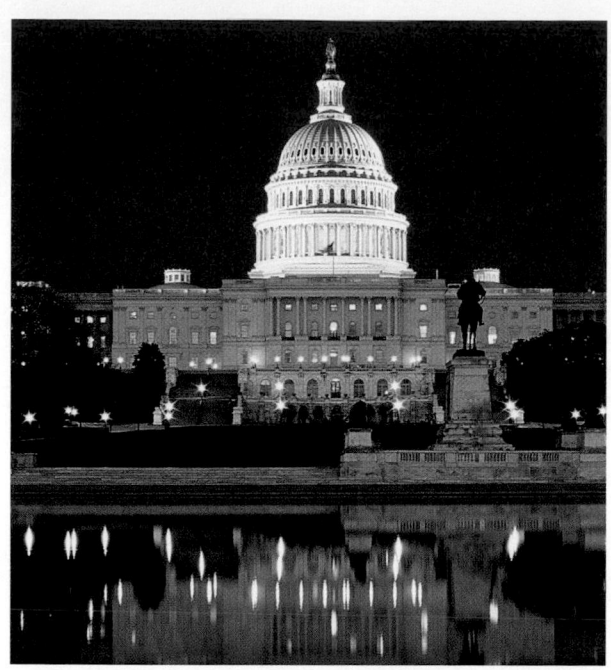
◀ *The U.S. Capitol building*

**CNNfyi.com** and other current events sources to inform you about key issues related to the section. Through this feature you will be able to see how civics affects your everyday life.

The material in this textbook will also show that there are several ways to be a good citizen. You probably already practice many actions of good citizenship, such as understanding and obeying the laws of your community. You will also learn how volunteer work and being active in your community strengthen our democracy. You might even run for political office some day. Through studying civics, you will come to understand that the most important element in a democratic society is the people—including you!

political system and its influences are two of the topics of civics. You will also learn about the U.S. economy and other economic systems. You will find out how a democratic government represents the various needs and interests of a diverse population. Finally, you will grow to understand the importance of the United States in the world political and economic system.

## Why Study Civics

You can help fulfill your civic responsibilities by staying informed and having your voice be heard. One way to stay informed is by using this textbook. The "Why Civics Matters" feature beginning every section of your textbook uses the vast resources of

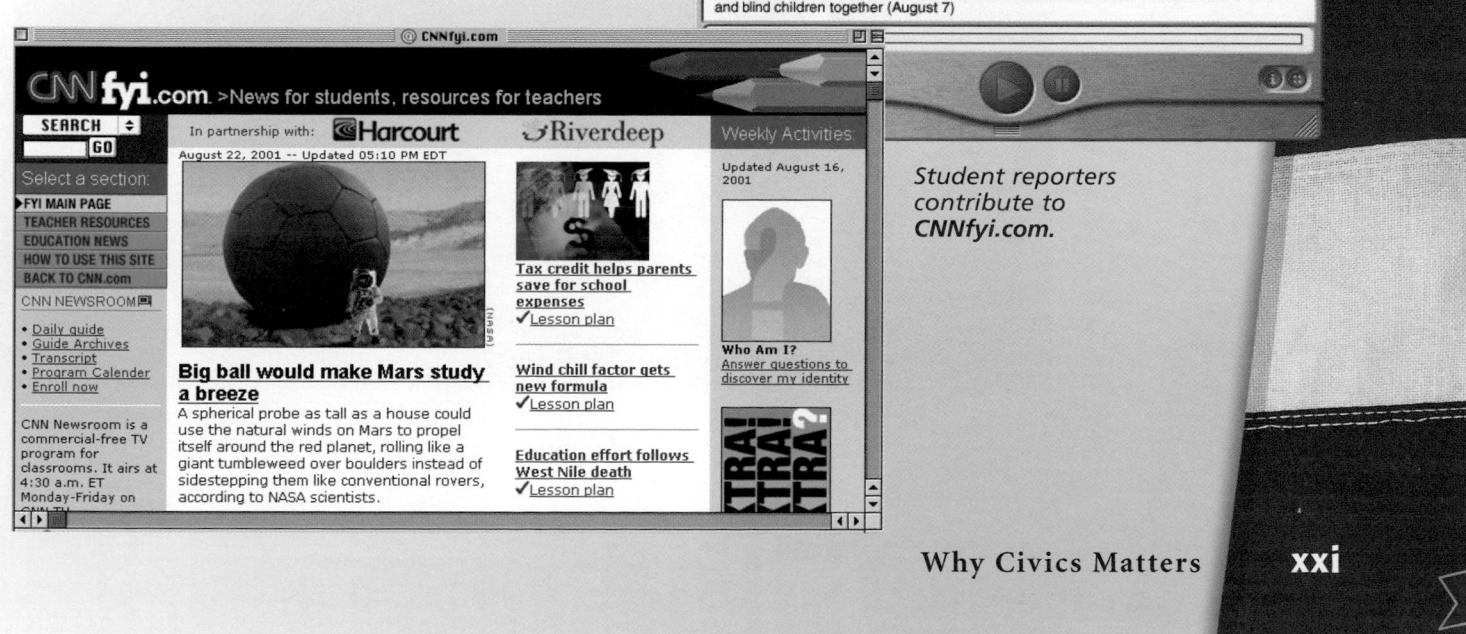

*Student reporters contribute to CNNfyi.com.*

# Skills Handbook

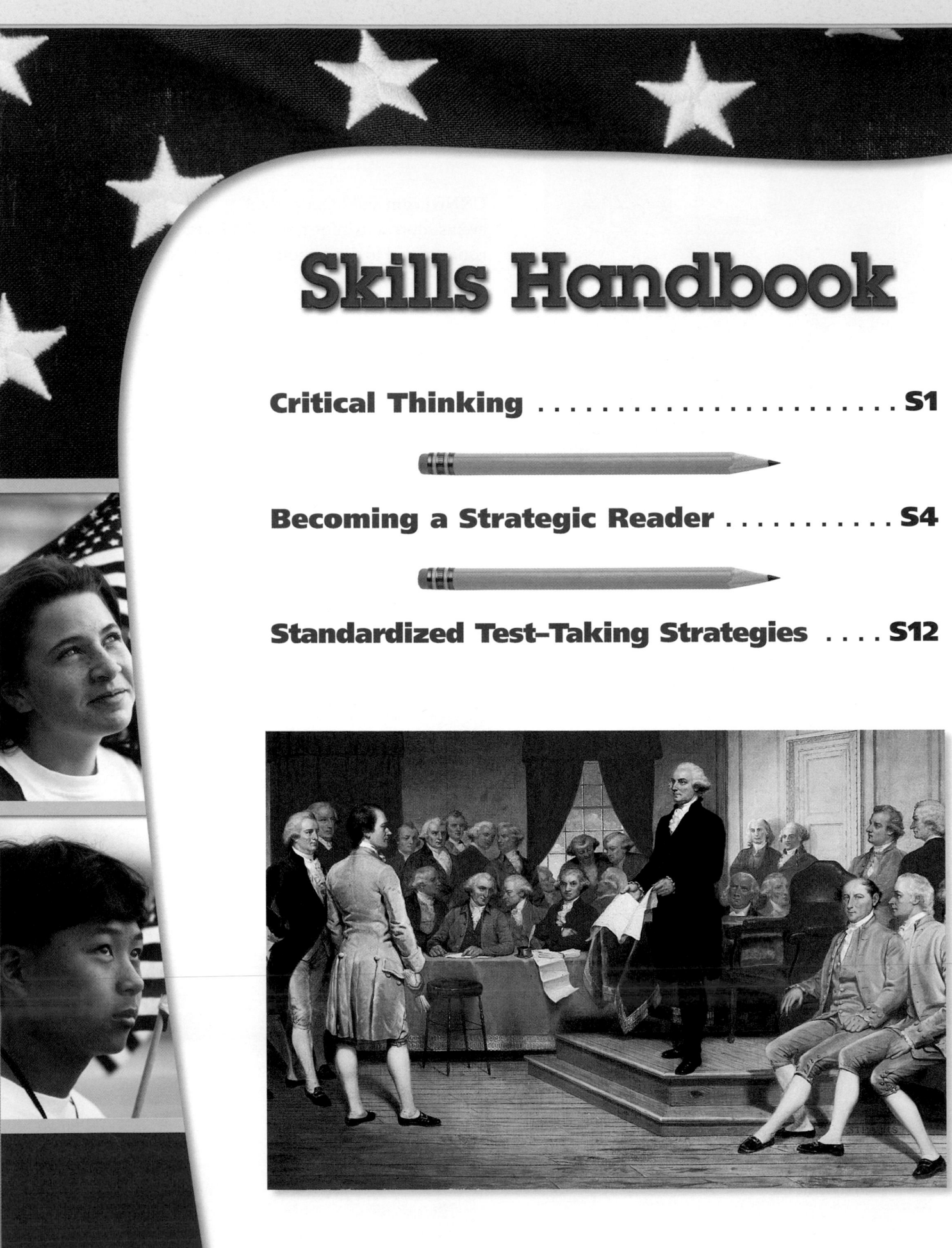

# Critical Thinking

Throughout your textbook, you will be asked to think critically about issues that affect your role as an American. Critical thinking is the reasoned judgment of information and ideas based on their merit. 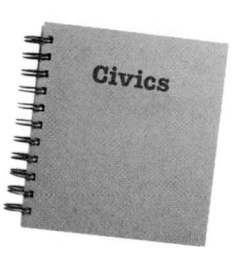 The development of critical thinking skills is essential to effective citizenship. Such skills empower you to exercise your civic rights and responsibilities. Helping you develop critical thinking skills is an important purpose of your textbook. The following critical thinking skills are exercised in the section reviews and chapter reviews of the book.

**1 Analyzing Information** is the process of breaking a concept down into sections and then examining the relationships between those parts. Analyzing enables you to better understand the information as a whole. For example, you may be asked to analyze how tradition and interpretation of the Constitution have influenced the U.S. federal government.

**2 Sequencing** is the process of placing events in their chronological order to better understand the relationships between those events. You can sequence events in two basic ways: according to absolute or relative chronology. Absolute chronology means that you pay close attention to the exact dates on which events took place. Relative chronology refers to the way events relate to one another. To put events in relative order, you only need to know which one happened first, which came next, and so forth.

**3 Categorizing** is the process of grouping things together by the characteristics they have in common. Putting things or events into categories makes it easier to see similarities and differences among them.

**4 Identifying Cause and Effect** is one way to interpret the relationships between events. A *cause* is a circumstance that leads to an action. The outcome of that action is an *effect*. When studying the text, you may discover multiple causes and effects. For example, the states' fear of a strong national government led to the creation of the Articles of Confederation. This in turn had far-reaching effects for the future of the U.S. federal government.

**5 Comparing and Contrasting** is the process of examining events, situations, or points of view for their similarities and differences. When *comparing*, you focus on both their similarities and their differences. When *contrasting*, you focus only on their differences. Studying similarities and differences between people and things can help you better understand a particular event or situation.

**6** **Finding the Main Idea** is the process of combining and sifting through information to determine the idea that is most important. To help illustrate a point, writers often use many examples and details to support their main ideas. Throughout your textbook, you will find numerous Reading Checks and questions in section reviews to help you focus on the main ideas in the text.

**7** **Summarizing** is the process of taking a large amount of information and boiling it down into a short and clear statement. Summarizing is particularly useful when you need to give a brief account of a longer story or event.

**8** **Making Generalizations and Predictions** is the process of interpreting information to form general statements and to guess what will happen next. A *generalization* is a broad statement that holds true for a variety of events or situations. Making generalizations can help you see the "big picture" of events rather than just focusing on details. However, it is very important that when making generalizations you try not to make statements that do not include all situations. When this occurs, you run the risk of creating a stereotype, or

overgeneralization. A *prediction* is an educated guess about an outcome. When you read your textbook, you should always be asking yourself questions like, "If the system were different, what would that mean for . . . ? How might my actions affect . . . ?", and so on. These types of questions help you draw on information you already know to see how changes in behavior or actions can influence an outcome.

**9** **Drawing Inferences and Conclusions** is forming possible explanations for an event, a situation, or a problem. When you make an *inference,* you take the information you know to be true and make an educated guess about what else you think may be true about that situation. A *conclusion* is a statement that can be made based on what you already know. For example, after reading about the powers of the legislative and executive branches of government, you might be asked who or what has authority over the president. You would then organize the evidence needed to support your conclusion.

**10** **Identifying Points of View** is the process of identifying factors that influence the outlook of an individual or group. A person's point of view includes beliefs and attitudes that are shaped by factors such as age, gender, religion, race, and economic status. This critical thinking skill helps you examine why people choose to act as they do, and it reinforces the fact that people's views may change over time or with a change in circumstances.

**11** **Supporting a Point of View** is a process that involves choosing a viewpoint on a particular event or issue and then arguing persuasively for that position. Your argument should be well organized and based on specific evidence that supports the point of view you have chosen. Supporting a point of view often involves working with controversial issues. For example, you might consider the point of view of a legislator who has been asked to consider ratifying the U.S. Bill of Rights. Whether you choose a position favoring the Bill of Rights or opposing it, you should state your opinion clearly and give reasons to defend it.

**12** **Identifying Bias** is the process of evaluating the opinions of others about events or situations. Bias is an opinion based on prejudice or strong emotions rather than on fact. It is important to identify bias when looking at historical sources, because biased sources often give you a false sense of what really happened. When looking at both primary and secondary sources, it is always important to keep the author's or speaker's point of view in mind and to adjust your interpretation of the source when you detect any bias.

**13** **Evaluating** is the process of assessing the significance, or overall importance, of something, such as the success of a reform movement, the actions of a president, or the results of a major conflict. You should base your judgment on standards that others will understand and that they are likely to share. For example, you might be asked to evaluate whether the Great Compromise was an effective agreement.

**14** **Problem Solving** is the process by which you pose possible solutions to difficult situations. The first step in the process is to identify a problem. Next you must gather information about the problem, such as its history and the various factors that contribute to the problem. Once you have gathered information, you should list and consider the options for solving the problem. For each of the possible solutions, weigh its advantages and disadvantages and choose and implement a solution based on your evaluation. Once the solution has been tried, go back and evaluate the effectiveness of the solution you selected.

**15** **Decision Making** is the process of reviewing a situation and then making decisions or recommendations for the best possible action. To complete the process, first identify a situation that requires a solution. Next, gather information that will help you reach a decision. You may need to do some background research to study the history of the situation. Once you have done your research, identify options that might resolve the situation. For each option, predict what the possible consequences might be if that option were followed. Once you have identified the best option, take action by making a recommendation and by following through on any tasks that option requires.

# Becoming a Strategic Reader

*by Dr. Judith Irvin*

Everywhere you look, print is all around us. In fact, you would have a hard time stopping yourself from reading. In a normal day you might read cereal boxes, movie posters, notes from friends, T-shirts, instructions for video games, song lyrics, catalogs, billboards, information on the Internet, magazines, the newspaper, and much, much more. Each form of print is read differently depending on your purpose for reading. You read a menu differently from the way you read poetry, and a motorcycle magazine is read differently than a letter from a friend. Good readers switch easily from one type of text to another. In fact, they probably do not even think about it; they just do it.

When you read, it is helpful to use a strategy to remember the most important ideas. You can use a strategy before you read to help connect information you already know to the new information you will encounter. Before you read, you can also predict what a text will be about by using a previewing strategy. During the reading you can use a strategy to help you focus on main ideas, and after reading you can use a strategy to help you organize what you learned so that you can remember it later. This textbook was designed to help you more easily understand the ideas you read. Important reading strategies employed in your textbook include the following:

**1** Methods to help you **anticipate** what is to come

**2** Tools to help you **preview and predict** what the text will be about

**3** Ways to help you **use and analyze visual information**

**4** Ideas to help you **organize the information** you have learned

# 1. Anticipate Information

## How Can I Use Information I Already Know to Help Me Understand What a New Chapter Will Be About?

**Anticipating** what a new chapter will be about helps you connect what you already know to the new information as you read it. By drawing on your background knowledge, you can build a bridge to the new material.

**①** Each chapter of your textbook asks you to consider the main themes of the chapter before you start reading by forming opinions based on your current knowledge.

**What's Your Opinion?**

Themes Journal — Do you **agree** or **disagree** with the following statements? Support your point of view in your journal.

- Families today live much like families always have in the United States.
- Increased stress upon the American family has placed increased demands on the field of family law.
- Citizenship skills should be taught in the family.

Create a chart like this one to help you analyze the statements.

| A<br>Before Reading<br>Agree/Disagree | | B<br>After Reading<br>Agree/Disagree |
|---|---|---|
| **②** | Families today live much like families always have in the United States. | **④** |
| | Increased stress upon the American family has placed increased demands on the field of family law. | |
| | Citizenship skills should be taught in the family. | |

**③** Read the text and discuss your answers with classmates.

**⑤** Refine your knowledge by answering the **What Did You Find Out?** questions in the chapter review.

### Anticipating Information

▶ **Step ①** Identify the major concepts of the chapter. In your textbook these are presented in the **What's Your Opinion?** feature at the beginning of each chapter.

▼

**Step ②** Agree or disagree with each of the statements and record your opinions in your journal.

▼

**Step ③** Read the text and discuss your responses with your classmates.

▼

**Step ④** After reading the chapter, revisit the statements and respond to them again based on what you have learned.

▼

**Step ⑤** Go back and check your knowledge by answering the **What Did You Find Out?** questions in the chapter review.

### What Did You Find Out?

1. How has the family in the United States changed over time?

2. How does the law protect family members, particularly children?

3. Why is learning and practicing good citizenship within the family important?

## 2. Preview and Predict

### How Can I Figure Out What the Text Is About Before I Even Start Reading a Section?

**Previewing and Predicting**

▶ **Step 1** Identify your purpose for reading. Ask yourself what you will do with this information once you have finished reading.

▼

**Step 2** Ask yourself what the main idea of the text is and what key vocabulary words you need to know.

▼

**Step 3** Use signal words to help identify the structure of the text.

▼

**Step 4** Connect the information to what you already know.

**Previewing** and **predicting** are good methods to help you prepare for reading the text. If you take the time to preview and predict before you read, the text will make more sense to you during your reading.

**1** Usually your teacher will state the purpose for reading. After reading some new information, you may be asked to write a summary, take a test, or complete some other type of activity.

"After reading about the roles of the president, you will write an article about…"

**2** As you preview the text, use *graphic signals,* such as headings, subheadings, and boldfaced type, to help you determine what is important in the text. Each section of your textbook begins by giving you important clues to help you preview the material.

Looking at the section's **main heading** and **subheadings** can give you an idea of what is to come.

**Read to Discover** questions give you clues as to the section's main ideas.

**Define and Identify** terms let you know the key vocabulary you will encounter in the section.

---

**SECTION 2**

## Powers and Roles of the President

**Read to Discover**
1. How is the president involved in the legislative process?
2. How does Congress limit the president's powers as commander in chief?
3. What are the president's duties as foreign-policy leader and as chief of state?

**Define**
- foreign policy
- diplomacy
- diplomatic notes
- treaties
- reprieve
- pardon
- commutation

**Identify**
- State of the Union Address

**WHY CIVICS MATTERS**

The Constitution charges the president with the responsibility of recommending laws to Congress. Use CNNfyi.com or other **current events** sources to read about a law that the president has recently recommended to Congress. Record your findings in your journal.

**3** Other tools that can help you while previewing are **signal words**. Signal words prepare you to think about a topic in a certain way. For example, when you see words such as *similar to, same as,* or *different from,* you know that the text will probably compare and contrast two or more ideas. Signal words indicate how the ideas in the text relate to each other. Look at the list below of some of the most common signal words. The words are grouped by the type of thoughts they indicate.

### Signal Words

| Cause and Effect | Compare and Contrast | Description | Problem and Solution | Sequence or Chronological Order |
|---|---|---|---|---|
| • because<br>• since<br>• consequently<br>• this led to…so<br>• if…then<br>• accordingly<br>• because of<br>• as a result of<br>• in order to<br>• may be due to<br>• for this reason | • different from<br>• same as<br>• similar to<br>• as opposed to<br>• instead of<br>• although<br>• however<br>• compared with<br>• as well as<br>• either…or<br>• but<br>• on the other hand<br>• unless | • for instance<br>• for example<br>• such as<br>• to illustrate<br>• in addition<br>• most importantly<br>• another<br>• furthermore<br>• first, second… | • the question is<br>• a solution<br>• one answer is | • not long after<br>• next<br>• then<br>• initially<br>• before<br>• after<br>• finally<br>• preceding<br>• following<br>• on (date)<br>• over time<br>• today<br>• when |

**4** Learning something new requires that you connect it in some way with something you already know. Learning requires you to think before you read and while you read. You may use a chart like this one to remind yourself of the information you are already familiar with and to come up with questions you want answered in your reading. The chart will also help you organize your ideas after you have finished reading.

| What I know | What I want to know | What I learned |
|---|---|---|
| | | |

## 3. Use and Analyze Visual Information

**How Can All the Pictures, Maps, Graphs, and Time Lines with the Text Help Me Be a Stronger Reader?**

### Analyzing Visual Information

▶ **Step 1** As you preview the text ask yourself how the visual information relates to the text.

▼

**Step 2** Generate questions based on the visual information.

▼

**Step 3** After reading the text, go back and review the visual information again.

▼

**Step 4** Make connections to what you already know.

**Using visual information** can help you understand and remember the information presented in your textbook. Good readers form a picture in their minds when they read. The pictures, charts, graphs, cartoons, time lines, and diagrams that occur throughout your textbook are placed strategically to increase your understanding.

**1** You might ask yourself questions like the following:

> Why did the author include this information with the text? What details about this visual are mentioned in the text?

After you have read the text, see if you can answer your own questions.

**2**

*Why is the chart important?*

*How is an amendment proposed?*

*Who approves an amendment?*

**Amending the Constitution**

| Proposed by | | Ratified by | | |
|---|---|---|---|---|
| Congress two-thirds vote in each house | → | Legislatures of three fourths of the states | → | Amendment added to the Constitution |
| **or** | | **or** | | |
| National convention called by Congress at the request of two thirds of the state legislatures | → | Conventions held in three fourths of the states | → | |

**3** After reading, take another look at the visual information.

**4** Try to make connections to what you already know.

## 4. Organize Information

Once I Learn New Information, How Do I Keep It All Straight So That I Will Remember It?

To help you remember what you have read, you need to find a way of **organizing information**. Two good ways of doing this are to use graphic organizers and concept maps. **Graphic organizers** help you understand important relationships—such as cause and effect, compare and contrast, sequence of events, and problem and solution—within the text. A **concept map** is a useful tool to help you focus on the text's main ideas and to help you organize supporting details.

## Identifying Relationships

Using graphic organizers will help you recall important ideas from the section. They are also study tools you can use to prepare for a quiz or test or to help with a writing assignment. Some of the most common types of graphic organizers are shown below.

### ▶ Cause and Effect

Events in our society cause people to react in certain ways. Cause-and-effect patterns show the relationships between results and the ideas or events that made the results occur. You may want to represent cause-and-effect relationships as one cause leading to multiple effects,

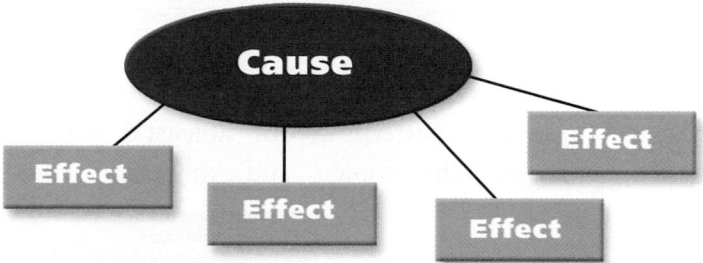

or as a chain of cause-and-effect relationships.

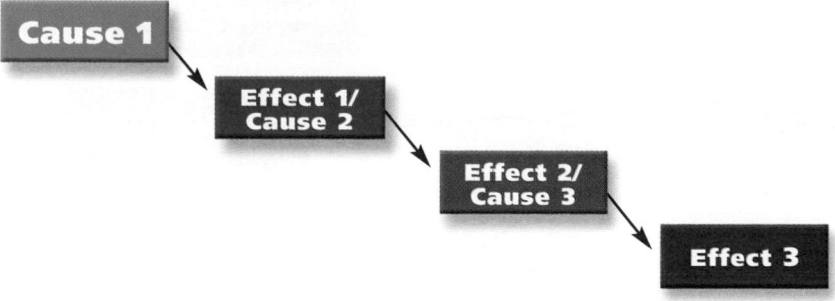

> **Constructing Graphic Organizers**
>
> ▶ **Step ❶** Preview the text, looking for signal words and main ideas.
>
> ▼
>
> **Step ❷** Form a hypothesis as to which type of graphic organizer would work best to display the information presented.
>
> ▼
>
> **Step ❸** Work individually or with your classmates to create a visual representation of what you read.

### ▶ Comparing and Contrasting

Graphic organizers are often useful when you are comparing or contrasting information. Compare-and-contrast diagrams point out similarities and differences between two concepts or ideas.

### ▶ Sequencing

Keeping track of dates and the order in which events took place is essential to understanding the relationships among events. Sequence, or chronological-order, diagrams show events or ideas in the order in which they happened.

### ▶ Problem and Solution

Problem and solution patterns identify at least one problem, offer one or more solutions to the problem, and explain or predict outcomes of the solutions.

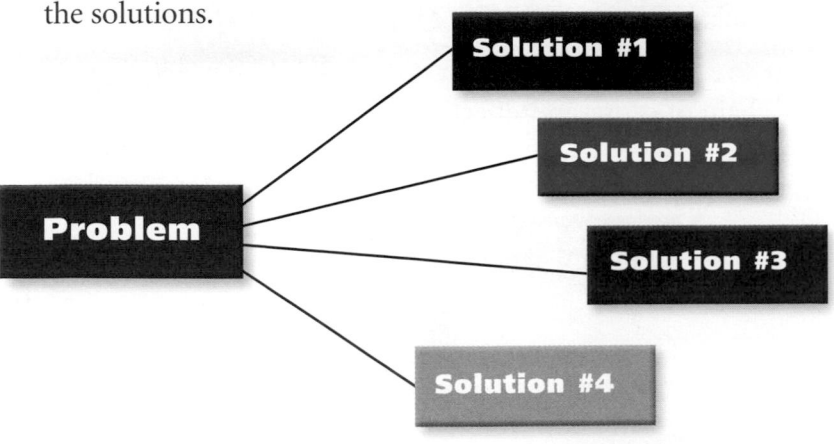

# Identifying Main Ideas and Supporting Details

One special type of graphic organizer is the concept map. A concept map, sometimes called a semantic map, allows you to zero in on the most important points of the text. The map is made up of lines, boxes, circles, and/or arrows. It can be as simple or as complex as you need it to be to accurately represent the text.

Here are a few examples of concept maps you might use.

## Constructing Concept Maps

▶ **Step ①** Preview the text, looking for what type of structure might be appropriate to display a concept map.

▼

**Step ②** Taking note of the headings, boldfaced type, and text structure, sketch a concept map you think could best illustrate the text.

▼

**Step ③** Using boxes, lines, arrows, circles, or any shapes you like, display the ideas of the text in the concept map.

# Standardized Test–Taking Strategies

A number of times throughout your school career, you may be asked to take standardized tests. These tests are designed to demonstrate the information and skills you have learned. It is important to keep in mind that in most cases the best way to prepare for these tests is to pay close attention in class and to take every opportunity to improve your general social studies, reading, writing, and mathematical skills.

## Tips for Taking the Test

1. Be sure that you are well rested.
2. Be on time and be sure that you have the necessary materials.
3. Listen to the instructions of the teacher.
4. Read directions and questions carefully.
5. **DON'T STRESS!** Just remember what you have learned in class, and you should do well.

▶ **Practice the strategies at go.hrw.com.**

**go.hrw.com STANDARDIZED TEST–PREP ONLINE**
keyword: SZ3 STP

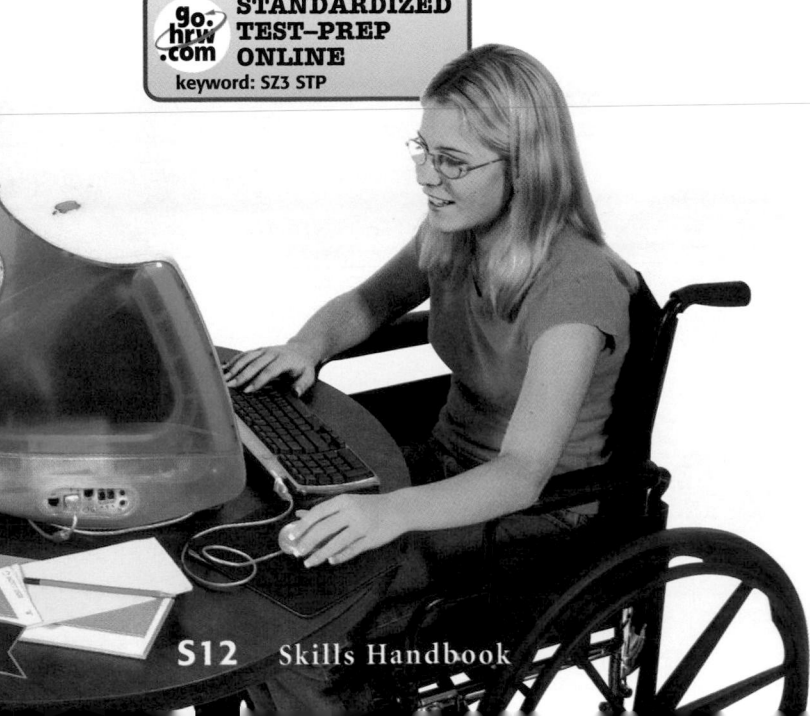

## Tackling Social Studies

The social studies portions of many standardized tests are designed to test your knowledge of the content and skills that you have been studying in one or more of your social studies classes. Specific objectives for the test vary, but some of the most common include the following:

1. Demonstrate an understanding of issues and events in history.
2. Demonstrate an understanding of geographic influences on issues and events.
3. Demonstrate an understanding of economic and social influences on issues and events.
4. Demonstrate an understanding of political influences on issues and events.
5. Use critical thinking skills to analyze social studies information.

Standardized tests usually contain multiple-choice questions and sometimes contain open-ended questions. The multiple-choice items are often based on maps, tables, charts, graphs, pictures, cartoons, and/or reading passages and documents.

## Tips for Answering Multiple-Choice Questions

1. If there is a written or visual piece accompanying the multiple-choice question, pay careful attention to the title, author, and date.
2. Then read through or glance over the content of the piece accompanying the question.
3. Next, read the multiple-choice question for its general intent. Then reread it carefully, looking for words that give clues. For example, words such as *most* or *best* tell you that there may be several correct answers, but you should look for the most appropriate answer.

4. Always read all of the possible answer choices, even if the first one seems like the correct answer. There may be a better choice farther down in the list.

5. Reread the accompanying information (if any is included) carefully to determine the answer to the question. Again, note the title, author, and date of primary-source selections. The answer will rarely be stated exactly as it appears in the primary source, so you will need to use your critical thinking skills to read between the lines.

6. Use your social studies knowledge to help limit the answer choices.

7. Finally, reread the question and your selected answer to be sure that you made the best choice and that you marked it correctly on the answer sheet.

## Strategies for Success

There are many strategies you can use to help you feel more confident about answering questions on social studies standardized tests. Here are a few suggestions:

1. Adopt an acronym—a word formed from the first letters of other words—that you will always use to analyze a document or visual that might accompany a question.

### Helpful Acronyms

For a document use **SOAPS**, which stands for

| **S** | Subject |
|---|---|
| **O** | Occasion |
| **A** | Audience |
| **P** | Purpose |
| **S** | Speaker/author |

For a picture, cartoon, map, or other visual piece of information, use **OPTIC**, which stands for

| **O** | Overview |
|---|---|
| **P** | Parts (labels or details of the visual) |
| **T** | Title |
| **I** | Interrelations (how the different parts of the visual work together) |
| **C** | Conclusion (what the visual means) |

2. Form visual images of maps and try to draw them from memory. The standardized test will most likely include important maps from the subjects you have been studying.

3. When you have finished studying any social studies topic, try to think of who or what might be important enough to be on the test. You may want to keep your ideas in a notebook so that you can refer to them when it is almost time for the test.

4. Pay particular attention to the Constitution and its development. Many standardized tests contain questions about this all-important document and the period during which it was written. Questions may include Magna Carta, the English Bill of Rights, the Declaration of Independence, *Common Sense*, as well as many other important historical documents.

5. For the skills area of the tests, practice putting major events and people in order in your mind. Sequencing people and events by dates can become a game you play with a friend who also has to take the test. Always ask yourself why each event is important.

6. Follow the tips under "Ready for Reading" on the next page when you encounter a reading passage in social studies, and remember that what you have learned in social studies classes can help you answer reading-comprehension questions.

## Ready for Reading

The main goal of the reading sections of most standardized tests is to determine your understanding of different aspects of a written passage. Basically, if you can grasp the main idea and the author's purpose, then pay attention to the details and vocabulary so that you are able to draw inferences and conclusions. You will then do well on the test.

### Tips for Answering Multiple-Choice Questions

1. Read the passage as if you were not taking a test.
2. Look at the big picture. Ask yourself questions like the following: What is the title? What do the illustrations or pictures tell me? and What is the author's purpose?
3. Read the questions. The questions will help you know what information to look for.
4. Reread the passage, underlining information related to the questions.

### Types of Multiple-Choice Questions

1. **Main Idea** This is the most important point of the passage. After reading the passage, locate and underline the main idea.
2. **Significant Details** You will often be asked to recall details from the passage. Read the question and underline the details as you read. But remember that the correct answers do not always match the wording of the passage precisely.
3. **Vocabulary** You will often need to define a word within the context of the passage. Read the answer choices and plug them into the sentence to see what fits best.
4. **Conclusion and Inference** There are often important ideas in the passage that the author does not state directly. Sometimes you must consider multiple parts of the passage to answer the question. If answers refer to only one or two sentences or details in the passage, they are probably incorrect.

5. Go back to the questions and try to answer each one in your mind before looking at the answers.
6. Read all the answer choices and eliminate the ones that are obviously incorrect.

### Tips for Answering Short-Answer Questions

1. Read the passage in its entirety, paying close attention to the main events and characters. Jot down information you think is important.
2. If you cannot answer a question, skip it and come back later.
3. Words such as *compare, contrast, interpret, discuss,* and *summarize* appear often in short-answer questions. Be sure you have a complete understanding of each of these words.
4. To help support your answer, return to the passage and skim the parts you underlined.
5. Organize your thoughts on a separate sheet of paper. Write a general statement with which to begin. This sentence will be your topic statement.
6. When writing your answer, be precise but brief. Be sure to refer to details from the passage in your answer.

## Targeting Writing

On many standardized tests, you will occasionally be asked to write an essay. In order to write a concise essay, you must learn to organize your thoughts before you begin writing the actual composition. Organization keeps you from straying too far from the essay's topic.

### Tips for Answering Composition Questions

1. Read the question carefully.
2. Decide what kind of essay you are being asked to write. Essays usually fall into one of the following types: persuasive, classificatory, compare/contrast, or "how to." To determine the type of essay, ask yourself questions like the following: Am I trying to persuade my audience? Am I comparing or contrasting ideas? or Am I trying to show the reader how to do something?
3. Pay attention to key words, such as *compare, contrast, describe, advantages, disadvantages, classify,* and *speculate.* They will give you clues as to the structure that your essay should follow.
4. Organize your thoughts on a separate sheet of paper. You will want to come up with a general topic sentence that expresses your main idea. Make sure this sentence addresses the question. You should then create an outline or some type of graphic organizer to help you organize the points that support your topic sentence.
5. Write your composition using complete sentences. Also, be sure to use correct grammar, spelling, punctuation, and sentence structure.
6. Be sure to proofread your essay once you have finished writing.

## Gearing up for Math

On most standardized tests you will be asked to solve a variety of mathematical problems that draw on the skills and information you have learned in class. If math problems sometimes give you difficulty, use the tips below to help yourself work through the problems.

### Tips for Solving Math Problems

1. Decide what the goal of the question is. Read or study the problem carefully and determine what information must be found.
2. Locate the factual information. Decide what information represents key facts—the ones you must use to solve the problem. You may also find facts you do not need to reach your solution. In some cases, you may determine that more information is needed to solve the problem. If so, ask yourself the following: What assumptions can I make about this problem? or Do I need a formula to help solve this problem?
3. Decide what strategies you might use to solve the problem, how you might use them, and what form your solution will be in. For example, will you need to create a graph or chart? Will you need to solve an equation? Will your answer be in words or numbers? By knowing what type of solution you should reach, you may be able to eliminate some of the choices.
4. Apply your strategy to solve the problem and compare your answer to the choices.
5. If the answer is still not clear, read the problem again. If you had to make calculations to reach your answer, use estimation to see if your answer makes sense.

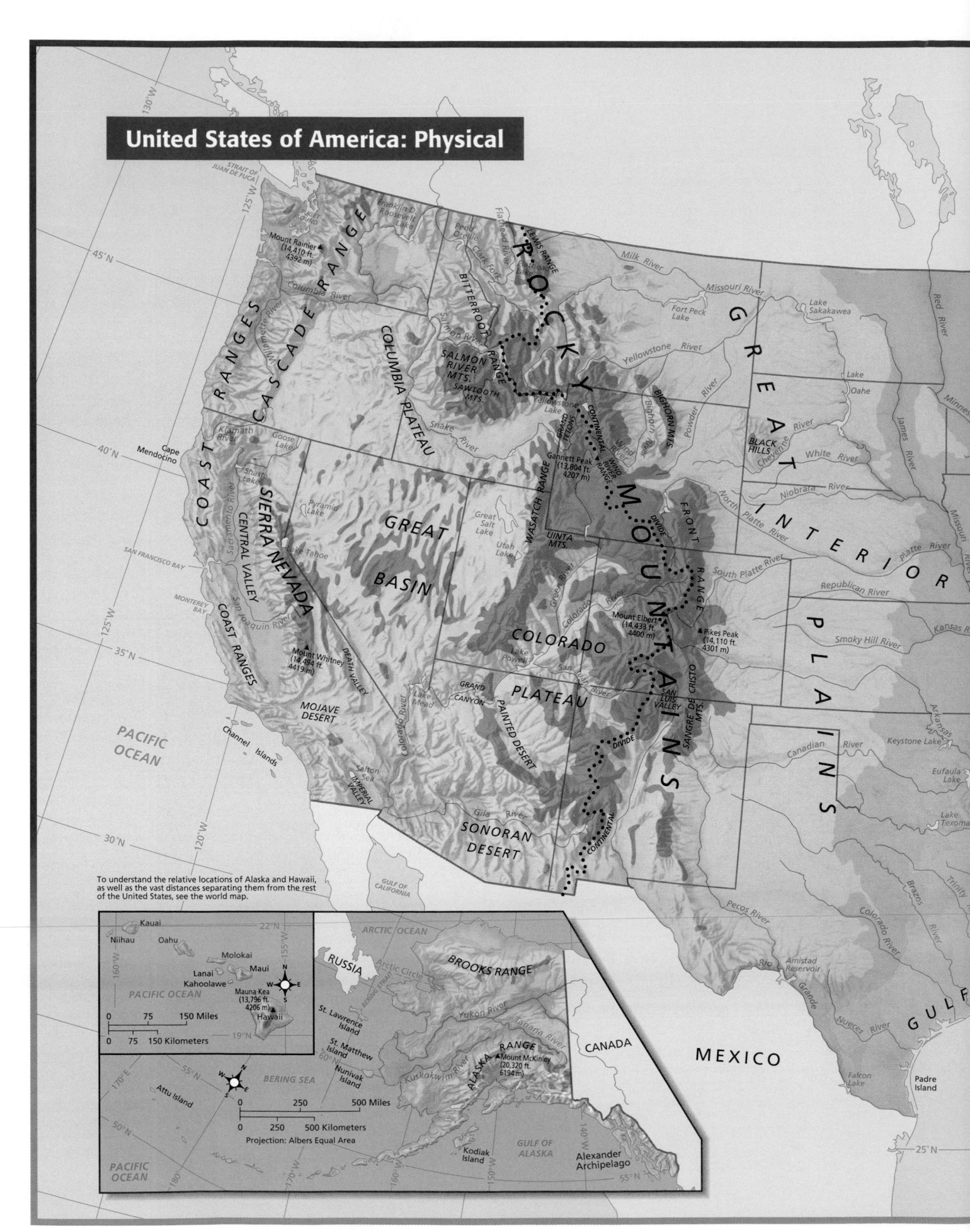

# United States of America: Physical

CANADA

MESABI RANGE
Isle Royale
Lake Superior
Lake Michigan
Lake Huron
Lake Ontario
Lake Erie

Mississippi River
Wisconsin River
Des Moines River
Illinois River
Lake of the Ozarks
Iowa River

P L A I N S

ZARK PLATEAU
OZARK PLATEAU
OUACHITA MTS.
Red River
White River
Sabine River
Toledo Bend Reservoir

Wabash River
Scioto River
Ohio River
Kentucky Lake
Lake Barkley
Cumberland River
Tennessee River
Pearl River
Alabama R.
Tombigbee River
Coosa River
Chattahoochee River
Oconee River
Altamaha River
Savannah River

ALLEGHENY PLATEAU
Allegheny River
Susquehanna River
Monongahela R.
Potomac River
Kanawha River
James River
Roanoke River
CUMBERLAND PLATEAU
GREAT SMOKY MTS.
BLUE RIDGE MOUNTAINS

A P P A L A C H I A N   M O U N T A I N S

CATSKILL MTS.
ADIRONDACK MTS.
Finger Lakes
Lake Champlain
GREEN MTS.
WHITE MTS.
LONGFELLOW MTS.
St. Lawrence River
St. Lawrence Seaway
Penobscot River
St. John River
Hudson R.
Connecticut River
Delaware River
Cape Cod
LONG ISLAND SOUND
Long Island
DELAWARE BAY
CHESAPEAKE BAY
PAMLICO SOUND
Cape Hatteras

P I E D M O N T

A T L A N T I C   C O A S T A L   P L A I N

C O A S T A L   P L A I N

Chandeleur Islands
Mississippi Delta
Sea Islands
Okefenokee Swamp

FLORIDA PENINSULA
Cape Canaveral
Lake Okeechobee
The Everglades
Cape Sable
Florida Keys
STRAITS OF FLORIDA

GULF OF MEXICO

ATLANTIC OCEAN

THE BAHAMAS

CUBA

50° N
45° N
40° N
35° N
30° N
25° N

65° W
60° W
55° W
70° W
75° W
80° W
85° W
90° W

**Elevation**

| Feet | | Meters |
|---|---|---|
| 13,120 | | 4,000 |
| 6,560 | | 2,000 |
| 1,640 | | 500 |
| 656 | | 200 |
| (Sea level) 0 | | 0 (Sea level) |
| Below sea level | | Below sea level |

Ice cap

ARCTIC OCEAN
NORTH AMERICA
EUROPE
ASIA
ATLANTIC OCEAN
AFRICA
Equator
PACIFIC OCEAN
SOUTH AMERICA
INDIAN OCEAN
AUSTRALIA
ANTARCTICA
Robinson Projection

N
W    E
S

0        250        500 Miles
0    250    500 Kilometers
Projection: Albers Equal Area

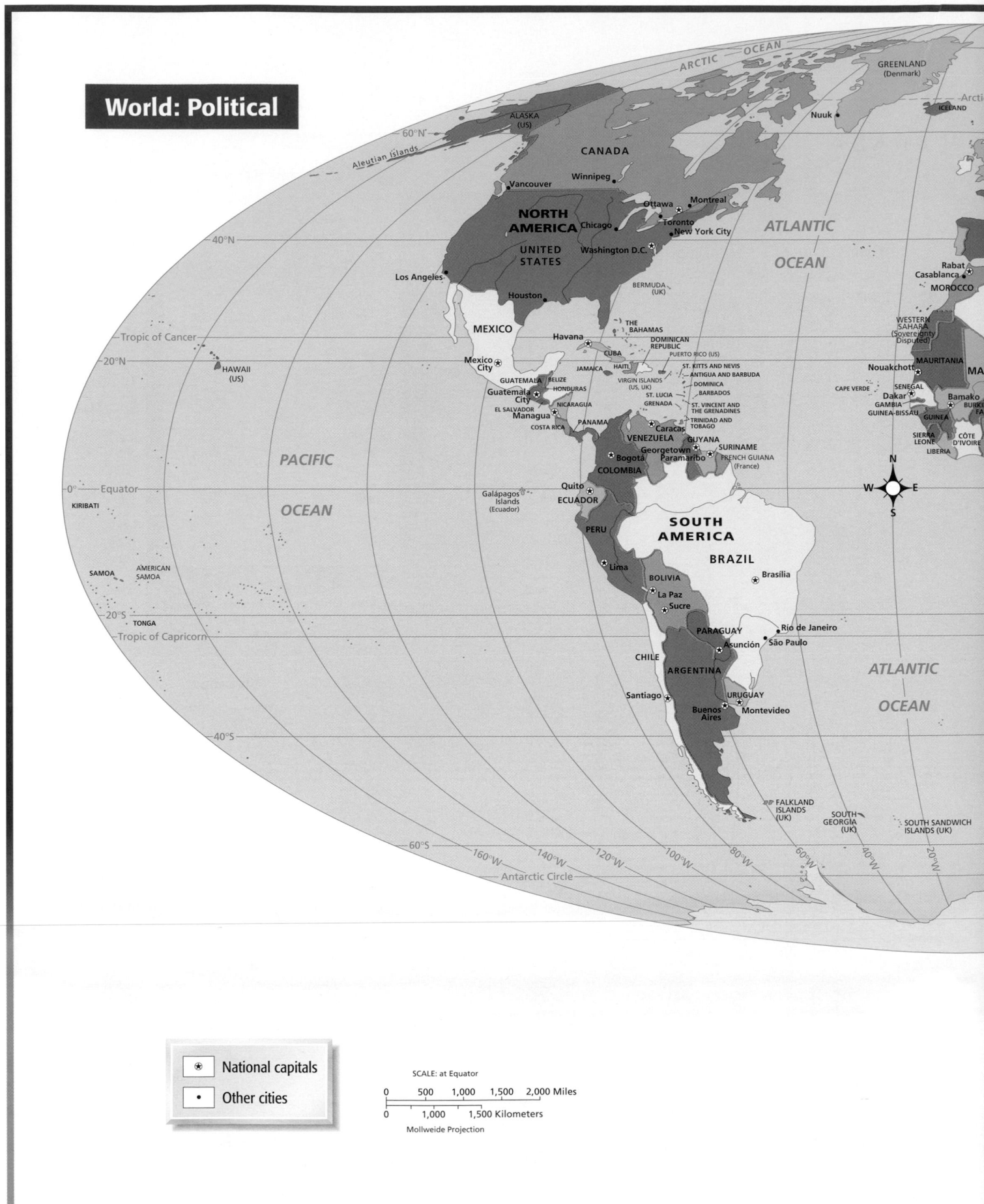

# World: Political

**National capitals**

**Other cities**

SCALE: at Equator

| 0 | 500 | 1,000 | 1,500 | 2,000 Miles |

| 0 | 1,000 | 1,500 Kilometers |

Mollweide Projection

| COUNTRY | CAPITAL |
|---|---|
| 1 Czech Republic | Prague |
| 2 Slovakia | Bratislava |
| 3 Slovenia | Ljubljana |
| 4 Croatia | Zagreb |
| 5 Bosnia and Herzegovina | Sarajevo |
| 6 Macedonia | Skopje |
| 7 Serbia and Montenegro | Belgrade |
| 8 Lithuania | Vilnius |
| 9 Latvia | Riga |
| 10 Estonia | Tallinn |

## A Tradition of Democracy

## UNIT OVERVIEW

The opening unit in *American Civics* sets the stage for an understanding of the rights and duties of U.S. citizenship. Beginning with the introduction to the first chapter, students learn about the American dream of freedom and learn about equal opportunity for all citizens. Specific information will be covered concerning the American people, their basic freedoms, and the nature of the government established to protect, promote, and defend those freedoms.

### In Their Own Words

*"The American dream that has lured tens of millions of all nations to our shores in the past century has not been a dream of merely material plenty, though that has doubtless counted heavily. It has been much more than that. It has been a dream of being able to grow to fullest development as man and woman, unhampered [unrestricted] by the barriers which had slowly been erected [built] in older civilizations, unrepressed by [free from] social orders which had developed for the benefit of classes rather than for the simple human being of any and every class. And that dream has been realized more fully in actual life here than anywhere else."*—James Truslow Adams

**Using the Quotation** Ask students to read the quotation by James Truslow Adams and have them identify what, in Adams's view, the American dream is.

**About the Author** James Truslow Adams (1878–1949) was an American historian and Pulitzer Prize-winning author of many scholarly and popular books. Born in Brooklyn, New York, Truslow worked for a time as a successful stockbroker before embarking on his writing career. His long list of books includes *The Founding of New England* (1921), for which he won a Pulitzer Prize, and *The Epic of America* (1931).

# UNIT 1
# A Tradition of Democracy

**CHAPTER 1  We the People**
**CHAPTER 2  Foundations of Government**
**CHAPTER 3  The U.S. Constitution**
**CHAPTER 4  Rights and Responsibilities**

Share the information in the chapter overviews with students. Ask them to brainstorm a list of challenges that any new government might face. Have students rank the answers that they suggested in order of importance. Organize students into groups and assign each group one of the problems that students decided was among the most important. Have each group think of at least three solutions that a government might use to meet the assigned challenge. After the students have completed the unit, ask students to look at their proposed solutions again to compare their ideas about how a new government might meet challenges with the actual responses that U.S. leaders had at the Constitutional Convention.

# Young Citizens

## IN ACTION

## Clothing People Living in Poverty

A group of New Yorkers huddle around an old table in a wind tunnel near a Port Authority bus terminal's busy entrance. On the table are stacks of thick socks, warm shirts, heavy sweaters, and other gear to shield against the bitter New York City winter. The people gathered around the table select a few items and thank the young people who are folding and arranging piles of clothing.

The leader of this volunteer team, Japheth Youmans, first began volunteering as a sixth grader with a community action organization called Fresh Youth Initiatives. As a volunteer at a food bank, Youmans noticed that many people receiving food also needed clothing. However, he could not find a space to house his clothing bank. Youmans quickly found a solution: the Washington Heights tunnel. This busy thoroughfare had plenty of pedestrian traffic from the bus station nearby—perfect for serving those in need.

One of Youmans's fellow volunteers, Heidi Lopez, has served on the board of Fresh Youth Initiatives. Heidi began volunteering as a junior high school student to complete a school assignment but continued after the assignment ended.

In recognition of their commitment to community service, Lopez and Youmans were honored at the 1998 National Basketball Association (NBA) All-Star Game. Although the event was exciting, these two teenagers remained focused on their original goal—improving their community.

Distributing clothing to people in need is one way to serve your community.

### You Decide

1. **How did Youmans first discover a need for a clothing bank in his community?**
2. **Find out what efforts are being made in your community to feed and clothe poor and homeless people. What can you and other teenagers in your community do to become involved in this effort?**

## What Can We Do?

After students research youth volunteer efforts within their community, organize them into groups. Then ask them to conduct research about community needs not being met. Have each group develop a proposal explaining how they might meet a community need that they have identified. Each group should incorporate the following into its proposal: an explanation of the need, a summary of how to meet that need, and an outline of how the plan should be implemented. As a class, discuss the various proposals and vote on the need and plan that the class would like to address. Encourage the class to begin steps to realize its plan and to meet a community need.

### YOU DECIDE ANSWERS
1. While volunteering at a food bank he recognized a need for a clothing bank as well.

2. Students' responses will vary.

# We the People

## CHAPTER RESOURCE MANAGER

| Objectives | Pacing Guide | Reproducible Resources |
|---|---|---|
| **SECTION 1:**<br>**Civics in Our Lives**<br>(pp. 3–7) | ⊞ Identify the meaning of the term *civics*.<br>⊞ Determine the ideals that form the basis of the U.S. government and the American way of life.<br>⊞ Explain the roles and qualities of a good citizen. | **Regular**<br>1 day<br>**Block Scheduling**<br>.5 day<br><br>*Block Scheduling Handbook with Team Teaching Strategies, Chapter 1* | **RS** Guided Reading Strategies 1.1<br>**RS** Readings in Economics and Government 9: "The Star-Spangled Banner"<br>**RS** Readings in Economics and Government 18: Documents of Patriotism: Pledge of Allegiance, American's Creed, Oath of Citizenship |
| **SECTION 2:**<br>**Who Are U.S. Citizens?**<br>(pp. 8–13) | ⊞ Identify North America's earliest inhabitants and when they arrived.<br>⊞ Explain the changes that have occurred in U.S. immigration policy since the early 1800s.<br>⊞ Describe how U.S. citizenship benefits people. | **Regular**<br>1.5 days<br>**Block Scheduling**<br>1 day<br><br>*Block Scheduling Handbook with Team Teaching Strategies, Chapter 1* | **RS** Guided Reading Strategies 1.2<br>**RS** Graphic Organizer Activity: Welcome to America<br>**PS** American Civics Political Cartoon: Attitudes Toward Immigration |
| **SECTION 3:**<br>**The American People Today**<br>(pp. 14–20) | ⊞ Evaluate why census information is important.<br>⊞ Explain the ways that a population grows.<br>⊞ Describe the changes that have come about in the movement of the American people from the early years of the country to the present. | **Regular**<br>1 day<br>**Block Scheduling**<br>.5 day<br><br>*Block Scheduling Handbook with Team Teaching Strategies, Chapter 1* | **RS** Guided Reading Strategies 1.3<br>**E** Creative Teaching Strategy: Learning Stations<br>**E** Challenge and Enrichment Worksheet 1: Completing a Census Form<br>**SM** Community Service and Participation Handbook: What Does the Government Know About Your Community? |

### Chapter Resource Key

| | | | | |
|---|---|---|---|---|
| **PS** | Primary Sources | **SM** | Skills Mastery |  CD–ROM |
| **RS** | Reading Support | **A** | Assessment |  Video |
| **IC** | Interdisciplinary Connections | **REV** | Review | Internet |
| **E** | Enrichment | **ELL** | Reinforcement and English Language Learners |  Holt Presentation Maker Using Microsoft® PowerPoint® |
| | | | Transparencies | |

 **One-Stop** Planner CD–ROM

See the *One-Stop Planner* for a complete list of additional resources for students and teachers.

## One-Stop Planner CD–ROM

It's easy to plan lessons, select resources, and print out materials for your students when you use the *One-Stop Planner CD–ROM with Test Generator*.

| Technology Resources | Reinforcement, Review, and Assessment |
|---|---|
| One-Stop Planner, Lesson 1.1 | REV Section 1 Review, p. 7 |
| Citizenship Skills Videocassette: The Roles of a Citizen | A Daily Quiz 1.1 |
| Homework Practice Online | ELL Main Idea Activity 1.1 |
| | ELL English Audio Summary 1.1 |
| | ELL Spanish Audio Summary 1.1 |
| One-Stop Planner, Lesson 1.2 | REV Section 2 Review, p. 13 |
| CNN. Presents: American Government | A Daily Quiz 1.2 |
| Homework Practice Online | ELL Main Idea Activity 1.2 |
| HRW Go site | ELL English Audio Summary 1.2 |
| | ELL Spanish Audio Summary 1.2 |
| One-Stop Planner, Lesson 1.3 | REV Section 3 Review, p. 20 |
| Holt Researcher CD–ROM | A Daily Quiz 1.3 |
| Homework Practice Online | ELL Main Idea Activity 1.3 |
| | ELL English Audio Summary 1.3 |
| | ELL Spanish Audio Summary 1.3 |

### internet connect

go.hrw.com

**HRW ONLINE RESOURCES**
GO TO: go.hrw.com
Then type in the keyword.

**TEACHER HOME PAGE**
KEYWORD: SZ3 Teacher

**CHAPTER INTERNET ACTIVITIES**
KEYWORD: SZ3 AC1
Choose an activity to:
- create thematic charts and graphs on demographic trends.
- write journal entries from the point of view of citizens that made a difference in their communities.
- make an oral presentation on immigration policy and the naturalization process.

**CHAPTER ENRICHMENT LINKS**
KEYWORD: SZ3 CH1

**ONLINE ASSESSMENT**
Homework Practice
KEYWORD: SZ3 HP1
Rubrics
KEYWORD: SS Rubrics

**ONLINE MAPS, CHARTS, AND GRAPHS**
KEYWORD: SZ3 MCG
- How an Alien Becomes a Citizen

**HOLT PRESENTATION MAKER**
KEYWORD: SZ3 PPT1

**CONTENT UPDATES**
KEYWORD: SS Content Updates

**ONLINE READING SUPPORT**
KEYWORD: SS Strategies

**CURRENT EVENTS**
KEYWORD: S3 Current Events

## Meeting Individual Needs

### Ability Levels

**Level 1** Basic-level activities designed for all students encountering new material

**Level 2** Intermediate-level activities designed for average students

**Level 3** Challenging activities designed for honors and gifted-and-talented students

**English Language Learners** Activities that address the needs of students with Limited English Proficiency

## Chapter Review and Assessment

- IC Vocabulary Activity 1
- Global Skill Builder CD–ROM
- HRW Go site
- REV Chapter 1 Tutorial for Students, Parents, Mentors, and Peers
- REV Chapter 1 Review, pp. 22–23
- A Standardized Test Practice
- A Chapter 1 Test Generator (on the One-Stop Planner)
- A Chapter 1 Test (Form A or B)
- A Alternative Assessment Handbook
- A Chapter 1 Test for English Language Learners and Special-Needs Students

Section 1    Civics in Our Lives

Section 2    Who Are U.S. Citizens?

Section 3    The American People Today

## What's Your Opinion?

To help students create their *Themes* Journal entries, provide the following examples of appropriate **agree**/**disagree** statements.

● **Agree**   All citizens must do their part to make democracy work.

**Disagree**   In a democratic society, one is free to choose not to perform his or her civic duties.

● **Agree**   The United States was founded by immigrants, therefore all immigrants should be welcome.

**Disagree**   Not all people seeking citizenship will have something to offer the country.

● **Agree**   The government can better serve the needs of its people with current census information.

**Disagree**   The census requires such a high expenditure of time, money, and effort that every decade is sufficient.

## Internet Activity

**Citizens Making a Difference**

**TOPIC:** Citizens Making a Difference
**GO TO:** go.hrw.com
**KEYWORD:** SZ3 AC1

Have students access the Internet through the HRW Go site to conduct research about incidents in which ordinary citizens made a difference in their communities, states, or nation. Then ask students to write a series of journal entries from the point of view of one of the people profiled at the Web site. As an extension, ask students to explain how the episodes illustrate American ideals, the roles of the citizen, and the qualities of good citizenship.

# 1 We the People

## Build on What You Know

Have you ever heard the term *American dream*? It refers to the hope of a better life for everyone. This dream began in colonial times and continues to draw thousands of people to the United States each year. For many people the American dream has meant freedom from religious persecution or from political upheavals and wars. For others it has meant freedom to achieve economic success. As an American, you have the freedom to pursue your own dream and a duty to protect this precious heritage of freedom.

## What's Your Opinion?

Do you **agree** or **disagree** with the following statements? Support your point of view in your journal.

- All citizens have the responsibility to participate in their government.

- Every person who comes to the United States seeking citizenship should be granted it.

- Census information is so important it should be collected every 5 years.

# SECTION 1

## OBJECTIVES

*After completing Section 1, students should be able to*

1 Identify the meaning of the term *civics.*

2 Determine the ideals that form the basis of the U.S. government and the American way of life.

3 Explain the roles and qualities of a good citizen.

## 🔊 LET'S GET STARTED!

As students enter the classroom, ask them the following question: What rights do you enjoy as an American? Compare students' responses to find the rights mentioned most often. *(Students' lists might include the right to an education or to speak freely.)* Explain to the class that in exchange for participation, people in a democracy receive certain rights. Tell students that in Section 1 they will learn more about civic rights and responsibilities and the privileges of freedom.

## SECTION 1

# Civics in Our Lives

### Read to Discover

1. What is civics?
2. What ideals form the basis of the U.S. government and the American way of life?
3. What are the roles and qualities of a good citizen?

### Define

- civics
- citizen
- government

#### WHY CIVICS MATTERS

People and the government continue to work together to preserve freedom and ensure equality for all Americans. Use **CNNfyi.com** or other **current events** sources to investigate suggested laws that seek to uphold these American ideals. Record your findings in your journal.

## SECTION 1 RESOURCES

### REPRODUCIBLE

- ▶ Guided Reading Strategies 1.1
- ▶ Readings in Economics and Government 9: "The Star-Spangled Banner"
- ▶ Readings in Economics and Government 18: Documents of Patriotism: Pledge of Allegiance, American's Creed, Oath of Citizenship

### TECHNOLOGY

- ▶ One-Stop Planner, Lesson 1.1
- ▶ Homework Practice Online
- ▶ Citizenship Skills Videocassette: The Roles of a Citizen

### REINFORCEMENT, REVIEW, AND ASSESSMENT

- ▶ Section 1 Review, p. 7
- ▶ Daily Quiz 1.1
- ▶ Main Idea Activity 1.1
- ▶ English Audio Summary 1.1
- ▶ Spanish Audio Summary 1.1

## *Reading Focus*

What is civics? Why do we study this subject in school? What does civics have to do with my life? These are some of the questions you may be asking as you begin your civics course.

Many of the subjects you study in school teach you about the priceless rights you enjoy as an American. The civics course you are about to begin will explain how you can help keep this heritage alive.

*The American flag features a star for every state and stripes representing the original 13 states of the Union.*

### ⭐ The Meaning of Civics

**Civics** is the study of what it means to be a U.S. **citizen**—a legally recognized member of the country. The word *civics* comes from the Latin *civis,* meaning "citizen." The concept of citizenship originated in ancient Greece and was then adopted by the Romans. The term has changed a great deal since the days of the ancient Romans. At that time, the Romans used the term to separate people living in the city of Rome from those born in territories that Rome had conquered. Today almost everyone is a citizen of a country. In the United States, people are citizens of both the country and the state in which they live.

The rights and responsibilities of being a citizen have also changed over time. Furthermore, they differ from country to country. They depend on a country's type of government. **Government** is the organizations, institutions, and individuals who exercise authority as a political unit over a group of people. Under the U.S. system of government,

# TEACH OBJECTIVE 1

**LEVEL 1:** Explain that the term *civics* comes from the Latin word *civis*, meaning "citizen," and is the study of the duties and responsibilities of citizenship. Discuss with students why it is important to study civics. Then ask students about real-life situations in which people use civics. Write students' responses on the chalkboard. (*Students might suggest that people use it when voting, when participating in volunteer activities, or when promoting a new law or issue that affects them.*)
**ENGLISH LANGUAGE LEARNERS**

**LEVEL 2:** Write the definition of the term *civics* on the chalkboard: *the study of the duties and responsibilities of citizenship*. Remind students that U.S. citizens have a variety of rights that citizens of other countries do not receive. In exchange for these rights, U.S. citizens have certain responsibilities to fulfill. Have students work in pairs to list some of the rights and responsibilities that they think U.S. citizens have. Tell them to prioritize their lists. Then call on volunteers to share their lists and to explain why they think it is important to study the rights and responsibilities of citizenship. **COOPERATIVE LEARNING**

## ★ Global Perspectives

**The Fight for Equality**
Throughout history, governments have limited the rights of some of their citizens (such as limiting an African American's right to vote using Jim Crow laws), in effect conferring upon them a sort of second-class citizenship. At various times in history, governments have come to see citizenship in more democratic terms. One result of the French revolution in 1789, for example, was the elimination of privileged classes in France. After the Revolution, people began to address everyone simply as "citizen." This equalizing title reflected their belief in the freedom and equality of all people.

**ACTIVITY:** Have students conduct research from outside sources to determine the reasons for the French Revolution. Then have them work in pairs to create a graphic organizer that compares the French Revolution's causes to those of the American Revolution. Display graphic organizers in the classroom.

## Visual Record Answer

*Students might suggest that they are building a house for charity.*

citizens have many rights and responsibilities. Your civics course will help you discover the most important ones.

You will discover that being a U.S. citizen means more than enjoying the rights that the U.S. system provides. It includes being a productive and sharing member of society. Americans participate in society in many ways. For example, almost all Americans belong to a family, go to school for several years, and work with other people. Americans are also members of their communities—villages, towns, and cities. Being an effective citizen of the United States means fulfilling your duties and responsibilities as a member of each of these various groups and communities.

✔ **Reading Check Summarizing** What topics will be covered in your civics course? the rights and responsibilities of U.S. citizenship

## ★ American Ideals

As a citizen of the United States, you have many different reasons to take pride in your country. It is a land of great natural beauty and of many hardworking creative people. You can also be proud of the ideals and beliefs that form the basis of this great country.

The U.S. government and the American way of life are based on the ideals of freedom and equality. As U.S. citizens, we are all guaranteed the same rights and freedoms. These rights and freedoms are protected by laws. Thus, they cannot be taken from any citizen who follows the laws of his or her community, state, and country. As a U.S. citizen, you must be willing to do your share to protect this heritage of liberty. It has been handed down from one generation of Americans to the next for more than 200 years.

✔ **Reading Check Analyzing Information** What ideals shape the American way of life? freedom and equality

**Interpreting the Visual Record**

Community participation *One of the strengths of any community is the willingness of its members to volunteer their time and effort to help others.* **What work are these volunteers doing in their community?**

**ALL LEVELS:** Copy the following graphic organizer onto the chalkboard, omitting the italicized answers. Ask each student to complete the organizer to determine the ideals that form the basis of the U.S. government and the American way of life. **ENGLISH LANGUAGE LEARNERS**

**American Ideals**
• *freedom*
• *equality*

**HOMEWORK** Have students refer to their copy of the graphic organizer created in the previous exercise. Ask students to illustrate examples of these ideals using words and pictures from magazines and newspapers as well as original drawings.

**LEVEL 3:** Organize the class into groups of four. Have each group create a children's book designed to teach elementary students about the ideals that form the basis of the U.S. government and the American way of life. *(Students' books should illustrate the ideals of freedom and equality.)* Encourage students to be creative in their depictions. **COOPERATIVE LEARNING**

## ★ A Heritage of Freedom

One important freedom protected in the United States directly concerns you as you read this textbook. It is the freedom to learn. Most Americans believe that every young citizen should learn about our country and the world by receiving a well-rounded education. To that end, our state and local governments provide free public schools for all young citizens. Each state also has public and private colleges and universities for those who wish to continue their education past high school.

Another important freedom is the freedom to choose a job or career. U.S. law guarantees that all persons qualified for a job have an equal opportunity to secure it.

Americans are fortunate to have many other freedoms as well. We may live as we wish, so long as we respect the rights of others. We are free to own a house, raise a family, and choose our own spiritual belief. We may start our own business, travel, and live anywhere in the country. We are free to speak and write what we wish, provided our words do not unjustly harm another person. We may not be arrested or imprisoned without just cause.

✔ **Reading Check Supporting a Point of View** Which one of the freedoms listed above do you think is the most important, and why? Answers will vary but should illustrate a knowledge of the freedoms listed above.

## ★ Government by the People

The leaders who planned our government created a system intended to guarantee freedom. The form of government that they established remains strong today. Under the U.S. form of government, the *people* rule through the officials they elect.

These officials are responsible to the people. If elected officials do not do their jobs properly, they can be voted out of office at election time. Officials can also be removed from office before the end of their terms if necessary. By creating this system, the founders of this country ensured that the government would continue to serve the American people.

As a U.S. citizen, you have many freedoms. Being a citizen involves many responsibilities as well. Voting in elections is one of the most important of these responsibilities.

You can also help in other ways to choose the men and women who will govern. You can work for a political party, for example. Anyone

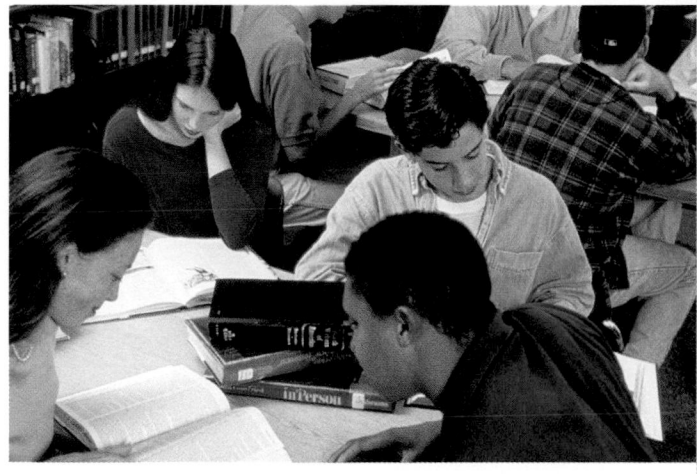

**Interpreting the Visual Record**

**Free schools** *Free public schools and the opportunity to learn are one of the major benefits our country provides to young Americans.* **How are these students spending their school time?**

## ★ The Democratic Process

**By the People for the People** "Government by the people" requires people capable of governing. In the 1800s, Thomas Jefferson believed that the new American country could succeed only if it had a well-informed electorate. Enlightened citizens, he thought, must be educated citizens. To that end, he introduced several education bills in Virginia. In the 2000s, government-backed education measures continue to support civics training in the United States. The National Assessment of Educational Progress (NAEP) tracks long-term trends in the basic achievement of American students in selected areas of study, including civics. Assessments are conducted on the state level. Information is then compiled to determine national trends.

**CRITICAL THINKING**

Why do you think it is important to monitor trends in civics education?

**ANSWER:** Students might observe the need for citizens to be aware of civics issues, beginning when they are students.

**Visual Record Answer**

*Students might suggest that they are learning.*

# TEACH OBJECTIVE 3

## TEACHER TO TEACHER

Don Timpel of Wisconsin recommends the following activity:

**LEVEL 1:** Lead a class discussion about the roles and qualities of a good citizen. *(Students' suggestions for roles might include voting, working for a political party, informing officials of one's needs; qualities may include being responsible, respectful and obedient, loyal, active in public life, and being well informed.)* Then ask each student to create a poster illustrating one thing that they can do to be "good citizens" both now and in the future.

**ENGLISH LANGUAGE LEARNERS**

**LEVEL 3:** Organize the class into two groups. Then have students use what they have learned about the roles and qualities of a good citizen to debate the following statement: *If you obey all laws, you have fulfilled your responsibilities as an American citizen.* Groups should address the question of whether being a good citizen means more than simply obeying laws.

**COOPERATIVE LEARNING**

## CLOSE

Ask students to list the rights of U.S. citizens. Write their responses on the chalkboard. Then ask what the responsibilities of a citizen are. Write the responses in a second list. Lead a discussion in which students compare the lists, emphasizing the give-and-take of citizenship.

---

### Interdisciplinary Connection

▶ **Sociology** ◀

**Amish Values** Various cultures and societies emphasize different aspects of good citizenship. Among the Old Order Amish, for example, devotion to family, the land, and "plain living" are marks of good citizenship. The Amish—the majority of whom live today in Pennsylvania, Ohio, and Indiana—are a strict religious group whose members avoid anything of a "worldly nature." They do not use automobiles, electricity, telephones, indoor plumbing, modern technology, or anything else from the non-Amish world. All aspects of the Amish culture revolve around the home and family life. Amish families are self sufficient. They produce their own food, clothing, soap, quilts, and furniture. Amish communities focus on intensive farming. Because modern farm equipment is forbidden, the work is difficult and demanding, yet hard work is expected of good citizens.

**CRITICAL THINKING**

How are Amish values reflected in Amish life?

**ANSWER:** Students might suggest that they focus on family, farming, and avoiding worldly things.

### Visual Record Answer

*Students' responses will vary.*

**Interpreting the Visual Record**

**Your role** *This young man is handing out information on an issue that he finds important. Staying informed on issues is a key part of being an active citizen.* **What issues might you want to share information on with others?**

who answers telephones, stuffs envelopes, or helps plan meetings of a political party is playing a part in the U.S. political system.

It is also your responsibility as a thoughtful citizen to inform officials of your needs or disagreements with government actions or policies. For example, you can write or call public officials or send letters to editors of newspapers. Knowing how your government works will help you carry out your duties and responsibilities as a citizen.

Studying civics is one key to understanding the workings of government. This text will introduce you to the organization and function of government at the national, state, and local levels. As you study the structure and purposes of government, you will learn what an important part it plays in your life. You will also learn your role in government.

✔ **Reading Check Summarizing** How does the U.S. system of government ensure that officials are responsible to the people, and how can citizens become involved in government? They depend upon the people to be elected, and they risk losing re-election if they do not do their jobs properly. Citizens can inform officials of their concerns and learn how government works.

## ★ Qualities of a Good Citizen

As a U.S. citizen and a future voter, you will play a vital role in determining the future of the country. Your participation is necessary for the U.S. form of government to work.

How can you become an effective citizen? What qualities will you need? Here is a list of 10 characteristics of a good citizen. You can probably think of several more. Good citizens

1. are responsible family members,
2. respect and obey the laws of the land,
3. respect the rights and property of others,
4. are loyal to their country and proud of its accomplishments,
5. take part in and improve life in their communities,
6. take an active part in their government,
7. use natural resources wisely,
8. are well informed on important issues and are willing to take a stand on these issues when conscience demands it,
9. believe in equality of opportunity for all people, and
10. respect individual differences, points of view, and ways of life that are different from their own.

✔ **Reading Check Drawing Inferences and Conclusions** What are some similarities among the characteristics of a good citizen? Students' responses may include consideration of others, loyalty, participation, responsibility, and respect.

## REVIEW AND ASSESS

Have students complete the **Section 1 Review** on page 7. Then have students complete **Daily Quiz 1.1**. As **Alternative Assessment**, you may want to use the children's book or profiling activities in this section's lessons.

## RETEACH

Have students complete **Main Idea Activity for English Language Learners and Special-Needs Students 1.1**. Then pair students and ask them to create an outline for this section. After they have finished their outlines, ask pairs to present their outlines to the class.

**ENGLISH LANGUAGE LEARNERS , COOPERATIVE LEARNING**

## EXTEND

Have students read the Declaration of Independence and the Preamble to the Constitution. Then ask each student to write an essay discussing how these documents reflect the ideals that form the basis of the U.S. government and the American way of life. Invite volunteers to discuss their essays with the class. **BLOCK SCHEDULING**

---

## ★ The Importance of Civics

Every American should understand how our system of government operates and why citizens must take part in it. Participation has always been a basic principle of the U.S. form of government.

In your study of civics, you will learn a great deal about U.S. government. Your study will also include many other topics that concern most U.S. citizens. You will study how communities serve their people and some of the challenges these communities face.

You will also read about the U.S. economic system and the opportunities it creates. You will learn why citizens must pay taxes. You will study jobs and careers and learn what training and abilities they require. You will discover how the education system works and how you can get the most from your school years. You will read about U.S. relations with other countries and learn how over the years the United States has become a world leader.

Being a U.S. citizen is something we often take for granted. However, becoming a responsible and effective citizen requires effort and training, just as becoming a good athlete or musician does. The country needs citizens who are well informed and who are willing to take part in determining how the government acts. Meeting the obligations of citizenship is an important challenge. This textbook was written to help you learn to meet that challenge.

**Interpreting the Visual Record**

**Civics and you** *Being a good citizen is an important responsibility and can be challenging.* **How are these young women expressing their civic pride?**

✔ **Reading Check** Supporting a Point of View Why do you think that studying civics is important? Students' responses will vary but should reflect an understanding that an informed citizen can better effect change in a democracy.

---

**go.hrw.com** **Homework Practice Online**

keyword: SZ3 HP1

## SECTION 1 Review

1. **Define** and explain:
   • civics
   • citizen
   • government

2. **Categorizing** Copy the graphic organizer to the right. Use it to identify the roles and qualities of a good U.S. citizen.

3. **Finding the Main Idea**
   a. What will you learn in your civics class?
   b. Upon what ideals is U.S. government based, and how are these ideals reflected in the American way of life?

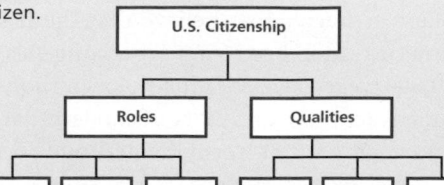

4. **Writing and Critical Thinking**
   **Summarizing** Imagine that you head a committee to encourage good citizenship in your community. Create a chart showing five goals you want your committee to achieve and suggestions for achieving each goal.

   **Consider:**
   • the roles of a U.S. citizen
   • the effect citizens can have on government

---

**Visual Record Answer**

*Students might suggest that they appear to be saying the pledge of allegiance.*

## Section 1 Review
### ANSWERS

**1. Define**
• civics, p. 3
• citizen, p. 3
• government, p. 3

**2.** roles: voting, taking an active role in a campaign for a candidate, to inform officials of your needs; qualities: responsible, respectful and obedient, loyal, active in public life, and well informed

**3. a.** the duties and responsibilities of citizenship

**b.** freedom and equality; included in everyday life in such areas as the availability of equal education in public schools and the freedom to choose a career

**4.** Students' answers will vary but may include increasing voter registration, encouraging community clean ups, circulating petitions, encouraging volunteerism, and starting community watch programs.

# SECTION 2

## OBJECTIVES

After completing Section 2, students should be able to

1 **Identify North America's earliest inhabitants and when they arrived.**

2 **Explain the changes that have occurred in U.S. immigration policy since the early 1800s.**

3 **Describe how U.S. citizenship benefits people.**

## LET'S GET STARTED!

Write the following statement on the chalkboard: *The United States is a country founded upon immigration.* Allow students time to share their reactions to the statement. Then ask students why they think some people might believe that it is necessary to limit immigration to the United States. *(Students might suggest scarcity of land or jobs as well as discrimination.)* Tell students that in Section 2 they will learn about the history of immigration to the United States.

# SECTION 2

# Who Are U.S. Citizens?

### Read to Discover

1. Who were North America's earliest inhabitants, and when did they arrive?

2. What changes have occurred in U.S. immigration policy since the early 1800s?

3. How does U.S. citizenship benefit people?

### WHY CIVICS MATTERS

Many people continue to migrate to the United States today. Use **CNNfyi.com** or other **current events** sources to research how the immigrant population in the United States has changed in recent years. Record your findings in your journal.

### Define

• immigrants
• quotas
• aliens
• refugees
• native-born citizen
• deport
• naturalization

*English colonists were encouraged to settle in areas such as Virginia by advertising.*

## Reading Focus

The heritage of freedom and equality in what is now the United States was formed bit by bit. Over time, groups from various parts of the world have settled here, contributing to American society. Today all Americans can be proud of the heritage we share. We are primarily **immigrants**—people who came here from other lands—or descendants of immigrants.

From their countries of origin, immigrants brought different languages, ideas, beliefs, customs, hopes, and dreams. These different ways of life mixed with the ideas and ways of life of people already present in North America. This multicultural heritage has given a special energy and richness to American society that would not be possible otherwise.

### ★ Early Americans

Archaeologists—scientists who study the remains of past cultures—have tried to discover where the first Americans originally came from. Many archaeologists believe that the first people to settle in North America came here from Siberia in Asia between about 12,000 and 40,000 years ago. Gradually, over thousands of years, these early Americans—the ancestors of modern-day American Indians—moved into many parts of North, Central, and South America.

The Vikings came to North America about A.D. 1000 but did not establish permanent settlements. In 1492 Christopher Columbus sailed

**LEVEL 1:** Organize the class into groups. Have each group prepare a glossary entry. Their entries should identify North America's earliest people and when they arrived. *(Students should identify that Native Americans were the first people in the United States, and that they came between 12,000 and 40,000 years ago.)* Ask a volunteer to read his or her group's glossary entry to the class.
**ENGLISH LANGUAGE LEARNERS , COOPERATIVE LEARNING**

**LEVEL 3:** Ask students to create a jacket cover for a book identifying the first people in the United States and when they arrived, as discussed in this section. Then have students write their title on the cover and create an illustration to accompany it. They should write an "excerpt" of the book on the back cover. On the left inside cover, have students create a mock table of contents and on the right inside cover have them write a brief summary about the book. *(See the Level 1 lesson for answers.)*

## Historical Document

### THE GETTYSBURG ADDRESS

*In November 1863, President Abraham Lincoln dedicated the national cemetery at Gettysburg, Pennsylvania, the scene of a bloody Civil War battle. His speech reaffirms our country's dedication to liberty and continues to inspire Americans today.*

"Fourscore and seven years ago our fathers brought forth on this continent a new nation, conceived in liberty, and dedicated to the proposition that all men are created equal. Now we are engaged in a great civil war, testing whether that nation, or any nation so conceived and so dedicated can long endure. We are met on a great battlefield of that war. We have come to dedicate a portion of that field as a final resting place for those who here gave their lives that that nation might live. It is altogether fitting and proper that we do this.

But, in a larger sense, we cannot dedicate—we cannot consecrate—we cannot hallow—this ground. The brave men, living and dead, who struggled here, have consecrated it far above our poor power to add or detract. The world will little note nor long remember what we say here, but it can never forget what they did here. It is for us, the living, rather, to be dedicated here to the unfinished work which they who fought here have thus far so nobly advanced. It is rather for us to be here dedicated to the great task remaining before us—that from these honored dead we take increased devotion to the cause for which they gave the last full measure of devotion; that we here highly resolve that these dead shall not have died in vain; that this nation, under God, shall have a new birth of freedom; and that government of the people, by the people, for the people, shall not perish from the earth.

**Analyzing Primary Sources**
1. What principles does Lincoln say the United States was founded or conceived upon?
2. What is the cause that Lincoln says his fellow Americans must be devoted to?

**internet connect**
go.hrw.com

**TOPIC:** Immigration and Naturalization
**GO TO:** go.hrw.com
**KEYWORD:**SZ3 AC1

Have students access the Internet through the HRW Go site to research the process of immigration and naturalization in the United States. Then have students give an oral presentation outlining the current policy regarding immigration, the process by which a person is granted legal alien status, and the process by which a person can become a naturalized citizen.

### ★★★★★★★★★★★★ That's Interesting! ★★★★★★★★★★★★

Christians were not the only European newcomers to the American colonies. There were also several large Jewish communities. The first such settlement was in the Dutch colony of New Amsterdam (now New York) in 1654. Groups of Jews also settled in Newport, Rhode Island, and Savannah, Georgia. In 1800 the 600 Jews of Charleston, South Carolina, comprised the largest Jewish population of any U.S. city.

to the Americas and claimed land for the Spanish crown. Columbus and his crew were the first Europeans to build lasting settlements. Spanish explorers settled in the Caribbean, Mexico, Central and South America, and what are now Florida, Texas, California, and the southwestern United States.

The original thirteen colonies were settled mostly by people from the British Isles. Colonists from other countries included Germans in Pennsylvania, Dutch along the Hudson River, Swedes along the Delaware River, and French in New York, Massachusetts, and South Carolina. Many Africans also came to the Americas. Unlike other immigrants, most of them were brought to the Americas as slaves. They and their children were forced to live in bondage for many years.

✔ **Reading Check Categorizing** What groups settled in the Americas, and in what region did each group settle? Siberians—many parts of North America; Spaniards—Caribbean, Mexico, Central and South America, and parts of North America; Germans—Pennsylvania; Dutch—Hudson River; Swedes—Delaware River; French—New York, Massachusetts, and South Carolina

### ★ U.S. Immigration Policy

Since its founding, the United States has been settled and populated by people from all over the world. During its early history, the new country provided economic opportunities for immigrants. In addition,

### ★★★★★★★★★★★★ That's Interesting! ★★★★★★★★★★★★

**The Americans** Why don't the people of Brazil, Canada, or Mexico call themselves Americans? After all, they are residents of either North or South America just like citizens of the United States. The reason the term *American* is generally reserved for U.S. citizens is that the United States of America was the first independent country in the Western Hemisphere. By the time Mexico and other countries achieved independence in the 1800s, the *American* label already had a specific meaning—a citizen of the United States of America.

**ANALYZING PRIMARY SOURCES ANSWERS**
1. liberty and equality
2. preserving the U.S. form of government

# TEACH OBJECTIVE 2

**ALL LEVELS:** Organize students into pairs. Then ask members of each pair to take turns playing the roles of an immigrant applying for citizenship and an immigration official—both in the 1800s and now. Ask pairs to present their dramatization to the class. (You might set up a mock immigration office.) Then lead the class in a discussion about the changes that have taken place in U.S. immigration policy since the 1800s. *(In the early 1800s the United States needed workers so it had an "open-shore" policy. In the late 1800s, competition for jobs and land increased, leading to restrictions in immigration that continue today.)* **ENGLISH LANGUAGE LEARNERS** , **COOPERATIVE LEARNING**

**LEVEL 3:** Organize the class into groups. Have each group use what it learned from the section to identify the conditions in the United States prior to the use of quotas in the early 1900s and again prior to 1990. Remind students that economic and political conditions are some of the reasons for limits to immigration. Have groups debate what they believe U.S. immigration policy should have been in the early 1900s and what it should be now. **COOPERATIVE LEARNING**

## ★ Global Perspectives

### The Plight of Refugees

Point out that many immigrants to the United States throughout the country's history have been refugees trying to escape from trouble spots around the world. Refugees flee the violence of war and persecution by oppressive governments. They are also a major part of the massive movement of people throughout the world. In fact, some officials put the total number of refugees in the world in 2000 at 14 million. It is estimated that about three quarters of refugees worldwide are currently from countries in the Middle East and Africa. Some reports indicate that 5 million people were displaced during the Persian Gulf conflict of 1990 and 1991 alone.

### CRITICAL THINKING

What are some reasons that people flee their country?

**ANSWER:** Students should suggest that people hope to escape violence and persecution.

### Visual Record Answer

*Students might suggest that if future immigrants hear of U.S. citizens that are of their culture, they will feel more comfortable in the United States.*

**Interpreting the Visual Record**

**Faces of America** *The faces of these young American citizens show the diversity of the U.S. population.* **How do you think such diversity might encourage future immigrants to come to the United States?**

agricultural workers and factory laborers were needed as the economy expanded and the country grew. As a result, there were few limitations on immigration during the first half of the 1800s.

Because some immigrants were willing to work for lower wages than many U.S. citizens were, some Americans wanted to change the country's immigration policy. During the 1880s the federal government placed some restrictions on immigration. In the 1920s the United States began limiting the number of immigrants who could be admitted to the country each year. The government also established **quotas**—set numbers—for how many immigrants could come from a particular country or region.

U.S. immigration policy today is guided by the Immigration Act of 1990. Under this law the cap on immigration for 1995 and beyond was set at 675,000 immigrants a year. Preference is given to spouses and children of U.S. citizens and permanent resident **aliens** and to people who have valuable job skills. Aliens are people in the United States who are citizens of another country. **Refugees,** or people fleeing persecution in their home countries, are not subject to this annual limit. Instead, the president works with Congress to set limits for the number of refugees allowed to enter the United States.

In recent decades many immigrants to the United States have come from Asia and Latin America. Some of these people immigrated to the United States to escape wars, political conflicts, and other crises in their home countries. Others come to meet family members already living in the United States or to expand their economic opportunities.

✔ **Reading Check** Comparing and Contrasting What are the similarities and differences between permanent resident aliens and refugees? They both have citizenship in another country, however refugees seek to escape persecution in their home country.

## ★ Citizenship by Birth

Millions of immigrants have become U.S. citizens. Some citizens belong to families that have lived in the United States for many generations. Other Americans were born in foreign countries. All citizens, regardless of their heritage, have the same legal rights and responsibilities.

Americans gain their citizenship either by birth or by a special legal process. Most of the population became U.S. citizens by birth. If you were born in any U.S. state or territory, you automatically became a **native-born citizen.** If one or both of your parents were U.S. citizens, you became a citizen by birth. This is the case even if they were living in a foreign country when you were born. Thus, citizenship can be acquired by people's place of birth or through their parents.

**ALL LEVELS:** Copy the following graphic organizer onto the chalkboard, omitting the italicized answers. Ask each student to complete the chart listing the benefits of U.S. citizenship. **ENGLISH LANGUAGE LEARNERS**

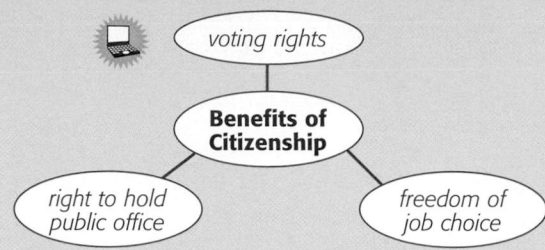

*voting rights*

**Benefits of Citizenship**

*right to hold public office*

*freedom of job choice*

**HOMEWORK** In the previous exercise students listed the benefits of U.S. citizenship. Tell them to write a few sentences to explain why they think these rights are reserved for citizens. *(Students might suggest that because citizens fulfill such responsibilities as paying taxes, they earn those rights.)*

**LEVELS 2 AND 3:** Organize students into small groups. Have each group imagine that they are on a "national citizenship committee." Then ask them to design and write poster-sized advertisements seeking U.S. citizens. Advertisements should highlight the benefits of U.S. citizenship. *(Posters should highlight voting, holding public office, and choosing any job.)* Also encourage students to incorporate other appropriate ideas or statements from the section into their posters. **COOPERATIVE LEARNING**

---

What about children born in this country whose parents are citizens of a foreign country? Are they citizens of the United States? In most cases they are.

What about children born here whose parents are officials representing a foreign country? They are not U.S. citizens because their parents are under the authority of another country. All cases involving claims of U.S. citizenship are handled by the Immigration and Naturalization Service (INS), an agency of the U.S. Department of Justice.

✔ **Reading Check Finding the Main Idea** Under what circumstances are children U.S. citizens by birth? if they are born in the United States or have at least one parent who is a U.S. citizen

## ★ Aliens in the United States

As you have learned, aliens are people in the United States who are citizens of a foreign country. Most of these people are here on a visit. Others live and work here or attend school but expect someday to return to their homelands. Many other aliens in the United States expect to live in the country permanently. In 2000 the number of foreign-born U.S. residents who were not citizens was about 18.7 million.

While they are in the United States, all aliens are subject to the laws of this country. If they violate the law, the government can **deport** them, or force them to leave the country. Aliens enjoy many of the benefits of U.S. citizenship. However, they cannot vote or hold public office. In addition, various state laws prohibit aliens from working at certain jobs, such as teaching in public schools.

All aliens living in the United States must register with the U.S. Immigration and Naturalization Service every year. They must also keep the agency informed of their current address.

✔ **Reading Check Contrasting** What restrictions do aliens face that citizens do not? cannot vote or hold public office; cannot work at certain jobs; must register with the INS

## ★ Illegal Immigration

Aliens who live in a country illegally are sometimes called undocumented residents. No one knows exactly how many undocumented residents live in the United States. However, a recent INS estimate suggested that the number may be as high as 7 million. In 1986 the Immigration Reform and Control Act was passed to legalize the status of undocumented residents who met certain requirements and to reduce the flow of illegal immigration into the United States. Yet the flow of illegal immigration remains high.

It is thought that about half of all undocumented residents come from Mexico. Most come to the United States to find work and a more

**BIOGRAPHY**

## Madeleine Albright
**(1937– )**

Madeleine Albright was born Marie Jana Korbel in Czechoslovakia. Her family settled in the United States in 1948. She became a naturalized citizen and began to pursue her political and academic interests. After graduating from college, Albright worked as an assistant for several Democratic politicians and for a number of nonprofit organizations. She also earned a Ph.D. in international affairs and taught classes at Georgetown University. President Bill Clinton named her U.S. ambassador to the United Nations in 1993. Her achievements in that position prompted her appointment as U.S. secretary of state in 1997. Albright was the first woman in U.S. history to hold that position. **How do Albright's achievements illustrate the contributions that immigrants have made to the United States?**

## ★ The Democratic Process

**Green Card Lottery** The Diversity Immigrant Visa Lottery (also known as the Green Card Lottery), established by the 1996 Immigration Act, hopes to provide people from countries with low U.S. immigration rates the opportunity to come here. These countries have included Guatemala, Taiwan, and Northern Ireland. With the lottery program, the U.S. government provides 55,000 permanent residence visas each year through a random computerized drawing. A permanent residence visa is commonly referred to as a green card. Green card holders are entitled to live and work in the United States permanently. Residents from some countries such as Vietnam, China, and Mexico are excluded due to their recent high rate of immigration to the United States.

**CRITICAL THINKING**

Why might the State Department wish to open a lottery to immigrants from underrepresented countries?

**ANSWER:** Students might suggest that it will help diversify the American population.

**BIOGRAPHY ANSWER**

Students might suggest that, like Albright, many immigrants have gotten an education, taught others, and participated in politics.

### SPOTLIGHT on Ancestry

Have students find out when one of their ancestors (or those of a friend or a famous American) entered this country and from what country that person originated. Students should use classroom and library resources to research conditions in the country of origin of their ancestors when the ancestors emigrated. Then have each student imagine that they are that immigrant and write personal journal entries describing the feelings he or she has about immigrating to the United States. **BLOCK SCHEDULING**

### CLOSE

On the chalkboard draw a chart with the following column headings: *Native-Born Citizen, Legal Alien, Illegal Alien, Naturalized Citizen.* Ask students for characteristics of each category. Write their answers in the appropriate columns. When the chart is complete, discuss the similarities and differences among the categories. Students may copy the chart as a study guide.

### ★ Profiles

**Mario Molina—U.S. Immigrant** Born in Mexico City, Mexico, in 1943, Mario Molina traveled extensively during his teens and young adulthood, mostly for educational purposes. Fascinated by science at an early age, Molina spent time in Switzerland, Germany, and France increasing his knowledge of physical chemistry. In 1968 Molina was accepted to the University of California at Berkeley. He began studying and performing experiments in physical chemistry that would bring him not only fame but also a family. Molina met his wife Luisa Tan on the research team he joined his first year at Berkeley. He went on to perform research at other universities over the years, eventually landing a position at the Massachusetts Institute of Technology (MIT). It was there that he joined the team with which he won the 1995 Nobel Prize in Chemistry for their work exploring the depletion of Earth's ozone layer.

**ACTIVITY:** Have students use the library and other resources to locate information about other famous U.S. immigrants. Ask them to select a person who interests them and to write a short biography to present to the class.

### Visual Record Answer

*Students might suggest that the United States wants to ensure that prospective citizens are committed to becoming a U.S. citizen.*

prosperous life. However, life is often difficult for these immigrants. Many become migrant workers, moving from farm to farm picking crops. Undocumented residents often have to work for very low wages under harsh working conditions. Some citizens resent these people, who they believe are benefiting illegally from government services and are taking jobs away from U.S. citizens. Undocumented residents also face the danger of being caught and deported.

✔ **Reading Check Summarizing** What are some of the difficulties facing undocumented residents? harsh working conditions, low pay, resentment from some citizens, the danger of deportation

### ★ Citizenship by Naturalization

Under certain circumstances, citizens of other countries may become U.S. citizens. The legal process by which an alien may become a citizen is called **naturalization.** The first part of the naturalization process is entering the United States legally.

To be eligible for naturalization, aliens must prove that they have been residents for at least five years. This period is reduced to three years for an alien married to a U.S. citizen. Aliens must be at least 18 years old to apply for citizenship in the United States. They must also prove that they can support themselves and that they can read, write, and speak English. They must be free from certain diseases and mental illnesses and cannot be drug addicts or criminals. There are several other restrictions that can bar people from naturalization or even immigration. One restriction bars persons who favor violent revolution—that is, the overthrow of the government by force.

Immigrants may file a declaration of intention if they eventually wish to apply for naturalization. This declaration states that the immigrant plans to become a citizen. A declaration of intention is not required by law. However, potential employers may ask for this document as evidence that the immigrant plans to stay in the country.

**Interpreting the Visual Record**

**Becoming citizens** *The Immigration and Naturalization Service oversees the process of becoming a naturalized citizen. The time and effort involved are no barrier to individuals such as these people taking the oath of citizenship.* **Why do you think the United States has the requirements it does for naturalization?**

## REVIEW AND ASSESS

Have students complete the **Section 2 Review** on p. 13. Then have students complete **Daily Quiz 1.2**. As **Alternative Assessment** you may want to use the book jacket or the citizenship poster activity in this section's lessons.

## RETEACH

Have students complete **Main Idea Activity for English Language Learners and Special-Needs Students 1.2**. Then give each student five index cards and have them write a test question about this section on one side of the card and the answer on the other side. Finally, pair students and have them quiz each other using the index cards as flash cards.

**ENGLISH LANGUAGE LEARNERS , COOPERATIVE LEARNING**

## EXTEND

Organize students into small groups. Have the groups conduct research outside of class to determine the major reasons that people come to the United States today seeking citizenship. Tell each group to design and create poster-sized advertisements encouraging people to become U.S. citizens. Advertisements might include several reasons people would want to become a U.S. citizen as well as the requirements of the naturalization process. Students might use other appropriate ideas or statements from the section as well. Encourage creativity.

**COOPERATIVE LEARNING , BLOCK SCHEDULING**

The second step to becoming a citizen is to fill out an application called a petition for naturalization. When immigration authorities receive this application, they set a date for the person to appear before a naturalization official for an interview.

During the interview the applicant must show that he or she is a person of good moral character who believes in the principles of the U.S. Constitution. The applicant must also prove that he or she can read, write, and speak English acceptably. In addition, an applicant must be familiar with U.S. history and government. The applicant then files the petition in a naturalization court.

Before they become citizens, applicants go through a background check and approval. Then they attend a final ceremony. There they take an oath of allegiance to the United States and are granted a certificate of naturalization. Minors—children under the age of 18—automatically become citizens when one of their parents is officially naturalized.

Naturalized citizens have the same rights and duties as native-born Americans. There is only one exception. Naturalized citizens are not eligible to become president or vice president of the United States.

*Learning English is a major goal for many immigrants wishing to become U.S. citizens.*

✔ **Reading Check Sequencing** What steps must a person take to become a naturalized U.S. citizen? must enter the United States legally, live here for the appropriate number of years, fill out a petition for naturalization, and attend an interview

## Section 2 Review
### ANSWERS

**1. Define**
- immigrants, p. 8
- quotas, p. 10
- aliens, p. 10
- refugees, p. 10
- native-born citizen, p. 10
- deport, p. 11
- naturalization, p. 12

**2.** Quotas were established to curb immigration; the Immigration Act of 1990 set the quota at 675,000 with preference given to spouses and children of U.S. citizens.

**3. a.** peoples from Siberia and Asia; between 12,000 and 40,000 years ago

**b.** voting, holding public office, working at any job for which they are qualified

**4.** Students' responses will vary but should reflect an understanding of the steps involved in the naturalization process.

## SECTION 2 Review

**go.hrw.com Homework Practice Online**
keyword: SZ3 HP1

**1. Define** and explain:
- immigrants
- quotas
- aliens
- refugees
- native-born citizen
- deport
- naturalization

**2. Evaluating** Copy the chart below. Use it to show how immigration policy has changed since the early 1800s and what caused these changes.

| Time Period | Characteristics of Immigration and Immigration Policy |
|---|---|
| Late 1800s to early 1900s | |
| Present day | |

**3. Finding the Main Idea**
a. Who were the first immigrants to America, and when did they come here?
b. What rights do U.S. citizens have that documented aliens do not?

**4. Writing and Critical Thinking**
**Identifying Points of View** Imagine that you have just become a naturalized citizen of the United States. Write a letter to a friend in the country in which you were born, explaining why and how you became a U.S. citizen.
**Consider:**
- the different ways an immigrant can become a citizen
- the rights of U.S. citizens

# SECTION 3

## OBJECTIVES

*After completing Section 3, students should be able to*

1 **Evaluate why census information is important.**
2 **Explain the ways that a population grows.**
3 **Describe the changes that have come about in the movement of the American people in the early years of the country to the present.**

## 📀 LET'S GET STARTED!

Write the word *census* on the chalkboard. As students enter the classroom, ask them to write down the meaning of the word. *(Students might write that a census is a way of documenting information about an area's people.)* Reinforce this definition. Tell students that in Section 3 they will learn about the uses of the census as well as trends that census information has shown in U.S. growth both historically and today.

## SECTION 3 RESOURCES

### REPRODUCIBLE

► Guided Reading Strategies 1.3
► Creative Teaching Strategy: Learning Stations
► Challenge and Enrichment Worksheet 1: Completing a Census Form
► Community Service and Participation Handbook: What Does the Government Know About Your Community?

### TECHNOLOGY

► One-Stop Planner, Lesson 1.3
► Holt Researcher CD–ROM
► Homework Practice Online

### REINFORCEMENT, REVIEW, AND ASSESSMENT

► Section 3 Review, p. 20
► Daily Quiz 1.3
► Main Idea Activity 1.3
► English Audio Summary 1.3
► Spanish Audio Summary 1.3

# SECTION 3

# The American People Today

## Read to Discover

1. Why is census information important?
2. In what ways does a population grow?
3. What has changed about the movement of the American people from the country's early years to the present?

### WHY CIVICS MATTERS

The U.S. population continues to change today. Use **CNNfyi.com** or other **current events** sources to identify examples of current trends in the U.S. population. Record your findings in your journal.

## Define

• census
• birthrate
• death rate
• rural areas
• urban areas
• suburbs
• metropolitan areas
• migration

## Identify

• Sunbelt

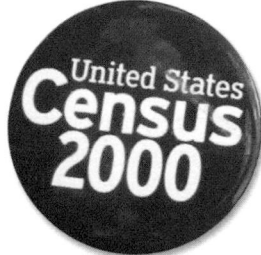

*Much of the data from the 2000 U.S. Census is available online through the Census Bureau.*

## Reading Focus

The leaders who created our system of government realized that they would need to know how many people lived in the country. They decided that every 10 years the federal government would take a count of U.S. residents. This count is called a **census.** The most recent census was conducted in 2000.

### ⭐ What the Census Tells Us

The main purpose of the census is to find out the size of each state's population. This information is used for many purposes, including the determination of how many people from each state will be elected to the House of Representatives.

The census also tells us a great deal about the United States and the people who live here. For example, it tells us how many children there are in each family. The census gives information about the growth or decline in population of a particular region or state. In addition, the census indicates the rate of population growth in the United States as a whole. This and other information gathered by census takers helps the government, businesses, and individuals plan for the future. It also helps us learn something about Americans and the United States.

✔ **Reading Check Making Generalizations and Predictions** How might businesses, government, and individuals use census information to plan for the future? Students might say that businesses may develop products and services related to population trends. Government can plan for city growth. Individuals may seek jobs in areas with migrating populations.

# TEACH OBJECTIVE 1

**LEVEL 1:** Lead a class discussion about the reasons that the census is important. Begin by asking each student to write on a slip of paper the different groups that use census information. *(Students' lists should include the government, businesses, and individuals.)* Then collect all of the responses and write the answers on the chalkboard. Remind students about the different types of information collected in a census. *(Types of data include age, gender, race, residency status, employment status, marital status, and so on.)* Have students suggest different ways that each group might use the information provided in a census. **ENGLISH LANGUAGE LEARNERS**

**ALL LEVELS:** Copy the following graphic organizer onto the chalkboard, omitting the italicized answers. Have students complete the chart to examine why census information is important. **ENGLISH LANGUAGE LEARNERS**

| Who Uses It | How They Use It |
| --- | --- |
| *government* | *to plan the budget* |
| *businesses* | *to fill the needs of the market* |
| *individuals* | *to write books and reports* |

## ★ Population Growth

When the first census takers counted the U.S. population in 1790, they reported fewer than 4 million people living in the original 13 states. Since that time, the country has grown in both size and population. According to current projections, the country's population will approach 300 million by 2010.

Countries can grow in three ways. One way is by the natural increase in population. A natural population increase occurs when the birthrate is greater than the death rate. The **birthrate** refers to the annual number of live births per 1,000 members of a population. The **death rate** refers to the annual number of deaths per 1,000 members of a country's population.

The second way a country grows is by adding new territory. The United States has gained new lands through war, purchase, and annexation. The people living in these new lands have added to the size of the country's population.

The third source of population growth is immigration. Since 1820, more than 60 million immigrants from all over the world have come to the United States. As you know, the United States has been called a country of immigrants.

✔ **Reading Check** Analyzing Information What are the three ways that a country's population can increase? Population increases when birthrate is greater than death rate, when territory is added, and because of immigration.

## ★ How the U.S. Population Grew

As the United States expanded from the Atlantic coast to the Pacific coast, its rapidly growing population made it possible to settle the land. In the early years of the country, the population grew at a relatively steady pace.

Between 1790 and 1830 the population of the country more than tripled, reaching almost 13 million. Most of this growth was the result of births in the United States. At that time, it was common for families to have many children. Large families were a practical necessity. Most people lived on farms, which required several people to maintain them. Thus, even though many children died young and the death rate was high because of hardships, the population grew significantly.

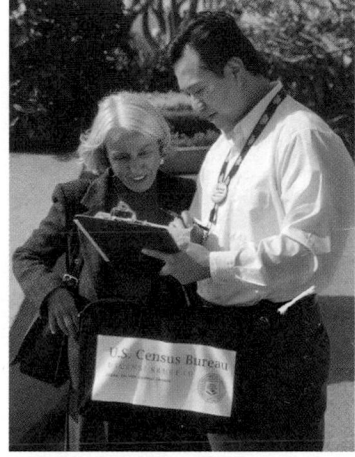

*Even with advances in technology, collecting census data requires many field-workers.*

### ★ ★ Historical Document ★ ★

## THE AMERICAN'S CREED

*William Tyler Page wrote the American's Creed during World War I. The House of Representatives adopted it in 1918 as "the best summary of the political faith of America."*

❝I believe in the United States of America as a
   government of the people, by the people, for
   the people;
whose just powers are derived from the consent of
   the governed;
a democracy in a Republic;
a sovereign nation of many sovereign States;
a perfect Union, one and inseparable;
established upon those principles of freedom,
   equality, justice, and humanity for which American
   patriots sacrificed their lives and fortunes.

I therefore believe it is my duty to my country to
   love it;
to support its Constitution;
to obey its laws;
to respect its flag;
and to defend it against all enemies."

**Analyzing Primary Sources**
What documents do you think may have influenced the words and ideas expressed in the creed?

LEVEL 3: Distribute figures from the latest census to students. *(The Bureau of Census provides many useful summary reports of the information that may be easier for your students to use for this exercise.)* Then organize the class into three groups. Assign each group one of the following categories: the government, business, or the individual. Ask students to evaluate the information from the point of view of their assigned group. Then reconvene and call on a volunteer from each group to give a class presentation about why the information is important to his or her assigned group. **COOPERATIVE LEARNING**

## TEACH OBJECTIVE 2

**LEVEL 1:** Write the following sentence on the chalkboard: *A country's population grows in several ways.* Tell students to write three sentences that support this main idea. Then call on volunteers to share their sentences. *(Students' sentences should note these three ways: naturally, by the addition of more territory, and by immigration.)* Conclude by having students use these sentences as an outline to write a paragraph about the three ways a population grows. **ENGLISH LANGUAGE LEARNERS**

## Interdisciplinary Connection

### ▶ Science and Technology ◀

**New Transportation Helps Migration** The location and growth of urban areas can be linked to the development of various technological advances. Early colonial cities sprang up along waterways to facilitate ship-bound transport of cargo. Steam-powered boats and factories gave rise to the Industrial Revolution in the late 1700s and early 1800s. The wealth of jobs in newly industrialized urban areas drew many people from farm life into the city. In the mid- to late-1800s the advent of the railroad and other innovations such as the harnessing of electricity and the manufacture of steel further increased the appeal of city life.

### CRITICAL THINKING

What technological innovations might affect peoples' choice about where to live today?

**ANSWER:** Students might suggest computer technology, cars, subways, or airplanes.

### ★ ★ ★ ★ ★ ★ ★ ★ ★ ★ ★
### *That's Interesting!*
### ★ ★ ★ ★ ★ ★ ★ ★ ★ ★ ★

In 1972 the United States experienced a period in which the population did not grow. This "zero-population growth" is attributed to the birthrate slipping temporarily below the death rate.

**Interpreting the Visual Record**

**Urban immigration** *By 1900 many of the immigrants to the United States were settling in large cities such as New York.* **What does this image suggest about crowding in the growing cities?**

### Holt Researcher

**go.hrw.com**
**KEYWORD: Holt Researcher**
**Freefind:** Immigration

Look up information on immigration on the Holt Researcher. Use this information to create a pie chart that answers the following question: What percentage of immigrants to the United States came from Africa, Asia, Europe, and South America in 1900 and 1990?

Beginning in the 1820s large numbers of immigrants started to arrive in the United States. Between 1831 and 1840 almost 600,000 immigrants came to this country, many from Ireland. Over the next 10 years some 1.7 million immigrants arrived. The population exceeded 23 million by 1850.

By 1920 the country's population had risen to nearly 106 million. Immigrants, particularly from southern and eastern Europe, accounted for a large part of this increase in total population. However, as you have read, after 1920 the United States began to limit the number of immigrants admitted into the country each year. By the mid-1920s most of the population growth was the result of natural increase.

✔ **Reading Check Summarizing** How has the U.S. population grown over the years? **Between 1790 and 1830 the population tripled. By 1850, 10 million more people were in the United States. By 1920 it had reached almost 106 million.**

### ★ Today's Population Growth

Today the population of the United States continues to grow. Yet the growth rate fluctuates from year to year and from decade to decade. For example, in 1970 some 205 million people lived in the country—at least 24 million more than in 1960. However, by 1980 a new trend had appeared. The population had increased by about 23 million over the decade, but this represented a change of only 11.4 percent. This was the second-smallest percent increase in any 10-year period since 1790. During the early 1990s, the rate of population growth rose. Later in the decade, however, it returned to the level of the 1980s.

**LEVEL 2:** Have students use newspapers and other periodicals to create collages illustrating the various ways that a population grows. *(See the Level 1 lesson for types of growth.)* For example, students might use articles about birthrates or pictures of maternity wards to illustrate natural increases in population. Use students' completed collages to prompt a discussion on the importance of accurate censuses. *(Students might discuss the fact that rapidly increasing birthrates mean increasing numbers of children and subsequent needs to improve and enlarge educational facilities.)*

**LEVEL 3:** Call on volunteers to explain the ways that a population grows. *(See the Level 1 lesson for the types of growth.)* Then ask volunteers to gauge the potential for population growth in their neighborhoods by describing the population that already lives there, perhaps by estimating the number of people by age group. As a class, discuss how these characteristics affect the potential population growth in the neighborhood. For example, if the neighborhood is populated mainly by older people, the most likely avenue for population growth might be new families moving into the neighborhood by immigration, rather than by births.

Population projections indicate that the rate of increase will continue to drop, falling to 0.9 percent by the decade beginning in 2000. One reason the U.S. population is growing at a slower rate is that many people are having smaller families.

✔ **Reading Check Comparing** How did growth trends in the 1980s compare to those of previous decades? The population had grown, but the percent increase was smaller than in the past.

## ★ A People on the Move

Where do the people of the United States live? The first census found most Americans living on farms, with a smaller number living in villages and in a few medium-sized cities. Over the years this changed significantly. The number of people living in **rural areas,** or regions consisting of a few farms and small towns, has become smaller each year. According to the 2000 census, only 59 million of the country's 281 million people lived in rural areas.

Beginning in the 1800s Americans began to move away from rural areas. Most of them went to live in **urban areas,** or cities. By 1830 the census showed that urban areas were growing faster than rural areas. With each census, the proportion of Americans living in or near cities continued to grow. The 1920 census found that more Americans lived in urban areas than in rural areas.

As the population continued to grow rapidly and people moved to the cities, urban areas became crowded. Many Americans could afford to buy automobiles, which made it possible to travel longer distances to work. As a result, in the mid-1900s people living in cities started moving in increasing numbers to surrounding areas. These areas are known as the **suburbs.**

They moved to the suburbs in search of larger homes, better quality schools, and quieter communities. Of the 25 largest cities in the United States in 1950, 14 had lost population by 1970. Today the people who live in the suburbs outnumber those who live in the cities.

Together cities and their suburbs account for the vast majority of the country's population. More than four fifths of the current U.S. population lives in **metropolitan areas,** or areas made up of cities and their suburbs. More than half of U.S. residents now live in areas with populations of 1 million or more.

✔ **Reading Check Identifying Cause and Effect** Why did rural populations decrease in the 1800s, and why did suburbs develop in the mid-1900s? People began to move to urban areas; urban areas became too crowded.

**Interpreting the Visual Record**

**Commuters** *The growth of suburbs has led to longer commutes for many Americans who work in cities but live outside of them.* **What is one side effect of having more cars on the road?**

# TEACH OBJECTIVE 3

**ALL LEVELS:** Organize the class into small groups. Have each group create a plan for a class bulletin-board display titled How the American Population Has Changed in the Past 20 Years. Each group should suggest drawings or found images, written captions, maps, or charts that would be used in the display. *(Students' plans should address the fact that most Americans once lived in farms and in rural areas. Now most people live in urban areas, including suburbs.)* Have the class vote on the elements from each groups' plan that they would like to use. Allow students time to decorate the bulletin board with the features selected by the class.
**ENGLISH LANGUAGE LEARNERS**

**LEVELS 2 AND 3:** Have students read this section to learn about the changes in the movement of the American people from the early years to the present. Have students work in pairs to answer the standard reporters' questions regarding this issue: Who? What? Where? When? Why? and How? (See the Level 1 lesson for movement.) Each student should then write a newspaper article reporting on efforts to help hungry and homeless people. Students may wish to gather their articles into a class newsletter. **COOPERATIVE LEARNING**

**HOMEWORK** Have each student create a graphic aid to enhance the information presented in the class newsletter.

**Interpreting the Visual Record**

**The Sunbelt** *Phoenix, Arizona, and other cities in the Sunbelt have experienced rapid growth in recent years.* **What qualities have attracted people to the Sunbelt?**

## Did You KNOW?

One of the key factors that encouraged people to move to the Sunbelt was the development of indoor air conditioning. First introduced in the 1920s, air conditioners had become affordable enough for home use by the 1950s. They helped make the hot summers of the Sunbelt bearable.

## ★ Another Population Shift

Throughout U.S. history, Americans have been on the move. This movement continues today, with many Americans moving to different parts of the country. The movement of large numbers of people from region to region is called **migration.**

States in the Midwest and older industrial areas in the Northeast have experienced relatively little growth, and some have lost population. Many Americans from these areas have moved to states in the South and West. These states are known as the **Sunbelt**. One of the main attractions of the Sunbelt is the region's warmer climate. In addition, as older industrial areas began facing tough economic times, job growth and better economic opportunities in the Sunbelt drew many migrants.

California has the largest population in the country. Arizona, Colorado, Nevada, and Texas are among the states growing at the fastest rates. These states showed large increases in population during the 1980s and 1990s. However, states such as Connecticut, North Dakota, and Rhode Island have shown little growth or have actually decreased in population in the past 10 years.

Because of the population shift to the Sunbelt, cities in the South and West are growing. According to the 2000 census, Las Vegas, Nevada, is one of the fastest growing cities in the United States. Six of the top 10 largest cities in the country are in the Sunbelt. These cities are Los Angeles and San Diego, in California; Dallas, Houston, and San Antonio, in Texas; and Phoenix, Arizona. Cities in the North and East such as Buffalo, New York; Newark, New Jersey; and Philadelphia, Pennsylvania, lost population between 1990 and 2000. Despite this population trend, however, New York City remains the country's most populous city.

✔ **Reading Check** **Making Generalizations and Predictions** If better jobs and opportunities arose in the Northeast and Midwest, what changes might occur? Students might say that people may migrate back and that cities would have to adjust their services to accommodate the growth.

## ★ A Diverse Population

People from all over the world have influenced the development of the United States. Today's Americans come from many different cultural backgrounds and represent a wide variety of ethnic groups. However, they are united by a common bond—they are all Americans.

**SPOTLIGHT** on **Homelessness in the United States** Have students research the history of homelessness in the United States. Students should focus their research to address the following questions: *What is the current situation of homeless people in the United States? Why is homelessness a difficult problem? How have state and local governments and private organizations tried to solve the problem?* Ask students to write editorials advocating possible remedies for homelessness in the United States. **BLOCK SCHEDULING**

**CLOSE**

Begin an outline on the chalkboard by writing the main headings throughout the section. Then have students complete the outlines at their desk, with each student listing the major points discussed under each heading. Encourage students to use the outlines as study guides.

White Americans make up the largest ethnic group in the United States. Hispanics are the country's second-largest and fastest-growing ethnic group. This group numbers more than 35 million and makes up 12.5 percent of the population. African Americans are the third-largest ethnic group. The 34.7 million African Americans living in the United States today make up 12.3 percent of the population. The fourth-largest ethnic group is Asian Americans. This group makes up 3.6 percent of the population. Between 1990 and 2000, the Asian American population has increased 48.3 percent—to more than 10.2 million. Much of this growth took place as a result of immigration.

✔ **Reading Check** Finding the Main Idea Why is the population of the United States said to be diverse? There are people from many cultural backgrounds and ethnic groups.

## ★ Changing Families

Recent statistics also show that other changes are taking place in the population of the United States. The size of U.S. households has decreased since 1970. Many people are having fewer children or are living alone. From 1970 to 2000, the total number of households increased from about 63 million to more than 105 million. The average number of people living in a household declined from four or more people to fewer than three people per household.

The number of one-parent households is also increasing. From 1970 to 2000, the number of one-parent families in the United States rose from 7 million to 16.5 million. Many of these households are headed by women. Today less than 25 percent of the country's households include a mother, father, and one or more children.

Changes have also taken place in the roles of men and women. Perhaps one of the most significant changes is that more families have both parents working outside the home. In recent years in the United States, more women than men have been entering and graduating from college. After receiving their education, a greater percentage of women have been entering the American workforce.

In 1970 about 31 million women worked outside the home. Today that number has risen to 65 million. Estimates show that this number will be nearly 73.5 million by the year 2008. Most women work for the same reason that most men do—economic necessity. Many single women depend on their jobs as a source of income. So do many married women. Today more than 60 percent of married women in the United States work outside the home. One result of the increased number of women in the workforce is that more women are entering professions that once were dominated by men.

✔ **Reading Check** Identifying Cause and Effect Why have more women entered the workforce, and what has resulted from this trend? Women are becoming educated, and they need the money. Women are entering previously male-dominated professions.

The number of one-parent households and families that have both parents working outside the home has increased. Working parents and caregivers need good day-care facilities for their children.

## REVIEW AND ASSESS

Have students complete the **Section 3 Review** on page 20. Then have them complete **Daily Quiz 1.3**. As **Alternative Assessment**, you may want to use the collage or newsletter activities in this section's lessons.

## RETEACH

Have students complete **Main Idea Activity for English Language Learners and Special-Needs Students 1.3**. Assign students one of the Read to Discover questions at the beginning of the section. Then have each student list at least five facts that could help other students identify the question. Create a master list of all the facts on the chalkboard. **ENGLISH LANGUAGE LEARNERS**

## EXTEND

Organize the class into groups and have students conduct research outside of class to determine the U.S. population's gradual shift westward over time. Each group member should find population information for specific states and cities and for specific years. Then have each group create sketch maps showing the changes. Some groups may want to show the location of large cities at different points in U.S. history, for example, while other groups might want to create maps showing the most populous states at various points in time. Display completed maps around the classroom.
**COOPERATIVE LEARNING , BLOCK SCHEDULING**

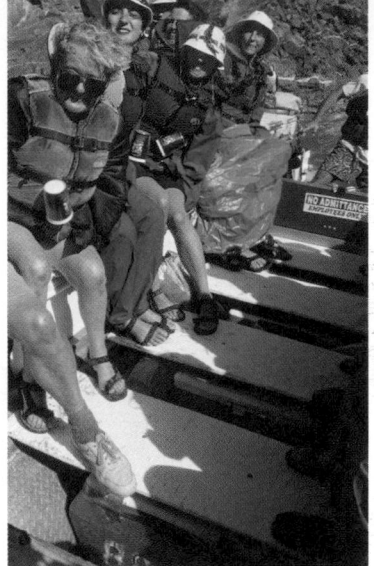

**Interpreting the Visual Record**

**Older Americans** *As Americans live longer and enjoy better health, many are remaining active well beyond retirement age.* **What activity are these older Americans participating in?**

## Section 3 Review
### ANSWERS

**1. Define**
- census, p. 14
- birthrate, p. 15
- death rate, p. 15
- rural areas, p. 17
- urban areas, p. 17
- suburbs, p. 17
- metropolitan areas, p. 17
- migration, p. 18

**2. Identify**
- Sunbelt, p. 18

**3.** the government, businesses, individuals

**4. a.** It can increase naturally, by adding more territory or due to immigration.

**b.** Most Americans once lived in farms and in rural areas. Now most people live in urban areas, including suburbs.

**5.** Students' descriptions should reflect an awareness of the increase in minority groups, smaller households and families, increased number of women in the workforce, and the aging population.

## ★ An Older Population

Statistics also show that the country is "growing older" every year. In the country's early years, when both birthrates and death rates were high, the country had a generally young population. For example, in 1850 half the population of the United States was under the age of 19. Until the 1980s half the population was under the age of 30.

Today people between the ages of 25 and 64 make up the largest sector of the population. In this group of almost 144 million people are most of the country's wage earners. However, an increasing part of the population consists of people who are 65 or older. This trend has resulted in part from a drop in both birthrates and death rates. The birthrate dropped steadily beginning in the 1960s before leveling off in the 1980s. The birthrate rose again in the early 1990s. However, it has dropped again in recent years, and experts believe that it will continue to decline. Also, Americans are living longer. In 1920 the average American lived to be 54 years old. Currently, the average life expectancy is about 77 years.

Today more than 35 million Americans are 65 or older. Because the typical retirement age is 65, many Americans are retired. However, some older people are eager to remain in the workforce. Some work part-time, and others have started new careers or returned to school.

Most older citizens continue to be active and productive. Still, many are troubled by the problems of low income and poor health. How to best use the experience and talents of older citizens offers both a challenge and an opportunity for the country.

✔ **Reading Check** Making Generalizations and Predictions How might the large number of people between the ages of 25 and 64 affect the population trends in the coming years? Students might say that they will continue the aging-population trend, which might cause issues with services such as Social Security and Medicare.

## SECTION 3 Review

**go.hrw.com Homework Practice Online**
**keyword: SZ3 HP1**

**1. Define** and explain:
- census
- birthrate
- death rate
- rural areas
- urban areas
- suburbs
- metropolitan areas
- migration

**2. Identify** and explain:
- Sunbelt

**3. Identifying Cause and Effect**
Copy the graphic organizer below. Use it to identify who makes use of census information to plan for the future.

Who uses census information?

**4. Finding the Main Idea**
a. What causes a country's population growth?
b. How have American migration patterns changed?

**5. Writing and Critical Thinking**
**Summarizing** Imagine that it is the year 2020 and you are a history textbook author. Describe for your readers the U.S. population in the mid-1990s.

**Consider:**
- population diversity and household size
- changing gender roles and the aging of the population

## TEACH

**LEVEL 1:** Organize the class into pairs. Provide each pair with copies of two Web pages covering the same topic from the Internet. Select one page that is informative and another that is not. Then instruct students to read the pages as if they were looking for information for a class report. Ask partners to discuss their observations about the pages with each other. Then call on volunteers to share their thoughts with the class. Lead a class discussion about the criteria that make a page useful for research. **ENGLISH LANGUAGE LEARNERS , COOPERATIVE LEARNING**

## EXTEND

Provide students with a Web page to evaluate. You may wish to use these search words to locate Web pages about chapter topics: civics, citizenship, naturalization, immigration, or census. Suggest that students develop criteria to determine the usefulness of the Web pages that you provided them. Then have students present their evaluations to a partner, explaining why they did or did not find the page to be informative. **COOPERATIVE LEARNING , BLOCK SCHEDULING**

---

# Civics Skills
## WORKSHOP

### Using the Internet

*There is a wealth of information on the Internet. However, it takes a careful approach to find information that is both accurate and useful for your needs.*

#### Finding the Information You Need

There are many types of search tools available. Directories, search engines, and subject guides are three of the major types of search tools. Each search tool is constantly changing. Be sure to examine the "Help" files of any search tool in order to get the full details on search information.

Some large Web sites—such as America Online, MSN, Netscape, and Yahoo!—offer links to a broad range of information. In addition, there are government sites such as the Library of Congress and Metroscope. Sites such as CNNfyi.com allow you to access up-to-the-minute news and information.

#### Check the Reliability of the Web Page

Users must be able to determine whether a Web page contains valuable information. Ask yourself these questions:
- Is the information unbiased, up-to-date, and easy to read?
- Is a well-respected organization sponsoring the site?

#### Use Keywords and Important Terms

Control your search by using keywords and key terms. Knowing how to use keywords can help you search more efficiently.

#### Searching Tips
- Use phrase searching and combine keywords.
- List terms that you want excluded from the search.
- Consider how your search tool treats capitalization.

#### Warnings to Students
The Internet contains a large amount of resources, making it an excellent tool for research. However, there is a lot of inappropriate material on the Web. Many sites have developed safe areas for youth, known as child-safe zones. Even at these sites you must be careful.

- Never give out any personal information or meet with strangers.
- If you get into an inappropriate area, get out immediately and tell your parent or teacher.

### Practicing the Skill

Search the Internet to find information on the U.S. economy. This could include information on employment, inflation, new jobs, or trade with foreign countries. Use this information to create an illustrated poster displaying the facts and figures you have found about the U.S. economy.

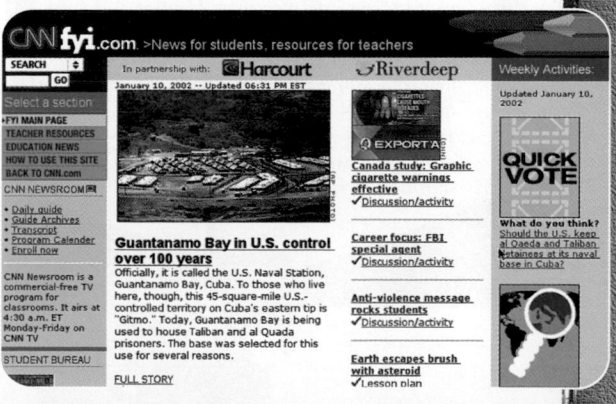

## SKILLS ANSWERS
Students' selections will vary, but their posters should accurately display their analysis of the facts and figures they have found.

## CHAPTER 1
### REVIEW ANSWERS

#### Define and Identify
Students should indicate an understanding of the following definitions:
1. civics, p. 3
2. immigrants, p. 8
3. aliens, p.10
4. deport, p. 11
5. naturalization, p. 12
6. birthrate, p. 15
7. death rate, p. 15
8. rural areas, p. 17
9. metropolitan areas, p. 17
10. Sunbelt, p. 18

# Review and Assessment Resources

**REPRODUCIBLE**

▶ Chapter 1 Review, pp. 22–23

▶ Vocabulary Activity 1

▶ Chapter 1 Tutorial for Students, Parents, Mentors, and Peers

▶ Chapter 1 Test (Form A or B)

▶ Alternative Assessment Handbook

**TECHNOLOGY**

▶ Chapter 1 Test Generator (on the One-Stop Planner)

▶ Global Skill Builder CD–ROM

▶ HRW Go site

**REINFORCEMENT, REVIEW, AND ASSESSMENT**

▶ Chapter 1 Test for English Language Learners and Special-Needs Students

## REVIEW

Have students complete the **Chapter 1 Review** on pages 22–23.

## ASSESS

Use one of the chapter tests to assess students' understanding of the content. For **Alternative Assessment**, see the **Alternative Assessment Handbook**.

---

### Understanding Main Ideas

**1.** to learn about the roles and responsibilities of U.S. citizenship

**2.** freedom and equality

**3.** Today there is a quota on immigration, whereas in the early 1800s immigration was unlimited.

**4.** They can vote, hold public office, and hold any job that they choose.

**5.** naturally, by the addition of more territory, or because of immigration

**6.** Most Americans once lived in farms and in rural areas. Now most people live in urban areas, including suburbs.

### What Did You Find Out?

**1.** Students should observe that people may contribute to their political party's campaign efforts, and people may be in contact with their political leaders regarding their needs.

**2.** Students may note that the number of people allowed to enter the United States is now controlled.

**3.** It helps the government to determine how many people from each state will be elected to Congress to make plans for the future.

---

# Chapter 1 Review

## Chapter Summary

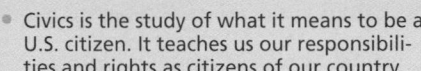

### Section 1

- Civics is the study of what it means to be a U.S. citizen. It teaches us our responsibilities and rights as citizens of our country.
- As citizens, we are guaranteed certain rights and freedoms.
- We must also fulfill our civic responsibilities by being active participants in our system of government and in our communities.

### Section 2

- The United States is a diverse nation filled with immigrants from many countries.
- U.S. immigration policy has changed over time. Today immigration is controlled by the Immigration Act of 1990.
- U.S. citizenship is gained by birth or by naturalization.
- Naturalized citizens enjoy the same rights as native-born citizens except the right to become president or vice president.

### Section 3

- The national government has taken a census every 10 years since 1790 to determine how many people live in the United States. The information tells us how the United States has grown and changed over the years.
- The United States has changed from a country of farms into a country of cities and suburbs.
- Recent statistics reveal that Americans are living longer, having smaller families, and moving to the Sunbelt.
- The number of African Americans, Hispanics, and Asian Americans is increasing, as is the number of women in the workforce.

---

### Define and Identify

1. civics
2. immigrants
3. aliens
4. deport
5. naturalization
6. birthrate
7. death rate
8. rural areas
9. metropolitan areas
10. Sunbelt

### Understanding Main Ideas

**Section 1** *(Pages 3–7)*
1. Why do people study civics?
2. What principles and ideals form the foundation of the American system of government?

**Section 2** *(Pages 8–13)*
3. How has U.S. immigration policy changed since the early 1800s?
4. What benefits do people derive from being a citizen of the United States?

**Section 3** *(Pages 14–19)*
5. Identify three ways that the populations of countries increase.
6. How have migration patterns shifted from the 1800s to the present?

### What Did You Find Out?

1. What responsibilities do U.S. citizens have to their government and their communities? What are some ways in which people perform these duties?
2. In what ways has immigration to the United States changed from the country's early history to today?
3. Why is the census an important tool for the U.S. government?

### Thinking Critically

1. **Supporting a Point of View** The founders of the United States made elected officials responsible to the people so that government would continue to serve the people. Do you think the people of the United States today are being adequately served by government? Explain your answer.
2. **Evaluating** Why do you think current immigration law gives preference to immigrants who are immediate relatives of U.S. citizens or who have certain job skills?
3. **Making Predictions and Generalizations** In what ways has the United States benefited from the diversity of its people?

## RETEACH

Organize the students into pairs. Have pairs scan the chapter and choose a picture that interests them. Ask them to describe what is happening in the picture, using as many Define words from the section openers as they can. One member of each pair should write down a description. The other member should read the description to the class. **ENGLISH LANGUAGE LEARNERS** , **COOPERATIVE LEARNING**

## Portfolio Extensions

**1. Interdisciplinary Connection to History** Ask each student to conduct research to obtain information about your community's origins. You may encourage students to visit their local historical society. Then have students use their research to create posters illustrating the community's early years. Ask volunteers to present their posters to the class and to discuss the significance of the people and events portrayed in their project.

**2. Cooperative Learning** Organize the class into six groups. Assign each group one of the questions addressed in the pupil's edition portfolio activity. Have each group conduct further research on its question to create a portion of a class bulletin-board display about the beginnings of your community. When groups have completed their research and design, reconvene as a class and create the bulletin-board display.

---

## Building Social Studies Skills

go.hrw.com **STANDARDIZED TEST PREP ONLINE** keyword: SZ3 STP1

### Interpreting Graphs

Study the line graph below, which shows the growth in the U.S. population from 1900 to 2000. Then answer the questions that follow.

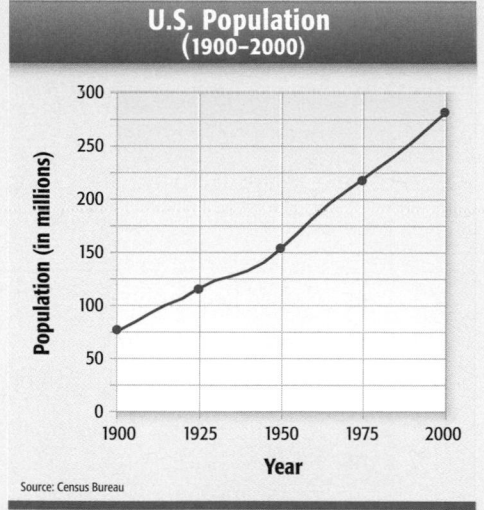

**U.S. Population**
(1900–2000)

Population (in millions) / Year

Source: Census Bureau

1. What is the largest increase in population in any 25-year period shown on the graph?
   a. About 25 million
   b. Slightly more than 50 million
   c. Slightly less than 50 million
   d. Slightly more than 60 million

2. About how many times greater was the U.S. population in 2000 than in 1925?
   a. About twice as large
   b. About three times as large
   c. About four times as large
   d. About the same size

3. Based on the patterns shown on this chart and your own knowledge, do you think the U.S. population will be greater than 325 million in 2025? Why or why not?

### Analyzing Primary Sources

Read the following excerpt from President Ronald Reagan's first inaugural address and then answer the questions that follow.

❝Freedom and the dignity of the individual have been more available and assured here than in any other place on earth. The price for this freedom has at times been high, but we have never been unwilling to pay that price. . . . It is time for us to realize that we are too great a nation to limit ourselves to small dreams. . . . We have every right to dream heroic dreams.❞

4. Which of the following statements best describes Reagan's point of view?
   a. Americans should act more heroically.
   b. Americans should be proud of their freedom and set high goals for themselves and their nation.
   c. The United States is the only country where freedom is important.
   d. The United States has protected its freedom easily.

5. What do you think the purpose of this speech was? Explain your answer.

### Thinking Critically

1. Students' responses will vary but should be based upon sound reasoning.

2. Immigrants with American relatives have a support system already in place. Skilled immigrants can contribute their knowledge and expertise to the labor force.

3. Students' responses will vary, but they may observe that America's culture has been expanded and that its people have learned to become more tolerant of those who are different from themselves.

### Skills Workshop

1. d

2. b

3. Students' responses will vary.

4. b

5. Students might suggest that Reagan was trying to inspire people to continue to fight for freedom.

---

## Alternative Assessment

### Building Your Portfolio

**Linking to Community**
Investigate the beginnings of your community. Who first settled the community? Where did the settlers come from? What cultural influences did they bring? What are the ethnic and cultural backgrounds of the people who live in your community today? Create a poster showing how the ethnic and cultural makeup of your community has changed over time.

### internet connect

**Internet Activity: go.hrw.com**
keyword: SZ3 AC1

Access the Internet through the HRW Go site to research population shifts, growth, and population diversity of the United States. Then use information from the 2000 census to create a thematic map, graph, or chart that illustrates trends in one of the above areas.

# Foundations of Government

## CHAPTER RESOURCE MANAGER

| Objectives | Pacing Guide | Reproducible Resources |
|---|---|---|
| **SECTION 1:**<br>**Why Americans Have Governments**<br>(pp. 25–29)<br><br>★ Describe what influences the form of a country's government.<br>★ Identify what distinguishes a democracy from other forms of government.<br>★ Examine the roles of government. | **Regular**<br>1.5 days<br><br>**Block Scheduling**<br>1 day<br><br>*Block Scheduling Handbook with Team Teaching Strategies, Chapter 2* | **RS** Guided Reading Strategies 2.1<br>**RS** Graphic Organizer Activity: You and Your Government<br>**SM** Community Service and Participation Handbook: And the Winner Is |
| **SECTION 2:**<br>**The First American Government**<br>(pp. 30–35)<br><br>★ Evaluate the significance of the Declaration of Independence.<br>★ Identify the limitations of the Articles of Confederation.<br>★ Describe the effect of a weak national government on the United States. | **Regular**<br>1.5 days<br><br>**Block Scheduling**<br>1 day<br><br>*Block Scheduling Handbook with Team Teaching Strategies, Chapter 2* | **RS** Guided Reading Strategies 2.2<br>**RS** Readings in Economics and Government 7: Articles of Confederation<br>**RS** Readings in Economics and Government 48: *Second Treatise of Civil Government*<br>**RS** Creative Teaching Strategy: Foundations of Government |
| **SECTION 3:**<br>**A New Constitution**<br>(pp. 40–46)<br><br>★ Identify the principles of Great Britain's government that influenced the ideas of the delegates to the Constitutional Convention.<br>★ Explain how the U.S. government became stronger under the Constitution.<br>★ Describe how the viewpoints of Federalists and Antifederalists differed and how they resolved their differences. | **Regular**<br>1 day<br><br>**Block Scheduling**<br>.5 day<br><br>*Block Scheduling Handbook with Team Teaching Strategies, Chapter 2* | **RS** Guided Reading Strategies 2.3<br>**RS** Readings in Economics and Government 6: The English Bill of Rights<br>**RS** Readings in Economics and Government 20: The Debate on the Proposed Constitution<br>**RS** Readings in Economics and Government 52 and 53: *Federalist Paper "No. 10"* and *Federalist Paper "No. 71"*<br>**PS** American Civics Political Cartoon: Ratifying the Constitution<br>**E** Challenge and Enrichment Worksheet 2: Understanding the Ideals of the Constitution |

## Chapter Resource Key

| | | | |
|---|---|---|---|
| **PS** | Primary Sources | **SM** | Skills Mastery |
| **RS** | Reading Support | **A** | Assessment |
| **IC** | Interdisciplinary Connections | **REV** | Review |
| **E** | Enrichment | **ELL** | Reinforcement and English Language Learners |

 CD–ROM

 Video

 Internet

Transparencies

Holt Presentation Maker Using Microsoft® PowerPoint®

 **One-Stop** Planner CD–ROM

See the *One-Stop Planner* for a complete list of additional resources for students and teachers.

**One-Stop** Planner CD–ROM

It's easy to plan lessons, select resources, and print out materials for your students when you use the **One-Stop Planner CD–ROM with Test Generator**.

## internet connect

**HRW ONLINE RESOURCES**
GO TO: go.hrw.com
Then type in the keyword.

**TEACHER HOME PAGE**
KEYWORD: SZ3 Teacher

**CHAPTER INTERNET ACTIVITIES**
KEYWORD: SZ3 AC2
Choose an activity to:
• create a chart on the strengths and weaknesses of the Articles of Confederation.
• write a feature story on types of governments in the world today.
• write a biography on notable Federalists and Antifederalists.

**CHAPTER ENRICHMENT LINKS**
KEYWORD: SZ3 AC2

**ONLINE ASSESSMENT**
**Homework Practice**
KEYWORD: SZ3 HP2

**Rubrics**
KEYWORD: SS Rubrics

**ONLINE MAPS, CHARTS, AND GRAPHS**
KEYWORD: SZ3 MCG
• Strengths and Weaknesses of the Articles of Confederation and the Constitution

**HOLT PRESENTATION MAKER**
KEYWORD: SZ3 PPT2

**CONTENT UPDATES**
KEYWORD: SS Content Updates

**ONLINE READING SUPPORT**
KEYWORD: SS Strategies

**CURRENT EVENTS**
KEYWORD: S3 Current Events

| Technology Resources | Reinforcement, Review, and Assessment |
|---|---|
| One-Stop Planner, Lesson 2.1<br>Homework Practice Online | REV Section 1 Review, p. 29<br>A Daily Quiz 2.1<br>ELL Main Idea Activity 2.1<br>ELL English Audio Summary 2.1<br>ELL Spanish Audio Summary 2.1 |
| One-Stop Planner, Lesson 2.2<br>CNN Presents: American Government<br>Homework Practice Online | REV Section 2 Review, p. 35<br>A Daily Quiz 2.2<br>ELL Main Idea Activity 2.2<br>ELL English Audio Summary 2.2<br>ELL Spanish Audio Summary 2.2 |
| One-Stop Planner, Lesson 2.3<br>Holt Researcher CD–ROM<br>Homework Practice Online<br>HRW Go site | REV Section 3 Review, p. 46<br>A Daily Quiz 2.3<br>ELL Main Idea Activity 2.3<br>ELL English Audio Summary 2.3<br>ELL Spanish Audio Summary 2.3 |

## Meeting Individual Needs

**Ability Levels**

**Level 1** Basic-level activities designed for all students encountering new material

**Level 2** Intermediate-level activities designed for average students

**Level 3** Challenging activities designed for honors and gifted-and-talented students

**English Language Learners** Activities that address the needs of students with Limited English Proficiency

## Chapter Review and Assessment

IC   Vocabulary Activity 2
   Global Skill Builder CD–ROM
   HRW Go site
REV   Chapter 2 Tutorial for Students, Parents, Mentors, and Peers
REV   Chapter 2 Review, pp. 48–49
A   Standardized Test Practice
A   Chapter 2 Test Generator (on the One-Stop Planner)
A   Chapter 2 Test (Form A or B)
A   Alternative Assessment Handbook
A   Chapter 2 Test for English Language Learners and Special-Needs Students

## What's Your Opinion?

*To help students create their **Themes** Journal entries, provide the following examples of appropriate **agree**/**disagree** statements.*

● **Agree** Consistency in the type of government makes international negotiations more productive.

**Disagree** There is not one government type that can work for all of the world's cultures.

● **Agree** Power should be equally shared between the states and the federal government.

**Disagree** The individual states that comprise a country should be more powerful than the federal government.

● **Agree** A country must have a strong foundation on which to build its government.

**Disagree** Too strong of a central government will result in too much power centered in one area.

# Internet Activity

## Around the World

## CHAPTER

# 2 Foundations of Government

## Build on What You Know

What do you think of when you hear the term *government*? Perhaps you think of the U.S. Capitol in Washington, D.C., or your state's capitol. Maybe the term brings to mind the president, your state governor, your city's mayor, or federal, state, or city laws. However, government is not only buildings, leaders, and laws. It is the entire system of authority that acts on behalf of the citizens of a particular city, state, or country. In the words of President Abraham Lincoln, the U.S. government is a government "of the people, by the people, and for the people." It has been established to serve us, protect our rights, and safeguard our freedom. The U.S. government is you—it is all of us.

## What's Your Opinion?

Do you **agree** or **disagree** with the following statements? Support your point of view in your journal.

- All countries should have the same kind of government.

- A federal government that gives the states too much power cannot operate effectively.

- A strong central government will help create a strong country.

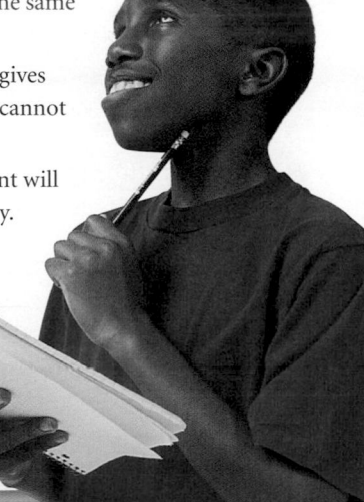

# SECTION 1

## OBJECTIVES

*After completing Section 1, students should be able to*

1 **Describe what influences the form of a country's government.**

2 **Identify what distinguishes a democracy from other forms of governments.**

3 **Examine the roles of government.**

## LET'S GET STARTED!

As students enter the classroom, ask them to describe what they believe to be the role of government in a society. *(Students might mention making laws, protecting people, or meeting with foreign officials.)* Then tell students that there are many different types of governments around the world, and the type of government a country has often determines what role the government will play in that society. Finally, tell students that in Section 1 they will learn about the types and roles of government.

## SECTION 1

# Why Americans Have Governments

### Read to Discover

1. What influences the form of a country's government?
2. What distinguishes a democracy from other forms of governments?
3. What are the roles of government?

### WHY CIVICS MATTERS

Government plays an essential role in every country. Use **CNNfyi.com** or other **current events** sources to find an example of how a country's government affects the lives of the people who live there. Record your findings in your journal.

### Define

- absolute monarchs
- dictatorship
- authoritarian
- totalitarian
- democracy
- direct democracy
- representative democracy
- republic
- laws
- constitution

## SECTION 1 RESOURCES

### REPRODUCIBLE

▶ Guided Reading Strategies 2.1

### TECHNOLOGY

▶ One-Stop Planner, Lesson 2.1
▶ The Holt Researcher
▶ Homework Practice Online

### REINFORCEMENT, REVIEW, AND ASSESSMENT

▶ Section 1 Review, p. 29
▶ Daily Quiz 2.1
▶ Main Idea Activity 2.1
▶ English Audio Summary 2.1
▶ Spanish Audio Summary 2.1

## Reading Focus

To govern means to rule. A government is any organization set up to make and enforce rules. You probably live under at least three different levels of government.

The city or town in which you live has a government. It makes and enforces rules for the people in your community. At the next level, your state government makes and enforces rules for you and the other people in your state. At the national level, the federal government makes and enforces rules for all the people in the United States.

### ★ Types of Governments

Every country in the world has a government. However, these governments are not all alike. There are many important differences in the way they govern. They differ in the way their leaders are chosen and in the amount of power held by the people. Each country's government has been shaped by the beliefs of the people and by their history.

**Monarchies** In times past, the governments of many countries were monarchies, which means they were controlled by monarchs, such as kings or queens. They often held all the power in their country's governments, and they were able to rule by force. Because they held absolute, or total, power, they were called **absolute monarchs.** Today there are few absolute monarchs left. Most countries that have monarchs greatly limit the monarchs' power. The monarch generally serves as a

*Kings and queens often possess crowns such as this one as symbols of their power.*

# TEACH OBJECTIVE 1

**LEVEL 1:** Have students create a description of a fictional country's government. The description should identify the factors that influence the form of a country's government and should determine what type of government it is. *(Students' descriptions should include a brief history of the people and characteristics of the particular type of government.)* Students should then read their descriptions to another student, and that student should guess what kind of government the fictional country has. **ENGLISH LANGUAGE LEARNERS** , **COOPERATIVE LEARNING**

**LEVEL 2:** Lead a class discussion on the various factors that influence the form of a country's government. Then organize students into groups and have each group create a guidebook for establishing a government. The guidebook should contain each form of government discussed in the section and should provide all the necessary influences that would lead to each particular form of government. *(For example, students might include that if a country has a king or a queen, a ruler who reigns by force, or a ceremonial head of state with little power, then that country will likely have a monarchy.)* **COOPERATIVE LEARNING**

## ★ The Democratic Process

**The Right to Rule** Leaders in all governments seek to justify their power. In democracies elections are the main justification. However, governments not chosen by popular vote must find other justifications. Communist dictatorships, for example, have often tried to justify their power by claiming to protect the working classes against what was a tyrannous wealthy class. Louis XIV of France, who ruled from 1643 to 1715, is a prime example of an absolute monarch. Like other European rulers of the time, Louis XIV believed his power came directly from God—that he ruled his country by divine right.

### CRITICAL THINKING

Why might an absolute monarch claim to have a divine right to rule?

**ANSWER:** Students might suggest that a divine right to rule is impossible to disprove and that it might make it more challenging for opposition to gain support against a divine ruler.

### Visual Record Answer

*The U.S. president is elected by citizens.*

**Interpreting the Visual Record** **Inauguration** *President George W. Bush and First Lady Laura Bush are escorted to the presidential inauguration.* **How is the selection of the U.S. president different from the process used in monarchies and dictatorships?**

ceremonial head of state. The power of the government lies elsewhere.

**Dictatorships** In some countries one person or a small group of people holds all the power. In an oligarchy a small group of people hold the power. The rulers have absolute control over the government. This type of government is called a **dictatorship.** Dictatorships are **authoritarian,** meaning their rulers answer only to themselves, not to the people they rule. Some dictatorships are considered **totalitarian.** In a totalitarian state, the rulers attempt to control all aspects of citizens' lives, including their religious, cultural, political, and personal activities. A theocracy is a form of government in which the rulers are religious leaders who claim to rule on behalf of God or the gods worshiped in their country.

**Democracies** Other countries have democratic governments. In a **democracy** the people of a nation either rule directly, or they elect officials who act on their behalf. The word *democracy* comes from an ancient Greek term meaning "rule of the people."

There are two forms of democracy. In a **direct democracy** all voters in a community meet in one place to make laws and decide what actions to take. Historically this form has been suited to only small communities. In a **representative democracy** the people elect representatives to carry on the work of government for them. The people consent to be ruled by their elected leaders. This system of government is called a **republic.** It is the form of government in the United States.

✔ **Reading Check Summarizing** Describe the three main types of governments and their characteristics. monarchies—kings and queens rule the country; dictatorships—person or a small group has absolute power and does not answer to the people; democracies—people of a country rule directly or indirectly

## ★ Purposes of Government

Would it be possible for all of us to live as we choose? Could we manage our own affairs without a government? Do we need rules for getting along with one another? Who would provide the basic services, like trash collection, that we use every day? To answer these questions, it is important to understand the basic purposes of government.

# TEACH OBJECTIVE 2

**ALL LEVELS:** Copy the following graphic organizer onto the chalkboard, omitting the italicized answers. Ask each student to complete the chart to identify what distinguishes a democracy from other forms of governments. Then have students expand the chart by adding the various sub-groups of government under the appropriate main type.

**ENGLISH LANGUAGE LEARNERS**

| Types of Governments | Characteristics of Governments |
|---|---|
| **Democracy**<br>• Direct<br>• Representative | *People rule directly or indirectly.*<br>• All voters make decisions together.<br>• People elect representatives. |
| **Monarchy**<br>• Absolute | *Ruled by a king or queen.*<br>• Monarchs have total control. |
| **Dictatorship** | *A person or small group has absolute power and does not answer to the people.* |

**HOMEWORK** Ask each student to write one or two sentences for each subsection of Section 1 to summarize the section's information. Then have students use their sentences to develop a five-question quiz about Section 1.

## Helping People Cooperate

One of the earliest lessons human beings learned was that cooperation was useful. It was easier to hunt and kill a large animal for food if the members of the group worked together. People could also better protect themselves against enemies when they were united. Government provides a means for people to unite and cooperate. Thus, whenever large groups of people have lived together, they have found it necessary and useful to have a government. Even simple forms of government helped to make life safer and easier.

## Providing Services

Over the years government has grown more and more complex. Yet its basic purposes have remained the same. Governments not only provide ways for people to live and work together but also enable large groups of people to get demanding jobs done. Each person in a group may be able to single-handedly do some of the things a government does. However, it would usually be much more difficult and expensive for each person to do so.

For example, what would happen if every family in your community had to educate its own children? Even if parents had time to teach, would they be able to teach all subjects well? By establishing schools, the government makes it possible for all children to receive a good education.

**Interpreting the Visual Record**

**Protecting citizens** *Fire departments are just one of the many essential services that governments provide for their citizens.* **How do services such as this one benefit the people in your community?**

# TEACH OBJECTIVE 3

**LEVEL 1:** Organize the class into groups. Have each group create a list of the four basic roles of a government. *(Groups should list helping people cooperate, providing services, providing rules, and putting ideals into practice.)* Then ask groups to write a position statement describing why people need the government to fulfill these purposes.

**ENGLISH LANGUAGE LEARNERS , COOPERATIVE LEARNING**

**LEVEL 3:** Have each student identify the four basic roles of a government *(See Level 1 activity for roles.)* Then ask students to each choose one purpose and to write an essay explaining how a government can achieve this purpose. Encourage students to use examples from their own experiences.

# CLOSE

Ask a volunteer to look up the meaning of the word anarchy. *(Anarchy comes from a Greek word meaning "having no ruler" and is a condition or situation characterized by disorder or an absence of authority)* Then ask the class what life might be like if there were no laws governing society. Have students identify specific rules in your school or laws in your community that help keep order. Conclude by discussing the advantages of living in a democracy.

## ★ Constitutional Heritage

**Constitutions** Not all constitutions are written. Great Britain, for example, from where many of the basic concepts of U.S. government came, has no written constitution. Instead, it has a collection of documents, judicial rulings, statutes, and customs that make up its constitution. One of the major differences between having such an unwritten constitution and a written one is that constitutional law in Great Britain can be changed or abolished without a lengthy amendment process to a written document.

### CRITICAL THINKING

Why might an unwritten constitution be considered much more flexible than a written one?

**ANSWER:** An unwritten constitution can change with the beliefs of the times as new laws and judicial rulings are made.

### Visual Record Answer

*Students might suggest that the students are conducting research online.*

---

**Interpreting the Visual Record**

**Education** *Public schools and libraries expand the educational opportunities available to all citizens.* **In what ways might these students be using library resources to further their education?**

*Local laws and regulations such as those that prohibit littering help keep communities safe and well maintained.*

DO NOT THROW LITTER $1000$^{00}$ FINE

---

Government also performs other services that would be difficult or impossible for individual citizens to provide for themselves. Government protects people from attacks by foreign countries. It provides police to protect lives and property and fire departments to protect homes and businesses.

Because of government, you can travel highways that stretch from border to border. A system of money makes it easy for you to buy and sell things and to know the price of these things. Your trash is collected, and health laws are enforced to protect you. You can go to public libraries. The government provides these and many more services.

✔ **Reading Check** Making Generalizations and Predictions What might happen if we had no government? Students might say that we would have no public education system, no defense from attacks by foreign countries, no protection of our property, and no system of money.

## ★ Providing Rules

Large groups of people need rules to help them live together in peace. When there are rules, all people know what they may and may not do. Without rules, any disagreement would probably end with the strongest members of the group forcing others to accept things their way.

Providing rules of conduct for a group is therefore one of the most important reasons for establishing governments. These rules are known as **laws.** They are recorded so that people can know and obey them. Laws are written by the government to guide and protect all of us.

For example, if you own a house on a city or village street, a law may require you to keep your sidewalk in good repair. If you fail to repair cracks, someone may fall and be injured. Such a law also protects you because you depend on your neighbors to keep their sidewalks in good condition.

The basic law under which Americans live is contained in a **constitution,** or a written plan of government. Americans have used constitutions to establish national and state governments. A constitution sets forth the purposes of the government and describes how the government is to be organized.

✔ **Reading Check** Summarizing What purposes do laws and constitutions serve in governments? Laws provide rules of conduct, and constitutions contain the plans of government.

## REVIEW AND ASSESS

Have students complete the **Section 1 Review** on page 29. Then have students complete **Daily Quiz 2.1**. As **Alternative Assessment**, you may want to use the government descriptions or the types of government organizer activities in this section's lessons.

## RETEACH

Have students complete **Main Idea Activity for English Language Learners and Special-Needs Students 2.1**. Then ask each student to make a list of the key terms found in the section. Have them write sentences that explain the significance of each term and its relation to the section material. **ENGLISH LANGUAGE LEARNERS**

## EXTEND

Have students use the library to locate magazine or newspaper articles about a foreign country's government. Then have them reference those articles to write a report that analyzes the similarities and differences between that country's system of government and U.S. representative democracy. **BLOCK SCHEDULING**

## ★ Putting Ideals into Practice

A democratic country's government helps put into practice the ideals of the people—that is, the things in which they believe. America was founded on the belief that the people should rule themselves. Americans also believe that each person is important and that no one should be denied his or her rights.

What are these rights? In the Declaration of Independence (discussed later in this chapter), these rights are described as "life, liberty, and the pursuit of happiness." All Americans have the right to live their lives in liberty, or freedom, and to seek happiness.

To safeguard each citizen's liberty, the basic laws of the United States guarantee certain freedoms, such as freedom of speech, freedom of the press, and freedom of religion. These freedoms can never be taken away from any U.S. citizen by the government. Nor can they be restricted, except to keep people from using these freedoms to violate the rights of others.

For example, free speech and a free press do not mean freedom to tell lies or write false statements about another person. Each citizen has the right to have his or her reputation protected from efforts to hurt it with untruths.

Most Americans believe that if any citizen is denied his or her rights, the liberty of all is endangered. Thus, the U.S. government passed and enforces laws that guarantee equal rights for all citizens. For example, U.S. laws require that all Americans have equal access to education and employment and have the right to vote.

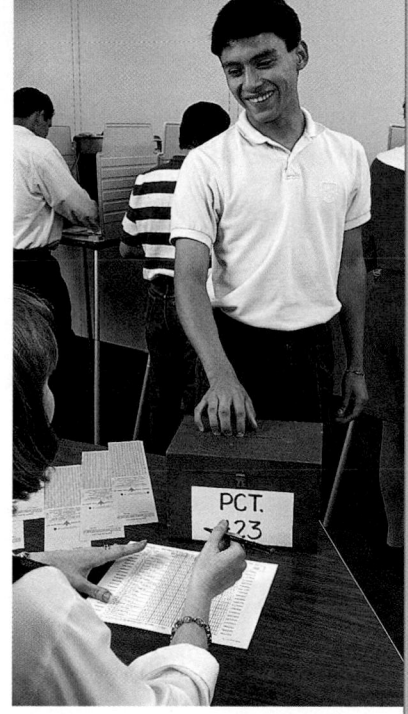

**Interpreting the Visual Record**

**Exercising our freedoms**
*Americans possess several fundamental rights that are protected by U.S. law.* **What basic right is this man exercising?**

✔ **Reading Check** Analyzing Information What are some of the freedoms guaranteed by U.S. laws? freedom of speech, freedom of the press, and freedom of religion, among others

## SECTION 1 Review

**go.hrw.com** Homework Practice Online
keyword: SZ3 HP2

1. **Define** and explain:
   • absolute monarchs
   • dictatorship
   • authoritarian
   • totalitarian
   • democracy
   • direct democracy
   • representative democracy
   • republic
   • laws
   • constitution

2. **Summarizing** Copy the chart below. Use it to identify four purposes of government in our society and to state how government fulfills each purpose.

| The Purposes of Government | | | |
|---|---|---|---|
| | | | |
| | | | |

3. **Finding the Main Idea**
   a. What factors shape the type of government a country forms?
   b. How does a democracy differ from other types of governments?

4. **Writing and Critical Thinking**
   **Supporting a Point of View**
   Write a three-paragraph essay explaining what you think are the most important functions of your local government. Be sure to explain how these functions affect members of your community.

   **Consider:**
   • public services available to your community
   • local laws

# SECTION 2

## OBJECTIVES

*After completing Section 2, students should be able to*

1 **Evaluate the significance of the Declaration of Independence.**
2 **Identify the limitations of the Articles of Confederation.**
3 **Describe the effect of a weak national government on the United States.**

**🎙 LET'S GET STARTED!**

As students enter the classroom ask them whether they think all human beings should have certain rights. Then have them make a list of those universal rights. *(Students' lists will vary.)* Tell students that Americans broke away from Great Britain partly because the British government violated certain human rights. Americans wanted to guarantee that their government would not have the power to deny peoples' basic rights. Finally, tell students that in Section 2 they will learn about how the United States declared independence and about their early attempts at establishing a government.

## SECTION 2 RESOURCES

### REPRODUCIBLE

▶ Guided Reading Strategies 2.2
▶ Readings in Economics and Government 7: *Articles of Confederation*
▶ Readings in Economics and Government 48: *Second Treatise of Civil Government*

### TECHNOLOGY

▶ One-Stop Planner, Lesson 2.2
▶ CNN Presents: American Government
▶ Homework Practice Online

### REINFORCEMENT, REVIEW, AND ASSESSMENT

▶ Section 2 Review, p. 35
▶ Daily Quiz 2.2
▶ Main Idea Activity 2.2
▶ English Audio Summary 2.2
▶ Spanish Audio Summary 2.2

# SECTION 2

# The First U.S. Government

## Read to Discover

1. What is the significance of the Declaration of Independence?
2. What were the limitations of the Articles of Confederation?
3. What was the effect of a weak national government on the United States?

## Define

• human rights
• confederation
• sovereignty

### WHY CIVICS MATTERS

The purpose of the U.S. government is to protect human rights. Use **CNNfyi.com** or other **current events** sources to find an example of how the U.S. government protects human rights. Record your findings in your journal.

## Reading Focus

As you know from your study of U.S. history, Great Britain founded and ruled the thirteen colonies that eventually became the United States. However, Great Britain and America are separated by the vast Atlantic Ocean. In part because of this great distance, American colonists governed themselves without interference from British leaders. Although royal officials controlled the colonies, the officials had little power. The colonies were for the most part self-governing.

When the British government under King George III began to enforce its rules and regulations in the colonies, many colonists became angry. Resentment grew as colonists were forced to obey British laws. Thus, they fought the Revolutionary War to maintain their freedom to govern themselves and to establish an independent country.

*This draft copy of the Declaration of Independence shows corrections and changes made by Thomas Jefferson.*

### ⭐ The Declaration of Independence

When fighting broke out between one of the American colonies and Great Britain in 1775, the colonists were not yet officially seeking independence. Nevertheless, the next year the Continental Congress—representatives from the thirteen colonies—met in Philadelphia. At this meeting, they named a committee to draw up the Declaration of Independence. Most of the Declaration was written by Thomas Jefferson. It was approved by members of the Continental Congress on July 4, 1776.

# TEACH OBJECTIVE 1

**LEVEL 1:** Lead a class discussion about the Declaration of Independence. Then organize the class into groups. Have each group prepare a mock radio news report on the Second Continental Congress and the significance of its outcome. Then have groups present their broadcasts to the class. **ENGLISH LANGUAGE LEARNERS**, **COOPERATIVE LEARNING**

**LEVEL 3:** Have students read the Declaration of Independence on page 36. Encourage them to pay close attention to the mention of human rights. Have students list the king's human-rights abuses alleged by the Second Continental Congress in the Declaration of Independence. Then ask students to imagine that they are colonists. Ask students to write journal entries evaluating the significance of the Declaration of Independence by explaining why declaring independence was justified because of these abuses.

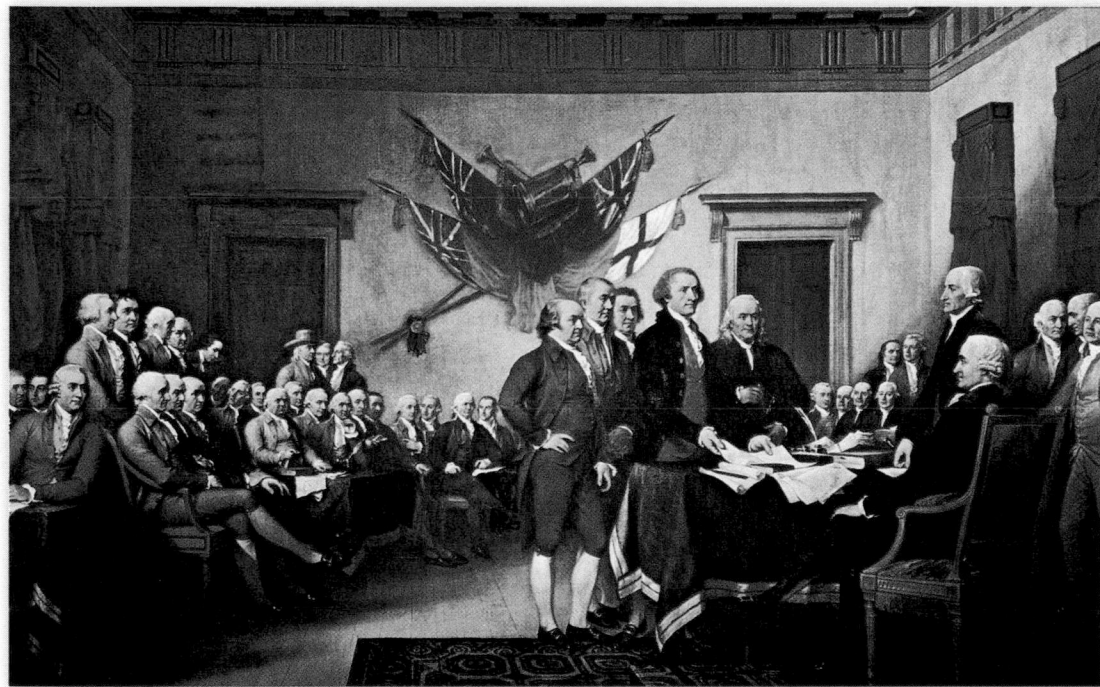

The Declaration of Independence explains the reasons the thirteen colonies decided to separate from Great Britain and to form an independent country. By doing so, the Declaration upholds the philosophy on which the United States is based. The colonists believed that the power of government comes from the consent of the governed—the people of the country. If a government ignores the will of the people, the people have a legitimate right to change the government.

Thus, the Declaration of Independence is much more than a document to justify independence. It is also a statement of American ideals. It explains to the world in clear language that the purpose of government is to protect **human rights.** These are the basic rights to which all people are entitled as human beings.

**Interpreting the Visual Record**

Independence *Members of the committee that drafted the Declaration of Independence present the document to the Continental Congress.* **How does this image convey the importance of this event?**

**Visual Record Answer**

*Students might suggest that the serious expressions of the participants indicates the significance.*

✔ **Reading Check Finding the Main Idea** What was the purpose and significance of the Declaration of Independence? It states why the colonies wanted independence from the rule of Great Britain and explains the American ideal that the purpose of government is to protect human rights.

## ★ Ideals of American Government

These basic human rights are clearly stated in the Declaration of Independence. "We hold these truths to be self-evident, that all men are created equal, that they are endowed by their Creator with certain unalienable Rights, that among these are Life, Liberty, and the pursuit of Happiness." This passage is one of the most famous in American writing.

★ ★ ★ ★ ★ ★ ★ ★ ★ ★ ★ ★
**That's Interesting!**
★ ★ ★ ★ ★ ★ ★ ★ ★ ★ ★ ★

**Signing the Declaration** Congress adopted the Declaration of Independence on July 4, 1776, the day we celebrate as Independence Day. However, there was no official ceremony for the signing of the Declaration. Only one delegate, John Hancock, signed his name on July 4. Other signers added their names later. The last signature may have been added as late as 1781!

Over the years this passage of the Declaration has come to mean that all Americans—members of all groups including both men and women—are equal under the law. For example, the right of each individual to life, liberty, and the pursuit of happiness must be equal to that of every other individual. No person has the right to act as though his or her own life and liberties are more important than those of others.

The leaders who signed the Declaration of Independence realized that these ideals would be difficult to achieve. Yet they believed such ideals were worth, as the Declaration states, "our lives, our fortunes, and our sacred honor."

The Declaration of Independence is considered one of the greatest documents in our country's history. Although it was written more than 225 years ago, it remains a lasting symbol of American freedom.

✔ **Reading Check Summarizing** What are the basic human rights stated in the Declaration of Independence? equality under the law and right to life, liberty, and pursuit of happiness

## ⭐ The Articles of Confederation

The Declaration of Independence was not meant to provide a government for the new country. In June 1776 the Continental Congress appointed a committee to draw up a plan of government—the Articles of Confederation. In 1781 it was approved by the 13 states, and the government under the Articles went into effect.

A **confederation** is a loose association, rather than a firm union, of states. The Articles of Confederation set up a "firm league of friendship" among the 13 states. Each state in the country was to have equal powers and in most ways was to be independent of the other states. The central, or national, government had very limited powers. The majority of people in the 13 states did not want a strong central government. They feared that such a government might use its power to limit the freedom of the separate states.

Under the Articles of Confederation, the national government consisted of a lawmaking body of one house, called Congress. The states sent representatives to Congress. Each state had one vote in Congress, regardless of the number of people living in the state.

The writers of the Articles of Confederation wanted to preserve the states' **sovereignty,** or absolute power. Thus, the Articles gave the power to enforce national laws to the states, rather than to the national government.

**LEVELS 2 AND 3:** On the chalkboard, draw a chart with three columns. Ask students to fill in the first column with the basic ideals and structures of the Articles of Confederation. For the second column, students should suggest how each of the items in the first column was a limitation of the Articles and contributed to a new government. Finally, have students complete the third column with suggestions on how the Articles could have been improved to strengthen the new government.

## TEACH OBJECTIVE 3

 **ALL LEVELS:** Have each student write three newspaper headlines expressing how a weak central government affected the United States. Students should address problems that resulted from the Articles of Confederation. (*Students might suggest problems with collecting taxes, not having enough money to run the government, or failing to regulate trade.*) Ask volunteers to present their headlines to the class.
**ENGLISH LANGUAGE LEARNERS**

This arrangement stemmed from the people's suspicion of strong leaders after their experience with King George III. The Articles also did not establish a national court system to interpret the laws and to punish lawbreakers.

During the Revolutionary War the 13 states were willing to work together and make sacrifices to achieve victory. Things were different in the years following the Revolution, however. Many Americans experienced difficult times after the war. Property had been destroyed. Trade with other countries, particularly Great Britain, where American merchants had enjoyed preferential treatment, had slowed. As a result, American businesses had suffered. Moreover, the war left the country deeply in debt. The Articles of Confederation did not give the new government the powers it needed to solve these problems.

✔ **Reading Check Identifying Cause and Effect** Why did the states prefer the Articles of Confederation, and how did this plan affect the national government? The states feared that a strong central government would limit their power. The Articles of Confederation did not give the new government needed powers.

## ★ Weaknesses of the Confederation

There were many reasons for the weakness of the national government under the Articles of Confederation. Congress had trouble passing laws because a vote of 9 of the 13 states was needed to pass important measures. In addition, without a president or an executive branch, there were no officials to ensure that the laws passed by Congress were carried out. Without national courts, there were no means of interpreting the laws or judging those who broke them.

In addition, changing the Articles of Confederation to make the national government stronger was difficult. Changes in the Articles required the unanimous vote of all 13 states.

Another weakness of the new government was that Congress lacked the power to collect taxes. Congress could ask the states to contribute money to pay the national government's expenses. Yet it had no power to force states to make these contributions.

Without money, Congress could not pay the country's debts or carry on any government activities that might be needed. Congress also could not pay the soldiers who had fought in the Revolutionary War. These limitations harmed relations with foreign nations and endangered America's national security.

Under the Articles of Confederation, the national government lacked other important powers. It could not control trade between the states or with foreign nations. Instead, each state regulated its own trade. This practice resulted in many disputes among the states and with other countries. In addition, most of the states issued their own money. There was no stable national currency or banking system.

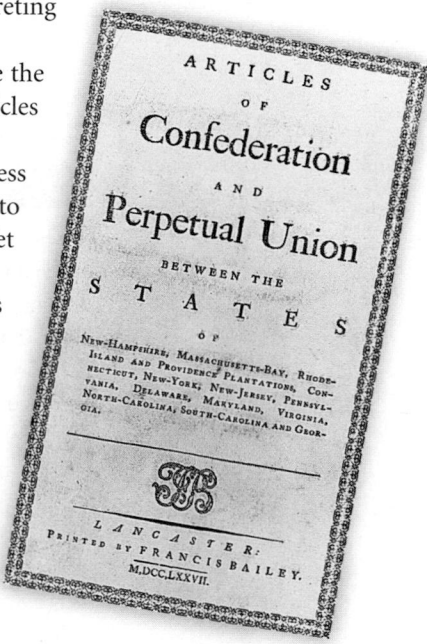
*The Articles of Confederation did not provide the central government with enough authority to address many problems faced by the new country.*

**LEVEL 3:** Lead a class discussion about how the weak central government under the Articles of Confederation led to many problems. *(The Articles placed most power with the states, provided little power to Congress, and did not provide an executive or judicial branch of government.)* Have students write a script for a public service announcement urging the need to change the Articles of Confederation. Students' scripts should fully state reasons for the needed changes as well as state the possible problems that might arise from having a weak central government.

## CLOSE

Organize the class into small groups and explain that each group is a committee of citizens appointed to critique the Articles of Confederation. Assign each group member an identity, such as a farmer, merchant, banker, ex-Revolutionary War soldier, or member of Congress. Each member should argue for or against the Articles. Then ask the groups to draft a consensus report for or against the Articles to present to the class.

**COOPERATIVE LEARNING**

---

## ★ Constitutional Heritage

**Shays's Rebellion** One of the major shortcomings of the Articles of Confederation was revealed during Shays's Rebellion. During the uprising in Massachusetts over taxation, the federal government was unable to properly handle the internal uprising. This rebellion, as well as many other weaknesses of the federal government under the Articles of Confederation, prompted delegates to gather again in 1787 to draft the Constitution.

**ACTIVITY:** Have students research the Articles of Confederation to obtain information about positive outcomes of this government. Ask them to prepare a brief oral report on one success of the Articles of Confederation.

### Visual Record Answer

*Students might suggest that they had to cross difficult terrain to reach their destinations.*

**Interpreting the Visual Record**

**Moving westward** *One of the most important actions of the Confederation Congress was the passage of the Northwest Ordinance of 1787. This law established rules for governing the Northwest Territory and created a system for bringing new states into the Union.* **What does this painting suggest about the difficulties faced by early pioneers?**

As a result of these weaknesses, the states acted more like small, separate nations than as members of a confederation. The states often refused to obey the laws of Congress. Relations between the states and Congress worsened.

✔ **Reading Check Analyzing Information** What were some of the weaknesses of the national government under the Articles of Confederation? Congress had trouble passing laws; there were no officials to enforce or interpret laws; changes in the Articles required unanimous vote of all 13 states; Congress lacked many powers.

## ★ The Need for Change

The Articles of Confederation succeeded in establishing a new country—a major achievement. However, the government set up by the Articles failed in a number of important ways.

The main trouble with the Articles was that they did not give the national government enough power to operate effectively. The states feared a strong central government and thus kept most of the real power in their own hands.

Another problem was that the citizens of the new country lacked a national identity. The residents of each state still tended to think of themselves as citizens of their particular state rather than as Americans. This mindset was natural because some of the states were separated by great distances, and transportation was poor. The colonies had been founded at different times and for different reasons. There had also been wide differences among the varying types of colonial governments.

## REVIEW AND ASSESS

Have students complete the **Section 2 Review** on page 35. Then have students complete **Daily Quiz 2.2**. As **Alternative Assessment**, you may want to use the mock radio news report or newspaper headlines activities in this section's lessons.

## RETEACH

Have students complete **Main Idea Activity for English Language Learners and Special-Needs Students 2.2**. Then ask them to create a comic strip that depicts the problems with the Articles of Confederation. Have volunteers present their comic strips to the class. **ENGLISH LANGUAGE LEARNERS**

## EXTEND

Ask students to imagine the United States today under the Articles of Confederation. Have each student write a brief essay explaining how one aspect of the Articles of Confederation might affect our current government and daily life. Have students conduct research on modern-day issues or events to provide a basis for hypothetical sitations. For example, one student might choose to write about how having no executive branch would affect a current U.S. foreign-policy issue. Ask volunteers to present their work to the class. **BLOCK SCHEDULING**

At first, independence did little to change this situation. Under the Articles many of the states continued to have only limited contact with each other. This made it difficult for them to agree on the common interests for which the government needed to work. It took years before the states began to think of themselves as part of a single country.

The weaknesses of the national government became clear as the young country began to face new problems. The states quarreled over the location of boundary lines. They became involved in disputes over trade. The national government was powerless to end these disagreements or to prevent new ones from arising. In addition to domestic troubles, the country looked weak to other nations.

Many leaders began to favor strengthening the national government. As a result, in 1787 Congress asked the states to send representatives to a meeting where revisions to the Articles could be discussed.

✔ **Reading Check** Identifying Points of View Why did people of the 13 states originally think of themselves as belonging to independent states rather than to one country? The states had little contact because some of them were separated by great distances and had varying forms of colonial government.

*Under the Articles of Confederation, each state printed its own currency.*

## Section 2 Review
### ANSWERS

**1. Define**
- human rights, p. 31
- confederation, p. 32
- sovereignty, p. 32

**2.** no national executive branch to enforce laws; no national courts to interpret laws or to judge those who broke them; change required unanimous vote of states; Congress not allowed to collect taxes to pay the country's debts or for necessary programs, not allowed to regulate trade, and not allowed to issue an official currency

**3. a.** It states why the colonies wanted independence from Great Britain and explains the American ideal that the purpose of government is to protect human rights.

**b.** states' fear of a strong central government and the lack of power to operate efficiently

**4.** Students' letters will vary but might mention the need for a strong central government in order to regulate trade and commerce between the states.

## SECTION 2 Review

go.hrw.com **Homework Practice Online**
keyword: SZ3 HP2

1. **Define** and explain:
   - human rights
   - confederation
   - sovereignty

2. **Summarizing** Copy the web diagram below. Use it to list the weaknesses of the Articles of Confederation.

   Weaknesses of the Articles of Confederation

3. **Finding the Main Idea**
   a. Why is the Declaration of Independence one of the most important documents written in U.S. history?
   b. What weakened the power of the national government under the Articles of Confederation?

4. **Writing and Critical Thinking**
   **Analyzing Information** Imagine that you are a farmer living in Virginia in the 1780s. In a letter to the editor of your local newspaper, describe the effect of the Articles of Confederation. Recommend what action must be taken to improve your situation.
   **Consider:**
   - trade disputes
   - lack of a strong central government

1776

★★★★★★★★★★★★
**That's Interesting!**
★★★★★★★★★★★★

Thomas Jefferson asked John Adams to draw up the first draft of the Declaration. Adams refused, saying, "Reason first—You are a Virginian, and a Virginian ought to appear at the head of this business. Reason second— I am obnoxious, suspected, and unpopular. You are very much otherwise. Reason third— You can write ten times better than I can."

**EXPLORING THE DOCUMENT ANSWER**
The Declaration shows that it is possible for people to change the government when it is no longer reflecting their will.

**Exploring the Document**

Thomas Jefferson wrote the first draft of the Declaration in a little more than two weeks. **How is the Declaration's idea about why governments are formed still important to our country today?**

[1]**impel:** force

[2]**endowed:** provided

[3]**usurpations:** wrongful seizures of power

[4]**evinces:** clearly displays

[5]**despotism:** unlimited power

# THE DECLARATION *of* INDEPENDENCE

*In Congress, July 4, 1776*
*The unanimous Declaration of the thirteen*
*united States of America,*

When in the Course of human events, it becomes necessary for one people to dissolve the political bands which have connected them with another, and to assume among the Powers of the earth, the separate and equal station to which the Laws of Nature and of Nature's God entitle them, a decent respect to the opinions of mankind requires that they should declare the causes which **impel**[1] them to the separation.

## Natural Rights

We hold these truths to be self-evident, that all men are created equal, that they are **endowed**[2] by their Creator with certain unalienable Rights, that among these are Life, Liberty, and the pursuit of Happiness. That to secure these rights, Governments are instituted among Men, deriving their just powers from the consent of the governed,

That whenever any Form of Government becomes destructive of these ends, it is the Right of the People to alter or to abolish it, and to institute new Government, laying its foundation on such principles and organizing its powers in such form, as to them shall seem most likely to effect their Safety and Happiness. Prudence, indeed, will dictate that Governments long established should not be changed for light and transient causes; and accordingly all experience hath shown, that mankind are more disposed to suffer, while evils are sufferable, than to right themselves by abolishing the forms to which they are accustomed. But when a long train of abuses and **usurpations**,[3] pursuing invariably the same Object **evinces**[4] a design to reduce them under absolute **Despotism**,[5] it is their right, it is their duty, to throw off such Government, and to provide new Guards for their future security.—

LEFT: *Thomas Jefferson*

## Colonists' Complaints against the King

Such has been the patient sufferance of these Colonies; and such is now the necessity which constrains them to alter their former Systems of Government. The history of the present King of Great Britain is a history of repeated injuries and usurpations, all having in direct object the establishment of an absolute **Tyranny**[6] over these States. To prove this, let Facts be submitted to a **candid**[7] world.

He has refused his Assent to Laws, the most wholesome and necessary for the public good.

He has forbidden his Governors to pass Laws of immediate and pressing importance, unless suspended in their operation till his Assent should be obtained; and when so suspended, he has utterly neglected to attend to them.

He has refused to pass other Laws for the accommodation of large districts of people, unless those people would **relinquish**[8] the right of Representation in the Legislature, a right **inestimable**[9] to them and **formidable**[10] to tyrants only.

He has called together legislative bodies at places unusual, uncomfortable, and distant from the depository of their Public Records, for the sole purpose of fatiguing them into compliance with his measures.

He has dissolved Representative Houses repeatedly, for opposing with manly firmness his invasions on the rights of the people.

He has refused for a long time, after such dissolutions, to cause others to be elected; whereby the Legislative Powers, incapable of **Annihilation**,[11] have returned to the People at large for their exercise; the State remaining in the mean time exposed to all the dangers of invasion from without, and **convulsions**[12] within.

He has endeavored to prevent the population of these States; for that purpose obstructing the Laws of **Naturalization of Foreigners**;[13] refusing to pass others to encourage their migration hither, and raising the conditions of new **Appropriations of Lands**.[14]

He has obstructed the Administration of Justice, by refusing his Assent to Laws for establishing Judiciary Powers.

He has made Judges dependent on his Will alone, for the **tenure**[15] of their offices, and the amount and payment of their salaries.

He has erected **a multitude of**[16] New Offices, and sent hither swarms of Officers to harass our people, and eat out their substance.

He has kept among us, in times of peace, Standing Armies without the Consent of our legislature.

He has affected to render the Military independent of and superior to the Civil Power.

He has combined with others to subject us to a jurisdiction foreign to our constitution, and unacknowledged by our laws; giving his Assent to their Acts of pretended legislation:

[6]**tyranny:** oppressive power exerted by a government or ruler

[7]**candid:** fair

### Exploring the Document

Here the Declaration lists the charges that the colonists had against King George III. **How might the language and content of the list appeal to people's emotions?**

[8]**relinquish:** release, yield

[9]**inestimable:** priceless

[10]**formidable:** causing dread

[11]**annihilation:** destruction

[12]**convulsions:** violent disturbances

[13]**naturalization of foreigners:** the process by which foreign-born persons become citizens

[14]**appropriations of land:** setting aside land for settlement

[15]**tenure:** term

[16]**a multitude of:** many

## Citizenship

**The Signers** The 56 signers of the Declaration of Independence shared many characteristics—almost all were Protestant white males and were fairly wealthy. Forty-eight of the signers were born in America.

### CRITICAL THINKING

How might the fact that 48 of the signers were born in America have influenced their decision to declare independence?

**ANSWER:** Students might suggest that these signers might have felt less loyalty to Great Britain and more loyalty to the colonies.

### EXPLORING THE DOCUMENT ANSWER

They were angry they were being taxed without representation.

---

[17]**quartering:** lodging, housing

### Exploring the Document

Colonists had been angry over British tax policies since just after the French and Indian War. **Why were the colonists protesting British tax policies?**

[18]**arbitrary:** not based on law

[19]**render:** make

[20]**abdicated:** given up

[21]**foreign mercenaries:** soldiers hired to fight for a country not their own

[22]**perfidy:** violation of trust

[23]**insurrections:** rebellions

[24]**petitioned for redress:** asked formally for a correction of wrongs

[25]**unwarrantable jurisdiction:** unjustified authority

[26]**magnanimity:** generous spirit

[27]**conjured:** urgently called upon

[28]**consanguinity:** common ancestry

[29]**acquiesce:** consent to

---

For **quartering**[17] large bodies of armed troops among us:

For protecting them, by a mock Trial, from Punishment for any Murders which they should commit on the Inhabitants of these States:

For cutting off our Trade with all parts of the world:

For imposing taxes on us without our Consent:

For depriving us in many cases, of the benefits of Trial by Jury:

For transporting us beyond Seas to be tried for pretended offences:

For abolishing the free System of English Laws in a neighboring Province, establishing therein an **Arbitrary**[18] government, and enlarging its Boundaries so as to **render**[19] it at once an example and fit instrument for introducing the same absolute rule into these Colonies:

For taking away our Charters, abolishing our most valuable Laws, and altering fundamentally the Forms of our Governments:

For suspending our own Legislature, and declaring themselves invested with Power to legislate for us in all cases whatsoever.

He has **abdicated**[20] Government here, by declaring us out of his Protection and waging War against us.

He has plundered our seas, ravaged our Coasts, burnt our towns, and destroyed the lives of our people.

He is at this time transporting large armies of **foreign mercenaries**[21] to complete the works of death, desolation and tyranny, already begun with circumstances of Cruelty & **perfidy**[22] scarcely paralleled in the most barbarous ages, and totally unworthy the Head of a civilized nation.

He has constrained our fellow Citizens taken Captive on the high Seas to bear Arms against their Country, to become the executioners of their friends and Brethren, or to fall themselves by their Hands.

He has excited domestic **insurrections**[23] amongst us, and has endeavored to bring on the inhabitants of our frontiers, the merciless Indian Savages, whose known rule of warfare, is an undistinguished destruction of all ages, sexes and conditions.

In every stage of these Oppressions We have **Petitioned for Redress**[24] in the most humble terms: Our repeated Petitions have been answered only by repeated injury. A Prince, whose character is thus marked by every act which may define a Tyrant, is unfit to be the ruler of a free People.

Nor have We been wanting in attention to our British brethren. We have warned them from time to time of attempts by their legislature to extend an **unwarrantable jurisdiction**[25] over us. We have reminded them of the circumstances of our emigration and settlement here. We have appealed to their native justice and **magnanimity,**[26] and we have **conjured**[27] them by the ties of our common kindred to disavow these usurpations, which, would inevitably interrupt our connections and correspondence. They too have been deaf to the voice of justice and of **consanguinity.**[28] We must, therefore, **acquiesce**[29] in the necessity, which denounces our Separation, and hold them, as we hold the rest of mankind, Enemies in War, in Peace Friends.

## An Independent and United Nation

We, therefore, the Representatives of the united States of America, in General Congress, Assembled, appealing to the Supreme Judge of the world for the **rectitude**[30] of our intentions, do, in the Name, and by Authority of the good People of these Colonies, solemnly publish and declare, That these United Colonies are, and of Right ought to be Free and Independent States; that they are Absolved from all Allegiance to the British Crown, and that all political connection between them and the State of Great Britain, is and ought to be totally dissolved; and that as Free and Independent States, they have full Power to levy War, conclude Peace, contract Alliances, establish Commerce, and to do all other Acts and Things which Independent States may of right do. And for the support of this Declaration, with a firm reliance on the Protection of Divine Providence, we mutually pledge to each other our Lives, our Fortunes and our sacred Honor.

[30]**rectitude:** rightness

John Hancock
President of Massachusetts

**GEORGIA**
Button Gwinnett
Lyman Hall
George Walton

**NORTH CAROLINA**
William Hooper
Joseph Hewes
John Penn

**SOUTH CAROLINA**
Edward Rutledge
Thomas Heyward, Jr.
Thomas Lynch, Jr.
Arthur Middleton

**MARYLAND**
Samuel Chase
William Paca
Thomas Stone
Charles Carroll of
  Carrollton

**VIRGINIA**
George Wythe
Richard Henry Lee

Thomas Jefferson
Benjamin Harrison
Thomas Nelson, Jr.
Francis Lightfoot Lee
Carter Braxton

**PENNSYLVANIA**
Robert Morris
Benjamin Rush
Benjamin Franklin
John Morton
George Clymer
James Smith
George Taylor
James Wilson
George Ross

**DELAWARE**
Caesar Rodney
George Read
Thomas McKean

**NEW YORK**
William Floyd
Philip Livingston
Francis Lewis
Lewis Morris

**NEW JERSEY**
Richard Stockton
John Witherspoon
Francis Hopkinson
John Hart
Abraham Clark

**NEW HAMPSHIRE**
Josiah Bartlett
William Whipple
Matthew Thorton

**MASSACHUSETTS**
Samuel Adams
John Adams
Robert Treat Paine
Elbridge Gerry

**RHODE ISLAND**
Stephen Hopkins
William Ellery

**CONNECTICUT**
Roger Sherman
Samuel Huntington
William Williams
Oliver Wolcott

### Exploring the Document

On July 4, 1776, Congress adopted the final draft of the Declaration of Independence. A formal copy written on parchment paper was signed on August 2, 1776. **From whom did the Declaration's signers receive their authority to declare independence in 1776?**

### Exploring the Document

The following is part of a passage that the Congress removed from Jefferson's original draft: "He has waged cruel war against human nature itself, violating its most sacred rights of life and liberty in the persons of a distant people who never offended him, captivating and carrying them into slavery in another hemisphere, or to incur miserable death in their transportation thither." **Why do you think the Congress deleted this passage?**

# SECTION 3

## OBJECTIVES

*After completing Section 3, students should be able to*

1. Identify the principles of Great Britain's government that influenced the ideas of the delegates to the Constitutional Convention.
2. Explain how the U.S. government became stronger under the Constitution.
3. Describe how the viewpoints of the Federalists and Antifederalists differed and how they resolved their differences.

## SECTION 3

# A New Constitution

### Read to Discover

1. What principles of Great Britain's government influenced the ideas of the delegates to the Constitutional Convention?
2. How did the U.S. government become stronger under the Constitution?
3. How did the viewpoints of Federalists and Antifederalists differ, and how did they resolve their differences?

### WHY CIVICS MATTERS

Compromise still plays an important role in the work of a government. Use CNNfyi.com or other **current events** sources to research how government officials have solved a recent problem by reaching a compromise. Record your findings in your journal.

### Define

- delegates
- bicameral
- federalism
- unitary system
- compromise
- legislature
- ratification

### Identify

- Parliament
- Federalists
- Antifederalists

# Reading Focus

In May 1787 a group of the country's most respected leaders from every state but Rhode Island met in Independence Hall in Philadelphia. They had been sent as **delegates**, or representatives, of their states to find ways to improve the national government. The delegates soon became convinced that changing the Articles of Confederation was not enough. They decided instead to create a completely new plan of government—a new constitution.

The meeting became known as the Constitutional Convention. The leaders who attended the Convention wrote a constitution that established a government for the United States. The form of government they created has endured for more than 210 years. The new plan of government drafted by the delegates is the current Constitution of the United States. It is the world's oldest written constitution still governing a country today.

*The Constitutional Convention took place in Independence Hall, Philadelphia.*

## ⭐ The Delegates

The 55 delegates to the Constitutional Convention included many of those who had aided the country's struggle for independence. George Washington had led the Continental Army to victory over the British in

**ALL LEVELS:** Organize the class into three groups. Assign each group either Magna Carta, the English Bill of Rights, or parliamentary government. Then have each group prepare flash cards that illustrate the historical significance of their assignment and how these ideas influenced the delegates to the Constitutional Convention. Finally, have a volunteer from each group present his or her group's cards to the class. **ENGLISH LANGUAGE LEARNERS , COOPERATIVE LEARNING**

**LEVEL 2:** Have students review this section for examples of how British law influenced the delegates to the Constitutional Convention. Then have each student create a menu listing British ideas and laws (as the dishes) and explaining each idea's significance (as a description of the dish). Have students base the price of each dish on the importance of the idea to the Constitution. Higher-priced dishes will represent ideas that were crucial to the Constitution while lower-priced dishes will represent ideas that were included but were not as crucial. *(Students could list Magna Carta; describe it as a charter written in 1215 that limited power of English monarchs; and give it a high price, such as $19.95, because it was a key influence on the Constitution.)* Encourage volunteers to discuss their menus with the class. Finally, review how British ideas and laws influenced early governments in America. **ENGLISH LANGUAGE LEARNERS**

---

the Revolutionary War. Respected by all, he was chosen to preside over the Convention. He called on speakers and kept the meetings running smoothly.

At 81 years of age, Benjamin Franklin—diplomat, inventor, writer—was the oldest delegate to the Constitutional Convention. Among the other delegates were James Madison, Alexander Hamilton, James Wilson, Roger Sherman, William Paterson, and Edmund Randolph. Thomas Jefferson was serving as U.S. ambassador to France and was not present.

✔ **Reading Check Comparing** What did many of the delegates attending the Constitutional Convention have in common? Many had been involved in the country's fight for independence.

## ★ An English Heritage

These leaders were familiar with history, and they had learned many important lessons from the past. The delegates wanted Americans to enjoy all of the rights the English people had fought for and had won during past centuries.

**Magna Carta** This heritage from England included the rights mentioned in Magna Carta (Great Charter). The English nobles had won these rights from King John in 1215. Magna Carta guaranteed that free people could not be arrested, put in prison, or forced to leave their nation unless they were given a trial by a jury of their peers. It guaranteed that the citizens of England were to be judged according to English law only. Magna Carta also protected the rights of Parliament against the monarch.

**English Bill of Rights** The delegates also wished to guarantee Americans the rights contained in the English Bill of Rights of 1689. One of these rights was the right to petition, or request, the government to improve or to change laws. Another was the right to a fair punishment if a citizen were to be found guilty of a crime.

**Parliamentary Government** The Convention delegates also carefully studied the example of parliamentary government in England. **Parliament**, the lawmaking body of Great Britain, is **bicameral.** That is, it consists of two parts, or houses. Parliament is made up of the House of Lords, appointed by the monarch, and the House of Commons, elected by the people. This system enables each house to check and improve the work of the other house. Today, however, the House of Lords holds less power than it once did.

The administration of the government is performed by the prime minister. This official is usually chosen from the political

## BIOGRAPHY

### James Madison
**(1751–1836)**

James Madison was born in Virginia. He attended the College of New Jersey, now Princeton University, before entering politics in Virginia. Early in his career, Madison became a strong supporter of religious freedom. He played a central role in framing the Constitution and adding the Bill of Rights. For these reasons he is often called the Father of the Constitution. Madison served in Congress until 1797. He became secretary of state in 1801 and later served two terms as president. His lengthy and distinguished career in politics gained him a place in American history as one of the country's founders. **Why is Madison called the Father of the Constitution?**

---

## Interdisciplinary Connection

### ▶ Literature ◀

**Preparing to Write the Constitution** James Madison began preparing for the Constitutional Convention in the fall of 1786 by rereading political history, works of classical republicanism, and works of contemporary political theory. With Thomas Jefferson's help, Madison had acquired a small library of the social and economic philosophies of the Enlightenment, including the 37-volume set of Denis Diderot's *Encyclopédie*—a compilation of knowledge and Enlightenment thought. In addition, Madison prepared two papers—one on the weaknesses of modern and ancient confederacies and another titled "Vices of the Political System of the United States," which outlined the political philosophy he applied when creating the Constitution.

**CRITICAL THINKING**

How could Madison's preparation have helped the delegates to the Constitutional Convention?

**ANSWER:** Students might suggest that his reading could provide delegates with inspirational new ideas while his writing analyzed previous political situations.

**BIOGRAPHY ANSWER**

He played a central role in framing the Constitution and adding the Bill of Rights.

## TEACH OBJECTIVE 2

 **LEVEL 1:** Compare government under the Articles of Confederation with that under the Constitution to explain how the U.S. government became stronger with the Constitution's ratification. Begin by drawing two "ships of state" on the chalkboard. Start with the Articles of Confederation. Ask students the following questions: *Did the government have the power to (1) make laws? (2) control trade? (3) collect taxes? (4) raise an army? (5) Did the government have a president to lead it?* Then ask the same questions about the Constitution. For each "yes" answer, draw (1) a hull, (2) masts, (3) sails, (4) cannons, and (5) the captain at the helm. (The final drawing should illustrate that the Articles of Confederation has only a hull while the Constitution is complete.)* **ENGLISH LANGUAGE LEARNERS**

party that holds most of the seats in the House of Commons. The prime minister chooses the top administrative officials in the government. Both the prime minister and his or her appointees can be replaced by Parliament if a majority vote is held.

✔ **Reading Check** Categorizing What parts of the British government did the delegates of the Constitutional Convention want to include in the new country's government? Magna Carta; English Bill of Rights of 1689; bicameral parliament

## ★ Secret Meetings

The delegates to the Constitutional Convention pledged to hold their meetings in secret. They agreed not to discuss any of the business of the Convention outside the Convention. This pledge was made so that the delegates could speak freely during their meetings. The Convention had drawn a great deal of public attention. Some delegates feared that if they spoke publicly on a particular issue, they would be pressured by out-siders. Taking a public stand might also make it more difficult for dele-gates to change their minds after debate and discussion.

Some delegates favored open public debate and criticized the idea of secrecy. Yet without secrecy, agreement on difficult issues might not have been possible.

If the meetings were held in secret, how do we know today what took place during the Convention? We know because of James Madison of Virginia. Madison kept a journal of the proceedings of each meeting. His journal, which was kept secret until after his death, is the chief source of information about the Convention. As Madison himself said of his record-keeping,

 66 It happened . . . that I was not absent a single day, nor more than a casual fraction of an hour in any day, so that I could not have lost a single speech, unless a very short one. 99

✔ **Reading Check** Identifying Points of View Why did the delegates decide to hold the Constitutional Convention secretly? They wanted to keep the meetings open to debate and discussion without outside pressure.

**Interpreting the Visual Record**

**Independence Hall** *The rooms where the Constitutional Con-vention delegates debated and created the Constitution have been preserved as historical landmarks.* **Why do you think this place has been preserved for future generations?**

```
              A STRONGER U.S.
                 GOVERNMENT
          ┌──────────┴──────────┐
```

**Powers of the National Government**
- *Print money*
- *Raise armed forces*
- *Regulate trade*
- *Set taxes*

**Powers Dealing with Laws**
- *Provide a president to carry out the country's laws*
- *Establish the Supreme Court and other national courts to interpret laws*

**LEVEL 3:** Lead a class discussion about the weaknesses of the Articles of Confederation. Then have students reflect on why the Articles were set up as they were in the first place. *(Students might suggest fear of a government that is too strong and so on.)* Organize the class into two groups. Have one group develop arguments for why the Constitution will make the United States stronger. Have the other group develop arguments for why the Articles are sufficient for governing the United States. Finally, have the two groups debate whether the Constitution or the Articles of Confederation is the best document on which to base the government. **COOPERATIVE LEARNING**

## The Articles of Confederation and the Constitution

| Articles (1781) | | Constitution (1789) |
|---|---|---|
| • States are given most powers; the central government is weak and ineffective. |  | • Central government is strong; states keep many powers but accept the Constitution as the supreme law of the land. |
| • No president exists to administer and enforce legislation.<br>• Executive committee oversees government when Congress is out of session. | **Executive Branch**<br> | • President administers and enforces federal laws. |
| • There is no national court system.<br>• Congress establishes temporary courts to hear cases of piracy. | **Judicial Branch**<br> | • National court system is headed by the Supreme Court. |
| • In the unicameral (one-house) legislature each state has one vote.<br>• Approval by 9 out of 13 states is required to pass laws.<br>• Congress has no power to collect taxes, regulate trade, coin money, or to establish armed forces. | **Legislative Branch**<br> | • A bicameral (two-house) legislature consists of the Senate, where each state has equal representation, and the House of Representatives, where each state is represented according to its population.<br>• Simple majority approval is required to pass laws.<br>• Congress can collect taxes, regulate interstate and foreign trade, coin money, and provide for national defense. |

**Interpreting Charts** *The Constitution addressed many of the weaknesses of the Articles of Confederation.* **What key position did the Constitution create that the Articles lacked?**

## Constitutional Heritage

**Constitutional Convention** Amazingly, the delegates to the Constitutional Convention managed to create the foundation of the country in just five months—May to September. More amazing still, they did it in spite of the heat, humidity, and bugs of a season some Philadelphians called the "worst summer since 1750." Commenting on the stifling heat, a French visitor wrote home, "At each inhaling of air, one worries about the next one. The slightest movement is painful."

**ACTIVITY:** Have students imagine that they are delegates to the Constitutional Convention. Then ask them to write a few diary entries from the perspective of a delegate to the convention.

**CHART ANSWER**
the president

## Writing the Constitution

The framers of the Constitution agreed that the national government had to be given greater power. At the same time, the framers agreed that the states should keep the powers needed to govern their own affairs. To achieve this balance, the framers established a system of government known as **federalism,** or a federal system. A federal system divides a government's powers between the national government, which governs the whole country, and state governments, which govern each state. This system is much different from a **unitary system,** in which the national government possesses all legal power. Local governments have no independent authority in a unitary system.

The framers worked out the plan for a federal system at their meetings during the hot summer months of 1787. There were some significant disagreements among the delegates, but they were committed to

**ALL LEVELS:** Organize the class into groups. Randomly assign groups to assume the role of either Federalists or Antifederalists. Ask each group to create a pamphlet in support of its view of the ratification issue. Using such things as slogans, headlines, articles, editorials, and political cartoons, the finished pamphlets should make an argument for or against the proposed strong national government. Finally, lead a class discussion about how the Federalists and Antifederalists resolved their differences on ratification.
**ENGLISH LANGUAGE LEARNERS , COOPERATIVE LEARNING**

**LEVEL 3:** Lead a class discussion about how the Federalists and Antifederalists could not agree about the Constitution. Tell students that it was not until the Bill of Rights was added that the Antifederalists agreed to support the Constitution. Then have students read the Bill of Rights. Ask each student to write a one to two sentence summary of each amendment explaining the rights that the amendment guarantees. Finally, have students rewrite each amendment in their own terms to guarantee certain rights that they feel need to be protected in today's society. (*Students' sentences will vary but may include the protection of privacy or security in schools.*)

## ★ Constitutional Heritage

**The Delegates** James Madison echoed the thoughts of most delegates when he said he hoped the Constitution would "last for ages." Benjamin Franklin stated this idea another way. "Our new Constitution is now established, and has an appearance that promises permanency," he declared, "but in this world nothing can be said to be certain, except death and taxes."

### CRITICAL THINKING

Why might Franklin have been skeptical that a constitution could last for ages?

**ANSWER:** Students might mention that the new United States had already created and then discarded one government and that it was possible that the Constitution would not meet with success.

### 💻 internet connect

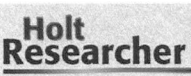

**TOPIC:** Federalists and Antifederalists
**GO TO:** go.hrw.com
**KEYWORD:** SZ3 AC2

Have students access the Internet through the HRW Go site to research noted Federalists and Antifederalists. Then have students write a biography about a Federalist or Antifederalist of their choice.

### Holt Researcher

**go.hrw.com**
**KEYWORD: Holt Researcher**

**Freefind:** Constitutional Convention

Search for information on delegates to the Constitutional Convention on the Holt Researcher. Pick at least two delegates and use the information to write a brief newspaper article that answers the following question: What roles did these delegates play in making the Constitutional Convention a success?

producing a constitution. George Washington explained the attitudes of many of the delegates.

> **Civics Voices**
> ❝To please all is impossible, . . . The only way, therefore, is . . . to form such a government as will bear the scrutinizing (questioning) eye of criticism, and trust it to the good sense and patriotism of the people. ❞

The delegates discussed many ideas and proposals and eventually settled many differences of opinion by a series of compromises. A **compromise** is an agreement in which each side gives up part of its demands in order to reach a solution to a problem.

The most serious disagreement arose over the question of representation in the new national **legislature,** or lawmaking body. The larger states favored a legislature in which representation would be based on the size of a state's population. The smaller states wanted each state to have an equal number of representatives in the legislature.

For weeks the framers debated this issue. Finally, both sides agreed to a compromise. Their agreement provided for a bicameral lawmaking body called Congress. In one house, the Senate, the states were to have equal representation. In the other house, the House of Representatives, each state was to be represented according to the size of its population. This agreement became known as the Great Compromise.

✔ **Reading Check** Evaluating How was the Great Compromise an effective agreement? It settled the disagreement between the large and small states over representation in the legislature by forming the Senate and House of Representatives.

## ★ A Strong New Country

Other compromises were reached as the delegates worked on the Constitution. The framers increased the powers of the national government. It could now coin and print money, raise armed forces, regulate trade among the states and with foreign nations, and set taxes. Provision was made for a president to carry out the country's laws. The Supreme Court and other national courts would interpret these laws. The chart on page 43 shows the major differences between the Articles of Confederation and the Constitution.

By September 1787 the delegates had completed their work. Probably no delegate was satisfied with each and every part of the document. For example, Benjamin Franklin did not approve of parts of the Constitution. Nevertheless, he believed that the framers had

**Interpreting the Visual Record** Ratification parade
*Federalists in New York celebrated the state's ratification of the Constitution with a parade.* **Why do you think these people felt that ratification of the Constitution was a cause for celebration?**

HOMEWORK Have students imagine that they were part of the Constitutional Convention. Then have each student write a journal entry about one of the compromises that were made during the drafting of the Constitution. Students' entries should also examine how this compromise affected the future government.

**CLOSE**

Have students outline this section. Suggest that each student write each of the headings from the section on a sheet of paper, followed by one or two sentences summarizing the material under each heading. Students should save their outlines to use as study guides.

written the best constitution possible. For this reason, he urged the delegates to sign the document.

Most of the delegates shared Franklin's belief. On September 17 the Constitution was signed by 39 of the 42 framers present. After a farewell dinner, the delegates left for home.

✔ **Reading Check** Finding the Main Idea What other key compromises were reached at the Constitutional Convention? The powers of the national government were increased. The executive and judicial branches were established.

## Approving the Constitution

The work of the members of the Constitutional Convention was not over when they left Philadelphia. The Constitution now had to be sent to the states for their **ratification,** or approval. Before the Constitution could go into effect, it had to be ratified by 9 of the 13 states. Each state set up a special convention of delegates to vote on the Constitution.

People quickly separated over whether or not to adopt the Constitution. Some people strongly supported the new plan of government. Others were opposed to it. The public was swamped with pamphlets, letters to newspapers, and speeches representing both sides of the debate.

✔ **Reading Check** Analyzing Information Why did the Constitution not go into effect after the Constitutional Convention ended? It still had to be ratified.

## Federalists and Antifederalists

Supporters of the Constitution, who favored a strong national government, were called **Federalists**. The Federalists argued that a strong national government was needed to keep the country united. They feared that unless the Constitution was adopted, the United States would break up into 13 separate countries. Alexander Hamilton, John Jay, and James Madison were leading Federalists. They published a series of articles known as the *Federalist Papers* to help increase support for the Constitution.

People who opposed the new Constitution and the federal system of government were called **Antifederalists**. They feared that a constitution that established such a strong national government defeated the purpose of the Revolutionary War. The Antifederalists believed that the proposed Constitution would protect neither the states' power nor the people's freedom.

✔ **Reading Check** Contrasting About what issues did Federalists and Antifederalists disagree? Federalists wanted a strong national government and supported approval of the Constitution. Antifederalists wanted the states to remain sovereign and believed the Constitution would not protect the states' power.

*Did You* **KNOW?**

The authors of the *Federalist Papers* all used the same pen name, Publius. Historians later determined that of the 85 essays, Alexander Hamilton wrote about 50, James Madison about 30, and John Jay the rest.

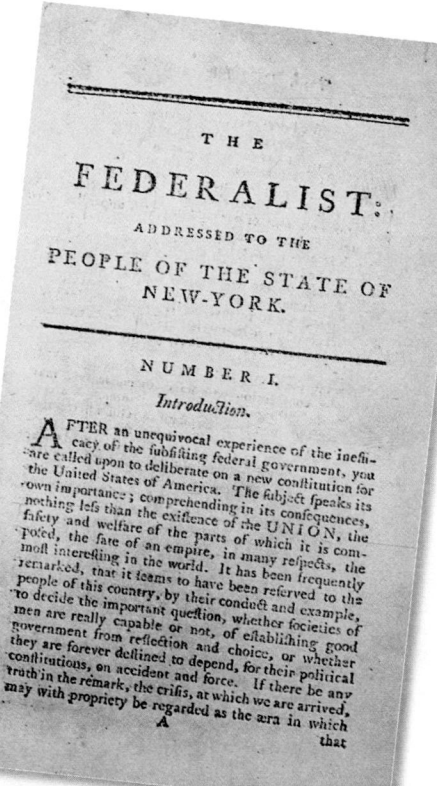
*Alexander Hamilton and James Madison wrote the majority of the* Federalist Papers.

THE
FEDERALIST:
ADDRESSED TO THE
PEOPLE OF THE STATE OF
NEW-YORK.

NUMBER I.
*Introduction.*

AFTER an unequivocal experience of the inefficacy of the subsisting federal government, you are called upon to deliberate on a new constitution for the United States of America. The subject speaks its own importance; comprehending in its consequences, nothing less than the existence of the UNION, the safety and welfare of the parts of which it is composed, the fate of an empire, in many respects, the most interesting in the world. It has been frequently remarked, that it seems to have been reserved to the people of this country, by their conduct and example, to decide the important question, whether societies of men are really capable or not, of establishing good government from reflection and choice, or whether they are forever destined to depend, for their political constitutions, on accident and force. If there be any truth in the remark, the crisis, at which we are arrived, may with propriety be regarded as the æra in which that

**Visual Record Answer**

*Students might suggest that it provided them with a stronger national government.*

## REVIEW AND ASSESS

Have students complete the **Section 3 Review** on page 46. Then have them complete **Daily Quiz 2.3**. As **Alternative Assessment**, you may want to use the menu or Bill of Rights activity in this section's lessons.

## RETEACH

Have students complete **Main Idea Activity for English Language Learners and Special-Needs Students 2.3**. Have each student create an annotated time line of the events in the section. Tell them to include specific information about each key event on their time lines. Ask volunteers to present their time lines to the class. **ENGLISH LANGUAGE LEARNERS**

## EXTEND

Have students conduct research about the similarities between the U.S. government under the Constitution and other world governments such as those of the Iroquois League, England, the Roman Republic and Empire, and ancient Greece. Then have each student design a poster to illustrate the various similarities as well as a time line to demonstrate when each government existed in relation to the U.S. government under the Constitution. **BLOCK SCHEDULING**

## Section 3 Review
### ANSWERS

**1. Define**
• delegates, p. 40
• bicameral, p. 41
• federalism, p. 43
• unitary system, p. 43
• compromise, p. 44
• legislature, p. 44
• ratification, p. 45

**2. Identify**
• Parliament, p. 41
• Federalists, p. 45
• Antifederalists, p. 45

**3.** Main Ideas—stronger central government, bicameral government; Influences—Magna Carta, English Bill of Rights; Compromises—bicameral legislature, delegates such as Franklin accepting Constitution despite disagreeing with some parts

**4. a.** freedoms and rights expressed in Magna Carta and English Bill of Rights of 1689 as well as the ideas of a bicameral legislature

**b.** Federalists—believed government under the Articles too weak to keep the country united; Antifederalists—feared that Constitution would not protect states or freedom of the people; settled by agreeing to add Bill of Rights

**5.** Students' speeches will vary but should stress how the Constitution will provide a stronger central government to deal with taxation, trade, laws, and currency.

This engraved poster shows George Washington surrounded by the seals of each of the original 13 states.

### ★ The Constitution Is Ratified

Gradually, Federalists gained support. However, many citizens were upset that the Constitution did not contain a list of the rights of the people. Some states suggested that such a list, or bill, of rights should be added if the new Constitution was ratified.

Most of the states ratified the Constitution in 1787 and 1788. The required ninth state ratified it in June 1788, and the new U.S. government began to operate in March 1789. Two states, North Carolina and Rhode Island, did not approve the Constitution until after it went into effect.

New York City was chosen as the country's temporary capital. Members of the new Senate and House of Representatives arrived to begin their work. On April 30, 1789, George Washington was sworn in as the first president of the United States. The country's new government was under way.

The U.S. Constitution is a remarkable and important document. Every American should read and study it carefully. You will learn more about the government established by the Constitution in Chapter 3.

✔ **Reading Check** Analyzing Information When did the required ninth state ratify the Constitution, and when did the new U.S. government begin operating? June 1788; March 1789

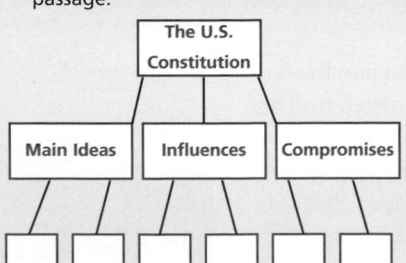

## SECTION 3 Review

go.hrw.com **Homework Practice Online**
keyword: SZ3 HP2

**1. Define** and explain:
• delegates
• bicameral
• federalism
• unitary system
• compromise
• legislature
• ratification

**2. Identify** and explain:
• Parliament
• Federalists
• Antifederalists

**3. Categorizing** Copy the chart below. Use it to show some of the Constitution's main ideas, its influences, and the compromises that allowed for its passage.

The U.S. Constitution
Main Ideas — Influences — Compromises

**4. Finding the Main Idea**
a. What ideas of government did the delegates to the Constitutional Convention borrow from Great Britain?
b. What ideas about government divided Federalists and Antifederalists?

**5. Writing and Critical Thinking**
**Contrasting** Write a speech that supports ratification of the Constitution. Compare the Constitution to the Articles of Confederation and explain how the Constitution will strengthen the national government.

**Consider:**
• taxes
• interstate and international trade
• the power of the national government

## TEACH

**LEVEL 1:** Have students choose another picture from this chapter. Then ask each student to apply the skill of interpreting pictures that is discussed on this page. Have students write down the four main observations needed to interpret their chosen pictures. *(Students' answers should include what or who is the subject, an examination of the details, a determination of the artist's point of view, and a determination of whether the information in the picture is accurate.)* **ENGLISH LANGUAGE LEARNERS**

**LEVEL 3:** Have students study the picture on this page and follow the guidelines to interpret the picture. Then have students use the picture to write a narrative of the scene. Students' narratives should provide the following information: what is happening in the picture; if the event is significant and why; who the people in the picture are; where this event is; what the outcome of the event might be; and what might happen if this event did not occur. Encourage students to present their narrative to the class.

# Civics Skills
## WORKSHOP

## Learning from Pictures

According to an old saying, "One picture is worth a thousand words." A painting or a photograph, however, does not speak for itself. You have to know how to examine and interpret a picture before you can fully grasp its meaning.

There are easy guidelines you can follow that will help you learn to get the most information from the paintings and photographs in your textbook.

## How to Learn from Pictures

1. **Determine the subject.** Look at the people who are portrayed in the picture and take note of any objects around these people. Determine what the people portrayed in the picture are doing. Read the title and caption of the picture for clues to its subject matter.

2. **Examine the details.** Study the details of the picture, including the picture's background. All of the visual evidence in a picture is important to understanding a historical event or time period. The picture's details are clues to its content, importance, and relevance.

3. **Determine the artist's point of view.** Most people think that a picture presents only facts. Any photograph or painting, however, also expresses the artist's ideas and feelings about a subject. Certain details are emphasized over the rest. Other details are left out. Determine whether the artist is portraying the events in the picture favorably or unfavorably.

4. **Put the data to use.** Determine whether the information presented in the picture is an accurate description of the actual events. Remember that a picture is an artist's interpretation of an event. Therefore, consider what you already know about the event or time period. Knowing whether the picture is accurate will give you clues about how to interpret and use the information.

## Applying the Skill

Examine the painting below, which shows a woman representing Liberty providing the gift of education to newly freed slaves. Then answer the questions that follow.

1. How does the artist portray Liberty and the freed slaves?

2. Why do you think the artist thought that education was an important right for free people?

3. What document might have encouraged some Americans to call for freeing the slaves?

Library Company of Philadelphia

---

### SKILLS ANSWERS

1. Students might suggest that Liberty is teaching the freed slaves.

2. Students might suggest that the artist may have felt that education was a right for all citizens.

3. Some students might suggest the Constitution.

## CHAPTER 2
### REVIEW ANSWERS

**Define and Identify**
1. dictatorship, p. 26
2. democracy, p. 26
3. republic, p. 26
4. constitution, p. 28
5. confederation, p. 32
6. sovereignty, p. 32
7. legislature, p. 44
8. ratification, p. 45
9. Federalists, p. 45
10. Antifederalists, p. 45

**Understanding Main Ideas**
1. beliefs and history of the people

2. In a democracy the people either rule directly or indirectly by electing representatives while in other forms of government the people have little to no control.

3. to declare the colonies' independence from Great Britain and to list the human-rights abuses of King George

4. no president or national court system; could not collect taxes, regulate trade, or issue official currency; no strong central government to foster national unity

**47**

## CHAPTER 2 — Review and Assessment Resources

### REPRODUCIBLE
▶ Chapter 2 Review, pp. 48–49
▶ Vocabulary Activity 2
▶ Chapter 2 Tutorial for Students, Parents, Mentors, and Peers
▶ Chapter 2 Test (Form A or B)
▶ Alternative Assessment Handbook, Chapter 2

### TECHNOLOGY
▶ Chapter 2 Test Generator (on the One-Stop Planner)
▶ Global Skill Builder CD–ROM
▶ HRW Go site

### REINFORCEMENT, REVIEW, AND ASSESSMENT
▶ Chapter 2 Test for English Language Learners and Special-Needs Students

## REVIEW

Have students complete the **Chapter 2 Review** on pages 48–49.

## ASSESS

Use one of the chapter tests to assess students' understanding of the content. For **Alternative Assessment**, see the **Alternative Assessment Handbook**.

---

**5.** provided ideas about parliamentary government and about the protection of human rights

**6.** the Constitution of the United States

**7.** Federalists—Articles were too weak to keep the country united; Antifederalists—Constitution would not protect the states or the people.

**What Did You Find Out?**
**1.** to make and enforce rules, provide services, help people cooperate, and to put ideals into practice

**2.** the Articles of Confederation; strengths—provided a government for the new nation, gave power to states instead of an absolute monarch; weaknesses—established a weak central government and allotted too much control to the states

**3.** gave the national government many of the powers previously reserved for the states as well as provided for an executive branch to enforce laws and for a judicial branch to interpret laws

---

# Chapter 2 Review

## Chapter Summary

### Section 1
- Several different types of government, including monarchies, dictatorships, and democracies, exist around the world. Governments frequently differ in the ways leaders are chosen and in the amount of power held by their people.
- Government serves several important functions. It helps people cooperate, provides services and rules, and puts ideals held by the country's people into practice.

### Section 2
- Because Americans believed that the people should rule themselves, the American colonies declared independence from Great Britain.
- The ideals of the American people are clearly set forth in the Declaration of Independence. The fundamental basis of the Declaration is that government should protect human rights.
- The Articles of Confederation established the first government of the 13 states. Under this plan, the national government was weak and ineffective.

### Section 3
- In 1787, delegates to the Constitutional Convention wrote a new plan of government for the United States.
- This plan, the Constitution of the United States, created a stronger national government and established a lawmaking body called Congress. The Constitution also provided for a president to carry out the laws and for national courts to interpret the laws.
- Supporters of the Constitution were called Federalists. Opponents of the Constitution were called Antifederalists. Most of the states ratified the Constitution between 1787 and 1789. It went into effect in 1789.

## Define and Identify
Use the following terms in complete sentences.
1. dictatorship
2. democracy
3. republic
4. constitution
5. confederation
6. sovereignty
7. legislature
8. ratification
9. Federalists
10. Antifederalists

## Understanding Main Ideas
**Section 1** *(Pages 25–29)*
1. What are two of the major factors that shape a country's government?
2. How are a democracy and other types of governments different?

**Section 2** *(Pages 30–35)*
3. What were the key purposes of the Declaration of Independence?
4. What were some of the problems the country faced after independence was declared?

**Section 3** *(Pages 40–46)*
5. In what ways did the colonists' English political heritage influence American ideas about government and individual rights?
6. What was the outcome of the Constitutional Convention?
7. What were the arguments of the Federalists and Antifederalists?

## What Did You Find Out?
1. Why do people have government?
2. What was the United States's first national plan of government called, and what were its strengths and weaknesses?
3. What did the Constitutional Convention do to create a strong new government?

## Thinking Critically
1. **Making Generalizations and Predictions** What might life be like for U.S. citizens today if government did not exist?
2. **Supporting a Point of View** Do you think that the United States would have grown from its original thirteen colonies if the country were still governed by the Articles of Confederation? Explain your answer.
3. **Analyzing Information** Explain the role of compromise in the Constitutional Convention. How have you used compromise to settle a disagreement about an issue?

**48**

## RETEACH

Organize students into three groups and assign each group one of the chapter's sections. Have groups create maps or diagrams illustrating the main ideas in their assigned section. Ask groups to illustrate each event and to include any relevant dates and captions. Finally, have each group present its work to the class.

**ENGLISH LANGUAGE LEARNERS ,
COOPERATIVE LEARNING**

## Portfolio Extensions

*American Civics*

### 1. Linking to Community
Remind students how important compromise was to the Constitutional Convention. Have students think of an issue in their community that was resolved by a compromise. Then have them write a detailed description of how the compromise was carried out.

**2. Cooperative Learning** Organize students into small groups. Ask groups to list some of the ideas about government that the convention delegates borrowed from Great Britain. Then assign groups a country that has modeled its constitution after the U.S. Constitution. Ask each group to conduct research on that country's constitution and to present a report about that constitution to the class.

---

## Building Social Studies Skills

STANDARDIZED TEST PREP ONLINE
keyword: SZ3 STP2

### Interpreting Charts
Study the chart below on the ratification of the U.S. Constitution. Use the information on the chart to answer the questions that follow.

### Ratifying the Constitution

| State | Ratification Date |
| --- | --- |
| Delaware | December 7, 1787 |
| Pennsylvania | December 12, 1787 |
| New Jersey | December 18, 1787 |
| Georgia | January 2, 1788 |
| Connecticut | January 9, 1788 |
| Massachusetts | February 6, 1788 |
| Maryland | April 28, 1788 |
| South Carolina | May 23, 1788 |
| New Hampshire | June 21, 1788 |
| Virginia | June 25, 1788 |
| New York | July 26, 1788 |
| North Carolina | November 21, 1789 |
| Rhode Island | May 29, 1790 |

1. About how many months passed between the times that the first and last states ratified the Constitution?
   a. 30
   b. 33
   c. 6
   d. 3
2. Based on your knowledge of the requirements for ratification, when did the Constitution go into effect?

### Analyzing Primary Sources
Read the following quotation from Federalist Paper No. 51, by James Madison, then answer the questions that follow.

❝But what is government but the greatest of all reflections on human nature? If men were angels, no government would be necessary. If angels were to govern men, neither external nor internal controls on government would be necessary. In framing a government which is to be administered [operated] by men over men, the great difficulty lies in this: you must first enable the government to control the governed; and in the next place oblige [force] it to control itself.❞

3. Which of the following best describes Madison's point of view?
   a. Government is not necessary because men are angels.
   b. There should be no controls on government so that it can run smoothly.
   c. The government must have the power to rule but limits must be placed on that power.
   d. Men should behave like angels.
4. Based on your knowledge of the period, why do you think that Madison thought it was important that the government be forced to control itself?

### Thinking Critically
1. Students' answers will vary.

2. Students' answers will vary, but some might suggest that the Articles were too weak to help the country grow from its original size.

3. Compromise permits people with opposing views to agree on a final conclusion. Students' answers will vary.

### Social Studies Skills
1. a

2. 1789

3. c

4. Students might say that the government must control itself because it is composed of human beings who must have rules.

---

## Alternative Assessment

### Building Your Portfolio

*American Civics*

#### Interdisciplinary Connection
Use your textbook or the library to research the Constitutional Convention. Then prepare interviews with delegates to the convention. Questions and answers should describe the Constitution itself, the convention, and the debate and compromises that took place. Present your interviews to the class and discuss how meetings like the Constitutional Convention take place in your community.

### internet connect

**Internet Activity: go.hrw.com
keyword: SZ3 AC2**

Access the Internet through the HRW Go site to research the Constitutional Convention. Then imagine you are one of the delegates. Create a series of journal entries outlining what you thought and how you voted. Make sure you reflect on the different plans for government and give your own view on which plans would have been best for the nation.

# THE CONSTITUTION

**The Preamble** Although short, the Preamble was hotly debated in the state ratifying conventions. The phrase "We the People" was particularly contentious because the delegates to the conventions had been appointed by states rather than elected by the people. Patrick Henry challenged this phrase during the ratifying process in Virginia saying, "The people gave them [the delegates to the Constitutional Convention] no power to use their name. That they exceeded their power is perfectly clear."

**CRITICAL THINKING**

How might someone have countered Henry's argument?

**ANSWER:** Students might suggest that people gave the states the right to appoint the delegates, so the people did actually give them power.

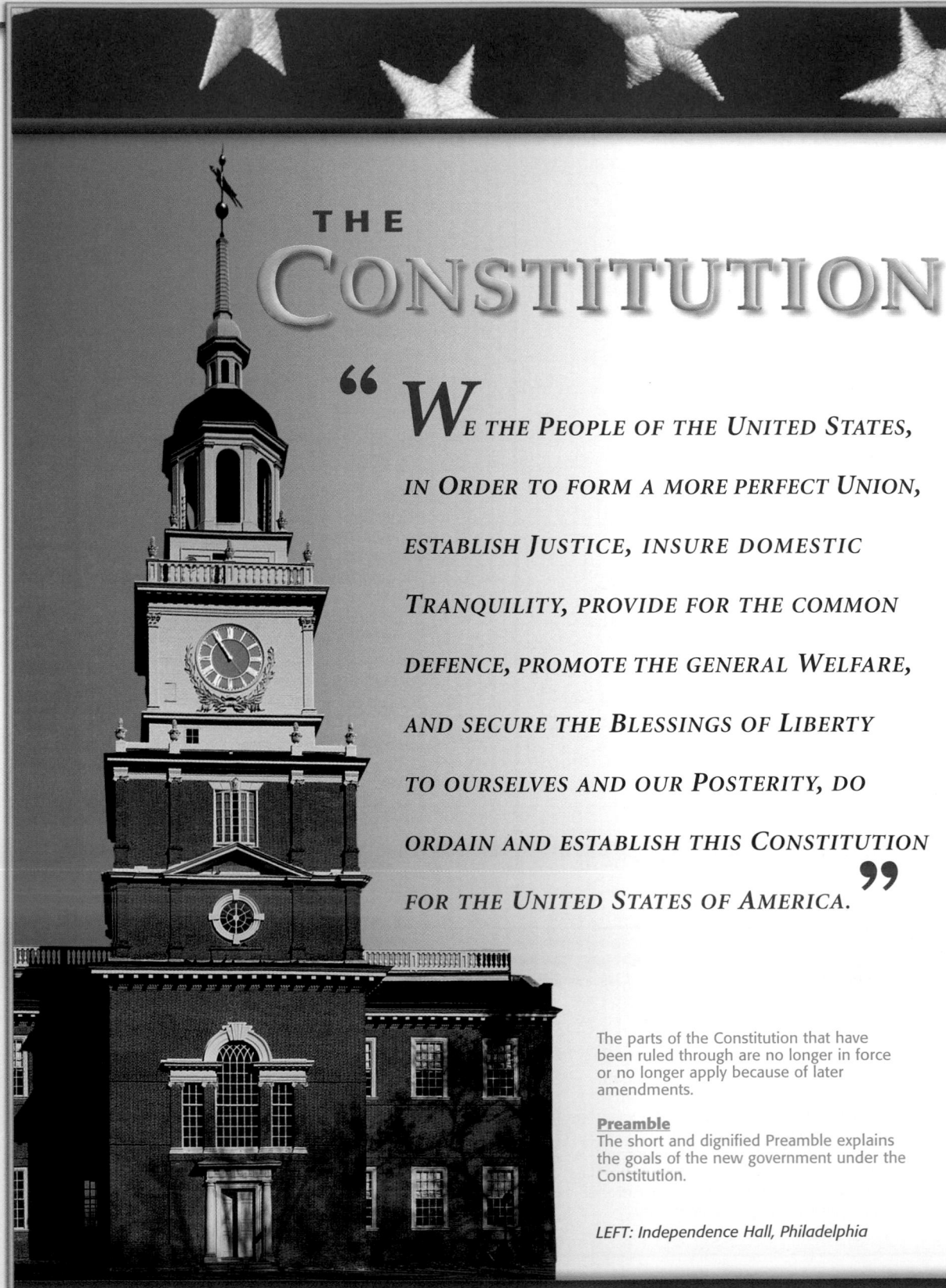

# THE CONSTITUTION

" *We the People of the United States,*

*in Order to form a more perfect Union,*

*establish Justice, insure domestic*

*Tranquility, provide for the common*

*defence, promote the general Welfare,*

*and secure the Blessings of Liberty*

*to ourselves and our Posterity, do*

*ordain and establish this Constitution*

*for the United States of America.* "

The parts of the Constitution that have been ruled through are no longer in force or no longer apply because of later amendments.

**Preamble**
The short and dignified Preamble explains the goals of the new government under the Constitution.

*LEFT: Independence Hall, Philadelphia*

## ARTICLE I

**Section 1.** All legislative Powers herein granted shall be vested in a Congress of the United States, which shall consist of a Senate and House of Representatives.

**Section 2.** The House of Representatives shall be composed of Members chosen every second Year by the People of the several States, and the Electors in each State shall have the Qualifications requisite for Electors of the most numerous Branch of the State Legislature.

No Person shall be a Representative who shall not have attained to the Age of twenty five Years, and been seven Years a Citizen of the United States, and who shall not, when elected, be an Inhabitant of that State in which he shall be chosen.

Representatives and direct Taxes shall be apportioned among the several States which may be included within this Union, according to their respective Numbers, which shall be determined by adding to the whole Number of free Persons, including **those bound to Service**[1] for a Term of Years, and excluding Indians not taxed, three fifths of **all other Persons**.[2] The actual **Enumeration**[3] shall be made within three Years after the first Meeting of the Congress of the United States, and within every subsequent Term of ten Years, in such Manner as they shall by Law direct. The Number of Representatives shall not exceed one for every thirty Thousand, but each State shall have at Least one Representative; and until such enumeration shall be made, the State of New Hampshire shall be entitled to chuse three; Massachusetts eight; Rhode Island and Providence Plantations one; Connecticut five; New York six; New Jersey four; Pennsylvania eight; Delaware one; Maryland six; Virginia ten; North Carolina five; South Carolina five; and Georgia three.

When vacancies happen in the Representation from any State, the Executive Authority thereof shall issue Writs of Election to fill such Vacancies.

The House of Representatives shall chuse their Speaker and other Officers; and shall have the sole Power of Impeachment.

**Section 3.** The Senate of the United States shall be composed of two Senators from each State, chosen by the Legislature thereof, for six Years; and each Senator shall have one Vote.

Immediately after they shall be assembled in Consequence of the first Election, they shall be divided as equally as may be into three Classes. The Seats of the Senators of the first Class shall be vacated at the Expiration of the second Year, of the second Class at the Expiration of the fourth Year, and of the third Class at the Expiration of the sixth Year, so that one third may be chosen every second Year; and if Vacancies happen by

**Legislative Branch**
Article I explains how the legislative branch, called Congress, is organized. The chief purpose of the legislative branch is to make the laws. Congress is made up of the Senate and the House of Representatives.

**The House of Representatives**
The number of representatives that each state has in the House is based on the population of the individual state. In 1929 Congress permanently fixed the size of the House at 435 members.

[1] **those bound to Service:** indentured servants
[2] **all other Persons:** slaves
[3] **Enumeration:** census or official population count

**The Vice President**
The only duty that the Constitution assigns to the vice president is to preside over meetings of the Senate. Modern presidents have usually given their vice presidents more responsibilities.

[4] **pro tempore:** temporarily
[5] **Impeachments:** official accusations of federal wrongdoing

## Exploring the Document

If the House of Representatives charges a government official with wrongdoing, the Senate acts as a court to decide if the official is guilty. **How does the power of impeachment represent part of the system of checks and balances?**

[6] **Quorum:** the minimum number of people needed to conduct business
[7] **adjourn:** to stop indefinitely

~~Resignation, or otherwise, during the Recess of the Legislature of any State, the Executive thereof may make temporary Appointments until the next Meeting of the Legislature, which shall then fill such Vacancies.~~

No Person shall be a Senator who shall not have attained to the Age of thirty Years, and been nine Years a Citizen of the United States, and who shall not, when elected, be an Inhabitant of that State for which he shall be chosen.

The Vice President of the United States shall be President of the Senate, but shall have no Vote, unless they be equally divided.

The Senate shall chuse their other Officers, and also a President **pro tempore,**[4] in the Absence of the Vice President, or when he shall exercise the Office of President of the United States.

The Senate shall have the sole Power to try all **Impeachments.**[5] When sitting for that Purpose, they shall be on Oath or Affirmation. When the President of the United States is tried, the Chief Justice shall preside: And no Person shall be convicted without the Concurrence of two thirds of the Members present.

Judgment in Cases of Impeachment shall not extend further than to removal from Office, and disqualification to hold and enjoy any Office of honor, Trust or Profit under the United States: but the Party convicted shall nevertheless be liable and subject to Indictment, Trial, Judgment and Punishment, according to Law.

**Section 4.** The Times, Places and Manner of holding Elections for Senators and Representatives, shall be prescribed in each State by the Legislature thereof; but the Congress may at any time by Law make or alter such Regulations, except as to the Places of chusing Senators.

~~The Congress shall assemble at least once in every Year, and such Meeting shall be on the first Monday in December, unless they shall by Law appoint a different Day.~~

**Section 5.** Each House shall be the Judge of the Elections, Returns and Qualifications of its own Members, and a Majority of each shall constitute a **Quorum**[6] to do Business; but a smaller Number may **adjourn**[7] from day to day, and may be authorized to compel the Attendance of absent Members, in such Manner, and under such Penalties as each House may provide.

Each House may determine the Rules of its Proceedings, punish its Members for disorderly Behaviour, and, with the Concurrence of two thirds, expel a Member.

Each House shall keep a Journal of its Proceedings, and from time to time publish the same, excepting such Parts as may in their Judgment require Secrecy; and the Yeas and Nays of the Members of either House on any question shall, at the Desire of one fifth of those Present, be entered on the Journal.

Neither House, during the Session of Congress, shall, without the Consent of the other, adjourn for more than three days, nor to any other Place than that in which the two Houses shall be sitting.

**Section 6.** The Senators and Representatives shall receive a Compensation for their Services, to be ascertained by Law, and paid out of the Treasury of the United States. They shall in all Cases, except Treason, Felony and Breach of the Peace, be privileged from Arrest during their Attendance at the Session of their respective Houses, and in going to and returning from the same; and for any Speech or Debate in either House, they shall not be questioned in any other Place.

No Senator or Representative shall, during the Time for which he was elected, be appointed to any civil Office under the Authority of the United States, which shall have been created, or the **Emoluments**[8] whereof shall have been encreased during such time; and no Person holding any Office under the United States, shall be a Member of either House during his **Continuance**[9] in Office.

**Section 7.** All **Bills**[10] for raising Revenue shall originate in the House of Representatives; but the Senate may propose or concur with Amendments as on other Bills.

Every Bill which shall have passed the House of Representatives and the Senate, shall, before it become a Law, be presented to the President of the United States; If he approve he shall sign it, but if not he shall return it, with his Objections to that House in which it shall have originated, who shall enter the Objections at large on their Journal, and proceed to reconsider it. If after such Reconsideration two thirds of that House shall agree to pass the Bill, it shall be sent, together with the Objections, to the other House, by which it shall likewise be reconsidered, and if approved by two thirds of that House, it shall become a Law. But in all such Cases the Votes of both Houses shall be determined by yeas and Nays, and the Names of the Persons voting for and against the Bill shall be entered on the Journal of each House respectively. If any Bill shall not be returned by the President within ten Days (Sundays excepted) after it shall have been presented to him, the Same shall be a Law, in like Manner as if he had signed it, unless the Congress by their Adjournment prevent its Return, in which Case it shall not be a Law.

Every Order, Resolution, or Vote to which the Concurrence of the Senate and House of Representatives may be necessary (except on a question of Adjournment) shall be presented to the President of the United States; and before the Same shall take Effect, shall be approved by him, or being disapproved by him, shall be repassed by two thirds of the Senate and House of Representatives, according to the Rules and Limitations prescribed in the Case of a Bill.

[8] **Emoluments:** salary

[9] **Continuance:** term

[10] **Bills:** proposed laws

**Exploring the Document**

The framers felt that because members of the House are elected every two years, representatives would listen to the public and seek its approval before passing taxes. **How does Section 7 address the colonial demand of "no taxation without representation"?**

**Exploring the Document**

The veto power of the president is one of the important checks and balances in the Constitution. **Why do you think the framers included the ability of Congress to override a veto?**

### Linking Past to Present

**Veto Power** In 1996 Congress passed the line-item veto, which gave the president the power to cancel specific items in spending bills. Proponents of the law hoped that it would help stop wasteful spending by allowing the president to prevent spending that he or she considered unnecessary. Soon a group of lawmakers challenged the line-item veto on constitutional grounds, however a federal court decided that the law was unconstitutional because it upset the system of checks and balances built into the Constitution. The judge claimed that the power to revoke spending appropriations after they are passed is a congressional one and "according to the framers' careful design, may not be delegated at all." In June 1998 the Supreme Court struck down the line-item veto, confirming the lower court's ruling that it was unconstitutional.

**CRITICAL THINKING**

Do you think the line-item veto would significantly change the system of checks and balances that the framers built into the Constitution?

**ANSWER:** Students' answers will vary, but some may suggest that it would grant the president too much power. Others may argue that it would be a useful way for the president to help Congress control spending.

### The First Postal Service

Before the Constitution was ratified, Congress had established a postal service under the Articles of Confederation. Benjamin Franklin served as the postmaster general. The postal service expanded rapidly, with revenue increasing from $37,935 in 1790 to $1,707,000 by 1829. By the early 1800s the government considered the post office so important that the postmaster general was made a cabinet member.

**ACTIVITY:** Have students use the school library to research the history of the postal service. Ask them to prepare a time line describing changes in postal service.

### EXPLORING THE DOCUMENT ANSWER
*(for page 53)*
Students might say that officials who are elected more frequently will be held more accountable for raising taxes.

### EXPLORING THE DOCUMENT ANSWER
*(for page 53)*
Students might suggest that this congressional power is included for checks and balances reasons.

[11] **Duties:** tariffs

[12] **Imposts:** taxes

[13] **Excises:** internal taxes on the manufacture, sale, or consumption of a commodity

[14] **Rule of Naturalization:** a law by which a foreign-born person becomes a citizen

[15] **Securities:** bonds

[16] **Letters of Marque and Reprisal:** documents issued by governments allowing merchant ships to arm themselves and attack ships of an enemy nation

### The Elastic Clause
The framers of the Constitution wanted a national government that was strong enough to be effective. This section lists the powers given to Congress. The last sentence in Section 8 contains the so-called elastic clause—which has been stretched (like elastic) to allow Congress to meet changing circumstances.

**Section 8.** The Congress shall have Power To lay and collect Taxes, **Duties,**[11] **Imposts**[12] and **Excises,**[13] to pay the Debts and provide for the common Defence and general Welfare of the United States; but all Duties, Imposts and Excises shall be uniform throughout the United States;

To borrow Money on the credit of the United States;

To regulate Commerce with foreign Nations, and among the several States, and with the Indian Tribes;

To establish an uniform **Rule of Naturalization,**[14] and uniform Laws on the subject of Bankruptcies throughout the United States;

To coin Money, regulate the Value thereof, and of foreign Coin, and fix the Standard of Weights and Measures;

To provide for the Punishment of counterfeiting the **Securities**[15] and current Coin of the United States;

To establish Post Offices and post Roads;

To promote the Progress of Science and useful Arts, by securing for limited Times to Authors and Inventors the exclusive Right to their respective Writings and Discoveries;

To constitute Tribunals inferior to the supreme Court;

To define and punish Piracies and Felonies committed on the high Seas, and Offences against the Law of Nations;

To declare War, grant **Letters of Marque and Reprisal,**[16] and make Rules concerning Captures on Land and Water;

To raise and support Armies, but no Appropriation of Money to that Use shall be for a longer Term than two Years;

To provide and maintain a Navy;

To make Rules for the Government and Regulation of the land and naval Forces;

To provide for calling forth the Militia to execute the Laws of the Union, suppress Insurrections and repel Invasions;

To provide for organizing, arming, and disciplining, the Militia, and for governing such Part of them as may be employed in the Service of the United States, reserving to the States respectively, the Appointment of the Officers, and the Authority of training the Militia according to the discipline prescribed by Congress;

To exercise exclusive Legislation in all Cases whatsoever, over such District (not exceeding ten Miles square) as may, by Cession of particular States, and the Acceptance of Congress, become the Seat of the Government of the United States, and to exercise like Authority over all Places purchased by the Consent of the Legislature of the State in which the Same shall be, for the Erection of Forts, Magazines, Arsenals, dock-Yards, and other needful Buildings;—And

To make all Laws which shall be necessary and proper for carrying into Execution the foregoing Powers, and all other Powers vested by this

Constitution in the Government of the United States, or in any Department or Officer thereof.

**Section 9.** ~~The Migration or Importation of such Persons as any of the States now existing shall think proper to admit, shall not be prohibited by the Congress prior to the Year one thousand eight hundred and eight, but a Tax or duty may be imposed on such Importation, not exceeding ten dollars for each Person.~~

The Privilege of the **Writ of Habeas Corpus**[17] shall not be suspended, unless when in Cases of Rebellion or Invasion the public Safety may require it.

No **Bill of Attainder**[18] or **ex post facto Law**[19] shall be passed.

No **Capitation**,[20] or other direct, Tax shall be laid, unless in Proportion to the Census or Enumeration herein before directed to be taken.

No Tax or Duty shall be laid on Articles exported from any State.

No Preference shall be given by any Regulation of Commerce or Revenue to the Ports of one State over those of another: nor shall Vessels bound to, or from, one State, be obliged to enter, clear, or pay Duties in another.

No Money shall be drawn from the Treasury, but in Consequence of Appropriations made by Law; and a regular Statement and Account of the Receipts and Expenditures of all public Money shall be published from time to time.

No Title of Nobility shall be granted by the United States: And no Person holding any Office of Profit or Trust under them, shall, without the Consent of the Congress, accept of any present, Emolument, Office, or Title, of any kind whatever, from any King, Prince, or foreign State.

**Section 10.** No State shall enter into any Treaty, Alliance, or Confederation; grant Letters of Marque and Reprisal; coin Money; emit Bills of Credit; make any Thing but gold and silver Coin a Tender in Payment of Debts; pass any Bill of Attainder, ex post facto Law, or law impairing the Obligation of Contracts, or grant any Title of Nobility.

No State shall, without the Consent of the Congress, lay any Imposts or Duties on Imports or Exports, except what may be absolutely necessary for executing its inspection Laws: and the net Produce of all Duties and Imposts, laid by any State on Imports or Exports, shall be for the Use of the Treasury of the United States; and all such Laws shall be subject to the Revision and Controul of the Congress.

No State shall, without the Consent of Congress, lay any Duty of Tonnage, keep Troops, or Ships of War in time of Peace, enter into any Agreement or Compact with another State, or with a foreign Power, or engage in War, unless actually invaded, or in such imminent Danger as will not admit of delay.

[17] **Writ of Habeas Corpus:** a court order that requires the government to bring a prisoner to court and explain why he or she is being held

[18] **Bill of Attainder:** a law declaring that a person is guilty of a particular crime

[19] **ex post facto Law:** a law that is made effective prior to the date that it was passed and therefore punishes people for acts that were not illegal at the time

[20] **Capitation:** a direct uniform tax imposed on each head, or person

### Exploring the Document

Although Congress has implied powers, there are also limits to its powers. Section 9 lists powers that are denied to the federal government. Several of the clauses protect the people of the United States from unjust treatment. **In what ways does the Constitution limit the powers of the federal government?**

## ★ Citizenship

***Gibbons v. Ogden*** The power to regulate interstate commerce was first tested in the Supreme Court case *Gibbons* v. *Ogden* (1824). Ogden and Gibbons operated two rival steamboat companies between New York and New Jersey. Ogden had been granted a monopoly by the state of New York, but Gibbons had been granted a federal license to operate a steamboat company. The Supreme Court held that Gibbons's license was valid because the federal government had the power to regulate interstate commerce. In the Court's decision Chief Justice John Marshall explained that if the states' powers were interpreted broadly and the federal government's were interpreted narrowly, the Constitution would be "a magnificent structure, indeed, to look at, but totally unfit for use."

### CRITICAL THINKING

Why might *Gibbons* v. *Ogden* be considered a landmark Supreme Court case?

**ANSWER:** Students might suggest that it not only established that federal law supersedes state law but also set a precedent for interpreting federal powers broadly.

### EXPLORING THE DOCUMENT ANSWER

The government cannot suspend the writ of habeas corpus or pass bills of attainder or ex post facto laws.

**The President** Initially, the writers of the Constitution agreed that the president would be chosen by the national legislature for a single seven-year term. Many delegates opposed a strong executive branch. However, when the Constitution was turned over to the Committee on Style, Gouverneur Morris, who wanted a stronger executive, reworded the article outlining the role of the president. He shortened the length of the president's term, allowed the president to run for more than one term, and altered the method by which the president would be elected. These changes passed with little debate, partly because the delegates were ready to go home and partly because many members believed that George Washington would be the first president—they felt that Washington would not abuse the power of the executive branch.

**CRITICAL THINKING**

Why might many of the delegates to the Constitutional Convention have opposed a one-person executive?

**ANSWER:** Students might suggest that they feared that they might create another monarchy.

**EXPLORING THE DOCUMENT ANSWER**
35 years old

**Executive Branch**
The president is the chief of the executive branch. It is the job of the president to enforce the laws. The framers wanted the president's and vice president's terms of office and manner of selection to be different from those of members of Congress. They decided on four-year terms, but they had a difficult time agreeing on how to select the president and vice president. The framers finally set up an electoral system, which varies greatly from our electoral process today.

**Presidential Elections**
In 1845 Congress set the Tuesday following the first Monday in November of every fourth year as the general election date for selecting presidential electors.

**Exploring the Document**

The youngest elected president was John F. Kennedy; he was 43 years old when he was inaugurated. (Theodore Roosevelt was 42 when he assumed office after the assassination of McKinley.) **What is the minimum required age for the office of president?**

## ARTICLE II

**Section 1.** The executive Power shall be vested in a President of the United States of America. He shall hold his Office during the Term of four Years, and, together with the Vice President, chosen for the same Term, be elected, as follows.

Each State shall appoint, in such Manner as the Legislature thereof may direct, a Number of Electors, equal to the whole Number of Senators and Representatives to which the State may be entitled in the Congress: but no Senator or Representative, or Person holding an Office of Trust or Profit under the United States, shall be appointed an Elector.

~~The Electors shall meet in their respective States, and vote by Ballot for two Persons, of whom one at least shall not be an Inhabitant of the same State with themselves. And they shall make a List of all the Persons voted for, and of the Number of Votes for each; which List they shall sign and certify, and transmit sealed to the Seat of the Government of the United States, directed to the President of the Senate. The President of the Senate shall, in the Presence of the Senate and House of Representatives, open all the Certificates, and the Votes shall then be counted. The Person having the greatest Number of Votes shall be the President, if such Number be a Majority of the whole Number of Electors appointed; and if there be more than one who have such Majority, and have an equal Number of Votes, then the House of Representatives shall immediately chuse by Ballot one of them for President; and if no Person have a Majority, then from the five highest on the List the said House shall in like Manner chuse the President. But in chusing the President, the Votes shall be taken by States, the Representation from each State having one Vote; A quorum for this Purpose shall consist of a Member or Members from two thirds of the States, and a Majority of all the States shall be necessary to a Choice. In every Case, after the Choice of the President, the Person having the greatest Number of Votes of the Electors shall be the Vice President. But if there should remain two or more who have equal Votes, the Senate shall chuse from them by Ballot the Vice President.~~

The Congress may determine the Time of chusing the Electors, and the Day on which they shall give their Votes; which Day shall be the same throughout the United States.

No Person except a natural born Citizen~~, or a Citizen of the United States, at the time of the Adoption of this Constitution~~, shall be eligible to the Office of President; neither shall any Person be eligible to that Office who shall not have attained to the Age of thirty five Years, and been fourteen Years a Resident within the United States.

In Case of the Removal of the President from Office, or of his Death, Resignation, or Inability to discharge the Powers and Duties of the said Office, the Same shall devolve on the Vice President, and the Congress may by Law provide for the Case of Removal, Death, Resignation or Inability, both of the President and Vice President, declaring what Officer shall then act as President, and such Officer shall act accordingly, until the Disability be removed, or a President shall be elected.

The President shall, at stated Times, receive for his Services, a Compensation, which shall neither be increased nor diminished during the Period for which he shall have been elected, and he shall not receive within that Period any other Emolument from the United States, or any of them.

Before he enter on the Execution of his Office, he shall take the following Oath or Affirmation:—"I do solemnly swear (or affirm) that I will faithfully execute the Office of President of the United States, and will to the best of my Ability, preserve, protect and defend the Constitution of the United States."

**Section 2.** The President shall be Commander in Chief of the Army and Navy of the United States, and of the Militia of the several States, when called into the actual Service of the United States; he may require the Opinion, in writing, of the principal Officer in each of the executive Departments, upon any Subject relating to the Duties of their respective Offices, and he shall have Power to grant **Reprieves**[21] and **Pardons**[22] for Offenses against the United States, except in Cases of Impeachment.

He shall have Power, by and with the Advice and Consent of the Senate, to make Treaties, provided two thirds of the Senators present concur; and he shall nominate, and by and with the Advice and Consent of the Senate, shall appoint Ambassadors, other public Ministers and Consuls, Judges of the supreme Court, and all other Officers of the United States, whose Appointments are not herein otherwise provided for, and which shall be established by Law: but the Congress may by Law vest the Appointment of such inferior Officers, as they think proper, in the President alone, in the Courts of Law, or in the Heads of Departments.

The President shall have Power to fill up all Vacancies that may happen during the Recess of the Senate, by granting Commissions which shall expire at the End of their next Session.

**Section 3.** He shall from time to time give to the Congress Information of the State of the Union, and recommend to their Consideration such Measures as he shall judge necessary and expedient; he may, on extraordinary Occasions, convene both Houses, or either of them, and in Case of Disagreement between them, with Respect to the Time of Adjournment, he may adjourn them to such Time as he shall think proper; he shall receive Ambassadors and other public Ministers; he shall take Care that the Laws be faithfully executed, and shall Commission all the Officers of the United States.

**Presidential Salary**
In 1999 Congress voted to set future presidents' salaries at $400,000 per year. The president also receives an annual expense account. The president must pay taxes only on the salary.

**Commander in Chief**
Today the president is in charge of the army, navy, air force, marines, and coast guard. Only Congress, however, can decide if the United States will declare war.

[21] **Reprieves:** delays of punishment
[22] **Pardons:** releases from the legal penalties associated with a crime

**Appointments**
Most of the president's appointments to office must be approved by the Senate.

**The State of the Union**
Every year the president presents to Congress a State of the Union message. In this message, the president introduces and explains a legislative plan for the coming year.

**John Marshall** The Supreme Court was considered a fairly unimportant institution in its early years. When John Marshall was appointed chief justice in 1801, he and his colleagues had to meet in the basement of the Capitol building because there was not a Supreme Court building. Having served in the Revolutionary War, Marshall was a committed nationalist. As chief justice, he established the Supreme Court as the final interpreter of the Constitution and made the Court into an important check on the power of the president and of Congress.

**CRITICAL THINKING**

How might Marshall's wartime experiences have shaped his ideas about the Constitution?

**ANSWER:** Students might suggest that having fought to gain independence, he would be particularly committed to making sure that the constitutional system worked fairly.

**EXPLORING THE DOCUMENT ANSWER**

In colonial courts, colonists could not have a trial by jury.

**Judicial Branch**
The Articles of Confederation did not set up a federal court system. One of the first points that the framers of the Constitution agreed upon was to set up a national judiciary. In the Judiciary Act of 1789, Congress provided for the establishment of lower courts, such as district courts, circuit courts of appeals, and various other federal courts. The judicial system provides a check on the legislative branch: it can declare a law unconstitutional.

**Exploring the Document**

In the Declaration of Independence, the colonists accused the British king of not allowing them trial by jury. **How does trial by jury differ from the courts that colonists had faced?**

[23] **Corruption of Blood:** punishing the family of a person convicted of treason

**Section 4.** The President, Vice President and all civil Officers of the United States, shall be removed from Office on Impeachment for, and Conviction of, Treason, Bribery, or other high Crimes and Misdemeanors.

## ARTICLE III

**Section 1.** The judicial Power of the United States, shall be vested in one supreme Court, and in such inferior Courts as the Congress may from time to time ordain and establish. The Judges, both of the supreme and inferior Courts, shall hold their Offices during good Behaviour, and shall, at stated Times, receive for their Services, a Compensation, which shall not be diminished during their Continuance in Office.

**Section 2.** The judicial Power shall extend to all Cases, in Law and Equity, arising under this Constitution, the Laws of the United States, and Treaties made, or which shall be made, under their Authority;—to all Cases affecting Ambassadors, other public Ministers and Consuls;—to all Cases of admiralty and maritime Jurisdiction;—to Controversies to which the United States shall be a Party;—to Controversies between two or more States;— between a State and Citizens of another State;— between Citizens of different States;—between Citizens of the same State claiming Lands under Grants of different States, and between a State, or the Citizens thereof, and foreign States, Citizens or Subjects.

In all Cases affecting Ambassadors, other public Ministers and Consuls, and those in which a State shall be Party, the supreme Court shall have original Jurisdiction. In all the other Cases before mentioned, the supreme Court shall have appellate Jurisdiction, both as to Law and fact, with such Exceptions, and under such Regulations as the Congress shall make.

The Trial of all Crimes, except in Cases of Impeachment, shall be by Jury; and such Trial shall be held in the State where the said Crimes shall have been committed; but when not committed within any State, the Trial shall be at such Place or Places as the Congress may by Law have directed.

**Section 3.** Treason against the United States, shall consist only in levying War against them, or in adhering to their Enemies, giving them Aid and Comfort. No Person shall be convicted of Treason unless on the Testimony of two Witnesses to the same overt Act, or on Confession in open Court.

The Congress shall have Power to declare the Punishment of Treason, but no Attainder of Treason shall work **Corruption of Blood,**[23] or Forfeiture except during the Life of the Person attainted.

## ARTICLE IV

**Section 1.** Full Faith and Credit shall be given in each State to the public Acts, Records, and judicial Proceedings of every other State. And the

Congress may by general Laws prescribe the Manner in which such Acts, Records and Proceedings shall be proved, and the Effect thereof.

**Section 2.** The Citizens of each State shall be entitled to all Privileges and Immunities of Citizens in the several States.

A Person charged in any State with Treason, Felony, or other Crime, who shall flee from Justice, and be found in another State, shall on Demand of the executive Authority of the State from which he fled, be delivered up, to be removed to the State having Jurisdiction of the Crime.

~~No Person held to Service of Labour in one State, under the Laws thereof, escaping into another, shall, in Consequence of any Law or Regulation therein, be discharged from such Service or Labour, but shall be delivered up on Claim of the Party to whom such Service or Labour may be due~~.

**Section 3.** New States may be admitted by the Congress into this Union; but no new State shall be formed or erected within the Jurisdiction of any other State; nor any State be formed by the Junction of two or more States, or Parts of States, without the Consent of the Legislatures of the States concerned as well as of the Congress.

The Congress shall have Power to dispose of and make all needful Rules and Regulations respecting the Territory or other Property belonging to the United States; and nothing in this Constitution shall be so construed as to Prejudice any Claims of the United States, or of any particular State.

**Section 4.** The United States shall guarantee to every State in this Union a Republican Form of Government, and shall protect each of them against Invasion; and on Application of the Legislature, or of the Executive (when the Legislature cannot be convened) against domestic Violence.

## ARTICLE V

The Congress, whenever two thirds of both Houses shall deem it necessary, shall propose Amendments to this Constitution, or, on the Application of the Legislatures of two thirds of the several States, shall call a Convention for proposing Amendments, which, in either Case, shall be valid to all Intents and Purposes, as Part of this Constitution, when ratified by the Legislatures of three fourths of the several States, or by Conventions in three fourths thereof, as the one or the other Mode of Ratification may be proposed by the Congress; Provided that ~~no Amendment which may be made prior to the Year One thousand eight hundred and eight shall in any Manner affect the first and fourth Clauses in the Ninth Section of the first Article; and that~~ no State, without its Consent, shall be deprived of its equal Suffrage in the Senate.

---

**Exploring the Document**

The framers wanted to ensure that the citizens could determine how the state governments would operate. **How does the need to respect the laws of each state support the principle of popular sovereignty?**

**The States**
States must honor the laws, records, and court decisions of other states. A person cannot escape a legal obligation by moving from one state to another.

**Exploring the Document**

In a republic, voters elect representatives to act in their best interest. **How does Article IV protect the practice of republicanism in the United States?**

**Exploring the Document**

America's founders may not have realized how long the Constitution would last, but they did set up a system for changing or adding to it. They did not want to make it easy to change the Constitution. **By what methods may the Constitution be amended? Under what sorts of circumstances do you think an amendment might be necessary?**

---

⭐ **Constitutional Heritage**

**Admission of New States** Although the framers of the Constitution wanted to allow new states to be admitted, many also wanted to preserve the power of the original states. One delegate suggested that the total number of representatives from the new states in the lower house should never exceed the total number from the original states.

**CRITICAL THINKING**
If this suggestion had become part of the Constitution, how might the current U.S. government be different?

**ANSWER:** Students might suggest that states along the Atlantic would have a greater amount of power than they currently do.

**EXPLORING THE DOCUMENT ANSWER**
It allows the people, rather than the federal government, to determine the laws of each state.

**EXPLORING THE DOCUMENT ANSWER**
It guarantees that every state will have a representative government.

**The Signers of the Constitution** At 27 years old, Jonathan Dayton was the youngest person to sign the Constitution. At the age of 81, Benjamin Franklin was the oldest. Franklin's signature was particularly important. As one of the most renowned men in America, he lent legitimacy to the new document.

**CRITICAL THINKING**

How might having people of varying ages draft the Constitution have helped to create a lasting document?

**ANSWER:** Students might suggest that it brought different perspectives and experiences to their efforts.

**EXPLORING THE DOCUMENT ANSWER**
*(for page 59)*

Two thirds of both Houses can propose amendments, or two thirds of the states can propose amendments; students' responses will vary.

**National Supremacy**
One of the biggest problems facing the delegates to the Constitutional Convention was the question of what should be done if a state law and a federal law conflicted. Which law would be followed? Who would decide? The second clause of Article VI answers those questions. When a federal law and a state law disagree, the federal law overrides the state law. The Constitution and other federal laws are the "supreme Law of the Land." This clause is often called the supremacy clause.

**Ratification**
The Articles of Confederation called for all 13 states to approve any revision to the Articles. The Constitution required that 9 out of the 13 states would be needed to ratify the Constitution. The first state to ratify was Delaware, on December 7, 1787. Almost two and a half years later, on May 29, 1790, Rhode Island became the last state to ratify the Constitution.

## ARTICLE VI

All Debts contracted and Engagements entered into, before the Adoption of this Constitution, shall be as valid against the United States under this Constitution, as under the Confederation.

This Constitution, and the Laws of the United States which shall be made in Pursuance thereof; and all Treaties made, or which shall be made, under the Authority of the United States, shall be the supreme Law of the Land; and the Judges in every State shall be bound thereby, any Thing in the Constitution or Laws of any State to the Contrary notwithstanding.

The Senators and Representatives before mentioned, and the Members of the several State Legislatures, and all executive and judicial Officers, both of the United States and of the several States, shall be bound by Oath or Affirmation, to support this Constitution; but no religious Test shall ever be required as a Qualification to any Office or public Trust under the United States.

## ARTICLE VII

The Ratification of the Conventions of nine States, shall be sufficient for the Establishment of this Constitution between the States so ratifying the Same.

Done in Convention by the Unanimous Consent of the States present the Seventeenth Day of September in the Year of our Lord one thousand seven hundred and Eighty seven and of the Independence of the United States of America the Twelfth. In witness whereof We have hereunto subscribed our Names,

*George Washington—*
**President and deputy from Virginia**

**NEW HAMPSHIRE**
*John Langdon*
*Nicholas Gilman*

**DELAWARE**
*George Read*
*Gunning Bedford, Jr.*
*John Dickinson*
*Richard Bassett*
*Jacob Broom*

**MASSACHUSETTS**
*Nathaniel Gorham*
*Rufus King*

**MARYLAND**
*James McHenry*
*Daniel of St. Thomas Jenifer*
*Daniel Carroll*

**CONNECTICUT**
*William Samuel Johnson*
*Roger Sherman*

**NEW YORK**
*Alexander Hamilton*

**VIRGINIA**
*John Blair*
*James Madison, Jr.*

**NEW JERSEY**
*William Livingston*
*David Brearley*
*William Paterson*
*Jonathan Dayton*

**NORTH CAROLINA**
*William Blount*
*Richard Dobbs Spaight*
*Hugh Williamson*

**PENNSYLVANIA**
*Benjamin Franklin*
*Thomas Mifflin*
*Robert Morris*
*George Clymer*

*Thomas FitzSimons*
*Jared Ingersoll*
*James Wilson*
*Gouverneur Morris*

**SOUTH CAROLINA**
*John Rutledge*
*Charles Cotesworth*
  *Pinckney*
*Charles Pinckney*
*Pierce Butler*

**GEORGIA**
*William Few*
*Abraham Baldwin*

*Attest:*
*William Jackson, Secretary*

## THE AMENDMENTS

Articles in addition to, and Amendment of the Constitution of the United States of America, proposed by Congress, and ratified by the Legislatures of the several States, pursuant to the fifth Article of the original Constitution.

*[The First through Tenth Amendments, now known as the Bill of Rights, were proposed to the states for ratification on September 25, 1789, and declared in force on December 15, 1791.]*

### First Amendment

Congress shall make no law respecting an establishment of religion, or prohibiting the free exercise thereof; or abridging the freedom of speech, or of the press; or the right of the people peaceably to assemble, and to petition the Government for a redress of grievances.

### Second Amendment

A well regulated Militia, being necessary to the security of a free State, the right of the people to keep and bear Arms, shall not be infringed.

### Third Amendment

No Soldier shall, in time of peace, be **quartered**[24] in any house, without the consent of the Owner, nor in time of war, but in a manner to be prescribed by law.

### Fourth Amendment

The right of the people to be secure in their persons, houses, papers, and effects, against unreasonable searches and seizures, shall not be violated, and no **Warrants**[25] shall issue, but upon probable cause, supported by Oath or affirmation, and particularly describing the place to be searched, and the persons or things to be seized.

### Fifth Amendment

No person shall be held to answer for a capital, or otherwise **infamous**[26] crime, unless on a presentment or **indictment**[27] of a Grand Jury, except in cases arising in the land or naval forces, or in the Militia, when in actual service in time of War or public danger; nor shall any person be subject for the same offence to be twice put in jeopardy of life or limb; nor shall be compelled in any criminal case to be a witness against himself, nor be deprived of life, liberty, or property, without due process of law; nor shall private property be taken for public use, without just compensation.

### Sixth Amendment

In all criminal prosecutions, the accused shall enjoy the right to a speedy and public trial, by an impartial jury of the State and district wherein the

---

**Bill of Rights**
One of the conditions set by several states for ratifying the Constitution was the inclusion of a bill of rights. Many people feared that a stronger central government might take away basic rights of the people that had been guaranteed in state constitutions.

### Exploring the Document

The First Amendment forbids Congress from making any "law respecting an establishment of religion" or restraining the freedom to practice religion as one chooses. **Why is freedom of religion an important right?**

[24] **quartered:** housed

[25] **Warrants:** written orders authorizing a person to make an arrest, a seizure, or search
[26] **infamous:** disgraceful
[27] **indictment:** the act of charging with a crime

**Rights of the Accused**
The Fifth, Sixth, and Seventh Amendments describe the procedures that courts must follow when trying people accused of crimes.

**Trials**
The Sixth Amendment makes several guarantees, including a prompt trial and a trial by a jury chosen from the state and district in which the crime was committed.

---

## ★ Global Relations

**Thomas Jefferson** At the time of the Constitutional Convention, Thomas Jefferson was in Paris as part of a diplomatic mission to France. Jefferson became increasingly convinced of the evils of monarchy as he saw the violations of civil liberties that the French people were experiencing. For example, the king could issue a *lettre du cachet*, which could order someone exiled or imprisoned without recourse. In addition, the aristocracy could destroy land without having to reimburse the owner for the damage. In his correspondence to delegates to the Constitutional Convention, Jefferson strongly advocated the inclusion of a bill of rights.

**CRITICAL THINKING**
How might Jefferson's experiences in France have driven him to insist on including a bill of rights in the Constitution?

**ANSWER:** Students might suggest that having seen what could happen if individual rights were violated, Jefferson would probably have been more convinced than many other U.S. lawmakers of the importance of protecting those rights.

**EXPLORING THE DOCUMENT ANSWER**
Students might suggest that it is a right on which the United States was founded.

## Linking Past to Present

**Civil Liberties** In the 1900s the Supreme Court extended the coverage of civil liberties in the Bill of Rights. For some time, justices ruled that the Bill of Rights did not override state laws. Although the Fourteenth Amendment stated that the states could not deprive citizens of their constitutional rights, few justices changed their opinions. In the mid-1900s, Justice Hugo Black began to reinterpret the Fourteenth Amendment. He believed that the guarantees in the Bill of Rights were absolute. Most justices have since tempered this position, believing that these guarantees are constrained by competing social interests.

**ACTIVITY:** Have students bring in newspaper articles that deal with the exercise of civil liberties. Using these articles to start discussion, have students describe what they think are proper and improper limitations of civil liberties.

---

**EXPLORING THE DOCUMENT ANSWER**
They extend rights to the people and to the states.

**28 ascertained:** found out

### Exploring the Document

The Ninth and Tenth Amendments were added because not every right of the people or of the states could be listed in the Constitution. **How do the Ninth and Tenth Amendments limit the power of the federal government?**

**29 construed:** explained or interpreted

**President and Vice President**
The Twelfth Amendment changed the election procedure for president and vice president.

crime shall have been committed, which district shall have been previously **ascertained**[28] by law, and to be informed of the nature and cause of the accusation; to be confronted with the witnesses against him; to have compulsory process for obtaining witnesses in his favor, and to have the Assistance of Counsel for his defence.

### Seventh Amendment

In Suits at common law, where the value in controversy shall exceed twenty dollars, the right of trial by jury shall be preserved, and no fact tried by a jury, shall be otherwise re-examined in any Court of the United States, than according to the rules of the common law.

### Eighth Amendment

Excessive bail shall not be required, nor excessive fines imposed, nor cruel and unusual punishments inflicted.

### Ninth Amendment

The enumeration in the Constitution, of certain rights, shall not be construed to deny or disparage others retained by the people.

### Tenth Amendment

The powers not delegated to the United States by the Constitution, nor prohibited by it to the States, are reserved to the States respectively, or to the people.

### Eleventh Amendment

*[Proposed March 4, 1794; declared ratified January 8, 1798]*
The Judicial power of the United States shall not be **construed**[29] to extend to any suit in law or equity, commenced or prosecuted against one of the United States by Citizens of another State, or by Citizens or Subjects of any Foreign State.

### Twelfth Amendment

*[Proposed December 9, 1803; declared ratified September 25, 1804]*
The Electors shall meet in their respective states, and vote by ballot for President and Vice-President, one of whom, at least, shall not be an inhabitant of the same state with themselves; they shall name in their ballots the person voted for as President, and in distinct ballots the person voted for as Vice-President, and they shall make distinct lists of all persons voted for as President, and of all persons voted for as Vice-President, and of the number of votes for each, which lists they shall sign and certify, and transmit sealed to the seat of the government of the United States, directed to the President of the Senate;—The President of the Senate shall, in the presence of the Senate and House of Representatives, open all the certificates and the votes

shall then be counted;—The person having the greatest number of votes for President, shall be the President, if such number be a majority of the whole number of Electors appointed; and if no person have such majority, then from the persons having the highest numbers not exceeding three on the list of those voted for as President, the House of Representatives shall choose immediately, by ballot, the President. But in choosing the President, the votes shall be taken by states, the representation from each state having one vote; a quorum for this purpose shall consist of a member or members from two-thirds of the states, and a majority of all the states shall be necessary to a choice. ~~And if the House of Representatives shall not choose a President whenever the right of choice shall devolve upon them, before the fourth day of March next following, then the Vice-President shall act as President, as in the case of the death or other constitutional disability of the President.~~ The person having the greatest number of votes as Vice-President, shall be the Vice-President, if such number be a majority of the whole number of Electors appointed, and if no person have a majority, then from the two highest numbers on the list, the Senate shall Choose the Vice-President; a quorum for the purpose shall consist of two-thirds of the whole number of Senators, and a majority of the whole number shall be necessary to a choice. But no person constitutionally ineligible to the office of President shall be eligible to that of Vice-President of the United States.

## Thirteenth Amendment

*[Proposed January 31, 1865; declared ratified December 18, 1865]*

**Section 1.** Neither slavery nor **involuntary servitude**,[30] except as a punishment for crime whereof the party shall have been duly convicted, shall exist within the United States, or any place subject to their jurisdiction.

**Section 2.** Congress shall have power to enforce this article by appropriate legislation.

## Fourteenth Amendment

*[Proposed June 13, 1866; declared ratified July 28, 1868]*

**Section 1.** All persons born or naturalized in the United States, and subject to the jurisdiction thereof, are citizens of the United States and of the State wherein they reside. No State shall make or enforce any law which shall abridge the privileges or immunities of citizens of the United States; nor shall any State deprive any person of life, liberty, or property, without due process of law; nor deny to any person within its jurisdiction the equal protection of the laws.

**Section 2.** Representatives shall be apportioned among the several States according to their respective numbers, counting the whole number of per-

**Abolishing Slavery**
Although some slaves had been freed during the Civil War, slavery was not abolished until the Thirteenth Amendment took effect.

**[30] involuntary servitude:** being forced to work against one's will

**Protecting the Rights of Citizens**
In 1833 the Supreme Court ruled that the Bill of Rights limited the federal government but not the state governments. This ruling was interpreted to mean that states were able to keep African Americans from becoming state citizens, and thus, the Bill of Rights did not protect them. The Fourteenth Amendment defines citizenship and prevents states from interfering in the rights of citizens of the United States.

★ **Citizenship**

**Postwar Amendments**
Three amendments—the Thirteenth, Fourteenth, and Fifteenth—were initially intended to respond to changes demanded by the northern victory in the Civil War. At the time it was passed, many southerners interpreted the Fourteenth Amendment as a way for the North to punish them for their rebellion by making the South extend civil rights to African Americans. Scholars have argued that the Fourteenth Amendment remains the most important addition to the Constitution since the Bill of Rights because of its inclusion of due process and equal protection clauses.

**CRITICAL THINKING**
Why might scholars feel the Fourteenth Amendment is so important?

**ANSWER:** Students might suggest that it redefined citizenship and that for the first time an attempt to guarantee African Americans their civil rights was made. It also made the Bill of Rights apply to state law.

**Suffrage** The passage of the Fourteenth and Fifteenth Amendments dramatically increased African Americans' political participation. Throughout the South, African American workers striked against their employers. The workers staged sit-ins on segregated carriages in Richmond, Virginia, and when police tried to stop their protests, angry crowds formed, demanding, "Let's have our rights." Almost every institution of black life, particularly the church, worked to mobilize the African American vote and to educate new voters. So many African American laborers attended the Republican state convention in Virginia that Richmond's tobacco factories had to close.

### CRITICAL THINKING

Why might African Americans after the Civil War have found the vote to be so important?

**ANSWER:** Students might suggest that since African Americans had been denied any form of political participation, they hoped that the vote would help them become full citizens of the United States and accepted members of their communities.

### EXPLORING THE DOCUMENT ANSWER

Students might suggest that in order to have equal representation under the law, all people must have the right to vote.

**Exploring the Document**

The Fifteenth Amendment extended the vote to African American men. **Why is the right to vote guaranteed by the Fifteenth Amendment important?**

sons in each State, ~~excluding Indians not taxed~~. But when the right to vote at any election for the choice of electors for President and Vice President of the United States, Representatives in Congress, the Executive and Judicial officers of a State, or the members of the Legislature thereof, is denied to any of the ~~male~~ inhabitants of such State, ~~being twenty-one years of age,~~ and citizens of the United States, or in any way abridged, except for participation in rebellion, or other crime, the basis of representation therein shall be reduced in the proportion which the number of such ~~male~~ citizens shall bear to the whole number of ~~male~~ citizens ~~twenty-one years of age~~ in such State.

**Section 3.** No person shall be a Senator or Representative in Congress, or elector of President and Vice President, or hold any office, civil or military, under the United States, or under any State, who, having previously taken an oath, as a member of Congress, or as an officer of the United States, or as a member of any State legislature, or as an executive or judicial officer of any State, to support the Constitution of the United States, shall have engaged in insurrection or rebellion against the same, or given aid or comfort to the enemies thereof. But Congress may by a vote of two-thirds of each House, remove such disability.

**Section 4.** The validity of the public debt of the United States, authorized by law, including debts incurred for payment of pensions and bounties for services in suppressing insurrection or rebellion, shall not be questioned. But neither the United States nor any State shall assume or pay any debt or obligation incurred in aid of insurrection or rebellion against the United States, ~~or any claim for the loss of emancipation of any slave~~; but all such debts, obligations and claims shall be held illegal and void.

**Section 5.** The Congress shall have power to enforce, by appropriate legislation, the provisions of this article.

### Fifteenth Amendment

*[Proposed February 26, 1869; declared ratified March 30, 1870]*

**Section 1.** The right of citizens of the United States to vote shall not be denied or abridged by the United States or by any State on account of race, color, or previous condition of servitude.

**Section 2.** The Congress shall have power to enforce this article by appropriate legislation.

### Sixteenth Amendment

*[Proposed July 12, 1909; declared ratified February 25, 1913]*

The Congress shall have power to lay and collect taxes on incomes, from whatever source derived, without apportionment among the several States, and without regard to any census or enumeration.

## Seventeenth Amendment

*[Proposed May 13, 1912; declared ratified May 31, 1913]*

The Senate of the United States shall be composed of two Senators from each State, elected by the people thereof, for six years; and each Senator shall have one vote. The electors in each State shall have the qualifications requisite for electors of the most numerous branch of the State legislatures.

When vacancies happen in the representation of any State in the Senate, the executive authority of such State shall issue writs of election to fill such vacancies: *Provided,* That the legislature of any State may empower the executive thereof to make temporary appointments until the people fill the vacancies by election as the legislature may direct.

This amendment shall not be so construed as to affect the election or term of any Senator chosen before it becomes valid as part of the Constitution.

## Eighteenth Amendment

*[Proposed December 18, 1917; declared ratified January 29, 1919; repealed by the Twenty-first Amendment December 5, 1933]*

**Section 1.** After one year from the ratification of this article the manufacture, sale, or transportation of intoxicating liquors within, the importation thereof into, or the exportation thereof from the United States and all territory subject to the jurisdiction thereof for beverage purposes is hereby prohibited.

**Section 2.** The Congress and the several States shall have concurrent power to enforce this article by appropriate legislation.

**Section 3.** This article shall be inoperative unless it shall have been ratified as an amendment to the Constitution by the legislatures of the several States, as provided in the Constitution, within seven years from the date of the submission hereof to the States by the Congress.

## Nineteenth Amendment

*[Proposed June 4, 1919; declared ratified August 26, 1920]*

The right of citizens of the United States to vote shall not be denied or abridged by the United States or by any State on account of sex.

Congress shall have power to enforce this article by appropriate legislation.

## Twentieth Amendment

*[Proposed March 2, 1932; declared ratified February 6, 1933]*

**Section 1.** The terms of the President and Vice-President shall end at noon on the 20th day of January, and the terms of Senators and Representatives

---

**Exploring the Document**

The Seventeenth Amendment requires that senators be elected directly by the people instead of by the state legislature. **What principle of our government does the Seventeenth Amendment protect?**

**Prohibition**
Although many people believed that the Eighteenth Amendment was good for the health and welfare of the American people, it was repealed 14 years later.

**Women's Suffrage**
Abigail Adams and others were disappointed that the Declaration of Independence and the Constitution did not specifically include women. It took almost 130 years and much campaigning before suffrage for women was finally achieved.

---

**Biography**

### Elizabeth Cady Stanton

The efforts of Elizabeth Cady Stanton, a tireless crusader for women's rights, contributed to the passage of the Nineteenth Amendment in 1920. Although she was active in the antislavery cause, she opposed passage of the Fourteenth and Fifteenth Amendments—which gave citizenship and the right to vote to African American men—because these laws did not include women. At her urging, in 1878 Senator Aaron A. Sargent of California introduced a women's suffrage amendment to the Constitution. This amendment was introduced and defeated repeatedly throughout Stanton's lifetime. She died in 1902, eighteen years before the passage of the amendment for which she had worked so hard.

**CRITICAL THINKING**

Do you think Stanton was right to oppose the Fourteenth and Fifteenth Amendments? Explain your answer.

**ANSWER:** Students' answers will vary.

**EXPLORING THE DOCUMENT ANSWER**
the principle of direct representation

---

**George W. Norris** During his long congressional career, George W. Norris not only created and worked to pass the Twentieth Amendment but also worked for the introduction of presidential primaries and for the direct election of senators. Though a Republican, Norris rarely voted along party lines. In defense of his independence, he claimed he "would rather be right than regular."

**ACTIVITY:** Have students find examples of recent political reform. Then have them draft bills or constitutional amendments that could be used to enact these reforms.

---

## EXPLORING THE DOCUMENT ANSWER

It had to be ratified by state conventions.

---

**Taking Office**
In the original Constitution, a newly elected president and Congress did not take office until March 4, which was four months after the November election. The officials who were leaving office were called lame ducks because they had little influence during those four months. The Twentieth Amendment changed the date that the new president and Congress take office. Members of Congress now take office during the first week of January, and the president takes office on January 20.

---

## Exploring the Document

The Twenty-first Amendment was the first amendment not ratified by state legislatures. **According to the crossed-out text, what method was used to ratify the Twenty-first Amendment?**

---

at noon on the 3d day of January, of the years in which such terms would have ended if this article had not been ratified; and the terms of their successors shall then begin.

**Section 2.** The Congress shall assemble at least once in every year, and such meeting shall begin at noon on the 3d day of January, unless they shall by law appoint a different day.

**Section 3.** If, at the time fixed for the beginning of the term of the President, the President elect shall have died, the Vice-President elect shall become President. If a President shall not have been chosen before the time fixed for the beginning of his term, or if the President elect shall have failed to qualify, then the Vice-President elect shall act as President until a President shall have qualified; and the Congress may by law provide for the case wherein neither a President elect nor a Vice-President elect shall have qualified, declaring who shall then act as President, or the manner in which one who is to act shall be selected, and such person shall act accordingly until a President or Vice-President shall have qualified.

**Section 4.** The Congress may by law provide for the case of the death of any of the persons from whom the House of Representatives may choose a President whenever the right of choice shall have devolved upon them, and for the case of the death of any of the persons from whom the Senate may choose a Vice-President whenever the right of choice shall have devolved upon them.

~~**Section 5.** Sections 1 and 2 shall take effect on the 15th day of October following the ratification of this article.~~

~~**Section 6.** This article shall be inoperative unless it shall have been ratified as an amendment to the Constitution by the legislatures of three-fourths of the several States within seven years from the date of its submission.~~

## Twenty-first Amendment
*[Proposed February 20, 1933; declared ratified December 5, 1933]*

**Section 1.** The eighteenth article of amendment to the Constitution of the United States is hereby repealed.

**Section 2.** The transportation or importation into any State, Territory, or possession of the United States for delivery or use therein of intoxicating liquors, in violation of the laws thereof, is hereby prohibited.

~~**Section 3.** This article shall be inoperative unless it shall have been ratified as an amendment to the Constitution by conventions in the several States, as provided in the Constitution, within seven years from the date of the submission hereof to the States by the Congress.~~

## Twenty-second Amendment

*[Proposed March 21, 1947; declared ratified February 26, 1951]*

**Section 1.** No person shall be elected to the office of the President more than twice, and no person who has held the office of President, or acted as President, for more than two years of a term to which some other person was elected President shall be elected to the office of the President more than once. ~~But this Article shall not apply to any person holding the office of President when this Article was proposed by the Congress, and shall not prevent any person who may be holding the office of President, or acting as President, during the term within which this Article becomes operative from holding the office of President or acting as President during the remainder of such term.~~

~~**Section 2.** This article shall be inoperative unless it shall have been ratified as an amendment to the Constitution by the legislatures of three-fourths of the several States within seven years from the date of its submission to the States by the Congress.~~

## Twenty-third Amendment

*[Proposed June 16, 1960; ratified March 29, 1961]*

**Section 1.** The District constituting the seat of Government of the United States shall appoint in such manner as the Congress may direct:

A number of electors of President and Vice-President equal to the whole number of Senators and Representatives in Congress to which the District would be entitled if it were a State, but in no event more than the least populous state; they shall be in addition to those appointed by the States, but they shall be considered, for the purposes of the election of President and Vice-President, to be electors appointed by a State; and they shall meet in the District and perform such duties as provided by the twelfth article of amendment.

**Section 2.** The Congress shall have power to enforce this article by appropriate legislation.

## Twenty-fourth Amendment

*[Proposed August 27, 1962; ratified January 23, 1964]*

**Section 1.** The right of citizens of the United States to vote in any primary or other election for President or Vice-President, for electors for President or Vice-President, or for Senator or Representative in Congress, shall not be denied or abridged by the United States or any State by reason of failure to pay any poll tax or other tax.

### Exploring the Document

From the time of President George Washington's administration, it was a custom for presidents to serve no more than two terms in office. Franklin D. Roosevelt, however, was elected to four terms. The Twenty-second Amendment restricted presidents to no more than two terms in office. **Why do you think citizens chose to limit the power of the president in this way?**

### Voting Rights

Until the ratification of the Twenty-third Amendment, the people of Washington, D.C., could not vote in presidential elections.

**Poll Tax** Congress began its attempt to end the poll tax in 1939. The tax had been instituted in some southern states after Reconstruction and was still in effect in five of those states in 1964. Oftentimes the poll tax was explicitly adopted to discriminate against African American voters. For example, when the poll tax was passed in Virginia in 1902, one representative said, "Discrimination! Why, that is precisely what we propose."

### CRITICAL THINKING

Why do you think an amendment was necessary for ending the poll tax?

**ANSWER:** Students may suggest an amendment was needed because Congress had no power over state election policies.

### EXPLORING THE DOCUMENT ANSWER

Students might suggest that citizens did not want an individual president to gain too much power.

**Woodrow Wilson** The realization of the need for the Twenty-fifth Amendment began during Woodrow Wilson's term. In 1919 Wilson suffered a stroke and could not meet with his cabinet for seven months. While the president was ill, his vice president, Thomas Marshall, made it clear that he did not want to serve as president. Instead, the seriously ill Wilson conducted government affairs through his wife, Edith.

**CRITICAL THINKING**

How can the U.S. government continue to function even when the head of state is ill?

**ANSWER:** The Constitution divides decision making and provides a framework for government activity to continue.

**Constitutional Heritage**

**Presidential Succession**
The rules for determining presidential succession have been amended, but the line of succession has never been tested past the vice president. Of the nine vice presidents who have succeeded presidents who have died or resigned, just four have been re-elected to a full term.

**ACTIVITY:** Have students research and draw a chart of the line of succession for the current presidency.

**Presidential Disability**
The illness of President Eisenhower in the 1950s and the assassination of President Kennedy in 1963 were the events behind the Twenty-fifth Amendment. The Constitution did not provide a clear-cut method for a vice president to take over for a disabled president or upon the death of a president. This amendment provides for filling the office of the vice president if a vacancy occurs, and it provides a way for the vice president—or someone else in the line of succession—to take over if the president is unable to perform the duties of that office.

**Section 2.** The Congress shall have power to enforce this article by appropriate legislation.

### Twenty-fifth Amendment
*[Proposed July 6, 1965; ratified February 10, 1967]*

**Section 1.** In case of the removal of the President from office or of his death or resignation, the Vice-President shall become President.

**Section 2.** Whenever there is a vacancy in the office of the Vice-President, the President shall nominate a Vice-President who shall take office upon confirmation by a majority vote of both Houses of Congress.

**Section 3.** Whenever the President transmits to the President pro tempore of the Senate and the Speaker of the House of Representatives his written declaration that he is unable to discharge the powers and duties of his office, and until he transmits to them a written declaration to the contrary, such powers and duties shall be discharged by the Vice-President as Acting President.

**Section 4.** Whenever the Vice-President and a majority of either the principal officers of the executive departments or of such other body as Congress may by law provide, transmit to the President pro tempore of the Senate and the Speaker of the House of Representatives their written declaration that the President is unable to discharge the powers and duties of his office, the Vice-President shall immediately assume the powers and duties of the office as Acting President.

Thereafter, when the President transmits to the President pro tempore of the Senate and the Speaker of the House of Representatives his written declaration that no inability exists, he shall resume the powers and duties of his office unless the Vice-President and a majority of either the principal officers of the executive department or of such other body as Congress may by law provide, transmit within four days to the President pro tempore of the Senate and the Speaker of the House of Representatives their written declaration that the President is unable to discharge the powers and duties of his office. Thereupon Congress shall decide the issue, assembling within forty-eight hours for that purpose if not in session. If the Congress, within twenty-one days after receipt of the latter written declaration, or, if Congress is not in session, within twenty-one days after Congress is required to assemble, determines by two-thirds vote of both Houses that the President is unable to discharge the powers and duties of his office, the Vice President shall continue to discharge the same as Acting President; otherwise, the President shall resume the powers and duties of his office.

## Twenty-sixth Amendment

*[Proposed March 23, 1971; ratified July 1, 1971]*

**Section 1.** The right of citizens of the United States, who are eighteen years of age or older, to vote shall not be denied or abridged by the United States or by any State on account of age.

**Section 2.** The Congress shall have power to enforce this article by appropriate legislation.

## Twenty-seventh Amendment

*[Proposed September 25, 1789; ratified May 7, 1992]*

No law, varying the compensation for the services of the Senators and Representatives, shall take effect, until an election of Representatives shall have intervened.

**Expanded Suffrage**
The Voting Act of 1970 tried to set the voting age at 18. However, the Supreme Court ruled that the act set the voting age for national elections only, not state or local elections. This ruling would make necessary several different ballots at elections. The Twenty-sixth Amendment gave 18-year-old citizens the right to vote in all elections.

## Separation of Powers and Checks and Balances

may reject appointments

may reject treaties

may withhold funding for presidential initiatives

may impeach president

may override a veto

**LEGISLATIVE BRANCH (Congress)**
writes the laws
confirms presidential appointments
approves treaties
grants money
declares war

may propose constitutional amendments to overrule judicial decisions

may impeach Supreme Court justices

may reject appointments to the Supreme Court

may adjourn Congress in certain situations

may veto bills

may declare laws unconstitutional

**EXECUTIVE BRANCH (President)**
proposes laws
administers the laws
commands armed forces
appoints ambassadors and other officials
conducts foreign policy
makes treaties

may declare executive actions unconstitutional

appoints judges

**JUDICIAL BRANCH (Supreme Court)**
interprets the Constitution and other laws
reviews lower-court decisions

**Congressional Pay Raises**
Ironically, one of the latest constitutional amendments to pass was proposed by one of the Constitution's framers, James Madison. Although amendments that have been passed in recent decades have included a deadline for passage, Madison never included one for what became the Twenty-seventh Amendment. The amendment states that congressional pay raises cannot take effect until a new Congress meets. After more than 200 years, Michigan became the required 38th state to approve the amendment. Madison had suggested the amendment in 1789, along with the other amendments that eventually made up the Bill of Rights. However, just 6 states ratified the amendment—out of the 11 needed to pass it—and it was largely forgotten until the 1980s, when an aide to a Texas legislator began a crusade to get it passed.

**CRITICAL THINKING**

Do you think the issue of congressional pay raises is more important now than it was in 1789?

**ANSWER:** Students' answers will vary, but some may say it is more important now because of budgetary concerns. Others may think that it was more important in 1789, when legislators may have needed guidance in allocating pay raises.

# The Constitution

## CHAPTER RESOURCE MANAGER

| Objectives | Pacing Guide | Reproducible Resources |
|---|---|---|
| **SECTION 1:**<br>**Ideals of the Constitution**<br>(pp. 71–76) | ★ Describe how the Pilgrims influenced the framers of the Constitution.<br>★ Identify the goals of the U.S. government as outlined in the Constitution.<br>★ Explain why the Constitution established the powers of the federal and state governments. | **Regular**<br>1.5 days<br><br>**Block Scheduling**<br>1 day<br><br>*Block Scheduling Handbook with Team Teaching Strategies, Chapter 3* | **RS** Guided Reading Strategies 3.1<br>**RS** Readings in Economics and Government 5: Fundamental Orders of Connecticut<br>**E** Creative Teaching Strategy: Ranking<br>**PS** American Civics Political Cartoon: Ratifying the Constitution<br>**E** Challenge and Enrichment Worksheet 3: Understanding the Ideals of the Constitution |
| **SECTION 2:**<br>**The Three Branches of Government**<br>(pp. 77–79) | ★ Analyze why the Constitution provides for the separation of powers.<br>★ Identify the main responsibilities of each of the three branches of government.<br>★ Explain how the system of checks and balances works. | **Regular**<br>1 day<br><br>**Block Scheduling**<br>.5 day<br><br>*Block Scheduling Handbook with Team Teaching Strategies, Chapter 3* | **RS** Guided Reading Strategies 3.2 |
| **SECTION 3:**<br>**A Flexible Document**<br>(pp. 82–84) | ★ Explain why the Constitution is called a "living document."<br>★ Analyze how the flexibility of the Constitution has benefited the United States.<br>★ Describe how amendments to the Constitution are proposed and passed. | **Regular**<br>1.5 days<br><br>**Block Scheduling**<br>1 day<br><br>*Block Scheduling Handbook with Team Teaching Strategies, Chapter 3* | **RS** Guided Reading Strategies 3.3<br>**RS** Graphic Organizer Activity: Power in the Constitution<br>**E** Community Service and Participation Handbook: The Equal Rights Amendment |

## Chapter Resource Key

| | | | | | |
|---|---|---|---|---|---|
| **PS** | Primary Sources | **SM** | Skills Mastery |  | CD–ROM |
| **RS** | Reading Support | **A** | Assessment |  | Video |
| **IC** | Interdisciplinary Connections | **REV** | Review |  | Internet |
| **E** | Enrichment | **ELL** | Reinforcement and English Language Learners | | Holt Presentation Maker Using Microsoft® PowerPoint® |
| | | | Transparencies | | |

 **One-Stop** Planner CD–ROM

**See the *One-Stop Planner* for a complete list of additional resources for students and teachers.**

## One-Stop Planner CD–ROM

It's easy to plan lessons, select resources, and print out materials for your students when you use the **One–Stop Planner CD–ROM with Test Generator**.

| Technology Resources | Reinforcement, Review, and Assessment |
|---|---|
| One-Stop Planner, Lesson 3.1 | REV Section 1 Review, p. 76 |
| Transparency 1: How Democracy Works | A Daily Quiz 3.1 |
| Homework Practice Online | ELL Main Idea Activity 3.1 |
| HRW Go site | ELL English Audio Summary 3.1 |
| | ELL Spanish Audio Summary 3.1 |
| One-Stop Planner, Lesson 3.2 | REV Section 2 Review, p. 79 |
| Holt Researcher CD–ROM | A Daily Quiz 3.2 |
| CNN Presents: American Government | ELL Main Idea Activity 3.2 |
| Homework Practice Online | ELL English Audio Summary 3.2 |
| | ELL Spanish Audio Summary 3.2 |
| One-Stop Planner, Lesson 3.3 | REV Section 3 Review, p. 84 |
| Homework Practice Online | A Daily Quiz 3.3 |
| | ELL Main Idea Activity 3.3 |
| | ELL English Audio Summary 3.3 |
| | ELL Spanish Audio Summary 3.3 |

### internet connect

**HRW ONLINE RESOURCES**
GO TO: go.hrw.com
Then type in the keyword.

**TEACHER HOME PAGE**
KEYWORD: SZ3 Teacher

**CHAPTER INTERNET ACTIVITIES**
KEYWORD: SZ3 AC3
Choose an activity to:
• propose an amendment and write a plan to get it ratified.
• create a diagram of the federal system.
• create a pamphlet on Watergate.

**CHAPTER ENRICHMENT LINKS**
KEYWORD: SZ3 CH3

**ONLINE ASSESSMENT**
Homework Practice
KEYWORD: SZ3 HP3
Rubrics
KEYWORD: SS Rubrics

**ONLINE MAPS, CHARTS, AND GRAPHS**
KEYWORD: SZ3 MCG
• The Federal System

**HOLT PRESENTATION MAKER**
KEYWORD: SZ3 PPT3

**CONTENT UPDATES**
KEYWORD: SS Content Updates

**ONLINE READING SUPPORT**
KEYWORD: SS Strategies

**CURRENT EVENTS**
KEYWORD: S3 Current Events

## Meeting Individual Needs

### Ability Levels

**Level 1** Basic-level activities designed for all students encountering new material

**Level 2** Intermediate-level activities designed for average students

**Level 3** Challenging activities designed for honors and gifted-and-talented students

**English Language Learners** Activities that address the needs of students with Limited English Proficiency

## Chapter Review and Assessment

IC Vocabulary Activity 3
 Global Skill Builder CD–ROM
HRW Go site
REV Chapter 3 Tutorial for Students, Parents, Mentors, and Peers
REV Chapter 3 Review, pp. 86–87
A Standardized Test Practice
A Chapter 3 Test Generator (on the One-Stop Planner)
A Chapter 3 Test (Form A or B)
A Alternative Assessment Handbook
A Chapter 3 Test for English Language Learners and Special-Needs Students

## Internet Activity

### Federalism

☞ **internet** connect

**go hrw .com**

**TOPIC:** Federalism
**GO TO:** go.hrw.com
**KEYWORD:** SZ3 AC3

Have students access the Internet through the HRW Go site to compare and contrast the roles, requirements, and powers of each branch of government. Then ask students to create an illustrated diagram that presents the information that he or she obtained in his or her research. Have students focus on issues such as term lengths, powers and responsibilities, ways in which the branches check and balance each other, and any other information that is unique to the executive, judicial, and legislative branches.

### What's Your Opinion?

📝 To help students create their **Themes** Journal entries, provide the following examples of appropriate **agree/disagree** statements.

• **Agree** The Constitution was written long ago and its ideals are not as relevant today.

**Disagree** The original ideals in the Constitution are general enough to continue to serve our country.

• **Agree** In order to fulfill its responsibilities, the more important branch of the government should have more power.

**Disagree** No one branch of the government is more important than any other branch.

• **Agree** If a country's constitution needs change, then it is no longer serving the country's needs and should be rewritten.

**Disagree** A constitution is the foundation of any society and should not be rewritten.

**CHAPTER** ★ ★ ★ ★ ★

# 3 The U.S. Constitution

### Build on What You Know

Although the framers of the U.S. Constitution lived in an age without our advanced technology, they created a plan of government that would accommodate it. They wrote a constitution based on fundamental ideals of democratic government. This constitution created a government flexible enough to change with the times while remaining true to its basic ideals. As a result, the Constitution is as relevant to your life today as it was to Americans who lived more than 225 years ago. The Constitution is the bond that unites all Americans—past, present, and future.

### What's Your Opinion?

**Themes Journal** Do you **agree** or **disagree** with the following statements? Support your point of view in your journal.

• The ideals that are expressed in the Constitution are different from the ideals that shape our government today.

• If one branch of the government is more important than the other two branches, it should have more power.

• It is better for the government of a country undergoing change to write a new constitution rather than change its existing constitution.

# SECTION 1

## OBJECTIVES

*After completing Section 1, students should be able to*

1 Describe how the Pilgrims influenced the framers of the Constitution.

2 Identify the goals of the U.S. government as outlined in the Constitution.

3 Explain why the Constitution established the powers of the federal and state governments.

## SECTION 1

# Ideals of the Constitution

### Read to Discover

1. How did the Pilgrims influence the framers of the Constitution?
2. What are the goals of the U.S. government as outlined in the Constitution?
3. Why does the Constitution establish the powers of the federal and state governments?

### Define

- popular sovereignty
- majority rule
- delegated powers
- reserved powers
- concurrent powers
- limited government

### Identify

- Preamble

#### WHY CIVICS MATTERS

Throughout U.S. history, political thinkers have discussed how power should be shared between the federal and state governments. Use  or other **current events** sources to investigate an issue that involves distribution of power between the states and the federal government. Record your findings in your journal.

## Reading Focus

The Declaration of Independence states that governments should receive their powers from "the consent [approval] of the governed [people]." This is one of the basic ideals on which the country was founded. This ideal can be traced in part to the Mayflower Compact. The Compact was drawn up on November 21, 1620, when the Pilgrims on the *Mayflower* reached North America. They had sailed far off course and had no charter from the king of England to settle in New England or to form a government. The Pilgrims wrote the Compact to create a new government based on the cooperation and consent of the people.

The Pilgrims arrived on the Mayflower.

### ★ Consent of the Governed

Government by **popular sovereignty,** or consent of the governed, is one of our most cherished ideals. It appears in the opening sentence of the Constitution, which is known as the **Preamble**. The Preamble is an introduction that explains why the U.S. Constitution was written.

The Preamble begins with the words "We the people." The framers of the Constitution wanted to emphasize the importance of the people. These words stress that our government was established by the people

# TEACH OBJECTIVE 1

**LEVEL 1:** Have a class discussion about the circumstances faced by the Pilgrims when they landed at Plymouth Rock. *(Students should note that no settlement or government awaited them in their new land.)* Ask students to identify the reasons the Pilgrims might have included the idea of popular sovereignty in their compact. *(Students may observe that they were tired of being ruled by the king.)* Ask them to explain how the Pilgrims' ideas influenced the framers of the Constitution. *(Students should note that the framers continued a tradition of popular sovereignty established in the Mayflower Compact.)* **ENGLISH LANGUAGE LEARNERS**

**LEVELS 2 AND 3:** Organize the class into small groups and then ask students to describe how the Pilgrims influenced the framers of the Constitution. *(Students should note that they established the idea of popular sovereignty in the Mayflower Compact.)* Then have each member offer a reason he or she thinks the framers included popular sovereignty when writing the Constitution. Have each group select the reason that its members feel is most plausible and present it to the class. Then have each group reconvene to prepare a proposal of its idea with a narrative support. If time permits, ask groups to present their proposals to the class. **COOPERATIVE LEARNING**

---

---

### Historical Document

## THE MAYFLOWER COMPACT

*In November 1620, the Pilgrim leaders aboard the Mayflower drafted the Mayflower Compact, the first guidelines for self-government in the English colonies. This excerpt describes the principles of the colony's government.*

"We whose names are underwritten, . . . do by these presents [this document] solemnly and mutually in the presence of God, and one of another, covenant [promise] and combine ourselves together into a body politic [government] for our better ordering and preservation and furtherance of the ends aforesaid; and by virtue hereof, to enact, constitute, and frame such just and equal laws, ordinances, acts, constitutions, and offices . . . as shall be thought most meet [fitting] and convenient for the general good of the colony unto which we promise all due submission and obedience."

**Analyzing Primary Sources**
1. Why do you think the colonists felt the need to establish a government for themselves?
2. How do you think the Mayflower Compact influenced later governments in America?

---

of the United States. As the Preamble clearly states, the American people "do ordain [order] and establish this Constitution."

✔ **Reading Check** **Finding the Main Idea** What is the significance of the Preamble of the Constitution? It introduces the Constitution, explaining why it was written.

## ★ Goals of the Constitution

The Preamble itself is not law. Rather, it is a statement of six goals for the government of the United States.

1. **To form a more perfect union** The new government should be a better union of states than the union created under the Articles of Confederation.
2. **Establish justice** The government should make laws and establish a system of courts that are fair to all.
3. **Insure domestic tranquillity** The government should preserve peace within the country.
4. **Provide for the common defense** The government should work to protect the country from its enemies.
5. **Promote the general welfare** The government should help provide for the well-being of all the people.
6. **Secure the blessings of liberty** The government should work to safeguard the freedom of the people.

*The U.S. government uses its military to help protect the country.*

**LEVEL 1:** Have each student make a chart with three columns. The first column should list the goals of the U.S. government as outlined in the Constitution. *(Students' first columns should include the following: to form a more perfect union, to establish justice, to insure domestic tranquility, to provide for the common defense, to promote the general welfare, and to secure the blessings of liberty.)* In the second column students should rank the goal in order of importance. *(Students' ranking will vary.)* When students have completed their charts, review information from volunteers' charts with the class. **ENGLISH LANGUAGE LEARNERS**

 **HOMEWORK** In the third column of the chart created in the previous exercise, have students provide reasons for their ranking. *(Students' reasons will vary but should be logically based.)*

**LEVELS 2 AND 3:** As a class, list the goals of the U.S. government as outlined in the Constitution. *(See the Level 1 activity for goals.)* Then organize the class into six groups and assign each group one of the goals. Ask each group to create a drawing to illustrate what its members believe to be the significance of the goal, the historical reasoning for it, and the present-day benefit it provides to the United States. Students may also wish to write a brief statement to accompany their illustration.
**COOPERATIVE LEARNING**

## Federalism

| Federal Government Powers (Delegated Powers) | Powers Shared by Federal and State Governments (Concurrent Powers) | State Government Powers (Reserved Powers) |
|---|---|---|
| • Declare war<br>• Maintain armed forces<br>• Admit new states<br>• Conduct foreign relations<br>• Regulate interstate and foreign trade<br>• Coin and print money<br>• Establish post offices<br>• Regulate immigration<br>• Make all laws necessary and proper for carrying out delegated powers | • Maintain law and order<br>• Collect taxes<br>• Establish courts<br>• Charter banks<br>• Provide for public health and welfare | • Establish local governments<br>• Regulate business and trade within the state<br>• Establish and maintain public schools<br>• Conduct elections<br>• Determine voter qualifications<br>• Make marriage laws<br>• License professional workers<br>• Assume other powers not delegated to the national government and not prohibited to the states |

**Interpreting Charts**
*The U.S. system of government divides powers among the national government and the state governments.* **What powers are shared by the federal government and the states?**

These goals reflect the belief that the U.S. government should serve its citizens. They remain the goals of the country today.

✔ **Reading Check Supporting a Point of View** Which one of the goals listed in the Preamble do you think is the most important and why? Students' responses will vary but should be reasonably supported.

## A Representative Democracy

The representative democracy, or republic, set up by the Constitution is based on the consent of the people who are governed. If the people become dissatisfied with the way their representatives are governing, they can let their representatives know what they believe should be done. They can also elect new representatives in the next election.

Our republic works successfully because most Americans believe in the idea of **majority rule.** This principle ensures that when people disagree, everyone accepts the decision of the majority, or more than half the people. However, the majority ideally must always respect the rights of the minority, or the smaller group of people. Moreover, the minority must be free to express its views on issues.

✔ **Reading Check Drawing Inferences and Conclusions** Why do you think majority rule is important in a democracy? Students may say that it keeps a small group from making decisions that the majority dislikes.

 **Did You KNOW?**

New York City was the first capital of the United States, followed by Philadelphia, Pennsylvania. The current capital, Washington D.C., was not completed until 1799. The federal government first met there in 1800.

## SPOTLIGHT
### on Constitution Goals

Remind students of the goals that the framers hoped to achieve as they wrote the Constitution. *(See the Level 1 activity for goals.)* Then ask students to conduct research at the library to obtain information about how those goals continue to be met today. Have each student write a paragraph on each goal that examines how relevant that goal remains today and why. Remind students to incorporate their research into their paragraphs. **BLOCK SCHEDULING**

## TEACH OBJECTIVE 3

**ALL LEVELS:** Copy the following graphic organizer onto the chalkboard, omitting the italicized answers. Ask each student to complete the organizer in order to explain why the Constitution established the separate powers of the federal and state governments.

**ENGLISH LANGUAGE LEARNERS**

| state government | *to keep each from getting too strong* | federal government |

## ★ Economics

**The Gold Standard** The delegated power of coining money was granted as a measure to prevent economic troubles that had occurred in the past. The standard system requires that any money made must be backed by an equal value, such as gold or silver. Prior to the standard system, states had printed and coined money at an unregulated rate. This unbacked currency resulted in a devaluation of the money, which led to inflation—an economic state in which the prices of goods and services rise while wages remain the same or decrease. Prior to the 1870s, most European countries operated under the silver standard, a system in which their currency was backed by the amount of silver held to match it. The gold standard was adopted by the U.S. Congress in 1900.

### CRITICAL THINKING

Why do you think it is important for money production to be regulated?

**ANSWER:** Students might suggest that it prevents economic problems.

### CHART ANSWER

those in executive departments and agencies; judicial positions

## ★ A Federal System

As noted in Chapter 2, the delegates to the Constitutional Convention agreed to establish a federal system of government. Under federalism the powers of government are divided between the national government and the state government. The national government governs the people of the whole country, and state governments govern the people living in each state.

The national government, which is usually referred to as the federal government, is centered in Washington, D.C. The term *federal system* refers to the country's entire system of government. This system includes both the federal government and the governments of each of the 50 states.

Under the U.S. federal system, the federal government has certain powers. All powers that the Constitution does not give to the federal government remain with the state governments.

✔ **Reading Check Summarizing** What groups make up the federal system?
the 50 state governments and the national government

**Federal Government Powers** The powers that the Constitution specifically gives to the federal government are called **delegated powers.** For example, only the federal government can coin money. Only the federal government has the power to control trade with foreign nations. The federal government alone has the power to provide for the country's defense because an attack on the United States could threaten all Americans.

## How Representative Democracy Works

**VOTE**

The people of the United States elect

**Legislative Branch (Congress)**

**Executive Departments and Agencies**

**Executive Branch (President)**

**Judicial Branch (Courts)**

**Interpreting Charts** *U.S. citizens rely on their elected officials to represent their interests wisely and effectively.* **Which positions in government are appointed?**

**LEVEL 2:** Remind students why the Constitution established the powers of the federal and state governments. *(See the Level 1 activity for the reason.)* Then organize the class into small groups. Distribute copies of current newspapers to each group. Have groups study the newspapers to locate articles that report on the checks and balances system between the federal and state government. After groups have located an article, ask each group to prepare an oral presentation that summarizes the current issue and explains how the checks and balances system works today. **COOPERATIVE LEARNING**

## CLOSE

Call on a volunteer to read the Preamble to the Constitution aloud. Tell students that the Preamble states the purposes of the Constitution. Ask students to draw an illustration of each of the American ideals incorporated into the Preamble.

You may recall that under the Articles of Confederation, the federal government did not exclusively hold these important powers. The Constitution delegated these powers solely to the federal government in order to strengthen it.

**State Government Powers** The U.S. Constitution leaves several important powers to the states, allowing them to manage their own affairs. The states or the people have all the powers that the Constitution does not specifically give to the federal government. These powers are known as **reserved powers** because they are reserved, or set aside, for the states or the people. The state governments, for example, conduct elections, regulate trade within the states and establish local governments.

**Shared Powers** The federal and state governments also share many powers. These powers are known as **concurrent powers.** For example, both the federal and state governments can raise funds through taxation. Both also have the power to borrow money. Moreover, they share the power to establish courts, to charter banks, to enforce laws and punish lawbreakers, and to provide for the health and welfare of the American people.

Whenever a state law disagrees with the Constitution or with a federal law, the state must give way to the federal government. The framers of the Constitution made this clear by stating that the Constitution and the laws of the federal government shall be "the supreme law of the land."

✔ **Reading Check Categorizing** Identify and summarize the powers granted to the federal and state governments and those that they share. federal—delegated: coin money and control foreign trade and defense; state—reserved: conduct elections and control intrastate trade and create local governments; both—concurrent: tax, borrow money, create courts and banks, enforce laws and punish lawbreakers, and provide for citizens' well being

## ⭐ Defining the Government's Powers

By establishing the federal system, the framers of the Constitution set up the stronger national government that the new country needed. However, the framers were also determined to keep the new federal government from becoming too powerful.

**Limited Government** In order to accomplish this task, the framers set up a system based on the principle of **limited government**—a government with defined restrictions to its power. As you learned in Chapter 2, the heritage of limited government dates back to Magna Carta. In 1215, English nobles forced King John to sign Magna Carta in order to restrict his power and provide certain rights to the people. English colonists brought the ideal of limited government with them when they settled in America.

### BIOGRAPHY

## John Marshall

**(1755–1835)**

John Marshall was born in Virginia. After only two years of formal education as a young man, he briefly studied law at the College of William and Mary before setting up a legal practice. He later entered Virginia politics and became a prominent Federalist. President John Adams appointed Marshall as chief justice of the Supreme Court in 1801, a post he held until his death in 1835. As chief justice, Marshall played a key role in many landmark Supreme Court decisions, including cases such as *Marbury* v. *Madison* and *McCulloch* v. *Maryland*. He helped establish the principle of judicial review and often acted to strengthen the power of the federal government. Marshall's actions and decisions made him one of the most influential Supreme Court justices in U.S. history. **How did Marshall increase the power of the Supreme Court?**

🔲 **internet** connect ☰  go.hrw.com

**TOPIC:** Comparing Constitutions
**GO TO:** go.hrw.com
**KEYWORD:** SZ3 AC3

Have students access the Internet through the HRW Go site to research the constitutions and governments of other countries. Then have students create a set of trading cards that profiles the constitution and form of government of a country featured on the Web site. Trading cards should have a picture or symbol for the country on one side and information or statistics regarding the constitution of that country on the other side. Encourage students to be creative. Students may want to model the format of their trading cards on baseball, football, or other collectible trading cards.

### BIOGRAPHY ANSWER
He helped establish the principle of judicial review.

Have students complete the **Section 1 Review** on p. 76. Then have students complete **Daily Quiz 3.1**. As **Alternative Assessment**, you may want to use the proposal or chart activities in this section's lessons.

## RETEACH

Have students complete **Main Idea Activity for English Language Learners and Special-Needs Students 3.1.** Organize the class into three groups. Have each group respond to one of the three Read to Discover questions by creating a magazine cover page that illustrates the answer.

**ENGLISH LANGUAGE LEARNERS , COOPERATIVE LEARNING**

## EXTEND

Have students research the goals of the Constitution as listed in the Preamble. They should find out the reasoning behind each of the goals. Then have them work in small groups to develop a list of goals for the school's student government. Each student should offer a proposed goal. Encourage students to use their research on the U.S. Constitution as a model. Have each group write its finished list on the board and present it to the class. Discuss similarities and differences in the lists, and vote on a final list of goals. Compare it with any existing list of student government goals, and discuss variations.

**COOPERATIVE LEARNING , BLOCK SCHEDULING**

## Section 1 Review
### ANSWERS

**1. Define**
• popular sovereignty, p. 71
• majority rule, p. 73
• delegated powers, p. 74
• reserved powers, p. 75
• concurrent powers, p. 75
• limited government, p. 75

**2. Identify**
• Preamble, p. 71

**3.** to form a more perfect union, to establish justice, to insure domestic tranquility, to provide for the common defense, to promote the general welfare, and to secure the blessings of liberty

**4. a.** The Pilgrims established the idea of popular sovereignty in the Mayflower Compact.

**b.** to maintain the strong functioning of the country without either the federal or state government becoming too strong

**5.** Students' poems or songs will vary but should refer to at least four constitutional ideals and reasonably demonstrate how these ideals relate to their lives.

*King John signed Magna Carta in 1215. This document stated that the king was subject to the rule of law. It also presented the ideas of a fair and speedy trial and due process of law.*

Before the signing of Magna Carta, England had an unlimited government. The monarchy could exercise its power in any way it pleased. A king could seize people's property and give it to those people who were loyal to him. Unlimited governments have existed in modern times as well. Prior to the overthrow of his regime in 2003, Saddam Hussein's control over Iraq was an example of unlimited government. Because we live in a democracy with a constitution, U.S. citizens know what powers the federal government possesses. They also know that their leaders must follow the same laws that the rest of the citizens do.

**Powers of the People** In the Bill of Rights (discussed in the next chapter), the Constitution also states that powers not belonging to the federal government are reserved for state governments or the people. The Bill of Rights also specifies certain powers that are forbidden to both the federal government and the states. It describes the many freedoms that belong to every citizen of the United States.

As you have read, the framers of the Constitution believed that all governments should have the consent of the people they govern. They made sure that the new government could have only as much power as the people wanted to give it. Those who drafted the Constitution wanted to limit, or to check, the powers of the federal government. As a result, the government of the United States would be responsible to the American people.

✔ **Reading Check** Drawing Inferences and Conclusions Why do you think Americans placed limits on their government and gave certain rights to the people? because of their experience with the monarchy's misuse of its power

## SECTION 1 Review

Homework Practice Online
keyword: SZ3 HP3

**1. Define** and explain:
• popular sovereignty
• majority rule
• delegated powers
• reserved powers
• concurrent powers
• limited government

**2. Identify** and explain:
• Preamble

**3. Summarizing** Copy the graphic organizer below. Use it to identify what the Preamble of the Constitution outlines as the goals of the U.S. government.

1.
2.
3.
4.
5.
6.

**4. Finding the Main Idea**
a. How can the Constitution be traced to the government of the Pilgrims?
b. Why is it important that the federal government and the state governments have separate as well as shared powers?

**5. Writing and Critical Thinking**
**Analyzing Information** Write a poem or song that describes how the ideals of the Constitution affect your life today.

**Consider:**
• the goals of the Constitution
• ways that the Constitution allows Americans to participate in government

# SECTION 2

## OBJECTIVES

*After completing Section 2, students should be able to*

1  **Analyze why the Constitution provides for the separation of powers.**
2  **Identify the main responsibilities of each of the three branches of government.**
3  **Explain how the system of checks and balances works.**

## 🔊 LET'S GET STARTED!

Write the terms *executive branch, judicial branch,* and *legislative branch* in a row on the chalkboard. As students enter the classroom, ask them to tell you to which branch the Congress, the president, and the courts belong. *(Students should note that Congress is legislative, the president is executive, and the Supreme Court is judicial.)* Position the answers beneath the terms. Then draw two "walls" with chalk to separate the terms, and explain that this shows the separation of powers between the branches. Tell students that in Section 2 they will learn about the responsibilities and limitations of each of the branches of the U.S. government as specified in the Constitution.

## SECTION 2

# The Three Branches of Government

### Read to Discover

1. Why does the Constitution provide for the separation of powers?
2. What are the main responsibilities of each of the three branches of government?
3. How does the system of checks and balances work?

### Define

- legislative branch
- executive branch
- judicial branch
- checks and balances
- veto

#### WHY CIVICS MATTERS

One way Congress can limit the power of the president is by overriding a presidential veto. Use CNNfyi.com or other **current events** sources to learn about a presidential veto that Congress might override in the near future. Record your findings in your journal.

### SECTION 2 RESOURCES

#### REPRODUCIBLE
▶ Guided Reading Strategies 3.2

#### TECHNOLOGY
▶ One-Stop Planner, Lesson 3.2
▶ Holt Researcher CD–ROM
▶ Homework Practice Online

#### REINFORCEMENT, REVIEW, AND ASSESSMENT
▶ Section 2 Review, p. 79
▶ Daily Quiz 3.2
▶ Main Idea Activity 3.2
▶ English Audio Summary 3.2
▶ Spanish Audio Summary 3.2

## *Reading Focus*

The Constitution contains provisions designed to prevent any person, or any part of the government, from taking too much power. In its first three articles, the Constitution creates three separate branches of the federal government and distributes power among them. It provides for a legislative branch to make the laws, an executive branch to carry out the laws, and a judicial branch to interpret the laws.

*Massachusetts senator Ted Kennedy meets with President George W. Bush.*

### ⭐ Legislative Branch

Article I of the Constitution established Congress as the **legislative branch,** or lawmaking branch, of the government. Congress is made up of two houses—the Senate and the House of Representatives.

The Constitution places great emphasis on the Congress. As James Madison stated in *Federalist Paper* "No. 51", "in republican government, the legislative authority necessarily predominates [holds the most power]." It is the first branch of government discussed in the Constitution. The workings of Congress are described in greater detail than either of the other two branches. Moreover, the other branches depend on Congress for the money they need to carry out their duties.

✔ **Reading Check Summarizing** Explain the makeup of the legislative branch. The legislative branch consists of the Senate and the House of Representatives.

# TEACH OBJECTIVES 1, 2, AND 3

**ALL LEVELS:** Copy the following graphic organizer onto the chalkboard, omitting the italicized answers. Have each student complete the organizer to analyze why the Constitution provides for the separation of powers. **ENGLISH LANGUAGE LEARNERS**

```
                    ┌───────────┐
                    │ Executive │
                    └───────────┘
                          │
        ┌─────────────────────────────────────┐
        │ to ensure that no one branch of the  │
        │ U.S. government becomes too powerful  │
        └─────────────────────────────────────┘
         │                                │
  ┌─────────────┐                  ┌──────────┐
  │ Legislative │                  │ Judicial │
  └─────────────┘                  └──────────┘
```

**LEVEL 1:** Assign each student one of the three branches of government. Then have students prepare and then present an enactment of the branches' main responsibilities in the form of a skit or pantomime. **ENGLISH LANGUAGE LEARNERS**

**LEVELS 2 AND 3:** Call on volunteers to explain how the system of checks and balances works. Then name each branch, one at a time, and have students suggest actions the branch could take in response to actions taken by other branches.

## CLOSE

Have students write a few sentences describing each group's portrayal of the main responsibilities of its branch.

### Holt Researcher

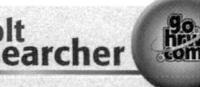

**go.hrw.com**
**KEYWORD:** Holt Researcher
**Freefind:** Checks and Balances
Read through the Supreme Court rulings on the Holt Researcher. Pick one example of a case where the Supreme Court upheld or overturned a federal law based on its constitutionality. Write a brief summary of the case that answers the following question: Do you agree or disagree with the Supreme Court's decision in the case? Why or why not?

## Checks and Balances in the Federal Government

| Powers | Branches | Checks on Powers |
|---|---|---|
| • Passes laws<br>• Can override presidential veto with a two-thirds majority in each house of Congress<br>• Appointments of federal court judges approved by Senate |  **Legislative** | • President can veto bills.<br>• The Supreme Court can rule that a law is unconstitutional. |
| • Can approve or veto laws<br>• Carries out the laws<br>• Appoints federal court judges |  **Executive** | • Congress can override presidential veto with a two-thirds majority in each house.<br>• Congress can impeach and remove the president for high crimes and misdemeanors.<br>• Senate approves the president's appointments to federal courts. |
| • Interprets the meaning of law<br>• Can rule that laws passed by Congress or actions taken by the executive branch are unconstitutional |  **Judicial** | • Congress or the states can propose an amendment to the Constitution to make a law constitutional.<br>• Senate can refuse to approve appointments to the federal courts.<br>• Congress can impeach and remove a federal judge from office. |

**Interpreting Charts** *Each branch of the federal government has certain powers that enable it to override or affect actions of the other branches.* **What checks are there on the powers of Congress?**

## ★ Executive Branch

The **executive branch,** created in Article II of the Constitution, is responsible for executing, or carrying out, the country's laws. It is headed by the president. This branch also includes the vice president and many other people who help the president enforce U.S. laws.

✔ **Reading Check Finding the Main Idea** What is the main responsibility of the executive branch? carrying out laws

## ★ Judicial Branch

Article III established the **judicial branch,** or federal court system, to interpret laws and punish lawbreakers. The Constitution makes the Supreme Court the head of the judicial branch. As such, the Court interprets the meaning of the Constitution. The Constitution also gives Congress the power to establish lower courts to help carry out the work of the judicial branch.

✔ **Reading Check Drawing Inferences and Conclusions** What are the functions of the judicial branch? to interpret laws and punish lawbreakers

## ★ Checks and Balances

To ensure that no branch of the federal government becomes too powerful, the Constitution provides for a system of **checks and balances.** Each branch has powers that check, or limit, the powers of the other two branches. Moreover, each branch has its own powers, which no other branch can assume. In this way the powers of government are balanced by being distributed among three branches.

How does the system of checks and balances in the U.S. government work? Consider lawmaking, for example. Congress has the power to make laws. However, the president has the power to **veto,** or turn down, proposed laws. With this veto power, the president can check the lawmaking power of Congress.

Does this power enable the president to stop any law passed by Congress from taking effect? If so, the president would have too much power. The Constitution, therefore, balances the president's power by also giving Congress the power to pass laws over the president's veto. Overriding a presidential veto requires a two-thirds vote of both houses of Congress. In this way Congress can check the lawmaking power of the president.

The Supreme Court can also become involved in lawmaking because it has the power to interpret the meaning of laws in its decisions. The Court can use this power to declare that certain laws are unconstitutional and cannot be enforced.

There are many other checks and balances in the federal government. You will learn more about how the three branches of the federal government check and balance each other in Chapters 5, 6, and 7.

✔ **Reading Check** Evaluating Why is the system of checks and balances important? to keep one branch of the government from gaining too much power

*Congress has the power to introduce legislation, as shown by the House bill above. Only the president can sign a bill into law. However, Congress can make a bill a law by overriding a presidential veto.*

---

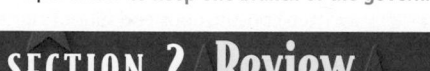

## SECTION 2 Review

**go.hrw.com** **Homework Practice Online**
keyword: SZ3 HP3

**1. Define** and explain:
- legislative branch
- executive branch
- judicial branch
- checks and balances
- veto

**2. Categorizing** Copy the graphic organizer below. Use it to list the powers of each branch of the U.S. government.

**3. Finding the Main Idea**
a. Explain why the separation of powers is part of the U.S. Constitution.
b. Describe the system of checks and balances.

**4. Writing and Critical Thinking**
**Identifying Points of View** Write a newspaper editorial explaining what might happen if the system of checks and balances were eliminated.

**Consider:**
- the power that each branch of the federal government has
- the limitations on the powers of each branch

**Powers of the U.S. Government Branches**

| Legislative | Executive | Judicial |
|---|---|---|
| | | |

**Historical Documents**

# ORIGINS OF THE REPUBLIC

*Did you know that some of the basic principles of government contained in the U.S. Constitution can be found in much earlier documents? The Charters of the Virginia Company of London (1606–1612), the Virginia Declaration of Rights (1776), and the Virginia Statute of Religious Freedom (1786) are three such documents. Together, these Virginia documents incorporate several of the basic principles of government and fundamental liberties and rights later included in the Declaration of Independence and the U.S. Constitution.*

## CHARTERS OF THE VIRGINIA COMPANY OF LONDON

*John Smith*

In the early 1600s, the Virginia Company of London was established as a joint-stock company. A joint-stock company is a business formed by a group of people who jointly share in a company's risks, profits, and losses. Shareholders in the company wanted to establish a colony in Virginia to search for gold and to profit from the natural wealth of the land. To establish their colony members of the Virginia Company obtained royal charters from King James I of England. These charters outlined the colony's formation and government. Included in the charters were some of the ideas that were growing increasingly popular in England. Government by consent of the governed and the right of people to enjoy the fruits of their labor, were two of the principles laid out in the charters.

In 1607, shareholders formed the colony of Jamestown in what is now Virginia. Colonists formed a General Assembly in 1619. This assembly is thought to be the first freely elected parliament of self-governing people in North America. The Jamestown colonists looked to the company charters for rules of government as well as for guarantees of fundamental rights and liberties. The charters provided a precedent, or example, for later generations of colonists who specified their rules for government and their rights in written constitutions and bills of rights.

## VIRGINIA DECLARATION OF RIGHTS

The Virginia Declaration of Rights accompanied the constitution that was drafted on behalf of Virginia colonists during the American Revolution. Drafted by George Mason, the Virginia declaration was the first of its kind in its statement of people's inherent rights, or rights derived from nature rather than government.

The declaration stated that "all men are by nature equally free and independent". It also argued that all people possess fundamental rights such as the enjoyment of life, liberty, property, and the pursuit of happiness. Do these words have a familiar ring to them?

According to the Declaration of Independence, which was adopted by American colonists about a month later, "all men are created equal . . . endowed by their Creator with certain inalienable Rights, that among these are Life, Liberty, and the pursuit of Happiness." Thomas Jefferson, author of the Declaration of Independence; James Madison; and George Mason—all of whom served in the Virginia legislature—were influenced by the idea that all people had the right to life and liberty. They also believed in freedom of religion.

Have students research the documents described on this page or other documents used by the framers when writing the Constitution. *(Students' alternate choices might include Magna Carta or the Articles of Confederation.)* Students should examine how these documents influenced and differed from the Constitution. Then have them report their findings in a comparison and contrast essay. Encourage students to include visual aids to clarify the information presented in their essays. Have students share their findings with the rest of the class.

**BLOCK SCHEDULING**

This scene shows an early meeting of Virginia's legislature.

## VIRGINIA STATUTE OF RELIGIOUS FREEDOM

Many of the founders also supported the separation of church and state. In 1779 Thomas Jefferson, then governor of Virginia, drafted the Virginia Statute of Religious Freedom. This document was based on the principle that church and state should be separate. Jefferson and James Madison, who greatly influenced Jefferson's efforts, were reacting against the Virginia legislature's attempts to make taxpayers provide for churches. Jefferson's statute, or bill, was designed to prevent the government establishment of religion. In 1786, after years of debate, the Virginia legislature finally passed the statute. It later provided the philosophical basis for the First Amendment to the Constitution, ratified in 1791 as part of the Bill of Rights. This document guarantees freedom of religion and the separation of church and state.

## TIES TO THE CONSTITUTION

Although the Virginia documents established many important rights, the U.S. Constitution guarantees many freedoms that were excluded from these earlier documents. Despite their differences, the Virginia documents, the Articles of Confederation, the Declaration of Independence, and the Constitution all embody the

*The Virginia Declaration of Rights*

principle of constitutionalism, or government according to the rules established in a written document. More importantly, perhaps, the earlier documents contain ideas about the inherent rights of life, liberty, the pursuit of happiness, and government by consent of the governed. These core values have shaped U.S. politics for more than two centuries.

**Understanding What You Read**
1. What is the significance of the General Assembly that met in Jamestown, Virginia, in 1619?
2. What basic ideas are outlined in the Virginia Declaration of Rights?
3. What prompted Thomas Jefferson to write the Virginia Statute of Religious Freedom?

**Thomas Jefferson** It is no wonder that the ideals of Virginia's early government resemble those ideals present in the Declaration of Independence—Thomas Jefferson played a role in establishing both. Jefferson was born and raised in the Virginia province, and he raised his family in the state. Jefferson spent his early years studying and then practicing law in Virginia, an interest that led him into public service. He was elected to the Virginia House of Burgesses when he was just 25 years old. Prior to that, he was a magistrate and county lieutenant in Abermarle, the county in which he was raised. Some historians believe that Jefferson's early experiences in local government formed his belief in the importance of protecting individual rights and limiting the reach of government.

**CRITICAL THINKING**

Why might Jefferson's early experiences have influenced his later contributions?

**ANSWER:** Students might suggest that he saw certain ideals succeed locally, leading him to assume that they would be useful on a national level.

# SECTION 3

## OBJECTIVES

*After completing Section 3, students should be able to*

1 **Explain why the Constitution is called a living document.**
2 **Analyze how the flexibility of the Constitution has benefited the United States.**
3 **Describe how amendments to the Constitution are proposed and passed.**

### 🔔 *LET'S GET STARTED!*

Write the following question on the chalkboard: *What technological innovations did not exist at the time the U.S. Constitution was written?* As students enter the classroom, allow them time to respond. *(Students' responses may include the following: television, telephone, CD player, airplane, electric lightbulb.)* Point out that these innovations and hundreds of other changes have taken place in the more than 200 years since the Constitution was written. Tell students that in Section 3 they will learn about how the Constitution has been able to govern the country successfully through such profound changes and developments.

## SECTION 3 RESOURCES

### REPRODUCIBLE

▶ Guided Reading Strategies 3.3
▶ Graphic Organizer Activity: Power in the Constitution
▶ Community Service and Participation Handbook: The Equal Rights Amendment

### TECHNOLOGY

▶ One-Stop Planner, Lesson 3.3
▶ Homework Practice Online

### REINFORCEMENT, REVIEW, AND ASSESSMENT

▶ Section 3 Review, p. 84
▶ Daily Quiz 3.3
▶ Main Idea Activity 3.3
▶ English Audio Summary 3.3
▶ Spanish Audio Summary 3.3

---

## SECTION 3

# A Flexible Document

### Read to Discover

1. Why is the Constitution called a living document?
2. How has the flexibility of the Constitution benefited the United States?
3. How are amendments to the Constitution proposed and passed?

#### WHY CIVICS MATTERS

The Constitution is an ever-changing document that meets the needs of a changing country. Use **CNNfyi.com** or other **current events** sources to investigate recent proposals to amend the Constitution. Record your findings in your journal.

### Define

• amendment
• repealed
• cabinet

*Every year people from around the world visit the National Archives in Washington, D.C., to view the U.S. Constitution.*

## Reading Focus

Changing times may call for changes in the government. In 1787, when the Constitution was written, the United States was a country of 13 states with fewer than 4 million people. Today the 50 states are home to more than 280 million people. The country has changed in other ways as well. How can the U.S. Constitution meet the needs of a changing country? The framers of the Constitution planned a system of government that could adapt to meet changing conditions and changing needs. The U.S. Constitution truly is a "living" document.

### ⭐ Providing for Change

One of the most important features of the U.S. Constitution is its flexibility. The framers of the Constitution knew that the plan of government they were creating would have to adapt to a growing nation.

The framers could not possibly foresee all of the changes the United States would undergo. Yet the government established by the Constitution has been able to adapt to new circumstances and challenges. There are three ways in which the Constitution and the government can be adapted to the changing needs and conditions of the country—amendment, interpretation, and custom.

✔ **Reading Check** Drawing Inferences and Conclusions What are some changes in modern times that the framers could not have foreseen?
Responses may include technology and the global economy.

# TEACH OBJECTIVE 1

 **ALL LEVELS:** Copy the following graphic organizer onto the chalkboard, omitting the italicized answers. Have students complete the organizer to explain why the Constitution is called a living document.

**ENGLISH LANGUAGE LEARNERS**

**Why the Constitution Is Called A Living Document**
*because its provisions enable government to change to meet changing conditions*

# TEACH OBJECTIVE 2

 **LEVEL 3:** Have students write, in their own words, a motivational speech describing how the flexibility of the Constitution has benefited the United States. Call on volunteers to present their speeches to the class and respond to any challenges to their arguments.

# TEACH OBJECTIVE 3

 **LEVELS 1 AND 2:** Review the amendment process as a class. As students provide the steps of the process, list them in a flowchart on the chalkboard. Then have students use the flowchart to organize their thoughts as they write short summaries of the process.

## Amending the Constitution

| Proposed by | Ratified by | |
|---|---|---|
|  Congress—two-thirds vote in each house |  Legislatures of three fourths of the states | 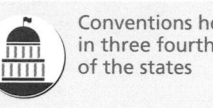 Amendment added to the Constitution |
| **or** | **or** | |
|  National convention—called by Congress at the request of two thirds of the state legislatures |  Conventions held in three fourths of the states | |

**Interpreting Charts**
*The process of amending the Constitution is intentionally difficult to make sure that only widely supported changes can be made.* **How many of the states must approve an amendment in order to ratify it?**

## ★ The Amendment Process

An **amendment** is a written change made to the Constitution. Article V of the Constitution outlines the process for making amendments. It is not easy to amend the Constitution. All proposed amendments require the approval of three fourths of the states. As a result, securing this approval for an amendment may take a long time.

An amendment may be proposed in two ways. The first way allows Congress to propose an amendment by a two-thirds vote in both houses. The second way of proposing an amendment begins with the states. The legislatures of two thirds of the states—34 out of 50—can ask Congress to call a national convention to propose an amendment. This method has never been used successfully. However, it could be used if Congress should refuse to propose an amendment that many Americans support.

After an amendment has been proposed, it must then be ratified, or approved, by three fourths, or 38, of the states. There are two ways an amendment may be ratified. The method of ratification used must be described in each proposed amendment.

One method involves sending the proposed amendment to the state legislatures for approval. All but one of the amendments to the Constitution were approved this way. The second method involves sending the proposed amendment to state conventions for consideration. After an amendment has been ratified by the required number of states, it becomes part of the written Constitution. If the people do not like the effects of an amendment it can be **repealed,** or canceled, by another amendment.

✔ **Reading Check** Summarizing How is the Constitution amended?
amendment proposed by Congress or states; ratified by states

★★★★★★★★★★★★
### That's Interesting!
★★★★★★★★★★★★

**Documents on Display** How do people preserve documents that are more than 200 years old? At the National Archives Building in Washington, D.C., the Bill of Rights, Constitution, and Declaration of Independence are displayed in a special glass case. This case protects the documents from air and moisture, which could damage the paper. Each evening, special machinery lowers the precious documents into a vault, where they are safe until they are raised for display the next morning.

## ★ Constitutional Heritage

**The Prohibition Amendment** The Eighteenth Amendment, ratified in 1919 and known as the Prohibition Amendment, made the manufacture, sale, or transportation of alcoholic beverages illegal. Over time, it became evident that prohibition was a failure. Gangsters thrived on the illegal business of bootlegging; millions of people continued to drink liquor; and with such widespread disregard for the law, the police could not enforce it. The Twenty-first Amendment, ratified in 1933, repealed prohibition.

**CRITICAL THINKING**

Do you think that an amendment should be repealed just because people do not obey it? Support your answer.

**ANSWER:** Students responses' will vary.

**CHART ANSWER**
two thirds; or 34 of the 50 states

## REVIEW AND ASSESS

Have students complete the **Section 3 Review** on page 84. Then have them complete **Daily Quiz 3.3**. As **Alternative Assessment**, you may want to use the motivational speech or summary activities in this section's lessons.

## RETEACH

Have students complete **Main Idea Activity for English Language Learners and Special-Needs Students 3.3**. Then ask them to make a word web for the term *U.S. Constitution*. Have them place the term in a center circle. Then, on lines radiating from the circle, have them write adjectives that describe the Constitution. **ENGLISH LANGUAGE LEARNERS**

## EXTEND

Have students conduct research outside of class to examine amendments to the Constitution that pertain to women, people with disabilities, and people of different ethnic origins. Suggest that students investigate how the interpretation of the Constitution has changed over the years with regard to addressing the equality of these groups. Then have each student prepare a three-to-five minute lesson to present his or her findings. Finally, have students present their lessons to the class. **BLOCK SCHEDULING**

## Section 3 Review
### ANSWERS

**1. Define**
• amendment, p. 83
• repealed, p. 83
• cabinet, p. 84

**2.** proposed: two-thirds vote in Congress or petition to Congress from two thirds of the states; passed: legislatures in three fourths of the states or by the conventions held in three fourths of the states

**3. a.** because its provisions enable government to change to meet changing conditions

**b.** Even though the founders could not foresee all of the changes that the United States would undergo, it did not limit growth of the structure that the country would need to support itself.

**4.** Students' speeches should demonstrate an understanding that making the Constitution flexible will enable it to serve the country's needs in the future.

**Interpreting the Visual Record**

**Washington's Cabinet** *Shown left to right are President Washington, and cabinet members Henry Knox, Alexander Hamilton, Thomas Jefferson, and Edmund Randolph.* **How do you think the Cabinet has changed since Washington was president?**

### ★ Changes in Government

The government also changes when some part of the Constitution is interpreted in a new way. Congress may interpret a certain clause in the Constitution as giving it the authority to pass a particular law. For example, Congress has passed laws setting minimum wages. A minimum wage is not mentioned anywhere in the Constitution. However, the Constitution does give Congress the power to control trade among the states. The goods made by workers usually travel from one state to another. Therefore, the Constitution has been interpreted to mean that Congress has the power to pass laws affecting working conditions, including wage rates. The Supreme Court has the power to decide if Congress has interpreted the Constitution correctly. The Court's rulings are final.

A number of changes in the federal government have also come about through custom and tradition. For example, the Constitution does not call for regular meetings of the leaders of the executive branch. However, President George Washington brought these leaders together regularly to serve as his advisers, or **cabinet.** Since that time, regular meetings between the president and the cabinet have become an accepted practice. Traditions like this one are seldom written down or passed into law. For this reason, they are sometimes referred to as part of the unwritten Constitution.

✔ **Reading Check** Analyzing Information How have interpretations of the Constitution and tradition influenced the federal government? Interpretation and tradition have allowed the government to do certain things that are not listed in the Constitution.

## SECTION 3 Review

keyword: SZ3 HP3

**1. Define** and explain:
   • amendment   • repealed   • cabinet

**2. Categorizing** Copy the graphic organizer below. Use it to identify the ways that constitutional amendments are proposed and passed.

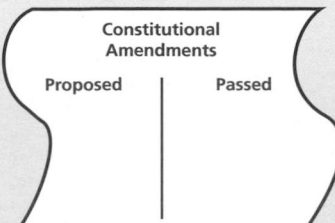

Constitutional Amendments

Proposed        Passed

**3. Finding the Main Idea**
   a. Why can it be said that the U.S. Constitution is a living document?
   b. What are the advantages of being able to change the U.S. Constitution?

**4. Writing and Critical Thinking**
   **Supporting a Point of View** Imagine that you are a delegate to the Constitutional Convention in Philadelphia. Write a short speech that will convince the other delegates that it is important to make the Constitution a flexible document.

   **Consider:**
   • the changes that may take place in the country over time
   • the varying needs of U.S. citizens

## TEACH

**LEVEL 1:** Call on a volunteer to list five steps he or she takes to get ready for school each day. *(The student might list the following: waking up, getting dressed, brushing teeth, eating breakfast, and so on.)* Write the student's responses on separate strips of paper and arrange them in order from the first to the last step on the chalkboard. As you connect the strips by drawing arrows between them, explain to the class that you are creating a flowchart. Tell them that flowcharts are used to show the movement of a process through time.
**ENGLISH LANGUAGE LEARNERS**

## EXTEND

Organize the class into four groups and assign each group one of the following processes to research: *how a student council member gets elected, how a school rule gets changed, how a textbook gets selected, or how a lesson gets planned.* Then have each group create a flowchart of the steps involved in their assigned process from start to finish. Encourage students to include places where the process may become stalled. Invite volunteers to share their group's flowchart with the class. **COOPERATIVE LEARNING** ,
**BLOCK SCHEDULING**

# Civics Skills
### WORKSHOP

### Reading Flowcharts

A flowchart is a diagram that presents information in a visual, easy-to-understand way. Its main purpose is to show the various steps that a process follows. Once you learn how to read a flowchart, you will be able to trace the movement of a process through time.

### How to Read Flowcharts

1. **Determine the subject.** Read the title of the chart to determine its subject matter. Look at any major headings for an overview of the process shown in the flowchart.

2. **Identify the beginning and the end points.** Study the arrows in the chart, noting their direction. They will tell you how the process begins and how it ends. A process on a flowchart may have more than one beginning and more than one end.

3. **Study the middle stages.** The middle stages show you movement through time by connecting all the stages in the order in which they take place. They also show you where the process may become stalled.

### Applying the Skill

Examine the flowchart below. Then answer the following questions.

1. What are the two ways in which an amendment to the Constitution can be proposed?

2. Based on the information in the flowchart, is the following statement true or false? "A majority of people must favor an amendment before it is added to the Constitution." Explain your answer.

## Amending the Constitution

| Proposed by | | Ratified by | | |
|---|---|---|---|---|
|  Congress—two-thirds vote in each house | → |  Legislatures of three fourths of the states | → |  Amendment added to the Constitution |
| **or** | | **or** | | |
|  National convention—called by Congress at the request of two thirds of the state legislatures |  |  Conventions held in three fourths of the states | | |

## Review and Assessment Resources

**REPRODUCIBLE**

▶ Chapter 3 Review, pp. 86–87

▶ Vocabulary Activity 3

▶ Chapter 3 Tutorial for Students, Parents, Mentors, and Peers

▶ Chapter 3 Test (Form A or B)

▶ Alternative Assessment Handbook

**TECHNOLOGY**

▶ Chapter 3 Test Generator (on the One-Stop Planner)

▶ Global Skill Builder CD–ROM

▶ HRW Go site

**REINFORCEMENT, REVIEW, AND ASSESSMENT**

▶ Chapter 3 Test for English Language Learners and Special-Needs Students

## REVIEW

Have students complete the **Chapter 3 Review** on pages 86–87.

## ASSESS

Use one of the chapter tests to assess students' understanding of the content. For **Alternative Assessment**, see the **Alternative Assessment Handbook**.

---

## CHAPTER 3
### REVIEW ANSWERS

**Define and Identify**
1. popular sovereignty, p. 71
2. Preamble, p. 71
3. delegated powers, p. 74
4. concurrent powers, p. 75
5. executive branch, p. 78
6. checks and balances, p. 79
7. veto, p. 79
8. amendment, p. 83
9. repealed, p. 83
10. cabinet, p. 84

**Understanding Main Ideas**

1. to form a more perfect union, to establish justice, to insure domestic tranquility, to provide for the common defense, to promote the general welfare, and to secure the blessings of liberty

2. legislative: makes laws; executive: carries out laws; judicial: interprets laws and punishes lawbreakers

3. by ensuring that no one branch wields too much power

4. Its provisions enable government to change to meet changing conditions.

5. process begins with proposal of an amendment by Congress or a national convention requested by 34 state legislatures; then amendment must be ratified by state legislatures or state conventions

**What Did You Find Out?**
1. It maintains control by the people through representation as well as by maintaining a balance of federal power with state power.

---

# Chapter 3 Review

## Chapter Summary

### Section 1

- The U.S. government is based on the ideal of popular sovereignty, or the consent of the people who are governed.

- The Preamble, or introduction of the Constitution, outlines the six goals of the document.

- The Constitution establishes a federal system of government. It gives certain powers to the federal and state governments and the people. Other powers are shared.

### Section 2

- The Constitution divides power among three separate branches of government—the legislative branch, the executive branch, and the judicial branch. This separation of powers is designed to prevent any branch from having too much power.

- Each branch of government has powers that check, or limit, the powers of the other two branches.

- The legislative branch makes laws and the executive branch carries them out. The judicial branch interprets the laws and punishes lawbreakers.

### Section 3

- The Constitution and the federal government have been able to meet the needs of a growing and changing country.

- The Constitution can be amended. The process for amending the Constitution involves two steps: proposal and ratification.

- Congress and the Supreme Court can interpret the Constitution in new ways.

- Changes can also come about through custom and tradition.

---

## Define and Identify

1. popular sovereignty
2. Preamble
3. delegated powers
4. concurrent powers
5. executive branch
6. checks and balances
7. veto
8. amendment
9. repealed
10. cabinet

## Understanding Main Ideas

**Section 1** *(Pages 71–76)*
1. What are the six goals of government as stated in the Preamble of the U.S. Constitution?

**Section 2** *(Pages 77–79)*
2. What are the three branches of the federal government, and what are their primary responsibilities?
3. How does the system of checks and balances in the federal government work?

**Section 3** *(Pages 82–84)*
4. What makes the Constitution of the United States a living document?
5. How can the Constitution be amended?

## What Did You Find Out?

1. How does the establishment of a federal system reflect the ideals of the Constitution and the United States?
2. How does the Constitution ensure that no one branch of government becomes too powerful?
3. How do interpretation, custom, and tradition affect the Constitution and the government of the United States?

## Thinking Critically

1. **Evaluating** The Constitution is based on many ideals of government. Which of these ideals do you consider most important to the American way of life? Why?
2. **Supporting a Point of View** The principle of majority rule means that sometimes the wishes of the minority go unfulfilled. Do you think this is fair? Why or why not?
3. **Analyzing Information** What experiences do you think led the framers of the Constitution to ensure that no one person or group in the government could gain too much power?

## RETEACH

Organize the class into three groups and assign each group one of the sections of Chapter 3. Have each group create a flowchart illustrating the section's main topics. Then instruct groups to link all of the section's Define and Identify terms to the appropriate main topics and offer a brief definition of each term.

**ENGLISH LANGUAGE LEARNERS ,**
**COOPERATIVE LEARNING**

## Portfolio Extensions

**1. Linking to Community** Ask students to read a copy your school district's mission statement. Then have each student interview a member of the school board about the member's goals as they relate to your school. Have volunteers present their interviews to the class.

**2. Cooperative Learning** Organize students into small groups. Then ask each group to write a composite Preamble that contains the group's favorite goals, explains its choices, and shows the benefits of including each. Have groups present their lists to the class.

---

## Building Social Studies Skills

go.hrw.com
STANDARDIZED TEST PREP ONLINE
keyword: SZ3 STP3

### Interpreting Political Cartoons

Study the political cartoon below. Then use the cartoon to help you answer the questions that follow.

**"Thanks–Thanks a lot–Thanks again– can I lean back now?"**

1. What does the illustration suggest that President Lyndon Johnson hopes to achieve?
   a. Johnson wants the Congressman to vote for his legislation.
   b. Johnson wants Congress to work harder.
   c. Johnson wants members of Congress to know how proud he is of their work.
   d. Johnson thinks Congress has too much power.
2. Based on your knowledge of the Constitution, why do you think a chief executive would rely on Congress to achieve his or her goals?

### Analyzing Primary Sources

Read the following quotation from Benjamin Franklin about the U.S. Constitution and then answer the questions that follow.

> **❝** I agree to this Constitution, with all its faults, if they are such, because I think a general government necessary for us. . . . I doubt, too, whether any other convention we can obtain [create] may be able to make a better constitution. . . . [It] astonishes me, sir, to find this system approaching so near to perfection as it does, and I think it will astonish our enemies. . . . Thus I consent [agree], sir, to this Constitution, because I expect no better, and I am not sure it is not the best. **❞**

3. Which of the following statements best describes Franklin's view of the Constitution?
   a. He thinks it is bad, but the delegates can probably do no better.
   b. He agrees to support it because of pressure from other delegates.
   c. He thinks it is very good and perhaps the best that can be written.
   d. He thinks America's enemies will be surprised that the Constitution is so poor.
4. What qualities of the Constitution do you think led Franklin to say it was "near to perfection"? Explain your answer.
5. Why do you think Franklin is willing to accept the Constitution "with all its faults"?
6. Based on what you have learned about the Constitution, do you agree or disagree with Franklin's assessment of the Constitution? Explain your answer.

2. It establishes a system of checks and balances.

3. by allowing the flexibility to change according to the needs of the times

### Thinking Critically

1. Students' responses will vary but should be well supported.

2. Students' responses should address the balance between majority rule and the rights of the minority to be heard.

3. Their experiences under British control made them wary of government.

### Skills Workshop

1. b

2. The system of checks and balances requires cooperation among the branches of government.

3. c

4. Students' responses will vary but should reflect accurate knowledge of the Constitution and logical reasoning.

5. Students might suggest that Franklin felt that the faults did not detract from the overall quality of the document.

6. Students' responses will vary, but they should support their answer.

---

## Alternative Assessment

### Building Your Portfolio

**Interdisciplinary Connection to Government**

Complete the following activity individually or in a group:

Examine the six goals of the Constitution that are laid out in the Preamble and are found on page 72. Then write out a Preamble for your work in this class. Make sure that your Preamble contains six goals and that you provide explanations for each.

### 🔲 internet connect

**Internet Activity: go.hrw.com**
**keyword: SZ3 AC3**

Access the Internet through the HRW Go site to research the process of amending the Constitution. Then propose a new amendment and draft a plan for getting your proposed amendment ratified. Your plan should account for all the steps in the amendment process. Include a short paragraph explaining your amendment and the reasons it should be added to the Constitution.

# Rights and Responsibilities

## CHAPTER RESOURCE MANAGER

| Objectives | Pacing Guide | Reproducible Resources |
|---|---|---|
| **SECTION 1:**<br>**The Bill of Rights**<br>(pp. 89–95) | **Regular**<br>1.5 days<br><br>**Block Scheduling**<br>1 day<br><br>*Block Scheduling Handbook with Team Teaching Strategies, Chapter 4* | **RS** Guided Reading Strategies 4.1<br><br>**RS** Readings in Economics and Government 3: English Petition of Rights<br><br>**PS** American Civics Political Cartoon: Principles of Democracy<br><br>**RS** Graphic Organizer Activity: The Bill of Rights |
| **SECTION 2:**<br>**Guaranteeing Other Rights**<br>(pp. 96–99) | **Regular**<br>1 day<br><br>**Block Scheduling**<br>.5 day<br><br>*Block Scheduling Handbook with Team Teaching Strategies, Chapter 4* | **RS** Guided Reading Strategies 4.2<br><br>**RS** Readings in Economics and Government, 11: Seneca Falls Declaration of Women's Rights<br><br>**RS** Readings in Economics and Government 24: Susan B. Anthony on Women's Suffrage<br><br>**E** Challenge and Enrichment Worksheet 4: Weighing<br><br>**SM** Community Service and Participation Handbook: Know Your Rights |
| **SECTION 3:**<br>**Citizens' Duties and Responsibilities**<br>(pp. 100–04) | **Regular**<br>1 day<br><br>**Block Scheduling**<br>.5 day<br><br>*Block Scheduling Handbook with Team Teaching Strategies, Chapter 4* | **RS** Guided Reading Strategies 4.3<br><br>**RS** Readings in Economics and Government 49: *The Social Contract,* Jean-Jacques Rousseau<br><br>**E** Creative Teaching Strategy: Resource Speaker |

(Section 1 objectives)
- Explain why the Bill of Rights was added to the Constitution.
- Examine how the First Amendment protects personal freedoms.
- Identify the other rights that the Bill of Rights guarantees.

(Section 2 objectives)
- Evaluate how the Thirteenth and Fourteenth Amendments extended civil rights.
- Indicate which amendments extended Americans' voting rights.

(Section 3 objectives)
- Explain the duties of citizenship.
- Identify where the duties of citizenship are described.
- Describe the responsibilities of citizenship.

## Chapter Resource Key

| | | | | |
|---|---|---|---|---|
| **PS** | Primary Sources | **SM** | Skills Mastery |  CD-ROM |
| **RS** | Reading Support | **A** | Assessment |  Video |
| **IC** | Interdisciplinary Connections | **REV** | Review | Internet |
| **E** | Enrichment | **ELL** | Reinforcement and English Language Learners |  Holt Presentation Maker Using Microsoft® PowerPoint® |
| | | | Transparencies | |

 **One-Stop** Planner CD–ROM

**See the *One-Stop Planner* for a complete list of additional resources for students and teachers.**

## One-Stop Planner CD–ROM

It's easy to plan lessons, select resources, and print out materials for your students when you use the **One-Stop Planner CD–ROM with Test Generator**.

## Meeting Individual Needs

### Ability Levels

**Level 1** Basic-level activities designed for all students encountering new material

**Level 2** Intermediate-level activities designed for average students

**Level 3** Challenging activities designed for honors and gifted-and-talented students

**English Language Learners** Activities that address the needs of students with Limited English Proficiency

## Chapter Review and Assessment

- **IC** Vocabulary Activity 4
- Global Skill Builder CD–ROM
- HRW Go site
- **REV** Chapter 4 Tutorial for Students, Parents, Mentors, and Peers
- **REV** Chapter 4 Review, pp. 106–07
- **A** Standardized Test Practice
- **A** Chapter 4 Test Generator (on the One-Stop Planner)
- **A** Chapter 4 Test (Form A or B)
- **A** Alternative Assessment Handbook
- **A** Chapter 4 Test for English Language Learners and Special-Needs Students

**CHAPTER 4**

Section 1    *The Bill of Rights*

Section 2    *Guaranteeing Other Rights*

Section 3    *Citizens' Duties and Responsibilities*

## What's Your Opinion?

*To help students create their Themes Journal entries, provide the following examples of appropriate agree/disagree statements.*

● **Agree**   Laws should clearly define citizens' rights so that they are always protected.

**Disagree**   The rights of citizens are inherent and therefore are automatically protected.

● **Agree**   It is the responsibility of all citizens to fulfill their civic duties in order to maintain a democratic society.

**Disagree**   In a democratic society, one is free to choose not to perform his or her civic duties.

● **Agree**   A constitution is the foundation of any society and should never be altered.

**Disagree**   Society changes throughout history; therefore, a constitution should be adaptable to the times.

## Internet Activity

**First Amendment Freedoms**

**internet** connect
**go.hrw.com**

**TOPIC:** First Amendment Freedoms
**GO TO:** go.hrw.com
**KEYWORD:** SZ3 AC4

Have students access the Internet through the HRW Go site to research the issues related to the First Amendment. Ask each student to find an example of a free speech case, a case involving symbolic speech, or a case involving freedom of the press. Students should review key court rulings on these issues and locate arguments that provide positive and negative views related to the issue. Then have students create a political cartoon or a drawing that reflects a point of view on his or her issue.

**CHAPTER**

# 4 Rights and Responsibilities

### Build on What You Know

Do you know how many years, months, and days are left until your 18th birthday? That time represents the countdown to the day you will receive the right to vote. Why is this day so important? From that day on, you will be able to participate fully in your government. You will have the right to vote on important issues and help elect your local, state, and national leaders. Just as the U.S. Constitution provides the foundation for our federal government, voting is the basis of our democratic system.

**What's Your Opinion?**

**Themes Journal**   Do you **agree** or **disagree** with the following statements? Support your point of view in your journal.

- A country's laws must outline citizens' basic rights so that they can be protected.

- Citizens must fulfill their duties and responsibilities to make the democratic system work.

- Once a constitution is written, it must never be changed.

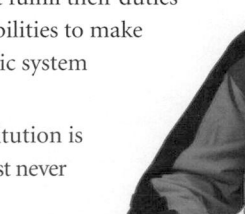

# SECTION 1

## OBJECTIVES

*After completing Section 1, students should be able to*

1 Explain why the Bill of Rights was added to the Constitution.
2 Examine how the First Amendment protects personal freedom.
3 Identify the other rights that the Bill of Rights guarantees.

## SECTION 1

# The Bill of Rights

### Read to Discover

1. Why was the Bill of Rights added to the Constitution?
2. How does the First Amendment protect personal freedoms?
3. What other rights does the Bill of Rights guarantee?

### WHY CIVICS MATTERS

The freedoms spelled out in the Bill of Rights are essential to our democratic system. Use **CNNfyi.com** or other **current events** sources to investigate a recent issue concerning the Bill of Rights. Record your findings in your journal.

### Define

• separation of church and state
• slander
• libel
• petition
• search warrant
• grand jury
• indict
• self-incrimination
• double jeopardy
• due process of law
• eminent domain
• bail

### Identify

• Bill of Rights

## *Reading Focus*

Most of the framers of the Constitution believed they had created enough safeguards to protect the rights of Americans. The Constitution was sent to the states in 1787 for ratification. The framers then learned that many Americans wanted a bill, or list, of rights added to the document. Upon ratification of the Constitution, a number of states made the strong recommendation that a bill of rights be added.

*A quill pen and silver inkstand similar to those used by the framers of the Constitution*

### ⭐ The First Amendment

Congress discussed more than 100 proposals for amendments before it presented 12 to the states for approval. The states ratified 10 of these amendments. These 10 amendments, known as the **Bill of Rights**, became part of the U.S. Constitution in 1791.

The rights described in the First Amendment of the Constitution are probably the most familiar to us because they are so close to our daily lives. The rights protected under the First Amendment are basic rights that are essential to a free people.

**Freedom of Religion** The first right, or freedom, guaranteed in the Bill of Rights is freedom of religion. Americans have the right to practice any religion—or to practice no religion at all.

The First Amendment forbids Congress from establishing an official national religion, or from favoring one religion in any way. Like all

**LEVEL 1:** Lead a class discussion about why the Bill of Rights was added to the Constitution. *(Students should indicate that upon ratification of the Constitution, a number of states recommended that a Bill of Rights be added.)* Ask students to imagine that they live in colonial America and are members of a committee urging the inclusion of a bill of rights. Have each student create a handbill listing five reasons why a bill of rights will be an essential part of the Constitution.

**ENGLISH LANGUAGE LEARNERS**

**LEVEL 1:** Discuss with students why the Bill of Rights was added to the Constitution. Then ask students about real-life situations in which various freedoms guaranteed in the Bill of Rights affect teenagers. On the chalkboard, write each of their suggestions as well as which of the first 10 amendments they correspond to. *(Students might indicate how freedom of the press affects their activities in working on the school newspaper. Students might also indicate how the freedoms of speech and of petition protect their right to have their concerns heard by their student government.)* **ENGLISH LANGUAGE LEARNERS**

## ★ Global Relations

### Universal Human Rights

The United States is not the only country with a Bill of Rights that guarantees the basic rights of its citizens. Delegates at the Constitutional Convention were influenced by the English Bill of Rights. In 1789 the French government, its society torn by revolution, passed the Declaration of the Rights of Man and of the Citizen in 1789. The Canadian Charter of Rights and Freedoms also guarantees basic rights. In 1948 the United Nations General Assembly adopted the Universal Declaration of Human Rights, which proclaims itself "as a common standard of achievement for all peoples and all nations."

**ACTIVITY:** Ask students to conduct research at the library to obtain information about countries that do not extend basic rights and freedoms to their citizens. Have students prepare a list of countries and annotate each entry with an example of how its citizens' freedoms are limited.

## Holt Researcher

**go.hrw.com**
**KEYWORD: Holt Researcher**
**Freefind:** Freedom of Speech
Scan through the Supreme Court cases on the Holt Researcher and find at least one that deals with freedom of speech. Use this information to write a short essay that answers the following question: Do you think the government should have the power to limit freedom of speech under certain circumstances? Why or why not?

*First Amendment rights are basic rights that are essential to a free people.*

rights listed in the Bill of Rights, freedom of religion has its origins in colonial times. Several colonies were established mainly by settlers seeking the freedom to practice their religion. The First Amendment eventually guaranteed this right to all Americans.

Over time, key Supreme Court decisions have interpreted the Constitution as requiring a strict **separation of church and state.** In other words, there should be a strict division between religion and government. For example, recent Supreme Court decisions have prevented people from holding school-sponsored prayers in public schools.

**Freedom of Speech** The right to express ideas and opinions through speech is called freedom of speech. Freedom of speech also includes the right to listen to the ideas and opinions of others. This freedom guarantees that Americans can openly express their thoughts and ideas. We may talk freely to friends and neighbors or deliver a speech in public to a group of people.

The First Amendment protects Americans' right to express opinions about the government and to criticize the actions of government officials. Such free-speech rights are not protected in some countries. People living under a totalitarian government, for example, have no right to speak freely. If they criticize the actions of the government, they may be punished.

Of course, people cannot use their right to freedom of speech to injure others. People do not have the right to tell lies or to spread false rumors about others. If they do, they may be sued in court for **slander**—knowingly making false statements that hurt another person's reputation.

Furthermore, the right of free speech cannot be exercised in a way that might cause physical harm to others. A person does not have the right to call out "Fire!" in a crowded room just to see what might happen. Such an action could cause panic, and people could be injured in the rush to escape.

In other words, like all freedoms, the right of free speech is not an absolute freedom. It has limits that are meant to protect the rights of others and to promote what is good for all. The government has tried to define these limits at various times in history. In the Supreme Court case *Schenck* v. *United States,* Justice Oliver Wendell Holmes wrote the majority opinion that established what has become known as the clear-and-present-danger rule. The clear-and-present-danger rule dictates that if an act of free speech can be closely linked to an unlawful act, government authority has the right to prevent it. However, it is

**ALL LEVELS:** Copy the following graphic organizer onto the chalkboard, omitting the italicized answers. Ask each student to complete the chart to list the rights that are guaranteed by the Bill of Rights. Then lead a class discussion about why the inclusion of the Bill of Rights was important.

**ENGLISH LANGUAGE LEARNERS**

| The Bill of Rights | |
|---|---|
| • *separation of church and state* | • *the inclusion of rights not specifically listed in the Constitution* |
| • *freedom of the press* | • *freedom of speech* |
| • *freedom of petition* | • *freedom of assembly* |
| • *no quartering of soldiers* | • *the right to bear arms* |
| • *protection for those accused* | • *protection from unreasonable search and seizure* |

# SUPREME COURT CASE STUDY

## Schenck v. United States

**Significance:** The Supreme Court ruling in *Schenck v. United States* established the "clear-and-present danger" test to decide what limits could be set on speech without violating individual freedom. The ruling states that speech that jeopardizes national security or the personal safety of others is not protected by the Constitution.

**Background:** Charles Schenck, a Socialist Party member, objected to the U.S. entry into World War I. He mailed pamphlets to those who had been drafted urging them not to participate in the fighting. The government charged Schenck with violating the Espionage Act of 1917, which made obstructing the draft illegal. Schenck was found guilty, and he appealed the verdict, claiming that the Espionage Act was unconstitutional because it

limited the First Amendment right to freedom of speech.

**Decision:** The case was argued on January 9–10, 1919, and decided on March 3, 1919, by a vote of 9 to 0. Justice Oliver Wendell Holmes spoke for the unanimous Court, which upheld the government's conviction of Schenck. The Court judged that the protection of free speech under the First Amendment had limits and that Schenck's actions had gone beyond those limits.

**How do you think Schenck's actions might have created a "clear and present danger" for the country?**

often difficult to determine when speech presents a clear and present danger to society or to the government. As a result, courts often consider the circumstances surrounding a statement when deciding whether it poses a real danger.

**Freedom of the Press** The right to express ideas in writing is freedom of the press. This freedom is closely related to freedom of speech and is also guaranteed by the First Amendment.

Americans of colonial times struggled for this important right. At that time newspapers were forbidden to criticize the government or public officials. These restrictions often applied even if what was written was known to be true. However, many colonists opposed the idea of preventing people from expressing their opinions about officials' actions. Such concerns led to the inclusion of freedom of the press in the Bill of Rights.

Freedom of the press gives all Americans the right to express their thoughts freely in writing. However, they do not have the right to engage in **libel**—the act of publishing falsehoods that damage a person's reputation. If people or companies knowingly or carelessly publish such falsehoods, they may be sued for libel.

As new technologies have been introduced, the courts have decided that freedom of the press applies to electronic media as well as to written works, such as books. Thus, television and radio broadcasts also are protected under the First Amendment.

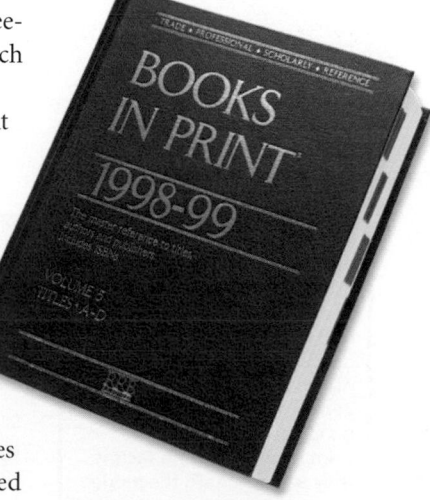

*Freedom of the press helps encourage the publication of thousands of books each year in the United States.*

## The Democratic Process

**Skokie Rally** In 1977 the National Socialist Party of America, a neo-Nazi group, wanted to hold a "white supremacy" rally in Skokie, Illinois. Skokie, a suburb of Chicago, was home to some 7,000 Jewish survivors of Nazi concentration camps. Town officials tried to block the rally, and the state courts backed their decision. The U.S. Supreme Court disagreed. In a five-to-four ruling, the Court said the ban violated the First Amendment, which guarantees the freedom of speech. As former justice Oliver Wendell Holmes once wrote, the Constitution protects not only "free thought for those who agree with us but freedom for the thought that we hate."

**CRITICAL THINKING**
Do you think that the Constitution should protect those U.S. citizens with unpopular or controversial viewpoints?

**ANSWER:** Students' responses may vary, but students should support their answers.

**CASE STUDY ANSWER**
Students might suggest that his encouragement of draftees to ignore their draft notice placed the country's interests at peril, both at home and abroad.

**LEVEL 1:** Lead a class discussion about how the First Amendment protects personal freedoms. Then organize students into small groups. Ask each group to create a poster that illustrates the freedoms that the First Amendment guarantees. *(Students' posters should depict the freedom of religion, freedom of speech, freedom of the press, freedom of assembly, and freedom of petition.)* Display the groups' posters around the classroom. **ENGLISH LANGUAGE LEARNERS** , **COOPERATIVE LEARNING**

**LEVELS 2 AND 3:** Review with the class the freedoms described in the First Amendment. *(See the Level 1 lesson for the freedoms.)* Then ask students to imagine that they have been assigned to work in a foreign country that does not enjoy the same freedoms that U.S. citizens do. Ask each student to write a letter to a family member back home, describing what it is like to live without particular rights that he or she possessed prior to moving abroad. Have volunteers read their letters to the class.

**HOMEWORK** Tell each student to create a political cartoon illustrating a freedom protected by the Bill of Rights.

## ★ The Democratic Process

**The Pentagon Papers** The U.S. courts have long struggled with First Amendment issues, particularly when the interest of national security is involved. It was in 1971 at the height of the Vietnam War when leaked information about the government's involvement in Vietnam found its way to the *New York Times* newspaper. After careful deliberation, the editors decided to publish portions of the classified documents. The U.S. government requested that the paper cease publication of the documents, arguing that it would result in "direct, immediate, and irreparable" harm to the country. The newspaper stood firm. The government won a temporary victory when a judge placed a restraining order on the paper, requiring it to cease publication of the documents. In the landmark *United States* v. *New York Times* decision, the Supreme Court overturned that restraint. Justice Hugo Black noted in his concurring opinion that "only a free and unrestrained press can effectively expose deception in government."

### CRITICAL THINKING

In what instances can the publication of information result in irreparable harm to the country?

**ANSWER:** Students might suggest that certain classified information should remain secret during times of war.

**Interpreting the Visual Record**

**Freedom of Assembly** *Americans have the right to meet in groups to express their views openly.* **What do you think the slogan "We will remember in November" means?**

★★★★★★★★★★★★
### That's Interesting!
★★★★★★★★★★★★

**A Free Press** Can you be locked up for criticizing a public official? Colonist John Peter Zenger was arrested in 1734 for criticizing the royal governor of New York in his paper. The judge in the case declared that trying to stir up dislike of government officials was a crime. But Zenger's lawyer argued that his client had the right to print even damaging facts if they were true. To the judge's dismay, the jury agreed and decided that Zenger was right about the governor's mistakes! The verdict was a victory for the right to express ideas openly.

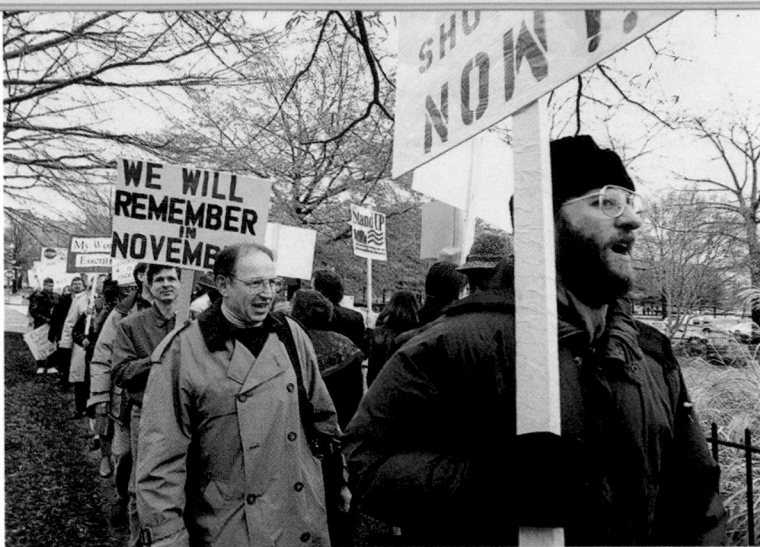

**Freedom of Assembly** Another of the priceless rights guaranteed by the First Amendment is freedom of assembly, or freedom to hold meetings. Americans have the right to meet to discuss problems and plan actions. They can gather to express their views about government decisions. Of course, such meetings must be peaceful.

**Freedom of Petition** The right to ask the government to do something or stop doing something is freedom of **petition.** A petition is a formal request. The First Amendment contains this guarantee. Freedom of petition gives you the right to contact your representatives in Congress and ask them to pass laws you favor. You are similarly free to ask your representatives to change laws you do not like. The right of petition helps government officials learn what citizens want done.

✔ **Reading Check Summarizing** What basic freedoms does the First Amendment guarantee? freedoms of religion, speech, the press, assembly, petition

## ★ The Second and Third Amendments

During the colonial period, Americans who served in militias, or volunteer armies, carried weapons to defend their communities. Colonial militias played an important part in the American Revolution.

Later, in the early years of the nation, Americans needed weapons to serve in the militias that were established to defend the states. The militias also provided protection during emergencies. Many Americans believed that without weapons they would be powerless if the government overstepped its powers and tried to rule by force. For these reasons, the Second Amendment to the Constitution protects Americans' right to bear arms.

Today, because of the increase of crime in the United States, gun control is widely debated. Some people demand that guns be regulated.

**LEVEL 3:** Have students exercise their freedom of petition by writing letters to school officials about issues important to them. Remind students to include in their letters how the First Amendment protects their right to petition.

**LEVEL 3:** Ask students to think about instances throughout history in which peaceful protest brought about a positive result. Then have each student write a one-page essay examining how peaceful protest is a protected personal freedom of the First Amendment. Students should include a paragraph about why this freedom is so essential to the First Amendment. *(Students might include historical events such as the women's suffrage movement or the civil rights movement.)*

# TEACH OBJECTIVE 3

**LEVEL 1:** Organize the class into small groups and then ask students about what other rights the Bill of Rights guarantees. *(right to bear arms, rights granted when accused of a crime, protection from illegal search or seizure, and so on)* Then have group members choose which amendment they believe to be the most important of the first 10 Amendments. Ask one member from each group to find more information about the amendment. Tell another member to provide real-life examples involving the amendment's guaranteed rights. One member should serve as a secretary to record the reasons the group chose its amendment as the most important one in the Bill of Rights. **COOPERATIVE LEARNING**

They say that gun control laws would lower the crime rate. Other people argue that the Second Amendment prevents the federal government from passing laws that limit the right to bear arms.

The Third Amendment states that the government cannot quarter, or give housing to, soldiers in private citizens' homes during peacetime without the owners' consent. Under British rule, the colonists were sometimes forced to house and feed British soldiers. As a result, Americans wanted a "no quartering" protection in the Bill of Rights.

✔**Reading Check Drawing Inferences and Conclusions** How did the American Revolution influence the Second and Third Amendments? Weapons to resist government tyranny; soldiers could not be quartered in homes without citizen consent.

## ⭐ The Fourth and Fifth Amendments

The Fourth Amendment protects people from unreasonable searches and seizures. This means that, unless there is just cause, our persons or property cannot be searched and our property cannot be taken from us by the government. A search is considered reasonable if a judge has issued a **search warrant**—a legal document that describes the place to be searched and the persons or things to be seized. A search warrant can be issued only if there is good reason to believe that evidence of a crime will be found. Although the Constitution does not refer to the rights to privacy, these rights generally fall under the Fourth Amendment.

The Fifth Amendment contains several provisions protecting the rights of a person accused of a crime. Before a person can be brought to trial, a **grand jury** must **indict,** or formally accuse, the individual of a crime. The grand jury decides if there is enough evidence to go to trial. This protects an accused person from hasty government action.

The Fifth Amendment protects an accused person from **self-incrimination,** or having to testify against oneself. It protects people from **double jeopardy,** or being tried twice for the same crime.

Another Fifth Amendment protection states that no person can be denied life, liberty, or property without **due process of law.** This means that a person cannot be punished for a crime until the law has been fairly applied to his or her case. Supreme Court interpretations of the amendment also require that the law itself be fair and reasonable.

The last clause of the Fifth Amendment guarantees all Americans the right to own private property. This is one of our most basic freedoms. The U.S. economic system is based on the principle of ownership of private property.

In some cases, the government has the authority to take private property for public use. For example, if the government needs to build

**Interpreting the Visual Record**

**The Fourth Amendment** *Authorities must obtain a search warrant from a court before searching private property.* **What type of information do you think would be important to include in a search warrant?**

**LEVELS 2 AND 3:** Bring several newspapers to class and then organize the class into groups. Ask groups to study the newspapers to find national and international stories that address one of the First Amendment rights. Have groups share their findings with the class. (*Students might present a story about a country that suppresses negative accounts of government policies.*) Finally, have students explain whether our rights guaranteed by the Bill of Rights ensure a better way of life and why.

**COOPERATIVE LEARNING**

## CLOSE

Have students compare the Bill of Rights to the list of 10 rights that the class created in the *Let's Get Started!* activity. Discuss the differences and have volunteers come to the chalkboard to create a chart with the 10 amendments of the Bill of Rights listed in one column and the class's 10 rights listed in a second column. Have students discuss which list best covers the most important rights of citizens.

### Freedoms Guaranteed by the Bill of Rights

**Freedom of Religion**
• Freedom to practice any religion, or none, with no official state religion

**Freedom of the Press**
• Freedom to publish ideas and opinions

**Right to Equal Justice**
• All persons accused of a crime must receive fair and equal treatment in court

**Right to Petition**
• Right to urge the government to pass laws or take certain actions

**Freedom of Assembly**
• Freedom to hold meetings

**Right to Freedom and Security**
• No unlawful search of homes or persons
• Troops may not be stationed in citizens' homes
• Right to bear arms

**Freedom of Speech**
• Freedom to express ideas and opinions

**Interpreting Charts**
*The Bill of Rights guarantees a set of basic freedoms and rights for all Americans.* **What freedoms listed above deal with expression of ideas and opinions?**

a road or a school, property owners may have to give up their property to meet a public need. The government's power to take citizens' private property for public use is known as **eminent domain.** The government must pay a fair price to the owner.

## ★ The Sixth, Seventh, and Eighth Amendments

The Sixth Amendment guarantees a person accused of a crime the right to a prompt public trial by a jury. Accused people must be informed of the crimes they are charged with committing. They have the right to hear and question all witnesses against them. Accused people can also call witnesses to appear in court.

The Sixth Amendment also guarantees a person accused of a crime the right to have the help of a lawyer. The Supreme Court has ruled that if an accused person cannot afford to hire a lawyer, one will be provided by the courts. The government pays the lawyer's fee.

The Seventh Amendment provides for a trial by jury in certain kinds of cases that involve conflicts over money or property. The Eighth Amendment states that the courts cannot set bail that is excessive, or too high. **Bail** is the money or property an accused person gives a court to hold. Bail serves as a guarantee that he or she will appear for trial. After the bail is paid, the accused person can leave jail. The bail is returned to the accused after the trial.

## REVIEW AND ASSESS

Have students complete the **Section 1 Review** on page 95. Then have students complete **Daily Quiz 4.1**. As **Alternative Assessment**, you may want to use the handbill or essay activities in this section's lessons.

## RETEACH

Have students complete **Main Idea Activity for English Language Learners and Special-Needs Students 4.1**. Then assign each student one of the sections in this chapter. Ask students to create a study guide for the sections that they have been assigned. After they have finished their study guides, ask volunteers to present their guides to the class. **ENGLISH LANGUAGE LEARNERS**

## EXTEND

Have students read the Ninth Amendment. Then ask each student to write an essay discussing how this amendment further establishes the flexibility of the Constitution. Students might name other basic rights and freedoms that are not specified in the Bill of Rights or the rest of the Constitution. Invite volunteers to discuss their essays with the class. **BLOCK SCHEDULING**

The Eighth Amendment also forbids "cruel and unusual" punishment. The exact meaning of what is "cruel and unusual" has been debated a great deal throughout U.S. history.

✔ **Reading Check** Analyzing Information How does the Bill of Rights protect the rights of the accused? requires search warrants and provides for trial by jury; prohibits unreasonable search and seizure, double jeopardy, cruel and unusual punishment, and excessive bail

## The Ninth and Tenth Amendments

The authors of the Bill of Rights did not want to imply that the people had only those rights that are specifically mentioned in the Constitution and in the first eight amendments. They wanted to ensure that Americans would enjoy every right and freedom possible. Thus, they added the Ninth Amendment. This amendment implies that the people of the United States enjoy many other basic rights that are not listed in the Constitution. These rights have not been specifically defined. Yet the Supreme Court has sometimes used the Ninth Amendment as a tool to support people's claims to specific rights, including the right to political activity and the right to privacy.

The Tenth Amendment serves as a final guarantee of citizens' rights. This amendment states that all powers not expressly given to the federal government nor forbidden to the states by the Constitution are reserved to the states or to the people. This provision gives the states the power to act to guarantee citizens' rights.

✔ **Reading Check** Evaluating How did the framers of the Constitution limit the power of the federal government in the Ninth and Tenth Amendments? expressed the idea that Americans enjoy other rights not stated in the Constitution and that states and the people retain powers not reserved to the federal government

### Interpreting the Visual Record

**Free Education** Although not specifically guaranteed by the Constitution, free public education is considered a basic right by many Americans. **Why do you think free public education is considered so important?**

### Visual Record Answer

*Students might suggest that it provides a form of equal opportunity for all citizens.*

## Section 1 Review
## ANSWERS

**1. Define**
- separation of church and state, p. 90
- slander, p. 90
- libel, p. 91
- petition, p. 92
- search warrant, p. 93
- grand jury, p. 93
- indict, p. 93
- self-incrimination, p. 93
- double jeopardy, p. 93
- due process of law, p. 93
- eminent domain, p. 94
- bail, p. 94

**2. Identify**
- Bill of Rights, p. 89

**3.** freedom of religion, speech, the press, assembly, petition

**4. a.** in order to guarantee their fundamental rights as citizens

**b.** Students' answers should include the right to bear arms, no quartering protection, protection from unreasonable searches and seizures, rights of the accused, right to a prompt public trial by a jury.

**5.** Students' speeches will vary but should include references to experiences while under British rule as well as the desire to define the powers of the government.

---

## SECTION 1 Review

**go.hrw.com** **Homework Practice Online** keyword: SZ3 HP4

**1. Define** and explain:
- separation of church and state
- slander
- libel
- petition
- search warrant
- grand jury
- indict
- self-incrimination
- double jeopardy
- due process of law
- eminent domain
- bail

**2. Identify** and explain:
- Bill of Rights

**3. Analyzing Information** Copy the web diagram below. Use the web to describe the freedoms guaranteed by the First Amendment.

First Amendment

**4. Finding the Main Idea**
a. Why did Americans want a bill of rights added to the Constitution?
b. List at least five rights guaranteed in the Second through Eighth Amendments.

**5. Writing and Critical Thinking**
**Supporting a Point of View** Imagine that you are a state legislator ratifying the Bill of Rights. Write a brief speech explaining why the Ninth and Tenth Amendments are necessary.

**Consider:**
- experiences under British rule
- the powers of government

# SECTION 2

## OBJECTIVES

*After completing Section 2, students should be able to*

1 Evaluate how the Thirteenth and Fourteenth Amendments extended civil rights.
2 Indicate which amendments extended Americans' voting rights.

## SECTION 2 RESOURCES

### REPRODUCIBLE

▶ Guided Reading Strategies 4.2
▶ Readings in Economics and Government, 11: Seneca Falls Declaration of Women's Rights
▶ Readings in Economics and Government 24; Susan B. Anthony on Women's Suffrage
▶ Challenge and Enrichment Worksheet 4: Weighing Conflicting Rights
▶ Community Service and Participation Handbook: Know Your Rights

### TECHNOLOGY

▶ One-Stop Planner, Lesson 4.2
▶ Homework Practice Online
▶ HRW Go site

### REINFORCEMENT, REVIEW, AND ASSESSMENT

▶ Section 2 Review, p. 99
▶ Daily Quiz 4.2
▶ Main Idea Activity 4.2
▶ English Audio Summary 4.2
▶ Spanish Audio Summary 4.2

## LET'S GET STARTED!

Write the following question on the chalkboard: *How is the term* civil *related to* civics *or* citizen? As students enter the classroom, ask them to respond to the question. *(Students might indicate that all Americans have civil rights—the rights and privileges of a citizen.)* Tell them that one of the most important civil rights is suffrage, which comes from a Latin word that means "political support." Then tell them that the poll tax prevented poor people, particularly poor African Americans, from exercising their right to vote. Tell students that in Section 2 they will learn about the amendments that ended slavery, protected citizens against unfair actions by state governments, and extended Americans' voting rights.

# SECTION 2

# Guaranteeing Other Rights

### Read to Discover

1. How did the Thirteenth and Fourteenth Amendments extend civil rights?
2. Which amendments extended Americans' voting rights?

### Define

• civil rights
• suffrage
• poll tax

### WHY CIVICS MATTERS

The right to vote is one of the greatest privileges of citizenship. Use **CNNfyi.com** or other **current events** sources to find information on recent or upcoming elections and how candidates have appealed to voters. Record your findings in your journal.

## Reading Focus

Since the passage of the Bill of Rights, other amendments have been added to the Constitution. These amendments were passed as new circumstances and changing beliefs in the country required changes in the government. Today the Constitution has a total of 27 amendments. Some of these amendments expanded the rights of U.S. citizens.

### ★ Extending Civil Rights

Rights guaranteed to all U.S. citizens are called **civil rights.** The U.S. Constitution, particularly the Bill of Rights, is the foundation for civil rights in this country. The protection of civil rights, however, was left largely to the individual states until after the Civil War. The Thirteenth and Fourteenth Amendments were added after the war to protect the rights of newly freed African Americans.

**The Thirteenth Amendment** The Thirteenth Amendment, ratified in 1865, outlawed slavery in the United States. President Abraham Lincoln had ordered an end to slavery in the Confederate states during the Civil War. But his order, called the Emancipation Proclamation, did not lead to the freedom of all slaves. The Thirteenth Amendment officially ended slavery in all the states and in all lands governed by the United States.

### Interpreting the Visual Record

*This poster celebrates the issuing of the Emancipation Proclamation.* **What was the effect of the Civil War and the proclamation on American society?**

**LEVEL 1:** Organize the class into groups. Have each group prepare two glossary entries—one entry dealing with the Thirteenth Amendment, the other with the Fourteenth Amendment. Entries should describe how the amendments extended civil rights. *(Students should include that the Thirteenth Amendment officially ended slavery and the Fourteenth Amendment protects citizens against unfair actions by state governments in all the states and in all lands governed by the United States.)* Ask a volunteer to read his or her group's glossary entries to the class.

**ENGLISH LANGUAGE LEARNERS**, **COOPERATIVE LEARNING**

**LEVEL 3:** Ask students to imagine that they are living during the period just following the Civil War. Have each student write a letter to a friend overseas, explaining the necessity of passing the Thirteenth and Fourteenth Amendments and how they will extend civil rights. *(See the Level 1 lesson for the reasons that the amendments were passed.)* Each letter should explain what rights and principles are behind the amendments, why the amendments are necessary, and what effects the amendments will have on all Americans. Encourage volunteers to share their letters with the class.

**HOMEWORK** Have students write a few stanzas of a song or a short poem about the amendments discussed in this chapter.

---

**The Fourteenth Amendment**  Ratified in 1868, the Fourteenth Amendment protects citizens against unfair actions by state governments. It is similar to the Fifth Amendment, which forbids unfair actions by the federal government. The Fourteenth Amendment was intended to protect the rights of African Americans. However, it contains rights to equal protection under the law that are important for all Americans.

The first part of the amendment grants full citizenship to African Americans. Then the amendment says that no state can take away a citizen's "life, liberty, or property, without due process of law." Also, no state can deny citizens equal protection of the law.

✔**Reading Check Summarizing** Why did Congress pass the Thirteenth and Fourteenth Amendments? to end slavery and to protect African Americans' civil rights

## ★ Extending Voting Rights

One of the most important civil rights is **suffrage,** or the right to vote. For some groups of Americans, including African Americans and women, the struggle to gain the right to vote was not won easily. Voting rights are the subject of six amendments to the Constitution.

At first the Constitution made no mention of voting rights. The states decided who could vote. Most states limited the vote to white men over the age of 21 who owned a certain amount of property. Some colonies had allowed only those people who held certain religious beliefs to vote, but states removed these restrictions at the end of the American Revolution. The states also gradually eliminated property qualifications for voting. Between the late 1800s and 1971, amendments to the Constitution extended suffrage to other U.S. citizens as well.

**The Fifteenth Amendment**  African American men were guaranteed the right to vote by the Fifteenth Amendment, ratified in 1870. It states that no person can be denied the right to vote because of race or color. However, in the late 1800s and early 1900s many states, particularly in the South, passed laws that kept African Americans from voting. In the 1960s, Congress finally passed civil rights laws that truly established equal voting rights for African Americans.

**The Seventeenth Amendment**  The Seventeenth Amendment gives a state's eligible voters the right to elect the state's U.S. senators. Before this amendment was ratified in 1913, U.S. senators were chosen by members of the state legislatures.

**BIOGRAPHY**

## Abraham Lincoln

### (1809–1865)

Abraham Lincoln was born in Kentucky. He entered politics in 1834, serving four terms in the state legislature of Illinois and one in the U.S. House of Representatives. Lincoln helped the new Republican Party increase its popularity in the late 1850s. He won the presidency in 1860. He led the Union during the difficult years of the Civil War, calling for unity and strength in speeches such as the Gettysburg Address. Lincoln's Emancipation Proclamation freed slaves in states rebelling against the Union. After the war he supported the ratification of the Thirteenth Amendment, which abolished slavery. He was assassinated in 1865 while attending a play.

Today Presidents' Day, a federal holiday, is held on the third Monday of every February, near Lincoln's birthday. Lincoln is also one of four presidents whose image is carved into the monument at Mount Rushmore, South Dakota. **What were some of Lincoln's major accomplishments as a political leader?**

**☑ internet** connect

**TOPIC:** Voting Rights and History
**GO TO:** go.hrw.com
**KEYWORD:** SZ3 AC4

Have students access the Internet through the HRW Go site to research the extension of voting rights and the history of the women's suffrage movement. Then ask students to create a pamphlet outlining which amendments, people, and political movements were involved in the extension of voting rights.

---

**BIOGRAPHY ANSWER**
Students might suggest his freeing of the slaves with the Emancipation Proclamation or his leadership abilities.

---

**Visual Record Answer**

*(for p.96)*
*Students should recognize the divisive effect of the Civil War, as well as the determination of the federal government to reunite the country. Students should also recognize that in the United States, the legal system is used to handle conflicts.*

# TEACH OBJECTIVE 2

**ALL LEVELS:** Copy the following graphic organizer onto the chalkboard, omitting the italicized answers. Have each student complete the list to identify which amendments extended Americans' voting rights.

**ENGLISH LANGUAGE LEARNERS**

| Amendments that Extended Voting Rights |
| --- |
| ✔ *Fifteenth Amendment* |
| ✔ *Seventeenth Amendment* |
| ✔ *Nineteenth Amendment* |
| ✔ *Twenty-third Amendment* |
| ✔ *Twenty-fourth Amendment* |
| ✔ *Twenty-sixth Amendment* |

**LEVELS 2 AND 3:** Organize the class into small groups and assign each group one of the amendments discussed in this section. Then have groups research the amendment's passage and ask each group to prepare a dramatization of its adoption process. Each group member should portray one of the people in the process. Finally, have groups present their dramatizations to the class. **COOPERATIVE LEARNING**

# CLOSE

Ask each student to create a book jacket about the constitutional amendments discussed in this chapter. Then tell students to write their titles on the jackets and to create illustrations to accompany them.

New Jersey's first constitution said that "any person" with property worth a certain amount of money could vote. At first, not many women voted. Soon, however, their votes began to decide some close elections. As a result, in 1807 the state's all-male legislature took away women's right to vote. New Jersey women would not vote again until the Nineteenth Amendment was ratified—more than a century later.

---

**ANALYZING PRIMARY SOURCES ANSWERS**

1. He wanted to end slavery.

2. The executive branch will enforce it.

---

## Historical Document

### THE EMANCIPATION PROCLAMATION

**P**resident Abraham Lincoln wrote the Emancipation Proclamation in September 1862 but did not officially issue it until January 1, 1863. Prior to the issuing of this Proclamation, the Civil War was being fought mainly to preserve the Union. After the Proclamation, the war also became a campaign to end slavery. Many historians believe the Proclamation greatly helped the Union cause. Its commitment to freedom remains a source of inspiration for Americans to the present day.

### JANUARY 1, 1863

Whereas on the twenty-second day of September, A.D. 1862, a proclamation was issued by the President of the United States, containing, among other things, the following, to wit:

"That on the first day of January, A.D. 1863, all persons held as slaves within any state or designated part of a state, the people whereof shall then be in rebellion against the United States, shall be then, thenceforward, and forever free; and the executive government of the United States, including the military and naval authority thereof, will recognize and maintain the freedom of such persons and will do no act or acts to repress such persons or any of them, in any efforts they may make for their actual freedom.

"That the Executive will on the first day of January aforesaid, by proclamation, designate the states and parts of states, if any, in which the people thereof, respectively, shall then be in rebellion against the United States; and the fact that any state or the people thereof shall on that day be in good faith represented in the Congress of the United States by members chosen thereto at elections wherein a majority of the qualified voters of such states shall have participated shall, in the absence of strong countervailing [opposing] testimony, be deemed conclusive evidence that such state and the people thereof are not then in rebellion against the United States. . . ."

**Analyzing Primary Sources**
1. Why did Lincoln issue the Proclamation?
2. How does Lincoln say that the Proclamation will be enforced?

**The Nineteenth Amendment** American women gained the right to vote with the passing of the Nineteenth Amendment. They won this right only after a long struggle. Courageous women such as Susan B. Anthony, Carrie Chapman Catt, Lucretia Mott, and Elizabeth Cady Stanton led the women's suffrage movement. They argued that women should not be treated as second-class citizens.

When Wyoming entered the Union in 1890, it became the first U.S. state to give women the right to vote. Gradually other states began to grant the vote to women. The suffragists—those who fought for women's right to vote—won their national struggle in 1920 when the Nineteenth Amendment was ratified.

**The Twenty-third Amendment** The Twenty-third Amendment, ratified in 1961, further extended citizens' voting rights. It gave citizens living in the District of Columbia (Washington, D.C.) the right to vote for president and vice president. Before this amendment was ratified, residents of the District of Columbia had not been able vote in national elections since the late 1700s.

*Did You* **KNOW?**

The first female governors took office in 1925. Both Nellie Tayloe Ross of Wyoming and Miriam Ferguson of Texas replaced their husbands in office. The first woman elected governor in her own right was Ella Grasso of Connecticut, elected in 1975.

## REVIEW AND ASSESS

Have students complete the **Section 2 Review** on page 99. Then have them complete **Daily Quiz 4.2**. As **Alternative Assessment**, you may want to use the voting-rights organizer or the book-jacket activity in this section's lessons.

## RETEACH

Have students complete **Main Idea Activity for English Language Learners and Special-Needs Students 4.2**. Then give each student a set of five index cards and have him or her write a test question about the Emancipation Proclamation on one side of the card and the answer on the other side.

**ENGLISH LANGUAGE LEARNERS**

## TEACHER TO TEACHER

Tim Bayne of Nebraska recommends the following activity:

## EXTEND

Organize the class into groups. Then ask each group to develop a Bill of Rights for its school or classroom. Have groups make a list of rights that it should receive from its school government, principal, teachers, office staff, and so on. *(Students might list rights such as safety in the halls, and so on.)* When groups are finished, have them post their lists on the chalkboard and as a class, develop a plan to have the most important rights followed.

**ENGLISH LANGUAGE LEARNERS , COOPERATIVE LEARNING**

**The Twenty-fourth Amendment** Beginning in the late 1800s some states required all people to pay a special tax, called a **poll tax,** before they could vote. Some of the American colonies had imposed poll taxes. These poll taxes were eliminated after the American Revolution only to be reintroduced during the period following the Civil War. Many Americans believed this tax was intended to discourage African Americans from voting. In 1964 the Twenty-fourth Amendment forbade the use of a poll tax as a qualification for voting in national elections. In 1966 the Supreme Court ruled that poll taxes are also unlawful in state elections.

**The Twenty-sixth Amendment** Another large group of Americans gained the right to vote in 1971. That year the Twenty-sixth Amendment lowered the voting age in national, state, and local elections to 18. Previously, most states had set 21 as the age at which people could vote for the first time. Supporters of the amendment pointed out that 18-year-olds were already considered responsible enough to be drafted to fight for their country. The Twenty-sixth Amendment gave young Americans a greater voice in government.

✔**Reading Check Analyzing Information** How has the right to vote expanded over time? Fifteenth Amendment—extended to men of all races; Seventeenth—direct election of senators; Nineteenth—extended to women; Twenty-third—extended to District of Columbia residents; Twenty-fourth—eliminated poll taxes; Twenty-sixth—voting age set at 18

## GLOBAL CONNECTIONS

### Women's Suffrage

Women in the United States were not the only women who struggled for the right to vote. Nor were they the first to achieve it. This distinction belongs to the women of New Zealand.

When a petition of signatures requesting women's suffrage was first sent to the New Zealand Parliament, the members of the all-male body did not take it seriously. It was not until a male supporter of women's suffrage presented the legislature with a 300-yard-long collection of petitions, signed by almost one fourth of all New Zealand women, that the women succeeded.

In 1893 New Zealand became the first self-governing country to grant women suffrage. American suffragists struggling for this right used the New Zealand victory as proof against the widespread notion that women did not really want the vote. It would be years, however, before women in the United States could vote. **How do you think the New Zealand example influenced American suffragists?**

## GLOBAL CONNECTIONS ANSWER

Students might suggest that it empowered them to seek the vote as well.

## Section 2 Review ANSWERS

**1. Define**
• civil rights, p. 96
• suffrage, p. 97
• poll tax, p. 99

**2.** Fifteenth, African American men; women; 1961, citizens living in the District of Columbia; Twenty-sixth, 18-year-olds

**3. a.** The Thirteenth Amendment officially ended slavery. The Fourteenth Amendment protects citizens against unfair actions by state governments in all the states and in all lands governed by the United States.

**b.** Voting was not limited to only those who could afford to pay the tax.

**4.** Students' narratives will vary but should include a discussion of the effect that the right to vote has had on them.

## SECTION 2 Review

go.hrw.com **Homework Practice Online**
keyword: SZ3 HP4

1. **Define** and explain:
   • civil rights
   • suffrage
   • poll tax

2. **Categorizing** Copy the graphic organizer below. Fill in the missing information about amendments that have expanded the right to vote.

| VOTING RIGHTS FOR AMERICANS | | |
|---|---|---|
| **Amendment** | **Year Ratified** | **Group Benefiting from Amendment** |
|  | 1870 |  |
| Nineteenth | 1920 |  |
| Twenty-third |  |  |
|  | 1971 |  |

3. **Finding the Main Idea**
   a. Describe the importance of the Thirteenth and Fourteenth Amendments.
   b. How did the elimination of poll taxes make elections more democratic?

4. **Writing and Critical Thinking**
   **Identifying Points of View** Write a brief narrative from the perspective of a person who has just received the right to vote. Make sure that your narrative explains the importance of the right.

   **Consider:**
   • the importance of voting to the individual
   • the importance of voting to the democratic system

# SECTION 3

## OBJECTIVES

*After completing Section 3, students should be able to*

1 **Explain the duties of citizenship.**
2 **Identify where the duties of citizenship are described.**
3 **Describe the responsibilities of citizenship.**

## SECTION 3 RESOURCES

### REPRODUCIBLE

▶ Guided Reading Strategies 4.3
▶ Readings in Economics and Government 49: *The Social Contract,* Jean-Jacques Rousseau
▶ Creative Teaching Strategy: Resource Speaker

### TECHNOLOGY

▶ One-Stop Planner, Lesson 4.3
▶ CNN Presents: American Government
▶ Homework Practice Online

### REINFORCEMENT, REVIEW, AND ASSESSMENT

▶ Section 3 Review, p. 104
▶ Daily Quiz 4.3
▶ Main Idea Activity 4.3
▶ English Audio Summary 4.3
▶ Spanish Audio Summary 4.3

---

# SECTION 3

# Citizens' Duties and Responsibilities

## Read to Discover

1. What are the duties of citizenship?
2. Where are the duties of citizenship described?
3. What are the responsibilities of citizenship?

## Define

• draft

### WHY CIVICS MATTERS

People across the nation help out to improve their communities. Use **CNN fyi.com** or other **current events** sources to find an example of how people are making a difference in their communities. Record your findings in your journal.

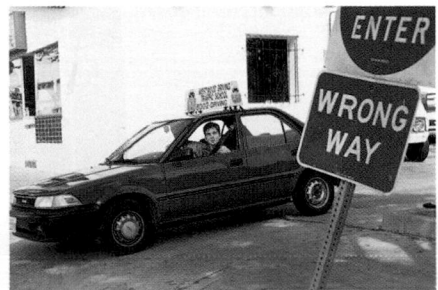
*Obeying the law means following posted signs and directions.*

## *Reading Focus*

You have been learning about the rights that are guaranteed to all U.S. citizens. Along with these rights, citizens also have important duties and responsibilities.

### ★ Duties of Citizenship

Certain actions are the duty of all citizens. These duties are the "musts" of citizenship. That is, all U.S. citizens are required by law to perform these actions. The duties required of all citizens are described in the Constitution and in the laws of the country and the states.

Most Americans are familiar with these duties of citizenship, but sometimes we forget how important they are. The success of our system of government depends on all citizens' fulfilling these duties.

**Obeying the Law**   One of the most important duties of citizenship is to obey the law. The U.S. system of government can work only if citizens respect and obey the laws. Of course, it is important to know what the laws are. For example, when you learn to drive a car, you must also learn the traffic laws. Ignorance of the law excuses no one.

**LEVEL 1:** Lead a class discussion about the duties of citizenship. Then ask each student to write on a slip of paper where he or she thinks these duties are described. *(Students should indicate that they are described in the Constitution and in the laws of the country and the states.)* Then collect all of the responses and write the different answers on the chalkboard. Remind students that they can find the duties of citizenship in the Constitution and in U.S. laws.

**ENGLISH LANGUAGE LEARNERS**

**LEVEL 2:** Refer students to the Constitution in this textbook. Then ask them to make lists of each instance in which the duties of citizenship are described. Ask volunteers to share their lists with the class.

*All Americans must fulfill certain duties and responsibilities of citizenship.*

**Attending School** One of the first duties of all Americans is to pursue an education. The United States places a high value on education. Public schools guarantee all young Americans the opportunity to study and learn in order to develop their talents and abilities. Education provides people with the knowledge they need to fulfill the duties and responsibilities of citizenship.

Education also helps ensure that citizens have the skills necessary to join the workforce and promote economic growth. To ensure freedom and the future of the country, citizens must be educated.

**Paying Taxes** Another important duty of citizenship is paying taxes. The federal government and almost all states tax their citizens in one or more ways. These taxes are sometimes unpopular, but they are needed to pay for the many different services provided by the government. By paying taxes, citizens provide for police and fire protection, paved streets, schools, electrical lines, wastewater treatment, and countless other services.

Tax money also pays the considerable costs of maintaining the country's military defenses. The United States must be able to defend itself in order to protect the rights and freedoms of its citizens.

**Serving in the Armed Forces** As a citizen, you have a duty to help the country if it is threatened. There are many different ways to contribute in times of need. To fulfill this obligation, you may be called to help defend the United States by serving in the armed forces.

## ★ Global Perspectives

**Women and the Draft** In most countries that draft their citizens into the armed forces, only men are called. But Israel, a small country surrounded by actual and potential enemies, has required service by both men and women since its founding in 1948. China did the same, starting in 1949, but with so many young people available each year, the Chinese draft has since become highly selective.

**CRITICAL THINKING**

Do you think that the United States should include women in the draft? Support your answer.

**ANSWER:** Students responses' will vary.

## ★ Economics

**State Income Tax** Wisconsin passed the first state income tax in 1911. Today 43 states have an individual income tax, although 2 of these only tax income from interest and dividends. In some states the income tax is a flat rate. That is, all people, regardless of how much money they earn, pay the same percentage of their income in taxes. In other states the rate is progressive.

**ACTIVITY:** Have students conduct research to determine the type or types of state taxes, if any, that are paid in their state.

# TEACH OBJECTIVE 2

**ALL LEVELS:** Organize the class into groups and assign each group a duty of citizenship. *(Assignments for groups should include the following: obeying the law, attending school, paying taxes, serving in the armed forces, and appearing in court.)* Then have each group compose a rap that encourages Americans to accept the duties of citizenship. Have students present their creations to the class.

**ENGLISH LANGUAGE LEARNERS , COOPERATIVE LEARNING**

**LEVEL 3:** Remind students of the duties and responsibilities that they have as citizens. Then ask each student to choose one duty or responsibility and to write a position paper presenting why it is important to fulfill that duty or responsibility as a U.S. citizen. Remind students that they have to support their reasoning. Call on volunteers to present their papers to the class and to answer any challenges to their positions.

During several periods in its history, the United States has instituted a **draft.** Draft laws require men meeting certain age and other qualifications to serve in the military. Such laws have generally been put into effect during times of war. Since 1973 the United States has used only volunteers in the armed forces. However, 18-year-old men must still register to serve if they meet all of the qualifications for service. Through the registration process the government keeps track of the names and addresses of all men of draft age. Registration ensures that if a war or other crisis requires that the country quickly expand its armed forces, the draft could be implemented again.

**Appearing in Court** Citizens must, if called, report to serve as members of a jury. Citizens must also testify in court if called as witnesses. Appearing in court can be inconvenient. Often citizens must take time off work to answer a jury summons or serve on a jury. However, the right to a trial by jury depends on citizens' fulfilling their duty to serve on juries and appear as witnesses.

✔ **Reading Check** **Making Predictions** What might happen if citizens did not perform the duties described above? Students might mention that the government could not function without taxes, the country could not defend itself, and the country would not prosper because of illiteracy.

## ★ Responsibilities of Citizenship

In addition to the duties of citizenship, Americans have many responsibilities of citizenship. These responsibilities are the "shoulds" of citizenship. That is, although citizens are not required by law to carry out these actions, most Americans accept these responsibilities. They recognize that these are important to the success of the country and the well-being of the people.

**Interpreting the Visual Record**

**Good Citizens** *The willingness of people to serve on juries is essential for the functioning of the U.S. court system.* ***Are these jurors fulfilling a duty or a responsibility?***

# TEACH OBJECTIVE 3

**ALL LEVELS:** Copy the following graphic organizer onto the chalkboard, omitting the italicized answers. Have students complete the organizer to list the responsibilities of citizenship.

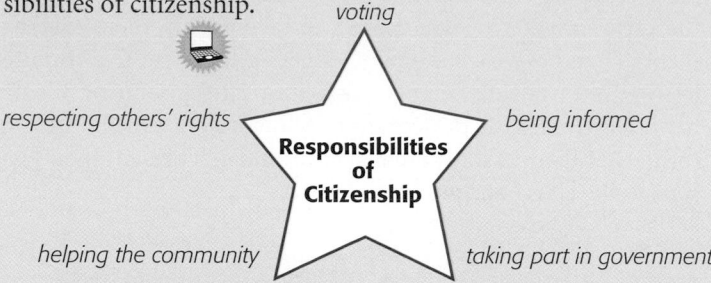

*voting*

*respecting others' rights*          *being informed*

**Responsibilities of Citizenship**

*helping the community*          *taking part in government*

**LEVELS 2 AND 3:** Lead a class discussion about the responsibilities of citizenship. Then have students prepare a mission statement that lists each of the responsibilities that they have at their school. Students should annotate each responsibility with why it is important to fulfill that responsibility.

## CLOSE

Organize the class into small groups and give each group a 6" by 6" sheet of paper. Assign each group a duty or responsibility of citizenship and have group members depict that duty or responsibility visually on their sheet of paper. After groups have finished their projects, assemble the pieces together to represent a quilt of civic responsibilities and duties.

---

## Responsibilities of Citizenship

### U.S. Citizens Should . . .

 **Vote** in elections

 **Obey laws** and **cooperate** with authorities

 **Help** in their communities and **respect** the rights of others

 **Be willing to serve** in the court system or in government if selected

 **Tell** their representatives what they think about issues

 **Stay informed** about current events and government

**Interpreting Charts**
*To help preserve the rights guaranteed by our form of government, Americans need to fulfill basic civic responsibilities. **What responsibilities of citizenship involve directly interacting with government?***

**Voting**   As you know, voting is one of the most important rights of U.S. citizens. Voting is also one of our most important responsibilities. By voting, each citizen plays a part in deciding who the leaders of government will be. Because the people we elect plan the government's activities, each voter is helping to determine what actions the government will take.

The vote of every citizen counts. Even national elections with millions of participating voters have been decided in the past by a few thousand votes. If you choose not to vote, you are giving up a vital way of expressing your political views. Only by exercising the right to vote can citizens carry out the constitutional ideal of government by consent of the governed. Voting is one of the great privileges citizens of the United States have.

**Being Informed**   To cast their votes wisely, citizens have a responsibility to be well informed. Education helps prepare citizens for this important responsibility. But the responsibility does not end there. Citizens should stay informed about current events so that they can better understand important issues.

Americans should take an active interest in the programs and activities of the government. They should also learn what policies are favored by each candidate running for office. Furthermore, Americans have a responsibility to tell their representatives what they think about issues of public concern.

**Taking Part in Government**   Citizens should be involved in their government either as members of a political party or as independent voters. A democratic government cannot truly represent the interests of the minority if too many people refuse to participate and will not share their viewpoints with government leaders. In addition, some citizens

## REVIEW AND ASSESS

Have students complete the **Section 3 Review** on page 104. Then have students complete **Daily Quiz 4.3**. As **Alternative Assessment**, you may want to use the rap or quilt activities in this section's lessons.

## RETEACH

Have students complete **Main Idea Activity for English Language Learners and Special-Needs Students 4.3**. Assign students one of the Read to Discover questions at the beginning of the section. Then have them work individually or in groups to create a graphic organizer showing how the text addresses the question. **ENGLISH LANGUAGE LEARNERS , COOPERATIVE LEARNING**

## EXTEND

Have students conduct research outside of class to determine the varied ways that Americans can take part in their government. Then have each student prepare a three- to five-minute lesson about government participation, incorporating his or her research into the presentation. Allow students to choose the formats of their lessons. Finally, have students present their lessons to the class. **BLOCK SCHEDULING**

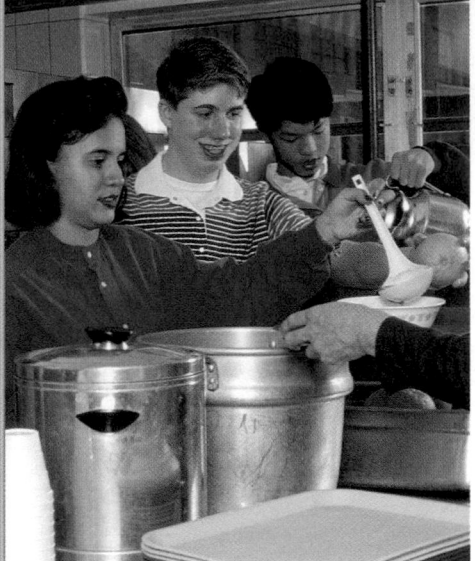

People can help their communities by volunteering at a local soup kitchen.

## Section 3 Review
### ANSWERS

**1. Define**
• draft, p. 102

**2.** obeying the law, attending school, paying taxes, helping the country if it is threatened, and appearing in court

**3. a.** voting, being informed, taking part in government, helping your community, and respecting and protecting others' rights

**b.** Duties are required by law, and responsibilities are necessary but not required by law. Citizens' duties are described in the Constitution.

**4.** Students' paragraphs will vary but should include various duties and responsibilities that help improve life for many in their community.

must be willing to serve as officials of government. The quality of any democratic government depends on the quality of the people who serve in it.

**Helping Your Community**   One of the most important ways to be a responsible citizen is to take pride in your community. In addition, you should make sure that your community can take pride in you. For example, it is essential that community members respect others' property.

It is also important to take an active part in the affairs of your community. Citizens should be willing to give their time to help improve their neighborhood, town, or city. People can volunteer their services and time at a public library, for example. They can work to help serve poor people or elderly residents who cannot care for themselves. Cooperating with the police through organizations such as Citizens on Patrol is another important way to help the community. When people volunteer they learn more about their communities and encourage others to participate as well.

**Respecting and Protecting Others' Rights**   The success of the United States depends on the protection of the rights of citizens. You can play an important role in protecting these priceless rights. By knowing what rights all people share, you can be sure to respect those rights. You will also know when people's rights are being violated, and you can act to help protect those rights. All Americans must take part in defending human rights. Only then can the country truly have, in Abraham Lincoln's words, a "government of the people, by the people, and for the people."

✔ **Reading Check** Making Generalizations How can individual citizens contribute to society? respect the rights of others, help in their communities, vote, serve on juries, help those less fortunate

## SECTION 3 Review

go. **Homework**
hrw **Practice**
.com **Online**
keyword: SZ3 HP4

**1. Define** and explain:
• draft

**2. Analyzing Information** Copy the graphic organizer below. Use it to list the duties of citizenship.

```
        Duties of
        Citizenship
   ┌────┬────┼────┬────┐
 [   ][   ][   ][   ][   ]
```

**3. Finding the Main Idea**
a. What are some of the responsibilities of U.S. citizenship?
b. What is the difference between a citizen's duties and a citizen's responsibilities, and where are citizens' duties described?

**4. Writing and Critical Thinking**
**Categorizing** Write a short paragraph identifying actions you could take on a daily basis to help your community.

**Consider:**
• responsibilities of citizenship
• possible effects of your contributions

## TEACH

**LEVEL 1:** Instruct each student to create a bar graph on the subject of his or her choosing. *(You may suggest that students can graph what each person will have or has had for lunch, the color of classmates' family cars, and so on.)* Encourage volunteers to present their graphs to the class.

**ENGLISH LANGUAGE LEARNERS**

## EXTEND

Have each student apply the bar graph skills that he or she studied in the workshop to create a bar graph displaying data related to another duty or responsibility of citizenship outlined in this chapter. For example, students may conduct outside research to determine how taxes have been paid over the course of the past 50 years. What group is responsible for paying either the most or least amount of taxes? How do corporate taxes factor into the visual picture? Are we paying a higher or lower percentage of income versus 20, 30, or 40 years ago, and so on. Encourage volunteers to draw their graphs on the chalkboard and then explain their findings to the class.

**BLOCK SCHEDULING**

# Civics Skills
## WORKSHOP

## Reading Bar Graphs

*Although the right to vote has been greatly expanded over the course of our country's history, not all citizens take advantage of this right.*

How often have you heard statements such as the one above? One effective way to illustrate such statements is to use graphs.

Graphs are important tools for understanding data. A single graph can condense large amounts of data into one easy-to-read diagram.

## How to Read Bar Graphs

1. **Identify the type of graph.** The graph shown on this page is called a bar graph because it uses bars to represent and compare amounts. Other graphs use different symbols, such as lines, pictures, or parts of circles, to display data.

2. **Determine the subject.** Read the title of the graph to determine the subject and purpose of the graph.

3. **Study the labels.** Bar graphs usually have two labels. One label reads across the bottom of the graph. This label identifies the data on the line called the horizontal axis. Now look at the label that runs along the side of the graph. This line is called the vertical axis. What information is indicated by the labels for the vertical axis and the horizontal axis? Often these labels indicate quantities or periods of time, as well as identifying the type of data shown. Studying the labels will help you understand the information presented in the graph.

4. **Analyze the data.** Compare the height of the bars in the graph. Use these bars to determine how the items or groups being compared on the horizontal axis differ.

5. **Put the data to use.** Use the data to draw conclusions about the subject of the graph.

## Applying the Skill

Examine the bar graph below. Then answer the following questions.

1. What conclusions can you draw about the relationship between presidential-election years and voter turnout? How might a candidate use the graph on this page?

2. Write a paragraph that summarizes the data presented in the bar graph. Which is more effective in describing the data—the bar graph or your paragraph? Explain your answer.

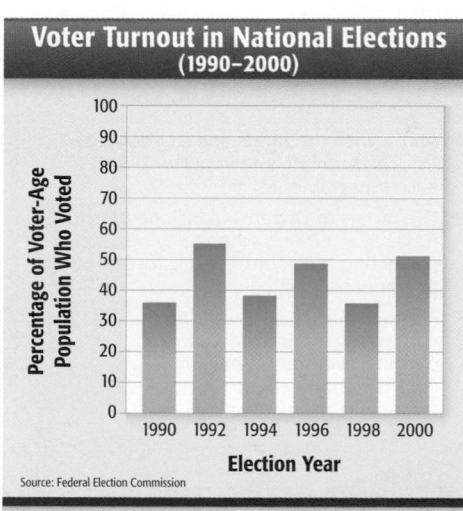

**Voter Turnout in National Elections (1990–2000)**

Percentage of Voter-Age Population Who Voted

Election Year

Source: Federal Election Commission

**CHAPTER 4**

**REVIEW ANSWERS**

**Define and Identify**
1. Bill of Rights, p. 89
2. petition, p. 92
3. indict, p. 93
4. double jeopardy, p. 93
5. eminent domain, p. 94
6. bail, p. 94
7. civil rights, p. 96
8. suffrage, p. 97
9. poll tax, p. 99
10. draft, p. 102

**REPRODUCIBLE**

▶ Chapter 4 Review, pp. 106–07
▶ Vocabulary Activity 4
▶ Chapter 4 Tutorial for Students, Parents, Mentors, and Peers
▶ Chapter 4 Test (Form A or B)
▶ Alternative Assessment Handbook

**TECHNOLOGY**

▶ Chapter 4 Test Generator (on the One-Stop Planner)
▶ Global Skill Builder CD–ROM
▶ HRW Go site

**REINFORCEMENT, REVIEW, AND ASSESSMENT**

▶ Chapter 4 Test for English Language Learners and Special-Needs Students

## REVIEW

Have students complete the **Chapter 4 Review** on pages 106-07.

## ASSESS

Use one of the chapter tests to assess students' understanding of the content. For **Alternative Assessment**, see the **Alternative Assessment Handbook**.

---

**Understanding Main Ideas**

**1.** Fourth—no unreasonable searches and seizures; Fifth—cannot go to trial unless indicted by grand jury, right to due process of law, protection against self-incrimination and double jeopardy; Sixth—speedy trial, trial by jury, hear charges, question witnesses, have a lawyer; Eighth—no excessive bail or cruel and unusual punishment

**2.** to give Americans every right and freedom possible

**3.** Thirteenth—outlawed slavery; Fourteenth—citizenship for African Americans, prevents states from taking away life, liberty, or property without due process, ensures that states provide equal protection under the law

**4.** by extending voting rights to men of all races, women, people age 18 and over, eliminating the poll tax, giving eligible voters the right to elect their state's senators, and allowing people in the District of Columbia to vote in presidential elections

**5.** obeying the law, attending school, paying taxes, protecting the country if necessary, and appearing in court

**6.** voting, being informed, taking part in government, helping your community, and respecting and protecting others' rights

---

# Chapter 4 Review

## Chapter Summary

### Section 1

- The first 10 amendments, known as the Bill of Rights, clearly define the rights of all Americans.
- These amendments guarantee such priceless rights as the freedoms of religion, speech, the press, assembly, and petition and the right to a speedy and fair trial by a jury.
- The Ninth Amendment states that the rights listed in the Constitution are not the only rights Americans hold.
- The Tenth Amendment reserves to the state governments and to the people all powers not specifically given to the federal government by the Constitution.

### Section 2

- Later amendments to the Constitution further expanded the civil rights of Americans.
- The Thirteenth and Fourteenth Amendments protected the rights of newly freed African Americans after the Civil War.
- Six other amendments to the Constitution expanded the voting rights of the American people.

### Section 3

- Along with the rights and freedoms of U.S. citizenship come important duties and responsibilities.
- The duties of citizenship include obeying the law, attending school, paying taxes, protecting the country if it is threatened, and appearing in court.
- Responsibilities of citizenship include voting, staying informed, taking part in government, helping your community, and respecting and protecting others' rights.

MR. PRESIDENT WHAT WILL YOU DO FOR WOMAN SUFFRAGE

## Define and Identify

1. Bill of Rights
2. petition
3. indict
4. double jeopardy
5. eminent domain
6. bail
7. civil rights
8. suffrage
9. poll tax
10. draft

## Understanding Main Ideas

**Section 1** *(Pages 89–95)*

1. Which amendments focus on the rights of people accused of crimes? What rights do these amendments guarantee?
2. Why was the Ninth Amendment included in the Bill of Rights?

**Section 2** *(Pages 96–99)*

3. How did the Thirteenth and Fourteenth Amendments extend the civil rights of Americans?
4. How have voting rights been expanded through constitutional amendments?

**Section 3** *(Pages 100–04)*

5. What are the duties of citizenship?
6. What are the responsibilities of citizenship?

## What Did You Find Out?

1. Why was the Bill of Rights added to the U.S. Constitution?
2. How might the country be affected if citizens failed to perform their duties and responsibilities?
3. Why has the Constitution been amended over time?

## Thinking Critically

1. **Supporting a Point of View** Unlike most of the amendments contained in the Bill of Rights, the Third Amendment's "no quartering" rule has never been tested in a court of law. Because this amendment seems to be far removed from Americans' modern-day lives, should it be repealed? Why or why not?
2. **Evaluating** Which freedom in the Bill of Rights do you consider to be the most important, and why?
3. **Identifying Cause and Effect** Why did Americans want to ensure that accused persons had the right to trial by jury? What might happen to our system of justice if citizens refused to serve on juries?

Organize students into three groups and assign each group one of the chapter's sections. Have members of each group create a visual presentation illustrating the main objectives in their assigned section. Then have each group present its work to the class. **ENGLISH LANGUAGE LEARNERS**, **COOPERATIVE LEARNING**

## Portfolio Extensions

**1. Linking to Community** Ask each student to interview a member of his or her town or city council. Students should ask the council members what they think are the most important duties and responsibilities of citizens in their community, and why. Then have volunteers present their interviews to the class.

**2. Cooperative Learning** Organize students into small groups. Ask each group to select a constitutional amendment. Groups should write a skit that explains the amendment, demonstrates the protections of the amendment, and shows what the consequences might be if the amendment was not included in the Constitution. Have groups perform their skits for the class.

---

## Building Social Studies Skills

**STANDARDIZED TEST PREP ONLINE** keyword: SZ3 STP4

### Interpreting Political Cartoons

Study the political cartoon below. Then use the information in the cartoon to help you answer the questions that follow.

LIBERTY'S CROWN

1. What do the words on the spikes of the Statue of Liberty's crown represent?
   a. the rights listed in the Declaration of Independence
   b. each of the rights guaranteed in the amendments that form the Bill of Rights
   c. rights that all Americans should have whether they are listed in the Constitution or not
   d. the rights that the cartoonist feels are some of the most treasured rights guaranteed by the Bill of Rights

2. Why do you think the artist chose the Statue of Liberty as the symbol to associate with these ideas?

### Analyzing Primary Sources

Read the following quote from President John F. Kennedy and then answer the questions that follow.

"The right to vote in a free American election is the most powerful and precious right in the world—and it must not be denied on the grounds of race or color. It is a potent [powerful] key to achieving other rights of citizenship. For American history—both recent and past—clearly reveals that the power of the ballot has enabled those who achieve it to win other achievements as well, gain a full voice in the affairs of their state and nation, and to see their interests represented in the governmental bodies which affect their future. In a free society, those with the power to govern are necessarily responsive to those with the right to vote."

3. Which of the following statements best describes President Kennedy's point of view?
   a. The only way that people can influence their government is by writing to elected officials.
   b. You are not a citizen if you do not vote.
   c. Voting affects everyone's future.
   d. Government officials are more likely to respond to citizens if they know that citizens can vote them out of office.

4. Based on what you know about the Constitution of the United States, what amendment is President Kennedy probably referring to when he says that people of any race or color should not be denied the right to vote?

### What Did You Find Out?
1. Upon ratification of the Constitution, a number of states made the strong recommendation that a bill of rights be added.

2. Students might say that a minority of people would make all decisions and that the government would be unable to provide basic services.

3. Amendments were passed as changing conditions and beliefs required changes in the country's government.

### Thinking Critically
1. Some students might point out that the quartering of soldiers is still possible.

2. Students' answers will vary, but they should use sound reasoning in their responses.

3. All Americans have a right to a trial by their peers. If citizens refused to serve on juries, this right could not be upheld.

### Skills Workshop
1. d

2. Students' answers will vary, but students should note that the Statue of Liberty is a widely recognized symbol of freedom.

3. d

4. the Fifteenth Amendment

---

### Alternative Assessment

## Building Your Portfolio

**Interdisciplinary Connection to Math** Research voter participation in your community. What are the statistics on voter registration? In what elections is voter participation highest? Is participation increasing or decreasing? Create a set of graphs that illustrate the answers to these questions. Present your findings to the class in an oral report. Include some suggestions for improving voter participation in your area.

**internet connect**

**Internet Activity: go.hrw.com** keyword: SZ3 AC4

Access the Internet through the HRW Go site to research the rights and responsibilities of citizenship. Then choose one of the responsibilities outlined in the chapter and create an action plan to increase your community's awareness of this responsibility. Your action plan should outline the responsibility on which you will focus and how you will increase awareness of it.

## TEACH

**LEVEL 1:** Organize the class into groups. Ask groups to read the text of the Constitution located in their textbooks. Then have each group choose one of the rights outlined in that document and to create a mission statement that explains how that right can be applied to its school environment. Have groups present their statements to the class. **ENGLISH LANGUAGE LEARNERS , COOPERATIVE LEARNING**

**ALL LEVELS:** Have students review the three-branches-of-education exercise which is outlined in the Civics Lab. Then have students take turns quizzing one another about the information found in the chart. **ENGLISH LANGUAGE LEARNERS**

**ALL LEVELS:** Have students create graphic organizers that incorporate the information that they included in their charts on students' rights and responsibilities. Ask volunteers to present their organizers to the class. **ENGLISH LANGUAGE LEARNERS**

## APPLYING THE SKILLS

Remind students that federal and local governments serve the people by ensuring that educational opportunities are available to all citizens. Point out that in a democracy it is the responsibility of each citizen to participate in government. Then ask students to consider ways that they think public education could be improved in their community. Have students write letters to the editor of a local newspaper that explain their ideas for improving education. Encourage students to be persuasive and to use facts to support their arguments.

# Civics Lab

## We the Students

Complete the following Civics Lab activity individually or in a group.

## Your Task

In Unit 1 you read about the country's long tradition of democracy under a government established to serve the people. Imagine that you are the U.S. representative at an international conference on education. The other delegates at the conference represent countries that have governments other than a democracy.

Your job is to explain to the other delegates that education under a democratic system of government serves the needs of students and the entire country. Your presentation to the delegates will consist of a report accompanied by visual materials. To prepare these materials, you will need to do the following.

## What to Do

**STEP 1** **Conduct research** to learn about the history of your school. Use this information to draw a large, illustrated time line showing how your school has changed over time, including changes in the number of students and teachers, changes in the ethnic makeup of the school population, curriculum changes, and changes in how students have shown their school spirit. Title your time line Our School: Then and Now.

Our School: Then and Now

| Then | Now |
| --- | --- |

## EXTEND

Have students gather copies of their Declarations of Education. As a class, create a poll about the Declaration. *(Students might include questions such as the following: Do you agree with the ideals? Does our school meet this ideal?)* Once the survey is created, instruct each student to pose the questions to at least five of their peers outside of class. During the next class period, evaluate the responses by asking students to raise their hands to tabulate the responses, and record the total number of positive and negative responses. Discuss the results with the class.

**STEP 2** **Write** a "Declaration of Education" statement. In your Declaration, express what you believe are the ideals of American education. Begin your Declaration of Education with the following phrase: "We, the American students, hold these truths to be self-evident. . . ." Your Declaration should then explain how your school upholds each of the educational ideals listed.

**STEP 3** **Create a chart** titled The Three Branches of Education. Write the following headings across the top of your chart: *Administration, Teachers, Students.* Under each heading, answer the following questions: What are the primary duties of this branch? What responsibilities does this branch share with the other branches? How does this branch work with the other branches? Then write a caption explaining why cooperation among the branches of education is a vital part of the U.S. educational system.

### The Three Branches of Education

| Administration | Teachers | Students |
|---|---|---|
| | | |

**STEP 4** **Create a chart** titled "Student Rights and Responsibilities." In one column of the chart, list the rights to which you are entitled as a student in the U.S. educational system. In the second column, list the responsibilities that accompany each of your rights. Then write a caption explaining why appreciating your rights and fulfilling your responsibilities help your school to operate more effectively.

### Student Rights and Responsibilities

| Rights | Responsibilities |
|---|---|
| | |

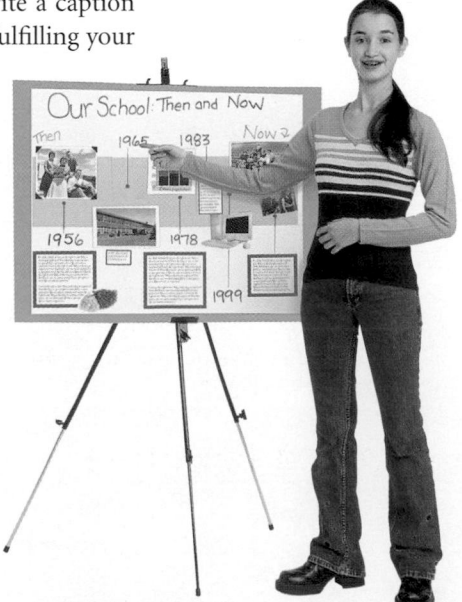

Organize your materials, and make your presentation to the other conference delegates (the rest of the class).

**A STEP FURTHER**

Ask students to imagine that they are delegates from a foreign country to a conference on education that is being held in the United States. Then have each student write a persuasive paper either praising the democratic system of education or explaining the flaws that exist within the system. Students' papers should support their positions with examples from the textbook. Ask volunteers to present their papers to the class.

## UNIT OVERVIEW

Unit 2 provides a detailed study of our federal system of government and the political machinery by which it operates. It also explains the functions and activities of each of the three branches of government: the legislative branch, the executive branch, and the judicial branch.

## In Their Own Words

*"This country, with its institutions, belongs to the people who inhabit it. Whenever they shall grow weary of the existing government, they can exercise their constitutional right of amending it, or their revolutionary right to dismember or overthrow it."*
—Abraham Lincoln

**Using the Quotation** Tell students that each of the three branches of government has offices in a number of buildings in Washington, D.C. These buildings as well as the memorials to former presidents, represent the federal government and honor the officials who have been a part of that government. Have students discuss the quotation, which speaks of the rights of the people to control their government and its institutions.

**About the Author** Although Abraham Lincoln (1809–1865) championed the right of the people to choose their government, he insisted on the preservation of the unity between the people and their government. Lincoln was assassinated just days after the Confederate surrender at Appomattox Courthouse ensured the preservation of the Union.

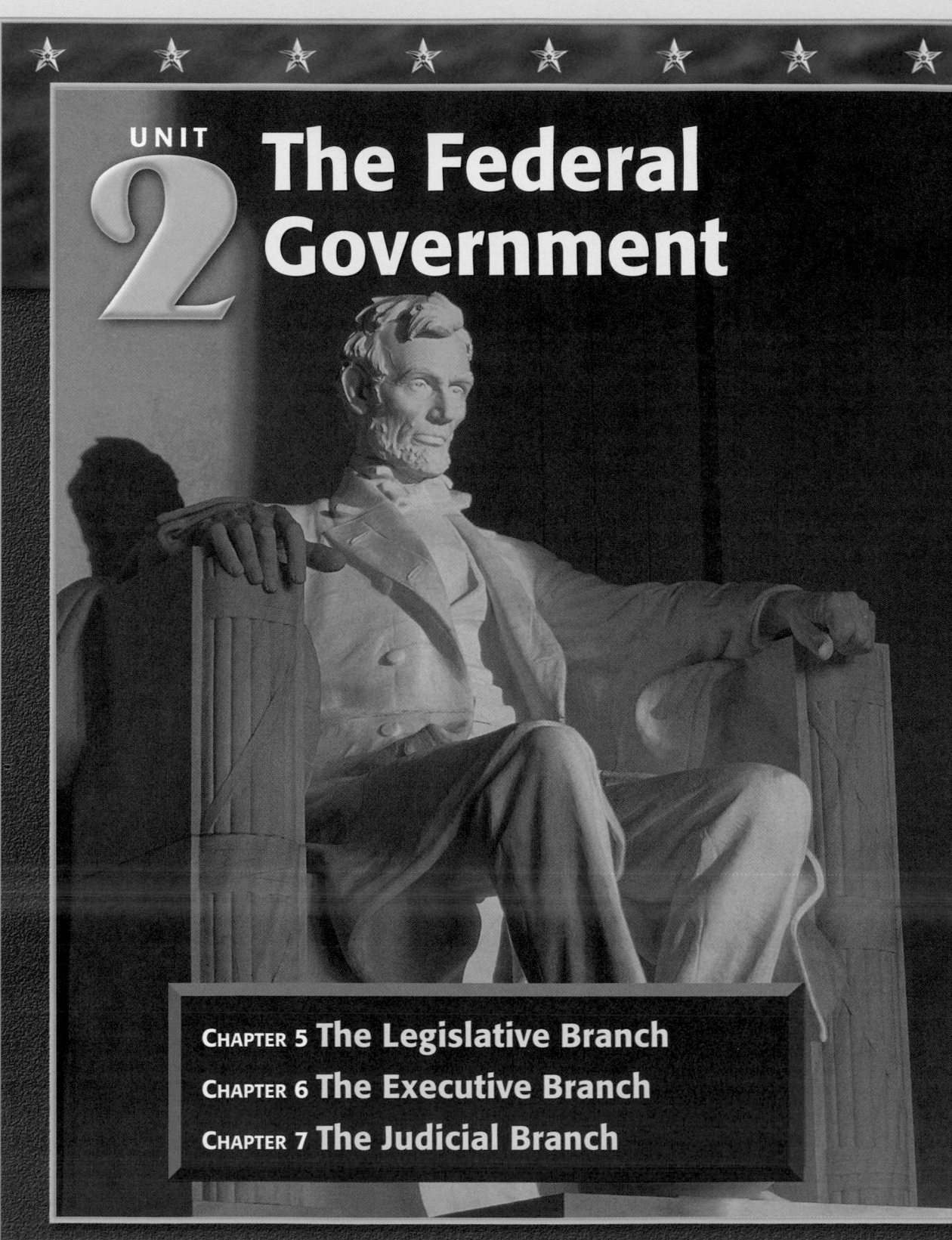

# UNIT 2 The Federal Government

Briefly discuss with students an overview of each chapter. Organize students into groups and ask each group to imagine that it is the democratic governing body of a place called Classroom Nation. Then ask each group to consider how it will organize itself so that no one member of the government holds too much power. Also ask students to consider what type of structure would best enable their group to meet the needs of all of the citizens of Classroom Nation. Have each group create a chart or diagram showing the balance of power in its government. After students have finished the unit, ask each group to evaluate how closely its plan for a government resembles the structure of the U.S. government.

# Young Citizens

## IN ACTION

### "Deaf President Now"

In March 1988 the students at Gallaudet University used their First Amendment right to free speech to change their school. The board of trustees at Gallaudet, a university for hearing-impaired people in Washington, D.C., had recently chosen a new president for the university. Students favored a deaf president, who they believed would better represent them. However, neither of the two deaf candidates was chosen. The students decided to protest the board's decision.

For a week, students protested peacefully but actively in a movement known as DPN, short for "Deaf President Now." They blocked the gates to the university and marched on the White House. Students rallied, gave speeches, and waved banners saying "Deaf President Now." Protest leaders met with the school's board of trustees, demanding that a deaf president be appointed. DPN gained the support of hearing and deaf people around the country and generated national media coverage. In response to the students' demands, I. King Jordan, an original candidate, was chosen to be the first deaf president of Gallaudet University. "Now we have respect; we have everything. It's just the beginning for all of us," said Greg Hlibok, Gallaudet's student body president. The students had won their fight.

By using their First Amendment right, the students of Gallaudet changed their university. The protest united the national deaf community. It showed "that deaf people are capable of leading themselves," remarked Truman Stelle, a Gallaudet faculty member. Above all, DPN's success was a victory for all people with disabilities and proved the value and power of free speech.

The slogan "Deaf President Now" expressed the goal of the Gallaudet students to have a president who would serve as their role model.

### You Decide

1. **What moved the students of Gallaudet University to speak out?**
2. **For what issues have people in your community used their First Amendment right to initiate change?**

## What Can We Do?

Have students research issues that have caused people in their community to use the First Amendment right to initiate change. Then organize students into groups. Ask groups to conduct research to identify a local problem that they would like to see corrected. Have each group develop a strategy for using their right to free speech as a means to bring about change. Groups should consider the following in their plans: an explanation of the problem, a description of how free speech could be used to help bring about a solution, and a list of the various methods that they might use to exercise their right to free speech. Students might suggest organizing a peaceful protest march, or suggest writing letters to local newspapers, magazines, or radio and television stations. Encourage students to design posters, banners, bumper stickers, T-shirts, or other media to promote their messages.

### YOU DECIDE ANSWERS

1. The board of trustees at Gallaudet, a university for hearing-impaired people, selected a new president who was not one of the deaf candidates favored by students.

2. Students' responses will vary.

# The Legislative Branch
## CHAPTER RESOURCE MANAGER

| | Objectives | Pacing Guide | Reproducible Resources |
|---|---|---|---|
| **SECTION 1:**<br>**The Senate and the House of Representatives**<br>(pp. 113–18) | ★ Identify how many members are in the House and Senate, respectively, and explain the term length for each position.<br>★ Describe the qualifications and salaries for members of the House and of the Senate.<br>★ Explain how Congress deals with misconduct by its members. | **Regular**<br>1 day<br>**Block Scheduling**<br>.5 day<br><br>*Block Scheduling Handbook with Team Teaching Strategies, Chapter 5* | **RS** Guided Reading Strategies 5.1<br>**RS** Readings in Economics and Government 66: Profiles in Courage<br>**RS** Readings in Economics and Government 73: The Contract with America |
| **SECTION 2:**<br>**How Congress Is Organized**<br>(pp. 119–24) | ★ Identify when a session of Congress begins and how long the session lasts.<br>★ Explain who leads the houses of Congress and how these leaders are chosen.<br>★ Describe the purpose of congressional committees, and tell how committee assignments are made. | **Regular**<br>1 day<br>**Block Scheduling**<br>.5 day<br><br>*Block Scheduling Handbook with Team Teaching Strategies, Chapter 5* | **RS** Guided Reading Strategies 5.2<br>**E** Challenge and Enrichment Worksheet 5: Researching Members of Congress<br>**RS** Creative Teaching Strategy: Open-Ended Statements |
| **SECTION 3:**<br>**The Powers of Congress**<br>(pp. 126–31) | ★ Identify the five major areas in which Congress has the power to make laws.<br>★ Analyze the significance of the elastic clause.<br>★ Describe the special powers of Congress, and explain how congressional powers are limited. | **Regular**<br>1 day<br>**Block Scheduling**<br>.5 day<br><br>*Block Scheduling Handbook with Team Teaching Strategies, Chapter 5* | **RS** Guided Reading Strategies 5.3<br>**SM** Community Service and Participation Handbook: Rate Your Legislator |
| **SECTION 4:**<br>**How a Bill Becomes a Law**<br>(pp. 132–39) | ★ Identify where ideas for bills originate.<br>★ Explain what happens to a bill once it is introduced in each house of Congress.<br>★ Determine the actions the president can take regarding a bill once it has passed both houses. | **Regular**<br>1 day<br>**Block Scheduling**<br>.5 day<br><br>*Block Scheduling Handbook with Team Teaching Strategies, Chapter 5* | **RS** Guided Reading Strategies 5.4<br>**RS** Readings in Economics and Government 29: Excerpt from a Filibuster |

## Chapter Resource Key

| | | | | | |
|---|---|---|---|---|---|
| **PS** | Primary Sources | **SM** | Skills Mastery |  | CD-ROM |
| **RS** | Reading Support | **A** | Assessment |  | Video |
| **IC** | Interdisciplinary Connections | **REV** | Review |  | Internet |
| **E** | Enrichment | **ELL** | Reinforcement and English Language Learners |  | Holt Presentation Maker Using Microsoft® PowerPoint® |
| | | | Transparencies | | |

 **One-Stop** Planner CD–ROM

**See the *One-Stop Planner* for a complete list of additional resources for students and teachers.**

## One-Stop Planner CD–ROM

It's easy to plan lessons, select resources, and print out materials for your students when you use the *One-Stop Planner CD–ROM with Test Generator*.

| Technology Resources | Reinforcement, Review, and Assessment |
|---|---|
| One-Stop Planner, Lesson 5.1<br>Transparency 3: Congressional Representation After the 2000 Census<br>Transparency 4: The Congress of the United States<br>Homework Practice Online | **REV** Section 1 Review, p. 118<br>**A** Daily Quiz 5.1<br>**ELL** Main Idea Activity 5.1<br>**ELL** English Audio Summary 5.1<br>**ELL** Spanish Audio Summary 5.1 |
| One-Stop Planner, Lesson 5.2<br>CNN Presents: American Government<br>Homework Practice Online | **REV** Section 2 Review, p. 124<br>**A** Daily Quiz 5.2<br>**ELL** Main Idea Activity 5.2<br>**ELL** English Audio Summary 5.2<br>**ELL** Spanish Audio Summary 5.2 |
| One-Stop Planner, Lesson 5.3<br>Holt Researcher CD–ROM<br>Homework Practice Online | **REV** Section 3 Review, p. 131<br>**A** Daily Quiz 5.3<br>**ELL** Main Idea Activity 5.3<br>**ELL** English Audio Summary 5.3<br>**ELL** Spanish Audio Summary 5.3 |
| One-Stop Planner, Lesson 5.4<br>Transparency 5: How Ideas for Bills Begin<br>Homework Practice Online | **REV** Section 4 Review, p. 139<br>**A** Daily Quiz 5.4<br>**ELL** Main Idea Activity 5.4<br>**ELL** English Audio Summary 5.4<br>**ELL** Spanish Audio Summary 5.4 |

## internet connect

### HRW ONLINE RESOURCES
GO TO: go.hrw.com
Then type in the keyword.

### TEACHER HOME PAGE
**KEYWORD: SZ3 Teacher**

### CHAPTER INTERNET ACTIVITIES
**KEYWORD: SZ3 AC5**
Choose an activity to:
- create a diagram on the roles and powers of houses of Congress.
- create a flyer for a congressional election.
- write a short story from the point of view of a bill going through Congress.

### CHAPTER ENRICHMENT LINKS
**KEYWORD: SZ3 CH5**

### ONLINE ASSESSMENT
**Homework Practice**
**KEYWORD: SZ3 HP5**

**Rubrics**
**KEYWORD: SS Rubrics**

### ONLINE MAPS, CHARTS, AND GRAPHS
**KEYWORD: SZ3 MCG**
- How Ideas for Bills Begin
- The Congress of the United States

### HOLT PRESENTATION MAKER
**KEYWORD: SZ3 PPT5**

### CONTENT UPDATES
**KEYWORD: SS Content Updates**

### ONLINE READING SUPPORT
**KEYWORD: SS Strategies**

### CURRENT EVENTS
**KEYWORD: S3 Current Events**

## Meeting Individual Needs

### Ability Levels

**Level 1** Basic-level activities designed for all students encountering new material

**Level 2** Intermediate-level activities designed for average students

**Level 3** Challenging activities designed for honors and gifted-and-talented students

**English Language Learners** Activities that address the needs of students with Limited English Proficiency

## Chapter Review and Assessment

**IC** Vocabulary Activity 5
Global Skill Builder CD–ROM
HRW Go site
**REV** Chapter 5 Tutorial for Students, Parents, Mentors, and Peers
**REV** Chapter 5 Review, pp. 140–41
**A** Standardized Test Practice
**A** Chapter 5 Test Generator (on the One-Stop Planner)
**A** Chapter 5 Test (Form A or B)
**A** Alternative Assessment Handbook
**A** Chapter 5 Test for English Language Learners and Special-Needs Students

## Internet Activity

### The Political Race

**internet connect** go.hrw.com

**TOPIC:** Running for Congress
**GO TO:** go.hrw.com
**KEYWORD:** SZ3 AC5

Have students access the Internet through the HRW Go site to research the role of a congressperson and congressional elections. Then ask students to imagine that they are running for Congress and to create a campaign poster, flyer, or commercial to publicize their campaign. Remind students to identify their personal beliefs in relation to important issues, the local political interests and interest groups that they support, and the party with which they are affiliated.

## What's Your Opinion?

*To help students create their **Themes** Journal entries, provide the following examples of appropriate **agree**/**disagree** statements.*

● **Agree**   In a democracy, all people share the same rights, including the right to run for Congress.

**Disagree**   Congressional membership is limited by age and state residency.

● **Agree**   The congressional workload is so burdensome, that committees are needed to handle it all.

**Disagree**   Committees are just one possible solution to the workload handled by Congress.

● **Agree**   Congressmembers are experts in government, hence they are qualified to judge federal officials.

**Disagree**   Elected leaders should not have the power to put elected officials on trial.

---

## CHAPTER

# 5   The Legislative Branch

**What's Your Opinion?**

### Build on What You Know

Every year on January 3, unless otherwise specified, representatives, senators, clerks, and congressional staff take their places in the Capitol Building in Washington, D.C., for the start of a new session of Congress. They reconvene to fulfill their constitutional responsibility of making the country's laws. Congress decides issues such as how large the U.S. armed forces will be and whether federal taxes will increase. Each session lawmakers make decisions that affect not only your life, your school, and your community but also national and world affairs.

**Themes Journal** Do you **agree** or **disagree** with the following statements? Support your point of view in your journal.

- Any U.S. citizen can become a congressmember.
- Congress would not be able to function without congressional committees.
- Congress should have the power to put federal officials on trial.

# SECTION 1

## OBJECTIVES

*After completing Section 1, students should be able to*

1. **Identify how many members are in the House and Senate, respectively, and explain the term length for each position.**

2. **Describe the qualifications and salaries for members of the House and of the Senate.**

3. **Explain how Congress deals with misconduct by its members.**

 **LET'S GET STARTED!**

As students enter the classroom, ask them to imagine that they have one of the most important jobs in government. Tell them that they work long hours to help people, and that they are paid well for their efforts. Ask students how they feel about this job. Now tell them that every two years they have to battle to keep their job for only another two years. How do they feel now? *(Students might express that they feel like a member of the House must feel.)* Tell students that in Section 1 they will learn more about the terms and requirements of congressmembers of the United States.

---

## SECTION 1

# The Senate and the House of Representatives

### Read to Discover

1. How many members are in the House and Senate, respectively, and what is the term length for each position?
2. What are the qualifications and salaries for members of the House and of the Senate?
3. How does Congress deal with misconduct by its members?

### Define

- apportioned
- gerrymandering
- term limits
- franking privilege
- immunity
- expulsion
- censure

#### WHY CIVICS MATTERS

Congress is organized to allow fair representation of all the states. Use **CNNfyi.com** or other **current events** sources to find out how your state is represented in Congress. Record your findings in your journal.

## *Reading Focus*

The legislative branch makes the country's laws. "Members of Congress are the human connection between the citizen and . . . government," noted one member of Congress. The framers discussed the legislative branch in Article I of the U.S. Constitution to emphasize that representatives of the people would govern the United States.

### ★ Two Houses of Congress

Congress is the lawmaking body of the federal government. The Constitution states that the Congress shall be composed of two houses—the Senate and the House of Representatives.

The leaders who drew up the U.S. Constitution in 1787 created a bicameral legislature, a lawmaking body of two houses. They did this in part to make sure that both small and large states would be fairly represented. Membership in the House of Representatives is based on state population, while each state is represented equally in the Senate. The system also allows each house to check the actions of the other. This system helps prevent Congress from passing laws in haste.

✔ **Reading Check Analyzing Information** Why does the Constitution specify a bicameral legislature? to ensure the equal representation of large and small states and to create a system of checks and balances within Congress

House members must follow strict rules of conduct while in session.

## SECTION 1 RESOURCES

### REPRODUCIBLE
► Guided Reading Strategies 5.1
► Transparency 3: Congressional Representation After the 2000 Census
► Transparency 4: The Congress of the United States
► Readings in Economics and Government 66: Profiles in Courage
► Readings in Economics and Government 73: The Contract with America

### TECHNOLOGY
► One-Stop Planner, Lesson 5.1
► Homework Practice Online

### REINFORCEMENT, REVIEW, AND ASSESSMENT
► Section 1 Review, p. 118
► Daily Quiz 5.1
► Main Idea Activity 5.1
► English Audio Summary 5.1
► Spanish Audio Summary 5.1

**LEVEL 1:** Lead a class discussion about the membership and term lengths for the House of Representatives and the Senate. Have students identify how many members are in the House and in the Senate and the term length for each position. *(Students should note that currently the House has 435 members and the Senate has 100. The term length for representatives is two years. It is six years for senators.)* Remind the class that the number of senators per state is fixed at two people, while House representation varies based on the population of each state as determined by the U.S. Census Bureau. **ENGLISH LANGUAGE LEARNERS**

**LEVEL 3:** Call on volunteers to identify how many members are in the House and in the Senate and the term length for members of each house. *(See the Level 1 lesson for answers.)* Then organize and lead the class in a panel discussion about the following topic: Do we really need limits for membership and term length? When the panel discussion is finished, organize students into groups and have each group create a pictorial montage that illustrates the information discussed. **COOPERATIVE LEARNING**

---

## ★ The Democratic Process

**Increased Representation** In January 1993, Congress changed its rules to allow delegates from the District of Columbia, Puerto Rico, Guam, American Samoa, and the U.S. Virgin Islands to have voting privileges in the House of Representatives, with the exception of final votes on legislation. Previously, those delegates could participate only in committee work because they did not meet the constitutional requirement that legislators represent states. Proponents of the new rules argued that initial votes on legislation and amendments from the floor actually take place in the "committee of the whole," which constitutes the entire House.

### CRITICAL THINKING

Why do you think these regions were given limited representation privileges?

**ANSWER:** Students might suggest that they are areas governed by the United States, which affords them some right to representation, but not full rights, because they are not states.

### Visual Record Answer

*Students might suggest that it shows him at the center of attention and with all of the participants' eyes focused on him.*

---

### Did You KNOW?

When Alaska and Hawaii became states in 1959, the membership of the House of Representatives was temporarily increased to 437. Since that time the membership has remained fixed at 435.

**Interpreting the Visual Record**

**Compromise** *The structure of Congress often makes it important for members to compromise with one another in order to pass legislation. Here Senator Henry Clay argues for the Compromise of 1850.* **How does this image show Clay's importance during the compromise discussions?**

---

## ★ The House of Representatives

The House of Representatives has 435 members. Members of the House are called representatives. According to the Constitution, the number of representatives each state can elect to the House is based on the state's population. Each state is entitled to at least one representative. Washington, D.C., Guam, American Samoa, and the Virgin Islands each have one non-voting delegate in the House.

**How Membership Is Divided** Every 10 years, after the census is taken, Congress determines how the seats in the House are to be **apportioned,** or distributed. Congress itself divides these seats among the states according to population. Originally, each state elected one representative for every 30,000 people living in the state. In the first Congress, which met in 1789, the Constitution allowed for 65 representatives in the House. As new states joined the Union and the country's population increased, membership in the House grew. In 1911, Congress limited the size of the House to 435 members. After the 2000 census, each member of the House represented about 646,000 people.

If a state's population decreases the number of its representatives may be reduced. States whose populations grow may be entitled to more representatives. The map on page 115 shows the number of representatives currently apportioned to each state.

**Congressional Districts** Each representative is elected by the voters in a congressional district. Each state legislature is responsible for dividing the state into as many congressional districts as it has members in the House of Representatives. District boundaries must be drawn so that each district is almost equal in population.

State legislators sometimes draw district lines that favor a particular political party, politician, or group of people. This practice is called **gerrymandering.** For example, a state legislature made up of mostly Democrats might draw district lines that place Democratic voters in a majority in as many districts as possible. Gerrymandering often results in oddly shaped districts.

**Electing Representatives** Regular elections for members of the House of Representatives are held in November of each even-numbered year. All representatives are elected for two-year terms. If a representative dies or resigns before the end of a term, the governor of the representative's home state must call a special election to fill the vacancy.

✔ **Reading Check Finding the Main Idea** What are the purposes of apportionment, gerrymandering, and regular elections? Apportionment ensures equal representation according to population. Gerrymandering is used to favor a political party, politician, or group. Regular elections allow people to choose or replace representatives.

# TEACH OBJECTIVE 2

**LEVEL 1:** Have students work in pairs to create a set of flash cards that list the qualifications and salaries for members of the House and of the Senate. Give each pair eight cards. They should write *House* on the back of half of the cards and *Senate* on the back of the other half. Then have them write qualifications and salaries on the appropriate cards. *(Students' cards should correctly identify the following qualifications: Representative—25 years or older, legal resident of state, U.S. citizen for 7 or more years, $154,700; Senate—30 years old, U.S. citizen for 9 or more years, legal resident of state, $154,700.)* Then have students quiz each other using their completed cards. **ENGLISH LANGUAGE LEARNERS , COOPERATIVE LEARNING**

**ALL LEVELS:** Have each student write a help-wanted ad. Ask half of the class to write one for a representative. Ask the other half to write an ad for the position of senator. The ads should include job requirements and qualifications for the positions. Encourage students to be creative in their attempts to attract people to work in the Congress of the United States. *(See the Level 1 lesson for qualifications.)* **ENGLISH LANGUAGE LEARNERS**

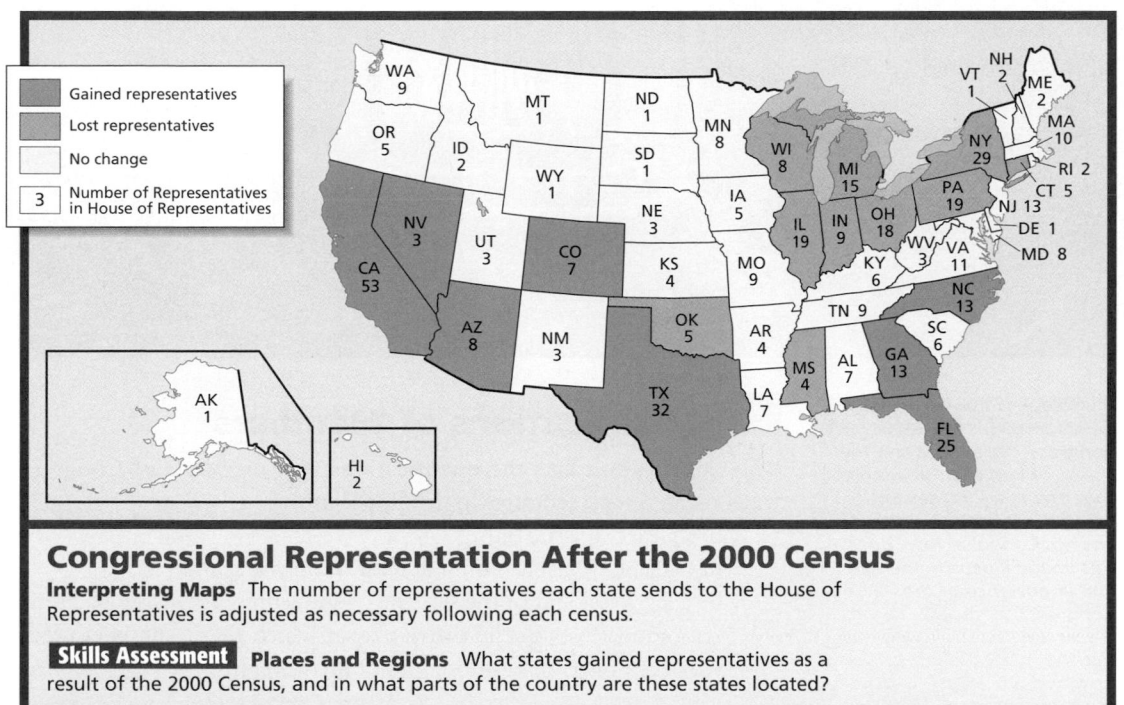

## Congressional Representation After the 2000 Census

**Interpreting Maps** The number of representatives each state sends to the House of Representatives is adjusted as necessary following each census.

**Skills Assessment** **Places and Regions** What states gained representatives as a result of the 2000 Census, and in what parts of the country are these states located?

## The Senate

The Senate is the smaller of the two houses of Congress. The Constitution requires each state, regardless of size, to be represented in the Senate by two senators. Today the Senate has 100 members—two senators from each of the 50 states. Each senator represents his or her entire state. Senators are elected to Congress for six-year terms. Elections for senators are held in November of each even-numbered year. Only one third of the Senate's membership comes up for election every two years. Therefore, a new Senate begins its work with at least two thirds of the members having prior experience.

The senator from each state who has served the longer period of time is the state's senior senator. If a senator dies or resigns before the end of a term of office, the seat must be occupied. Most states allow the governor to appoint someone to fill the vacancy until the next regular election or until a special state election is held.

Recently, many people have supported limiting the number of terms that members of Congress can serve. However, in 1995 the Supreme Court ruled that such **term limits** for federal offices are unconstitutional. The Constitution reserves to the people the right to choose their federal lawmakers, and term limits would infringe upon this right.

✔ **Reading Check Contrasting** How does the number of senators representing a state differ from the number of representatives? Each state has two senators. The number of representatives is based on state population.

---

**The Democratic Process**

**Gerrymandering** State legislatures responsible for drawing the boundaries of congressional districts have often been accused of gerrymandering. The term is a cross between *Gerry* and *salamander*. In 1812 political opponents criticized (perhaps unfairly) Governor Elbridge Gerry of Massachusetts for the creative drawing of congressional district boundaries in a way that benefited his party. The bizarre shape of one congressional district reminded some observers of a salamander, and was called "gerrymander" by some people.

**ACTIVITY:** Have students use outside resources such as the almanac or census reports to determine the boundaries of your congressional district. Then have them map the district. In the margins, encourage students to include facts, such as the number of representatives in your state.

**MAP ANSWER**
Arizona, California, Colorado, Florida, Georgia, Nevada, North Carolina, Texas; the South and West

**LEVELS 2 AND 3:** Organize the class into pairs. Have each pair draw a two-column chart, with each student taking one column. One student should list the qualifications of a member of the House of Representatives. The other should list those of a senator. *(See the Level 1 lesson for qualifications.)* Then have each pair use the chart to develop qualifications for student government representatives. **COOPERATIVE LEARNING**

## TEACH OBJECTIVE 3

**ALL LEVELS:** Copy the following graphic organizer onto the chalkboard, omitting the italicized answers. Ask each student to complete the chart to identify the means by which Congress can deal with misconduct by its members and how each measure is enacted.

**ENGLISH LANGUAGE LEARNERS**

| Legislative Misconduct | |
|---|---|
| **How** | **Description** |
| *censure* | *written reprimand* |
| *expulsion* | *removing a member from Congress* |

**HOMEWORK** Tell each student to create a political cartoon illustrating each of the ways that Congress deals with the misconduct of its members.

**Congressional Profile**
As mentioned in the text, most members of Congress have traditionally been educated, white men in their mid- to late-fifties with backgrounds in law or business. The 108th Congress showed some variation in gender and ethnic background among its members, while their age and occupational background remains similar to tradition. There were 76 female members of Congress—a record number. Twenty-two members were Hispanic American, thirty-seven were African Americans, seven were Asian American or Pacific Islanders, and two were American Indian. Still as in previous Congresses, most members were male, had a background in law or business, and were in their mid- to late-fifties.

**ACTIVITY:** Have students select a congressperson from your state and find more information about his or her background. Tell them to research the representative's work history, education, and prior political experience. Create a chart on the chalkboard to compare the information on each representative.

**Visual Record Answer**

*Students might suggest that the size of the room and the number of people present illustrate the size and importance of Congress.*

**Interpreting the Visual Record**

**Congress** *The Senate and the House of Representatives meet together in a joint session when the president wishes to address Congress.* **How does this image illustrate the size and importance of the Congress?**

*The desks used in the Senate today are based on a design that is more than 100 years old.*

## ★ Qualifications of Members

The Constitution lists the qualifications that members of Congress must meet. A representative in the House must
1. be at least 25 years old;
2. have been a U.S. citizen for at least seven years; and
3. be a legal resident of the state he or she represents. (Usually a representative lives in the district from which he or she is elected. However, the Constitution does not require this.)

The qualifications for members of the Senate differ slightly from those for members of the House. The Constitution lists the following qualifications for senators. A senator must
1. be at least 30 years old;
2. have been a U.S. citizen for at least nine years; and
3. be a legal resident of the state he or she represents.

In addition to these qualifications, members of Congress traditionally have shared other characteristics. For example, they usually have had previous political experience, often in their state legislatures. Most members of Congress also have been active members of community and volunteer organizations.

Many members of Congress are lawyers, businesspeople, public servants, or educators. Senators tend to be older than representatives. In 2001 the average age for representatives was 54. The average age for senators was 59.

In the past, most members of Congress have been white men. Yet, in recent years, the number of women, African Americans, Hispanic Americans, Asian Americans, and American Indians in Congress has increased. In 2001, for example, there were 61 women in the House and 13 women in the Senate. Thirty-eight African Americans served as representatives. However, the numbers of women and ethnic minorities in Congress remain well below their percentages in the population.

✔ **Reading Check** **Drawing Inferences and Conclusions** Why do you think so many educators, public servants, lawyers, and businesspeople become congressmembers? *Students might say that congressmembers use their experiences and contacts from these professions and apply them to their work in Congress.*

**LEVEL 3:** Call on volunteers to identify and explain the ways that Congress deals with misconduct by its members. *(Students should identify censure and expulsion.)* Then have students organize their thoughts to write a position paper that addresses this statement: *Our country's leaders are role models and should set an example with their behavior.* Students' papers should discuss why we expect good conduct from our civil leaders.

# CLOSE

List the six subsections of this section on the chalkboard. *(Subheads include Two Houses of Congress, The House of Representatives, The Senate, Qualifications of Members, Salary and Benefits, and Rules of Conduct.)* Have students discuss the main idea of each one. Then help students create a one- or two-sentence summary of each subsection.

## ★ Salary and Benefits

Each member of Congress receives a yearly salary of $154,700. For years the power of Congress to set its own salary was a controversial matter. In response to this debate, the Twenty-seventh Amendment to the Constitution was ratified in 1992. This amendment states that no increase in congressional pay can take effect until after the next congressional election. This condition allows voters to respond to the proposed increase by voting for or against those members who supported a pay increase.

All members of Congress have offices in the Capitol Building and receive an allowance to pay staff members. Members receive free trips to their home states, an allowance for local district offices, and a stationery allowance. In addition, they have the **franking privilege**—the right to mail official letters or packages free of charge.

Members of Congress also have **immunity,** or legal protection. Immunity means that members of Congress cannot be arrested in or on their way to or from a meeting in Congress. This protection ensures that congressmembers are not unnecessarily kept from performing their duties. In addition, members of Congress cannot be sued for anything they say while they are speaking in Congress. This provision of the Constitution is intended to protect their freedom to debate.

✔ **Reading Check** Analyzing Information What are the benefits of being a congressmember, and why do congressmembers receive these benefits? These benefits include an allowance to pay staffmembers, free trips to their home states, an allowance for district offices, a stationery allowance, franking privilege, and congressional immunity. These benefits enable congressmembers to perform their duties.

### The Congress of the United States

| The Senate<br>100 Senators<br>(2 from each state) | | The House of Representatives<br>435 Representatives<br>(Based on state populations) |
|---|---|---|
| 6 years | **Length of Term** | 2 years |
| One third of Senate elected every 2 years | **When Elected** | Entire House elected every 2 years |
| At least 30 years old | **Required Age** | At least 25 years old |
| U.S. citizen at least 9 years | **Citizenship** | U.S. citizen at least 7 years |
| Resident of state where elected | **Legal Residence** | Resident of state where elected |

**Interpreting Charts** *Each house of Congress has specific requirements for membership. How often are senators and representatives elected?*

## ★ Profiles

**The First Congresswoman** Several years before women were even allowed to vote, the first woman was elected to Congress. In 1916 Jeannette Rankin, a leader in the suffrage movement, was sent to the House of Representatives for the state of Montana. While there, she helped draft an early version of an amendment to give women the right to vote. It was turned down at that time, but the issue resurfaced, and the amendment was passed in 1919. Women still lead in Congress today. In the 108th Congress, 62 of the 435 members of the House are women and 14 out of 100 senators.

**ACTIVITY:** Have students use these figures to determine what percentage of House and Senate leaders were female. *(Just over 14 percent of the House and 14 percent of the Senate are female.)*

**CHART ANSWER**
senators—every 6 years; representatives—every 2 years

★★★★★★★★★★★★★
### That's Interesting!
★★★★★★★★★★★★★

**The Franking Privilege** Every member of Congress has the franking privilege—the right to send official mail without paying postage. Instead of a stamp, a copy of the congressperson's signature appears on the envelope. In the past, the franking privilege was sometimes abused. The most extreme example of this abuse involved a senator in the 1800s. He declared his horse to be a "public document" and put his signature on the horse's bridle. In this way he had his horse shipped home for free.

## ★ Rules of Conduct

Both houses of Congress have the right to decide who shall be seated as members. If the Senate or the House questions the constitutional qualifications of a newly elected member of Congress, the member may not be seated in Congress until an investigation of the charges is made. The Supreme Court may review the actions of Congress in this regard. Congress seldom has to refuse to seat one of its members.

The House and Senate have passed codes of conduct for their members. For example, members of Congress may not use campaign funds for personal expenses. There is also a limit to the amount of outside income they may earn. In addition, members of Congress are required to make a full disclosure of their financial holdings.

Serious misconduct by a member of the Senate or House may result in **expulsion** from office, which requires a vote of two thirds of the senators or representatives. Expulsion of a member means that the person must give up his or her seat in Congress. Grounds for expulsion are limited to serious offenses, such as treason or other conduct unbecoming a member of Congress.

Less serious offenses may bring a vote of **censure,** or formal disapproval of a member's actions. A censured member must stand alone at the front of the House or Senate and listen as the charges against him or her are read.

✔ **Reading Check Comparing and Contrasting** How are expulsion and censure both alike and different? They are both responses to congressional misconduct. Expulsion is more serious, requiring a member to give up his or her seat.

go.hrw.com **Homework Practice Online**

keyword: SZ3 HP5

## SECTION 1 Review

**1. Define** and explain:
- apportioned
- gerrymandering
- term limits
- franking privilege
- immunity
- expulsion
- censure

**2. Comparing** Copy the graphic organizer below. Use it to compare the qualifications and salaries of members of the House and Senate.

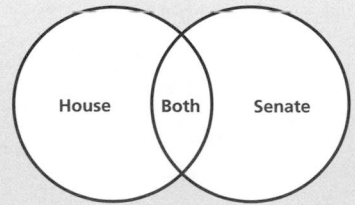

House  Both  Senate

**3. Finding the Main Idea**
  a. How many members sit in the Senate and the House of Representatives, and how long do members of each house of Congress serve?
  b. What might members of Congress do if a congressmember engages in inappropriate behavior?

**4. Writing and Critical Thinking**
  **Supporting a Point of View** Write a position statement agreeing or disagreeing with the Supreme Court's decision on the issue of congressional term limits.

  **Consider:**
  - how term limits help Congress better serve the people
  - how limits hurt the ability of Congress to serve the people

# SECTION 2

## OBJECTIVES

*After completing Section 2, students should be able to*

**1** Identify when a session of Congress begins and how long the session lasts.

**2** Explain who leads the houses of Congress and how these leaders are chosen.

**3** Describe the purpose of congressional committees and tell how committee assignments are made.

## 🔊 LET'S GET STARTED!

Write the following instructions on the chalkboard: *List strategies that a large group might use to handle a heavy workload.* As students enter the classroom, allow them time to write down their responses. *(Students' responses may include to divide up the work, to select leaders to monitor the workload, and so on.)* Briefly discuss students' responses. Then tell students that in Section 2 they will learn about the ways Congress is organized to handle its heavy workload.

---

# SECTION 2

# How Congress Is Organized

## Read to Discover

1. When does a session of Congress begin, and how long does the session last?
2. Who leads the houses of Congress, and how are these leaders chosen?
3. What is the purpose of congressional committees, and how are committee assignments made?

### WHY CIVICS MATTERS

The leaders of the House and Senate play important roles in Congress. Use **CNN fyi.com** or other **current events** sources to discover who the current congressional leaders are and what issues they support. Record your findings in your journal.

## Define

- sessions
- caucuses
- majority party
- minority party
- floor leader
- party whip
- president *pro tempore*
- bills
- committees
- standing committees
- subcommittees
- select committees
- joint committees
- conference committee
- seniority system

## Identify

- Speaker

## SECTION 2 RESOURCES

### REPRODUCIBLE

▶ Guided Reading Strategies 5.2

▶ Challenge and Enrichment Worksheet 5: Researching Members of Congress

▶ Creative Teaching Strategies Handbook: Open-Ended Statements

### TECHNOLOGY

▶ One-Stop Planner, Lesson 5.2

▶ CNN Presents: American Government

▶ Homework Practice Online

### REINFORCEMENT, REVIEW, AND ASSESSMENT

▶ Section 2 Review, p. 124
▶ Daily Quiz 5.2
▶ Main Idea Activity 5.2
▶ English Audio Summary 5.2
▶ Spanish Audio Summary 5.2

## *Reading Focus*

Beginning with the First Congress in 1789, each Congress has been identified by number. The Congress that began its term in 2004 is called the 108th Congress Second Session.

### ⭐ Terms and Sessions

In each term of Congress, there are two regular **sessions,** or meetings. The first session usually begins the first week of January in the odd-numbered year following the congressional election in the previous November. The second session begins in January of the next year.

Each session may last as long as Congress wishes. In the past, sessions usually lasted from January until August or September. In recent years, the growing workload has led to longer sessions. Both houses of Congress agree on the date to adjourn, or end, the session.

Occasionally, serious problems arise after Congress has adjourned its regular session. In such cases, the president of the United States can ask Congress to meet in a special session. The president can call both houses into special session, or may call only one of the two houses.

Under certain circumstances, the House of Representatives and the Senate will meet together. This is known as a joint session of Congress. For example, a joint session will be called if the president wants to

*The laws that Congress passes each year can fill many volumes of books.*

**LEVEL 1:** Organize the class into groups. Have each group prepare an encyclopedia entry that identifies when a session of Congress begins and how long the session lasts. *(Students should write that the first session begins January 3 in the odd-numbered year following the congressional election in November. The second session begins January 3 of the following year. Sessions last as long as Congress wishes—adjournment dates are selected by Congress.)* Encourage students to include other details about congressional sessions as well. Call on a volunteer to read his or her group's entry to the class.
**ENGLISH LANGUAGE LEARNERS , COOPERATIVE LEARNING**

**ALL LEVELS:** Copy the following graphic organizer onto the chalkboard, omitting the italicized answers. Have each student complete the list to identify when a session of Congress begins and how long it lasts. **ENGLISH LANGUAGE LEARNERS**

| When Sessions Begin | How Long They Last |
|---|---|
| *The first session begins January 3 in odd-numbered years following the congressoinal election in November. The second session begins January 3 of the following year.* | *Sessions last as long as Congress wishes. Adjournment dates are selected by Congress.* |

## The Democratic Process

**Caucuses** Besides party caucuses, the Congress is also home to several unofficial caucuses. Among the most powerful has been the Congressional Black Caucus, formed in 1969 to further the interests of African Americans. Other caucuses include the Congressional Hispanic Caucus and the Older Americans Caucus. These caucuses combine the clout of individual members of Congress, often providing political pressure to pursue the interests of their members. The Congressional Black Caucus, for example, often provides support for African American nominees to government posts and to policies that may directly affect African Americans.

**ACTIVITY:** Have small groups of students hold majority or minority party caucuses. With Congress as a model, each group should draw up a list of school government leadership positions and elect members to the positions. Each "leader" should develop a list of qualifications and responsibilities for his or her office. Have the group present its leaders, each of whom should explain the qualifications and responsibilities of his or her office.

---

**BIOGRAPHY ANSWER**
as a soldier, as a representative, and as a senator

---

**BIOGRAPHY**

### Daniel Inouye
**(1924– )**

Daniel Inouye was born in Hawaii while it was still a U.S. territory. Inouye served his country bravely during World War II, sustaining an injury that cost him his right arm. He received the Medal of Honor, the Bronze Star, and the Purple Heart for his actions.

After the war Inouye studied law. In 1954 he was elected to Hawaii's territorial House of Representatives. Four years later he joined the Hawaiian Senate. When Hawaii was granted statehood in 1959, Inouye became the first Japanese American to serve in Congress. Today Inouye sits on multiple Senate committees and continues to serve as a respected legislator. **What are some of the ways in which Daniel Inouye has served his country?**

address both houses of Congress. These sessions and many others are often televised.

✔ **Reading Check Contrasting** What is the difference between a regular session and a special session of Congress? A regular session is held each year to consider legislation. A special session is only called if Congress must reconvene to address a specific issue.

## Organization

The Constitution provides for only three congressional officers. First, it directs the House of Representatives to select a presiding officer. Second, it names the vice president of the United States as president of the Senate. Third, it calls for the selection of a senator to preside in the vice president's absence. These are the only directions the Constitution gives about the organization of Congress.

Over the years, Congress has developed procedures to organize itself. Shortly after the opening day of each term, the Republican and Democratic members in each house gather separately in private meetings. These private meetings are called party **caucuses.** At these caucuses, the Republican members of each house choose their own leaders, and the Democratic members do the same.

The political party that has the most members in each house is known as the **majority party.** The political party that has fewer members is called the **minority party.**

✔ **Reading Check Analyzing Information** What are the three congressional officers that the Constitution provides for, and what other procedures does Congress use to organize itself? The Constitution allows for a presiding officer for the House, president of the Senate, which is filled by the vice president, and a senator to preside in the vice president's absence. The Republican and Democratic members hold caucuses to choose their own leaders.

## Leaders of the House and Senate

According to the Constitution, the presiding officer of the House of Representatives is the **Speaker** of the House. The Speaker is the most powerful officer in the House. No representative may speak until called on, or recognized, by the Speaker. The Speaker also greatly influences the order of business in the House. The Speaker, because of these important responsibilities, is paid about $40,000 more per year than other representatives. The Speaker is always a member of the majority party. Like other leaders in the House and Senate, the Speaker is usually a long-time member of Congress. House members also choose a number of other leaders. At their private caucuses, House Democrats and Republicans each choose a **floor leader** that guides the party's proposed laws through Congress. The floor leader of the majority party is called the majority leader. The floor leader of the minority party is the minority leader. Each floor leader is assisted by a **party whip,** whose job it is to persuade members to vote for party-sponsored legislation.

# TEACH OBJECTIVE 2

**LEVEL 1:** Ask the class to identify the leaders of the houses of Congress. *(Students should identify the Speaker, floor leaders, and party whips as the House leaders and the vice president, president pro tempore, and the majority and minority leaders for the Senate.)* Then help students create their own charts that list the ways in which these leaders are chosen. *(Students' charts should note that the Speaker, the president of Senate, and the president pro tempore of Senate are selected as determined in the Constitution. The others are chosen by party caucuses.)* **ENGLISH LANGUAGE LEARNERS**

**LEVEL 3:** Have students write a memorandum informing their classmates about who leads the houses of Congress and how they are chosen. Tell them to include a section evaluating the effectiveness of the seniority system. *(Students' essays should note the following leaders and processes: House—Speaker, floor leaders, and party whips; Senate—president, president pro tempore, majority leader, and minority leader party whips. The Speaker, the president of the Senate, and the president pro tempore of the Senate are selected as determined in the Constitution. The others are chosen by party caucuses.)* Then have students exchange their memos with a partner. Ask students to read their partner's work and to discuss their views about the seniority system. **COOPERATIVE LEARNING**

The Constitution provides for the vice president to serve as the presiding officer of the Senate. The vice president, however, cannot take part in Senate debates and may vote only in the case of a tie.

In recent years, the vice president has taken on many additional responsibilities and has generally spent little time in the Senate. In the event of the vice president's absence, the Senate is presided over by the **president *pro tempore,*** a president "for the time being." This leader is elected by the members of the Senate. The president *pro tempore* is by custom the longest-serving member of the majority party.

The most powerful officers of the Senate are the majority leader and the minority leader. Like the floor leaders of the House, the majority leader and the minority leader are elected in party caucuses. They too are assisted by party whips.

✔ **Reading Check Summarizing** Who are the most important leaders of the House and Senate, and what are their responsibilities? the Speaker of the House—allows others to speak and greatly influences House agenda; the House and the Senate majority and minority leaders—guide party's proposed laws through Congress; and the party whips—try to persuade members to vote for party-sponsored legislation

## ★ Committees

Every year Congress has to consider thousands of **bills,** or proposed laws. It would be impossible for all members of each house to consider every bill that is proposed. Therefore, the members divide their work among many **committees,** or smaller groups.

Most of the work of Congress is done in committees. The congressional committees study all bills before they are considered by Congress. To obtain information needed to do their work, committees hold hearings—special meetings—and conduct investigations.

✔ **Reading Check Finding the Main Idea** Why are congressional committees necessary? They enable Congress to handle the heavy workload of reviewing and passing legislation.

# TEACH OBJECTIVE 3

**ALL LEVELS:** Have students use the information in this section to create a poster that could be used to announce the upcoming committee selection process to members of Congress. Tell them to illustrate the purpose of congressional committees. *(Students' posters should show that they help divide the heavy workload.)* Encourage students to also depict the process by which committee selections are made. *(Party committees in each house nominate party members. Then a party caucus reviews the nominations and makes the selections.)* Encourage volunteers to explain their posters to the class.

**ENGLISH LANGUAGE LEARNERS**

**LEVEL 2:** As a class, discuss the purpose of congressional committees. *(See the All Levels lesson for purpose.)* Then play this sequencing game with students to help them recall how committee assignments are made. State one step in the process and have a volunteer name an adjoining step. Then have another student determine whether the adjoining step comes before or after the step you named. *(Students should note that committee assignments are made in the following order: the party committee nominates party members, a party caucus reviews the nominees, then the caucus selects committee members.)*

---

## ★ Culture

**Native American Governments** Some Native American peoples had complex systems of government. For example, the Cheyenne were governed by a civil council comprised of 44 chiefs. The highest ranking of these 44 chiefs were the five priestly chiefs, one of whom (called the Prophet) presided over the council meetings. Two council members were designated as doormen, whose duties included moving the council toward decisions on issues before it. A separate council of 24 war chiefs was responsible for the Cheyenne's military affairs. The war chiefs appointed the war leader for a single military operation.

**ACTIVITY:** Have students write an essay that compares and contrasts the Cheyenne system of government with the U.S. government.

★★★★★★★★★★★★★
### That's Interesting!
★★★★★★★★★★★★★

The term party *whip* was first used in the Parliament, applying the name to officials whose job it was to keep party members in line with the party's leadership. The term derives from the word "whipper-in." In fox hunting the job of a whipper-in is to keep fox-sniffing dogs from straying during a hunt. To do so, the whipper-in literally *whips* the dogs back into the pack.

---

**Standing Committees** Each house of Congress has a number of **standing committees,** or permanent committees. The Senate has 16 standing committees, and the House has 19. Each committee is responsible for a special area of congressional business. In the House of Representatives, for example, the Ways and Means Committee handles all matters concerning taxes. In the Senate, bills related to taxes are handled by the Finance Committee.

Before Congress considers a bill, it is studied carefully by an appropriate standing committee in each house. The committee holds hearings to gather information on the positive and negative aspects of the proposed legislation. Committee members may also revise a bill to address any other issues of concern. The bill is then sent to the entire membership for consideration, along with the committee's recommendation for or against it. This recommendation usually determines whether the members will approve the bill.

**Subcommittees** Each standing committee is divided into **subcommittees.** These subcommittees deal with specific issues that fall within the area handled by the committee as a whole. For example, the the Senate Foreign Relations Committee has subcommittees on African, East Asian and Pacific, and European Affairs.

**Select Committees** From time to time, each house of Congress will appoint **select committees** to deal with issues that are not handled by the standing committees. Select committees have investigated government scandals, for example. After holding hearings to discuss a specific problem area, a select committee recommends solutions that may lead to new laws. Select committees are disbanded when they have finished their work.

**Joint Committees** Congress also has two committees made up of an equal number of representatives and senators. The two houses of Congress have set up these **joint committees** to better handle certain matters by working together.

> **Interpreting the Visual Record**
>
> **Hearings** *Congressional committees often hold special hearings on complex issues in order to hear expert testimony.* **Why are hearings an important part of the legislative process?**

LEVEL 3: Organize the class into three groups. Have each group storyboard a television program about congressional committees. One group should explain why congressional committees are useful. Another group should identify the selection process. The third group should examine the benefits and drawbacks of the seniority system. *(The first group should note that committees divide the large workload. The second should mention that party committees in each house nominate members. Then a party caucus reviews them and makes the selections. The third group should note experience as a plus but lack of new ideas as a downfall.)* Encourage students to divide tasks evenly among group members. Ask each group to present its segment to the class. **COOPERATIVE LEARNING**

 **HOMEWORK** Have students write a short song that could be used to recall the information listed in their charts.

## CLOSE

Have students discuss whether they would prefer to be a newer member of Congress or a senior member and to provide reasons for their opinions. Use the discussion to review congressional organization as presented in this section.

**Conference Committees** Another kind of House-Senate committee is known as a **conference committee.** Conference committees are frequently formed to work out compromises when the House and Senate pass different versions of the same bill. Each conference committee is temporary and considers only one bill.

✔ **Reading Check Evaluating** What do you think is the most important type of committee? Explain your answer. Students' responses will vary but should be logically reasoned.

## Committee Membership

Each member of the House can serve on only two of the major standing committees. This rule enables each representative to specialize in one subject area. In the Senate, each senator serves on at least two major standing committees. Members of Congress seek assignment to these major standing committees to increase their political influence.

The membership of the standing committees is divided in proportion to the number of members each party has in each house. If the Senate contains 60 Republicans and 40 Democrats, a 10-member committee would include 6 Republicans and 4 Democrats. Thus, the majority party has a great advantage over the minority party. Through this system the majority party is able to control much of the work done in any given committee.

Each party in the House of Representatives meets in a committee to decide committee assignments. This group nominates, or names, members of the party to serve on the various standing committees. A party caucus then reviews the nominations. Loyal party members and longtime members of Congress are usually rewarded with important committee assignments.

✔ **Reading Check Drawing Inferences and Conclusions** Why does the majority party have an advantage over the minority party under the committee system? The majority party's larger membership in Congress gives it larger membership in the committees and increased control over what bills will be considered.

## Committee Chairpersons

Because congressional committees are so important, their chairpersons are very powerful. Chairpersons decide when committees will meet and when they will hold hearings. They create subcommittees and hire and fire committee staff. These responsibilities give committee chairpersons great influence in Congress.

How does someone reach this position? For many years, the post of committee chairperson automatically went to the majority party member with the most years of service on the committee. This **seniority system** was a long-established custom.

**GRIN AND BEAR IT**

WHITE HOUSE STAFF
HAIL TO THE CHIEF

"The only way we can get an energy bill through is to tack a congressional pay raise to it."

**Interpreting Political Cartoons**

**Passing bills** *Proposed laws can face many challenges when moving through Congress.* **What do you think the cartoonist is suggesting about politicians' motivations?**

## REVIEW AND ASSESS

Have students complete the **Section 2 Review** on page 124. Then have students complete **Daily Quiz 5.2**. As **Alternative Assessment** you may want to use the encyclopedia entry or the congressional committee poster activity in this section's lessons.

## RETEACH

Have students complete **Main Idea Activity for English Language Learners and Special-Needs Students 5.2**. Then have each student write five fill-in-the-blank sentences that can each be completed by one of the section's Define and Identify terms. **ENGLISH LANGUAGE LEARNERS**

## EXTEND

Assign one congressional committee to each student. Have students obtain newspaper and magazine articles about their assigned committee and its work. Students should list specific bills that their assigned committee considers. Then have each student identify the committee's counterpart in the other chamber. Call on volunteers to report their findings to the class. **BLOCK SCHEDULING**

## Section 2 Review
### ANSWERS

**1. Define**
- sessions, p. 119
- caucuses, p. 120
- majority party, p. 120
- minority party, p. 120
- floor leader, p. 120
- party whip, p. 120
- president *pro tempore*, p. 121
- bills, p. 121
- committees, p. 121
- standing committees, p. 122
- subcommittees, p. 122
- select committees, p. 122
- joint committees, p. 122
- conference committee, p. 123
- seniority system, p. 123

**2. Identify**
- Speaker, p. 120

**3.** House—Speaker, floor leaders, and party whips; Senate— president, president *pro tempore*, majority leader, and minority leader; Speaker, president of the Senate, and president *pro tempore* of the Senate selected per the Constitution; others chosen by party caucuses

**4. a.** last as long as Congress determines; first session begins January 3 in odd-numbered years after November elections; second session begins January 3 of the following year

**b.** to divide the large workload; each party in each house has a committee that nominates party members; party caucus makes selections

**5.** Students' statements will vary.

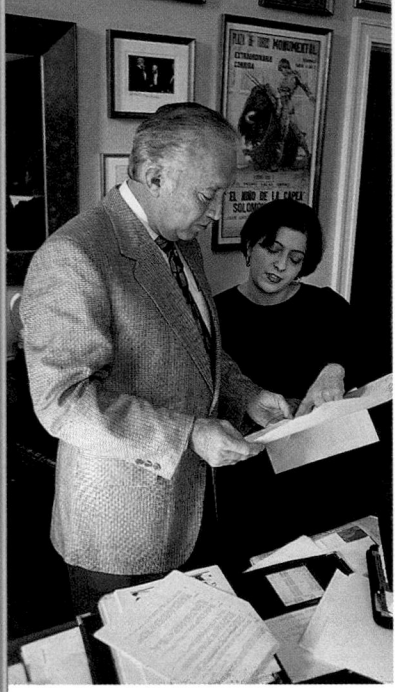

*Members of Congress rely on their staff members to help keep them informed on a wide range of issues.*

Some people believe the seniority system works well. They say it assures experienced leadership. However, in recent years others have questioned the use of seniority in choosing committee chairpersons. Critics of the seniority system believe that younger members with fewer years of service might provide new ideas and more active leadership.

As a result of such criticism, Congress has changed its method of selecting chairpersons. The majority party in each house now chooses the heads of committees by secret vote in a party caucus. However, the person with the longest service in Congress is almost always selected by this method as well.

✔ **Reading Check Contrasting** How is the current method of selecting committee chairpersons different from the method used in the past? Today the majority party in each house chooses the heads of committees by a secret vote. In the past, the seniority system was used to select committee chairpersons.

## ★ Congressional Staffs

Congressional staff members include special assistants, clerks, and secretaries. Members of Congress need large staffs to help run their offices in Washington, D.C., and in their home districts or states. Their staffs also provide information on bills being considered by Congress and help keep senators and representatives informed on a variety of important issues. Furthermore, congressional staffs keep members of Congress informed on what the people they represent think about issues under consideration.

✔ **Reading Check Finding the Main Idea** What are the responsibilities of congressional staffs? to support congressmembers by running their offices and providing them with information on key issues and on the thoughts of their constituents

## SECTION 2 Review

go.hrw.com **Homework Practice Online**
keyword: SZ3 HP5

**1. Define** and explain:
- sessions
- caucuses
- majority party
- minority party
- floor leader
- party whip
- president *pro tempore*
- bills
- committees
- standing committees
- subcommittees
- select committees
- joint committees
- conference committee
- seniority system

**2. Identify** and explain:
- Speaker

**3. Categorizing** Copy the graphic organizer below. Use it to identify the leaders of the houses of Congress and describe how they are selected.

House

Senate

**4. Finding the Main Idea**
a. When does each session of Congress begin, and how long does each regular session last?
b. Explain why Congress has committees and how a congressmember can serve on a committee.

**5. Writing and Critical Thinking**
**Decision-Making** Write a statement that outlines what you believe is the best method for choosing chairpersons.

**Consider:**
- the seniority system
- requests for participation from newer congressmembers

## TEACH

**LEVEL 1:** Call on volunteers to identify various political symbols that they have seen used in political cartoons. *(Students might have seen a donkey, an elephant, an eagle, Uncle Sam, and so on.)* Briefly discuss the meanings of these symbols. Then have students identify the symbols used in the cartoon on this page and their meanings. *(Students might identify the capitol building or the monarch.)* Ask the class why they think that cartoonists rely upon symbols to convey their viewpoints rather than simply stating them directly.

**ENGLISH LANGUAGE LEARNERS**

## EXTEND

Provide each student with cartoons from the editorial section of your newspaper. Then have them follow the steps listed on this page to interpret one of them. Encourage students to write down their observations as they complete each step. Then pair students who have the same cartoon and have them compare each other's interpretations. Finally, have partners work together to create a political cartoon that addresses the same issue as the cartoon they interpreted, but from a different point of view. Display students' analyses and cartoons around the classroom.

**COOPERATIVE LEARNING , BLOCK SCHEDULING**

# Civics Skills
## WORKSHOP

## Interpreting Political Cartoons

Political cartoons are typically found in the editorial sections of newspapers. These cartoons use pictures to express a point of view. They often make use of political symbols or characters. Because the pictures are often humorous, your first reaction might be to laugh. It is important, however, to look beyond the humor. Every political cartoon has an underlying message.

## How to Interpret Political Cartoons

1. **Identify the symbols.** As you look at the cartoon, keep in mind that the artist often uses symbols, or drawings with special meanings. Some symbols, such as Uncle Sam, represent countries, groups of people, or places. Other symbols represent ideas. Justice, for example, is often shown as a blindfolded, robed woman holding a set of scales.

2. **Identify the caricatures.** Caricatures are sketches that exaggerate, or distort, a person's features. Caricatures can be positive or negative, depending on the cartoonist's point of view. Determine whether the cartoonist is portraying the subject in a favorable or unfavorable manner.

3. **Read the labels.** Editorial cartoons often use labels to identify people, objects, events, or ideas. How do the labels help express the cartoonist's point of view?

4. **Read the caption.** Many cartoons have a caption. If the cartoon has a caption, note how it relates to the cartoon. Identify whose point of view is being expressed in the caption—that of the cartoonist, the cartoon figure, or some other person.

## Applying the Skill

Examine the political cartoon below. Then answer the following questions.

1. What is the subject of the cartoon?

2. Why do you think the cartoonist chose to portray the seniority system of Congress as an old king?

3. What is the cartoonist's opinion of the seniority system? Do you agree with this opinion? Why or why not?

American Revolution Bicentennial

Copyright 1975 by Herblock in The Washington Post

# SECTION 3

## OBJECTIVES

*After completing Section 3, students should be able to*

1. **Identify the five major areas in which Congress has the power to make laws.**
2. **Analyze the significance of the elastic clause.**
3. **Describe the special powers of Congress and explain how congressional powers are limited.**

## SECTION 3 RESOURCES

### REPRODUCIBLE
▶ Guided Reading Strategies 5.3

### TECHNOLOGY
▶ One-Stop Planner, Lesson 5.3
▶ Holt Researcher CD–ROM
▶ Homework Practice Online

### REINFORCEMENT, REVIEW, AND ASSESSMENT
▶ Section 3 Review, p. 131
▶ Daily Quiz 5.3
▶ Main Idea Activity 5.3
▶ English Audio Summary 5.3
▶ Spanish Audio Summary 5.3

## 🔊 LET'S GET STARTED!

As students enter the classroom, provide each student with a copy of the Reading in Economics on Government 66, Profiles in Courage. Then ask students to take a few moments to think of a list of powers that they think senators should have. List students' responses on the chalkboard. *(Students' responses may include making treaties, passing laws, and approving Supreme Court candidates.)* Then ask students to explain how a senator should balance those powers with obligations to their constituents as well as various interests. Tell students that in Section 3 they will learn more about congressional powers as well as the limits placed on them.

---

## SECTION 3

# The Powers of Congress

### Read to Discover

1. What are the five major areas in which Congress has the power to make laws?
2. What is the significance of the elastic clause?
3. What are the special powers of Congress, and how are congressional powers limited?

### WHY CIVICS MATTERS

Laws passed by Congress affect life nationwide and in your state. Use **CNN fyi.com** or other **current events** sources to investigate the latest bills supported by your state's congressmembers. Record your findings in your journal.

### Define
- elastic clause
- implied powers
- treason
- impeachment
- *ex post facto* law
- bill of attainder
- writ of *habeas corpus*
- constituents

## *Reading Focus*

The U.S. Congress is the most powerful representative body in the world. Under the Constitution, Congress's most important responsibility is to make laws. These laws do not simply tell us what we can and cannot do. They affect us in other ways as well. For example, laws passed by Congress determine how high taxes will be. They provide for the building of highways and dams. They determine what military equipment the United States will sell to other countries. The actions of Congress affect the lives of millions of people in the United States and throughout the world.

*Congress is responsible for collecting money to finance national defense.*

### ★ Powers Granted to Congress

Article I, Section 8, of the Constitution lists the powers granted to Congress. As you know, these powers are called delegated powers because they are granted, or delegated, to Congress by the Constitution. Delegated powers give Congress the authority to make laws in five important areas.

**Financing Government** Congress has the authority to raise and collect taxes, borrow money, and print and coin money. It can use the funds it collects to pay the debts of the United States and to provide for the country's defense and general welfare.

# TEACH OBJECTIVE 1

**ALL LEVELS:** Copy the following graphic organizer onto the chalkboard, omitting the italicized answers. Have students complete the organizer to identify the five major areas in which Congress has the power to make laws.

**ENGLISH LANGUAGE LEARNERS**

*defending the country*

*providing for growth*

**Congressional Powers**

*financing government*

*enforcing laws*

*regulating and encouraging U.S. trade and industry*

**LEVEL 2:** Have students list the five major areas in which Congress has the power to make laws. *(See the All Levels lesson for powers.)* Then ask them to place the powers in order of importance. On the chalkboard, tally students' rankings. Then lead a discussion with the class regarding the prioritization of congressional powers.

**Regulating and Encouraging American Trade and Industry** Congress can regulate trade with foreign countries and among the states. It can also help American businesses by setting a uniform standard of weights and measures and by passing laws that protect the rights of inventors. Congress makes laws authorizing the establishment of post offices. It regulates the building of roads, which in turn helps American businesses and industries. Congress can set punishments for piracy and other major crimes committed against American ships on the high seas.

**Defending the Country** Congress has the power to declare war and to maintain an army and a navy. It can also provide for a citizen army that can be called to duty during wartime or national emergencies.

**Enforcing Laws** Congress can pass laws concerning such crimes as counterfeiting and treason. To ensure that these and other federal laws are upheld, Congress has established a system of national courts.

**Providing for Growth** Congress has the power to regulate immigration and to pass naturalization laws. Naturalization laws make it possible for immigrants to become U.S. citizens. In Article IV, Section 3, Congress is also given the power to govern the country's territories and to provide for the admission of new states.

✔**Reading Check** Supporting a Point of View Which of these five powers do you think is the most important? Explain your answer. Students' responses will vary but should be logically reasoned.

## ⭐ Implied Powers

The last power that is listed in Section 8 of Article I is among the most important and far-reaching. It states that Congress has the power "to make all laws which shall be necessary and proper for carrying into execution [carrying out] the foregoing powers."

This statement is known as the necessary and proper clause. It is also called the **elastic clause,** because it allows Congress to stretch the delegated powers listed in the Constitution to cover many other subjects. The elastic clause has permitted Congress to

☑ **internet** connect

**TOPIC:** How a Bill Becomes a Law
**GO TO:** go.hrw.com
**KEYWORD:** SZ3 AC5

Have students access the Internet through the HRW Go site to research the process by which a bill becomes a law. Then ask students to assume the point of view of a bill, and have them write a short story that traces its progress through Congress. The story should be told from the point of view of the bill, should include the sponsor and why the bill was drafted, and should directly refer to students' research.

**CHART ANSWER**
powers to collect taxes, print and coin money, regulate interstate and foreign trade, and borrow money

### Powers of Congress

| Delegated Powers | • Collect taxes<br>• Print and coin money<br>• Regulate interstate and foreign trade<br>• Borrow money |
| --- | --- |
| | • Declare war and make peace<br>• Raise armed forces for defense |
| | • Admit new states to the Union<br>• Govern the District of Columbia and the nation's territories |
| | • Establish a national court system<br>• Establish post offices and roads<br>• Make laws on immigration and naturalization<br>• Grant patents and copyrights |
| Implied Powers | • Make all laws necessary and proper to carry out delegated powers<br>• Provide for the general welfare of the United States |

**Interpreting Charts** *Congress has a wide range of powers specifically granted by the Constitution, as well as some implied powers.* **What congressional powers are directly involved with money and trade?**

**LEVEL 3:** Organize the class into five groups. Assign each group one of the five delegated powers of Congress. *(See the All Levels lesson for powers.)* Have each group prepare a dramatic scene that illustrates its assigned power. The power itself must not be mentioned. Have the groups perform their scenes in front of the class. Then ask the rest of the class to guess which power is being illustrated. **COOPERATIVE LEARNING**

## TEACH OBJECTIVE 2

 **LEVEL 1:** Lead a class discussion about the powers of Congress, including its special powers. Then discuss the elastic clause. Ask students to write a dictionary description of the purpose of the elastic clause. *(Students should note that it allows Congress to stretch the delegated powers listed in the Constitution to address situations that developed long after the Constitution was written.)* **ENGLISH LANGUAGE LEARNERS**

 **HOMEWORK** Have students write an editorial that addresses the following question: *Does Congress have too much power?*

## Global Perspectives

**Impeachment** Many countries have the ability to impeach their leaders. As in the United States, leaders facing impeachment react in a variety of ways. A few leaders have faced the hearing and were eventually impeached. This was the case with Brazil's president Fernando Collor de Mello in 1992. Other leaders have survived impeachment attempts and have kept their jobs. These include U.S. presidents Andrew Johnson (in 1868) and Bill Clinton (in 1999), Sri Lanka's President Ranasinghe Premadasa in 1991, and Russian president Boris Yeltsin in 1993. Still others have taken preventive measures—they left office to avoid the proceedings. Among this list are U.S. president Richard Nixon in 1974 and Venezuela's president Carlos Andrés Pérez in 1993.

**ACTIVITY:** Ask students to conduct research about impeachment and to write an essay reporting the circumstances surrounding one of these leader's impeachment cases. You might assign leaders to students to ensure that the class researches each of the various cases.

### Visual Record Answer

*Students might suggest that they were established to train young men to serve their country.*

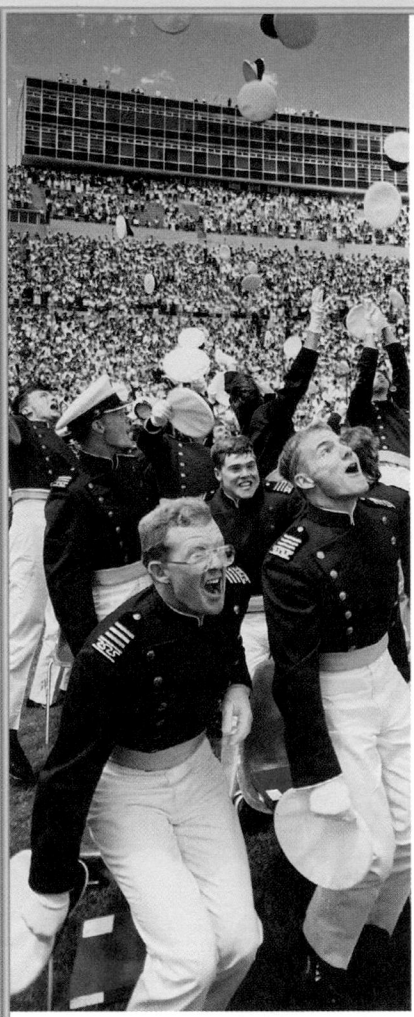

**Interpreting the Visual Record**

**Military academies** *These cadets are celebrating following their graduation from the United States Air Force Academy in Colorado Springs.* **Why do you think Congress felt it necessary to create the military academies?**

pass laws related to situations that developed long after the Constitution was written.

For example, Congress has set up national military academies to train officers who can serve in the army, navy, and air force. The Constitution does not specifically give Congress this power. However, Congress argues that establishing the academies is "necessary and proper" to ensure the defense of the United States. Congress has claimed that the elastic clause implies, or suggests, that Congress has the right to establish military academies to train military officers. For this reason, the powers that Congress has claimed under the elastic clause are called **implied powers.**

✔ **Reading Check Analyzing Information** Why is the elastic clause important? The elastic clause allows Congress to pass laws regarding situations that developed long after the Constitution was written.

## Power to Impeach

The Constitution gives Congress other powers in addition to lawmaking. One of Congress's most important powers is its power to accuse high federal officials of serious crimes against the country. Congress also has the power to bring them to trial. The federal officials that Congress can bring to trial include the president, vice president, and federal judges. Congress may remove these officials from office if they are found guilty of serious crimes such as **treason.** Treason is an act that betrays or endangers one's country.

The charges against an accused official must be drawn up in the House of Representatives. The list of charges is read before the entire House. Then the representatives vote. If a majority of them vote in favor of the list of charges, the official is impeached, or formally accused. The individual will then be put on trial. The procedure of drawing up and passing the list of charges in the House is called **impeachment.**

The trial on the impeachment charges is held in the Senate. During the impeachment trial, the Senate becomes a court. The vice president usually acts as the judge. However, if the president is impeached the chief justice of the Supreme Court presides over the trial instead. The vice president cannot act as judge because he or she would become president if the president were found guilty. This possibility might bias his or her judgement.

The members of the Senate act as the jury. They hear the evidence and examine all witnesses. They then vote on the guilt or innocence of the official. Two thirds of the Senate must find the official guilty before he or she can be dismissed from office.

The impeachment process has rarely been used. Altogether, 17 federal officials have been impeached. Only seven of them, all judges, were found guilty of the charges brought against them and dismissed from office. Two presidents, Andrew Johnson and Bill Clinton, have been

**LEVEL 3:** Organize the class into four groups. Tell group members to imagine that they are a government think tank. Have them write a report that analyzes the significance of the elastic clause. *(Students should explain that it allows Congress to stretch the delegated powers listed in the Constitution to address situations that developed long after the Constitution was written.)*
**COOPERATIVE LEARNING**

## TEACH OBJECTIVE 3

**ALL LEVELS:** Organize the class into pairs. Then have pairs of students write lists including the special powers of Congress. *(Students' lists should contain the following— House—can start impeachment hearings, originates all bills for*

*raising money, if no candidate for president receives the number of votes needed to be elected it elects the president; Senate—holds impeachment trials, if no candidate for vice president receives the number of votes needed to be elected it chooses the vice president, it approves all agreements with foreign countries with a two-thirds vote, approves certain elected officials appointed by the president.)* Then have the students find newspaper and magazine articles that illustrate each of the powers of Congress. Have the students present their examples to the class.
**ENGLISH LANGUAGE LEARNERS , COOPERATIVE LEARNING**

impeached. At his impeachment trial in the Senate in 1868, President Johnson was found not guilty by only one vote. President Clinton was impeached in December 1998 on charges that he lied under oath and obstructed justice. The Senate found Clinton not guilty of both charges. In 1974 the threat of impeachment led President Richard M. Nixon to resign from office.

✔**Reading Check** Sequencing List the steps necessary for removing a high official from office. The House draws up charges against the accused official and votes on them. If the majority of the House approves the list of charges, the Senate then holds court to decide whether the official will be dismissed.

### ★ Special Powers

The Constitution gives each house of Congress a number of special powers. The House of Representatives has three special powers.

1. The House alone can start impeachment proceedings.
2. All bills for raising money must begin in the House.
3. If no presidential candidate receives the number of electoral votes needed to be elected, House members choose the president.

The Senate has four special powers.

1. All impeachment trials must be held in the Senate.
2. If no vice-presidential candidate receives the number of electoral votes needed to be elected, then senators choose the vice president.
3. All treaties, or written agreements, with foreign nations must be approved in the Senate by a two-thirds vote.
4. Certain high officials appointed by the president must be approved in the Senate by a majority vote. Such officials include justices of the Supreme Court.

✔**Reading Check** Drawing Inferences and Conclusions How do the special powers granted to the House of Representatives and the Senate balance the two houses of Congress? Students might say that neither house can monopolize any actions related to impeachment or to elections and appointments of high officials.

*Richard Nixon was the only president to resign from office.*

**Interpreting the Visual Record**

**Impeachment** *Chief Justice William Rehnquist, seated at the back, presides over the impeachment trial of President Bill Clinton.* **Why do you think the chief justice of the Supreme Court was selected to preside over the trial?**

### ★ Constitutional Heritage

**Limiting the Legislature**
The inclusion of Article I, Section 9, of the U.S. Constitution marked the first time in history that a legislative body had limits placed upon its powers. Historically kings had been legally curbed by various provisions in documents such as charters, but never had a parliamentary body had these limits placed on its powers. When arguing in support of this portion of the Constitution, Jefferson wrote: "An elective despotism was not the government we fought for." James Madison concurred, arguing that "... the people ought to indulge all their jealousy and exhaust all their precautions."

**CRITICAL THINKING**
Do you think the framers' experience with Parliament led them to place limits on the legislative branch? Support your answer.

**ANSWER:** Some students might suggest that parliamentary abuses may have led to such a measure, while others might suggest that the founders were simply being cautious.

**Visual Record Answer**

*Students might suggest that he was chosen for impartiality.*

**LEVELS 2 AND 3:** Have each student create a chart. In the first column students should identify the special powers designated to Congress. *(See the All Levels lesson for powers.)* Then have them name the limits on the powers of Congress and write their responses in the second column, beside the list of powers. Then reconvene as a class and have students debate the following question: *Do congressmembers have too much power or do these limits "tie their hands"?*

## CLOSE

Have students use newspapers and other periodicals to create collages illustrating the powers of Congress. Students should be prepared to discuss how each part of their collages represents these powers. Call on volunteers to present their collages to the class. Have the class suggest ways in which powers illustrated in the collages are limited.

### Interdisciplinary Connection

#### ▶ Language ◀ Arts

*Habeas Corpus* The Latin words *habeas corpus* literally mean "you should have the body." In practice, the court is saying to law-enforcement officials, "bring us the accused person" so that the person can be charged with a specific crime. The right of *habeas corpus* helps prevent unlawful imprisonment and thus protects the rights of all individuals.

**ACTIVITY:** Have students use outside resources (such as a dictionary, encyclopedia, or thesaurus) to investigate the etymology of other terms used in this section. Suggest they find the origins of the term *ex post facto laws.* Ask students to write down their findings and share them with a partner.

**Holt Researcher**

**go.hrw.com**
**KEYWORD:** Holt Researcher
**Freefind:** Watergate

Look up information on President Richard Nixon and the Watergate scandal on the Holt Researcher. Use the information to write a short editorial that answers the following question: Do you think it was appropriate for President Nixon to resign from office rather than face possible impeachment? Why or why not?

## ★ Limits on Powers

The powers of Congress are limited in several important ways. The Supreme Court has the power to decide when Congress has overstepped the powers granted to it by the Constitution. (You will read more about this in Chapter 7.) When the Court rules that Congress has passed a law that exceeds Congress's constitutional powers, this law has no force. The Tenth Amendment to the Constitution reserves those powers not specifically granted to the national government for the state governments. These reserved powers include the states' authority with regard to elections, education, and marriage.

In addition, Article I, Section 9, of the Constitution denies certain powers to Congress. The Constitution specifically forbids Congress from the following actions.

**Passing Ex Post Facto Laws**  A law that applies to an action that occurred before the law was passed is called an *ex post facto* **law.** For example, Congress cannot pass a law banning the use of foreign cars and then have people arrested who used foreign cars *before* the law was passed.

**Passing Bills of Attainder**  A law that sentences a person to prison without a trial is called a **bill of attainder.** The Constitution provides that anyone accused of a crime must be given a trial in a court of law.

**Suspending the Writ of *Habeas Corpus***  A person accused of a crime has the right to a **writ of *habeas corpus.*** This writ is a court order requiring that the accused person be brought to court. The court can then determine if there is enough evidence to hold the person for trial. This system prevents a person from being kept in jail indefinitely. The only exception to this rule can occur in times of rebellion or invasion.

**Taxing Exports**  Goods that are sent to other countries are called exports. A tax on exports would harm the country's foreign and domestic trade. However, Congress can pass taxes on imports.

**Passing Laws that Violate the Bill of Rights**  The Bill of Rights spells out the rights and freedoms of all U.S. citizens. Congress may not pass any law that violates these rights.

**Favoring Trade of a State**  Congress cannot pass laws giving a state or group of states an unfair trade advantage. Laws regulating trade must apply equally to all states.

**Granting Titles of Nobility**  Americans believe that all people are created equal. They are opposed to establishing a noble class, or small group of persons with rights superior to those of other citizens.

# REVIEW AND ASSESS

Have students complete the **Section 3 Review** on page 131. Then have them complete **Daily Quiz 5.3**. As **Alternative Assessment**, you may want to use the dramatic scene or think-tank report activities in this section's lessons.

## RETEACH

Have students complete **Main Idea Activity for English Language Learners and Special-Needs Students 5.3**. Then organize the class into four teams and assign each team one topic covered in this section. *(Topics include congressional powers, elastic clause, special powers, and limits on congressional power.)* Then have each team list at least five facts that could help other students understand their assigned topic. Create a master list of all the facts on the chalkboard.

**ENGLISH LANGUAGE LEARNERS , COOPERATIVE LEARNING**

## EXTEND

Organize the class into groups and have each group create an outline, web, or chart illustrating the events discussed in this section. Have students use the library or other resources to obtain additional information on the topics covered in this section. Ask groups to use this information to add details about the events that they have selected to their graphic organizer. Then ask groups to write a paragraph to accompany their visual aid. Have each group present its completed project to the class.

**COOPERATIVE LEARNING , BLOCK SCHEDULING**

---

**Withdrawing Money Without a Law**  Congress must pass a law indicating how money shall be spent. It must also specify the amount to be spent before public funds are made available. This limitation means that Congress must pass additional laws to provide the money for carrying out any new laws it passes.

✔**Reading Check** Summarizing Describe each of the constitutional limits placed on Congress. The Constitution specifically forbids Congress from passing *ex post facto* laws, passing bills of attainder, suspending the writ of *habeas corpus,* taxing exports, passing laws violating the Bill of Rights, favoring trade of a state, granting titles of nobility, and withdrawing money without a law.

## ★ Other Roles of Congress

Over the years, the responsibilities of Congress have expanded to include roles that were not anticipated in the Constitution. One of the congressmembers' most important duties is to serve their **constituents,** or the people in their home districts or states.

Members of Congress receive thousands of e-mails, faxes, and letters from their constituents every week. Some of this mail gives opinions on issues. Other letters ask a representative or senator to vote for or against a certain piece of legislation. Most mail is from people asking for help. For example, the owner of a small company may ask how to apply for a government contract.

Another essential responsibility of Congress is its power to conduct investigations. Either house of Congress may investigate national issues. The purpose of these investigations may be to determine whether a new law is needed. At times an investigation is necessary to decide whether an existing law is being carried out as Congress intended.

✔**Reading Check** Finding the Main Idea What do congressmembers do besides make laws? They help their constituents and investigate national issues.

**Interpreting the Visual Record**

**Congressional Mail** *Members of Congress receive thousands of letters from constituents each year.* **What other means of contacting your congressperson might you use?**

# SECTION 3 Review

**go.hrw.com Homework Practice Online**
**keyword: SZ3 HP5**

1. **Define** and explain:
   - elastic clause
   - implied powers
   - treason
   - impeachment
   - *ex post facto* law
   - bill of attainder
   - writ of *habeas corpus*
   - constituents

2. **Categorizing** Copy the chart below. Use it to explain the special powers of Congress and how congressional powers are limited.

| Special Powers | Limits on Powers |
|---|---|
|  |  |
|  |  |
|  |  |

3. **Finding the Main Idea**
   a. In what five major areas does Congress have the power to make laws?
   b. Why is the elastic clause useful?

4. **Writing and Critical Thinking**
   **Evaluating** Imagine that you are a congressmember who supports building a new military academy. Write a speech that explains why Congress has the power to set up this academy. Be sure to address the fact that the Constitution does not specify that Congress can do this.

   **Consider:**
   • Article I, Section 8, of the Constitution
   • why the academy may be necessary

**Visual Record Answer**

*Students might suggest telephone calls, e-mails, or faxes.*

# Section 3 Review
## ANSWERS

1. **Define**
   • elastic clause, p. 127
   • implied powers, p. 128
   • treason, p. 128
   • impeachment, p. 128
   • *ex post facto* law, p. 130
   • bill of attainder, p. 130
   • writ of *habeas corpus*, p. 130
   • constituents, p. 131

2. House Powers—can start impeachment hearings, originates bills for raising money, elects president if needed; Senate Powers—holds impeachment trials, if needed chooses vice president, approves all agreements with foreign countries, approves certain high officials appointed by the president; Limits—no passing *ex post facto* laws or bills of attainder, no suspending the writ of *habeas corpus*, no taxing exports, no passing laws against Bill of Rights, no favoring trade of a state, no granting titles of nobility, no withdrawing money without a law

3. a. financing government, regulating and encouraging U.S. trade and industry, defending the country, enforcing laws, and providing for growth

b. It allows Congress to stretch the delegated powers listed in the Constitution to address situations that developed long after the Constitution was written.

4. Students' speeches should demonstrate an understanding of the elastic clause and how it allows Congress to handle issues that the framers could not have otherwise foreseen.

# SECTION 4

## OBJECTIVES

*After completing Section 4, students should be able to*

1 **Identify where ideas for bills originate.**

2 **Explain what happens to a bill once it is introduced in each house of Congress.**

3 **Determine the actions the president can take regarding a bill once it has passed both houses.**

## SECTION 4 RESOURCES

### REPRODUCIBLE

▶ Guided Reading Strategies 5.4

▶ Transparency 5: How Ideas for Bills Begin

▶ Readings in Economics and Government 29: Excerpt from a Filibuster

### TECHNOLOGY

▶ One-Stop Planner, Lesson 5.4

▶ Homework Practice Online

▶ HRW Go Site

### REINFORCEMENT, REVIEW, AND ASSESSMENT

▶ Section 4 Review, p. 139

▶ Daily Quiz 5.4

▶ Main Idea Activity 5.4

▶ English Audio Summary 5.4

▶ Spanish Audio Summary 5.4

## LET'S GET STARTED!

As students enter the classroom, have them identify a law they would like to see passed which has some bearing upon their lives. *(Students' suggestions will vary but should be reasonable.)* Explain to students that in the United States, voting citizens are among the groups who can originate a bill in the process of becoming a law. Ask them who else they think can originate a bill. *(Students might suggest the president and congressmembers.)* Tell students that in Section 4 they will learn more about who can propose a bill and how one is passed as law.

## SECTION 4

# How a Bill Becomes a Law

### Read to Discover

1. Where do ideas for bills originate?
2. What happens to a bill once it is introduced in each house of Congress?
3. Once a bill is passed by both houses, what actions can the president take regarding the bill?

### WHY CIVICS MATTERS

Many bills pass before Congress each year. Use **CNNfyi.com** or other **current events** sources to investigate bills currently being considered by Congress. Record your findings in your journal.

### Define

- appropriation bill
- act
- quorum
- roll-call vote
- filibuster
- cloture
- pocket veto

## *Reading Focus*

Each day that Congress is in session, an interesting scene unfolds. As the members of the House enter their legislative hall, some of them approach the front of the chamber. They drop papers into a box on the clerk's desk. This box is called the hopper. The papers dropped into it by the members are bills, or written proposals for laws.

Of course, not all of these proposals become laws. Because getting a law passed is a long and difficult process, people sometimes think that government is not responsive enough. In the long run, however, this careful process helps ensure that the country's laws will be sound ones.

*Representative Christopher Shays speaks to a group of citizens who support a bill limiting campaign contributions.*

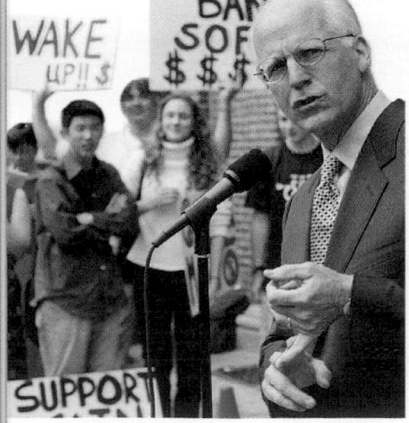

## ★ The Idea for a Bill Begins

Each year the Senate and the House of Representatives consider thousands of bills. These bills may be introduced in either house. The only exception to this rule is an **appropriation bill,** or bill approving the spending of money. It is a long-standing custom that an appropriation bill originates in the House of Representatives. Every bill must be passed by both houses of Congress. Then it can be signed by the president and become a law. A law is also known as an **act.**

Where do the ideas for these bills begin, or originate? Ideas can come from the following sources: from U.S. citizens, organized groups, congressional committees, members of Congress, and the president.

**LEVEL 1:** Lead a class discussion about the types of bills that students would like to see passed into law. Then ask each student to write on a slip of paper where he or she thinks ideas for bills originate. *(Students should indicate that ideas start with voters, individual congressmembers, groups of Americans, congressional investigating committees, or the president.)* Then collect all of the responses and write the different answers on the chalkboard. **ENGLISH LANGUAGE LEARNERS**

**LEVEL 2:** Organize the class into small groups. Have students imagine that they are members of an advertising team that has been asked to create a public service announcement explaining to the public how ideas for bills originate. *(See the Level 1 lesson for how bills originate.)* Have each group create an advertising jingle to accompany its announcement. Remind students that jingles should be informative and easy to remember. Have volunteers share their jingles with the class. *(Students' jingles should identify voters, individual congressmembers, groups of Americans, congressional investigating committees, or the president.)* **COOPERATIVE LEARNING**

**From U.S. Citizens** The people are a powerful force in influencing laws and lawmakers. When a large number of constituents requests a particular law, their congressmember usually introduces a bill that contains the constituents' ideas.

**From Organized Groups** Members of Congress sometimes introduce bills because certain groups ask them to do so. For example, businesspeople may want to limit competition from industries in other countries. Labor groups may call for laws establishing improved working conditions or higher hourly wages.

**From Committees of Congress** Many ideas for bills begin in Congress itself. Suppose that a congressional investigating committee conducts a study of certain kinds of crime. The committee may determine that the federal government needs to make a new law on crime control. The members can then draw up a bill and introduce it in Congress.

**From Members of Congress** Members of Congress often become experts in certain fields. A member who has experience with farming issues, for example, may introduce a bill to fund an agriculture program.

**From the President** The president has great influence on bills introduced in Congress. Early in each session, the president appears before a joint session of Congress to deliver the State of the Union address. In

## How Ideas for Bills Begin

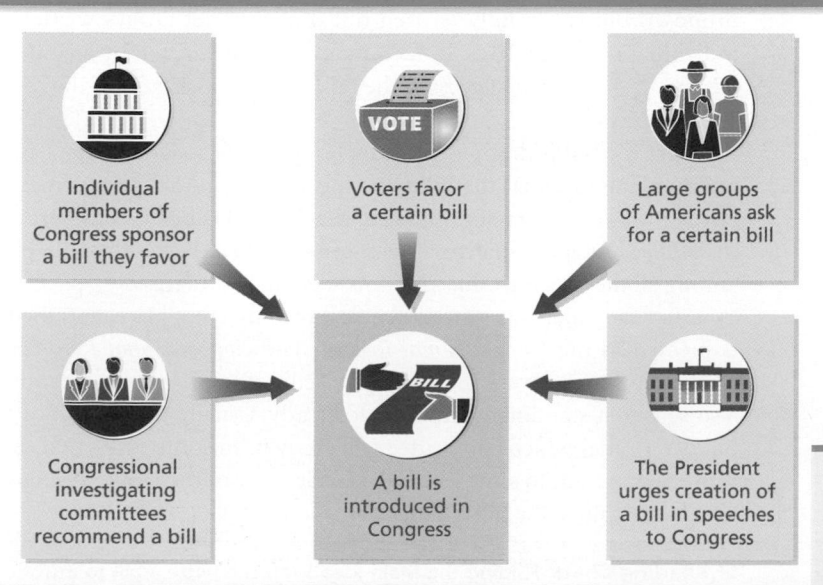

Individual members of Congress sponsor a bill they favor

Voters favor a certain bill

Large groups of Americans ask for a certain bill

Congressional investigating committees recommend a bill

A bill is introduced in Congress

The President urges creation of a bill in speeches to Congress

**Interpreting Charts**
*The ideas for new bills come from a variety of sources.* **What are ways in which Congress introduces bills?**

**Youth Voting Rights** In 1971 the U.S. Constitution was amended to lower the voting age from 21 to 18 years of age. Supporters successfully argued that if 18 years olds were old enough to be drafted to fight in a war, they were old enough to vote. Today youth groups in both Canada and the United States seek laws that give voting rights to citizens of all ages. These citizens reason that they pay sales and employment taxes and that they are affected by policy decisions made by the government. As such, they believe they should have the right to vote. Several bills regarding these issues have made it to the floors of state legislatures and city councils. Most recently, bills appeared before the 1999 Minnesota state legislature and the Cambridge, Massachusetts, city council. Both measures were defeated, however.

**CRITICAL THINKING**
Do you think a bill should be passed to lower the voting age? Support your answer.

**ANSWER:** Some students will agree with the arguments stated above. Others might suggest that young people might be influenced by their parents or might not know enough about the issues to vote.

**CHART ANSWER**
Students might suggest that Congress introduces bills at constituents' request, by investigating committees, and so on.

**LEVEL 3:** Organize the class into five groups. Assign each group one of the sources of ideas for bills listed in the textbook. Then have groups assume the identity of that source and submit an idea for a bill. (*The "voter" and "organized group" should write letters to their representatives. The "committee" and "member of Congress" might write memos. The "president" might prepare a speech.*) Remind students that they have to support their reasoning. Have groups present their ideas to the class and respond to any challenges. **COOPERATIVE LEARNING**

# TEACH OBJECTIVE 2

**LEVEL 1:** Have students work in pairs to explain what happens to a bill once it is introduced in each house of Congress. (*Students' lists should show that a new bill is given a letter and a number to indicate the house it was introduced in and the order. Then it goes to a standing committee. If it is not set aside, hearings are held about the bill. Changes are made after careful study, then the bill is sent to the floor to be considered by the House.*) Then have them write a series of newspaper headlines that track a fictitious bill's progress following its introduction. Pairs should present and explain their headlines to the class. **ENGLISH LANGUAGE LEARNERS**

**Interpreting the Visual Record**

**New laws** *The president has a responsibility to suggest and approve or oppose legislation proposed by Congress.* **How does this image of President Reagan illustrate the heavy workload that the president must take on?**

this speech the president recommends laws that he or she believes are needed to improve the country's well-being. Many of these ideas are soon introduced as bills by members of Congress.

✔ **Reading Check** Summarizing What groups or individuals might come up with ideas for bills? U.S. citizens, organized groups, committees of Congress, members of Congress, the president

## ★ An Idea Becomes a Bill

Although anyone can suggest an idea for a bill, only members of Congress can introduce a bill. Suppose that a group of citizens favors the creation of a new national park. The citizens write to the congressmembers for their state or district to explain their idea. The group's leader arranges a meeting with a congressmember to discuss the idea.

At this meeting the leader provides facts and figures on the subject and urges that a bill be introduced. If the senator or representative is convinced that the group's idea is a good one, he or she may agree to introduce or sponsor the bill in Congress. To learn how a bill becomes a law, follow the progress of the national park bill. It goes first to the House of Representatives and then to the Senate for consideration.

## ★ The Bill Is Introduced in the House

How does the representative introduce this bill in the House? First, the proposed bill is carefully written out. Bills are not always written by individual representatives. In fact, many bills are written by a committee, by the group that suggested the bill, or by an assistant on the representative's staff.

After the bill is dropped into the hopper, it is assigned letters and a number. Suppose that the bill to create a new national park is marked H.R. 1215. The letters *H.R.* indicate that the bill is being considered by the House of Representatives. The number *1215* indicates the bill's place among all the bills introduced in this session of Congress.

After the bill is introduced, the first reading takes place, and the bill is printed in the *Congressional Record*. The *Congressional Record* is a publication that covers the daily proceedings of Congress. The bill is also sent to a standing committee for study. Usually the subject of the bill determines which committee will study it. In some cases, two committees may want to study the bill. The Speaker of the House decides to which committee the bill will be sent.

✔ **Reading Check** Finding the Main Idea Who can write a bill to introduce in Congress and what happens to the bill after it is introduced? A representative, a committee, the group that suggested it, or the representative's assistant may write a bill. An introduced bill is named, printed in the Congressional Record, and then sent to a standing committee for consideration.

## The Bill Is Sent to Committee

In the case of H.R. 1215, the Speaker sends the bill to the House Resources Committee. The committee then refers the bill to the appropriate subcommittee for review. In this case, the House Subcommittee on National Parks, Recreation, and Public Lands will receive the bill for consideration.

Each bill is given careful attention by the committee and subcommittee to which it is sent. In many cases, members of the committee or subcommittee decide that the bill is unnecessary. Such a bill is set aside and is never returned to the House for action. By setting aside bills that they consider unnecessary, the committees reduce the amount of legislation Congress must consider.

H.R. 1215 is not set aside. Instead, the House Resources Committee holds hearings on the bill. Most committee hearings like this one are open to the public. Many important congressional hearings are shown on television. Televising hearings and keeping them open to the public allows voters to stay informed about various bills. People can also learn about the issues surrounding a particular piece of legislation.

At the hearings the committee calls witnesses to testify for and against the bill. These witnesses give committee members the information they need to recommend that the bill be accepted, rejected, or changed. Aside from this testimony, letters from citizens and evidence gathered by committee members from many other sources will be considered. All of this evidence will help the committee reach a decision on the bill.

In the case of H.R. 1215, the Resources Committee decides to change parts of the bill in certain ways. Members rewrite paragraphs and add new sections. When they are finished, the bill is very different from the one they originally received. The majority of committee members decide to recommend that the House pass the bill as amended by the standing committee.

*Congress holds hearings on issues touching all areas of American life. Here the House Judiciary Committee investigating baseball asks questions of the commissioner of baseball (far left).*

✔ **Reading Check Identifying Cause and Effect** Why are committees necessary, and what happens to a bill during committee hearings? to determine whether a bill should be accepted, rejected or changed; witnesses testify for or against the bill

## The House Considers the Bill

When the House Resources Committee recommends H.R. 1215, it is officially reported out of committee. The bill is then sent back to the House of Representatives lend placed on the House calendar. The calendar is the schedule that lists the order in which bills have been reported out of committee. However, bills do not usually come to the floor in the same order in which they appear on the schedule. The Speaker of the House

**LEVEL 3:** Lead a class discussion about the process a bill must go through to become a law. Emphasize the point at which a bill goes to committee. *(See the Level 1 lesson for process.)* Then have a group of students draw up an imaginary bill that would accomplish a worthy goal to submit to a "class congress." Organize the rest of the class into a number of committees relevant to the goal of the bill. Then have the first group present its bill to each group for consideration. Each committee must decide whether it will support the bill and then should explain its decision to the class. **COOPERATIVE LEARNING**

## TEACH OBJECTIVE 3

**LEVEL 1:** Have students create pantomimes that depict the actions a president can take regarding a bill once it has passed both houses. *(Students' pantomimes should illustrate that the president can sign the bill, veto it, or keep it for 10 days without signing it. This is called a pocket veto if Congress is out of session.)* Encourage students to refer to their textbooks for more information. Call on volunteers to act out their pantomimes and have the class identify which action they are demonstrating. **ENGLISH LANGUAGE LEARNERS**

---

## The Democratic Process

### Emergency Legislation

World events can frequently affect the workload of Congress. For example, following the September 11, 2001, attacks on the World Trade Center and the Pentagon, over 250 bills were submitted to Congress. Bills that passed into law cover such areas as providing benefits to public servants who helped maintain order during the crisis, tightening security and extending intelligence-gathering measures, and declaring the date "Patriot Day."

### CRITICAL THINKING

What type of bills regarding this issue might be promoted by citizen groups? By U.S. leaders?

**ANSWER:** Students will note the likelihood of citizens to ask for protections of their person and rights and governments' desire to take measures to oversee the country as a whole.

### Visual Record Answer

*Students should say the Democrats.*

---

determines when or if a bill will reach the floor and where it will be debated.

H.R. 1215 must be given three readings in the House of Representatives. By the time it comes up on the calendar, the first reading has already occurred. It took place when the title of the bill was first read to the House before sending it to the appropriate standing committee. The second reading will occur when the bill is considered on the floor.

The House Rules Committee decides how much time will be given to debate this bill. The time to be spent in debate, or discussion, is divided evenly between supporters and opponents of the bill.

For the debate, the House can act as a Committee of the Whole. As one large committee, the House can act less formally and turn the meeting into a work session. The bill is now given its second reading. A clerk reads either the entire bill or portions of it, and then amendments may be offered. Debate on each amendment is usually limited to several minutes for each member who speaks. A vote is then taken on the amendment. It is usually a voice vote with all members in favor saying "yea" and all those opposed saying "nay."

Each paragraph of the bill is read and amended in similar fashion until the entire bill has been considered. Either during the Committee of the Whole or when the House meets again in formal session, a member may demand a "quorum call." A **quorum,** or majority of the members, must be present in order to do business. During the Committee of the Whole, a quorum is equal to 100 members.

✔ **Reading Check Summarizing** How does the House go about considering a bill? The bill is read a second time on the floor and debated. Then amendments are offered and voted on.

**Interpreting the Visual Record**

**Voting on bills** *After hearings, committee recommendations, and changes are completed, the time comes to vote on a bill.* **Based on this vote count, which party appears to support the bill being voted on?**

## ★ The House Votes on the Bill

When action has been completed on amendments, the House is ready for the third reading. This reading is usually by title only. A member may occasionally demand, however, that the bill be read in its entirety. The vote is then taken. In most cases a majority is needed to pass a bill.

On important bills a **roll-call vote** is usually taken. Each member's name is called, and a record is made of his or her vote. The bill to create a new national park, as amended, passes the House. But it is not yet a law. Like all bills, it must now be considered by the other house of Congress, the Senate.

✔ **Reading Check Analyzing Information** If a bill passes the House, does it become a law? No, the bill must pass both houses to become a law.

**ALL LEVELS:** Copy the following graphic organizer onto the chalkboard, omitting the italicized answers. Have students complete the organizer to describe the actions the president can take regarding a bill once it has been passed.
**ENGLISH LANGUAGE LEARNERS**

**LEVEL 2:** Tell students to imagine that they have been asked to create a bulletin board display describing the actions the president can take regarding a bill once it has been passed. Students should begin by listing the actions. Then suggest they work in pairs to design graphic depictions of each action. Tell students that they may refer to their texts for ideas. *(See the Level 1 lesson for actions.)* **COOPERATIVE LEARNING**

Presidential Actions Regarding a Passed Bill

*sign it*  |  *veto it*  |  *keep it for 10 days without signing it*

## The Senate Acts on the Bill

In the Senate, the bill is called S. 2019. The way in which a bill is handled in the Senate is similar to the process followed in the House of Representatives. Bill S. 2019 is read by title, for its first reading. It is then sent to the Senate Energy and Natural Resources Committee. After holding hearings, the committee revises S. 2019. The committee then recommends that the bill be passed by the Senate.

The senators usually are not limited in their debate of the bill, unlike members of the House of Representatives. In the Senate, speeches may last a long time. To prevent the Senate from taking a vote on a bill, some senators have talked for many hours, thereby "talking the bill to death." This method of delay by making lengthy speeches is called a **filibuster.** Debate in the Senate can be limited only if at least three fifths of the full Senate vote to limit it. Limit on debate in the Senate is called **cloture.**

After the members of the Senate finish their debate on S. 2019, a roll call is taken. Bill S. 2019 passes. What happens next?

**Interpreting the Visual Record**

**Filibuster** *This 1965 photo shows Senate leader Everett Dirksen as he prepares materials to read in a filibuster.* **Why do you think the senator has collected so much reading material for the filibuster?**

✔ **Reading Check Comparing and Contrasting** How is the process that the Senate uses to handle a bill similar to and different from that of the House of Representatives? similar—bill reviewed by a committee and hearings are held; different—senators usually not limited in their debate and can filibuster

## The House and the Senate Agree on the Final Bill

When a bill passes the House and Senate in identical form, it is ready to be sent to the president for his signature. However, the two houses usually pass different versions of the same bill. If a bill is changed, it must be sent back to the house that originated it for another vote. In the example of the national park bill, suppose the House of Representatives does not agree to the Senate changes. When this happens, a conference committee must be called.

A conference committee meets to reach an agreement on the bill. The committee is made up of an equal number of senators and representatives. The committee members from each house may have to give up something to reach a compromise.

Finally, a compromise bill is sent back to both houses. Usually both houses approve the work of the conference committee.

✔ **Reading Check Summarizing** Once each house passes a bill, what steps must be followed? If it is not identical, it returns to the originating house for another vote. If the revised bill is not accepted by its original house, it is sent to a conference committee. The conference committee must create a compromise bill that must then be passed by both houses.

## The Democratic Process

**Filibuster Tactics** Some senators have read telephone books, almanacs, and baseball statistics in their filibuster attempts. These efforts to prolong debate have irritated many senators, particularly those in the majority, who want to pass the bill. Yet others, such as Illinois senator Everett Dirksen, have taken a different view. He once called the filibuster "the only weapon which the minority has to protect itself."

**ACTIVITY:** Obtain a copy of the movie *Mr. Smith Goes to Washington.* After viewing it with the class, lead a debate over the fairness of using a filibuster with the students. Focus the debate around this question: *Under what conditions, if any, should congressmembers have a right to filibuster?*

**Visual Record Answer**

*Students might suggest that he will need a great deal of reading material with which to filibuster.*

*The Legislative Branch* **137**

**LEVELS 2 AND 3:** Organize the class into three groups. Assign each group one of the three actions a president can take on a bill once it has been passed. *(Group actions will include signing a bill, vetoing it, and pocket vetoing it.)* Then have students obtain information on a bill that the president acted on in their assigned way. Have each group create a poster that features information about the bill, including reasons why the president acted on it the way that he did. Have students use a combination of pictures and their own drawings to complete their projects. Have groups present their posters to the class.

**COOPERATIVE LEARNING**

## CLOSE

Provide students with paper and markers to create a hand-rolled movie about the procedure a bill follows from introduction through passage into law. Instruct students to include before-and-after scenes involving its origins and the president's actions as well as narration of the scenes. Have volunteers present their movies to the class.

---

### ★ Civics Sidelight

**ABC Teaches Civics** In the 1970s the American Broadcasting Company (ABC) television network created a series of public service segments that were aired during children's programs. The segments sought to instruct students on a variety of topics. One segment "I'm Just a Bill," which aired in 1975, details the complex process a bill goes through to become a law. The first few lines begin:

"I'm just a bill,

Yes, I'm only a bill,

And I'm sitting here on Capitol Hill."

**ACTIVITY:** Have students write their own song from the point of view of a bill submitted to Congress. Students should use the first person. The song should also address what happens to the bill after it has been passed and reaches the president's desk.

---

**CHART ANSWER**

The conference committee irons out the differences between the House and Senate versions of the bill and then returns the revised bill to both houses for approval.

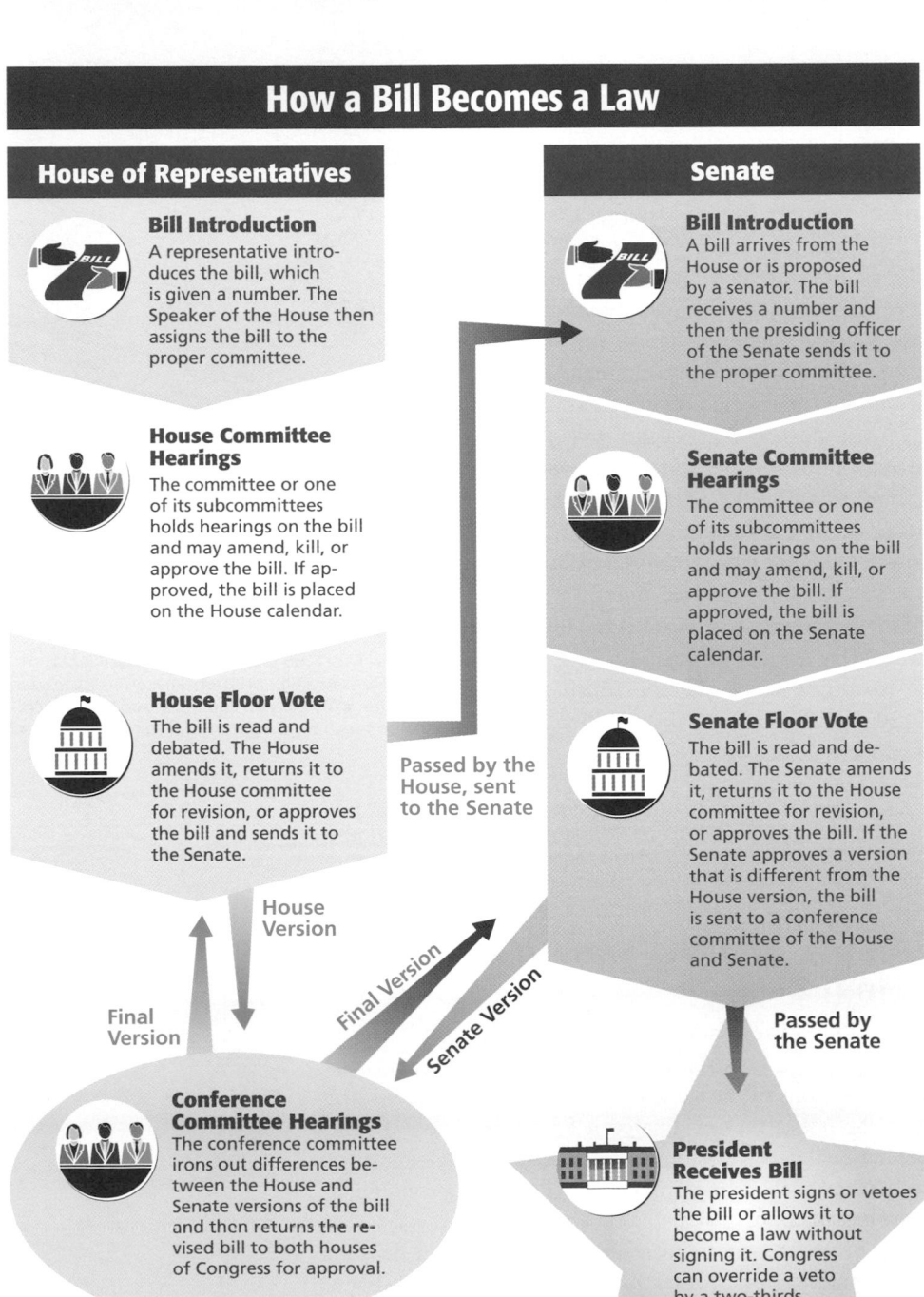

## How a Bill Becomes a Law

### House of Representatives

**Bill Introduction**
A representative introduces the bill, which is given a number. The Speaker of the House then assigns the bill to the proper committee.

**House Committee Hearings**
The committee or one of its subcommittees holds hearings on the bill and may amend, kill, or approve the bill. If approved, the bill is placed on the House calendar.

**House Floor Vote**
The bill is read and debated. The House amends it, returns it to the House committee for revision, or approves the bill and sends it to the Senate.

### Senate

**Bill Introduction**
A bill arrives from the House or is proposed by a senator. The bill receives a number and then the presiding officer of the Senate sends it to the proper committee.

**Senate Committee Hearings**
The committee or one of its subcommittees holds hearings on the bill and may amend, kill, or approve the bill. If approved, the bill is placed on the Senate calendar.

**Senate Floor Vote**
The bill is read and debated. The Senate amends it, returns it to the House committee for revision, or approves the bill. If the Senate approves a version that is different from the House version, the bill is sent to a conference committee of the House and Senate.

Passed by the House, sent to the Senate

House Version

Final Version

Final Version

Senate Version

Passed by the Senate

**Conference Committee Hearings**
The conference committee irons out differences between the House and Senate versions of the bill and then returns the revised bill to both houses of Congress for approval.

**President Receives Bill**
The president signs or vetoes the bill or allows it to become a law without signing it. Congress can override a veto by a two-thirds vote of each house.

**Interpreting Charts** *The House and Senate use similar procedures to approve or kill new bills.* **What is the purpose of the conference committee?**

## ★ The President Approves the Bill

Once both houses have agreed upon and passed a final version of the bill, it is ready for the next step. The bill is sent to the president of the United States for approval. The president may take one of three possible actions on a bill from Congress.

1. The president may sign the bill and declare it to be a law.
2. The president may refuse to sign the bill. Instead, the bill is sent back to Congress with a message giving the president's reasons for rejecting it. This action is called a veto.
3. The president may choose to keep the bill for 10 days without signing or vetoing it. If Congress is in session during this 10-day period, the bill becomes a law without the president's signature. However, if Congress is not in session and the president does not sign the bill within 10 days, it does not become a law. Instead, the bill has been killed by a **pocket veto.** Presidents do not use the pocket veto often.

Congress has the power to pass a bill over a presidential veto by a two-thirds vote of both houses. However, it is usually difficult to obtain the necessary votes to override a presidential veto. In the case of this national park bill, the president signs it into law and it goes into effect afterward.

The long and involved process of making laws may be slow. Yet it does prevent hasty legislation while providing a way for the federal government to pass needed laws.

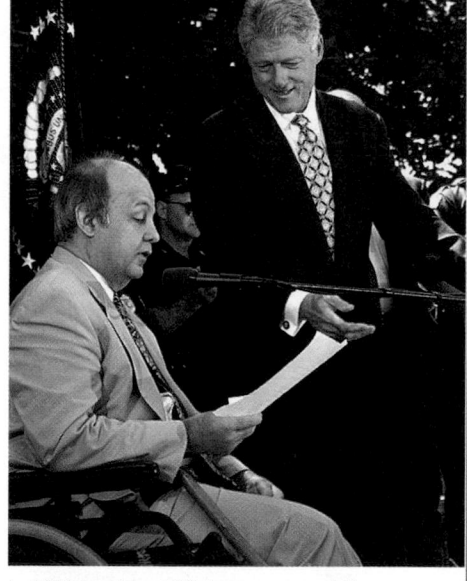

*In 1993 President Clinton approved the Handgun Violence Prevention Act, also called the Brady Bill, after former presidential press secretary James Brady, shown at left.*

✔ **Reading Check Drawing Inferences and Conclusions** Why is it important for the president to have final approval over congressional legislation? Why is political conflict in the United States generally less divisive than in other nations? Students might say to keep a balance of power and to make sure the national interest is being served. All parties respect the Constitution, use the legal system to manage conflicts, and respect checks and balances.

## SECTION 4 Review

**go.hrw.com Homework Practice Online**
keyword: SZ3 HP5

1. **Define** and explain:
   - appropriation bill
   - act
   - quorum
   - roll-call vote
   - filibuster
   - cloture
   - pocket veto

2. **Summarizing** Copy the graphic organizer below. Use it to identify the various sources for new legislation.

Ideas for a Bill

3. **Finding the Main Idea**
   a. What happens after a bill is introduced in the House?
   b. Explain the actions that the president can take on a bill that has been passed by both houses of Congress.

4. **Writing and Critical Thinking**
   **Sequencing** Imagine that you are a senator who has been invited to visit your class. Write a presentation explaining the process a bill follows to become a law.
   **Consider:**
   - the stages through which the bill must pass to become a law
   - how citizens can become involved in the process

## Review and Assessment Resources

### REPRODUCIBLE
- Chapter 5 Review, pp. 140–141
- Vocabulary Activity 5
- Chapter 5 Tutorial for Students, Parents, Mentors, and Peers
- Chapter 5 Test (Form A or B)
- Alternative Assessment Handbook, Chapter 5

### TECHNOLOGY
- Chapter 5 Test Generator (on the One-Stop Planner)
- Global Skill Builder CD–ROM
- HRW Go site

### REINFORCEMENT, REVIEW, AND ASSESSMENT
- Chapter 5 Test for English Language Learners and Special-Needs Students

### REVIEW
Have students complete the **Chapter 5 Review** on pages 140–141.

### ASSESS
Use one of the chapter tests to assess students' understanding of the content. For **Alternative Assessment**, see the **Alternative Assessment Handbook**.

---

### Understanding Main Ideas

**1.** to check and balance the work of each house and to ensure the equal representation of large and small states.

**2.** expulsion and censure

**3.** House—Speaker, floor leaders, and party whips; Senate—president, president *pro tempore*, majority leader, minority leader, and party whips. The House Speaker, Senate president, and president *pro tempore* are named in the Constitution, and the party leaders are chosen in caucuses.

**4.** to divide the large workload

**5.** House—can start impeachment hearings, originates all bills for raising money, if there are not enough votes it elects the president; Senate—holds impeachment trials, if there are not enough votes it chooses the vice president, approves all agreements with foreign countries with a two-thirds vote; approves certain appointed high officials.

**6.** They are introduced, sent to committee, heard and debated on by full house, sent to other house if passed, possibly sent to conference committee, then sent to president if passed by both houses.

**7.** The president can sign the bill, veto it, or keep it for 10 days without signing it. (This is called a pocket veto if Congress is out of session.)

---

## Chapter 5 Review

### Chapter Summary

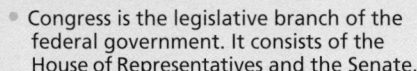

#### Section 1
- Congress is the legislative branch of the federal government. It consists of the House of Representatives and the Senate.
- Representation in the House is based on state population. Each state is represented in the Senate by two senators.
- Senators and representatives must meet certain qualifications to be elected.

#### Section 2
- Congress meets for two regular sessions in each of its terms. Much of the work of Congress is done by committees.
- The leader of the House is called the Speaker. The vice president leads the Senate. In the vice president's absence the president *pro tempore* leads the Senate.

#### Section 3
- The Constitution grants Congress the law-making authority to finance government, regulate trade and industry, defend the country, enforce laws, and provide for growth.
- The elastic clause allows Congress to exercise implied powers not specifically granted to it.
- The Constitution reserves certain powers for the states and specifically forbids some powers to Congress.

#### Section 4
- Congress considers thousands of bills each year that come from U.S. citizens, organized groups, congressional committees, congressmembers, and the president.
- The legislative process is long and involves many steps. To become a law, each bill must be passed by both houses before being signed by the president.

### Define and Identify
Use the following terms in complete sentences.
1. gerrymandering
2. expulsion
3. caucuses
4. Speaker
5. party whip
6. committees
7. implied powers
8. bill of attainder
9. quorum
10. pocket veto

### Understanding Main Ideas
**Section 1** *(Pages 113–18)*
1. Why did the framers of the Constitution create a bicameral national legislature?
2. What two methods does Congress have to deal with misconduct by its members?

**Section 2** *(Pages 119–24)*
3. Who leads the houses of Congress, and how are these leaders chosen?
4. Why is most of the work of Congress done through committees?

**Section 3** *(Pages 126–31)*
5. What special powers does each house of Congress have?

**Section 4** *(Pages 132–39)*
6. How do bills become laws?
7. What can the president do with a bill passed by Congress?

### What Did You Find Out?
1. What qualifications must a person meet to run for Congress?
2. How do committees affect the work of Congress?
3. Describe the impeachment process.

### Thinking Critically
1. **Drawing Inferences and Conclusions** Why do you think that the House limits debate on a bill, but the Senate does not?
2. **Supporting a Point of View** The Senate has fewer members than the House, and senators have longer terms of office than representatives. The Senate also receives more media attention than the House. Do you think these factors affect how responsive the Senate is to the needs of the people? Explain your answer.
3. **Comparing and Contrasting** What are the advantages and disadvantages of having Congress follow a lengthy and complex lawmaking process?

## RETEACH

Have students assign visual symbols to as many vocabulary terms for this chapter as time permits. They should find terms that lend themselves to graphic representation. For example, bicameral might be symbolized by two houses within a diagram of the Capitol. For each vocabulary term, students should draw the symbol, write the term, and define the term.

**ENGLISH LANGUAGE LEARNERS ,
COOPERATIVE LEARNING**

## Portfolio Extensions

**1. Linking to Community** Invite a staff member from a Senate or House office to speak to your class about the day-to-day business of getting a bill through Congress, including the sources of ideas for bills. Have each student prepare a list of appropriate questions to ask the speaker. For example, they might ask the staff member to explain the process of researching and preparing the bill to be introduced—who does the research—staff or outside groups?

**2. Cooperative Learning** Organize students into small groups. Ask each group to conduct research outside of class to find a local group that is petitioning its representative to propose a new law. Then have each group prepare a three- to five-minute lesson about government participation, incorporating its research into the presentation. Allow students to choose the format of their lesson. Finally, have students present their lessons to the class.

---

## Building Social Studies Skills

**STANDARDIZED TEST PREP ONLINE** keyword: SZ3 STP5

### Interpreting Tables

Study the table on Standing Committees of Congress below. Then use the information in the table to answer the questions that follow.

#### Standing Committees of Congress

**House**

Agriculture; Appropriations; Banking and Financial Services; Budget; Commerce; Economic and Educational Opportunities; Government Reform and Oversight; House Oversight; International Relations; Judiciary; National Security; Resources; Rules; Science; Small Business; Standards of Official Conduct; Transportation and Infrastructure; Veterans' Affairs; Ways and Means

**Senate**

Agriculture, Nutrition, and Forestry; Appropriations; Armed Services; Banking, Housing and Urban Affairs; Budget; Commerce, Science, and Transportation; Energy and Natural Resources; Environment and Public Works; Finance; Foreign Relations; Governmental Affairs; Indian Affairs; Judiciary; Labor and Human Resources; Rules and Administration; Small Business; Veterans' Affairs

1. Which of the following committees exist in both the House of Representatives and the Senate?
   a. Appropriations and Government Reform and Oversight
   b. Finance and Ways and Means
   c. Small Business and Standards of Official Conduct
   d. Budget and Veterans' Affairs
2. Based on your knowledge of Congress and the names of the committees shown in the table, would you say that economic issues are or are not an important subject of congressional affairs? Explain your answer.

### Analyzing Primary Sources

Read the following quotation from Senate Majority Leader and Democrat Tom Daschle as he calls for a vote on a special resolution in response to the September 11, 2001, terrorist attacks. Then answer the questions that follow.

"Mr. President, as I think certainly everyone on the floor knows, but for those who may be viewing our proceedings, and should know, our caucuses have been meeting for the last hour to review the work which has been done by colleagues on both sides of the aisle in concert with the administration and with the House of Representatives. This work has been ongoing now for several days. . . . Let me say, . . . how much I appreciate, once again, the leadership of our Republican leader [the president]. . . . I commend him, and I thank all of our colleagues for their remarkable participation during this difficult week."

3. Which of the following statements best expresses Daschle's point of view?
   a. He is happy that the Senate and the president have worked together against the House of Representatives.
   b. He appreciates the cooperation that Congress, the president, and members of both political parties have shown.
   c. He appreciates how the president has led both houses of Congress.
   d. He is upset at the lack of progress that has been made during a difficult week.
4. How does this quotation demonstrate the importance of cooperation between the executive branch, political parties, and both houses of Congress during times of crisis?

---

### Alternative Assessment

## Building Your Portfolio

**Interdisciplinary Connection to Government**

Choose one person who serves your state as a representative or senator in Congress. Write a profile of this person. Be sure to provide background information, such as place of birth, education, and occupation. Also provide information on the person's political experience such as offices held, length of service in Congress, political party membership, and positions on key issues.

**internet connect**

**Internet Activity: go.hrw.com**
keyword: SZ3 AC5

Access the Internet through the HRW Go site to compare and contrast the roles, requirements, and powers of both houses of Congress. Then create an illustrated diagram to present your information. Focus on issues such as term lengths, number of members, and any other information that is unique to either the House or the Senate.

---

### What Did You Find Out?

1. House—at least 25 years old, U.S. citizen for seven years, and a legal resident of state to represent; Senate—at least 30 years old, a U.S. citizen for nine years, and a legal resident of state to represent

2. They lighten the workload of each individual congressmember.

3. The House draws up charges if the majority agrees, the impeachment is approved, and the leader is brought to trial.

### Thinking Critically

1. Students might note that the Senate has fewer members.

2. Students should explain how these factors do or do not affect the speed and effectiveness with which the Senate meets the public's needs.

3. Pros may include that bills will be fully considered before becoming law. Cons may include that it is too slow and difficult to understand to fully meet the needs of the citizens.

### Skills Workshop

1. d

2. Some students may note that they are important because they appear in 2 to 3 committees of each house. Others may note that this is a relatively small number of committees compared to the overall variety.

3. b

4. Students may suggest that the process is complex and the workload is time-consuming as it is, without cooperation it would be even more so.

| Objectives | Pacing Guide | Reproducible Resources |
|---|---|---|
| **SECTION 1:**<br>**The Presidency**<br>(pp. 143–46)<br><br>★ Identify the qualifications and terms of office for the presidency.<br>★ Describe the duties of and terms of office for the vice president.<br>★ Explain the order of presidential succession. | **Regular**<br>1 day<br><br>**Block Scheduling**<br>.5 day<br><br>*Block Scheduling Handbook with Team Teaching Strategies, Chapter 6* | **RS** Guided Reading Strategies 6.1<br>**RS** Readings in Economics and Government 17: U.S. Presidential Oath of Office<br>**RS** Readings in Economics and Government 31: John F. Kennedy's Inaugural Address |
| **SECTION 2:**<br>**Powers and Roles of the President**<br>(pp. 147–52)<br><br>★ Describe how the president is involved in the legislative process.<br>★ Explain how Congress limits the president's powers as commander in chief.<br>★ Identify the president's duties as foreign-policy leader and as chief of state. | **Regular**<br>1 day<br><br>**Block Scheduling**<br>.5 day<br><br>*Block Scheduling Handbook with Team Teaching Strategies, Chapter 6* | **RS** Guided Reading Strategies 6.2<br>**RS** Readings in Economics and Government 28: Woodrow Wilson's "Fourteen Points"<br>**PS** American Civics Political Cartoon: Watergate<br>**E** Creative Teaching Strategy: Role-Playing<br>**RS** Graphic Organizer Activity: The President's Many Hats |
| **SECTION 3:**<br>**Executive Departments and the Cabinet**<br>(pp. 153–61)<br><br>★ Define the Executive Office of the President and explain its purpose.<br>★ Describe how heads of the executive departments and members of the cabinet are related.<br>★ Name the 14 executive departments. | **Regular**<br>1 day<br><br>**Block Scheduling**<br>.5 day<br><br>*Block Scheduling Handbook with Team Teaching Strategies, Chapter 6* | **RS** Guided Reading Strategies 6.3<br>**E** Challenge and Enrichment Worksheet 6: Identifying the President's Cabinet<br>**SM** Community Service and Participation Handbook: "Ask What You Can Do" |
| **SECTION 4:**<br>**Independent Agencies and Regulatory Commissions**<br>(pp. 163–65)<br><br>★ Identify the independent agencies and explain why they are separate from the executive departments.<br>★ Evaluate the purpose of regulatory commissions and explain who runs them.<br>★ Describe the federal bureaucracy. | **Regular**<br>1.5 days<br><br>**Block Scheduling**<br>1 day<br><br>*Block Scheduling Handbook with Team Teaching Strategies, Chapter 6* | **RS** Guided Reading Strategies 6.4 |

## Chapter Resource Key

**PS** Primary Sources
**RS** Reading Support
**IC** Interdisciplinary Connections
**E** Enrichment

**SM** Skills Mastery
**A** Assessment
**REV** Review
**ELL** Reinforcement and English Language Learners
 Transparencies

 CD–ROM
 Video
 Internet
Holt Presentation Maker Using Microsoft® PowerPoint®

**One-Stop Planner CD–ROM**

**See the *One-Stop Planner* for a complete list of additional resources for students and teachers.**

## One-Stop Planner CD–ROM

It's easy to plan lessons, select resources, and print out materials for your students when you use the **One-Stop Planner CD–ROM with Test Generator**.

| Technology Resources | Reinforcement, Review, and Assessment |
|---|---|
| One-Stop Planner, Lesson 6.1<br>Homework Practice Online | **REV** Section 1 Review, p. 146<br>**A** Daily Quiz 6.1<br>**ELL** Main Idea Activity 6.1<br>**ELL** English Audio Summary 6.1<br>**ELL** Spanish Audio Summary 6.1 |
| One-Stop Planner, Lesson 6.2<br>Transparency 6: Powers of the President<br>Holt Researcher CD–ROM<br>Homework Practice Online | **REV** Section 2 Review, p. 152<br>**A** Daily Quiz 6.2<br>**ELL** Main Idea Activity 6.2<br>**ELL** English Audio Summary 6.2<br>**ELL** Spanish Audio Summary 6.2 |
| One-Stop Planner, Lesson 6.3<br>Homework Practice Online<br>HRW Go site | **REV** Section 3 Review, p. 161<br>**A** Daily Quiz 6.3<br>**ELL** Main Idea Activity 6.3<br>**ELL** English Audio Summary 6.3<br>**ELL** Spanish Audio Summary 6.3 |
| One-Stop Planner, Lesson 6.4<br>**CNN** Presents: American Government<br>Homework Practice Online | **REV** Section 4 Review, p. 165<br>**A** Daily Quiz 6.4<br>**ELL** Main Idea Activity 6.4<br>**ELL** English Audio Summary 6.4<br>**ELL** Spanish Audio Summary 6.4 |

## internet connect

### HRW ONLINE RESOURCES
GO TO: go.hrw.com
Then type in the keyword.

### TEACHER HOME PAGE
KEYWORD: SZ3 Teacher

### CHAPTER INTERNET ACTIVITIES
KEYWORD: SZ3 AC6
Choose an activity to:
• write a newspaper classified advertisement for the president.
• create a flowchart on presidential succession.
• create a database on information related to the executive departments.

### CHAPTER ENRICHMENT LINKS
KEYWORD: SZ3 CH6

### ONLINE ASSESSMENT
**Homework Practice**
KEYWORD: SZ3 HP6
**Rubrics**
KEYWORD: SS Rubrics

### ONLINE MAPS, CHARTS, AND GRAPHS
KEYWORD: SZ3 MCG
• Powers of the President

### HOLT PRESENTATION MAKER
KEYWORD: SZ3 PPT6

### CONTENT UPDATES
KEYWORD: SS Content Updates

### ONLINE READING SUPPORT
KEYWORD: SS Strategies

### CURRENT EVENTS
KEYWORD: S3 Current Events

## Meeting Individual Needs

### Ability Levels

**Level 1** Basic-level activities designed for all students encountering new material

**Level 2** Intermediate-level activities designed for average students

**Level 3** Challenging activities designed for honors and gifted-and-talented students

**English Language Learners** Activities that address the needs of students with Limited English Proficiency

## Chapter Review and Assessment

| | |
|---|---|
| **IC** | Vocabulary Activity 6 |
| | Global Skill Builder CD–ROM |
| | HRW Go site |
| **REV** | Chapter 6 Tutorial for Students, Parents, Mentors, and Peers |
| **REV** | Chapter 6 Review, pp. 166–67 |
| **A** | Standardized Test Practice |
| **A** | Chapter 6 Test Generator (on the One-Stop Planner) |
| **A** | Chapter 6 Test (Form A or B) |
| **A** | Alternative Assessment Handbook |
| **A** | Chapter 6 Test for English Language Learners and Special-Needs Students |

## Internet Activity

**Succeeding to the Presidency**

**internet connect**

go.hrw.com

**TOPIC:** Presidential Succession
**GO TO:** go.hrw.com
**KEYWORD:** SZ3 AC6

**ACTIVITY:** Have students access the Internet through the HRW Go site to research presidential succession and the Twenty-fifth amendment. Then have each student create a flowchart illustrating the order of succession and the names of government officials that presently occupy offices that are involved in presidential succession.

### What's Your Opinion?

To help students create their **Themes** *Journal* entries, provide the following examples of appropriate **agree**/**disagree** statements.

● **Agree**   U.S. citizens should be able to re-elect a president as many times as they want.

**Disagree**   In order to prevent a president from becoming too powerful, he or she should be allowed no more than two terms in office.

● **Agree**   If a president ran the government single-handedly, it would be easier to get things done.

**Disagree**   The United States is not a monarchy; the president should not have the absolute authority of a king.

● **Agree**   Special departments and agencies help the federal government perform specific duties.

**Disagree**   Too many departments and agencies in the executive branch complicate and slow down the federal government's business.

**CHAPTER**

# 6 The Executive Branch

**What's Your Opinion?**

### Build on What You Know

Every four years Inauguration Day attracts thousands of visitors to Washington, D.C. The ceremony is held at the Capitol Building and watched by millions of people. The president-elect is sworn in with these words from the Constitution. "I do solemnly swear (or affirm) that I will faithfully execute the office of the President of the United States, and will, to the best of my ability, preserve, protect, and defend the Constitution of the United States."

By taking this oath, the president becomes one of the world's most powerful people. The new president delivers an inaugural speech and goes on to lead the United States for the next four years.

 Do you **agree** or **disagree** with the following statements? Support your point of view in your journal.

● A president should be able to run for re-election for as many consecutive terms as he or she wants to.

● The president should be able to single-handedly run the entire U.S. government.

● Special departments and agencies are an efficient way for the government to do business.

# SECTION 1

## OBJECTIVES

*After completing Section 1, students should be able to*

1. **Identify the qualifications and terms of office for the presidency.**
2. **Describe the duties of and terms of office for the vice president.**
3. **Explain the order of presidential succession.**

## 🎙 LET'S GET STARTED!

Write the following quotation from President Harry Truman on the chalkboard: *"My first five days in the White House were like five lifetimes. Within the first few months, I discovered that being a president is like riding a tiger. A man has to keep on riding or be swallowed."* As students enter the classroom, ask them what personal strengths they think a president must possess to keep from being "swallowed" politically. *(Students' responses will vary.)* Make a list of these qualities on the chalkboard and ask students to explain their answers. Tell students that in Section 1 they will learn more about the qualifications that a person must have to hold the office of president.

---

# SECTION 1

## The Presidency

### Read to Discover

1. What are the qualifications and terms of office for the presidency?
2. What are the duties of and terms of office for the vice president?
3. What is the order of presidential succession?

### Define

• presidential succession

#### WHY CIVICS MATTERS

The significance of the office of vice president has changed in recent years. Use **CNNfyi.com** or other **current events** sources to investigate the responsibilities of the current vice president. Record your findings in your journal.

## Reading Focus

The executive branch of the federal government, described in Article II of the Constitution, is responsible for carrying out the country's laws. The president of the United States heads the executive branch and is the country's most powerful elected official. In 1789 George Washington became the first U.S. president. Since then only 42 others have served as president.

### ★ Qualifications

The Constitution sets forth certain qualifications that the president of the United States must meet. The president must

1. be a native-born U.S. citizen,
2. be at least 35 years of age, and
3. have been a resident of the United States for at least 14 years.

These are the only qualifications for president mentioned in the Constitution. However, the people who have been elected up to this point have shared similar traits. For example, all U.S. presidents have been white men. All have been Christian. Most presidents have attended college. Many have been lawyers. Most have held other political offices at the state or national level before becoming president.

Yet these tendencies can change. For example, for most of the country's history, only Protestants were elected president. The election of John F. Kennedy, a Roman Catholic, broke that tradition in 1960.

*President George W. Bush served as governor of Texas before being elected president.*

## SECTION 1 RESOURCES

### REPRODUCIBLE

▶ Guided Reading Strategies 6.1
▶ Readings in Economics and Government 17: U.S. Presidential Oath of Office
▶ Readings in Economics and Government 31: John F. Kennedy's Inaugural Address

### TECHNOLOGY

▶ One-Stop Planner, Lesson 6.1
▶ Homework Practice Online

### REINFORCEMENT, REVIEW, AND ASSESSMENT

▶ Section 1 Review, p. 146
▶ Daily Quiz 6.1
▶ Main Idea Activity 6.1
▶ English Audio Summary 6.1
▶ Spanish Audio Summary 6.1

# TEACH OBJECTIVE 1

**LEVEL 1:** Lead a class discussion about the qualifications and terms of office for the presidency. *(Students should indicate that the Constitution sets forth only three qualifications for the president and that the president can serve only two terms.)* Ask students to list the additional traits commonly shared by presidents in the past. Have students discuss whether they think that the United States will one day elect a president who is not white, Christian, or male. **ENGLISH LANGUAGE LEARNERS**

**LEVEL 3:** Remind students about the qualifications and terms of office for the presidency. Then ask students to imagine that they are at least 35 years old and are running for president. Have each student prepare a short campaign speech explaining the qualifications that he or she possesses. *(Students might list personal qualities, such as honesty, reliability, etc., or they might imagine future accomplishments, such as having a college degree, holding other political offices, and so on.)* If time permits, have the class hold a mock election based on the campaign speeches.

# TEACH OBJECTIVE 2

**ALL LEVELS:** Copy the graphic organizer on the following page onto the chalkboard, omitting the italicized answers. Have students complete the organizer to indicate the term of office and the duties of the vice president. **ENGLISH LANGUAGE LEARNERS**

---

## ★ Culture

### Of Poets and Presidents

On January 20, 1993, writer Maya Angelou read her poem "On the Pulse of Morning" at the presidential inauguration of Bill Clinton. She stirred the crowd with her call for peace and harmony among all ethnic groups and cultures. Her poem ends with a hopeful appeal: "Here, on the pulse of this new day / You may have the grace to look up and out / And into your sister's eyes, and into / Your brother's face, your country / And say simply / Very simply / With hope— / Good morning."

**ACTIVITY:** Have students conduct research to learn about other poets or writers who have read at presidential inaugurations. Then have each student write a brief report about his or her findings.

---

### ★★★★★★★★★★★
### *That's Interesting!*
### ★★★★★★★★★★★

The ages of presidents have varied widely. John F. Kennedy, at 43, was the youngest person ever elected president. However, Theodore Roosevelt—who succeeded to the presidency at the age of 42 upon William McKinley's assassination in 1901—was actually the youngest president. Ronald Reagan, at 69, was the oldest person elected president.

---

## BIOGRAPHY

### *George Washington*
### (1732–1799)

Many people consider George Washington to be the Father of Our Country. He entered the presidency as one of the great heroes of the American Revolution. He felt a great sense of responsibility to the nation. Washington wanted to be a dignified leader who listened to the needs of the people. He also felt the tremendous pressure of other people's expectations.

Washington presided over many key moments in the establishment of the national government. These include the creation of the federal court system and the selection of Washington, D.C., as the site of the new national capital. He also faced challenges in foreign relations and helped put down the Whiskey Rebellion at home. Before he left office in 1797, he gave a farewell address that advised the nation on many future issues. Today Presidents' Day, a federal holiday, is held on the third Monday of every February, near Washington's birthday. He is also one of four presidents whose image is carved into the monument at Mount Rushmore, South Dakota. **Why do many people consider George Washington to be the Father of Our Country?**

---

Recently, more women and members of minority groups have become involved in presidential politics. In 1984 Geraldine Ferraro was the first female Democratic nominee for vice president. There have also been more African Americans campaigning for presidential nomination in recent years. Republican Alan Keyes sought his party's nomination in 1996 and 2000. In 2004 Carol Moseley Braun and the Reverend Alfred C. "Al" Sharpton sought the Democratic Party nomination.

✔ **Reading Check Summarizing** What qualifications does the Constitution require of the president of the United States, and what additional characteristics have presidents shared? Native-born U.S. citizens, 35 years of age, U.S. residents for 14 years; white Christian men, most have been college-educated.

## ★ Term of Office, Salary, and Benefits

The president is elected to a four-year term and may be re-elected for a second term of office. The U.S. Constitution did not originally state how many terms the president could serve.

George Washington set the precedent of a limit of two terms. He refused to run for the presidency a third time when he was urged to do so. This two-term tradition was not broken until Franklin D. Roosevelt was elected to a third term as president in 1940. In 1944 he won a fourth and final term.

In 1951 the number of terms a president can serve was limited by passage of the Twenty-second Amendment. This amendment set a two-term limit to the presidency.

Congress sets the presidential salary and benefits. However, Congress cannot change the salary during a president's term of office. This restriction prevents Congress from punishing or rewarding a president.

Today the president is paid a salary of $400,000 a year plus a $50,000 non-taxable allowance. Since the president must travel frequently, there is also an annual allowance for travel costs.

The president is provided with many additional benefits. The president's family lives in the White House. This building has been the home of all U.S. presidents since John Adams. The White House is also the site of the president's office and the offices of the president's closest assistants.

For special meetings and for relaxation time, the president can use Camp David, located in the hills of nearby Maryland. A large fleet of cars, helicopters, and planes—including the special jet *Air Force One*—is also available to the president.

✔ **Reading Check Evaluating** What benefits do presidents receive during their terms of office? a $400,000 a year salary, an allowance, personal transportation, residency in the White House, and a recreation area at Camp David

## TEACH OBJECTIVE 3

**ALL LEVELS:** Remind students that the cabinet members in line to succeed the president are appointed, not elected, officials. Then point out that in 1973 a situation arose in which neither the president nor vice president had been elected. Have students write position statements answering the following question: Should a nation be run by appointed officials? Ask volunteers to present their positions to the class. **ENGLISH LANGUAGE LEARNERS**

## CLOSE

Organize students into three groups and assign each group an objective from this chapter. Then have groups create flash cards about their objectives. Collect the finished cards and use them to quiz the class on this chapter's objectives. **COOPERATIVE LEARNING**

**Interpreting the Visual Record**

**White House guests** *The President and First Lady receive and entertain many special guests at the White House. Why do you think the President opens the White House to such guests?*

## The Vice President

The Constitution provides that if the president dies, resigns, or is removed from office, the vice president becomes president. The vice president has only one other job—to preside over the Senate. Because the vice president's power is so limited, John Adams, the first to hold the position, called the office "the most insignificant" ever invented.

In recent years, however, presidents have given their vice presidents more responsibilities. Vice presidents must be fully informed and prepared to take over the important job that could become theirs. The vice president must meet the same constitutional qualifications as the president and also serves a four-year term. The vice president receives a salary of $186,300 a year plus a $10,000 taxable expense allowance. Vice presidential candidates are often chosen for their ability to help the presidential candidates win the election. Increasingly, political parties have also chosen vice presidential nominees who are fully qualified to succeed to the presidency.

Eight U.S. presidents have died while in office. One president resigned. In each case, the vice president took the oath of office and became president as provided by the Constitution.

✔ **Reading Check Contrasting** How are vice presidential duties different than they were in the time of John Adams? Initially, the vice president's only job was to preside over the Senate. In recent years, presidents have given their vice presidents more responsibilities.

## The Rules of Succession

If the president dies or resigns and is succeeded by the vice president, who then becomes vice president? Until 1967 the office of the vice president remained empty. Adopted in 1967, the Twenty-fifth Amendment to the U.S. Constitution provides that the new president nominates a new vice president. The nomination of the vice president must then be approved by a majority vote of both houses of Congress.

### Constitutional Heritage

**The Lame Duck** A president's final months in office can be frustrating. Presidents become "lame ducks," lacking political clout because they are soon to leave office. Before the Twentieth Amendment was passed in 1933, presidents were lame ducks between the November election and the new president's inauguration in March of the next year. The four-month interval gave newly elected officials time to travel the often great distances from their homes to the capital. The Twentieth ("Lame Duck") Amendment, passed in the era of the automobile, moved the inauguration up to January, thus cutting the lame-duck period in half.

**ACTIVITY:** Lead students in a discussion about what the term *lame duck* means and why it might be difficult for a president in this position to get important work done.

### Visual Record Answer

*Students' responses will vary.*

### BIOGRAPHY ANSWER
(for page 144)
Students might suggest because he was the first president.

# REVIEW AND ASSESS

Have students complete the **Section 1 Review** on page 146. Then have students complete **Daily Quiz 6.1**. As **Alternative Assessment**, you may want to use the campaign speech or the position statement exercises in this section's lessons.

## RETEACH

Have students complete **Main Idea Activity for English Language Learners and Special-Needs Students 6.1**. Then assign each student one of the sections in this chapter. Ask students to create study guides for the sections that they have been assigned. After they have finished their study guides, ask volunteers to present their guides to the class. **ENGLISH LANGUAGE LEARNERS**

## EXTEND

Have students refer to an encyclopedia to create a chart showing the nine vice presidents who had to assume the office of the presidency. The chart should also indicate the dates and circumstances under which these vice presidents were required to become president. **BLOCK SCHEDULING**

 For example:

| Vice President | President | Date | Reason |
|---|---|---|---|
| John Tyler | William Harrison | 1841 | died |
| Millard Fillmore | Zachary Taylor | 1850 | died of cholera |

146

## Section 1 Review
### ANSWERS

**1. Define**
• presidential succession, p. 146

**2.** the Speaker of the House of Representatives, president pro tempore of the Senate, members of the president's cabinet in the order in which their departments were created

**3. a.** The president must be a native-born U.S. citizen, be at least 35 years of age, and have been a resident of the United States for at least 14 years. The president is elected to a four-year term and is limited to two terms.

**b.** The function of the vice president is to succeed the president and to preside over the Senate. The vice president also serves a four-year term.

**4.** Students should suggest that George Washington and the other framers of government wanted to ensure that the president did not become too powerful. Students might cite Franklin D. Roosevelt's four terms as evidencing the popularity of Roosevelt as a leader and of his response to the demands of the Great Depression and World War II.

Gerald Ford became the first vice president and later president to hold office without being elected.

The first use of the Twenty-fifth Amendment occurred in 1973 when Gerald Ford replaced the resigning Vice President Spiro Agnew. The amendment was used again in 1974. When President Nixon resigned because of the Watergate scandal, Vice President Ford became president. Nelson A. Rockefeller was then chosen as vice president. For the only time in its history, the country had a president and a vice president whom the people had not elected.

The Twenty-fifth Amendment also provides that the vice president will serve as acting president until the president is able to perform his duties. Suppose the president wants to resume the duties of office, but the vice president and the cabinet do not think the president is fit to do so. Then Congress must decide by a two-thirds vote who will serve as president.

What would happen if both the president and the vice president died or left office? The Constitution gave Congress the right to decide who should become president. The order in which the office of president is to be filled is known as **presidential succession.** According to a law passed by Congress in 1947, the Speaker of the House of Representatives is first in line for the office. If the Speaker dies or is removed from office, then the president *pro tempore* of the Senate succeeds to the presidency. Following them in succession to the presidency are the members of the president's cabinet, in the order in which their departments were created.

✔ **Reading Check Summarizing** What is the order of presidential succession? vice president, Speaker of the House, president *pro tempore*, cabinet heads in the order they were created

# SECTION 1 Review

**go.hrw.com** **Homework Practice Online** keyword: SZ3 HP6

**1. Define** and explain:
• presidential succession

**2. Sequencing** Copy the chart below, adding more boxes as necessary. Use it to fill in the missing levels of presidential succession.

| Vice President |
|---|

**3. Finding the Main Idea**
a. What are the qualifications and terms of office for the president?
b. What is the function and term of office of the vice president?

**4. Writing and Critical Thinking**
**Making Generalizations and Predictions** Write a two-paragraph essay describing the advantages and disadvantages of the limit the Twenty-second Amendment places on the number of terms that a president can serve in office.

**Consider:**
• why George Washington set a two-term tradition
• why Franklin D. Roosevelt was elected to four terms

# SECTION 2

## OBJECTIVES

*After completing Section 2, students should be able to*

1  **Describe how the president is involved in the legislative process.**

2  **Explain how Congress limits the president's powers as commander in chief.**

3  **Identify the president's duties as foreign-policy leader and as chief of state.**

## SECTION 2

# Powers and Roles of the President

### Read to Discover

1. How is the president involved in the legislative process?
2. How does Congress limit the president's powers as commander in chief?
3. What are the president's duties as foreign-policy leader and as chief of state?

### WHY CIVICS MATTERS

The Constitution charges the president with the responsibility of recommending laws to Congress. Use **CNN fyi.com** or other **current events** sources to read about a law that the president has recently recommended to Congress. Record your findings in your journal.

### Define
- foreign policy
- diplomacy
- diplomatic notes
- treaties
- reprieve
- pardon
- commutation

### Identify
- State of the Union Address

## SECTION 2 RESOURCES

### REPRODUCIBLE
- ▶ Guided Reading Strategies 6.2
- ▶ Readings in Economics and Government 28: Woodrow Wilson's "Fourteen Points"
- ▶ American Civics Political Cartoon: Watergate
- ▶ Creative Teaching Strategy: Role-Playing
- ▶ Graphic Organizer Activity: The President's Many Hats

### TECHNOLOGY
- ▶ One-Stop Planner, Lesson 6.2
- ▶ Transparency 6: Powers of the President
- ▶ Holt Researcher CD–ROM
- ▶ Homework Practice Online

### REINFORCEMENT, REVIEW, AND ASSESSMENT
- ▶ Section 2 Review, p. 152
- ▶ Daily Quiz 6.2
- ▶ Main Idea Activity 6.2
- ▶ English Audio Summary 6.2
- ▶ Spanish Audio Summary 6.2

## *Reading Focus*

Article II, Section 1, of the Constitution provides that "the executive power shall be vested in [given to] a President of the United States of America." This clause means that the president, as head of the executive branch, is responsible for executing, or carrying out, the laws passed by Congress. As a result, the president is often called the nation's chief executive. The president must participate in all phases of government.

## ★ Legislative Leader

As you know, the president recommends, or suggests, needed laws to Congress. In fact, the Constitution requires that the president "shall from time to time give to the Congress information of [about] the state of the Union, and recommend to their [Congress's] consideration such measures as he shall judge necessary."

To carry out this constitutional provision, the president delivers several messages to Congress each year. These messages may be delivered as speeches before Congress or be sent in writing. Every year, usually in late January, the president delivers a **State of the Union Address** to Congress. This televised speech sets forth the programs and policies that the president wants Congress to put into effect as laws. These programs and policies usually address the country's most pressing concerns.

*The Oval Office is where the president conducts much of the day-to-day business of the presidency.*

# TEACH OBJECTIVE 1

**LEVEL 1:** Lead a class discussion about how the president is involved in the legislative process. Then organize the class into groups and have each group divide a sheet of paper into two columns. In the first column, have students prepare a list of important issues or problems that they think the president should discuss in the State of the Union Address. Then, in the second column, have students make a corresponding list of programs and policies that the president should encourage Congress to enact to solve these problems. *(Students should indicate that the Constitution requires that the president recommend needed laws or policies to Congress. Students might suggest such new policies as increasing funding for education and* health care, enacting stricter regulations to control air pollution, or developing programs to reduce crime.) Ask a volunteer to read his or her group's list of policy suggestions to the class.
**ENGLISH LANGUAGE LEARNERS , COOPERATIVE LEARNING**

**LEVEL 2:** Ask students to consider whether or not the president should have the legislative power to veto bills passed by Congress. Have each student write a brief argument supporting his or her position.

**Interpreting the Visual Record**

**Special address** *Following the terrorist attacks of September 11, 2001, President George W. Bush addressed the country at a special joint session of Congress.* **Why do you think a joint session of Congress was held for this address?**

★★★★★★★★★★★★
### That's Interesting!
★★★★★★★★★★★★

**His Highness?** When George Washington became the nation's first president, no one knew what to call him. Vice President John Adams wanted to call him His Highness, the President of the United States and Protector of the Rights of the Same.

The Senate supported the title, but the House of Representatives did not. Washington also wanted a simpler title. Leaders of the new government agreed to simply call their new president Mr. President. All U.S. presidents since then have gone by this title.

The president also sends Congress an economic message, recommending how the federal government should raise and spend its money. In the economic message to Congress, the president reviews the country's economic condition and recommends various laws and programs to help the economy.

The president also influences legislation by using his veto power. Sometimes the threat of a presidential veto discourages Congress from passing a bill. Congress knows how difficult it is to pass a bill after it has been vetoed by the president. For this reason, members of Congress carefully consider the issues before passing a bill the president does not favor.

✔ **Reading Check Summarizing** How does the president shape legislation?
recommends plans for legistation and uses veto power

## ★ Commander in Chief

As head of the U.S. armed forces, or commander in chief, the president has important powers. All military officers, in a time of war or in peacetime, ultimately answer to the president. The president does not actually lead U.S. forces into battle. The president is, however, in constant contact with U.S. military leaders. The president also has the final say in planning how a war is to be fought.

Under the Constitution, only Congress can declare war. However, as commander in chief of the armed forces, the president may send U.S. forces into any part of the world where danger threatens. Presidents have sent troops into action in foreign lands many times throughout U.S. history.

Sending U.S. troops into certain situations sometimes involves the risk of war. Therefore, Congress passed the War Powers Act in 1973 to limit the president's military power. This act requires that the president recall troops sent abroad within 60 days, unless Congress approves the

# TEACH OBJECTIVE 2

 **ALL LEVELS:** Lead a class discussion about the types of situations that could lead a president to deploy troops prior to congressional approval. (*Students should cite situations such as maintaining peace between foreign nations, protecting U.S. citizens abroad, defending U.S. allies, and so on.*) Remind students that the War Powers Act, which is one of the ways that Congress limits the president's powers as commander in chief, requires that troops be recalled unless Congress approves the action within 60 days. Then ask students to provide specific examples from recent times when the president sent U.S. military forces abroad. **ENGLISH LANGUAGE LEARNERS**

**LEVEL 3:** Tell students to imagine that they are members of Congress in 1973 and that they are trying to pass the War Powers Act. Have each student write a brief speech arguing for the necessity of an act to limit the president's power as commander in chief. (*Students should give reasons the president should not have unlimited authority over the military, and they should cite historical events to support their arguments.*) Ask volunteers to read their speeches in class as if they were addressing Congress.

---

## Historical Document

### JOHN F. KENNEDY'S INAUGURAL ADDRESS

*John F. Kennedy, at age 43, was the youngest person ever elected president. His inaugural address inspired many Americans.*

"My Fellow Citizens: We observe today not a victory of party but a celebration of freedom—symbolizing an end as well as a beginning—signifying renewal as well as change. . . .

Let the word go forth from this time and place, to friend and foe alike, that the torch has been passed to a new generation of Americans—born in this century, tempered by war, disciplined by a hard and bitter peace, proud of our ancient heritage—and unwilling to witness or permit the slow undoing of those human rights to which this nation has always been committed, and to which we are committed today at home and around the world.

Let every nation know, whether it wishes us well or ill, that we shall pay any price, bear any burden, meet any hardship, support any friend, oppose any foe in order to ensure the survival and the success of liberty. This much we pledge—and more.

And so, my fellow Americans: Ask not what your country can do for you—ask what you can do for your country.

My fellow citizens of the world: Ask not what America will do for you, but what together we can do for the freedom of man.

Finally, whether you are citizens of America or citizens of the world, ask of us the same high standards of strength and sacrifice which we ask of you. With a good conscience our only sure reward, with history the final judge of our deeds, let us go forth."

**Analyzing Primary Sources**
1. What does Kennedy ask Americans and world citizens to ask themselves?
2. What does Kennedy pledge that the United States will do on behalf of liberty?

---

action. The 60 days may be extended to 90 days if needed to ensure the safe removal of U.S. troops.

✔ **Reading Check Contrasting** What different military powers do the president and Congress have? Only Congress can declare war, but the president has the power to send U.S. forces anywhere danger threatens. The War Powers Act requires that the president recall troops sent abroad within 60 days, unless Congress approves the action.

## ★ Foreign-Policy Leader

The president, as chief executive of one of the most powerful countries in the world, must give constant attention to U.S. **foreign policy.** Foreign policy is the government's plan for interacting with the other countries of the world. As the person in charge of conducting U.S. foreign policy, the president seeks to secure friendly relations with foreign governments while preserving national security.

To conduct relations with other governments, the president appoints officials to represent the U.S. government in foreign countries. The president also meets with leaders and representatives of other countries. These meetings are held both in the United States and in the officials' home nations. Traveling to foreign nations is an important part of the president's job as foreign-policy leader.

Great skill and tact are required in dealing with both friendly and unfriendly countries. The art of interacting with foreign governments is called **diplomacy.** The president is the country's chief diplomat.

---

## ★ The Democratic Process

**Declaring War** After negotiations to bring peace to the war-torn city of Kosovo collapsed, President Bill Clinton, in his role as commander in chief, committed U.S. military forces to lead a 78-day air war against Yugoslavia in 1999. U.S. forces and forces from other allied countries belonging to the North Atlantic Treaty Organization (NATO) remained in the Kosovo region as part of a peacekeeping mission.

**ACTIVITY:** Ask students to research other conflicts that prompted a U.S. president to send troops abroad to maintain or restore peace. Ask each student to choose one such conflict and to create a chart with four columns showing (1) the date and place, (2) the reasons for military involvement, (3) the number and types of troops sent abroad, and (4) the result of U.S. military action.

---

**ANALYZING PRIMARY SOURCES ANSWERS**
1. Americans should ask themselves what they can do for their country, and world citizens should ask themselves what they can do for the freedom of man.

2. Kennedy says that the United States will "pay any price, bear any burden, meet any hardship, support any friend, oppose any foe in order to ensure the survival and the success of liberty."

# TEACH OBJECTIVE 3

**ALL LEVELS:** Copy the graphic organizer to the right onto the chalkboard, omitting the italicized answers. Have each student complete the list to identify the duties of the president as foreign-policy leader and as chief of state.

**ENGLISH LANGUAGE LEARNERS**

**LEVELS 1 AND 2:** Ask students to draw a wagon wheel on the chalkboard with the president at the center of the spokes. At the end of each spoke, have students draw a symbol representing a different presidential role. *(For example, a pair of clasped hands could represent the role of chief diplomat, or a helmet could represent the role of commander in chief.)* The drawing should contain as many spokes as the students find necessary.

| **President's Duties as Foreign Policy Leader and Chief of State** |
| --- |
| • *secure friendly relations with foreign governments* |
| • *preserve the security of the United States* |
| • *appoint officials to represent the United States in foreign countries* |
| • *meet with leaders of foreign countries* |
| • *travel abroad to meet with foreign leaders* |
| • *assume responsibility for treaties with foreign countries* |

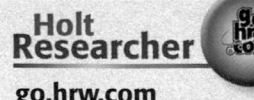

**Holt Researcher**

**go.hrw.com**
**KEYWORD: Holt Researcher**
**Freefind: Foreign Policy**
Scan through the listings of presidents on the Holt Researcher. Choose three presidents and create a table that describes each president's key contributions to international relations.

## Powers of the President

Approves or vetoes all bills passed by Congress

Prepares the federal government's budget

Is commander in chief of the armed forces

Proposes laws and programs to Congress

**The President of the United States**

Can pardon those guilty of crimes against the federal government

Keeps Congress informed about the state of the country and the economy

Appoints cabinet members, ambassadors, and federal judges

Conducts U.S. foreign relations, makes treaties, and receives foreign ambassadors

**Interpreting Charts**
*The Constitution provides the president with a wide-ranging set of powers to carry out his duties.* **In what ways does the president interact with Congress?**

Presidential visits to foreign countries build international friendship and security and promote U.S. interests.

As the nation's chief diplomat, the president often corresponds with the leaders of foreign governments. Written communications among diplomats are called **diplomatic notes.** The president also has access to a computerized communications system. This system enables the president to make a direct connection with other governments in an emergency.

The U.S. government also makes written agreements, called **treaties,** with other countries. Many officials work to reach these agreements. The president, however, assumes the final responsibility for the agreements. All treaties must be made with the advice and consent of the Senate. The Senate must approve a treaty by a two-thirds vote before it becomes effective. The president must see that the treaty is carried out.

✔ **Reading Check Drawing Inferences and Conclusions** Why do you think treaties require the work of both the president and the Senate? Students might say that this is part of the federal government's system of checks and balances.

 **Judicial Powers**

The Constitution gives the president the power to appoint Supreme Court justices and other federal judges. These judicial appointments must be approved by a majority vote of the members of the Senate before they are final.

The president also has the power to grant reprieves and pardons to those who have committed certain federal crimes. A **reprieve** postpones the carrying out of a person's sentence. It gives a convicted person the opportunity to gather more evidence to support his or her case or to appeal for a new trial. A **pardon** forgives a person convicted of a crime and frees him or her from serving out the sentence. The president also has the judicial power of **commutation,** or making a convicted person's sentence less severe.

✔ **Reading Check** Summarizing What are some of the judicial powers held by the president? the power to grant reprieves, pardons, and commutations and to appoint Supreme Court justices and other federal judges

## Other Presidential Roles

Over the years the president has assumed other roles that are not mentioned in the Constitution. These roles include chief of state and political party leader.

As chief of state, the president is the symbol of the United States and its people. It is the president who greets visiting foreign heads of state and travels to other countries to strengthen ties and improve relations. The president performs many ceremonial duties as well. These include awarding medals to honor worthy citizens, lighting the nation's Christmas tree, and throwing out the first baseball to open the baseball season.

The president is also the leader of a political party. Members of the president's political party work hard to help elect the president. In return, the president makes speeches in favor of other party members who are running for public office. The president also helps the party raise money for its political campaigns, candidates, and programs.

✔ **Reading Check** Evaluating How does the president act as a symbol of the United States? by greeting and visiting foreign leaders to strengthen ties and improve relations and by performing ceremonial duties

## Presidential Daily Life

The president must find time to carry on a wide range of activities from day to day. At all times the president's office must be in touch with other key government officials. Thus, the president can never be far from a telephone.

The activities that occupy the president's time are varied. Many hours of the day are spent in meetings with presidential advisers. When Congress is in session, the president may have breakfast or luncheon meetings with congressional leaders. Meetings are

**Did You KNOW?**

The first jet plane known as *Air Force One* was introduced in 1962 and used by President John F. Kennedy. The name comes from the call sign used by the Air Force for any plane carrying the president. Today there are two planes that serve the president, each fully equipped for work, entertaining, and communications.

**Interpreting the Visual Record**

**Presidential leadership** *President George W. Bush visited U.S. military troops stationed in Baghdad on Thanksgiving Day, 2003.* **How does this visit demonstrate the role of the president as commander in chief of the United States?**

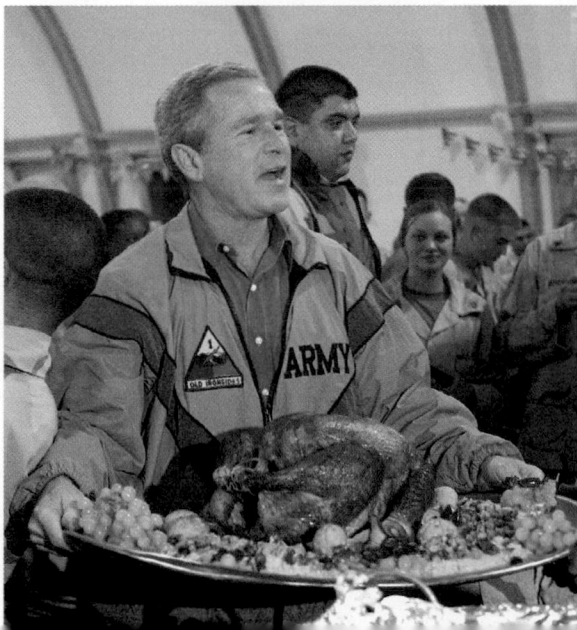

**Global Perspectives**

**Keeping the Peace** On March 26, 1979, President Jimmy Carter, in his role as chief of state, convinced Anwar el-Sadat of Egypt and Menachem Begin of Israel to sign a peace treaty. The agreement was called the Camp David Accords, named after the presidential retreat in Maryland, where the leaders met. It was the first peace treaty between Israel and an Arab state. As part of the agreement, Israel returned the Sinai to Egypt in 1982, and the two countries promised to negotiate Palestinian autonomy in the Israeli-occupied West Bank and Gaza Strip. Unfortunately, violence still plagues the region today, while Israelis and Palestinians continue difficult negotiations.

**CRITICAL THINKING**

Should the U.S. president mediate between other nations or encourage other countries to sign treaties that do not directly involve the United States?

**ANSWER:** Some students may cite that world peace benefits all nations and that the United States as a superpower should take a leading role. Other students may argue that the United States should not get involved in the affairs of other countries.

**Visual Record Answer**

*Students might suggest that the president's visit signified a gesture of support and leadership to the troops.*

151

## REVIEW AND ASSESS

Have students complete the **Section 2 Review** on page 152. Then have students complete **Daily Quiz 6.2**. As **Alternative Assessment**, you may want to use the State of the Union Address activity or the veto-power debate in this section's lessons.

## RETEACH

Have students complete **Main Idea Activity for English Language Learners and Special-Needs Students 6.2**. Then give each student a set of five index cards and have him or her write a different presidential role on one side of each card. Next, tell students to write descriptions of the duties of the specific roles on the opposite side. Pair students and have them quiz each other, using the index cards as flash cards. **ENGLISH LANGUAGE LEARNERS , COOPERATIVE LEARNING**

## EXTEND

Have students conduct research outside of class on how the president's power as legislative leader, commander in chief, or foreign policy leader is limited, or balanced, by Congress. Tell students to find at least one specific example where the president and Congress disagreed over a specific issue or policy, and then ask each student to write an essay explaining how this example illustrates the importance of having a system of "checks" and "balances" on presidential power. Invite volunteers to present their findings to the class. **BLOCK SCHEDULING**

**GLOBAL CONNECTIONS ANSWER**

power concentrated under the executive branch; National Assembly is not accountable to voters; Council of State issues laws that cannot be challenged by the Cuban Supreme Court

## Section 2 Review
### ANSWERS

**1. Define**
- foreign policy, p. 149
- diplomacy, p. 149
- diplomatic notes, p. 150
- treaties, p. 150
- reprieve, p. 151
- pardon, p. 151
- commutation, p. 151

**2. Identify**
- State of the Union Address, p. 147

**3.** recommends needed laws to Congress; head of all U.S. armed forces, can send military forces abroad; secures friendly relations with foreign governments, signs treaties; symbol of the United States, greets foreign visitors, travels to foreign countries; appoints Supreme Court justices and federal judges, grants reprieves and pardons, and has power of commutation

**4. a.** recommends legislation, gives State of the Union Address, sends economic messages to Congress, may veto bills

**b.** Only Congress can declare war, and under the War Powers Act of 1973, any military forces that the president sends abroad must be recalled within 60 days unless approved by Congress.

**5.** Students' speeches should address suggested solutions to problems.

## GLOBAL CONNECTIONS

### Executive Power

The U.S. Constitution divides power among three branches. So does the government of Cuba. Under the Cuban constitution, however, power is concentrated within the executive branch under the authority of Fidel Castro, the nation's chief of state. The political rights of Cuban citizens, including freedom of speech, freedom of association, and the right to vote, depend on their loyalty to the Communist Party and its goals.

Unlike the U.S. Congress, Cuba's legislative body—the National Assembly—is not accountable to voters. The Assembly also meets rarely and has little practical power. The nation is run by the Council of Ministers or the Council of State, which has fewer members than the National Assembly and is headed by the president, Fidel Castro. The council proposes and issues laws. The Cuban Supreme Court, unlike the U.S. Supreme Court, does not have the power to consider whether these laws are constitutional. **In what ways do Cuba's branches of government differ from those of the United States?**

also held with members of the president's political party. Party members discuss bills before Congress, appointments of officials, or political plans and strategies important to the party. In addition, the president meets regularly with members of the cabinet.

The president delivers a great number of speeches. President Franklin D. Roosevelt established the custom of reporting directly to the American people. He did so by giving radio talks, which he called fireside chats.

Today the president still delivers radio talks to the public, usually every week. However, presidents also rely on television broadcasts. The president appears on television to speak directly to the American people, to inform them of proposed new programs, and to ask for their support. The president also holds press conferences to explain government decisions and to answer questions from reporters.

The president must also attend to many other important duties. The president must sign (or veto) bills submitted by Congress, prepare speeches, appoint officials, and examine budget figures. The president must deal with matters of foreign policy and reach decisions on national defense issues. To stay informed on events, the president must find time to read newspapers and magazines and to study reports received from government officials at home and abroad.

✔ **Reading Check Analyzing Information** What types of activities might make up the president's day? Answers might include attending meetings, preparing and giving speeches, giving press conferences, signing bills, appointing officials, and reading up on current events.

go.
hrw
.com
**Homework Practice Online**
keyword: SZ3 HP6

## SECTION 2 Review

**1. Define** and explain:
- foreign policy
- diplomacy
- diplomatic notes
- treaties
- reprieve
- pardon
- commutation

**2. Identify** and explain:
- State of the Union address

**3. Categorizing** Copy the chart below. Use it to list the duties that accompany each presidential role.

| Presidential Role | Duty |
| --- | --- |
| Legislative Leader | |
| Commander in Chief | |
| Foreign-Policy Leader | |
| Chief of State | |
| Judicial Powers | |

**4. Finding the Main Idea**
   a. What is the president's influence on the legislative process?
   b. In what ways is the president's military power limited?

**5. Writing and Critical Thinking**
   **Problem Solving** Using the president's State of the Union Address as a model, write a State of the School Address. In your speech identify some of the challenges facing your school, suggest possible solutions, and provide a plan to resolve them.

   **Consider:**
   - the purpose of the State of the Union Address
   - the school's most pressing problems
   - policies and programs that can improve your school

# SECTION 3

## OBJECTIVES

*After completing Section 3, students should be able to*

1 Define the Executive Office of the President and explain its purpose.
2 Describe how heads of the executive departments and members of the cabinet are related.
3 Name the 15 executive departments.

## 🔔 LET'S GET STARTED!

Write the word *cabinet* on the chalkboard. As students enter the classroom, ask them to write down what advice and information a president might need to seek from the cabinet. (*Students might write that the president could discuss issues regarding defense, national security, the economy, education, the environment, foreign policy, and so on.*) Explain to students that the president's cabinet has grown since the time of George Washington, whose cabinet consisted of only three executive departments: the Postmaster General, the Attorney General, and the Departments of State, Treasury, and War. Tell students that in Section 3 they will learn about the Executive Office of the President, the cabinet, and the 14 executive departments.

## SECTION 3

# Executive Departments and the Cabinet

### Read to Discover

1. What is the Executive Office of the President, and what is its purpose?
2. How are heads of the executive departments and the members of the cabinet related?
3. What are the 15 executive departments?

#### WHY CIVICS MATTERS

The executive departments have significant and specific responsibilities in the federal government. Use **CNNfyi.com** or other **current events** sources to illustrate the unique role that one of the executive departments plays in the U.S. government. Record your findings in your journal.

### Define

• budget
• executive departments
• secretary
• attorney general
• ambassadors
• embassy
• ministers
• consul
• consulate
• passports
• visas
• counterfeiting
• civilian

### Identify

• Joint Chiefs of Staff

## SECTION 3 RESOURCES

### REPRODUCIBLE

▶ Guided Reading Strategies 6.3
▶ Challenge and Enrichment Worksheet 6: Identifying the President's Cabinet
▶ Community Service and Participation Handbook: "Ask What You Can Do"

### TECHNOLOGY

▶ One-Stop Planner, Lesson 6.3
▶ Homework Practice Online
▶ HRW Go site

### REINFORCEMENT, REVIEW, AND ASSESSMENT

▶ Section 3 Review, p. 161
▶ Daily Quiz 6.3
▶ Main Idea Activity 6.3
▶ English Audio Summary 6.3
▶ Spanish Audio Summary 6.3

## Reading Focus

The duties of the executive branch of the federal government have grown significantly since George Washington served as the country's first chief executive. During the country's early years, presidents carried out their executive duties with the help of a few assistants. Today there are thousands of people who assist the president.

### ⭐ Executive Office of the President

The president's closest advisers and aides are part of the Executive Office of the President. The Executive Office was established in 1939. Every president has reorganized the office. The agencies and offices that make up the Executive Office advise the president on current issues, including important domestic and international matters.

The Council of Economic Advisers, for example, gives the president information about the nation's economy. This agency recommends programs to promote economic growth and stability. Another agency of the Executive Office is the Office of Management and Budget. This agency assists in the preparation of the federal budget, which the president presents to Congress. A **budget** is a plan of income and spending.

The National Security Council (NSC) is the president's top-ranking group of advisers on all matters concerning defense and security. The Office of National Drug Control Policy coordinates federal, state, and

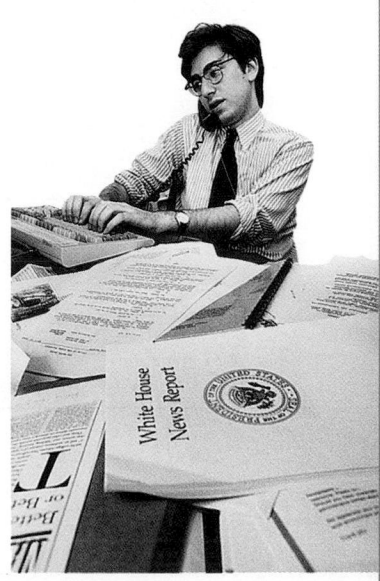

*Members of the Executive Office provide the president with important information and guidance on many issues.*

**LEVEL 1:** Organize the class into groups and ask each group to create its own Executive Office, using some of the agencies and offices mentioned on pages 153–154. Remind students that every president has reorganized the Executive Office. Ask each group to add any offices or agencies that it thinks might be useful in running the country. *(Students should include offices that might address specific contemporary issues.)* Have students organize the individual offices according to their importance. Then ask volunteers to explain the purpose of the Executive Office and to describe why their group ordered the offices the way that it did. **ENGLISH LANGUAGE LEARNERS** , **COOPERATIVE LEARNING**

**ALL LEVELS:** Lead a class discussion about the purpose of the Executive Office of the President. Remind students that the U.S. Constitution leaves plenty of room for growth in its plan for the government. Then ask students to imagine that they are helping the framers of the Constitution determine whether or not to specify who should assist the president. Have each student write a brief paragraph explaining why the number and types of assistants should not be specified. **ENGLISH LANGUAGE LEARNERS**

## The Democratic Process

**"The President Needs Help"** The genesis of the Executive Office of the President was the Report of the President's Committee on Administrative Management in 1937. "The president needs help," concluded the committee upon its review of the administrative needs of an executive branch whose policy authority had been greatly expanded. Indeed, the Great Depression and the New Deal programs that were instituted to battle it were important factors in the growth of the executive branch. Congressional action also lent a hand in the expansion of the executive branch. For example, Congress created the Bureau of the Budget as part of the Treasury Department in 1921. The Bureau of the Budget (later changed to the Office of Management and Budget) moved to the Executive Office of the President in 1939. Congress also expanded the president's role in areas such as labor, national security, and atomic-energy policy.

### CRITICAL THINKING

What other departments have become part of the Executive Office since 1939, and what conditions do you think necessitated their creation?

**ANSWERS:** Students' answers will vary but should be supported.

**Interpreting the Visual Record**

**National Security Council** *President George W. Bush appointed Condoleezza Rice as national security advisor— a key position on the National Security Council. Here Rice gives a press briefing.* **Under what sorts of circumstances do you think briefings on national security would be necessary?**

local activities designed to stop the use of illegal drugs. The Council on Environmental Quality monitors the environment and makes recommendations about it to the president.

The White House Office includes the president's closest personal and political advisers. This office also includes researchers, clerical staff, social secretaries, and the president's doctor. Members of the White House staff perform many important jobs for the president. They schedule the president's appointments and write speeches. They help maintain good relations with Congress and with other departments and agencies of the government. A press secretary represents the president to the news media and the public.

✔ **Reading Check** Summarizing What is the main function of the agencies and offices of the Executive Office of the President? to advise the president on current issues

## Executive Departments

The leaders who wrote the U.S. Constitution drew up a plan of government with plenty of room for growth. They did not try to work out every detail of government. For example, they did not try to designate the responsibilities of all the people who would later assist the president. Thus, the Constitution makes no mention of the president's assistants except that "he may require the opinion, in writing, of the principal officer in each of the executive departments."

In 2003 there were 15 **executive departments** in the federal government. Each department has specific areas of responsibility. The chart on page 158 shows the principal duties of each executive department. On the next few pages, you will read about each of the 15 executive departments. All of these departments work to improve the lives of all Americans.

Congress has the power to establish executive departments, to reorganize and combine different departments, or even to eliminate a department. For example, the Department of Defense was created in 1949 to combine the War and Naval Departments into a single structure. The ability to reorganize the executive departments helps the presidency and the nation adapt to changing times.

As chief executive, the president has a great deal of influence on these changes. Congress listens carefully to the president's wishes and requests regarding the executive departments. The president also has the power to direct the executive departments, working within the structure established by Congress.

✔ **Reading Check** Finding the Main Idea Who has power over the executive departments? Congress and the president

## ★ The Cabinet

George Washington had the help of only five executive departments—the Postmaster General, the Attorney General, and the Departments of State, Treasury, and War. He met frequently with the heads of these departments to discuss policy. The heads of these executive departments, as you recall, became known as the president's cabinet. Every president since Washington has held cabinet meetings.

The cabinet consists of the heads of the 15 executive departments and any other officials the president chooses. The president often invites other key government officials, such as the vice president, to attend cabinet meetings. Cabinet meetings are led by the president.

The president appoints the members of the cabinet. However, the Senate must approve these appointments by a majority vote. The title of most cabinet members is **secretary.** For example, the head of the Department of State is called the secretary of state. The head of the Department of the Treasury is called the secretary of the treasury. The head of the Department of Justice, however, is known as the **attorney general.**

✔ **Reading Check Contrasting** How was George Washington's cabinet different from modern presidential cabinets? Washington's cabinet consisted of only five executive departments. Today the cabinet is composed of 15.

## ★ Department of State

Foreign policy is the special responsibility of the Department of State. The secretary of state heads a large staff of officials in Washington, D.C., who direct the worldwide work of the department. U.S. officials sent abroad to represent the country also report to the Department of State.

**Ambassadors** are the highest-ranking U.S. representatives in foreign countries. The official residence and offices of an ambassador in a foreign country are called an **embassy.** In a few smaller countries, **ministers,** or diplomatic ministers ranked below ambassadors, represent the United States.

**ALL LEVELS:** Copy the following graphic organizer onto the chalkboard, omitting the italicized answers. Ask each student to complete the chart by listing the 14 department secretaries that are included in the president's cabinet. **ENGLISH LANGUAGE LEARNERS**

| Cabinet Members | |
| --- | --- |
| *Secretary of State* | *Secretary of Defense* |
| *Secretary of Treasury* | *Secretary of Health and Human Services* |
| *Attorney General* | *Secretary of Housing and Urban Development* |
| *Secretary of the Interior* | *Secretary of Transportation* |
| *Secretary of Agriculture* | *Secretary of Energy* |
| *Secretary of Commerce* | *Secretary of Education* |
| *Secretary of Labor* | *Secretary of Veterans Affairs* |

**LEVEL 2:** Organize the class into groups and ask each group to imagine that it comprises one of the 14 executive offices. Have each group choose one student to be its head, and then ask each group to create a list of important items that will become the department head's responsibility to discuss with the president. Have the department heads present their lists to the president during a mock cabinet meeting. **COOPERATIVE LEARNING**

## ★ Economics

**The New Greenbacks**
In March 1996 the U.S. Department of the Treasury began issuing new versions of its paper currency, starting with a redesigned hundred-dollar bill. The new bills incorporate state-of-the-art technology to protect U.S. currency from counterfeiters.

**ACTIVITY:** Ask students to find information on the new designs and security measures used in the redesigned U.S. currency and to compare these advancements to the old security measures. Have students share their research in class.

★★★★★★★★★★★★
### That's Interesting!
★★★★★★★★★★★★

*Ambassador* and *embassy* come from the same root word meaning "service." Explain that the residence of an ambassador in a foreign country is an embassy.

### Visual Record Answer

*Students' responses will vary.*

*U.S. citizens require passports to travel abroad to most countries.*

**Interpreting the Visual Record**

**Printing money** The Bureau of Engraving and Printing is responsible for printing U.S. paper currency. Recent changes in the design of U.S. currency have made it more difficult to counterfeit. **Why is preventing counterfeiting important for the U.S. economy?**

There is another kind of representative, called a **consul,** who represents U.S. commercial interests in foreign countries. A U.S. consul's office, or **consulate,** can be found in most large foreign cities. The consuls and the members of their staffs work hard to improve trade between the United States and other countries. They also help protect U.S. citizens who conduct business and own property in foreign countries. U.S. citizens traveling in foreign lands may go to U.S. consulates if they need assistance.

At home the Department of State is the keeper of the Great Seal of the United States. The Great Seal is put on all laws and treaties. The Department of State also issues documents known as **passports** and **visas.** Passports are formal documents that allow U.S. citizens to travel abroad. Visas allow foreigners to come to the United States.

✔ **Reading Check** Summarizing What are some of the duties of the Department of State? to represent the United States abroad through ambassadors, ministers, and consuls; to put the Great Seal on all laws and treaties; to issue passports and visas

## ★ Department of the Treasury

The Department of the Treasury manages the country's money. It collects taxes from citizens and businesses and pays out the money owed by the federal government. When necessary, the Department of the Treasury borrows money for the government. It also supervises the coining and printing of money, and it keeps the president informed about the economic condition of the country.

There are several divisions within the Department of the Treasury. The Internal Revenue Service (IRS) collects individual and corporate income taxes. The Customs Service collects taxes on goods brought into the country. The Secret Service protects the president and helps prevent **counterfeiting**—the making or distributing of fake money.

✔ **Reading Check** Comparing What do the IRS, Customs Service, and Secret Service have in common? all are part of the Department of the Treasury

**LEVEL 3:** Ask students to think of a significant issue or problem in their local community and to identify which one of the 14 executive departments oversees programs or agencies relevant to that issue. Tell each student to write a letter to a specific cabinet member, describing the issue and explaining how that cabinet member's executive department can help the president. *(For example, students interested in improving mass transit in their community should write to the secretary of transportation.)* Ask volunteers to read their letters to the class.

## TEACH OBJECTIVE 3

 **LEVEL 1:** Lead the class in a discussion about why the number of executive departments has grown to 14 over the years. Encourage students to think about changes that have occurred in the United States and in the world that may have necessitated these new offices. Organize students into groups and assign one or two departments to each group. Then have each group write down possible reasons for the creation of the departments that it has been assigned. *(Students might suggest a need to improve education, streamline energy mandates, and so on.)* **ENGLISH LANGUAGE LEARNERS** , **COOPERATIVE LEARNING**

## ★ Department of Defense

Until 1947 the U.S. armed forces were directed by two separate departments—the Department of War and the Department of the Navy. In 1947 Congress began the task of reorganizing the armed forces. It eventually placed the army, navy, and air force under one department, the Department of Defense. The department's head, the secretary of defense, is always a **civilian,** or nonmilitary person. However, the secretary does have many military officers as assistants. These officers help the secretary plan military defense and provide for the training and equipping of the armed forces.

There are three major divisions within the Department of Defense. The Department of the Army commands land forces. The Department of the Navy has charge of seagoing forces. This department also includes the U. S. Marine Corps. During times of war, the Department of the Navy supervises the Coast Guard. During times of peace, the Coast Guard falls under the jurisdiction of the Department of Transportation. The Department of the Air Force is responsible for air defenses. Each of these three divisions is headed by a civilian secretary.

The highest-ranking military officers of the army, navy, and air force form the **Joint Chiefs of Staff**. This group has the responsibility of advising the president on military affairs. While not officially a member, the head of the marine corps attends all meetings of the Joint Chiefs. He or she also takes part as an equal member when matters concerning the marines are discussed.

The Department of Defense is also responsible for four officer-training schools. These are the U.S. Military Academy at West Point, New York; the U.S. Naval Academy at Annapolis, Maryland; the U.S. Air Force Academy at Colorado Springs, Colorado; and the U.S. Coast Guard Academy at New London, Connecticut.

With the exception of the Coast Guard Academy, academy candidates must be nominated for admission. Candidates usually obtain nominations from their district representatives or from their state senators and face a very competitive admission process. All candidates must have good high school academic records and must pass scholastic and physical tests.

The successful candidate receives a free four-year college education from the academy. Upon graduation he or she becomes an officer in one of the military services. Since 1976, women have been admitted into all the service academies on an equal basis with men.

✔ **Reading Check** Categorizing Who are some of the civilian and military leaders of the Department of Defense? civilian—secretaries of defense, of the army, the navy, and the air force; military—Joint Chiefs of Staff

*An increasing number of American women have joined the armed forces in the past 10 years.*

## ★ Culture

**President Bush's Cabinet** President George W. Bush's cabinet appointments in 2001 represented a mix of racial and ethnic groups. These appointments included African Americans Colin Powell (secretary of state) and Rod Paige (secretary of education), Asian Americans Norman Mineta (secretary of transportation) and Elaine Chao (secretary of labor), and Cuban American Mel Martinez (secretary of housing and urban development).

**ACTIVITY:** Break students into groups and assign each group a different member of President Bush's cabinet. Ask students to write one-paragraph biographies of their assigned cabinet members and to present these biographies to the class.

## The Democratic Process

### Expanding the Cabinet

Following the terrorist attacks of September 11, 2001, President George W. Bush created the cabinet-level position of Director of Homeland Security and named Pennsylvania governor Tom Ridge as director. The executive order creating the Office of Homeland Security instructs the office to "develop and coordinate the implementation of a comprehensive national strategy to secure the United States from terrorist threats or attacks."

**ACTIVITY:** Have students conduct research to find out what steps the Department of Homeland Security has taken to improve security in the United States. Ask students to present their findings to the class.

### internet connect

**TOPIC:** Executive Departments Online
**GO TO:** go.hrw.com
**KEYWORD:** SZ3 AC6

Have students access the Internet through the HRW Go site to research present-day executive departments. Then have students create charts that include the following information: the responsibilities of each department, who heads it, the department's Web site, and the kinds of online services the department offers citizens.

**158**

## Principal Duties of the Executive Departments

**Department of State**
• Conducts foreign relations
• Protects U.S. citizens abroad
• Issues passports and visas

**Department of Defense**
• Maintains U.S. armed forces
• Operates military bases

**Department of Housing and Urban Development**
• Helps urban-housing programs

**Department of Labor**
• Determines standards of labor
• Publishes employment information
• Directs public-employment services

**Department of the Interior**
• Controls public lands and water resources
• Maintains public parks
• Supervises American Indian reservations

**Department of Energy**
• Helps develop the nation's energy policies
• Promotes conservation of energy
• Regulates energy resources

**Department of Treasury**
• Mints, coins and prints money
• Collects taxes and pays bills
• Manages government funds

**Department of Health and Human Services**
• Directs public health services
• Sees that foods and medicines are safe

**Department of Agriculture**
• Directs soil conservation programs
• Manages food stamps and school lunch programs

**Department of Transportation**
• Helps develop the nation's transportation policy
• Supervises federal-aid highway program
• Promotes transportation safety

**Department of Veterans Affairs**
• Administers medical and disability benefits to veterans and their families
• Provides pensions and death benefits for veterans

**Department of Homeland Security**
• Prevents terrorist attacks within the United States
• Minimizes damage from potential attacks and natural disasters

**Department of Commerce**
• Encourages and regulates foreign trade
• Publishes reports on business and trade
• Sets standards for weights and measures

**Department of Justice**
• Investigates violations of federal laws
• Prosecutes cases before courts
• Administers naturalization laws
• Enforces immigration laws

**Department of Education**
• Sets guidelines for granting financial aid to schools
• Administers federal education programs
• Conducts research on education

**Interpreting Charts** *The executive departments carry out most of the work of the executive branch. What department is responsible for maintaining public parks?*

## Department of Justice

The Department of Justice, led by the attorney general, enforces federal laws. This department also defends the United States in court when a lawsuit is brought against the federal government.

The Federal Bureau of Investigation (FBI) is within the Department of Justice. The FBI investigates crimes in which federal government laws are broken and arrests those accused of crimes against the United States. The Immigration and Naturalization Service (INS) and the Federal Bureau of Prisons are agencies that are part of the Department of Justice.

✔ **Reading Check** Finding the Main Idea What is the function of the Department of Justice, and what agencies help it fulfill its duties?
to enforce federal law; the Federal Bureau of Investigation, the Immigration and Naturalization Service, and the Federal Bureau of Prisons

**LEVEL 3:** Write the names of each cabinet position on separate slips of paper and have students draw them at random. Tell students that they have just been named secretary of the department that they have chosen. Have each student write a speech in which he or she accepts the position and describes the policies and plans the department should enact. *(Students should take time to think carefully about any current events or issues that their departments should address.)* Ask volunteers to read their speeches to the class.

**ENGLISH LANGUAGE LEARNERS**

**LEVEL 3:** Ask each student to choose one of the 15 executive departments and to create a brochure about it. The brochure should include information about the department's history, duties, and structure as well as information about issues affecting the department. Students might need to refer to other classroom resources, such as encyclopedias. Collect the brochures to create a Guide to the Executive Departments.

**ENGLISH LANGUAGE LEARNERS**

## ★ Department of the Interior

The Department of the Interior manages the nation's natural resources. It encourages the wise use of U.S. land, minerals, water, fish, and wildlife. The department also manages national parks and federal dams.

There are several important divisions within the department. The Bureau of Indian Affairs handles matters involving American Indians, and there are 562 federally recognized tribal governments. The Bureau of Reclamation sponsors irrigation, flood control, and hydroelectric power projects. Other divisions include the National Park Service, the Office of Surface Mining Reclamation and Enforcement, and the U.S. Fish and Wildlife Service.

✔ **Reading Check** Summarizing How does the Department of the Interior manage the nation's natural resources? Through its several divisions the department encourages the wise use of U.S. land, minerals, water, fish, and wildlife.

## ★ Department of Agriculture

The Department of Agriculture helps farmers in the important task of raising and marketing crops. Special agencies in the department, such as the Agricultural Research Service and the Natural Resources Conservation Service, encourage better methods of farming. The department also prepares reports on market conditions for crops and livestock to help farmers in their planning and planting.

Other divisions within the Department of Agriculture include the Farm Service Agency (FSA), which provides loans for buying and operating farms, and the USDA Forest Service, which helps protect the nation's woodlands. The Food and Nutrition Service manages the Food Stamp and National School Lunch programs.

✔ **Reading Check** Drawing Inferences and Conclusions How do you think the work of the Department of Agriculture affects most Americans? Students might say that it affects the quality of agricultural products available to American consumers.

## ★ Department of Commerce

The Department of Commerce encourages American trade and business. There are many important agencies within this department. For example, the Bureau of Economic Analysis studies business conditions in the United States. The Minority Business Development Agency assists in creating and strengthening minority-owned businesses. The Patent and Trademark Office protects the rights of inventors. The International Trade Administration promotes world trade and seeks to strengthen the U.S. position in such trade.

**Interpreting the Visual Record**

**High tech** *The Commerce Department tries to promote the development of cutting-edge industries in areas such as computers and medical science.* **How does the work of the Patent Office help encourage technological innovation in the private sector?**

### ★ Civics Sidelight

**Keeping America Beautiful** In 1872 Congress established Yellowstone National Park. By 1916 the number of national parks and monuments under the care of the Department of the Interior had grown to 40, so Congress created the National Park Service as a bureau within the Department of the Interior. Congress entrusted the National Park Service to "conserve the natural and historic objects in such manner as will leave them unimpaired for the enjoyment of future generations." Today there are more than 83 million acres of land in the care of the National Park Service.

**ACTIVITY:** Tell students to identify the five national parks closest to their school and to find out the history of each. Ask each student to make a poster showing highlights and information about the parks and to explain his or her poster to the class.

**CHART ANSWER**
(for page 158)
Department of the Interior

**Visual Record Answer**

*Students might suggest that it works to ensure that inventors receive credit for their work.*

**LEVEL 3:** Tell students that each of the 14 executive departments employs many people to help the president run the country. Ask each student to choose one executive department and to conduct research to learn about what opportunities are available in that department. (*Students might describe how the Department of Health and Human Services employs scientists, doctors, and counselors.*) Have each student write a brief summary of five different career opportunities that can be found within a specific executive department. Ask volunteers to tell the class about the jobs that they thought sounded the most interesting. **ENGLISH LANGUAGE LEARNERS**

## CLOSE

Have each student create a detailed chart showing the organization and duties of the presidency, the Executive Office, the cabinet, and the executive departments. Students should include a brief description of the duties and powers of each office or department and should arrange the departments in a way that shows the hierarchy within the executive branch.

### ★ Citizenship in Action

**Operation Head Start**

Many senior citizens volunteer in an educational program called Head Start, which helps prepare preschool children for elementary school. The Economic Opportunity Act of 1964 established this program for financially disadvantaged children, and the program was later expanded to assist children above the poverty level as well. In 1969 responsibility for the program was transferred to the Department of Health, Education, and Welfare, and now Head Start is overseen by the Department of Health and Human Services.

**ACTIVITY:** Ask students to find out whether there is a Head Start center near their community. Have them conduct research to learn what programs Head Start offers preschool children, and ask each student to create a poster depicting these services. Display these posters around the classroom.

### Visual Record Answer

*Students might suggest that the department will become more important as Americans age and become more dependent on the health care system.*

Also within the Commerce Department is the U.S. Census Bureau. The Census Bureau counts the U.S. population every 10 years. The National Oceanic and Atmospheric Administration, which monitors and forecasts the country's weather, is also part of the Department of Commerce.

## ★ Department of Labor

The Department of Labor gathers information on working conditions in various businesses and industries. The Employment Standards Administration is responsible for carrying out federal laws that regulate the wages and hours of workers. This division also seeks to improve working conditions.

Another division of the Department of Labor is the Bureau of Labor Statistics, which collects information about and reports on employment and labor-management relations. The Women's Bureau is responsible for promoting the employment opportunities and personal well-being of working women.

✔ **Reading Check Summarizing** How are the Departments of Commerce and Labor involved with business and employment issues? commerce—promotes American trade and business; labor—collects information and enforces laws regarding employment

## ★ Other Executive Departments

The remaining executive departments have all been created since the end of World War II. Each deals with a set of social or economic needs.

**Health and Human Services** The Department of Health and Human Services runs programs to promote the health and well-being of all citizens. It was created out of the Department of Health, Education, and Welfare (HEW) in 1979. Its largest division, the Social Security Administration, became independent early in 1995.

**Housing and Urban Development** The Department of Housing and Urban Development (HUD) seeks to improve the housing conditions in U.S. cities. It runs programs to help people buy homes, and it helps city and state governments provide public housing and improve neighborhoods.

**Transportation** The Department of Transportation helps coordinate and develop the country's ground-, water-, and air-transportation systems. It also promotes public safety and deals with mass transitation issues. The Coast Guard is part of the Department of Transportation in peacetime. In wartime it becomes part of the Navy and the Department of Defense.

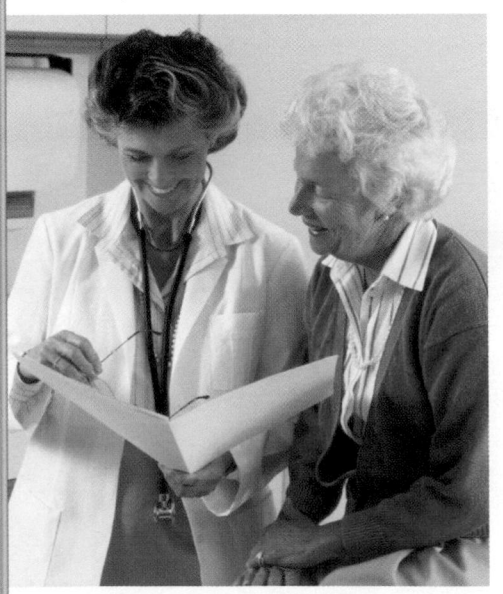

**Interpreting the Visual Record**

**Public health** *The Department of Health and Human Services promotes the health of U.S. citizens.* **In what ways does the growing number of elderly Americans make the role of this department increasingly important?**

## REVIEW AND ASSESS

Have students complete the **Section 3 Review** on page 161. Then have students complete **Daily Quiz 6.3**. As **Alternative Assessment**, you may want to use the ambassador's memo activity or the executive-departments brochure activity in this section's lessons.

## RETEACH

Have students complete **Main Idea Activity for English Language Learners and Special-Needs Students 6.3**. Assign students one of the Read to Discover questions at the beginning of the section. Then have them work individually or in groups to create a graphic organizer showing how the text addresses the question. **ENGLISH LANGUAGE LEARNERS › COOPERATIVE LEARNING**

## EXTEND

Point out to students that the 15 executive departments are also made up of smaller offices. Assign an executive department to each student and have him or her research at least three smaller offices that fall under the jurisdiction of the department. Then have each student prepare a five-minute lesson describing the roles that these smaller offices play in the government. Finally, have students present their lessons to the class. **BLOCK SCHEDULING**

**Energy** The Department of Energy helps plan and manage U.S. energy policy. It enforces energy laws and regulates the development and use of nuclear and hydroelectric power, gas and oil pipelines, and other energy resources.

**Education** The Department of Education provides advice and information to the country's school systems. It is also responsible for distributing federal funds and administering federal school programs throughout the United States.

**Veterans Affairs** The Department of Veterans Affairs administers government benefits, including health care, pensions, and education loans, to U.S. veterans and their families.

**Homeland Security** The Department of Homeland Security was established after the terrorist attacks of September 11, 2001. Its primary mission is to protect the nation against further terrorist attacks. It also helps to provide better public services, including federal assistance, when natural disasters occur in the United States.

*The Department of Energy is responsible for regulating the development and safety of nuclear power facilities.*

✔ **Reading Check Summarizing** What services do the seven Executive Departments created after World War II provide? **See text above and chart on page 158.**

## SECTION 3 Review

**go.hrw.com Homework Practice Online**
keyword: SZ3 HP6

**1. Define** and explain:
- budget
- executive departments
- secretary
- attorney general
- ambassadors
- embassy
- ministers
- consul
- consulate
- passports
- visas
- counterfeiting
- civilian

**2. Identify** and explain:
- Joint Chiefs of Staff

**3. Categorizing** Copy the diagram below. Use it to identify the responsibilities of the following six departments.

**4. Finding the Main Idea**
a. How can the Executive Office of the President and its purpose be described?
b. How are the chiefs of executive departments and cabinet members alike?

**5. Writing and Critical Thinking**
**Problem Solving** You are a newly appointed secretary to an executive department (of your choice). Your first duty is to write a memo to the president. In two paragraphs describe the most pressing national issue facing your department and explain your department's plan to address it.

**Consider:**
- the specific role of the 15 executive departments
- your department's work to improve the lives of all Americans

| State | Treasury | Defense | Justice | Commerce | Interior |
|---|---|---|---|---|---|
| ↓ | ↓ | ↓ | ↓ | ↓ | ↓ |
|  |  |  |  |  |  |

## Section 3 Review
## ANSWERS

**1. Define**
- budget, p. 153
- executive departments, p. 154
- secretary, p. 155
- attorney general, p. 155
- ambassadors, p. 155
- embassy, p. 155
- ministers, p. 155
- consul, p. 156
- consulate, p. 156
- passports, p. 156
- visas, p. 156
- counterfeiting, p. 156
- civilian, p. 157

**2. Identify**
- Joint Chiefs of Staff, p. 157

**3.** State—foreign relations, protects U.S. citizens abroad, passports and visas

Treasury—issues money, collects taxes, pays bills, manages government funds

Defense—maintains armed forces, conducts military studies, operates bases

Justice—investigates violations of federal law, prosecutes cases, administers naturalization laws, enforces immigration laws

Commerce—sets standards for weights and measures, regulates foreign trade, reports on business and trade

Interior—controls public lands, maintains public parks, supervises American Indian reservations, controls water resources

**4. a.** It is composed of agencies and offices that advise the president on domestic and foreign matters.

**b.** Chiefs of executive departments are all members of the cabinet.

**5.** Memos will vary, but students should demonstrate an understanding of their department's purpose.

## TEACH OBJECTIVE 1

 **LEVEL 1:** Have each student draw a chart to represent the organization of the business or place of employment where a family or friend works. Point out the similarities between the students' charts and the organizational chart of the Department of Defense shown on this page. Tell students that such charts can help to sort out the complex chain of command in many types of organizations.

**ENGLISH LANGUAGE LEARNERS**

## EXTEND

Have students review the organizational-chart skills that they studied in the workshop. Then ask them to create data related to another organization, such as their school or their local government. Ask each student to draw a small chart on a piece of notebook paper, showing the lines of communication and authority that exist between the various members or departments of the organization he or she has chosen to represent. Then encourage volunteers to draw their organizational charts on the chalkboard and to explain their findings to the class.

**BLOCK SCHEDULING**

## SKILLS ANSWERS

1. secretary of the air force

2. secretaries of the army, air force, and navy and the Joint Chiefs of Staff (advisory role); secretary of defense

3. Civilians hold all the top positions to ensure that the military remains accountable to the people.

# Civics Skills
## WORKSHOP

### Reading Organizational Charts

An effective way to visualize the executive branch is to use an organizational chart. Organizational charts have two basic parts: boxes and lines. The boxes represent certain offices or people. The lines that connect the boxes represent lines of communication. Generally, the offices or people with the most authority are at the top of the chart.

### How to Read Organizational Charts

1. **Determine the subject.** Read the title of the chart to learn which organization is being diagrammed.

2. **Identify the symbols and colors.** Most organizational charts include a key explaining the symbols and colors in the chart.

3. **Analyze the chart.** Read the labels of the various boxes, and notice how the lines of authority and communication connect the boxes.

4. **Put the data to use.** Draw conclusions about the organization from the chart.

### Applying the Skill

Examine the organizational chart below. Then answer the following questions.

1. To whom does the chief of staff of the Air Force report?

2. Who reports to the secretary of defense? Who reports directly to the commander in chief?

3. What role is played by civilians in the Department of Defense? Why do you think this is so?

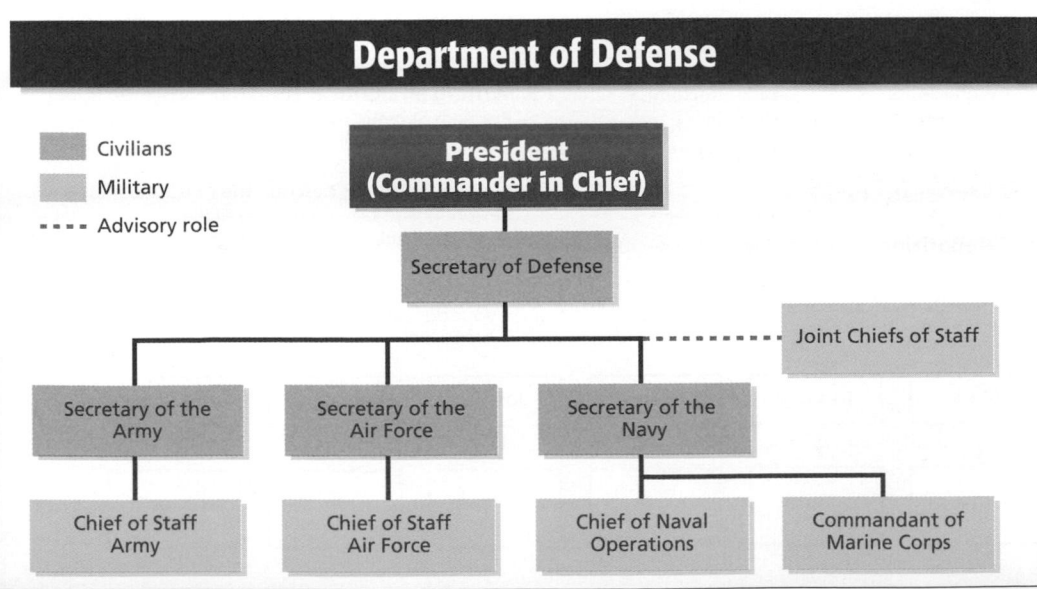

**Department of Defense**

Civilians
Military
- - - - Advisory role

President (Commander in Chief) → Secretary of Defense

Joint Chiefs of Staff

Secretary of the Army — Secretary of the Air Force — Secretary of the Navy

Chief of Staff Army — Chief of Staff Air Force — Chief of Naval Operations — Commandant of Marine Corps

# SECTION 4

## OBJECTIVES

After completing Section 4, students should be able to

1 **Identify the independent agencies and explain why they are separate from the executive departments.**

2 **Evaluate the purpose of regulatory commissions and explain who runs them.**

3 **Describe the federal bureaucracy.**

### 🔊 LET'S GET STARTED!

Write the word *bureaucracy* on the chalkboard. As students enter the classroom, invite them to write on the chalkboard the name of government agencies that are a part of the federal bureaucracy. *(Students might list the Small Business Administration, the Internal Revenue Service, the Food and Drug Administration, and so on.)* Explain that the federal bureaucracy comprises all of the agencies and departments in the executive branch of government. Tell students that in Section 4 they will learn more about the agencies and regulatory commissions of the federal bureaucracy.

## SECTION 4

# Independent Agencies and Regulatory Commissions

### Read to Discover

1. What are independent agencies, and why are they separate from the executive departments?
2. What is the purpose of regulatory commissions, and who runs them?
3. What is the federal bureaucracy?

### Define

- independent agencies
- regulatory commissions
- bureaucracy

#### WHY CIVICS MATTERS

The federal bureaucracy employs millions of people and has many rules and regulations for completing a broad scope of activities. Use CNNfyi.com or other **current events** sources to illustrate what steps can be involved in the bureaucratic process. Record your findings in your journal.

## SECTION 4 RESOURCES

### REPRODUCIBLE
▶ Guided Reading Strategies 6.4

### TECHNOLOGY
▶ One-Stop Planner, Lesson 6.4
▶ CNN Presents: American Government
▶ Homework Practice Online

### REINFORCEMENT, REVIEW, AND ASSESSMENT
▶ Section 4 Review, p. 165
▶ Daily Quiz 6.4
▶ Main Idea Activity 6.4
▶ English Audio Summary 6.4
▶ Spanish Audio Summary 6.4

## Reading Focus

In addition to the executive departments, Congress has set up a number of **independent agencies.** These agencies help the president carry out the duties of office.

The independent agencies are separate from the executive departments because they perform specialized duties that often do not fit into any regular department. In addition, some of these agencies serve all the departments. Therefore, they function best as separate and independent organizations.

### ⭐ Independent Agencies

There are more than 65 independent agencies. Each was created by Congress to perform a specific job. For example, the U.S. Commission on Civil Rights collects information about discrimination. The Farm Credit Administration helps farmers obtain loans. The Small Business Administration makes loans to small businesses. The National Aeronautics and Space Administration (NASA) runs the U.S. space program.

Several independent agencies assist the work of the entire government. For example, the Office of Personnel Management gives

*Applicants for some positions with U.S. government agencies must take a written exam.*

**LEVEL 1:** Lead a class discussion about the independent agencies and why they are separate from the executive departments. Tell each student to choose one of the agencies and to draw a picture illustrating one of that agency's responsibilities. **ENGLISH LANGUAGE LEARNERS**

**ALL LEVELS:** Lead a class discussion about the effectiveness and ineffectiveness of the federal bureaucracy. Ask each student to write a sentence about whether the bureaucratic system is the best way for the government to do its business.
**ENGLISH LANGUAGE LEARNERS**

**ALL LEVELS:** Copy the following graphic organizer onto the chalkboard, omitting the italicized answers. Have students complete the organizer by writing the names of independent agencies in the larger oval and the regulatory commissions in the smaller oval. **ENGLISH LANGUAGE LEARNERS**

**Independent Agencies**
*Commission on Civil Rights*
*Farm Credit Administration*

**Regulatory Commissions**
*Federal Election Commission*
*Consumer Product Safety Commission*
*Securities and Exchange Commission*
*National Labor Relations Board*

*National Aeronautics and Space Administration*
*Small Business Administration*
*Office of Personnel Management*
*General Services Administration*

---

## Civics Sidelight

**Regulating the Regulators** Some people believe that independent agencies are sometimes influenced by outside interest groups. For example, the Nuclear Regulatory Commission (NRC)—an independent regulatory agency— inspects and licenses nuclear reactors. Some critics have argued that the NRC has been too lax. In 1979, mechanical problems and human errors caused a serious accident at the Three Mile Island nuclear power plant in Pennsylvania, and this accident highlighted problems with the NRC's regulations. Since that time, however, industry and government officials have worked together to improve safety standards at nuclear power facilities.

**ACTIVITY:** Ask students to conduct research to find other examples of how industry and independent government agencies have worked together to maintain and improve safety standards. Ask each student to write a description of what he or she has learned and to share this with the class.

### Visual Record Answer

*Students' responses will vary.*

**Interpreting the Visual Record**

NASA *The National Aeronautics and Space Administration maintains the U.S. fleet of space shuttles. Here a space shuttle launches into orbit.* **Why do you think the space program has its own agency?**

tests to people who want to apply for jobs with the federal government. The General Services Administration buys supplies for the federal government. It also builds and maintains federal buildings.

✔ **Reading Check Summarizing** What is the purpose of independent agencies, and what are some of the specific jobs that they perform? They help the president by performing specialized duties that often do not fit into any regular department. See preceding text for duties.

## Regulatory Commissions

Some independent agencies have the power to make rules and bring violators to court. These agencies are called **regulatory commissions.** Their decisions often have the force of law.

The Federal Election Commission (FEC), for example, was created in 1975 to enforce the Federal Election Campaign Act. This act determines how federal elections are financed. The FEC enforces election laws, provides finance information for campaigns, and controls public funding of presidential elections.

The Consumer Product Safety Commission (CPSC) sets and enforces safety standards for consumer products. It also conducts safety research and provides education programs. The Securities and Exchange Commission (SEC) helps enforce laws regulating the buying and selling of stocks and bonds. This helps protect Americans' investments. The National Labor Relations Board (NLRB) helps enforce federal labor laws. It also works to prevent and remedy unfair labor practices among businesses.

✔ **Reading Check Contrasting** What distinguishes a regulatory commission from other independent agencies? has the power to make rules and bring violators to court

## Who Runs the Regulatory Commissions?

The regulatory commissions are independent so that they have the freedom they need to do their jobs. The heads of these commissions are appointed by the president and approved by the Senate. However, these officials serve long terms. Because of these long terms, a single president cannot appoint more than a few commission leaders. This system was put in place to help keep the commissions from being too influenced by party politics.

Some people have criticized the independence of the regulatory commissions on the grounds that it makes them too powerful. Some critics feel that these commissions over-regulate and interfere too much in our lives. Other people defend these commissions. They say that the commissions' regulations are needed to protect the public.

✔ **Reading Check Identifying Points of View** Why have regulatory commissions been criticized? *Some say they over-regulate and interfere too much in our lives.*

### ⭐ The Federal Bureaucracy

The departments and agencies in the executive branch of the government form the federal **bureaucracy.** Almost 3 million people work in the bureaucracy. They include administrators, lawyers, scientists, doctors, engineers, secretaries, and clerks. They work in Washington, D.C., in other cities throughout the United States, and in foreign countries.

The bureaucracy has many rules and regulations for carrying out a wide range of activities. Often these rules and regulations lead to bureaucratic delay, or "red tape." Sometimes people dealing with a government agency must spend time filling out forms or standing in long lines. They might have to go from department to department before getting the help they need. Despite these problems, the people in the bureaucracy keep the executive branch functioning under every president.

✔ **Reading Check Identifying Cause and Effect** What does bureaucracy use to carry out activities, and what is often the result? *rules and regulations; bureaucratic delay*

GRIN AND BEAR IT        by Lichty & Wagner

©Field Enterprises, Inc., 1979

"Sorry. . .You'll have to go through the red tape like everyone else."

**Interpreting Political Cartoons**

**Red tape** *This cartoon pokes fun of the difficulties that the federal bureaucracy can cause when trying to raise money.* **What is the politician in the cartoon saying?**

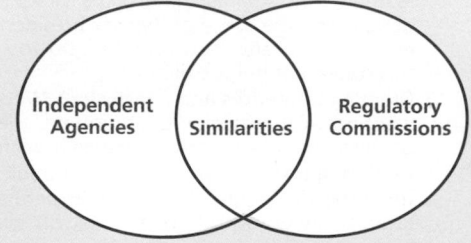

## SECTION 4 Review

**go.hrw.com Homework Practice Online**
keyword: SZ3 HP6

**1. Define** and explain:
• independent agencies
• regulatory commissions
• bureaucracy

**2. Comparing** Copy the chart below. Use it to explain the similarities and differences between independent agencies and regulatory commissions.

Independent Agencies | Similarities | Regulatory Commissions

**3. Finding the Main Idea**
a. What purpose do independent agencies serve, and why are they set up independently from the executive departments?
b. What parts of the executive branch make up the federal bureaucracy?

**4. Writing and Critical Thinking**
**Supporting a Point of View** Imagine that you are an individual trying to get federal aid. Write a three-paragraph speech that either supports or criticizes the role of the federal bureaucracy.

**Consider:**
• the wide range of activities that the bureaucracy performs
• criticisms of the bureaucracy

## Review and Assessment Resources

**REPRODUCIBLE**
▶ Chapter 6 Review, pp. 166–67
▶ Vocabulary Activity 6
▶ Chapter 6 Tutorial for Students, Parents, Mentors, and Peers
▶ Chapter 6 Test (Form A or B)
▶ Alternative Assessment Handbook

**TECHNOLOGY**
▶ Chapter 6 Test Generator (on the One-Stop Planner)
▶ Global Skill Builder CD–ROM
▶ HRW Go site

**REINFORCEMENT, REVIEW, AND ASSESSMENT**
▶ Chapter 6 Test for English Language Learners and Special-Needs Students

## REVIEW

Have students complete the **Chapter 6 Review** on pages 166–67.

## ASSESS

Use one of the chapter tests to assess students' understanding of the content. For **Alternative Assessment**, see the **Alternative Assessment Handbook**.

---

## CHAPTER 6

### REVIEW ANSWERS

**Define and Identify**
Students should indicate an understanding of the following definitions:

1. presidential succession, p. 146
2. diplomacy, p. 149
3. treaties, p. 150
4. reprieve, p. 151
5. pardon, p. 151
6. commutation, p. 151
7. attorney general, p. 155
8. consulate, p. 156
9. Joint Chiefs of Staff, p. 157
10. bureaucracy, p. 165

**Understanding Main Ideas**

1. succeeds president if president dies, resigns, or is removed from office and presides over the Senate

2. two-term limit

3. keep Congress informed and set forth programs and policies that the president wants Congress to put into effect

4. recommends laws, sends Congress a budget, has the power to veto bills passed by Congress

5. advises the president on current domestic and international issues

6. members of the cabinet

7. because they perform specialized duties that do not fit into any regular department and some of these agencies serve all of the departments

---

# Chapter 6 Review

## Chapter Summary

### Section 1

- As the head of the executive branch, the president is responsible for seeing that the country's laws are carried out.
- The president must be a native-born citizen, be at least 35 years old, and have been a U.S. resident for at least 14 years.
- The president may be elected to no more than two four-year terms.
- The vice president must meet the same constitutional requirements as the president.
- The order of presidential succession is as follows: vice president, Speaker, president *pro tempore* of the Senate, and members of the cabinet in the order in which their departments were created.

### Section 2

- The president must provide leadership in such vital areas as setting an agenda for legislation, heading the armed forces, setting foreign policy, dealing with foreign governments, appointing judges, and promoting the country's prosperity.

### Section 3

- There are 15 executive departments in the federal government. These departments carry on much of the work of the executive branch of the federal government.

### Section 4

- A number of independent agencies also assist in the day to day work of the executive branch. Some of these agencies are regulatory commissions, with the power to make rules and bring violators to court.
- The many departments and agencies of the executive branch form the federal bureaucracy.

---

## Define and Identify

Use the following terms in complete sentences.

1. presidential succession
2. diplomacy
3. treaties
4. reprieve
5. pardon
6. commutation
7. attorney general
8. consulate
9. Joint Chiefs of Staff
10. bureaucracy

## Understanding Main Ideas

**Section 1** *(Pages 143–46)*
1. What is the vice president's role in the government?
2. What limitation did the Twenty-second Amendment place on the terms of the presidency?

**Section 2** *(Pages 147–52)*
3. What is the purpose of the State of the Union Address?
4. How does the president participate in the legislative process?

**Section 3** *(Pages 153–61)*
5. How does the Executive Office of the President serve the president?
6. What other position do the executive department heads hold?

**Section 4** *(Pages 163–65)*
7. Why are the independent agencies separate from the executive departments?

## What Did You Find Out?

1. What qualifies a presidential candidate for the presidency, and how long can the president serve?
2. How is the executive branch organized?
3. What are the arguments supporting and opposing regulatory commissions?

## Thinking Critically

1. **Supporting a Point of View** As you have learned, John Adams, the first U.S. vice president, called the office of the vice president "the most insignificant" ever invented. Do you think this statement holds true today?
2. **Drawing Inferences and Conclusions** Who or what has authority over the president, the most powerful member of the executive branch?
3. **Analyzing Information** Why do you think only three specific requirements for president are listed in the Constitution? Why do you think those qualifications were listed?

## RETEACH

Organize students into four groups and assign each group one of the chapter's sections. Have each group create a poster or chart illustrating the main objectives in its assigned section. Then have groups present their work to the class.

**ENGLISH LANGUAGE LEARNERS ,**
**COOPERATIVE LEARNING**

## Portfolio Extensions

**1. Interdisciplinary Connection to Art and Literature** Ask students to identify local artistic or literary programs that have been supported or funded by a specific department or agency of the federal bureaucracy, such as the National Endowment for the Humanities. *(Students might identify radio and television programs, book festivals, museum shows, school programs in the arts, and so on.)* Then have each student create a poster showing

how his or her community has been enriched by these programs in art and literature.

**2. Linking to Community** Ask students to identify programs in their community that are under the direction of an executive department or one of its smaller offices. Tell each student to interview someone who has been directly involved in one of these programs and to ask why the support of the federal government is important. Have volunteers present their interviews to the class.

---

## Building Social Studies Skills

STANDARDIZED TEST PREP ONLINE keyword: SZ3 STP6

### Interpreting Political Cartoons

Study the political cartoon of President Theodore Roosevelt below and answer the questions.

1. Why do you think the artist drew Roosevelt as a king?
   a. American presidents have the same powers as kings.
   b. The artist thinks Roosevelt is so talented that he should be crowned king .
   c. The artist thinks Roosevelt is trying to stay in power for life like a king.
   d. Roosevelt does not listen to the people.
2. The crown Roosevelt is placing on his head is labeled "third term." Why would it be unusual for Roosevelt to be seeking a third term?

### Analyzing Primary Sources

Read the following quotation from President George W. Bush's address to Congress and the country after the September 11, 2001, terrorist attacks. Then answer the questions that follow.

> ❝We have suffered great loss. And in our grief and anger we have found our mission and our moment. Freedom and fear are at war. The advance of human freedom—the great achievement of our time, and the great hope of every time—now depends on us. Our nation—this generation—will lift a dark threat of violence from our people and our future. We will rally the world to this cause by our efforts, by our courage. We will not tire, we will not falter, and we will not fail.❞

3. Which of the following statements best describes Bush's view of the U.S. role in the world?
   a. The example and the actions of the United States play an important role in leading the struggle for freedom around the world.
   b. The United States must protect only itself.
   c. The United States is the strongest nation in the world and has nothing to fear.
   d. Other countries do not practice democracy.
4. Why do you think President Bush chose to address the country about national defense and foreign-policy goals?

### What Did You Find Out?

1. native-born citizen, at least 35 years old, U.S. resident for at least 14 years; no more than two four-year terms

2. There are 15 executive departments, the heads of which are members of the president's cabinet

3. for: needed to protect the public; against: interfere too much in our daily lives

### Thinking Critically

1. Some students might point out that the responsibilities of the vice president have increased since Adams's time.

2. The War Powers Act and the power of impeachment are some ways that Congress and the judiciary can exercise authority over the president. Congress can also reject the budget and policies proposed by the president.

3. Answers will vary, but students should point out that the Constitution makes it possible for people of many different backgrounds to run for the office of the presidency.

### Skills Answers
1. c

2. because of the two-term precedent set by George Washington

3. a

4. Students might suggest that the American people needed a message of strength and hope.

---

## Alternative Assessment

### Building Your Portfolio

**Cooperative Learning**
Complete the following activity in small groups. Gather newspaper and magazine photographs that illustrate the president's daily activities. Determine how each of the president's activities affects your community and create a collage. What policies or laws has the president carried out that affect your daily life and/or the lives of other members of your community? Present the collage to the class.

### internet connect

**Internet Activity: go.hrw.com**
**keyword: SZ3 AC6**

Access the Internet through the HRW Go site to research the qualifications, daily job requirements, and personal qualities needed in a successful president. Than write a newspaper classified advertisement for the president of the United States. Be sure to include qualifications, a brief job description, salary, and benefits. Make it as realistic as possible by looking in a local newspaper for examples of what the ad might look like.

# The Judicial Branch

## CHAPTER RESOURCE MANAGER

| Objectives | Pacing Guide | Reproducible Resources |
|---|---|---|
| **SECTION 1:**<br>**Equal Justice**<br>**under the Law**<br>(pp. 169–73)<br><br>✪ Describe how majority rule affects the making of laws, and explain why obeying laws is important.<br>✪ Identify the four types of U.S. law.<br>✪ Define the roles played by courts in the United States. | **Regular**<br>1.5 days<br><br>**Block Scheduling**<br>1 day<br><br>*Block Scheduling Handbook with Team Teaching Strategies, Chapter 7* | **RS** Guided Reading Strategies 7.1<br>**RS** Readings in Economics and Government 70: "A Theory of Justice," by John Rawls<br>**E** Creative Teaching Strategy: Music, Poetry, and Law<br>**PS** American Civics Political Cartoon: Lawsuits<br>**SM** Community Service and Participation Handbook: Reaching a Verdict |
| **SECTION 2:**<br>**The Federal**<br>**Court System**<br>(pp. 174–80)<br><br>✪ Determine which cases are tried in federal courts.<br>✪ Explain how federal courts are organized.<br>✪ Describe the Supreme Court's role in the judicial system. | **Regular**<br>1 day<br><br>**Block Scheduling**<br>.5 day<br><br>*Block Scheduling Handbook with Team Teaching Strategies, Chapter 7* | **RS** Guided Reading Strategies 7.2<br>**RS** Readings in Economics and Government 37: Judiciary Act of 1789 |
| **SECTION 3:**<br>**The Supreme**<br>**Court**<br>(pp. 182–89)<br><br>✪ Examine the process through which cases are tried in the Supreme Court.<br>✪ Explain how justices get appointed to the Supreme Court and tell how long they serve.<br>✪ Analyze how judicial review has strengthened the Court's power and how Congress limits this power. | **Regular**<br>1.5 days<br><br>**Block Scheduling**<br>1 day<br><br>*Block Scheduling Handbook with Team Teaching Strategies, Chapter 7* | **RS** Guided Reading Strategies 7.3<br>**E** Challenge and Enrichment Worksheet 7: Identifying Members of the Supreme Court<br>**RS** Graphic Organizer Activity: Some Landmark Decisions |

## Chapter Resource Key

| | | | | |
|---|---|---|---|---|
| **PS** Primary Sources | **SM** Skills Mastery |  CD-ROM | | **One-Stop** Planner CD-ROM |
| **RS** Reading Support | **A** Assessment |  Video | | |
| **IC** Interdisciplinary Connections | **REV** Review |  Internet | | **See the *One-Stop Planner* for** |
| **E** Enrichment | **ELL** Reinforcement and English Language Learners |  Holt Presentation Maker Using Microsoft® PowerPoint® | | **a complete list of additional resources for students and teachers.** |
| | Transparencies | | | |

## One-Stop Planner CD-ROM

It's easy to plan lessons, select resources, and print out materials for your students when you use the *One-Stop Planner CD-ROM with Test Generator*.

| Technology Resources | Reinforcement, Review, and Assessment |
|---|---|
| One-Stop Planner, Lesson 7.1 | **REV** Section 1 Review, p. 173 |
| Homework Practice Online | **A** Daily Quiz 7.1 |
|  | **ELL** Main Idea Activity 7.1 |
|  | **ELL** English Audio Summary 7.1 |
|  | **ELL** Spanish Audio Summary 7.1 |
| One-Stop Planner, Lesson 7.2 | **REV** Section 2 Review, p. 180 |
| Transparency 7: The U.S. Court System | **A** Daily Quiz 7.2 |
| CNN. Presents: American Government | **ELL** Main Idea Activity 7.2 |
| Homework Practice Online | **ELL** English Audio Summary 7.2 |
|  | **ELL** Spanish Audio Summary 7.2 |
| One-Stop Planner, Lesson 7.3 | **REV** Section 3 Review, p. 189 |
| Holt Researcher CD-ROM | **A** Daily Quiz 7.3 |
| Homework Practice Online | **ELL** Main Idea Activity 7.3 |
| HRW Go site | **ELL** English Audio Summary 7.3 |
|  | **ELL** Spanish Audio Summary 7.3 |

## internet connect

### HRW ONLINE RESOURCES
GO TO: go.hrw.com
Then type in the keyword.

### TEACHER HOME PAGE
KEYWORD: SZ3 Teacher

### CHAPTER INTERNET ACTIVITIES
KEYWORD: SZ3 AC7
Choose an activity to:
- create a mobile to display the federal court system.
- create a pamphlet on landmark Supreme Court cases.
- create a map or diagram illustrating Supreme Court rules and procedures.

### CHAPTER ENRICHMENT LINKS
KEYWORD: SZ3 CH7

### ONLINE ASSESSMENT
**Homework Practice**
KEYWORD: SZ3 HP7
**Rubrics**
KEYWORD: SS Rubrics

### ONLINE MAPS, CHARTS, AND GRAPHS
KEYWORD: SZ3 MCG
- The Right to a Fair Trial

### HOLT PRESENTATION MAKER
KEYWORD: SZ3 PPT7

### CONTENT UPDATES
KEYWORD: SS Content Updates

### ONLINE READING SUPPORT
KEYWORD: SS Strategies

### CURRENT EVENTS
KEYWORD: S3 Current Events

## Meeting Individual Needs

### Ability Levels

**Level 1** Basic-level activities designed for all students encountering new material

**Level 2** Intermediate-level activities designed for average students

**Level 3** Challenging activities designed for honors and gifted-and-talented students

**English Language Learners** Activities that address the needs of students with Limited English Proficiency

## Chapter Review and Assessment

| | |
|---|---|
| **IC** | Vocabulary Activity 7 |
|  | Global Skill Builder CD-ROM |
|  | HRW Go site |
| **REV** | Chapter 7 Tutorial for Students, Parents, Mentors, and Peers |
| **REV** | Chapter 7 Review, pp. 190–91 |
| **A** | Standardized Test Practice |
| **A** | Chapter 7 Test Generator (on the One-Stop Planner) |
| **A** | Chapter 7 Test (Form A or B) |
| **A** | Alternative Assessment Handbook |
| **A** | Chapter 7 Test for English Language Learners and Special-Needs Students |

## CHAPTER 7

**Section 1**   Equal Justice under the Law

**Section 2**   The Federal Court System

**Section 3**   The Supreme Court

### What's Your Opinion?

*To help students create their **Themes** Journal entries, provide the following examples of appropriate **agree/disagree** statements.*

● **Agree**   U.S. laws are created to protect the rights of all citizens.

**Disagree**   Inequalities in justice occur despite guaranteed equal protection under U.S. law.

● **Agree**   Impartial judges and balanced juries are selected to ensure fair trials.

**Disagree**   Judges are human; hence, they are subject to making mistakes.

● **Agree**   All citizens have equal access to the judgment of the highest court in the land.

**Disagree**   Only cases that satisfy certain requirements are heard before the Supreme Court.

## Internet Activity

**The Supreme Court**

**internet connect**

**TOPIC:** Supreme Court Procedures
**GO TO:** go.hrw.com
**KEYWORD:** SZ3 AC7

Have students access the Internet through the HRW Go site to research how the Supreme Court functions, when it accepts cases for hearing, and who the justices are. Then ask them to create a map that illustrates how a case gets through the Supreme Court. The map should be annotated and should reflect the current Supreme Court.

### CHAPTER

# 7 The Judicial Branch

**What's Your Opinion?**

### Build on What You Know

The actions of the U.S. government and its citizens are governed by laws. The government relies on a special set of officials to interpret these laws and to punish lawbreakers. These functions are the responsibility of the judicial branch of the federal government. In interpreting the laws, the judicial branch is guided by the ideal of equal justice for all. This ideal, essential to a free society, protects your rights and the rights of all Americans.

Do you **agree** or **disagree** with the following statements? Support your point of view in your journal.

- U.S. laws guarantee equal justice for all citizens.

- The courts always make fair decisions.

- Any person can take a trial directly to the Supreme Court.

# SECTION 1

## OBJECTIVES

*After completing Section 1, students should be able to*

1  **Describe how majority rule affects the making of laws and explain why obeying laws is important.**

2  **Identify the four types of U.S. law.**

3  **Define the roles played by courts in the United States.**

📢 *LET'S GET STARTED!*

As students enter the classroom, call on a volunteer to quote the last six words of the Pledge of Allegiance. *(Students should respond, "with liberty and justice for all.")* Explain to the class that the word *liberty* comes from the Latin word for "free." Then ask students, "What does justice have to do with freedom?" Allow students time to respond. *(Students might suggest that justice guarantees freedom.)* Tell students that in Section 1 they will learn about U.S. laws and the role that the courts play in the system.

## SECTION 1

# Equal Justice under the Law

### Read to Discover

1. How does majority rule affect the making of laws, and why is obeying laws important?
2. What are the four types of U.S. law?
3. What roles do the courts play in the United States?

### WHY CIVICS MATTERS

Although the Constitution was created to protect all Americans equally, citizens still have the right to seek a new verdict if they believe that they have not received a fair trial. Use **CNNfyi.com** or other **current events** sources to research a case that is being re-examined by the courts. Record your findings in your journal.

### Define

- statutory laws
- precedent
- common law
- administrative laws
- constitutional law
- petit jury
- jurors
- jury duty
- verdict
- hung jury
- cross-examine
- testimony
- appeal

## SECTION 1 RESOURCES

### REPRODUCIBLE

▶ Guided Reading Strategies 7.1

▶ Readings in Economics and Government 70: "A Theory of Justice" by John Rawls

▶ Creative Teaching Strategy: Music, Poetry, and Law

▶ American Civics Political Cartoon: Lawsuits

▶ Community Service and Participation Handbook: Reaching a Verdict

### TECHNOLOGY

▶ One-Stop Planner, Lesson 7.1

▶ Homework Practice Online

### REINFORCEMENT, REVIEW, AND ASSESSMENT

▶ Section 1 Review, p. 173

▶ Daily Quiz 7.1

▶ Main Idea Activity 7.1

▶ English Audio Summary 7.1

▶ Spanish Audio Summary 7.1

## *Reading Focus*

Carved in marble over the entrance of the Supreme Court Building in Washington, D.C., is the motto "Equal Justice Under Law." This motto means that in the United States all citizens are considered equal and are protected by the rule of law. In other words, the country's laws restrict the power of government. As a result, citizens are protected from the arbitrary, or unreasoned, rule of public officials.

### ★ Laws for the Good of All

U.S. citizens enjoy freedom because the United States has laws to protect their rights, yet some laws, of course, limit freedom. For example, a law against robbery denies the robber's freedom to steal. However, this law guarantees other citizens the freedom to use and enjoy their personal property. A system of law provides citizens with predictable rules by which they must live. Without such rules, a country could fall into a state of political disorder, known as anarchy.

Laws usually represent majority rule, or what the majority of citizens believe to be right or wrong. When most of the people believe strongly that something should or should not be done, a law is passed on this issue. If voters later change their position on the issue, the law can be changed. Thus, laws grow and adapt to the country's needs.

*A blindfolded woman holding a set of scales is often used as a symbol for justice.*

**LEVEL 1:** Lead a class discussion about how majority rule affects the making of laws. *(Students should observe that laws usually reflect the beliefs of the majority of the population.)* Then tell students that when followed, laws ensure the safety of citizens and the protection of their freedoms. Call on volunteers to provide an example that supports this point. *(Students might suggest that a law against robbery limits the robber's freedom but safeguards the freedom of other citizens.)* **ENGLISH LANGUAGE LEARNERS**

**LEVEL 3:** Organize students into pairs. Then have pairs review how majority rule affects the making of laws. *(See the Level 1 lesson for the answer.)* Ask pairs to suggest a "law" for their school based on this concept. *(Students might suggest maintaining quiet during testing periods.)* Lead a debate on each proposed law and then vote on each law. Ask students why it would be important for everyone, including those who voted against the laws, to obey the new school laws. *(Students should note that, when followed, laws ensure the safety of citizens and the protection of their freedoms.)* **COOPERATIVE LEARNING**

## ★ Culture

**Common Law** Common law has roots in England during the Middle Ages, after the Norman Conquest in 1066. Before that time, local custom—strongly influenced by the church—formed the basis for law in England. The Normans established a central judiciary in England. Judges' decisions began to be recorded so that other judges could read and profit by them. This practice led to the development of the common-law legal tradition that later spread throughout the British Empire, including the British colonies in North America.

### CRITICAL THINKING

Why would judges benefit from reading the rulings of other judges?

**ANSWER:** Students might suggest that judges could learn from each other's thinking.

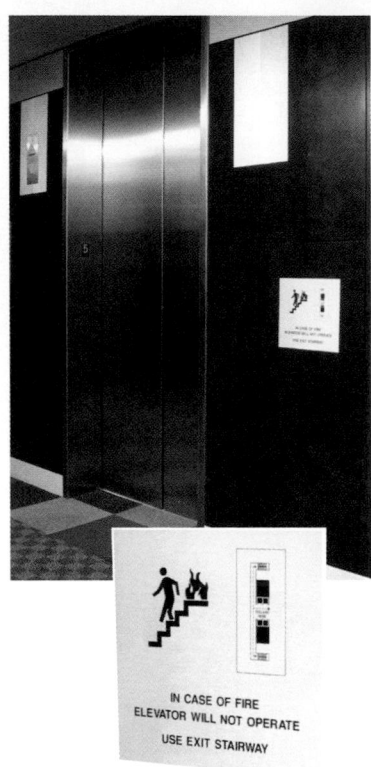

The presence of fire exits is an example of statutory laws in effect. This sign tells people to use stairs instead of the elevator to reach fire exits.

Every U.S. citizen has the duty to know and obey the laws, particularly those concerning activities he or she undertakes. If you ride a bicycle, for example, you must learn about road signs and traffic regulations. Law-abiding citizens understand that laws are passed for the good of all. By learning and obeying the country's laws, you are practicing good citizenship.

✔ **Reading Check** Finding the Main Idea What factor is usually the basis for making a law in the United States? majority rule

## ★ Kinds of Law

There are several kinds of law in the United States. The four principal types of law include statutory law, common law, administrative law, and constitutional law. All these laws must follow the principles set forth in the Constitution, which is the supreme law of the land.

**Statutory Law** Laws that are passed by lawmaking bodies are known as **statutory laws.** Congress and state and local governments pass these laws. For example, a state law that requires all public buildings to contain fire exits is a statutory law.

**Common Law** What happens if there is no existing statutory law covering a specific situation? Then Americans follow certain rules that we have accepted as the proper ways in which to act. Some of these rules are based on common sense. Others are based on experience and common practice.

For example, before automobiles became a major form of transportation, there were no laws about driving them. Suppose that someone was driving an automobile at its top speed and ran into a horse-drawn wagon, crushing the wagon and injuring the horse. The driver of the automobile might argue that the case should be dismissed because there were no existing laws regulating the speed of automobiles. The judge might reply that there is an established principle that people cannot use their property to injure others. Thus, the judge would apply the rule of common sense and common practice in such a case.

The judge's decision might be remembered by another judge hearing a similar case. Eventually, most judges might follow the same **precedent,** or earlier decision, when considering such cases. In time, those guilty of driving their automobiles recklessly would be punished according to this customary rule. This rule would become a part of the country's customary, or common, law. Thus, **common law** is a type of law that comes from judges' decisions.

In time, most common law is passed as statutory law by the country's lawmaking bodies. In this way, a law is written down so that all citizens may know it.

# TEACH OBJECTIVE 2

**LEVEL 1:** Create a four-column chart on the chalkboard. Then have students copy the chart onto a sheet of paper. Instruct them to complete the chart by identifying and describing the four types of U.S. law. (*Students' charts should include: statutory—passed by lawmaking bodies; common—guided by common sense and common rule; administrative—made by government agencies; constitutional—based on the Constitution and the Supreme Court's interpretation of it.*) Encourage volunteers to present their answers to the class.
**ENGLISH LANGUAGE LEARNERS**

**HOMEWORK** Have students refer to the chart they made in class and then use your local newspaper to find articles that illustrate the types of law being discussed.

**LEVEL 3:** Organize the class into four groups. Assign each group one of the four types of law on which to present a class lesson. Each group member should find at least one example of the assigned type of law. Then members should work together to illustrate the group's examples and to present them to the class. (*See the Level 1 lesson for types of laws and descriptions.*)
**COOPERATIVE LEARNING**

**Administrative Law**   Many of the laws that affect our daily lives are created by government agencies. These laws are known as **administrative laws.** For example, the Consumer Product Safety Commission (CPSC) makes an administrative law when it rules that a particular toy is unsafe and must be taken off the market immediately.

**Constitutional Law**   The U.S. Constitution, as you know, is the supreme law of the United States. **Constitutional law** is based on the Constitution of the United States and on Supreme Court decisions interpreting the Constitution.

✔ **Reading Check Summarizing** List and describe the types of law that exist in the United States. statutory—passed by lawmaking bodies; common—guided by common sense and common rule; administrative—made by government agencies; constitutional—based on the Constitution and on Supreme Court decisions interpretating it

## ★ Roles of the Courts

Courts use the different kinds of law to settle disputes. Disputes between people, disputes between people and the government, and disputes between governments are brought before a court. The court applies the law and reaches a decision in favor of one side or the other.

To be just, a law must be enforced fairly. What might happen if an FBI agent found a U.S. citizen who worked in a nuclear power plant talking to a foreign spy? Could the federal government arrest and imprison this citizen for years on suspicion of treason? The answer is no. Even though the crime is serious, under the U.S. system of justice the employee, like any accused person, must be given a fair public trial.

To guarantee justice, U.S. law assumes that a person is innocent until proven guilty. The proper way to determine whether a person is guilty is to hold a trial in a court of law. The courts are made up of persons who have been given the authority to administer justice. Most Americans believe that only a system of courts can assure equal justice for all people.

✔ **Reading Check Analyzing Information** What is the role of the courts, and how do they guarantee justice? The courts uphold the law by deciding whether the accused is guilty of breaking it. A person is innocent until proven guilty in a court of law.

**Interpreting the Visual Record**

**Representation in Court** *In the U.S. court system individuals often hire lawyers to represent their side in a dispute.* **What do you think is the advantage of having legal representation in court?**

## TEACH OBJECTIVE 3

**ALL LEVELS:** Copy the following graphic organizer onto the chalkboard, omitting the italicized answers. Ask each student to complete the organizer to define the roles that the courts play in the United States.
**ENGLISH LANGUAGE LEARNERS**

**The Roles that Courts Play**

*provide fair public trials*

*ensure equal justice for all*

**LEVEL 3:** Have students imagine that they are correspondents for a court television network. Organize the class into small groups. Then ask each group to prepare a 1–2 minute broadcasting segment that defines for the viewer the roles played by courts in the United States. Finally, have groups present their segments to the class. **COOPERATIVE LEARNING**

## CLOSE

On the chalkboard begin a flowchart that shows the rights of accused persons as they move through the court process. Prompt students to complete the chart by asking the question, "If you were accused of a serious crime, what is the first thing you would do?" Continue prompting students throughout the process.

---

---

## ⭐ Right to a Fair Trial

The Constitution guarantees every American the right to a fair public trial. But just what does the right to a fair trial mean?

**Right to Have a Lawyer** All persons accused of crimes who face a jail sentence for their crimes are entitled to the services of a lawyer. If the accused cannot afford a lawyer, the court will appoint one and pay the lawyer's fees out of public funds.

**Right to Be Released on Bail** Usually a person accused of a crime may be released if he or she can put up bail. Bail, as you have learned, is money deposited with the court as a pledge that the accused will appear in court. The amount of bail is set by a judge. However, a person accused of a serious crime, such as murder or treason, may be denied bail by the court and have to remain in jail until the trial is held.

✔ **Reading Check Making Generalizations and Predictions** How do the rights to a fair trial, a lawyer, and release on bail assist citizens? These rights protect the citizens' access to freedom and support the idea that people are innocent until proven guilty.

**Indictment by a Grand Jury** There must be enough evidence against someone to justify bringing that person into court for trial. The group that decides this issue is the grand jury. In federal courts, the grand jury is made up of between 12 and 23 citizens who live in the court district where the trial will be held.

The grand jury examines the evidence against the accused person. It questions witnesses and investigates the facts. If a majority of grand jury members agree that the evidence against the accused is strong enough, the person is indicted, or formally accused of a crime.

**Right to a Jury Trial** The Sixth Amendment to the Constitution guarantees an accused person the right to be tried before a trial jury. A trial

### Interpreting the Visual Record

**Jury selection** *Lawyers try to select jury members who are unbiased concerning the individuals and issues in a case.* **How might a lawyer try to determine if a potential jury member is biased about the case being tried?**

## REVIEW AND ASSESS

Have students complete the **Section 1 Review** on page 173. Then have students complete **Daily Quiz 7.1.** As **Alternative Assessment**, you may want to use the school-law or correspondent activities in this section's lessons.

## RETEACH

Have students complete **Main Idea Activity for English Language Learners and Special-Needs Students 7.1.** Then refer students to the terms in the Define portion of the Section Review. Ask students to choose a partner and to split the list between them. Have pairs write two related facts about each term. Then have students take turns reading their facts and having their partners identify the terms. **ENGLISH LANGUAGE LEARNERS , COOPERATIVE LEARNING**

## EXTEND

A part of the U.S. court process is the actual trial at which the accused person is to be found innocent or proven guilty *beyond a reasonable doubt.* Have each student write a position paper about how the court process helps ensure that the accused person will be found innocent or guilty beyond a reasonable doubt. **BLOCK SCHEDULING**

jury is also called a **petit jury.** It is usually made up of between 6 and 12 persons—known as **jurors.**

Jurors on trial juries and grand juries are selected from a list of people who live in the community. A court official selects the names at random and sends notices ordering the people to report for **jury duty.** From this group, or panel of jurors, the required number of jurors is chosen for the trial.

The trial jury must try to reach a decision, or **verdict,** in the case. Usually the jury's verdict must be a unanimous vote, with all members agreeing on whether the accused is guilty or innocent of the charges. If a jury cannot reach a verdict, it is called a **hung jury.** When a trial results in a hung jury, a new trial with a new jury is usually held.

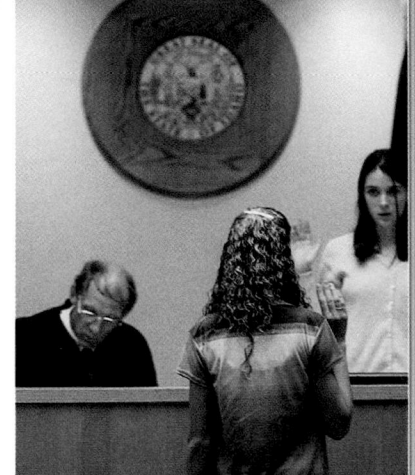

*Witnesses appearing during a trial take an oath to tell the truth in their testimony.*

✔ **Reading Check** Comparing and Contrasting How are grand juries and petit juries similar and different? Both are made up of people from the community. Grand juries decide if there is enough evidence for a trial. Petit juries must reach a decision on the defendants' guilt or innocence.

**Innocent until Proven Guilty** The burden of proof in a jury trial rests with those people who bring charges against the person on trial. They must prove their case "beyond a reasonable doubt." Accused persons cannot be forced to testify against themselves. Their lawyers have the right to **cross-examine,** or question, witnesses to ensure that the **testimony,** or evidence given in court, is accurate. Accused persons also have the right to call their own witnesses in order to defend themselves.

**Right of Appeal** Because courts are made up of human beings, they sometimes make mistakes. To ensure that cases are tried fairly, convicted individuals may **appeal,** or ask for a review of the court's decision.

✔ **Reading Check** Evaluating Why do you think the accused is considered innocent until proven guilty? Students might say that this requirement helps prevent innocent people from being convicted of crimes that they did not commit.

## SECTION 1 Review

go.hrw.com **Homework Practice Online**
keyword: SZ3 HP7

1. **Define** and explain:
   - statutory laws
   - precedent
   - common law
   - administrative laws
   - constitutional law
   - petit jury
   - jurors
   - jury duty
   - verdict
   - hung jury
   - cross-examine
   - testimony
   - appeal

2. **Categorizing** Copy the web diagram below. Use it to identify and describe the four types of law that govern Americans.

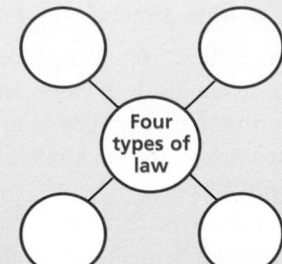

Four types of law

3. **Finding the Main Idea**
   a. Explain the effects of majority rule on U.S. laws and the importance of obeying these laws.
   b. How do courts help the U.S. government?

4. **Writing and Critical Thinking**
   **Problem Solving** Imagine that you live in a country in which there is no rule of law. Write a descriptive paragraph about life in such a country and how it might be improved by establishing a permanent legal system.
   **Consider:**
   - the benefits laws bring to citizens
   - how laws are created in the United States

**Section 1 Review**
## ANSWERS

**1. Define**
- statutory laws, p. 170
- precedent, p. 170
- common law, p. 170
- administrative laws, p. 171
- constitutional law, p. 171
- petit jury, p. 173
- jurors, p. 173
- jury duty, p. 173
- verdict, p. 173
- hung jury, p. 173
- cross-examine, p. 173
- testimony, p. 173
- appeal, p. 173

**2.** statutory laws—passed by lawmaking bodies; common laws—guided by common sense and common rule; administrative laws—made by government agencies; constitutional laws—based on the Constitution and on Supreme Court decisions supporting it

**3. a.** Laws usually reflect the beliefs of the majority of the population. If a majority of voters disagree with a law, it might be changed. When followed, laws ensure the safety of citizens and the protection of their freedoms.

**b.** by providing fair public trials and by assuring equal justice for all

**4.** Students' paragraphs will vary but should display an understanding of the purpose of laws and the procedures for creating them in the United States.

# SECTION 2

## OBJECTIVES

*After completing Section 2, students should be able to*

1 **Determine which cases are tried in federal courts.**
2 **Explain how federal courts are organized.**
3 **Describe the Supreme Court's role in the judicial system.**

## SECTION 2 RESOURCES

### REPRODUCIBLE

▶ Guided Reading Strategies 7.2
▶ Transparency 7: The U.S. Court System
▶ Readings in Economics and Government 37: Judiciary Act of 1789

### TECHNOLOGY

▶ One-Stop Planner, Lesson 7.2
▶ CNN Presents: American Government
▶ Homework Practice Online

### REINFORCEMENT, REVIEW, AND ASSESSMENT

▶ Section 2 Review, p. 180
▶ Daily Quiz 7.2
▶ Main Idea Activity 7.2
▶ English Audio Summary 7.2
▶ Spanish Audio Summary 7.2

# SECTION 2

# The Federal Court System

## Read to Discover

1. Which cases are tried in federal courts?
2. How are federal courts organized?
3. What is the Supreme Court's role in the judicial system?

### WHY CIVICS MATTERS

The U.S. court system is organized to adequately meet the needs of each state. Use **CNNfyi.com** or other **current events** sources to investigate cases being tried in your state's district court(s). Record your findings in your journal.

## Define

• jurisdiction
• original jurisdiction
• appellate jurisdiction
• district courts
• marshal
• subpoenas
• magistrate judges
• courts of appeals
• circuit
• territorial courts
• court-martial

*John Jay was the first chief justice of the Supreme Court.*

## Reading Focus

Under the federal system of government, the United States has two court systems. One is the federal court system and the other is the system of state courts. (You will read about the state court system in Chapter 8.) Article III of the U.S. Constitution provides that "the judicial power of the United States shall be vested in one Supreme Court, and in such inferior [lower] courts as the Congress may from time to time . . . establish." The First Congress used this constitutional power to set up a system of federal courts.

In 1789 Congress passed the Judiciary Act, which established what has grown into one of the great court systems of the world. This system of federal courts makes up the judicial branch of the federal government.

### ⭐ Cases Tried in Federal Courts

The Constitution grants the federal courts **jurisdiction** in several different kinds of cases. The jurisdiction of a court is the authority that court has to interpret and administer the law. Listed below are the kinds of cases that are brought to trial in federal courts.

1. any person accused of disobeying any part of the U.S. Constitution, including its amendments;
2. anyone accused of violating a U.S. treaty;

# TEACH OBJECTIVE 1

**ALL LEVELS:** Copy the following graphic organizer onto the chalkboard, omitting the italicized answers. Have each student complete the list to reveal which cases are tried in federal courts. **ENGLISH LANGUAGE LEARNERS**

| **Federal Court Cases** |
| --- |
| **1.** *constitutional violations* |
| **2.** *U.S. treaty violations* |
| **3.** *congressional law violations* |
| **4.** *cases between a foreign government and a U.S. citizen or the government* |
| **5.** *crimes committed on U.S. ships at sea* |
| **6.** *cases involving U.S. ambassadors and consuls who broke laws in their stationed countries* |
| **7.** *crimes committed on certain types of federal property* |
| **8.** *disagreements between states or citizens of different states* |

3. anyone accused of breaking laws passed by Congress;

4. charges brought by a foreign country against the U.S. government or a U.S. citizen;

5. crimes committed on U.S. ships at sea;

6. ambassadors and consuls accused of breaking the laws of the country in which they are stationed;

7. crimes committed on certain types of federal property;

8. disagreements between the states (although the Eleventh Amendment provides that any lawsuit against a state brought by a citizen of another state or of a foreign country shall be tried in a state court); and

9. lawsuits between citizens of different states (Most federal court cases are of this type.)

The federal courts are organized into several levels. They are also classified according to their jurisdiction. The lowest courts are trial courts, which have **original jurisdiction.** They have the authority to be the first courts in which most federal cases are heard.

Above trial courts are courts that have **appellate jurisdiction.** These courts review decisions made by lower courts. The word *appellate* means "dealing with appeals." Every convicted person has the right to appeal to an appellate court. An appeal is usually made when lawyers believe the law was not applied correctly in the lower court. A case can also be appealed if new evidence is found.

✔ **Reading Check** Supporting a Point of View Select an area of jurisdiction and explain why you believe it was granted to the federal courts. Responses will vary, but students should recognize that the areas address issues of national concern or issues best handled in the national sphere.

## ★ U.S. District Courts

There are three main levels of federal courts. See the organizational chart of the courts in the federal system on page 177. At the base of the federal court system are the **district courts.** There is at least one district court in each of the 50 states and in the District of Columbia. Some states are divided into as many as four federal court districts, each with its own district court. Today there are 94 federal district courts in the United States and its territories.

The district court is the only federal court in which jury trials are held. District courts have original jurisdiction in most federal cases. They cannot hear appeals from other courts.

The Constitution specifies where federal cases shall be tried. Article III, Section 2, states that "such trial shall be held in the State where the said crimes shall have been committed."

**Interpreting the Visual Record**

**District courts** *Every state has at least one district court, such as this one in Boston, Massachusetts.* **Why do you think district courts are distributed in this fashion?**

## ★ The Democratic Process

***Gibbons v. Ogden*** Federal courts help settle conflicts of authority between federal and state law. One of the most famous cases in a federal court was a dispute between two steamboat operators—Thomas Gibbons and Aaron Ogden—that went all the way to the Supreme Court. Gibbons sued Ogden to keep him from carrying passengers between ports in New York and New Jersey. The issue was whether interstate commerce should be controlled by states or by the federal government. In *Gibbons* v. *Ogden* (1824), the Supreme Court decided that the commerce clause of the Constitution (Article I, Section 8) gave control over interstate commerce to Congress.

**CRITICAL THINKING**

Do you think that states have a right to control waterways, or should they share them? Support your answer.

**ANSWER:** Students' answers will vary, but students should support their answer.

**Visual Record Answer**

*Students might suggest that a court located in the state is more convenient to the accused and witnesses. Also, state judges might be more familiar with a region's citizens and issues, enabling them to decide on a fairer punishment.*

**LEVEL 2:** Organize the class into four groups. Assign each group two of the types of cases tried in federal courts. *(See the All Levels lesson for case types.)* Then have each group provide in writing an example of each type of case it was assigned. Distribute a copy of the groups' examples to each student and have students identify which types of cases the examples represent. **COOPERATIVE LEARNING**

**LEVEL 3:** Have students list the types of cases tried in federal courts. *(See the All Levels lesson for case types.)* Then ask each student to devise one reason supporting federal jurisdiction in these areas and one reason against it. Have the class debate students' arguments; on the chalkboard list reasons for consensus on each side of the issue.

# TEACH OBJECTIVE 2

**LEVELS 1 AND 2:** Review with students how the federal courts are organized. As a class, examine the organizational chart in this section. Call on a volunteer to identify the subject of the chart. *(Students should identify the subject as the federal court system.)* Ask students to describe the lines of authority. Then have them pose and answer questions. For example, a student might ask which court would hear an appeal from a district court. *(Students should respond that it is a U.S. court of appeals or the U.S. Court of Appeals for the Federal Circuit.)* **ENGLISH LANGUAGE LEARNERS**

## Global Perspectives

**A Panel of Judges** In the United States and a number of other countries, a single judge presides over a trial court. But in continental Europe, a panel of three or more judges is the norm. Many European judges do not sit as independent arbiters between the defense and the prosecution. They are more likely to take an active role in determining guilt or innocence than are judges in the United States. For example, a French judge may take witnesses with conflicting testimony to his or her office for a confrontation. During this procedure, the judge aggressively questions, or confronts, the witnesses in an attempt to judge the truth of the competing versions of a story.

**ACTIVITY:** Organize the class into two groups and have each group research one type of judicial rule: single or panel. Then lead the class in a debate about which method is more effective overall and which is best for the United States.

**Visual Record Answer**

*Students might suggest that witnesses or the accused might be in danger from suspects or victims related to the case.*

The reason for this provision is to ensure that the accused person receives a fair and convenient trial. The witnesses who will testify are usually close at hand. No one has to travel long distances to be heard. Furthermore, the jury will be familiar with the location of the crime, and it can judge the truth of the evidence more fairly.

✔ **Reading Check** Analyzing Information What is unique about district courts? They are the only federal courts that have jury trials and cannot hear appeals from other courts.

## ★ District Court Officials

Each district court has from 1 to 28 judges, depending on the caseload of the individual court. All district court judges, except those in U.S. territories, are appointed for life. District court judges decide matters of court procedure and explain the law involved in a case to the jury. They also decide the punishment if the accused person is found guilty.

A number of other officials help the district courts work smoothly. Each district court has a U.S. **marshal.** Marshals arrest persons accused of breaking federal laws. They also deliver official court orders, called **subpoenas,** that require persons to appear in court. In addition, U.S. marshals keep order in the district courtrooms and see that the courts' verdicts are carried out.

District court officials also include **magistrate judges.** These officials hear the evidence against accused persons and decide whether the cases should be brought before a grand jury. Magistrate judges also hear some minor cases.

Another district court official is the U.S. attorney. This official is a lawyer for the federal government. It is the job of the U.S. attorney to prove to a jury that the accused person is guilty of the federal crime he or she is charged with committing.

✔ **Reading Check** Summarizing Who are the officials in the district court system, and what are their roles? justices—rule in cases; marshals—perform arrests and deliver subpoenas; magistrate judges—hear and rule on pretrial evidence; U.S. attorneys—try defendants

**Interpreting the Visual Record**

**U.S. Marshals** *Marshals are often responsible for transporting witnesses or accused criminals to testify in federal trials.* **Why might it be necessary to protect some witnesses or accused individuals from harm?**

## The U.S. Court System

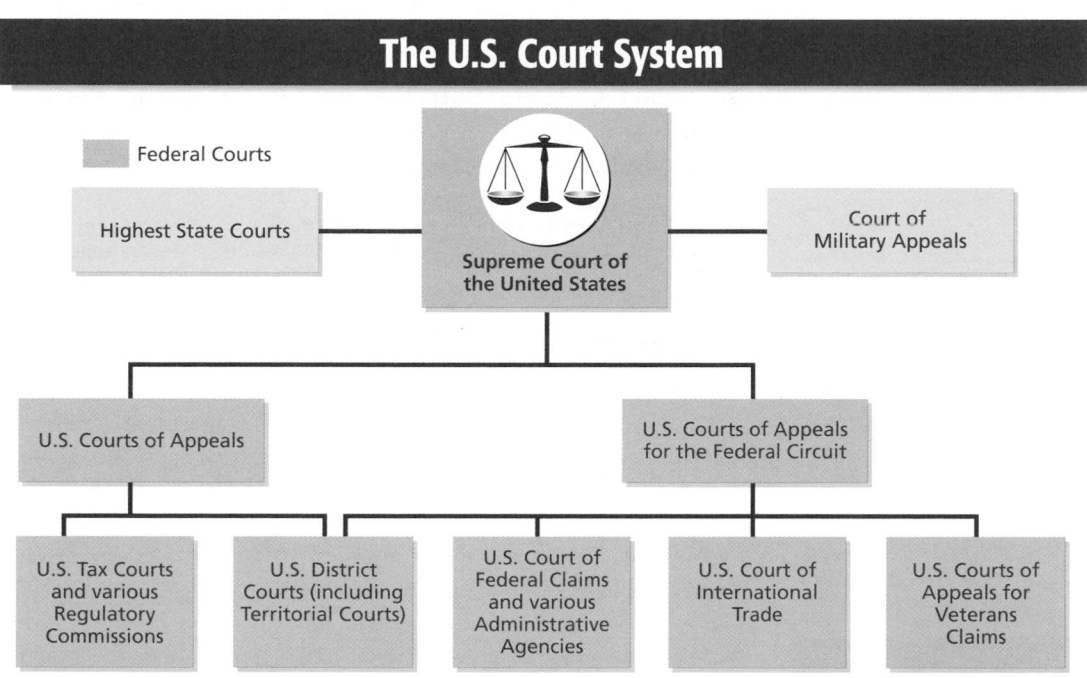

Federal Courts

Highest State Courts

Supreme Court of the United States

Court of Military Appeals

U.S. Courts of Appeals

U.S. Courts of Appeals for the Federal Circuit

U.S. Tax Courts and various Regulatory Commissions

U.S. District Courts (including Territorial Courts)

U.S. Court of Federal Claims and various Administrative Agencies

U.S. Court of International Trade

U.S. Courts of Appeals for Veterans Claims

**Interpreting Charts**
*The Supreme Court hears cases originating in the state court system and the federal courts.* **What route would a case originating in the U.S. Court of International Trade take to reach the Supreme Court?**

### ★ U.S. Courts of Appeals

The next level of the federal court system consists of **courts of appeals.** These courts review cases that are appealed from the district courts. Courts of appeals also hear appeals of federal regulatory commission decisions. For example, a cable-services company might believe that the limit on rates for cable services set by the Federal Communications Commission is unfair. If so, the company can ask a court of appeals to review the commission's decision.

There are 12 U.S. courts of appeals. Each court of appeals covers a large judicial district known as a **circuit.** The 50 states are divided into 11 circuits. The twelfth circuit is the District of Columbia. There is also a court of appeals for the federal circuit. This court of appeals has national jurisdiction.

Each court of appeals has between 6 and 28 judges. The judge of each circuit who has served the longest and is under 65 years of age serves as the chief judge. The judges of the courts of appeals are appointed for life.

Jury trials do not take place in the courts of appeals. Instead, a panel of at least three judges makes the decision. The judges examine the records of the district court trial and hear arguments by the lawyers for both sides. The judges do not determine whether the accused person is guilty or innocent. Their job is to determine if the person who appealed the case was granted full legal rights during the trial.

**LEVEL 1:** Call on volunteers to describe the Supreme Court's role in the judicial system. *(Students should mention that it functions as the last word in cases that have been appealed from lower federal courts. It also has original jurisdiction in several types of cases.)* Then review with students the three types of cases in which the Supreme Court has original jurisdiction. *(Students should identify cases involving foreign diplomats, disputes between states, and cases involving a state and the federal government.)* Finally, pair students and have them quiz each other on the information covered in this lesson.
**ENGLISH LANGUAGE LEARNERS , COOPERATIVE LEARNING**

**LEVEL 2:** To continue students' study of the Supreme Court's role in the judicial system, organize the class into four groups. Assign each group one of the types of cases heard by the Supreme Court. *(Group assignments include appeals cases and the three special cases listed in the Level 1 lesson.)* Then have each group create an illustration of its assigned case type. For example, a group assigned cases involving disputes between states might draw the two states as if they were boxers. Have students title and describe their illustrations and present them to the class. **COOPERATIVE LEARNING**

---

## ★ The Democratic Process

**The Power of Judicial Review** According to Alexis de Tocqueville, "pronouncing a statute to be unconstitutional forms one of the most powerful barriers that have ever been devised against the tyranny of political assemblies." De Tocqueville should know—he was a Frenchman who came to the United States to study the effectiveness of its democratic process. His purpose was to determine which aspects of American government worked and why, as a means of providing a blueprint for European countries. At the time, some European countries frequently found themselves at the will of legislative bodies and their politically based decisions. The American system, on the other hand, not only used judicial review to check the legislature, it used the power of the people to check the Court—the Court could not review any law unless the people first brought the case there.

### CRITICAL THINKING

What problems might arise if judicial review did not exist?

**ANSWER:** Students might suggest that the legislature could abuse its power by making laws that suited personal interests and did not necessarily serve the people.

### Visual Record Answer

*It declares the final word in cases that come before it.*

---

The judges reach their decision by majority vote. The court of appeals may send the case back to the district court for a new trial or it may uphold the district court's decision. In most cases the decision of the court of appeals is final. Sometimes, however, yet another appeal is made to the U.S. Supreme Court.

✔ **Reading Check** Identifying Cause and Effect Why are cases sent to the court of appeals, and what are the possible results? Cases are appealed when one party feels that the outcome of the trial was not legally just. An appeals court panel reviews each case. The panel rules to keep the judgment as is or to send it back for a new trial.

## ★ The U.S. Supreme Court

The highest court in the land is the U.S. Supreme Court, which meets in Washington, D.C. The Supreme Court works chiefly as an appeals court, reviewing cases that have been tried in lower federal courts and in state courts. The decisions of the Supreme Court are final and cannot be appealed.

In addition, the Constitution gives the Supreme Court original jurisdiction in the following three types of cases:

1. cases involving diplomatic representatives of other countries;
2. cases involving disputes between states (For example, the Supreme Court once settled a dispute between Arizona and California over the use of water from the Colorado River basin.); and
3. cases involving a state and the federal government. (For example, the ownership of public lands has often been a source of conflict between the states and the federal government.)

✔ **Reading Check** Drawing Inferences and Conclusions Why might the Supreme Court have been given special jurisdiction in the areas listed above? The Supreme Court is the national court of the United States, and these are national issues.

**Interpreting the Visual Record**

**Justices of the Supreme Court** *Here, the U.S. Supreme Court justices assemble for a portrait. Standing (left to right): Ruth Bader Ginsburg, David Souter, Clarence Thomas, and Stephen Breyer. Sitting (left to right): Antonin Scalia, John Paul Stevens, William Rehnquist, Sandra Day O'Connor, and Anthony Kennedy. **What role does the Supreme Court play in the U.S. court system?***

**LEVEL 3:** Organize the class into small groups and assign each group one of the types of Supreme Court cases discussed in this section. *(Students' assignments will include appeals cases and each of the three special cases.)* You may wish to use the same four groups as in the previous exercise. Then have groups review the description of their case type in the textbook and illustrate the Court's role in the judicial system by preparing a dramatization of their case type. Have groups present their skits to the class. **COOPERATIVE LEARNING**

## CLOSE

Have each student write a scenario about one of the types of federal cases covered in this section. Then call on volunteers to describe their scenarios to the class.

### ★ Other Federal Courts

Congress also set up a number of special courts to handle specific types of cases. These courts are identified in the chart on page 177.

**Court of Federal Claims** This court hears cases involving money claims against the federal government. If the court rules against the government, the person bringing the suit is usually granted a sum of money. Congress must then authorize the payment of the claim.

**U.S. Court of International Trade** This court hears cases involving taxes on imports. People who think that the tax on their imported goods is too high, for example, may take their cases to the Court of International Trade. This court is in New York City, but it also hears cases in other port cities.

**Territorial Courts** **Territorial courts** were established by Congress to administer justice to the people living in U.S. territorial possessions. There is one territorial court in each of the following U.S. territories: the Northern Mariana Islands, Guam, the Virgin Islands, and Puerto Rico. These courts handle the same kinds of cases as district courts. They also hear the types of cases that would go to a state court.

**U.S. Tax Court** This court hears appeals from taxpayers who disagree with rulings of the Internal Revenue Service (IRS) concerning their payment of federal taxes. The Tax Court is actually an independent agency, but it has the powers of a court.

**Court of Appeals for the Armed Forces** This court is the appeals court for the country's armed services. People in the armed services who are accused of breaking a military law are tried at a **court-martial.**

179

★★★★★★★★★★★★★
### That's Interesting!
★★★★★★★★★★★★★

**"Oyez, oyez, oyez!"** The words *Oyez, oyez, oyez!* are called out as the Supreme Court justices file in to the courtroom. Oyez sounds like "Oh, yes." An odd way to open a court? Actually, the word means "Hear ye" and it comes from the French language. In fact, several French words are used in conducting U.S. government business. Many of our country's founders were heavily influenced by the ideas some French philosophers had about government.

Court of Federal Claims—people who have money claims against the federal government; Court of International Trade—individuals or businesses importing goods into the United States; territorial courts—people living in U.S. territorial possessions; Tax Court—taxpayers; Court of Appeals for the Armed Services—people in the armed services; Court of Appeals for Veterans Claims—people with claims for veterans benefits

This is a trial conducted by military officers. The Court of Appeals for the Armed Forces consists of five civilian judges. Appeals of this court's decisions can be, but rarely are, heard by the Supreme Court.

**U.S. Court of Appeals for Veterans Claims** This court hears appeals brought by military veterans against the Department of Veterans Affairs. Cases brought before this court always involve claims for veterans benefits.

✔ **Reading Check Categorizing** List the different special federal courts and who they serve.

## ★ Federal Court Judges

All the federal courts are presided over by judges. The president appoints these judges. The Senate must approve these appointments by a majority vote.

With the exception of those judges who preside over territorial courts, federal judges are appointed for life. They can be removed from office only by impeachment by Congress. Congress may not lower a judge's salary during her or his time in office. These guarantees were written into the U.S. Constitution to ensure that judges are not punished or rewarded for their decisions in cases. Judges are assisted in their work by many other people, including clerks and court reporters.

✔ **Reading Check Finding the Main Idea** Why are federal judges appointed for life at a fixed salary? to ensure that judges are not rewarded or punished for their decisions

go.hrw.com **Homework Practice Online**
keyword: SZ3 HP7

# SECTION 2 Review

**1. Define** and explain:
• jurisdiction
• original jurisdiction
• appellate jurisdiction
• district courts
• marshal
• subpoenas
• magistrate judges
• courts of appeals
• circuit
• territorial courts
• court-martial

**2. Summarizing** Copy the graphic organizer on the left. Use it describe which types of cases are tried in federal courts.

**3. Finding the Main Idea**
a. Explain the organization of federal courts.
b. What role does the Supreme Court play in the federal court system?

**4. Writing and Critical Thinking**
**Supporting a Point of View** Write a position statement supporting or opposing a constitutional amendment to end the system of lifetime appointments for federal judges.

**Consider:**
• how lifetime appointments benefit the U.S. justice system
• how such appointments are harmful to the system

**Federal Court Cases**

| 1. | 4. | 7. |
|----|----|----|
| 2. | 5. | 8. |
| 3. | 6. | 9. |

## TEACH

**LEVEL 1:** Ask the class how decision making relates to the role of a U.S. justice. (*Students might suggest that a justice's job is based upon deciding whether the law has been broken and deciding how to punish people who have broken the law.*) Tell the class that justices also make decisions on a daily basis. Then organize the class into pairs and have each pair make a list of the types of decisions that students make. Ask pairs to select one of their examples and to apply the steps listed in this workshop to their decision.

**ENGLISH LANGUAGE LEARNERS , COOPERATIVE LEARNING**

**LEVELS 2 AND 3:** Organize students into the same pairs as in the previous lesson. Have students refer to the lists that they made in the Level 1 lesson. Ask them to create a three-column chart that categorizes their decisions into two types—short- and long-term decisions. When students have completed the first two columns of their charts, have them add a third column that lists examples of each type of decision that they have listed. Call on volunteers to share their charts with the class. **COOPERATIVE LEARNING**

# Civics Skills
## WORKSHOP

## Making Decisions

It is important that you make the right decisions about important issues in your life. You must decide how best to study for your tests. You must decide what extracurricular clubs to join. Many of the decisions you make have important effects not only on you but also on the people around you.

## How to Make Decisions

1. **Define the problem.** It helps to identify the problem and then write the decision facing you in the form of a question, such as "Should I take an after-school job?" Writing the question down helps clarify the problem. It may also help you see if you are asking the right question. For example, to decide if you need an after-school job, you might analyze the problem. Do you need more money?

2. **Determine the importance of the decision.** Many decisions are simple, such as deciding what you will wear each day. Other decisions are much more complex and important, such as deciding where you will go to college. Take more time and care when making important decisions.

3. **Identify your options.** For some decisions, your options are limited. For example, if the question is "Should I write a research paper on the Supreme Court?" your only options are yes or no. However, if the question is "What should be the topic of my research paper?" then you are faced with many more options. Make a list of all your options. Then write down the advantages and disadvantages that each option offers. Gather the information you

need to make an informed decision. You may want to discuss your options with your family, teachers, or friends.

4. **Choose an option.** Take your time studying the lists you have made. Narrow your choices by ruling out less desirable options until you are left with the one best option for you. Select the most appropriate option from your choices.

5. **Carry out your decision.** Once you have made your decision, make a plan of action. Follow it through.

6. **Evaluate your decision.** After you have carried out your decision, decide if you made the correct one. Judging whether you made a mistake will help you make wise decisions in the future.

## Applying the Skill

Read the situation below. Then answer the questions that follow.

*Should Rosa take a part-time job at the ice cream shop? She needs to save at least $1,000 a year for college, and she might not find work this summer. The hours could be a problem—three hours every day after school and all day every Saturday. She would have to miss basketball practice. And she would have less time to study. Her grades might drop, and she might not be accepted into college. What should she do?*

1. What are Rosa's options in this situation?

2. What are the advantages and disadvantages of each of her options?

3. If you were in Rosa's position, which choice would you make? Explain the reasoning behind your choice.

## SKILLS ANSWERS

1. to take the job or not to take it

2. Students might suggest that by taking the job she will earn the money she needs for college, but she will miss basketball and lose study time. Conversely, by not taking it she will have time for basketball and studying, but she may not find another job to earn the money she needs for college.

3. Students who choose to take the job will note that the benefits mentioned in the last response outweigh the disadvantages, and vice versa.

# SECTION 3

## OBJECTIVES

After completing Section 3, students should be able to

**1** Examine the process through which cases are tried in the Supreme Court.

**2** Explain how justices get appointed to the Supreme Court and tell how long they serve.

**3** Analyze how judicial review has strengthened the Court's power and how Congress limits this power.

## SECTION 3 RESOURCES

### REPRODUCIBLE

▶ Guided Reading Strategies 7.3

▶ Challenge and Enrichment Worksheet 7: Identifying Members of the Supreme Court

▶ Graphic Organizer Activity: Some Landmark Decisions

### TECHNOLOGY

▶ One-Stop Planner, Lesson 7.3

▶ Holt Researcher CD–ROM

▶ Homework Practice Online

▶ HRW Go site

### REINFORCEMENT, REVIEW, AND ASSESSMENT

▶ Section 3 Review, p. 189

▶ Daily Quiz 7.3

▶ Main Idea Activity 7.3

▶ English Audio Summary 7.3

▶ Spanish Audio Summary 7.3

## LET'S GET STARTED!

Write the following statement on the chalkboard: *Every case is eligible to be tried before the Supreme Court.* As students enter the classroom, ask them whether they agree or disagree with this statement and why. *(Students who agree may claim it is a right within our democratic system; those who disagree might observe that only certain cases are tried before the Court.)* Explain to students that the Supreme Court tries only cases that are on appeal. Tell students that in Section 3 they will learn more about how the Supreme Court functions.

# SECTION 3

# The Supreme Court

## Read to Discover

1. What is the process through which cases are tried in the Supreme Court?

2. How do justices get appointed to the Supreme Court, and how long do they serve?

3. How has judicial review strengthened the Court's power, and how does Congress limit this power?

## Define

- justices
- judicial review
- unconstitutional
- docket
- remand
- brief
- opinion
- concurring opinion
- dissenting opinion
- segregated

### WHY CIVICS MATTERS

Supreme Court justices hold their positions for life or until they resign. Use CNNfyi.com or other **current events** sources to discover who currently sits on the U.S. Supreme Court, their ages, and how long each justice has been there. Record your findings in your journal.

*William Howard Taft was the only person to serve as both president of the United States and chief justice of the Supreme Court.*

## Reading Focus

The Supreme Court is the head of the judicial branch of the federal government. It is the only court specifically established by the Constitution. Its decisions affect the lives of all Americans.

### ⭐ Supreme Court Justices

The size of the Supreme Court is determined by Congress. The number of **justices,** or judges, of the Supreme Court has been set at nine since 1869. The Court has a chief justice, who is the principal judge, and eight associate justices.

Supreme Court justices, like other federal judges, are appointed by the president. The Senate must approve their appointments by a majority vote. Justices are appointed for life and can be forcibly removed from office only by the impeachment process. The annual salary of the chief justice is $181,400. Associate justices are paid $173,600 per year.

The Constitution does not set any requirements for Supreme Court justices. However, all have been lawyers, and many have served as judges on lower courts. Others have taught law or held public office. Until 1981, all justices were men. In that year Sandra Day O'Connor became the first woman to serve on the Supreme Court. A second woman, Ruth Bader Ginsburg, joined the Court in 1993.

# TEACH OBJECTIVE 1

**LEVEL 1:** Have students create a diagram that illustrates the process through which cases are tried in the Supreme Court. *(Students' diagrams should show the following steps: the Court decides whether it will hear a case; rejected cases stand as decided; written and oral evidence for accepted cases is examined and debated, and the case is voted on; the majority and dissenting opinions are written by one justice on each side of the argument.)* **ENGLISH LANGUAGE LEARNERS**

**ALL LEVELS:** Invite students to imagine that they are lawyers arguing before the Supreme Court. Ask them the following questions: *How would you prepare? What process would the case have to go through?* Have each student write brief journal entries as if he or she were a lawyer arguing a case in front of the highest court in the land. *(See the Level 1 lesson for a description of the process.)* **ENGLISH LANGUAGE LEARNERS**

Presidents generally try to appoint justices who share their political beliefs. Once appointed, however, a justice of the Supreme Court is free to make decisions regardless of the president's opinion.

✔ **Reading Check** Drawing Inferences and Conclusions Why do you think the Senate has been given the power to approve presidential appointments to the Supreme Court? to maintain a balance of power among the three branches

## Power of Judicial Review

A unique feature of the U.S. court system is the courts' power of **judicial review.** The courts have the power to determine whether a law or a presidential action is in accord with the Constitution. The Supreme Court holds the ultimate authority to make this determination. If a court decides that a law conflicts with the Constitution, that law is declared **unconstitutional.** Before a law is declared unconstitutional, however, someone must challenge the law and bring a case to court.

The Constitution does not specifically give the judicial branch the power of judicial review. John Marshall established the power when he served as chief justice of the Supreme Court from 1801 to 1835.

✔ **Reading Check** Evaluating How did Marshall increase the Supreme Court's power? by establishing the power of judicial review, which is not outlined in the Constitution

## Influence of John Marshall

During his 34 years as chief justice, John Marshall established three basic principles of U.S. law. Marshall promoted the idea of judicial review for the first time in 1803 in the case of *Marbury* v. *Madison.* The case involved William Marbury, who had been promised appointment as a justice of the peace, and Secretary of State James Madison.

Marbury claimed that the Judiciary Act of 1789 gave the Supreme Court the power to order Secretary of State Madison to give him the promised appointment. In his now-famous opinion, Chief Justice Marshall found that the Judiciary Act was in conflict with the Constitution. The act gave the Supreme Court powers not granted by the Constitution. Because the Constitution is the supreme law of the land, the Judiciary Act passed by Congress was declared unconstitutional.

Under Chief Justice Marshall, the Supreme Court also established the principle that the Constitution is superior to laws passed by state legislatures if a legal conflict between the two arises. The third principle established by Marshall is that the Supreme Court has the power to reverse the decisions of state courts. Therefore, over the years the Supreme Court has become the final interpreter of the Constitution.

✔ **Reading Check** Summarizing What are the three principles that John Marshall outlined for the Supreme Court while he was chief justice? Supreme Court has the right to declare an act of Congress unconstitutional; Constitution is superior to state laws that may conflict with it; Supreme Court has the power to reverse the decisions of state courts

## Did You KNOW?

The Supreme Court's rulings have not always been followed. In 1832 John Marshall ruled that the state of Georgia could not evict Cherokee living on tribal lands. But President Andrew Jackson disagreed and refused to enforce the ruling.

**Interpreting the Visual Record**

**John Marshall** *As Chief Justice, John Marshall greatly expanded the power and influence of the Supreme Court.* **How do you think the balance of powers in the federal government would be different without Marshall's influence?**

## The Democratic Process

**Chief Justice Appointments** The president's nominee for chief justice of the Supreme Court must undergo Senate confirmation even if the nominee is already an associate justice on the Court. For example, President Ronald Reagan, with Senate approval, elevated Associate Justice William Rehnquist to chief justice in 1986. The appointment is for life.

**ACTIVITY:** Have students use the library or other resources to obtain information about the selection and approval process of Justice Rehnquist. Then ask them to prepare a news story about the event. Encourage students to use the 5W-How? questions to organize their reports.

★ ★ ★ ★ ★ ★ ★ ★ ★ ★ ★
## That's Interesting!
★ ★ ★ ★ ★ ★ ★ ★ ★ ★ ★

Do you know what eventually happened to William Marbury? In spite of its declaration that the Judiciary Act was unconstitutional, the Supreme Court said that Marbury deserved the job on other grounds. The Court, however, did not have the power to force Madison to act. Marbury did not receive the appointment.

**LEVEL 2:** Organize the class into pairs. Have each pair write on strips of paper the steps in the process by which cases are tried in the Supreme Court. *(See the Level 1 lesson for steps.)* Then have one partner shuffle the strips and ask the other partner to place them in the correct order. When both students have mastered ordering the steps, challenge pairs to add steps that do not belong or to leave out steps that do belong.
**COOPERATIVE LEARNING**

**LEVEL 3:** Organize the class into four groups and assign each group a case from the homework assignment. Assign two groups the same case. Explain to students that each group will examine its assigned case as a mock Supreme Court. Acting as the Court, groups should follow the process by which high court cases are tried. Have them begin by deciding whether to hear the case and explaining their reasoning. Discuss the rulings made in each case. **COOPERATIVE LEARNING**

 **HOMEWORK** Prepare students for the next exercise with this assignment. Have each student create names and descriptions of cases that might be appealed to the Supreme Court.

## SUPREME COURT CASE STUDY

### *Marbury v. Madison*

**Significance:** This ruling established the Supreme Court's power of judicial review, by which the Court decides whether laws passed by Congress are constitutional. This decision greatly increased the prestige of the Court and gave the judiciary branch a powerful check against the legislative and executive branches.

**Background:** William Marbury and several others were commissioned as judges by Federalist president John Adams during his last days in office. This act angered the new Democratic-Republican president, Thomas Jefferson. Jefferson ordered his secretary of state, James Madison, not to deliver the commissions. Marbury took advantage of a section in the Judiciary Act of 1789 that allowed him to take his case directly to the Supreme Court. He sued Madison, demanding the commission and the judgeship.

**Decision:** This case was decided on February 24, 1803, by a vote of 5 to 0. Chief Justice John Marshall spoke for the court, which decided against Marbury. The court ruled that although Marbury's commission had been unfairly withheld, he could not lawfully take his case to the Supreme Court without first trying it in a lower court. Marshall said that the section of the Judiciary Act that Marbury had used was actually unconstitutional, and that the Constitution must take priority over laws passed by Congress.

How did Marshall increase the power of the Supreme Court by declaring that it did not have the power to try Marbury's case directly?

## ⭐ Hearing Cases

As you know, the Supreme Court cannot begin a case itself. It serves mainly as an appeals court. All cases heard by the Court involve real legal disputes. A person cannot simply ask the Supreme Court for an opinion about whether or not a law is constitutional.

The Supreme Court decides what cases it will hear. Thousands of cases are appealed to the Court each year. The Court, however, chooses only about 100 to 200 of these cases to place on its annual **docket,** or calendar, for review. If the Supreme Court had to review all cases that were appealed to it, the justices would still be deciding cases that had originated decades ago.

How, then, does the Supreme Court decide what cases to hear? The justices accept only those cases that involve issues of significant public interest. Cases heard by the Court generally deal with important constitutional or national questions. At least four of the nine justices must vote to hear a case. If the Supreme Court refuses to review a case, the decision of the lower court remains in effect. The Court may also **remand,** or return, a case to a lower court for a new trial.

*A real legal dispute must occur and then be appealed to the Court. The justices examine petitions and then select from between 100 and 200 cases a year. If they refuse a case, the original decision stands. They may also remand a case to a lower court for a new trial.*

✔ **Reading Check** Identifying Cause and Effect How do cases come before the Supreme Court, and how does the Court's decision affect a case?

## TEACH OBJECTIVE 2

**LEVEL 1:** Lead a class discussion about appointments and terms of Supreme Court justices. *(Students should display knowledge that the president appoints Supreme Court justices and that Congress approves them. Justices are seated for life or until they choose to resign.)* Have students set up a "Supreme Court" for your school's student government by using the U.S. Supreme Court as a model. Call on volunteers to explain the process. **ENGLISH LANGUAGE LEARNERS**

**ALL LEVELS:** Have each student write a want ad for the position of Supreme Court justice. The ad should explain the appointment process and the length of the term. Students should also include job requirements and qualifications. Encourage students to be creative in their attempts to attract people to work for the Supreme Court of the United States. *(See the Level 1 lesson for appointment process and length of term.)* **ENGLISH LANGUAGE LEARNERS**

---

## ★ The Court in Action

The Supreme Court begins its session each year on the first Monday in October. The Court usually adjourns in late June. The justices spend much of their time reading written arguments, hearing oral arguments, and holding private meetings. Each justice has one vote, and decisions are reached by a simple majority.

After the Supreme Court has agreed to hear a case, the lawyers for each side prepare a **brief.** This is a written statement explaining the main points of one side's arguments about the case. Each justice studies the briefs.

The next step takes place in a public session. The lawyers for each side appear before the Court to present an oral argument. Each presentation is limited to 30 minutes, and the time limit is strictly enforced. The justices often question the lawyers about the case. The entire procedure is designed to bring out the facts in each case as quickly as possible.

One of the justices who supported the majority decision is assigned to write the opinion of the Court. An **opinion** explains the reasoning that led to the decision. The Court's opinion is binding on all lower courts.

Sometimes a justice agrees with the decision of the majority, but for different reasons. In that case the justice may decide to write a **concurring opinion.**

Justices who disagree with the decision of the Court may explain their reasoning in a **dissenting opinion.** Although dissenting opinions have no effect on the law, they are still important. Many dissenting opinions have later become the law of the land when the beliefs of society and the opinions of the justices changed.

✔ **Reading Check** **Making Generalizations and Predictions** What might happen if the full panel of justices, instead of just one justice, was responsible for writing the opinion of the court together? Students may suggest that it would bring much debate, requiring more effort and time than the current method which could result in a reduced caseload or an extended session.

## ★ Checking the Court's Power

The Supreme Court has gained great power over the years. How do the other branches of government check the powers of the Court?

Consider what happens when the Supreme Court rules that a law passed by Congress is unconstitutional. As you know, this means that the law has no force. Congress, however, may pass a new law that follows the Constitution and that the Supreme Court may uphold. In this way, laws can be improved while the rights of U.S. citizens under the Constitution remain protected.

Another way to make a desired law constitutional is to amend the Constitution. For example, in 1895 the Supreme Court declared that an

**Interpreting the Visual Record**

**The Supreme Court** *Cameras are not allowed to be present while Supreme Court cases are being heard. Instead, artists provide illustrations of courtroom proceedings.* **Why do you think cameras are not allowed in the courtroom during cases?**

**LEVEL 2:** Have each student prepare a chart that demonstrates the role played by each branch of the government in the selection process for Supreme Court members. Charts should have two columns labeled *Branch* and *Role*. Have students begin by listing the three branches in the first column. Then students should fill in the Role column. *(For example, students should annotate the Judicial Branch column with the term length for Court justices.)* Encourage volunteers to present their charts to the class. *(Students' charts should show that the president appoints Supreme Court justices and that Congress approves them. They are seated for life or until they choose to resign.)*

**LEVEL 3:** Use this exercise to reinforce students' knowledge of how justices are appointed to the Supreme Court and how long they serve. Tell students that they have been chosen to select the next justices of the Court. Organize the class into three groups and assign groups these roles: the president, Congress, and the departing Supreme Court members. Ask each group to describe the process that it will experience. *(Students should display knowledge that the president appoints Supreme Court justices and that Congress approves them. Justices are seated for life or until they choose to resign.)* **COOPERATIVE LEARNING**

**The Evolving Court** The Supreme Court's choice to postpone the *Brown* v. *Board of Education* decision until reargument the following year may have led to one of the most important decisions of all time. During initial hearings, Chief Justice Fred Vinson encouraged the justices to uphold segregation, and it is claimed that the vote may have been 5 to 4 in favor of maintaining segregation. During the postponement, however, Vinson died and Earl Warren was named chief justice. During reargument of the case, Chief Justice Warren appealed to the justices to vote against segregation. He presented the issue in terms of morality. The justices may well have taken Warren's comments to heart. The final vote in the case was 9 to 0 in favor of ending segregation.

**ACTIVITY:** Have students conduct research at the library to obtain information about other Supreme Court cases. Have them choose one case and research the history of the case as well as the decision, and prepare an oral report to teach the class about their case.

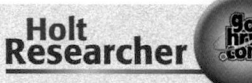

**Holt Researcher**

**go.hrw.com**
**KEYWORD:** Holt Researcher
**Freefind:** Civil Rights Cases

Examine the information on civil-rights-related Supreme Court cases on the Holt Researcher. Choose one case and create a brief encyclopedia entry that answers the following questions: What was the topic of the case and why was it important?

*Public transportation in the South was commonly segregated during the late 1800s and much of the 1900s.*

income tax law passed by Congress was unconstitutional. The Court pointed out that the Constitution (Article I, Section 9, Clause 4) states that direct taxes must be apportioned according to the population of each state. In other words, such taxes must fall evenly on all people.

The income tax law taxed some individuals at a higher level than others, and so did not meet this constitutional requirement. The Court declared the law unconstitutional. However, in 1913 the states ratified the Sixteenth Amendment, which gave Congress the power to tax a person's income. The income tax then became legal and constitutional.

✔ **Reading Check Summarizing** What are the different ways to correct a law that the Supreme Court has declared unconstitutional? pass a new law that abides by the Constitution or amend the Constitution

## ★ Changing Court Opinions

The Supreme Court has helped make the Constitution a flexible document by interpreting it differently at different times. In this way, the Court helps the Constitution meet the demands of changing times. Supreme Court justices are aware of changing social, political, and economic conditions. In reaching decisions, they consider the beliefs of the people and the changing ideas of justice for all.

The following example illustrates how the Court can change its opinion to meet changing times. In the late 1800s many states passed segregation laws. These laws **segregated,** or separated, African Americans in society. As a result, African Americans and whites could not share the use of public services such as trains, schools, hotels, and hospitals.

**A Decision for Segregation** In 1896 an important case about segregation was brought before the Supreme Court. The case, *Plessy* v. *Ferguson*, challenged a Louisiana law that required African Americans and whites to ride in separate railroad cars. Homer Plessy, who was part African American, had taken a seat in a passenger car that had a sign reading "For Whites Only." When Plessy refused to move to a car for African Americans, he was arrested.

Plessy was found guilty of breaking the Louisiana law and appealed the decision to the Supreme Court. He argued that Louisiana's segregation laws denied him the "equal protection of the law" guaranteed by the Fourteenth Amendment to the Constitution.

The Supreme Court did not accept Plessy's argument. The Court ruled that segregation laws did not violate the Fourteenth Amendment if the separate facilities provided for African Americans were equal to those for whites. This decision established the "separate but equal" principle in American law. The Court's decision in *Plessy* v. *Ferguson* legalized separate but equal facilities for African Americans and whites in all areas of life.

## TEACH OBJECTIVE 3

**LEVEL 1:** To help students analyze how judicial review has strengthened the Court's power and how Congress limits this power, draw a large balance scale on the chalkboard. Label one side *Supreme Court* and the other side *Congress*. Have students take turns explaining judicial review, established by the Marshall Court, on one side and Congress's actions to check the Court on the other. *(Students should note that judicial review asserted the Court's power to declare congressional laws and presidential acts unconstitutional. Congress may pass a similar law that abides by the Constitution or may work to amend the Constitution.)* Discuss this example of checks and balances. **ENGLISH LANGUAGE LEARNERS**

**ALL LEVELS:** Copy the following graphic organizer onto the chalkboard, omitting the italicized answers. Have students complete the organizer to analyze how judicial review has strengthened the Court's power and how Congress limits this power. **ENGLISH LANGUAGE LEARNERS**

**Judicial Review**

**Strengthen**
*It asserted the Court's power to declare laws of Congress and presidential acts unconstitutional.*

**Limit**
*Congress may pass a similar law abiding by the Constitution or may try to amend the Constitution.*

**Congress**

**A Decision against Segregation** In most places, however, facilities for African Americans clearly were not equal to those for whites. For example, schools for African American students were often overcrowded and lacked much of the equipment provided in schools for white students.

After World War II, conditions in the country began to change. Many people began to realize that African American citizens were not being treated fairly under the system of segregation.

In 1954 the Court decided another important segregation case. The case of *Brown* v. *Board of Education* concerned seven-year-old Linda Brown, an African American girl living in Topeka, Kansas. The school located close to Linda's home was for whites only. Linda traveled across town to a school for African Americans. Her father sued the school district, claiming segregated schools were unconstitutional.

In a unanimous decision, the Supreme Court agreed. The Court ruled that segregated schools were not equal and therefore violated the Fourteenth Amendment. Segregated schools, argued the Court, denied students equal protection under the law. Therefore, the Court ruled that public schools in the United States should be desegregated "with all deliberate speed." The Supreme Court had reversed its earlier decision.

✔ **Reading Check** **Contrasting** How were the rulings in *Plessy* v. *Ferguson* and *Brown* v. *Board of Education* different? *Plessy* v. *Ferguson*—Court ruled that segregation did not violate the Fourteenth Amendment; *Brown* v. *Board of Education*—Court ruled that segregated schools violated the Fourteenth Amendment

**Interpreting the Visual Record**

**Segregated schools** *The photo on the left shows Thurgood Marshall (center) and other NAACP leaders who helped bring* Brown *v. Board of Education to the Supreme Court. Linda Brown is shown with her class in the second photo below.* **How might the ruling in this case have affected the school children shown in the photo below?**

**Visual Record Answer**

*Students might suggest that it offered them the opportunity to meet new classmates and expand their experiences.*

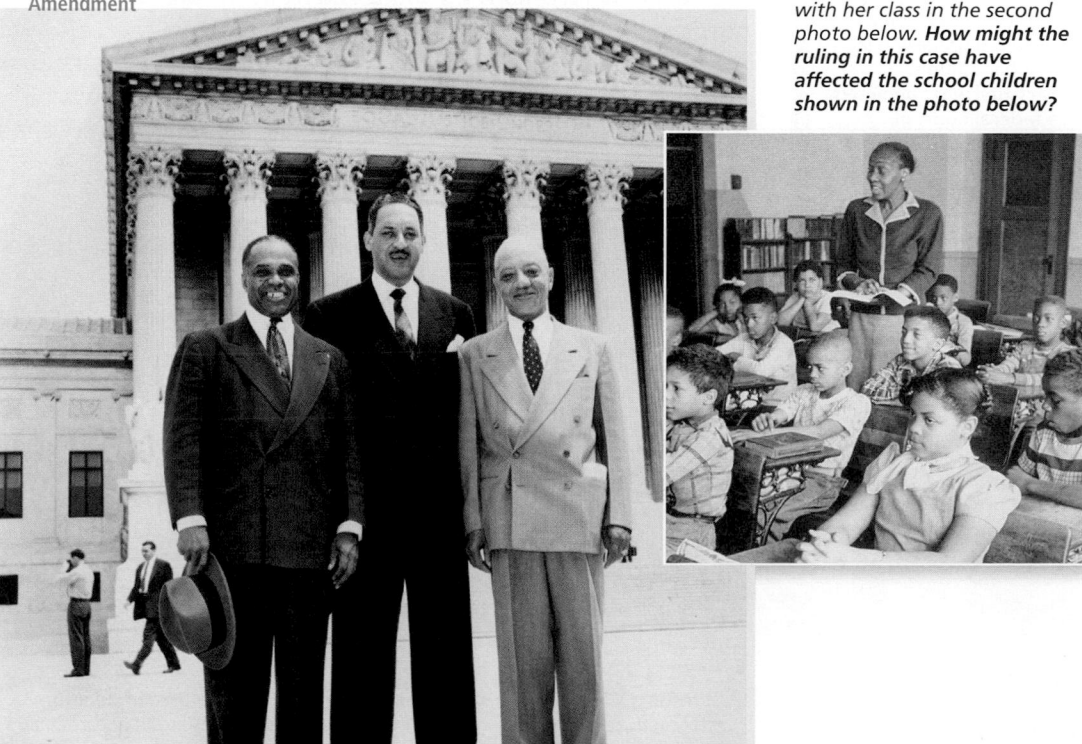

**LEVEL 3:** Have small groups of students role-play an interview with the Supreme Court about judicial review. Have one student act as the interviewer and others act as Supreme Court justices on opposite sides of the following issue. Have students analyze how judicial review has strengthened the Court's power and how Congress limits this power. Have each group conduct its mock interview for the class. **COOPERATIVE LEARNING**

## SPOTLIGHT
### on *Plessy* and *Brown*
Have students use the library and other resources to research the history of the *Plessy* v. *Ferguson* and *Brown* v. *Board of Education of Topeka* cases and the Supreme Court's rationale

for its ruling in both decisions. Then have students write newspaper editorials about these two landmark civil rights cases that address these questions: What principle did the Supreme Court address in these cases? Why is it important that the Supreme Court be able to change its opinion? **BLOCK SCHEDULING**

## CLOSE
Ask students to brainstorm adjectives to describe Supreme Court justices. Have a volunteer list the words on the chalkboard. Discuss how the adjectives describe students' feelings about the Supreme Court.

---

## Section 3 Review
### ANSWERS

**1. Define**
• justices, p. 182
• judicial review, p. 183
• unconstitutional, p. 183
• docket, p. 184
• remand, p. 184
• brief, p. 185
• opinion, p. 185
• concurring opinion, p. 185
• dissenting opinion, p. 185
• segregated, p. 186

**2.** The case is accepted; written arguments are examined; the case is debated and voted on; opinions are written up. The case is not accepted or is remanded to a lower court.

**3. a.** The president appoints Supreme Court justices, and the Senate approves these appointments. Justices are seated for life or until they choose to resign.

**b.** Judicial review asserted the Court's power to declare congressional laws and presidential acts unconstitutional. If the Court declares a law unconstitutional, Congress may pass a similar law that abides by the Constitution or may work to amend the Constitution.

**4.** Students' opinions will vary but should reflect an understanding of the significance of the case.

### BIOGRAPHY
## Thurgood Marshall
### (1908–1993)

Thurgood Marshall was born in Baltimore, Maryland. Marshall graduated first in his class from Howard Law School in 1933. He soon became a key legal counsel for the National Association for the Advancement of Colored People (NAACP). He helped the NAACP win several important civil rights cases. Perhaps his most famous victory was *Brown v. Board of Education* in 1954, which outlawed segregation in U.S. public schools.

Marshall was appointed as a federal Court of Appeals judge in 1961. He became the first African American justice on the Supreme Court in 1967, serving for more than twenty years. Marshall retired from the court in 1991 and died two years later. He left behind a legacy of defending individual rights and demanding equal justice for all Americans. **How did Thurgood Marshall contribute to the legal system of the United States?**

## ★ Strengthening Constitutional Rights

In recent years, Supreme Court decisions have made far-reaching changes in three areas of American life—the rights of accused persons, voting rights, and civil rights.

**Rights of Accused Persons** A number of Supreme Court decisions in the 1960s greatly strengthened the rights of accused persons. In the 1966 case of *Miranda* v. *Arizona*, the Supreme Court declared that the police must inform arrested suspects of their rights before questioning them. Suspects must be told that they have the right to remain silent, that anything they say may be used against them, and that they have the right to have a lawyer present during questioning. If a suspect cannot afford a lawyer, a lawyer will be appointed for the suspect.

The Supreme Court's rulings on the rights of the accused raise a difficult question. What is the proper balance between the rights of the individual and the rights of society? This issue continues to be debated as new cases come before the courts.

✔ **Reading Check** **Identifying Points of View** What did the Supreme Court rule in *Miranda* v. *Arizona?* The ruling states that police must inform arrested suspects of their rights before questioning them. Answers will vary.

**"One Person, One Vote"** The Supreme Court also made several decisions in the 1960s concerning voting and representation in state legislatures and the House of Representatives. A result of these court cases was the ruling that election districts for choosing representatives to Congress and the state legislatures must be divided by population as equally as possible. This means that each state must make every effort to ensure that every citizen's vote is equal in value.

✔ **Reading Check** **Evaluating** How does the concept of "one person, one vote" increase the fairness of elections? Each person's vote has equal value.

**Civil Rights and Civil Liberties** The third area in which the Supreme Court's rulings have had important results is in civil rights and civil liberties. The 1954 Brown decision against segregated schools did not completely eliminate segregation in American schools or in American life. The Court's decision, however, struck a blow against segregation by suggesting that these laws were unconstitutional.

The civil rights movement and civil rights laws followed. Segregation laws were removed, and laws guaranteeing African Americans the right to vote were passed. In its decisions, the Court established that the rights guaranteed in the Constitution apply to all Americans.

✔ **Reading Check** **Analyzing Information** How did the *Brown* decision affect segregation? It suggested that segregation laws were unconstitutional, which led to the civil rights movement and legislation outlawing segregation.

## REVIEW AND ASSESS

Have students complete the **Section 3 Review** on page 189. Then have them complete **Daily Quiz 7.3.** As **Alternative Assessment**, you may want to use the Supreme Court lawyer's journal entry or job announcement activities in this section's lessons.

## RETEACH

Have students complete **Main Idea Activity for English Language Learners and Special-Needs Students 7.3.** Then have students refer to their texts to find two related facts for each of the section's Define terms. Call on volunteers to share their facts with the rest of the class. **ENGLISH LANGUAGE LEARNERS**

## TEACHER TO TEACHER

Heather Verdi of Connecticut recommends the following activity:

Ask students to conduct research at the library or through other sources to obtain the names of the elected officials in your state. Their research should include learning to what political party the representatives belong. Have students compile their research into a directory. If possible, you might invite one or more of the officials to your class for a question-and-answer session. **BLOCK SCHEDULING**

## ★ The Court's Prestige

Throughout U.S. history, the prestige and dignity of the Supreme Court have grown. Supreme Court justices, for the most part, have remained uninvolved in politics and have not been influenced by favors or bribes. Most Americans believe the Court is an important part of our democratic system. The decisions of the Supreme Court have not, however, been free of controversy. Some have criticized the Court for being too liberal or too conservative.

In the late 1930s President Franklin D. Roosevelt attempted to change the nature of the Supreme Court by adding more justices to the Court. Yet public outcry caused Roosevelt's plan to be dropped. Americans did not want to change the balance of power among the federal government's executive, legislative, and judicial branches.

The debate over the Supreme Court's power continues today. Limits on the Court's power do exist. Although the Court makes important decisions that affect U.S. policies and American life, it cannot enforce these decisions. The Court must depend on the executive branch to carry out its decisions.

**Interpreting Political Cartoons**

**Pressuring the Court** *In the 1930s President Franklin D. Roosevelt attempted to influence the decisions of the Supreme Court by adding justices who agreed with his views.* **How does this cartoon portray Roosevelt and his allies and the Supreme Court?**

✔ **Reading Check** Supporting a Point of View Would you limit or increase the power of the Supreme Court? Explain your answer. Students should explain why they think the Supreme Court is too powerful or too weak.

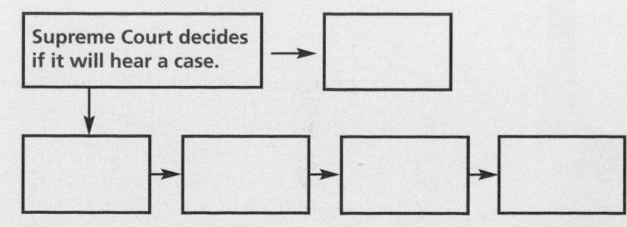

# SECTION 3 / Review

go.hrw.com **Homework Practice Online**
keyword: SZ3 HP7

1. **Define** and explain:
   - justices
   - docket
   - opinion
   - segregated
   - judicial review
   - remand
   - concurring opinion
   - unconstitutional
   - brief
   - dissenting opinion

2. **Sequencing** Copy the flowchart below. Use it to identify the steps for a case in the Supreme Court.

**The Supreme Court in Action**

```
Supreme Court decides
if it will hear a case.  →  [    ]
         ↓
[    ]  →  [    ]  →  [    ]  →  [    ]
```

3. **Finding the Main Idea**
   a. How are appointments to the Supreme Court made, and what are the justices' terms of office?
   b. How did the power of judicial review strengthen the Supreme Court, and how is the power of the Supreme Court limited by Congress?

4. **Writing and Critical Thinking**
   **Identifying Points of View** Imagine that it is 1954 and you are a justice of the Supreme Court. The Court has just made a ruling in the case of *Brown* v. *Board of Education,* and you have been assigned to write the Court's opinion on the case.

   **Consider:**
   - why the Court has decided to overturn *Plessy* v. *Ferguson*
   - why segregated schools are unconstitutional

---

**POLITICAL CARTOON ANSWER**
Roosevelt and his allies are portrayed as doctors seeking to cure a healthy patient, while the Supreme Court is shown as a reluctant patient.

## CHAPTER 7
### REVIEW ANSWERS

**Define and Identify**
1. precedent, p. 170
2. constitutional law, p. 171
3. testimony, p. 173
4. original jurisdiction, p. 175
5. appellate jurisdiction, p. 175
6. subpoenas, p. 176
7. magistrate judges, p. 176
8. circuit, p. 177
9. judicial review, p. 183
10. brief, p. 185

**Understanding Main Ideas**
1. statutory—passed by lawmaking bodies; common—guided by common sense and common rule; administrative—made by government agencies; constitutional—based on the Constitution and the Supreme Court's interpretation of it

2. providing fair public trials and ensuring equal justice for all

3. constitutional violations, U.S. treaty violations, congressional law violations, cases between a foreign government and a U.S. citizen, crimes committed on U.S. ships at sea, cases involving U.S. ambassadors and consuls who break laws in their stationed countries, crimes committed on certain types of federal property, and disagreements between states or citizens of different states

# Review and Assessment Resources

**REPRODUCIBLE**
▶ Chapter 7 Review, pp. 190–91
▶ Vocabulary Activity 7
▶ Chapter 7 Tutorial for Students, Parents, Mentors, and Peers
▶ Chapter 7 Test (Form A or B)
▶ Alternative Assessment Handbook

**TECHNOLOGY**
▶ Chapter 7 Test Generator (on the One-Stop Planner)
▶ Global Skill Builder CD–ROM
▶ HRW Go site

**REINFORCEMENT, REVIEW, AND ASSESSMENT**
▶ Chapter 7 Test for English Language Learners and Special-Needs Students

## REVIEW

Have students complete the **Chapter 7 Review** on pages 190–91.

## ASSESS

Use one of the chapter tests to assess students' understanding of the content. For **Alternative Assessment**, see the **Alternative Assessment Handbook**.

---

**4.** Federal courts are classified according to jurisdiction—original and appellate. Original jurisdiction courts hear cases for the first time. Appellate courts hear appeals.

**5.** appointed by the president and approved by the Senate; for life or until they resign

**6.** judicial review by declaring congressional laws and presidential acts unconstitutional; Congress may pass a similar law that abides by the Constitution or may work to amend the Constitution

### What Did You Find Out?
**1.** They safeguard the freedoms and rights of all citizens, including those accused of a crime.

**2.** if there is reason to doubt that a person did not receive a fair trial

**3.** The Court hears appeals, cases involving diplomatic representatives of other countries, cases involving disputes between states, and cases involving a state and the federal government; the lawyers for each side submit a brief and then present oral arguments, after which the justices vote and then draft the opinion, adding concurring and dissenting opinions if necessary.

---

# Chapter 7 Review

## Chapter Summary

### Section 1

- All citizens are considered equal and are protected by the rule of law.
- There are four different kinds of law in the United States. These are statutory law, common law, administrative law, and constitutional law.
- The U.S. court system uses the different kinds of law to settle disputes by applying the law and reaching a decision in favor of one side or the other.
- U.S. citizens are guaranteed certain legal rights. These are the right to a lawyer, the right to be released on bail, the right to indictment by a grand jury, the right to a jury trial, the assumption of innocence until guilt is proven, and the right of appeal.

### Section 2

- The Constitution gives the federal courts jurisdiction to hold trials in a wide variety of cases.
- There are three main levels of federal courts—district courts, courts of appeals, and the U.S. Supreme Court.
- There are additional federal courts that deal with specific issues such as international trade or military appeals.

### Section 3

- The U.S. Supreme Court is the only court specifically established by the Constitution. It currently has nine justices who were appointed by U.S. presidents.
- Through its power of judicial review, the Supreme Court can decide if laws and presidential actions are constitutional.
- Supreme Court decisions may change over time to reflect changing social, political, or economic decisions.

---

## Define and Identify
Use the following terms in complete sentences.
1. precedent
2. constitutional law
3. testimony
4. original jurisdiction
5. appellate jurisdiction
6. subpoenas
7. magistrate judges
8. circuit
9. judicial review
10. brief

## Understanding Main Ideas

**Section 1** *(Pages 169–73)*
1. Describe the types of laws that exist in the United States.
2. What services do U.S. courts provide?

**Section 2** *(Pages 174–80)*
3. Which cases are tried in federal courts?
4. How is the federal court system organized?

**Section 3** *(Pages 182–89)*
5. How are appointments made to the Supreme Court, and how long do justices serve?
6. How does the Supreme Court limit Congress's power, and how does Congress reassert it?

## What Did You Find Out?
1. In what ways do U.S. laws ensure justice for all?
2. When might a person appeal a case?
3. What kinds of cases come to the Supreme Court, and what happens to a case once the Court agrees to hear it?

## Thinking Critically
1. **Supporting a Point of View** When the Supreme Court hears a case, it limits the lawyers for each side to a 30-minute presentation. Argue persuasively whether you think this is enough time to present all the facts of a case. Be sure to explain why you think such a time limit exists.
2. **Analyzing Information** Some people believe that the rights guaranteed to the accused offer too much protection to criminals. Other people believe that these rights are needed to protect those who are unjustly accused. Explain whether you think there are too many or too few protections.
3. **Evaluating** Justices of the Supreme Court vote to decide which cases they will review. What issues might arise from using this system, and could they be solved by using an impartial panel instead? Explain your answer.

## RETEACH

Organize students into three groups and assign each group one of the chapter's sections. Have members of each group create a visual presentation illustrating the main objectives in their assigned section. Then have each group present its work to the class. **ENGLISH LANGUAGE LEARNERS** , **COOPERATIVE LEARNING**

## Portfolio Extensions

**1. Interdisciplinary Connection to Art and Literature** Have students conduct research at the library to obtain a copy of a book that profiles a case heard before the Supreme Court. Ask each student to read the book and then write a book report that addresses the following issues—the significance of the case; why the Supreme Court chose to hear that specific case; the final ruling and its resulting effect on the country; whether the student agrees with the Court's decision and why.

**2. Cooperative Learning** Organize students into small groups. Ask each group to select a constitutional amendment. Groups should write a skit that explains the amendment, demonstrates the protections of the amendment, and shows what the consequences might be if the amendment were not included in the Constitution. Have groups perform their skits for the class.

---

## Building Social Studies Skills

### Interpreting Political Cartoons

Study the political cartoon below. Then answer the following questions.

BUT CAPTAIN!

1. If the ship's captain represents the president of the United States, what does the cartoon suggest about the relationship between the Supreme Court and the president?
   a. The Supreme Court exists for the president's protection.
   b. The president holds the most powerful political office in the United States.
   c. The president and the Supreme Court justices must work together on many issues.

d. The president would like to limit the Supreme Court's power.

2. Why do you think the individual representing the American people is shown with a shocked expression?

### Analyzing Primary Sources

Read the following quotation from Chief Justice John Marshall's ruling in the *Marbury* v. *Madison* case. Then answer the questions that follow.

❝The powers of the legislature are defined and limited; and that those limits may not be mistaken or forgotten, the Constitution is written. . . . It is, emphatically [without question] the province and duty of the Judicial Department to say what the law is. . . . So if a law be in opposition to the Constitution. . . . [and] the Constitution is superior to any ordinary act of the legislature, the Constitution, and not such ordinary act, must govern the case to which they both apply.❞

3. Which of the following statements best describes Marshall's view of the Supreme Court's authority?
   a. The legislature has less power than the Supreme Court, which can ignore new laws it does not like.
   b. The Constitution is superior to any acts of the legislature that conflict with it, and it is the Supreme Court's duty to identify such laws.
   c. The Supreme Court can change the Constitution as needed to adjust to new laws.
   d. The Supreme Court cannot rule on whether a law is unconstitutional or not.

4. How do the principles stated by Marshall above help establish an important power of the Supreme Court?

### Alternative Assessment

#### Building Your Portfolio

**Linking to Community**
With the supervision of an adult, interview a member of your local police force. Ask the officer how the force protects the rights of the accused. Does the officer believe that these rules help or hinder the work of the police? Next, interview a local, state, or federal judge in your community about the ways in which the courts protect the rights of the accused. Finally, write a paragraph comparing the views of these two sources.

**internet** connect

**Internet Activity: go.hrw.com**
keyword: SZ3 AC7

Access the Internet through the HRW Go site to research the structure of the federal court system. Then create a mobile that displays your information. Focus on the jurisdictions of various courts and the cases that each court handles.

### Thinking Critically

1. Students who think it is may suggest that a well-informed, articulate lawyer can present a case in this amount of time; students who disagree may point out the complexity of such issues as those that reach the Supreme Court. The time limit exists because of the heavy workload of the Court.

2. Students who think there is too much protection may suggest that most accused persons turn out to be guilty. Students who disagree may say that equality under the law requires protecting the rights of all.

3. Students who like the current system may reason that justices have the necessary experience to do such a review and that it gives them a chance to get to know cases and watch for litigation trends. Students who prefer a panel may feel that a justice may select or refuse a case based on bias.

### Social Studies Skills

1. d

2. Students' responses will vary.

3. b

4. Students should note that Marshall saw that the Court has the power to review all laws and reject those that are unconstitutional; they should note that this is the power of judicial review.

## TEACH

**LEVEL 1:** Remind students that the Constitution specifies the organization of the U.S. government. Then explain to students that Congress must approve any proposed changes to the government's structure. Organize students into pairs and ask pairs to draw cartoons illustrating the process that a bill would have to go through in order to be passed by Congress. **ENGLISH LANGUAGE LEARNERS , COOPERATIVE LEARNING**

**ALL LEVELS:** Organize students into groups and have each group create a set of trading cards depicting the president in the different roles required by the executive office. Ask students to describe the responsibilities of each role on the back of the cards. Then ask each group to list tasks that they think do not require the president's attention and to make a separate pile of the executive responsibility cards that they would eliminate from the set. Ask students to explain who would handle these responsibilities if they were no longer the president's responsibility. **ENGLISH LANGUAGE LEARNERS**

## APPLYING THE SKILLS

Ask students to design billboards in support of their Civics Lab proposing changes to the way that the government is organized. Tell students that each billboard should contain the phrase "Reinventing Government." Encourage students to make their billboards persuasive and easy to understand.

# Civics Lab

### Reinventing Government
**Complete the following Civics Lab activity individually or in a group.**

## Your Task

In Unit 2 you have read about the structure of the U.S. federal government. Imagine that you are a member of a group of American citizens who feel that the size and complexity of the federal government are interfering with its effectiveness. These concerns have led your group to work on "reinventing" government—to make it more efficient and responsive to the people.

Your job is to prepare a proposal titled Reinventing Government. In your proposal explain what changes you wish to make to each branch of the federal government. Be sure to explain why these changes are needed and how they can be made within a democratic system. Any changes you propose must uphold the Constitution's principles and ideals, such as checks and balances, the separation of powers, and the accountability of government to the people. Your proposal will need visual and written materials. To prepare these materials, you will need to do the following.

## What to Do

**STEP 1** Write a bill outlining the changes you propose to make Congress more efficient and responsive. Create a two-column chart that shows your proposed changes. In one column, titled *Current,* list current membership requirements, procedures, and organizational structures for Congress. In the second column, titled *Proposed,* describe how you would

| Proposed Changes | |
| --- | --- |
| Current | Proposed |
| | |

**ALL LEVELS:** Have students create graphic organizers with the following horizontal headings: *Legislative Branch, Executive Branch, Judicial Branch*. Have students chart the organization of each branch of government beneath these headings. Then ask students to explain why the Constitution specifies that the government should be organized in this manner. Have students indicate the advantages and disadvantages of this organization.

**ENGLISH LANGUAGE LEARNERS**

**LEVEL 3:** Ask students to list the responsibilities of the Supreme Court. Then ask each student to consider which responsibility is the most important for maintaining the rights and freedoms of democracy. Ask each student to write a position paper defending his or her opinions. Remind students to support their arguments with evidence and careful reasoning.

change (or keep) each item in the first column. Your bill should summarize the chart's information and explain the purpose and reasoning behind each change.

**STEP 2** **Create a list** of the responsibilities of the executive branch. Next to each item, indicate which part of the executive branch takes care of that responsibility— the president and the Executive Office, an executive department, or an independent agency. Analyze your list. Do responsibilities overlap, causing conflict and inefficiency? Are there too many departments and agencies? Too few? Write a paragraph explaining any changes you would make to the executive branch. If no changes are needed, explain why.

*Executive Responsibilities*

FOREIGN POLICY →
- *President*
- *Secretary of State*
- *State Department*

**STEP 3** **Draw** an organizational chart of the federal court system. Then draw a second organizational chart showing any changes you would make to the system. Consider how judges are chosen, the terms judges serve, the number of judges in each court, the types of cases each court handles, and each court's power to review other courts' and other federal branches' decisions. In a caption, explain the reasoning behind each change or the lack of changes.

**The Federal Court System**

Supreme Court

- State Courts
- U.S. Court of Appeals
- U.S. Court of Appeals for the Federal Circuit

Organize your materials and present your proposal to a local citizens' group (the rest of the class).

**A STEP FURTHER**

Ask students to imagine that they are members of Congress who must vote on whether to make changes to the government. Have each student write a speech that argues whether the Congress should adhere strictly to the Constitution as it is written or administer changes to it to meet the changing needs of the country. Students' papers should support their positions with examples from the various presentations in the Civics Lab or the textbook. Ask volunteers to debate their positions in front of the class.

**UNIT OVERVIEW**

Unit 3 describes how state and local governments function in the United States. By examining the powers, duties, and organization of each of these levels of government, students receive a clearer understanding of how the federal system works. They also gain insight into the importance of state and local governments in meeting the special needs of all their citizens.

**In Their Own Words**

"... The genius of the United States is not best or most in its executives or legislatures, nor in its ambassadors or authors, or colleges or churches or parlors, nor even in its newspapers or inventors—but almost most in the common people, south, north, west, east, in all its states, through all its mighty amplitude [range]."—Walt Whitman

**Using the Quotation** Have students read the quotation by Walt Whitman. Ask them to think about Whitman's words and then to give a short answer to the following question: Of all the components that make up the U.S. system of government, which one is the most important? *(Students should respond that people are the most important component.)*

**About the Author** Walt Whitman (1819–1892) was born on Long Island in New York. Whitman's varied career included work as a journalist, teacher, house builder, and poet. He cared for wounded soldiers during the U.S. Civil War and produced a number of well-known poems about the war and President Abraham Lincoln's death. He first published *Leaves of Grass*, a widely read book of his poems, in 1855. Revised editions of the book were published up to Whitman's death in 1892.

UNIT

3

# State and Local Government

**CHAPTER 8** State Government

**CHAPTER 9** Local Government

Ask students to list the basic government services that they make use of on a daily basis. Then have students consider what government agencies or offices make these services possible. Ask students to consider what would happen if one of these services were suddenly unavailable. Also ask students to determine whether these services are best provided by federal, local, or state governments. After students finish reading this unit, have them compare these answers with what they have learned.

# Young Citizens

## IN ACTION

### Practicing Citizenship

When Ben Johnson first arrived at Nevada Boys State, he was not sure what to expect. "The only thing anyone at my school could tell me was that it involved a mock government," Ben said. Created by the American Legion in 1935, Boys State is attended by young men the summer after their junior year of high school. The American Legion Auxiliary sponsors Girls State, a similar program for young women.

During the week-long program, participants learn about government and democracy. However, the young citizens are not attending another class. Instead, they participate in a two-party government. Delegates have the opportunity to create party platforms, prepare speeches, and run for elected office. Their activities include legislative sessions and trials. Other delegates have responsibilities such as law enforcement.

Boys State enables delegates to participate more actively in a democratic society. In addition, delegates acquire experience and skills that they can use in a variety of careers. Some famous Boys State participants include Vice President Dick Cheney, news anchor Tom Brokaw, and astronaut Neil Armstrong.

No matter how delegates use their experience, many believe the program was worth a week of their summer vacations. Johnson described his memories of Boys State: "Having two of my bills signed by the Boys State governor and participating in the speech contest are just a few of the memories that I cherish from my time at Boys State. I knew that after my experience at Boys State my life would never be the same again."

*Boys State offers participants the opportunity to learn about democracy in action.*

### You Decide

1. *How does Boys State teach participants about democracy?*
2. *Why are programs like Boys State and Girls State important?*
3. *If you were a Boys State or Girls State delegate, what would be the goal of the first bill you introduced in the Senate, and why?*

## What Can We Do?

Ask students to research youth programs available in their own community that offer hands-on experience in the processes of government. Then have students find other ways that they can become involved in their local government, such as through letter writing, attending public meetings, participating in community organizations, and so on. Encourage students to identify issues that concern them and ask them to write proposals explaining how they can participate in the democratic process to bring these issues to the attention of their local government.

### YOU DECIDE ANSWERS

1. Participants in Boys State learn about government through direct involvement in creating party platforms, preparing speeches, running for office, and passing and enforcing laws.

2. They give high school students hands-on experiences in the processes of government, and they help students become good citizens.

3. Students' responses will vary.

# State Government

## CHAPTER RESOURCE MANAGER

| Objectives | Pacing Guide | Reproducible Resources |
|---|---|---|
| **SECTION 1:**<br>**The States**<br>(pp. 197–202) | ✪ Identify the powers reserved to the states.<br>✪ Describe the components of a state constitution.<br>✪ Explain how states cooperate with each other and with the federal government. | **Regular**<br>1.5 days<br><br>**Block Scheduling**<br>1 day<br><br>*Block Scheduling Handbook with Team Teaching Strategies, Chapter 8* | **RS** Guided Reading Strategies 8.1<br><br>**RS** Readings in Economics and Government 65: Why Alaska Needs Statehood<br><br>**SM** Community Service and Participation Handbook: This Building Has a Name? |
| **SECTION 2:**<br>**State Legislatures**<br>(pp. 203–08) | ✪ Analyze why the populations in state election districts must be as equal as possible.<br>✪ Identify the qualifications and explain the terms of office for state legislators.<br>✪ Describe how presiding officers are chosen and analyze how the work of the state legislatures is carried out in most states. | **Regular**<br>1 day<br><br>**Block Scheduling**<br>.5 day<br><br>*Block Scheduling Handbook with Team Teaching Strategies, Chapter 8* | **RS** Guided Reading Strategies 8.2<br><br>**PS** Graphic Organizer Activity: Your State Government |
| **SECTION 3:**<br>**The State Executive Branch**<br>(pp. 210–14) | ✪ Describe the qualifications, terms of office, duties, and powers of most governors.<br>✪ Identify the other officials of state executive branches.<br>✪ Explain the purpose of the state executive agencies and officials. | **Regular**<br>1 day<br><br>**Block Scheduling**<br>.5 day<br><br>*Block Scheduling Handbook with Team Teaching Strategies, Chapter 8* | **RS** Guided Reading Strategies 8.3<br><br>**E** Challenge and Enrichment Worksheet 8: Researching Your State Executive Branch |
| **SECTION 4:**<br>**State Courts**<br>(pp. 215–19) | ✪ Describe the kinds of cases that state courts handle.<br>✪ Explain the areas of responsibility of each of the four types of state courts.<br>✪ Evaluate how overcrowding causes problems for the courts. | **Regular**<br>1.5 days<br><br>**Block Scheduling**<br>1 day<br><br>*Block Scheduling Handbook with Team Teaching Strategies, Chapter 8* | **RS** Guided Reading Strategies 8.4<br><br>**E** Creative Teaching Strategy: Learning Stations |

## Chapter Resource Key

| | | | |
|---|---|---|---|
| **PS** | Primary Sources | **SM** | Skills Mastery |
| **RS** | Reading Support | **A** | Assessment |
| **IC** | Interdisciplinary Connections | **REV** | Review |
| **E** | Enrichment | **ELL** | Reinforcement and English Language Learners |
| | | | Transparencies |

 CD-ROM

 Video

 Internet

💻 Holt Presentation Maker Using Microsoft® PowerPoint®

 **One-Stop** Planner CD–ROM

**See the *One-Stop Planner* for a complete list of additional resources for students and teachers.**

## One-Stop Planner CD–ROM

It's easy to plan lessons, select resources, and print out materials for your students when you use the **One-Stop Planner CD–ROM with Test Generator**.

| Technology Resources | Reinforcement, Review, and Assessment |
|---|---|
| One-Stop Planner, Lesson 8.1<br>Holt Researcher CD–ROM<br>Homework Practice Online | **REV** Section 1 Review, p. 202<br>**A** Daily Quiz 8.1<br>**ELL** Main Idea Activity 8.1<br>**ELL** English Audio Summary 8.1<br>**ELL** Spanish Audio Summary 8.1 |
| One-Stop Planner, Lesson 8.2<br>Transparency 8: State Government<br>CNN Presents: American Government<br>Homework Practice Online | **REV** Section 2 Review, p. 208<br>**A** Daily Quiz 8.2<br>**ELL** Main Idea Activity 8.2<br>**ELL** English Audio Summary 8.2<br>**ELL** Spanish Audio Summary 8.2 |
| One-Stop Planner, Lesson 8.3<br>Transparency 9: The Powers and Duties of the Governor<br>Homework Practice Online | **REV** Section 3 Review, p. 214<br>**A** Daily Quiz 8.3<br>**ELL** Main Idea Activity 8.3<br>**ELL** English Audio Summary 8.3<br>**ELL** Spanish Audio Summary 8.3 |
| One-Stop Planner, Lesson 8.4<br>Homework Practice Online<br>HRW Go Site | **REV** Section 4 Review, p. 219<br>**A** Daily Quiz 8.4<br>**ELL** Main Idea Activity 8.4<br>**ELL** English Audio Summary 8.4<br>**ELL** Spanish Audio Summary 8.4 |

### internet connect

**HRW ONLINE RESOURCES**
GO TO: go.hrw.com
Then type in the keyword.

**TEACHER HOME PAGE**
KEYWORD: SZ3 Teacher

**CHAPTER INTERNET ACTIVITIES**
KEYWORD: SZ3 AC8
Choose an activity to:
- create a dossier on principal elected officials in your state.
- create a model or visual display on the structure of your state government.
- create a legal newspaper on issues before state court systems.

**CHAPTER ENRICHMENT LINKS**
KEYWORD: SZ3 CH8

**ONLINE ASSESSMENT**
Homework Practice
KEYWORD: SZ3 HP8
Rubrics
KEYWORD: SS Rubrics

**ONLINE MAPS, CHARTS, AND GRAPHS**
KEYWORD: SZ3 MCG
- The Federal System

**HOLT PRESENTATION MAKER**
KEYWORD: SZ3 PPT8

**CONTENT UPDATES**
KEYWORD: SS Content Updates

**ONLINE READING SUPPORT**
KEYWORD: SS Strategies

**CURRENT EVENTS**
KEYWORD: S3 Current Events

### Meeting Individual Needs

**Ability Levels**

**Level 1** Basic-level activities designed for all students encountering new material

**Level 2** Intermediate-level activities designed for average students

**Level 3** Challenging activities designed for honors and gifted-and-talented students

**English Language Learners** Activities that address the needs of students with Limited English Proficiency

### Chapter Review and Assessment

**IC** Vocabulary Activity 8
Global Skill Builder CD–ROM
HRW Go site
**REV** Chapter 8 Tutorial for Students, Parents, Mentors, and Peers
**REV** Chapter 8 Review, pp. 220–21
**A** Standardized Test Practice
**A** Chapter 8 Test Generator (on the One-Stop Planner)
**A** Chapter 8 Test (Form A or B)
**A** Alternative Assessment Handbook
**A** Chapter 8 Test for English Language Learners and Special-Needs Students

# CHAPTER 8

Section 1    The States

Section 2    State Legislatures

Section 3    The State Executive
             Branch

Section 4    State Courts

## What's Your Opinion?

To help students create their **Themes** Journal entries, provide the following examples of appropriate **agree**/**disagree** statements.

● **Agree**   State governments affect the lives of their citizens in more ways than the federal government.

**Disagree**   The federal government has greater responsibilities than state governments.

● **Agree**   To create more efficient interaction, all state governments should be organized the same way.

**Disagree**   As long as state governments reflect a republican government, their organization can vary.

● **Agree**   State courts interpret the law similarly in order to ensure a standard rule of law.

**Disagree**   There are a variety of state courts, different in both their jurisdiction and types of cases heard.

## Internet Activity

**A Closer Look at State Government**

internet connect

**TOPIC:** Your State Government
**GO TO:** go.hrw.com
**KEYWORD:** SZ3 AC8

Have students access the Internet through the HRW Go site to conduct research about the structure, agencies, and branches of your state government. Then have each student create a visual display or model based upon his or her research. Student models or displays should include information on the power and authority of each branch or agency.

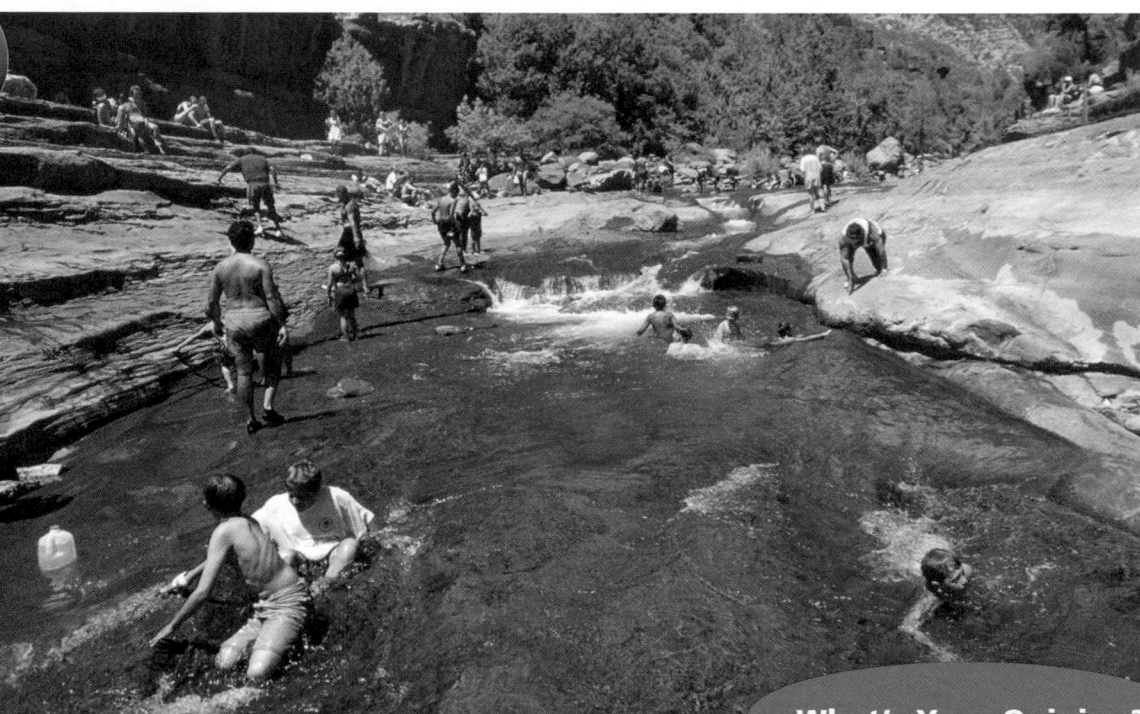

## What's Your Opinion?

## Build on What You Know

Have you ever wondered who decides how many days you must attend school each year? Your state government does. Your state government passes laws that affect the people living in your state. It also helps pay for public education and state parks like the one shown above. It provides hospitals and builds and maintains state roadways. Your state government does all this and more because, like the federal government, it has been established to serve the people.

Do you **agree** or **disagree** with the following statements? Support your point of view in your journal.

● State governments have more responsibilities than the federal government.

● All state governments should be organized the same way.

● All state courts perform the same duties.

# SECTION 1

## OBJECTIVES

*After completing Section 1, students should be able to*

1. **Identify the powers reserved to the states.**
2. **Describe the components of a state constitution.**
3. **Explain how states cooperate with each other and with the federal government.**

## LET'S GET STARTED!

As students enter the classroom, organize the class into three groups and give each group a large sheet of paper and a marker. Ask members of one group to draw their state, identifying anything that borders their state. Ask members of the second group to write down any facts or trivia that they know about their state. Instruct members of the third group to list any laws that might be particular to their state. (*Students' answers might include differences in education requirements, testing requirements in schools, speed limits, legal age to marry or drive, and so on.*) Have each group explain the results of its assignment to the class. Tell students that in Section 1 they will learn more about the rights and duties of states.

## SECTION 1

# The States

### Read to Discover

1. What powers do states have?
2. What are the components of a state constitution?
3. How do states cooperate with each other and with the federal government?

#### WHY CIVICS MATTERS

State governments provide many services to the citizens of their state. Use **CNNfyi.com** or other **current events** sources to find three examples of different services your state government offers its residents. Record your findings in your journal.

### Define

• territory
• full faith and credit clause
• extradition

### SECTION 1 RESOURCES

#### REPRODUCIBLE

▶ Guided Reading Strategies 8.1
▶ Readings in Economics and Government 65: Why Alaska Needs Statehood
▶ Community Service Participation Handbook: This Building Has a Name?

#### TECHNOLOGY

▶ One-Stop Planner, Lesson 8.1
▶ Holt Researcher CD–ROM
▶ Homework Practice Online

#### REINFORCEMENT, REVIEW, AND ASSESSMENT

▶ Section 1 Review, p. 202
▶ Daily Quiz 8.1
▶ Main Idea Activity 8.1
▶ English Audio Summary 8.1
▶ Spanish Audio Summary 8.1

## Reading Focus

When the American colonies won their independence, the original 13 states acted like small, separate countries. Each state regulated trade crossing its borders and often treated neighboring states as if they were foreign countries. For the first few years of the republic it seemed that the United States would break up into 13 small, weak countries. The Constitution addressed these problems by creating a federal system with a strong national government.

### ★ Division of Powers

In the U.S. federal system, the powers of government are divided between the 50 states and the federal government. How was the division of these powers decided?

The Constitution gave the federal government those powers that affected all U.S. citizens. For example, only the federal government can regulate trade between the states, coin money, and conduct foreign affairs. The federal government alone can set up a postal service and maintain an army and a navy.

The states, meanwhile, have considerable power to govern the people who live within their borders. State governments are closer to the people and can better provide them with many needed services.

*The 13 states represented on this early U.S. flag had little in common with each other.*

✔ **Reading Check** Contrasting How are the powers of federal government and state governments divided? The federal government has those powers that affect all the people of the country. State governments have the power to govern the people who live within their borders.

**ALL LEVELS:** Lead a class discussion about the Constitution. Tell students that Article I, Section 8, defines powers given to the federal government and that Article I, Section 10, lists those powers that are prohibited to the states. Tell students that the Tenth Amendment reserves to the states all powers not given to the federal government or prohibited to the states. Organize the class into small groups and assign each group one of the following topics: powers belonging to the federal government, powers prohibited to the states, or powers reserved to the states. Ask each group to create a collage illustrating the powers involved in its assigned topic. Have groups present their work to the class.

**ENGLISH LANGUAGE LEARNERS , COOPERATIVE LEARNING**

**ALL LEVELS:** Copy the following graphic organizer onto the chalkboard, omitting the italicized answers. Organize the class into small groups and have each group complete the diagram with the types of powers reserved for the states.

**ENGLISH LANGUAGE LEARNERS , COOPERATIVE LEARNING**

Powers Reserved for the States

*Federal* ∩ *State*
*concurrent*

Every now and then lawmakers review old case law and find laws that today seem foolish, silly, or strange. The following are samples of such laws that were once—and in some cases still are—on the books in their respective states.

Alabama: It is illegal to wear a fake mustache that causes laughter in church.

Alaska: While it is legal to shoot bears, waking a sleeping bear for the purpose of taking a photograph is prohibited.

Georgia: It is illegal to change the clothes on a storefront mannequin unless the shades are down.

Illinois: In Chicago it is illegal to fish in one's pajamas.

Indiana: In Gary it is illegal to attend the theater within four hours of eating garlic.

Kansas: In Natoma it is illegal to throw a knife at anyone wearing a striped shirt.

Tennessee: In Memphis it is illegal for a woman to drive by herself "a man must walk or run in front of the vehicle, waving a red flag in order to warn approaching pedestrians and motorists."

Texas: In Mesquite it is illegal for children to have unusual haircuts.

Utah: In Monroe daylight must be visible between partners on a dance floor.

## ★ Reserved State Powers

As you have read, the Tenth Amendment reserves certain powers—those not granted to the federal government or prohibited to the states—to state governments. For example, states are responsible for conducting local, state, and national elections. They also decide most of the qualifications for voting not otherwise specified in the U.S. Constitution. The federal system depends on the states to ensure that Americans are given the opportunity to elect their representatives.

State governments also have the authority to establish and maintain schools. The states can decide what kinds of schools they will provide. However, state school regulations cannot conflict with the U.S. Constitution or with the rulings of the Supreme Court.

State laws deal with health, safety, welfare, and the regulation of business within state borders. Therefore, states can make laws about various aspects of their residents' lives—ranging from marriage and divorce to traffic regulations. In addition, state governments have control over all local governments within their boundaries—districts, cities, towns, townships, and counties. Local governments receive their powers from the states.

✔ **Reading Check** Summarizing What are some of the states' reserved powers, and what are the limitations of these powers? powers—hold elections, run schools, make laws concerning marriage and traffic, address health, safety, and business within state; limitations—states cannot pass laws that conflict with the U.S. Constitution or Supreme Court rulings

## Division of Powers

**The Nation**

**The federal government has authority over the whole nation.**

Major Powers
- Foreign Relations
- National Defense
- Interstate and Foreign Trade
- Money System

**The States**

**State governments have authority over most affairs within state borders.**

Major Powers
- Election Oversight
- Education
- Police Protection
- Public Building Programs
- Health and Safety
- Highways

**Local Communities**

**Local governments have authority over the affairs of their communities.**

Major Powers
- Schools and Libraries
- Police Protection
- Fire Protection
- Zoning and Building Codes
- Parks and Playgrounds
- Sewage Systems
- Public Utilities
- Streets and Traffic

**Interpreting Charts** *Under the federal system, different levels of government have responsibility for different areas of daily life.* **Over what affairs do state and local governments both have responsibilities?**

**LEVEL 3:** Tell students that when our Constitution was written, there were some who feared the increasing power of the federal government and wanted the Tenth Amendment to say, "The powers not expressly delegated to the United States by the Constitution, nor prohibited by it to the States, are reserved by the States respectively, or to the people." James Madison said "it was impossible to confine a government to the exercise of expressed powers." Instruct each student to write a position paper justifying his or her belief concerning this topic and outlining the powers reserved to the states.

# TEACH OBJECTIVE 2

**LEVEL 1:** Lead a class discussion about the components of a state constitution. Then organize the class into small groups and assign each group one of the components of state constitutions. *(The components include a preamble, a bill of rights, an outline containing the duties of the branches, provisions for elections, provisions for maintaining state affairs, and methods of amending the state constitution.)* Obtain copies of your state's constitution and distribute one to each group. Have groups create a visual illustrating their assigned topic. **ENGLISH LANGUAGE LEARNERS** ,

**COOPERATIVE LEARNING**

## ★ Concurrent Powers

The states also share many powers with the federal government. These shared powers, as you recall, are called concurrent powers. Even if certain powers are granted to the federal government in the Constitution, state governments may also have these powers. Unless a power is forbidden to the states by the U.S. Constitution, state governments may exercise that power.

A good example of a shared, or concurrent, power is the power of taxation. Both the federal government and the state governments have the power to tax their citizens. Federal and state governments must collect various kinds of taxes to carry on their activities. State governments may raise money by taxing items such as gasoline, liquor, and cigarettes, or through income and property taxes. The money raised through state taxes pays for education, highways, health and safety programs, and other state services. Other shared powers include establishing court systems, borrowing and spending money, and making and enforcing laws.

✔ **Reading Check** Finding the Main Idea Define concurrent powers and give examples of these powers. Concurrent powers are shared between the federal and state governments. Examples include taxation, establishing court systems, borrowing and spending money, and making and enforcing laws.

## ★ From 13 States to 50 States

The 13 original states became part of the United States when they approved the Constitution. The states that joined the country later had to apply for statehood. Most of these states were once U.S. territories. A **territory** is an area, governed by the United States, that is eligible to become a state.

In 1787, under the Articles of Confederation, Congress passed an important law called the Northwest Ordinance. This law provided a way for territories to join the country as new and equal states.

Under the Northwest Ordinance a territory was eligible to petition Congress for statehood once it had a population of 60,000. If Congress agreed to the request, it asked the territory's lawmakers to write a state constitution. This constitution had to be approved by the people of the territory and by the U.S. Congress. Congress then voted on whether to admit the territory as a new state.

The United States has admitted 37 states since it became an independent country. In 1959 Hawaii became the 50th state. The United States could grow larger still. U.S. territorial possessions include Puerto Rico, Guam, American Samoa, the U.S. Virgin Islands, and various Pacific islands. In 1993 and 1998 Puerto Rican voters rejected the opportunity to petition the U.S. Congress for statehood.

✔ **Reading Check** Sequencing List in order the steps that the Northwest Ordinance outlines for a territory to become a state. See preceding text for answer.

### ★★★★★★★★★★★ That's Interesting! ★★★★★★★★★★★

**The State that Never Was** "Franklin, the fourteenth state." Sound strange? The first attempt to create a new state took place in 1784. The people of what is today the northeastern portion of Tennessee appealed to Congress for statehood. They wanted to call this new state Franklin after Benjamin Franklin. But the residents of Franklin and the state of North Carolina disputed control over the territory. Finally, the land was given to the national government in 1790, and in 1796 Franklin became part of the new state of Tennessee.

## ★ Economics

**"Sin Taxes"** All states have the power to tax, and each government approaches the issue with an eye towards its own domestic realities. So-called sin taxes serve as an example. The taxes on cigarettes and alcohol are known as sin taxes, which implies that some people believe that those who smoke and consume alcohol should suffer economically for their habits. To some Americans raising sin taxes is much more acceptable than raising taxes on income or property. Also, in an era of health consciousness, asking Americans to pay more for products that can lead to health problems makes sense to many politicians. On the other hand, some politicians and other Americans, particularly in states where the liquor and tobacco industries are important to local economies, oppose sin taxes. They argue that such taxes endanger jobs in those industries.

**CRITICAL THINKING**

Do you think the state governments should be able to sue cigarette or liquor companies for damages to recover some of the health costs that states have had to spend to medically assist individuals suffering from tobacco or alcohol related diseases?

**ANSWER:** Students should support their answers.

---

**CHART ANSWER**
(for page 198) police protection

**LEVEL 2:** Organize students into small groups and have each group write an advertisement for selling a "new and improved" state constitution. The advertisement should boast about the constitution's components and elements as listed in the textbook. Advertisements might also describe the document's value as an instrument of government. Some students might wish to turn their work into posters. Display groups' work and ask students which state constitutions they would "buy" and why.

**COOPERATIVE LEARNING**

 **HOMEWORK** Ask each student to cut out a newspaper article that illustrates an example of a state power and to explain in a written paragraph the state power that is illustrated.

**LEVEL 3:** Obtain copies of your state's constitution and distribute them to students. Have students write a paper comparing their state constitution to the components that are contained in most constitutions. Finally, ask students to present their papers to the class.

## ★ The Democratic Process

**Act 60** In 1996 the U.S. Supreme Court, in *Amanda Brigham* v. *State of Vermont*, declared that Vermont's system for funding public education—with its substantial dependence on local property taxes and wide disparities in money available to the various school districts—"deprived children of an equal educational opportunity in violation of the Vermont Constitution." In response, the legislature passed Act 60, which led to a statewide $1.10 property tax rate and to state block grants that provided equal access to revenues per pupil. Other provisions were also passed to ensure overall educational quality in Vermont schools.

**ACTIVITY:** Tell students to conduct research about how schools are financed in your state and to create a poster to illustrate their findings.

**MAP ANSWER**
5

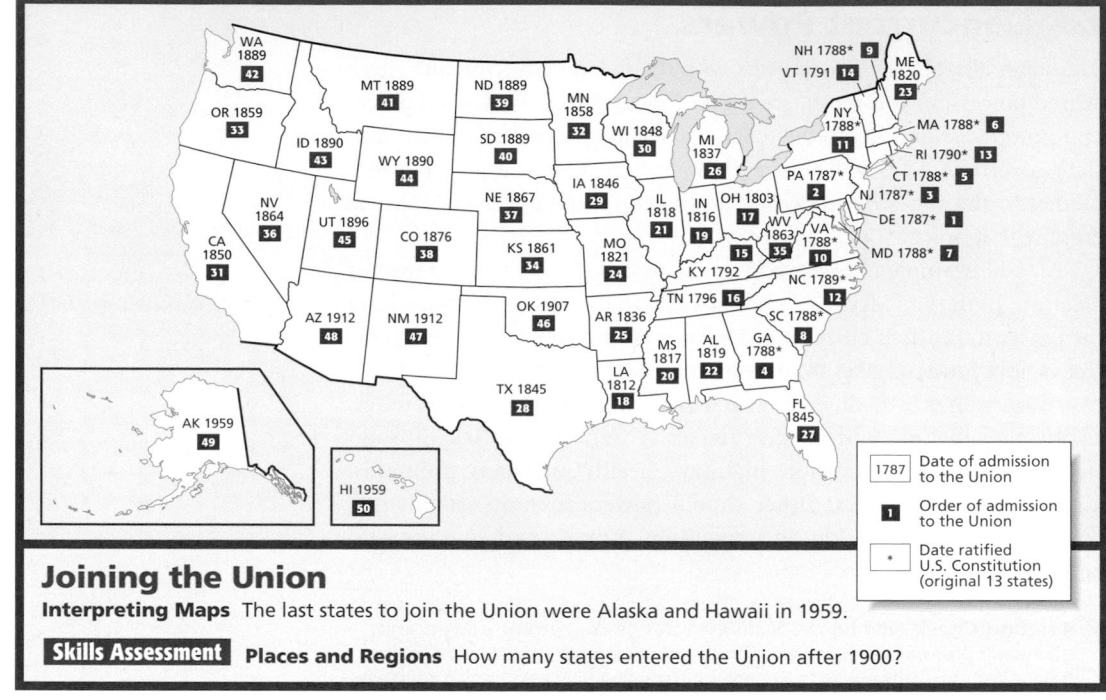

## Joining the Union

**Interpreting Maps** The last states to join the Union were Alaska and Hawaii in 1959.

**Skills Assessment** **Places and Regions** How many states entered the Union after 1900?

 **Did You KNOW?**

In 2001 the Greater North Dakota Association proposed changing the state's name from North Dakota to Dakota. Supporters hoped the change would help improve the state's image and its economy. Changing the name would require approval by voters, the state legislature, and Congress.

## ★ State Constitutions

Each of the 50 states has its own constitution that contains the rules that direct how the state government will be organized and carry out its work. Most state constitutions contain the following:

- a preamble, or beginning, that states the basic ideas and ideals on which the state government is founded;
- a bill of rights that lists the rights and freedoms guaranteed to all citizens who live in the state;
- an outline of the organization of the state's government, with the duties of the legislative, executive, and judicial branches carefully spelled out;
- provisions for elections, including qualifications for voting that must be met by the citizens of the state, as well as rules for conducting elections;
- provisions for managing state affairs, including education, keeping law and order, building highways, regulating business, and raising money by means of taxes; and
- methods of amending, or changing, the state constitution, and a list of the amendments passed.

Amendments to state constitutions have been necessary because the powers and duties of state governments have changed since their constitutions were written. The Texas state constitution has been

# TEACH OBJECTIVE 3

**LEVELS 1 AND 2:** Discuss with students how states cooperate with each other and with the federal government. (*Students might suggest the full faith and credit clause; extradition; cooperation on projects such as bridges that border states, and so on.*) Organize the class into groups and assign each group one of the topics explained above. Tell students to create handbills explaining their topics and illustrating examples of their topics in action. **ENGLISH LANGUAGE LEARNERS , COOPERATIVE LEARNING**

**LEVEL 3:** Lead a class discussion about how the states cooperate with each other and with the federal government. Then tell students that one of the responsibilities the federal government has to the states is to protect against domestic insurrection. Ask each student to conduct research on and write a report about an incident in our country's history in which the president has called out the National Guard against the wishes of the state governor. Then have students share their findings with the class.

## CLOSE

Write the following statements on the chalkboard and discuss with students if each statement is an advantage or a disadvantage of state control over federal control. *Encourages local unity and a spirit of community responsibility and self reliance.* (*advantage*) *Results in extreme differences in standards of public service and protection of civil rights.* (*disadvantage*)

**Interpreting the Visual Record**

**Constitutional Amendments**
*An Alaskan voter speaks against a ballot measure that will amend the Alaskan constitution by adding wildlife management to a list of issues that cannot be decided by a voter initiative.* **Why might voters oppose such an amendment?**

amended almost 400 times. Amendments can be proposed in a number of ways, including a two-thirds vote of the legislature, a constitutional convention, or an election in which citizens vote to ratify a proposed amendment. Alabama's state constitution was ratified in 1901. Although it has been amended more than 650 times, it has consistently kept state taxes and government spending low. Other states have drawn up new constitutions.

✔ **Reading Check** Comparing What do all 50 states have in common?
Each state has its own constitution that outlines how the state government will be organized and carry out its work.

## ⭐ States Working Together

In joining the Union, the states agreed to work together in harmony. Article IV, Section 1, of the U.S. Constitution states that "Full faith and credit [acceptance] shall be given in each State to the public acts, records, and judicial proceedings of every other State."

The **full faith and credit clause** ensures that each state will accept the decisions of civil courts in other states. For example, if a court in California decides that one of its citizens owns a certain piece of land, the other states will accept this legal decision. Another example of the full faith and credit clause is the acceptance of the official records of other states. A marriage certificate, birth certificate, will, contract, or deed issued by any state is accepted by all other states.

States work together in other ways, as well. Fugitives cannot escape justice by fleeing to another state. For example, a person who commits a crime in Utah and flees to Arizona can be returned to Utah for trial. This method of returning fugitives is called **extradition.**

States cooperate on many projects. A bridge that crosses a river bordering two states is built and maintained by the governments of both states. States also work together to reduce water and air pollution.

✔ **Reading Check** Drawing Inferences and Conclusions Why do you think the states agree to cooperate? Students might say that officials want decisions made in the courts of one state to be honored by all other states. Students may also say that officials want to share responsibility for projects that affect neighboring states or all states combined.

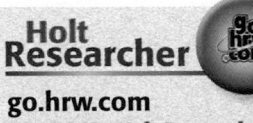

**Holt Researcher**

**go.hrw.com**
**KEYWORD: Holt Researcher**

**Freefind:** Governors

Scan the entries on state governors on the Holt Researcher. Choose one governor who went on to become president of the United States and write a brief biographical note that answers the following question: How do you think this person's experience as a governor helped prepare him for the presidency?

**Suffrage Requirements**
Article I, Section 2, of the Constitution left voting qualifications to the states, but since the Civil War, the federal courts and Congress have imposed national standards that prevent states from disenfranchising certain citizens who are otherwise qualified to vote. The registration of voters and some suffrage requirements are still determined by each state. All states require that voters be U.S. citizens, and most states require state residency for a certain period before individuals are allowed to vote. Today federal guidelines allow a residency period of no more than 30 days, but it can be less. States also differ in their registration requirements. Forty-nine states require voters to officially register with local election boards.

**CRITICAL THINKING**
Why do you think that some sort of voter registration should be required?

**ANSWER:** Students might suggest that registration prevents voter fraud.

**Visual Record Answer**

*Students might suggest that wildlife management could be an important issue to many voters.*

## REVIEW AND ASSESS

Have students complete the **Section 1 Review** on page 202. Then have students complete **Daily Quiz 8.1**. As **Alternative Assessment**, you may want to use the collage or advertisement exercises found in this section's lessons.

## RETEACH

Have students complete **Main Idea Activity for English Language Learners and Special-Needs Students 8.1**. Then have each student create flash cards using the information found in this section. Students can use their cards as study guides. **ENGLISH LANGUAGE LEARNERS**

## EXTEND

Organize the class into groups. Then instruct each group to create a debate page and to mount the components of the project on a poster board. The first component is an essay concerning background information on the topic. The second component is to write two editorials—one in favor of Puerto Rico becoming a state, the other against it becoming a state. The third component is to create a political cartoon that illustrates the ideas behind either of the two editorials. The final component consists of writing and executing a public-opinion poll in which the student composes one question and records the responses of at least five individuals. **BLOCK SCHEDULING** ,
**BLOCK SCHEDULING**

## Section 1 Review
### ANSWERS

**1. Define**
• territory, p. 199
• full faith and credit clause, p. 201
• extradition, p. 201

**2.** concurrent powers: to tax, to establish courts, to make laws, to borrow money

state powers: education, marriage and divorce laws, highway traffic laws

**3. a.** preamble, a bill of rights, an outline of the organization of the state's government, provisions for elections, provisions for managing state affairs, methods of amending the state constitutions, and a list of amendments passed

**b.** According to the full faith and credit clause, each state will accept the decisions of courts in other states as well as official records of other states. States extradite fugitives and share services, such as highway building, etc. The federal government guarantees each state a republican government and is responsible for the state's protection against invasion or domestic violence.

**4.** Students' essays will vary but should include references to problems such as obtaining marriage and birth certificates, driver's licenses, motor vehicle registration, and so on.

**Interpreting the Visual Record**

**Head Start** *Government programs like the Head Start program for preschool-age children are one way federal and state governments work together.* **Why do you think federal and state governments would collaborate on early childhood education?**

Constitution—republican form of government, protection from invasion, and help controlling domestic violence; federal and state governments—help fund services offered to citizens

## ★ The States and the Federal Government

For the federal system to work well, it is important that the 50 states and the federal government cooperate. For example, the U.S. Constitution, in Article IV, Section 4, promises that "The United States shall guarantee to every State in this Union a republican government." Every state, as it joined the Union, has been required to provide for a republican form of government in its state constitution.

The Constitution also states that the federal government must help any state put down "domestic violence" within its borders. An example of domestic violence might be rioting in a town. The governor may call on the National Guard of the state if local police cannot control the riot. In extreme cases, the governor may ask the federal government for assistance.

The federal and state governments share the costs of furnishing a number of services to the American people. Federal and state governments work together to build highways, assist the unemployed, help people with low incomes, and conserve natural resources. Together the federal and state governments provide low-cost lunches for schoolchildren and offer job training to people with disabilities.

✔ **Reading Check Summarizing** What does the Constitution promise to the states, and in what additional ways do state and federal governments cooperate with each other?

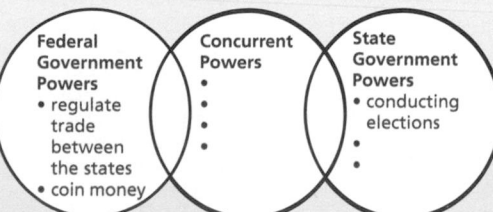

## SECTION 1 Review

go.hrw.com **Homework Practice Online**
keyword: SZ3 HP8

**1. Define** and explain:
• territory
• full faith and credit clause
• extradition

**2. Comparing and Contrasting** Copy the graphic organizer below. Use it to show some of the differences and similiarities between state and federal powers.

Federal Government Powers
• regulate trade between the states
• coin money

Concurrent Powers
•
•
•

State Government Powers
• conducting elections
•
•

**3. Finding the Main Idea**
a. Describe the different parts of state constitutions.
b. What are some of the ways that state governments work together and work with the federal government?

**4. Writing and Critical Thinking**
**Making Generalizations and Predictions** Imagine that the Constitution has no full faith and credit clause and that your family intends to move to another state. In a three-paragraph essay, explain how the lack of this clause will affect your family in your new state of residence.

**Consider:**
• the purpose of the full faith and credit clause
• how states cooperate with each other under the clause

# SECTION 2

## OBJECTIVES

*After completing Section 2, students should be able to*

1 **Analyze why the populations in state election districts must be as equal as possible.**

2 **Identify the qualifications and explain the terms of office for state legislators.**

3 **Describe how presiding officers are chosen and analyze how the work of state legislatures is carried out in most states.**

### 🔊 LET'S GET STARTED!

As students enter the classroom, show them a picture of your state's capital and ask them if they can identify the photo. Then ask students if they have been to their state capital and if so, ask students what they remember most about their visit. *(Students' responses will vary.)* If someone actually sat in during a legislative session, ask him or her to explain to the class what he or she saw. Tell students that in Section 2 they will learn about their state legislature, its composition, and how the legislature passes laws to protect citizens of the state.

---

## SECTION 2

# State Legislatures

### Read to Discover

1. Why must the populations in state election districts be as equal as possible?
2. What are the qualifications and terms of office for state legislators?
3. How are presiding officers chosen, and how is the work of state legislatures carried out in most states?

### WHY CIVICS MATTERS

State legislatures have the responsibility of making state laws. Use **CNNfyi.com** or other **current events** sources to show how your state legislatures works and what kinds of laws it is passing. Record your findings in your journal.

### Define

- unicameral
- item veto
- initiative
- proposition
- referendum
- recall

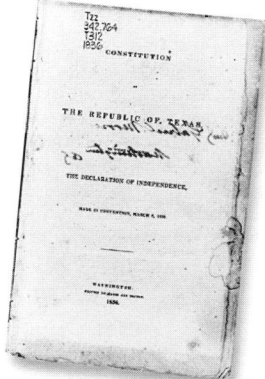

## SECTION 2 RESOURCES

### REPRODUCIBLE

▶ Guided Reading Strategies 8.2

▶ Graphic Organizer Activity: Your State Government

### TECHNOLOGY

▶ One-Stop Planner, Lesson 8.2

▶ Transparency 8: State Government

▶ Homework Practice Online

### REINFORCEMENT, REVIEW, AND ASSESSMENT

▶ Section 2 Review, p. 208

▶ Daily Quiz 8.2

▶ Main Idea Activity 8.2

▶ English Audio Summary 8.2

▶ Spanish Audio Summary 8.2

## *Reading Focus*

Each state has a lawmaking body elected by the people of the state. In 27 states this lawmaking body is called the legislature. The term *general assembly* is used in 19 states. In North Dakota and Oregon, the lawmaking body is the legislative assembly. In Massachusetts and New Hampshire, it is known as the general court. In this chapter we will use the general term *state legislature*.

## ★ Organization

All but one of the states have a bicameral legislature. The larger of the two houses is usually called the House of Representatives. The smaller house is known as the Senate. Only Nebraska has a **unicameral,** or one-house, legislature called the Senate.

State legislatures vary greatly in size. Alaska has the smallest legislature, with 40 representatives and 20 senators. New Hampshire's legislature is the largest in the United States. It has 400 representatives and 24 senators.

The people of the state elect the members of each state legislature. Each member represents the people who live in a particular district of that state. The state legislature divides the state into districts.

Originally, the upper house (Senate) of the state legislature usually had one senator from each county or from each election district.

*The New Hampshire state seal*

**LEVEL 1:** Discuss with students why legislative districts need to be as equal in population as possible. *(District apportionment should be as equal as possible to ensure that each citizen's vote carries the same weight.)* Then tell students that after the census is taken and the population is determined, it is up to the state legislature to add, drop, or redraw districts. Ask students to list the problems that might occur as the state legislature redraws the districts.

**ENGLISH LANGUAGE LEARNERS**

**LEVEL 3:** Lead a class discussion about why the populations in state election districts must be as equal as possible and about the significance of the principle of "one person, one vote." *(See the Level 1 lesson for significance.)* Then have students research the population sizes of each of the state congressional districts in their state. Ask each student to create a map of his or her state, that defines the congressional districts and their population sizes. Ask volunteers to present their maps to the class.

## The Democratic Process

**Nebraska's Unicameral Legislature** After 68 years of using a bicameral legislature, in 1934 Nebraska legistators voted to get rid of half of their state legislature. They instituted a unicameral legislature, which consists of one house. Those who argued for a unicameral legislature said that one legislative house would be more efficient and less costly, while those who argued against a unicameral legislature said there would be a greater potential for abuse of power.

**CRITICAL THINKING**

Which argument do you most agree with and why?

**ANSWER:** Students' answers will vary but must be supported with sound reasoning.

**CASE STUDY ANSWER**
The states were ordered to redraw their districts so that every district had approximately equal population.

## SUPREME COURT CASE STUDY

### *Reynolds* v. *Sims*

**Significance:** This ruling upheld the principle of "one person, one vote." It firmly established that representation in state legislatures must be based mainly on population so that each citizen's vote has as equal a value as possible. The ruling led to widespread changes in state voting districts throughout the country.

**Background:** Residents of Jefferson County, Alabama, filed a complaint challenging the apportionment of the Alabama state legislature. This apportionment was based on the 1900 federal census, making it extremely out of date with changes in state population. The residents argued that Alabama's unequal apportionment system violated the Equal Protection Clause of the Fourteenth Amendment.

**Decision:** This case was argued on November 13, 1963, and decided on June 15, 1964, by a vote of 8 to 1. Chief Justice Earl Warren spoke for the majority, stating that "the achievement of fair and effective representation for all citizens is concededly the basic aim of legislative apportionment." The Court ruled that the state of Alabama had established a system that did not fairly represent a large number of its citizens.

**How did the Court's ruling affect the political processes of the United States?**

However, the counties or districts were often unequal in population. Under this system sparsely populated areas of the state often had the same number of senators as heavily populated areas.

In the 1964 case of *Reynolds* v. *Sims,* the U.S. Supreme Court ruled that all state election districts must be equal in population—or as equal as possible. This is the famous ruling that upheld the principle of "one person, one vote." The states are now required to establish election districts that are almost equal in population.

✔ **Reading Check Contrasting** What are some of the differences among the ways that state legislatures are organized? There are both bicameral and unicameral legislatures. Legislatures also vary significantly in size.

## Qualifications, Terms, and Compensation

In many states members of a state legislature must be U.S. citizens. In almost all states senators and representatives must live in the district that they represent. In most states a state senator must be at least 25 years of age. Most states require state representatives to be at least 21 years old. Some states, however, have lowered the age requirement to 18 for senators and representatives.

In most states senators are elected for four years and representatives for two years. However, in a few states both senators and representatives are elected for four-year terms. In some states senators and representatives both serve two years. The senators who serve in Nebraska's one-house legislature are elected for four-year terms.

# TEACH OBJECTIVE 2

**LEVEL 1:** Assign each student a state and provide him or her with information about the makeup of that state's legislature and the term of office for its representatives. You might also tell students when sessions meet and what qualifications are necessary for members of the states' legislatures. Then ask each student to compose a fact sheet about his or her information and share it with the rest of the class.
**ENGLISH LANGUAGE LEARNERS**

**ALL LEVELS** Copy the following graphic organizer onto the chalkboard, omitting the italicized answers. Then have each student complete the help-wanted ad to list the qualifications and terms of office for a state legislator.
**ENGLISH LANGUAGE LEARNERS**

---

### HELP WANTED
# LEGISLATOR

**Job qualifications include:** *[qualifications will vary according to state]*

**Terms of Office:** *[terms will vary according to state]*

---

In 1995 the Supreme Court ruled that term limits for federal lawmakers were unconstitutional. At that time 23 states had already adopted such term limits for state legislators. Although the Court's ruling does not apply to state legislators, these term limits are also being challenged in some states.

The salaries and benefits received by state legislators vary widely from state to state. Even so, the salaries of nearly all state legislators are surprisingly low, considering the important work that they do. In Rhode Island, for example, state legislators each receive only $10,000 a year. New York's legislators are among the highest paid in the country, each receiving an annual salary of $79,500, plus $138 a day for expenses.

✔ **Reading Check Summarizing** What did the Supreme Court rule about term limits in 1995, and how did the ruling affect the terms of state legislators? The Supreme Court ruled that term limits for federal legislators were unconstitutional, but the ruling does not apply to state legislators.

## ★ State Legislatures at Work

Most state legislatures meet in regular sessions every year. Other state legislatures meet once every two years. The California legislature has a two-year session that meets for that entire period. In North Carolina the legislature holds a regular length session in odd-numbered years and a shorter session in even-numbered years. In other states a session can last from 30 days to more than six months.

## State Government

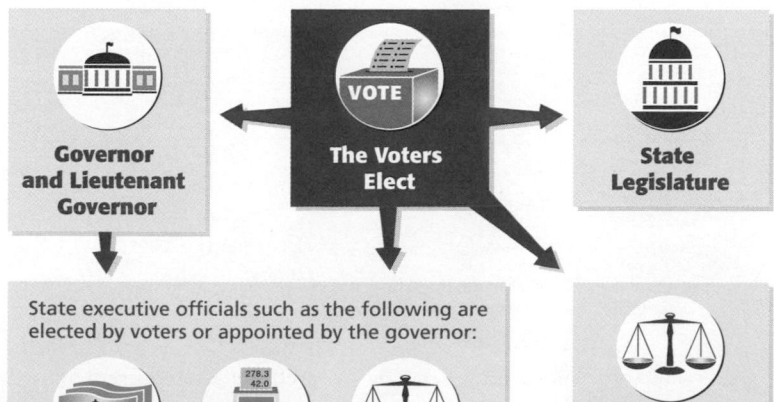

The Voters Elect

Governor and Lieutenant Governor

State Legislature

State executive officials such as the following are elected by voters or appointed by the governor:

Treasurer

Auditor

Attorney General

State Courts*
*In some states some judges may be appointed.

**Interpreting Charts** *State governments divide power among executive, judicial, and legislative branches.* **What state positions are always elected offices?**

---

HOMEWORK Instruct students to create an opinion poll. Students should ask the interviewee whether he or she supports, or opposes, term limitations and why. Tell students that they must poll 10 people, 5 of whom must be adults.

## TEACH OBJECTIVE 3
## TEACHER TO TEACHER

Heather Verdi of Connecticut recommends the following activity:

**LEVELS 1 AND 2:** Organize the students into small committees. Tell each committee that it may brainstorm to create a new law that it would like to initiate. *(Students' laws could involve a school initiative such as longer school lunches or increased safety in schools.)* Then each committee will write a brief informative proposal apprising the legislature (the class) about its proposed rule. The legislature will then vote on whether to approve the proposed rule. **ENGLISH LANGUAGE LEARNERS , COOPERATIVE LEARNING**

### Constitutional Heritage

**1780 Massachusetts Constitution** Primarily written by John Adams, the Massachusetts Constitution did not rely on legislative supremacy but instead created three branches with a system of checks and balances to prevent possible abuse or misuse of power. The governor was elected by the people and had the power to veto laws made by the legislature, which could then be overridden by a two-thirds vote of the legislature. The governor could also appoint officials to the executive and judicial branches. The Massachusetts Constitution also separated the powers among different classes of people. For example, only people who owned a large amount of property could elect the governor, people who had a little less property could elect members to the upper house, and people who had the minimum amount of property necessary to vote could elect members of the lower house.

#### CRITICAL THINKING

Why do you think property ownership was necessary to vote?

**ANSWER:** Students might suggest that property ownership was a sign of status in the process.

#### Visual Record Answer

*Students might suggest that it speeds up the process.*

At the beginning of the session, the presiding officer and other leaders are chosen. Committees are appointed. The organization and offices of most state legislatures are similar to those of the U.S. Congress.

In most states the lieutenant governor presides over the Senate. In other states the Senate chooses its own presiding officer. Members of the lower house in all states choose their own presiding officer, usually called the Speaker.

As in the U.S. Congress, most of the work of the state legislatures is done in committees that specialize in certain areas, such as agriculture or budget. In the upper house, committee members are chosen by the presiding officer or by all the upper house members. In the lower house the Speaker usually has the responsibility of appointing committee members. Seniority often plays a key role in determining committee membership and leadership.

✔ **Reading Check Contrasting** How do the lengths of state sessions and the salary amounts of state legislators differ from state to state? Some sessions occur annually, and others every two years. Sessions can last for an entire two-year period, 30 days, or more than six months. Salaries vary widely.

### Passing State Laws

The lawmaking process in state legislatures is similar to the procedure followed in Congress. (See Chapter 5.) The following summarizes the way in which a bill becomes a state law.

**A Bill Is Introduced.** A member of either house may introduce a bill. It is first handed to the clerk and given a number. The presiding officer reads the title of the bill and sends it to the appropriate committee.

**Interpreting the Visual Record**

State legislatures *State legislators, such as these New York representatives, must read through bills carefully before deciding to vote for or against them.* **How do you think the electronic voting device on the desk in front of the representatives might assist the legislative process?**

**LEVELS 2 AND 3:** Organize the class into two groups of slightly unequal size. Designate one group as Republican members of your lower state legislature and the other group as Democratic members of your lower state legislature. Distribute blue tags for the Democrats to wear and red tags for the Republicans to wear. Tell students that they must select the presiding officer for the lower house. Designate one student from each group as the leader of his or her party. Then hold an election. *(The elected presiding officer should come from the group with the most members.)* Then list 5 to 10 of your state's standing committees on the chalkboard and instruct your presiding officer to make the committee assignments. Secretly tell the officers to ensure that the committee chairperson, as well as the majority of committee members should come from the major-

ity party. After the assignments are made, instruct students to group themselves according to the committee assignments. Ask the minority party members in each committee how they feel about their party's chances of passing partisan legislation. Then ask each group to write a congressional summary about how the work of the state legislature is to be carried out.
**COOPERATIVE LEARNING**

## CLOSE

Draw two columns on the chalkboard, and have students compare your state's legislature to the U.S. Congress. Ask students to write an item on the board for comparison. *(Students might compare qualifications, terms of office, length of sessions, and so on.)*

**The Bill Is Sent to Committee.** The committee listens to various witnesses for and against the bill and then questions them to obtain necessary information. The members may discuss the bill for many hours. The committee may vote to pass the bill, to change it, or to kill it.

**The Bill Reaches the Floor.** If the committee approves the bill, it is returned to a full meeting of the house. The bill is read aloud, line by line. The members of the house discuss each part of the bill. Amendments may be offered and if passed, they become part of the bill. The members then vote on the bill. Bills that are passed are signed by the presiding officer and sent to the second house.

**The Bill Is Sent to the Second House.** When the bill is introduced in the second house of the state legislature, it is sent to a committee. If the bill survives this committee, it is sent back to the floor of the second house. Here it is debated, can be amended again, and then is put to a vote.

Bills that pass one house and fail in the second house are dead. If both houses pass a bill in the same form, it is then sent to the governor to be signed. Frequently, however, both houses pass the bill, but in different forms. In this case, it is sent to a joint-conference committee to resolve the differences.

**The Bill Is Sent to a Joint-Conference Committee.** Joint-conference committees are made up of members selected from both houses. Committee members must try to reach a compromise that will be acceptable to both houses. The compromise bill of the joint-conference committee is then voted on by the two houses. Each house usually accepts this final version of the bill.

**The Bill Is Sent to the Governor.** The final step in making a state law is to send the bill to the governor. If the governor signs the bill, it becomes a law. In all states, the governor may veto a bill he or she does not support. (North Carolina did not give this power to its governor until 1997.) In most states the governor also has the power to veto only one part, or item, of an appropriation bill. This power is called an **item veto.** The legislature can pass a bill over the governor's veto by a two-thirds vote in each house.

✔ **Reading Check** Sequencing List in order the steps required for a bill to become a law. A bill is introduced and sent to committee. If the committee approves the bill, it is returned to the house for a vote. If the bill passes, it is sent to the second house. If an amended bill is passed, the bill is sent to a joint-conference committee. An approved bill is sent to the governor to be signed.

**Interpreting the Visual Record**

**Discussing Issues** *North Carolina governor Mike Easley (right), speaks with a North Carolina state representative (center) about a bill proposal.* **Why is communication between the governor and members of the state legislature important?**

### ★ Constitutional Heritage

**Direct Democracy at Work** During the late 1800s a group of reformers known as the progressives, began working to improve American society. Concerned about political corruption, they worked to pass reform measures that gave voters a chance to participate directly in state and local governments. These reform measures are known as the recall, initiative, and referendum. These measures were first practiced at the state level in Oregon during the early 1900s and are used today by many states. Currently about one fifth of the states allow citizen initiatives; over one third of the states provide for the referendum; and removal by recall occurs primarily in the western states.

**ACTIVITY:** Have students conduct research on any reform measures that his or her state practices and write a position paper concerning a specific use of this practice.

### Visual Record Answer

*Students might suggest that it ensures that all of the key players are involved in making the best decisions for their state.*

## REVIEW AND ASSESS

Have students complete the **Section 2 Review** on page 208. Then have students complete **Daily Quiz 8.2.** As **Alternative Assessment**, you may want to use the map or fact sheet activities in this section's lessons.

## RETEACH

Have students complete **Main Idea Activity for English Language Learners and Special-Needs Students 8.2.** Then ask students to create a web design covering the information they learned in this section. Ask volunteers to share their designs with the class. **ENGLISH LANGUAGE LEARNERS**

## EXTEND

Ask students to conduct research at the library to obtain information about the following: the initiative, proposition, referendum, and recall. Have students write an encyclopedia entry for each term, including a real-life example of each. Ask volunteers to present their entries to the class. **BLOCK SCHEDULING**

## Section 2 Review
### ANSWERS

**1. Define**
- unicameral, p. 203
- item veto, p. 207
- initiative, p. 208
- proposition, p. 208
- referendum, p. 208
- recall, p. 208

**2.** The committee can pass the bill as is, change the bill, or kill it; bill reaches the floor for debate; bill is voted on and passed without amendments; bill is voted on and passed; bill dies.

**3. a.** U.S. citizen, resident of the state and district, certain minimum age; four year for senators in most states, two years for representatives in most states

**b.** In most states the lieutenant governor presides over the Senate. In other states, senators choose presiding officer. Members of lower houses in all states choose officers. Most of the work is done in specialized committees.

**4.** Students' speeches will vary but should include a reference to Supreme Court decisions and the effect of unequal populations in state election districts.

*California's Proposition 13, which reduced state taxes, was one of the most influential initiatives ever passed.*

### ★ Citizen Action

Some state constitutions allow the people to take a direct part in making laws. Citizens are able to initiate, or start, new legislation through a process called the **initiative.**

To begin an initiative, citizens must first draw up a petition describing the proposal. A required number of voters—the number varies from state to state—must then sign the petition. If this occurs, then the **proposition,** or proposed law, appears on the ballot at the next general election. If enough people vote for the bill, it becomes law. Some states have indirect initiatives. In these states initiatives are sent to the state legislatures for approval.

In many states certain bills passed by the legislature must be approved by the voters before the bills can become laws. This method of referring potential laws directly to the people for approval is called a **referendum.**

Some states also provide voters with the means to remove elected officials from office. This process, known as a **recall,** begins when a required number of voters signs a petition. A special election on the petition is then held. If a majority of voters favors the recall, the official is removed.

✔ **Reading Check** Summarizing What is one way that citizens are able to take a direct part in making laws? Through a process called the initiative, citizens can draw up a petition describing a proposed law. If signed by enough voters, the proposition will appear on the ballot. If it receives enough votes, it becomes law.

---

## SECTION 2 Review

**go.hrw.com Homework Practice Online**
keyword: SZ3 HP8

**1. Define** and explain:
- unicameral
- item veto
- initiative
- proposition
- referendum
- recall

**2. Sequencing** Copy the flowchart below. Use it to show how a bill becomes a law in state legislatures.

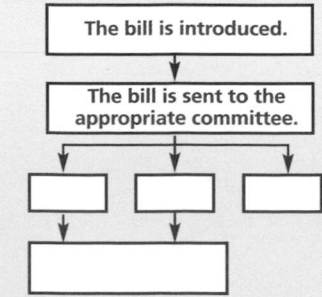

The bill is introduced.

The bill is sent to the appropriate committee.

**3. Finding the Main Idea**
a. What qualifications must be met to serve as a state legislator, and how long can members of state legislatures hold office?
b. When do state legislatures select their presiding officers, and how do most legislatures complete their work?

**4. Writing and Critical Thinking**
**Supporting a Point of View** Write a short speech that supports creating electoral districts that are all equal in population.

**Consider:**
- what would happen if areas of high and low population had the same number of senators
- U.S. Supreme Court decisions on the matter

## TEACH

**LEVEL 1:** Ask each student to create a one-sheet directory containing the names, titles, and addresses of his or her local, state, and national representatives. Underneath the title of each office, have students record the proper term of address for each official.
**ENGLISH LANGUAGE LEARNERS**

**LEVEL 3:** Have students write a letter to a state official concerning a topic that they feel strongly about. Then have students exchange their letters with a classmate to peer edit the letter before sending it. **COOPERATIVE LEARNING**

# Civics Skills
## WORKSHOP

## Writing to Your Legislator

One of the best ways to let your legislator know what you are thinking is to write a letter. You can find the names of your federal, state, and local legislators in the newspaper or by going online to the official federal, state, county, or city Web site. There are some basic rules to follow to make yours the kind of letter that receives an answer.

## How to Write Your Legislator

1. **Include your return address.** Make sure that your return address is on the letter. This will allow your legislator to respond to you.

2. **Use the proper term of address.** Always address a legislator as "The Honorable (*name*)." This applies to both the inside address and the address on the envelope.

3. **Use the correct opening and closing.** In the salutation, or greeting, use the person's correct title. For members of the U.S. House of Representatives, "Dear Representative (*last name*)," "Dear Congresswoman (*last name*)," or "Dear Congressman (*last name*)" are all acceptable. For members of the Senate, "Dear Senator (*last name*)" is the usual style. Titles of state officials vary. End your letter with the proper closing, such as "Respectfully yours" or "Sincerely yours." Then add your signature.

4. **Use your writing skills.** Keep the body, or main part, of the letter as brief as possible. Clearly state your position or request

in the first paragraph. Point out the relevant facts that will help your legislator understand your concerns.

5. **Be considerate of your reader.** Put yourself in the legislator's place. Be polite—even if you are angry. Also, your letter will receive more attention if it is neatly typed or handwritten.

## Applying the Skill

Read the letter below. Then answer the following questions.

1. To whom is the letter addressed? What closing does the writer use?

2. What issue is Aaron Campbell concerned about in his letter?

3. Why might a letter be more convincing than a telephone call?

415 Sleepy Hollow
Roanoke, VA 24022
February 12, 2004

The Honorable Jane Doe
The State House
Richmond, VA 23218

Dear Representative Doe:

As you know, there is a bill currently before the legislature that would create 3,000 summer jobs for teenagers in our state. I strongly urge you to support this bill. Passage of Bill HR 1099 will give many teenagers the chance to earn money for school. It will also provide them with experience for future jobs. Finally, the state stands to benefit from all the work these teenagers will be doing in our parks, hospitals, and civic centers. I would appreciate knowing your position on this important issue.

Sincerely yours,

*Aaron Campbell*

Aaron Campbell

# SECTION 3

## OBJECTIVES

*After completing Section 3, students should be able to*

1 **Describe the qualifications, terms of office, duties, and powers of most governors.**

2 **Identify the other officials of state executive branches.**

3 **Explain the purpose of state executive agencies and officials.**

## SECTION 3 RESOURCES

### REPRODUCIBLE

▶ Guided Reading Strategies 8.3

▶ Challenge and Enrichment Worksheet 8: Researching Your State Executive Branch

### TECHNOLOGY

▶ One-Stop Planner, Lesson 8.3

▶ Transparency 9: Powers and Duties of the Governor

▶ Homework Practice Online

### REINFORCEMENT, REVIEW, AND ASSESSMENT

▶ Section 3 Review, p. 214

▶ Daily Quiz 8.3

▶ Main Idea Activity 8.3

▶ English Audio Summary 8.3

▶ Spanish Audio Summary 8.3

## 📀 LET'S GET STARTED!

As students enter the classroom, show them photographs of five individuals. *(Photographs should be of a celebrity, a sports figure, a local personality, one that they will not be able to identify, and one of the state governor.)* Ask students to identify each of the photographs. If they can identify the governor, ask them to share what they know about the governor. *(Have students guess his/her age, years in office, political party, and so on.)* Then ask students if they can name any previous governors. If they cannot identify the governor, introduce them to the governor by discussing some of the personal information suggested above. Tell students that in Section 3 they will focus on the executive branch of the state government, examining its purpose and its officials.

# SECTION 3

## The State Executive Branch

### Read to Discover

1. What are the qualifications, terms of office, duties, and powers of most governors?
2. Who are the other officials of state executive branches?
3. What is the purpose of state executive agencies and officials?

### Define

- governor
- executive orders
- lieutenant governor
- warrant
- patronage

#### WHY CIVICS MATTERS

Governors have many responsibilities to the people living in their states. Use **CNNfyi.com** or other **current events** sources to learn how the governor of your state is trying to help you and other residents. Record your findings in your journal.

## Reading Focus

A state's legislative branch makes the laws for that state. These laws are then carried out by the state's executive branch. The executive branch is headed by the **governor.** It also includes other officials and agencies who assist the governor.

### ★ Qualifications and Terms of Governors

The governor is the chief executive in each state. He or she is elected by the people of the state in a statewide election. The qualifications for governor are listed in each state constitution. In general, a candidate for governor must be a U.S. citizen and must have lived in the state for a certain number of years. Most states require a governor to be at least 30 years old. A few states, such as California and Ohio, allow persons at least 18 years of age to run for governor.

Most governors serve four-year terms. In some states they are elected for two years. About half of the states limit their governors to one or two terms in office.

The salaries of governors vary greatly from state to state. For example, the governor of New York receives $177,000 a year, the governor of North Carolina receives $118,430, and the governor of Nebraska is paid $65,000 per year. In addition, governors usually

*Most governors live in a state-owned home such as the governor's mansion in Virginia.*

# TEACH OBJECTIVE 1

**LEVEL 1:** Obtain a photograph of your state's governor and make enough copies of it to pass out to all of the students. Then instruct each of the students to write along the sides of the photograph the following: the qualifications for the office of governor, the term of office, and his or her powers and duties. **ENGLISH LANGUAGE LEARNERS**

**ALL LEVELS:** After discussing the qualifications, terms of office, and powers and duties of most governors, copy the following graphic organizer onto the chalkboard, omitting the italicized answers. Then ask students to complete the organizer by labeling the powers and duties of the governor. **ENGLISH LANGUAGE LEARNERS**

**Powers and Duties of the Governor** →
1. *Chief Legislator*
2. *Chief Executive*
3. *Political Party Leader*
4. *Other Powers*

receive an allowance for expenses. In most states governors and their families live in an official residence in the state capital.

✔ **Reading Check Comparing and Contrasting** How are the qualifications for governor similar among the U.S. states, and how are they different? similar—must be a U.S. citizen and live in the states that they govern; different—must have lived in the state for a specified number of years and meet age requirement

## ★ Powers and Duties of Governors

The main job of a governor, as chief executive of the state, is to carry out the laws. However, like the president of the United States, many governors also have legislative and judicial responsibilities.

**Chief Legislator** Only the state legislature can pass laws. Nevertheless, the governor plays an important part in proposing new laws. The governor usually appears before the state legislature at one of its early meetings. At this meeting, the governor outlines laws he or she thinks should be passed. The governor talks to leaders of the legislature, urging them to pass specific bills and oppose others. State legislators know that if they pass a bill the governor opposes, it may be vetoed.

After the legislature has passed a law, it is the responsibility of the governor to put it into force. Imagine that the legislature has passed a new tax law. It will be the duty of the governor to issue orders that will determine how the taxes should be collected. The orders that set up methods of enforcing laws are called **executive orders.** Almost every new law requires an executive order.

**Chief Executive** In most states one of the governor's most important responsibilities is to draw up a budget for the state. A budget director or a budget bureau usually assists the governor in this task. For example, Virginia has a budget director who must help create budgets every two years. Long hours are spent by budget officials in each state determining how much money the state will need during the next one- or two-year period. The governor and budget director or budget bureau must also decide what taxes will be required to meet this need. The completed budget is sent to the legislature for approval.

The governor may also appoint a number of state officials with the approval of the state senate. The governor works with these officials to carry out state laws.

**Political Party Leader** The governor is the head of his or her political party in the state. State senators and representatives within the

## BIOGRAPHY

### *Ruth Ann Minner*
#### (1935– )

Ruth Ann Minner became Delaware's first female governor in 2000. Born and raised on a small farm, she quit high school to help support her family. After returning to school at the age of 32, Minner went on to a career in politics. She got her start as the governor's receptionist and moved on to positions as a senator in the state legislator and lieutenant governor. Minner's key achievements include the Delaware Land and Water Conservation Act and her continuing commitment to adult education and child welfare. In her inaugural address she declared, "I treasure families. . . . Just as I sacrificed for my family, we must all be willing to put the children of this state first." In her career Governor Minner has been honored in Delaware as Mother of the Year and Woman of the Year. **How might issues such as adult education and child welfare be related?**

## ★ Civics Sidelight

**Stepping-Stone to the Presidency** The state legislature is a common breeding ground for gubernatorial hopefuls. There, governors-to-be can learn the ins and outs of state government. In the same way, the position of governor can be a stepping-stone to the presidency. As of 2001, ten presidents had moved directly from a governorship to the White House, the most recent being George W. Bush from Texas. In addition, twelve presidents began their political careers as state legislators.

**CRITICAL THINKING**

What president since 1900 did not have any state or national political experience prior to being elected, and why do you think that person was elected president?

**ANSWER:** Dwight D. Eisenhower; Students might suggest that Eisenhower proved his leadership abilities as the commander of the Allied forces during the D-Day invasion in World War II.

**BIOGRAPHY ANSWER**
Students might suggest that educated parents have more opportunities to provide for the welfare of their children.

## Powers and Duties of the Governor

### The Governor carries out state laws and also...

 Approves or vetoes all bills passed by legislature

 Controls state police and militia

 Proposes laws and programs to the legislature

 Can pardon criminals and grant reprieves

 Appoints and removes certain state officials

 Supervises state executive branch

 Acts as a political party leader

**Interpreting Charts**
*Governors have powers similar to those of the president.* **Which of the governor's powers relate to law enforcement?**

governor's party pay close attention to his or her opinions and policies. They know the governor can help them during their campaigns.

**Other Powers** A governor has many other powers. The heads of the state police force and state militia report to the governor. In times of emergency, such as during floods or hurricanes, the governor may call out the National Guard to help keep order and assist with relief efforts. The governor also has the judicial power to pardon certain prisoners.

✔ **Reading Check** Summarizing What are three roles of governors, and what responsibilities does each role entail? chief legislator—proposes new laws, encourages legislators to support or oppose pieces of legislation, and vetoes legislation; chief executive—draws up state budget and appoints state officials; political party leader—leads party and helps party members during their election campaigns

### ★ Other State Executive Officials

Each state also has a number of other officials to help run the state government and enforce state laws. The following officials are the most important members of each state's executive branch. In most states these officials are elected by the voters. In some states, however, they are appointed by the governor. In these states officials are a part of the governor's cabinet. In other states they are not considered members of the cabinet unless they are appointed by the governor.

**ALL LEVELS:** Lead a class discussion about the purposes and functions of the state executive branch. Then tell students that a number of state agencies, sometimes referred to as boards, commissions, or departments, help the governor perform his/her duties. *(Examples of state agencies may be the state board of health, the department of human services, or the civil service commission.)* Ask each student to refer to his or her textbook to create a chart of state agencies and officials and list their primary functions. **ENGLISH LANGUAGE LEARNERS**

**LEVELS 1 AND 2:** Discuss with students the purpose and function of state executive agencies and officials. Ask students the following question: *Other than appointed heads of state executive agencies, how do most state employees get their positions? (Students might suggest that they apply through a government office.)* Then ask students to explain how the rest of the jobs are filled. *(Students might suggest that party leaders recommend some candidates.)* Invite students to imagine that they are the head of one of the state executive branches or agencies. Have each student create a comprehensive job description to fill the position of an assistant.

## CLOSE

Bring newspapers to class. Then have students locate a newspaper article concerning either the governor or a state executive agency. Have students summarize the article in a current events discussion.

---

**Lieutenant Governor** All but seven of the states have a **lieutenant governor.** The lieutenant governor becomes head of the state executive branch if the governor dies, resigns, or is removed from office. In some states it is possible for the lieutenant governor and the governor to belong to different political parties. The lieutenant governor often serves as presiding officer of the state senate.

**Secretary of State** The secretary of state keeps state records and carries out election laws. This official is sometimes called the secretary of the commonwealth. Only Alaska, Hawaii, and Utah do not have this official. In states without a lieutenant governor, the secretary of state may take over as governor if the office of governor becomes vacant.

**Attorney General** The attorney general is in charge of the state's legal business, or matters concerning the law. If a state official wants advice about the meaning of a law, the attorney general provides it. The attorney general or an assistant represents the state in court when the state is involved in a lawsuit. The attorney general may also assist local officials in the prosecution of criminals.

**State Treasurer** In some states the state treasurer is in charge of handling all state funds. Sometimes this official supervises the collection of taxes and pays the state's bills as well.

**State Auditor** The state auditor ensures that no public funds from the state treasury are used unless the payment is authorized by law. Usually the state treasurer cannot pay any bills without a written order that is signed by the state auditor. This order to pay out money is called a **warrant.** The auditor also regularly examines the state's financial records to make sure that they are correct. The auditor is sometimes called the comptroller.

**Superintendent of Public Instruction** The superintendent of public instruction carries out the policies of the state board of education. (The state board of education is known by other titles in some states.) The state board makes regulations, under state law, that govern the various local school districts. The superintendent is in charge of the distribution of state funds to local school systems according to state and federal laws. In some states this official is called the superintendent of public schools or the state commissioner of education.

✔ **Reading Check** Supporting a Point of View Which official do you think has the most important responsibilities and why? Answers will vary, but students should indicate a clear understanding of the selected official's duties.

**Interpreting the Visual Record**

**Succession** *Former lieutenant governor of Texas Rick Perry became his state's governor after George W. Bush was elected to the presidency.* **What other state official may succeed a departing governor in some states?**

---

### ★ Culture

**The First African American Governor** In 1990 Lawrence Douglas Wilder of Virginia became the first African American to be elected governor of a state. A Korean War veteran and an attorney, Wilder later became the first African American to be elected to the Virginia Senate in the 1900s. He was also the first to be elected to a statewide office, that of lieutenant governor. Four years later Wilder was elected governor, and more recently he was a candidate for the Democratic nomination for president.

**CRITICAL THINKING**

How does Wilder's election as governor illustrate the changes that have occurred in Virginia and in the country?

**ANSWER:** Students might refer to various past restrictions that prevented minorities from not only holding office but also from voting.

**Visual Record Answer**

*Students might suggest the secretary of state.*

---

**CHART ANSWER**
*(for page 212)* controls state police and militia; pardons criminals and grants reprieves

## REVIEW AND ASSESS

Have students complete the **Section 3 Review** on page 214. Then have them complete **Daily Quiz 8.3**. As **Alternative Assessment**, you may want to use the Spotlight essay or state executive branch graphic organizer activities in this section's lessons.

## RETEACH

Have students complete **Main Idea Activity for English Language Learners and Special-Needs Students 8.3**. Then organize the class into small groups and instruct groups to produce a brochure illustrating the state's executive branch. Each group should share its brochure with the class.

**ENGLISH LANGUAGE LEARNERS , COOPERATIVE LEARNING**

## EXTEND

Tell students that some state governments are structured to disperse power, resulting in many elected state officials, a weak governor, and a part-time legislature. Others are structured to concentrate power, resulting in few elected officials, a strong governor, and a full-time professional legislature. Ask each student to write an essay analyzing your state's structure and comparing it to a state with the opposing structure. *(Indiana and Texas are examples of dispersed power, while California and Wisconsin are examples of concentrated power.)*

**BLOCK SCHEDULING**

---

## Section 3 Review
### ANSWERS

**1. Define**
- governor, p. 210
- executive orders, p. 211
- lieutenant governor, p. 213
- warrant, p. 213
- patronage, p. 214

**2.** lieutenant governor: next in line if governor dies, resigns, or is removed; often serves as presiding officer of the state senate

secretary of state: keeps state records and carries out election laws

attorney general: in charge of state's legal business

state treasurer: in charge of handling all state funds

state auditor: ensures that no public funds from the state treasury are used unless payment is authorized by law and regularly examines the state's financial records

superintendent of public instruction: carries out the policies of the state board of education

**3. a.** U.S. citizen, resident of the state for a certain number of years, certain minimum age; four-year term for most, two-year term for some, one or two term limits for about half the states; carries out the laws, proposes and vetoes laws, prepares the state budget, heads own political party, can call out the National Guard and state police force, and can grant pardons and reprieves

**b.** lieutenant governor, secretary of state, attorney general, state treasurer, state auditor, and superintendent of public instruction

**4.** Students' paragraphs will vary.

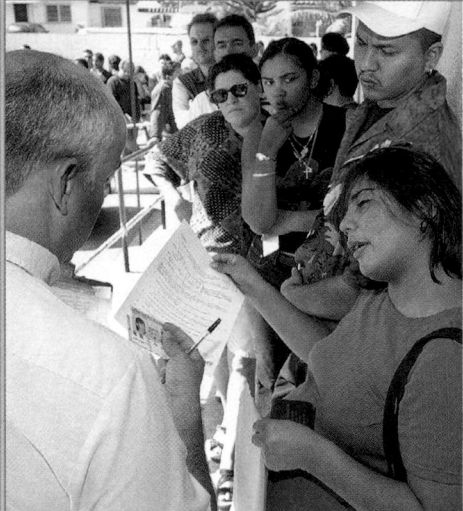

*Most states have a department of motor vehicles that handles vehicle titles and driver's licenses.*

## ★ State Executive Agencies

A number of state agencies help the governor carry out the laws. Most state agencies are headed by officials appointed by and responsible to the governor. In some states agency heads are appointed by and responsible to the state legislature.

Most states have the following executive departments: agriculture, justice, labor, public safety (which includes the state police), public works, and transportation. Each state agency has a specific area of responsibility. The state board of health enforces health laws and recommends measures to improve the health of state citizens. The department of human services supervises programs that help people who are disabled, poor, or unemployed. Other state agencies administer state laws on agriculture, conservation, and highways or regulate banks and public utilities.

The 50 state governments employ more than 4.7 million people. Most state-government jobs are open to any qualified citizen who passes a state examination. However, some state jobs are filled through **patronage.** That is, the jobs are given to people recommended by political-party leaders. Such jobs often go to people who provided valuable help during the election campaign.

✔ **Reading Check** Summarizing Describe how state agencies assist governors in carrying out state laws. by addressing a specific area of responsibility, enforcing laws, recommending measures to improve services, and providing services to state residents

---

## SECTION 3 Review

**go.hrw.com** **Homework Practice Online** keyword: SZ3 HP8

**1. Define** and explain:
- governor
- executive orders
- lieutenant governor
- warrant
- patronage

**2. Categorizing** Copy the chart below. Use it to identify the role of each state official.

### STATE EXECUTIVE OFFICIALS

| Position | Duties |
| --- | --- |
| Lieutenant Governor | |
| Secretary of State | |
| Attorney General | |
| State Treasurer | |
| State Auditor | |
| Superintendent of Public Instruction | |

**3. Finding the Main Idea**
a. Identify the qualifications, term limitations, and functions of state governors.
b. What six state officials assist the governor in performing the duties of the executive branch?

**4. Writing and Critical Thinking**
Analyzing Information Imagine that you are a political consultant. Write a two-paragraph presentation that explains the purpose of state executive agencies. Include your thoughts on why agencies at both the state and federal levels handle many of the same sorts of issues.

**Consider:**
- the main job of the governor
- the specific responsibilities of each agency

# SECTION 4

## OBJECTIVES

*After completing Section 4, students should be able to*

1 Describe the kinds of cases that state courts handle.

2 Explain the areas of responsibility of each of the four types of state courts.

3 Evaluate how overcrowding causes problems for the courts.

## 📶 LET'S GET STARTED!

As students enter the classroom, read to the class a local newspaper article concerning either a trial, a lawsuit, or a particular crime that was committed. Ask the students if the trial is being held in a federal court or in a state court and why it is being held in that particular court. Also, ask students if the case is an example of a criminal case or a civil case. *(Students' responses will depend on the article read.)* Discuss their responses. Tell students that in Section 4 they will learn more about state courts and their jurisdiction.

## SECTION 4

# State Courts

### Read to Discover

1. What kinds of cases do state courts handle?
2. What are the areas of responsibility of each of the four types of state courts?
3. How does overcrowding cause problems for the courts?

### Define

- penal code
- criminal cases
- civil cases
- complaint
- plaintiff
- justice of the peace
- municipal courts
- small claims courts
- general trial courts

#### WHY CIVICS MATTERS

The state court system is instrumental in interpreting state laws and bringing people who break them to justice. Use **CNNfyi.com** or other **current events** sources to investigate a case recently tried in state court. Identify how the court brought lawbreakers to justice. Record your findings in your journal.

## SECTION 4 RESOURCES

### REPRODUCIBLE

▶ Guided Reading Strategies 8.4

▶ Creative Teaching Strategy: Learning Stations

### TECHNOLOGY

▶ One-Stop Planner, Lesson 8.4

▶ Homework Practice Online

▶ HRW Go site

### REINFORCEMENT, REVIEW, AND ASSESSMENT

▶ Section 4 Review, p. 219

▶ Daily Quiz 8.4

▶ Main Idea Activity 8.4

▶ English Audio Summary 8.4

▶ Spanish Audio Summary 8.4

## *Reading Focus*

Each state government has the authority to maintain peace and order within its boundaries and to establish a **penal code.** A penal code is a set of criminal laws. This power is shared by all three branches of state government. The legislature passes laws to provide for the welfare and safety of the state's residents. The executive branch ensures that these laws are enforced. The judicial branch—the state court system—is responsible for interpreting state laws and for punishing those who break them.

*Penal codes like this one from the state of Texas list punishments for various crimes.*

### ★ The Work of the State Courts

Federal and state courts handle both criminal and civil law cases. **Criminal cases** deal with violations of the law. Such cases involve acts that harm individuals or the community as a whole. A criminal act is considered an offense against society. Breaking a state law is a crime committed against the people of the state. In such a case, an attorney for the state presents the evidence against the accused.

**Civil cases** deal with disputes between individuals or businesses. They may also involve disputes between a business and the government or between an individual and the government. These disputes usually focus on property or money. For example, imagine that one person

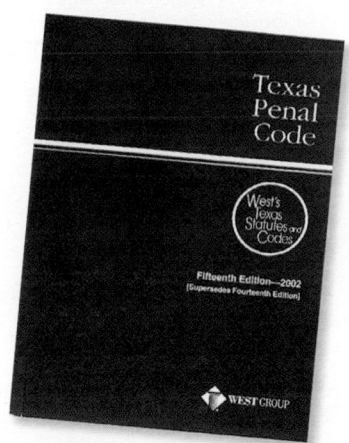

Texas Penal Code

West's Texas Statutes and Codes

Fifteenth Edition—2002
[Supersedes Fourteenth Edition]

WEST GROUP

# TEACH OBJECTIVE 1

**LEVELS 1 AND 2:** Describe the kinds of cases that state courts handle, reminding students of the differences between a civil suit and a criminal suit. Then organize students into groups. Have each group create a mock court docket that includes both civil and criminal cases and a brief description of each. **ENGLISH LANGUAGE LEARNERS**, **COOPERATIVE LEARNING**

**LEVELS 2 AND 3:** Reintroduce the kinds of cases state courts handle, discussing the differences between a civil suit and a criminal suit. *(State courts handle both civil and criminal cases.)* Then read an example to the class of a scenario involving a criminal offense and a scenario involving a civil action. Ask the class to differentiate between a scenario involving a civil action and one involving a criminal offense. Also, ask what led them to that conclusion. Finally, organize the class into small groups and instruct each group to write two scenarios: one involving a criminal offense and another involving a civil action. When finished, ask students to share their scenarios with the class and quiz the class concerning the type of law illustrated by each scenario. **COOPERATIVE LEARNING**

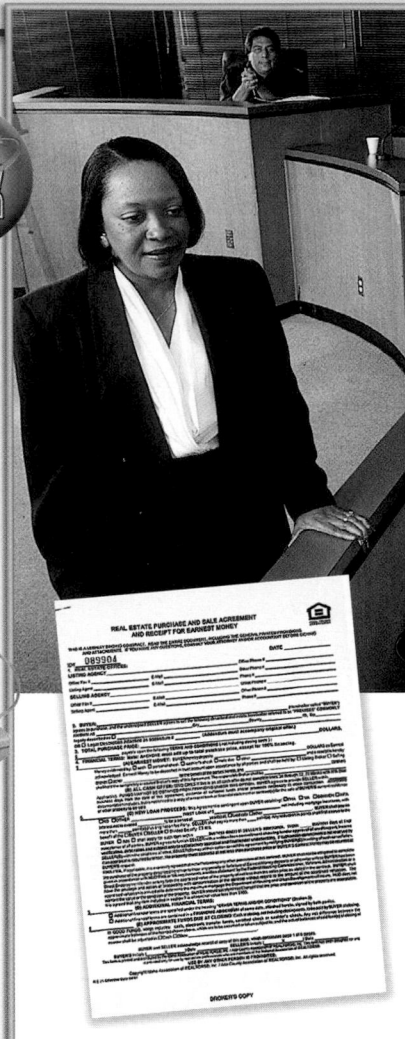

**internet** connect

**TOPIC:** State Courts
**GO TO:** go.hrw.com
**KEYWORD:** SZ3 AC8

Have students access the Internet through the HRW Go site to conduct research about legal and administrative issues presently before state court systems. Then have each student create a legal newspaper that outlines the issues, cites evidence from their research, and discusses how the states are attempting to solve problems related to the court system.

## Visual Record Answer

*Students might suggest that it ensures that the signer of the contract knows the exact contents of the contract before he or she signs.*

### Interpreting the Visual Record

**Civil court** *Civil court cases often involve disputes over contracts and other types of business agreements. Why do you think it is important to read through contracts carefully?*

claims that another person owes him or her money. He or she asks a state court for help in collecting this money. Another example of a civil case is a lawsuit brought by one company against another for not carrying out its part of a contract. Torts, wrongful acts that result in one party suing another for damages, are heard in civil courts. Torts do not include breach of contract cases.

In a civil case the person or company filing the **complaint,** or lawsuit, is referred to as the **plaintiff.** The state court must decide who is right according to the law and must award damages in civil cases.

✔ **Reading Check Contrasting** How do criminal cases and civil cases differ? Criminal cases deal with violations of the law that are considered offenses against society. Civil cases deal with disputes between individuals, businesses, an individual and the government, or a business and the government that tend to focus on property or money.

## ★ Organization

Each state has its own system of courts to interpret the law and punish lawbreakers. Four types of courts are found in most states—lower courts, general trial courts, appeals courts, and a state supreme court.

**Lower Courts** The lower courts generally hear minor cases, including misdemeanors and civil cases involving small amounts of money. In most rural areas and small towns these cases are heard by a **justice of the peace** who presides over a justice court. For misdemeanors the justice of the peace can hand down fines or short jail sentences. In larger towns and small cities such cases are handled by a magistrate's court or police court. An elected judge usually presides over these courts.

**ALL LEVELS:** After discussing the four types of state courts, copy the following graphic organizer onto the chalkboard, omitting the italicized answers. Then ask students to complete the organizer by labeling the courts and indicating their areas of responsibility.

**ENGLISH LANGUAGE LEARNERS**

**HOMEWORK** Have students study a newspaper to find examples of 5 of the 9 *Define* terms found on page 215. Students should bring the newspaper and their examples to class.

**General Trial Courts:**
*These courts hear major civil and criminal cases. Most involve a jury with a judge presiding.*

**Lower Courts:**
*These courts hear minor cases, including misdemeanors and civil cases involving small amounts of money. They may also handle traffic violations, family disputes, and juvenile cases.*

**Appeals Courts:**
*These courts hear cases on appeal, deciding if the lower court handled the trial properly and gave the accused the rights guaranteed under the Constitution.*

**State Courts**

**State Supreme Courts:**
*These courts are the highest court in most states, hearing cases on appeal.*

---

Many large cities have **municipal courts.** These courts are often divided into smaller courts that handle specific types of cases. Traffic courts, for example, hear cases involving traffic violations. Family-relations courts hear cases involving family disputes. Juvenile courts hear cases involving young persons.

Judges with special legal training usually preside over the lower courts. These judges conduct hearings without a jury. They are interested in discovering the cause of the trouble and preventing further difficulty. Judges in juvenile and family-relations courts work closely with social workers to help families who are in trouble. In some cases the decision of the judge may be appealed to a trial court.

Most states have also established special courts that hear civil cases involving small amounts of money. These **small claims courts** usually handle cases involving less than $5,000. No lawyers are needed. Each person involved in the dispute explains his or her side of the argument to the judge. After questioning each side to discover all the facts, the judge makes a decision in the case.

✔ **Reading Check** **Analyzing Information** How are most cases conducted in the lower courts? Judges with special legal training usually preside over the lower courts and conduct hearings without a jury.

**General Trial Courts** Major criminal and civil cases are handled in **general trial courts.** Most cases are heard by a jury, and a judge presides. Larger cities usually have several general trial courts. Sometimes one of these courts hears only civil cases and another hears only criminal cases. In many states, the general trial court judges are elected by the people of the county or district in which they serve.

Some states have trial courts called county courts. The county court is located in the county seat, which is the center of county government in most states. In other states, such as North Carolina, trial courts are called district courts. In some states there are also circuit courts. In the circuit court the trial judge travels a circuit (complete route) from one county to another to hold court trials. However, in Virginia the term circuit court refers to general trial courts that serve counties or cities. These courts may try both civil and criminal cases. The judges are elected by the General Assembly. Other names for trial courts in some states are superior courts and courts of common pleas.

✔ **Reading Check** **Summarizing** What five types of trial courts are there? county courts, district courts, circuit courts, superior courts, and courts of common pleas

**Appeals Courts** Sometimes a person believes his or her case was not handled fairly in a trial court. That person may appeal the decision to an appeals court. These courts are often called intermediate courts of

**Interpreting the Visual Record**

**Municipal Courts** *Many cities have established various special lower courts, including family-relations court.* **Why might a judge, instead of a jury, make decisions in a family-relations case?**

---

## The Democratic Process

**Small Claims Court** *The People's Court,* a popular television show that first aired in 1981, showed millions of viewers how a small-claims court operates. The litigants and their cases were real, and the judge—Joseph A. Wapner—was a veteran of the California court system. In a no-nonsense way, Judge Wapner persuaded viewers that the best means to win in a small-claims court is to be prepared. He and others—"Judge Judy," "Judge Brown," and "Judge Mills Lane"—have all instructed litigants to have on hand all pertinent receipts, canceled checks, photographs, contracts, and any other documented evidence. Litigants should then relate the events of their story in chronological order, making sure that all dates are accurate. These T.V. shows illustrate not only how the court works but also that there is a remedy to a dispute, other than securing an attorney.

**CRITICAL THINKING**

Why is the use of a small-claims court a necessity in the state judicial branch?

**ANSWER:** People who may not have the funds to hire an attorney have an opportunity to seek a remedy to a problem, and the problem is settled.

**Visual Record Answer**

*Students might suggest that judges need to use their experience to handle sensitive family cases.*

LEVEL 3: Discuss with students how the areas of responsibility of each of the four types of courts differ and how each level has its own purpose. Then set up a small claims court in class. Organize the class into small groups and have each group create a dispute that would involve a small-claims court. The groups will also provide the plaintiff, the defendant, and any witnesses. Assign members of the class to serve as the presiding judges. Finally, have students role-play each of the case scenarios. The presiding judges should deliberate and render a decision.
**COOPERATIVE LEARNING**

# TEACH OBJECTIVE 3

 **ALL LEVELS:** Discuss with students how overcrowding causes problems for the courts. Invite the district attorney, a local judge, a police officer, or a defense attorney to speak to your class. Ask the speaker to explain not only his or her role in the trial process, but also why the conditions that exist in your town or community that result in the delay of trials, the settling of cases out of court, and so on.
**ENGLISH LANGUAGE LEARNERS**

## CLOSE

Have students create a word puzzle using the Define words from this section.

## ★ Civics Sidelight

**Sentences Versus Time Served** The following table compares the maximum sentence lengths, excluding life and death sentences, and the actual time served for various convictions at the state level.

| Type of Offense | Average Sentence | Time Served |
|---|---|---|
| All violent | 7 yr 1 mth | 3 yr 3 mth |
| Homicide | 15 yr | 7 yr |
| Rape | 9 yr 8 mth | 5 yr 1 mth |
| Robbery | 7 yr 8 mth | 3 yr 4 mth |
| Negligent manslaughter | 8 yr 1 mth | 3 yr 5 mth |
| Assault | 5 yr 1 mth | 2 yr 4 mth |

**ACTIVITY:** Have students research the process by which a person in their state is paroled. Also, ask students to research if the victims or relatives of the victims are allowed to address the parole board, are notified of the release of the parolee, and so on. After researching the topic, have each student write an essay on the parole process in your state.

**CHART ANSWER**
lower courts

## State Court System

Most state court systems are organized in the following fashion. Judges at different levels may be elected or appointed depending upon the state.

**State Supreme Courts**

**Appeals Courts**
• Intermediate Courts of Appeals

**General Trial Courts**
• County Courts          • District Courts
• Circuit Courts         • Superior Courts
      • Courts of Common Plea

**Lower Courts**
• Justice Courts          • Traffic Courts
   • Magistrate or Police Courts
   • Juvenile and Family Courts
• Small Claims Courts     • Probate Courts

**Interpreting Charts** *Most states have many levels of courts specializing in different types of cases. To what level of the system do probate, small claims, and traffic courts belong?*

appeals. The usual basis for an appeal is that the right to a fair trial guaranteed to all citizens was somehow violated during a person's trial.

Appeals courts do not use juries. Instead, a group of judges examines the trial record of the lower court and hears arguments from the lawyers on both sides.

The group of judges then decides the case by majority vote. The judges must decide whether the lower court trial gave the accused all the rights guaranteed under the Constitution. If the accused is still not satisfied with the appeals court's decision, he or she can appeal to the state supreme court.

✔ **Reading Check** Analyzing Information How do appeals courts decide the outcome of a case? Judges examine the trial record of the lower court, hear arguments, and decide the case by majority vote.

**State Supreme Court** The state supreme court is the highest court in most states. The judges who sit on the state supreme court hear cases on appeal in much the same way as the U.S. Supreme Court. In some states the supreme court is called the court of appeals or the supreme judicial court.

State supreme court judges are elected in most states. In other states they are appointed by the governor with the consent of the state senate. Decisions of the state supreme court are final unless a federal law or a question about the U.S. Constitution is involved. Then the case may be appealed to the U.S. Supreme Court for review.

✔ **Reading Check** Finding the Main Idea What is the purpose of the state supreme court? As the highest court in the state, it hears cases on appeal from the intermediate courts of appeals and is the last court a case goes to before the U.S. Supreme Court.

### ★ Overcrowded Courts

There have been many proposals in recent years for the reform of state court systems. The primary reason for these efforts is that the state courts are overburdened with work. So many cases come before them that the court calendar is often a year or more behind schedule. It is not unusual to find automobile accident cases that have waited two or three years for a court settlement.

In many large cities the jails are crowded with accused persons who are awaiting trial. Some of these people have waited for more than a year. They have remained in jail because they do not have the money to post bail. These individuals may or may not be guilty. They have not been brought to trial because there are so many other cases ahead of theirs on the court schedules.

This backlog of cases makes it impossible to fulfill every American's constitutional guarantee of a speedy public trial. Critics give three reasons for this situation. First, there are more cases than ever before and not enough judges to handle the increasing caseload. Second, trials are long and slow. The very guarantees that protect U.S. citizens often cause trials to take a long time. Third, some courts are not run efficiently. Judges may call frequent recesses, or breaks, in a trial. Lawyers sometimes use delaying tactics to help their clients.

Some people believe that many state and local court systems are behind the times. They suggest that all courts should use modern technological tools. Many people believe that using technology such as computers would help make the courts work more efficiently. However, upgrading existing court equipment and facilities to take advantage of new technologies would be expensive.

The problems that courts face are serious. Currently many courts cannot fulfill the constitutional obligation of providing a speedy trial. Their improvement is a pressing concern to all citizens in our democratic society.

**Interpreting the Visual Record**

**Court backlog** *These West Virginia Supreme Court judges are looking over the backlog of cases that have flooded their court.* **How do such backlogs interfere with the functioning of the court system?**

✔ **Reading Check** Identifying Points of View What accounts for the courts' inability to guarantee a speedy public trial? not enough judges to handle the increasing caseload; trials long and slow; inefficient use of court time; and lack of sufficient technology

**SECTION 4 Review**

go.hrw.com **Homework Practice Online**

keyword: SZ3 HP8

**1. Define** and explain:
- penal code
- criminal cases
- civil cases
- complaint
- plaintiff
- justice of the peace
- municipal courts
- small claims courts
- general trial courts

**2. Summarizing** Copy the graphic organizer below. Use it to identify the problems that result from overcrowded state courts.

```
          Overcrowded state courts
   ┌──────┬──────┬──────┬──────┐
   ▼      ▼      ▼      ▼
 ┌────┐ ┌────┐ ┌────┐ ┌────┐
 └────┘ └────┘ └────┘ └────┘
```

**3. Finding the Main Idea**
a. What types of lawsuits do state courts hear?
b. Identify the four types of state courts and the types of cases each oversees.

**4. Writing and Critical Thinking**
**Problem Solving** Invent a court case in which either the defendant or plaintiff disagrees with the court's ruling. In two paragraphs describe the person's next course of action in the court system and the person's arguments for an appeal.

Consider:
- the hierarchy of the court system
- the fairness and constitutionality of the ruling

**REPRODUCIBLE**

- ▶ Chapter 8 Review, pp. 220–21
- ▶ Vocabulary Activity 8
- ▶ Chapter 8 Tutorial for Students, Parents, Mentors, and Peers
- ▶ Chapter 8 Test (Form A or B)
- ▶ Alternative Assessment Handbook

**TECHNOLOGY**

- ▶ Chapter 8 Test Generator (on the One-Stop Planner)
- ▶ Global Skill Builder CD–ROM
- ▶ HRW Go site

**REINFORCEMENT, REVIEW, AND ASSESSMENT**

- ▶ Chapter 8 Test for English Language Learners and Special-Needs Students

## REVIEW

Have students complete the **Chapter 8 Review** on pages 220–21.

## ASSESS

Use one of the chapter tests to assess students' understanding of the content. For **Alternative Assessment,** see the **Alternative Assessment Handbook.**

---

4. referendum, p. 208
5. executive orders, p. 211
6. warrant, p. 213
7. patronage, p. 214
8. penal code, p.215
9. plaintiff, p. 216
10. small-claims court, p. 217

**Understanding Main Ideas**

1. reserved powers; conducting elections, making rules on voting, making laws on education, marriage, and highway traffic laws, and so on.

2. organized under a state constitution; full faith and credit clause

3. U.S. citizen, resident of state and district, and certain minimum age

4. initiative—involves creating and signing petitions; referendum—involves voting; recall—involves creating and signing petitions and voting

5. state governors propose and can veto legislation, issue executive orders, prepare state budgets, appoint officials, head the state political party, oversee the state police, call on the National Guard, and grant pardons

6. state officials—lieutenant governor, secretary of state, attorney general, state treasurer, state auditor, and superintendent of public instruction; and state agencies

7. lower courts—misdemeanors and minor civil cases; general trial courts—major criminal and civil cases; appeals courts—cases from people dissatisfied with lower court trials; and the state supreme court

# Chapter 8 Review

## Chapter Summary

### Section 1

- The Tenth Amendment guarantees the states certain reserved powers. State governments have power over areas such as public education, elections, highways, and the establishment of local governments.

- The states and the federal government share powers such as taxation, law enforcement, and the protection of the health, safety, and welfare of the American people.

### Section 2

- Each state has a legislative branch. Most state legislatures have two houses. The process of passing state laws is similar to that used in Congress. Legislatures in most states meet every year; some meet every two years.

- In some states citizens can take a direct part in making laws through initiatives, propositions, or referenda.

### Section 3

- The laws made by a state's legislative branch are carried out by its executive branch.

- Governors are the chief executive officers of the state governments. They ensure that state laws are enforced.

- Other executive officials and state executive agencies assist governors in their work.

### Section 4

- The court system in the states includes lower courts, general trial courts, appeals courts, and state supreme courts.

## Define and Identify

Use the following terms in complete sentences.

1. full faith and credit clause
2. extradition
3. proposition
4. referendum
5. executive orders
6. warrant
7. patronage
8. penal code
9. plaintiff
10. small claims courts

## Understanding Main Ideas

**Section 1** *(Pages 197–02)*

1. What is the term for the powers granted to state governments, and what are some examples?
2. How are the rules of state governments organized, and under what rule did they agree to cooperate with each other?

**Section 2** *(Pages 203–08)*

3. What conditions must be met in order for someone to serve as a state lawmaker?
4. How can citizens take direct action in legislation and state government?

**Section 3** *(Pages 210–14)*

5. Who heads the state executive branch, and what does the job require?
6. Who helps the governor run the state government?

**Section 4** *(Pages 215–19)*

7. What types of courts exist in most states, and what does each do?
8. How does the appeals process work?

## What Did You Find Out?

1. How do the states' powers compare to those of the federal government?
2. How is the organization of most state legislatures similar to that of the U.S. Congress?
3. How do state court systems work?

## Thinking Critically

1. **Supporting a Point of View** It has been said that the initiative, referendum, and recall are the three basic instruments of direct democracy. Do you agree or disagree and why?
2. **Evaluating** What steps do you think state courts could take to reduce their backlog?
3. **Drawing Inferences and Conclusions** As you have learned, there are a variety of state governments. Why do you think this is the case?

## RETEACH

Organize students into small groups and assign each group one of the chapter sections. Have groups create a visual illustrating the content of their assigned section. Each group will then share its illustration with the class.

**ENGLISH LANGUAGE LEARNERS ,
COOPERATIVE LEARNING**

## Portfolio Extensions

**1. Linking to Community** Ask students to interview people connected with one of the branches in state government. Students should ask the interviewees about their job, their qualifications, and the future of their particular job. Then have each student write an essay covering the information he or she learned in the interview.

**2. Cooperative Learning** Organize students into small groups. Ask each group to take one of the branches of the state government and design a Web page illustrating the composition, function, and uniqueness of its assigned branch of government. Ask volunteers to discuss and show their pages.

---

## Building Social Studies Skills

go.hrw.com STANDARDIZED TEST PREP ONLINE keyword: SZ3 STP8

### Interpreting Maps

Study the map of the Northwest Territory below. Then answer the questions that follow.

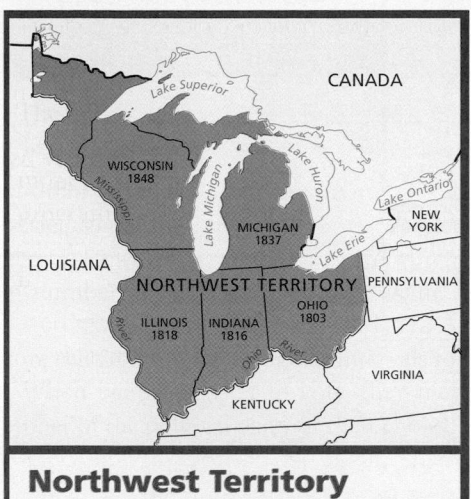

**Northwest Territory**

1. In what order did the states of the Northwest Territory join the Union?
   a. Ohio, Michigan, Illinois, Indiana, and Wisconsin
   b. Ohio, Illinois, Indiana, Michigan, and Wisconsin
   c. Ohio, Indiana, Illinois, Michigan, and Wisconsin
   d. Indiana, Ohio, Illinois, Wisconsin, and Michigan
2. Which of the new states bordered Lake Erie?

### Analyzing Primary Sources

Read the following quotation from the State of the State address of Governor Michael F. Easley of North Carolina, then answer the questions that follow.

"I am proud to stand here before you tonight—at the beginning of a bright new age for North Carolina. We leave behind a decade that will long be remembered as one of the most rewarding in our history. . . . The people of North Carolina rallied together like never before—for our schools, for our communities, for our families. . . . I want to personally thank you for putting people first and putting party differences aside. Good government is not about Democrats and Republicans. It is about children, seniors and working families. You put them first. . . . You are the first Legislature of the new century. You have a chance to be remembered as the group that brought sustained progress to North Carolina. You have a chance to make history and be remembered for it. . . . Any state can make progress in good times. It's the great states that make progress in the tough times."

3. To what does Governor Easley attribute the success and progress of the previous 10 years in North Carolina?
   a. the efforts of children and seniors to improve living conditions in the state
   b. cooperation between Democrats and Republicans who put the people of their state first
   c. The past 10 years were actually not successful.
   d. good times which made progress easy
4. What does Governor Easley ask the state legislature to do in the future?

8. If the accused is dissatisfied with the general trial court's ruling, the case can be taken to an appeals court. If the accused is still dissatisfied, then the case can be taken to the state supreme court. Cases involving constitutional issues can be taken to the U.S. Supreme Court.

### What Did You Find Out?

1. Some powers are concurrent powers. Also, the powers of both the state and federal governments are protected under the U.S. Constitution.

2. bicameral

3. A case begins in the lower court; may go to a trial court; can be appealed to an appeals court; may in some instances be appealed to the state supreme court.

### Thinking Critically

1. Students should indicate that these processes are a means for citizens to influence government. Viewpoints agreeing or disagreeing may vary as may explanations supporting them, but students should indicate a clear understanding of each process and the role each plays in state government.

2. Students' responses will vary.

3. Students might suggest that different states require various types of government.

### Social Studies Skills

1. c

2. Michigan and Ohio

3. b

4. to unite and make history; cooperate because times are tough

---

## Alternative Assessment

### Building Your Portfolio

**Interdisciplinary Connection to Government**

Complete the following activity individually or in a group. Use the library, local government organizations, and other sources to find out about the structure of your state's court system. Find a case being heard in your community and show the route it has taken in the courts and where it stands. Summarize your findings in a brief report and present your report to the class.

### internet connect

**Internet Activity: go.hrw.com
keyword: SZ3 AC8**

Access the Internet through the HRW Go site to research the principal executive officials in your state. Then make a list of the officials in your state that contains their names, principal duties and responsibilities, salaries, and whether the officials were elected by the citizens or appointed by the governor.

# Local Government

## CHAPTER RESOURCE MANAGER

| Objectives | Pacing Guide | Reproducible Resources |
|---|---|---|
| **SECTION 1:**<br>**Units of Local Government**<br>(pp. 223–27)<br><br>★ Explain how local governments are established and why they are needed.<br>★ Describe how the county system of government began in the United States.<br>★ Analyze the organization of county government and define the main purposes of its levels. | **Regular**<br>1.5 days<br><br>**Block Scheduling**<br>1 day<br><br>*Block Scheduling Handbook with Team Teaching Strategies, Chapter 9* | **RS** Guided Reading Strategies 9.1<br>**E** Challenge and Enrichment Worksheet 9: Researching Local Government |
| **SECTION 2:**<br>**Town, Township, and Village Governments**<br>(pp. 228–33)<br><br>★ Locate where town government began and describe how it has changed.<br>★ Explain why townships and special districts developed, and describe how each functions.<br>★ Determine why villages and boroughs are created, and describe how they operate. | **Regular**<br>1 day<br><br>**Block Scheduling**<br>.5 day<br><br>*Block Scheduling Handbook with Team Teaching Strategies, Chapter 9* | **RS** Guided Reading Strategies 9.2<br>**RS** Readings in Economics and Government 55: *Democracy in America,* by Alexis de Tocqueville |
| **SECTION 3:**<br>**City Government**<br>(pp. 234–39)<br><br>★ Define the term *city,* and identify the services city governments provide for their residents.<br>★ Examine how city governments are established.<br>★ Identify the different types of city governments and their functions. | **Regular**<br>1 day<br><br>**Block Scheduling**<br>.5 day<br><br>*Block Scheduling Handbook with Team Teaching Strategies, Chapter 9* | **RS** Guided Reading Strategies 9.3<br>**RS** Graphic Organizer Activity: How Governments Work Together |
| **SECTION 4:**<br>**How Governments Work Together**<br>(pp. 241–45)<br><br>★ Analyze why there is a division of powers among different levels of government.<br>★ Explain why the federal government became involved in the building of roads.<br>★ Identify the government functions that require the cooperation of different levels of government. | **Regular**<br>1.5 days<br><br>**Block Scheduling**<br>1 day<br><br>*Block Scheduling Handbook with Team Teaching Strategies, Chapter 9* | **RS** Guided Reading Strategies 9.4<br>**SM** Community Service and Participation Handbook: Adopt-a-Highway |

## Chapter Resource Key

| | | | |
|---|---|---|---|
| **PS** Primary Sources | **SM** Skills Mastery |  CD-ROM | |
| **RS** Reading Support | **A** Assessment |  Video | |
| **IC** Interdisciplinary Connections | **REV** Review | Internet | |
| **E** Enrichment | **ELL** Reinforcement and English Language Learners |  Holt Presentation Maker Using Microsoft® PowerPoint® | |
| | Transparencies | | |

 **One-Stop** Planner CD–ROM

**See the *One-Stop Planner* for a complete list of additional resources for students and teachers.**

**One-Stop** Planner CD–ROM

It's easy to plan lessons, select resources, and print out materials for your students when you use the **One-Stop Planner CD–ROM with Test Generator**.

**internet** connect

| Technology Resources | Reinforcement, Review, and Assessment |
|---|---|
|  One-Stop Planner, Lesson 9.1 <br>  Transparency 10: County Government <br> Homework Practice Online | **REV** Section 1 Review, p. 227 <br> **A** Daily Quiz 9.1 <br> **ELL** Main Idea Activity 9.1 <br> **ELL** English Audio Summary 9.1 <br> **ELL** Spanish Audio Summary 9.1 |
|  One-Stop Planner, Lesson 9.2 <br>  Homework Practice Online | **REV** Section 2 Review, p. 233 <br> **A** Daily Quiz 9.2 <br> **ELL** Main Idea Activity 9.2 <br> **ELL** English Audio Summary 9.2 <br> **ELL** Spanish Audio Summary 9.2 |
|  One-Stop Planner, Lesson 9.3 <br>  Holt Researcher CD–ROM <br>  Transparency 11: Plans of City Government <br>  Homework Practice Online <br>  HRW Go site | **REV** Section 3 Review, p. 239 <br> **A** Daily Quiz 9.3 <br> **ELL** Main Idea Activity 9.3 <br> **ELL** English Audio Summary 9.3 <br> **ELL** Spanish Audio Summary 9.3 |
|  One-Stop Planner, Lesson 9.4 <br>  Transparency 12: Sources of Government Laws and Powers <br>  **CNN** Presents: American Government <br>  Homework Practice Online | **REV** Section 4 Review, p. 245 <br> **A** Daily Quiz 9.4 <br> **ELL** Main Idea Activity 9.4 <br> **ELL** English Audio Summary 9.4 <br> **ELL** Spanish Audio Summary 9.4 |

**HRW ONLINE RESOURCES**
  GO TO: go.hrw.com
  Then type in the keyword.

**TEACHER HOME PAGE**
  KEYWORD: SZ3 Teacher

**CHAPTER INTERNET ACTIVITIES**
  KEYWORD: SZ3 AC9
  Choose an activity on state and local government to:
  • create a labeled diagram on the organization of your local government.
  • write a proposal for a federal grant to improve your community.
  • create a pamphlet on the effects of the Galveston hurricane on local government.

**CHAPTER ENRICHMENT LINKS**
  KEYWORD: SZ3 CH9

**ONLINE ASSESSMENT**
  **Homework Practice**
  **KEYWORD: SZ3 HP9**
  **Rubrics**
  **KEYWORD: SS Rubrics**

**ONLINE MAPS, CHARTS, AND GRAPHS**
  KEYWORD: SZ3 MCG
  • County Government

**HOLT PRESENTATION MAKER**
  KEYWORD: SZ3 PPT9

**CONTENT UPDATES**
  KEYWORD: SS Content Updates

**ONLINE READING SUPPORT**
  KEYWORD: SS Strategies

**CURRENT EVENTS**
  KEYWORD: S3 Current Events

## Meeting Individual Needs

### Ability Levels

**Level 1** Basic-level activities designed for all students encountering new material

**Level 2** Intermediate-level activities designed for average students

**Level 3** Challenging activities designed for honors and gifted-and-talented students

**English Language Learners** Activities that address the needs of students with Limited English Proficiency

## Chapter Review and Assessment

**IC** Vocabulary Activity 9
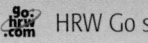 Global Skill Builder CD–ROM
HRW Go site
**REV** Chapter 9 Tutorial for Students, Parents, Mentors, and Peers
**REV** Chapter 9 Review, pp. 246–47
**A** Standardized Test Practice
**A** Chapter 9 Test Generator (on the One-Stop Planner)
**A** Chapter 9 Test (Form A or B)
**A** Alternative Assessment Handbook
**A** Chapter 9 Test for English Language Learners and Special-Needs Students

221b

**CHAPTER 9**

**Section 1** Units of Local Government

**Section 2** Town, Township, and Village Governments

**Section 3** City Government

**Section 4** How Governments Work Together

## Internet Activity

**Your Local Government**

### What's Your Opinion?

To help students create their **Themes** *Journal* entries, provide the following examples of appropriate **agree**/**disagree** statements.

● **Agree** It takes an individual more time and effort to complete a task than it takes local government.

**Disagree** Individuals can work more quickly and less expensively because they are not hindered by bureaucracy.

● **Agree** Similar rules and procedures can reduce the time and effort required for cooperation between cities.

**Disagree** Cooperative projects can be organized similarly allowing cities to maintain the uniqueness of their government.

● **Agree** Federal, state, and local governments have their own duties and jurisdiction.

**Disagree** To meet citizens' needs, governments on all levels must work together.

# CHAPTER
# 9 Local Government

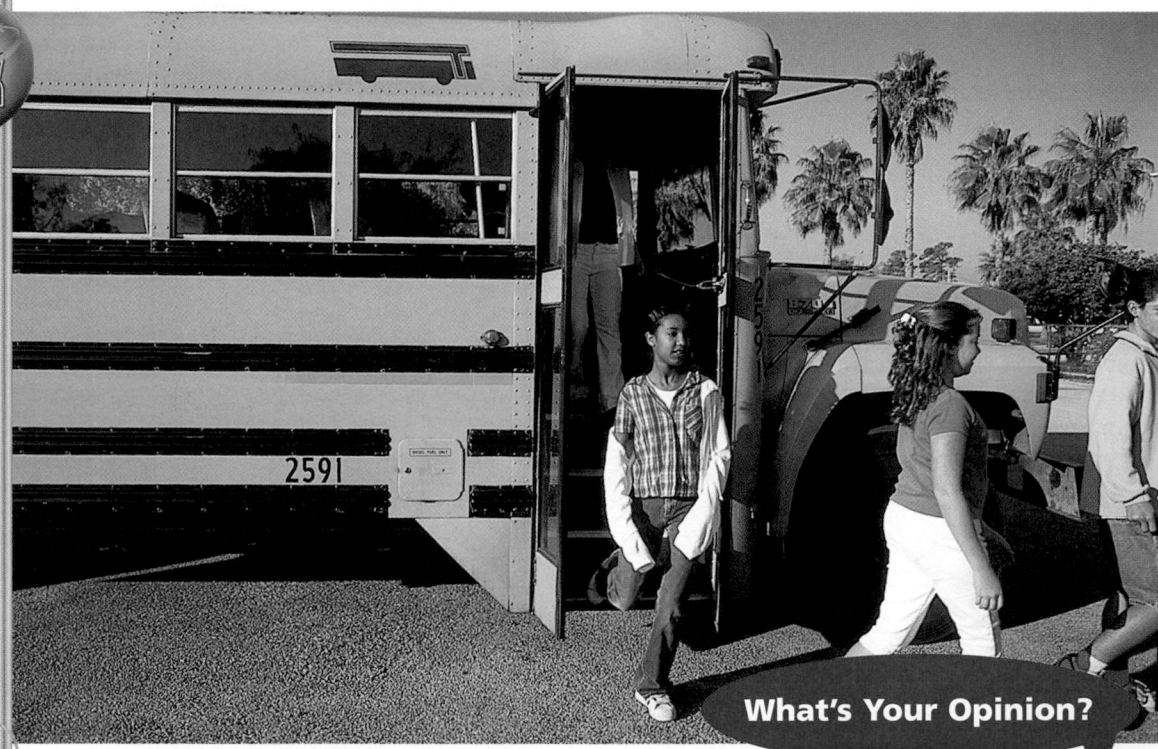

**What's Your Opinion?**

### Build on What You Know

Your local government is the government closest to your daily life. It makes rules that protect you and the people of your community and provides services that improve your life. Your local government manages your community's road system, its water supply, and its school system. You can see the work of your local government all around you every day.

 **Themes Journal** Do you **agree** or **disagree** with the following statements? Support your point of view in your journal.

● Local governments provide services more efficiently than individuals working alone can.

● Cities can cooperate more efficiently if they are organized the same way.

● Federal, state, and local governments all operate independently.

# SECTION 1

## OBJECTIVES

*After completing Section 1, students should be able to*

1 **Explain how local governments are established and why they are needed.**

2 **Describe how the county system of government began in the United States.**

3 **Analyze the organization of county government and define the main purposes of each of its levels.**

## 🔊 LET'S GET STARTED!

As students enter the classroom, ask them which of the following things would affect their daily lives most directly: closing the nearest national park, closing the state parks, or closing all of the local parks. Allow students time to respond. *(Students will likely respond that closing the local park would affect them most.)* Explain that local government provides these parks. Then have students suggest other facilities and services provided by local government. Tell students that in Section 1 they will learn more about the history of local governments and the services that they provide.

## SECTION 1

# Units of Local Government

### Read to Discover

1. How are local governments established, and why are they needed?
2. How did the county system of government begin in the United States?
3. How is county government organized, and what are the main purposes of each level of county government?

### Define

- charters
- municipalities
- ordinances
- counties
- county seat
- sheriff
- county clerk
- district attorney

### WHY CIVICS MATTERS

Local governments provide and oversee many services for the people in their communities. Use **CNNfyi.com** or other **current events** sources to learn more about a service provided by a local government. Record your findings in your journal.

## SECTION 1 RESOURCES

### REPRODUCIBLE
- ▶ Guided Reading Strategies 9.1
- ▶ Challenge and Enrichment Worksheet 9: Researching Local Government

### TECHNOLOGY
- ▶ One-Stop Planner, Lesson 9.1
- ▶ Transparency 10: County Government
- ▶ Homework Practice Online

### REINFORCEMENT, REVIEW, AND ASSESSMENT
- ▶ Section 1 Review, p. 227
- ▶ Daily Quiz 9.1
- ▶ Main Idea Activity 9.1
- ▶ English Audio Summary 9.1
- ▶ Spanish Audio Summary 9.1

## Reading Focus

Local governments have grown as the country has grown. As the American people settled in rural communities, towns, cities, and suburbs, they set up local governments.

## ⭐ Establishing Local Governments

All local governments are established by and receive their powers from the state governments. State constitutions direct the state legislatures to set up a government for each village, town, city, and county within the state borders.

Most local governments receive **charters** from the state. A charter is a basic plan for a local governmental unit that defines its powers, responsibilities, and organization. Some units of local government are incorporated by the state, which means they have the legal status of corporations. These units, known as **municipalities,** usually include cities, villages, and boroughs. Municipalities, established by the residents, have a large degree of self-government. As corporations, municipalities may own property, make contracts, and sue or be sued in court.

*Towns and other local governments usually have clearly defined boundaries.*

✔ **Reading Check** Drawing Inferences and Conclusions Why do you think state governments establish local governments? Students might say that this practice allows people at a local level to address their needs and problems directly and more efficiently.

*Local Government* **223**

**ALL LEVELS:** Copy the following graphic organizer onto the chalkboard, omitting the italicized answers. Ask each student to complete the chart to explain how local governments are established and why they are needed.

**ENGLISH LANGUAGE LEARNERS**

| How Local Governments Are Established | Why Local Governments Are Needed |
|---|---|
| *State governments establish local governments and grant them powers.* | *They provide and manage services to the community.* |

**LEVEL 3:** Ask students to imagine that they have been selected to write a proposal that outlines the creation of a new local government. Tell students to write a public relations piece intended to gather support for their project. Suggest that students include an explanation of how local governments are established and why they are needed in their public relations piece. *(See the Level 1 lesson for description.)*

---

## ★ Civics Sidelight

**Competition Creates Conflict** Conflict between local and state governments can sometimes involve the courts. School funding is one example. Although the federal government provides some funding, public education is primarily a responsibility of state and local government. Courts in a number of states have declared that inequalities in funding between rich and poor school districts violate state constitutions. In fact, the Texas Supreme Court made such a ruling in 1989. Some recommended remedies have included forcing wealthy school districts to share some of their funds with poorer districts. A number of states continue to grapple with the problem of equitable education funding.

### CRITICAL THINKING

How might such problems be resolved cooperatively among local and state governments?

**ANSWER:** Students might suggest that funds could be distributed more equitably when handed down from the state.

---

### BIOGRAPHY ANSWER
She has sought to end poverty and discrimination by leading the Cherokee Nation to set up Head Start programs, health-care clinics, and job-training programs.

---

### BIOGRAPHY
## Wilma Mankiller
### (1945– )

Wilma Mankiller was born in Oklahoma in 1945. When she was 11 years old, Mankiller and her family were relocated to San Francisco, California, by the U.S. Bureau of Indian Affairs. City life was difficult for Mankiller, who missed her friends and family, and sense of community in Oklahoma. In 1976, after studying sociology, Mankiller returned to Oklahoma to live near the headquarters of the Cherokee Nation. She took classes in community planning and was soon writing applications for federal funds for Cherokee projects and programs.

In 1983 Mankiller was elected Deputy Chief of the Cherokee Nation. By 1987 she became the first woman ever elected Principal Chief. She was re-elected to the position in 1991, with 82 percent of the vote. She eventually resigned in 1995 for health reasons.

As leader of her tribal government, Mankiller governed 150,000 people and managed a budget of some $78 million. Her efforts to end poverty and discrimination among American Indians led the Cherokee Nation to set up Head Start programs, health-care clinics, and job-training programs. For her efforts on behalf of her people, Mankiller was inducted into the National Women's Hall of Fame in 1993. **What contributions has Mankiller made as an American Indian leader?**

---

## ★ Why We Need Local Government

There are many kinds of local governments, including boroughs, cities, counties, towns, townships, and villages. The main job of all these different forms of local government is to provide services for citizens.

The people who live in each community depend on local government to serve them in many ways. We often take for granted such conveniences as roads, running water, sewage systems, sidewalks, street cleaning, and trash collection. However, all these services depend on a well-run local government. Some services, such as electricity and public transportation, may be provided by privately owned companies. Nevertheless, local government must make sure these services are economical, efficient, and well managed.

It might be possible for individuals working alone to perform all the services local governments provide. Each person might hire someone to haul trash away. Each person might be able to guard against fire by keeping a fire extinguisher in the home. Yet life would be more difficult, if every citizen had to do all of these things alone. People find that by working together they can secure better and more efficient services than by working alone.

✔ **Reading Check Summarizing** What sorts of services do local governments provide? provide and manage services such as transportation, roads, running water, sewage systems, sidewalks, street cleaning, trash collection, and other utilities

## ★ Local and State Cooperation

Local governments work closely with state governments to make communities better places to live. Local lawmaking bodies have the power to pass **ordinances,** or regulations that govern the community. An ordinance has the force of a law but must not conflict with state and national laws. Local governments also enforce the laws that are passed by the state government.

Which state laws are enforced by local governments? State governments rely on local governments to make sure that elections are carried out according to state rules. Local government officials supervise the voting process. Local governments also provide their communities with polling places, or locations where citizens can vote. State governments also rely on local governments to enforce laws that concern weights and measures. In most states

# TEACH OBJECTIVE 2

 **LEVEL 1:** Lead a class discussion about how the county system of government began in the United States. *(Students should note that southern colonies were divided into counties with county seats where owners of scattered plantations could meet regularly to make laws.)* Ask students to imagine that they live in the southern colonies. Then have each student provide an explanation of why this system of government helps to meet the community's needs.
**ENGLISH LANGUAGE LEARNERS**

**LEVEL 3:** Organize the class into small groups. Have each group create a special section of a newspaper in honor of the county system of government. Tell students to include a description of how the county system of government began in the United States. *(See Level 1 lesson for the description.)* Roles for group members include reporter, editor, headline writer, and editorial or column writer. Have groups present their "pages" to the class for discussion. **COOPERATIVE LEARNING**

 **HOMEWORK** Ask each student to create a political cartoon to accompany his or her group's editorial page.

County seats served as the central points for county government.

the scales that grocery stores use to weigh meat and produce must meet certain standards required by state law. These standards are often enforced by local inspectors. Local police departments enforce state laws as well as local ordinances.

✔ **Reading Check** Summarizing How do local and state governments cooperate? Local ordinances must not conflict with state or national laws, and local governments help enforce state laws.

## ★ County Governments

Most states are divided into parts called **counties.** The number and size of these counties vary from state to state. While the state of Texas has 254 counties, Delaware has only 3. Altogether the United States has more than 3,000 counties. Louisiana calls its county-level units of government parishes. Alaska refers to its counties as boroughs.

In many states the county government is the largest unit of local government. In Connecticut and Rhode Island, however, counties are only geographical areas, without actual county governments. In the New England states, most counties serve as judicial districts. In these states the functions of county governments are usually performed by town governments.

The county form of government began in the southern colonies. In this region, agriculture was the main industry, and the population was scattered. Cotton, rice, and tobacco plantations were often located far from each other. The county form of government, borrowed from England, seemed well suited to the settlers' needs.

Each southern colony was divided into a number of counties. The plantation owners who lived in each county met regularly in a centrally located town, which became known as the **county seat.** At these meetings the plantation owners discussed issues and passed the laws of the county government.

## ★ Economics

**Finding Funding for Cities** Outside influences sometimes tighten bonds between state and local governments. For example, declining federal aid to cities in the 1990s meant that states had to increase their support to cities. In 1998, federal aid covered nearly 20 percent of state and local government expenditures. Although expenditures had risen by over $113 billion by the year 2000, federal aid had only increased by $24 billion. No doubt public education was the hardest hit. The largest portion of state and local government budgets—about 25 percent—is dedicated to funding education.

**CRITICAL THINKING**

How do you think local governments compensate for reduced federal support?

**ANSWER:** Students might suggest that they cut the budget, raise taxes, or seek state funding.

# TEACH OBJECTIVE 3

**LEVEL 1:** Organize the class into small groups and assign each group one level of county government. Have each group write a paragraph explaining how county government is organized and the main purpose of its assigned level. *(Students' paragraphs will show the following: county board—legislative branch; sheriff—enforces the law; county clerk—records the actions and decisions of the county board; county treasurer—manages the county's funds; county auditor—examines tax records and expenditures; district attorney—represents the state government in county trials.)* **ENGLISH LANGUAGE LEARNERS , COOPERATIVE LEARNING**

**LEVEL 3:** Organize the class into small groups and assign each group one level of county government. Have groups interview a member of their assigned level of government in your county to find out how the job has changed over the years. Ask volunteers to share their findings in an oral report that defines the purpose of the group's level and shares the main ideas from the interview. *(See the Level 1 lesson for purposes.)* **COOPERATIVE LEARNING**

## CLOSE

Organize the class into two groups. Have the two sides debate this statement: *Each county should have a single leader just as each state and the nation do.* Call on volunteers to share their opinions and state their reasoning. **COOPERATIVE LEARNING**

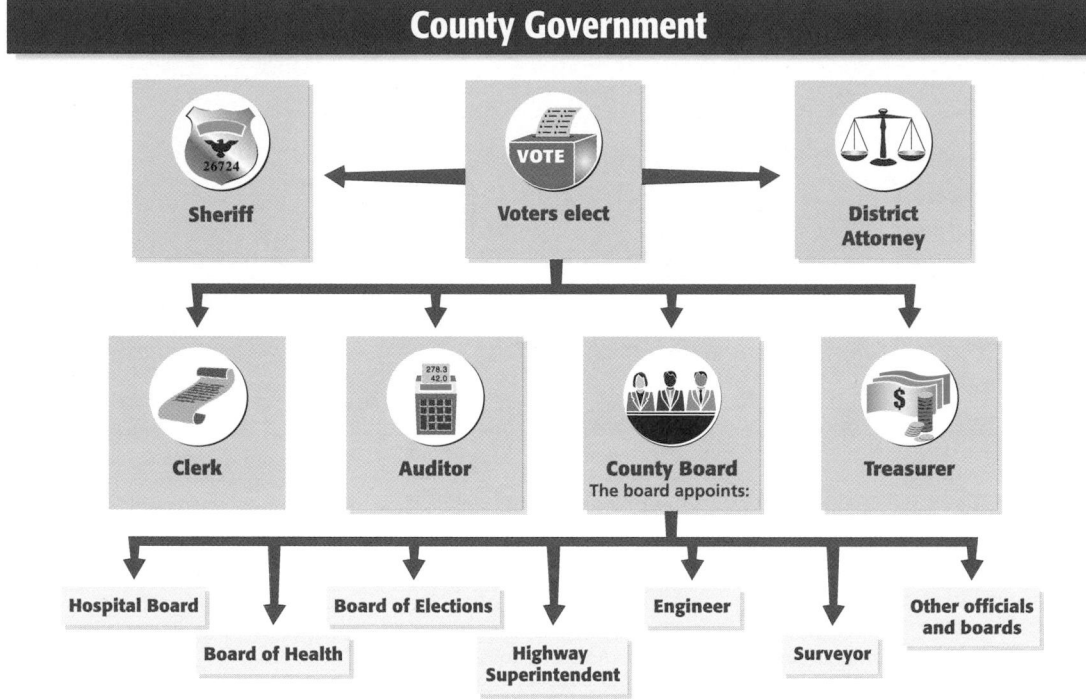

**County Government**

Voters elect → Sheriff · District Attorney

Clerk · Auditor · County Board *The board appoints:* · Treasurer

Hospital Board · Board of Health · Board of Elections · Highway Superintendent · Engineer · Surveyor · Other officials and boards

**Interpreting Charts** *Counties can have many different officials depending on their size and population.* **What county officials are typically elected by voters?**

The chief official in this early form of government was known as the sheriff. This title had originally been used for a similar official in England. The sheriff's job was to see that all of the laws of the county were enforced.

Today, in states where counties are important, county governments serve two main purposes. First, they help the state government collect various state taxes, supervise elections, and enforce state laws. Second, they serve the county residents by providing them with health and welfare services, law enforcement, libraries, roads, and schools. Counties also serve as boundaries for court districts in many states.

✔ **Reading Check** Analyzing Information How did the county form of government originate in the United States? It originated in the South and was borrowed from England. Southern colonies were divided into counties, and plantation owners in each county met regularly to pass laws.

## ★ County Officials

At the head of a county government is a group of officials elected by the voters. This governing body is often called the county board. Other names include board of commissioners, county court, or board of county supervisors. The county board is the county's legislative body. It may pass local laws regulating health and safety. It may collect taxes on

## REVIEW AND ASSESS

Have students complete the **Section 1 Review** on page 227. Then have students complete **Daily Quiz 9.1**. As **Alternative Assessment**, you may want to use the government proposal or interview activities in this section's lessons.

## RETEACH

Have students complete **Main Idea Activity for English Language Learners and Special-Needs Students 9.1**. Then have students work in pairs to write five fill-in-the-blank sentences that can each be completed by one of the section's Define terms. Have pairs exchange sentences, complete the ones they receive, and then return them for grading.

**ENGLISH LANGUAGE LEARNERS , COOPERATIVE LEARNING**

## EXTEND

Have students use the library and other resources to obtain information about how their county government serves their state. Then have students create informational pamphlets offering their opinions on whether county government should be abolished in their state. Students should consider whether the services county governments offer could be provided just as well by towns and cities, or directly by the state. Pamphlets should also consider how dense or scattered the population is.

**BLOCK SCHEDULING**

real estate or personal property in the county. The county board also supervises county buildings such as the courthouse and jail.

Many counties have no individual leader for the executive branch of their government. Instead, they have several county officials, each with separate responsibilities. These officials are frequently elected by the people of the county.

The **sheriff** enforces the law. He or she selects deputies to help with law enforcement. The sheriff arrests lawbreakers and carries out the orders of the courts. The **county clerk** keeps a record of the actions and decisions of the county board. The clerk also keeps records of births, deaths, election results, and marriages. The county treasurer takes care of the county's funds. The treasurer sees that no money is spent unless the county board approves. The county auditor examines the official records of taxes received and money spent to make sure all transactions are recorded properly. The **district attorney** represents the state government in county trials. He or she is also known as the county prosecutor. The number of county officials varies greatly.

In some places, the traditional form of county government has been viewed as inefficient. With the approval of the voters and the state legislature, a number of counties have established the positions of county manager and county executive.

The county executive is elected by the voters and the county manager is appointed by the county board. The county manager supervises the county government and organizes it in a businesslike manner.

✔ **Reading Check** Categorizing List three county official positions and their responsibilities. See highlighted terms and names of officials above for typical positions and responsibilities.

**Interpreting the Visual Record**

**Surveying** *Surveyors are needed to map out the boundaries of local governments and their property holdings.* **Why would accurate measurements be important to surveying?**

---

## SECTION 1 Review

**go.hrw.com** **Homework Practice Online**
keyword: SZ3 HP9

1. **Define** and explain:
   - charters
   - municipalities
   - ordinances
   - counties
   - county seat
   - sheriff
   - county clerk
   - district attorney

2. **Categorizing** Copy the chart below. Use it to explain the duties of each level of county government.

| | |
|---|---|
| County Board | |
| Sheriff | |
| County Clerk | |
| County Treasurer | |
| County Auditor | |
| District Attorney | |

3. **Finding the Main Idea**
   a. Why and how are local governments formed?
   b. How did the county system of local government begin?

4. **Writing and Critical Thinking**
   **Supporting a Point of View** Imagine that you are on a state board that is deciding how to organize a new local government. Persuade your peers to adopt the form of county management—either county board or county manager—that you think would most benefit the county.

   **Consider:**
   - how each method divides power
   - how officials are selected under each method

---

**Visual Record Answer**

*Students might say that accurate measurements are needed to ensure correct boundaries.*

## Section 1 Review
### ANSWERS

**1. Define**
- charters, p. 223
- municipalities, p. 223
- ordinance, p. 224
- counties, p. 225
- county seat, p. 225
- sheriff, p. 227
- county clerk, p. 227
- district attorney, p. 227

**2.** County Board—the county's legislative body, may pass local laws regulating health and safety, collect taxes on real estate or personal property, and supervise county buildings; Sheriff—enforces the law and selects deputies; County Clerk—keeps a record of actions and decisions of the county board, as well as records of births, deaths, marriages, and election results; Treasurer—takes care of the county's funds; Auditor—examines official records of taxes and money spent; District Attorney—represents the state government in county trials

**3. a.** to provide and manage services to the community; established and given powers by their state governments

**b.** Southern colonies were divided into counties with centrally located county seats where owners of widely scattered plantations could meet regularly to decide laws.

**4.** Students' explanations will vary but should reflect an understanding that the county-manager approach concentrates authority into an executive position and that the county board is elected while the county manager is appointed.

# SECTION 2

## OBJECTIVES

*After completing Section 2, students should be able to*

1 **Locate where town government began and describe how it has changed.**

2 **Explain why townships and special districts developed and describe how each functions.**

3 **Determine why villages and boroughs are created and describe how they operate.**

## SECTION 2 RESOURCES

### REPRODUCIBLE

▶ Guided Reading Strategies 9.2
▶ Readings in Economics and Government 55: *Democracy in America* by Alexis de Tocqueville

### TECHNOLOGY

▶ One-Stop Planner, Lesson 9.2
▶ Homework Practice Online

### REINFORCEMENT, REVIEW, AND ASSESSMENT

▶ Section 2 Review, p. 233
▶ Daily Quiz 9.2
▶ Main Idea Activity 9.2
▶ English Audio Summary 9.2
▶ Spanish Audio Summary 9.2

## 🔊 LET'S GET STARTED!

Write the following question on the chalkboard: *Do you think it is possible for an entire town to attend a town meeting?* As students enter the classroom, ask them to respond to the question. *(Students might indicate that it is or is not possible depending upon the purpose of the meeting and the size of the town.)* Tell them that town meetings are one type of governmental process used in towns. Then tell students that in Section 2 they will learn about the structure of government in towns, townships, and villages.

---

## SECTION 2

# Town, Township, and Village Governments

### Read to Discover

1. Where did town government begin, and how has it changed?
2. Why did townships and special districts develop, and how does each function?
3. Why are villages and boroughs created, and how do they operate?

### WHY CIVICS MATTERS

Local governments assist the federal government by handling smaller issues. Use **CNNfyi**.com or other **current events** sources to investigate a federal issue and explain why it might not be resolved as effectively by a local government. Record your findings in your journal.

### Define

• town
• village
• town meeting
• townships
• constables
• special district

## Reading Focus

Although counties are the largest unit of local government, they are not always the most influential government. In some states, counties serve only as election districts, and the real work of local government is performed by other units. In all states, counties must share the job of governing with other units of local government.

### ★ Development of Towns and Villages

The **town** form of government began in the New England colonies. Each colony received a grant of land from the king of England. The colonists established small towns, where they built their homes and churches. At the edges of the towns, the settlers established their farms. Each day they left their homes and worked on the farms. The colonists considered these outlying farms to be part of their towns. Later, some of the settlers moved to the farms. As long as these farms were located within the town limits, people living on them were considered residents of that town. As a result, New England towns stretched out into the surrounding countryside.

In some areas the settlers set up a **village** form of government. Only the village itself, which included the homes of the settlers and other buildings, was overseen by the village government. The

*This book outlining the laws and charters of Pennsylvania was written by Benjamin Franklin.*

# TEACH OBJECTIVE 1

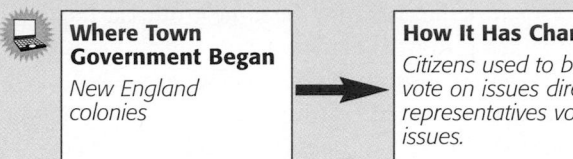

**ALL LEVELS:** Copy the following graphic organizer onto the chalkboard, omitting the italicized answers. Have each student complete the organizer to locate where town government began and describe how it has changed. **ENGLISH LANGUAGE LEARNERS**

| **Where Town Government Began** *New England colonies* | → | **How It Has Changed** *Citizens used to be able to vote on issues directly, now representatives vote on issues.* |

**LEVEL 2:** Have students draw a plan for a class exhibit about town government. In their plan, students should explain how the class would depict where town government began and describe how it has changed.

**LEVEL 3:** Ask students to imagine that they are government officials who have been alive since the founding of the New England colonies. Acting as the town government official, each student should write a series of business diary entries about the local government. Students' entries should mention where town government began and how it has changed. *(See the All Levels lesson for origins and changes.)* Encourage volunteers to share their diary entries with the class.

Colonial Williamsburg Foundation

outlying parts of the settlement were not considered part of the village. These areas later came under the rule of the county government.

As other people pushed farther west, they established new settlements. Some of them called their settlements towns. In Pennsylvania, settlements were often called boroughs. Thus, many different names were used for these small settlements.

✔ **Reading Check Comparing and Contrasting** How were early towns and villages alike and different? They were both small governed areas. Town governments considered outlying areas to be under their rule, but villages did not.

## ⭐ Early Town Government

The people of the early New England towns created a simple yet effective form of local government—the **town meeting.** Town residents and people from surrounding farms met regularly in the town hall. At these public meetings, citizens discussed issues and problems and decided how they should be handled.

Citizens had the opportunity to speak on any issue. After all opinions were heard, the people at the meeting voted on the issue. In this way, each citizen had a direct vote in the government. A New England town meeting was direct democracy in action. Some small New England towns still manage their business in this manner. Town meetings are also held in several states in the Midwest.

✔ **Reading Check Finding the Main Idea** Why could early town meetings be considered "direct democracy in action"? All citizens could debate and vote on issues.

---

**Interpreting the Visual Record**

**Jamestown** *The original English settlers at the Jamestown colony built a triangular fort to protect their settlement.* **Why do you think the settlers constructed this fort near a river?**

---

### ⭐ Civics Sidelight

**New Amsterdam's Government** Prior to its existence as a village, the colony of New Amsterdam was a company-run town. In 1647 the Dutch West India Company sent Peter Stuyvesant to take charge of the colony. As colonial governor, Stuyvesant selected nine men to serve as a council of advisers and judges. Two years later, the same nine men requested that the company release its control of the town and grant the people the right to self-government. Stuyvesant resisted their request but was ordered to honor it in 1652. He finally complied in 1653. Ironically, with the establishment of a local government, the council was relieved of its duties and replaced by magistrates.

**CRITICAL THINKING**

Why do you think the council was disbanded?

**ANSWER:** Students might suggest that the type of government changed enough to warrant a replacement of those officials.

---

**Visual Record Answer**

*Students might suggest that they needed water for drinking and transportation.*

## TEACH OBJECTIVE 2

**LEVEL 1:** Call on volunteers to explain why townships and special districts developed. *(Students should note that townships developed to manage the needs of local citizens and that special districts are created to handle special needs.)* Then organize the class into groups and have each group prepare two glossary entries. Each entry should describe how the different organization functions. *(Students should include that townships have an elected chairperson, a board of commissioners, constables, an assessor, treasurer, tax collector, and school board members. The organization of special districts varies depending on their function.)* **ENGLISH LANGUAGE LEARNERS**, **COOPERATIVE LEARNING**

**LEVEL 2:** Lead a class discussion about why townships and special districts developed. *(See the Level 1 lesson for reasons.)* Then organize students into small groups. Instruct each group to create a series of clues that indicate a characteristic of either the township or special district. When groups are finished, combine two groups together to take turns playing a game with the clues and answers. **COOPERATIVE LEARNING**

**LEVEL 3:** Organize the class into the same groups as the Level 2 lesson. Have each group take turns acting out its clues for the class. To start, have the group share its clues as a whole. When the class has determined the group's identity, have members provide clues to help the class guess their individual roles. **COOPERATIVE LEARNING**

### ⭐ Global Relations

**Direct Democracy in Ancient Greece** The direct democracy of the town meeting has its roots in ancient Greece. In the 400s B.C., the city-state of Athens developed a true democracy. The citizens of Athens—free adult males—ruled themselves. In the Athenian Assembly, which met 40 times a year, citizens could speak their minds on any subject, not unlike citizens at town meetings today. However, a council of 500 Athenian men did set an agenda for each meeting in order to maintain order and keep meetings moving along.

**ACTIVITY:** Have students conduct research outside of class to find out more about the citizenry and government of ancient Greek city-states. Ask them to evaluate their findings by writing a position paper that addresses this question: *Should a "true democracy" serve all of the people under its rule?*

### Visual Record Answer

*Students might suggest that it would take too much time to hear everyone's opinion, reach consensus, and take votes.*

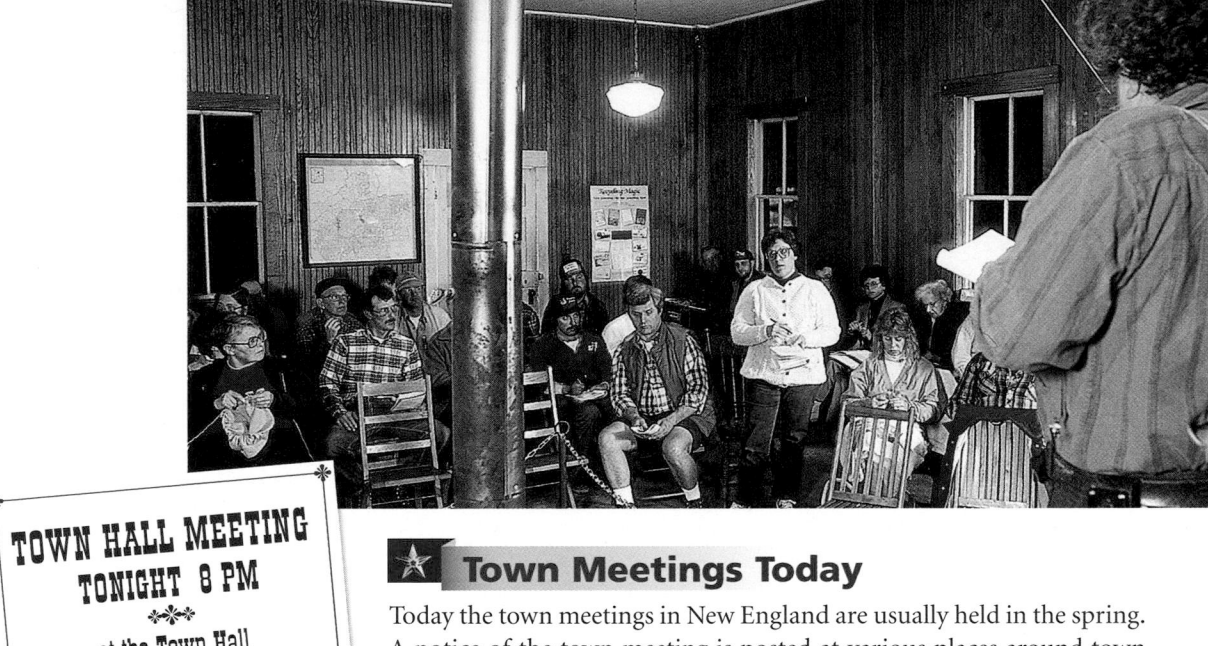

TOWN HALL MEETING
TONIGHT 8 PM
at the Town Hall
*Everyone invited!*

**Interpreting the Visual Record**

**Town Meeting** *Many smaller communities in New England still hold town meetings to deal with local affairs.* **How would a large town population make a meeting such as this one more difficult?**

### 💡 Did You KNOW?

In recent years a variation of the town meeting system known as the electronic town meeting or town hall has become increasingly popular. Officials appear on television before a live audience whose members can phone in or e-mail comments.

## ⭐ Town Meetings Today

Today the town meetings in New England are usually held in the spring. A notice of the town meeting is posted at various places around town before the meeting. This notice states the time of the meeting and lists the business to be discussed by the voters.

On meeting day the voters gather in the town hall. Town elections may be held before or after the meeting, depending on the town. The voters typically elect some three to five officials, called selectmen and selectwomen. These people manage the town's affairs during the period between regular town meetings. The voters also elect the other town officials who deal with specific town needs. These officials include a town clerk, members of the school board, a tax collector, a tax assessor, and fish and game wardens.

During the town meeting, voters discuss the town's business. They elect a moderator to preside over this part of the meeting. The selectmen and selectwomen report on their activities of the past year. The treasurer gives the financial report, explains the town's debts, and asks the citizens to vote to pay these debts.

Next, the officials discuss the town business for the coming year. The voters may be asked to give their opinions on such matters as street lighting or the building of a new school. After the discussion ends, a vote is taken on each item. Voting is usually by voice vote rather than by written ballot.

✔ **Reading Check Summarizing** How are town meetings organized today? Voters elect town officials and a moderator. After hearing reports from officials and discussing the next year's business, a vote is taken on each issue.

## ⭐ Representative Town Meetings

The town meeting form of government works well in areas that have small populations. Direct democracy—of which the traditional town meeting is an excellent example—is practical in such towns because it is

# TEACH OBJECTIVE 3

**LEVEL 1:** Explain to the class that villages and boroughs are created to deal with the needs that arise from a growing area. Call on volunteers to provide examples of villages or boroughs that they know. *(Students might suggest a village in their community or a borough of New York City such as Brooklyn or Queens.)* Ask a volunteer to read the paragraphs in this section that explain how a village or borough operate. *(Students will read that they have an elected 3- to 9-member council that makes laws and an elected president who carries them out. Other officials such as a clerk, constable, street commissioner, and engineer may be included.)*
**ENGLISH LANGUAGE LEARNERS**

**LEVEL 2:** Organize the class into two groups. Assign one group the role of a potential village and the other group the role of a potential borough. Have each group write up a list of reasons why its community needs to become a village or borough. *(Students' lists should mention increasing size and offer some needs arising from that growth.)* Then have each group create an organizational chart that demonstrates how its members intend to set up their government if approved. *(See the Level 1 lesson for organization.)* **COOPERATIVE LEARNING**

**HOMEWORK** Have students draw illustrations and include annotations that identify where town government began and describe how it has changed.

easy for all the voters to gather in one central location. For many other towns, however, increases in population have made it impractical to gather all the town's citizens at one meeting. In addition, growth has led to a need for more local services. As a result, larger towns have changed their system of government.

Some towns no longer hold town meetings. Instead, they have hired town managers to run the day-to-day affairs of the community. Other towns have turned to representative town meetings. In this type of town government, the voters elect representatives to attend the town meetings and to make decisions for them.

✔ **Reading Check Analyzing Information** Why did some towns stop holding town meetings, and what have they replaced them with? population growth; town managers or representative town meetings

## ★ Early Township Governments

In a number of the Middle Atlantic states (New York, Pennsylvania, and New Jersey), counties were divided into smaller units of local government called **townships.** These townships served many of the same purposes as the towns in New England. For example, they maintained local roads and rural schools and assisted poor residents.

As county governments grew in the Middle Atlantic states, township governments became less important. Eventually, these states developed a form of local government known as county-township government. In this mixed form of local government, county and township officials worked side by side.

Another type of township developed in the midwestern states that were carved out of the old Northwest Territory between the Ohio and Mississippi Rivers. In 1785 Congress developed a system of surveying, or measuring, this vast area. Congress divided the Northwest Territory into areas called congressional townships that were each 6 miles square.

Early congressional townships were not units of government. They were only divisions of land. As settlers from New England moved into this territory, they set up governments similar to town governments. These units of government were called civil townships. Sometimes a civil township occupied the same area as a congressional township, but usually it included more territory.

✔ **Reading Check Summarizing** How were congressional townships formed, and how were they different from civil townships? Congressional townships were formed out of a division of the Northwest Territory. They were divisions of land, not units of government.

## Swiss Cantons

Like the United States, the European country of Switzerland has a system in which power is divided among national, state, and local governments. The Swiss "states" are called cantons, and local governments are referred to as communes. Each canton has a great deal of political independence in terms of the policies and programs it establishes. Some cantons have high taxes and public welfare programs, while others have low taxes and rely on public charity. Swiss citizens who favor one set of policies over another can move about, creating a competition between cantons to support the best policies.

Swiss citizens also make frequent use of referendums and initiatives to introduce new legislation or show their views on national laws. This involvement of citizens in the functioning of local and national government is an important key to Switzerland's economic success and high standard of living. In both Switzerland and the United States, active participation by citizens is an essential part of making democracy work. **In what ways other than elections do Swiss citizens influence government policies?**

**GLOBAL CONNECTIONS ANSWER**
through referendums and initiatives

★ ★ ★ ★ ★ ★ ★ ★ ★ ★ ★
## *That's Interesting!*
★ ★ ★ ★ ★ ★ ★ ★ ★ ★ ★

In the 1980s, presidential candidates began to hold town meetings as part of their campaigns. These meetings took place in midsized towns throughout the country. The candidates met with a group of citizens, gave a short speech, and answered questions. Unlike early town meetings, however, these meetings were simply held to discuss issues, not to resolve them with a direct vote. Another difference was that the meetings were sometimes televised.

**LEVEL 3:** In the same groups as the Level 2 lesson, have students create their respective governments. Members should assign each other different roles, depending upon the type of government their group represents. Have each member refer to the textbook to write a brief description of his or her job responsibilities. Then have the groups create a special "Government Handbook" that explains why their governments were created and how they operate.

**COOPERATIVE LEARNING**

## TEACHER TO TEACHER

Rich Rosenow of Missouri recommends the following activity:

## CLOSE

Using the section objectives, Define terms, and additional section information, create a review game for the class. Answers are to be phrased in the form of a question. For example, *Clue: It began in the New England colonies. Student answer: Where did town government begin?* Organize the students into groups of three. Then, providing the three students from each group with a bell, begin the game. Each group should have an opportunity to play by answering at least one question.

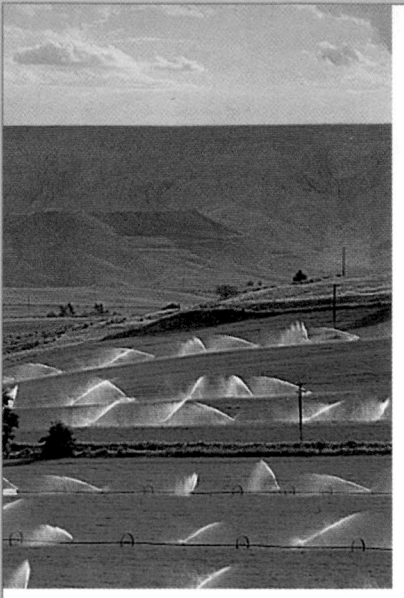

**Interpreting the Visual Record**

**Special Districts** *Many special districts are set up to provide irrigation for farming, such as this district in Idaho.* **How might an irrigation district benefit people who do not live in that district?**

## ★ Township Government Today

Generally, township government has decreased in importance. In many areas municipal and county governments now provide the services once provided by townships. Found today in 20 states—mostly states in the Midwest and Northeast—townships mainly serve rural areas.

Township governments vary from state to state. Usually the township is headed by a chairperson, or township supervisor. This official is elected by the voters. The voters also elect a township board of commissioners, or board of trustees, which makes the laws or regulations for the township. **Constables** enforce the laws, and a justice of the peace tries minor cases. Most townships also elect an assessor, a tax collector, a treasurer, and members of the school board.

✔ **Reading Check** Finding the Main Idea Describe how townships are organized. They generally have an elected board to make laws, a constable to enforce them, and other officials as needed, such as an assessor and a clerk.

## ★ Special Districts

People living in a certain area may have a special need. In such cases these people may go directly to the state legislature and ask for a charter to set up a **special district** addressing that need.

For example, farmers in part of a county may wish to have an irrigation system installed to water their crops. To pay for the pipes, ditches, and other equipment to supply this need, the state legislature may create an irrigation district. This special district's only purpose would be to supply water to residents of the district. The residents' land would be taxed at a rate sufficient to pay the costs. All other local government services would remain in the hands of the county. This allows the farmers in the special district to meet their needs without placing a tax burden on the other residents of the county.

Special districts are the most numerous of the country's local governments. Special districts have been formed to meet many different needs. These needs include fire protection, libraries, parks and recreation centers, public transportation, and sewage disposal. The state legislature usually sets up a commission to handle the details of establishing and operating the special district. The commission members may be elected or appointed.

School districts are considered special districts by some researchers. These districts are created by states to provide funds for local schools. There are nearly 15,000 school districts in the United States. Each district has its own governing body called a board of education. An executive, usually called a superintendent of schools, manages the schools' day-to-day operations.

✔ **Reading Check** Making Generalizations and Predictions What might happen if a local government did not make use of special districts? Students may deduce that the needs of the people would not be met as efficiently and that the local government would be overburdened by problems.

# REVIEW AND ASSESS

Have students complete the **Section 2 Review** on page 233. Then have students complete **Daily Quiz 9.2**. As **Alternative Assessment**, you may want to use the organizational chart or the government handbook activity in this section's lessons.

## RETEACH

Have students complete **Main Idea Activity for English Language Learners and Special-Needs Students 9.2**. Then organize the class into three teams and assign each team one topic covered in this section. *(Topics include towns, townships, and villages.)* Then have each team list at least five facts that could help other students understand its topic. Create a master list of all the facts on the chalkboard.
**ENGLISH LANGUAGE LEARNERS , COOPERATIVE LEARNING**

## EXTEND

Have students find two articles in your local newspaper about a special district in the community. *(Remind the class that your school is part of a special district called a school district.)* Then ask students to write a summary of their two articles. When students have completed their articles, compile them in a booklet titled Special Districts in Our State. Call on volunteers to present sample reports to the class. **BLOCK SCHEDULING**

## ★ Village and Borough Governments

When rural communities grow to a population of 200 to 300, their residents often encounter problems that require them to work together. The residents may then decide to organize their community as a village or borough and to create their own local government.

A request to establish a village or borough form of government must be sent to the state legislature. If the legislature approves, it permits the village or borough to establish itself as a self-governing municipality. As a municipality, the village or borough can collect taxes, set up fire and police departments, and provide other services.

The village or borough is often governed by a small council, or board of trustees. The voters also elect an executive or president of the board of trustees to carry out the laws. This person is sometimes called the mayor of the village.

In small boroughs or villages, most of the local officials serve on a part-time basis. There is usually not enough local government business to occupy them full-time. However, there may be a full-time clerk, constable, street commissioner, and engineer.

If the population of a village or borough becomes large enough, the people may ask the state legislature to grant the community a city charter. The number of people needed to qualify as a city varies from state to state. Many states require a population of several thousand before a city charter is granted.

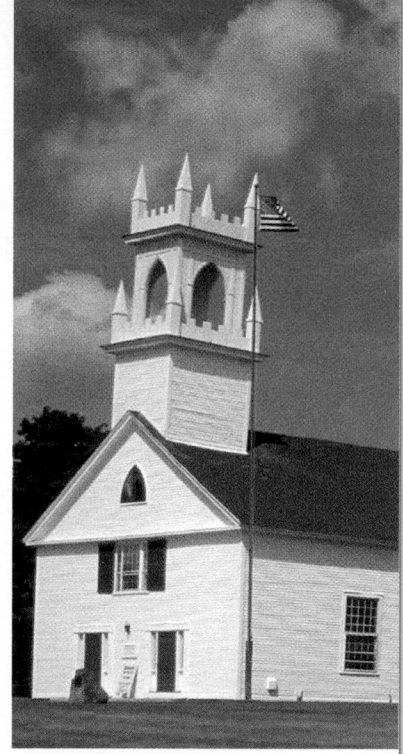

*Meeting houses likes this one in Washington, New Hampshire, provide village officials and community members with places to meet and make decisions.*

✔ **Reading Check Analyzing Information** Why do you think an increase in population requires the formation of a government? As population grows, the need for community services and cooperation increases. Villages and boroughs are formed to serve these needs.

---

## SECTION 2 Review

go.hrw.com **Homework Practice Online**
keyword: SZ3 HP9

1. **Define** and explain:
   • town
   • village
   • town meeting
   • townships
   • constables
   • special district

2. **Summarizing** Copy the graphic organizer below. Use it to explain why townships and special districts develop, and how each is organized.

| Townships | Special Districts |
|---|---|
| Why: | Why: |
| | |
| Organization: | Organization: |

3. **Finding the Main Idea**
   a. Where did the town form of local government begin, and how has it changed over time?
   b. When do rural areas become villages or boroughs, and how do these systems of local government function?

4. **Writing and Critical Thinking**
   **Evaluating** As you have learned, the New England town meeting is a form of local government that invites the participation of all the townspeople. Investigate your community's form of government and evaluate how well you think the town meeting concept would work in your community. Explain your answer.
   **Consider:**
   • the size and needs of your community
   • the benefits and problems of your community's current form of government

---

## Section 2 Review ANSWERS

**1. Define**
• town, p. 228
• village, p. 228
• town meeting, p. 229
• townships, p. 231
• constables, p. 232
• special district, p. 232

**2.** townships: why—to manage the everyday needs of local citizens; organization—an elected chair-person, a board of commissioners, constables, an assessor, treasurer, tax collector, and school board members; special districts: why—to handle special needs; organization—organization varies depending on the district's function

**3. a.** began in the New England colonies; citizens used to be able to vote on issues directly, but now they elect representatives to vote on issues for them

**b.** when population increases to about 200 to 300 people and more organization is needed to address community needs; an elected council makes laws, an elected president carries them out, and other officials, such as a clerk, constable, street commissioner, and engineer may be included

**4.** Students' evaluations should demonstrate an understanding of local government's organization as related to the needs of the community.

# SECTION 3

## OBJECTIVES

*After completing Section 3, students should be able to*

1 **Define the term *city* and identify the services city governments provide for their residents.**

2 **Examine how city governments are established.**

3 **Identify the different types of city governments and their functions.**

## SECTION 3 RESOURCES

### REPRODUCIBLE

▶ Guided Reading Strategies 9.3
▶ Transparency 11: Plans of City Government
▶ Graphic Organizer Activity: How Governments Work Together

### TECHNOLOGY

▶ One-Stop Planner, Lesson 9.3
▶ Holt Researcher CD–ROM
▶ Homework Practice Online
▶ HRW Go site

### REINFORCEMENT, REVIEW, AND ASSESSMENT

▶ Section 3 Review, p. 239
▶ Daily Quiz 9.3
▶ Main Idea Activity 9.3
▶ English Audio Summary 9.3
▶ Spanish Audio Summary 9.3

## 📀 LET'S GET STARTED!

Write the following scenario on the chalkboard: *Imagine that our community doubled in size overnight. What types of issues might result?* As students enter the classroom, ask them to write down several issues. *(Students might suggest overcrowding in schools, greater demand on social services, the need for more public transportation, and so on.)* Explain to students that cities are larger than towns and as such usually operate within a more complicated government framework. Tell students that in Section 3 they will learn about how city governments are organized to serve their residents' needs.

## SECTION 3

# City Government

### Read to Discover

1. What is a city, and what services do city governments provide for their residents?
2. How are city governments established?
3. What are the different types of city governments and their functions?

### Define

- city
- home rule
- city council
- mayor
- wards
- council members at large
- commission

### WHY CIVICS MATTERS

The local media often covers city council meetings and other local government activities. Use **CNNfyi.com** or other **current events** sources to investigate how the media in your community reports on the work of your local government officials. Record your findings in your journal.

## *Reading Focus*

A **city** is usually larger than other forms of local government, such as towns or villages. Some cities, such as New York, Los Angeles, and Chicago, have millions of residents. Often the city's large population is crowded into a relatively small area, creating many challenges. The city government must manage a variety of problems dealing with education, health, and safety. Transportation systems, sanitation, water supply, fire and police protection—all these and hundreds of other services—are the daily business of city governments.

*Some modern cities have much higher populations than the rest of the state in which they are located.*

### ★ Organization

City governments are established by and receive charters from state legislatures. Increasingly, however, states have been granting to cities an authority referred to as **home rule.** Under home rule, a city can write and amend its own municipal charter. Usually, the charter is written by a commission and must be approved by the voters. In addition, it cannot conflict with the state constitution or with the U.S. Constitution.

**LEVEL 1:** Call on a volunteer to define the term *city*. Then ask each student to quickly write on a slip of paper the types of services that city governments provide for their residents. *(Students should list services that deal with citizens' health, education, and safety.)* Then collect all of the responses and write the answers on the chalkboard. Remind students that the city provides these services as part of its responsibility to its citizens. **ENGLISH LANGUAGE LEARNERS**

**LEVELS 2 AND 3:** Have pairs of students work together to make a collage called City. Ask them to define the term at the top of their collages and to find pictures that illustrate the services city governments provide for their residents. Tell students to categorize the pictures according to service type. Suggest that students look through the textbook for illustration ideas. Have students write a caption for each picture. Students should stretch their imaginations to think of any possible way that a picture might connect to services provided by local government. **COOPERATIVE LEARNING**

---

Home rule gives cities the power to manage their own affairs and to deal with their own local problems. Many people believe that home rule strengthens local government. Some states provide cities with a more limited degree of independence. For example, all Virginian cities are independent of the counties in which they are located. This helps prevent duplication of offices and services.

Depending on its charter, a city government may take one of three forms: a mayor-council government, a commission government, or a council-manager government.

✔ **Reading Check** **Identifying Cause and Effect** What services do city governments provide, and how does this make running a city difficult?
City governments must provide hundreds of services, involving education, health, and fire and police protection. Large populations, small areas, and so many services make administration difficult.

## ⭐ Mayor-Council Government

The oldest and most common form of city government is the mayor-council system. In this kind of government, the lawmaking body is called the **city council.** The chief executive of the city government is the **mayor,** who sees that ordinances, or city laws, are enforced. The mayor and members of the city council are elected by the voters of the city, usually to terms of either two or four years in length.

Under the mayor-council form of government, the city is divided into several districts called **wards.** The people who live in each ward elect one person to represent them in the city council. In some cities, several **council members at large** are elected by all the voters in the city. Almost all city councils are unicameral. That is, they consist of only one legislative body.

### Interpreting the Visual Record

**City Council Meetings** *City council meetings give voters the opportunity to tell council members their viewpoints on many issues.* **How do these meetings illustrate democracy in action?**

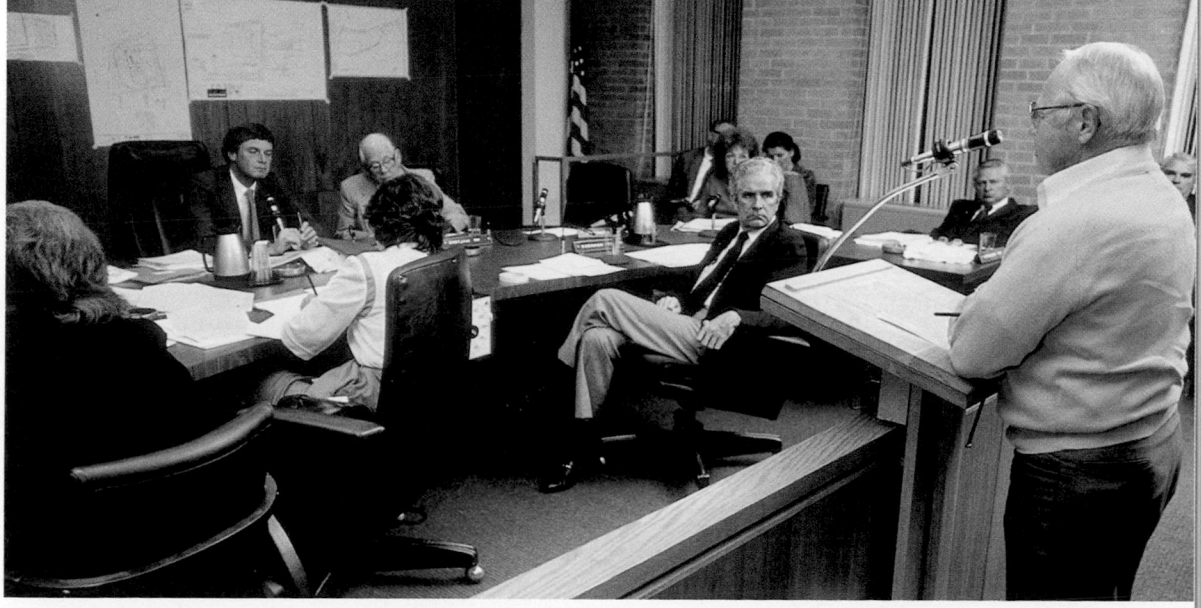

**Defining City** The point at which a town becomes a city is a matter of debate. Some people use population as a measure. The U.S. Bureau of the Census defines the term *urban* as "all territory, population, and housing units in urbanized areas and in places of 2,500 or more persons outside urbanized areas." The United Nations classifies a big city as having 500,000 or more inhabitants; a city as having 100,000 or more; an urban locality as having 20,000 or more; and a rural locality as having fewer than 20,000. Other people prefer more qualitative measures. Some people might define a city as a place that is large, culturally varied, and socially diverse.

### CRITICAL THINKING

How would you describe the community in which you live?

**ANSWER:** Students' responses will vary.

### Visual Record Answer

*Students might suggest that it shows government and the public interacting.*

**ALL LEVELS:** Copy the following graphic organizer onto the chalkboard, omitting the italicized answers. Have students complete the organizer to explain how city governments are established.

**ENGLISH LANGUAGE LEARNERS**

**LEVEL 3:** Provide students with the names of two different types of cities in your state: one that received its charter from the state government and another that wrote its own charter under home rule. Then have students create a triptych display that explains the steps followed in each process and the story behind the establishment of each city's government. Display students' projects in the classroom.

```
              How City Governments Are Established

      ┌──────────────────────┐      ┌──────────────────────────┐
      │  charter granted by  │      │  the state gives the city │
      │  state government    │      │  permission to write its own │
      └──────────────────────┘      │  charter under home rule  │
                                     └──────────────────────────┘
```

## The Democratic Process

**Party Politics** In the mid-1800s many mayors and council members in large U.S. cities owed their positions to powerful party bosses, such as the notorious William Marcy Tweed (1823–1878), who ruled New York's Democratic party. "Boss Tweed" was smug about his power. He reportedly once said, "You may elect whichever candidates you please to office, if you allow me to select the candidates." He scoffed at his critics, saying, "As long as I count the votes, what are you going to do about it?" Tweed and his associates cheated New York City out of millions of dollars. Justice finally caught up with the boss of Tammany Hall, however. Tweed, who had called himself a statesman, died in prison.

**ACTIVITY:** Ask students to conduct research on corruption in city politics during the Gilded Age. Have students incorporate their research into the format of their choice and then ask them to present their findings to the class.

**CHART ANSWER**
mayor-council plan and commission plan

## Major Types of City Government

**Mayor-Council Plan of City Government**

**Commission Plan of City Government**

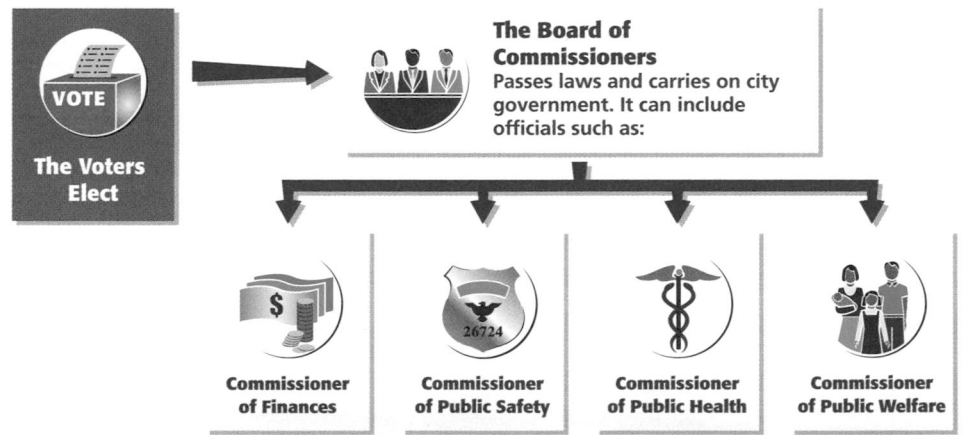

**Council-Manager Plan of City Government**

**Interpreting Charts** *Most cities use one of the plans outlined here to run their affairs.* **Which plans feature appointed heads of city departments?**

**LEVEL 1:** Make a three-column chart on the chalkboard with *Government Type, Advantages,* and *Disadvantages* heading the top three columns. Call on students to identify the different types of city governments and their functions. *(Students should suggest the following: mayor-council/weak mayor—the council holds more power than the mayor, often resulting in conflict; mayor-council/strong mayor—the mayor has more power than the council; commission—three to nine elected officials make and carry out the city's laws; council-manager—an elected council appoints a manager, helping the executive remain impartial.)* Make a copy of the chart for students to use as a study guide. **ENGLISH LANGUAGE LEARNERS**

**LEVELS 2 AND 3:** Organize the class into four groups. Assign each group the role of one of the types of city governments. *(Group assignments will include a mayor-council/weak mayor, mayor-council/strong mayor, commission, and council-manager.)* Then have each group prepare for a panel discussion regarding the most effective type of city government. When students have become well versed in the advantages and disadvantages of their assigned government type, facilitate the discussion between volunteers from each group. *(See the Level 1 lesson for advantages and disadvantages.)* **COOPERATIVE LEARNING**

**Interpreting the Visual Record**

**Local Cooperation** *New York governor George Pataki and New York City mayor Rudolph Giuliani spoke to the public after the attacks on the World Trade Center in September 2001.* **Why was it important for these two officials to work together?**

**internet** connect

**TOPIC:** The Galveston Hurricane
**GO TO:** go.hrw.com
**KEYWORD:** SZ3 AC9

Have students access the Internet through the HRW Go site to conduct research on how the Galveston hurricane of 1900 affected the political, economic, and social development of Texas. Then have students assume the point of view of someone writing an article on the five-year anniversary of the storm and ask them to create a pamphlet that shows the various ways in which the hurricane changed Galveston's people, infrastructure, and government.

City voters also elect other officials, including a treasurer, judges of the municipal courts, tax assessors, and a city attorney, or solicitor. Other officials may be elected or appointed. These include the heads of departments for fire fighting, police, health and welfare, housing, parks and playgrounds, traffic, water, and so on.

✔ **Reading Check Summarizing** How is a mayor-council government organized? The city council is the lawmaking body, and the chief executive of the city government is the mayor, who enforces laws.

**Weak-Mayor Plan** During the country's early years, Americans still remembered British governors who had abused their powers. For this reason some cities developed the weak-mayor plan to limit the power of city officials. Under this plan of city government, the city council holds more power than the mayor. For example, the council appoints the heads of city departments who report directly to the city council. In addition, the mayor must obtain the consent of the council before spending money or taking other actions. The weak-mayor plan often results in conflicts between the mayor and the council.

**Strong-Mayor Plan** Recently, most city governments using the mayor-council system have tried to become more efficient by following the strong-mayor plan. Under the strong-mayor plan, the mayor has chief responsibility for running the city's government. The mayor appoints most of the city officials and can dismiss them if they do not do a good job. The mayor can veto bills passed by the council and must draw up the city budget. When the council has approved the budget, the mayor must ensure that the city's money is spent properly.

✔ **Reading Check Contrasting** What is the difference between a weak-mayor and a strong-mayor plan? In the weak-mayor plan the council holds more power. In the strong-mayor plan the mayor is chiefly responsible for managing the city's business.

**Visual Record Answer**

*Students might say that cooperation was important because government officials needed to respond to the attacks as quickly as possible.*

**LEVEL 3:** Have students think of a crisis that a city might encounter. *(Students' selections might include flooding, fire, riots, or earthquakes.)* Then have students refer to the chart created in the Level 1 lesson and have them write a "Crisis Plan" depicting how each form of city government might deal with the situation. Call on volunteers to share their approaches and have the class discuss the effectiveness of each type of government in handling such a situation. *(See the Level 1 lesson for government types and functions.)*

 **HOMEWORK** Have students write a paragraph explaining which form of city government they think is the most effective and why. Encourage students to support their choice with information provided during the panel discussion.

## CLOSE

Have each student write several sentences relating each picture and graphic in this section to an organization and function of city government. Call on volunteers to share their sentences with the class.

## ⭐ Global Perspectives

**Bürgermeisters** Germany uses a local system of government similar to the U.S. council-manager plan. The mayor of a German town or city is called the Bürgermeister, or "town master." Bürgermeisters are elected by the voters or by a council, and their power varies from place to place. They are usually skilled public administrators, like city managers in the United States. Besides their local government duties, bürgermeisters also function as state government officials.

**ACTIVITY:** Ask students to conduct research on Germany's bürgermeisters and U.S. city managers. Ask them to determine the similarities and differences between the systems. Have students write an essay that compares and contrasts the systems. Then ask them to present their findings to the class.

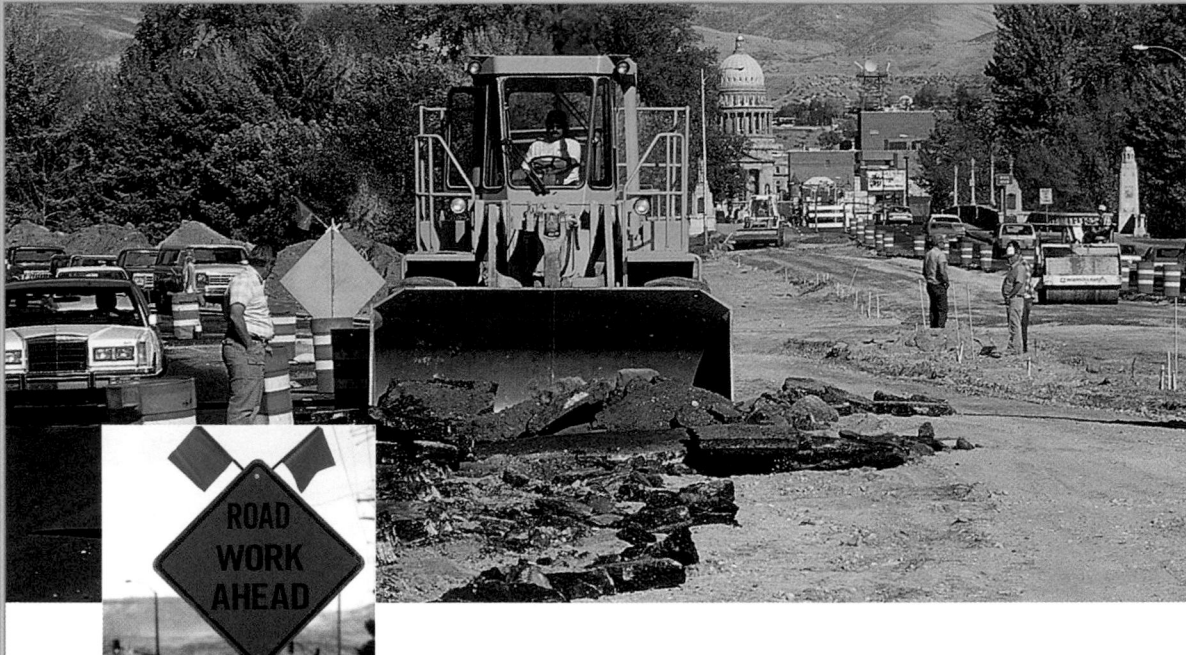

*Building and maintaining local roads is a major responsibility and expense faced by city governments.*

★★★★★★★★★★★★
### That's Interesting!
★★★★★★★★★★★★

**The Galveston Hurricane**
There are a lot of ways that new governments can be created. But government created by a hurricane? That's unusual! In 1900 a hurricane struck Galveston, Texas. Thousands died and much of the city was destroyed. The city's mayor and council were unable to handle the disaster. As a result, leading citizens in Galveston set up a new form of city government. It was called the commission plan. Although Galveston has since switched to a council-manager government plan, it inspired several hundred cities to adopt commission plans in the early 1900s.

## ⭐ Commission Government

The **commission** form of government was introduced in Galveston, Texas, around 1900. Several hundred other cities soon adopted this plan of government. Under the commission plan, a city is governed by a commission, usually consisting of three to nine elected officials. The commission acts as the city's lawmaking and executive body. The commission passes all city ordinances and each commissioner heads a department of city government.

Usually one commissioner heads the department of public safety, which includes the police and firefighters. Another commissioner oversees public works. This official sees that the city has an adequate supply of clean water and that the streets are kept in good repair. A third commissioner oversees the city's finances, including tax collections. Another runs the public welfare department, which helps the city's disadvantaged citizens. The health department is managed by a commissioner who supervises hospitals, clinics, and health inspectors.

The commissioners meet as a group to make the city's laws. Each commissioner carries out the laws that apply to his or her own department. Either the citizens or the commissioners choose one of the commissioners to be mayor and preside over meetings of the commission.

The commission form of city government has certain disadvantages. Sometimes voters find it difficult to elect officials who know how to run a department of the city's government. In addition, commissioners may disagree about who should manage activities that fall under the jurisdiction of different departments.

✔ **Reading Check** Summarizing How is the commission plan of city government structured? A commission of elected officials, each heading a department of city government, acts as the city's lawmaking and executive body.

## REVIEW AND ASSESS

Have students complete the **Section 3 Review** on page 239. Then have them complete **Daily Quiz 9.3**. As **Alternative Assessment**, you may want to use the collage or panel discussion activities in this section's lessons.

## RETEACH

Have students complete **Main Idea Activity for English Language Learners and Special-Needs Students 9.3**. Then organize students into three groups and have each group make a crossword puzzle using the Define terms from this lesson. Then have groups try to complete each others' puzzles.

**ENGLISH LANGUAGE LEARNERS , COOPERATIVE LEARNING**

## EXTEND

Have students use the library or other resources to conduct research on the way your city is governed and the problems and issues its officials face today. Then invite a government official from your area to discuss city government with your class. Have students refer to their findings to ask questions about the city's approach to various issues. Then have each student write a newspaper article about the interview with the official.

**BLOCK SCHEDULING**

## ⭐ Council-Manager Government

In 1912 the citizens of Sumter, South Carolina, were the first to set up a council-manager plan of government. Today a growing number of cities use this plan of government. Under this system, a city is run much like a big business firm, employing specially trained professionals to handle city affairs.

Under the council-manager plan, voters elect a city council to act as the city's lawmaking body. The council then appoints a city manager. The city manager, as the city's chief executive, appoints the heads of the city departments. These officials report directly to the city manager, who may also remove them from office.

City managers are appointed, not elected, so that they will not take part in party politics or face any political pressure. They are given the freedom to run city governments efficiently and economically. If a city manager does not do a good job, the council may dismiss him or her and appoint a new manager.

The council-manager plan of government has certain disadvantages. Some smaller cities cannot afford the salary required to hire a good manager. In addition, some critics argue that cities are better governed when the officials who run their city's government are directly accountable to the voters who elect them.

✔ **Reading Check Analyzing Information** What are the benefits and drawbacks of a council-manager government? benefits—managers do not participate in party politics, efficient and economic management; drawbacks— small cities unable to afford good managers

**Holt Researcher**

**go.hrw.com**
KEYWORD: Holt Researcher
Freefind: City Manager
Look up the entry on the city manager career on the Holt Researcher. Use the information provided to answer the following question: What responsibilities does a typical city manager have, and what are the standard educational requirements for the job?

## SECTION 3 Review

**Homework Practice Online**
keyword: SZ3 HP9

1. **Define** and explain:
   • city
   • home rule
   • city council
   • mayor
   • wards
   • council members at large
   • commission

2. **Comparing and Contrasting** Copy the chart below. Use it to explain the advantages and disadvantages of each type of city government.

| Type of City Government | Advantages | Disadvantages |
|---|---|---|
| Mayor-Council (weak-mayor plan) | | |
| Mayor-Council (strong-mayor plan) | | |
| Commission | | |
| Council-Manager | | |

3. **Finding the Main Idea**
   a. What is a city, and how do cities provide for their residents?
   b. What is the process for establishing city governments?

4. **Writing and Critical Thinking**
   **Comparing** Imagine that you are part of a committee establishing a new city. Write a short speech explaining which of the three plans you believe is the most effective form of city government and why.

   **Consider:**
   • how each form of government works
   • the strengths and weaknesses of each plan
   • the varying needs of people and cities

## Section 3 Review
### ANSWERS

**1. Define**
• city, p. 234
• home rule, p. 234
• city council, p. 235
• mayor, p. 235
• wards, p. 235
• council members at large, p. 235
• commission, p. 238

**2.** mayor-council/weak mayor— no danger of dictatorial mayor; often results in conflict; mayor-council/strong mayor—reduced conflict; too much power may be given to the mayor; commission— specialists head the departments; interested specialists are hard to find; council-manager—reduction in party politics; small cities unable to pay manager well

**3. a.** A city is the largest type of municipality. City governments provide services that deal with their citizens' health, education, and safety.

**b.** State governments may grant cities a charter or cities may write their own charters under home rule.

**4.** Students' speeches will vary but should clearly state their position and support it logically.

## TEACH

**LEVEL 1:** Call on volunteers to explain the difference between a news article and an editorial. *(Students should note that a news article is impartial, while an editorial states a point of view.)* Tell students that the same newspaper may carry a news story and an editorial about an important event. Ask them to write a few sentences explaining why this might be a useful way to inform the public of issues. *(Students might write that reading both facts and opinions enables the public to develop a fuller picture of the event.)* Call on volunteers to share their paragraphs with the class. **ENGLISH LANGUAGE LEARNERS**

## EXTEND

Pair students and provide each pair with a copy of a recent newspaper from your state or community. Ask students to read the paper and to locate an article and an editorial that discuss the same issue. Have students find the answers to the *5W-How?* questions in each piece. Suggest that they discuss their observations with each other after completing this task. *(Students may observe that the article addresses the questions while the editorial may not.)* Then have pairs present their findings to the class in a three-minute oral presentation. **BLOCK SCHEDULING**

## SKILLS ANSWERS

1. The story takes place locally.

2. what happened, where, and when; no

3. Students should note that the body says that the cleanup has been a tradition since 1976. The first cleanup was so successful that officials have decided to make it an annual tradition.

# Civics Skills
## WORKSHOP

### Reading Newspaper Articles

It is important for all citizens to stay informed about what is happening in their country and around the world. One source of information concerning current events is the newspaper. Generally, newspaper articles are written according to a standard format. Learning to understand that format is one key to becoming an informed citizen.

### How to Read Newspaper Articles

1. **Read the headline.** A headline is the short statement printed in large bold type above the article. It contains key words designed to capture your attention and to present the main topic of the article.

2. **Notice the dateline and the byline.** The dateline and the byline are located just below the headline. If the event discussed in the news story occurs outside of the area in which you live, the article will probably contain a dateline telling you where and when the article was written. The byline tells you who wrote the article—naming either a reporter or a news service. Two of the largest news services are Associated Press (AP) and Reuters.

3. **Read the lead.** The lead, or first sentence, of a news article is designed to tell you who did what, where, when, and how.

4. **Read the body.** The paragraphs following the lead make up the body of the newspaper article. The body usually contains the "why" of the story, including quotations and details.

5. **Distinguish between news and editorials.** What you should *not* find in a news article is the writer's opinion or point of view. Writers present their opinions in editorials, found on the editorial pages of the newspaper. Citizens who disagree with editorials or who want to express their own opinions may write letters to the editor.

### Applying the Skill

Read the article below. Then answer the following questions.

1. What does the byline tell you?

2. What questions are answered by the facts given in the lead? Does the article present an opinion?

3. What details does the body of the article provide?

## Lakeville Cleans Up

*by Maria López*

LAKEVILLE, Mich.—The city's annual July Fourth cleanup was a great success, city officials said Tuesday.

"It was the most successful celebration we've ever seen," said Mayor Tamara Patterson.

In what has become a tradition, Lakeville residents once again did more than watch parades on Independence Day. Residents also swept sidewalks, planted flowers, and picked up litter.

The tradition began in 1976 when Lakeville residents decided to do something different for the nation's 200th birthday, Patterson said. Response to a citywide cleanup was so enthusiastic, the city council decided to make it a regular event, she said.

# SECTION 4

## OBJECTIVES

*After completing Section 4, students should be able to*

1 **Analyze why there is a division of powers among different levels of government.**

2 **Explain why the federal government became involved in the building of roads.**

3 **Identify the government functions that require the cooperation of different levels of government.**

## 🔊 LET'S GET STARTED!

Write the word *cooperation* on the chalkboard. As students enter the classroom, ask them to write down the meaning of the word. *(Students might suggest that it means "sharing resources and responsibilities to accomplish a common goal.")* Explain to students that although different levels of government have different powers, they must cooperate to serve the needs of the community. Tell students that in Section 4 they will learn about the division of powers and cooperation among the different levels of government.

---

# SECTION 4

# How Governments Work Together

### Read to Discover

1. Why is there a division of powers among different levels of government?
2. Why did the federal government become involved in the building of roads?
3. What government functions require the cooperation of different levels of government?

### Define

• grants-in-aid
• block grants

### WHY CIVICS MATTERS

Different levels of government work together to provide services, such as education, to U.S. residents. Use **CNNfyi.com** or other **current events** sources to investigate current educational issues and identify which level of government is managing them. Record your findings in your journal.

### SECTION 4 RESOURCES

**REPRODUCIBLE**
▸ Guided Reading Strategies 9.4
▸ Transparency 12: Sources of Government Laws and Powers
▸ Community Service and Participation Handbook: Adopt-a-Highway

**TECHNOLOGY**
▸ One-Stop Planner, Lesson 9.4
▸ CNN Presents: American Government
▸ Homework Practice Online

**REINFORCEMENT, REVIEW, AND ASSESSMENT**
▸ Section 4 Review, p. 245
▸ Daily Quiz 9.4
▸ Main Idea Activity 9.4
▸ English Audio Summary 9.4
▸ Spanish Audio Summary 9.4

## *Reading Focus*

You live under three levels of government—local, state, and federal. If these levels did not cooperate, life would become difficult and confusing. City governments could pass city laws that would conflict with state laws. State governments might ignore federal laws. Citizens would not know which set of laws to obey.

### ★ Division of Powers

Fortunately, under the U.S. federal system of government, the powers of each level of government are clearly defined and understood. The U.S. Constitution is the supreme law of the land. All levels of government must obey it. State constitutions set up rules that govern the people of each state. These state constitutions must not, of course, take from the people any of the rights guaranteed in the U.S. Constitution.

Local units of government, as you have read, have their powers defined for them in charters by the state legislatures. Therefore, each level of government has its own work to do. Each level has the powers needed to do its job.

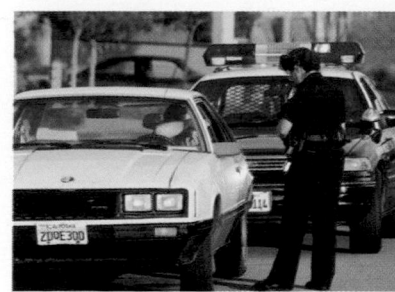

*Local police officers must enforce state and local laws.*

✔ **Reading Check Making Generalizations and Predictions** What might happen if there were no division of power among different levels of government? Students might say that life would become difficult and confusing because each level might create laws and provide services that overlap or conflict with another.

# TEACH OBJECTIVE 1

**LEVEL 1:** Draw a chart on the chalkboard that illustrates the division of powers among different levels of government. The chart should have the following column headings: *Federal, State,* and *Local.* Call on volunteers to suggest the powers specific to each level of government and to add the answers under the appropriate column heading. Then lead a class discussion about why this division of powers is necessary. *(Students should note that it ensures that there are no conflicts among laws passed by different levels of government.)* **ENGLISH LANGUAGE LEARNERS**

**LEVEL 3:** Remind students of the reason that there is a division of powers among different levels of government. *(The division of powers is to ensure that there are no conflicts about laws passed by different levels of government.)* Then have students draw political cartoons that demonstrate what might happen if the division of powers did not exist. *(Students might illustrate state government and local government clashing over taxes or control of local affairs.)* Display students' cartoons around the classroom.

**Interpreting the Visual Record**

**The National Road** *The most important of the early federal roads was the National Road, also known as the Cumberland Road. It started at Cumberland, Maryland, and continued as far west as Wheeling, West Virginia. The road was later extended on both ends.* **Why do you think people built towns and shops along this road as seen in the painting?**

## ★ Why Governments Work Together

Many issues call for cooperation among local, state, and federal governments. Consider, for example, the way the country's modern highway system was built.

In colonial days the building of a road was a local project. If the people of a town wanted a road, they had to build it themselves. As settlements spread westward, each county assumed the responsibility of building connecting roads. These early roads were often twisting and rutted, dusty in dry weather, and muddy after rain. However, they were cheap to build and repair. Local governments could easily plan and pay for such roads.

As the United States grew, large roads—and later, highways—were needed to connect the East with the growing West. In response, Congress voted to have the federal government build the main roads that extended westward.

Still, for a long time local governments and private companies built most of the roads in the United States. The people who used these roads funded their construction by paying tolls, or fees. However, when first bicycles and then automobiles became more popular, people began to demand dependable well-maintained highways.

In the late 1800s New Jersey became the first state to use state funds to help its counties improve their local roads. Massachusetts went a step further in 1893 when it established a state highway commission to build a statewide highway system. Other states soon established state highway departments to build main roads. Today most well-traveled roads are built and maintained by the states. Each year state governments spend billions of dollars to build and improve roads.

The federal government pays a large part of the cost of new state highways. It does so because good roads contribute to the safety and well-being of all U.S. citizens. Good roads make it easier for people and products to move across the country.

# TEACH OBJECTIVE 2

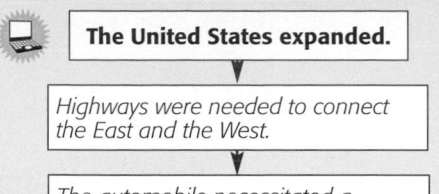

**ALL LEVELS:** Copy the following graphic organizer onto the chalkboard, omitting the italicized answers. Have students complete the organizer to explain why the federal government became involved in the building of roads. **ENGLISH LANGUAGE LEARNERS**

> The United States expanded.
>
> ↓
>
> *Highways were needed to connect the East and the West.*
>
> ↓
>
> *The automobile necessitated a complex system of national highways.* →

> **The federal government became involved in the planning, building, and maintenance of the highway system to facilitate the movement of people and goods.**

**LEVELS 2 AND 3:** Organize the class into groups. Have each group write and illustrate a children's book that explains why the federal government became involved in the building of roads. *(See the All Levels lesson for explanation.)* Encourage students to make their stories informative and entertaining. Students should begin their tales with "Once upon a time . . ." Arrange for each group to share its book with a group of younger students. **COOPERATIVE LEARNING**

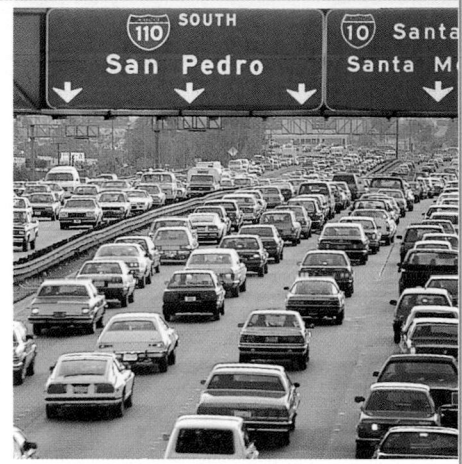

The interstate highway system, planned by the federal government, now connects all parts of the country. This system is a joint project of the federal and state governments. In general, the state governments plan the routes and supervise the construction of the roads. The federal government pays 90 percent of the cost of building and maintaining most of the country's interstate highways. This money comes from a highway trust fund to which motorists contribute through taxes they pay on gasoline and tires. The federal government also assists state and local governments in building and maintaining other highways, bridges, and tunnels.

✔ **Reading Check** **Analyzing Information** How is the road system an example of cooperation between state and federal government? *federal government contributes to maintenance and construction of roads and sets requirements; state governments plan the routes and supervise construction*

## ⭐ Cooperation in Education

Public education is one of the most important areas in which governments cooperate to serve the public. State governments grant funds to communities to help them operate their schools. State boards of education provide services for local school districts and see that they obey state laws. However, actual control of the schools is left to local boards of education. These local boards are more familiar with the needs of the students in their schools.

The federal government cooperates with local governments by contributing special funds for schools. Schools with many students from low-income families receive special federal aid to enrich educational programs. The federal government also provides school lunch programs for students from low-income families. In addition, the federal government supports research in education.

✔ **Reading Check** **Drawing Inferences and Conclusions** Why do you think it is necessary for the federal government to help state and local governments with education? *Students might suggest that federal involvement results in more funds and a consistent educational system throughout the country.*

## ⭐ Other Forms of Cooperation

Local, state, and federal governments work together to perform many other activities. For example, local and state police cooperate with the Federal Bureau of Investigation (FBI) to capture suspects. Most states have crime laboratories, whose services are also used by local police officials. Suspects arrested and convicted by local governments are often sent to prisons maintained by state governments.

Stores and businesses must obey many state laws that require good business practices. Workers in local factories and mines are protected by state inspectors who ensure that the

**Interpreting the Visual Record**

**Highways** *The modern U.S. interstate highway system is the product of cooperation between the states and the federal government. It depends heavily on federal funding.* **What benefits does the highway system provide for your community?**

*Another area of state and federal cooperation is law enforcement. The FBI cooperates with state and local police.*

## ⭐ Economics

**The Costs of Building a Highway** Today the federal government funds the majority of highway construction and repair costs. Expense was among the leading factors that caused the federal government to get involved in highway construction during the early 1800s. The National Road, also known as the Cumberland Road (which is now part of U.S. Route 40), was the first federally funded highway. It cost $6,825,000 to build—a monumental sum at the time of its completion in the 1830s. The National Road was the first highly engineered highway, measuring 20 feet (6.1 m) wide, with a thick surface of broken stone. Today the cost of building a new highway can be astronomical, depending on where it is located. A new rural interstate could cost $2 million per mile, not including interchanges. However, a complex highway through a major city could cost hundreds of millions of dollars per mile of roadway.

**CRITICAL THINKING**

Why do you think it costs more to build a highway in the city than it does in rural areas?

**ANSWER:** There are more obstacles to consider, such as increased traffic and more complex construction.

**Visual Record Answer**

*Students might suggest that it enables companies across the country to deliver products to customers and offers people a safe road upon which to travel.*

# TEACH OBJECTIVE 3

**LEVELS 1 AND 2:** Have each student look at the photos in this section and list examples for each photo that illustrate the cooperation between different levels of government. Then have students draw a chart identifying the government functions requiring this cooperation and to correctly categorize each photo and activity in the appropriate section. *(Possible categories are education, road building, law enforcement, and business practices.)* **ENGLISH LANGUAGE LEARNERS**

**LEVELS 1 AND 2:** Organize the class into four groups. Assign each group one of the government functions that require cooperation among levels. *(See the Levels 1 and 2 lesson for functions.)* Have each group create a puppet show that demonstrates the importance of its function and the need for cooperation to complete it. Encourage students to be creative. Arrange for groups to present their puppet shows at a local elementary school to teach young children about the importance of cooperation between different levels of government. **COOPERATIVE LEARNING**

## CLOSE

Discuss how the three levels of government are separate and distinct but also connected. Then have students list examples of intergovernmental cooperation that directly affect their lives and those of other citizens.

## ★ Civics Sidelight

**The Block Grant at a Glance** Since 1982 the Virginia Community Development Block Grant (CDBG) Program has provided funding to eligible areas of local government that address key community development needs. These development needs may include housing, infrastructure, and economic development. The state of Virginia is able to allocate this money because the U.S. Department of Housing and Urban Development makes available to the state up to $24 million annually through its Planning Grants and Community Improvement Grants.

**ACTIVITY:** Ask students to conduct research to discover if there are any local community programs that directly benefit from a block grant. Then have each student present a brief oral report on that program and how the block grant has benefitted it.

## Visual Record Answer

*Students might suggest that such cooperation reduces costs and increases efficiency.*

industries obey all safety regulations. State bank inspectors help ensure that bank accounts are safe.

State governments also establish state licensing boards. These boards administer examinations and issue licenses to accountants, dentists, doctors, engineers, lawyers, nurses, and teachers. This service helps ensure that communities have qualified professional workers.

The federal government provides state and local governments with funds to help them implement important programs. **Grants-in-aid** are federal funds given to state and local governments for specific projects, such as airport construction or pollution control. The receiving government must meet certain standards and conditions and must often provide some money of its own for the project. Grant-in-aid projects are subject to supervision by the federal government.

**Block grants** are funds given by the federal government for broadly defined purposes. State and local governments develop and carry out the programs on which the funds will be spent. However, they must develop a spending plan and report to the federal government how the funds were spent.

✔ **Reading Check Summarizing** What are some other ways that different levels of government cooperate? by enforcing laws, maintaining prisons, capturing suspects, requiring good business practices, ensuring qualifications of professional workers, and providing funds for block grants and grants-in-aid

## ★ City Governments Working Together

Cities face many common challenges. For example, all city governments are concerned about increasing funds for police departments, fire departments, and education. They look for ways to lessen air pollution and to safely dispose of trash. The U.S. Conference of Mayors meets regularly so that the country's mayors may compare problems and discuss possible solutions.

As neighboring cities grow closer together, they often begin to share problems. Consider the many villages and townships that lie in Nassau County on Long Island, New York, for example. The population of this area grew from about 300,000 in 1930 to more than 1.4 million in 1970. Soon it was impossible to distinguish where one community ended and another one began. The officials of the various local units realized that cooperation among Nassau County communities was needed.

For greater efficiency and better service, the officials of the various localities agreed that their communities should combine and share certain services. Fire alarms in one community may now be answered by the fire departments of the several

**Interpreting the Visual Record**

**Public Services** *Neighboring communities often find it helpful to cooperate when providing services such as fire protection. **What might be the benefits of such cooperation?***

## REVIEW AND ASSESS

Have students complete the **Section 4 Review** on page 245. Then have them complete **Daily Quiz 9.4**. As **Alternative Assessment**, you may want to use the children's book or puppet show activities in this section's lessons.

## RETEACH

Have students complete **Main Idea Activity for English Language Learners and Special-Needs Students 9.4**. Then organize the class into three groups and assign one of this section's Read to Discover questions to each group. First, have each group find information in the section that could be used to formulate an answer to its question. Then have each group pass its answers to you. Read each answer to the class and have students from the other groups identify the question to which it applies.

**ENGLISH LANGUAGE LEARNERS** , **COOPERATIVE LEARNING**

## EXTEND

Have each student research a major local project that required the help or guidance of the local government. *(Students might select the construction of a major road or a public hospital, for example.)* Ask students to find the answers to such questions as *Which levels of government were involved? How did these various levels of government cooperate?* and *Where did the funding come from?* Then have students report their findings to the class.

**BLOCK SCHEDULING**

neighboring communities. The costs of trash collection, water, and other services may be shared.

✔ **Reading Check Finding the Main Idea** How do city governments benefit from working together? by achieving greater efficiency and providing better and more consistent service

### ⭐ Government Competition

Governments also compete with one another. For example, governments compete for citizens' tax dollars in the form of various income, property, and sales taxes.

States compete with each other to attract industry. They may offer lower taxes, a good supply of labor, efficient highway systems, and favorable laws to encourage industries to move to their state. Cities compete for trade and industry in similar fashion.

The federal government and federal laws sometimes seem to interfere or compete with local laws and customs. For example, the federal government may challenge state election procedures if such procedures conflict with federal laws.

The combined system of federal, state, and local governments is complex. Conflicts between the different governments are to be expected at times. Only by working together can the country's three levels of government fulfill their duty to serve the American people.

✔ **Reading Check Analyzing Information** What are some of the areas in which governments compete? taxes, attracting business, local laws and customs.

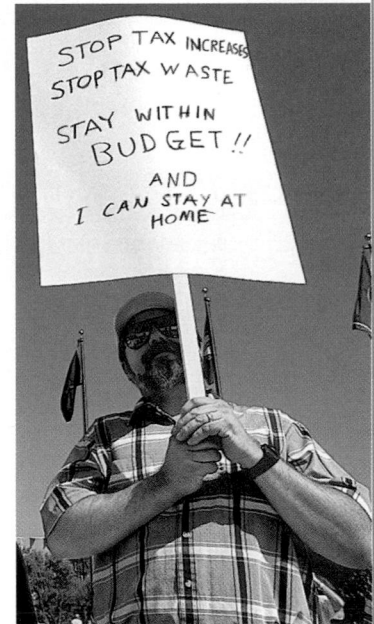

*The competition between different levels of government for tax dollars can frustrate taxpayers.*

## SECTION 4 Review

go. **Homework**
hrw **Practice**
.com **Online**

keyword: SZ3 HP9

1. **Define** and explain:
   • grants-in-aid   • block grants

2. **Categorizing** Copy the graphic organizer below. Use it to list some of the ways different levels of government cooperate and provide examples of each type of cooperation.

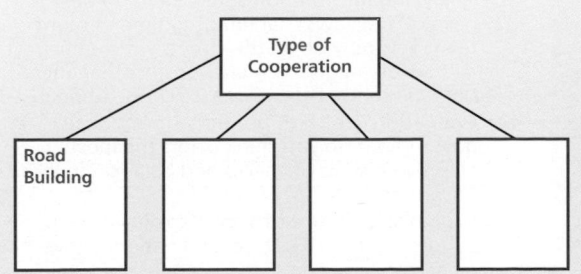

3. **Finding the Main Idea**
   a. What is the purpose of the division of powers among different levels of government?
   b. Explain why the federal government became involved in the building of roads.

4. **Writing and Critical Thinking**
   **Analyzing Information** Imagine that you have been invited by your local government to give a short speech entitled How Governmental Cooperation Serves Our Community. In your speech explain how the three levels of government work together to improve life in your community.
   **Consider:**
   • the areas of cooperation covered in this lesson
   • the needs of your community

## Section 4 Review
### ANSWERS

**1. Define**
• grant-in-aid, p. 244
• block grant, p. 244

**2.** road building—state highway departments manage the road system; the federal department develops plans for building and maintenance; education—state and federal governments grant funds for local schools; local boards run the schools; law enforcement—state and local governments collect evidence for federal cases; state and local police conduct arrests; business—state governments certify professionals; the federal government provides aid.

**3. a.** to ensure that there are no conflicts among laws passed by different levels of government

**b.** As the United States expanded, highways were needed to connect the East and the West. The automobile necessitated a complex system of national highways. The federal government became involved in the planning, building, and maintenance of the highway system to facilitate the movement of people and goods.

**4.** Students' speeches will vary but should display their knowledge of the ways governments work together to provide local services.

# Review and Assessment Resources

**REPRODUCIBLE**
▶ Chapter 9 Review, pp. 246–47
▶ Vocabulary Activity 9
▶ Chapter 9 Tutorial for Students, Parents, Mentors, and Peers
▶ Chapter 9 Test (Form A or B)
▶ Alternative Assessment Handbook

**TECHNOLOGY**
▶ Chapter 9 Test Generator (on the One-Stop Planner)
▶ Global Skill Builder CD–ROM
▶ HRW Go site

**REINFORCEMENT, REVIEW, AND ASSESSMENT**
▶ Chapter 9 Test for English Language Learners and Special-Needs Students

## REVIEW

Have students complete the **Chapter 9 Review** on pages 246–47.

## ASSESS

Use one of the chapter tests to assess students' understanding of the content. For **Alternative Assessment**, see the **Alternative Assessment Handbook**.

---

## CHAPTER 9
### REVIEW ANSWERS

**Define and Identify**
1. charters, p. 223
2. municipalities, p. 223
3. county seat, p. 225
4. town meeting, p. 229
5. special district, p. 232
6. home rule, p. 234
7. mayor, p. 235
8. council members at large, p. 235
9. grants-in-aid, p. 244
10. block grants, p. 244

**Understanding Main Ideas**
1. The state establishes local governments and grants them their powers.

2. Southern colonies were divided into counties with centrally located county seats, where plantation owners could meet to decide laws.

3. It began in New England colonies; citizens once voted on issues directly but now elect representatives to vote for them.

4. when their population exceeds 200 or 300 and the needs of the area increase; elected council makes laws, elected president carries them out, and other officials may be included

5. largest type of municipality; provide services that address health, education and safety

6. State governments grant cities a charter or cities write charters under home rule.

7. education, road building, law enforcement, and business regulations

8. confusion about conflicting

---

# Chapter 9 Review

## Chapter Summary

### Section 1

- Local governments are established by and receive their powers from the state governments. Most local governments receive charters from the state that define their powers, responsibility, and organization.

- The governments of our country's cities, towns, townships, and counties provide fire and police protection, trash removal, and other necessary services.

- There are many kinds of local governments, including towns, townships, villages, boroughs, counties, and cities.

### Section 2

- In early New England towns, town meetings served as the local government. Some of the American colonies organized into governed areas called townships.

- People living within a certain area who have a special need can ask their state government to form a special district.

- When rural communities reach a population of 200 to 300, they may request to form a borough or village.

### Section 3

- There are three major forms of city government: the mayor-council plan, the commission plan, and the council-manager plan of government.

### Section 4

- Federal, state, and local governments cooperate in many areas, such as education, road construction, law enforcement, and business practices.

- Sometimes the various governments compete for taxes, trade, and industry.

---

## Define and Identify

Use the following terms in complete sentences.
1. charters
2. municipalities
3. county seat
4. town meeting
5. special district
6. home rule
7. mayor
8. council members at large
9. grants-in-aid
10. block grants

## Understanding Main Ideas

**Section 1** *(Pages 223–27)*
1. How are local governments established?
2. What are the origins of the county system of government in the United States?

**Section 2** *(Pages 228–33)*
3. Explain where town government began and how it has changed over time.
4. When are villages and boroughs created, and how do they operate?

**Section 3** *(Pages 234–39)*
5. Define the term *city* and explain the services city governments provide for their residents.
6. How do city governments get their power and structure?

**Section 4** *(Pages 241–45)*
7. In which areas do the three levels of government—local, state, and federal—cooperate?
8. What difficulties could occur if different levels of government did not cooperate?

## What Did You Find Out?

1. What purposes do local governments serve?
2. Explain the different forms of city government.
3. In what areas do the three levels of government sometimes compete?

## Thinking Critically

1. **Analyzing Information** Some communities have curfew laws that limit the time of night teenagers may be on the streets without an adult. How might such laws protect teenagers? Do you feel that such laws are constitutional?
2. **Evaluating** Which of the three forms of city government do you think offers the most effective system of checks and balances in local government?
3. **Supporting a Point of View** Explain why it is important that city, state, and national governments cooperate on such projects as road building.

## RETEACH

Organize the class into four groups and assign each group one of the four sections of Chapter 9. Then have the groups review their assigned section to identify its main ideas. Ask each group to present the information in the form of a graphic organizer to the class. **ENGLISH LANGUAGE LEARNERS**, **COOPERATIVE LEARNING**

## Portfolio Extensions

American Civics

**1. Interdisciplinary Connection to Sociology** After groups have completed their research on their community's government, ask each group to interview a variety of citizens regarding their feelings about the government. *(Students' questions should address feelings about when and how the community was founded, how it has changed, and statistics on the current organization.)* Then have students compile their findings into a class report that generalizes the citizens' feelings about the community government.

**2. Cooperative Learning** Organize students into small groups. Ask each group to create a board game called Our Community Government. Students might include game cards for funding or regulations that help (or limit) them in building such things as bridges, roads, civic centers, and parks on their properties. The purpose of the game is to illustrate how your community government works. Have groups play each others' games.

---

## Building Social Studies Skills

go.hrw.com STANDARDIZED TEST PREP ONLINE keyword: SZ3 STP9

### Interpreting Charts

Examine the chart on levels of government below. Then answer the questions that follow.

#### Levels of Government

| Level | Source of Authority |
|---|---|
|  Federal Government | • The People of the United States<br>• The Constitution |
|  State Governments | • The People of the United States<br>• The Constitution<br>• State constitutions |
|  Local Governments | • The People of the United States<br>• The Constitution<br>• State constitutions<br>• State charters |

1. What source of authority shown on the chart applies only to local governments?
   a. state charters
   b. state constitutions
   c. the people of the United States
   d. There is no source of authority that applies only to local governments.
2. Why do you think all levels of government shown on the chart derive some of their authority from the people and the Constitution?

### Analyzing Primary Sources

Read the following quotation from the Alexandria, Virginia, city government publication "Know Your City." Then answer the questions that follow.

> "Alexandria is an independent city (Virginia cities have no county affiliation), which derives its governing authority from a charter granted by the Virginia General Assembly. . . . By referendum in 1921, an overwhelming majority of the voters approved the adoption of the council-manager form of city government, which went into effect in September 1922. This form of government centralizes legislative authority and responsibility in the elected City Council. Administrative authority and responsibility are held by the City Manager, who is appointed by the City Council. The City Council is composed of a Mayor and six Council members who are elected at-large for three-year terms."

3. Who has administrative authority and responsibility for the city of Alexandria?
   a. The Virginia General Assembly
   b. The City Council of Alexandria
   c. The Mayor of Alexandria
   d. The City Manager of Alexandria
4. What form of city government does the city of Alexandria use? When was this system of government adopted?
5. Based on your knowledge of city government types, what are some reasons why the citizens of Alexandria might have adopted this particular form of city government? What advantages and disadvantages would they face as a result?

---

## Alternative Assessment

American Civics

### Building Your Portfolio

**Linking to Community**
With your group, research the history and current operations of your local government. You should use your library for research and conduct interviews with local government officials. In your report, discuss when and how your community was founded, the type of government that was established, how that government has changed over the years, and the number, type, and name of local officials serving today.

📡 internet connect

**Internet Activity: go.hrw.com**
keyword: SZ3 AC9

Access the Internet through the HRW Go site or use your library to research the organization, sources of revenue, and property tax rate for your county or city government. Then create a labeled diagram to illustrate your research.

go.hrw.com

---

laws and which ones to follow

### What Did You Find Out?

**1.** They provide services to the local community, such as fire and police protection, education, libraries, and hospitals.

**2.** mayor-council/weak mayor—council holds more power than mayor; mayor-council/strong mayor—mayor has chief responsibility; commission—three to nine elected officials make and carry out city's laws; council-manager—an elected council appoints manager

**3.** taxes, trade, and industry

### Thinking Critically

**1.** Some students may note that these laws may reduce teenage crime and protect young people. Others may feel they infringe on teens' freedoms.

**2.** Students' responses should reflect an understanding of city government.

**3.** Students' answers may refer to the history of road building or may predict the results of road building without cooperation.

### Skills Workshop

**1.** a

**2.** Students might suggest that the Constitution is the supreme law of the land and that Americans have a direct influence on government.

**3.** d

**4.** council-manager; 1921

**5.** Students' responses will vary.

## TEACH

**LEVEL 1:** Remind students that local government is responsible for many of the services that they use on a daily basis. Then organize students into pairs. Ask each pair to design a mural for their town or city hall that depicts the various services provided by local government.

**ENGLISH LANGUAGE LEARNERS**

**ALL LEVELS:** Organize students into small groups. Ask groups to design a Web page explaining the organization of their state government. Remind students that the Web page should make use of graphics and illustrations to present information. Encourage students to include links on their Web page to sites explaining the responsibilities that the state government shares with local or federal agencies.

**ENGLISH LANGUAGE LEARNERS , COOPERATIVE LEARNING**

### APPLYING THE SKILLS

Organize students into small groups. Ask each group to write a brief skit based on one of the Utopian communities created in the Civics Lab. Students' skits should depict the problems and concerns addressed by the founding citizens of Utopia as they work together to design their government. Have each group also show how the new government functions to solve a particular public crisis.

# Civics Lab

## Creating a Government
Complete the following Civics Lab activity individually or in a group.

## Your Task

In Unit 3 you learned about how state and local governments are organized and the responsibilities they carry out. Imagine that you are a citizen of the newly independent island nation of Utopia. The citizens of Utopia want to establish their own government, but the people are not sure what type of government would best serve them.

Your job is to develop a two-tiered plan of government for Utopia based on the most effective aspects of Earth's state and local governments. The plan should include legislative, executive, and judicial aspects of government. The Utopians have agreed to accept your plan of government, but they insist on knowing the reasoning behind your recommendations. Your plan will need to include visual and written materials. To prepare these materials, you will need to do the following.

## What to Do

**STEP 1** **Create a reference document** explaining how typical state governments are organized. First, write a summary of the typical form of state government. Include an organizational chart to show how duties and powers are divided among the different parts of this government. Your chart should address issues such as how leaders are chosen and how the government serves the needs of the people.

**ALL LEVELS:** Have each student create a graphic organizer with three overlapping circles. Have students label the circles with the following headings: *Federal Government, State Government,* and *Local Government.* Have students list the responsibilities of each level of government within the appropriate circle. In the areas where these circles overlap, have students fill in the responsibilities that are shared by the different levels of government. **ENGLISH LANGUAGE LEARNERS**

**LEVEL 3:** Ask students to consider what would happen if there were no local governments. What services would be overlooked, and how would the federal government meet the needs of all citizens? Ask each student to write a short story describing what day-to-day life would be like if there were no state or local governments. Encourage students to consider specific services that would be missing.

**STEP 2** **Write** a second summary that describes how some state governments differ from the typical form of state government. Then create an organizational chart that shows how these state governments are different from a typical state government.

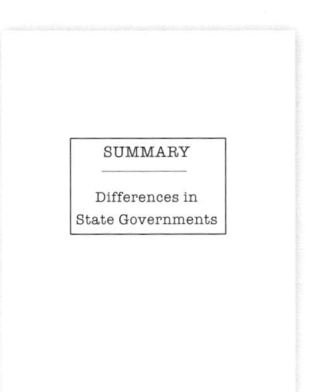

SUMMARY

Differences in
State Governments

**STEP 3** **Create a chart** that lists the advantages and disadvantages of the various forms of state government. Consider the following issues: how leaders are chosen, what types of areas are governed, and the governments' goals.

**STEP 4** **Use** the two summaries and the chart that you have created to write the Utopia Constitution's section on organization. Be sure to explain why you have organized the government in this way. You should answer questions such as: How will this form of government be more efficient? How will it divide power fairly and represent the people's interests?

### Other Forms of State Government

| Governor | Legislature | Courts |
|----------|-------------|--------|
| ↓ | ↓ | ↓ |

### Comparing State Governments

| Advantages | Disadvantages |
|------------|---------------|
|            |               |

Organize your materials and present your plan to the Utopians (the rest of the class).

Ask students to imagine that they are members of the United Nations representing the island country Utopia. Then have each student write a speech explaining the philosophy and organization of the Utopian government. Students' speeches should also point out the strengths of the Utopian government compared to other governments. Students' papers should support their positions with examples from the Civics Lab. Ask volunteers to read their speeches to the class.

### UNIT OVERVIEW

The material in Unit 4 presents an in-depth look at the key elements of the American political system—elections, political parties, interest groups, public opinion, and the media. The unit also stresses the importance of participatory democracy, noting the ways in which Americans can influence the decisions of their elected leaders.

### In Their Own Words

*"A nation is formed by the willingness of each of us to share in the responsibility for upholding the common good. A government is invigorated when each one of us is willing to participate in shaping the future of this nation. . . . We must . . . begin again to shape a common future. Let each person do his or her part. If one citizen is unwilling to participate, all of us are going to suffer. For the American idea, though it is shared by all of us, is realized in each of us."*
— Barbara Jordan

**Using the Quotation** Have students read the quotation by Barbara Jordan, who was the first African American congresswoman from the South. Ask them to summarize the quotation in their own words. Then have students read the titles of the chapters in this unit. Encourage students to suggest connections between Jordan's ideas and the subjects in this unit.

**About the Author** Barbara Jordan (1936–1996) served in the Texas Senate for six years before her election to the U.S. House of Representatives in 1972. She served in Congress until 1979, when she became a professor at the Lyndon B. Johnson School of Public Affairs at the University of Texas at Austin.

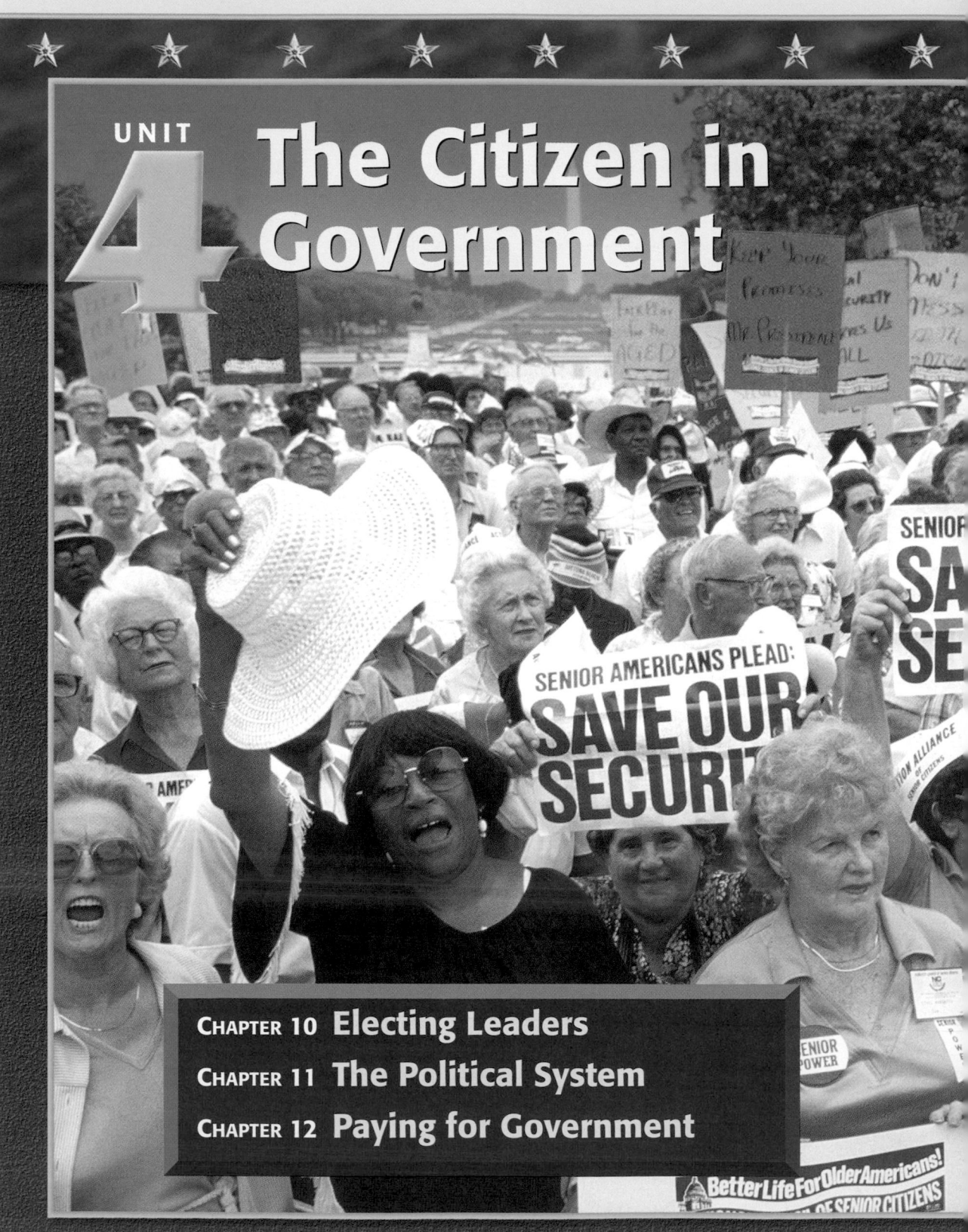

# UNIT 4 The Citizen in Government

Remind students that the Twenty-sixth Amendment lowered the voting age to 18. Have students suggest what they might do to start preparing themselves for the decisions that they will have to make when they become eligible to vote. Then ask students to consider other ways, in addition to voting, that they can influence government policies and decisions. Have students make a list of reasons that voting and public opinion are an important part of democracy.

# Young Citizens

## IN ACTION

### Making a Difference

Have you ever wondered how young people can shape opinions and influence lives around them? Such is the goal of SADD, or Students Against Destructive Decisions. SADD members try to make a difference in the lives of young people by raising awareness about potential consequences of underage drinking and drug use. The group also promotes positive decision making.

SADD was started in 1981 by hockey coach Robert Anastas at Wayland High School in Massachusetts when two of his students died in separate alcohol-related car accidents. Since then, it has grown into a national organization with chapters across the United States. SADD also has chapters in foreign countries. Chapters can be found wherever students are present—in schools, community centers, and youth groups.

SADD members work to spread the message of "no use" of alcohol and drugs.

To spread SADD's message of "no use" of alcohol and other drugs, chapters sponsor a number of activities in their communities. For example, SADD's substance-free parties create a social environment that is free from alcohol and drugs. Chapters are supported by and remain in close contact with the SADD National Office. Together chapters work to promote SADD's cause nationally. For example, 500 SADD members from 34 states organized with U.S. Department of Transportation secretary Norman Mineta to celebrate SADD's 20th anniversary with the launch of "Think About It . . . The Power of SADD." "By emphasizing shared responsibility among students for their decisions and the decisions of their friends, this campaign will encourage teens to consider the effect their choices will have on others," said Student Leadership Council member Jared Davis.

Through its programs, SADD actively works to shape the opinions of young people and their families about teen safety. The actions of each SADD member show how young people can change the lives of others.

WE RECYCLE

**You Decide**

1. What is the purpose of SADD?
2. How is SADD an example of how young people can change society?

## What Can We Do?

Ask students to research youth organizations that are trying to make a difference within their community. Then organize students into groups and ask each group to identify a specific problem facing young people that is not being addressed in their community. Have each group propose the creation of an organization designed to address the specific problem it identified. Each group's proposal should include the following: a description of the problem, a summary of how to address that problem, and an outline of what its proposed organization plans to do. As a class, discuss the proposals and vote on the program that the class would most like to develop. Encourage the class to take the necessary steps to establish the program and to make a difference in the community.

**YOU DECIDE ANSWERS**

1. The purpose of SADD is to make a difference in the lives of young people by raising awareness about the potential consequences of underage drinking and drug use.

2. Students' responses will vary, but they should cite specific examples.

# Electing Leaders

## CHAPTER RESOURCE MANAGER

| | Objectives | Pacing Guide | Reproducible Resources |
|---|---|---|---|
| **SECTION 1:**<br>**A Two-Party System**<br>(pp. 253–58) | ★ Explain the role of political parties in the United States.<br>★ Describe how political parties developed in the United States.<br>★ Explain the differences between a one-party and a two-party system. | **Regular**<br>1.5 days<br><br>**Block Scheduling**<br>1 day<br><br>*Block Scheduling Handbook with Team Teaching Strategies, Chapter 10* | **RS** Guided Reading Strategies 10.1<br>**RS** Readings in Economics and Government 59: *Communist Manifesto,* Karl Marx and Friedrich Engels |
| **SECTION 2:**<br>**Political Party Organization**<br>(pp. 259–63) | ★ Name the committees that help major political parties and define their responsibilities.<br>★ Explain where political parties get their money and examine why Congress regulates political contributions.<br>★ Describe how the Federal Election Campaign Act regulates federal campaigns. | **Regular**<br>2 days<br><br>**Block Scheduling**<br>1.5 days<br><br>*Block Scheduling Handbook with Team Teaching Strategies, Chapter 10* | **RS** Guided Reading Strategies 10.2<br>**RS** Readings in Economics and Government 72: "Congress: The First Two-Hundred Years," Thomas P. O'Neill Jr.<br>**PS** American Civics Political Cartoon: Party Politics |
| **SECTION 3:**<br>**The Right to Vote**<br>(pp. 264–68) | ★ Determine who can vote in U.S. elections and describe how this right is protected.<br>★ Describe the differences between primary elections and general elections.<br>★ Explain how the voting process has changed over the years. | **Regular**<br>1 day<br><br>**Block Scheduling**<br>.5 day<br><br>*Block Scheduling Handbook with Team Teaching Strategies, Chapter 10* | **RS** Guided Reading Strategies 10.3<br>**RS** Readings in Economics and Government 45: Voting Rights Act of 1965<br>**RS** Graphic Organizer Activity: Politics and the Vote |
| **SECTION 4:**<br>**Nominating and Electing Our Leaders**<br>(pp. 270–75) | ★ Explain the purpose of national nominating conventions and describe how convention delegates are chosen.<br>★ Examine the nomination process at the national conventions.<br>★ Describe some of the methods of presidential campaigning.<br>★ Determine the main purpose of the electoral college. | **Regular**<br>1.5 days<br><br>**Block Scheduling**<br>1 day<br><br>*Block Scheduling Handbook with Team Teaching Strategies, Chapter 10* | **RS** Guided Reading Strategies 10.4<br>**E** Creative Teaching Strategy: Quick Survey<br>**E** Challenge and Enrichment Worksheet 10: Interpreting Election Results<br>**SM** Community Service and Participation Handbook: Electing Leaders |

## Chapter Resource Key

| | | | | | |
|---|---|---|---|---|---|
| **PS** | Primary Sources | **SM** | Skills Mastery |  CD-ROM | |
| **RS** | Reading Support | **A** | Assessment |  Video | |
| **IC** | Interdisciplinary Connections | **REV** | Review |  Internet | |
| | | **ELL** | Reinforcement and English Language Learners | 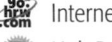 Holt Presentation Maker Using Microsoft® PowerPoint® | |
| **E** | Enrichment | |  Transparencies | | |

 **One-Stop** Planner CD-ROM

**See the *One-Stop Planner* for a complete list of additional resources for students and teachers.**

**One-Stop** Planner CD–ROM

It's easy to plan lessons, select resources, and print out materials for your students when you use the *One-Stop Planner CD–ROM with Test Generator*.

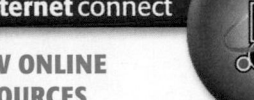
| Technology Resources | Reinforcement, Review, and Assessment |
|---|---|
|  One-Stop Planner, Lesson 10.1 <br>  Holt Researcher CD–ROM <br> Homework Practice Online <br> HRW Go site | REV Section 1 Review, p. 258 <br> A Daily Quiz 10.1 <br> ELL Main Idea Activity 10.1 <br> ELL English Audio Summary 10.1 <br> ELL Spanish Audio Summary 10.1 |
| One-Stop Planner, Lesson 10.2 <br> Transparency 13: Organization of Political Parties <br> Homework Practice Online | REV Section 2 Review, p. 263 <br> A Daily Quiz 10.2 <br> ELL Main Idea Activity 10.2 <br> ELL English Audio Summary 10.2 <br> ELL Spanish Audio Summary 10.2 |
|  One-Stop Planner, Lesson 10.3 <br>  **CNN** Presents: American Government <br> Homework Practice Online | REV Section 3 Review, p. 268 <br> A Daily Quiz 10.3 <br> ELL Main Idea Activity 10.3 <br> ELL English Audio Summary 10.3 <br> ELL Spanish Audio Summary 10.3 |
|  One-Stop Planner, Lesson 10.4 <br>  Transparency 14: Electoral Map of the United States <br> Citizenship Skills Videocassette Segment 4: On the Campaign Trail <br> Homework Practice Online | REV Section 4 Review, p. 275 <br> A Daily Quiz 10.4 <br> ELL Main Idea Activity 10.4 <br> ELL English Audio Summary 10.4 <br> ELL Spanish Audio Summary 10.4 |

### HRW ONLINE RESOURCES
GO TO: go.hrw.com
Then type in the keyword.

**TEACHER HOME PAGE**
KEYWORD: SZ3 Teacher

**CHAPTER INTERNET ACTIVITIES**
KEYWORD: SZ3 AC10
Choose an activity to:
• deliver an oral report on local political parties.
• write a public service announcement on voting methods.
• create a party brochure on a historical third party.

**CHAPTER ENRICHMENT LINKS**
KEYWORD: SZ3 CH10

**ONLINE ASSESSMENT**
Homework Practice
KEYWORD: SZ3 HP10
Rubrics
KEYWORD: SS Rubrics

**ONLINE MAPS, CHARTS, AND GRAPHS**
KEYWORD: SZ3 MCG
• Functions of Political Parties

**HOLT PRESENTATION MAKER**
KEYWORD: SZ3 PPT10

**CONTENT UPDATES**
KEYWORD: SS Content Updates

**ONLINE READING SUPPORT**
KEYWORD: SS Strategies

**CURRENT EVENTS**
KEYWORD: S3 Current Events

## Chapter Review and Assessment

IC Vocabulary Activity 10
 Global Skill Builder CD–ROM
HRW Go site
REV Chapter 10 Tutorial for Students, Parents, Mentors, and Peers
REV Chapter 10 Review, pp. 276–77
A Standardized Test Practice
A Chapter 10 Test Generator (on the One-Stop Planner)
A Chapter 10 Test (Form A or B)
A Alternative Assessment Handbook
A Chapter 10 Test for English Language Learners and Special-Needs Students

## Meeting Individual Needs

### Ability Levels

**Level 1** Basic-level activities designed for all students encountering new material

**Level 2** Intermediate-level activities designed for average students

**Level 3** Challenging activities designed for honors and gifted-and-talented students

**English Language Learners** Activities that address the needs of students with Limited English Proficiency

## What's Your Opinion?

 To help students create their *Themes* Journal entries, provide the following examples of appropriate **agree**/**disagree** statements.

● **Agree**   Joining a political party is the only way that a person can become a part of the collective action.

**Disagree**   We can also influence government by developing petitions, serving on bipartisan committees, and getting the issues out to the public.

● **Agree**   Today's voting systems have made elections fairer and more honest.

**Disagree**   Paper ballots are still used today, as they were in the past.

● **Agree**   The preliminary steps to presidential elections are presidential primaries or state conventions, the national nominating conventions, and the campaign itself.

**Disagree**   Candidates have been able to "throw their hat into the ring" much later in the campaign.

# Internet Activity

**Third Party Politics**

**☑ internet connect**

**TOPIC:** Third Parties
**GO TO:** go.hrw.com
**KEYWORD:** SZ3 AC10

**ACTIVITY:** Have students access the Internet through the HRW Go site to conduct research about a significant third party of the 1900s such as the Reform Party. Ask them to find reasons for the party's existence and the ways it affected the two major parties. Then create a party brochure in which you take the point of view of a member of the third party and publicize your candidates and issues.

## CHAPTER

★ ★ ★ ★ ★

# 10 Electing Leaders

## What's Your Opinion?

### Build on What You Know

Will you be ready to vote? The Twenty-sixth Amendment to the U.S. Constitution gives U.S. citizens the right to vote at age 18. At that time you will be faced with the challenge of casting your vote wisely for national, state, and local officials. Voting is a responsibility that all citizens should take seriously. Learn all you can about the U.S. political process and become involved in that process now. What you learn now will help you become a well-informed and intelligent voter.

**Themes Journal**   Do you **agree** or **disagree** with the following statements? Support your point of view in your journal.

- Joining a political party is the only way that a person can influence the government.

- Voting procedures today differ from those in the past.

- Presidential elections involve many preliminary steps.

# SECTION 1

## OBJECTIVES

After completing Section 1, students should be able to

1 **Explain the role of political parties in the United States.**

2 **Describe how political parties developed in the United States.**

3 **Explain the differences between a one-party and a two-party system.**

## ((•)) LET'S GET STARTED!

As students enter the classroom, show an illustration of an elephant and a donkey. Ask them what the illustrations might represent. *(Students might suggest that the elephant represents the Republican Party and the donkey represents the Democratic Party.)* Ask them what political candidates in the last presidential election represented each of those parties. Then ask students to list any other political parties that had a candidate for president. Finally, ask the students what it means when someone says they are a Democrat or a Republican. Tell students that in Section 1 they will learn about the role of political parties in the United States, the history of their development, and the various types of political party systems.

# SECTION 1

## A Two-Party System

### Read to Discover

1. What is the role of political parties in the United States?
2. How did political parties develop in the United States?
3. How do one-party and two-party political systems differ?

### WHY CIVICS MATTERS

American political parties play an important role in the passage of legislation in the United States. Use **CNNfyi.com** or other **current events** sources to identify a bill that the Democratic or Republican Party is supporting. Record your findings in your journal.

### Define

• political party
• nominate
• candidates
• two-party system
• multiparty system
• coalition
• third parties
• one-party system

## SECTION 1 RESOURCES

### REPRODUCIBLE

▶ Guided Reading Strategies 10.1
▶ Readings in Economics and Government 59: *Communist Manifesto,* Karl Marx and Friedrich Engels

### TECHNOLOGY

▶ One-Stop Planner, Lesson 10.1
▶ Holt Researcher CD–ROM
▶ Homework Practice Online
▶ HRW Go site

### REINFORCEMENT, REVIEW, AND ASSESSMENT

▶ Section 1 Review, p. 258
▶ Daily Quiz 10.1
▶ Main Idea Activity 10.1
▶ English Audio Summary 10.1
▶ Spanish Audio Summary 10.1

## *Reading Focus*

Nowhere in the Constitution is there a provision calling for political parties. However, political parties play an important role in the American democratic process. As party members, Americans put their political ideas to work at all levels of government. Political parties play a significant role in helping the American people govern themselves.

## ★ Role of Political Parties

A **political party** is an organization made up of citizens who have similar ideas on public issues. Party members work together to put their ideas into effect through government action. To achieve their purposes, political parties encourage voters to elect to office those people that the party favors. Parties also work to pass laws that they support.

In the United States, political parties are voluntary. Citizens are free to join the party of their choice. They also may decide not to join any party. Americans who join a political party usually do so because they agree with most of that party's ideas. Of course, not all members of a political party agree on every issue. If members strongly disagree with their party on important issues, they are free to leave the party.

This banner supporting Thomas Jefferson was one of the first political party advertisements.

**LEVEL 1:** Ask students what roles or purposes political parties serve in the United States. *(Students might suggest that they encourage voters to elect to office those candidates the party endorses, they work to have laws passed, and so on.)* Write their responses on the chalkboard and discuss the importance of each response. Add any other purposes that the students might have omitted. Then have the class rank the order of importance and discuss the results.

**ENGLISH LANGUAGE LEARNERS**

**ALL LEVELS:** Lead a discussion about the role of political parties in the United States. Tell students that our two major political parties developed during George Washington's presidency and that even though they were called the Federalists and the Democratic-Republicans, many of their beliefs are similar to those shared by either the Democrats or the Republicans today. Invite members of the local Democratic and Republican parties (and others if appropriate) to speak to the class. Before their visits, have students prepare pertinent questions for each speaker, covering such subjects as the founding of his or her party, the role of their party in the United States, the party's philosophy, and any similarities between their party and the Federalists and Democratic-Republicans (Anti-Federalists).

**ENGLISH LANGUAGE LEARNERS**

## ★ Constitutional Heritage

**Are Political Parties Dangerous Factions?** The founding fathers had not made any provisions for a party system in the Constitution because they belived that political parties were bad for democracy. They inherited this belief from British thinkers such as Jonathan Swift, who had declared, "Party is the madness of the many, for the gain of the few." Benjamin Franklin accused parties of "tearing to pieces the best of characters," while John Adams maintained that a two-party system was "to be dreaded as the greatest political evil." The perception at the time that parties represented dangerous factionalism led the founding fathers to overlook the benefits that parties can bring to a democracy.

**CRITICAL THINKING**

Do you think political parties are dangerous factions?

**ANSWER:** Students' responses will vary but should be adequately supported.

**CHART ANSWER**

ensure that they do a good job

Political parties offer an effective way for large numbers of people with similar ideas to get things done. Political parties are interested in practical politics. In other words, parties are concerned with the actions that government should take.

Practical politics affects every one of us. For example, when you voice a concern about the high cost of living, you are taking a practical interest in politics. However, if you alone act on your concern, you will not be very effective. If instead you join a group that shares your concern, your voice can be heard in a way that gets results. Political parties serve this purpose.

Political parties also **nominate,** or select, **candidates** to run for public office. Candidates are the men and women who run for election to offices at various levels of the government. Most Americans who serve as public officials have been elected to their offices as candidates of political parties. Although not impossible, it is difficult for a person to run for national office without the support of a political party.

Political parties also take positions on public issues and work to have laws passed. During election campaigns, each political party tries to convince the voters that it offers the best program.

After an election, the winning candidates become the leaders of the government. The political party to which these leaders belong tries to make sure that the leaders do a good job. In this way the party hopes to ensure that its candidates will win again in the next election.

The party whose candidates lose the election will seek to regain leadership of the government. That party's leaders will watch for and point out any mistakes the winning party's leaders may make while in office. However, it is important for both parties to compromise and work in the public interest.

✔ **Reading Check Finding the Main Idea** What are the purposes of political parties in the United States? They organize voters with similar views, nominate candidates, and support positions on public issues.

## ★ Beginnings of the Two-Party System

The first political parties began during President George Washington's administration. As you read in Chapter 2, those people who favored a strong federal government were called Federalists. Those who favored limiting the power of the central government were called Antifederalists. Antifederalists later became known as Democratic-Republicans.

Alexander Hamilton was a leading member of the Federalist Party. He proposed policies that would strengthen the federal government. Thomas Jefferson,

## What Political Parties Do

 Parties point out weaknesses in other parties and their candidates.

 Parties recommend programs and laws that guide the actions of government.

 Parties keep members informed and help keep all citizens interested in their government.

 Parties ensure that public officials do a good job so voters will re-elect them.

 Parties select candidates to run for election to public offices in the government.

**Interpreting Charts** *Political parties play an important role in organizing and directing the political process.* **How do parties help government by watching their officials and officials of other parties?**

## Historical Document

### WASHINGTON'S FAREWELL ADDRESS

On September 19, 1796, President George Washington's Farewell Address first appeared in a Philadelphia newspaper. In it, he wrote about the potential dangers posed by political parties.

"Let me . . . warn you in the most solemn manner against the baneful effects of the Spirit of Party, generally. . . . This spirit, unfortunately, is inseparable from our nature, having its root in the strongest passions of the human mind. It exists under different shapes in all governments. . . . [Party loyalty] agitates the Community with ill-founded jealousies and false alarms; kindles the animosity of one part against another, foments [causes] occasionally riot and insurrection

[revolt]. It opens the door to foreign influence and corruption, which find . . . access to the government itself through the channels of party passions. . . . There is an opinion, that parties in free countries are useful checks upon the administration of the Government, and serve to keep alive the spirit of Liberty. This within certain limits is probably true. . . . [But] there [is a] constant danger of excess."

**Analyzing Primary Sources**
1. According to Washington, what are the dangers of political parties?
2. What benefits does Washington agree that parties may provide?

leader of the Democratic-Republicans, opposed Hamilton and the Federalist Party. Jefferson and the Democratic-Republicans tried to limit the power of the federal government.

President Washington became worried as he watched these two different points of view lead to the establishment of political parties. He feared that the growth of parties would weaken the new country. In his farewell address as president, Washington warned Americans that political parties were dangerous because they could divide the country.

Washington's warnings went unheeded, however. Political parties became a lasting part of the American form of government. Throughout most of its history, the United States has had a **two-party system,** or two strong political parties.

✔ **Reading Check** Summarizing How did the two-party system develop in the United States? Federalists, led by Alexander Hamilton, wanted a strong federal government; Thomas Jefferson led the Antifederalists, later called the Democratic-Republicans, who wanted to limit the power of the federal government.

## ★ The Democratic and Republican Parties

For more than 140 years, the Democratic Party and the Republican Party have been the country's two major political parties. The current Democratic Party traces its roots to Jefferson's Democratic-Republican Party. In the 1820s that party split into several groups.

One group, led by Andrew Jackson, became the Democratic Party. Jackson believed that the federal government was acting to benefit the wealthy. He was determined that the federal government should represent frontier settlers, farmers, and city laborers—the common people.

**Holt Researcher**

go.hrw.com
KEYWORD: Holt Researcher
Freefind: Political Parties

Read through the Holt Researcher's entries on political organizations aimed at young Americans. Use the information to write a short press release that answers the following question: What do these organizations do to keep their members informed on political issues?

## ★ The Democratic Process

**The Platform** One manner in which political parties help citizens is by presenting them with a party platform, which is a product of the party's presidential nominating convention. The platform declares the party's principles and objectives. It also offers a critical evaluation of the policies of the opposing party. Some critics complain that party platforms are vague documents that do not actually give any real sense of a party's concerns, but many political scientists believe that party platforms reveal a great deal about the compromises among interest groups within a party. Despite their limitations, party platforms serve the voter by providing insight into the goals of the party and its candidates during an election year.

**ACTIVITY:** Have students conduct research to obtain more information about party platforms either today or in the past. Then have students prepare a written representation of their chosen platform and present it to the class.

### ANALYZING PRIMARY SOURCES ANSWERS

1. Washington believed that party loyalty caused animosity, jealousy, and even occasionally a revolt.

2. Washington does agree that political parties are useful checks on the administration and serve to keep the spirit of liberty alive.

## TEACHER TO TEACHER

Christie Hutchins of Missouri recommends the following activity:

**ALL LEVELS:** Lead a class discussion about how political parties developed in the United States. *(Tell students that Alexander Hamilton served as George Washington's secretary of the treasury and Thomas Jefferson served as his secretary of state. These two men had different views concerning the role of government in peoples' lives, which led to the development of the Federalist and Democratic-Republican Parties.)* Then inform students about the two main parties' beliefs. Do not tell them the name of the party, only the main ideas. Ask each student to try to guess with which party the idea belongs and to write several sentences about why they feel that idea belongs to that party. Then reveal the answers and ask students to volunteer whether they guessed correctly. **ENGLISH LANGUAGE LEARNERS**

 **HOMEWORK** Have each student develop a manifesto for a new political party. *(See the Level 1 lesson for development.)* Students should expand on their views and intentions for the party by outlining what their new party will offer the country.

---

★★★★★★★★★★★★
## That's Interesting!
★★★★★★★★★★★★

John F. Kennedy liked to tell the following story about himself and the other 1960 Democratic candidates for president, Lyndon Johnson and Stu Symington. "Several nights ago," he said, "I dreamed that the good Lord touched me on the shoulder and said, 'Don't worry, you'll be the Democratic Presidential nominee in 1960. What's more, you'll be elected.' " Kennedy told Stu Symington about the dream. "Funny thing," said Stu, "I had exactly the same dream about myself." Both Kennedy and Symington told their dreams to Lyndon Johnson, and Johnson said, "That's funny. For the life of me, I can't remember tapping either of you two boys for the job."

---

**BIOGRAPHY ANSWER**
the Democratic Party

---

## BIOGRAPHY

### Andrew Jackson
#### (1767–1845)

Andrew Jackson was born in South Carolina. By the time he was 13 years old both his parents had died. Jackson grew to be a man with a reputation for toughness. He became a lawyer and later earned respect as a military leader during the War of 1812. He represented Tennessee in the U.S. Senate before winning the presidency in 1828 in a landslide.

Jackson's supporters formed the Democratic Party and helped him win two terms in office. Jackson himself was an aggressive leader who vetoed more bills during his presidency than all the previous presidents combined. Although he made political enemies, he was popular with the common people. They saw Jackson as a simple man who had gained great influence and respect through hard work. **What political party did Jackson's supporters form?**

---

Andrew Jackson was elected president in 1828, and the Democratic Party that he helped establish began its long history.

Today's Republican Party was formed in 1854 by people who opposed slavery and its spread into U.S. territories. The various small groups that represented these antislavery interests joined together to oppose the Democratic Party. In 1860 Abraham Lincoln became the first candidate nominated by the Republican Party to be elected president of the United States.

✔ **Reading Check** Contrasting How do the histories of the Democratic and Republican Parties differ? The Democratic Party developed in the 1820s, and the Republican Party was formed in 1854. Democrats championed the cause of common people. The Republican Party was created by people who opposed slavery.

## ★ Advantages of Two-Party Systems

Since the mid-1800s the Democratic and Republican Parties have had almost equal strength, making the two-party system work remarkably well. When one party fails to please a majority of voters, there is another strong party ready to take over. The newly elected party often tries different programs and policies in dealing with the country's problems. Governments formed in two-party systems also tend to be quite stable.

Several European countries have a **multiparty system**—one in which there are more than two strong political parties. If all the parties are of about equal strength, no one party can win a majority of votes. To run the government, two or more of the political parties must often agree to compromises and to work together. This agreement between two or more political parties to work together to run the government is called a **coalition.**

In the Netherlands and other countries, coalition governments have worked well. However, this system has certain disadvantages. Often the political parties disagree and the coalition breaks apart, weakening the government and the country. As a result, some countries, such as Italy, have had great difficulty in forming stable governments.

✔ **Reading Check** Summarizing What are the advantages of two-party political systems? Two-party systems provide two strong political platforms to choose from, and they tend to be stable.

## ★ Third Parties

There are a number of minor political parties, or **third parties,** in the United States. At certain times in the country's history, third parties have had great influence.

In 1912 Theodore Roosevelt was denied the presidential nomination of the Republican Party. As a result, he organized a third party called the Progressive Party. Roosevelt ran for president as the nominee of this party. Although he was not elected, Roosevelt took many votes

**ALL LEVELS:** Copy the graphic organizer on the right onto the chalkboard, omitting the italicized answers. Then ask students to complete the chart by listing the differences between a one-party and a two-party system.

**ENGLISH LANGUAGE LEARNERS**

## CLOSE

Tell students that George Washington's Farewell Address warned the country of the "baneful effects of the Spirit of Party." Discuss with students his concerns and ask them to write a paragraph analyzing whether Washington's beliefs still ring true today.

| One-Party System | Two-Party System |
|---|---|
| • *Usually a totalitarian government* | • *Usually forms a stable government* |
| • *Usually an unlimited government* | • *Usually a limited government* |
| • *A government unrestrained by the people* | • *Composed of a diverse group of people who share similar political beliefs* |
| • *Opposition parties are illegal* | • *Elections are based on a "winner take all" format* |
| • *Usually restrictive of civil and political rights* | • *Usually civil and political rights are protected* |

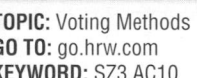

from Republican candidate William Taft. In this way, Roosevelt actually helped Democratic candidate Woodrow Wilson win the presidency.

The strongest showing of any third-party or independent presidential candidate since Theodore Roosevelt occurred in 1992. Independent Ross Perot ran against Democrat Bill Clinton and Republican George Bush. Although election results gave the country's highest office to Clinton, Perot won an impressive 19 percent of the vote.

Third-party candidates have run for office throughout U.S. history, but few have done as well as Roosevelt and Perot. Among the most notable third-party candidates are George Wallace and John Anderson. Wallace, former governor of Alabama, ran for president in 1968 as the candidate of the American Independent Party. He received 9.9 million votes, or 13.5 percent of the vote. Representative John Anderson of Illinois, an independent presidential candidate in 1980, won almost 7 percent of the vote. Throughout U.S. history, third parties have proposed new ideas that the major political parties first opposed but later adopted. For example, in the late 1800s a group of Americans who favored several new ideas formed the Populist Party. One of these ideas was the election of U.S. senators directly by the voters. Democratic and Republican Party leaders favored the election of senators by the state legislatures as provided in the Constitution.

Populist ideas soon began to gain public support. The major parties then adopted and put into effect some of these ideas, including the direct election of senators. The passage of the Seventeenth Amendment to the Constitution officially changed the method of electing U.S. senators.

**Interpreting the Visual Record**

**Three-way race** *In 1992 independent candidate Ross Perot (seated at left) appeared in two televised debates with the Republican and Democratic presidential candidates.* **Why would such exposure be unusual for a third-party candidate?**

**Visual Record Answer**

*Third-party candidates usually do not have enough support to warrant participation in the presidential televised debates.*

✔ **Reading Check** **Analyzing Information** How have third parties affected U.S. politics? At times third parties have affected the outcome of presidential elections and forced the two major parties to adopt their issues.

## REVIEW AND ASSESS

Have students complete the **Section 1 Review** on page 258. Then have students complete **Daily Quiz 10.1**. As **Alternative Assessment**, you may want to use the briefing sheet or manifesto exercises in this section's lessons.

## RETEACH

Have students complete **Main Idea Activity for English Language Learners and Special-Needs Students 10.1**. Then assign each student one of the objectives in this section. Ask students to prepare flash cards concerning the important information contained in their objective. Ask students to quiz the class, using their flash cards. **ENGLISH LANGUAGE LEARNERS**

## EXTEND

Have students conduct research at the library about the development of the Federalist and Democratic-Republican Parties. Then instruct students to write an essay analyzing the differences and similarities between these parties. Tell students to focus on the differences and similarities concerning federalism, a republican government, separation of powers, checks and balances, and a need for a bill of rights. **BLOCK SCHEDULING**

## Section 1 Review
### ANSWERS

**1. Define**
- political party, p. 253
- nominate, p. 254
- candidates, p. 254
- two-party system, p. 255
- multiparty system, p. 256
- coalition, p. 256
- third parties, p. 256
- one-party system, p. 258

**2.** Democratic-Republicans; Alexander Hamilton; 1854, Abraham Lincoln; Democratic, 1820s

**3. a.** a way for people with similar ideas to accomplish things, help people make voices heard, nominate candidates, take stand on issues, ensure that officeholders do good jobs, check conduct of opposing party

**b.** A one-party system is one in which there is only one political party in the country and that party controls the government. A two-party system is one in which two parties share the control of the government, usually election-oriented parties.

**4.** Students' responses should include the advantages and disadvantages of both types of systems as well as rationale for their choice.

*Cuban dictator Fidel Castro is the living symbol of that country's communist government.*

## ★ One-Party Governments

In countries with more than one political party, the voters have a choice. They can decide which party to join and which party to vote for. They may even change parties or choose not to join any party.

In some countries, however, governments are based on a **one-party system.** In this system, the country has only one political party. All other political parties are forbidden by law. As you know, such governments are sometimes called dictatorships or totalitarian governments.

In this type of government, all power is in the hands of one person or one group of people. In a one-party government, a single party controls the government. The people must obey its dictates, or commands.

Italy under Benito Mussolini and Germany under Adolf Hitler had such a form of government. Today several communist countries, such as Cuba, North Korea, and the People's Republic of China, have one-party governments. Some noncommunist countries, such as Libya and Syria, also have only one official political party.

The United States and other democratic countries have traditionally opposed most dictatorships and totalitarian governments. They have done so because such systems do not allow citizens freedom of speech and action. Most Americans and citizens of other democratic countries consider these freedoms essential. They believe that a government should serve and be responsible to its people.

✔ **Reading Check** Contrasting What is the major difference between one-party and two-party systems? In a two-party system, voters have a choice of candidates and political parties. In a one-party system, voters can choose only the government's candidates or policies.

go.hrw.com **Homework Practice Online**
keyword: SZ3 HP10

## SECTION 1 Review

**1. Define** and explain:
- political party
- nominate
- candidates
- two-party system
- multiparty system
- coalition
- third parties
- one-party system

**2. Summarizing** Copy the chart below. Then fill in the missing information about political parties in the United States.

**3. Finding the Main Idea**
a. What purposes do political parties serve?
b. What are the differences between one-party and two-party systems?

**4. Writing and Critical Thinking**
**Supporting a Point of View**
Imagine that you are a political leader advising citizens on their country's future. Tell the citizens whether you think their country should have a two-party or multiparty political system.

**Consider:**
- characteristics of a two-party system
- characteristics of a multiparty system
- advantages and disadvantages of a coalition government

| Party | Founded | Leader |
|---|---|---|
|  | 1800s | Thomas Jefferson |
| Federalist | 1800s |  |
| Republican |  |  |
|  |  | Andrew Jackson |

# SECTION 2

## OBJECTIVES

*After completing Section 2, students should be able to*

1 **Name the committees that help major political parties and define their responsibilities.**
2 **Explain where political parties get their money and examine why Congress regulates political contributions.**
3 **Describe how the Federal Election Campaign Act regulates federal campaigns.**

## 🔊 *LET'S GET STARTED!*

As students enter the classroom, ask them whom they supported in the last presidential election and why they supported that particular candidate. *(Students' answers will vary.)* Also ask if any students were directly involved in their candidate's political campaign or have been involved in any other political campaign and discuss their involvement. Finally, ask students how they or their parents can become directly involved, other than by exercising their right to vote. Tell students that in Section 2 they will focus on the organization of political parties, how candidates' campaigns are financed, and the regulations imposed by the government.

---

## SECTION 2

# Political Party Organization

### Read to Discover

1. What are the committees that help major political parties, and what are their responsibilities?
2. Where do political parties get their money, and why does Congress regulate political contributions?
3. How does the Federal Election Campaign Act regulate federal campaigns?

### Define

• precincts
• polling place

#### WHY CIVICS MATTERS

The major U.S. political parties get their funds from a variety of sources. Use **CNNfyi.com** or other **current events** sources to learn about how a political party is raising money. Record your findings in your journal.

### SECTION 2 RESOURCES

#### REPRODUCIBLE

▶ Guided Reading Strategies 10.2
▶ Readings in Economics and Government 72: "Congress: The First Two-Hundred Years," Thomas P. O'Neill, Jr.
▶ American Civics Political Cartoon: Party Politics

#### TECHNOLOGY

▶ One-Stop Planner, Lesson 10.2
▶ Transparency 13: Organization of Political Parties
▶ Homework Practice Online

#### REINFORCEMENT, REVIEW, AND ASSESSMENT

▶ Section 2 Review p. 263
▶ Daily Quiz 10.2
▶ Main Idea Activity 10.2
▶ English Audio Summary 10.2
▶ Spanish Audio Summary 10.2

## *Reading Focus*

To work effectively, a political party must be well organized. It must have leaders, committees, and workers able to carry out the party's program. It must be organized at the local, state, and national levels. The party must also be able to raise money to pay its expenses. The party must nominate its candidates for office and plan its campaign strategies to get these candidates elected.

Over the years, party members have established procedures for carrying out all of the above activities. Both major parties are organized in much the same way.

### ★ Party Committees

The planning for each political party is done through a series of committees. Each political party has a national committee and state central committees in each state. Each party also has local committees at the county, city, and sometimes at township levels.

Each of these party committees is headed by a chairperson. The committee members are usually elected by the party supporters at election time. Sometimes, however, the members are chosen at meetings of party leaders. These meetings of political party leaders are called caucuses.

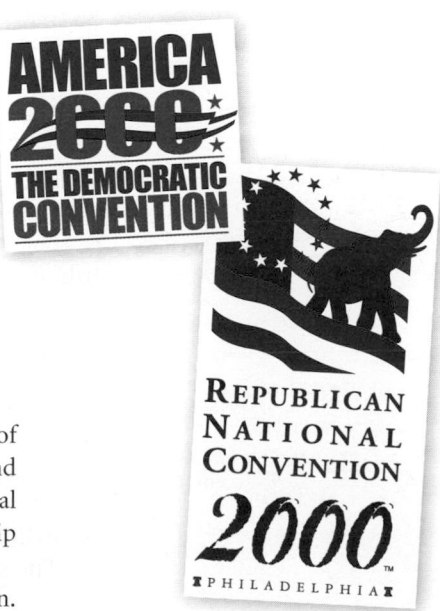

*A major function of party committees is organizing national party conventions during presidential election years.*

**ALL LEVELS:** Copy the graphic organizer to the right onto the chalkboard, omitting the italicized answers. Then ask each student to complete the rectangles by listing and describing the responsibilities of each of the committees and the ways they help their major political party. **ENGLISH LANGUAGE LEARNERS**

**LEVEL 3:** Remind students that there are certain responsibilities required at each of the levels of party committees. *(See the All Levels lesson for responsibilities.)* Then organize the class into small groups and assign one of the three levels of party committees to each group. Have each group create a planning

document of the committee's responsibilities and goals during an imaginary election campaign. **COOPERATIVE LEARNING**

**National Committee**
- *Selects the site and date for the national nominating convention*
- *Sets rules for convention*
- *Helps presidential candidate with election*

**State Central Committees**
- *Supervises party's operations within each state*
- *Maintains party harmony*
- *Helps raise money for political campaigns*

**Local Committees**
- *Conducts campaigns at the local level*
- *Raises money for the party and party candidates*
- *Makes recommendations for political appointments*
- *Precinct captains are responsible for getting voters out to vote*

## The Democratic Process

**Soft Money** When the Federal Election Commission was drafted in 1978, the intent was to ban individual contributions of more than $1,000 for a specific federal candidate and cap campaign contributions at $25,000. However, a loophole in the law existed for several decades; this loophole was known as "soft money." Soft money, which was money given to a party for the purpose of "party-building activities" such as voter registration, get-out-the-vote drives, and issue ads, proved difficult to regulate. The Bipartisan Campaign Reform Act of 2002 closed the soft-money loophole.

**CRITICAL THINKING**

Why do you think it took lawmakers several decades to ban soft money?

**ANSWER:** Students might point out that some lawmakers were elected with the help of soft money.

**Visual Record Answer**

*Students might suggest that it elects representatives that will explain those interests to others.*

**Interpreting the Visual Record**

**State convention** *In each state political parties hold conventions to elect the delegates who will represent the party at the national convention.* **How does such a system help ensure that the special interests of each state will be represented at the national party convention?**

**The National Committee** The largest party committee is the national committee. For many years it consisted of one committeeman and one committeewoman from each state and U.S. territory and the District of Columbia. However, in the 1970s each party enlarged the membership of its national committee.

Members of the national committee may be chosen in three ways. They may be elected by a state convention, elected by voters in a statewide election, or chosen by the state central committee. The national committee chairperson is often chosen by the party's presidential candidate.

The national committee selects the city in which the national nominating convention will be held. At this official party meeting, the party's presidential and vice presidential candidates are chosen. The national committee is responsible for setting the date and drawing up rules for the convention.

During an election year, the national committee publishes and distributes party literature and arranges for campaign speakers. The committee also helps the presidential candidate to plan, conduct, and raise money for the election campaign.

**State Central Committees** Each political party has a state central committee to supervise the party's operation within each of the 50 states. The state central committee chairperson is one of the party's most prominent members in the state. He or she is often a member of the national committee.

The state central committee represents the party organization in each state. Like the national committee, it is busiest at election time. The state central committee chairperson works with committee members to maintain party harmony and a strong state organization. The committee works to raise money for campaigns and to help candidates win elections.

**ALL LEVELS:** Explain to students where political parties get their money and why Congress regulates political contributions. (*Political parties receive money through private fundraising events and donations from business groups, individuals, or labor unions. Congress regulates these contributions in order to lessen the possibility of corruption.*) Tell students about the 1972 Federal Election Campaign Act and the 2002 Bipartisan Campaign Reform Act. Have students write a letter to the editor supporting or opposing campaign finance reforms or regulations.
**ENGLISH LANGUAGE LEARNERS , COOPERATIVE LEARNING**

**LEVELS 2 AND 3:** Discuss the differences between "hard money" and "soft money" contributions and why Congress regulates contributions. Then organize students into groups and instruct each group to produce a debate page concerning the pros and cons of placing further limits on soft money. Tell students that the debate page is created on a sheet of posterboard that contains the following items: background information detailing the origin of political campaign finances and why and how Congress regulates contributions, a political cartoon illustrating the topic, an editorial supporting further campaign limits on soft money, an editorial opposing campaign limits on soft money, and a political opinion poll in which students formulate a question about the topic and ask five individuals for their responses. **COOPERATIVE LEARNING**

**Local Committees** At the local level are county committees and city committees. Township committees are sometimes found in rural areas. Members of local committees are elected by party members. Committee chairpersons are elected by committee members and serve as local party leaders.

The party's successes or failures often depend on the local committees and their leaders. The county or city committee is responsible for conducting all campaigns on the local level. It raises money for the party and party candidates. Through the local chairperson, the committee makes recommendations for political appointments and for candidates for office. A strong chairperson may stay in office for many years and become quite powerful in the party.

✔ **Reading Check** Categorizing What are the functions of national, state, and local political party committees? All levels raise money. National committees also arrange national nominating conventions and publish political literature. State committees maintain state organizations. Local committees conduct campaigns and make political recommendations.

## ★ Local Party Organization

To make voting easier for citizens and more efficient for election officials, all counties, cities, and wards are divided into voting districts called **precincts.** The voters in each precinct vote at the same **polling place.** A rural precinct may cover large areas of countryside. A precinct in a crowded city may cover just a few blocks. The party leader in the precinct is called the precinct captain. The precinct captain encourages all voters to cast their ballots for the party's candidates.

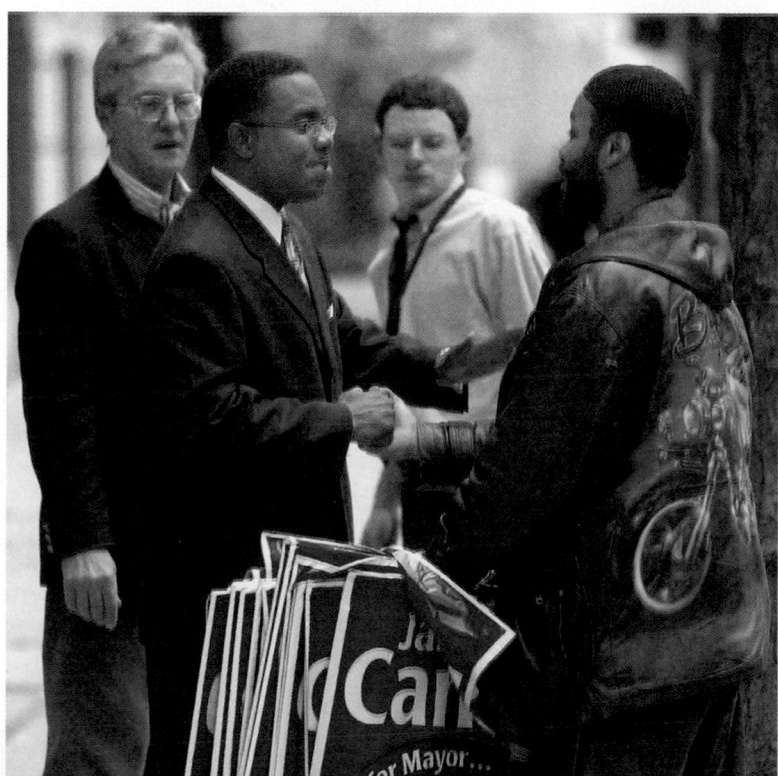

**Interpreting the Visual Record**

Local politics *On the local level, political parties play a key role in conducting campaigns and informing voters about candidates and their issues.* **How is this politician getting out his message?**

### The Democratic Process

**Campaign Slogans** During the course of a presidential campaign, either the candidate or the media will prescribe a particular slogan that illustrates a policy or a set of programs that are proposed by the candidate. The following are some of those campaign slogans.

1844—James K. Polk
"Fifty-Four Forty or Fight"

1884—James Blaine
"Ma, Ma, Where's My Pa, Gone to the White House, Ha, Ha, Ha"

1916—Woodrow Wilson
"He kept us out of War"

1920—Warren G. Harding
"Cox and Cocktails"

1928—Herbert Hoover
"A chicken in every pot and a car in every garage"

1952—Dwight Eisenhower
"I Like Ike"

1992—Ross Perot
"Ross for Boss"

1996—Bill Clinton
"Building a Bridge to the 21st Century"

2000—George W. Bush
"Real Plans for Real People"

**ACTIVITY:** Have students research the meaning behind one of the slogans listed above and then have them write an essay explaining the message behind the slogan.

### Visual Record Answer

*Students might suggest he is talking directly with the public.*

**LEVEL 1:** Discuss the Federal Election Campaign Act and the ways campaigns are regulated. *(Candidates must first raise $5,000 from private contributions in each of at least 20 states to receive up to a certain amount in matching public funds. To receive these public funds, however, a candidate must agree to certain stipulations such as agreeing to limit spending, using public funds only for campaign expenses, and if they receive the nomination, they must agree that their campaign will be paid only with public funds.)* Then ask each student to create a graphic organizer reflecting these regulations and stipulations.
**ENGLISH LANGUAGE LEARNERS**

**LEVELS 2 AND 3:** Lead a class discussion about the Federal Election Campaign Act and the ways federal campaigns are regulated. *(See the Level 1 lesson for regulations and stipulations.)* Then organize students into four large groups and instruct each group to produce a commercial asking the public to contribute $3 of their taxes to the election fund. Roles for group members include narrator, scriptwriters, and on-air personalities. Have groups present their commercials to the class.
**COOPERATIVE LEARNING**

## CLOSE

Using key terms, ideas, and phrases from this section, play a game of hangman with the class.

## ★ Economics

### Political Action Committees

Under the current campaign laws individuals can only contribute up to $1,000 to a specific candidate's primary or general election campaign, but that same individual can contribute $5,000 to a PAC (Political Action Committee). PACs are organizations that represent special interest groups and support their cause by raising and spending money on behalf of their organization. The first PAC, formed by the Congress of Industrial Organization, began in 1943. PACs can contribute to as many campaigns as they want, whereas individuals are limited to a maximum of $25,000 in campaign contributions. Two of the top PAC spenders in 2001 were Emily's List, a PAC supporting women and women's issues, and the NRA Political Victory Fund, a PAC opposing gun control legislation.

### CRITICAL THINKING

Do you think incumbents have an unfair advantage concerning raising campaign funds because of their ties to PACs?

**ANSWER:** Students might suggest that an incumbent who has established ties with PACs will find fund-raising much easier than will his or her challenger.

### Visual Record Answer

*Students might suggest that it puts people in more of a festive and therefore, giving mood.*

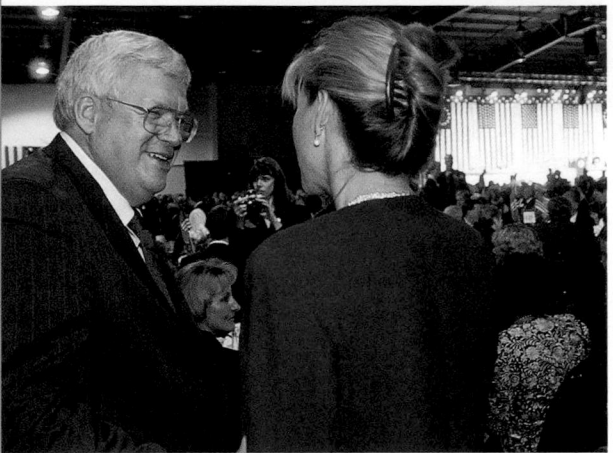

**Interpreting the Visual Record**

**Fundraising** *Political fundraisers often include music, food, and other entertainment as well as speeches from leading party members.* **Why do you think party officials include entertainment at fund-raising events?**

Precinct captains are busy at election time. They organize volunteers to distribute campaign literature. They see that pictures of the party's candidates are displayed in local shops. Precinct captains may arrange to have voters with disabilities driven to the polling place. They may have party workers telephone voters and urge them to vote for party candidates. Between elections, precinct captains get to know the people in the neighborhood.

✔ **Reading Check** Finding the Main Idea What role do precincts play in the voting process? Precincts are voting districts that enable residents to vote at polling places near them.

## ★ Political Party Finances

Running for political office is expensive. Candidates for president need millions of dollars to run their campaigns. Their costs include office rent, assistants, campaign literature, radio and television broadcasts, and traveling expenses. Where does all this money come from?

Until 1974 political campaigns were paid for entirely with private contributions. Many campaigns are still paid for this way. Voters are urged to contribute to the political party of their choice. Business groups, labor unions, and many other groups also contribute to the political party that they believe best represents their interests.

Political parties work hard to raise money. Several times a year, they hold large fund-raising events. The money raised at these events goes into the party's treasury and is used to pay election campaign expenses.

Whenever large campaign contributions are made, however, people worry about corruption. Will a big contributor receive special favors in return for helping the winning candidate? To lessen the possibility of political corruption, the U.S. Congress passed the Federal Election Campaign Act in 1972.

The Federal Election Campaign Act (FECA) requires every political candidate in federal elections (campaigns for Congress or president) to report the name of every person who contributes $200 or more in a year. The law also limits individual contributions to candidates to $1,000 for primary elections and another $1,000 for general elections. These provisions are enforced by the Federal Election Commission. However, much attention has been given recently to what is known as soft money. The FECA still allows various individuals and groups to make huge contributions to political parties. In theory, such soft-money contributions cannot be spent on federal campaigns. However, it is very difficult to monitor how these contributions are actually spent.

✔ **Reading Check** Analyzing Information How do political parties raise money, and what rules must they follow? Parties raise money through large fund-raising events and campaign contributions. They must follow the FECA, which limits individual contributions.

## REVIEW AND ASSESS

Have students complete the **Section 2 Review** on page 263. Then have students complete **Daily Quiz 10.2.** As **Alternative Assessment**, you may want to use the debate page or commercial activity in this section's lessons.

## RETEACH

Have students complete **Main Idea Activity for English Language Learners and Special-Needs Students 10.2.** Write questions and answers covering the three objectives to be used in a Jeopardy-type game. Write the questions and answers in a format with the answers given first, followed by the questions. After the questions and answers are created, organize the class

into groups of four and have groups play the game.
**ENGLISH LANGUAGE LEARNERS , COOPERATIVE LEARNING**

## EXTEND

Have students work together in small groups to research a historical campaign or political issue that drew young people into the political process. Issues might include the Twenty-sixth Amendment, the civil rights movement, or the Vietnam War. Then have each group explore which candidates seemed to attract the most young people to the political process and why. Then have students write a script for a play concerning their research and depicting involvement by young people.
**COOPERATIVE LEARNING , BLOCK SCHEDULING**

---

## ★ Public Financing

The Federal Election Campaign Act also introduced public financing of presidential elections. Through public financing, money is made available to candidates from the Presidential Election Campaign Fund in the U.S. Treasury. By checking a box on their federal income tax forms, Americans can contribute $3 of their taxes to the election fund. This neither raises nor lowers the amount of tax a person pays.

The U.S. Treasury distributes the fund's money to the candidates. To be eligible to receive this money, a candidate trying to win a party's nomination for president must first raise at least $5,000 from private contributions in each of at least 20 states. The candidate then can receive up to a certain amount in matching public funds. Minor-party candidates may qualify to receive public funds after the election if they win at least 5 percent of the vote during the election. The more money a candidate raises, the more matching funds he or she can receive. To receive public funds, however, candidates must agree to limit their spending in nomination campaigns. They must also promise to use public funds only for campaign expenses.

After winning the nomination of their party, presidential candidates who accept public financing cannot accept private contributions. Their campaigns must be paid for only with the public funds they receive.

✔ **Reading Check** Finding the Main Idea How are presidential elections publicly financed? **Qualifying candidates receive matching funds from the U.S. Treasury. If they win the nomination, candidates who accept public funds cannot take private contributions.**

**Interpreting Political Cartoons**
**Campaign funding** This cartoon shows the Republican and Democratic Parties stuffing themselves on campaign contributions. **What type of contribution are the parties shown receiving?**

In the 2000 election, George W. Bush did not accept federal matching funds. Free to raise as much money as he could, he spent a record $100 million on his campaign.

## Section 2 Review
### ANSWERS

**1. Define**
• precincts, p. 261
• polling place, p. 261

**2.** National—selects city and date for national nominating convention, draws up rules for the convention, publishes and distributes party literature and arranges campaign speakers, helps presidential candidate plan, conduct, and raise money; State Central—supervises party operation in state, raises money and helps candidates win elections; Local—conducts campaigns on the local level

**3. a.** private contributions, fundraisers, and government matching funds

**b.** the Federal Election Campaign Act and the Revenue Act

**4.** Students' pamphlets will vary but should include rationale for guidelines and the present campaign funding guidelines.

---

## SECTION 2 Review

**go.hrw.com** Homework Practice Online
keyword: SZ3 HP10

**1. Define** and explain:
• precincts   • polling place

**2. Summarizing** Copy the graphic organizer below. Use it to identify the committees that run each of the major political parties and the functions of each committee.

COMMITTEES → FUNCTIONS
COMMITTEES →
COMMITTEES →

**3. Finding the Main Idea**
a. How do political candidates and parties fund campaigns?
b. How does Congress regulate financial contributions?

**4. Writing and Critical Thinking**
**Summarizing** Create a pamphlet explaining the guidelines you would suggest for federal financing of presidential campaigns.

Consider:
• how presidential campaigns are publicly funded
• the advantages and disadvantages of federal financing

# SECTION 3

## OBJECTIVES

*After completing Section 3, students should be able to*

1. Determine who can vote in U.S. elections and describe how this right is protected.

2. Describe the differences between primary elections and general elections.

3. Explain how the voting process has changed over the years.

## SECTION 3 RESOURCES

### REPRODUCIBLE

▶ Guided Reading Strategies 10.3

▶ Readings in Economics and Government 45: Voting Rights Act of 1965

▶ Graphic Organizer Activity: Politics and the Vote

### TECHNOLOGY

▶ One-Stop Planner, Lesson 10.3

▶ CNN Presents: American Government

▶ Homework Practice Online

### REINFORCEMENT, REVIEW, AND ASSESSMENT

▶ Section 3 Review, p. 268

▶ Daily Quiz 10.3

▶ Main Idea Activity 10.3

▶ English Audio Summary 10.3

▶ Spanish Audio Summary 10.3

## LET'S GET STARTED!

As students enter the classroom, ask them if they ever accompanied their parents to the polls and watched as they went through the procedure of voting. If they did, ask them what they remember about the process. *(Students' responses will vary.)* Using props and students as election officials, take students through the procedure of voting, beginning with presenting the voter registration card or some other form of identification to the polling place officials. Tell students that in Section 3 they will learn what qualifications are necessary to exercise the right to vote, as well as the protections that ensure our right to vote. The section will also discuss how voting has changed over the years.

## SECTION 3

# The Right to Vote

### Read to Discover

1. Who can vote in U.S. elections, and how is this right protected?

2. What is the difference between primary elections and general elections?

3. How has the voting process changed over the years?

### Define

- independent voters
- primary election
- general election
- closed primary
- open primary
- runoff
- grassroots
- secret ballots
- straight ticket
- split ticket

### WHY CIVICS MATTERS

Despite having the right to vote, U.S. citizens often fail to exercise their power to influence government. Use **CNNfyi**.com or other **current events** sources to learn what the voter participation figures were in a recent election. Record your findings in your journal.

## Reading Focus

At the age of 18, all U.S. citizens become eligible to vote in national, state, and local elections. The right to vote is one of the most important rights held by U.S. citizens. It is the means through which citizens can most directly affect the actions of government.

*All U.S. citizens become eligible to vote at the age of 18.*

### ★ State Qualifications for Voting

Each state decides qualifications for registering to vote and voting in state elections. To register to vote in most states, a person must be 18 within a certain time period before the next election or simply by the time of the next election.

All states must follow the provisions about voting contained in the U.S. Constitution. Specifically, the Constitution forbids any state to deny a citizen the right to vote on the basis of race, color, or sex. To ensure these voting rights, Congress passed the Voting Rights Act in 1965 and expanded it in 1970, 1975, and 1982.

Many states disqualify certain people from voting. In most states a prison inmate who is convicted of a serious crime loses the right to vote. Most states also deny the right to vote to mentally incompetent persons, election-law violators, and persons with no established residence.

✔ **Reading Check** Drawing Inferences and Conclusions Why might states disqualify some citizens from voting? Students may suggest that losing the right to vote might be a result of how voter registration records are kept, questioned competency, residency restrictions, or intended as a punishment.

# TEACH OBJECTIVE 1

**ALL LEVELS:** Lead a class discussion about who can vote in U.S. elections and describe how that right is protected. *(Outline the qualifications regarding age, citizenship, and residency requirements. Also explain the importance of the Voting Rights Acts, beginning with the Voting Rights Act of 1965.)* Refer students to information on the Voting Rights Act of 1965 on page 265. Then organize the class into groups and ask groups to create a pamphlet designed for elementary-age students that explains the Voting Rights Act of 1965. The pamphlet should restate each important idea in simple terminology. Arrange to deliver the pamphlets to an elementary class that is interested in learning more about voting. **ENGLISH LANGUAGE LEARNERS**

**LEVELS 2 AND 3:** Lead a class discussion about who can vote in U.S. elections and how the right to vote is protected. Then ask students why some people, though qualified, do not exercise their right to vote. Organize the class into small groups and tell each group to formulate solutions that would increase voter participation. After groups have finished, have them share their solutions with the class. Then select the top 10 solutions and have the class rank them in order of their preference. **COOPERATIVE LEARNING**

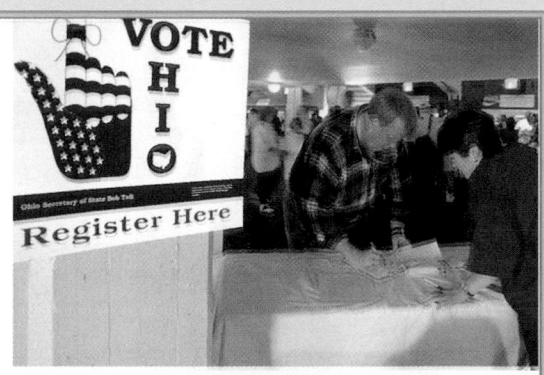

## ★ Registering to Vote

When a person goes to a polling place to vote, officials must be able to tell that he or she is a qualified voter. Most states require voters to register before the day of an election. Registering to vote places a voter's name on the official roll of eligible voters. When people register, they give their name, address, date of birth, and other information showing that they meet the voting qualifications. They may be given cards showing that they are registered voters.

Almost all states have permanent registration. This means that people need to register only once as long as they do not move out of their precinct. However, some states require voters who do not vote in a certain number of elections to register again. A few states have periodic registration in some or all areas. This means that voters must register before each election or at regular intervals to remain qualified.

When people register to vote, they may be asked to register as a member of the political party of their choice. Party membership may be changed later by registering again. Citizens may also register as **independent voters,** or as voters who are not members of a political party. However, if a person does not register as a member of a political party, that person may not be allowed to vote in primary elections in some states.

**Interpreting the Visual Record**

**Voter registration** *Most communities encourage their residents to register to vote. Why is registering to vote important?*

✔ **Reading Check** Summarizing How do states verify qualified voters? States require voters to register ahead of time, giving their name, address, date of birth, and other information.

---

### Historical Document

### VOTING RIGHTS ACT OF 1965

*The Voting Rights Act of 1965 banned voting discrimination based on race or color in federal, state, and local elections. The act also made the use of practices such as literacy tests for voters illegal. As a result of the new law, the number of people who were eligible to vote increased.*

"To assure that the right of citizens of the United States is not denied or abridged on account of race or color, no citizen shall be denied the right to vote in any Federal, State, or local election because of his failure to comply with any test or device in any State . . . .

The phrase "test or device" shall mean any requirement that a person as a prerequisite for voting or registration for voting (1) demonstrate the ability to read, write, understand, or interpret any matter, (2) demonstrate any educational achievement or his knowledge of any particular subject, (3) possess good moral character, or (4) prove his qualifications by the voucher of registered voters or members of any other class."

**Analyzing Primary Sources**
1. What was the intent of the Voting Rights Act of 1965?
2. Why do you think legislators found it necessary to specify what "test or device" means?

---

## ★ Global Perspectives

**The Minimum Voting Age** The first requirement one must meet to register to vote is age. The minimum voting age in the United States, 18, is a fairly common requirement in many other countries. The minimum age does vary, however. Iranians may vote at age 15, but Malaysians must wait until they are 21. Japanese are eligible to vote when they are 20. The minimum voting age in most European countries is 18. The following is a selection of countries and their minimum voting ages as of 2002: Nigeria, 21; Kenya, 18; Israel, 18; Argentina, 18; Chile, 18; Philippines, 15.

**CRITICAL THINKING**

Why do you think that the U.S. voting age was changed from 21 to 18 in 1971?

**ANSWER:** Students might suggest that many felt that if soldiers were old enough to fight in Vietnam, they were old enough to vote.

---

**ANALYZING PRIMARY SOURCES ANSWERS**

1. to prevent voter discrimination based on race or color in any federal, state, or local election

2. Students might suggest because legislators did not want to leave an opportunity to circumvent the meaning of the act.

---

**Visual Record Answer**

*Registration helps ensure that voters are legally qualified to vote.*

265

*Electing Leaders* **265**

**ALL LEVELS:** Explain the differences between a primary election and a general election. *(The primary election takes place first, usually in the late spring or summer, and the general election is the one in which voters choose their leaders.)* Then organize the class into two groups and tell one group that they are members of the Democratic Party. Tell the other one that they are members of the Republican Party. Then choose four students from each party to stand up and announce their candidacy for state representative. Have each party then select its winner. Tell the winners to remain standing and to explain to the class that now they will run against each other in the general election. **ENGLISH LANGUAGE LEARNERS , COOPERATIVE LEARNING**

**LEVEL 3:** Discuss with students the differences between primary and general elections and tell them that the winners of the Democratic and Republican primaries are automatically placed on the ballot. *(See the All Levels lesson for differences.)* Then tell students that independent candidates are not automatically placed on the ballot and are required to obtain a certain number of signatures on a petition before they can be placed on the ballot. Then have each student imagine that they are independent candidates running for a seat in the legislature. Students should create a leaflet or a fact sheet explaining to prospective voters why they should vote for an independent candidate.

## Civics Sidelight

### If the Horseshoe Fits
Many terms used to describe elections were first used to describe horse races. Elections are often referred to as *races*. This is natural, since candidates run to see who will win. A nominee for high office, such as the presidency, has a *running mate*, who is running for vice president. In horse racing a stable owner might use another horse, a running mate, to set the pace for another of his or her horses in a race. In politics and horse racing, a *dark horse* (or long shot) is a contender who seems to have little chance of winning. The candidate or horse who is ahead is called the *front runner*—but the *finish* may be *neck and neck* after all.

### CRITICAL THINKING
Can you think of any other terms that are used to describe other political or governmental situations?

**ANSWER:** Students might suggest terms such as *lame duck*, *pork barrel*, and others.

### Visual Record Answer
*Students might suggest that it narrows the field of candidates, therefore making it easier to make a final decision.*

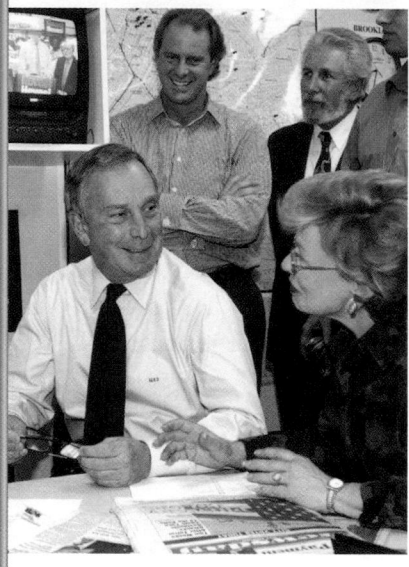

**Interpreting the Visual Record**

**Primaries** *Winning the party primary is a candidate's first step toward election. Here mayoral candidate Michael Bloomberg watches results indicating his victory in the New York City Republican primary.* **Why do you think parties hold primaries instead of letting all party candidates run for an office in the general election?**

## Primary Elections

Two separate elections are held in most states. The **primary election** takes place first and is usually held in the late spring or early summer. The primary election allows voters to choose the candidates from each party who will run in the later **general election.** The general election is the election in which voters actually choose their leaders.

There are two types of primary elections—the **closed primary** and the **open primary.** In the closed primary, only those voters who are registered in the party can vote to choose the party's candidates. Most states use the closed primary. Thus, in most states, only registered Democrats can vote for Democratic candidates, and only registered Republicans can vote for Republican candidates. Those people who have registered as independent voters cannot vote in a closed primary. In the open primary, voters may vote for the candidates of either major party, whether or not the voters belong to that party.

In most states, the candidate who receives the highest number of votes is the winner of the primary election. The winning candidate does not have to receive a majority, or more than 50 percent, of the vote. In some states, however, the winner must receive a majority of the votes. If no candidate receives a majority, a **runoff** between the two leading candidates decides the winner. The winning candidate in the primary election then becomes the party's candidate in the general election.

In some states, political parties choose their candidates in a nominating convention. Delegates to the convention are elected by the various committees in the state's political organization. In a state convention, the county and city committees select the delegates. State committees select the delegates to national conventions.

✔ **Reading Check** **Contrasting** How do primaries differ from general elections? In the primaries, voters choose their party's candidates to run for public office in the later general election.

## Independent Candidates

An independent candidate can have his or her name printed on the general election ballot if enough supporters sign a petition. Independent candidates usually receive only **grassroots** support. Grassroots support is support from many individuals at the local level rather than from national parties and other large organizations. Independent candidates are not elected as often as major-party candidates, but they do win some elections, mostly for local offices.

It is even possible, however difficult, for a person to be elected to an office when his or her name is not printed on the ballot. In some states, voters may write in the name of an unofficial candidate.

✔ **Reading Check** **Analyzing Information** How do independent candidates run for office? They must get enough supporters to sign a petition to have their name placed on the general election ballot.

# TEACH OBJECTIVE 3

**ALL LEVELS:** Explain how the voting process has changed over the years. Copy the following graphic organizer onto the chalkboard, omitting the italicized answers. Have students complete the organizer with some of the voting method alternatives, other than a paper ballot, that are currently used across the country.
**ENGLISH LANGUAGE LEARNERS**

## CLOSE

Organize students into small groups and give each group a long sheet of butcher paper and colored markers. Have groups design a mural illustrating the barriers that prevented certain groups from exercising their right to vote and illustrating the protections that now exist to protect voting rights.

## General Elections

Congress has set the date for the general elections of the president and Congress. It is the first Tuesday following the first Monday in November of an election year. Presidential elections take place every four years. Congressional elections occur every two years. Most general elections for state officials are also held in November. The president and members of Congress are elected in even-numbered years. Some states elect their state officials in odd-numbered years, but the timing of state elections varies from state to state.

On election day, the American voter faces both the great responsibility and privilege of citizenship. The voter must choose wisely among the candidates of the various parties. The informed voter has studied hard to identify the candidate whose views most closely resemble his or her own.

There are many resources available to American voters. Nonpartisan organizations like the League of Women Voters provide information about national and local election issues. Voters can also read newspapers and magazines and find information about candidates on the Internet. They can listen to the candidates on the radio and on television and can discuss the candidates with other people.

As voters enter the polling place, they may see several of their neighbors working. These people are acting as inspectors, or poll watchers. Each party has its own poll watchers to ensure that elections are conducted fairly.

✔ **Reading Check** Finding the Main Idea What are some ways that voters can educate themselves about candidates and election issues? They can consult organizations, read articles in newspapers and magazines, find information on the Internet, listen to the radio, watch television, and discuss the candidates with other people.

## Voting in the Past

During the first part of the 1800s, voting in the United States was usually by voice vote. Voters announced aloud to the election official their choice of candidate.

This system of voice voting made it easier to pressure a person to vote a certain way. Suppose a person's boss were standing nearby. The boss could hear how the employee voted and might fire the employee who did not vote the way the boss wanted.

In 1888 a new system of voting with **secret ballots** was adopted. Paper ballots contain the names of the candidates and a place for the voter to mark a choice. This ballot is marked in secret to guarantee that a person's vote remains private. This method of voting helps make elections fair and honest.

### Voting in Australia

Even though voting is a right and responsibility of U.S. citizenship, some Americans choose not to vote. Not all nations give their citizens this choice. In Australia, for example, voting is compulsory.

All Australian citizens age 18 and over are required by law to register as voters. Citizens must vote in all national and state elections and in most local elections. People too ill to go to the polls on election day are allowed to mail in their ballots. Australians who fail to vote may have to pay a fine of $50. Not surprisingly, Australia has one of the highest voter turnout rates of any industrialized nation in the world. **Do you agree or disagree with compulsory voting? Explain your answer.**

## The Democratic Process

**Voting—2000 Style** On presidential-election night 2000, many election officials were using blow-dryers to dry out punchcard ballots because the humidity in the air was causing the vote-counting machines to reject numerous ballots. Thousands of ballots are discarded each year because of imperfect voting methods. Just what methods were used across the United States in the 2000 presidential election? The punchcard, with its "hanging chads" or "dimpled marks" was used by 34 percent of the population, the optical scan was used by 27 percent, the lever machines by 19 percent, electronic voting by 9 percent, and paper ballots were used by 2 percent of the population. Combinations of these methods made up the rest of the percentage.

**CRITICAL THINKING**

The Constitution left election procedures to the states, but do you think there should be a uniform national voting technology that should be required for all states to implement?

**ANSWER:** Students' answers will vary.

**GLOBAL CONNECTIONS ANSWERS**
Students' answers will vary.

## REVIEW AND ASSESS

Have students complete the **Section 3 Review** on page 268. Then have them complete **Daily Quiz 10.3**. As **Alternative Assessment**, you may want to use the pamphlet or petition activities in this section's lessons.

## RETEACH

Have students complete **Main Idea Activity for English Language Learners and Special-Needs Students 10.3**. Organize students into small groups and assign each group one of the three objectives of this section. Groups should create a visual that illustrates their objective. Groups will then share their visuals with the class. **ENGLISH LANGUAGE LEARNERS** , **COOPERATIVE LEARNING**

## EXTEND

Have students research your state's residency voting requirements and your state's registration requirements for voting. Compare your state's requirements to the requirements of neighboring states. Then have students create a chart that illustrates the requirements for all 50 states. **BLOCK SCHEDULING**

## Section 3 Review
### ANSWERS

**1. Define**
• independent voters, p. 265
• primary election, p. 266
• general election, p. 266
• closed primary, p. 266
• open primary, p. 266
• runoff, p. 266
• grassroots, p. 266
• secret ballots, p. 267
• straight ticket, p. 268
• split ticket, p. 268

**2.** secret ballot, voting machines

**3. a.** Most states require that a person must be 18 and satisfy some time of residency requirement. The Constitution and the various voting rights acts prevent the government (local, state, or federal) from preventing a legal voter from exercising his or her right.

**b.** Voters are required to register to help prevent voter fraud. Most states have permanent registration, so that once voters are registered, they do not have to register again unless they move.

**4.** Students' paragraphs will vary but should include the information required.

**Interpreting the Visual Record**

**Ballots** *This ballot from the 2000 presidential election shows all of the official candidates.* **How many different political parties are listed on this ballot?**

## ★ Voting Today

Today many states offer alternatives to the paper ballot. Other voting mechanisms include mechanical lever machines, punchcards, marksense, and direct recording electronic (DRE) systems. Mechanical lever machines were the most common form of voting in the 1960s but are now being replaced by other voting mechanisms. Lever machines are large, curtained booths. On the front of the voting machines, the voter sees several small rows of levers with the name of a candidate or issue near the lever.

Voters using punchcards use a hole punch to indicate what candidate or issue they support. The marksense or optical scan system requires voters to fill in little black circles or arrows with a pencil. A special machine called an optical scanner then counts the votes. The DRE system provides voters with the ballot on a special touch screen. Voters select their candidates by touching the person's name on the screen.

Many voters choose to vote a **straight ticket** —that is, they vote for all of the candidates of one party. Other voters choose to vote a **split ticket** —choosing candidates of more than one political party.

On election day, polling places are usually open from early in the morning until evening. In most states, the law provides that all employers must give time off to employees to vote.

✔ **Reading Check** Summarizing How has voting changed during the past 200 years? The secret ballot has replaced the voice vote; voting machines, punchcards, marksense and direct electronic systems have replaced paper ballots.

## SECTION 3 Review

**1. Define** and explain:
• independent voters
• primary election
• general election
• closed primary
• open primary
• runoff
• grassroots
• secret ballots
• straight ticket
• split ticket

**2. Contrasting** Copy the graphic organizer below. Use it show the ways that voting has changed since the first part of the 1800s.

| Past | | Present |
|------|------|---------|
| Voice Vote | replaced by | |

| Past | | Present |
|------|------|---------|
| Paper Ballot | replaced by | |

**3. Finding the Main Idea**
**a.** What are the qualifications for voting, and how do the Constitution and the Voting Rights Act protect voters?
**b.** Why are voters required to register? How do people register to vote?

**4. Writing and Critical Thinking**
**Contrasting** Write a brief paragraph describing the different types of primary elections and the difference between primaries and general elections.

**Consider:**
• the types of primary elections
• the purpose of primary elections and general elections

## TEACH

**LEVEL 1:** Obtain from your local voter election administrator a copy of the voter registration form. Make an overhead transparency of the form and explain the form to your class. Then ask them why the address on the form must be specific. (*Students might suggest that if people put down a post office box number or a rural route number, the election administrator will not be able to assign them to the appropriate precinct.*) Then ask students if they think only citizens should be allowed to vote. (*Students' answers will vary.*) Ask if there are any circumstances in which they think resident aliens should be allowed to vote. Have students list any advantages or disadvantages to allowing resident aliens the right to vote. **ENGLISH LANGUAGE LEARNERS**

## EXTEND

Have students research the various methods that had been used in the past to prevent those legally qualified to vote, from voting. Also have students research the court cases or congressional legislation passed that prohibited the above practices. Have students present their findings to the class in the form of a 30-second news report. **BLOCK SCHEDULING**

---

# Civics Skills
## WORKSHOP

### Registering to Vote

Voting for candidates is a right we enjoy as U.S. citizens. Under the U.S. Constitution you must be at least 18 years old to vote. In addition, some states require you to live in the state for a certain period of time before you can register to vote. Many states require you to register in person; other states allow you to register by mail. Whatever the requirements in your state, it is important that you fulfill them so that you, too, can exercise your right to vote.

### How to Register to Vote

1. **Learn the registration procedure.** The registration process varies from state to state. To find out how to register, contact your state or local election office. You should request a registration form and ask what deadlines you must meet.

2. **Follow the procedure.** Usually, registering to vote is as simple as filling out a form. The forms in most states ask for basic information: your name, your age, your residence, and whether you are a citizen of the United States. You must also sign the form, swearing that the information you have given is correct.

### Applying the Skill

Study the voter registration form below. Then answer the following questions.

1. What information does this registration form require you to provide about yourself?

2. Why must you sign a voter registration form?

3. Why do you think this form is printed in Spanish as well as English?

---

**Prescribed by the Secretary of State 17.97 BPM1.1-97** | **VOTER REGISTRATION APPLICATION (SOLICITUD DE INSCRIPCION DE VOTANTE)** | Additional Information | For Official Use Only PCT    Cert. Num.    EDR

Last Name (Apellido usual) | First Name (NOT HUSBAND'S) (Su nombre de pila) (Siendo mujer: no el del esposo) | Middle/Maiden Name (If any) (Segundo Nombre/Apellido de Soltera) (si tiene)) | Former Name (Nombre anterior)

Residence Address: Street Address and Apartment Number, City, State, and ZIP. If none, describe where you live. (Do not include P.O. Box or Rural Rt.) (Domicilio: Calle y número, número de apartamento, Ciudad, Estado, y Código Postal; A falta de estos datos, describa la localidad de su residencia.) (No incluya su apartado postal ni su ruta rural.)

Mailing Address, City, State and ZIP: If mail cannot be delivered to your residence address. (Dirección postal, Ciudad, Estado y Código Postal) (Si es imposible entregarle correspondencia a domicilio.) | Gender (Optional) (Sexo) (Optativo) ☐Male (Hombre) ☐Female (Mujer)

Date of Birth: month, day, year (Fecha de Nacimiento): (mes, día, año) | City, County, and State of Former Residence (Ciudad, Condado, Estado de su residencia anterior) | Social Security No. (Optional) (Número de Seguro Social)(optativo)

Check appropriate box: I AM A UNITED STATES CITIZEN ☐Yes ☐No (Marque el cuadro apropiado: Soy Ciudadano/a de los Estados Unidos) (Sí) (No) | TX Driver's License No. or Personal I.D. No. (Issued by TX Dept. of Public Safety) (Optional) (Número de su licencia tejana de manejar o su Cédula de Identidad expedida por el Departamento de Seguridad Pública de Tejas) (optativo)

I understand that giving false information to procure a voter registration is perjury, and a crime under state and federal law. (Entiendo que el hecho de proporcionar datos falsos a fin de obtener inscripción en el registro de votantes, constituye el delito de perjurio o declaración falsa y es una infracción sancionable por ley federal y estatal.) | Telephone Number (Optional) (Número telefónico) (optativo)

I affirm that I (Declaro que soy)
• am a resident of this county; (residente del condado)
• have not been finally convicted of a felony or if a felon I am eligible for registration under section 13.001, Election Code; and (que no he sido condenado/a por un delito penal, o en caso de tal condena, que estoy habilitado/a para inscribirme, a tenor de lo dispuesto por la sección 13.001 del Código Electoral) | Check one (Marque el cuadro) ☐New (Nuevo) ☐Change (Cambiar) ☐Replacement (Reemplazar)

X | Date (fecha) /    /

• have not been declared mentally incompetent by final judgment of a court of law. (no se me ha declarado mentalmente incapacitado por orden judicial.) | Signature of Applicant or Agent and Relationship to Applicant or Printed Name of Applicant if Signed by Witness and Date. (Firma débile la solicitante o de su apoderado/a y que parezxca su nombre si/la apoderado con el/la solicitante. Si la firma es de un(a) testigo, escriba el nombre del/de la solicitante usando letra de molde y ponga la fecha.)

---

---

**SKILLS ANSWERS**

1. name, maiden name, former name, address, mailing address, date of birth, former residence, affirmation of eligibility

2. to attest to the truth of the information provided

3. It is required by law if a certain percentage of the people in the state or district speak a second language.

# SECTION 4

## OBJECTIVES

*After completing Section 4, students should be able to*

1 **Explain the purpose of national nominating conventions and describe how convention delegates are chosen.**

2 **Examine the nomination process at the national conventions.**

3 **Describe some of the methods of presidential campaigning.**

4 **Determine the main purpose of the electoral college.**

## ((( ○ LET'S GET STARTED!

As students enter the classroom, ask them if the popular vote or the electoral vote determines the winner in a presidential election? *(Students should suggest that the electoral vote determines the president.)* Then ask which state's electoral vote in the 2000 presidential election determined the winner. *(Students should respond with Florida.)* Using the chalkboard, tell students to list examples of problems that Florida election officials encountered when trying to declare a winner. *(Students might suggest the problems with the butterfly ballots, problems with hanging chads, and so on.)* Once the list is completed and the discussion finished, tell students that in Section 4 they will learn more about nominating and electing our leaders.

## SECTION 4

# Nominating and Electing Our Leaders

### Read to Discover

1. What is the purpose of national nominating conventions, and how are convention delegates chosen?
2. What is the nomination process at the national conventions?
3. What are some methods of presidential campaigning?
4. What is the main purpose of the electoral college?

### Define

- presidential primaries
- party platform
- favorite sons or daughters
- popular vote
- electors
- electoral college
- electoral votes

#### WHY CIVICS MATTERS

Presidential elections are exciting national events. Use **CNNfyi.com** or other **current events** sources to learn about the major issues in the most recent U.S. presidential election. Record your findings in your journal.

## Reading Focus

Every four years the country stirs with excitement as the presidential election draws near. Americans generally like a good, hard-fought battle, and the election of the president is one of the best. Informed voters follow the presidential election campaign every step of the way in newspaper, magazine, radio, and television reports.

### ★ Convention Delegates

In each state, members of each political party choose delegates to go to their party's nominating convention to nominate candidates for president and vice president. Convention delegates may either be elected in presidential primaries or selected by party leaders.

In recent years, **presidential primaries** have grown in importance. Today most states and the District of Columbia hold presidential primaries. In these primaries, voters indicate which candidate they want the delegates to vote for at the national nominating convention.

In some states the candidate who receives the most votes in the presidential primaries wins all the delegate votes from that state. In other states each candidate wins some of the delegate votes based on the proportion of primary votes received. In still other states delegates may vote as they wish at the convention.

*During the 2000 election, Bill Bradley competed with Al Gore for the Democratic nomination at the early presidential primaries.*

**ALL LEVELS:** Discuss with students the purpose of the national nominating convention and describe how convention delegates are chosen. (*It nominates the party's candidate for president and vice president. Delegates are either elected in presidential primaries or selected by primary leaders.*) Ask students to suggest some of the methods used to grab the attention of voters and other delegates. (*Students might suggest slogans, songs, pictures, slide shows, testimonials, and so on.*) Organize students into small groups and tell each group that their task is to drum up support for a candidate at a fictional national convention by writing a song or a rap to introduce their candidate's views. Call on volunteers to present their finished songs to the class. **ENGLISH LANGUAGE LEARNERS , COOPERATIVE LEARNING**

**LEVELS 2 AND 3:** Discuss with students the fact that most states today hold party primaries, not only to demonstrate voter preference concerning candidates but also to choose delegates to the national nominating conventions. Also tell students that the procedure differs from state to state and inform them how your state chooses delegates. Discuss with students the purpose of the national nominating conventions. (*See the All levels lesson for purpose.*) Then have each student design a brochure describing the purpose of the national nominating conventions and detailing the selection process for your state.

Some states do not hold primaries. In these states party leaders usually choose the delegates in state or local party conventions. State committees may also select delegates.

States with larger populations send more delegates to the national nominating convention than states with smaller populations do. The Democratic and Republican Parties have different formulas for determining how many delegates a state may send to the convention. As a result, the number of delegates at each party's convention also differs.

A state's political party may send additional delegates if the party's candidate won in that state in the last presidential election. Both parties use complicated formulas to choose these extra delegates. States also send alternates who vote if regular delegates become ill.

✔ **Reading Check Finding the Main Idea** Why do parties hold national nominating conventions, and how do the states choose delegates for these conventions? National conventions are held to nominate candidates for president and vice president. Delegates may either be elected in presidential primaries or selected by party leaders.

## ★ National Nominating Conventions

Each party's national nominating convention is held during the summer of the presidential election year. Party conventions are huge, lively events filled with tradition. The only formal business is agreeing on a party's platform and nominating presidential and vice presidential candidates. Because national conventions are televised, party leaders use them to try to win the support of voters across the country for their platform and candidate.

**Selecting a Platform** On the convention's opening day, the delegates from each state are seated in the vast convention hall. After a keynote speaker delivers an opening address, a special committee presents the **party platform.** This written statement outlines the party's views on important issues and sets forth a proposed program for the nation. Each part of the platform is called a plank. For example, the party

**Interpreting the Visual Record**

National conventions *Thousands of delegates and supporters may attend a convention such as the 2000 Republican National Convention in Philadelphia. How might attending a convention such as this one help unify party members with differing views?*

## ★ Culture

**Reflecting Diversity** The number and importance of primaries have fluctuated over the years since they were established in 1905. The parties have made efforts to diversify their convention delegations by ethnicity and gender. For example, a Democratic Party commission formed in 1969 proposed reforms that required state delegations to include members from ethnic groups and both genders in proportion to their numbers in the general electorate. Although these requirements have been modified over the years, the result has been increasingly diverse delegations to national conventions. In 1992 the Republican Party continued its efforts toward diversification by adopting rules that instructed state party organizations to "endeavor to have equal representation" of both genders among their national convention delegations.

**CRITICAL THINKING**

Why would both parties want to continue their efforts toward diversification of convention delegates?

**ANSWER:** to reflect the diversity of the United States of America so that all viewpoints are presented

**Visual Record Answer**

*Students might suggest that they come to the convention with the spirit of cooperation.*

**ALL LEVELS:** After discussing how the nomination process works at the national nominating convention, organize a mock national nominating convention in class. *(A roll call of the states is held and then the task of choosing the candidates begins.)* Assign each student various roles, such as speakers, convention delegation members that nominate a favorite son or daughter, delegation members that nominate a major candidate, acceptance-speech writers, and party nominees. Then organize the class into "states" and conduct a roll-call vote for the nomination. Have students create political hats and signs that support the fictional party nominees.
**COOPERATIVE LEARNING**

**HOMEWORK** Have each student choose a book to read that covers a political campaign and election. Then ask each student to write a report about his or her book.

## TEACH OBJECTIVE 3

 **ALL LEVELS:** Discuss with students some of the methods of presidential campaigning. *(Some of the methods are television and other media, newspapers, radio, and personal appearances.)* Obtain a video clip of a presidential debate and show portions of it to the class, discussing the history behind this method and its effectiveness in getting the issues to the public. As a class, devise a checklist of items an

## Civics Sidelight

**"Minority Presidents"**
In the 1860 presidential election Abraham Lincoln received just 39.9 percent of the popular vote in a hotly contested, four-way race. However, he won the presidency with 59.4 percent of the votes in the electoral college. Lincoln is one of the 17 such "minority presidents," a list that also includes John F. Kennedy, Richard M. Nixon, Bill Clinton, and George W. Bush. Clinton won the presidency with a little more than 43 percent of the popular vote. However, he won 68.8 percent of the votes in the electoral college. George W. Bush claimed a little more than 47 percent of the popular vote but won the presidency after Florida's 25 electoral votes awarded him the edge.

**CRITICAL THINKING**

Why is the popular vote rarely in the same proportion as the electoral vote?

**ANSWER:** Students might suggest that the Senate-based electors distort the numbers as does the "winner take all" system.

platform may include a plank calling for an increase in environmental protections. Sometimes there are heated debates before delegates vote on and adopt a platform.

✔ **Reading Check** Summarizing What happens at national nominating conventions? State delegates are seated, the keynote speaker delivers an address, a special committee presents the party platform, delegates debate the platform and then vote to adopt it.

## Presidential Candidates

The candidates for each party are usually determined after the primaries. However, candidates are officially chosen at the national nominating conventions. A roll call of the states is held, and then the task of choosing the candidate begins.

**Nominations** Because presidential nominees are usually chosen by the end of the primaries, nominations allow party delegates to formally endorse the candidate. First there is a state-by-state roll call.

As each state is called, one of its delegates may give a speech nominating, or naming, a candidate. Each nominating speech is followed by one or more seconding speeches. When the political party has a president in power who is eligible to run again, the convention almost always nominates this person for a second term.

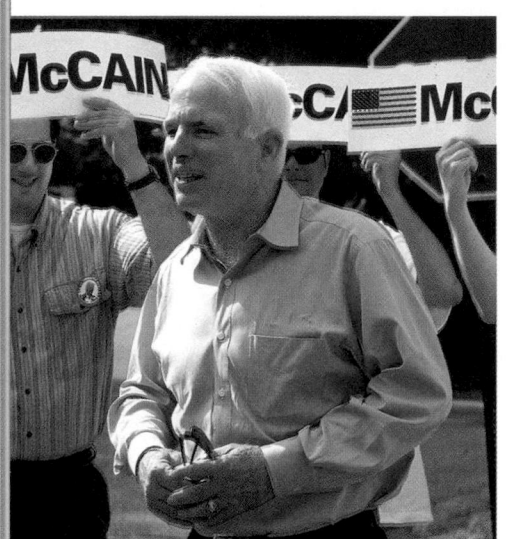
*Arizona senator John McCain ran a strong race for the Republican presidential nomination in the 2000 election.*

**Favorite Sons and Daughters** Some of the candidates named are **favorite sons or daughters.** They are the party leaders who are popular in their home states. In most cases, favorite sons and daughters have little chance of winning their party's presidential nomination. Instead, most delegates will support the candidate with the strongest showing in the primaries.

Why, then, do states nominate them? Sometimes the name of a favorite son or daughter is presented to honor that state's party leader. Delegates also might name a favorite son or daughter to delay their decision on which well-known candidate to support.

**Balloting** After all candidates are nominated, the balloting begins. To win the nomination, a candidate must receive a majority of the convention delegates' votes. A roll call of the states is taken again. A delegate from each state announces how many votes the delegation is casting for each candidate. In recent decades, one of the candidates has almost always been nominated on the first ballot. However, if no candidate is strong enough to win a majority many ballots may be needed.

✔ **Reading Check** Sequencing What is the order of events in the nominating process at party conventions? State delegates give nominating speeches for a candidate. A balloting roll call of the states is taken, asking how many votes the delegation is casting for each candidate.

informed citizen would look for when watching a debate. Now rewatch the video clip of the presidential debate and have students analyze the debate, according to the checklist.

**ENGLISH LANGUAGE LEARNERS**

**LEVELS 2 AND 3:** Tell students that one of the most effective campaign devices available to candidates is television. Also, explain that certain propaganda techniques used to sway the audience are patriotic music, colors, and symbols. Organize students into small groups and have each group produce a presidential campaign commercial for a candidate of its choice. Have volunteers present their commercials to the class.

**COOPERATIVE LEARNING**

## TEACH OBJECTIVE 4

 **ALL LEVELS:** Discuss with students the purpose of the electoral college. (*The electoral college is the group of electors who cast the official votes that elect the president and vice president.*) Copy the graphic organizer below onto the chalkboard, omitting the italicized answers. Then ask students to complete the flowchart by listing the steps between announcing candidacy and the inauguration.

```
Announces          National Nominating     Presidential-        Votes counted before
candidacy          Conventions             Election Day         a Joint Session of
                                                                Congress

Presidential       Campaigning             Electors Vote        Inauguration
Primaries
```

## ★ Vice Presidential Candidates

Next, the delegates nominate the vice president. Vice presidential candidates are chosen for their ability to win votes. Sometimes they are from a state whose support the party needs. The vice presidential candidate must also possess the qualifications to be president.

The nominee for president has the strongest voice in deciding who will be the vice presidential candidate. In 1984 Democratic presidential candidate Walter Mondale made a historic choice. He selected Geraldine Ferraro, a congresswoman from New York, making her the first female vice presidential candidate for a major party.

✔ **Reading Check Drawing Inferences** Why do you think the presidential nominee has the most influence selecting a vice presidential candidate? Students may suggest that the presidential candidate will be working most closely with this person and therefore should have the most influence over the choice.

## ★ The Election Campaign

The presidential election campaign becomes very serious soon after the convention ends. Candidates use television and other media to advertise their views. Since the 1960s presidential candidates have participated in televised debates. Computers have also become a campaigning tool. The 1996 presidential campaign marked the first time Americans could use online computer services to learn about the candidates.

Another widely used method of campaigning is the personal-appearance tour. Jet planes enable the candidates to crisscross the country many times during an election campaign. However, candidates also choose more old-fashioned forms of travel. In the 2000 presidential election, Republican candidate George W. Bush traveled by train through several U.S. states, meeting with voters along the way.

Election day itself is busy for party workers who are telephoning citizens and urging them to vote. On election night, many Americans watch the election returns on television. Because of the different time zones, the first election returns come from the eastern states.

The last reports usually come in from California, Hawaii, and Alaska. Sometimes the final results are not known until the next morning. In 2000 the election was so close that the final results were not known until five weeks after the election.

✔ **Reading Check Summarizing** What are some methods of campaigning, and when does a campaign end? Campaigning methods include personal-appearance tours, televised debates, and online computer services; campaigning ends on the night before the election.

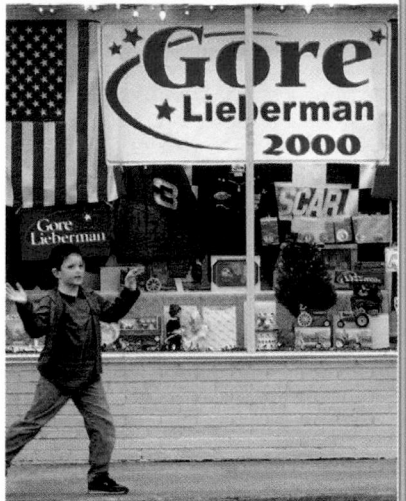

*In the 2000 election, Senator Joseph Lieberman became the first Jewish candidate for U.S. vice president.*

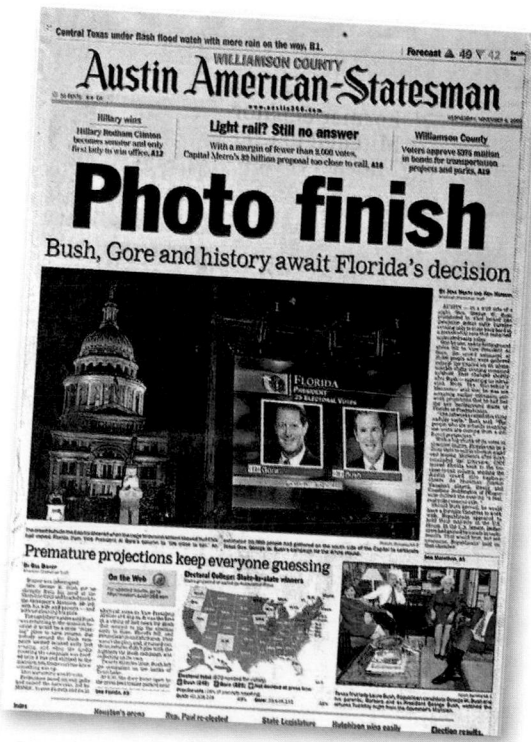

*The closeness of the 2000 presidential election made it very difficult to predict the eventual results.*

## ★ The Democratic Process

**Women and Politics**

Geraldine Ferraro's nomination was a milestone in women's political history, but she is not the only woman to try for high office. Several minor parties have nominated women to run for president and vice president. Prominent among the parties are those that supported women's suffrage in the late 1800s and early 1900s. More recently, Elizabeth Dole sought the Republican nomination in 2000. Before dropping out of the race, Lenora Fulani of the New Alliance Party ran a distant sixth (with 73,714 votes) in her bid for the presidency in 1992. Also in 1992, the Libertarian Party nominated Nancy Lord, a doctor and lawyer, for vice president. In 1972 the Libertarian ticket, which included vice presidential nominee Tonie Nathan, received an electoral vote from Virginia.

**CRITICAL THINKING**

In the past, why were third parties more likely to select a woman as a presidential candidate than were either one of the two major parties?

**ANSWER:** Students might answer that third parties were more likely than major parties to take a chance.

**LEVEL 3:** After discussing the purpose of the electoral college, ask students to explain what they remember about the problems that occurred in Florida concerning the 2000 presidential election. Hand out copies of the Supreme Court case, *Bush* v. *Gore*, butcher paper, and markers. Organize the class into four groups and instruct each group to create a visual concerning one of the following parts of a case study: group 1—facts of the case; group 2—arguments of the petitioner (one who brings the suit); group 3—arguments of the respondent; and group 4—the decision of the Supreme Court and its rationale. Ask each group to present its portion of the case study and to discuss the case in detail. **COOPERATIVE LEARNING**

## CLOSE

Using the "Electoral Map of the United States" found on page 274, ask students if they were campaigning for president, what states would be a must to visit along the campaign trail. Have them list the states on a sheet of paper.

## REVIEW AND ASSESS

Have students complete the **Section 4 Review** on page 275. Then have them complete **Daily Quiz 10.4.** As **Alternative Assessment,** you may want to use the campaign trail or campaign song activities found in this section's lessons.

---

## ★ The Democratic Process

**Electoral College Reforms** After the 2000 presidential election, people across the United States began questioning our current system of selecting the chief executive. Several proposals are currently suggested, each having their own merits. The District Plan, in which electors would be chosen from congressional districts, would eliminate the "winner take all" system and make the electoral vote a more accurate reflection of the popular vote. Using the Proportional Plan, each candidate would receive the same share of a state's electoral vote as he or she received of the state's popular vote. However, the number of electors that each state is guaranteed is based on the number of members their state has in both the House and the Senate. Thus, there is still a chance that the winner of the popular vote may not win the electoral vote. A third plan calls for abolishing the electoral college in favor of the direct popular election.

**CRITICAL THINKING**
Which proposal do you support, and why?

**ANSWER:** Students should support their answers.

---

**MAP ANSWER**
California; 3

---

## ★ The Electoral College

In a presidential election, Americans do not vote directly for the president. The votes they cast are known as the **popular vote.** This vote is actually for people called **electors.** Electors cast the official votes for president. A vote for the Democratic candidate is a vote for the Democratic electors. A vote for the Republican candidate is a vote for the Republican electors.

The names of the electors may or may not appear on the ballot. Each state has a number of electors equal to the total number of senators and representatives it has in Congress. In addition, the District of Columbia (Washington, D.C.), which has no representatives in Congress, has three electoral votes. The nation's 538 electors are referred to as the **electoral college.** In each state the electors usually gather in the state capital on the first Monday after the second Wednesday in December. The party electors of the winning candidate cast all the state's electoral votes at this December meeting.

If the Democratic candidate wins a majority of the state's votes, the Democratic electors cast the state's **electoral votes.** If the Republican candidate wins, it is the Republican electors who cast the official votes. The electors are not required by law to vote for their party's candidate. However, only rarely do electors cast their votes for a candidate who does not belong to their party.

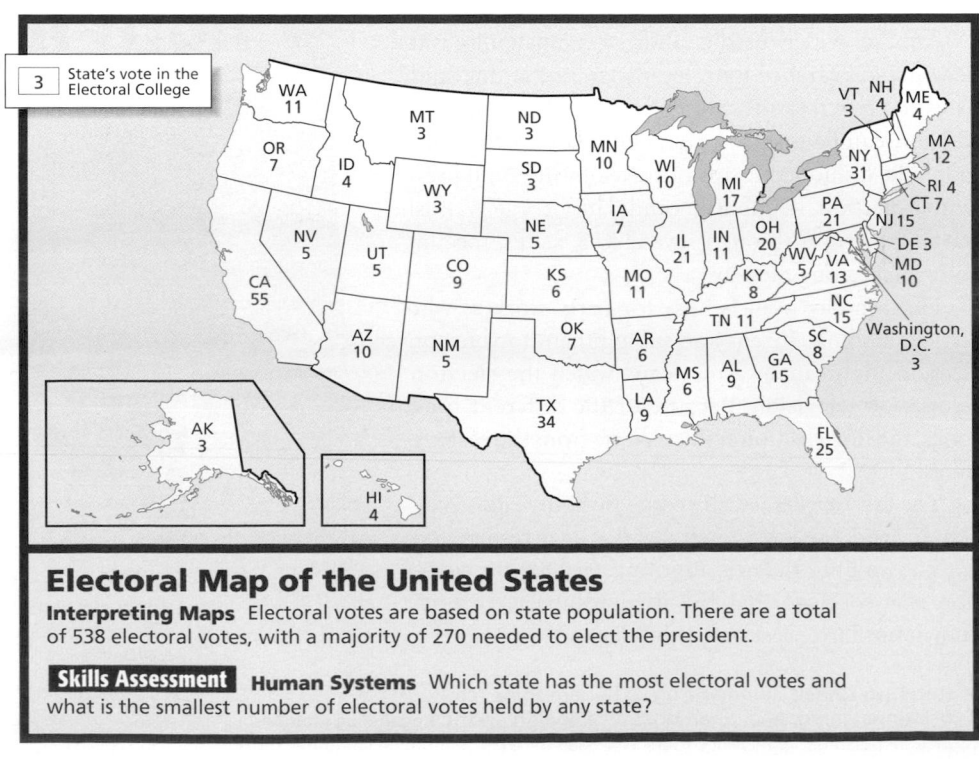

**Electoral Map of the United States**
**Interpreting Maps** Electoral votes are based on state population. There are a total of 538 electoral votes, with a majority of 270 needed to elect the president.

**Skills Assessment** **Human Systems** Which state has the most electoral votes and what is the smallest number of electoral votes held by any state?

## RETEACH

Have students complete **Main Idea Activity for English Language Learners and Special-Needs Students 10.4**. Then organize the class into small groups and assign each group one of the four objectives. Tell groups that they must outline the information that covers their objective. When finished, create new groups of four, containing one member from each of the first four groups. Have group members share their outlines with their new group. **ENGLISH LANGUAGE LEARNERS**, **COOPERATIVE LEARNING**

## EXTEND

Have students conduct research to obtain information about the controversy surrounding the electoral college system. Then have them submit a proposal in narrative form either supporting their position regarding a change or retention of the current system. As an option, students can then debate the topic. **BLOCK SCHEDULING**

The electoral votes are then sent to the president *pro tempore* of the Senate. In early January, following the presidential election, both houses of Congress gather in a joint session. The electoral votes are opened and officially counted. The candidate who receives a majority (270) of the electoral votes is declared the next president of the United States.

What happens if no presidential candidate receives a majority of the votes in the electoral college? In that case, the president is chosen by the House of Representatives from among the three leading candidates. If no candidate receives a majority of votes for vice president, that official is chosen by the Senate. The choice is made from among the two candidates with the highest number of electoral votes. Congress has had to choose the president only twice—in 1800 and 1824—and the vice president only once—in 1836.

The framers of the Constitution originally set up the electoral college. They worried that the citizens of the new republic would have difficulty choosing wise leaders. They also provided for senators to be elected by state legislatures rather than by the people.

In recent years, many plans have been proposed to replace the electoral college with a system of direct election by popular vote. During the 2000 presidential election, Democratic candidate Al Gore won the popular vote for president. Republican candidate George W. Bush won the electoral college, and thus the presidency. These results intensified the debate over the future of the electoral college.

★ ★ ★ ★ ★ ★ ★ ★ ★ ★ ★
**That's Interesting!**
★ ★ ★ ★ ★ ★ ★ ★ ★ ★ ★

**Electoral Oversights**
Did you know that the runner-up in a presidential election used to become vice president? It's true! Even if the top two finishers were from different political parties, the candidate in second place served as vice president. To solve this problem, parties began choosing both a presidential and vice presidential candidate to run on the same ticket. But because electors still cast only one ballot for both candidates, the two Democratic-Republican candidates in 1800 ended up in a tie for president! In 1804, Congress passed the Twelfth Amendment, which directs electors to cast separate ballots for president and vice president.

✔ **Reading Check** **Finding the Main Idea** How does the electoral college work, and how many electors serve in it? The popular vote for president elects people called electors who cast the official vote for president; 538 electors are in the electoral college.

**go.hrw.com** **Homework Practice Online**
keyword: SZ3 HP10

## SECTION 4 Review

1. **Define** and explain:
   - presidential primaries
   - party platform
   - favorite sons or daughters
   - popular vote
   - electors
   - electoral college
   - electoral votes

2. **Summarizing** Copy the web diagram below. Use it to show the different ways that presidential candidates share their viewpoints during campaigns.

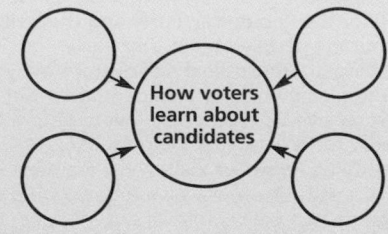
How voters learn about candidates

3. **Finding the Main Idea**
   a. Why do parties hold national nominating conventions, and how are delegates to each party's national convention chosen?
   b. What happens at the national nominating conventions?

4. **Writing and Critical Thinking**
   **Supporting a Point of View** Write an editorial arguing whether the president should be elected by the electoral college or by popular vote.
   **Consider:**
   - the main purpose of the electoral college
   - the potential differences between the popular vote and the electoral college

## Section 4 Review
### ANSWERS

**1. Define**
- presidential primaries, p. 270
- party platform, p. 271
- favorite sons or daughters, p. 272
- popular vote, p. 274
- electors, p. 274
- electoral college, p. 274
- electoral votes, p. 274

**2.** television, computers, personal appearance tours, debates

**3. a.** to choose their parties' candidate for president and to write party platforms; presidential primary elections or selected by party leaders

**b.** State delegations are seated, the keynote speaker delivers an address, the party platform is presented, and delegates debate.

**4.** Students' editorials will vary.

## CHAPTER 10
### REVIEW ANSWERS

**Define and Identify**
1. candidates, p. 254
2. coalition, p. 256
3. one-party system, p. 258
4. precincts, p. 261
5. independent voters, p. 265
6. closed primary, p. 266
7. grassroots, p. 266
8. secret ballots, p. 267
9. party platform, p. 271
10. electoral votes, p. 274

# Review and Assessment Resources

**REPRODUCIBLE**

▶ Chapter 10 Review, pp. 276–77

▶ Vocabulary Activity 10

▶ Chapter 10 Tutorial for Students, Parents, Mentors, and Peers

▶ Chapter 10 Test (Form A or B)

▶ Alternative Assessment Handbook

**TECHNOLOGY**

▶ Chapter 10 Test Generator (on the One-Stop Planner)

▶ Global Skill Builder CD–ROM

▶ HRW Go site

**REINFORCEMENT, REVIEW, AND ASSESSMENT**

▶ Chapter 10 Test for English Language Learners and Special-Needs Students

## REVIEW

Have students complete the **Chapter 10 Review** on pages 276–77.

## ASSESS

Use one of the chapter tests to assess students' understanding of the content. For **Alternative Assessment**, see the **Alternative Assessment Handbook.**

### Understanding What You Read

**1.** give large numbers of people with similar ideas a practical way to get things done; nominate candidates for public office and support positions on public issues; advantage—when one party fails to please a majority of voters, there is another strong party ready to take over and try new policies

**2.** form when two or more political parties agree to compromises and work together; often unstable because the parties forming the coalition often disagree, and the coalition breaks apart and weakens the government

**3.** through large fundraising events and campaign contributions; must follow the FECA

**4.** Candidates who accept public funds cannot take private contributions. Minor party candidates can receive public funding after the election if they win at least 5 percent of the popular vote.

**5.** Constitution forbids any state to deny a citizen the right to vote on the basis of race, color, or gender. The Voting Rights Act prohibits any state from using literacy tests, or reading tests, as a requirement for voting.

**6.** Candidates are nominated formally at the national nominating conventions.

**7.** Several times the winner of the popular vote did not win the electoral vote and therefore did not win the presidency.

# Chapter **10** Review

## Chapter Summary

### Section 1

- Although political parties are not mentioned in the Constitution, the United States has developed a strong two-party system.
- Political parties help organize voters around certain ideas and programs. Parties also choose most political candidates.

### Section 2

- The planning for each political party is done through a series of committees, which also help raise campaign funds.
- The U.S. Congress passed the Federal Election Campaign Act to lessen the chance of corruption in campaign funding.

### Section 3

- U.S. citizens become eligible to vote at the age of 18.
- The Constitution provides that the states set most of the qualifications for voting, subject to the restrictions established by the U.S. Constitution and by Congress.
- The U.S. Congress passed the Voting Rights Act of 1965 to ensure the voting rights of all citizens.
- Two separate elections are held in most states—the primary election and the general election.

### Section 4

- Presidential elections are held every four years. Each party's candidates for president and vice president are chosen by party delegates in national nominating conventions.
- Candidates use methods of campaigning such as personal appearances, television, and computers to reach U.S. voters.
- On election day, citizens cast the popular vote, which selects the members of the electoral college, who in turn choose the president.

## Define and Identify

Use the following terms in complete sentences.

1. candidates
2. coalition
3. one-party system
4. precincts
5. independent voters
6. closed primary
7. grassroots
8. secret ballots
9. party platform
10. electoral votes

## Understanding What You Read

**Section 1** *(Pages 253–58)*

1. What purposes do political parties serve, and what are the advantages of a two-party system?
2. What are coalition governments, and why are they often unstable?

**Section 2** *(Pages 259–63)*

3. How do political parties raise money, and how does Congress regulate fund-raising?
4. How do presidential candidates use public funds for their campaigns?

**Section 3** *(Pages 264–68)*

5. What protections do voters receive from the Constitution and the Voting Rights Act of 1965?

**Section 4** *(Pages 270–75)*

6. How do the major political parties select their presidential candidates?
7. Why do some people want to replace the electoral college?

## What Did You Find Out?

1. How do political parties function in the U.S. political system?
2. How is the voting process today different from voting in the past?
3. What are the major stages of a presidential election?

## Thinking Critically

1. **Supporting a Point of View** Imagine that you are living in the late 1800s. Write a political slogan that reflects the views of either the Democratic Party or the Republican Party and that will encourage people to join that party.
2. **Drawing Inferences and Conclusions** Why do you think minor-party presidential candidates must receive 5 percent of the vote before they qualify for federal matching funds?
3. **Identifying Points of View** If the framers of the U.S. Constitution were alive today, would they view the two-party political system as beneficial or harmful to the country? Explain the reasoning behind your answer.

## RETEACH

Organize students into small groups and assign each group one of the chapter's sections. Have members of each group create a poster or a brochure illustrating the main objectives in their assigned section. Have each group present its work to the class.

**ENGLISH LANGUAGE LEARNERS ,**
**COOPERATIVE LEARNING**

## Portfolio Extensions

**1. Interdisciplinary Connection to Drama** Have each student choose a movie to watch that dramatizes an election campaign or profiles a candidate running for office. After students have watched their video, ask them to prepare a brief synopsis reviewing the movie. Students can give it a thumbs-up or thumbs-down rating or choose their own form of evaluating the movie.

**2. Cooperative Learning** Organize students into small groups and have each group create its own political party. Groups must give their party a name, write a platform, design a bumper sticker, and create one commercial. Have groups present their party to the class.

---

### Building Social Studies Skills

go.hrw.com STANDARDIZED TEST PREP ONLINE keyword: SZ3 STP10

## Interpreting Graphs

Study the bar graph on recent voter registration and voter turnout below. Then answer the questions that follow.

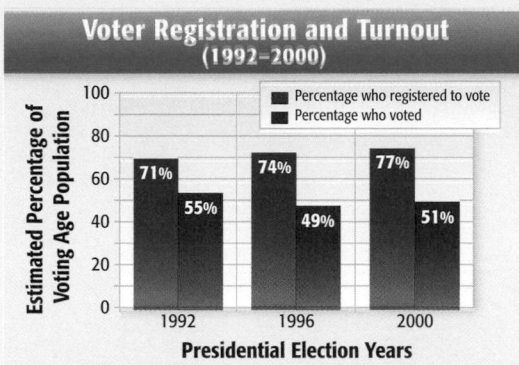

**Voter Registration and Turnout (1992–2000)**

Estimated Percentage of Voting Age Population

- ■ Percentage who registered to vote
- ■ Percentage who voted

1992: 71% / 55%
1996: 74% / 49%
2000: 77% / 51%

Presidential Election Years

Source: Federal Election Commission

1. What was the difference between the percentage of the voting age population who registered to vote in 1996 and the percentage of those who actually voted?
   a. 15 percent
   b. 25 percent
   c. 16 percent
   d. 2 percent
2. What trend do you see in the voting figures for the past three presidential elections?
3. Based on your understanding of the voting process, why do you think so many of the people who register to vote do not actually vote? What steps do you think might help address this problem?

## Analyzing Primary Sources

Read the following quotation from President Thomas Jefferson's first inaugural address, in which he discusses the change from a Federalist to a Republican administration. Then answer the questions that follow.

❝All, too, will bear in mind this sacred principle, that though the will of the majority is in all cases to prevail, that will to be rightful must be reasonable; that the minority possess their equal rights, which equal law must protect, and to violate would be oppression. Let us, then, fellow-citizens, unite with one heart and one mind. Let us restore . . . that harmony and affection without which liberty and even life itself are but dreary things. . . . Every difference of opinion is not a difference of principle. We have called by different names brethren [brothers] of the same principle. We are all Republicans, we are all Federalists.❞

4. Which of the following statements best represents Jefferson's point of view?
   a. The will of the majority is the most important principle of republican government.
   b. It is important not to have differences of opinion in politics.
   c. There should only be one political party made up of former Republicans and Federalists.
   d. The will of the majority rules, but the rights and interests of the minority must be protected.
5. What do you think Jefferson means when he says that "every difference of opinion is not a difference of principle"?
6. Why do you think Jefferson claimed "We are all Republicans, we are all Federalists"?

## What Did You Find Out?

1. Political parties allow a collective voice to be heard, they nominate candidates for political office, they take positions on public issues and work to get laws passed, and they serve as a "watchdog" regarding the party in power.

2. The voice vote, used before the late 1800s, was changed during the Progressive movement to a secret ballot.

3. presidential primaries, national nominating conventions, campaign itself, general election, electoral college election, counting of the ballots before a joint session of Congress, and inauguration

### Thinking Critically
1. Students' slogans will vary.

2. Students might suggest that minor parties have to wait until after the election to see if the public considers them legitimate contenders.

3. Students' responses will vary.

### Social Studies Skills
1. b

2. Only approximately half of the eligible voters actually vote.

3. Students' responses will vary.

4. d

5. Students might suggest that we are all Americans who share the same beliefs in common principles.

6. because both sides have the same common goal—the public good.

---

### Alternative Assessment

## Building Your Portfolio

**Connecting to Community**
Attend a political rally or other meeting of voters in your community. Observe the meeting, talk to the people in attendance, and record enough information so that you will be able to answer the questions *who, what, when, where,* and *why*. Use this information and supporting details to write a newspaper article about the meeting. You may wish to submit the article to your school newspaper.

**■ internet** connect

**Internet Activity: go.hrw.com**
**keyword: SZ3 AC10**

Access the Internet through the HRW Go site to find information about the local party structures of the Republican or Democratic party in your community. Then gather information on this and create an oral report to present to your class. With your teacher's permission, you might want to invite local party leaders to class to answer questions you had during your research.

| Objectives | Pacing Guide | Reproducible Resources |
|---|---|---|
| **SECTION 1:**<br>**Shaping Public Opinion**<br>(pp. 279–85)<br><br>★ Identify what influences people's opinions and explain what makes a well-informed citizen.<br>★ Define the term *propaganda* and describe some of the most common propaganda methods.<br>★ Examine how public opinion is measured. | **Regular**<br>1.5 days<br><br>**Block Scheduling**<br>1 day<br><br>*Block Scheduling Handbook with Team Teaching Strategies, Chapter 11* | **RS** Guided Reading Strategies 11.1<br>**E** Creative Teaching Strategy: Analyzing Political Cartoons<br>**PS** American Civics Political Cartoon: Public Opinion |
| **SECTION 2:**<br>**Interest Groups**<br>(pp. 287–90)<br><br>★ Define *interest groups,* and explain how they differ from political parties.<br>★ Identify the different types of interest groups and determine why such groups have been criticized.<br>★ Describe the ways that lobbyists try to influence government and public opinion. | **Regular**<br>1.5 days<br><br>**Block Scheduling**<br>1 day<br><br>*Block Scheduling Handbook with Team Teaching Strategies, Chapter 11* | **RS** Guided Reading Strategies 11.2<br>**RS** Graphic Organizer Activity: The American Political System |
| **SECTION 3:**<br>**Taking Part in Government**<br>(pp. 291–95)<br><br>★ Identify the four ways that all citizens can participate in government.<br>★ Explain why voting is important and analyze why so few U.S. citizens vote.<br>★ Describe how volunteers and interest groups help political campaigns. | **Regular**<br>1.5 days<br><br>**Block Scheduling**<br>1 day<br><br>*Block Scheduling Handbook with Team Teaching Strategies, Chapter 11* | **RS** Guided Reading Strategies 11.3<br>**SM** Community Service and Participation Handbook: Don't Believe the Hype<br>**E** Challenge and Enrichment Worksheet 11: Registering to Vote |

## Chapter Resource Key

| | | | |
|---|---|---|---|
| **PS** Primary Sources | **SM** Skills Mastery |  CD–ROM |  **One-Stop** Planner CD–ROM |
| **RS** Reading Support | **A** Assessment |  Video | |
| **IC** Interdisciplinary Connections | **REV** Review |  Internet | **See the *One-Stop Planner*** for a complete list of additional resources for students and teachers. |
| **E** Enrichment | **ELL** Reinforcement and English Language Learners | Holt Presentation Maker Using Microsoft® PowerPoint® | |
| | Transparencies | | |

## One-Stop Planner CD–ROM

It's easy to plan lessons, select resources, and print out materials for your students when you use the **One-Stop Planner CD–ROM with Test Generator**.

| Technology Resources | Reinforcement, Review, and Assessment |
|---|---|
| One-Stop Planner, Lesson 11.1 | REV Section 1 Review, p. 285 |
| Holt Researcher CD–ROM | A Daily Quiz 11.1 |
| Transparency 15: Propaganda Techniques | ELL Main Idea Activity 11.1 |
| Homework Practice Online | ELL English Audio Summary 11.1 |
| | ELL Spanish Audio Summary 11.1 |
| One-Stop Planner, Lesson 11.2 | REV Section 2 Review, p. 290 |
| Homework Practice Online | A Daily Quiz 11.2 |
| | ELL Main Idea Activity 11.2 |
| | ELL English Audio Summary 11.2 |
| | ELL Spanish Audio Summary 11.2 |
| One-Stop Planner, Lesson 11.3 | REV Section 3 Review, p. 295 |
| CNN Presents: American Government | A Daily Quiz 11.3 |
| Homework Practice Online | ELL Main Idea Activity 11.3 |
| HRW Go site | ELL English Audio Summary 11.3 |
| | ELL Spanish Audio Summary 11.3 |

## internet connect

### HRW ONLINE RESOURCES
GO TO: go.hrw.com
Then type in the keyword.

**TEACHER HOME PAGE**
KEYWORD: SZ3 Teacher

**CHAPTER INTERNET ACTIVITIES**
KEYWORD: SZ3 AC11
Choose an activity to:
- present a skit on business groups and lobbyists.
- create a brochure on popular opinion and American politics.
- create a plaque or graph related to historic elections.

**CHAPTER ENRICHMENT LINKS**
KEYWORD: SZ3 CH11

**ONLINE ASSESSMENT**
Homework Practice
KEYWORD: SZ3 HP11
Rubrics
KEYWORD: SS Rubrics

**ONLINE MAPS, CHARTS, AND GRAPHS**
KEYWORD: SZ3 MCG
- Propaganda Techniques

**HOLT PRESENTATION MAKER**
KEYWORD: SZ3 PPT11

**CONTENT UPDATES**
KEYWORD: SS Content Updates

**ONLINE READING SUPPORT**
KEYWORD: SS Strategies

**CURRENT EVENTS**
KEYWORD: S3 Current Events

## Chapter Review and Assessment

- IC Vocabulary Activity 11
- Global Skill Builder CD–ROM
- HRW Go site
- REV Chapter 11 Tutorial for Students, Parents, Mentors, and Peers
- REV Chapter 11 Review, pp. 296–97
- A Standardized Test Practice
- A Chapter 11 Test Generator (on the One-Stop Planner)
- A Chapter 11 Test (Form A or B)
- A Alternative Assessment Handbook
- A Chapter 11 Test for English Language Learners and Special-Needs Students

## Meeting Individual Needs

### Ability Levels

**Level 1** Basic-level activities designed for all students encountering new material

**Level 2** Intermediate-level activities designed for average students

**Level 3** Challenging activities designed for honors and gifted-and-talented students

**English Language Learners** Activities that address the needs of students with Limited English Proficiency

**Section 1** *Shaping Public Opinion*

**Section 2** *Interest Groups*

**Section 3** *Taking Part in Government*

## What's Your Opinion?

*To help students create their Themes Journal entries, provide the following examples of appropriate agree/disagree statements.*

● **Agree** Governments that promote freedom will not try to influence public opinion.

**Disagree** The public will form its own opinion on issues, regardless of a government's intent.

● **Agree** Special interest groups with ample resources frequently influence government actions.

**Disagree** Government leaders have a responsibility to the people and therefore are not heavily influenced by special interest groups.

● **Agree** The role of political leaders is to be the primary influence on governmental proceedings.

**Disagree** Citizens and interest groups can be a powerful force in determining what the government does.

## Internet Activity

**Measuring Public Opinion**

**internet** connect

**TOPIC:** Public Opinion and Politics
**GO TO:** go.hrw.com
**KEYWORD:** SZ3 AC11

Have students access the Internet through the HRW Go site to conduct research about ways that public opinion is influenced and measured in American politics. Then ask students to create a brochure in which to display their research.

**CHAPTER**

# 11 The Political System

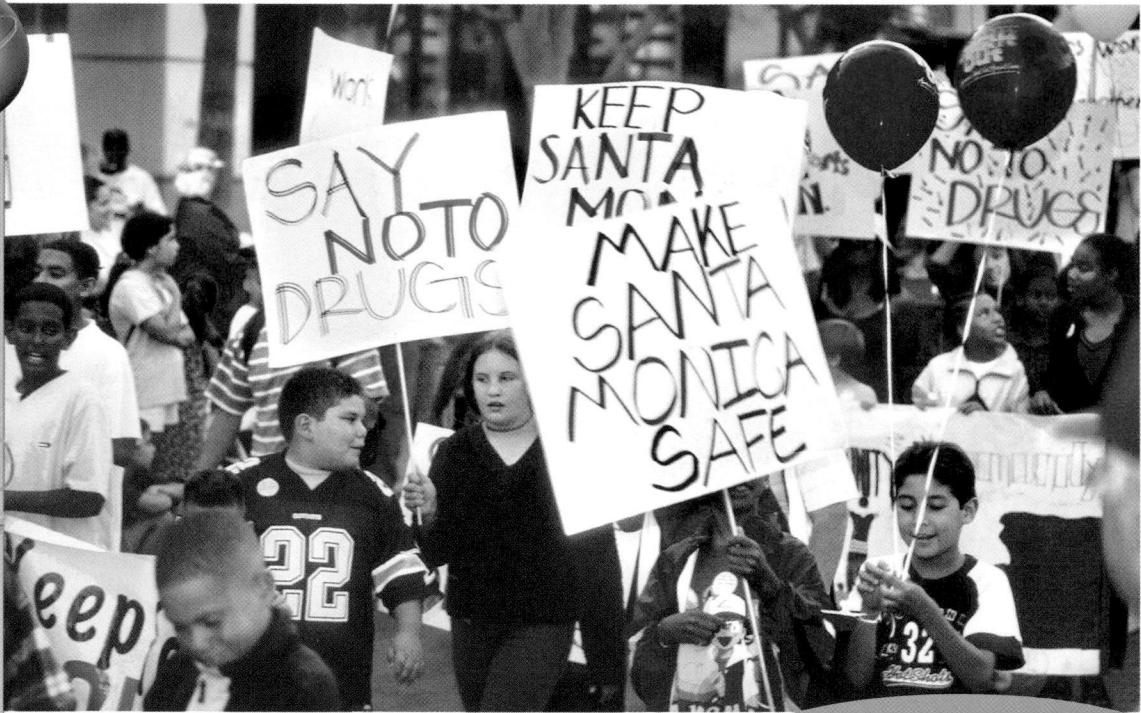

### Build on What You Know

There are many ways for citizens to participate in the political system. No matter how a person chooses to participate, action is the key to democracy. A democratic country such as the United States relies on citizens who are active participants in the political system. It is not enough for Americans to simply receive the benefits of living in a free society. Citizens must also be willing to contribute their time and effort to the preservation of this freedom.

**What's Your Opinion?**

 Do you **agree** or **disagree** with the following statements? Support your point of view in your journal.

• The type of government a country has determines how public opinion is influenced.

• Special interests have too much power over government.

• Political leaders are the only people who can influence what the government does.

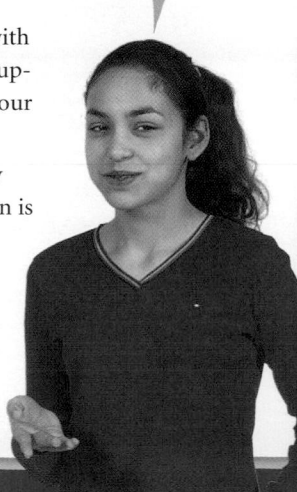

# SECTION 1

## OBJECTIVES

*After completing Section 1, students should be able to*

1. **Identify what influences people's opinions and explain what makes a well-informed citizen.**

2. **Define the term *propaganda* and describe some of the most common propaganda methods.**

3. **Examine how public opinion is measured.**

Write the following quotation from Abraham Lincoln on the chalkboard: *"Our government rests in public opinions. Whoever can change public opinion can change government."* As students enter the classroom, ask them if they agree or disagree with Lincoln's statement. *(Students who agree might mention the influence the media has on the public. Those who disagree might suggest that people make up their own minds about issues.)* Tell students that in Section 1 they will learn more about public opinion, its power, and the factors that can affect it.

## SECTION 1

# Shaping Public Opinion

### Read to Discover

1. What influences people's opinions, and what makes a well-informed citizen?
2. What is propaganda, and what are some of the most common propaganda methods?
3. How is public opinion measured?

### Define

- public opinion
- mass media
- propaganda
- concealed propaganda
- revealed propaganda
- poll

### WHY CIVICS MATTERS

Political leaders and interest groups find many ways to shape public opinion. Use **CNNfyi.com** or other **current events** sources to locate a political advertisement that is being aired to influence the beliefs of American citizens. Record your findings in your journal.

## *Reading Focus*

What is your opinion? You have probably been asked this question many times. Our opinions can influence what others believe or how they act. In the United States the opinions of the people greatly influence government affairs. For example, an elected public official who ignores the opinions of the people is not likely to be elected again. But what are the opinions of the people?

### ★ What Is Public Opinion?

We have all heard such statements as "Public opinion demands that something be done." People sometimes think that public opinion is one opinion shared by all Americans. However, there are very few issues on which all Americans agree.

On any particular issue, there are a number of opinions held by a number of separate groups. Each group is made up of people who share the same opinion. Each group, therefore, makes up a "public." Because each issue has many interested publics, **public opinion** is the total of the opinions held concerning a particular issue. Thus, the term *public opinion* really refers to many opinions.

*Political candidates are very interested in learning about and influencing the opinions of young Americans on key issues.*

✔ **Reading Check Contrasting** What do some people mistakenly think public opinion is, and what does public opinion really refer to? Some people mistakenly believe that public opinion is one opinion shared by all Americans. However, it is really the total of the opinions held concerning a particular issue.

**LEVEL 1:** Have each student identify what can influence people's opinions. *(Students should identify family, friends, teachers, clubs, and mass media.)* Then organize the class into pairs and have members of each pair list an example of how each influence might shape their opinions on topics such as the importance of education. Reconvene to share lists and explain to students that thinking critically about the information they receive from these sources can help keep them well informed as citizens. **ENGLISH LANGUAGE LEARNERS** , **COOPERATIVE LEARNING**

**ALL LEVELS:** Discuss with students what makes a citizen well informed. *(Students should note that thinking critically about what is seen, heard, and read helps people separate fact from opinion and remain well informed.)* Then create a chart with two columns. In the first column, list what influences people's opinions. *(The influences are friends, family, teachers, clubs, and mass media.)* Call on volunteers to write examples of each type of influence in the second column.

## The Democratic Process

**Praise and Scorn for Newspapers** Thomas Jefferson saw the value not only of public opinion but also of the newspapers that printed it. In 1787 he wrote: "The basis of our government being the opinion of the people, the very first object should be to keep that right; and were it left to me to decide whether we should have a government without newspapers, or newspapers without a government, I should not hesitate a moment to prefer the latter."

French writer and politician Alexis de Tocqueville saw the issue differently. In Volume 2 of *Democracy in America*, he wrote: "I shall not deny that in democratic countries newspapers frequently lead the citizens to launch together into very ill-digested schemes; but if there were no newspapers there would be no common activity. The evil which they produce is therefore much less than that which they cure."

**ACTIVITY:** Ask students to paraphrase Jefferson and de Tocqueville's opinions on newspapers in a paragraph.

## Visual Record Answer

*Students might suggest that having more than one daily newspaper increases the chance that differing opinions on issues will be made available to the public.*

280

**Interpreting the Visual Record**

**Getting information** *Many large cities have more than one daily newspaper, such as the two Seattle papers shown here.* **What might be the benefits of having more than one newspaper reporting on local politics and issues?**

## What Shapes Opinions?

Opinions are shaped by influences from many sources. The first influence on our opinions is our family. It is only natural for the ideas and beliefs of our family members to play a major part in shaping our own attitudes and values. Because we share so many of the same experiences with our family, we often have similar responses to many issues. As we grow older, other people and experiences that we encounter begin to influence what we believe. Friends, teachers, and clubs play a major role in shaping our opinions.

Information is also important in shaping opinions. Much of the information we need to make wise decisions about public issues comes from the mass media. The **mass media** are made up of various forms of communication that transmit information to large numbers of people. These forms include printed media such as books, magazines, and newspapers as well as electronic media like film, radio, television, and the Internet.

Today there are huge amounts of information available to the public on many issues. Simply having access to information, however, does not always mean being well informed. Sometimes the information that we receive is inaccurate or one-sided. A newspaper, for example, might give more favorable coverage to political candidates it supports and less favorable coverage to candidates it opposes. Magazine articles might express an opinion rather than simply report the facts.

Effective citizenship requires us to think critically about what we see, hear, and read. To participate fully in the democratic process, it is essential that we be well informed. We must, therefore, learn to recognize the difference between fact and opinion and to gather information from reliable sources.

✔ **Reading Check** Summarizing What shapes people's beliefs? family, friends, teachers, clubs, and mass media

**LEVELS 2 AND 3:** Have students list all of the ways that their opinions have been influenced recently, noting the source of each influence. *(See the Level 1 lesson for influences.)* Then have each student create a collage (with explanatory captions) illustrating the sources of the influences he or she listed. A picture or sketch of a family, for example, could represent the influence of a student's family on his or her opinions. Have students explain along the bottom of their collage, how to remain well informed as citizens.

## TEACH OBJECTIVE 2

**LEVEL 1:** Tell students that the word *propaganda* is related to the root word *propagate* meaning to encourage public awareness. Tell students to locate the term in their text and to relate its definition to this root. Then pair students. Have each student in a pair describe some of the different methods of propaganda. *(Students should describe testimonials, bandwagon, name-calling, glittering generalities, plain-folks appeal, and card stacking.)* When each student has finished, partners should compare their responses and reach agreement on descriptions by referring to their textbooks.
**ENGLISH LANGUAGE LEARNERS , COOPERATIVE LEARNING**

**HOMEWORK** Tell each student to create two pieces of propaganda that use two different methods to promote education.

## ★ Propaganda and Public Opinion

Many of the ideas in the mass media have been directed at us for a purpose. Someone or some group is urging us to do something—to buy something, to believe something, or to act in a certain way. Ideas that are spread to influence people are called **propaganda.**

It has been said that we live in the propaganda age. Propaganda is certainly nothing new, but it has become increasingly influential in recent years. Two reasons for this development are the tremendous growth of the mass media and advances in communications technology. Communications satellites, computer networks, and television broadcasts all help spread propaganda farther and faster than ever before.

There are always many people, groups, and advertisers using propaganda to influence public opinion. Advertisers use propaganda to urge consumers to buy their products. Political candidates use propaganda to convince voters to support them.

Propaganda can be thought of as a technique to sway people's attitudes, opinions, and behaviors. However, people often think of propaganda as negative. For example, under a dictatorship or a totalitarian government, the government controls propaganda. In these societies the government uses propaganda techniques to control people's actions and limit their freedoms. In contrast, in democratic societies many groups, not just the government, use propaganda. These groups compete to influence the public. The propaganda they use is mostly neutral— neither good nor bad. It is simply a technique designed to sway people's attitudes, opinions, and behaviors.

✔ **Reading Check** Finding the Main Idea Why has the use of propaganda grown in recent years? The tremendous growth in mass media and advances in technology have led to the increased use of propaganda.

## ★ Kinds of Propaganda

Citizens must be alert to propaganda. They must be able to recognize it and be aware of the various methods used by propagandists. When propaganda is presented as being factual and its sources are kept secret, it is called **concealed propaganda.** Concealed propaganda is used to fool people without letting them know that its purpose is to influence their views.

Sometimes concealed propaganda is relatively harmless. For example, press agents may make up interesting stories about television actors to give these actors publicity. At other times, concealed propaganda may be used to create a harmful impression. For example, a photograph may be taken in a certain way or may be digitally enhanced or altered to portray a political candidate in a negative light. False rumors may be spread to harm someone or to mislead people about a proposed program or policy.

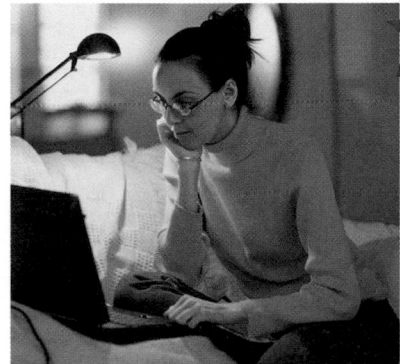
**Interpreting the Visual Record**

**Information technology** *Computers and the World Wide Web make huge amounts of information available to citizens. However, much of this information can be biased or inaccurate and must be interpreted carefully.* **What are some ways that you can check the accuracy of information you find on the Internet?**

*Advertising is commonly used in local campaigns. Such advertisements can be as simple as a sign placed in a supporter's yard.*

*Beverly Griffith*
*City Council*

**Interdisciplinary Connection**

▶ **Psychology** ◀

**The Nixon-Kennedy Debates** The effect that a candidate's media presence has on his or her electability has long been debated. In 1960 the first televised presidential debate took place, many say to the detriment of Richard Nixon's campaign. Experts say that when compared with John F. Kennedy's pleasant and outgoing appearance Nixon's gaunt appearance and placid demeanor were key determinants in the outcome of election. This televised debate, the first of its kind, was meant simply to complement the race as a form of additional coverage. It became far more significant, however. Prior to the debate, Kennedy was struggling to keep up with his opponent in the polls. After the debate, many voters felt that Kennedy "looked more presidential." Nixon lost the race. Today televised presidential debates are an important aspect of the presidential race.

**CRITICAL THINKING**

Does a candidate's personality have a bearing on his or her performance as a political leader?

**ANSWER:** Students' responses will vary.

**Visual Record Answer**

*Students might suggest that they can compare it to primary and secondary sources that are known to be reliable.*

**Holt Researcher**

**go.hrw.com**
**KEYWORD: Holt Researcher**
**Freefind:** Advertising and the Law

Read through the Supreme Court Cases on the Holt Researcher that address the rights of advertisers. Use the information to write a brief report that answers the following question: What are some examples of advertising that the Supreme Court has said are or are not protected as free speech?

Revealed propaganda is common in the United States and in other democracies. **Revealed propaganda** makes readers or listeners aware that someone is trying to influence them. Almost all advertising is revealed propaganda. You know when you see most advertisements that somebody wants you to buy something, to believe something, or to feel a certain way.

Television and radio commercials are direct appeals to the public to buy products. During an election campaign political parties often run commercials in an effort to get voters to support their candidates. These commercials must be clearly labeled as paid advertisements.

✔ **Reading Check Comparing and Contrasting** How are concealed and revealed propaganda alike and different? Both are intended to sway public opinion. However, concealed propaganda is hidden whereas revealed propaganda is apparent.

## ★ Propaganda Techniques

Some propaganda techniques are difficult to spot. Others can be easily recognized by people who carefully examine what they see, read, and hear. What are some common propaganda techniques?

**Testimonials** Political candidates and advertisers often seek endorsements from famous people. For example, advertisers know that people admire sports heroes. Therefore, advertisers pay famous athletes to say they use and like their products.

Advertisers know that if a football hero says he drives a certain automobile, many people will believe the automobile must be good. Because these people admire the football hero, they trust his judgment. People who think for themselves, however, know that this testimonial by a famous athlete proves little. A football player may be a good quarterback, but his talent on the field does not make him an expert on automobiles.

**Bandwagon** People who write propaganda know that if you say something often enough and loud enough, many people will believe it. If you can win some people over to your ideas, eventually more and more people will come over to your side. This is known as the bandwagon technique. "Everybody's doing it! Jump on the bandwagon!" This method of propaganda appeals to people's desire to do what their friends and neighbors are doing. It takes advantage of the "peer pressure" factor.

**Name-Calling** Another propaganda technique is name-calling. Name-calling is the use of an unpleasant label or description to harm a person, group, or product. During an election campaign, both sides often use name-calling. For example, you may hear that one candidate favors

*Popular athletes like Tiger Woods are often in demand for advertising testimonials.*

**ALL LEVELS:** Copy the following graphic organizer onto the chalkboard, omitting the italicized answers. Ask students to complete the organizer to examine how public opinion is measured. **ENGLISH LANGUAGE LEARNERS**

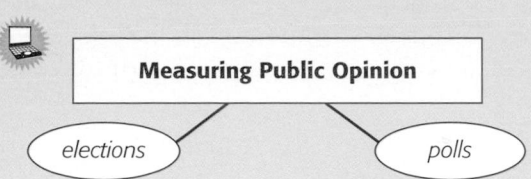

**LEVEL 2:** Organize the class into pairs and provide each pair with newspapers and other periodicals from late October and early November. Have them locate articles with references to the two ways that public opinion is measured. *(Students should find articles that mention elections and polls.)* For example, pairs might find newspaper articles speculating about why a candidate lost an election or why he or she has fallen in the polls. Then have each pair write an analysis of one of the articles identifying how measurement of public opinion is demonstrated. **COOPERATIVE LEARNING**

## Propaganda Techniques

**Bandwagon**
"The latest polls show a growing majority of people support candidate Smith!"

**Card Stacking**
"Candidate Smith is clearly the most qualified."

**Glittering Generalities**
"A vote for Smith is a vote for values."

**Name-Calling**
"Candidate Jones is corrupt and caters to special interests!"

**Plain-Folks Appeal**
"Vote for candidate Smith, who understands the problems of our town."

**Testimonials**
"Candidate Smith is someone you can trust. He has our vote."

**Interpreting Charts**
*Politicians can use a variety of advertising methods to gain the support of voters. Which techniques encourage you to consider the views of other voters?*

"reckless spending" or that another is "opposed to progress." You must ask yourself what proof is given and whether these charges are supported by any facts.

**Glittering Generalities** Another technique used to influence people's thinking is the glittering generality. This technique uses words that sound good but have little real meaning. Many advertising slogans are glittering generalities. For example, statements such as "It contains a miracle ingredient!" or "It's new and improved to be better than ever!" tell nothing about the product or its ingredients.

Political candidates often use vague statements with which everyone can agree. These glittering generalities tell voters nothing about what a candidate really believes. This type of propaganda often uses words such as *home, country, freedom, patriotism,* and *American*. These words are chosen because they spark positive images with which most people in the country identify.

**Plain-Folks Appeal** During election campaigns, many candidates describe themselves as plain, hardworking citizens. They stress that they understand the problems of average Americans. This plain-folks appeal is designed to show people that, as one of them, the candidate can best represent their interests.

**Card Stacking** Another propaganda technique is card stacking. This technique uses facts in a way that favors a particular product, idea, or candidate. For example, newspapers may give front-page attention to the activities of the candidates they favor. The activities of the opposing party's candidates may be given less coverage.

✔ **Reading Check Summarizing** Identify and explain the six different types of propaganda techniques. See preceding paragraphs for each technique and its definition.

---

### The Democratic Process

**Those Glittering Generalities** The propaganda method of glittering generality is, in effect, name-calling in reverse. While name-calling seeks to make us form a judgment to reject or condemn without examining the evidence, the glittering generality device seeks to make us approve and accept without examining the evidence. The Institute for Propaganda Analysis suggests a number of questions that people should ask themselves when confronted with this technique:

- What does the glittering generality really mean?
- Does the idea in question have a legitimate connection to the real meaning of the word?
- Is an idea that does not serve my best interests being "sold" to me merely through its being given a name that I like?
- Leaving the glittering generality out of consideration, what are the merits of the idea itself?

**ACTIVITY:** Have students conduct research to obtain examples of glittering generality.

---

**CHART ANSWER**
bandwagon and testimonials

**LEVEL 3:** Review with students the ways that public opinion is measured. *(Public opinion is measured by elections and polls.)* Then ask students to imagine that they are interviewing to be the campaign manager of an imaginary incumbent's re-election campaign. Have them write proposals explaining how they will use these devices to determine the candidate's current standing and to gauge public opinion throughout the campaign. *(Students' proposals should demonstrate an understanding that election results and poll findings both indicate public opinion regarding a politician's actions and policies.)*

## CLOSE

Have each student write a letter to the editor regarding an issue important to him or her. The letter should critique how the media has covered the issue, such as how propaganda techniques and polls were used to influence or inform the public. Suggest that students address how they felt propaganda affected the issue. Encourage them to explain in their letters why it is important for citizens to remain well informed.

## ★ Measuring Public Opinion

Government officials are responsible for carrying out the wishes of the people. How do government officials find out what the public wants? The most obvious test of public opinion is an election. Another way to measure public opinion is to conduct a public opinion **poll,** or survey.

Polls are used to find out what people think about specific issues and about politicians and their policies. A poll attempts to measure public opinion by asking the opinions of a sample, or portion, of the public.

Great care must be taken to choose a sample that is representative of the public being measured. An unrepresentative sample can cause serious errors in a poll's results. Suppose that your school conducts a poll to find out whether people want the cafeteria to remain open during the entire school day. A poll of only teachers and cafeteria workers would have different results than a poll that included students.

A well-known sampling error occurred in 1936. A popular magazine called *Literary Digest* conducted a public opinion poll to predict the outcome of the presidential election. President Franklin D. Roosevelt, the Democratic candidate, ran against Republican candidate Alfred M. Landon.

The *Digest* mailed 10 million ballots to people chosen at random from telephone directories and automobile registration lists. Approximately 2 million people filled out these ballots and mailed them back to the magazine. Based on the poll results, the *Digest* predicted that Landon would be elected. The election results were very different, however. Roosevelt won by a landslide, with 60 percent of the vote.

What went wrong? The poll failed because in 1936 only people with high incomes could afford to own telephones and automobiles. The sample did not represent the entire voting population.

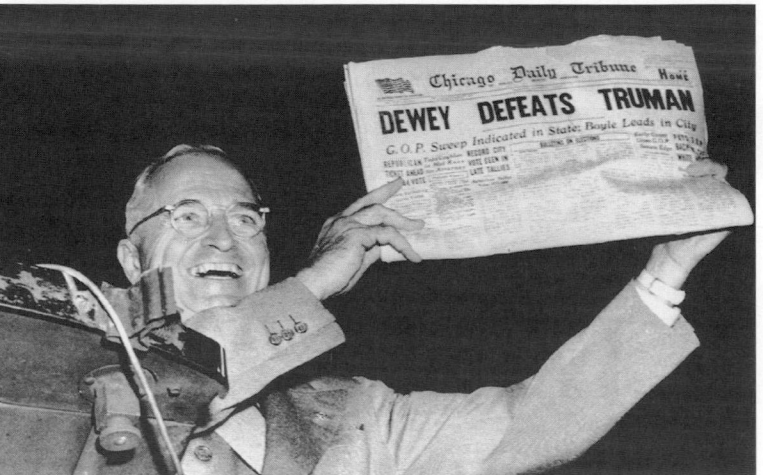

**Interpreting the Visual Record**

**Upset victory** *Another famous polling error took place in the 1948 presidential campaign. Many people believed that Thomas Dewey would win, and some newspapers even printed headlines declaring him the winner. But Harry Truman, shown here, won instead.* **What does the newspaper that Truman is holding say?**

# REVIEW AND ASSESS

Have students complete the **Section 1 Review** on page 285. Then have students complete **Daily Quiz 11.1**. As **Alternative Assessment**, you may want to use the collage or propaganda essay exercises in this section's lessons.

## RETEACH

Have students complete **Main Idea Activity for English Language Learners and Special-Needs Students 11.1**. Then list the major influences on public opinion on the chalkboard. Have each student create one page of a picture book that will explain the concepts of propaganda and public opinion to next year's class. **ENGLISH LANGUAGE LEARNERS**

# TEACHER TO TEACHER

Ben Ward of North Carolina recommends the following activity:

## EXTEND

Bring several examples of propaganda to class. Then lead a class discussion about the term *propaganda. (See the Level 1 lesson for the definition.)* Ask each student to conduct research to obtain examples of propaganda. Students may locate either printed materials or video examples. Then have students prepare oral reports using their examples as visual aids and explaining what their piece of propaganda is meant to influence and the degree to which that tool is successful. **BLOCK SCHEDULING**

---

Once a representative sample has been chosen, care must be taken in deciding what questions to ask. The way questions are phrased often affects the answers that will be given. For example, the neutral question "Should more firefighters be hired?" might receive one answer. The question "Should taxes be raised to hire more firefighters?" might receive a different answer.

✔ **Reading Check** Identifying Cause and Effect What went wrong with the *Digest* poll, and what was the result? **It only sampled people with high incomes. The poll showed candidate Alfred M. Landon as the favorite, but Franklin D. Roosevelt won the election.**

## ★ Using Polls Carefully

Polls are a valuable tool for measuring public opinion. However, some critics fear that polls influence public opinion as well as measure it. For example, some people want to be on the winning side. Imagine that two days before the election, a poll predicts that candidate Z will win by 15 percent. The possibility exists that some voters will decide in favor of candidate Z in order to support a winner.

Polls can help us evaluate public opinion only if we look at more than just the percentages given in the results. We must also look at the wording of the questions, the number of people responding, and the sample population surveyed. Particularly important is the number of people responding to a polling question as "undecided." Often, the number of people who are undecided is so large that no prediction is possible. In election campaigns, candidates usually try to address their strongest appeal to undecided voters, hoping to gain their votes.

✔ **Reading Check** Identifying Points of View What do critics mean when they say that polls can influence public opinion? **They mean that people may side with the predicted winner in order to be associated with the winning side.**

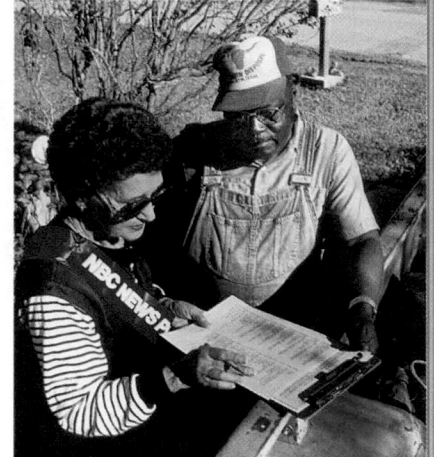

**Interpreting the Visual Record**

**Polling** *Some polls are conducted in person rather than by phone or mail-in questionnaire.* **Do you think there would be any advantages or disadvantages to conducting polls in person?**

## Section 1 Review ANSWERS

**1. Define**
- public opinion, p. 279
- mass media, p. 280
- propaganda, p. 281
- concealed propaganda, p. 281
- revealed propaganda, p. 282
- poll, p. 284

**2.** testimonials—uses endorsements from famous people; bandwagon—uses the "peer pressure" factor; name-calling—uses an unpleasant name or description to harm a person; glittering generalities—uses words that sound good but that have little meaning; plain-folks appeal—presents candidate as a regular person; card stacking—uses facts in a way that favors a particular product, idea, or person

**3. a.** family, friends, teachers, clubs, and mass media; by thinking critically about what we see, hear, and read in order to help us separate fact from opinion.

**b.** through elections and polls

**4.** Students' advertisements and analyses will vary but should reflect an understanding of the techniques explained in this section.

---

# SECTION 1 Review ★

**go.hrw.com** **Homework Practice Online**
keyword: SZ3 HP11

**1. Define** and explain:
- public opinion
- mass media
- propaganda
- concealed propaganda
- revealed propaganda
- poll

**2. Categorizing** Copy the chart below. Use it to identify and describe the different propaganda techniques.

| Technique | Description |
|---|---|
|  |  |
|  |  |
|  |  |
|  |  |
|  |  |

**3. Finding the Main Idea**
a. What influences people's opinions, and how is it possible to remain well informed?
b. How do politicians and researchers measure public opinion?

**4. Writing and Critical Thinking**
**Identifying Bias** Find an advertisement that uses some or all of the propaganda techniques covered in this section. Write a paragraph analyzing the message the advertisement promotes and explaining the techniques it uses to do so.

**Consider:**
- the different techniques presented in this section
- the purpose of the advertisement

## TEACH

**LEVEL 1:** Ask students to classify the following poll questions as neutral or leading: Do you agree with the new policy? Do you disagree with the new policy? How do you feel about the new policy? Then ask students to explain their responses. *(Students' responses should be leading, leading, and neutral.)* Remind students that pollsters rarely ask people to supply their own answers. Then ask them to suggest rephrasings of the neutral question. Write their responses on the chalkboard. *(Students might suggest the following: Do you agree or disagree with the new policy, and why?)* Conclude with a discussion about the importance of examining the questions, answers, and generalizations provided in polls.
**ENGLISH LANGUAGE LEARNERS**

## EXTEND

Have pairs of students develop a poll for the entire school. Students should ensure that their polls include representative samples of the student body. Then have the students conduct two polls—one with a representative sample and one without—and write short reports identifying their results.
**COOPERATIVE LEARNING , BLOCK SCHEDULING**

## SKILLS ANSWERS

1. Students who say "yes" may cite the presence of neutrality evidenced in the choice of answers given in the question. Students who say "no" may point out that the order of the choices might influence peoples' selections.

2. how much of the time people think they can trust government in Washington to do what is right

3. most of the time

4. Yes. Only 1 percent of the people polled responded that they never trust the government to do the right thing.

# Civics Skills
## WORKSHOP

## Understanding Polls

Each year millions of Americans participate in public-opinion polls. In fact, someday a pollster may call to ask your opinion on a topic. Poll results are often reported in the media. By learning to understand polls you can gain insight into what Americans think about important issues.

## How to Understand Polls

1. **Examine the questions.** Questions must be worded in such a way that they mean the same thing to every person in the poll. Confusing questions often result in inaccurate answers. Questions must also be neutral. If a question leads respondents toward any one answer, it does not truly measure public opinion.

2. **Examine the answers.** Pollsters rarely ask people to supply answers of their own. Rather, they provide a limited set of answers and let people choose the ones that apply to them. Pollsters use a limited set of answers so that they can put large numbers of people into a few answer categories. Otherwise, if pollsters questioned 1,000 people, they might receive 1,000 different responses.

3. **Examine the results.** When a poll is complete, the pollsters compute the percentage of people who selected each answer. These figures are the poll's facts. Pollsters use these facts to make generalizations, or broad statements, that describe the patterns and relationships among the facts.

Every generalization must be supported by the facts. If any of the facts do not fit, the generalization is not valid, or correct. For example, consider this statement: "I like spaghetti, lasagna, and ravioli." This statement lists the facts. A generalization supported by these facts is "I like pasta."

## Applying the Skill

Study the poll results below. Then answer the following questions.

1. Does the question posed by the pollster meet the standards for a good question? Why or why not?

2. What are the facts collected and presented by the poll?

3. Which response was given by the largest number of the respondents to the poll?

4. "There are few people who never trust the government in Washington." According to the poll's results, is this a valid generalization? Explain your answer.

*How much of the time do you think you can trust government in Washington to do what is right—just about always, most of the time, only some of the time, or never?*

| | |
|---|---|
| **Just about always** | 13% |
| **Most of the time** | 47% |
| **Only some of the time** | 38% |
| **Never** | 1% |
| **No opinion** | 1% |

Source: Gallup Poll News Service, October 2001

# SECTION 2

## OBJECTIVES

*After completing Section 2, students should be able to*

1 Define *interest groups* and explain how they differ from political parties.

2 Identify the different types of interest groups and determine why such groups have been criticized.

3 Describe the ways that lobbyists try to influence government and public opinion.

## SECTION 2

# Interest Groups

### Read to Discover

1. What are interest groups, and how do they differ from political parties?
2. What are the different types of interest groups, and why have such groups been criticized?
3. How do lobbyists try to influence government and public opinion?

### Define
- interest groups
- lobby
- lobbyist
- public interest groups

### WHY CIVICS MATTERS

Interest groups work to persuade the government to adopt particular policies and address specific issues. Use **CNNfyi.com** or other **current events** sources to find an example of an interest group working to influence Congress today. Record your findings in your journal.

## *Reading Focus*

Americans can express their opinions to government officials in many ways. As you know, they can call, e-mail, fax, or write their government representatives. One of the most effective ways to express an opinion is by becoming part of an interest group.

### ⭐ What Is an Interest Group?

Many Americans are members of one or more **interest groups.** These groups are organizations of people with a common interest that try to influence government policies and decisions. An interest group is also known as a pressure group or **lobby.** A person who is paid by a lobby or interest group to represent that group's interests is called a **lobbyist.**

Interest groups differ from political parties. While both seek to influence government, interest groups are more interested in influencing public policies than in electing candidates.

There are many different kinds of interest groups. They include business associations, labor unions, farm organizations, veterans' organizations, teachers' associations, and consumer groups. Each group works to promote the interests of its members.

Many interest groups represent the economic interests of their members. These interest groups include the National Association of

*Lobbyists can be very persistent when trying to convince politicians to support their issues.*

## TEACH OBJECTIVE 1

**LEVEL 1:** Have each student write the definition of the term *interest group.* (*It is an organization of people with a common interest that tries to influence government policy and decisions.*) Then have each student write a few sentences explaining how these groups differ from political parties. (*Students' sentences should reflect that an interest group's main purpose is to influence public policy, not to elect candidates to office.*) **ENGLISH LANGUAGE LEARNERS**

**LEVEL 3:** Have each student write an essay examining the problems that might occur if interest groups were allowed to conduct business as political parties do. In their essays, students should include a definition of the term *interest group* as well as an explanation of the difference between interest groups and political parties.

## TEACH OBJECTIVE 2

**LEVELS 1 AND 2:** Write the three types of interest groups on the chalkboard:—*economic, issue-oriented,* and *public interest.* Ask students to write down two examples of each group type as well as an issue that might interest each group. Then call on a volunteer to explain why such groups have been criticized. (*Critics say they play too great a role in the lawmaking process; groups lacking money and organization are overshadowed by better-funded groups.*)

**ENGLISH LANGUAGE LEARNERS**

---

## The Democratic Process

**Taking a Stand Against Slavery** The interest groups who opposed slavery in the 1800s included both whites and African Americans. William Lloyd Garrison (1805–1879), who published an antislavery newspaper called *The Liberator*, saw himself as a radical crusader: "I do not wish to think, or speak, or write, with moderation. . . . I am in earnest—I will not equivocate—I will not excuse—I will not retreat a single inch—AND I WILL BE HEARD." Garrison's African American counterpart in the abolition movement was Frederick Douglass, an escaped slave. Douglass (1817–1895) believed in political action, and he used his own antislavery newspaper, *North Star*, to that end. After the Civil War, Douglass's interest turned to the fight for civil rights for African Americans and women.

### CRITICAL THINKING

What did these two men have in common?

**ANSWER:** Students might suggest that they both openly objected to slavery in the press.

---

**BIOGRAPHY ANSWER**
discrimination because of her physical disability

---

### BIOGRAPHY

## Judy Heumann
### (1948– )

Judy Heumann was born in New York City, where she contracted polio when she was 1 1/2 years old. The illness left her confined to a wheelchair. Because public schools were not equipped to meet the needs of disabled students, she was home-schooled until the fourth grade. After graduation, Heumann studied to become a school teacher. However, the state of New York would not certify her as a teacher due to her physical disability. Heumann won a lawsuit against the state and later helped found Disabled in Action, a disabled-rights organization. She also served with the Centre for Independent Living, which helps integrate disabled individuals into their local communities.

Heumann went on to become Assistant Secretary of the Office of Special Education and Rehabilitative Services in the U.S. Department of Education in the Clinton administration. In this office she worked on improving school conditions for disabled children. Today she works as a consultant on disabled rights and education issues. **What challenges did Heumann overcome to make a difference in society?**

---

Manufacturers, the United Mine Workers of America, and the American Farm Bureau Federation. Members of these and other economic interest groups seek to influence government policies that affect their industry or profession. For example, the American Farm Bureau Federation is a national organization of farmers. It works to have bills passed that help farmers recover losses from natural disasters and falling crop prices.

Some interest groups consist of people whose concerns are issue-oriented. That is, they focus on a specific issue or cause. For example, the National Association for the Advancement of Colored People (NAACP) works to promote racial equality. The National Organization for Women (NOW) seeks to protect the rights of women.

Other groups, referred to as **public interest groups,** seek to promote the interests of the general public rather than just one part of it. They include groups working to protect consumers, wildlife, and the environment.

Interest groups vary in size, goals, and budgets. However, most interest groups use similar methods to influence government decisions. They encourage members to write to the president or to their senators or representatives about specific bills. Many interest groups also hire lobbyists to speak for them and to represent their interests. Lobbyists work at all levels of government, although most are located in Washington, D.C.

Most lobbyists today are highly skilled people with a staff of research assistants. Some lobbyists are former members of the legislatures or public agencies they now seek to influence. Other lobbyists are lawyers, public-relations experts, journalists, or specialists in particular fields.

✔ **Reading Check Finding the Main Idea** What are interest groups? They are organizations of people with a common interest that try to influence government.

## ★ Influencing Government

Many national, state, and local laws are the result of a struggle among various interest groups. One example is the minimum wage law. This law states that workers may not be paid less than a certain amount of money per hour. Labor groups often seek an increase in the minimum wage. Business groups generally oppose such an increase. Lobbyists for both interest groups present their arguments to Congress. After listening to both sides and considering all the facts, Congress makes its decision. The result is usually a compromise.

288

## TEACH OBJECTIVE 3

**ALL LEVELS:** Copy the following graphic organizer onto the chalkboard, omitting the italicized answers. Have each student complete the checklist to identify how lobbyists try to influence government and public opinion. **ENGLISH LANGUAGE LEARNERS**

| How Lobbyists Influence Opinions |
|---|
| • *Argue for or against legislation* |
| • *Ask congressmembers to sponsor bills* |
| • *Supply information, help write bills* |
| • *Testify at hearings* |
| • *Advertise* |
| • *Provide workers and contributors for candidates* |
| • *Urge people to contact public officials* |

**LEVEL 3:** Organize the class into seven groups. Assign each group one of the lobbyists' strategies listed in the All Levels exercise. Then have each group prepare and present a dramatization of its strategy to the class. **COOPERATIVE LEARNING**

## CLOSE

Invite a member of a teacher's association (or another interest group) to meet with the class. Ask the speaker to bring along any pamphlets or other literature the group uses to influence government or public opinion. Help students use what they have learned in this section to prepare critical questions to ask the speakers.

---

Lobbyists use a number of different methods to promote the actions they seek. They argue in support of bills they favor and against bills they oppose. Sometimes lobbyists ask members of Congress to sponsor bills favored by members of the lobbyist's interest group. They supply information for the bill and may help write the bill. Government officials often contact lobbyists to learn what interest groups think about issues affecting those groups.

Lobbyists testify at committee hearings as well. In fact, lobbyists from different interest groups often present evidence on opposite sides of the issue. Each lobbyist comes to the hearings prepared with facts and well-developed arguments.

Supplying lawmakers with information is one of a lobbyist's most important responsibilities. As you read in Chapter 5, members of Congress are faced with thousands of bills each year covering many different subjects. No lawmaker can be fully informed in all these areas. Lawmakers appreciate the help provided by lobbyists.

Interest groups attempt to influence not only the government but public opinion as well. For example, interest groups place advertisements in the mass media in support of their positions. The groups often promise to help government officials in their next election campaigns by supplying workers and contributions. Sometimes lobbyists urge local groups and individuals to send letters and telegrams to public officials. They hope that public support will influence the lawmakers' decisions.

✔ **Reading Check Summarizing** How do lobbyists try to influence government and public opinion? They argue for or against legislation, ask Congress members to sponsor bills, supply information, give contributions, help write bills, and testify at hearings.

### Did You KNOW?

Lobbyists get their name from the way they operated many years ago. In the past, they waited for lawmakers in the lobbies outside the legislatures' meeting rooms. There they talked to lawmakers and tried to influence their decisions on the issues of the day.

## SUPREME COURT CASE STUDY

### Muller v. Oregon

**Significance:** A landmark for cases involving social reform, this decision established the Court's recognition of social and economic conditions (in this case, women's health) as a factor in making laws.

**Background:** In 1903 Oregon passed a law limiting workdays to 10 hours for female workers in laundries and factories. In 1905 Curt Muller's Grand Laundry was found guilty of breaking this law. Muller appealed, claiming that the state law violated his freedom of contract (the Supreme Court had upheld a similar claim that year in *Lochner* v. *New York*). When this case came to the Court, the National Consumers' League hired lawyer Louis D. Brandeis to present Oregon's argument. Brandeis argued that the Court had already defended the state's police power to protect its citizens' health, safety, and welfare.

**Decision:** This case was decided on February 24, 1908, by a vote of 9 to 0 upholding the Oregon law. The Court agreed that women's well-being was in the state's public interest and that the 10-hour law was a valid way to protect their well-being.

**How might this decision affect the labor or social reform cases that followed it?**

# REVIEW AND ASSESS

Have students complete the **Section 2 Review** on page 290. Then have students complete **Daily Quiz 11.2**. As **Alternative Assessment**, you may want to use the graphic organizer or the dramatization exercises in this section's lessons.

## RETEACH

Have students complete **Main Idea Activity for English Language Learners and Special-Needs Students 11.2**. Then give each student a set of five index cards and have him or her write a test question about the section material on one side of the card and the answer on the other side. Finally, pair students and have them use the index cards as flash cards to quiz each other.

**ENGLISH LANGUAGE LEARNERS , COOPERATIVE LEARNING**

## EXTEND

Have students select and research a bill that Congress recently passed. Then ask each student to write a newspaper account of its passage. (A local congressperson's office might be able to provide information about a particular bill.) Students' articles should include information about the ways that interest groups for and against the bill tried to influence government and public opinion, and about how the bill was passed.

**BLOCK SCHEDULING**

---

**Visual Record Answer**

*Mothers Against Drunk Driving*

## Section 2 Review
### ANSWERS

**1. Define**
• interest groups, p. 287
• lobby, p. 287
• lobbyist, p. 287
• public interest groups, p. 288

**2.** Economic Interest Groups— seek to further the economic interests of their supporters, National Association of Manufacturers; Issue-Oriented Interest Groups— focus on specific issues or causes, National Association for the Advancement of Colored People (NAACP); Public Interest Groups— seek to promote interests of general public, consumer advocacy groups

**3. a.** An interest group's main purpose is to influence public policy, not to elect candidates to office.

**b.** They argue for or against legislation, ask congressmembers to sponsor bills, supply information, help write bills, testify at hearings, advertise, provide workers and contributions for candidates, and urge people to contact public officials.

**4.** Students' paragraphs will vary but should address the right of all groups in a democracy to be equally heard.

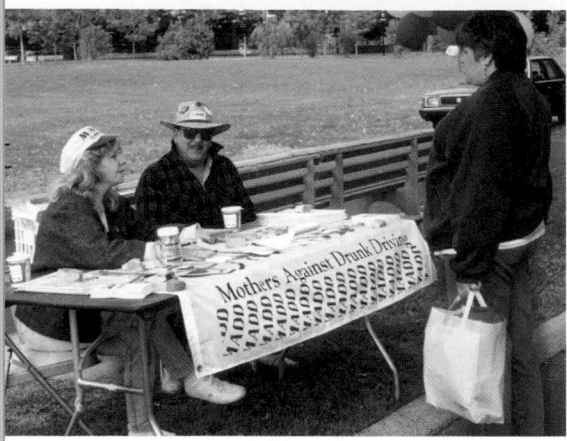

**Interpreting the Visual Record**

**Public interest** *Many interest groups depend on the labor and contributions of local members to stir up support for their causes.* **What interest group do these people represent?**

## ★ Regulating Interest Groups

Interest groups may use any legal means to influence public officials and the public itself. To keep a record of groups, federal and state governments require lobbyists to register. They must indicate for whom they are working and how much money they spend on their lobbying efforts. The Lobbying Disclosure Act of 1995 tightened regulations by closing many loopholes, or ways of evading the law.

Some people are critical of interest groups and their lobbyists. They believe these groups play too great a role in the lawmaking process. Critics charge that too much attention is paid to the interest group that is the most organized and best funded. As a result, some important interests—such as those of disadvantaged citizens—do not always receive the same amount of attention from government officials.

Despite this suggested imbalance, interest groups play an important role in the political process. Although you may not be aware of it, you probably belong to one or more interest groups. We the people—in our roles as students, consumers, workers, and veterans—make up interest groups. In a free society, citizens have the right to make their opinions known to government leaders. Interest groups are evidence of this political freedom.

✔ **Reading Check** Identifying Points of View Why do some critics feel that lobbyists are too powerful in American politics? They fear that groups with less money are not receiving equal attention.

---

## SECTION 2 Review

**go.hrw.com Homework Practice Online**
**keyword: SZ3 HP11**

**1. Define** and explain:
• interest groups
• lobby
• lobbyist
• public interest groups

**2. Categorizing** Copy the graphic organizer below. Use it to give an example of and describe each type of interest group.

**3. Finding the Main Idea**
a. How are interest groups different from political parties?
b. What methods do lobbyists use to influence government and public opinion?

**4. Writing and Critical Thinking**
**Supporting a Point of View** Do you agree or disagree with the statement that "interest groups are evidence of political freedom"? Write a paragraph explaining your point of view. Be sure to include a suggestion for what might be done to better serve the interests of groups that lack money and representation.

**Consider:**
• the function of interest groups
• the role of freedom in a democracy

# SECTION 3

## OBJECTIVES

*After completing Section 3, students should be able to*

1 **Identify the four ways that all citizens can participate in government.**

2 **Explain why voting is important and analyze why so few U.S. citizens vote.**

3 **Describe how volunteers and interest groups help political campaigns.**

### LET'S GET STARTED!

Write the word *volunteers* on the chalkboard. As students enter the classroom, ask them to write down the meaning of the word. *(Students might write that it means people who perform a service of their own free will, without pay.)* Explain to students that the origin of the word comes from the Latin root meaning "will." A person who volunteers does so willingly. Tell students that in Section 3 they will learn about the ways that citizens can participate in government as volunteers.

## SECTION 3

# Taking Part in Government

### Read to Discover

1. What are the four ways that all citizens can participate in government?
2. Why is voting important, and why do so few U.S. citizens vote?
3. How do volunteers and interest groups help political campaigns?

### Define

- volunteers
- political action committees (PACs)

#### WHY CIVICS MATTERS

Americans can participate in government by speaking out on issues that matter to them. Use **CNNfyi.com** or other **current events** sources to find an example of a citizen raising public awareness about an important problem. Record your findings in your journal.

## SECTION 3 RESOURCES

### REPRODUCIBLE
- ▶ Guided Reading Strategies 11.3
- ▶ Community Service and Participation Handbook: Don't Believe the Hype
- ▶ Challenge and Enrichment Worksheet 11: Registering to Vote

### TECHNOLOGY
- ▶ One-Stop Planner, Lesson 11.3
- ▶ CNN Presents: American Government
- ▶ Homework Practice Online
- ▶ HRW Go site

### REINFORCEMENT, REVIEW, AND ASSESSMENT
- ▶ Section 3 Review, p. 295
- ▶ Daily Quiz 11.3
- ▶ Main Idea Activity 11.3
- ▶ English Audio Summary 11.3
- ▶ Spanish Audio Summary 11.3

## Reading Focus

Americans can participate in government in many ways. We can vote in local, state, and national elections. We can work for political parties. We can speak out on public issues and help make our communities better places to live. As good citizens, it is our responsibility to participate in these activities. They are vital to the preservation of a democratic government.

### ★ Voting—Democracy in Action

Voting is the most important opportunity for citizens to participate in government. Because society relies on people performing a variety of duties, only a small percentage of citizens can actually serve in the government. Therefore, we elect officials to represent us. All citizens can take part in selecting the leaders who will represent and serve them.

Elections offer every citizen the chance to be involved in governing the country. Each voter helps determine what actions the government will take. We are making our opinions on public issues known when we vote. When we choose candidates, we are expressing our opinions about their leadership abilities as well as their programs.

Voting is not only a right, it is an important responsibility. Yet millions of U.S. citizens do not vote. In fact, the United States has one of the lowest voter turnouts of any democratic country in the world. In

*On election day most communities have multiple locations open where citizens can cast their votes.*

# TEACH OBJECTIVE 1

 **ALL LEVELS:** Copy the following graphic organizer onto the chalkboard, omitting the italicized answers. Have students complete the organizer to identify the five ways that all citizens can participate in government.
**ENGLISH LANGUAGE LEARNERS**

| How Citizens Can Participate in Government |
| --- |

| *Voting* | *Speaking out on issues* | *Working for a political party* |
| --- | --- | --- |

| *Contacting public officials* | *Volunteering in the community* |
| --- | --- |

**LEVEL 3:** Organize the class into five groups and assign each group one of the ways that all citizens can become involved in government. *(Assignments include voting, working for a political party, speaking out on public issues, contacting public officials, and volunteering in the community.)* Then have each group develop and perform a pantomime of its assigned method of participation. Call on volunteers to identify the method being performed. **COOPERATIVE LEARNING**

---

**internet connect**

**TOPIC:** Elections in America
**GO TO:** go.hrw.com
**KEYWORD:** SZ3 AC11

Have students access the Internet through the HRW Go site to find information on historic elections in U.S. history. Then have students create a plaque commemorating one of the elections featured on the Web site. As an extension, ask students to use the Holt Grapher to create a graph or chart that represents the vote counts for each candidate.

In the historic 2000 presidential election, only about half of eligible voters went to the polls to vote.

**Election Drama** Can you imagine waiting five weeks for election results? Well, it happened! On November 7, 2000, all major television networks first predicted that the state of Florida's 25 electoral votes would go to Al Gore. A few hours later, however, the networks changed their position and said the Florida vote was too close to name a winner. About 2:00 A.M. EST, most networks announced that George W. Bush had won the Florida vote and was now the president-elect. Believing the networks, Gore called Bush to concede the election. But as more results from Florida were posted on the Internet, Bush's lead narrowed. Gore called Bush again—this time to take back his concession. It would be another five weeks before George W. Bush would officially win by only 537 votes.

recent presidential elections about half the voting-age population voted. In 1996 only about 49 percent of the voting-age public voted for the country's president. In nonpresidential elections the percentage of voters is even smaller. For example, in 1998 only 36.4 percent of the voting-age public voted. This low voter turnout leaves the selection of government officials to a small percentage of the country's people.

Why do so few people vote? Apathy, or a lack of interest or concern about the issues, discourages people from voting. Some people do not register and thus are not eligible to vote. Others may not like any of the available candidates. Some are ill and cannot reach the polling places on election day. Still others may be unexpectedly away from home and cannot reach the polling places where they are registered to vote. Others move and do not meet residency requirements for voting.

✔ **Reading Check** **Problem Solving** What are some ways that people might be persuaded to vote? *Students might suggest a public service campaign, providing better access to election facilities, or helping people become better informed about the candidates and issues.*

## ★ Every Vote Counts

Another reason for not voting is a person's belief that his or her vote does not count. Many people who do not vote think that their votes will not make a difference in the election's outcome. Of course, this is not true. The vote of every individual helps determine who wins or loses an election. By voting we influence the laws and policies that greatly affect our lives. The importance of every vote is demonstrated by the results of two presidential elections in the 1900s.

**Woodrow Wilson and Charles Evans Hughes** In 1916, election results indicated that Charles Evans Hughes, the Republican candidate, would win the presidential election. Hughes would have won if 3,773 Californians had voted for him instead of for the Democratic candidate, Woodrow Wilson. Because Wilson received a majority of California's popular vote he was awarded all of that state's electoral votes. California's electoral votes gave Wilson enough votes to win the election.

**The 2000 Presidential Election** The most famous close call in recent election history is the 2000 presidential election. Republican candidate George W. Bush and Democratic candidate Al Gore had been neck and neck in the polls for months. As polls closed across the country, the news networks began to project the election results in several states. Votes and tallies rose throughout the evening. Americans began to realize that the outcome in Florida—and that state's 25 electoral votes—would decide the winner.

At 7:50 P.M. EST the networks announced that Al Gore had won Florida. The networks based these projections on exit polls—surveys of voters after they leave the polls. However, polls in the largely Republican

# TEACH OBJECTIVE 2

**LEVEL 1:** Call on volunteers to explain why voting is important. *(Students should note that when there is a low voter turnout, selection of public officials is left to a small percentage of the population.)* Then organize students into pairs and have them list reasons people do not vote. *(People may believe their votes do not matter, they do not register, they do not like the candidates, they are too ill to go to the polls, they are not home on election day, or they move and do not meet residency requirements.)* Call on volunteers to share their lists with the class.
**ENGLISH LANGUAGE LEARNERS , COOPERATIVE LEARNING**

**LEVELS 2 AND 3:** Organize the class into six groups and assign each group one of the reasons that people do not vote. *(See the Level 1 lesson for reasons.)* Ask each group to create a public-service advertising campaign geared toward getting its target audience to vote. Remind students to include in their ads an explanation of why voting is important. Have groups present their campaigns to the class. **COOPERATIVE LEARNING**

**HOMEWORK** Have each student create a slogan addressing one of the reasons that people do not vote. Students may wish to base their slogans on an explanation of why voting is important.

Florida panhandle remained open. As votes came in from these areas, the networks eventually admitted that the race was too close to call.

The Florida results were so close that Florida state law required recounts. After machine recounts revealed a narrow Bush lead, Gore requested manual recounts in four counties. The Bush campaign challenged these manual recounts in court. Each campaign also challenged how votes in various parts of the state had been counted.

Eventually, the legal debate was heard before the Supreme Court. The Court ruled that hand recounts in several Florida counties were not valid. Florida's electoral votes went to Bush, making him the winner. However, the final results nationwide showed that Gore had won 50,999,897 popular votes and Bush had won 50,456,002 popular votes. Bush thus became the first president in more than 100 years who did not win the popular vote.

✔ **Reading Check** Drawing Inferences and Conclusions  Why might the results of the 2000 presidential election encourage more Americans to vote? Students might suggest that the closeness of the election results in Florida might help convince citizens that every vote is very important.

## ★ Taking Part in Political Campaigns

Another way to influence political decisions is to take part in election campaigns. Although you must be 18 years old to vote, people of any age can work as volunteers in political campaigns. **Volunteers** are people who work without pay to help others. Working as a campaign volunteer is an effective way to have a say in who represents you in the government. You can also learn firsthand how the American political system works.

There are many jobs for volunteers during an election campaign. You can ring doorbells or make phone calls to inform voters about your

---

**Interpreting the Visual Record**

**Volunteers** *Volunteers, such as these women calling voters, play a critical role in most political campaigns. People often also show their support by displaying bumper stickers, lawn signs, and other advertisements.* **Why do you think volunteers play such an important role in politics?**

---

**Visual Record Answer**

*Students might suggest that they make valuable contributions of time and that through their participation, demonstrate to politicians which issues matter to citizens.*

**LEVELS 1 AND 2:** Call on volunteers to identify the ways in which volunteers and interest groups can help political campaigns. *(Students should identify that volunteers can ring doorbells, make phone calls, encourage others to vote, distribute campaign literature, address and stuff envelopes, and baby-sit for voters; interest groups can provide volunteers and donate money through PACs.)* Write students' responses on the chalkboard. Then have them vote on which contribution they think is the most important. Reorder the list according to the results and lead the class in a discussion regarding the ranking.

**LEVELS 2 AND 3:** Have students imagine that they are volunteer coordinators for a political campaign. Ask students to make a list of jobs that a volunteer might perform. Encourage them to include a description. Then have them write several sentences that might be used to convince a potential volunteer to take on one of the jobs. *(See the Level 1 lesson for jobs.)*

## CLOSE

Have students reflect on the thoughts a volunteer might have at the end of a hard-fought political campaign. Ask each student to write a journal entry reflecting the volunteer's thoughts after the election has been decided. Students might review what the volunteer did and discuss feelings about his or her contribution.

### Visual Record Answer

*Students might suggest through protesting.*

## Section 3 Review
### ANSWERS

**1. Define**
- volunteers, p. 293
- political action committees (PACs), p. 294

**2.** Volunteers—ring doorbells, make phone calls, encourage others to vote, distribute campaign literature, address and stuff envelopes, baby-sit for voters; Both—donate necessary support; Interest Groups—provide volunteers, give money through PACs

**3. a.** Students may suggest four of the following: voting, working for a political party, speaking out on public issues, contacting public officials, and volunteering in the community.

**b.** When there is a low voter turnout, selection of public officials is left to a small percentage of the population. Some people believe their votes do not matter. They do not register, do not like the candidates, are too ill to go to the polls, are not home on election day, or move and do not meet residency requirements.

**4.** Students' speeches will vary but should demonstrate their knowledge of the importance of voting and of the things that keep people from doing it.

*Collecting petition signatures is a common activity for many interest groups.*

### Interpreting the Visual Record

**Expressing ideas** *Citizens can use many different methods of making their views known to their politicians.* **How is this woman expressing her views?**

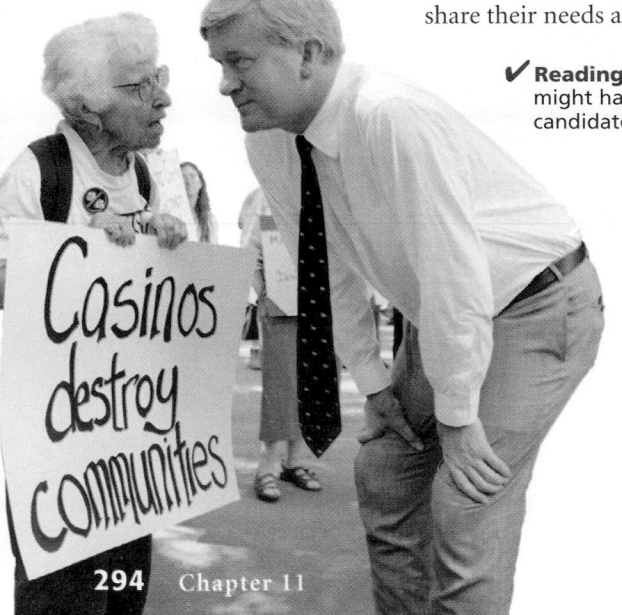

candidate and his or her ideas. You can encourage your friends and family members to vote. Campaigns always need people to distribute literature to passersby on the street. Addressing, stuffing, and mailing envelopes are also important duties for volunteers. On election day, campaign workers urge people who support their candidate to vote. They baby-sit young children to allow voters to go to the polling places. All these efforts can make quite a difference in the outcome of an election.

✔ **Reading Check** **Finding the Main Idea** What are some ways that volunteers support political campaigns? They ring doorbells, make phone calls, encourage others to vote, distribute campaign literature, address and stuff envelopes, and baby-sit for voters.

### ★ Interest Groups and Political Campaigns

Interest groups take part in political campaigns. They sometimes provide volunteers to help candidates who are sympathetic to their causes. They can also make financial contributions to election campaigns.

Although interest groups are prohibited by law from contributing money directly to candidates, they may contribute through **political action committees (PACs).** PACs collect voluntary contributions from members and use this money to fund candidates that the committees favor. The number of PACs has risen dramatically in recent years—from 608 in 1974 to about 3,800 in 2000. PACs contributed nearly $260 million to candidates running in the 2000 national election.

As the number of PACs has increased, so has the variety of groups that exist. Some of the more influential PACs include the United Auto Workers Voluntary Community Action Program, the National Education Association PAC, the American Medical Association PAC, and the Realtors PAC. These groups give people the opportunity to share their needs and concerns with elected officials.

✔ **Reading Check** **Making Generalizations and Predictions** What might happen if interest groups could donate money directly to candidates? Students might say that the interest groups with the most money would give large donations to candidates, thus gaining undue influence.

### ★ Contacting Public Officials

Suppose the street corner near your home needs a traffic light. Or suppose you are against a proposed 15-cent increase in your city's bus fare. Or suppose the House of Representatives will vote soon on an issue important to you. How can you make your opinion on these issues known quickly?

Writing letters to local officials or Congressmembers is an excellent way to let them know what

# REVIEW AND ASSESS

Have students complete the **Section 3 Review** on page 295. Then have them complete **Daily Quiz 11.3**. As **Alternative Assessment**, you may want to use the pantomime or public service ad exercises in this section's lessons.

# RETEACH

Have students complete **Main Idea Activity for English Language Learners and Special-Needs Students 11.3**. Organize the class into teams and assign each team one Read to Discover question. Then have each team list at least three points that could help other students to answer the question.

**ENGLISH LANGUAGE LEARNERS , COOPERATIVE LEARNING**

# EXTEND

Have students create a list of criteria that describe an involved citizen. Then ask each student to select a community member who fits those criteria. Have students conduct research outside of class about their "good citizen." Then have each student prepare a three-to-five-minute oral report about his or her chosen person, incorporating their research into the presentation. Have students present their reports to the class.

**BLOCK SCHEDULING**

---

is on your mind. As you read in Chapter 5, members of Congress receive a lot of mail. They welcome these letters as a way of learning what the people they represent think about the issues.

You can also contact public officials by telephone, e-mail, fax, or telegram. A visit to an official's office is another way to express your opinions. Many officials have regular office hours for scheduled meetings with their constituents.

✔ **Reading Check** Summarizing What are some of the ways that voters can share their viewpoints with a lawmaker? Voters can send letters, e-mails, or faxes as well as make telephone calls to or visit their Congressmember in person.

## ★ Community Action

The quality of life in towns and cities depends largely on how well local governments serve their citizens. It is therefore important for all Americans to actively participate in their communities.

Citizens often work together in community groups. For example, in many cities people working to improve their neighborhoods have formed block associations. Residents of an apartment building might form a tenants' group to improve the condition of their building. Citizens in a town might organize to raise money for new library books or to repair the school's baseball field.

Community groups are active in large and small cities and in towns. Working together makes it easier for citizens to bring about needed improvements and changes in their communities. Citizen involvement helps make democracy work.

✔ **Reading Check** Identifying Cause and Effect Why do people form community groups, and how do these groups make a difference? Working together makes it easier to effect necessary changes. Community groups make a difference by organizing in response to a local issue.

**Interpreting the Visual Record**

**Community groups** The Neighborhood Watch is one of the most common community organizations around the country. **What is the purpose of the Neighborhood Watch according to the sign?**

---

**CHAPTER 11**
**REVIEW ANSWERS**

**Define and Identify**
1. public opinion, p. 279
2. mass media, p. 280
3. concealed propaganda, p. 281
4. revealed propaganda, p. 282
5. interest groups, p. 287
6. lobby, p. 287
7. lobbyist, p. 287
8. public interest groups, p. 288
9. volunteers, p. 293
10. political action committees (PACs), p. 294

**Understanding Main Ideas**
1. In totalitarian societies, propaganda is used to control people's actions and limit their freedoms. In a democracy, many groups use propaganda, and most of it is neutral.

2. to measure public opinion; to be more accurate.

3. An interest group's main purpose is to influence public policy, not to elect candidates to office.

---

## SECTION 3 Review

**Homework Practice Online**
keyword: SZ3 HP11

1. **Define** and explain:
   - volunteers
   - political action committees (PACs)

2. **Comparing and Contrasting** Copy the graphic organizer below. Use it to compare and contrast the ways that volunteers and interest groups help political campaigns.

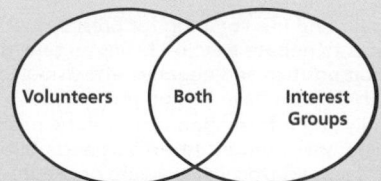

3. **Finding the Main Idea**
   a. Identify four ways that citizens can participate in government.
   b. Why is it important for all eligible citizens to vote, and why do so few U.S. citizens vote?

4. **Writing and Critical Thinking**
   **Problem Solving** Imagine that the president of the United States has invited you to the White House to deliver a speech titled How to Encourage Citizen Participation in Politics. Write a draft of the speech.

   **Consider:**
   - the results of low voter turnout
   - the reasons people do not vote

### REPRODUCIBLE
▶ Chapter 11 Review, pp. 296–97
▶ Vocabulary Activity 11
▶ Chapter 11 Tutorial for Students, Parents, Mentors, and Peers
▶ Chapter 11 Test (Form A or B)
▶ Alternative Assessment Handbook, Chapter 11

### TECHNOLOGY
▶ Chapter 11 Test Generator (on the One-Stop Planner)
▶ Global Skill Builder CD–ROM
▶ HRW Go site

### REINFORCEMENT, REVIEW, AND ASSESSMENT
▶ Chapter 11 Test for English Language Learners and Special-Needs Students

### REVIEW
Have students complete the **Chapter 11 Review** on pages 296–97.

### ASSESS
Use one of the chapter tests to assess students' understanding of the content. For **Alternative Assessment**, see the **Alternative Assessment Handbook**.

---

**4.** They argue for or against legislation, ask congressmembers to sponsor bills, supply information, help write bills, testify at hearings, advertise, provide workers and contributions for candidates, and urge people to contact public officials.

**5.** by voting, working for a political party, speaking out on public issues, contacting public officials, and volunteering in the community

**6.** When there is a low voter turnout, selection of public officials is left to a small percentage of the population. Some people believe their votes do not matter. They do not register, do not like the candidates, are too ill to go to the polls, are not home on election day, or move and do not meet residency requirements.

### What Did You Find Out?
**1.** Public opinion is the total of opinions held concerning a particular issue. Propaganda is used to convince the public to believe something, buy something, or act in a certain way.

**2.** An interest group is an organization of people with a common interest that tries to influence policy and decisions. They lobby lawmakers, influence public opinion, and rally public support.

**3.** to influence government decisions and to make government more responsive to their needs

---

# Chapter 11 Review

## Chapter Summary

### Section 1
- Public opinion is the total of the opinions held concerning a particular issue. One way to measure public opinion is by using public-opinion polls.
- Many different sources, including family, friends, teachers, and clubs, shape people's opinions. Information provided by the mass media also plays a major role in shaping people's opinions.
- Propaganda is often used to try to influence people. Citizens must be able to recognize propaganda.
- Common propaganda techniques include testimonials, bandwagon, name-calling, glittering generalities, plain-folks appeal, and card stacking.
- Polls are a common method of measuring public opinion. Pollsters must be careful to choose representative samples and ask carefully worded questions.

### Section 2
- Interest groups play an important role in influencing government decisions and in shaping public opinion.
- Interest groups often hire lobbyists to promote the policies they favor.
- Congress has passed laws restricting the activities of interest groups and requiring lobbyists to identify who they are working for and how their money is spent.

### Section 3
- Responsible citizens take an active part in public affairs.
- By voting in elections, citizens can help select the officials who will represent them.
- Citizens can also take part in political campaigns and work with community groups.

---

## Define and Identify
Use the following terms in complete sentences.
1. public opinion
2. mass media
3. concealed propaganda
4. revealed propaganda
5. interest groups
6. lobby
7. lobbyist
8. public interest groups
9. volunteers
10. political action committees (PACs)

## Understanding Main Ideas
**Section 1** *(Pages 279–85)*
1. How does the use of propaganda differ in totalitarian societies and democratic societies?
2. What is the purpose of polls? Why must polls use representative samples?

**Section 2** *(Pages 287–90)*
3. How do interest groups differ from political parties?
4. Identify the ways that lobbyists try to influence public policy and opinion.

**Section 3** *(Pages 291–95)*
5. How can citizens take part in the political system?
6. Why is voting important? Why do so few Americans vote?

## What Did You Find Out?
1. What is public opinion, and how does propaganda attempt to influence it?
2. What are interest groups, and how do they work to influence the government?
3. Why is it important for all Americans to take an active part in government?

## Thinking Critically
1. **Supporting a Point of View** Do you think that elected officials should use their own best judgment when voting on the issues? Or should they follow the public opinion positions of the voters? Explain your answer.
2. **Evaluating** It is common for presidential candidates to debate election issues on television. What positive and negative effects do you think such debates have had on presidential politics?
3. **Analyzing Information** Describe the propaganda techniques used by advertisers and politicians. Why should citizens be aware of these methods and their uses?

## RETEACH

Organize students into groups of three. Assign each group one section of the chapter to summarize. Then ask each group to identify and define the vocabulary terms in its assigned section. Have the groups exchange their summaries. You might make copies to create a chapter study guide for all the students. **ENGLISH LANGUAGE LEARNERS , COOPERATIVE LEARNING**

## Portfolio Extensions

**1. Interdisciplinary Connection to Art** Have each student acquire and analyze the press kit of the community interest group selected for the Student's Edition activity. Ask them to analyze the materials to determine propaganda methods used by the group. Suggest that students prepare short papers explaining their findings and including their opinion regarding the effectiveness of the techniques applied. Ask volunteers to read their papers and present items from their press kits to the class.

**2. Cooperative Learning** Organize students into small groups. Then ask each group to select a national interest group. Each group should write a skit that explains the purpose of the interest group, demonstrates the methods commonly employed by the group, and shows what the effect has been on public policy and opinion. Have groups perform their skits for the class.

---

## Building Social Studies Skills

STANDARDIZED TEST PREP ONLINE
keyword: SZ3 STP11

### Interpreting Political Cartoons

Look at the political cartoon about public opinion polls below and use it to answer the questions that follow.

NEWS

"OUR LATEST POLL SHOWS THAT 68% OF THE VOTERS THINK THAT 91% OF THE POLLS ARE INACCURATE 71% OF THE TIME.— PLUS OR MINUS THREE PERCENTAGE POINTS."

1. Which of the following statements best describes the message in the political cartoon?
   a. Polls always contain important information that the public can use.
   b. Polls have too much influence on public opinion.
   c. Once a person considers the way poll information is presented and the possibility of error, the information may not be useful.
   d. For a poll to be accurate, the poll takers must choose a careful sample.
2. What makes the information presented by the newscaster difficult to understand? What is the subject of the poll?
3. Based on what you have read about polls, why do you think the cartoonist has chosen to send this particular message about them?

### Analyzing Primary Sources

Read the following quotation by Becky Cain, President of the League of Women Voters, and then answer the questions that follow.

❝Do people discuss the independent expenditure loophole law [law allowing interest groups to spend money in support of an election campaign without actually contributing money to a particular candidate] over coffee in the morning? No, probably not. But does this mean that they don't care about campaign finance reform? The ballooning activity occurring on this issue at the grassroots level disproves the notion that people don't care.

How is it then that campaign finance reform has stalled at the federal level while it's succeeding at the state level? Why should citizens expect less from the federal government than from state governments?❞

4. Which of the following statements best describes Cain's point of view?
   a. People do not make the effort to monitor campaign contributions and therefore do not care about the issue.
   b. Papers must publish more information about campaign funding.
   c. Because people are participating in activities that show their support for campaign finance reform, a federal campaign finance reform law should be passed.
   d. People should address issues of concern at the state level rather than at the local level.
5. Based on what you have read about influencing government policy, why do you think that reform might be easier to achieve at a state level than at a federal level?

### Thinking Critically

1. Some may feel that politicians are specialists and can trust their own thinking. Others may think that politicians are elected to represent public opinion.

2. positive—people become informed about the candidates' opinions and familiar with their candidate's abilities; negative—some candidates may be good leaders but have bad television presence

3. Students should describe testimonials, bandwagon, name-calling, glittering generalities, plain-folks appeal, and card stacking; unaware citizens may become misinformed by them.

### Social Studies Skills

1. c.

2. the long list of percentages; polls

3. Students might suggest to show the importance of paying attention to more than just poll results when making a decision about an issue.

4. c.

5. Students might suggest that affecting change in state and local government is easier than doing it at the national level.

---

## Alternative Assessment

### Building Your Portfolio

**Linking to Community**
Select an interest group that is active in your community to research. Find out the answers to these questions: *What is the purpose of the group? How many members does the group have? How long has the group been in existence? How does the group try to achieve its goals? What problems has the group encountered in its work toward these goals?* Then create a poster illustrating the goals and activities of the interest group.

### internet connect

**Internet Activity: go.hrw.com**
**keyword: SZ3 AC11**

Access the Internet through the HRW Go site to find information about selected interest groups and lobbyists. Then determine how and why these groups try to influence legislation and elections. Include both positive and negative viewpoints on the work of interest groups and lobbyists. Then present a skit portraying lobbyist activity.

# Paying for Government

## CHAPTER RESOURCE MANAGER

| | Objectives | Pacing Guide | Reproducible Resources |
|---|---|---|---|
| **SECTION 1:** **Raising Money** (pp. 299–03) | ✪ Analyze why the cost of government is high. <br> ✪ Examine how government officials decide how to spend the government's money. <br> ✪ Describe the guidelines governments use when taxing citizens. | **Regular** 1.5 days <br><br> **Block Scheduling** 1 day <br><br> *Block Scheduling Handbook with Team Teaching Strategies, Chapter 12* | **RS** Guided Reading Strategies 12.1 <br> **E** Creative Teaching Strategy: Decision Tree <br> **RS** Graphic Organizer Activity: Types of Taxes |
| **SECTION 2:** **Types of Taxes** (pp. 304–08) | ✪ Examine the different types of taxes. <br> ✪ Describe the difference between progressive and regressive taxes. <br> ✪ Define tariffs and explain how they can be used to help the U.S. economy. | **Regular** 1.5 days <br><br> **Block Scheduling** 1 day <br><br> *Block Scheduling Handbook with Team Teaching Strategies, Chapter 12* | **RS** Guided Reading Strategies 12.2 <br> **E** Challenge and Enrichment Worksheet 12: Reading a Map <br> **SM** Community Service and Participation Handbook: Pay Your Taxes! |
| **SECTION 3:** **Managing the Country's Money** (pp. 310–15) | ✪ Describe how governments collect public money. <br> ✪ Identify the steps involved in creating the federal budget. <br> ✪ Identify and explain the size of the national debt. | **Regular** 1.5 days <br><br> **Block Scheduling** 1 day <br><br> *Block Scheduling Handbook with Team Teaching Strategies, Chapter 12* | **RS** Guided Reading Strategies 12.3 <br> **RS** Readings in Economics and Government Reading 25: William Jennings Bryan, "Cross of Gold" <br> **PS** American Civics Political Cartoon: Congressional Budget |

## Chapter Resource Key

| | | | | | |
|---|---|---|---|---|---|
| **PS** | Primary Sources | **SM** | Skills Mastery |  | CD–ROM |
| **RS** | Reading Support | **A** | Assessment |  | Video |
| **IC** | Interdisciplinary Connections | **REV** | Review |  | Internet |
| **E** | Enrichment | **ELL** | Reinforcement and English Language Learners |  | Holt Presentation Maker Using Microsoft® PowerPoint® |
| | | | Transparencies | | |

 **One-Stop** Planner CD–ROM

**See the *One-Stop Planner* for a complete list of additional resources for students and teachers.**

## One-Stop Planner CD–ROM

It's easy to plan lessons, select resources, and print out materials for your students when you use the **One-Stop Planner CD–ROM with Test Generator**.

### Technology Resources

- One-Stop Planner, Lesson 12.1
- Civics Transparency 16: Why the Costs of the Federal Government Have Increased
- CNN Presents: American Government
- Homework Practice Online

- One-Stop Planner, Lesson 12.2
- Holt Researcher CD–ROM
- Civics Transparency 17: State Sales and Income Taxes
- Homework Practice Online
- HRW Go site

- One-Stop Planner, Lesson 12.3
- Civics Transparency 18: The National Debt
- Homework Practice Online

### Reinforcement, Review, and Assessment

- REV  Section 1 Review, p. 303
- A  Daily Quiz 12.1
- ELL  Main Idea Activity 12.1
- ELL  English Audio Summary 12.1
- ELL  Spanish Audio Summary 12.1

- REV  Section 2 Review, p. 308
- A  Daily Quiz 12.2
- ELL  Main Idea Activity 12.2
- ELL  English Audio Summary 12.2
- ELL  Spanish Audio Summary 12.2

- REV  Section 3 Review, p. 315
- A  Daily Quiz 12.3
- ELL  Main Idea Activity 12.3
- ELL  English Audio Summary 12.3
- ELL  Spanish Audio Summary 12.3

### internet connect

**HRW ONLINE RESOURCES**
GO TO: go.hrw.com
Then type in the keyword.

**TEACHER HOME PAGE**
KEYWORD: SZ3 Teacher

**CHAPTER INTERNET ACTIVITIES**
KEYWORD: SZ3 AC12
Choose an activity to:
- create a graph or chart illustrating expenditures in the current federal budget.
- create a poster on the history and structure of the Internal Revenue Service.
- make mnemonic devices related to types of taxes.

**CHAPTER ENRICHMENT LINKS**
KEYWORD: SZ3 CH12

**ONLINE ASSESSMENT**
**Homework Practice**
KEYWORD: SZ3 HP12
**Rubrics**
KEYWORD: SS Rubrics

**ONLINE MAPS, CHARTS, AND GRAPHS**
KEYWORD: SZ3 MCG
- Why the Costs of the Federal Government Have Increased

**HOLT PRESENTATION MAKER**
KEYWORD: SZ3 PPT12

**CONTENT UPDATES**
KEYWORD: SS Content Updates

**ONLINE READING SUPPORT**
KEYWORD: SS Strategies

**CURRENT EVENTS**
KEYWORD: S3 Current Events

### Meeting Individual Needs

#### Ability Levels

**Level 1** Basic-level activities designed for all students encountering new material

**Level 2** Intermediate-level activities designed for average students

**Level 3** Challenging activities designed for honors and gifted-and-talented students

**English Language Learners** Activities that address the needs of students with Limited English Proficiency

### Chapter Review and Assessment

- IC  Vocabulary Activity 12
-  Global Skill Builder CD–ROM
- HRW Go site
- REV  Chapter 12 Tutorial for Students, Parents, Mentors, and Peers
- REV  Chapter 12 Review, pp. 316–17
- A  Standardized Test Practice
- A  Chapter 12 Test Generator (on the One-Stop Planner)
- A  Chapter 12 Test (Form A or B)
- A  Alternative Assessment Handbook
- A  Chapter 12 Test for English Language Learners and Special-Needs Students

## What's Your Opinion?

*To help students create their* **Themes** *Journal entries, provide the following examples of appropriate* **agree**/**disagree** *statements.*

● **Agree**   All citizens should equally contribute to the government.

**Disagree**   Citizens should be taxed according to their level of income.

● **Agree**   The purpose of a government is to ensure that its citizens have the basic necessities.

**Disagree**   A government should not have to support individuals simply because they lack money or means.

● **Agree**   A government should be able to provide services without the need of outside assistance.

**Disagree**   A government has a responsibility to provide services regardless of whether it collects enough tax revenue.

## Internet Activity

**All About Taxes**

**internet** connect

**TOPIC:** Types of Taxes
**GO TO:** go.hrw.com
**KEYWORD:** SZ3 AC12

Have students access the Internet through the HRW Go site to research types of taxes levied by local, state, and federal governments. Then have students create a series of drawings or mnemonic devices that include information on how the tax is levied, who pays the tax, and what is done with the revenue raised from the tax. As a review, ask students to share their drawings or mnemonic devices with the class.

# CHAPTER

# 12 Paying for Government

## Build on What You Know

Try to imagine a stack of $1,000 bills that reaches 100 miles (160.9 km) into the sky. This is less than the amount of money that the federal government spent in 2000— just under $1.8 trillion. State and local governments also spend many billions of dollars each year. Where does all this money come from? It comes from the American people.

The costs of government are paid with public funds. Thus, it is important to understand how the government raises and spends money. Making sure that the government manages money wisely is a serious responsibility faced by all citizens, including you.

### What's Your Opinion?

 **Themes Journal**   Do you **agree** or **disagree** with the following statements? Support your point of view in your journal.

- Governments should raise money by taxing all people the same amount.

- Governments should provide programs and services to people who cannot afford them.

- Governments should not borrow money to pay for services that they cannot pay for with tax dollars.

# SECTION 1

## OBJECTIVES

*After completing Section 1, students should be able to*

1 **Analyze why the cost of government is high.**

2 **Examine how government officials decide how to spend the government's money.**

3 **Describe the guidelines governments use when taxing citizens.**

## SECTION 1

# Raising Money

### Read to Discover

1. Why is the cost of government high?
2. How do government officials decide how to spend the government's money?
3. What guidelines do governments use when taxing citizens?

#### WHY CIVICS MATTERS

Every year, the federal government must decide how it will spend the revenue it receives from taxes. Use **CNNfyi.com** or other **current events** sources to investigate the budget priorities of the federal government. Record your findings in your journal.

### Define

- interest
- national debt
- revenue
- fees
- fine
- bond

Bull Shoals State Park

## Reading Focus

Each year, the local, state, and federal governments spend huge amounts of money on many needed services. For example, local governments provide their citizens with police officers, firefighters, and schools. Local governments also provide paved streets, sewers, trash removal, parks, and playgrounds. State governments fund highways and state police. They provide money for public schools and unemployment benefits. The federal government funds the country's defense. It helps agriculture, business, and labor and serves U.S. residents in hundreds of other ways. All these services cost money.

### ★ The High Cost of Government

It costs an enormous amount of money today to run the government. One reason it costs so much is that the United States serves a larger population than ever before—more than 281 million people. In addition, the cost of living continues to rise. Today a dollar will not buy as much as in earlier years. Finally, the government provides many more programs and services than in the past.

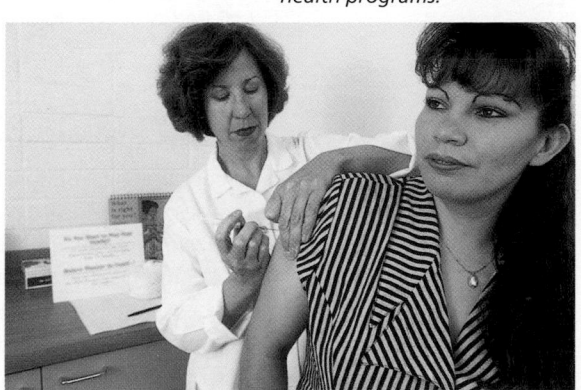

*Local governments and the federal government share much of the cost for public health programs.*

# TEACH OBJECTIVE 1

**LEVEL 1:** Have students design a cover for a news magazine featuring stories about the cost of government. Ask students to design a cover that identifies the reasons why the cost of government is high.

**ENGLISH LANGUAGE LEARNERS**

**LEVEL 2:** Discuss with students the reasons for the high cost of government. (*Students might suggest the rising population, the shrinking value of the dollar, growth in services and benefits, growing costs for national defense, and paying the national debt.*) Then have each student write a brief essay explaining how each of these factors has contributed to higher government costs. Invite volunteers to present their essays to the rest of the class.

# TEACH OBJECTIVE 2

**LEVEL 1:** Have small groups of students create collages prioritizing and illustrating various areas of government spending. (*Areas of government spending might include programs, services, benefits, national defense, and the national debt.*) Then ask each group member to be responsible for illustrating at least one example. Groups should place their images on the collages in order from top to bottom according to their priorities. Ask groups to present their collages to the class and to explain how they decided on prioritizing the spending.

**ENGLISH LANGUAGE LEARNERS , COOPERATIVE LEARNING**

---

## ★ The Democratic Process

**Tax Cuts** Californians began a wave of "taxpayer revolts" in 1978 when they approved Proposition 13, which cut property taxes 57 percent. "Prop 13," an initiative amending the California Constitution, significantly reduced the funds available to public schools and local governments. By 1980, 38 states had followed California's lead and reduced or stabilized their tax rates.

**ACTIVITY:** Have students conduct research to obtain information about the most recent legislation regarding taxes. Ask students to write a brief summary of the legislation and the proposed purpose of the new law.

---

**CHART ANSWER**
Students might mention some of the historical reasons for increased services or some of the demands of modern life.

---

## Some Causes of Increased Federal Spending

 The U.S. population has grown.

 Prices have increased, and the cost of living has risen.

 The national debt has grown and requires huge interest payments.

 The federal government now provides more services.

 The number of people receiving benefits has increased.

 Large sums are spent for U.S. defense.

**Interpreting Charts**
*The federal government spends much more today than it did when the country was founded.* **Why do you think the government provides more services now than it did in the past?**

These programs and services are expensive. The largest cost to the federal government is in benefit payments to people who are elderly, disabled, or living in poverty. The numbers who receive these benefits have been growing and will continue to rise.

A large amount of money is also spent by the government on national defense. From 1990 to 1998, defense spending decreased. After 1998 it began to rise. Following terrorist attacks in 2001, government leaders pushed for even greater increases. In December 2001 Congress approved a $318 billion defense bill. Defense will continue to account for a large portion of government spending.

Another reason for the high cost of government is debt. Over the years, the government has spent more money than it has raised. To make up the difference, the government has had to borrow money. The government must pay **interest** on this money. Interest is the payment made for the use of borrowed money. It is generally a certain percentage of the amount of money borrowed. When a large amount of money is borrowed, as is the case here, the amount of interest is also large. This interest plus the total amount of money that the U.S. government has borrowed is known as the **national debt.** You will read more about the national debt later in this chapter.

✔ **Reading Check** Summarizing What are some of the expenses of the U.S. government? benefit payments to individuals, expenditures on services and programs for an increasing population, defense, and debt

## ★ Establishing Priorities

Federal, state, and local governments all raise most of the money to pay for services and programs by collecting taxes. Taxes are compulsory—citizens and businesses are required to pay them.

Some people question the amount of taxes they pay. They think that the costs of government are too high. Others believe the government should spend more on public services. All citizens have the right to expect that the government will spend the taxpayers' money wisely.

**HOMEWORK** Ask students to imagine that they have to prioritize their family's budget. Then have each student create a list of prioritized items in order of importance that will need to be paid with the family income. *(Students might list rent or a mortgage payment as most important, and cable television access as less important.)*

# TEACH OBJECTIVE 3

**ALL LEVELS:** Copy the following graphic organizer onto the chalkboard, omitting the italicized answers. Have students complete the chart to describe the guidelines governments use when taxing citizens.
**ENGLISH LANGUAGE LEARNERS**

*ability to pay*

**Principles of Taxation**

*equal application*     *scheduled payments*

Government officials, therefore, face difficult decisions. What government programs most need money? What programs will bring the greatest benefits to the most people?

Government officials must decide which activities need funding, in order of their urgency and need. This process is called establishing priorities. Programs with highest priority get funded first. Programs with a lower priority may not receive funds. In recent years there has been much debate over the country's priorities.

✔ **Reading Check** Drawing Inferences and Conclusions Why do you think paying taxes is compulsory? Students might say that if it were voluntary, many people might choose not to pay, and the government would not have enough money to operate effectively.

## ⭐ The Purpose of Taxes

The chief purpose of taxes is to raise **revenue,** or money. This revenue pays the costs of government. Another purpose of taxes is to regulate, or control, some activities.

For example, taxes on imports are sometimes fixed at a high level. Their aim is not to raise large sums of money but to discourage imports and to encourage business activity in the United States. High taxes on cigarettes and alcoholic beverages are partly intended to discourage their use.

✔ **Reading Check** Supporting a Point of View Do you think it is fair for the government to tax certain products at a high rate to discourage their use? Answers may vary. Supporting answers might say that the government should regulate products that could be harmful to citizens. Opposing answers might suggest that the government should treat all businesses equally.

## ⭐ Principles of Taxation

Governments try to follow certain principles, or rules, when they set up taxes. These rules aim to raise the funds necessary to run the government without creating too great a burden for taxpayers.

**Ability to Pay** Taxes are set at different rates to make it possible for citizens to pay. Taxes on people's earnings are lower for those with low incomes and higher for those with high incomes. People with very low incomes do not pay income taxes.

**Equal Application** The principle of equal application of taxes is part of the U.S. tax structure. This means that taxes are applied at the same rate for similar taxable items. For example, a local tax on property is the same for all property worth the same amount of money. Sales taxes and other taxes collected on the goods we buy are the same for everyone purchasing these goods.

---

**Interpreting the Visual Record**

**An important expense** *Funding schools is an expensive but vital budget item for local governments.* **What might happen if schools received little or no money in the government's budget?**

---

## ⭐ Civics Sidelight

**Alternative Taxation**
Taxes have not always been paid in money. For example, some governments have taxed agricultural production by requiring farmers to turn over a portion of their grain to the government. In early frontier communities in the United States, some citizens paid their taxes by working to construct roads, schools, and other community facilities.

**CRITICAL THINKING**

Why might government today require that taxes be paid only in money?

**ANSWER:** Students might say that the high cost of government operation requires money, which comes from taxes.

**Visual Record Answer**

*Students might suggest that many schools would be forced to close.*

**LEVEL 3:** Lead a class discussion on the guidelines governments use when taxing citizens. Then have students identify which principle of taxation is applied to a hypothetical situation. Suggest that workers in Ohio and Iowa with the same level of income also pay the same federal income tax rate. *(Students should answer that the principle of equal application is being applied.)* Then have students create their own situations that address the principles of taxation. Finally, have students use these examples to create a poster showing the principles of the U.S. tax system.

## CLOSE

Have each student draw a picture or a political cartoon characterizing how a government obtains revenue or spends money. Students might want to illustrate one aspect of government funding or spending. Encourage students to be creative. Students should be prepared to explain how their cartoons depict government funding, spending, or both.

## ⭐ Constitutional Heritage

**Asset Forfeiture** One controversial new source of government revenue is asset forfeiture. In 1984 law-enforcement agencies began seizing not just drug dealers but also their assets—boats, cars, planes, even houses. The agencies can then resell the property to help pay for the tools, weapons, and personnel needed to fight the war on drugs. In 1997 local law enforcement agencies received $648 million worth of cash goods and property from drug asset forfeiture. In 1985 Congress allowed the proceeds from these asset seizures to be shared with state and local law-enforcement agencies. Almost any property alleged to have a connection with a person's illegal drug-related activities might be seized, even if the person is not convicted of a crime. For this reason, some critics have condemned the practice as unconstitutional.

### CRITICAL THINKING

Which constitutional amendments might the practice of asset forfeiture violate?

**ANSWER:** Students might suggest the Fifth Amendment, which protects the rights of persons accused of crimes.

### Visual Record Answer

*Students might suggest to track motorists.*

**Scheduled Payment** Taxes are paid on a set schedule. Employers withhold a portion of taxes from workers' paychecks. This tax money is sent directly to the government. Self-employed people are responsible for withholding the necessary funds for their taxes from the money they earn. They also send this money directly to the government.

Imagine that all taxes had to be paid during the Christmas holidays. This is a time of year when many people have extra bills to pay. Most Americans would find paying taxes then difficult. Instead, governments collect taxes at a time when it is easier for people to pay them. The federal government requires payment in full by an April 15 deadline. However, taxpayers can request to pay any taxes that they still owe in installments, or chunks spread throughout the year on a set schedule. These payments are charged interest and penalty fees.

✔ **Reading Check** **Drawing Inferences and Conclusions** Why are some taxes set at different rates? The government sets a tax rate based on people's ability to pay so that people pay what they can afford.

## ⭐ Other Methods of Raising Revenue

Governments also raise money through fees, fines, and payments for special services. **Fees,** or small payments, are charged for various licenses, such as hunting licenses and marriage licenses. State governments raise large sums of money from the fees paid for driver's licenses and automobile license plates. The federal government raises billions of dollars annually from fees. The federal government receives fees for trademark registration, grazing rights on federal land, and entrance to national parks.

Money charged as a penalty for breaking certain laws is called a **fine.** Local governments in particular raise revenue by charging fines for actions such as illegal parking, speeding, and other traffic violations.

**Interpreting the Visual Record**

**Government fees** *State governments collect fees for automobile license plates and for the use of services such as toll roads.* **What use do license plates have other than as a way for governments to collect money?**

# REVIEW AND ASSESS

Have students complete the **Section 1 Review** on page 303. Then have students complete **Daily Quiz 12.1**. As **Alternative Assessment**, you may want to use the tax situations activity or the guidelines for taxation organizer in this section's lessons.

## RETEACH

Have students complete **Main Idea Activity for English Language Learners and Special-Needs Students 12.1**. Then ask each student to make a list of the key terms found in the section. Have them write sentences that explain the significance of each term and its relation to the section material.
**ENGLISH LANGUAGE LEARNERS**

## EXTEND

Have students research a publicly funded project created in their community in the last decade. Ask students to develop a chart that displays the following information: what the project was, how much it cost, how the money for the project was appropriated, and what effect the project has had on the community. **BLOCK SCHEDULING**

Governments provide some special services that are paid for directly by those who use these services. For example, the federal government sells timber from national forest reserves and electricity from certain federal dam projects. State governments collect payments from drivers who use certain toll roads and bridges. Many local governments install parking meters to collect payments from individuals who park their cars along city streets.

✔ **Reading Check Contrasting** What is the difference between fees and fines? A fee is a payment in exchange for a license or other service. A fine is a payment made as a punishment for violating a law.

## ★ Government Borrowing

As you have read, governments raise most of their funds through taxes and other revenue. Occasionally, governments raise more money than they need, ending in a budget surplus. More often, they must borrow money to meet their expenses. Large projects, such as bridges or schools, cost a lot to build. State and local governments usually cannot pay for them in full out of the government's income for a single year. Therefore, state and local governments must borrow from citizens the additional money needed.

Governments borrow money by issuing bonds. A government **bond** is a certificate stating that the government has borrowed a certain sum of money from the owner of the bond. The government promises to repay the loan on a certain date and to pay interest on the amount borrowed. Bonds thus allow governments to raise money for public projects while giving investors an opportunity to make a profit.

✔ **Reading Check Analyzing Information** Why do governments borrow money? to pay for large projects that exceed a single year's budget; to provide services above what the government can afford under the existing budget

**Interpreting the Visual Record**

**Borrowing money** *Bonds are a common way for governments to raise money. Some bonds require public approval before they can be issued; otherwise the money cannot be borrowed.* **Why do you think some bonds require public approval?**

Election 2001

## Travis voters approve bonds

■ $185 million will be used for road and park projects, land purchases

BY ALEX TAYLOR
American-Statesman Staff

---

# SECTION 1 Review

go.hrw.com **Homework Practice Online**
keyword: SZ3 HP12

1. **Define** and explain:
   • interest
   • national debt
   • revenue
   • fees
   • fine
   • bond

2. **Analyzing Information** Copy the chart below. Use it to list the three principles of taxation and to explain why each one is important.

   | Principle | | | |
   |---|---|---|---|
   | Importance | | | |

3. **Finding the Main Idea**
   a. What are six reasons for the high cost of government?
   b. How do government priorities affect government spending?

4. **Writing and Critical Thinking**
   **Decision Making** Imagine that you are part of a review board examining the cost of government. Write a proposal explaining what government programs and services you think should have the highest priority and why.

   **Consider:**
   • the sources of funding
   • the needs of the general public

---

**Visual Record Answer**

*Students might suggest because they require a tax increase for funding.*

## Section 1 Review
### ANSWERS

**1. Define**
• interest, p. 300
• national debt, p. 300
• revenue, p. 301
• fees, p. 302
• fine, p. 302
• bond, p. 303

**2.** Principle—ability to pay, equal application, scheduled payments; importance—set taxes at different rates to make it possible for citizens to pay, taxes applied at the same rate for similar taxable items, ensures taxes are paid on a set schedule

**3. a.** growing population, growing numbers of people receiving benefits, defense spending, growing number of government programs, federal debt, and growing cost of living

**b.** The programs that have the highest priority will be funded first.

**4.** Students' answers will vary but could include national defense, general health and welfare, and education.

# SECTION 2

## OBJECTIVES

*After completing Section 2, students should be able to*

1 **Examine the different types of taxes.**

2 **Describe the difference between progressive and regressive taxes.**

3 **Define tariffs and explain how they can be used to help the U.S. economy.**

## 🔔 LET'S GET STARTED!

As students enter the classroom, ask them to list as many different types of taxes as they can. *(Students might name sales and income taxes.)* Inform students that there are many different types of taxes, but all taxes serve the same purpose—to raise revenue for the government. Finally, tell students that in Section 2 they will learn more about the various types of taxes.

## SECTION 2 RESOURCES

### REPRODUCIBLE

▶ Guided Reading Strategies 12.2

▶ Civics Transparency 17: State Sales and Income Taxes

▶ Challenge and Enrichment Worksheet 12: Reading a Map

▶ Community Service Participation Handbook: Pay Your Taxes!

### TECHNOLOGY

▶ One-Stop Planner, Lesson 12.2

▶ Holt Researcher CD–ROM

▶ Homework Practice Online

▶ HRW Go site

### REINFORCEMENT, REVIEW, AND ASSESSMENT

▶ Section 2 Review, p. 308

▶ Daily Quiz 12.2

▶ Main Idea Activity 12.2

▶ English Audio Summary 12.2

▶ Spanish Audio Summary 12.2

---

## SECTION 2

# Types of Taxes

### Read to Discover

1. What are the different types of taxes?
2. What is the difference between progressive and regressive taxes?
3. What are tariffs, and how can they be used to help the U.S. economy?

### Define

- income taxes
- exemptions
- deductions
- taxable income
- progressive tax
- profit
- Social Security tax
- sales tax
- regressive tax
- excise taxes
- property tax
- real property
- personal property
- estate tax
- inheritance tax
- gift tax
- tariff

> **WHY CIVICS MATTERS**
>
> Increases in property taxes at the state and local levels are usually a source of debate. Use **CNNfyi.com** or other **current events** sources to investigate a property tax controversy in your state or area. Record your findings in your journal.

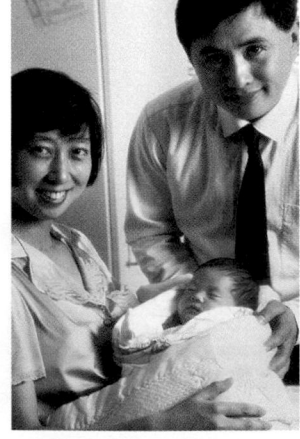

*Children, such as this baby, are considered dependents.*

## Reading Focus

As you have learned, taxes are the main source of revenue for the federal, state, and local governments. All levels of government depend on many types of taxes to raise the large sums of money they need.

### ★ Individual Income Taxes

The largest source of revenue for the federal government is **income taxes.** These are taxes on the earnings of individuals and companies.

**How Much Do We Pay?** All taxpayers are allowed to deduct, or subtract, a certain amount of money for themselves and for each dependent. A dependent is a person who relies on another person, usually a family member, for support. These amounts are called **exemptions.** The amount of the exemption is adjusted, or changed, according to the inflation rate. If prices increase, the amount of the exemption also increases. In 2002 the exemption was $3,000.

Taxpayers also are allowed to deduct certain expenses. These amounts are called **deductions.** For example, taxpayers can deduct charitable contributions, most business expenses, and the interest paid on home mortgages.

304

**LEVEL 1:** Lead a class discussion about the different types of taxes. Then have students create a crossword puzzle using the definitions as clues and the different types of taxes as answers. *(For example, students might use for the answer* Social Security tax *that the clue is a tax used mainly to provide income for retired people.)* **ENGLISH LANGUAGE LEARNERS**

**ALL LEVELS:** Have each student list the kinds of taxes discussed in this section. Then have students consult dictionaries to look up each tax name. Have the students create charts with dictionary definitions or sketches of the terms in one column and textbook descriptions of each tax in a second column. **ENGLISH LANGUAGE LEARNERS , COOPERATIVE LEARNING**

**LEVEL 2:** Pair students and have each pair play a vocabulary game using the different kinds of taxes discussed in this section. Have pairs make flash cards and then take turns quizzing each other. **COOPERATIVE LEARNING**

**HOMEWORK** Have students create flowcharts illustrating the ways in which sales taxes; excise taxes; property taxes; tariffs; and estate, inheritance, and gift taxes affect various people.

---

The amount of income left after all subtractions are made from the total income is called **taxable income.** This is the amount from which individual income tax is paid. The individual income tax is a progressive tax. A **progressive tax** is a tax that takes a larger percentage of income from higher-income groups than from lower-income groups. Thus, it is based on ability to pay. Congress changes tax rates when it wants to help the economy.

**How Do We Pay?** As you have read, the deadline for paying federal taxes is April 15. U.S. taxpayers must fill out and mail their tax forms on or before this date each year. Some taxpayers take advantage of electronic filing systems.

Most taxpayers do not pay all their income tax at the time they file tax returns. Income tax payments have already been taken out of each paycheck by their employers. Their employers then forward the tax money on to the government. This system of making small tax payments each payday makes it easier for the government to collect the payments. It also makes payment easier for most Americans.

Filling out the tax forms shows taxpayers how much they owe in taxes for the previous year. Sometimes people learn they will receive a refund. This means they will get back some of the tax money withheld by their employers during the year. Sometimes people find they owe the government more money. Additional tax payments or refunds depend on the amount contributed to taxes over the year, as well as on deductions and exemptions.

**State and Local Taxes** All but a few of the state governments and some city governments also collect an individual income tax. Each of these states and cities has its own income tax laws and rates. Such tax rates are much lower than those for the federal income tax.

**Corporate Income Taxes** Like individual income taxes, corporate income taxes are an important source of revenue for state governments. This tax is based on a corporation's profits. **Profit** is the income a business has left after paying its expenses. Like individuals, corporations may deduct certain amounts to lower their taxable income. For example, they may subtract money paid to buy new machinery or for employee salaries. Also like individuals, corporations with higher taxable incomes are usually taxed at a higher rate.

**Social Security Taxes** Another type of income tax that Americans pay is the **Social Security tax.** Money collected from this tax is used mainly to provide income to retired people and people with disabilities. The

**Holt Researcher**

**go.hrw.com**
**Keyword: Holt Researcher**
**Free Find:** The Federal Budget

Search for information on federal receipts on the Holt Researcher. Use the information provided to create a bar graph that shows how much revenue the federal government received from each major type of tax for the most recent year listed on the Researcher. Your graph should answer the following question: What form of tax provided the federal government with the most revenue?

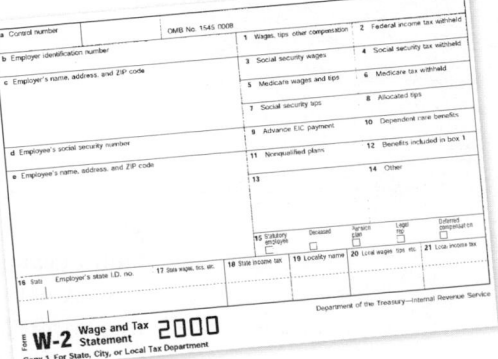

*The W-2 form provided by most employers indicates how much of your paycheck has been withheld for tax purposes.*

---

## ★ Constitutional Heritage

**The Tax Man** The first income taxes were not levied until the Civil War. The initial tax rate was 3 percent on incomes of more than $800 for U.S. residents. This income tax was repealed in 1872. Efforts in the 1890s by several progressive organizations led to a second federal income tax law in 1894, but the Supreme Court declared it unconstitutional a year after its enactment. In 1913 the addition of the Sixteenth Amendment to the Constitution permitted Congress to pass an income tax.

**CRITICAL THINKING**
Why might progressive organizations in the 1890s want to institute an income tax?

**ANSWER:** to help fund progressive programs

---

**internet** connect

**TOPIC:** The Internal Revenue Service
**GO TO:** go.hrw.com
**KEYWORD:** SZ3 AC12

Have students access the Internet through the HRW Go site to research the Internal Revenue Service (IRS). Then have each student create a poster that includes information on the major operating divisions of the IRS, the number of employees, and a brief history of the bureau.

**Progressive Tax** *takes a larger percentage of income from higher-income groups.*

**Regressive Tax** *takes a larger percentage of income from lower-income groups.*

tax paid by each worker is matched by the employer. You will read more about Social Security in Chapter 19.

✔ **Reading Check Summarizing** What are the different types of income taxes? individual: federal, state, and local; corporate; and Social Security

## Sales and Excise Taxes

Most states and many cities have a **sales tax.** This tax is collected on most products sold. For example, if the sales tax is 5 percent, buyers must pay $1.05 for an item that costs $1.00. Sellers send the extra 5 percent they collect to the state or city government.

A sales tax is a regressive tax. A **regressive tax** is a tax that takes a larger percentage of income from low-income groups than from high-income groups. For example, a wealthy person and a poor person both buy the same television. A sales tax on the television will take a higher percentage of the poor person's money. However, people with high incomes typically buy more than people with low incomes. This means they contribute more in sales tax.

**Excise taxes** are similar to sales taxes. Yet excise taxes are collected only on certain services and goods, usually "luxury" items, sold in the United States. Some of the items on which excise taxes are collected are air travel, alcoholic beverages, gasoline, luxury automobiles, and tobacco. Excise taxes are collected by the federal government and by several state governments.

✔ **Reading Check Comparing and Contrasting** How are sales taxes and excise taxes similar and different? Both are taxes on purchased goods, but excise taxes are limited to specific items, usually luxury goods.

## Property Taxes

The chief source of income for most local governments is the **property tax.** This is a tax on the value of the property owned by a person or by a business. Property taxes are collected on two different types of property—real property and personal property.

**Types of Property** **Real property** consists of land, buildings, and other structures. **Personal property** includes such items as stocks, bonds, jewelry, cars, and boats. It is often difficult to determine the value of an individual's personal property. Thus, most governments apply the property tax only to real property. If personal property is taxed, the rate is usually very low.

**Taxing Real Property** To determine the value of property for tax purposes, local governments depend on local officials called tax assessors. These assessors visit the property and assess it, or make a judgment of its value.

**Interpreting the Visual Record**

**Shopping and taxes** *Sales taxes contribute a considerable amount of money to states and many cities.* **What do you think happens to sales tax revenues during the Christmas holidays?**

# TEACH OBJECTIVE 3

**LEVEL 1:** Organize students into groups and have each group write a radio commercial script for a pro-tariff organization. Scripts should define what a tariff is and explain how tariffs can be used to help the U.S. economy. Have groups present their commercials to the class. **ENGLISH LANGUAGE LEARNERS , COOPERATIVE LEARNING**

**LEVEL 3:** Have students imagine that they are advisers to the U.S. president. Then have each student develop a list of foreign goods that should have a tariff placed on them. In their lists, students should define reasons why that item should be taxed and how tariffs can be used to help the U.S. economy.

# CLOSE

Review with students the principles of taxation. Then list on the chalkboard all the kinds of taxes discussed in this section. Pair students and have them apply the principles to each of the taxes to determine how each tax meets the fairness standards. Have the pairs create charts to illustrate the relationships between these principles and each tax. **COOPERATIVE LEARNING**

The local government adds up the assessed value of all the property in a certain area, or locality. The local government then determines the total amount of money it must raise by the property tax. To determine the tax rate, it divides this amount by the total assessed value of property in the locality.

For example, consider a small town that needs revenue of $100,000 from its property tax assessments. Suppose that the total assessed value of property within the boundaries of the town is $5 million. To determine the amount that property owners must pay, divide $100,000 by $5 million. This gives a tax rate of 2 cents on each dollar, or $2 on each $100 of assessed property value. At this 2 percent tax rate, a house and land assessed at $60,000 would be taxed $1,200 a year.

Much of the funding for public schools in the United States comes from local property taxes. This method of funding public education has met with controversy in recent years. Critics charge that this system allows wealthier communities to provide their students with higher-quality education and materials. Because property values are high in wealthier communities, these communities can collect greater amounts of property taxes. Thus, they have more money to spend on their local schools.

✔ **Reading Check Summarizing** How is a local property tax determined? The local government determines the total amount of revenue needed by the property tax, and it divides that by the total assessed value of real property in the area.

## ★ Estate, Inheritance, and Gift Taxes

When a person dies, that person's heirs may have to pay taxes on property left by the deceased. This property may include real estate, money, and personal property. An **estate tax** is a federal tax on all the wealth a person leaves. The rate at which the tax is paid by the heirs depends on the value of the estate. In 2004 estates valued under $1,500,000 were not taxed. This limit is scheduled to rise to $2,000,000 in 2006.

Individuals may also be taxed on the share of the estate that they inherit, or receive. Note the difference between this **inheritance tax** and the estate tax. The inheritance tax is based on the portion of the estate received by an individual. The estate tax is based on the value of the entire estate before it is divided.

Even a gift of money may be subject to a tax by the federal government. A **gift tax** must be paid by any person who gives a gift worth more than $10,000.

✔ **Reading Check Contrasting** What is the difference between the estate and inheritance taxes? Estate taxes are based on the value of the entire estate before it is divided. Inheritance taxes are based on the portion of the estate received by an individual.

**Interpreting the Visual Record**

**Real estate** *The owners of expensive properties, such as this mansion, must contribute more in property tax than most Americans.* **How would the assessment of this property's value affect the amount it was taxed?**

## REVIEW AND ASSESS

Have students complete the **Section 2 Review** on page 308. Then have them complete **Daily Quiz 12.2.** As **Alternative Assessment**, you may want to use the tax vocabulary game or the progressive/regressive tax organizer activities in this section's lessons.

## RETEACH

Have students complete **Main Idea Activity for English Language Learners and Special-Needs Students 12.2.** Then ask students to create an acrostic puzzle using all the different types of taxes discussed in this section.
**ENGLISH LANGUAGE LEARNERS**

## TEACHER TO TEACHER

Michelle Bierman of Minnesota recommends the following activity:

## EXTEND

Give each student a particular salary. Then ask students to conduct research in order to obtain information about federal taxes. Have students calculate the federal taxes on their salary, and if a state tax is levied, have them calculate that as well. As a class, discuss how they would spend their tax dollars if they were the government. Finally, have them rank their decisions from most important to least important. **BLOCK SCHEDULING**

## Section 2 Review
### ANSWERS

**1. Define**
• income taxes, p. 304
• exemptions, p. 304
• deductions, p. 304
• taxable income, p. 305
• progressive tax, p. 305
• profit, p. 305
• Social Security tax, p. 305
• sales tax, p. 306
• regressive tax, p. 306
• excise taxes, p. 306
• property tax, p. 306
• real property, p. 306
• personal property, p. 306
• estate tax, p. 307
• inheritance tax, p. 307
• gift tax, p. 307
• tariff, p. 308

**2.** individual income—tax on income; sales and excise—on products sold; property—on real or personal property; estate, inheritance, gift—on estate after death, on inheritance, or on gifts over $10,000, respectively; import tariff—goods imported from foreign countries

**3. a.** income after allowed deductions are made; through payroll deduction and then final payment by April 15

**b.** by making imported goods as expensive as, or more expensive than, U.S. goods

**4.** Students' answers will vary, but students should present well-reasoned arguments.

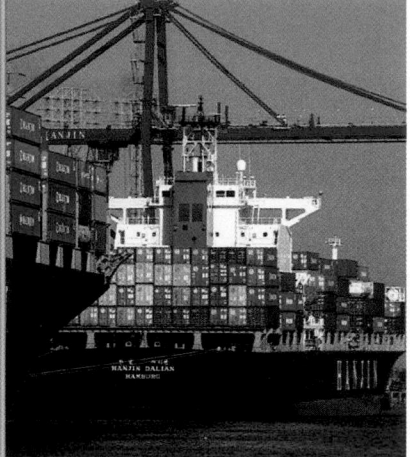

**Interpreting the Visual Record**

**Imports** *Taxes on imported goods raise money for the federal government and can be used to protect domestic industries from foreign competition.* **How would import taxes affect consumers who buy imported goods?**

## ★ Import Taxes

The U.S. government collects taxes on many products imported from foreign countries. This import tax is called a **tariff,** or sometimes a customs duty. In the early years of the country, tariffs were an important source of revenue for the federal government. At that time the federal government did not collect any personal income taxes.

Today the United States uses tariffs primarily to regulate trade rather than to raise money. The government places tariffs on certain products to retaliate against foreign tariffs on U.S. goods or to protect American industries against foreign competition.

Workers in many foreign countries are paid less than those in the United States. As a result of lower labor costs, these foreign countries can manufacture goods less expensively than the United States can. Lower manufacturing costs mean that those countries could sell their goods here for far less money than American manufacturers would charge. With such competition, American industry would lose business, and some jobs in the United States would be lost.

In such cases tariffs can be used to raise the prices of imported goods, making them as expensive as, or more expensive than, American-made products. In this way tariffs can protect American industry from competition that is seen as unfair. Yet in some cases tariffs hurt American consumers by raising the prices of certain products.

✔ **Reading Check** **Making Generalizations and Predictions** How might a high tariff on German automobiles affect the number of American automobiles purchased in the United States? Students should say that high tariffs on German cars would probably make them more expensive than American cars. As a result, purchases of American cars should go up.

---

## SECTION 2 Review

**go.hrw.com Homework Practice Online**
keyword: SZ3 HP12

**1. Define** and explain:
• income taxes
• exemptions
• deductions
• taxable income
• progressive tax
• profit
• Social Security tax
• sales tax
• regressive tax
• excise taxes
• property tax
• real property
• personal property
• estate tax
• inheritance tax
• gift tax
• tariff

**2. Categorizing** Copy the graphic organizer below. Fill in each box with a type of tax and an example of something to which that tax could be applied.

**Types of Taxes**

| | |
|---|---|
| | |
| | |
| | |
| | |

**3. Finding the Main Idea**
a. On what are income taxes based, and how do citizens and corporations pay income taxes?
b. How can tariffs be used to help the U.S. economy?

**4. Writing and Critical Thinking**
**Supporting a Point of View** Write a position statement in which you argue for or against making all U.S. taxes progressive taxes. Be sure to explain why you have taken this position.

**Consider:**
• the effect of regressive taxes on both poor and rich taxpayers
• the amount of income that can be generated by progressive and regressive taxes

## TEACH

**LEVEL 1:** Suggest to students that they can use a pie graph to represent nearly anything that is composed of various elements. For example, the contents of a refrigerator might be broken down by percentage into meats, vegetables, drinks, and so on. Tell students that pie graphs are helpful because of their visual representation. In complex areas such as budgeting, people can see at a glance where their money is going. Ask students to keep track of their spending for a week. Then have them determine a category for each sum spent and show the categories as different-sized sections of a pie graph. **ENGLISH LANGUAGE LEARNERS**

**LEVEL 3:** Have students refer to the pie graph that they created in the Level 1 activity. Then tell students that they must now reduce at least half of their weekly spending. Have students write proposals on which category or categories they would reduce, how they would reduce them, and why they would reduce spending in the category or categories they selected.

# Civics Skills
## WORKSHOP

## Reading Pie Graphs

The federal government collected more than $2 trillion in revenue in 2000. It uses the money to pay for the hundreds of federal programs and services it provides for U.S. citizens. Because the government handles so much money, it can be difficult to visualize how the huge government budget operates. Where does all of this money go each year?

One effective way to visualize this information is to use a pie graph. Like other graphs, pie graphs summarize large amounts of information in easy-to-read diagrams.

Every pie graph equals 100 percent of something. The pie graph on this page, for example, represents 100 percent of the federal government's expenses for one year. Each slice of the pie represents a part of those expenses. Because national defense accounts for 16 percent of the government's expenses, 16 percent of the pie, or circle—little more than one seventh—is colored to represent this expenditure.

## How to Read Pie Graphs

1. **Determine the subject.** Read the title of the graph to determine its subject and purpose.

2. **Study the labels.** The graph's labels indicate the main categories, or "slices," into which the circle has been divided.

3. **Analyze the data.** Compare the sizes of the various sections of the graph. The size of each section is determined by the percentage of the total it represents. The larger the section in the graph, the greater the percentage of the total that section represents.

4. **Put the data to use.** Use the data to draw conclusions about the subject of the graph.

## Applying the Skill

Study the pie graph entitled Federal Government Spending below. Then answer the following questions.

1. What is the federal government's largest expense?

2. What percentage of the federal budget is used to make interest payments on the national debt?

3. Based on the information presented in this graph, what conclusions can you draw about government spending priorities?

4. What are the advantages and disadvantages of using a pie graph to display information such as this?

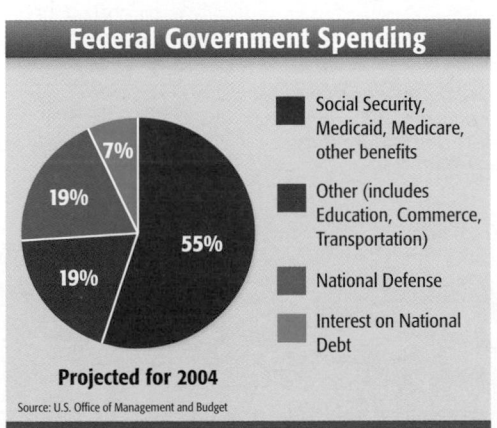

**Federal Government Spending**

- Social Security, Medicaid, Medicare, other benefits
- Other (includes Education, Commerce, Transportation)
- National Defense
- Interest on National Debt

7%
19%
19%
55%

**Projected for 2004**
Source: U.S. Office of Management and Budget

## SKILLS ANSWERS

1. benefits payments

2. 7 percent

3. Answers will vary but might mention the fact that benefits payments account for more than half of government spending.

4. A pie graph summarizes the large amount of information in an easy-to-read diagram. A pie graph cannot reflect the particulars that comprise the data in the graph.

# SECTION 3

## OBJECTIVES

*After completing Section 3, students should be able to*

1. **Describe how governments collect public money.**
2. **Identify the steps involved in creating the federal budget.**
3. **Identify and explain the size of the national debt.**

## SECTION 3 RESOURCES

### REPRODUCIBLE

▶ Guided Reading Strategies 12.3

▶ Civics Transparency 18: The National Debt

▶ Readings in Economics and Government Reading 25: William Jennings Bryan, "Cross of Gold"

▶ American Civics Political Cartoon: Congressional Budget

### TECHNOLOGY

▶ One-Stop Planner, Lesson 12.3

▶ Homework Practice Online

### REINFORCEMENT, REVIEW, AND ASSESSMENT

▶ Section 3 Review, p. 315

▶ Daily Quiz 12.3

▶ Main Idea Activity 12.3

▶ English Audio Summary 12.3

▶ Spanish Audio Summary 12.3

## 🔔 *LET'S GET STARTED!*

Draw a vertical rule on the chalkboard. Mark the top end of the rule "+$" and the bottom end of the rule "–$." Mark the midpoint " 0. " Draw a horizontal line from the midpoint out to the right. As students enter the classroom, ask them the following question: Would you show a surplus above the line or below it? *(Students should suggest above the line.)* Discuss why and then have a student label the area. Ask the same question for a deficit. Finally, tell students that in Section 3 they will learn about the federal deficit and the national debt.

---

## SECTION 3

# Managing the Country's Money

### Read to Discover

1. How do governments collect public money?
2. What steps are involved in creating the federal budget?
3. How large is the national debt, and why?

### Define

- balanced budget
- surplus
- deficit
- audit

> #### WHY CIVICS MATTERS
>
> The importance of having a balanced federal budget has increased each year as the national debt has gradually increased. Use **CNNfyi.com** or other **current events** sources to investigate the debate over balancing the federal budget. Record your findings in your journal.

## *Reading Focus*

As you know, the federal, state, and local governments collect and spend many billions of dollars each year. Each level of government has established within itself separate divisions to manage public funds.

### ★ Collecting Public Money

Each level of government has a department whose responsibility it is to collect taxes. At the federal level, the collection of taxes is handled by the Internal Revenue Service (IRS). The IRS is an agency of the U.S. Department of the Treasury. The IRS collects many types of taxes. These include individual income taxes, corporate income taxes, Social Security taxes, excise taxes, estate taxes, and gift taxes. This agency has offices throughout the country. Another agency of the federal government, the U.S. Customs Service, collects tariffs on imported goods.

State and local governments have established their own tax collection agencies. State tax collection agencies collect taxes such as state income taxes and inheritance taxes. Taxes collected by local tax collection agencies include local property taxes.

*The Main Treasury Building in Washington, D.C., is the headquarters of the Treasury Department.*

# TEACH OBJECTIVE 1

**ALL LEVELS:** Copy the following graphic organizer onto the chalkboard, omitting the italicized answers. Have students complete the chart to describe how governments collect public money. **ENGLISH LANGUAGE LEARNERS**

**LEVELS 2 AND 3:** Have each student draw political cartoons to portray the collection of public money for one level of government. Because such activities are often portrayed negatively, you might ask some students to portray positive aspects of how each level of government accomplishes the task. Display the cartoons around the classroom.

---

### Government Collection of Public Money

**Federal "collection agency"**
*Internal Revenue Service*

**Role of the "collection agency"**
*collects individual income taxes, corporate income taxes, Social Security taxes, excise taxes, estate taxes, and gift taxes*

**State and local "collection agencies"**
*collects state income and inheritance taxes as well as local property taxes*

---

After tax money is collected, it is sent to the treasuries of the various governments. The U.S. Treasury Department spends federal tax dollars under the authorization of Congress. In state and local governments the comptroller acts as the "watchdog of the treasury." The comptroller is responsible for ensuring that public funds are spent only as authorized by the state legislature or city council.

✔ **Reading Check Summarizing** What agencies collect government revenue, and who keeps track of it? The IRS, state, and local tax collection agencies collect revenue. Federal, state, and local comptrollers track the money.

##  Planning Government Spending

All governments have budgets. As you know, a budget lists the amount of expected revenue, or money income. It also lists the sources from which this revenue will be collected. A budget also specifies the proposed expenditures, or money to be spent, for various public purposes. A budget is usually intended to pay for the government's operations for one year.

The function of managing public funds is divided between the executive and legislative branches of government. The chief executive of each level of government is responsible for drawing up the budget. In municipalities the mayor, the city manager, or another executive officer plans and draws up the budget. In most state governments the governor prepares the yearly budget of the state's income and spending. The president is responsible for budget planning in the federal government.

The legislative branch must turn the budget into law before any public money can be spent. Once the budget has been passed, the head of the executive branch must ensure that the money is spent according to the approved budget. The courts of the judicial branch settle any disputes over the collection and spending of public money.

✔ **Reading Check Categorizing** How are the budget responsibilities divided among the executive and legislative branches of government? The executive branch proposes the budget, and the legislative branch turns the budget into law.

## Preparing the Federal Budget

In the federal government the president recommends how public funds should be raised and how they should be spent. The job of planning the federal budget is so large and so complicated that the president needs the help of several government agencies.

---

**BIOGRAPHY**

### Eliot Ness
#### (1903–1957)

Eliot Ness was born in Chicago, Illinois. An excellent student, Ness studied business and political science at the University of Chicago. Soon after graduation he went to work for the Treasury Department. At that time the Treasury Department was in charge of enforcing prohibition. Ness transferred to the Prohibition Bureau and quickly made a name for himself as a tough opponent of organized crime in Chicago. After transferring to the Justice Department, Ness created a team that became known in the newspapers as the "Untouchables," because they could not be bribed or intimidated. Due in part to his efforts, in 1931 organized crime boss Al Capone was sent to jail for income tax evasion and failure to file a tax return. Ness later went on to serve in the city administration of Cleveland, Ohio, and helped run several businesses. After his death the story of Ness's crimefighting exploits inspired a popular television series called *The Untouchables*. **In what ways do you think Ness's career was unusual for an agent of the Treasury Department?**

---

### ✦ Economics

**The Federal Budget** The budget for the federal government is determined not for the calendar year but for the fiscal year. The government's fiscal year begins on October 1 and ends on September 30. Thus, the budget for 2002 actually covers the period from October 2001 through September 2002. The reason for the late start of the fiscal year is that the period must accommodate the government's budgeting and appropriating processes.

**CRITICAL THINKING**

What other benefits might exist for having a delayed fiscal year?

**ANSWER:** Students might suggest that it also allows time for the government to determine how much revenue has been collected and is available for use.

---

**BIOGRAPHY ANSWER**
He helped fight organized crime.

---

# TEACH OBJECTIVE 2

**LEVEL 1:** To help students identify the steps in creating the federal budget, have them create a fictional budget for their student government. First, list on the chalkboard the ways government raises money. Then call on volunteers to suggest how the student government might raise money and for what purposes. Have students also decide how much money should be spent for each purpose. To conclude, lead a class discussion about the additional steps necessary to create the federal budget. **ENGLISH LANGUAGE LEARNERS**

**LEVEL 2:** Organize the class into groups. Have groups create a flowchart to show the main steps in creating the federal budget. Group members should illustrate one part of the flowchart and draw an arrow from one item to the next. In addition, each part of the flowchart should be explained in a short caption. Groups should begin with the Office of Management and Budget's forecast of tax income. The flowcharts should end with the approved budget becoming law. Display the completed flowcharts around the classroom. **COOPERATIVE LEARNING**

## ⭐ Economics

### The Democratic Process

The Advisory Council on Social Security was created to investigate problems with the Social Security system. Economists working for the council in 1994 concluded in their 1994–1996 report that as of the year 2020, Social Security will hit a deficit. In addition, there will be only enough payroll taxes to pay 75 percent of the Social Security benefits. A contributing factor to this problem will be paying benefits to baby boomers, who comprise one-third of the U.S. population. The council has not been able to agree on one plan to remedy the situation, and the attacks of September 11 further threaten the funds in Social Security.

### CRITICAL THINKING

What do you think should be done to save Social Security?

**ANSWER:** Student's responses will vary.

### CHART ANSWER

public welfare/benefits, education, transportation

## How Government Spends Its Money

| | Sources of Income | Expenditures |
|---|---|---|
|  **Federal Government** | • Individual income taxes<br>• Corporate income taxes<br>• Social Security taxes<br>• Excise taxes<br>• Import taxes<br>• Estate and gift taxes<br>• Borrowing (public debt) | • Benefits payments<br>• National defense<br>• Interest on debt<br>• Grants to states and local areas<br>• Foreign relations<br>• Health and education<br>• Transportation and commerce<br>• Energy and the environment<br>• Science, space, and technology |
| 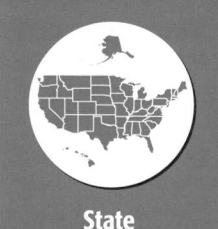 **State Governments** | • Federal government<br>• Individual income taxes<br>• Corporate income taxes<br>• General sales taxes<br>• Cigarette, gasoline, and liquor taxes<br>• Inheritance taxes<br>• Licenses and fees<br>• Borrowing (public debt) | • Education<br>• Public welfare<br>• Highways<br>• Health and hospitals<br>• Police<br>• Natural resources<br>• Housing and community development |
|  **Local Governments** | • Federal and state governments<br>• Property taxes<br>• Licenses and payments<br>• Fines<br>• Utilities<br>• Borrowing (public debt) | • Schools and libraries<br>• Public welfare<br>• Fire and police protection<br>• Health and hospitals<br>• Utilities<br>• Highways<br>• Sewers and sanitation<br>• Parks and recreation |

**Interpreting Charts** *Each level of government in the federal system has certain special sources of income.* **What types of expenses are common to all levels of government?**

The chief agency that helps the president prepare the federal budget is the Office of Management and Budget (OMB). This important agency evaluates the effectiveness and efficiency of executive agencies. It also forecasts the amount of tax income the government will receive in the coming year.

Each of the executive departments makes a careful estimate of how much money it plans to spend the following year. All these estimates are submitted to the OMB. The president and the director of the OMB study the many requests and establish priorities for the various departments' needs. Some requests may be cut to bring the total expenditures closer to estimated revenues.

**HOMEWORK** Tell students that governments can reduce the federal budget deficit by either increasing revenues or decreasing expenditures. Have students write a letter to the president with recommendations for lowering the federal budget by either increasing revenues or decreasing expenditures.

## TEACH OBJECTIVE 3

**ALL LEVELS:** Lead a class discussion about the size of the national debt. Write a 6 with 12 zeros on the chalkboard to help illustrate how large $6 trillion is. Organize the class into groups. Then have groups imagine that they are writing a letter to one of the founders of our government. Ask students to explain in their letters how the national debt grew so large. **ENGLISH LANGUAGE LEARNERS**

After the budget is prepared each year, it is published in book form. The budget is actually several books and is thousands of pages long, listing thousands of separate items.

✔ **Reading Check** Summarizing How does the president set the priorities in the federal budget? With the help of the OMB, the president reviews funding requests and then ranks them in importance.

## Congress and the Budget

The president sends the finished federal budget to Congress. Along with the budget, the president sends a message explaining the budget and urging that it be passed. Often the president addresses a joint session of Congress to seek support for the federal budget.

Congress makes its own study of the proposed budget. As you have learned, only Congress has the power to raise and spend money. The House of Representatives and the Senate debate the various items in the budget and make changes. Both houses of Congress must approve the final version of the federal budget. The budget is passed in the form of 13 appropriations bills. Appropriations bills are those that actually authorize the spending of funds. These bills are then sent back to the president to be approved or vetoed.

The process of preparing the federal budget takes many months. There is often much heated debate before the final budget is approved. When finally completed, the federal budget becomes the law under which public money will be spent during the coming year.

✔ **Reading Check** Drawing Inferences and Conclusions Why do you think the responsibility for developing the budget is divided between the president and the Congress? Students might say that this form of checks and balances ensures that no one person (or party) has undue influence over the budget priorities.

## The National Debt

When a government has a **balanced budget,** its revenue equals its expenditures. That is, the amount of money it collects equals the amount of money it spends. However, frequently a government budget is not balanced. When a government collects more money than it spends, it has a **surplus,** or an excess of money. When a government spends more money than it collects, it has a **deficit,** or a shortage of money.

From 1970 to 1997, the government of the United States operated at a deficit each year. That is, the federal government spent more money than it collected in revenue. To make up this difference, the federal government each year had to borrow increasing amounts of money. The

"...Comes unassembled. Does not include batteries or instructions...."

**Interpreting Political Cartoons**

**Budget woes** *Creating a budget is a yearly struggle for the federal government.* **What difficulties are these members of Congress encountering?**

★★★★★★★★★★★★
**That's Interesting!**
★★★★★★★★★★★★

**Watching Every Dime** Keeping a budget requires careful records. Would you notice if you underpaid a bill by three cents? President James Buchanan was this precise in his everyday accounting. Throughout his life, he kept books in which he carefully recorded every penny that he earned or spent.

## ▶ Global Perspectives

**Budget Concerns in Great Britain** Unlike the U.S. federal budget, which considers revenue and expenditures in one document, the proposed budget of the United Kingdom is comprised of many documents. Expenditure plans are presented in a White Paper, usually in February or March. The full budget is presented in March in several volumes, titled *Financial Statement and Budget Report.*

**CRITICAL THINKING**

Which budget might be easier to approve, the U.S. budget or the United Kingdom's budget?

**ANSWER:** Students might suggest that the United Kingdom's budget might be easier to approve because spending and revenues are not discussed at the same time.

**POLITICAL CARTOON ANSWER**

Students might suggest how to operate the tools involved with the "Budget Machine," which represents the complex nature of the federal budget.

**LEVEL 3:** Ask each student to imagine that he or she is a member of Congress who has been invited to appear on a national news show to discuss a bill that he or she has introduced. The bill will eliminate the national debt over a period of 10 years. Have students write the dialogue for the interview. The interview should cover the following topics—what the amount of the national debt is, how it grew so large, why it is a problem, and why it is important to pass legislation eliminating it.

## CLOSE

Have students create pamphlets encouraging citizens to take seriously their responsibility to ensure that public money is managed well and spent wisely. The pamphlets should include ways citizens can exert influence on the management of public money (such as through voting). Encourage students to be creative, using graphics, cartoons, or other visuals. Remind students to title their pamphlets.

## *Did You* KNOW?

The lowest recorded figure for the public debt of the United States was $33,733 in 1835. Of course, the value of a dollar was greater then. In December 2003 the public debt was estimated to be $6,915,121,384,308!

The deficit occurs when the government spends more money than it collects. There is a national debt, which requires interest payments.

government balanced the budget from 1998 to 2000, ending up with a surplus. However, at the end of 2001, congressional leaders predicted that spending increases would once again lead to a deficit. Borrowing money contributes more to the national debt, which by 2003 had reached almost $7 trillion.

The chart on this page shows how the national debt has grown over time. The enormous growth of this debt has been one of the most controversial public issues in recent years. Many people charge that the government's practice of operating under a budget deficit is harmful to the country. In 1997 Congress and President Bill Clinton reached an agreement to balance the federal budget by 2002. Cuts in defense and domestic spending were part of this plan. However, an economic slowdown and the terrorist attacks of September 11, 2001, led to increased spending in these areas.

Part of the revenue collected each year must be used to pay the interest on the national debt. This portion cannot be used to fund programs and services for the people. The interest on the debt is so high that future generations will be repaying the money that is borrowed now. In addition, the government borrows much of the money it needs to make up for the deficit by issuing government bonds. Increasingly, these bonds are being bought by foreign investors. This means public tax dollars are going overseas to pay interest on these bonds.

There is no constitutional limit on the size of the national debt. Congress establishes a limit above which the debt cannot go. However, it periodically raises this limit as the need for more spending arises.

✔ **Reading Check** Identifying Cause and Effect What causes the federal budget deficit, and what has been the result?

**Interpreting Graphs**
*The size of the national debt has grown immensely as the national population and government expenditures have grown.* **What historical event do you think might have contributed to the jump in national debt from 1940 to 1950?**

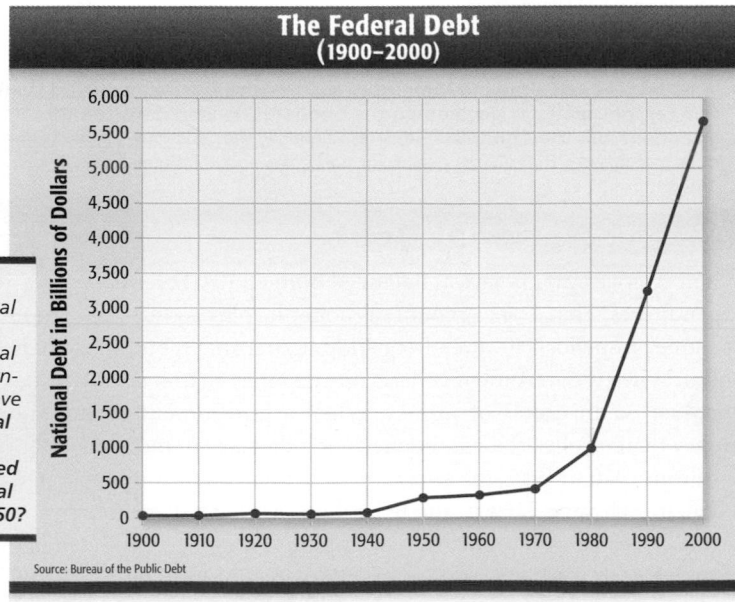

**The Federal Debt**
(1900–2000)

National Debt in Billions of Dollars

Source: Bureau of the Public Debt

## REVIEW AND ASSESS

Have students complete the **Section 3 Review** on page 315. Then have them complete **Daily Quiz 12.3**. As **Alternative Assessment**, you may want to use the political cartoon or the national debt letter activity in this section's lessons.

## RETEACH

Have students complete **Main Idea Activity for English Language Learners and Special-Needs Students 12.3**. Then have students create a list of advantages and disadvantages of reducing the federal budget by either increasing revenues or decreasing expenditures. **ENGLISH LANGUAGE LEARNERS**

## EXTEND

Have students research attempts since the 1970s to eliminate or shrink the federal budget. Then have each student create an outline that addresses the following questions: What methods were used to pare the deficit—spending cuts or freezes, raising taxes, or others? How successful have these efforts been? What were the general public's reactions to methods employed to cut the deficit? Call on volunteers to present their findings to the class.
**BLOCK SCHEDULING**

---

### ★ Public Money Is a Public Trust

To ensure that funds are spent according to law, all levels of government provide for an **audit** of their accounts. An audit is a careful examination by trained accountants of every item of income and every expenditure.

A department of the state government usually audits expenditures of local governments. State departments of education require that local school districts submit audit reports of their spending. In state governments an independent agency of the state under the comptroller's direction usually conducts state audits. The General Accounting Office examines federal expenditures.

### ★ Citizen Responsibility

The well-being of the country depends on how wisely our governments handle public funds. If wise policies of raising and spending money are to be followed, citizens must take an active part. They must understand taxes, the use of public funds, and the national debt. They must also make their voices heard on these issues.

*The General Accounting Office plays a critical role in the budget process by reviewing the expenditures of the federal government.*

✔ **Reading Check Finding the Main Idea** How do governments and citizens ensure that public funds are being spent properly? Independent government agencies audit the finances of the government on a regular basis. Citizens are expected to stay informed and to express their concerns about how public funds are managed.

---

## SECTION 3 Review

**go.hrw.com Homework Practice Online**
**keyword: SZ3 HP12**

**1. Define** and explain:
- balanced budget
- surplus
- deficit
- audit

**2. Categorizing** Copy the graphic organizer below. Fill in the missing information about the responsibilities of different branches of government in creating the federal budget. Add boxes to the organizer as necessary.

| The executive branch . . . | The legislative branch . . . | The judicial branch . . . |
|---|---|---|
| | | |
| | | |

**3. Finding the Main Idea**
a. How do the three levels of government collect public money?
b. How large is the national debt today, and why is it so large?

**4. Writing and Critical Thinking**
**Supporting a Point of View** Write a letter to the president with your recommendations for keeping the federal budget balanced. Be sure to tell the president why you think your recommendations will be effective.

**Consider:**
- the advantages and disadvantages of increasing revenue
- the advantages and disadvantages of reducing spending

---

**REPRODUCIBLE**
► Chapter 12 Review, pp. 316–17
► Vocabulary Activity 12
► Chapter 12 Tutorial for Students, Parents, Mentors, and Peers
► Chapter 12 Test (Form A or B)
► Alternative Assessment Handbook, Chapter 12

**TECHNOLOGY**
► Chapter 12 Test Generator (on the One-Stop Planner)
► Global Skill Builder CD–ROM
► HRW Go site

**REINFORCEMENT, REVIEW, AND ASSESSMENT**
► Chapter 12 Test for English Language Learners and Special-Needs Students

## REVIEW
Have students complete the **Chapter 12 Review** on pages 316–17.

## ASSESS
Use one of the chapter tests to assess students' understanding of the content. For **Alternative Assessment**, see the **Alternative Assessment Handbook**.

---

## Understanding Main Ideas

**1.** population growth, more government services, rising cost of living, growth in benefit payments, higher defense spending, interest on national debt

**2.** ability to pay—taxes based on the amount of money people earn; equal application—taxes are applied at the same rate for similar taxable items; scheduled payment—taxes paid on a set schedule

**3.** to provide funds to make up for the deficit; issue government bonds

**4.** income after allowed deductions are made; fill out income tax forms to determine proper amount to send to the government

**5.** A progressive tax is a tax that takes a larger percentage of income from higher-income groups, such as individual income tax; a regressive tax is a tax that takes a larger percentage of income from low-income groups, such as sales tax.

**6.** surplus—excess of money; deficit—shortage of money

**7.** It is the total amount of money owed by the U.S. government, plus the interest that must be paid on this borrowed money; if it continues to increase, so will the interest payments required, which means the government will have to raise increasing amounts of money to cover all of its costs.

---

# Chapter 12 Review

## Chapter Summary

### Section 1
- Running a government costs a great deal of money. This money must be provided by citizens—each of us shares the costs of government and benefits from its expenditures.
- Over the years the costs of running the government have increased greatly.
- Governments raise revenue through taxes, fees, fines, special payments, and borrowing.

### Section 2
- There are many kinds of taxes. Americans pay taxes on individual income, property, purchases, imported goods, corporate profits, gasoline, and many other items.
- Federal, state, and local governments all collect a share of these taxes.
- Progressive taxes take a greater percentage of income from high-income groups. Regressive taxes take a greater percentage of income from low-income groups.

### Section 3
- Various agencies collect tax revenue and ensure that it is spent properly.
- The executive branches of governments work closely with the legislative branches to plan revenue collection and spending.
- In addition to relying on tax revenue, governments also borrow large sums of money to help pay their expenses.
- Federal borrowing has created a large national debt, a problem that concerns many Americans. As taxpayers, we must play an active role in understanding how the government collects and spends money.

Bull Shoals State Park

## Define and Identify
Use the following terms in complete sentences.
1. national debt
2. revenue
3. income taxes
4. progressive tax
5. sales tax
6. regressive tax
7. tariff
8. balanced budget
9. deficit
10. audit

## Understanding Main Ideas
**Section 1** *(Pages 299–03)*
1. Identify six reasons for the high cost of government.
2. Identify and explain the principles the government uses to try to make taxation fair.
3. Why must governments borrow money? How do they borrow money?

**Section 2** *(Pages 304–08)*
4. How is individual income tax calculated, and how do citizens pay individual income taxes?
5. What is the difference between a progressive tax and a regressive tax, and what is an example of each?

**Section 3** *(Pages 310–15)*
6. What is the difference between a surplus and a deficit?
7. What is the national debt, and how might it be harmful to the country?

## What Did You Find Out?
1. What are the different kinds of taxes?
2. What are some of the services that governments use their revenue to provide?
3. How does the government manage money, and why is there a national debt?

## Thinking Critically
1. **Identifying Points of View** In recent years some federal officials and members of the public have sought a constitutional amendment to require a balanced federal budget each year. However, Congress and many citizens have strongly resisted such an action. What are the reasons for supporting or opposing a balanced budget amendment?
2. **Evaluating** Do you think that the income tax should be a progressive tax? Why or why not?
3. **Analyzing Information** From what you have read in this chapter, do you think our tax system is too complicated or that the system works well? Explain your answer.

## RETEACH

Assign each student one or more of the charts and maps in Chapter 12. Then have them study these visual guides and write a summary of the content of each one. Then call on volunteers to lead discussions about each of the charts and maps.

**ENGLISH LANGUAGE LEARNERS**

## Portfolio Extensions

*American Civics*

### 1. Linking to Community
Have students research taxing and spending in their community. Then have them interview local officials about the taxes, fees, and fines paid by citizens. Ask students to determine how their local government sets priorities, how it decides how to spend local revenue, and whether citizens are allowed to participate in this process. Finally, have students create a poster showing the community projects and services that are paid for by public money. In a caption, have students explain how each is funded.

### 2. Cooperative Learning
Organize students into small groups. Ask groups to design a mock Web site on government taxation. Have one member of the group design the home page, while the other members design the remaining pages. The Web sites should fully explain how and why the government taxes citizens, and what are the various types of taxes. The Web sites should also provide examples of where each tax is used.

---

## Building Social Studies Skills

go.hrw.com — STANDARDIZED TEST PREP ONLINE — keyword: SZ3 STP12

### Interpreting Maps
Study the map below. Then use the information on the map to answer the questions that follow.

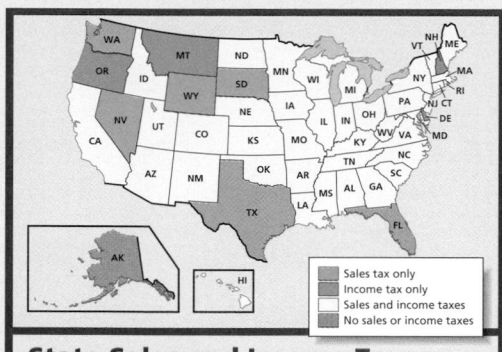

**State Sales and Income Taxes**

- Sales tax only
- Income tax only
- Sales and income taxes
- No sales or income taxes

1. How many states have no sales tax?
   a. 4
   b. 7
   c. 5
   d. 10
2. How many states have an income tax?
   a. 43
   b. 42
   c. 4
   d. 40
3. How many states have only a sales tax?
   a. 2
   b. 6
   c. 7
   d. 44
4. Why do you think so many states have both a sales and an income tax?

### Analyzing Primary Sources
Read the following quotation from Representative Earl Pomeroy. Then answer the questions that follow.

❝Back where I come from and across the country, Americans wanted the parties to work together to iron out the most difficult problems facing this country. They wanted a balanced budget. They have to do it as individual families. Collectively they wanted to do it on behalf of the country. But they also wanted our values reflected. Those values include protecting the health care that our seniors depend upon, committing to a bright educational future for our young people, and the opportunity for people at a midcareer track to go back [to school] and get the skills training they need to compete in the work force today. It means working and middle-income families find it just a little easier to make ends meet.❞

5. Which of the following statements best represents Pomeroy's viewpoint?
   a. The American people want a balanced budget but recognize that it is not possible due to the number of government expenses.
   b. Americans want a balanced budget that still provides for their basic interests.
   c. Americans are willing to cut expenses such as health care to balance the budget.
   d. Balancing the budget is not a priority for most Americans.
6. How does this quotation help demonstrate some of the difficulties involved in balancing the federal budget?

---

## Alternative Assessment

### Building Your Portfolio
*American Civics*

**Interdisciplinary Connection to Economics**
Conduct research to find out what rules apply to raising and spending money in a club or organization in your school. Ask the organization for copies of its budget. How is money raised? How is money spent? Summarize your findings in a flow-chart that shows the process of raising and spending money for the organization. Include captions that explain each step.

### internet connect
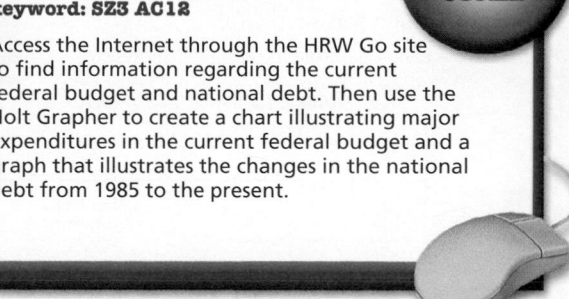

**Internet Activity: go.hrw.com**
**keyword: SZ3 AC12**

Access the Internet through the HRW Go site to find information regarding the current federal budget and national debt. Then use the Holt Grapher to create a chart illustrating major expenditures in the current federal budget and a graph that illustrates the changes in the national debt from 1985 to the present.

---

## What Did You Find Out?

1. income tax, Social Security tax, sales tax, excise tax, property tax, tariff, estate tax, inheritance tax, gift tax, and import tax

2. Students' answers will vary but might include benefit payments to individuals, health care and education, transportation, grants to states and local areas, or advancements in science and technology.

3. The government establishes a budget for the money; however, the budget may have more expenditures than revenue. Therefore, the budget results in a deficit. The budget deficit and interest paid on borrowed money have contributed to the national debt.

### Thinking Critically
1. Students' answers will vary but some might suggest that some people believe actions to eliminate the deficit might hurt the economy.

2. Students' answers will vary but should be logically presented.

3. Students' answers will vary but should be logically presented.

### Social Studies Skills
1. c
2. a
3. b
4. because an income tax and sales tax can provide a large amount of revenue
5. b
6. It mentions many of the programs provided by the government that must be addressed when balancing the budget.

## TEACH

**LEVEL 1:** Explain to students that voting is one of the most important responsibilities of citizens living in a democracy. Ask students to consider the reasons that voting is important. Then organize students into pairs and ask pairs to imagine that they have been hired by both political parties to promote voter turnout at the next election. Ask each pair to design a series of bumper stickers that encourage people to vote. **ENGLISH LANGUAGE LEARNERS**

**ALL LEVELS:** Have each student create a graphic organizer that uses a web design to depict the ways that U.S. citizens can get involved in the political process. Students' graphic organizers should consider how the government is influenced by voting, public opinion, interests groups, and so on.
**ENGLISH LANGUAGE LEARNERS**

## APPLYING THE SKILLS

Ask students to use the information that they have researched in the Civics Lab exercise to create an effective advertisement for a candidate running for student council. Encourage students to make use of visual images while presenting important information about the candidate. Ask volunteers to present their advertisements to the class.

# Civics Lab

## Election Campaign
**Complete the following Civics Lab activity individually or in a group.**

## Your Task

In Unit 4 you read about the important role that active citizens play in our form of government. Imagine that the superintendent of public schools has asked you to make a presentation to a group of students from schools in your state. The group is made up of students who are considering running for Student Council president in their schools. The title of your presentation will be How to Run an Effective Election Campaign. Your presentation should consist of both written and visual materials. To prepare these materials, you will need to do the following.

## What to Do

**STEP 1** Choose a U.S. president whom you admire, and research that person's presidential campaign. What people were important to the campaign's success? How did volunteers help the campaign? How did the president raise campaign contributions? What kind of relationship did the president have with the media? Organize your findings in an illustrated time line titled, The Election Campaign of President                    .
Below your time line explain why this campaign was successful.

**John F. Kennedy's Campaign**

| January 1960 | | | | | | | November 1960 |
|---|---|---|---|---|---|---|---|

Wins the Presidency

**LEVELS 1 AND 2:** Remind students that political parties in the United States have changed over time. Ask students to create a chart that traces the development of the two-party political system since the beginning of the United States. Have students include descriptions of the major positions of each party. **ENGLISH LANGUAGE LEARNERS**

**LEVEL 3:** Remind students that citizens fund the operation of the government by paying taxes. Then ask each student to draw a political cartoon illustrating the positive and negative aspects of paying taxes. Students' cartoons should consider how the growth of the United States and its government has also resulted in increased expenses.

**STEP 2** **Conduct** a poll in which you ask a representative sample of students in your school to identify the problems and issues facing students today. Show the results in a bar graph that indicates what percentage of poll respondents identified each issue or problem as a concern. Title the bar graph Student Concerns. Use your poll results to create a list of campaign goals that will address students' concerns.

**STEP 3** **Conduct** research to learn what financial rules apply to Student Council elections in your school. Are there rules concerning the sources of campaign funds? How do Student Council candidates spend the money for their campaigns? Then ask to see the Student Council budget for the past five years. How does the Student Council raise money? How are decisions made about how the money will be spent? Summarize your findings in a flow-chart that shows how and where campaign funds flow in a campaign. Include captions that explain each step and any restrictions concerning the raising and use of the funds.

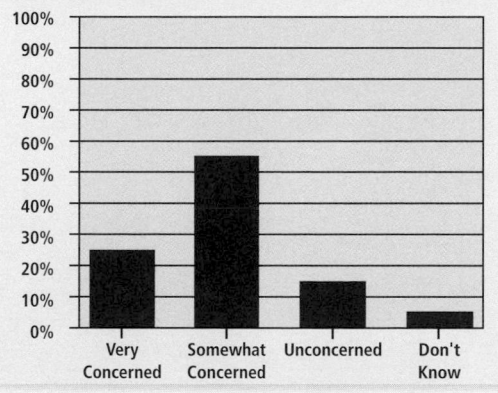

**SAMPLE CHART**

**How Concerned Are You by the Amount of Homework You Are Assigned?**

(Bar graph with y-axis 0% to 100% in 10% increments. Categories: Very Concerned ~25%, Somewhat Concerned ~55%, Unconcerned ~15%, Don't Know ~5%)

$ Student Council Expenses → Homecoming Dance
→ After School Tutoring Program
→

Organize your materials and make your presentation to the prospective Student Council candidates (the rest of the class).

**A STEP FURTHER**

Ask students to imagine that they are running the election campaign of a fictional student running for Student Council president. Have each student prepare a press packet of information about the candidate's views and plans. Students' press packets should also include brief quotes or slogans that represent their candidates' positions on various issues. Students might also include flyers or handouts that explain their candidates' campaign strategies. Ask volunteers to present their press packets to the class.

# UNIT 5

## The Citizen in Society

### UNIT OVERVIEW

Unit 5 focuses on the basic characteristics of good citizenship at home, at school, and in the community. It also encourages good citizenship through a complete understanding of and a respect for the law. The unit depicts present-day problems realistically and invites students to look for solutions that will protect our basic social institutions.

### In Their Own Words

*"Volunteerism still combines the best and most powerful values in our society—pride in the dignity of work, the opportunity to get involved in things that affect us, the freedom of choice and expression, the chance to put into practice an ethic of caring, and the realization that one person can make a difference."*— Charlotte J. Lunsford-Berry

**Using the Quotation** Have students read the quotation and find pictures in this unit that show people working together. Ask: What does volunteering have to do with the idea of citizenship? Invite students to share their own experiences with volunteering.

**About the Author** Charlotte J. Lunsford-Berry (1931– ) served as National Chairperson of Volunteers for the American Red Cross from 1986 to 1989. She was re-elected to a second three-year term on the Board of Governors of the National Red Cross in 1993. Lunsford-Berry, a graduate of Mary Baldwin College in Staunton, Virginia, and a resident of Columbia, South Carolina, has served in a wide variety of roles for the Red Cross since the early 1970s. She also has served on numerous boards, including the Mary Baldwin College Board of Trustees.

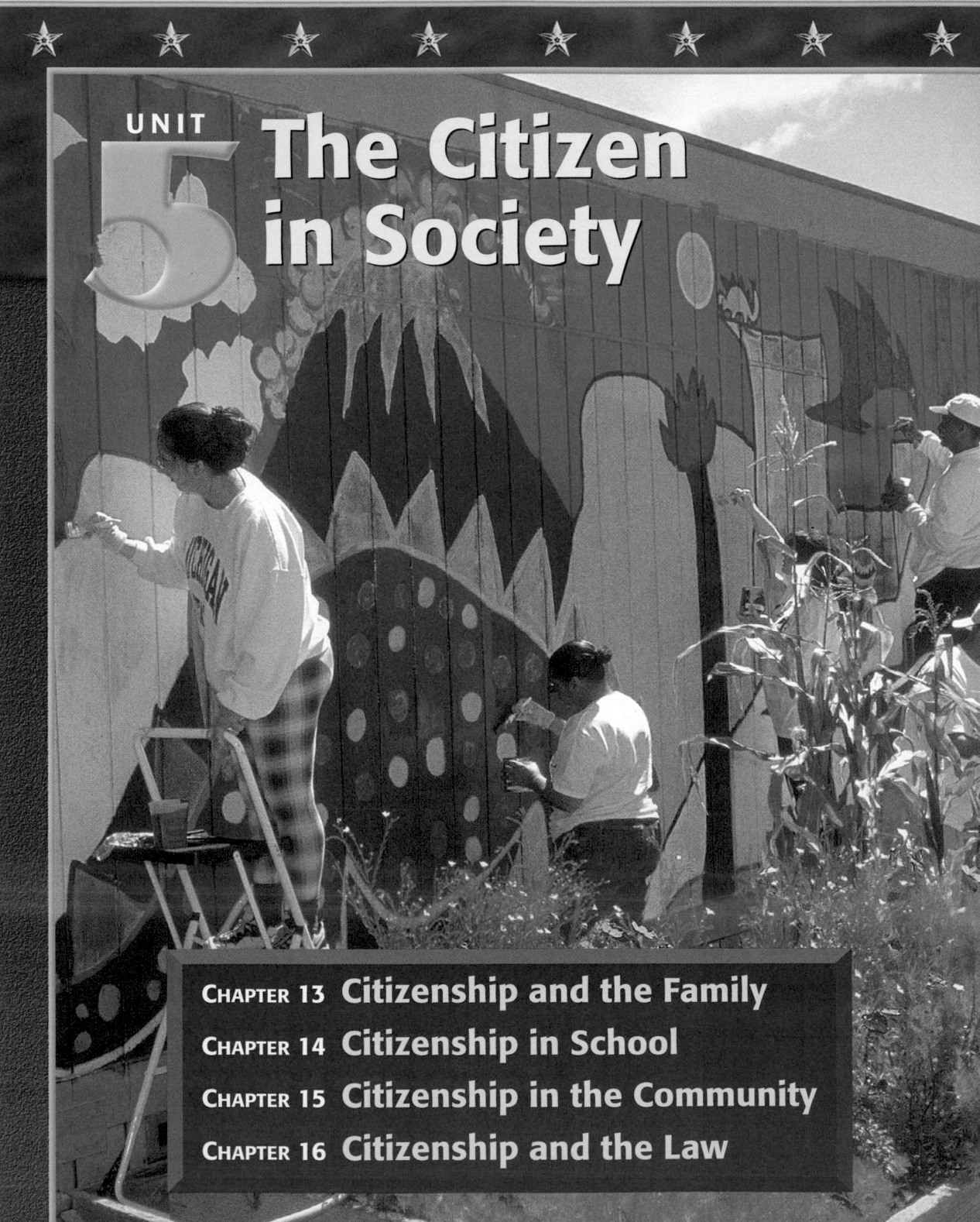

# UNIT 5 The Citizen in Society

Share the information in the chapter overviews with students. Then organize students into three groups and ask each group to brainstorm a list of specific actions that members might perform to be good citizens at home, at school, and in the community. Have each group vote on the five actions that it thinks are most important. Then ask groups to outline plans for good citizenship that explain why the five actions that they have chosen are important and how they might put these actions into effect. Later, when students have finished the unit, ask them to look at their plans again and have students compare their ideas about how to be good citizens with the ideas presented in this unit.

# Young Citizens

## IN ACTION

### Volunteering

Kay Lauren Miller, a student at James Madison High School in Vienna, Virginia, struggled with a reading disorder known as dyslexia when she was younger. Overcoming this challenge helped her recognize the importance of literacy. "Reading is the basis of knowledge," she said. "I wanted to help make sure that needy children would have books to read." Miller organized her first book drive in 1997. Several homeless shelters in Miller's community received the used books that were collected during the drive.

With the success of her first drive, Miller was encouraged to expand her efforts. She brought in student volunteers to organize larger book drives. After sorting and organizing the books, these volunteers distributed them to children who needed them. By 2001, her efforts had developed into ROAR, the Reach Out and Read program. ROAR student volunteers collect books and distribute them to homeless shelters, hospitals, and other places where children might not have access to books.

*Organizing a book drive for children in need is one way to make a difference in your community.*

So far, Miller's organization has collected more than 30,000 books. It has also set up libraries at shelters, day-care centers, and elementary schools in Virginia, Maryland, and the District of Columbia. Miller even sent 400 books to a small town in South Dakota after a tornado destroyed its local library. Miller's long-term goal is to set up ROAR programs in all 50 states.

Miller has received national attention and awards for her efforts. Through these efforts, she has demonstrated that it is never too early to practice good citizenship.

### You Decide

1. Why did Miller start her first book drive?
2. Why is volunteering an important part of being a good citizen?

## What Can We Do?

Ask students to conduct research to obtain more information about book drives or similar volunteer programs intended to promote literacy and education in their community. Then organize students into groups and ask them to conduct research to learn more about specific literacy needs that are not being met in the community. Have each group develop a proposal that describes how it might meet this need by collecting books for a local homeless shelter, by raising money for a community library, or by participating in a similar volunteer activity. As a class, discuss the various proposals and vote on the proposal that the class would most like to adopt. Encourage students to take the steps necessary to make their proposal's goal a reality.

### YOU DECIDE ANSWERS

1. She started her first book drive because she realized the importance of literacy after overcoming dyslexia when she was younger.

2. Students' answers will vary, but they might point out that citizens can improve their communities by volunteering.

WE RECYCLE

# Citizenship and the Family

## CHAPTER RESOURCE MANAGER

| Objectives | Pacing Guide | Reproducible Resources |
|---|---|---|
| **SECTION 1:**<br>**The Changing Family**<br>(pp. 323–28)<br><br>⊞ Describe how the move from rural areas to urban areas changed the American family.<br>⊞ Explain why people are delaying marriage and define the term *blended family*.<br>⊞ Identify the additional stresses that single-parent families face, and determine why the number of two-income families is increasing. | **Regular**<br>1 day<br><br>**Block Scheduling**<br>.5 day<br><br>*Block Scheduling Handbook with Team Teaching Strategies, Chapter 13* | **RS** Guided Reading Strategies 13.1 |
| **SECTION 2:**<br>**Law and the Family**<br>(pp. 329–32)<br><br>⊞ Explain the purpose of a waiting period for marriage licenses, and explain why some states require couples to take a medical test.<br>⊞ Describe how state laws work to protect children.<br>⊞ Identify the types of decisions that must be made by couples who are planning to divorce. | **Regular**<br>1 day<br><br>**Block Scheduling**<br>.5 day<br><br>*Block Scheduling Handbook with Team Teaching Strategies, Chapter 13* | **RS** Guided Reading Strategies 13.2<br><br>**E** Challenge and Enrichment Worksheet 13: Researching Your State's Marriage Laws |
| **SECTION 3:**<br>**Your Family and You**<br>(pp. 334–37)<br><br>⊞ Identify five important functions served by the family.<br>⊞ Explain why it is important to respect the rights of other family members and for family members to compromise.<br>⊞ Evaluate why it is useful for a family to budget its money. | **Regular**<br>1.5 days<br><br>**Block Scheduling**<br>1 day<br><br>*Block Scheduling Handbook with Team Teaching Strategies, Chapter 13* | **RS** Guided Reading Strategies 13.3<br><br>**E** Creative Teaching Strategy: Structured Discussion<br><br>**PS** American Civics Political Cartoon: The Spread of Suburbia<br><br>**RS** Graphic Organizer Activity: Factors Influencing the American Family<br><br>**E** Community Service and Participation Handbook: Drowning in Debt |

## Chapter Resource Key

**PS** Primary Sources
**RS** Reading Support
**IC** Interdisciplinary Connections
**E** Enrichment

**SM** Skills Mastery
**A** Assessment
**REV** Review
**ELL** Reinforcement and English Language Learners
📚 Transparencies

💿 CD-ROM
📼 Video
 Internet
💻 Holt Presentation Maker Using Microsoft® PowerPoint®

 **One-Stop** Planner CD–ROM

See the *One-Stop Planner* for a complete list of additional resources for students and teachers.

## One-Stop Planner CD–ROM

It's easy to plan lessons, select resources, and print out materials for your students when you use the **One-Stop Planner CD–ROM with Test Generator**.

| Technology Resources | Reinforcement, Review, and Assessment |
|---|---|
| One-Stop Planner, Lesson 13.1 | REV Section 1 Review, p. 328 |
| Holt Researcher CD–ROM | A Daily Quiz 13.1 |
| Homework Practice Online | ELL Main Idea Activity 13.1 |
| | ELL English Audio Summary 13.1 |
| | ELL Spanish Audio Summary 13.1 |
| One-Stop Planner, Lesson 13.2 | REV Section 2 Review, p. 332 |
| Homework Practice Online | A Daily Quiz 13.2 |
| HRW Go site | ELL Main Idea Activity 13.2 |
| | ELL English Audio Summary 13.2 |
| | ELL Spanish Audio Summary 13.2 |
| One-Stop Planner, Lesson 13.3 | REV Section 3 Review, p. 337 |
| CNN. Presents: American Government | A Daily Quiz 13.3 |
| Homework Practice Online | ELL Main Idea Activity 13.3 |
| | ELL English Audio Summary 13.3 |
| | ELL Spanish Audio Summary 13.3 |

### internet connect

**HRW ONLINE RESOURCES**
GO TO: go.hrw.com
Then type in the keyword.

**TEACHER HOME PAGE**
KEYWORD: SZ3 Teacher

**CHAPTER INTERNET ACTIVITIES**
KEYWORD: SZ3 AC13
Choose an activity to:
• create a collage that shows the way in which the family serves the country.
• make thematic graphs and charts related to the changing American family.
• organize an oral report on current issues in family law.

**CHAPTER ENRICHMENT LINKS**
KEYWORD: SZ3 CH13

**ONLINE ASSESSMENT**
**Homework Practice**
KEYWORD: SZ3 HP13
**Rubrics**
KEYWORD: SS Rubrics

**ONLINE MAPS, CHARTS, AND GRAPHS**
KEYWORD: SZ3 MCG
• Largest Cities, 1900

**HOLT PRESENTATION MAKER**
KEYWORD: SZ3 PPT13

**CONTENT UPDATES**
KEYWORD: SS Content Updates

**ONLINE READING SUPPORT**
KEYWORD: SS Strategies

**CURRENT EVENTS**
KEYWORD: S3 Current Events

## Meeting Individual Needs

### Ability Levels

**Level 1** Basic-level activities designed for all students encountering new material

**Level 2** Intermediate-level activities designed for average students

**Level 3** Challenging activities designed for honors and gifted-and-talented students

**English Language Learners** Activities that address the needs of students with Limited English Proficiency

## Chapter Review and Assessment

IC Vocabulary Activity 13

Global Skill Builder CD–ROM

HRW Go site

REV Chapter 13 Tutorial for Students, Parents, Mentors, and Peers

REV Chapter 13 Review, pp. 338–39

A Standardized Test Practice

A Chapter 13 Test Generator (on the One-Stop Planner)

A Chapter 13 Test (Form A or B)

A Alternative Assessment Handbook

A Chapter 13 Test for English Language Learners and Special-Needs Students

# CHAPTER 13

Section 1    The Changing Family

Section 2    Law and the Family

Section 3    Your Family and You

## What's Your Opinion?

 *To help students create their **Themes** Journal entries, provide the following examples of appropriate agree/disagree statements.*

● **Agree**   Basic family values remain the same over time because people's core values do not change.

**Disagree**   Circumstances in the United States have changed, and therefore families have changed in response to them.

● **Agree**   The field of family law has grown to meet the needs of stressed families.

**Disagree**   There is not an increased need for legal assistance because stress-related problems in the family are easily resolved at home.

● **Agree**   The family is a person's primary reference for how to behave, hence citizenship skills must be modeled at home.

**Disagree**   Society is responsible for building values, and therefore values should be taught in many places.

# CHAPTER
# 13 Citizenship and the Family

 **What's Your Opinion?**

## Build on What You Know

Being a good citizen does not only mean taking part in politics and government. To be a good citizen, you also must fulfill your duties and responsibilities to society. One way you can do this is by being a responsible family member. The family teaches children the basic skills, values, beliefs, and behavior patterns of society. From your family you learn what it means to be a good citizen. This process is called socialization.

**Themes Journal**   Do you **agree** or **disagree** with the following statements? Support your point of view in your journal.

- Families today live much like families always have in the United States.
- Increased stress upon the American family has placed increased demands on the field of family law.
- Citizenship skills should be taught in the family.

# SECTION 1

## OBJECTIVES

*After completing Section 1, students should be able to*

1 **Describe how the move from rural areas to urban areas changed the American family.**

2 **Explain why people are delaying marriage and define the term *blended family*.**

3 **Identify the additional stresses that single-parent families face, and determine why the number of two-income families is increasing.**

As students enter the classroom, invite them to describe television shows that portray families. Ask them the following question: Do you think these programs present an accurate picture of family life today? Write students' responses on the chalkboard. Explain to the class that the American family has been portrayed in many different ways, particularly in the past few decades. Tell students that in Section 1 they will learn more about different types of American families.

---

## SECTION 1

# The Changing Family

### Read to Discover

1. How did the move from rural areas to urban areas change the American family?
2. Why are people delaying marriage, and what is a blended family?
3. What additional stresses do single-parent families face, and why is the number of two-income families increasing?

#### WHY CIVICS MATTERS

Families exist in many different forms today, resulting in a variety of issues related to the diversity of the American family. Use **CNN fyi.com** or other **current events** sources to investigate issues that face the current American family. Record your findings in your journal.

### Define

- delayed marriage
- remarriages
- blended families
- two-income families
- single-parent families

---

## SECTION 1 RESOURCES

### REPRODUCIBLE
▶ Guided Reading Strategies 13.1

### TECHNOLOGY
▶ One-Stop Planner, Lesson 13.1
▶ Holt Researcher CD–ROM
▶ Homework Practice Online

### REINFORCEMENT, REVIEW, AND ASSESSMENT
▶ Section 1 Review, p. 328
▶ Daily Quiz 13.1
▶ Main Idea Activity 13.1
▶ English Audio Summary 13.1
▶ Spanish Audio Summary 13.1

---

## *Reading Focus*

The family has always played an important economic and social role in the history of the United States. The American family exists in many different forms and has undergone many changes in the past few decades. As a result, there is no typical American family.

Some American families have two parents and any number of children. Others have one parent and one or more children. Still other families are made up of couples who have no children. Some families are formed when divorced people marry and bring children from their previous marriages into their new marriage. Sometimes three or more generations of a family share a home. The fact that the American family can exist in many forms is evidence of its strength.

### ★ The Colonial Family

How different was the structure of the colonial family from the family structure of today? Because much of the country at the time was rural, most colonial families lived on farms. Colonial families also tended to be larger than modern American families.

*Members of colonial families, like these women spinning cloth, often worked together to provide for their needs.*

**ALL LEVELS:** Have students create drawings of rural and urban scenes depicting the changes brought about by industrialization and the migration of families to urban areas. Then have students use captions to describe how the move from rural areas to more urban areas changed the American family. Allow students the option of combining their own illustrations with images from newspapers and magazines. *(Students' illustrations should show that the migration changed families from mostly self-sufficient units to consumers, or people who had to earn money to buy the things that they once made.)*

**ENGLISH LANGUAGE LEARNERS**

**LEVEL 3:** Have each student create two journal entries about the typical day of a rural family before heavy migration to the cities began. Then have them write two additional entries from the point of view of an urban family during the same time period. Explain to students that the entries should work together to describe how the move from rural areas to more urban areas changed the American family. *(See the Level 1 lesson for description.)* Invite volunteers to read their journal entries to the class.

## Global Perspectives

**The Move to Chinese Cities** The rapid pace of economic and social change in China has brought more than prosperity to some Chinese cities—it has brought people. As of 2000, 32 percent of China's population lived in urban areas. That may not seem like much, considering that nearly 70 percent remained in rural settings. However, China's overall population exceeds 1 billion people. Therefore, the 32 percent of the people living in urban settings is equal to about 320 million people. That figure is more than 40 million more people than live in the entire United States. These figures reflect a trend in migration from China's rural areas to its urban centers. Between 1995 and 2000, 2.47 percent of rural occupants migrated to cities. In other words, during those 5 years, nearly 25 million Chinese moved from the country to the city.

#### CRITICAL THINKING

Why do you think there are more jobs in urban areas than in rural ones?

**ANSWER:** Students might suggest that the country's economy is based on commerce rather than agriculture.

#### GLOBAL CONNECTIONS ANSWER

because they conflict with the American ideal of freedom

### The One-Child Family in China

American families today are smaller than families of the past. For a number of reasons, Americans are choosing to have fewer children. For more than 20 years, China's government has encouraged its citizens to limit their family size to one child per family.

In 1981 China's population reached one billion. Believing that this rapid population growth would interfere with plans for modernization, Chinese officials began a program to limit family size. The government provides strong economic incentives. Couples that agree to have only one child receive payments for food, free health care and schooling for the child, and access to better jobs and housing. The government also uses educational programs and peer pressure to convince couples to have only one child. **Why might citizens in the United States protest against such population control measures?**

The growth of cities in the late 1800s could be very rapid. In 1850 the population of Chicago was just 29,963. By 1890 the city had a population of 1,099,850!

Children were economic assets to the colonial family, for many hands were needed to do all the work required on a farm. Daughters worked alongside their mothers. They learned to cook and sew, and to make soap and candles. They were also taught to can fruits and vegetables that they grew themselves and to preserve meat. Older boys learned from their fathers how to plow the soil, plant seeds, and harvest the crops. They also learned to care for the animals, repair barns and fences, and do other daily chores.

Life on early American farms was difficult. There was little time for play or schooling. Some farm children attended a one-room schoolhouse. However, many children received a basic education at home.

The early farm family was the basic work unit in the colonies. Families themselves produced most of what they needed to survive. The family depended on all its members to do their part. As children got older and married, they did not always move away from home. Often they brought their wives or husbands with them to live on the family farm.

In these large families everyone lived and worked together. As a man grew older, he took on lighter chores while his son or son-in-law did the heavier work. As a woman grew older, she too spent less time on heavy household chores. She spent more time sewing or looking after her grandchildren.

Young or old, family members contributed what they could and received the care they needed. The need to work together developed a strong spirit of cooperation and family pride.

✔ **Reading Check Summarizing** What was daily life like for early farm families? They all pitched in to provide for the family's needs. Married children often brought their families with them to the farm.

### ★ The Move to Cities

During the 1800s American life began to change rapidly. One hundred years ago, 6 of every 10 Americans lived on farms or in rural areas. Today only 1 in 4 Americans lives in a rural area. This change came about because of the remarkable progress in science and technology that took place during the 1800s.

New inventions and improved methods of production led to the rise of factories. These factories used new technology and work methods to produce large quantities of goods. In turn, the growth of factories encouraged the growth of cities, as people moved to urban areas seeking factory jobs. At the same time, fewer people were needed to work on the farms because of improvements in farm machinery and equipment.

**ALL LEVELS:** Copy the following graphic organizer onto the chalkboard, omitting the italicized answers. Ask each student to complete the organizer to explain why people are delaying marriage and to describe the meaning of the term *blended family*. **ENGLISH LANGUAGE LEARNERS**

| People are delaying marriage because | The term *blended family* means |
|---|---|
| • *being single is more accepted*<br>• *they want to finish their education and start a career* | *families that are formed when one or both partners bring children from a previous relationship into the new marriage* |

**LEVEL 3:** Organize the class into four groups. Each group will represent one of the reasons that people are delaying marriage, or the creation of the blended family. *(See the All Levels lesson for assignments.)* Then have each group create a case study of fictional Americans who fit the description of their assignment. Have one member from each group present the group's case study to the class, in a mock-documentary style. **COOPERATIVE LEARNING**

**HOMEWORK** Tell each student to create an editorial cartoon illustrating why being single is more widely accepted today.

This movement of Americans from the farms to the cities resulted in vast changes in family life.

✔ **Reading Check** Analyzing Information What motivated many farm families to move to cities? factory-job opportunities, decreased need for farmworkers

## ★ The City Family

Life in the cities was much different for families than farm life had been. For example, families could no longer spend as much time living and working together. Fathers often worked long hours outside the home to earn money to buy things they once produced on their farms. In addition, many children—even those who were very young—worked in factories to earn money for their families. This remained the case until national child labor laws were passed in the 1930s.

On the farm, the family tended to be a self-sufficient unit. Family members produced what they consumed, and the family was largely responsible for the educational and religious training of children. Thus, the family tended to be the major influence in the lives of children. However, in the cities the family had to share these responsibilities with other institutions.

The public schools, for example, took on a greater responsibility for educating children. The urban family also became part of the social and economic life of the city rather than a self-sufficient unit. For example, city families had to take jobs and earn money to buy food produced by farm families.

The family continues to be the main influence in the lives of children. Teachers, friends, and the mass media are also strong influences.

✔ **Reading Check** Contrasting How did moving to the city change family life? Families became less self-sufficient and had to buy many personal goods they once produced. Families also faced greater competition for influence on their children.

---

**Interpreting the Visual Record**

**City schools** *As a result of the movement of families to urban areas, a greater number of children attended public schools.* **How does this early urban school look similar to or different from your school?**

---

***A New England Girlhood*** During her childhood in the 1830s and following her father's death, author Lucy Larcom worked in the mills of Lowell, Massachusetts. She eventually left the mill and became a teacher and an author of children's books. In her autobiographical book *A New England Girlhood*, Larcom weaves a story that describes how work and the Puritan faith influenced her childhood in Lowell in the 1830s. The early days at the mill were not terribly strenuous, as Larcom recalls. For many children, however, working in mills was very tedious, and in some instances, dangerous.

**CRITICAL THINKING**

Why were children like Larcom put to work?

**ANSWER:** Students might suggest that they worked to help support the family.

**Visual Record Answer**

*Students' responses will vary.*

**LEVEL 1:** Tell students that families come in many forms today. Then have them name some types of families. Have students suggest a meaning for the terms *single-parent family* and *two-income family.* Discuss each term and invite students to provide examples of additional stresses that such families face, as well as reasons for the increasing number of two-income families. *(Students should note that single-parent families are more likely to be headed by an economically disadvantaged single parent who must handle the responsibility of supporting and raising a family alone. The number of two-income families is increasing because more women are working outside of the home.)* **ENGLISH LANGUAGE LEARNERS**

**LEVEL 2:** Have students use material from this section to create an illustrated chart depicting the additional stresses that single-parent families face. *(See the Level 1 lesson for stresses.)* Ask students to create a caption for each entry, suggesting ways for families to handle such stresses. Then have students write a few sentences explaining why the number of two-income families is increasing. *(See the Level 1 lesson for the reason.)*

**Interpreting the Visual Record**

**Older parents** *An increasing number of couples are waiting until their 30s or later to have their first children.* **What might be some advantages and disadvantages to this approach?**

## Changing Marriage Trends

Family life has changed a great deal since the time when most Americans lived on farms. Social scientists who study the family are interested in the ways in which the family continues to change. Marriage customs often have a direct effect on family life. Social scientists have noted a number of marriage trends in recent years. These trends include delayed marriage and remarriage.

**Delayed Marriage** The average age at which people marry has risen steadily for several decades. For example, in 1960 the average age at first marriage for women was 20.3 years. The average age for men was 22.8. By 1998 the average age at first marriage had risen to 25 for women and 26.7 for men.

According to social scientists, there are several reasons for **delayed marriage,** or marrying at an older age. First, remaining single has become a more widely accepted way to live. Second, many young people have chosen to delay marriage to finish their educations and start their careers. This is particularly true for women. Third, there is a large increase in the number of couples who live together without being married. Although most people who live with someone for a long period of time eventually get married, this arrangement contributes to delayed marriage.

In addition to delaying marriage, couples are delaying having children. In the past, married women usually had their first child when they were in their 20s. This pattern remains true for most women having children today. However, an increasing percentage of women are having their first child after the age of 30. Couples who delay childbearing usually wait until both spouses are established in their careers before they have children.

✔ **Reading Check** Summarizing Why are people delaying marriage and waiting to have children? People are delaying marriage because remaining single is more widely accepted, to finish their education and start a career, and because more people are living together without being married.

**Remarriages** The United States has one of the highest divorce rates in the world. Despite this fact, Americans continue to believe strongly in marriage and the family. More than 40 percent of the marriages taking place today are **remarriages.** This means that one or both of the partners have been married before.

In some 65 percent of remarriages, one or both of the partners bring children from previous relationships into the new marriage. These new families are called **blended families,** or stepfamilies.

**LEVEL 3:** Organize the class into two groups. Students in one group should imagine that they are parents in a single-parent family, and students in the other group should imagine that they are parents in a two-income family. Students should write humorous essays describing their fictional families, detailing the stresses and advantages family members have. Encourage volunteers to turn their essays into one-person skits or monologues. Have these volunteers present their dramas to the class. (*See the Level 1 lesson for definitions, reasons, and stresses.*) **COOPERATIVE LEARNING**

## CLOSE

Create a two-column chart about the changing American family. On the chalkboard list the social trends regarding families today in the first column. (*Trends include delayed marriage, two-income families, single-parent families, blended families, and remarriage.*) Then have students suggest the reasons for each of these trends and write their descriptions in the second column.

The people who become part of a stepfamily must often undergo a period of adjustment. For the marital partners this means taking on roles formerly occupied by biological parents. For stepchildren this period of adjustment means learning to share a parent's attention with new stepbrothers and stepsisters.

Adjusting to life in a stepfamily sometimes brings conflict. It is important for all members of the new family to remember that they are undergoing a period of transition. They should try to communicate openly and honestly with one another. To build a strong family unit, all members must have patience, understanding, and a willingness to cooperate.

✔ **Reading Check** Finding the Main Idea How are blended families formed? One or both marital partners bring children from a previous relationship into a new marriage.

### ★ Two-Income Families

In recent decades, the number of **two-income families,** or families in which both partners work, has increased. This increase is the result of the large number of married women who work outside the home. In 1950 about 25 percent of married women worked outside the home. But that number has risen steadily since 1950. In 1998, for example, approximately 62 percent of all married women in the United States worked outside the home.

Economic necessity has led many married women to enter the workforce. It has become more difficult for many families to enjoy the standard of living that they desire when only one parent is working. Also, as more women pursue higher education, more of them choose to put their skills to use in the workplace. Many women are finding success in fields once considered the domain of men—fields such as business, engineering, medicine, and law.

---

**Holt Researcher**

**go.hrw.com**
**Keyword:** Holt Researcher
**Freefind:** Social Work

Look up the entry on careers in social work on the Holt Researcher. Use the information in that entry to create a short want ad that answers the following question: What qualifications are typically needed for a career in social work?

---

**Interpreting the Visual Record**

**Child care** As the number of two-income and single-parent families increases, there is an even greater need for daycare facilities to help parents care for their children. **What are these children doing?**

---

### ★ Economics

**Women in the Workforce** Statistics for 1999 indicated that nearly 46 percent of all women in the United States over the age of 15 were in the workforce. This figure compares with 49 percent in the Russian Federation and 41 percent in Japan. Some cultures, however, do not encourage women to work outside the home. In Guatemala, for example, only 28 percent of women have officially entered the workforce. In Iraq the figure is just 19 percent. Statistics, however, can be misleading because of the high percentage of work that women perform without pay. In Bangladesh, for example, an estimated 90 percent of women are involved in producing food. In Africa women do most of the agricultural work. Worldwide, this phenomenon of unpaid labor contributes to women continuing to earn less than men.

**CRITICAL THINKING**

Why might a culture discourage women from working?

**ANSWER:** Students might suggest tradition, law, or religious practices.

**Visual Record Answer**

*Students might suggest that they are playing together with toy dinosaurs.*

## REVIEW AND ASSESS

Have students complete the **Section 1 Review** on page 328. Then have students complete **Daily Quiz 13.1.** As **Alternative Assessment**, you may want to use the journal entry or case study exercises in this section's lessons.

## RETEACH

Have students complete **Main Idea Activity for English Language Learners and Special-Needs Students 13.1.** Then refer students to the terms in the Define portion of the Section Review. Have students write down two related facts about each term. Ask students to choose a partner and have them take turns reading their facts and identifying the terms.

**ENGLISH LANGUAGE LEARNERS , COOPERATIVE LEARNING**

## EXTEND

Have each student use the library or other resources to conduct research on American family life in previous eras. Students might focus on the mill workers of New England, freed slaves in the South, farmers in the Midwest, or any other group that interests them. Each student should then write a descriptive essay about the daily life, configuration, and stresses of the family life that he or she studied and present it to the class.

**BLOCK SCHEDULING**

---

### Visual Record Answer

*Students might suggest that in a family that cooperates, members would learn that they have support.*

## Section 1 Review
### ANSWERS

**1. Define**
- delayed marriage, p. 326
- remarriages, p. 326
- blended families, p. 326
- two-income families, p. 327
- single-parent families, p. 328

**2.** cause: the move to cities; effect: families became consumers, having to earn money to purchase goods they once made

**3. a.** Economic necessity is leading more married women to work outside the home.

**b.** Single-parent families are more likely to be poor; the single parent must handle the responsibility of supporting and raising a family alone. Blended families are formed when one or both partners bring children from a previous relationship into the new marriage.

**4.** Students' articles should mention that singlehood is more widely accepted; some people delay marriage to finish their education and start a career; and more people are living together without being married.

### Interpreting the Visual Record

**Helping out** *In many families, parents depend on children to help with chores and to help take care of their siblings.* **How might such cooperation strengthen family bonds?**

---

There has also been an increase in the amount of time that husbands devote to childcare and household tasks. Although women still assume the major responsibility for these tasks, more men are sharing this responsibility with their wives. Men who help with household tasks and childcare tend to be younger than men who do not share such tasks.

✔ **Reading Check Summarizing** Why is the number of two-income families increasing? Economic necessity is leading more married women to work outside the home.

## ★ Single-Parent Families

Another trend noted in recent years is a large increase in the number of single-parent families. **Single-parent families** are formed through divorce, widowhood, adoption by single people, and births to single women.

Many single-parent families in the United States are the result of divorce. More than 27 percent of American families with children under the age of 18 are single-parent families.

Although every family has its difficulties, the single-parent household is subject to added stresses. For example, single-parent families are more likely than two-parent families to be poor. In fact, nearly 30 percent of all single-parent families headed by women live in poverty. Also, parents in single-parent families must handle the responsibilities shared in two-parent families.

✔ **Reading Check Analyzing Information** What are some of the challenges that single-parent families face? a greater likelihood of poverty, added stress, reduced support for parental responsibilities

---

## SECTION 1 Review

**go.hrw.com Homework Practice Online**
**keyword: SZ3 HP13**

**1. Define** and explain:
- delayed marriage
- remarriages
- blended families
- two-income families
- single-parent families

**2. Identifying Cause and Effect**
Copy the graphic organizer below. Use it to explain the reason American families began to change in the 1800s and the results of these changes.

**Family Changes**

Cause → Effect

**3. Finding the Main Idea**
a. What has led to the increase in the number of two-income families?
b. What are the added stresses experienced by single-parent families, and how are blended families formed?

**4. Writing and Critical Thinking**
**Summarizing** Imagine that you are a reporter assigned to investigate the increase in the average age at first marriage. Write a short article that explains the major reasons for this trend.

**Consider:**
- the status of single adults
- economic and educational factors
- alternative living arrangements

---

# SECTION 2

## OBJECTIVES

*After completing Section 2, students should be able to*

1  Identify the purpose of a waiting period for marriage licenses, and explain why some states require couples to take a medical test.

2  Describe how state laws work to protect children.

3  Identify the types of decisions that must be made by couples who are planning to divorce.

## 📢 LET'S GET STARTED!

Write the following question on the chalkboard: *Do you think that children need protection when there is stress in their home lives?* As students enter the classroom, ask them to respond to the question. *(Students might indicate that all citizens, including children, need and deserve protection.)* Explain that family laws help ensure the protection of children in a variety of ways. Tell students that in Section 2 they will learn about the laws, regulations, and decisions that relate to marriage, child protection, and divorce.

---

## SECTION 2

# Law and the Family

### Read to Discover

1. What is the purpose of a waiting period for a marriage license, and why do some states require couples to take a medical test?
2. How do state laws work to protect children?
3. What types of decisions must be made by couples who are planning to divorce?

### WHY CIVICS MATTERS

U.S. law is set up to protect the well-being of children whose families are experiencing difficult times. Use **CNNfyi.com** or other **current events** sources to find reports concerning child welfare and protection. Record your findings in your journal.

### Define

- family law
- child abuse
- foster homes
- guardian
- adopt
- divorce
- no-fault divorce

## SECTION 2 RESOURCES

### REPRODUCIBLE
▶ Guided Reading Strategies 13.2
▶ Challenge and Enrichment Worksheet 13: Researching Your State's Marriage Laws

### TECHNOLOGY
▶ One-Stop Planner, Lesson 13.2
▶ Homework Practice Online
▶ HRW Go site

### REINFORCEMENT, REVIEW, AND ASSESSMENT
▶ Section 2 Review, p. 332
▶ Daily Quiz 13.2
▶ Main Idea Activity 13.2
▶ English Audio Summary 13.2
▶ Spanish Audio Summary 13.2

---

## *Reading Focus*

As you have learned, there are many different kinds of families in the United States today. Family life may differ depending on whether you live in a big city, a suburb, or a small town. Your family's life may be affected by your ethnic, cultural, and religious background. Family life may also be affected by factors such as income and age at marriage. Although life within the family may vary, all families are subject to certain laws. These laws are designed to benefit everyone.

### ★ Marriage Laws

Because everyone is part of a family at some point in his or her life, many laws have been passed to protect the rights and define the responsibilities of people in families. These laws have been passed by state legislatures because state governments have the power to regulate **family law.** Family law regulates marriage, divorce, and the responsibilities and the rights of adults and children in the family.

The more than 2 million marriages that take place each year must follow the laws of the state in which they are performed. For example, state laws establish the earliest age at which residents of a particular state may get married.

Most states require people to be at least 18 to marry without parental consent. In many states, boys and girls may marry at age 16

*In addition to laws, each society has several customs regarding marriage.*

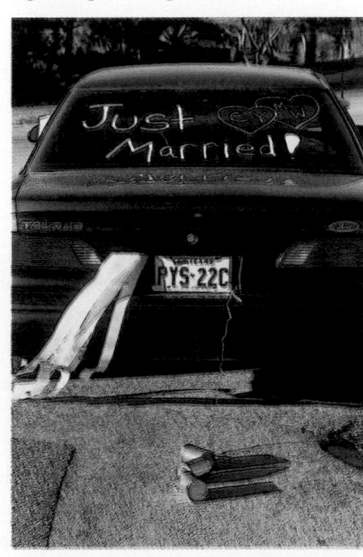

*Citizenship and the Family*  **329**

# TEACH OBJECTIVE 1

 **LEVELS 1 AND 2:** Have small groups of students design an application for a marriage license. Encourage discussion of the purpose of a waiting period for marriage licenses, and explain why some states require couples to take a medical test. *(Students should observe that the waiting period is intended to discourage hasty marriages; medical tests are used to check for infectious diseases.)* Obtain a copy of a real marriage-license application from your local government to compare with the application created by the class.

# TEACH OBJECTIVE 2

 **ALL LEVELS:** Copy the following graphic organizer onto the chalkboard, omitting the italicized answers. Have each student complete the list to describe how state laws work to protect children. **ENGLISH LANGUAGE LEARNERS**

| Laws allow children to be placed in foster care or with guardians when . . . | | |
|---|---|---|
| *they have been abused.* | *they have been orphaned.* | *parents are unable to support them.* |

## That's Interesting!

In some states, support payments continue for children beyond the age of 18. Sixteen states have provisions that may require a parent to make college support payments.

### Visual Record Answer

*Students might suggest that the presence of witnesses ensures that someone can prove that the ceremony took place and that both parties agreed to it.*

**Interpreting the Visual Record**

**Getting married** *Weddings might be large events with many families and friends in attendance, or they might be small gatherings. As long as they meet legal requirements, all such weddings, regardless of size, are equally valid before the law.* **Why do you think witnesses are required at a wedding?**

*Adoption plays an important role in helping some children find happy homes.*

with the consent of their parents. In a few states the couple also needs the consent of the court. Some states allow people to marry at even younger ages.

About half the states require that couples wait for one to five days before the license is issued. This waiting period is intended to discourage hasty marriages by allowing couples time to "think it over." Some states also require that a man and woman applying for a marriage license have a medical examination. Such examinations check for certain diseases that can be passed on to another person.

Most states require that marriages be performed by civil officials such as a justice of the peace, judge, or mayor. Religious officials such as ministers, priests, or rabbis may often perform marriages as well. Witnesses must be present at the ceremony to testify that a legal marriage was performed.

✔ **Reading Check Finding the Main Idea** What is family law, and why is it needed? Family law is law that regulates marriage, divorce, and the responsibilities and rights of parents and children in a family. Millions of Americans belong to families, thus making laws regulating them important.

## ★ Protecting Family Members

When the marriage ceremony is completed, the newly married couple is considered a family unit. The husband and wife both have certain rights guaranteed by law. If the rights of either the husband or wife are violated, the courts may be asked to intervene, or take action.

Most cases of nonsupport, physical abuse, desertion, and other marital problems are tried in a family-relations court. The court usually recommends that couples seek counseling to try to work out their problems before proceeding with a trial.

**LEVEL 1:** Organize the class into four groups, and assign each group one of the types of decisions that must be made by couples who are planning to divorce. *(Assignments include decisions about the division of property, child custody, visitation rights, and spouse and child support payments.)* Then have each group prepare and present a written description of its assigned decision.

**ENGLISH LANGUAGE LEARNERS , COOPERATIVE LEARNING**

**LEVEL 3:** Organize the class into four groups and assign each group one of the types of decisions that must be made by couples who are planning to divorce. *(See the Level 1 lesson for decisions.)*

Then have each group prepare and present a puppet show that depicts a family dealing with its assigned decision.

**COOPERATIVE LEARNING**

## CLOSE

Have each student write a brief summary of marriage laws, child protection laws, and factors divorcing couples must consider. Have students include several sentences indicating their opinion about legal involvement in family matters. Ask students to use the section to support their opinion.

---

Children, too, have certain legal rights as members of a family. If a child is not given proper care by the parents, the authorities can step in to protect the child. Every state requires doctors, teachers, and other people to report suspected instances of **child abuse.** Child abuse is emotional abuse, physical injury, or sexual abuse inflicted on a child by another person. An act or failure to act that creates a risk of serious harm to a child is also considered child abuse under the law. For example, leaving a very young child unattended for a long period of time would be considered dangerous neglect. Children who are mentally, physically, or sexually abused by their parents or other family members may be taken from them by the state.

These children may be placed in **foster homes**—homes of people who are unrelated to the children but who agree to act as their caregivers. The state pays the foster parents to care for the children. Parents who abuse their children may also have criminal charges filed against them. Parents who cannot care for a child may ask the state to place the child in a foster home for a while.

If a child's parents die, a judge may appoint a relative or family friend to act as the child's **guardian.** A guardian is a person appointed by a state court to care for an individual who is not an adult or who is unable to care for himself or herself.

Sometimes the guardian will **adopt** the child, which means that he or she has legally established the child as his or her own. If no relative or family friend can be found to act as a guardian, the state may put the child up for adoption.

✔ **Reading Check Sequencing** What steps are typically taken to care for children whose parents die? The child lives with an appointed guardian. Sometimes the guardian will adopt the child. If no guardian is available, the child may be put up for adoption.

### ★ Divorce Laws

The final legal ending of a marriage is called **divorce.** Each state makes its own laws concerning divorce. Some states require a waiting period before granting couples a divorce. Beginning with California in 1969, every state enacted some form of **no-fault divorce.** Under this system, people seeking divorce do not have to charge their partners with grounds such as desertion or abuse. Instead, couples must simply state that their marriages have problems that cannot be resolved.

All couples who divorce must make many decisions, often following the advice of their lawyers. Depending upon the length of the marriage and whether or not the couple has children, there can be many issues to

### BIOGRAPHY

## Marian Wright Edelman

**(1939– )**

Marian Wright Edelman was born in Bennettsville, South Carolina. The daughter of a Baptist minister, she was encouraged not only to pursue her education but to use her abilities to help others. Her parents set an example by opening the Wright Home for the Aged. In addition, over time her parents cared for 12 foster children.

Edelman graduated from law school and became active in the National Association for the Advancement of Colored People's struggle against segregation. She then turned her efforts toward protecting the rights of children. In 1973 she founded the Children's Defense Fund. This organization aims to help children and addresses children's issues in public policy. Edelman has testified before Congress several times on children's issues.

Today Edelman continues her lobbying efforts on behalf of children's health care, nutrition, education, and employment issues. The home where she was born in South Carolina is now a youth development center of the Children's Defense Fund. The Fund continues to help hundreds of children in need. **How have Edelman's efforts aided children?**

---

**Setting Child Support**
Since the 1980s, state governments have been responsible for setting guidelines regarding child support. The guidelines provide formulas that weigh several factors to determine a fair amount for one parent to pay another to provide for the child's basic needs. Factors include the parents' incomes, the number of children, and estimates of how much families tend to pay to support children when married. Since the laws have been put into place, child support payments have increased by almost 50 percent. As of 1995, the average child support payment was just over $300 per month. Unfortunately, it is estimated that about half the parents who are entitled to receive child support do not receive the full amount. Half of those receive none at all.

**CRITICAL THINKING**

Why do you think it is necessary for states to be involved in setting child support guidelines?

**ANSWER:** Students might suggest that it keeps the requirements uniform and fair.

**BIOGRAPHY ANSWER**
Students might suggest that she has testified before Congress and otherwise lobbied on behalf of children's health care, nutrition, education, and employment issues.

## REVIEW AND ASSESS

Have students complete the **Section 2 Review** on page 332. Then have students complete **Daily Quiz 13.2**. As **Alternative Assessment** you may want to use the foster care organizer or the marriage license application exercises in this section's lessons.

## RETEACH

Have students complete **Main Idea Activity for English Language Learners and Special-Needs Students 13.2.** Then begin an outline on the chalkboard by writing the three main headings from this section on laws concerning marriage, the protection of family members, and divorce. Have volunteers complete the outline on the chalkboard by describing the laws under each heading. **ENGLISH LANGUAGE LEARNERS** , **COOPERATIVE LEARNING**

## EXTEND

Organize the class into groups and have each group conduct research on the legal requirements regarding marriage, children, and divorce in your state. Have groups of students use their findings to create a Family Guidebook that explains the laws pertaining to families in these various situations. Guidebooks may be in pamphlet or brochure form. Encourage students to illustrate their group's guidebooks. **COOPERATIVE LEARNING** , **BLOCK SCHEDULING**

---

### Visual Record Answer

*Students might suggest that it raises concerns because the family plays a valuable role in providing stability in a child's life.*

## Section 2 Review
### ANSWERS

**1. Define**
- family law, p. 329
- child abuse, p. 331
- foster homes, p. 331
- guardian, p. 331
- adopt, p. 331
- divorce, p. 331
- no-fault divorce, p. 331

**2.** division of property, child custody, visitation rights, and spouse and child support payments

**3. a.** The waiting period is intended to discourage hasty marriages; medical examinations are used to check for diseases that might be passed on to others.

**b.** There are laws that allow children to be placed in foster homes with guardians when they have been abused or orphaned or when their parents are unable to support them.

**4.** Students' suggestions will vary but should reflect their understanding of the reasons for the high divorce rate and should offer sufficient explanation of why their proposals would be effective.

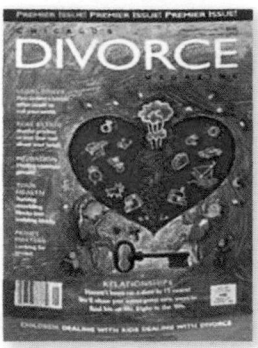

### Interpreting the Visual Record

**Divorce** *This magazine discusses some of the challenges faced by divorced couples and their children.* **Why do you think the high U.S. divorce rate concerns some Americans?**

resolve. These include issues such as division of property, custody of children, visitation rights, and spousal and child support payments. These decisions are reviewed by a judge. If the judge finds that the decisions are fair, the divorce agreement is approved. If the couple cannot agree on these issues, the judge will decide for them.

The United States has one of the highest divorce rates in the world. More than 1 million marriages in this country end in divorce each year, affecting more than 1 million children annually.

Social scientists who study the family note several reasons for the high divorce rate in the United States. The divorce process has become less complicated over the past few decades. Also, as more women work outside the home, they are gaining the financial independence to leave unhappy marriages. Furthermore, American society in general has become more tolerant and accepting of divorce.

Some Americans believe that the best way to reduce the number of divorces is to pass stricter marriage laws. Others believe that more preparation for marriage would result in better family life and fewer divorces. Many high schools and colleges now offer courses in marriage and the family. They hope to help young people understand the realities of marriage.

However, laws designed to protect marriage partners and their children and to keep families together do not always succeed. Many people believe that the best way to achieve a happy and productive family life is to encourage family members to share and work together for the good of the family.

✔ **Reading Check Contrasting** How does no-fault divorce differ from the traditional system of divorce? No-fault divorce does not require people to charge partners with grounds for divorce. They must simply state that their marriages have problems that cannot be resolved.

---

## SECTION 2 Review

**Homework Practice Online**
keyword: SZ3 HP13

1. **Define** and explain:
   - family law
   - child abuse
   - foster homes
   - guardian
   - adopt
   - divorce
   - no-fault divorce

2. **Categorizing** Copy the graphic organizer below. Use it to identify the types of decisions that must be made by couples who are planning to divorce.

Decisions in a Divorce

3. **Finding the Main Idea**
   a. Why do many states have a waiting period before issuing marriage licenses? What is the purpose of a medical examination before marriage?
   b. What legal measures do states put into place to protect children?

4. **Writing and Critical Thinking**
   **Evaluating** Imagine that you are part of a national committee attempting to reduce the high American divorce rate. List three of your suggestions and explain why you believe they will be effective.
   **Consider:**
   - the reasons for the high divorce rate
   - the effects of your suggestions on families

## TEACH

**LEVEL 1:** Provide each student with a copy of a television or cablevision program schedule. Have students use the guides to identify the many types of programs that provide information on a given day. For example, students should list the number of news programs, general interest and investigative features, and children's programs. Then lead the class in a discussion about the proportion of news and informational programming to general interest programming and entertainment. Ask the question: *Is television a valuable source of information?* **ENGLISH LANGUAGE LEARNERS**

## EXTEND

Organize the class into groups and have each group conduct research on two forms of news media. *(Students might select radio, television, Internet, newspapers, periodicals, and so on.)* Then have each group create a visual display that explains how to best use each source as a resource for becoming well informed. Groups should also include an analysis of which of the two selected media is best suited to providing information to citizens. Allow students to set up their displays in the classroom. **BLOCK SCHEDULING**, **COOPERATIVE LEARNING**

## SKILLS ANSWERS

1. *Great Inventors* and *Biography;* they each list the name of a famous person in the subtitle.

2. *Current News, House Recordings,* and *Budget Debate;* insight on today's issues and discussions of current public policy developments

# Civics Skills
## WORKSHOP

## Using Television as a Resource

Imagine it is New York in 1929. Engineers focus a camera on a statue of cartoon hero Felix the Cat. In Kansas, other engineers see his face flicker on a tiny screen.

Now imagine the Moon in 1969. A camera sends pictures back to Earth. Millions of people all over the world hold their breath as astronaut Neil Armstrong takes humankind's first steps on the Moon.

In the 40 years between these two events, television became the country's main source of news and entertainment. Today more than 98 percent of American households have televisions. News agencies operate independently of the government and their right to freedom of the press is protected by the First Amendment. Because so much of our news comes from television, it is important to watch it with a critical eye.

Most news programs follow definite formats. Once you become familiar with these formats, it will be easier for you to interpret what you see and hear.

## How to Use Television as a Resource

1. **Listen for the important events of the day.** Regularly scheduled news programs shown each evening are organized like a newspaper. The opening stories are the headline news, or the most important events of the day.

2. **Distinguish between hard news and features.** Features are human-interest stories meant to amuse and entertain you. Features usually follow the hard news and often appeal more to emotions than to intellect.

3. **Watch the close of the program.** News programs usually close with sports and weather reports. Sometimes the last report is a commentary—a journalist's personal interpretation of an event.

4. **Recognize types of news programs.** In addition to the evening news, there are other types of news programs. The most popular are newsmagazines and documentaries. A newsmagazine usually studies several issues in one program. A documentary focuses on a single topic for the entire program.

## Applying the Skill

Study the television schedule below. Then answer the following questions.

1. In which programs would you expect to find information about a famous person in U.S. history? Explain your answer.

2. Which programs discuss news and current events? What information might you expect to gain from these programs?

| TUE December 11 | | 7:00 P.M. | 7:30 P.M. | 8:00 P.M. |
|---|---|---|---|---|
| **DISC** Discovery | 32 | The Galapagos Islands | Great Inventors: Thomas Edison | |
| **HIST** History Channel | 33 | World War II: D-Day | | Biography: Theodore Roosevelt |
| **ESPN** Sports | 34 | College Basketball : University of Texas at Kansas | | |
| **CNN** Headline News | 35 | Current News | | |
| **CSPAN** Public Service | 36 | House Proceedings | | Budget Debate |

# SECTION 3

## OBJECTIVES

*After completing Section 3, students should be able to*

1 **Identify five important functions served by the family.**

2 **Explain why it is important to respect the rights of other family members and for family members to compromise.**

3 **Evaluate why it is useful for a family to budget its money.**

As students enter the classroom, tell them to think about the types of items that might appear in a family budget. *(Students might suggest rent, food, clothes, and entertainment.)* Explain to students that budgeting and instilling values are some of the functions of a family. Tell students that in Section 3 they will learn about financial values as well as other influences that family members have on each other.

## SECTION 3 RESOURCES

### REPRODUCIBLE

▶ Guided Reading Strategies 13.3

▶ Creative Teaching Strategy: Structured Discussion

▶ American Civics Political Cartoon: The Spread of Suburbia

▶ Graphic Organizer Activity: Factors Influencing the American Family

▶ Community Service and Participation Handbook: Drowning in Debt

### TECHNOLOGY

▶ One-Stop Planner, Lesson 13.3

▶ CNN Presents: American Government

▶ Homework Practice Online

### REINFORCEMENT, REVIEW, AND ASSESSMENT

▶ Section 3 Review, p. 337

▶ Daily Quiz 13.3

▶ Main Idea Activity 13.3

▶ English Audio Summary 13.3

▶ Spanish Audio Summary 13.3

---

## SECTION 3

# Your Family and You

### Read to Discover

1. What are five important functions served by the family?
2. Why is it important to respect the rights of other family members and for family members to compromise?
3. Why is it useful for a family to budget its money?

### Define

• fixed expenses

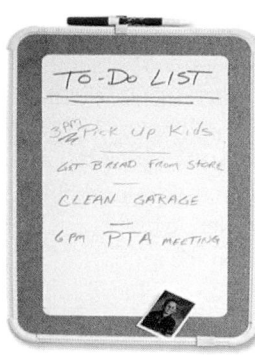

### WHY CIVICS MATTERS

Budgets are used to manage the funds of different groups, including families and the entire country. Use **CNNfyi.com** or other **current events** sources to find examples of federal budgeting. Record your findings in your journal.

## Reading Focus

The family continues to be the most important group in American society. It is the foundation on which the country is built. Regardless of whether a family is large or small, rich or poor, it performs many important functions for its members and for the country.

### ★ The Family Serves the Country

There are more than 70 million families in the United States. We depend on these families to teach their children the skills they need to become responsible adults. What are some of the family's chief functions as it teaches these skills?

*These family members are camping together.*

**Ensuring the Country's Future** A country is only as strong as its people. The family helps keep the country strong when it provides a stable environment for children to learn and grow. In this way families shape the country's future.

**Educating Its Members** Children learn many things from their families. It is in the home that children learn to walk, talk, and dress themselves. The family also teaches children to get along with others and to share in household work.

# TEACH OBJECTIVE 1

 **ALL LEVELS:** Lead a class discussion about the five main functions of the family. Write students' responses on the chalkboard. *(Functions include ensuring the future of the country, educating its members, teaching good behavior, helping manage money, and teaching good citizenship.)* Then have students draw five pictures, each depicting a family performing one of these functions. **ENGLISH LANGUAGE LEARNERS**

**LEVEL 3:** Assign each student one of the five chief functions of a family. *(See the All Levels lesson for assignments.)* Have students write an editorial outlining the importance of the assigned functions. Invite at least one student from each group to read aloud his or her editorial. **ENGLISH LANGUAGE LEARNERS**

# TEACH OBJECTIVE 2

 **LEVELS 1 AND 2:** Call on volunteers to explain why it is important to respect the rights of other family members and for family members to compromise. *(Students should note that if people believe that their rights are respected, then they are more likely to respect the rights of others. Compromise helps people find solutions to problems because everyone gives up something but also obtains something.)* Organize the class into groups and have each group write a one-act play showing what can happen when respect and compromise do not occur in a family. **ENGLISH LANGUAGE LEARNERS , COOPERATIVE LEARNING**

**Interpreting the Visual Record**

**Family lessons** *Eating together, as this family is doing, provides an opportunity to teach good behavior and gives family members a chance to talk about their day.* **Why are communication and manners important to family life?**

**Teaching Good Behavior** The child's earliest ideas of right and wrong are taught in the home. Within the family, children learn how to behave.

**Helping Manage Money** The family earns and spends money to provide food, clothing, a place to live, and other things for its members. Some parents give their children an allowance, or a small sum of money, every week to encourage them to learn to manage money and to share financial responsibilities.

**Teaching Good Citizenship** The family must teach children to respect the rights of others and to fulfill their responsibilities as good citizens.

✔ **Reading Check Summarizing** What are some key ways that the family serves the country? ensuring the future of the country, educating its members, teaching good behavior, money management, and good citizenship

## ★ Good Citizenship at Home

A home is more than just a building. When most Americans think of home, they picture a place where the family lives together. The word *home* means "the familiar place that members of the same family share." The ideal home is loving and secure. Of course, no family can live up to the ideal all the time. Any group of people living together will disagree at times and need to find ways to resolve their differences.

Using self-restraint and considering other people's points of view help prevent serious conflict. Remember that each member of the family is a person worthy of respect. Each person has rights. If people's rights are respected, they are more likely to respect the rights of others.

Members of a family should take a sincere interest in one another's activities. They should take every opportunity to discuss the events of the day and to share their thoughts. Sharing problems and events of interest teaches family members to give and receive praise, advice, support, and criticism.

## ★ Economics

**The Rising Costs of Homeownership** In 2000 just over 66 percent of Americans owned their own homes. The percentage of income that Americans spend on housing has been rising steadily over the years. In 2000, for example, American homeowners with mortgages spent a median of $1085 per month on housing costs. And for more than half of these people, these payments comprised nearly 25 percent or more of their annual income. Comparatively, in 1990, Americans with mortgages spent only $737 per month on housing costs. Although the price for a home has increased in the past decade, the actual size of American homes has not. The average American home in both 1990 and 2000 had 5 rooms.

**CRITICAL THINKING**

Why do you think that Americans are paying more money but getting the same sized houses?

**ANSWER:** Students might observe that the cost of living has increased.

**Visual Record Answer**

*Students might suggest that they contribute to a peaceful and respectful home environment.*

# TEACH OBJECTIVE 3

**ALL LEVELS:** Copy the following graphic organizer onto the chalkboard, omitting the italicized answers. Have each student complete the organizer to evaluate why it is useful for a family to budget its money. **ENGLISH LANGUAGE LEARNERS**

*to provide food,*

*a place to live,*

*clothing,*

*and to reduce their financial worries*

*to share financial responsibilities*

**LEVEL 3:** Organize the class into small groups and have each group create a family budget. Call on volunteers to present their family's budget to the class and to explain the importance of budgeting. **COOPERATIVE LEARNING**

**HOMEWORK** Have students ask their family members why they think it is important to budget their money.

## CLOSE

Have students write a brief ode singing the praises of the family. Encourage students to include the functions served by the family as well as the benefits of respect and cooperation within a family. Call on volunteers to read their odes to the class.

---

## Civics Sidelight

**Mediation** When groups in conflict cannot come to a resolution, a mediator can help. Mediators are people trained in helping two sides reach an agreement. A mediator remains objective and helps find a compromise that suits both sides. Some couples who are going through a divorce choose a mediator rather than using lawyers and taking their conflict to court. State agencies, such as the New York State Council on Divorce Mediation, regulate divorce mediators and raise public awareness of mediation as an option during divorce. Additionally, many schools have added conflict resolution programs to their curricula. These programs teach basic mediation skills. Such programs can equip students with a cooperative, nonviolent means of resolving their conflicts.

**ACTIVITY:** Have students locate articles in newspapers and other periodicals about issues facing families or students today that might require mediation. Call on volunteers to summarize these articles for the class and to explain how they think a mediator could assist with resolving their conflict.

### ★★★★★★★★★★★
### That's Interesting!
### ★★★★★★★★★★★

**Saving Lady Liberty** What would you think if the United States had never placed the Statue of Liberty in New York Harbor? It might have happened without the efforts of American family members. The statue was a gift to the United States from France in 1885. But money was needed to build a pedestal for the statue to rest upon. Neither the U.S. Congress nor the state of New York would pay for the work. Finally, newspaper publisher Joseph Pulitzer called upon working-class families to donate the needed funds. "Let us not wait for the millionaires to give this money," he declared. In amounts as small as a few pennies given by schoolchildren, the contributions from American families poured in. After more than 120,000 donations, the goal was reached and a symbol of American freedom had a proper resting place.

*Creating a family budget helps ensure that there is money available to pay bills.*

## ★ Solving Conflicts

Although conflicts can be unpleasant, family members can often benefit from disagreements. Arguments, if kept in hand, can teach you how to present your ideas effectively. They can also help you understand the other person's point of view.

Conflicts can occur between parents, between parents and children, or among the children in a family. These disagreements require members of the family to make compromises—to give a little and take a little. A sign of a well-adjusted family is that members of the family work together to find solutions to minor problems. If not dealt with properly, small concerns can develop into crises.

By talking over ideas with members of your family, you learn to be understanding and patient. These traits are important in getting along with other people—friends, classmates, teachers, neighbors, and, later, coworkers.

✔ **Reading Check Finding the Main Idea** Why are respect and compromise important to family harmony? These qualities help prevent and resolve family conflicts.

## ★ Managing Family Funds

One issue all families face is how to spend the family's money. Adults try to earn enough money to pay for all the things the family needs and wants. They are concerned about feeding, clothing, and providing shelter for the family. Members of the family want money for lunches, transportation, entertainment, and many other things that seem important at the time.

When there is only so much money to divide among the family members, compromises must be worked out. This way, each family member's needs can be provided for appropriately. Doing your share in handling family funds will help you learn about spending and saving money. Learning to manage money now will be a valuable skill to you as an adult.

Many families operate on some kind of a budget. The very thought of a budget discourages some people. When they think of a budget, they imagine a complicated bookkeeping system with column after column of figures. They also believe it usually means "pinching pennies" and having less fun.

In reality, a budget should not discourage anyone. It is simply a plan for spending or saving the family's income. In fact, if a budget is carefully planned and followed, it can help reduce a family's worries about money.

Each family must decide how to budget its money. Financial advisers may make suggestions and explain ways to handle money. However, a family's own special interests and needs require that the family make the final decisions about its spending plan.

The first step is to gather information about family expenses and income and to make a plan based on these facts. The starting point in any budget is the total amount of money available to spend. Families must keep their spending within this limit.

First on a family's budget are certain **fixed expenses.** These are regular expenses that must be paid. They include rent on an apartment or mortgage payments on a house. The cost of food and regular bills must also be considered. The remaining money pays for health care, transportation, entertainment, and other items. Families should also try to save some money.

✔ **Reading Check** Analyzing Information Why should families use a budget? There are many people's needs to consider, and budgeting helps families make good decisions about which needs to meet. Budgeting can also reduce the stress on the family.

### ★ Preparing for the Future

You can help your family follow its budget plan. One important way to do this is to help prevent waste in your home. In addition, try not to ask for things outside your family's budget. Talk to your parents or guardian before you agree to activities that cost money.

If you receive an allowance or earn money on your own, draw up your own budget. Decide how much money you need for transportation, lunches, and other fixed expenses. Then, if you can, set aside some money for future expenses or emergencies.

Handling money is just one of the skills you will need for the future. By learning to get along with your family, you are preparing for the day when you manage your own home.

✔ **Reading Check** Summarizing How can you help your family stay within its budget plan? by preventing waste, living within the family budget, and making your own budget

**Interpreting the Visual Record**

**Working together** *The family is an excellent place to first learn skills such as cooperation and teamwork.* **How can such skills help you later in life?**

## Section 3 Review
### ANSWERS

**1. Define**
• fixed expenses, p. 337

**2.** ensuring the future of the country, educating its members, teaching good behavior, helping manage money, teaching good citizenship

**3. a.** If people believe that their rights are respected, they are more likely to respect the rights of others. Compromise helps people find solutions to their problems because everyone gives up or obtains something.

**b.** Staying within a budget helps families reduce their financial worries.

**4.** Students' paragraphs will vary but should reflect an awareness that saving is important to good money management.

---

## SECTION 3 Review

go.hrw.com **Homework Practice Online**
keyword: SZ3 HP13

1. **Define** and explain:
   • fixed expenses

2. **Summarizing** Copy the graphic organizer below. Use it to explain the five important functions that a family serves.

Important Functions of the Family

3. **Finding the Main Idea**
   a. In what ways are respect and compromise helpful for family members?
   b. How does having a budget help a family?

4. **Writing and Critical Thinking**
   **Evaluating** Write out a personal budget. First, list your weekly expenses. Next, list your weekly sources of income. Finally, write a paragraph evaluating your current use of money and setting goals for your future use of it.
   **Consider:**
   • how to prioritize your spending
   • whether you are able to save any money
   • ways you can improve your money-managing skills

**REPRODUCIBLE**
- ▶ Chapter 13 Review, pp. 338–39
- ▶ Vocabulary Activity 13
- ▶ Chapter 13 Tutorial for Students, Parents, Mentors, and Peers
- ▶ Chapter 13 Test (Form A or B)
- ▶ Alternative Assessment Handbook

**TECHNOLOGY**
- ▶ Chapter 13 Test Generator (on the One-Stop Planner)
- ▶ Global Skill Builder CD–ROM
- ▶ HRW Go site

**REINFORCEMENT, REVIEW, AND ASSESSMENT**
- ▶ Chapter 13 Test for English Language Learners and Special-Needs Students

## REVIEW
Have students complete the **Chapter 13 Review** on pages 338–39.

## ASSESS
Use one of the chapter tests to assess students' understanding of the content. For **Alternative Assessment**, see the **Alternative Assessment Handbook**.

---

# CHAPTER 13
## REVIEW ANSWERS

**Define and Identify**
1. delayed marriage, p. 326
2. remarriages, p. 326
3. two-income families, p. 327
4. family law, p. 329
5. child abuse, p. 331
6. foster homes, p. 331
7. guardian, p. 331
8. adopt, p. 331
9. divorce, p. 331
10. fixed expenses, p. 337

**Understanding Main Ideas**
1. City families had to earn money to buy things that they had once produced themselves on farms.

2. Singlehood is more widely accepted, some people delay marriage to finish their education and start a career, and more people are living together without being married.

3. to discourage hasty marriages

4. division of property, custody arrangements, visitation rights, spousal and child support; they can make the decisions more complicated

5. ensuring the future of the country, educating its members, teaching good behavior, helping manage money, teaching good citizenship

6. Staying within a budget helps families reduce their financial worries.

---

# Chapter 13 Review

## Chapter Summary

### Section 1
- Families are groups in which young people learn lessons that stay with them for the rest of their lives.
- The family's economic role has changed over time. The United States has changed from a country of self-sufficient farm families to a country of city-dwelling consumers.
- As the country has changed, so has family life. People are marrying later in life, and the number of two-income families, single-parent families, and remarriages has increased. There is no typical American family.

### Section 2
- To protect family members, states pass laws regulating marriage, divorce, and the rights of parents and children.
- The United States has one of the world's highest divorce rates. Contributing factors include a less-complicated divorce process, greater financial independence for women, and a higher social tolerance for divorce.

### Section 3
- Many solutions have been offered for keeping the family together. There may be no one answer. All those who achieve a happy family life work hard at it.
- You can help your family by connecting with family members, respecting others' rights, making compromises, and staying within the family budget.

## Define and Identify
Use the following terms in complete sentences.
1. delayed marriage
2. remarriages
3. two-income families
4. family law
5. child abuse
6. foster homes
7. guardian
8. adopt
9. divorce
10. fixed expenses

## Understanding Main Ideas
**Section 1** (Pages 323–28)
1. How did the move to cities bring changes to American families?
2. Why has the average age at first marriage increased in recent years?

**Section 2** (Pages 329–32)
3. Why do most states have a waiting period for couples applying for marriage licenses?
4. What types of issues do divorced spouses need to resolve? How does having children affect the decisions that need to be made?

**Section 3** (Pages 334–37)
5. Identify five important family functions.
6. How can a budget help a family manage its income and spending?

## What Did You Find Out?
1. How has family life in the United States changed over time?
2. How does the law protect family members, particularly children?
3. Why is learning and practicing good citizenship within the family important?

## Thinking Critically
1. **Evaluating** How might developing strong, respectful relationships with other family members benefit people in their lives outside the family?
2. **Comparing and Contrasting** Research or watch an episode of a family-centered television program from the 1950s or 1960s, such as *Leave It to Beaver* and *Father Knows Best*. Compare and contrast these programs with current programs that focus on families. How are they similar or different in their representations of family life?
3. **Supporting a Point of View** Do you think that the government has the right to make and enforce laws that affect family life? Explain your answer.

## RETEACH

Organize students into nine groups and assign each group one of the chapter's Read to Discover questions. Have each group find the answer to its assigned question. Then have groups take turns being the teacher. Each group should ask the others for responses to its assigned Read to Discover question. Remind students that they are responsible for leading the discussion to find the possible answers.

**ENGLISH LANGUAGE LEARNERS**, **COOPERATIVE LEARNING**

## Portfolio Extensions

**1. Cooperative Learning** Organize the class into pairs and have each pair of students find articles about families in local newspapers and magazines. Partners should characterize each family in as many ways as they can, using descriptive phrases from the chapter such as "one- parent family" or "two-income family." Pairs should also identify details about other family circumstances, such as whether any of the children are adopted. Then have each pair design a bulletin-board display with a picture of each family type they found to accompany a summary of their findings.

**2. Interdisciplinary Connection to Sociology** Have students conduct research about television shows from the 1950s and 1960s. Then ask each student to write a report about the portrayal of families in shows from this era and explain how those shows reflected thoughts and collective attitudes about family life during those periods.

## Building Social Studies Skills

go.hrw.com STANDARDIZED TEST PREP ONLINE keyword: SZ3 STP13

### Interpreting Graphs

Study the line graph below. Then use the information in the graph to answer the questions that follow.

**Men and Women in the Workforce (1960–2000)**

Millions of Civilian Workers / Year

Male Workers / Female Workers

Source: Statistical Abstract of the United States

1. About how many more male workers than female workers were there in 1980?
   a. 15 million
   b. 25 million
   c. 5 million
   d. 1 million
2. In what year did the number of female workers first exceed the number of male workers who were in the workforce in 1960?
   a. 1960
   b. 1980
   c. 1983
   d. 1999
3. Based on the information displayed in this graph, what trend in employment has taken place over the past 40 years?

### Analyzing Primary Sources

Read the following quotation from historian Stephanie Coontz and then answer the questions that follow.

❝Most people react to these conflicting claims and contradictory trends with understandable confusion. They know that family ties remain central to their own lives, but they are constantly hearing about people who seem to have *no* family feeling. Thus, at the same time as Americans report high levels of satisfaction with their *own* families, they express a pervasive [serious] fear that other people's families are falling apart. In a typical recent poll, for example, 71 percent of respondents said they were 'very satisfied' with their own family life, but more than half rated the overall quality of family life as negative: 'I'm okay; you're not.' . . . Americans understand that along with welcome changes have come difficult new problems.❞

4. Which of the following statements best describes Coontz's point of view?
   a. Americans are very concerned about their own families and the changes that have taken place in family life.
   b. Most Americans are not concerned about family issues.
   c. Americans are happy with their own families but concerned about problems faced by families in general.
   d. Americans think family life is not complicated.
5. Based on what you have read, what types of changes in family life do you think Coontz is referring to in this quotation?

### Alternative Assessment

### Building Your Portfolio

*American Civics*

#### Linking to Community

In a small group, conduct a poll in your community that asks the following question: What do you think is the greatest problem facing families today? Organize your group so that each member asks this question of a different group of people. Then tally the results and evaluate them. Which problems are mentioned most or least often? How do the various groups differ in their opinions? Write a report and share it with the class.

### internet connect

**Internet Activity: go.hrw.com keyword: SZ3 AC13**

Access the Internet through the HRW Go site to research the ways in which the American family serves the country. Then create a collage to illustrate your research. Include a written description explaining how the photographs you chose for your collage represent the role of the family in citizenship and society.

### What Did You Find Out?

1. It has evolved from a self-sufficient farm family into consumers who live in cities. Family size and configuration has also changed.

2. by defining the responsibilities of parents and the rights of children

3. because citizenship learned in the family will be applied to everyday life

### Thinking Critically

1. Students might suggest that learning values such as cooperation, respect, and honesty in the family can help people behave appropriately outside of the family.

2. Students should note the similarities and differences in family forms and values.

3. Some students may feel that it does because children need to be protected and groups need to be regulated. Others may feel that families should manage their own relationships.

### Social Studies Skills

1. a

2. c

3. More women work outside of the home.

4. c

5. Students might suggest the increase in divorce rates, which has resulted in more single-parent families.

# Citizenship in School

## CHAPTER RESOURCE MANAGER

| Objectives | Pacing Guide | Reproducible Resources |
|---|---|---|
| **SECTION 1:**<br>**The U.S. School System**<br>(pp. 341–48)<br><br>★ Summarize why Americans value education.<br>★ Explain how the U.S. school system began.<br>★ Identify the different levels in the U.S. school system and explain why higher education has become more important.<br>★ Examine the values that have guided American education and identify the challenges that today's schools face. | **Regular**<br>2 days<br><br>**Block Scheduling**<br>1.5 days<br><br>*Block Scheduling Handbook with Team Teaching Strategies, Chapter 14* | RS  Guided Reading Strategies 14.1<br>E   Challenge and Enrichment Worksheet 14: Thinking About Education |
| **SECTION 2:**<br>**The Best Education for You**<br>(pp. 349–53)<br><br>★ Identify the seven goals of education.<br>★ Describe how you can best prepare for class work and tests.<br>★ Explain what you can learn from extracurricular activities. | **Regular**<br>1 day<br><br>**Block Scheduling**<br>.5 day<br><br>*Block Scheduling Handbook with Team Teaching Strategies, Chapter 14* | RS  Guided Reading Strategies 14.2<br>RS  Graphic Organizer Activity: Education and You<br>SM  Community Service and Participation Handbook: Each One, Reach One, Teach One |
| **SECTION 3:**<br>**Developing Your Life Skills**<br>(pp. 354–58)<br><br>★ Describe how learning relates to experience.<br>★ Determine the steps involved in critical thinking.<br>★ Describe how people can be influenced by the thinking of others and explain the need for people to think for themselves. | **Regular**<br>1 day<br><br>**Block Scheduling**<br>.5 day<br><br>*Block Scheduling Handbook with Team Teaching Strategies, Chapter 14* | RS  Guided Reading Strategies 14.3<br>E   Creative Teaching Strategy: Poetic Expressions<br>RS  Readings in Economics and Government 34: Spiro T. Agnew's "The Television News Medium" |

## Chapter Resource Key

| | | | |
|---|---|---|---|
| **PS** Primary Sources | **SM** Skills Mastery |  CD–ROM | |
| **RS** Reading Support | **A** Assessment |  Video | |
| **IC** Interdisciplinary Connections | **REV** Review |  Internet | |
| **E** Enrichment | **ELL** Reinforcement and English Language Learners |  Holt Presentation Maker Using Microsoft® PowerPoint® | |
| |  Transparencies | | |

 **One-Stop** Planner CD–ROM

**See the *One-Stop Planner* for a complete list of additional resources for students and teachers.**

**One-Stop Planner CD–ROM**

It's easy to plan lessons, select resources, and print out materials for your students when you use the *One-Stop Planner CD–ROM with Test Generator*.

## Technology Resources

- One-Stop Planner, Lesson 14.1
- Transparency 19: Local School Districts
- Transparency 20: Education and Income Average
- Holt Researcher CD–ROM
- Homework Practice Online
- HRW Go site

- One-Stop Planner, Lesson 14.2
- CNN. Presents: American Government
- Citizenship Skills Videocassette Segment 8: Building the Future
- Homework Practice Online

- One-Stop Planner Lesson 14.3
- Homework Practice Online

## Reinforcement, Review, and Assessment

- REV Section 1 Review, p. 348
- A Daily Quiz 14.1
- ELL Main Idea Activity 14.1
- ELL English Audio Summary 14.1
- ELL Spanish Audio Summary 14.1

- REV Section 2 Review, p. 353
- A Daily Quiz 14.2
- ELL Main Idea Activity 14.2
- ELL English Audio Summary 14.2
- ELL Spanish Audio Summary 14.2

- REV Section 3 Review, p. 358
- A Daily Quiz 14.3
- ELL Main Idea Activity 14.3
- ELL English Audio Summary 14.3
- ELL Spanish Audio Summary 14.3

**HRW ONLINE RESOURCES**
GO TO: go.hrw.com
Then type in the keyword.

**TEACHER HOME PAGE**
KEYWORD: SZ3 Teacher

**CHAPTER INTERNET ACTIVITIES**
KEYWORD: SZ3 AC14
Choose an activity to:
- make an oral report on ways to study for a test.
- create a brochure on the history of the American school system.
- role play a council member and employ a problem solving process to decide on a course of action.

**CHAPTER ENRICHMENT LINKS**
KEYWORD: SZ3 CH14

**ONLINE ASSESSMENT**
Homework Practice
KEYWORD: SZ3 HP14
Rubrics
KEYWORD: SS Rubrics

**ONLINE MAPS, CHARTS, AND GRAPHS**
KEYWORD: SZ3 MCG
- Local School Districts

**HOLT PRESENTATION MAKER**
KEYWORD: SZ3 PPT14

**CONTENT UPDATES**
KEYWORD: SS Content Updates

**ONLINE READING SUPPORT**
KEYWORD: SS Strategies

**CURRENT EVENTS**
KEYWORD: S3 Current Events

## Meeting Individual Needs

**Ability Levels**

**Level 1** Basic-level activities designed for all students encountering new material

**Level 2** Intermediate-level activities designed for average students

**Level 3** Challenging activities designed for honors and gifted-and-talented students

**English Language Learners** Activities that address the needs of students with Limited English Proficiency

## Chapter Review and Assessment

- IC Vocabulary Activity 14
- Global Skill Builder CD–ROM
- HRW Go site
- REV Chapter 14 Tutorial for Students, Parents, Mentors, and Peers
- REV Chapter 14 Review, pp. 360–61
- A Standardized Test Practice
- A Chapter 14 Test Generator (on the One-Stop Planner)
- A Alternative Assessment Handbook
- A Chapter 14 Test for English Language Learners and Special-Needs Students

## What's Your Opinion?

To help students create their **Themes** Journal entries, provide the following examples of appropriate **agree/disagree** statements.

● **Agree**   Since the first public schools were organized, public schools have educated children.

**Disagree**   Women and minorities had to turn to other education sources early in our history.

● **Agree**   Schools adopt mission statements and campus improvement plans to set goals for students.

**Disagree**   Schools and their curricula are not effectively linked across grade levels or between disciplines to achieve optimum success.

● **Agree**   Teachers are best prepared to foster the development of critical thinking and other life skills.

**Disagree**   Some individuals have learned that school is not the only place to learn life skills.

## Internet Activity

**Taking a Walk in Their Shoes**

**🔲 internet connect** ≡

**TOPIC:** Council Member for a Day
**GO TO:** go.hrw.com
**KEYWORD:** SZ3 AC14

Have students access the Internet through the HRW Go site to conduct research to employ a problem-solving process. Ask students to imagine they are members of the town council, and they must decide on a course of action regarding the expansion of the town hall. Each student's process should include these steps: identifying the problem, gathering background information, listing and considering options, considering advantages and disadvantages, choosing and implementing a solution, and evaluating the effectiveness of the solution.

## Build on What You Know

H ave you thought about the kind of work you want to do when you become an adult? No matter what future you choose for yourself, you will profit from getting a good education. Not only will you benefit from developing your talents and abilities, but the country will benefit as well. In this increasingly complex and technologically oriented world, the future of the United States depends on well-educated citizens. The country needs people who can make valuable contributions to its progress. The future depends on you.

### What's Your Opinion?

**Themes Journal**   Do you **agree** or **disagree** with the following statements? Support your point of view in your journal.

- Public schools have always been the main method of education in the United States.

- Schools are designed to achieve certain goals.

- Developing thinking skills and other life skills can only take place in school.

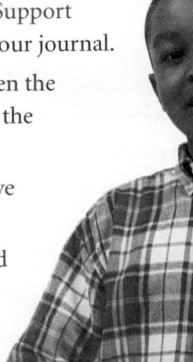

# SECTION 1

## OBJECTIVES

*After completing Section 1, students should be able to*

1 **Summarize why Americans value education.**

2 **Explain how the U.S. school system began.**

3 **Identify the different levels in the U.S. school system and explain why higher education has become more important.**

4 **Examine the values that have guided American education, and identify the challenges that today's schools face.**

### 🔊 LET'S GET STARTED!

Write the following quote by James Madison in 1822, on the chalkboard: "A popular Government, without popular information, or the means of acquiring it, is but a Prologue to a Farce or a Tragedy; or perhaps both. Knowledge will forever govern ignorance: And a people who mean to be their own Governors, must arm themselves with the power which knowledge gives." As students enter the classroom, ask them what this quotation means. Ask them to give examples of how, when, and where they learned about what it means to be a U.S. citizen. *(Students might suggest that Madison is referring to the importance of an educated citizenry.)* Tell students that in Section 1 they will learn about the U.S. school system.

## SECTION 1

# The U.S. School System

### Read to Discover

1. Why do Americans value education?
2. How did the U.S. school system begin?
3. What are the different levels in the U.S. school system, and why has higher education become more important?
4. What values have guided American education, and what challenges do today's schools face?

### Define

- community colleges
- colleges
- university
- graduate school
- mainstreaming

### WHY CIVICS MATTERS

Education is central to American society. Use CNNfyi.com or other **current events** sources to find out what issues educators and others citizens face in the field of education today. Record your findings in your journal.

*The Department of Education helps state and local school systems carry out their responsibilities.*

## Reading Focus

There are about 69 million students enrolled in public and private schools and colleges in the United States. The cost of running these educational enterprises has risen to nearly $745 billion a year, or about $10,800 per student. About 9 million teachers, administrators, and staff handle the day-to-day tasks of education in this country. This vast educational system affects every U.S. citizen.

### ⭐ Purposes of Education

Americans place a high value on education for two main reasons. They believe it is important for citizens' development as well as for the development of the country.

**Development of Individual Citizens** From the earliest days of U.S. history, Americans have placed great value on the individual. One important purpose of education, therefore, is to serve the individual. Americans believe that all citizens should be given the opportunity to study and learn in order to develop their talents and abilities.

The Declaration of Independence sets forth the American belief "that all men are created equal, that they are endowed by their Creator

## SECTION 1 RESOURCES

### REPRODUCIBLE

▶ Guided Reading Strategies 14.1

▶ Challenge and Enrichment Worksheet 14: Thinking About Education

### TECHNOLOGY

▶ Transparency 19: Local School Districts

▶ Transparency 20: Education and Average Income

▶ One-Stop Planner, Lesson 14.1

▶ Holt Researcher CD–ROM

▶ Homework Practice Online HRW Go site

### REINFORCEMENT, REVIEW, AND ASSESSMENT

▶ Section 1 Review, p. 348

▶ Daily Quiz 14.1

▶ Main Idea Activity 14.1

▶ English Audio Summary 14.1

▶ Spanish Audio Summary 14.1

**LEVEL 1:** Lead a class discussion about the value of education. *(Students might suggest that education gives people the power to change their lives and those of the people around them.)* Tell students that before the Civil War, slaves in most southern states were forbidden by law to learn to read or write. Ask students to discuss possible reasons for this denial. Discuss with students the value of an education in reaching both educational and career goals. Then ask students to list their educational and career goals and to write a plan of action for each goal in a journal. On a scale of 1 to 10, ask them to rate the importance of education in obtaining each of their goals. **ENGLISH LANGUAGE LEARNERS**

**ALL LEVELS:** Discuss with students the value placed on education. *(Students should respond that education is responsible for the development of individual citizens and the country.)* Then write the following quotation on the chalkboard and circle around the word knowledge: "Knowledge is Power." Draw rays coming off the circle and ask students to identify examples of power that knowledge provides. *(Students might suggest that knowledge provides them with the means to distinguish between fact and opinion, the power to think for themselves, and so on.)* Record student responses on the rays of the circle. **ENGLISH LANGUAGE LEARNERS**

 **HOMEWORK** Have students create a collage that includes captions that illustrate the value of education.

---

## The Democratic Process

### "No Child Left Behind"

President George W. Bush signed into law an educational reform act that not only redefines the role of the federal government in K–12 education, but also attempts to close the achievement gap between the special populations students and their peers. The No Child Left Behind Act of 2001, makes education a national priority. It is based on the following four principles: increased accountability, meaningful choices for parents and students, greater flexibility for state and local control, and an emphasis on proven teaching methods. Under this program if schools continue to fail to meet state standards, disadvantaged students will have an option to obtain supplemental services, such as tutoring, or to participate in a public school choice program.

**ACTIVITY:** Develop a public opinion poll concerning the use of state standardized testing, asking respondents to state advantages and disadvantages for such testing.

### BIOGRAPHY ANSWER

Students might suggest that his personal experience might better provide him with answers to the challenges that face our school systems today.

---

### BIOGRAPHY

## Rod Paige
### (1933– )

Rod Paige was born in Monticello, Mississippi. His father was a school principal and his mother a school librarian. Paige followed his parents into public education. He earned a bachelor's degree at Jackson State University and his doctorate at Indiana University. He served as dean of the College of Education at Texas Southern University before being named superintendent of the Houston Independent School District in 1994. Paige helped reform and restructure the Houston school system, improving test scores, rewarding outstanding teachers, and reducing operating costs. "At HISD . . . we are leaving no one behind," he declared.

Paige was named national superintendent of the year by the American Association of School Administrators. In 2001 President George W. Bush chose Paige as his secretary of education. **How might Secretary Paige's experience help him perform the duties of his office?**

---

with certain unalienable rights, that among these are life, liberty, and the pursuit of happiness." Americans have come to believe that all citizens—men and women of all ethnic groups—should have the same opportunities to succeed through equal access to education.

**Development of the Country** The well-being of all Americans depends on the willingness and ability of individuals to use their talents for the welfare of the entire country. One aim of education is to teach young citizens how to contribute to society through good citizenship. Schools try to show students how the well-being of each citizen and the country's future depend on all Americans learning to work together for the common good.

✔ **Reading Check** Finding the Main Idea What are the two main reasons Americans value education? They believe individuals should be given the opportunity to develop their abilities and talents; education teaches young citizens how to contribute to society.

### ★ Beginnings of the U.S. School System

The American system of education has been growing for more than 350 years. The first major step in developing public education was taken in Massachusetts in 1647. In that year, a law was passed requiring all but the smallest towns in the colony to set up public schools.

This law stated that every town of 50 families or more must hire a schoolteacher, who would be paid by the town. By doing so, Massachusetts shifted the responsibility for schooling from the home to the community.

In many of the other colonies, however, the education of some children was neglected. Although children of the wealthy were sent to private schools or were taught by tutors, children of poor parents often worked at an early age and received little or no schooling.

Many of the framers of the Constitution, including Thomas Jefferson, believed a system of public education should be established. Jefferson thought that in order for a democracy to operate effectively, its citizens had to be educated. Jefferson took steps to establish a public-education system in Virginia. His plans were rejected, however.

It was not until the first half of the 1800s that leaders such as Horace Mann worked to establish a system of public schools for all children. The developing public-school system helped many children receive an education. Initially, however, most girls were not educated beyond elementary school and the system did not include most minority students.

Public education faced many challenges. Many Americans in those days were opposed to tax-supported public schools. Some taxpayers did not want to pay to educate other people's children. Owners of some private schools argued that public schools would lead to decreased private

**LEVELS 2 AND 3:** After you summarize the value of an education, explain to students that one of the values is the development of good citizens—a necessary component for the success of our country. Then suggest that one of the purposes of education is to introduce the virtues of citizenship, such as honesty, perseverance and loyalty. Organize students into small groups and have each group select a virtue and then write a children's story or poem that illustrates its topic. Each group will create a visual highlighting both the virtue and a segment of the story or poem that best illustrates their topic. Ask volunteers to share their selections with the class.
**COOPERATIVE LEARNING**

# TEACH OBJECTIVE 2

 **ALL LEVELS:** Discuss with students how the U.S. school system began. Then organize students into pairs. Distribute the following puzzle pieces to pairs and ask them to sequence the pieces into the correct order. *(The five puzzle pieces are: (3) Horace Mann and others urge public schools for all children. (1) Massachusetts law requires all but the smallest towns to set up public schools. (2) Thomas Jefferson tries to establish a public education system in Virginia, but fails. (5) Public secondary schools began to increase. (4) Most northern states and some southern states set up public school systems.)* After checking their finished sequencing, discuss the proper order with the class. **ENGLISH LANGUAGE LEARNERS, COOPERATIVE LEARNING**

school enrollment. Some people who ran church-supported schools claimed that education should be under the control of the church and the home.

Public-education supporters believed that a successful democratic society requires citizens who can read and write. For this reason, government should pay for schools. By the time of the Civil War, the struggle for public, tax-supported schools was gaining ground. Most northern states and some southern states had set up public-school systems. However, these school systems were usually limited to elementary education. There were few secondary schools in the United States in 1850. Only after the Civil War did a system of public secondary schools, or high schools, begin to appear in the United States.

✔ **Reading Check Sequencing** What is the early history of the U.S. public-school system? Public schools were first started in colonial Massachusetts, but in most colonies children received little or no schooling. In the 1800s an elementary public-school system was established in many states, but most girls and minority students lacked equal access. By the late 1800s public high schools began to appear.

## The Educational Ladder

Most Americans spend many years receiving an education. There are several levels in the U.S. system of education. Schools range from preschools for young children to universities for adult higher education.

**Preschool** Many children attend preschool. Preschools usually accept children who are three and four years old. In these schools, children learn to play and get along with other children. Most preschools are private. However, some communities support preschools as part of their public-school system. The federal government also grants funds for preschool programs in some communities.

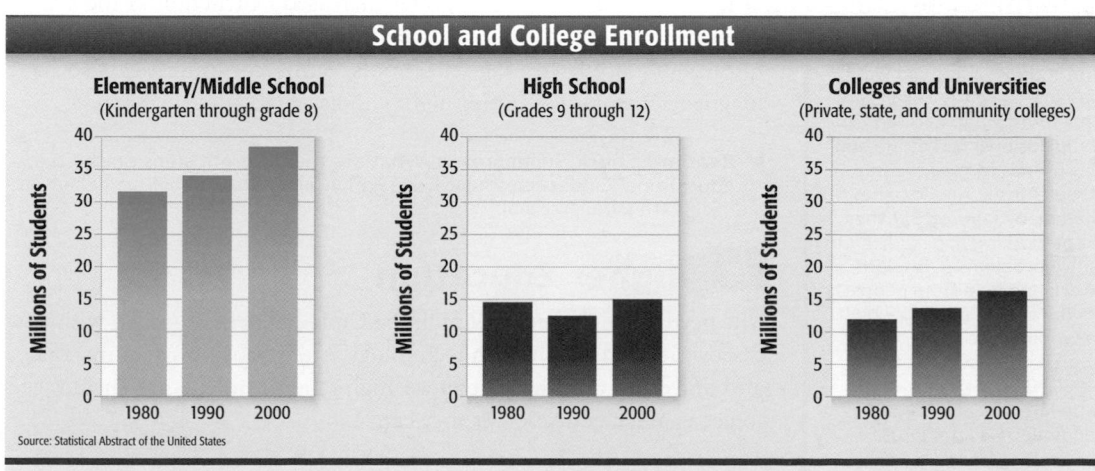

**School and College Enrollment**

**Elementary/Middle School** (Kindergarten through grade 8) — Millions of Students — 1980, 1990, 2000
**High School** (Grades 9 through 12) — Millions of Students — 1980, 1990, 2000
**Colleges and Universities** (Private, state, and community colleges) — Millions of Students — 1980, 1990, 2000

Source: Statistical Abstract of the United States

**Interpreting Graphs** *Private and public schools in the United States educate millions of students each year.* **At what educational levels did enrollment increase in both 1990 and 2000?**

**LEVEL 3:** Lead a class discussion about the history behind the U.S. school system. *(See the All Levels lesson for history.)* Then tell students that one of the earliest pieces of legislation that required setting aside land for public schools was the Northwest Ordinance. Explain that later legislative acts either added to this requirement or promoted additional educational opportunities. Ask students to write an essay describing the effects of the Northwest Ordinance, the Morrill Federal Land Grant of 1863, and the Smith-Hughes Act of 1917 on public education. *(These legislative acts set aside land for schools in the Northwest Territory, funded a system of state colleges and universities for teaching agriculture and mechanics, and provided federal grants to support vocational education, respectively.)*

## TEACH OBJECTIVE 3

**ALL LEVELS:** Discuss with students the different levels within the U.S. K–12 school system. *(The different levels are preschool, kindergarten, elementary school, junior high school, and high school.)* Ask students to identify the various levels of education available after high school. Explain that a university may contain one or more colleges as well as a graduate school, that provides advanced degrees. Organize the class into small groups and tell each group to choose a university or junior college in their state. Then tell groups that they must produce a poster for their assigned institution of higher learning. **ENGLISH LANGUAGE LEARNERS** ,

**COOPERATIVE LEARNING**

📃 **internet** connect ≣  **go hrw .com**

**TOPIC:** The American School System
**GO TO:** go.hrw.com
**KEYWORD:** SZ3 AC14

Have students access the Internet through the HRW Go site to conduct research about the history, development, and reform movements of the American school system. Then ask each student to create a brochure that presents his or her research.

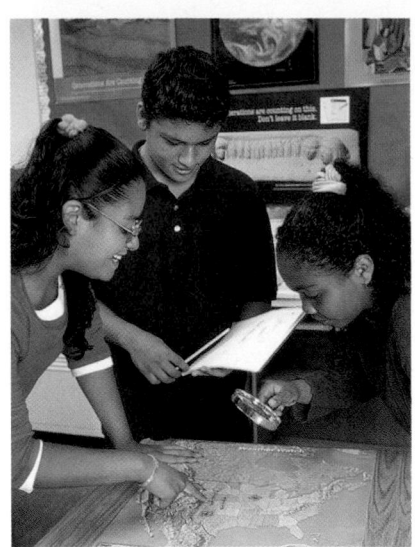

*The public-school system is designed so that each level builds upon the skills and knowledge taught at previous levels.*

**Kindergarten** Many public-school systems start with kindergarten classes for five- and six-year-old children. The word *kindergarten* is German and means "garden for children." Kindergarten children spend a year learning how to get along with others and preparing for first grade. In many areas, kindergartens teach the basics of reading and writing and number recognition.

**Elementary School** Most children enter the first grade of elementary school at the age of six. In elementary school, students learn the building blocks of education—reading, writing, arithmetic, and citizenship. The curriculum also includes subjects such as history, science, health, art, music, and physical education. Children attend elementary school for five to eight years, depending on how the school system is arranged.

**Junior High School** Grades seven, eight, and nine usually make up junior high school. Many school systems have replaced junior high schools with middle, or intermediate, schools. Middle schools range in structure from grades four through eight.

**High School** Students who have completed the first eight or nine grades enter high school. There are generally three kinds of high schools. Academic high schools prepare students for college. Technical and vocational high schools enable students to learn a trade or occupation. Comprehensive high schools offer both educational options. Some high schools have been designed as magnet schools—schools that present a specialized curriculum designed to attract certain students. Many of these schools, for example, offer increased instruction in the arts or sciences while still providing basic instruction. All students in a community can apply to magnet schools. Some communities also have magnet elementary or junior high schools.

✔ **Reading Check Summarizing** What are the different steps on the U.S. educational ladder? preschool, kindergarten, elementary school, junior high or middle school, high school

⭐ **Higher Education**

The need for higher education in the United States has grown with new discoveries and advances in technology. Many jobs now require college and university training. Therefore, high school students are encouraged to get as much education as they can.

**Community Colleges** The growing demand for higher education is being met in part by two-year **community colleges.** These schools are sometimes called junior colleges. They are often supported by taxpayers

★★★★★★★★★★★★
**That's Interesting!**
★★★★★★★★★★★★

**"Rocket Boys"** Can you imagine building your own rocket from scratch as an extracurricular project? That's what high school student Homer Hickham and his friends did in the 1950s. Hickham was fascinated by the Soviet satellite *Sputnik* and decided to build his own rocket. He and his friends formed the Big Creek Missile Agency. They had many failures. But they kept working and studying to solve problems. With hard work and help from people in the community, they built a working rocket. Hickham won a gold medal at the 1960 National Science Fair and later became a NASA engineer. He later wrote a bestselling book about his experiences, *Rocket Boys*, that was made into the movie *October Sky*.

**LEVELS 1 AND 2:** Tell students that a school board, elected by the citizens of the community, oversees five levels of the U.S. school system. Ask students what levels come under the control of the school board? *(See the All Levels lesson for levels.)* Then ask a member of the school board to talk to your class concerning the responsibilities of the school board and some of the problems that they face in providing opportunities for all students. Also ask the school board members to describe what steps your school system has taken to promote the importance of a higher education. After the discussion, have students design an agenda for a mock school board meeting, detailing what they think should be discussed and implemented at each of the levels to promote the importance of higher education. **ENGLISH LANGUAGE LEARNERS**

## TEACHER TO TEACHER
Christie Hutchins of Missouri recommends the following activity:

**LEVEL 2:** Have each student make a list of three jobs that they would like to have as an adult. Try to ensure that the chosen jobs are realistic. Then ask the students to create a personal educational time line and a list of steps needed to accomplish each stage in achieving those professional goals.

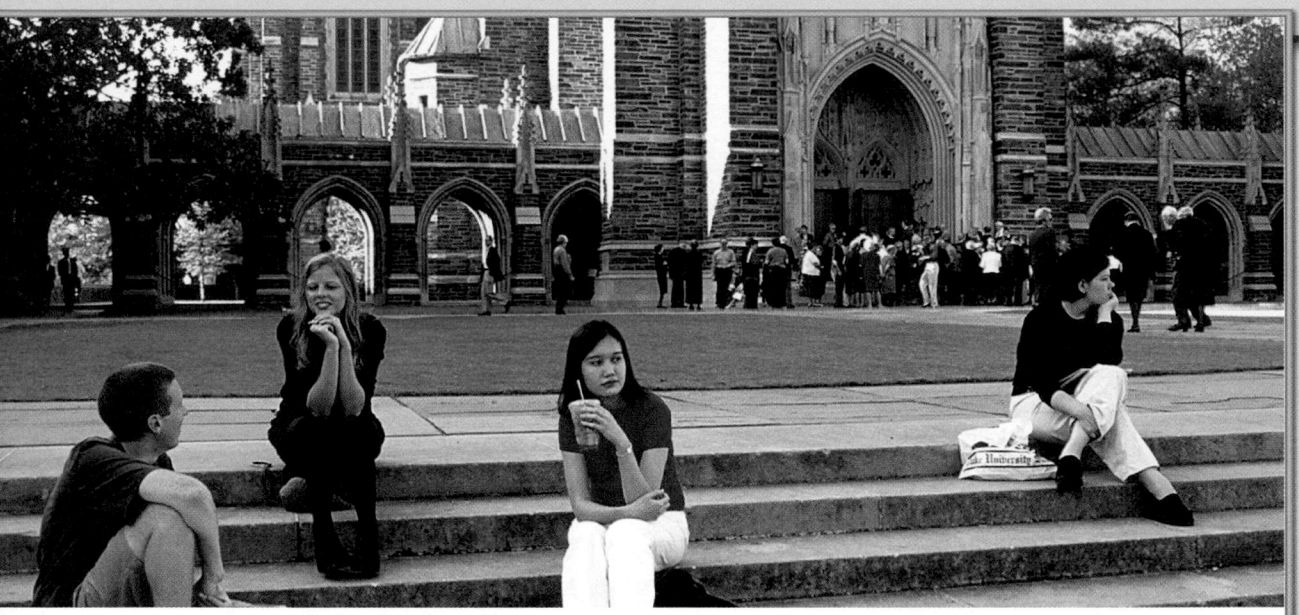

and offer courses at low tuition to local high school graduates. Courses include training for specialized fields and preparation for more advanced study. Many community-college graduates transfer to four-year colleges or universities to complete their education.

**Colleges and Universities** There are roughly 1,500 colleges and universities in the United States. Most **colleges** offer four-year degrees in a variety of fields and are coeducational. Coeducational colleges are open to both male and female students. They range in size from small private colleges with only a few hundred students to large institutions with 10,000 students or more. The federal and state governments contribute about $69 billion to help support higher-education institutions.

Some institutions of higher learning are organized as universities. A **university** includes one or more colleges. It also has graduate programs in professional fields of learning, such as business, medicine, engineering, and law. A university also provides advanced studies in most of the subjects that are offered in colleges. After graduation from college, students may go on to **graduate school** to study for an advanced degree.

It pays to stay in school and get as much education as you can. In addition to helping you to become a well-educated person, a higher level of education will usually increase your income. For example, professional careers in medicine and law usually require advanced degrees. This holds true for both men and women. However, regardless of their level of education women have traditionally been paid less money than men for the same work.

✔ **Reading Check** **Drawing Inferences and Conclusions** What are the different types of higher education institutions, and why have they recently increased in importance for American students? Higher education includes community college, college, university, and graduate school; new discoveries and advances in technology have resulted in many jobs in the United States now requiring higher education.

**Interpreting the Visual Record**

**College** *Enrollment in American colleges and universities has increased steadily over the past 20 years.* **What are some of the benefits offered by a college education?**

The first coeducational college in the United States was Oberlin College, which began admitting women in 1833. Today most colleges in the country are coeducational.

### Civics Sidelight

**Adult Education** An additional rung on the educational ladder is adult education, which is booming in the United States. In 1991, 34 percent of all adults took adult education courses to acquire new skills or knowledge. In 1995, 40 percent of the adult population signed up for an educational activity and in 1999 the percentage rose to 46 percent. Adults 25 to 34 years of age accounted for the greatest percentages, with 56 percent of that age group enrolled in an adult education class in 1999. (This does not include full-time enrollment in a higher education credential program). Finally, adults between the ages of 55 to 64 and 65 and older accounted for percentage rates of 37 percent and 19 percent, respectively.

**ACTIVITY:** Instruct students to poll at least 10 adults concerning any educational activity they participated in during the last year. If the adults respond with a yes, tell students to ask what kind of activity they participated in and for what reasons.

### Visual Record Answer

*Students might suggest career training.*

**LEVEL 1:** After leading a class discussion about the values that have guided American education, remind students that one of those values is "equal schooling open to everyone." *(The values that have guided American education are free public education, equal schooling open to all, local control, compulsory attendance, and an enriching environment.)* Then tell students that one of the challenges that our school system faces today is ensuring that equal educational opportunities are available to all students, including students that have special needs. Discuss with students the Americans with Disabilities Act and other legislation that pertains to students with special needs. Ask students to list how your school meets those requirements. Then ask students how your school can better help those students with special needs.

**ENGLISH LANGUAGE LEARNERS**

**HOMEWORK** After discussing the challenge of providing equal educational opportunities for all students, especially those with special needs, have students turn in a list of a required number of examples in which your community complies with the Americans with Disabilities Act.

---

## ⭐ Culture

**Just the Facts** In 1999, more than one-fourth of the U.S. population was enrolled in school, 15 million of which were in college, 16 million in high school, 33 million in elementary school, and 8 million in nursery school or kindergarten. Diversity in education also increased, as 63 percent of all schoolchildren were non-Hispanic whites, compared to 79 percent in 1972, and in 1999 one in five children had at least one parent who was foreign born. It is also estimated that 1.7 percent of children in the United States were home-schooled, and that over 50 percent of 3- and 4-year-olds went to nursery school in 1999 as compared to 5 percent in 1964.

### CRITICAL THINKING

Why do you think more 3- and 4-year-olds go to nursery school today than in 1964?

**ANSWER:** Students might suggest that in today's society both parents usually work, whereas in 1964 fewer women worked outside of the home.

---

### CASE STUDY

*Brown* v. *Board of Education* reversed the "separate but equal" principle established in *Plessy* v. *Ferguson*, ruling that racial segregation in public education was by nature unequal, even if the school facilities were equal.

---

## SUPREME COURT CASE STUDY

### Brown v. Board of Education

**Significance:** This ruling reversed the Supreme Court's earlier position on segregation set by *Plessy* v. *Ferguson* (1896). The decision also inspired Congress and the federal courts to help carry out further civil rights reforms for African Americans.

**Background:** Beginning in the 1930s, the National Association for the Advancement of Colored People (NAACP) began using the courts to challenge racial segregation in public education. In 1952 the NAACP took a number of school segregation cases to the Supreme Court. These included the Brown family's suit against the school board of Topeka, Kansas, over its "separate-but-equal" public-school policy.

**Decision:** This case was decided on May 17, 1954, by a vote of 9 to 0. Chief Justice Earl Warren spoke for the unanimous court, which ruled that segregation in public education created inequality. The Court held that racial segregation in public schools was by nature unequal, even if the school facilities were equal. The Court noted that such segregation created feelings of inferiority that could not be undone. Therefore, enforced separation of the races in public education is unconstitutional.

**How did the Court reverse its earlier ruling with the Brown decision?**

---

### Holt Researcher

**go.hrw.com**
**KEYWORD: Holt Researcher**
Freefind: Courts and Education

Read through the Supreme Court cases on the Holt Researcher that involve education. Use the information to create a table that answers the following question: What are some of the key educational rights for parents and students that the Supreme Court has supported?

---

## ⭐ Students with Special Needs

Most U.S. citizens believe in equal educational opportunities for everyone. In the past, however, students with special needs were isolated in separate classrooms or separate schools. Students with special needs include gifted students and students with physical, mental, or learning disabilities. Today the law demands that students with special needs be taught in regular classrooms whenever possible. This practice is called **mainstreaming,** or inclusion in some schools.

Many students with disabilities attend regular classes for most of the day. They also work with specially trained teachers for a few hours each day or each week. Others receive special instruction for much of the day and then join regular classes in subjects such as art and music. Gifted students may receive expanded enrichment instruction.

✔ **Reading Check Evaluating** What are the advantages of mainstreaming students? Answers may vary, but students may suggest that attending regular classes allows students with special needs to interact and share experiences with other students.

## ⭐ American Values in Education

Certain values have influenced the development of the U.S. public-school system. The following are some of the traditional values that have become part of the American educational process.

**Free Public Education** Citizens are entitled to a free public education from kindergarten through high school. This means that instruction is

**ALL LEVELS:** Copy the following graphic organizer onto the chalkboard, omitting the italicized answers. Have each student complete the organizer by adding a current value that is guiding American education for each ray of the sun.

**ENGLISH LANGUAGE LEARNERS**

## CLOSE

Across the top of the chalkboard list the American values in education. Then have students suggest why they think each of these values is important. List their reasons beneath the appropriate value heading on the chalkboard.

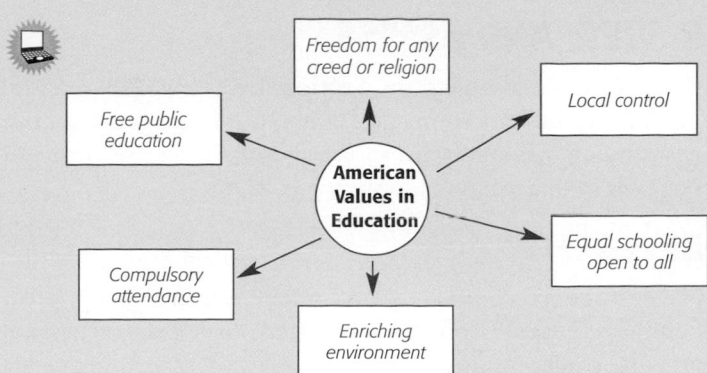

Free public education

Freedom for any creed or religion

Local control

**American Values in Education**

Compulsory attendance

Enriching environment

Equal schooling open to all

---

## Local School Districts

VOTE

The voters of the school district or the community elect the Board of Education.

Some school boards are appointed rather than elected.

The Board of Education hires:

Superintendent of Schools

Principals

Teachers

Custodians, secretaries, and other staff

Coaches

Counselors

**Interpreting Charts**
*School districts are separate units of local government. In some states, schools are governed by city, county, or town governments.* **What are some of the school positions hired by the Board of Education?**

provided at no cost to students. Public education costs American taxpayers around $326 billion a year, including expenditures by the federal government of about $22 billion.

**Equal Schooling Open to All** No one should be discriminated against because of race, sex, religion, or financial status.

**Freedom for Any Creed or Religion** U.S. schools are open to all Americans, regardless of their religious beliefs. The Supreme Court has held that no school-sponsored prayer or Bible reading shall be allowed during the school day in the public-school system.

**Local Control** Local school boards operate public schools under laws passed by the state legislature. State boards or departments of education assist local schools and often determine policy. Actual day-to-day control of the schools rests with the local school district.

**Compulsory Attendance** Each state requires school attendance by young people, usually between the ages of 7 and 16. However, some families educate their children at home. Laws on homeschooling vary from state to state.

**Enriching Environment** Schools should be places where young people can grow in mind, body, and spirit. Sports, clubs, social events, and creative arts are a part of each person's education. Schools should be places where individuals can develop to their full potential.

✔ **Reading Check Summarizing** What are the values that have guided the development of the American educational system? American education is based on the following principles: free education for all citizens, separation of religion and public education, local control, compulsory attendance, and an enriching environment.

---

### ★ Constitutional Heritage

***Plyer v. Doe*** In 1975 the Texas legislature passed a law authorizing school districts to deny enrollment to illegal alien children. Schools could also opt to charge tuition to those children, and the Tyler Independent School District chose this course of action. In 1977 a class action suit was filed against the district questioning the constitutionality of treating children of undocumented parents differently than children who were legal residents of the United States. Attorneys for the undocumented students said their clients were being denied equal protection under the law as guaranteed by the Fourteenth Amendment. The U.S. Supreme Court ruled in 1982 that the equal protection clause applies equally to citizens as well as noncitizens residing in the United States. The Fourteenth Amendment says "... nor shall any State ... deny to *any person* within its jurisdiction the equal protection of the laws."

**CRITICAL THINKING**
Why do you think the U.S. Supreme Court ruled as it did?

**ANSWER:** Students might suggest that the Fourteenth Amendment protects all persons, not only citizens.

**CHART ANSWER**
Superintendent of Schools, principals, teachers, counselors, coaches, and other staff members, such as custodians, secretaries, and cafeteria workers

## REVIEW AND ASSESS

Have students complete the **Section 1 Review** on page 348. Then have students complete **Daily Quiz 14.1**. As Alternative Assessment you may want to use the puzzle or the proposal exercises in this section's lessons.

## RETEACH

Have students complete **Main Idea Activity for English Language Learners and Special-Needs Students 14.1**. Then organize students into small groups and have each group create a rap, poem, or song that best exemplifies the educational ladder, both its values and its challenges.

**ENGLISH LANGUAGE LEARNERS , COOPERATIVE LEARNING**

## EXTEND

Organize students into small groups and have each group research one of the following court cases concerning schools. Tell each group to prepare a case study information sheet for its assigned case. The information sheet should contain the following items: the name and date of the case, the facts of the case, the issue or question that the Court decided, the arguments for the plaintiff, the arguments for the respondent, and the decision of the Court and its rationale. Groups should then share their information sheets with the class. Court cases: *Plyer* v. *Doe, San Antonio I.S.D.* v. *Rodriguez, Sweatt* v. *Painter,* and *Brown* v. *Board of Education*. **COOPERATIVE LEARNING**

### Interpreting the Visual Record

**Science education** *One of the many educational reforms being pursued in the United States is improved education in science.* **What type of activity are these students performing?**

---

**Visual Record Answer**

*Students might suggest a chemistry lab experiment.*

## Section 1 Review
### ANSWERS

**1. Define**
• community colleges, p. 344
• colleges, p. 345
• university, p. 345
• graduate school, p. 345
• mainstreaming, p. 346

**2.** college/university, high school, junior high school, elementary school, kindergarten

**3. a.** free public education, equal schooling for all, freedom of creed or religion, local control, compulsory attendance, enriching environment

**b.** Public schools were first started in Massachusetts in 1647. In the early 1800s, leaders such as Horace Mann worked to establish a public school system for all children, but girls were only educated through elementary school and minorities were excluded. By the Civil War, tax-supported elementary schools were becoming more common, but public high schools were uncommon until the late 1800s.

**4.** Students' answers will vary but should mention ways to provide more money to poor school districts, improve test scores, and decrease violence.

---

### ⭐ Challenges in Today's School System

Americans have long believed that education is the backbone of democracy. Because education is so important, all citizens must be aware of and meet the challenges facing the U.S. educational system.

One issue that currently challenges the public-education system is the distribution of resources. The money used to fund schools comes from property taxes. Areas with low property-tax revenue have less money for schools than areas with high revenue. In addition, some school districts attract more qualified teachers than others. Ensuring that public education is of equal quality from place to place is a difficult job.

Another challenge is the need for educational reform. American students' science, math, and reading test scores are lower at most levels than those in other industrial countries. Many fear that this problem will lead to a shortage of highly skilled workers, weakening the U.S. economy.

To help young people meet some of these challenges, Congress passed the Goals 2000: Educate America Act in 1994. This $458 million program sets goals for U.S. education and encourages the states to develop stricter educational standards. It includes grants to states and local school agencies to help fund educational reforms.

The U.S. educational system also faces an alarming increase in school violence. In some schools, teachers must spend more time trying to maintain discipline than teaching. Some schools have installed metal detectors to prevent students from bringing in weapons. Others have police officers stationed in the hallways and rules against students carrying backpacks. Many U.S. schools now offer violence-prevention programs that teach students how to settle disputes peacefully.

✔ **Reading Check** Finding the Main Idea What challenges does the American educational system face? unequal distribution of resources; falling test scores in math, reading, and science; school violence

---

## SECTION 1 Review

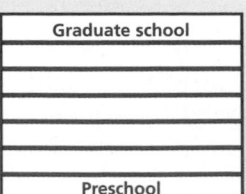
go.hrw.com **Homework Practice Online**
keyword: SZ3 HP14

**1. Define** and explain:
• community colleges
• colleges
• university
• graduate school
• mainstreaming

**2. Categorizing** Copy the graphic organizer to the right. Then fill in the missing levels on the U.S. educational ladder.

| Graduate school |
| --- |
| |
| |
| |
| |
| Preschool |

**3. Finding the Main Idea**
a. What are the values guiding public education in the United States?
b. Briefly describe how the public-school system developed in the United States.

**4. Writing and Critical Thinking**
**Problem Solving** What solutions would you propose to the challenges facing American education today?

**Consider:**
• the values that have guided American education
• areas of education that need improvement

# SECTION 2
## OBJECTIVES

After completing Section 2, students should be able to
1. **Identify the seven goals of education.**
2. **Describe how you can best prepare for class work and tests.**
3. **Explain what you can learn from extra-curricular activities.**

## 🔊 LET'S GET STARTED!

On the chalkboard write the following quotation, *"Success is when preparation meets opportunity."* As students enter the class-room, ask what the quotation means to them. *(Students might suggest that when opportunity strikes, if someone has prepared for success, success is usually achieved.)* Continue the discussion by describing to your students what requirements you had to fulfill to obtain a teaching degree. Then ask students to list some of the requirements for other professions. As you list the requirements on the chalkboard, ask students what preparations are needed to achieve each requirement. Tell students that in Section 2 they will learn about the opportunities school can offer them and how they can best prepare to take advantage of those opportunities.

## SECTION 2

# The Best Education for You

### Read to Discover
1. What are the seven goals of education?
2. How can you best prepare for class work and tests?
3. What can you learn from extracurricular activities?

### WHY CIVICS MATTERS
Public education has a considerable influence on most American children. Use **CNNfyi.com** or other **current events** sources to learn more about the range of activities students take part in at their schools. Record your findings in your journal.

### Define
• extracurricular activities

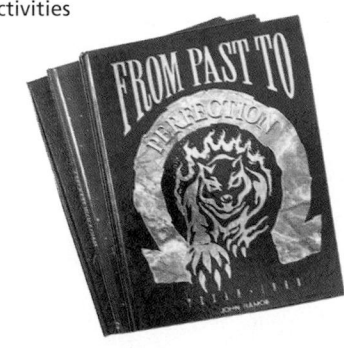

## *Reading Focus*

Luck has been defined as being in the right place at the right time. A lucky person is also usually able to see opportunities and make good use of them. This is true in school and in studying as well. You must be aware of and take advantage of the opportunities offered in school. What are these opportunities?

## ★ What Your School Has to Offer

In 1929 an organization of teachers, parents, and school officials adopted a list of educational goals for U.S. schools. These principles still apply to the skills schools try to teach you today. As you study these goals, ask yourself if you are taking advantage of the opportunities offered by your school.

**Using Basic Learning Skills** One of the main goals of schools is to teach students the skills of reading, writing, arithmetic, and citizenship. In addition, schools teach other skills that help students learn and study. These learning skills include listening, public speaking, and organizing and expressing ideas. They also include supporting a point of view, computing, using a dictionary, and conducting research. The ability to read and interpret maps, graphs, charts, pictures, and cartoons are other important skills. You can use these skills in many different courses in school. You will also discover that you will use these skills throughout your life.

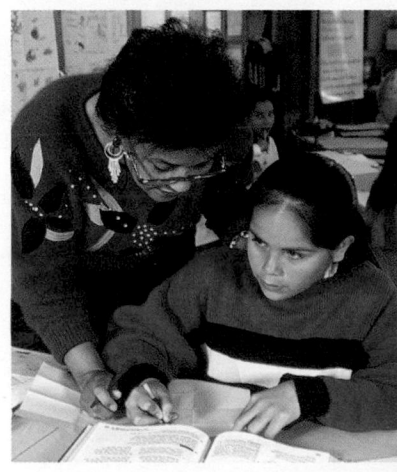

*Teachers play a critical role in providing basic skills instruction to young children.*

### SECTION 2 RESOURCES

#### REPRODUCIBLE
▶ Guided Reading Strategies 14.2
▶ Graphic Organizer Activity: Education and You
▶ Community Service Participation Handbook: Each One, Reach One, Teach One

#### TECHNOLOGY
▶ One-Stop Planner, Lesson 14.2
▶ CNN Presents: American Government
▶ Citizenship Skills Videocassette Segment 8: Building the Future
▶ Homework Practice Online

#### REINFORCEMENT, REVIEW, AND ASSESSMENT
▶ Section 2 Review, p. 353
▶ Daily Quiz 14.2
▶ Main Idea Activity 14.2
▶ English Audio Summary 14.2
▶ Spanish Audio Summary 14.2

# TEACH OBJECTIVE 1

**LEVEL 1:** Identify the seven goals of education with students. *(The seven goals are using basic learning skills, learning to work with others, health education, training for you life's work, active citizenship, considerate behavior, and the wise use of leisure time.)* Then organize the class into small groups of two to three students and have groups write a paragraph about their ideal school—one that meets or exceeds the seven goals listed in the textbook. Groups should include examples of how the goals are achieved in their ideal school. Ask volunteers to present their paragraphs to the class.
**ENGLISH LANGUAGE LEARNERS , COOPERATIVE LEARNING**

**LEVELS 2 AND 3:** After discussing the seven goals of education, tell students that many schools develop a mission statement explaining the school's overall goal, as well as steps or objectives that need to be met in order to achieve that goal. *(See the Level 1 lesson for goals.)* Have small groups compose a mission statement for their school, including the objectives that are necessary to achieve the mission statement. Ask volunteers to present their mission statements to the class. If time permits, invite one of your administrators to discuss the results of the assignment. **COOPERATIVE LEARNING**

## ★ Profiles

### Washington and DuBois

Booker T. Washington (1856–1915), founder of the Tuskegee Institute in Alabama, believed education should include moral values and should train a person for his or her life's work. He favored teaching vocational skills and "the everyday practical things of life." W.E.B. DuBois (1868–1963) thought this approach was too limited. He believed higher education should be the goal. DuBois believed that African Americans with advanced training would lead all African Americans to full equality. The arguments of these two famous African Americans reflect general questions that are still being asked: What kind of education best promotes equality and opportunity? Is the role of schooling to produce skilled workers or to encourage scholarship, or both?

#### CRITICAL THINKING

Ask students how they would answer the above questions and why.

**ANSWER:** Students' answers will vary but should include a rationale for their choices.

#### Visual Record Answer

*Students might suggest that good health and physical fitness habits make a person feel better about themselves, reduce the risk of heart attacks, diabetes, and other diseases later in life, as well as promote healthy habits as a person ages.*

**350**

**Interpreting the Visual Record**

**Good health** *Health education, including physical fitness and sports programs, is offered at most schools.* **How do good health and physical fitness benefit you in life?**

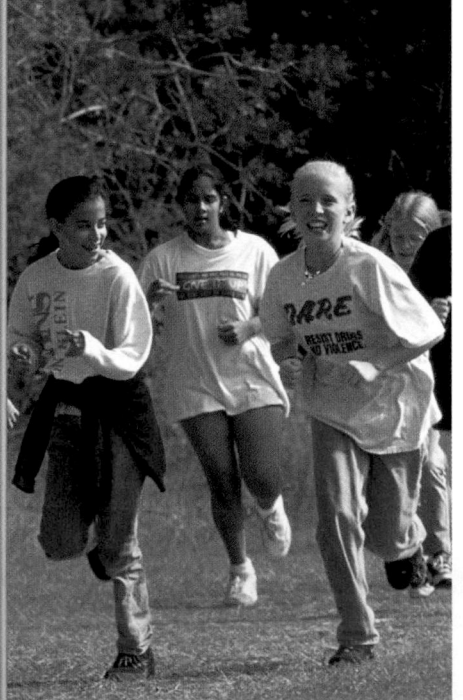

**Learning to Work with Others** Many of your school activities require you to work with other students. This cooperation is good practice for working with members of your family. It will also help you work with other people in your community and your future workplace.

**Health Education** Most schools have a program in health education to teach students to develop good health habits. Health education usually also offers programs of physical fitness and sports. You will benefit from the exercise these programs provide. Moreover, the practice in school will help you take care of your health and keep physically fit throughout your life.

**Training for Your Life's Work** Your school provides the educational foundation on which specialized job training can be based. Your school also helps you prepare for job opportunities after you graduate. Employers need well-educated, skilled workers. School makes it possible for you to become that kind of employee. In using your education, you can prepare for a job that contributes to the country and also gives you personal satisfaction.

**Active Citizenship** To help you become a good citizen, your school seeks to develop your interest in community life. It teaches you about the history of the United States, its institutions, and the problems it faces today. Your classes and school activities help you develop a sense of loyalty and an understanding of democratic principles. They also teach you citizenship skills, good judgment, and a willingness to do your fair share for the good of all.

**Considerate Behavior** Your school teaches students to adapt to accepted standards of behavior. It also tries to develop in all students a feeling of consideration for the people around them. These people include their families, teachers, classmates, friends, and other members of the community. Your school also stresses the importance of respecting the privacy and property of other citizens.

**Wise Use of Leisure Time** Your school introduces you to good books, art, and music so that they may enrich your life. Your teachers encourage you to develop interesting hobbies and to participate in school activities such as athletics and drama.

By encouraging you to undertake such activities, your school is trying to help you find a hobby or special interest to enjoy now and in the future. In this way your school helps make you a well-rounded person.

✔ **Reading Check** Summarizing What goals do schools work to achieve?
Schools teach basic skills, cooperation, job and life skills, wise use of leisure time, and good citizenship, manners, and health habits.

**ALL LEVELS:** Copy the following graphic organizer onto the chalkboard, omitting the italicized answers. Then ask students to complete the organizer by filling in the circles with how one can best prepare for class work and tests. **ENGLISH LANGUAGE LEARNERS**

- Select *a quiet place to study.*
- Take *notes while you read.*
- Keep *materials you need close at hand.*
- Make *effective use of your textbook.*

**How to Study**

**ALL LEVELS:** Remind students how to best prepare for class work and tests. *(See the All Levels lesson for preparation.)* Then organize the class into pairs and tell each pair to list all the parts of a textbook that can be used to help students prepare for class work and tests. **ENGLISH LANGUAGE LEARNERS , COOPERATIVE LEARNING**

**HOMEWORK** Hand out a blank time log to each student. Ask students to fill out the time log for the following week, making sure that they take time during the day to write down entries. After time logs are completed, ask students to categorize their activities, such as schoolwork, exercise, socializing, sleep, and so on. Then ask them to prioritize their categories on the basis of what is necessary to achieve their future goals.

## Getting the Most out of School

To make the best use of the opportunities your school offers, you must remember the goals of your education. Your years in school are very important. The success you enjoy in school and the study and learning habits you develop may play a role in the person you will become. They will also influence the kind of job you will have. What kinds of study and learning habits should you try to develop?

One of the first and most important study habits all students must learn is the wise use of time. A well-organized student finds time in his or her daily schedule for study, school activities, exercise, relaxation, and the proper amount of sleep.

Just as your family budgets its money, it is wise to budget your time. Work out a daily schedule for your more important activities, and try to finish things on time.

✔ **Reading Check Drawing Inferences and Conclusions** Why is the wise use of time an important study habit? Finding the right balance between time spent studying, participating in school activities, exercising, relaxing, and sleeping will help students produce better quality schoolwork.

## How to Study

Study your schoolwork with care and concentration. If possible, select a regular place to study that is quiet and has enough light and space to work. Keep the materials you need close at hand.

Take notes while you read. You will soon find that writing down important ideas on paper or typing them with a computer will help you understand and remember these ideas. Make sure you understand your assignment before you start. Then do the best job you can.

**Interpreting the Visual Record**

**School play** *Extracurricular school activities, such as drama, can help you create a more well-rounded school experience.* **What skills are these students developing by practicing their performance?**

### ★ Civics Sidelight

**AVID** Founded by Mary Catherine Swanson in 1980 at Clairemont High School in San Diego, California, AVID (Advancement Via Individual Determination) is an organization that helps students complete their college preparatory requirements. It focuses on students in the middle, especially low-income, underachieving and minority students who have academic potential. AVID seeks to increase the number of students who complete the college-prep pathway through a support system consisting of an AVID curriculum based on writing, inquiry, and collaboration; formally trained college tutors; motivational activities and speakers; and a site team that coordinates this special elective class. AVID serves students throughout a number of states. Over 93 percent of AVID graduates enroll in college.

**CRITICAL THINKING**

Why do you think AVID has been so successful?

**ANSWER:** Students might suggest that AVID provides a support structure that enhances student success.

**Visual Record Answer**

*Students might suggest that the students practicing the play are learning cooperation skills, considerate behavior skills, as well as other interpersonal skills.*

## TEACH OBJECTIVE 3

**ALL LEVELS:** Ask students what they can learn from extracurricular activities and discuss their responses. *(Students might suggest that besides developing special abilities, special interests, and social skills, activities may help them gain admission to college or obtain a scholarship.)* Ask students to generate a chalkboard list of all the extracurricular activities available in your school and community. Next to each activity, have them list service projects offered by that activity. Then hand out a blank resumé to each student and have them complete the form. Tell students that they should update the resumé as they participate in activities. *(Sample resumés might include the following items: name, address, phone, email address, GPA, rank in class, school activities, awards and recognitions, leadership activities, community service activities, work experience, and so on.)* **ENGLISH LANGUAGE LEARNERS**

## CLOSE

Review with students the importance of being prepared for class work and taking tests. Then have students make a list of other aspects of life in which they could benefit by being prepared—or would be at a disadvantage if they were unprepared. Ask volunteers to present their lists to the class.

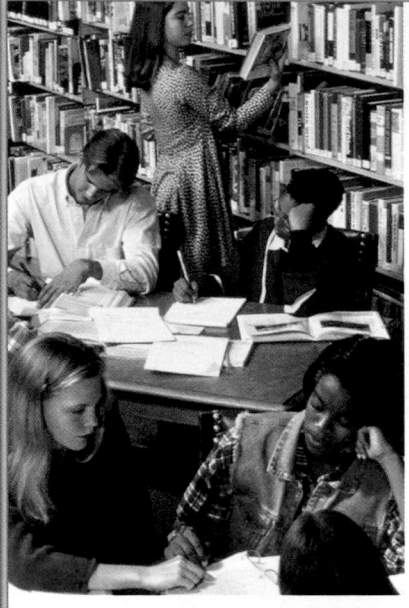

**Interpreting the Visual Record**

**Studying** *Proper studying requires focus, organization, and effort.* **Why do you think these students are studying in their school library?**

*Participating in class is an important responsibility for all students.*

Your textbooks are written to help you learn quickly and efficiently. Here are some useful hints to help you get the most from your textbooks.

- Learn how to use the study guides in the book. Use the table of contents, index, glossary, maps, charts, appendices, and captions.
- Note the chapter title, the section headings, and other subheadings within the chapter. They give you clues to the chapter's most important ideas.
- Read through the assigned text carefully, noting topic sentences and summarizing paragraphs.
- Reread the assigned text. This time, make written notes on the important ideas and facts included in the material.
- Answer the questions at the end of each section of the chapter. If you find a question you cannot answer, turn to the page in your textbook where the subject is discussed and find the correct answer.
- Some people find using an index-card file helpful. They create a file of index cards containing definitions, formulas, important facts, and answers to key questions. These cards are helpful when reviewing for a test.

✔ **Reading Check Decision Making** What factors will improve your study skills? Which study skills work best for you? Study skills will improve by studying in a quiet place, taking notes, using the textbook's study guides, summarizing, answering review questions, and creating review cards. Answers will vary.

## ★ Participating in Class

When you go to class, bring the materials you will need to take an active part in that day's lesson. Pay careful attention to what is being taught in class. Think about the lessons and do not be afraid to ask questions. Learn to form your own ideas and opinions. If you fall behind or fail to understand part of a lesson, ask for help.

If you come to class unprepared, neither you nor your classmates will benefit from what you might have contributed. A class is like any group that depends on each member to function at its best. The group performs well when everyone does his or her part. The group performs poorly if its members fail to carry out their responsibilities.

✔ **Reading Check Identifying Cause and Effect** What is class participation, and how does it affect your classmates? Class participation means taking an active part in class; it affects classmates positively if students come to class prepared and negatively if they are unprepared.

## ★ How to Do Well on Tests

When preparing to take a test, review your notes carefully. Some students find it helpful to have classmates ask them questions that might appear on the test. This review process helps them discover whether they really know the material.

When taking a test, it is a good idea to read each question carefully before trying to answer it. Before you begin, look over the

## REVIEW AND ASSESS

Have students complete the **Section 2 Review** on page 353. Then have students complete **Daily Quiz 14.2**. As **Alternative Assessment**, you may want to use the paragraph about their ideal school or the resumé activities in this section's lessons.

## RETEACH

Have students complete **Main Idea Activity for English Language Learners and Special-Needs Students 14.2**. Then organize students into three groups and assign each group one of this section's objectives. Have groups create a political cartoon that illustrates the main idea behind their assigned objective.

**ENGLISH LANGUAGE LEARNERS , COOPERATIVE LEARNING**

## EXTEND

Have students research the No Child Left Behind Act signed by President George W. Bush in 2001. After discussing the act, ask each student to conduct additional research and write a position paper concerning the right of parents and students to obtain supplemental educational services from the public school system or a private sector provider.

**BLOCK SCHEDULING**

---

entire test. How many questions are there, and how much time should be spent on each question? If there is time left at the end of the test period, reread your answers. Also check carefully that you have answered each question to the best of your ability.

✔ **Reading Check Finding the Main Idea** What skills can help you succeed on tests? Students should review their notes carefully, work with other students to review the material, read questions carefully and budget time, answer questions to the best of their ability, and reread answers if time is left.

### ★ Taking Part in Activities

School is more than classes, homework, tests, and class projects. School clubs, student government, sports teams, cheerleading, drama, dances, and other social events are also part of your education. These **extracurricular activities**—activities you participate in outside of the classroom—can teach you how to work with others toward a goal.

Extracurricular activities add to your fun in school. At the same time, they help you develop your own special abilities and interests. You may learn new skills or new ways to express yourself. You may also make new friends. In addition, your involvement in extracurricular activities may help you gain admission to college or aid you in getting scholarships.

Students who take part in class work and activities are not satisfied by merely showing up and "getting by" in school. They know that they must be active participants in school to gain a rewarding education and the opportunities that provide for a richer future.

✔ **Reading Check Drawing Inferences and Conclusions** How might extracurricular activities enhance your educational experience? They teach you to work with others, help to develop your personal abilities and interests, provide opportunities to make new friends, and to have fun.

*Marching band is a popular extracurricular activity at many schools.*

---

## SECTION 2 Review

**go.hrw.com**
**Homework Practice Online**
keyword: SZ3 HP14

1. **Define** and explain:
   • extracurricular activities

2. **Categorizing** Copy the chart below. Then use it to identify the seven goals of education and give one example of each goal in action at your school.

| Goal | Example |
|------|---------|
| 1. | |
| 2. | |
| 3. | |
| 4. | |
| 5. | |
| 6. | |
| 7. | |

3. **Finding the Main Idea**
   a. What can you do to improve your performance in school?
   b. How can you best prepare for tests?

4. **Writing and Critical Thinking**
   **Supporting a Point of View** Write a persuasive paragraph explaining how extracurricular activities are valuable sources of learning.

   **Consider:**
   • the skills that extracurricular activities teach
   • the value of working with other students in these activities

---

## Section 2 Review
### ANSWERS

**1. Define**
• extracurricular activities, p. 353

**2.** Schools work to teach students basic skills in reading, writing, math, and citizenship; to be cooperative with students, family, and community members; and to practice good health habits. They provde students with the educational foundation to become skilled workers and good citizens, to behave in a considerate manner toward others in school and the community, and to use leisure time wisely. Students' answers will vary.

**3. a.** Find the right balance between time spent studying, participating in school activities, exercising, relaxing, and sleeping; study in a quiet place with proper materials, take notes, use the textbook's study aids, note topic sentences and summarizing paragraphs, answer the questions at the end of each section, and create a card file that can later be used to study for tests.

**b.** Review notes carefully, work with other students to review, read questions carefully and budget time, and reread answers if time is left.

**4.** Students' paragraphs will vary but should include opportunities for learning, fun, development of special interests and abilities, and socializing experiences.

# SECTION 3

## OBJECTIVES

*After completing Section 3, students should be able to*

1 **Describe how learning relates to experience.**

2 **Determine the steps involved in critical thinking.**

3 **Describe how people can be influenced by the thinking of others and explain the need to think for yourself.**

## 🔊 LET'S GET STARTED!

Write the term *motivation* on the board and ask students to explain its meaning. *(Students might suggest that it has something to do with "motor.")* Tell students that the Latin root, *movere*, means "to move" and is used in other words, such as motor or motion. Now ask students to break down the word *prejudice* by separating it into parts: *-pre*, meaning "before" and *judice*, meaning "judgment." Discuss with students that pre-judging someone often leads to incorrect and uninformed conclusions. Finally, have students break apart the word *insight* "seeing within." Tell students that in Section 3 they will learn about how learning takes place, how we think, and the need to think for ourselves.

# SECTION 3

## Developing Your Life Skills

### Read to Discover

1. How are learning and experience related?
2. What are the steps involved in thinking critically?
3. How can people be influenced by others' thinking, and why should people learn to think for themselves?

### Define

- experience
- conditioning
- habit
- motivation
- insight
- creativity
- critical thinking
- prejudice

### WHY CIVICS MATTERS

Social scientists study how people learn. Use **CNNfyi.com** or other **current events** sources to find out more about recent research on learning. Record your findings in your journal.

## Reading Focus

A main purpose of education is to teach people life skills, such as how to think. The dictionary tells us that to think is to form ideas in the mind. This sounds simple enough, but how do we form these ideas?

We start by gathering information. When faced with a problem, thinking people try to consider all the facts. They then consider possible solutions and their consequences. Then they decide which solution seems best. How do we obtain the facts we need? We learn them.

### ⭐ How We Learn

Almost everything we do—the way we act, think, pass along information, even the way we show emotion—is learned. People learn in many ways. However, all learning is the result of some kind of **experience,** or the direct observation of or participation in events.

The simplest kind of learning is the result of experience that involves the motor nerves—those nerves that control muscles. For example, you will pull back your hand from a hot stove because of the pain. Next time you will avoid a hot stove. Now suppose someone said "Hot!" when you were reaching for the stove. In the future, that warning will cause you to draw back your hand when near a stove. This kind of learning is called **conditioning.**

Much of our behavior, or the way we act, is conditioned. People learn to do things because they expect to be rewarded or to gain satisfaction. Children will wash their hands before meals if they expect to

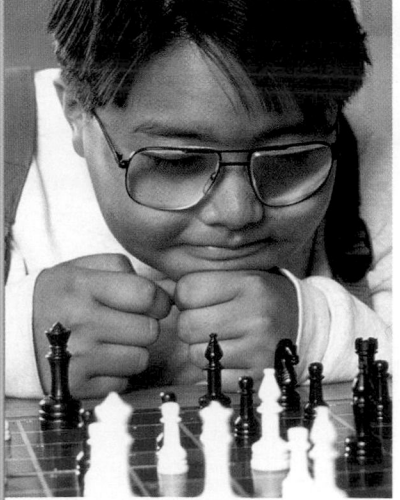

*Chess requires careful observation, logic, and the ability to anticipate possible events.*

**LEVEL 1:** Lead a class discussion about how learning relates to experience. *(Learning results from some kind of experience or from the direct observation of or participation in events.)* Explain to students that habits are conditioned responses, actions that we perform automatically without thinking. Ask students to list examples of habits on the chalkboard—both positive and negative. Referring to the list of habits on the chalkboard, ask students what could be done to change the negative habits to positive ones. **ENGLISH LANGUAGE LEARNERS**

**LEVELS 1 AND 2:** Explain that a computer programmer learns how to create a computer program in part by relying on her or his experience in working on other programs. Solutions to special problems in creating a new program, however, often come from insight. Organize students into pairs and ask each pair to think of other specific examples that illustrate the relationship between learning, experience, and insight. Pairs should illustrate and present their examples to the class.
**ENGLISH LANGUAGE LEARNERS , COOPERATIVE LEARNING**

**LEVEL 3:** Organize the class into small groups and have each group write a script for a play illustrating the positive and negative consequences of imitating others. Ask for volunteers to either read or act out their group's script.

receive praise or a hug. They will continue to behave in the desired way if they are rewarded occasionally. Behavior that is often repeated usually becomes a **habit**—an action that is performed automatically without thinking.

People also learn by copying, or imitating, others. Young children imitate their parents or guardians and other members of their family. They repeat their family's opinions and habits. As adults, people often imitate their friends and others they admire.

✔ **Reading Check** Finding the Main Idea How is experience related to learning? All learning is a direct result of some kind of experience.

## ★ Learning in School

Much of what we know is also learned by looking and listening. Every day of our lives we learn through our senses and by taking in different kinds of information. We also learn by role-playing—imagining ourselves in a particular place, time, or job. In today's complex society, there is an overflow of information. This information has to be organized, or arranged in groups, to be usable. A large part of the organized information we learn is taught in school and in books. We also learn from what we see on television or on the Internet.

Schools teach students how to best use information by analyzing and putting facts together and by drawing conclusions about the facts. They also teach students where to find information.

The ability to learn depends on maturity, experience, and intelligence. It also depends on a person's degree of motivation. **Motivation** is the internal drive that pushes people to achieve their goals and directs their behavior and attitudes.

✔ **Reading Check** Summarizing What factors affect the ability to learn?
maturity, experience, intelligence, and motivation

### Interpreting the Visual Record

**Learning** *Subjects such as math have complex sets of rules and principles that must be learned in order to use the skills successfully.* **How are these students working together with their teacher to learn?**

### Interdisciplinary Connection

▶ **Psychology** ◀

**Pavlov's Experiment**
Russian physiologist Ivan Pavlov's experiment involved classical conditioning, in which the critical part of the conditioning occurs before the response. The stimulus actually causes the response. Psychologist B.F. Skinner believed that our personalities are the result of what we learn. This theory, called operant conditioning, states that the critical part of the conditioning occurs after the response—determined by what kind of reinforcement is given. The reinforcement determines whether the response will occur again.

**CRITICAL THINKING**

Ask students to reflect on the kinds of reinforcement they give family members or friends and how changes can be made to achieve better relationships.

**ANSWER:** Students' answers will vary.

### Visual Record Answer

*Students might suggest that the students are working cooperatively with the teacher to learn math skills.*

**ALL LEVELS:** Lead the class in a discussion on the steps involved in critical thinking. Then organize the class into small groups and distribute newspapers to each group. Have groups locate articles on current local or state problems. Tell students to gather information about one of the problems and then to apply the steps for critical thinking to reach some conclusions about possible solutions. (*The critical thinking steps include defining the issue, distinguishing fact from opinion, weighing the evidence, and reaching a conclusion.*) Groups might summarize this activity in a flowchart. Ask volunteers to share their group's findings with the class. **ENGLISH LANGUAGE LEARNERS , COOPERATIVE LEARNING**

**LEVELS 2 AND 3:** After discussing the steps involved in critical thinking, ask students if any are in the process of making important decisions in their life, such as what college they should go to, whether to pursue college or some other form of advanced training, or whether to go to work after graduating from high school. Ask students to list their options and to write positive and negative consequences for each choice. Then have them share their choices and consequences with a classmate or with you to get feedback or possibly consider some other options or consequences. Then have them write a paragraph explaining why one option might be better than the others. **COOPERATIVE LEARNING**

## The ★ Democratic Process

**Political Views** Researchers studying the influences on adolescents' political views have found few clear patterns. Although political views of parents do influence those of their children, such influence is believed to be limited. The political views of young people often diverge from those of their parents. Many researchers agree that once political views are established in adolescence, however, those views tend to remain stable over time.

### CRITICAL THINKING

Develop a public opinion poll that would compare students' political views to those of their parents. Conduct the poll and compute the findings. Ask students what other factors might influence their political philosophy.

**ANSWER:** Student answers will vary but might include friends, teachers, or the media.

### Visual Record Answer

*Students might suggest that the person in the picture is using the visual arts medium to express her creativity.*

**Interpreting the Visual Record**

**Creativity** *Artistic expression is one of the most obvious examples of creativity at work.* **What method is this student using to express her creativity?**

## ★ How We Think

Thinking is a complex process. It involves awareness, understanding, and interpretation of what we see and know. We are thinking when we solve problems by considering all possible solutions.

Sometimes we cannot find an answer, no matter how hard we try. Then, suddenly, the answer will spring to mind. This is called **insight.** The answer seems to come out of nowhere. Actually, it comes to mind only after we have studied the problem and ruled out several possible answers. Without realizing it, people often take their own knowledge and apply it to the problem they are trying to solve.

Sometimes the solutions we come up with are original. The ability to find new ways of thinking and doing things is called **creativity.** Everyone can think creatively. We have other thinking abilities as well. Other ways of thinking include the abilities to reason, question, and weigh information.

✔ **Reading Check Comparing** What roles do insight and creativity play in the thinking process? insight—people take knowledge and apply it to a problem; creativity—people come up with original solutions to problems

## ★ Critical Thinking

There is no simple way to learn the truth about an issue or to solve a problem. The search for the truth about many subjects is long and hard. How can we learn to think clearly in order to find solutions and make decisions? The kind of thinking we do to reach decisions and solve problems is called **critical thinking.** This type of reasoning, or clear thinking, is made up of a number of steps.

**Defining the Issue** The first step is to make sure that the issue or question is clearly defined in your mind. That is, you need to make certain that you fully understand it and any terms that might be involved. You may find it helpful to write down the issue or question. If it is a difficult one, you might outline the main ideas. Look for relationships between the ideas. Are some of the ideas causes and others effects?

**Distinguishing Fact from Opinion** Once you have determined the question, look for evidence that will help you understand and judge the issues involved. What are the facts? It may surprise you to discover that there are often disagreements about facts. One side may say one thing, and the other side may claim something very different. Therefore, it is important in critical thinking to always distinguish between fact and opinion.

To illustrate how difficult it can be to determine what is fact, consider the following example. A newspaper reporter may write that a person "angrily pounded on a neighbor's door until he broke it down." The

# TEACH OBJECTIVE 3

**ALL LEVELS:** Tell students how people can be influenced by the thoughts of others and explain the need to think for oneself. Then copy the following graphic organizer onto the chalkboard, omitting the italicized answers. Ask students to complete the organizer by filling in the choices.
**ENGLISH LANGUAGE LEARNERS**

## CLOSE

Have students write autobiographical sketches of how they see themselves in their mid-twenties, incorporating examples of how they might apply the thinking skills described in this section.

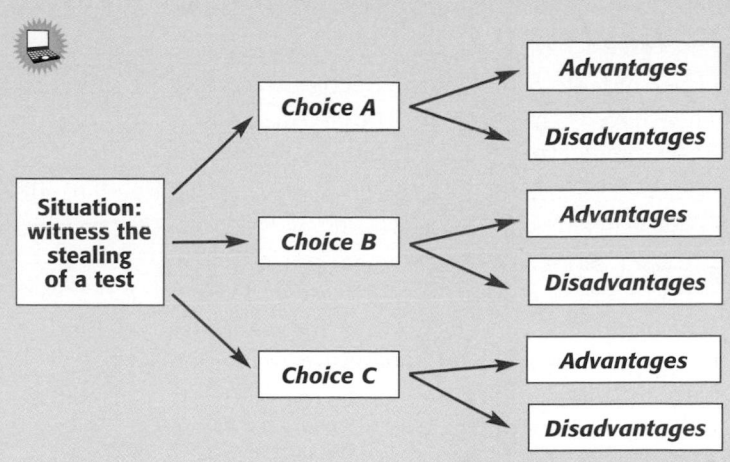

fact that the door pounding took place can be proved. Several witnesses may have seen it. But was the person angry? This is the reporter's judgment. The person may have pounded on the door not in anger, but to warn the neighbor of a fire.

A person's emotions, such as anger or happiness, are difficult to judge or measure accurately. Therefore, it is important to always distinguish between facts and information colored by judgments.

**Weighing the Evidence** In thinking through an issue, it also is important to learn to weigh all the evidence. Are the facts provided the facts you need to know? Are important facts missing? Have you studied all the tables, graphs, maps, and other available sources? In learning to think clearly, you must also learn to judge whether the given facts fit the problem. You must learn to judge which side of the argument the facts seem to support.

**Reaching a Conclusion** After you have weighed the evidence, you can reach your own conclusion. Try to keep an open mind. Remember that if new evidence is found, it may be necessary to change your conclusion.

Sometimes there is more than one possible answer to a question or solution to a problem. In trying to decide which solution is best, you may want to test how each solution might work. You may do this by mentally checking the facts against each possible solution. You might imagine the problem in a real-life setting. Determine which of the possible solutions would work best in such a situation. Knowing which solution is most appropriate to the circumstances is an important part of making decisions and solving problems.

✔ **Reading Check Summarizing** What are the steps involved in thinking critically? defining the issue, distinguishing fact from opinion, weighing the evidence, reaching a conclusion

## ⭐ Who Influences Your Thinking?

Critical thinking also demands that you realize how other people influence your thinking. How much does what others say or do influence you?

No one can do our thinking for us. However, other people do help determine what we think. Families, teachers, and friends have a great influence on our opinions. Sometimes we are influenced by some well-known person we admire. As you recall, we also receive ideas from the mass media. Many of these ideas are propaganda. That is, they are used to try to influence us.

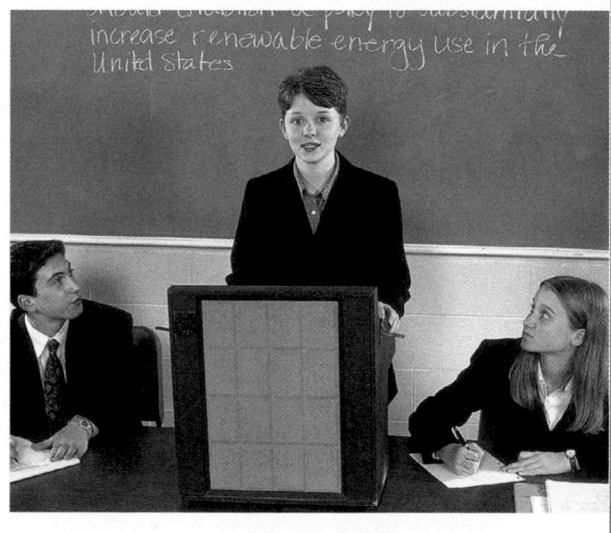

**Interpreting the Visual Record**

**Influencing opinions** *Abilities such as evaluating facts, forming arguments, and persuading others are essential to success for activities such as debate.* **How might these skills be useful in other activities?**

**Visual Record Answer**

*Students' responses will vary.*

# REVIEW AND ASSESS

Have students complete the **Section 3 Review** on page 358. Then have them complete **Daily Quiz 14.3**. As **Alternative Assessment**, you may want to use the critical thinking-flowchart activity or the autobiographical sketch found in this section's lessons.

# RETEACH

Have students complete **Main Idea Activity for English Language Learners and Special-Needs Students 14.3**. Then have students outline this section, emphasizing the key points.
**ENGLISH LANGUAGE LEARNERS**

# EXTEND

Organize students into small groups and have each group conduct research at the library to obtain information about one of the four types of learning: classical conditioning, operant conditioning, social learning, and the cognitive approach. Have students share their findings with the class. Then have each group perform a socio-drama, acting out each type of learning so that the other students can get a visual image of that learning process. **BLOCK SCHEDULING** , **COOPERATIVE LEARNING**

## Section 3 Review
### ANSWERS

**1. Define**
• experience, p. 354
• conditioning, p. 354
• habit, p. 355
• motivation, p. 355
• insight, p. 356
• creativity, p. 356
• critical thinking, p. 356
• prejudice, p. 358

**2.** Answers will vary but could include children learning to cover their mouths when they yawn for a reward of a hug or other sign of approval.

**3. a.** insight is a sudden answer to a problem that comes to mind only after the mind has studied the problem and ruled out other possible answers; creativity is the ability to find new ways of thinking and doing things.

**b.** The steps involved in critical thinking are defining the issue, distinguishing fact from opinion, weighing the evidence, and reaching a conclusion.

**4.** Students should consider that families, teachers, friends, mass media, and members of particular groups may influence people's opinions, potentially leading to prejudice. Individual thinking allows you to vote wisely, understand current issues, and solve problems.

*Our system of government relies on the active participation of educated, clear-thinking citizens.*

Sometimes people think and behave in certain ways because they are members of particular groups in society. In a labor dispute, for example, employers may have opinions that differ from those of workers.

Because of these influences, people often have opinions that favor one side or the other. Few people can be impartial, or completely objective, all the time. All of us have certain fixed feelings, or prejudices. **Prejudice** is an opinion that is not based on a careful and reasonable investigation of the facts. We must be careful not to be ruled by our prejudices or those of others.

✔ **Reading Check** Identifying Cause and Effect  Who might influence your opinions, and what negative effect could this influence have?
family, teachers, friends, well-known people we admire, mass media; lack of objectivity

## ★ Think for Yourself

You live in a country that values and constitutionally protects the freedom of independent thought and expression. Take advantage of this freedom to learn how to think for yourself. Study the way that you make decisions. Try to be objective and free from unfair bias in your judgments. Learn how to gather information and how to interpret it. Most importantly, believe in yourself enough to arrive at and stand by your own conclusions.

Our system of government only works if citizens think for themselves and do not simply accept what others tell them. Your school can help you learn to think critically. When you examine information you acquire in class and make up your own mind, you will acquire key life skills. You need these skills to vote wisely, understand current issues, and solve problems.

✔ **Reading Check** Summarizing  Why is it important to think for yourself?
so you can vote wisely, understand current issues, and solve problems with reasoned judgement

---

## SECTION 3 Review

**go.hrw.com Homework Practice Online**
keyword: SZ3 HP14

**1. Define** and explain:
• experience
• conditioning
• habit
• motivation
• insight
• creativity
• critical thinking
• prejudice

**2. Summarizing** Copy the graphic organizer below. Then use it to demonstrate the relationship between learning and experience.

☐ → ☐

**3. Finding the Main Idea**
a. What role do insight and creativity play in the thinking process?
b. How does one learn to think critically?

**4. Writing and Critical Thinking**
**Supporting a Point of View** Why should you learn to think for yourself? Give an example of a situation in which thinking for yourself would be important.

**Consider:**
• the influence of others on your opinions
• the functioning of our country

## TEACH

**ALL LEVELS:** After discussing how to distinguish fact from opinion, distribute copies of newspapers to each student. Have students locate an article that illustrates the distinguishing of fact from opinion. Using a highlighter, have students mark the information that answers the questions *who, what, where, when,* and *how.* Then have students, using a different-color highlighter, mark any loaded words that carry an emotional appeal. Finally, have students circle phrases that change a statement from a fact to an opinion. When they are finished, have students mount their articles on a colored sheet of paper and display them around the classroom. Ask students to circulate around the room, reading the articles, and noting which articles are more factual and which ones contain loaded words and opinions. **ENGLISH LANGUAGE LEARNERS**

**LEVEL 3:** Have students write 10 statements that might appear in a political campaign, some of which are fact and some of which are opinion. Then have students exchange papers. Ask each student to categorize as fact or opinion the statements made in the other student's list. Papers should then be returned to their originators to be "graded." **COOPERATIVE LEARNING**

# Civics Skills
## WORKSHOP

## Distinguishing Fact from Opinion

One of the keys to evaluating what you read and hear is the ability to distinguish between fact and opinion. A fact is something that can be proven. Facts can be counted, measured, or documented in some way. In contrast, opinions are personal beliefs about what is true. Because people often use facts to support their opinions, it is important to learn how to distinguish between the two.

## How to Distinguish Fact from Opinion

1. **Determine if the information can be proved.** You can begin to identify facts by asking the same questions a reporter uses to write a good news story. If the information answers the questions *who, what, when, where,* or *how,* it probably contains facts. Next, determine if these facts can be documented, perhaps through other types of sources. Facts can be verified. Opinions cannot be proven.

2. **Note how the facts are used.** Keep in mind that a single word can often change a statement from fact to opinion. Certain phrases, such as "In our judgment . . . ," "I believe that . . . ," or "I think that . . . ," clearly signal that the speaker or writer is about to give an opinion.

3. **Identify loaded words.** Loaded words are words that carry an emotional appeal, such as *beautiful, boring, exciting,* and *extremely.* These descriptive words signal an opinion because they express the speaker's or writer's personal viewpoint. Do not allow loaded words to color your judgment about the facts.

## Applying the Skill

Read the campaign flyer below. Then answer the questions that follow.

1. If you were a reporter writing an article on Green's campaign, what information from the flyer would you include in your news story as being factual? Explain why you chose this information.

2. Use the information in the flyer to write a brief editorial about Green that includes the key issues that she is interested in.

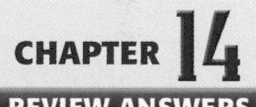

**JANICE GREEN FOR CITY COUNCIL**

**Janice Green** is determined to improve our city. If elected Green will:

★ **Increase** the number of buses running during rush hour. Thirty percent of public buses do not run during rush hour.

★ **Ensure** that our city taxes are reasonable. Over the past 10 years, city taxes have been increased six times.

★ **Add** to and improve facilities for the elderly. At present, there are over 100 persons waiting to take part in this city's programs for the elderly.

Janice Green knows our city well. She is a dedicated educator who has served successfully on the school board for more than 12 years.

**Elect Janice Green**
She will make this a better city in which to live!

## SKILLS ANSWERS

1. Reporters would first have to verify the accuracy of the flyer's statements. If their accuracy is verified, the following statements are facts: Thirty percent of public buses do not run during rush hour; city taxes have increased six times over a 10-year period; more than 100 people are waiting to take part in the city's programs for the elderly; Green has served on the school board for more than 12 years.

2. Students should make careful use of the facts to support their opinions and to influence the opinions of others.

## CHAPTER 14
### REVIEW ANSWERS

**Define and Identify**
1. community colleges, p. 344
2. graduate school, p. 345
3. mainstreaming, p. 346
4. extracurricular activities, p. 353
5. conditioning, p. 354
6. motivation, p. 355
7. insight, p. 356
8. creativity, p. 356
9. critical thinking, p. 356
10. prejudice, p. 358

**REPRODUCIBLE**
► Chapter 14 Review, pp. 360–61
► Vocabulary Activity 14
► Chapter 14 Tutorial for Students, Parents, Mentors, and Peers
► Chapter 14 Test (Form A or B)
► Alternative Assessment Handbook

**TECHNOLOGY**
► Chapter 14 Test Generator (on the One-Stop Planner)
► Global Skill Builder CD–ROM
► HRW Go site

**REINFORCEMENT, REVIEW, AND ASSESSMENT**
► Chapter 14 Test for English Language Learners and Special-Needs Students

**REVIEW**
Have students complete the **Chapter 14 Review** on pages 360–61.

**ASSESS**
Use one of the chapter tests to assess students' understanding of the content. For **Alternative Assessment**, see the **Alternative Assessment Handbook.**

## Understanding Main Ideas

**1.** They believe that individuals should have the opportunity to develop their abilities and talents and that young citizens should be taught how to contribute to society

**2.** Public schools were first started in Massachusetts in 1647. In the early 1800s, leaders such as Horace Mann worked to establish a public-school system for all children. By the time of the Civil War, tax-supported elementary schools were becoming more common, but public high schools were uncommon until the late 1800s.

**3.** Finding the right balance between time spent studying, participating in school activities, exercising, relaxing, and sleeping will help students produce better quality schoolwork. Study skills will improve by studying in a quiet place with the proper materials, taking notes, using the textbook's study guides, noting topic sentences and summarizing paragraphs, re-reading and taking notes on the assigned text, answering the questions at the end of each section, and creating a card file that can later be used to study for tests.

**4.** Extracurricular activities teach you to work with others toward a goal, add to fun in school, help to develop your personal abilities and interests, give you new skills or ways to express yourself, and provide opportunities to make new friends.

**5.** The steps involved in critical thinking are defining the issue, distinguishing fact from opinion, weighing the evidence, and reaching a conclusion.

# Chapter 14 Review

## Chapter Summary

### Section 1

* The U.S. educational system is multi-leveled, beginning at preschool and ending with higher education in college or graduate school.
* Americans support core educational values, including free public education.
* The U.S. educational system faces many challenges, including violence in schools and low test scores in some subjects.

### Section 2

* Educators have developed seven educational goals that schools should try to meet. Most schools should teach basic skills, cooperation, health education, citizenship, job and life skills, manners, and the wise use of leisure time.
* Learning how to study, taking part in class work, studying for tests, and participating in activities are all key parts of getting an education.

### Section 3

* Two of the most important skills taught in school are how to learn and think clearly.
* Thinking for yourself is an important citizenship skill. In learning to think for yourself, you need to consider how opinions are formed.
* You must also be aware that people are sometimes biased because they are members of particular groups in society.

## Define and Identify
Use the following terms in complete sentences.

1. community colleges
2. graduate school
3. mainstreaming
4. extracurricular activities
5. conditioning
6. motivation
7. insight
8. creativity
9. critical thinking
10. prejudice

## Understanding Main Ideas

**Section 1** *(Pages 341–48)*
1. What are the two main reasons Americans value education?
2. Where did public schooling begin in the United States, and when did it become widespread?

**Section 2** *(Pages 349–53)*
3. What approaches to learning and studying will make you more successful in school?
4. How can extracurricular activities enhance your education?

**Section 3** *(Pages 354–58)*
5. What must a student do to develop and exercise critical thinking skills?
6. What are the benefits of thinking through problems and issues for yourself?

## What Did You Find Out?

1. How were children educated in the United States before the development of public schools?
2. What goals guide public schools?
3. How do people develop critical thinking and other life skills?

## Thinking Critically

1. **Drawing Inferences and Conclusions** Why do you think some families wish to educate their children at home? What might be the advantages and disadvantages of doing so?
2. **Problem Solving** As you have learned, efforts are being made to reform the U.S. educational system. What problems does the educational system currently face, and what recommendations would you make to reform American education?
3. **Supporting a Point of View** Which do you think is more important to the learning process—critical thinking or creative thinking? Explain your answer, using examples of each type of thinking.

## RETEACH

Organize students into three groups and assign each group one of the chapter's sections. Have each group create a visual presentation illustrating the main objectives in their assigned section. Have each group present its work to the class.

**ENGLISH LANGUAGE LEARNERS ,**
**COOPERATIVE LEARNING**

## Portfolio Extensions

**1. Linking to Community** Invite a representative from an area junior college or university to speak to your class concerning opportunities for higher education and what students can do now to prepare for the rigors of college academics. Ask students to prepare a list of questions they think might be beneficial for the representative to answer.

**2. Interdisciplinary Connection to Language Arts** Explain to students that one effective method of taking notes is called Cornell notetaking, which helps maximize learning in the classroom. Ask students to conduct research to learn more about Cornell notetaking. Then have volunteers instruct the class on its use and background.

**STANDARDIZED TEST PREP ONLINE**
keyword: SZ3 STP14

### Interpreting Political Cartoons

Study the political cartoon below. Then answer the questions that follow.

Bruce Beattie, ©2001 Daytona Beach News-Journal, Copley News Service

1. What is the young man in the cartoon doing?
   a. Playing games instead of doing his homework.
   b. Using the Internet to do research.
   c. Using the Internet to download answers to a school assignment.
   d. Talking to another student using the computer.
2. Which of the following is not an appropriate way to use the Internet for research?
   a. Looking up current economic information on a government Web site.
   b. Copying a research paper from the Internet.
   c. Reading news stories on a news Web site.
   d. Looking up a presidential speech in a historical archive.
3. What message do you think the cartoonist is trying to present about the use of the Internet for schoolwork? Do you agree or disagree with this message? Explain your answer.

### Analyzing Primary Sources

Read the following quotation from former National Education Association president Bob Chase. Then answer the questions that follow.

"While American society has changed enormously in recent decades, children's needs have not changed at all. Children still crave the security of knowing someone really cares about them and will be there for them. . . . Now, we have come a long way from the days when the message from the school to the parent was: 'You raise them, and we will teach them.' But we still have much further to go. Too many schools are still too isolated from the families and communities that they serve. . . . When schools work together with families to support learning, very good things happen. Student attitudes, attendance, homework, and report cards improve. . . . Teachers and parents, my friends! We're two peas from the same pod. And if we work together, there is no telling how much our children will achieve!"

4. Which of the following statements best represents Chase's point of view?
   a. Parents and schools have separate responsibilities and should interact little.
   b. Changes in society have made it impossible for schools to educate children.
   c. Parents and teachers need to work together to ensure the best possible education for America's youth.
   d. Families are more important than schools.
5. Why do you think Chase referred to parents and teachers as "peas from the same pod"?

6. Individual thinking helps prevent prejudice and allows you to vote wisely, understand current issues, and solve problems.

### What Did You Find Out?
1. Some students had private tutors or went to private schools, but many children received little or no schooling.

2. Schools work to teach students basic skills in reading, writing, math, and citizenship; to be cooperative with students, family, and community, and to practice good health habits. They also teach students how to become skilled workers and good citizens, to be considerate of others, and to make wise use of leisure time.

3. All learning is the result of experience—the direct observation of or participation in events—which takes place inside and outside of school.

### Thinking Critically
1. Students may mention the advantage of individual attention and the disadvantage of a lack of interaction with other students.

2. Students might mention the distribution of resources, the challenges of improving American students' performance in math, reading, and science, and creating a safe school environment.

3. Students' responses will vary.

### Social Studies Skills
1. c

2. b

3. Students' responses will vary.

4. c

5. Students might suggest that he meant that parents and teachers share the same goal of educating and molding children.

---

### Building Your Portfolio

**Cooperative Learning**
With a group, interview older members of your families to learn about their school experiences. What courses were required? What problems were present in the schools? What extracurricular activities were available? Based on the responses, each group member should write a paragraph comparing being a student today to earlier times. Collect your group's work into an anthology titled Working for a Diploma: Then and Now.

**internet** connect

**Internet Activity: go.hrw.com**
**keyword: SZ3 AC14**

Access the Internet through the HRW Go site to research different ways of studying and preparing for tests. Then choose one method you found in your research and prepare a short report or oral presentation that describes the method and explains why you think it could be effective and useful.

go.hrw.com

# CHAPTER 15

# Citizenship in the Community

## CHAPTER RESOURCE MANAGER

| | Objectives | Pacing Guide | Reproducible Resources |
|---|---|---|---|
| **SECTION 1:**<br>**Kinds of Communities**<br>(pp. 363–68) | ★ Describe how transportation, resources, and climate affect the location of communities.<br>★ Identify the kinds of communities that exist in rural areas.<br>★ Explain what both an urban area and a metropolitan area are. | **Regular**<br>1.5 days<br><br>**Block Scheduling**<br>1 day<br><br>*Block Scheduling Handbook with Team Teaching Strategies, Chapter 15* | **RS** Guided Reading Strategies 15.1<br>**E** Challenge and Enrichment Worksheet 15: Making a Profile of Your Community<br>**E** Creative Teaching Strategy: Open-Ended Statements |
| **SECTION 2:**<br>**Purposes of Communities**<br>(pp. 369–72) | ★ Identify the different methods of communication used in communities.<br>★ Examine how communities help people enjoy their lives.<br>★ Explain why local communities need laws and regulations. | **Regular**<br>2 days<br><br>**Block Scheduling**<br>1 day<br><br>*Block Scheduling Handbook with Team Teaching Strategies, Chapter 15* | **RS** Guided Reading Strategies 15.2 |
| **SECTION 3:**<br>**Citizens Serve Communities**<br>(pp. 374–77) | ★ Identify the challenges that American communities face.<br>★ Evaluate how volunteer groups improve the communities in which we live.<br>★ Analyze how good citizenship is related to developing good communities. | **Regular**<br>3 days<br><br>**Block Scheduling**<br>1 day<br><br>*Block Scheduling Handbook with Team Teaching Strategies, Chapter 15* | **RS** Guided Reading Strategies 15.3<br>**SM** Community Service and Participation Handbook: Host a Special Olympian<br>**RS** Graphic Organizer Activity: Doing Your Part |

## Chapter Resource Key

| | | | | | |
|---|---|---|---|---|---|
| **PS** | Primary Sources | **SM** | Skills Mastery |  | CD-ROM |
| **RS** | Reading Support | **A** | Assessment |  | Video |
| **IC** | Interdisciplinary Connections | **REV** | Review |  | Internet |
| **E** | Enrichment | **ELL** | Reinforcement and English Language Learners | | Holt Presentation Maker Using Microsoft® PowerPoint® |
| | | | Transparencies | | |

 **One-Stop** Planner CD–ROM

**See the *One-Stop Planner* for a complete list of additional resources for students and teachers.**

**One-Stop** Planner CD–ROM

It's easy to plan lessons, select resources, and print out materials for your students when you use the **One-Stop Planner CD–ROM with Test Generator**.

| Technology Resources | Reinforcement, Review, and Assessment |
|---|---|
| One-Stop Planner, Lesson 15.1 | **REV** Section 1 Review, p. 368 |
| **CNN** Presents: American Government | **A** Daily Quiz 15.1 |
| Homework Practice Online | **A** Main Idea Activity 15.1 |
| HRW Go site | **A** English Audio Summary 15.1 |
| | **A** Spanish Audio Summary 15.1 |
| One-Stop Planner, Lesson 15.2 | **REV** Section 2 Review, p. 372 |
| Homework Practice Online | **A** Daily Quiz 15.2 |
| | **A** Main Idea Activity 15.2 |
| | **A** English Audio Summary 15.2 |
| | **A** Spanish Audio Summary 15.2 |
| One-Stop Planner, Lesson 15.3 | **REV** Section 3 Review, p. 377 |
| Holt Researcher CD–ROM | **A** Daily Quiz 15.3 |
| Citizenship Skills Videocassette Segment 1: The Roles of a Citizen | **A** Main Idea Activity 15.3 |
| Homework Practice Online | **ELL** English Audio Summary 15.3 |
| | **ELL** Spanish Audio Summary 15.3 |

## Meeting Individual Needs

### Ability Levels

**Level 1** Basic-level activities designed for all students encountering new material

**Level 2** Intermediate-level activities designed for average students

**Level 3** Challenging activities designed for honors and gifted-and-talented students

**English Language Learners** Activities that address the needs of students with Limited English Proficiency

## 🔲 internet connect

**HRW ONLINE RESOURCES**
GO TO: go.hrw.com
Then type in the keyword.

**TEACHER HOME PAGE**
KEYWORD: SZ3 Teacher

**CHAPTER INTERNET ACTIVITIES**
KEYWORD: SZ3 AC15
Choose an activity to:
• create a plan to volunteer in your community.
• create thematic graphs and charts on demographic information on your community or state.
• create an annotated diagram on sources of revenue for your local government.

**CHAPTER ENRICHMENT LINKS**
KEYWORD: SZ3 CH15

**ONLINE ASSESSMENT**
**Homework Practice**
KEYWORD: SZ3 HP15
**Rubrics**
KEYWORD: SS Rubrics

**ONLINE MAPS, CHARTS, AND GRAPHS**
KEYWORD: SZ3 MCG
• The Purposes of Communities

**HOLT PRESENTATION MAKER**
KEYWORD: SZ3 PPT15

**CONTENT UPDATES**
KEYWORD: SS Content Updates

**ONLINE READING SUPPORT**
KEYWORD: SS Strategies

**CURRENT EVENTS**
KEYWORD: S3 Current Events

## Chapter Review and Assessment

| | |
|---|---|
| **IC** | Vocabulary Activity 15 |
|  | Global Skill Builder CD–ROM |
| | HRW Go site |
| **REV** | Chapter 15 Tutorial for Students, Parents, Mentors, and Peers |
| **REV** | Chapter 15 Review, pp. 378–79 |
| **A** | Standardized Test Practice |
| **A** | Chapter 15 Test Generator (on the One-Stop Planner) |
| **A** | Chapter 15 Test (Form A or B) |
| **A** | Alternative Assessment Handbook |
| **A** | Chapter 15 Test for English Language Learners and Special-Needs Students |

## Internet Activity

**Abolitionists**

✈ **internet** connect

**TOPIC:** Abolitionist Newspapers
**GO TO:** go.hrw.com
**KEYWORD:** SZ3 AC15

Have students access the Internet through the HRW Go site to conduct research about the influence of abolitionist newspapers written by William Lloyd Garrison and Frederick Douglass. Then ask each student to create a visual display for his or her research. Students should include primary sources and biographical information about each abolitionist. Finally, tell students that their displays should also illustrate how these abolitionists represented the abolitionist point of view in their newspapers.

### What's Your Opinion?

To help students create their **Themes** *Journal* entries, provide the following examples of appropriate **agree**/**disagree** *statements.*

● **Agree** All communities develop for basically the same reasons.

**Disagree** There are a variety of reasons that towns and cities form.

● **Agree** An individual can meet his or her own needs better than a community can.

**Disagree** A community provides connection and support that individuals do not receive alone.

● **Agree** In exchange for the benefits of living communally, members should contribute by maintaining harmony within the community.

**Disagree** Individuals are responsible for their own well-being, whether they live in a community or not.

**CHAPTER** ★★★★★

# 15 Citizenship in the Community

### Build on What You Know

A community is a group of people who have common interests and live in the same area. They are also governed by the same laws. A community provides goods and services that citizens cannot easily provide for themselves. In addition, communities offer the opportunity for their citizens to communicate and to get to know each other. In return for the benefits of community life, it is your responsibility to make your community a good place to live.

### What's Your Opinion?

 **Themes Journal** Do you **agree** or **disagree** with the following statements? Support your point of view in your journal.

- All communities form for the same reasons.

- People are just as well off living individually as they are living in a community.

- Community members should take responsibility for making things go well for everyone.

# SECTION 1

## OBJECTIVES

*After completing Section 1, students should be able to*

1. **Describe how transportation, resources, and climate affect the location of communities.**
2. **Identify the kinds of communities that exist in rural areas.**
3. **Explain what both an urban area and a metropolitan area are.**

## 🔊 LET'S GET STARTED!

Write the following question on the chalkboard: *What are some of the differences between living in the city and living in the country?* As students enter the classroom, ask them to respond to the question. *(Students might suggest that city living is more crowded, busy, and impersonal and that country living is less crowded, less hectic, and more personable.)* Tell them that cities are called urban areas and that rural areas are those outside of cities that are less developed. Then tell students that in Section 1 they will learn about different types of urban and rural communities.

---

## SECTION 1

# Kinds of Communities

### Read to Discover

1. How do transportation, resources, and climate affect the location of communities?
2. What kinds of communities exist in rural areas?
3. What is an urban area, and what is a metropolitan area?

### Define

- crossroads
- megalopolis

#### WHY CIVICS MATTERS

As metropolitan areas expand, changes must be made. Use **CNNfyi**.com or other **current events** sources to investigate changes that have arisen in a metropolitan area. Record your findings in your journal.

EST. 1873
**WELCOME TO**
**CLAY CITY**
**INDIANA**
"MAYBERRY OF THE MIDWEST"

## *Reading Focus*

Early American settlers chose locations for their settlements that had natural advantages. Farmers were attracted to the fertile river valleys and later to the plains. Those interested in trade knew that settings in a place with a good harbor would help them build a prosperous business. A natural dam site along a river would provide power for factories. A bend in the river would make a good landing place for riverboats. Even today the natural advantages of a warm sunny climate or snowcapped mountains can determine where a new community is located.

## ★ Crossroads Settlements

As people moved farther inland, they often settled where two main roads met. A **crossroads** was generally a good place to sell supplies to local farmers and travelers. An enterprising settler might build an inn at the crossroads. A blacksmith found business there shoeing horses and repairing wagons. Farmers came to these small settlements to trade. In time, a crossroads settlement could grow and become a thriving town and then perhaps a city.

✔ **Reading Check Finding the Main Idea** Why did people settle near crossroads? More people were likely to come to their shops, which would increase their economic opportunities.

*A good harbor for shipping was a major asset for early colonial settlements.*

## SECTION 1 RESOURCES

### REPRODUCIBLE
▶ Guided Reading Strategies 15.1
▶ Challenge and Enrichment Worksheet 15: Making a Profile of your Community
▶ Creative Teaching Strategy: Open-Ended Statements

### TECHNOLOGY
▶ One-Stop Planner, Lesson 15.1
▶ CNN Presents: American Government
▶ Homework Practice Online
▶ HRW Go site

### REINFORCEMENT, REVIEW, AND ASSESSMENT
▶ Section 1 Review, p. 368
▶ Daily Quiz 15.1
▶ Main Idea Activity 15.1
▶ English Audio Summary 15.1
▶ Spanish Audio Summary 15.1

# TEACH OBJECTIVE 1

**LEVELS 1 AND 2:** Lead a class discussion about the ways that transportation, resources, and climate affect the location of communities. *(Students should note that available transportation gives access to and within a location; natural resources shape economic livelihoods; and climate helps determine economic livelihoods and lifestyles.)* Ask students to imagine that they are business owners searching for a city location for their businesses. Have each student create a plan that includes his or her considerations regarding these factors.
**ENGLISH LANGUAGE LEARNERS**

**HOMEWORK** Tell each student to create a poster that shows how transportation, climate, or resources have affected the location of your community.

**LEVEL 3:** Organize the class into small groups, and have each group determine how transportation options, availability of resources, or climate affected development of a city in your state. *(See the Levels 1 and 2 lesson for the ways these factors affect city development.)* Have each group create a brochure about the city's location that might be used to encourage businesses to move there. Encourage groups to include visual guides such as maps and illustrations or photos of the city.
**COOPERATIVE LEARNING**

---

### Visual Record Answer

*Students might suggest that it would give them better access to goods and services.*

---

## ★ Transportation Centers

Many American communities grew because they were located on transportation routes. The American colonies depended largely on ships and boats for transportation. The country's waterways thus helped determine the location of many cities. The largest cities in the American colonies were deepwater ports on the Atlantic coast. Boston, New York, Philadelphia, and Charleston were such cities.

Most of the large inland cities grew up at lake ports or along major rivers. For example, St. Paul and Minneapolis are located at easy-to-reach stopping points on the upper Mississippi River. New Orleans prospered because it is at the mouth of the Mississippi River. Goods coming down the river were loaded onto oceangoing vessels. These cities became important transportation centers because of their locations on major bodies of water.

The coming of the railroad also helped cities grow. After 1840, railroad lines began to crisscross the country, connecting its many regions. The railroads contributed to the development of existing towns and cities and also created new cities. Inland cities that were not on rivers or lakes sprang up as the railroads provided a new method of transportation. Indianapolis, Dallas, Denver, and many other cities grew prosperous because they were located along busy railroad lines.

Today Americans depend heavily on automobiles for transportation. As a result, new communities have appeared along the country's highways. Some of these communities provide services to travelers. Others are home to people who commute along the highways to jobs in the cities. As these communities have grown, people have formed local governments to provide laws and services.

✔ **Reading Check** **Analyzing Information** What role did transportation play in determining the location of early American communities? People settled in areas accessible by various means of transportation.

**Did You KNOW?**

In 1865 there were only about 35,000 miles of railroad track in the entire United States. By 1890 there were nearly 200,000 miles, and railroads were the largest industry in the country.

**Interpreting the Visual Record**

**Railroads** *This early railroad poster celebrates the ability of rail lines to connect people around the United States. Why would it be beneficial for communities to be located along railroad lines?*

**LEVEL 1:** Ask students to identify the kinds of communities that exist in rural areas. (*Students might suggest a rural farm, small country town, and newer rural America.*) Write their responses on the chalkboard as column heads for a three-column chart. Then have volunteers describe features of each kind of rural community. **ENGLISH LANGUAGE LEARNERS**

**LEVELS 2 AND 3:** Organize the class into three groups and assign each group one of the kinds of communities found in rural America. (*See the Level 1 lesson for types.*) Have each group create a diorama of its assigned type. Call on volunteers to explain what features characterize their area, as shown in the group's model. **COOPERATIVE LEARNING**

**ALL LEVELS:** Copy the following graphic organizer onto the chalkboard, omitting the italicized answers. Ask each student to complete the chart to define what both an urban area and a metropolitan area are.
**ENGLISH LANGUAGE LEARNERS**

| Urban Area | Metropolitan Area |
|---|---|
| • *village*<br>• *town*<br>• *borough*<br>• *city*<br>• *population of 2,500 or more* | • *large city*<br>• *unclear where city ends and the surrounding towns and suburbs begin* |

## ★ Resources and Climate

The United States is a country with rich natural resources. It has a variety of climates that are good for recreation such as outdoor sports or hiking. Its broad lakes and rivers and long coastlines provide many good ports and harbors. The country also has vast stretches of fertile soil, adequate rainfall, good pastureland, and abundant forests. Beneath the soil are rich deposits of coal and petroleum, as well as copper, gold and other metals.

Climate and natural resources have encouraged the growth of many American communities. For example, Duluth, Minnesota, is a port city on Lake Superior. It owes much of its growth to the great iron-ore deposits located nearby in the Mesabi Range. Central California provides another example. At first, the region's good soil and mild climate attracted farmers, who could grow many types of crops there. Today the pleasant climate is a major attraction for people who wish to live in the area's cities.

Many New England factory communities were established near waterfalls. The early textile mills needed waterpower to turn machines that spun thread and wove cloth. Meanwhile, many settlers moved to the Midwest because of the rich, fertile soil—one of nature's most important resources.

A community's climate and resources can affect the types of government services needed by people living there. For example, communities with rich ore deposits might rely on their governments to help develop these resources. Local government might persuade a mining company to access these resources by offering economic incentives such as low taxes. Such incentives and development might create local jobs. Citizens might also expect elected officials to pass laws to protect their community's natural resources.

✔ **Reading Check** Finding the Main Idea What natural factors affect city growth, and how? Natural resources and climate affect city growth. Rich resources enable economic growth. Climate type facilitates economic growth and determines lifestyle and the type of government services needed.

**Interpreting the Visual Record**

**Farmland** *A suitable climate and natural resources such as good soil and a steady water supply are critical factors for farming.* **Do you think an area with good farmland is more or less likely to develop near large cities?**

### ★ Global Perspectives

**A Global Move to Cities**
The percentage of the world's population that lives in urban areas has steadily risen in the past two centuries. In 1800 only three percent of people in the world lived in urban areas. In 1900 that percentage climbed to 14 percent. The new millennium saw a huge jump—more than 45 percent of people in the world lived in cities at the turn of the most recent century. As of 2000, there were 411 cities worldwide with more than 1 million people living in them. Some sources list Tokyo, Japan, as the most populous "urban agglomeration" in the world, at 26.4 million people in 2000. It is estimated that this city's population increased 34 percent between 1975 and 2000.

**ACTIVITY:** Have students conduct research to create a list of the 10 most populous cities in the world.

**Visual Record Answer**

*Students might suggest that it is less likely because the land would be better used for farming.*

**Visual Record Answer**

*(for p. 366)*
*Students might suggest that they can help people get to know each other, share information, and inspire them to cooperate to reach community goals.*

**LEVEL 2:** Organize students into pairs. Instruct each pair to create a Web site on poster board that informs the browser about the difference between urban and metropolitan areas. Tell pairs that their Web sites should include definitions, photographs, illustrations, and data, as well as imaginary links to other sites. Ask volunteers to present their Web sites to the class.

**COOPERATIVE LEARNING**

**LEVEL 3:** Obtain from a local automobile association, airline, or travel agent information about the cities in the Boston-Washington, Chicago-Pittsburgh, or San Francisco-San Diego megalopolises. Have students write a travelogue as if they were driving through one of these metropolitan areas. Students should begin at one city and work their way to the other, commenting on the urban landscape as they travel. The travelogues should be written for visitors from urban areas and should describe the differences between an urban area and a metropolitan area. *(See the All Levels lesson for the definition of each term.)*

**Interpreting the Visual Record**

**Small towns** *Gatherings such as this one give residents of rural communities a chance to sell goods, discuss local events, and socialize with neighbors.* **How might such activities help draw communities together?**

## ★ Rural Communities

As you know, a rural area is a region of farms and small towns. When you travel along the country's highways, you see many different kinds of rural communities. One way to classify them is by their size. They may also be classified by the kinds of buildings in the community and how the people make their living.

**Rural Farm Communities** The people who live and work on farms make up America's smallest kind of community—the rural farm community. In many parts of the United States, you will pass farm after farm as you travel through the countryside. All parts of the United States have farms. However, farms differ from region to region because of climate differences.

In Pennsylvania there are farms where a variety of crops are grown and some pigs, cows, and chickens are raised. These farms are called mixed farms. In Wisconsin you will see a large number of dairy farms. Farther west, in Wyoming, you will see large ranches that raise herds of cattle or sheep.

In southern states you will pass tobacco and cotton farms and cattle ranches. West of the Mississippi River, you will see large wheat farms. In the Imperial Valley of California, there are farms that grow fruits and vegetables for city markets. In Hawaii you will see sugarcane and pineapple plantations.

Today there are about 2 million farms in the United States. Some farms are located near other farms, main highways, or roads. Other farms are isolated and are a long distance from their nearest neighbors.

✔ **Reading Check** *Summarizing* What are some of the different rural farm communities that exist in the United States? mixed farms, wheat farms, dairy farms, cattle and sheep ranches, farms growing nonfood items like cotton and tobacco, fruit and vegetable farms, tropical plantations

**Small Country Towns** There is another kind of rural community—the small country town. It has a population of less than 2,500 and is usually located near open farmland. Most country towns have served as

## SPOTLIGHT
### on Rural Communities

Ask students to select a particular rural community for a research project. Then have each student conduct research about that community to create a community profile in a format of his or her choice. *(Profiles might be a report, brochure, poster, and so on.)* Tell students that their profile should include the history of the place, a study of daily rural life, the advantages and disadvantages of life in a rural community, and illustrations if they are available. Ask volunteers to present their profiles to the class. **BLOCK SCHEDULING**

## CLOSE

Invite students to write a quiz that consists of one statement describing each of the following types of communities: rural farm community, small country town, suburb, metropolitan area, and megalopolis. Each student should develop an answer key for his or her quiz. Have students exchange papers in order to take each other's quizzes.

---

places where farmers could buy supplies. People in more rural areas could shop, go to the movies, and send mail in these towns. Small towns have also served as marketing centers for farm crops.

During the 1930s many of the rural areas in the United States experienced severe droughts and became known as the Dust Bowl. The United States was also suffering from a major economic downturn known as the Great Depression. As farmers were unable to make a living growing crops, many of them moved to the cities to find jobs.

However, recently some rural areas have begun to grow again. The newcomers are not farmers but workers who commute to new businesses in the countryside. Rural land is cheaper, and many operating costs are lower. As a result, there are now two rural Americas. One consists of the old rural farm communities and small country towns. The other includes farms in addition to businesses that have left the cities.

✔ **Reading Check Contrasting** How have small country towns changed since the 1930s? In the 1930s they declined in population because of droughts and economic problems. Today these towns are growing. They are home to new businesses and many commuters who have left the city.

### ★ Suburbs

As you have read, a town, village, or community located on the outskirts of a city is called a suburb. People who live in the suburbs often work in the city. They travel from their homes to their city offices or other places of employment.

Suburbs attract many people. Suburbs are smaller than cities, and some people prefer life in a smaller community. Others want their children to grow up in a community with more open spaces, trees, and places to play. They want a house with a backyard. Some families want to get away from city crowds, noise, pollution, and traffic.

Suburbs allow people to live away from the city even though they earn their living in the city. However, suburbs have been growing rapidly and are now facing many of the same challenges as cities, including crime and traffic jams. Suburban residents have the responsibility of telling their local government how they want to manage growth. They should also work to create solutions to crime and traffic problems.

✔ **Reading Check Summarizing** What are some advantages to living in the suburbs, and what challenges do residents face? The communities are smaller, quieter, and more spacious. Suburbs have been growing rapidly and face many of the same challenges as cities.

### ★ Urban Areas

Boroughs, towns, villages, and cities of 2,500 or more people are called urban areas. Urban areas vary greatly in size. For example, Camilla, Georgia, has about 5,669 people, making it an urban area.

**Interpreting the Visual Record**

Suburban communities *The suburbs were developed primarily as residential areas, although most suburbs also have shopping areas and smaller businesses.* **What do you notice about the homes in this suburb?**

---

## ★ Civics Sidelight

### Cities of the 1900s, Megacities of the 2000s

At the beginning of the 1900s cities such as New York and London, England, each experienced a huge rate of growth. Infrastructure problems increased rapidly. Sanitation, employment, job safety, and disease caused these urban centers to suffer a higher rate of mortality than rural areas. At the beginning of the 2000s megacities in the world's poorest areas are forecasted to suffer a similar plight. Others disagree. They say that the growth of megacities in poor areas can give a much-needed boost to the economic growth of the area. Further, they cite the ability of modern technology to help city managers deal with modern problems.

**CRITICAL THINKING**

Do you think the megacities of 2000 will have different problems than cities of the 1900s?

**ANSWER:** Students might suggest that new technologies and larger populations result in different problems.

**Visual Record Answer**

*(for p.366)* Students should recognize the importance of friendships and good relationships with neighbors.

**Visual Record Answer**

Students might suggest that they all look alike.

*Citizenship in the Community* **367**

Have students complete the **Section 1 Review** on page 368. Then have students complete **Daily Quiz 15.1**. As **Alternative Assessment**, you may want to use the travelogue or business plan exercises in this section's lessons.

## RETEACH

Have students complete **Main Idea Activity for English Language Learners and Special-Needs Students 15.1**. Then assign students one of the subsections in this section. Ask each student to create a study guide for his or her assigned subsection. After they have finished their study guides, ask volunteers to present their guides to the class.

**ENGLISH LANGUAGE LEARNERS**

## EXTEND

Have students conduct research using the library or other resources to obtain information about what the local area was like when your community was founded. Students should identify whether the community was rural or urban and find out how your community has changed in size and configuration since its early days. Tell students to prepare a list of pertinent facts to present to the class in a brief oral report.

**BLOCK SCHEDULING**

---

### Visual Record Answer

*Students might suggest that people who enjoy exploring cultural and entertainment opportunities might choose to live in a city.*

---

## Section 1 Review
### ANSWERS

**1. Define**
- crossroads, p. 363
- megalopolis, p. 368

**2.** Traditional rural America is made up of regions with rural farm communities and small country towns. Newer rural America has farms but also has factories and businesses built in the countryside, as well as commuting workers.

**3. a.** Available transportation gives access to and within a location; natural resources shape economic livelihoods; and climate helps determine economic livelihoods and lifestyles.

**b.** a village, town, borough, or city with a population of 2,500 or more; a city that has become so large that it is difficult to tell where the city ends and the surrounding towns and suburbs begin

**4.** Students' editorials will vary but should demonstrate their knowledge of the advantages and disadvantages of living in each location.

---

### Interpreting the Visual Record

**Urban culture** *Big cities offer many cultural activities to their residents, including art museums like the Guggenheim Museum in New York City. Urban areas also tend to have major sports teams, theaters, and a variety of restaurants.* **Why might such features attract residents to cities?**

---

In contrast, New York City, another city classified as an urban area, has a population of more than 8 million. Most urban areas in the United States have populations between the sizes of Camilla and New York City.

According to the 2000 census, 80 percent of all Americans live in urban communities. Those who live in the large cities are near theaters, restaurants, museums, art galleries, and other cultural activities that cities offer. They enjoy the hustle and bustle of city living. However, recent studies show that suburbs are growing faster than cities. More than half the urban population lives outside the central cities. A number of large cities have actually shown a loss in population in recent years.

Some cities, such as Chicago, Dallas, Los Angeles, and New York City, have become very large, expanding beyond the former city limits. It has become difficult to tell where these cities end and where the surrounding towns and suburbs begin. As you have read, a large city and its surrounding towns and suburbs are referred to as a metropolitan area, or a metropolis. For example, the metropolitan area of Chicago, Illinois, includes several large cities in neighboring states, such as Gary, Indiana. There are about 200 metropolitan areas in the United States. Of these, 44 have a population of at least 1 million.

Some metropolitan areas have grown so large that they form a continuous urban chain. This type of giant urban area is referred to as a **megalopolis.** The metropolitan areas of Boston, New York City, Philadelphia, Baltimore, and Washington, D.C., form a megalopolis along the Atlantic coast.

✔ **Reading Check Identifying Points of View** Why do some people choose to live in cities? There are a variety of activities as well as more cultural activities, excitement, and action.

---

## SECTION 1 Review

**go.hrw.com** Homework Practice Online
keyword: SZ3 HP15

**1. Define** and explain:
- crossroads
- megalopolis

**2. Contrasting** Copy the graphic organizer below. Use it identify the two types of communities that exist in rural America and how they are different.

> Traditional Rural America
> ↕
> Newer Rural America

**3. Finding the Main Idea**
a. How do transportation, resources, and climate help determine the kind and location of a community or settlement?
b. What kind of community can be called an urban area, and what is a metropolitan area?

**4. Writing and Critical Thinking**
**Evaluating** Write an editorial describing the advantages and disadvantages of living in the suburbs compared to living in a metropolitan area. Tell which area you would prefer to live in and why.

**Consider:**
- the advantages and disadvantages of life in the suburbs
- the advantages and disadvantages of living in a metropolis

# SECTION 2

## OBJECTIVES

*After completing Section 2, students should be able to*

**1** Identify the different methods of communication used in communities.

**2** Examine how communities help people enjoy their lives.

**3** Explain why local communities need laws and regulations.

## 🔊 LET'S GET STARTED!

Create an empty word web on the chalkboard. As students enter the classroom, call their attention to the word web, telling them it will be used to describe the word *community*. Ask students to contribute words and phrases to help build the web. *(Students might suggest cooperation, groups, home, school, city, suburb, country, and so on.)* Then explain to them that there are different sizes and types of communities. Tell students that in Section 2 they will learn about the different features and benefits of community living.

---

## SECTION 2

# Purposes of Communities

### Read to Discover

1. What different methods of communication are used in communities?
2. How do communities help people enjoy their lives?
3. Why do local communities need laws and regulations?

#### WHY CIVICS MATTERS

Citizens rely on their communities to provide several important services. Use **CNNfyi.com** or other **current events** sources to find examples of services that a community provides. Record your findings in your journal.

### Define

- communication
- recreation

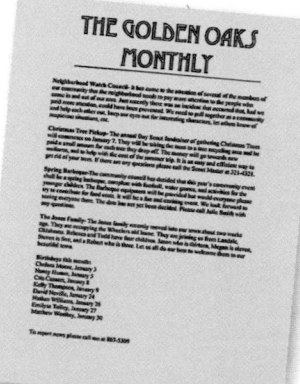

THE GOLDEN OAKS MONTHLY

## SECTION 2 RESOURCES

### REPRODUCIBLE

▶ Guided Reading Strategies 15.2

### TECHNOLOGY

▶ One-Stop Planner, Lesson 15.2

▶ Homework Practice Online

### REINFORCEMENT, REVIEW, AND ASSESSMENT

▶ Section 2 Review, p. 372

▶ Daily Quiz 15.2

▶ Main Idea Activity 15.2

▶ English Audio Summary 15.2

▶ Spanish Audio Summary 15.2

## *Reading Focus*

One of the most important things communities do is teach people how to live and work together. The first lessons in living and getting along with others are learned in the home. As we grow up, we also learn from teachers, schoolmates, neighbors, and friends. The people of our communities teach us values, respect for the law, and many other things.

### ⭐ Communication

We continue to learn as long as we live. Almost every day we share information we have learned with others. This passing along of information, ideas, and beliefs from one person to another is known as **communication.**

One reason people live in communities is to be able to communicate with each other easily. People can often ease the problems they face by talking them over with someone else. People also enjoy hearing about the latest events and learning new ideas from other people in the community.

Every community has several means of communication. The most common one, as mentioned above, is conversation. Such devices as telephones, e-mail, the Internet, radios, and televisions have increased our ability to learn and share information. We also communicate in writing through letters and notes.

*This PTA meeting is helping to improve communication between parents and teachers.*

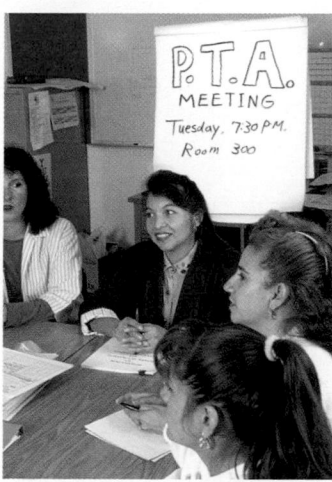

P.T.A. MEETING
Tuesday, 7:30 P.M.
Room 300

**ALL LEVELS:** Organize the class into groups. Assign each group one of the ways people communicate in communities. *(Assignments include in person, by telephone and through computer, radio, television, letters, notes, newspapers, books, and magazines.)* Choose a prominent issue currently being discussed in your community. Then have each group communicate the story in its assigned way. In its demonstration, each group should show how its method of communication imparts the information to an audience. Have the class guess each group's assigned method. **COOPERATIVE LEARNING**

**ALL LEVELS:** Call on volunteers to explain how communities help people enjoy their lives. Write their responses on the chalkboard. *(Students might mention that they provide the company of others, provide for better health and safety, and fulfill a need for goods and services.)* Then organize the class into small groups and invite students to imagine that they live in a community that is not doing these things. Have each group write a letter to the editor of the local newspaper explaining the value of these qualities. Letters should include proposals for the establishment of facilities that enable such services. **ENGLISH LANGUAGE LEARNERS , COOPERATIVE LEARNING**

## ★ Civics Sidelight

### Informing Americans

Americans have a wide choice of sources for getting information, and fewer are choosing newspapers. By the end of 1999, only 55 million U.S. residents subscribed to a daily newspaper. That figure was down from 60 million in 1994. Over the same time period, the U.S. population increased by more than 20 million people, from about 261 million in 1994 to more than 281 million in 2000. So where are Americans getting their information? In 1999, 99 percent of U.S. households had at least one radio, 98.2 percent had at least one television, and 68 percent received cable television service. Also in 1999, 22.2 percent of U.S. households had access to the Internet in their homes. An additional 17 percent accessed the Internet elsewhere, such as in school, at the library, or at work.

**ACTIVITY:** Have students use the library or other resources to conduct research on Americans' use of the Internet as a news source. Have students create a Web page to present their findings.

### CHART ANSWER

Students' responses will vary.

**The Purposes of Communities**

| | |
|---|---|
| **Learning to Live Together** | Communities teach their citizens how to live and work together. |
| **Services** | Communities provide important services to citizens, including:<br>• Police forces • Utilities<br>• Public libraries • Schools<br>• Fire departments |
| **Communication** | Communities make it easier to share information and ideas. |
| **Local Government** | Communities provide rules and enforce law and order. |
| **Recreation** | Communities provide public facilities to help citizens enjoy being with other people. |

*Interpreting Charts Communities provide valuable benefits to their citizens.* **Which of the benefits shown above do you enjoy in your community?**

One of the main means of communication is the newspaper. Newspapers report events happening around the world. They also provide community news, such as what laws are passed, election information, and when public meetings are held. In addition, newspapers tell us about births, marriages, and deaths in the community. Books and magazines are other important ways of communicating ideas and facts. Most American communities provide free public libraries so that citizens have easy access to news, information, and ideas. These different forms of communication allow citizens to stay informed about what their government is doing. In return, citizens can use these means of communication to express their ideas to their leaders.

✔ **Reading Check Finding the Main Idea** How do people in communities communicate with each other, and why is communication important? People use conversation, print, and electronic media. Communication helps people express ideas and stay informed.

## ★ Recreation

One important reason people form communities is to enjoy the company of other people. Nearly every U.S. city and town has bowling alleys, movie theaters, parks, skating rinks, and other public places of recreation. **Recreation** is relaxation or amusement that comes from playing or doing something different from one's usual activities. Sporting events provide one popular form of recreation.

Many recreational facilities are maintained at public expense. Taxes support public playgrounds, athletic fields, picnic grounds, basketball courts, and golf courses. There are also worthwhile activities sponsored by groups of citizens willing to volunteer their own time and money. The YMCA, Boy Scouts, Girl Scouts, Big Brothers/Big Sisters, and 4-H Clubs are examples of groups that help the members of the community relax and learn together.

Many communities have learned to take advantage of an unusually good climate or geographical location. They have promoted and developed these advantages not only for their own residents but also to attract tourists. Lake communities and seaside towns have developed boating, swimming, and water-skiing as special attractions. Rural communities promote hunting and fishing opportunities in their areas. Other communities have developed hiking, horseback riding, rock climbing, and skiing facilities.

# TEACH OBJECTIVE 3

 **ALL LEVELS:** Copy the following graphic organizer onto the chalkboard, omitting the italicized answers. Explain to students that other than safety and protection, communities also pass laws to enhance the well-being and morals of a community. Have each student complete the organizer, listing some of the laws and regulations that exist in your community and whether their purpose is safety, protection, well-being, or morals. **ENGLISH LANGUAGE LEARNERS**

```
        Why Communities Need Laws and Regulations

   to maintain peace              to maintain order
```

**LEVEL 3:** Organize the class into small groups, and have each group create a skit that demonstrates why local communities need laws and regulations. *(See the All Levels lesson for the reasons.)* Have each group present its skit to the class.
**COOPERATIVE LEARNING**

## CLOSE

Refer students to the chart on page 370. Invite students to imagine what life would be like if one of these purposes of communities were missing. Have students write a short paragraph explaining the importance of each of the purposes of community shown in the chart.

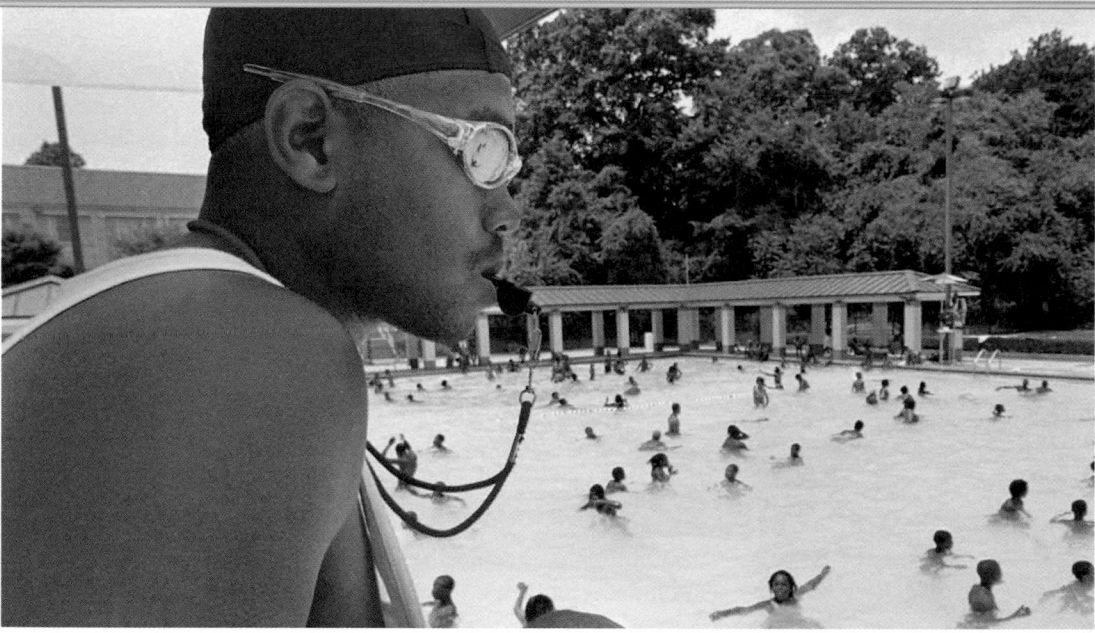

Good community recreational facilities serve a number of purposes:

1. They provide worthwhile ways for Americans to use their leisure time by giving people interesting and healthy things to do.

2. They help members of the community keep physically fit. Well-managed playgrounds, swimming pools, and recreation centers encourage good health habits.

3. They expand people's knowledge and may help develop new interests and hobbies. For example, a community cooking class or reading club can teach a participant much about culture and history.

4. They give people places to relax and have fun in the company of others. Recreation helps "re-create" the individual—it makes him or her feel like a new person.

✔ **Reading Check Analyzing Information** What purposes do recreational facilities serve? **They give people interesting and healthy things to do, enable people to keep physically fit, expand the mind through new interests and hobbies, and enable people to spend time in the company of others.**

## ★ Community Services

People also form communities to provide better services to citizens. The people of a community can meet certain needs more effectively by working together than by working separately. This was a major reason why many early communities were formed. By pooling their resources and labor, members of these communities could improve the quality of life for everyone. For example, residents can work to maintain a good police force and fire department, which helps ensure public safety. Public schools help meet the need to provide education to a community's young people.

---

**Interpreting the Visual Record**

**Summer fun** *Many communities support recreational facilities such as this public pool.* **What are the benefits of providing such facilities to community members?**

---

★★★★★★★★★★★★
**That's Interesting!**
★★★★★★★★★★★★

**Learning to Play** Can you imagine a city without public playgrounds? Until the early 1900s such recreational areas were rare. Some reformers noticed that many urban children were playing in parking lots and other unsafe areas. As a result, they formed the Playground Association of America (PAA) in 1906. The PAA built play areas and published a magazine called Playground. The PAA later merged with other groups to form the National Recreation and Park Association (NRPA). The NRPA continues to support park and recreation projects today.

---

### ★ Citizenship in Action

**Play Ball** For many young people, youth baseball and softball organizations provide the focus of summer recreation. Little League Baseball, Inc., for example, operates throughout the United States as well as internationally. It is a quasi-governmental agency (with a charter from the federal government), and most of its functions are performed by volunteers. Parents volunteer as coaches, umpires, and groundskeepers. Leagues often operate on community-owned property, relying on player registration fees, local business sponsorships, and earnings from concessions to pay their bills. Little League, like many other organizations that are youth-oriented, is a prime example of the positive aspects of volunteer contributions and the benefits of community life.

**CRITICAL THINKING**

Why do you think that parents commonly volunteer to help with Little League?

**ANSWER:** Students might suggest that it benefits their children.

**Visual Record Answer**

*Students might suggest that it enhances the quality of community life.*

---

# REVIEW AND ASSESS

Have students complete the **Section 2 Review** on page 372. Then have students complete **Daily Quiz 15.2**. As **Alternative Assessment**, you may want to use the collage or skit exercises in this section's lessons.

# RETEACH

Have students complete **Main Idea Activity for English Language Learners and Special-Needs Students 15.2**. Then give each student a set of five index cards, and have students write a test question about this section on one side of the card and the answer on the other side. Finally, pair students and have them quiz each other using the index cards as flash cards.

**ENGLISH LANGUAGE LEARNERS , COOPERATIVE LEARNING**

# EXTEND

Invite students to imagine that a federal official wants to tour your community. Students should plan a field trip that will best show your community's strengths. Have students work together to plan the itinerary and make all the arrangements. If feasible, take the trip that students planned and have students write down their impressions as if they were visitors to the community. Afterward, ask students to identify the community's strengths and weaknesses. **BLOCK SCHEDULING**

---

## Visual Record Answer

*Students might suggest that people may choose to move to a community where the service is provided.*

## Section 2 Review
### ANSWERS

**1. Define**
• communication, p. 369
• recreation, p. 370

**2.** by providing for the company of others, fulfilling a need for community services, and by providing laws and regulations to maintain peace and order.

**3. a.** conversation, telephones, computers, radios, television, letters, notes, newspapers, books, and magazines

**b.** to maintain peace and order

**4.** Students' recommendations will vary but might mention additional recreational services, youth centers, enhanced police and fire protection, and improved transportation services.

---

**Interpreting the Visual Record**

**Services** *Communities and local governments must work together to provide basic services for residents.* **What might happen if the service shown here was not provided in your community?**

---

People living as neighbors in a community also need pure water, an efficient sewage system, and regular trash removal. Dependable gas and electric services are also necessities. Sometimes the people of a community join together and vote to have the local government furnish these services. In other cases, private companies can perform the necessary tasks. However these services are provided, citizens usually pay for them with some combination of local taxes and fees.

✔ **Reading Check Summarizing** What types of services do communities provide? police and fire protection, clean water, good sewage systems, trash removal, and gas and electric services

## ★ Local Government

In addition to providing basic services, local governments provide ordinances and laws. When people live together in a community, laws and regulations are needed to keep order.

Suppose that two neighbors argue over the location of the boundary that separates their properties. If there were no laws or local government, these neighbors might use force to settle their difficulties. Fortunately, communities help citizens avoid conflicts. Local courts, judges, and law enforcement officers help maintain peace and order in our communities. Local governments also provide citizens with a forum to discuss and address problems before they get out of hand.

✔ **Reading Check Supporting a Point of View** Do you think laws and regulations are necessary for a community? Explain your reasoning. Some may feel that rules are needed to ensure fairness and equality. Others may say that people can cooperate without laws.

**Homework Practice Online** keyword: SZ3 HP15

---

## SECTION 2 Review

**1. Define** and explain:
• communication
• recreation

**2. Summarizing** Copy the graphic organizer below. Use it to explain how communities help people enjoy their lives.

How Communities Bring Enjoyment

**3. Finding the Main Idea**
a. What methods do people use to communicate with each other?
b. Why is it important that communities have laws and regulations?

**4. Writing and Critical Thinking**
**Problem Solving** Imagine that you have just been named to head the community services division of your local government. Write a recommendation to the mayor for ways to improve the existing services in your community.

**Consider:**
• what new services might benefit your community
• how these new services would be funded

---

## TEACH

**LEVEL 1:** Review the guidelines in the Civics Skills Workshop on how to work in groups. *(Students should review these steps: identifying the group's purpose, creating an agenda, choosing a group leader, being a good communicator, and compromising to reach a decision.)* Then call on volunteers to provide examples of how they have used each of these guidelines in past group situations. Conclude the lesson by leading a class discussion about what problems might arise if any one of the guidelines is not met. **ENGLISH LANGUAGE LEARNERS**

## EXTEND

Organize the class into groups. Have each group follow the guidelines on this page to complete the following project. Ask groups to research and report on a volunteer organization that works for the betterment of society. Such groups include volunteer fire departments, literacy projects, and Meals on Wheels. Have each group present its findings to the class in an oral report. Students should also include an analysis of how their group used the guidelines for working in groups found in the workshop on this page. **COOPERATIVE LEARNING ,**
**BLOCK SCHEDULING**

# Civics Skills
## WORKSHOP

## Working in Groups

Chances are that you will work with some group of people nearly every day of your life. That group may be your family, your classmates, your friends, or your co-workers. It is important that you know how to work effectively as a member of all these groups.

## How to Work in Groups

1. **Identify the group's purpose.** Groups are usually formed to accomplish a particular task. For example, your teacher may organize the class into groups to complete a project. To avoid confusion, it is important that the members of each group understand the group's goal, or purpose.

2. **Create an agenda.** An agenda is an itemized plan of the topics to be covered in a meeting. It is useful for keeping group members on task. It should also include the assignment of individual tasks.

3. **Choose a group leader.** The agenda for the first meeting of a group might include the election of the group's leader. A leader can help keep the discussion focused on the group's goal and agenda. The leader also ensures that all group members have the opportunity to contribute their ideas.

4. **Be a good communicator.** Communication in a group means speaking *and* listening. Organize your thoughts before you speak. Do not interrupt other members of the group. When other group members are speaking, listen closely to what they have to say. Ask questions if you are unclear on their ideas.

5. **Compromise to reach a decision.** Groups are made up of a number of people who usually have different ideas about how things should be done. How do groups agree on what action to take? Group members compromise to reach an agreement. For people to compromise, each side needs to make sure the other side receives something in return. In this way all members of a group will accept a proposal even though it might not completely satisfy everyone.

## Applying the Skill

Answer the following questions.

1. Why is it important to know how to work with a group of people?

2. Why is having a leader important to a group? What qualities do you think a leader should have?

3. Why is compromise vital when trying to achieve group goals?

# SECTION 3

## OBJECTIVES

*After completing Section 3, students should be able to*

1. Identify the challenges that American communities face.
2. Examine how volunteer groups help improve the communities in which we live.
3. Analyze how good citizenship is related to developing good communities.

## SECTION 3 RESOURCES

### REPRODUCIBLE

▶ Guided Reading Strategies 15.3
▶ Community Service and Participation Handbook: Host a Special Olympian
▶ Graphic Organizer Activity: Doing Your Part

### TECHNOLOGY

▶ One-Stop Planner, Lesson 15.3
▶ Holt Researcher: American Government
▶ Citizenship Skills Videocassette Segment 1: The Roles of a Citizen
▶ Homework Practice Online

### REINFORCEMENT, REVIEW, AND ASSESSMENT

▶ Section 3 Review, p. 377
▶ Daily Quiz 15.3
▶ Main Idea Activity 15.3
▶ English Audio Summary 15.3
▶ Spanish Audio Summary 15.3

## LET'S GET STARTED!

Write the following statement on the chalkboard: *I live in many communities.* As students enter the classroom, ask them to write a short opinion statement supporting or opposing the statement on the board. *(Students who agree may list school, home, and town. Others may only list the town and state that they live in as one community.)* Then share this definition of community with students: a community is a group of people who have common interests, live in the same area, and are governed by the same laws. Tell students that in Section 3 they will learn about the different types of communities people live in and how members can contribute to them.

---

## SECTION 3

# Citizens Serve Communities

### Read to Discover

1. What challenges do American communities face?
2. How do volunteer groups help improve the communities in which we live?
3. How is good citizenship related to developing good communities?

### WHY CIVICS MATTERS

Volunteer groups perform many useful services in communities across the country. Use **CNNfyi.com** or other **current events** sources to identify examples of volunteer organizations that are serving your community. Record your findings in your journal.

### Define

• compulsory

## Reading Focus

For communities to remain healthy, it is vital that people work to improve society. Communities also depend on cooperation among people.

*Obeying laws such as this reserved-parking restriction is compulsory for all members of a community.*

### ★ Your Communities

To encourage cooperation, some citizenship services are **compulsory,** or required by law. For example, members of a community must obey traffic rules or suffer the penalty established. Furthermore, young citizens must attend school. Yet, communities rely on their members to respect the rights of others simply because it is the right thing to do.

Each of us lives in a number of different communities. We benefit from their services, and we owe certain duties and responsibilities in return. The family is the smallest community. We should cooperate with and respect our family members. This cooperation and respect should extend to the larger communities of our neighborhood, town or city, state, and country. Every community faces challenges that must be met so that life in that community can be pleasant.

✔ **Reading Check Making Generalizations and Predictions** Why do you think that some responsibilities of citizenship are compulsory and others are voluntary? Students might say that government can only enforce basic laws that establish order. Leaders cannot force citizens to take an interest in their community, but society will benefit if they do.

# TEACH OBJECTIVE 1

**ALL LEVELS:** Organize the class into five groups. Assign each group one of the challenges that American communities face. *(Assignments include infrastructure repair, pollution, traffic congestion, crime, and declining neighborhoods.)* Have each group use newspapers and other periodicals to identify examples of its challenge. Each group should then develop a course of action for meeting that challenge. Plans should include general goals and proposals for achieving them. The group should appoint a chairperson and a recording secretary. Another member should illustrate the plan of action with a flowchart or other graphic device.
**ENGLISH LANGUAGE LEARNERS , COOPERATIVE LEARNING**

# TEACH OBJECTIVE 2

**ALL LEVELS:** Explain how volunteer groups help improve the communities in which we live. *(Students should note that they help people who are sick or living in poverty, older citizens, and people with disabilities. They collect money for charities and assist emergency personnel. They help in schools, libraries, sports groups, and other organizations.)* Write each of these qualities on the chalkboard in the first column of a two-column chart. Then have each student write a paragraph discussing the volunteer groups in your community that meet these qualities. **ENGLISH LANGUAGE LEARNERS**

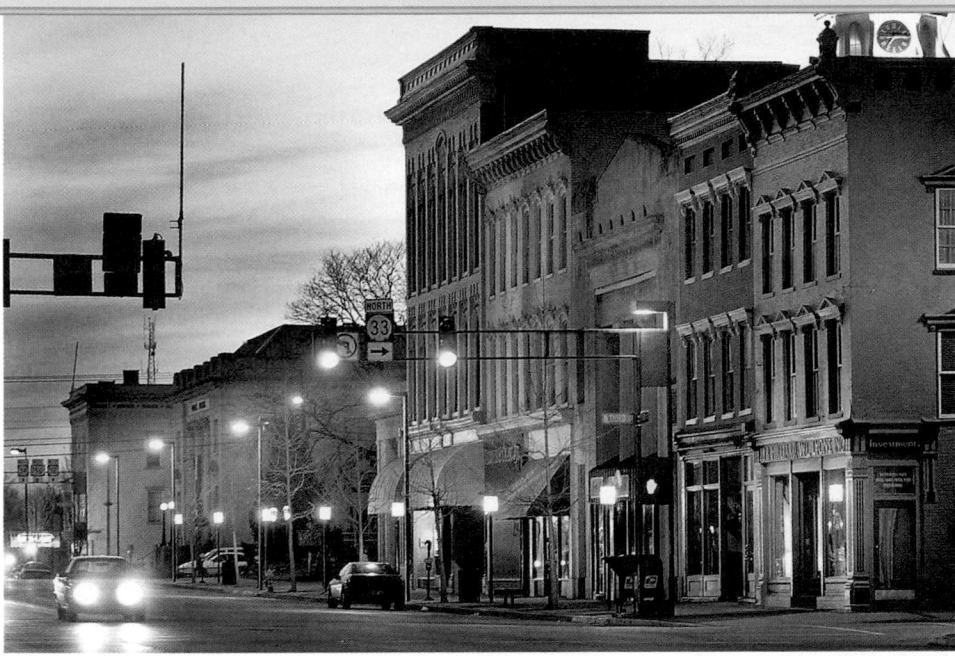

## ★ Improving Communities

Groups of concerned citizens are taking action on many issues in their communities. Consider Las Vegas, New Mexico, a town of about 15,000 people. Residents of Las Vegas were concerned about the limited opportunities that were available for the town's young people. The citizens of Las Vegas wanted to address this problem.

An advisory board was created and staff was hired to study the risks that the youth faced and offer possible solutions. The board decided to focus on the risks of drug use, firearms, and crime, as well as family management problems. The Las Vegas City Council ratified the plan in May 1999. The board's plan, a program called Communities That Care, is still being implemented. The board's goals include the creation of a youth commission to create better communication between youth and city leaders. The board also hopes to offer parenting classes and to create community policing programs.

Each year other American communities face similar issues and do something about them. The citizens of Decatur, Illinois, undertook a program to improve their downtown areas, clear slums, and reduce traffic jams. Decatur cleared and rebuilt a large part of its business district. The city of Worcester, Massachusetts, established a successful new program to better its schools, playgrounds, and museums.

At one time the people of Pittsburgh, Pennsylvania, were not pleased with some aspects of the city. The smoke from the steel mills and factories was so thick that Pittsburgh was known as the Smoky City. Traffic jams choked city streets, and the central city was in poor repair.

The people of Pittsburgh voted to spend the money needed to improve their city. New skyscrapers were built. A successful campaign

### Interpreting the Visual Record

**Renewal** *Many communities have taken steps to revitalize and rebuild older downtown areas, such as this main street.* **How do such renewal efforts benefit community members?**

**Holt Researcher**

**go.hrw.com**
**KEYWORD: Holt Researcher**
**Freefind: Volunteer Groups**
Read through the entries on volunteer groups and careers with volunteer organizations on the Holt Researcher. Use the information you find to create a chart listing several groups and describing what they do. Your descriptions should help answer the following question: How do these groups assist communities?

### ★ Global Relations

**Expanded Visions of Urban Renewal** At the beginning of the 2000s, England began to expand its urban renewal program beyond mere physical improvements. Under Prime Minister Tony Blair, the government has developed a 20-year plan that seeks to improve many aspects of the quality of community life in 1,300 of England's most poverty-stricken neighborhoods. The plan includes an organization of 18 teams, each focused on an aspect of urban renewal, such as housing management or financial services. These teams conduct studies of the needs of the areas to be renewed and create strategies to be enacted cooperatively by local strategic partnerships. Additionally, neighborhood managers will assist these groups in maintaining awareness of the needs of each local neighborhood to be renewed.

### CRITICAL THINKING

What might be the benefits of expanding urban renewal programs beyond physical improvements?

**ANSWER:** Students might suggest that directly helping community members improve their quality of life can help make the renewal have long-term effects.

### Visual Record Answer

*Students might suggest that such efforts can bring in new businesses and consumers and increase safety in a community.*

**375**

**ALL LEVELS:** Copy the following graphic organizer onto the chalkboard, omitting the italicized answers. Have each student complete the organizer to describe how good citizenship relates to developing good communities.

**ENGLISH LANGUAGE LEARNERS**

Have students create posters encouraging young people to volunteer in their communities. The posters should show the connection between good citizenship and good communities. Invite your school principal to view the posters. Then arrange to have them placed around the school as part of a campaign to promote volunteerism.

| How Good Citizenship Relates to Developing Good Communities |
| --- |

*When citizens fulfill their duties and responsibilities* → *the quality of life in communities improves.*

## Citizenship in Action

### A Presidential Example

Former president Jimmy Carter has spent years volunteering his time in his work with Habitat for Humanity International. Habitat is a Georgia-based nonprofit organization that helps people in need build homes for themselves. Carter and his wife, Rosalynn, have on numerous occasions rolled up their sleeves and worked side by side with other volunteers and the future homeowners. They pounded nails, sawed lumber, and otherwise made direct contributions to the well-being of less fortunate individuals. Carter has also served in a variety of roles around the world since he left office, including as an election observer and a negotiator in international disputes.

**ACTIVITY:** Remind students that Habitat for Humanity is an international nonprofit organization. Ask them to locate a chapter in your state and to find out what opportunities exist for volunteers. Have students present their findings in a persuasive speech intended to recruit volunteers for their selected organization.

### BIOGRAPHY ANSWER

She lobbied to create an American chapter of the Red Cross, and she was its president for 22 years.

## BIOGRAPHY

### Clara Barton
#### (1821–1912)

Clara Barton was born in North Oxford, Massachusetts. Her parents encouraged her to become a schoolteacher to overcome her shyness as a child. Barton was a great success as a teacher and gained an interest in women's rights and social reform. She moved on to work as a clerk in the U.S. Patent Office in Washington, D.C. When the Civil War began, Barton volunteered to serve as a nurse. She insisted on being stationed at the battlefield to give aid to the suffering.

Barton's wartime experiences convinced her that more needed to be done to help wounded soldiers and civilians. She worked with the Red Cross in Europe for several years before returning to the United States in 1873. Barton lobbied for many years to create an American chapter of the Red Cross, achieving success at last in 1881. Barton served as the president of the American Red Cross for 23 years, making tremendous contributions to its size, organization, and effectiveness. Under her direction the Red Cross also began aiding disaster victims. She received many international awards for her work, including the International Red Cross Medal. Barton resigned from the Red Cross at the age of 83 and lived the rest of her life in quiet retirement. **How did Clara Barton contribute to volunteer organizations in America?**

against air pollution reduced the smoke in the air. More roads were built, a new water system was planned, and parks and recreation centers were added.

Proud of their efforts, the citizens of Pittsburgh learned that their city must continue to plan, build, and change. The city must meet its citizens' needs in the future. Across the country, cities such as Baltimore, Denver, Houston, Philadelphia, and St. Paul have rebuilt older areas of their cities. These improvement programs have turned the areas into business and entertainment centers.

✔ **Reading Check Finding the Main Idea** What are some issues that American communities face, and how have citizens helped address these problems? Problems include poor streets, lack of good community facilities, pollution, traffic congestion, crime, and slums. Citizens can vote for and participate in improvement programs.

## ★ Community Volunteers

Another way citizens can improve their communities is by becoming volunteers. Many Americans do not realize how much work is done by volunteers. Volunteers help sick people, those in poverty, older citizens, and people with disabilities. They collect money for charities. In some areas volunteers put out fires and drive ambulances. Communities rely on the help of volunteers because no government can know all the needs of local areas. Volunteers also help provide services a community might otherwise be unable to afford.

The United States has many different kinds of volunteer groups. Some are small local groups. Others are large national organizations that depend on local volunteers to carry out their work. A small group may be formed for a specific purpose, such as cleaning up the neighborhood. After the problem is solved, the group disbands. However, some areas have permanent neighborhood groups that meet regularly to discuss community needs.

Many towns, cities, and counties have permanent volunteer groups. They include hospital volunteers, volunteer firefighters, and student-parent-teacher associations. Such groups rely on the help of citizens of all ages. For example, some high school students take older citizens to doctor appointments. Retired people may spend a few hours each week helping in libraries, hospitals, and other community facilities.

Some groups require that volunteers take short courses to learn specific skills, such as first aid and operating special equipment. Those people who take part in these programs have the satisfaction of performing a valuable service for their community. In addition to that, they learn useful new skills.

## REVIEW AND ASSESS

Have students complete the **Section 3 Review** on page 377. Then have them complete **Daily Quiz 15.3**. As **Alternative Assessment**, you may want to use the plan of action or volunteer chart exercises in this section's lessons.

## RETEACH

Have students complete **Main Idea Activity for English Language Learners and Special-Needs Students 15.3**. Then assign students one of the Read to Discover questions. Have each student create a graphic organizer showing how the text addresses the question. **ENGLISH LANGUAGE LEARNERS**

## TEACHER TO TEACHER

Lynn Southern of North Carolina recommends the following activity:

## EXTEND

Organize the class into groups of four students. Tell groups to research the background and purpose of a volunteer organization, identifying the community needs that are met. Assign each member one of the following tasks: assuming the task of group leader, writing a report, drawing a poster advertising the purpose of the organization, and presenting the information to the class in a brief 30-second public service announcement. **BLOCK SCHEDULING , COOPERATIVE LEARNING**

Among the large national volunteer groups are the League of Women Voters, the American Cancer Society, and Volunteers of America. These associations are supported by money from private contributors and depend on the services of volunteers. A large group such as the American Red Cross has more than 1 million volunteers working for it. Local branches of these organizations are usually started by concerned citizens. Community members can support these groups with their time, ideas, and money.

✔ **Reading Check Summarizing** How do volunteer groups help improve communities? They help sick people, those in poverty, older citizens, and people with disabilities. They collect money for charities, serve as firefighters, and drive ambulances. They help in schools, libraries, sports groups, and other organizations.

### ⭐ Helping Your Community

Right now you are an active member of your local community. You attend its schools, and you enjoy its parks and recreation centers. You are protected by its police and fire departments. You depend on your community to provide you with many other services. Someday you may work and raise a family in your community.

It is important that you be a good citizen in all the communities in which you live. These communities include your town, state, and country. Enjoying the benefits of the communities of which you are a member makes it your responsibility to help these communities. These responsibilities range from picking up litter to offering your services as a volunteer. It is up to you to take pride in your communities and practice good citizenship wherever you are.

✔ **Reading Check Finding the Main Idea** What makes good communities? Good citizens make good communities.

**Interpreting the Visual Record**

**Volunteering** *Volunteering in your community can involve something as simple as helping pick up trash in a city park.* **What types of volunteer work could you provide in your community?**

### Visual Record Answer

*Students might suggest that they can help read to children in the hospital, visit people at a retirement home, or help pass out food at a soup kitchen.*

## Section 3 Review
### ANSWERS

**1. Define**
• compulsory, p. 374

**2.** They help people who are sick or poor, older citizens, and people with disabilities. They collect money for charities, serve as fire fighters, drive ambulances and assist emergency personnel. They help in schools, libraries, sports groups, and other organizations.

**3. a.** If citizens did not fulfill their duties and responsibilities, the quality of life in communities would suffer.

**b.** Student answers will vary, but might include infrastructure repair, pollution, traffic congestion, crime, and slums.

**4.** Students' applications will vary but should reflect an understanding that students' contributions would help make their communities better places to live.

## SECTION 3 Review

**go.hrw.com** **Homework Practice Online**
keyword: SZ3 HP15

**1. Define** and explain:
• compulsory

**2. Analyzing Information** Copy the graphic organizer below. Use it to identify ways in which volunteer groups provide services that communities could otherwise not afford.

| Volunteer Services |
|---|
| • |
| • |
| • |
| • |
| • |

**3. Finding the Main Idea**
a. How is good citizenship related to good communities?
b. What are some of the problems that American communities are trying to solve?

**4. Writing and Critical Thinking**
**Decision Making** Identify a variety of volunteer groups in your community. Write an application essay to the group that you are most interested in joining.
**Consider:**
• why you want to join the group
• what skills and services you can offer the group
• how the group helps the community

## REPRODUCIBLE

▶ Chapter 15 Review, pp. 378–79

▶ Vocabulary Activity 15

▶ Chapter 15 Tutorial for Students, Parents, Mentors, and Peers

▶ Chapter 15 Test (Form A or B)

▶ Alternative Assessment Handbook

## TECHNOLOGY

▶ Chapter 15 Test Generator (on the One-Stop Planner)

▶ Global Skill Builder CD–ROM

▶ HRW Go site

## REINFORCEMENT, REVIEW, AND ASSESSMENT

▶ Chapter 15 Test for English Language Learners and Special-Needs Students

## REVIEW

Have students complete the **Chapter 15 Review** on pages 378–79.

## ASSESS

Use one of the chapter tests to assess students' understanding of the content. For **Alternative Assessment**, see the **Alternative Assessment Handbook**.

---

## CHAPTER 15
### REVIEW ANSWERS

**Define and Identify**
1. crossroads, p. 363
2. megalopolis, p. 368
3. communication, p. 369
4. recreation, p. 370
5. compulsory, p. 374

**Understanding Main Ideas**
1. They help determine the accessibility, economy, and lifestyle of an area.

2. Traditional rural America is made up of regions with rural farm communities and small country towns. Newer rural America has farms but also has factories and businesses built in the countryside, as well as commuting workers.

3. in person, by telephone, by computer, and through radio, television, letters, notes, newspapers, books, and magazines

4. They maintain peace and order.

5. They provide services the community cannot afford; they help sick or poor people, older citizens, and people with disabilities; they serve as firefighters and other emergency personnel; they help in schools, libraries, and various organizations.

6. infrastructure repair, pollution, traffic congestion, and slums

---

## Chapter 15 Review

### Chapter Summary

#### Section 1

- The United States is a country of many communities. These communities differ greatly in location, size, and population. They face many common challenges despite these vast differences.
- The prosperity of each community depends on its location, climate, and natural and industrial resources.
- Communities generally fall into one of the following categories: rural, suburban, or urban.

#### Section 2

- Communities serve many important purposes. These include fostering communication among residents, helping people learn to live together, providing recreation, and offering residents the opportunity to earn a living.
- Communities, through the efforts of local government, volunteers, and local businesses, also provide needed services and maintain law and order.

#### Section 3

- Many communities are carrying out planned programs of improvement. Projects include infrastructure development, pollution control, and traffic-congestion solutions.
- Citizens can help to improve their communities by becoming volunteers. Common volunteer efforts include hospital volunteers, volunteer firefighters, and student-parent-teacher associations.
- Citizens can also help their communities by being good citizens who are respectful of others.

---

### Define and Identify

Use the following terms in complete sentences.
1. crossroads
2. megalopolis
3. communication
4. recreation
5. compulsory

### Understanding Main Ideas

**Section 1** *(Pages 363–68)*
1. How do natural factors and transportation influence the development of communities?
2. What are the "two rural Americas," and how do they differ?

**Section 2** *(Pages 369–72)*
3. How do people communicate in communities?
4. What roles do laws and regulations play in communities?

**Section 3** *(Pages 374–77)*
5. In what ways are volunteer organizations essential to a community's success?
6. What problems do communities in the United States face?

### What Did You Find Out?

1. How do communities develop, and what kinds of communities exist?
2. What special advantages do people enjoy by living in communities?
3. How do people make life better in their communities?

### Thinking Critically

1. **Supporting a Point of View** Some American communities require students to do some community service to pass particular courses or to graduate from school. Do you think being required to volunteer adds to or detracts from the spirit of volunteerism?
2. **Evaluating** People who commit minor crimes sometimes are ordered to perform community service rather than go to jail or pay a fine. What is the purpose of such a sentence? Do you think this type of sentencing is more beneficial to a community than jail time or fines? Explain your answer.
3. **Analyzing Information** How is it possible to live in several communities at the same time?

# RETEACH

Organize students into pairs and then have pairs work together to complete a chapter outline that lists the important points found under each subhead in the sections throughout the chapter.

**ENGLISH LANGUAGE LEARNERS ,
COOPERATIVE LEARNING**

## Portfolio Extensions

### 1. Cooperative Learning

Organize the class into pairs and have each pair contact historical associations in your area to learn about the history of the community problem researched in the Student's Edition exercise. Have pairs find the answers to these questions: Did your community have to deal with this problem in the past? If so, how did the problem arise and how was it solved? If not, why do you think that the problem did not arise in the past, and what do you think its presence now indicates about the city?

### 2. Interdisciplinary Connection to Sociology

Have students conduct a survey of their classmates to determine the reasons classmembers might or might not be inclined to perform volunteer work. Encourage them to ask such questions as: Have you ever volunteered? Why or why not? What organizations would you consider volunteering for now? Why would you prefer them? What types of organizations do not interest you? Why? Then have them create an illustrated report that presents their findings.

---

## Building Social Studies Skills

STANDARDIZED TEST PREP ONLINE
keyword: SZ3 STP15

### Interpreting Charts

Study the chart below. Use the information in the chart to answer the questions that follow.

**How Many U.S. Communities Grew**

Nearby small towns

Apartments

Small stores

Private homes

Suburbs

Original downtown center

Suburbs

Private homes

Small stores

Duplexes

Nearby small towns

1. Which of the following types of buildings are found in the outermost region surrounding a typical U.S. city?
   a. small stores
   b. apartments
   c. factories
   d. suburban homes
2. Based on what you have learned in this chapter, how is the population of a typical U.S. urban area distributed between the city center and the suburbs?

### Analyzing Primary Sources

Read the following quotation by Henry Cisneros, former secretary of Housing and Urban Development and former mayor of San Antonio, Texas. Then answer the questions that follow.

"In alarming numbers, citizens are becoming increasingly disengaged [separated] from public affairs, uninterested in the political process and public institutions, and skeptical that government has the talent, resources, and moral courage to solve problems. . . . The problems confronting us as a nation and as communities require immediate attention. The solutions will not come from government alone. The society we want and can have will be achieved only through the combined effort of involved and concerned citizens and the public, private, and voluntary sectors."

3. Which of the following statements best describes Cisneros's point of view?
   a. Government does not have the talent or courage to solve problems.
   b. People are uninterested in politics so officials should make decisions for them.
   c. A successful society requires cooperation between citizens, government, and businesses.
   d. Power should be taken away from government and put into the hands of volunteers and businesses.
4. Do you agree or disagree with Cisneros's argument?
5. Based on what you have learned in this chapter, create a list of volunteer organizations that are making or could make important contributions to your community.

### What Did You Find Out?

1. around transportation systems, resources, and useful climates; rural, suburban, and urban

2. They enjoy the company of others, access to a wide range of services, and the order and protection provided by laws and regulations.

3. by volunteering and fulfilling their duties and responsibilities as community members

### Thinking Critically

1. Some may feel it builds it by teaching participation. Others may feel the requirement dampens the spirit of volunteerism. Students should have sound reasoning.

2. Students may suggest that community service may teach offenders responsibility and respect for others.

3. People can be a part of a family, a local area, state, a country, and the world. These are all communities.

### Social Studies Skills

1. d

2. Students might suggest that a high percentage of the population of people who work in the city live in the suburbs.

3. c

4. Students' responses will vary.

5. Students' lists will vary but should reflect an understanding of your community's needs and the type of help available.

---

Alternative Assessment

### Building Your Portfolio

**Connecting to Community**
Use the Internet or a local newspaper to learn about a problem that citizens and elected officials are trying to solve. When you have finished your research, create a presentation with the following information: what the problem is, how citizens and government are trying to solve it, who is creating the plans, and how the solution will affect the community. Share the completed presentation with your class.

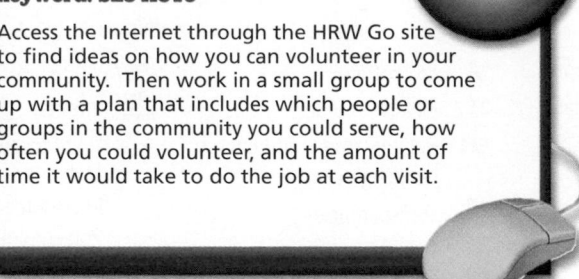

**internet connect**

**Internet Activity: go.hrw.com**
**keyword: SZ3 AC15**

Access the Internet through the HRW Go site to find ideas on how you can volunteer in your community. Then work in a small group to come up with a plan that includes which people or groups in the community you could serve, how often you could volunteer, and the amount of time it would take to do the job at each visit.

# Citizenship and the Law

## CHAPTER RESOURCE MANAGER

| Objectives | Pacing Guide | Reproducible Resources |
|---|---|---|
| **SECTION 1:**<br>**Crime in the United States**<br>(pp. 381–86)<br><br>✦ Distinguish the difference between a crime against a person and a crime against property.<br>✦ Identify the different types of crime.<br>✦ Analyze some of the causes of crime and how crime is fought. | **Regular**<br>2 days<br><br>**Block Scheduling**<br>1.5 days<br><br>*Block Scheduling Handbook with Team Teaching Strategies, Chapter 16* | **RS** Guided Reading Strategies 16.1<br>**E** Creative Teaching Strategy: Continuum<br>**RS** Graphic Organizer Activity: Causes of crime |
| **SECTION 2:**<br>**The Criminal Justice System**<br>(pp. 387–93)<br><br>✦ Identify the duties of police officers, and explain how people become police officers.<br>✦ Describe what happens to a suspect after he or she is arrested.<br>✦ Determine how criminals are punished. | **Regular**<br>2 days<br><br>**Block Scheduling**<br>1.5 days<br><br>*Block Scheduling Handbook with Team Teaching Strategies, Chapter 16* | **RS** Guided Reading Strategies 16.2<br>**E** Challenge and Enrichment Worksheet 16: Interpreting a Poll on Capital Punishment |
| **SECTION 3:**<br>**Juvenile Crime**<br>(pp. 395–99)<br><br>✦ Identify some of the possible causes of juvenile crime.<br>✦ Analyze how the judicial system has changed the way it handles juveniles.<br>✦ Explain what happens when juveniles are charged and found guilty of breaking the law. | **Regular**<br>1 day<br><br>**Block Scheduling**<br>.5 day<br><br>*Block Scheduling Handbook with Team Teaching Strategies, Chapter 16* | **RS** Guided Reading Strategies 16.3<br>**RS** Readings in Economics and Government 69: Abe Fortas's Opinion In *re Gault*<br>**SM** Community Service and Participation Handbook: Back Away From Crime |

## Chapter Resource Key

| | | | | |
|---|---|---|---|---|
| **PS** | Primary Sources | **SM** | Skills Mastery |  CD–ROM |
| **RS** | Reading Support | **A** | Assessment | Video |
| **IC** | Interdisciplinary Connections | **REV** | Review |  Internet |
| **E** | Enrichment | **ELL** | Reinforcement and English Language Learners |  Holt Presentation Maker Using Microsoft® PowerPoint® |
| | | | Transparencies | |

 **One-Stop** Planner CD–ROM

**See the *One-Stop Planner* for a complete list of additional resources for students and teachers.**

## One-Stop Planner CD–ROM

It's easy to plan lessons, select resources, and print out materials for your students when you use the **One-Stop Planner CD–ROM with Test Generator**.

### internet connect

**HRW ONLINE RESOURCES**
GO TO: go.hrw.com
Then type in the keyword.

**TEACHER HOME PAGE**
KEYWORD: SZ3 Teacher

**CHAPTER INTERNET ACTIVITIES**
KEYWORD: SZ3 AC16
Choose an activity to:
• write a report on teen court.
• create a display on the FBI.
• conduct a mock trial.

**CHAPTER ENRICHMENT LINKS**
KEYWORD: SZ3 CH16

**ONLINE ASSESSMENT**
**Homework Practice**
KEYWORD: SZ3 HP16
**Rubrics**
KEYWORD: SS Rubrics

**ONLINE MAPS, CHARTS, AND GRAPHS**
KEYWORD: SZ3 MCG
• Jurisdiction of the Lower Courts

**HOLT PRESENTATION MAKER**
KEYWORD: SZ3 PPT16

**CONTENT UPDATES**
KEYWORD: SS Content Updates

**ONLINE READING SUPPORT**
KEYWORD: SS Strategies

**CURRENT EVENTS**
KEYWORD: S3 Current Events

| Technology Resources | Reinforcement, Review, and Assessment |
|---|---|
| One-Stop Planner, Lesson 16.1<br>Homework Practice Online | REV  Section 1 Review, p. 386<br>A  Daily Quiz 16.1<br>A  Main Idea Activity 16.1<br>A  English Audio Summary 16.1<br>A  Spanish Audio Summary 16.1 |
| One-Stop Planner, Lesson 16.2<br>Holt Researcher CD–ROM<br>Homework Practice Online<br>HRW Go site | REV  Section 16 Review, p. 393<br>A  Daily Quiz 16.2<br>A  Main Idea Activity 16.2<br>ELL  English Audio Summary 16.2<br>ELL  Spanish Audio Summary 16.2 |
| One-Stop Planner, Lesson 16.3<br>CNN. Presents: American Government<br>Homework Practice Online | REV  Section 3 Review, p. 399<br>A  Daily Quiz 16.3<br>A  Main Idea Activity 16.3<br>ELL  English Audio Summary 16.3<br>ELL  Spanish Audio Summary 16.3 |

## Meeting Individual Needs

### Ability Levels

**Level 1** Basic-level activities designed for all students encountering new material

**Level 2** Intermediate-level activities designed for average students

**Level 3** Challenging activities designed for honors and gifted-and-talented students

**English Language Learners** Activities that address the needs of students with Limited English Proficiency

## Chapter Review and Assessment

IC  Vocabulary Activity 16
  Global Skill Builder CD–ROM
HRW Go site
REV  Chapter 16 Tutorial for Students, Parents, Mentors, and Peers
REV  Chapter 16 Review, pp. 400–401
A  Standardized Test Practice
A  Chapter 16 Test Generator (on the One-Stop Planner)
A  Chapter 16 Test (Form A or B)
A  Alternative Assessment Handbook
A  Chapter 16 Test for English Language Learners and Special-Needs Students

★★★★
**CHAPTER 16**

Section 1    Crime in the
             United States

Section 2    The Criminal
             Justice System

Section 3    Juvenile Crime

## What's Your Opinion?

*To help students create their **Themes** Journal entries, provide the following examples of appropriate **agree**/**disagree** statements.*

● **Agree**  Victimless crimes are not true criminal acts.

**Disagree**  Any illegal act, whether committed against a person or not, is a criminal act.

● **Agree**  Accused criminals should not be given the same rights as innocent citizens.

**Disagree**  All citizens deserve the same rights until they are proven guilty in a court of law.

● **Agree**  Children cannot be expected to receive the same treatment and punishment as adults.

**Disagree**  All criminals should be treated equally, regardless of age.

## Internet Activity

### FBI Story

**TOPIC:** The Federal Bureau of Investigation
**GO TO:** go.hrw.com
**KEYWORD:** SZ3 AC16

Have students access the Internet through the HRW Go site to conduct research about the many aspects of the Federal Bureau of Investigation. Ask each student to choose the aspect of the FBI that most interests them and to create a visual displaying their findings.

# CHAPTER ★★★★
# 16 Citizenship and the Law

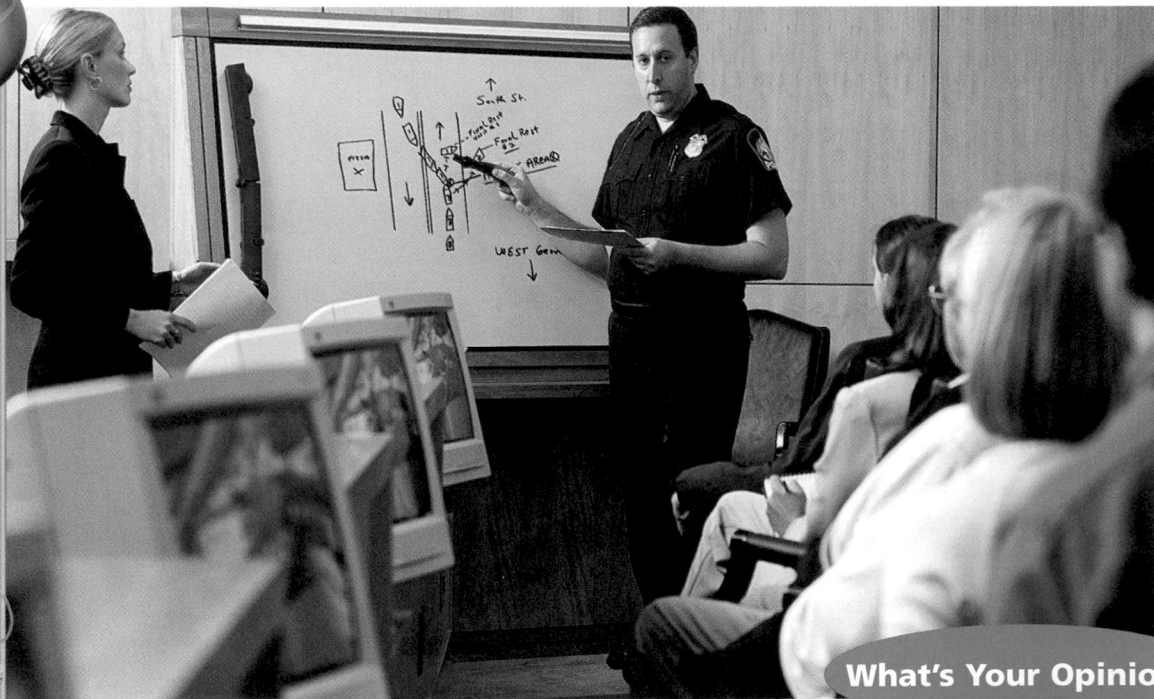

### Build on What You Know

The Declaration of Independence, the Constitution, and the Bill of Rights guarantee basic rights and freedoms to all Americans and establish the rule of law in American society. Although it is the duty of all citizens to obey the law, some people choose to break the law. We, therefore, must rely on a system of police, courts, and prisons to protect us. But you also need to do your part. You must learn and obey the laws and encourage others to do the same. Only if all Americans work toward stopping crime can we feel safe in our homes, communities, and country.

### What's Your Opinion?

**Themes Journal**  Do you **agree** or **disagree** with the following statements? Support your point of view in your journal.

● In order for an act to be criminal, it must be committed against another person.

● People who are accused of committing crimes should not have rights.

● Children who commit crimes should be treated differently than adults who commit crimes.

# SECTION 1

## OBJECTIVES

*After completing Section 1, students should be able to*

1 **Distinguish the difference between a crime against a person and a crime against property.**

2 **Identify the different types of crime.**

3 **Analyze some of the causes of crime and how crime is fought.**

### 🔊 LET'S GET STARTED!

As students enter the classroom explain that state laws distinguish between the seriousness of crimes, categorizing some crimes as felonies and less serious crimes as misdemeanors. Then have students categorize school rules according to seriousness. Ask students to label serious rule violations as felonies and less serious violations as misdemeanors. *(Students might label fighting at school as a felony, and being tardy as a misdemeanor.)* Finally, tell students that in Section 1 they will learn more about crime in the United States.

## SECTION 1

# Crime in the United States

### Read to Discover

1. What is the difference between a crime against a person and a crime against property?
2. What are some different types of crime?
3. What are some causes of crime, and how is crime fought?

### WHY CIVICS MATTERS

A variety of factors cause the national crime rate to rise or fall. Use CNNfyi.com or other **current events** sources to investigate trends in the national crime rate. Record your findings in your journal.

### Define

- crime
- criminal
- felonies
- misdemeanors
- homicide
- aggravated assault
- forcible rape
- burglary
- larceny
- petty larceny
- grand larceny
- robbery
- vandalism
- arson
- victimless crimes
- white-collar crimes
- embezzlement
- fraud

## SECTION 1 RESOURCES

### REPRODUCIBLE

▶ Guided Reading Strategies 16.1
▶ Creative Teaching Strategy: Continuum
▶ Graphic Organizer Activity: Causes of Crime

### TECHNOLOGY

▶ One-Stop Planner, Lesson 16.1
▶ Homework Practice Online

### REINFORCEMENT, REVIEW, AND ASSESSMENT

▶ Section 1 Review, p. 386
▶ Daily Quiz 16.1
▶ Main Idea Activity 16.1
▶ English Audio Summary 16.1
▶ Spanish Audio Summary 16.1

## Reading Focus

The Federal Bureau of Investigation (FBI) provides information on crime in the United States. From 1990 to 2000 an average of 1.8 million violent crimes were reported each year. Although crime rates have dropped in the past decade, crime continues to be a problem for many U.S. communities.

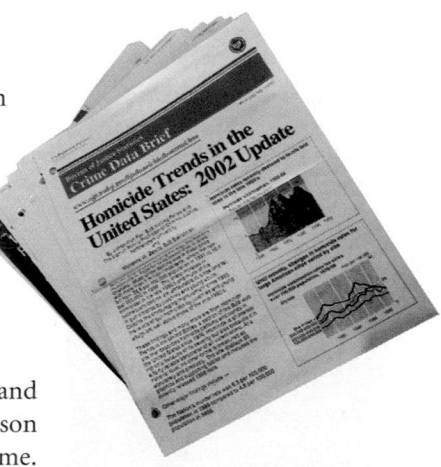

*Government officials and law enforcement agencies carefully review annual crime statistics to help determine the success of their programs.*

## ★ Types of Crime

What is considered a crime? A **crime** is any act that breaks the law and for which a punishment has been established. A **criminal** is a person who commits any type of crime. The FBI identifies 29 types of crime. Serious crimes, such as homicide and kidnapping, are called **felonies.** Less serious offenses, such as traffic violations and disorderly conduct, are known as **misdemeanors.**

The 29 types of crime can be categorized in other ways as well. Five main crime categories are crimes against persons, crimes against property, victimless crimes, white-collar crimes, and organized crimes.

**Crimes against Persons** Crimes against persons are violent crimes. They include acts that harm a person, end a person's life, or that threaten to do so. The most serious of such crimes is **homicide,** or the killing of one person by another person. From 1995 to 2000, an average of 17,000 homicides were committed in the United States each year.

# TEACH OBJECTIVE 1

**LEVEL 1:** Lead a class discussion about the difference between a crime against a person and a crime against property. *(Crimes against a person are violent crimes, or acts that harm or end a person's life or threaten to do so. Most crimes committed in the United States are crimes against property, which include actions such as stealing or destroying property.)* Then have students write a position statement arguing that one type of crime is more damaging to society than the other. Ask volunteers to present their statements to the class.
**ENGLISH LANGUAGE LEARNERS**

**LEVEL 3:** Organize students into groups and have each group create a public service announcement about the risks and dangers of crimes against people and crimes against property. *(See the Level 1 lesson for differences.)* In their announcements, groups should discuss the differences between the two types of crime and list specific examples of both. Finally, have groups present their public service announcements to the class.
**COOPERATIVE LEARNING**

**WARNING:**

**SHOPLIFTERS WILL BE PROSECUTED TO THE FULLEST EXTENT OF THE LAW.**

*Many stores post signs like this as warnings to potential criminals.*

**Interpreting the Visual Record**

**Stolen cars** *Car thieves often break up the stolen vehicles and sell the parts.* **How do you think such criminal acts make the job of police more difficult?**

Some homicides can also be classified as hate crimes. Hate crimes are violent crimes committed against people because of particular prejudices. Hate crimes include those committed against someone for racial or religious reasons. They also include crimes committed against people because of their disabilities.

The most common type of violent crime is aggravated assault. **Aggravated assault** is any kind of physical injury that is done intentionally to another person. Such assault is often committed during the act of robbing someone. The FBI records about 1 million cases of aggravated assault each year.

Another type of violent crime is the sexual violation of a person by force and against the person's will. The FBI terms this type of crime **forcible rape**. In the past five years an average of 90,000 forcible rapes have taken place in the United States each year.

✔ **Reading Check** **Summarizing** What are some examples of violent crime? homicide, aggravated assault, forcible rape

## Crimes against Property

Most crimes committed in the United States are crimes against property. This type of crime includes actions that involve stealing or destroying someone else's property. The forcible or illegal entry into someone's home or other property with the intention to steal is called **burglary.** In recent years about 2 million burglaries were reported annually.

**Larceny** is the theft of property without the use of force or violence against another person. Examples of larceny include stealing from a cash register and shoplifting. A theft of goods valued under a certain amount of money is called **petty larceny.** A theft of goods worth more than a certain amount of money is called **grand larceny.** The amount of money used to determine whether a theft is petty or grand larceny varies from state to state.

The theft of automobiles, or motor-vehicle theft, is a common crime against property and a serious national problem. In recent years, about 1.2 million cars have been reported stolen annually. Many cars are taken by organized gangs that resell them or strip them and sell the parts. Other cases typically involve young people who steal the cars, drive them for a while, and then abandon them.

**Robbery** is a crime that involves both property and persons. It may be defined as taking something from a person by threatening the person with injury. The robber may demand the person's property and back the threat with a weapon. Some 400,000 robberies take place in the United States each year. Many of them involve the use of firearms.

**ALL LEVELS:** Copy the following graphic organizer onto the chalkboard, omitting the italicized answers. Have students complete the web to identify the different types of crime. **ENGLISH LANGUAGE LEARNERS**

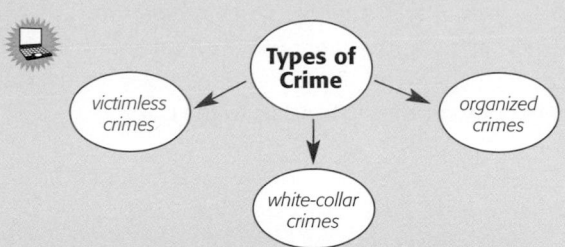

**LEVEL 2:** Have students bring a week's worth of newspapers to class and then have them read the newspapers to find articles about crime. Ask students to list on the chalkboard the different kinds of crime written about in the newspapers. Then have students write a position statement for the following question: Is anyone in society not affected by crime? Explain. Finally, lead a brief discussion on the different types of crimes listed. *(See the All Levels lesson for types.)*

Another kind of crime against property is **vandalism,** or the willful destruction of property. **Arson** is the destruction of property by setting fire to it. The damaging of schools and other public property by vandalism and arson hurts all citizens in a community.

✔ **Reading Check Comparing and Contrasting** How are burglary, larceny, and robbery the same, and how are they different? All three crimes involve the theft of property. Burglary involves entering a home or other property, larceny is nonviolent theft, and robbery is violent theft.

## ⭐ Victimless Crimes and White-Collar Crimes

Some crimes, such as gambling and the use of illegal drugs, are called **victimless crimes.** In such crimes, the criminal does not violate another person's rights. There is no victim involved. These crimes mainly harm the lawbreakers themselves. Nevertheless, victimless crimes are harmful to society. The sale and possession of illegal drugs increases the death rate and often leads to other types of crime, such as robbery. Gamblers who lose their money may turn to stealing and other crimes. People who use drugs may also hurt their family members if they become violent.

Crimes committed by people in the course of their work are called **white-collar crimes.** These crimes range from stealing office supplies to **embezzlement** and **fraud.** Embezzlement is taking money that has been entrusted to one's care for one's own use. Fraud is cheating someone out of their money or property. A person commits fraud when charging for services that were not performed, for example.

**Interpreting the Visual Record**

**Arson** *Arson is one of the most destructive crimes against property. It is also very dangerous and can cause severe injuries or death.* **How do such crimes harm the community?**

## TEACH OBJECTIVE 3

**LEVEL 1:** Have students list on the chalkboard the reasons that people commit crimes. *(Students might list poverty, illegal drug use, or population shifts as possible reasons.)* To help them understand these reasons, ask students to make up specific examples, or scenarios, of fictional characters who turn to crime—one example for each reason listed on the chalkboard. Ask volunteers to present their fictional scenarios to the class. **ENGLISH LANGUAGE LEARNERS**

**LEVELS 2 AND 3:** Have students write newspaper editorials on how to decrease crime rates. Editorials should include references to the causes of crime, although students are free to argue that one (or more) of these causes has less to do with crime than others do. Each editorial should include proposals for addressing the causes of crime and other methods for reducing crime. *(Students might suggest stricter penalties for violent offenders, new prisons, and more police officers.)* Some students might want to focus on efforts to fight organized crime. Call on volunteers to present their editorials to the class.

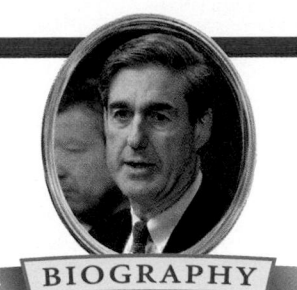

### BIOGRAPHY

## Robert S. Mueller III
### (1944– )

Robert S. Mueller III lives in San Francisco, California. He studied International Studies and law in college. He also served for three years in the marines, earning medals that include the Bronze Star and the Purple Heart. Beginning in 1976 he served in various states as a prosecutor and supervisor. In those positions he investigated and prosecuted cases involving narcotics, tax violations, and public corruption.

In 1990 Mueller was named assistant attorney general in the Department of Justice. He served in several positions within the Department of Justice, supervising and taking part in investigations covering subjects such as organized crime, computer crime, and terrorist attacks. He also practiced law privately for a brief period as a partner in a Boston law firm.

In 2001 President George W. Bush appointed Mueller as director of the Federal Bureau of Investigation. One of his first responsibilities was coordinating FBI efforts to combat terrorism in the wake of the September 11 terrorist attacks on the United States. Among his key priorities have been improving the FBI's computer network and its communication with other law enforcement agencies. **How has Mueller's previous experience helped prepare him for his position as director of the FBI?**

It is impossible to know exactly how much money such crimes cost American businesses each year. However, experts estimate that it may cost them billions of dollars. The financial costs of white-collar crimes are then passed on to consumers in the form of higher prices. Thus, everyone in society ends up paying for the costs that result from white-collar crimes.

Many white-collar crimes involve computers, which most businesses and government offices use to store essential and sensitive information. Some criminals, often called hackers, break into these computer systems to commit electronic theft, fraud, and embezzlement.

✔ **Reading Check Drawing Inferences and Conclusions** How does society ultimately end up paying for victimless crimes and white-collar crimes? Students might say that victimless crimes often lead to other types of crime. White-collar crimes increase costs for consumers and businesses.

## ⭐ Organized Crime

When most people think of criminals, they think of individuals who act on their own to commit crimes. This is not always the case. Some criminals are part of organized crime. That is, they belong to a crime syndicate, or a large organization of career criminals.

Organized crime syndicates specialize in providing illegal goods and services. These include gambling, drug trafficking, prostitution, and loan-sharking, or lending money at extremely high interest rates. Often these crime syndicates engage in legal business pursuits that serve as a front, or cover, for illegal activities. They often use the threat of violence to keep people from going to the police.

✔ **Reading Check Summarizing** What are the most common criminal activities for organized crime syndicates? prostitution, gambling, drug trafficking, and loan-sharking

## ⭐ Determining the Crime Rate

National statistics on crime are collected from local police departments by the FBI. The U.S. Bureau of Justice Statistics, meanwhile, collects information on crime from crime victims. Even with all of this information, it is impossible to know how many crimes are committed each year. Many crimes go undetected, and citizens do not always report crimes to the police. For these reasons, the crime rate is undoubtedly higher than statistics indicate.

✔ **Reading Check Finding the Main Idea** Why is the crime rate higher than what statistics indicate? Some crimes go either undetected or unreported.

**HOMEWORK** Have each student create a vocabulary quiz using this section's Define terms. Tell students that they may choose the format of the quiz. After they return to class with their finished assignments, organize students into pairs. Have pairs exchange quizzes, complete them, and return them to their authors for grading.

## CLOSE

Have students create anticrime posters. Each student should determine whether his or her poster's audience is comprised of children, teenagers, adults, or the general public. The posters should address such topics as ways to prevent crime and how to avoid being a crime victim.

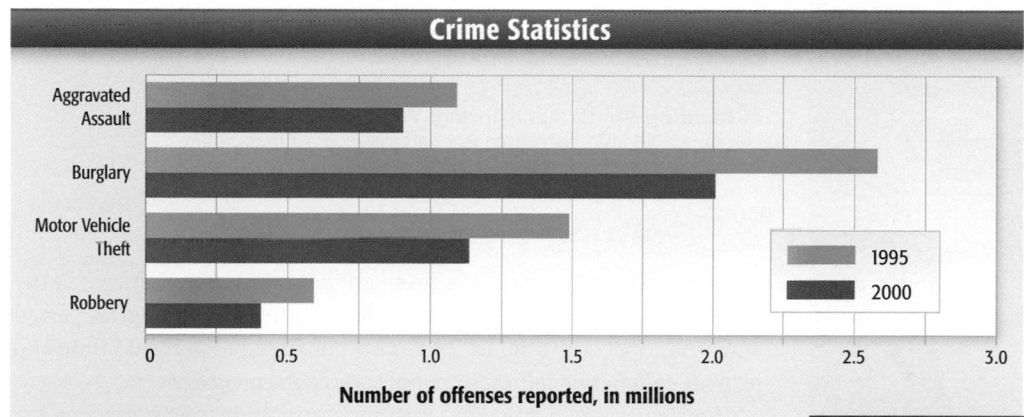

**Crime Statistics**

Source: Federal Bureau of Investigation

**Interpreting Graphs**
*The Federal Bureau of Investigation keeps extensive records on reported crimes in the United States.* **What general trend in crime took place between 1995 and 2000 according to these figures?**

## ★ Causes of Crime

Although no one really knows why people commit crimes, many theories exist. The causes usually given for crime and its increase are poverty, illegal drug use, and certain trends in society.

**Poverty** One cause of crime is poverty. Many poor people live in overcrowded, rundown areas. They may be poorly educated and have unstable family lives. Under these conditions, many people do not receive the training they need for good jobs. As a result, some feel helpless and may turn to breaking the law to try to obtain things they do not have.

**Illegal Drug Use** In recent years the use of illegal drugs has risen in the United States. Between 1984 and 2000, drug offense charges in federal courts rose from almost 12,000 to over 32,000. Arrests related to drug use add to the crime rate, and people who use illegal drugs often turn to other types of crime to support expensive drug habits.

**Permissive Society** Some people believe that a permissive society contributes to crime. They say many parents spoil their children and permit them to do anything they want. These children sometimes find it difficult to control their behavior when they are older. They have not learned to act responsibly in their own lives and toward others. Other people believe the courts are too permissive. They say judges often are too lenient with convicted criminals.

**Urbanization** Some experts suggest that urbanization plays a role in crime. More offenses are committed in cities than in rural areas. As the United States has become urbanized, the crime rate has also risen. There are many reasons for this. More people live in cities, thus providing more opportunities for criminals. In addition, there are more young

## Interdisciplinary Connection

► **Science** ◄

**Computer Crime** A growing area of criminal activity is computer crime. Computers have been used in various crimes ranging from theft, burglary, larceny, fraud, embezzlement, extortion, sabotage, espionage, kidnapping, and murder. Computer systems can also fall victim to attacks, such as a computer virus—a portion of a program that is designed to destroy data and program code. More serious crimes involving computers occur in the banking-financial industry, where financial records can be altered to enhance, decrease, or delete a person's account.

**CRITICAL THINKING**
What technological advancement might have contributed to an increase in computer crime?

**ANSWER:** Students might suggest that the Internet may play an important role in increasing computer crime.

**GRAPH ANSWER**
It decreased.

**BIOGRAPHY ANSWER**
(for page 384)
He had an extensive background in law enforcement.

## REVIEW AND ASSESS

Have students complete the **Section 1 Review** on page 386. Then have students complete **Daily Quiz 16.1**. As **Alternative Assessment**, you may want to use the types of crime organizer or the causes of crime editorials in this section's lessons.

## RETEACH

Have students complete **Main Idea Activity for English Language Learners and Special-Needs Students 16.1**. Then have students list the different types of crimes on the chalkboard. Have one volunteer provide an example of each type of crime listed and have another volunteer provide a possible cause for the crime. Continue this exercise for each type of crime. **ENGLISH LANGUAGE LEARNERS** , **COOPERATIVE LEARNING**

## EXTEND

Have students conduct research to determine the latest crime statistics. Have students identify whom they should contact to find the most recent statistics. (*The FBI is the most reliable source.*) Then have students imagine that they are newspaper reporters writing a story on the crime rate in their community. Have each student write a dialogue that might take place between a reporter and the FBI. **BLOCK SCHEDULING**

## Section 1 Review
### ANSWERS

**1. Define**
- crime, p. 381
- criminal, p. 381
- felonies, p. 381
- misdemeanors, p. 381
- homicide, p. 381
- aggravated assault, p. 382
- forcible rape, p. 382
- burglary, p. 382
- larceny, p. 382
- petty larceny, p. 382
- grand larceny, p. 382
- robbery, p. 382
- vandalism, p. 383
- arson, p. 383
- victimless crimes, p. 383
- white-collar crimes, p. 383
- embezzlement, p. 383
- fraud, p. 383

**2.** Crimes against persons—murder, aggravated assault, forcible rape; Crimes against property—burglary, larceny, robbery, vandalism, arson; Victimless crimes—sale and possession of illegal drugs; White-collar crimes—embezzlement, fraud; Organized crime—drug trafficking

**3. a.** crimes against persons—acts that harm or end a person's life or that threaten to do so; crimes against property—stealing or destroying someone else's property

**b.** poverty, illegal drug use, permissive society, urbanization

**4.** Students' speeches will vary but should include various methods that can be used to reduce crime.

### Interpreting the Visual Record

**Preventing crimes** *An important aspect of crime prevention is education. Young people commit much of the crime reported in the United States, so police participate in school programs to encourage young Americans to obey the law.* **What is taking place in this image?**

people in cities. People under the age of 25 account for about half of all of those arrested in the United States.

✔ **Reading Check Summarizing** What are some of the main causes of crime? poverty, illegal drug use, permissiveness, urbanization

### ⭐ Fighting Crime

Whatever its causes, crime is a problem that harms every citizen. Partly in response to the growing public outcry about crime, Congress passed a new national crime bill in 1994. This bill aimed to prevent crime and provide tougher penalties for people who commit crimes.

Strategies for achieving these goals include life sentences for three-time violent offenders, grants to build new prisons, and grants to state and local communities to hire more police officers. Providing crime-prevention education in the schools is another tool in the fight against crime.

The crime rate has decreased since these new strategies have been in place. However, putting an end to crime requires citizen involvement. Citizens must report all crimes that they see and take precautions to ensure their safety and the safety of others. Citizens must also lend their support to the police officers who work to serve and protect their communities.

✔ **Reading Check Analyzing Information** What can government and citizens do to fight crime? Government can increase criminal penalties and police funding, build new prisons, and educate citizens. Citizens can report criminal activity and work with police.

go.
hrw.com
**Homework Practice Online**
keyword: SZ3 HP16

## SECTION 1 Review

**1. Define** and explain:
- crime
- criminal
- felonies
- misdemeanors
- homicide
- aggravated assault
- forcible rape
- burglary
- larceny
- petty larceny
- grand larceny
- robbery
- vandalism
- arson
- victimless crimes
- white-collar crimes
- embezzlement
- fraud

**2. Categorizing** Copy the chart below. Fill in the boxes with different types of crime on the left and examples of each type of crime on the right.

| Type of Crime | Examples |
| --- | --- |
|  |  |
|  |  |
|  |  |
|  |  |
|  |  |
|  |  |
|  |  |
|  |  |

**3. Finding the Main Idea**
a. How are crimes against persons and crimes against property different?
b. What are the main causes of crime?

**4. Writing and Critical Thinking**
**Problem Solving** Imagine that you are the police commissioner for a city. Write a speech discussing how government and citizens can work to reduce crime.

**Consider:**
- steps that have already been taken
- the responsibilities of citizens and government

# SECTION 2

## OBJECTIVES

*After completing Section 2, students should be able to*

1 Identify the duties of police officers, and explain how people become police officers.
2 Describe what happens to a suspect after he or she is arrested.
3 Determine how criminals are punished.

## 🔔 LET'S GET STARTED!

Write the term *parole* on the chalkboard. As students enter the classroom, ask them what they think this word means. *(Students might suggest that it means being released from prison early but promising not to get in trouble again.)* Tell students that the word *parole* comes from the French word for "promise" or "word." Then ask students what *capital* means in the term *capital punishment*? Tell students that the Latin root *capit* means "head." In the past some people were executed by decapitation—having one's head cut off. Finally, tell students that in Section 2 they will learn more about the criminal justice system in the United States.

---

## SECTION 2

# The Criminal Justice System

### Read to Discover

1. What are the duties of police officers, and how do people become police officers?
2. What happens to a suspect after he or she is arrested?
3. How are criminals punished?

#### WHY CIVICS MATTERS

Many states have laws permitting capital punishment, or the death penalty. Use **CNNfyi.com** or other **current events** sources to investigate capital punishment in your state or neighboring states. Conduct research on what type of punishment is used and how often it is applied. Record your findings in your journal.

### Define

• criminal justice system
• community policing
• probable cause
• arrest warrant
• own recognizance
• arraignment
• defense
• prosecution
• defendant
• acquit
• sentence
• plea bargain
• corrections
• deterrence
• rehabilitation
• parole
• capital punishment

## *Reading Focus*

Society depends on responsible citizens who obey the law. It also needs officials to help achieve the constitutional goal of "domestic tranquillity." For this reason, police forces have been established at the local, state, and national levels.

### ★ Role of the Police

Keeping the peace requires more than hiring police officers to arrest criminals. Once arrested, an accused person must be tried and, if found guilty, punished. The three-part system of police, courts, and corrections used to bring criminals to justice is known as the **criminal justice system.**

The police have a number of duties. These include protecting life and property, preventing crime, and arresting people who violate the law. They also include protecting the rights of the individual, maintaining peace and order, and controlling the flow of traffic on streets and highways.

It is not a police officer's job to punish suspects or to decide whether they are guilty. Deciding questions of guilt and innocence is the function of courts of law. Rather, good police officers use their trained judgment about whom to arrest and on what grounds. They try to avoid the use of undue force and to be patient in the face of

## SECTION 2 RESOURCES

### REPRODUCIBLE

▶ Guided Reading Strategies 16.2
▶ Challenge and Enrichment Worksheet 16: Interpreting a Poll on Capital Punishment

### TECHNOLOGY

▶ One-Stop Planner, Lesson 16.2
▶ Holt Researcher CD–ROM
▶ Homework Practice Online
▶ HRW Go site

### REINFORCEMENT, REVIEW, AND ASSESSMENT

▶ Section 2 Review, p. 393
▶ Daily Quiz 16.2
▶ Main Idea Activity 16.2
▶ English Audio Summary 16.2
▶ Spanish Audio Summary 16.2

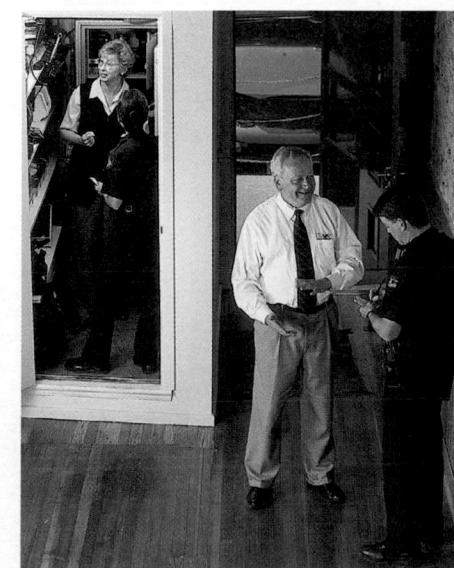

*The police work with citizens to gain clear information about crimes after they have been committed.*

**LEVEL 1:** Ask students to imagine that they are new police officers beginning their first day walking a beat in a major city. Ask them to write a journal entries expressing the anxiety or anticipation they might feel. As part of the journal entries, students should describe their duties as a police officer and also recall how they became an officer. *(Students' entries should indicate that before they were hired, their background was fully investigated, they had to take tests, and they had to pass difficult physical and psychological examinations. Their duties include protecting life and property, preventing crime, arresting those who violate the law, and maintaining peace and order.)* **ENGLISH LANGUAGE LEARNERS**

**ALL LEVELS:** Organize students into four groups. Have each group create an episode for a crime drama (or comedy) television show. Each episode should be written about a rookie police officer in his or her first week on the job, chronicling what he or she had to undergo to become an officer and what his or her duties as a uniformed police officer are now. *(See the Level 1 lesson for requirements and duties.)* When groups have created their episodes, have them perform them before the class. **ENGLISH LANGUAGE LEARNERS ,COOPERATIVE LEARNING**

## ★ Civics Sidelight

**The First Female Police Chief** More and more women have joined police forces in recent years, but the job of police chief has traditionally gone to a man. In 1990 Elizabeth M. Watson became the first woman to be named police chief of one of the country's 20 largest cities. Watson's appointment to head the Houston Police Department came after 17 years on the force. She worked her way up through the ranks, becoming Houston's first female captain in 1984 and the city's first female deputy chief in 1987. Watson, who comes from a family of police officers, said, "I am deeply committed to policing, and if in the course of doing that I serve as a role model to other women, I am doubly honored."

### CRITICAL THINKING

What positive effect might a female police chief have on recruiting officers?

**ANSWER:** Students might suggest that Watson might serve as a role model for other women, encouraging more female applicants.

### Visual Record Answer

*advantages—quicker response and mobility around crowded areas; disadvantages—difficult to pursue criminals in vehicles.*

**★★★★★★★★★★★★**
### That's Interesting!
**★★★★★★★★★★★★**

**Where Are the Police?** Can you imagine a city of more than 500,000 people without a permanent police force? Well, that's just what New York City was like before 1853. A volunteer night watch patrolled the city. During the day an officer known as a constable was on duty. He and his assistants were paid a fee for each crime they helped stop. Private citizens were often asked to catch criminals. This system was used in other cities as well. As cities grew larger, this system could not keep up with crime. Cities began creating permanent forces of paid and trained police officers.

### Interpreting the Visual Record

**On patrol** *In some crowded urban areas the police use bicycle patrols to improve their response time and mobility.* **What might be some advantages and disadvantages of using bicycle patrols?**

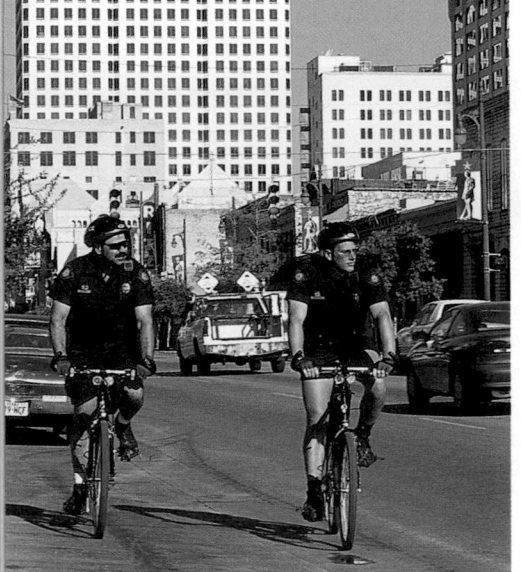

insults and threats of personal injury. Police officers act as peacemakers, advisers, protectors, and community members as well as law enforcers. The job of a police officer is not an easy one. It can also be a frustrating job because of the overextension of court resources and other problems in the U.S. court system.

✔ **Reading Check Summarizing** What are some of the duties of police officers? protecting life and property, arresting people who violate the law, maintaining peace and order, and directing traffic

## ★ Training Police Officers

Today's police officers are carefully selected and trained. Before they are hired, their backgrounds are fully investigated. They must pass aptitude and intelligence tests as well as written tests. They also must complete difficult physical and psychological examinations. Most cities require police officers to be high-school graduates. Some cities seek college graduates.

New police officers attend police academies. There they learn about law, community relations, gathering evidence, arrest procedures, and record keeping. They also receive on-the-job training that includes the use of weapons and other physical skills. They are taught how to deal calmly with the public, how to handle emergencies, and how to give first aid. When trouble occurs, they must be ready to arrest suspects, prepare reports for the courts, and appear in court as witnesses.

✔ **Reading Check Finding the Main Idea** How are police officers selected and trained? Police officers must pass mental, physical, and psychological tests and learn about law, community relations, arrest procedures, and other job-specific skills.

## ★ Police Patrols

Some police officers may make communities safer "walking a beat," or patrolling an assigned area. Because such foot patrols are an effective way to prevent crime, many experienced police officers are returning to foot patrols. These patrols, combined with small local police stations, are experiments in **community policing.** In community policing, officers are encouraged to get to know the people who live and work in the neighborhood. Community members are encouraged to rely on the officers for help, to report crimes, and to become involved in crime-prevention programs.

Most communities add to the strength and mobility of their police forces by using patrol cars. Radio-equipped police cars can be sent to any part of the city when trouble is reported or suspected. Many patrol cars now carry computers that give officers immediate access to crime information.

# TEACH OBJECTIVE 2

**ALL LEVELS:** Copy the following graphic organizer onto the chalkboard, omitting the italicized answers. Have students complete the chart to describe what happens after a suspect is arrested. **ENGLISH LANGUAGE LEARNERS**

A police officer's main responsibility is to prevent crime. A well-trained officer knows the factors that invite crime—burned-out streetlights, unlocked doors, broken windows. By preventing crime, officers save lives, money, and property. They also make the community a better and safer place to live.

When a crime is committed, police officers question suspects and witnesses, collect evidence, and recover property whenever possible. At the same time, officers must take care to protect the rights of suspects and witnesses.

✔ **Reading Check** Analyzing Information Why do police officers patrol neighborhoods? **Police patrol neighborhoods to prevent crimes before they happen, making neighborhoods safer and better places to live.**

## ★ From Arrest to Sentencing

A police officer must have **probable cause** to arrest a suspect. Probable cause means that the officer must have witnessed the crime or have gathered enough evidence to make an arrest. If the suspect has not been seen committing a crime, an **arrest warrant** may be necessary. An arrest warrant is an authorization by the court to make the arrest.

According to the Bill of Rights, all arrested suspects are entitled to due process and must be informed of their rights before they are questioned. They must be told that they have the right to remain silent and to have a lawyer present during questioning. Arrested suspects must also be told that anything they say can be used against them in a court of law. If a suspect is not given this information before questioning, any statements he or she makes cannot be used as evidence in court.

After the arrest, the suspect is taken to the police station for "booking"—record of the arrest is made. An officer writes down the name of the suspect, the time of the arrest, and the charges involved. If the person is suspected of a felony or a serious misdemeanor, he or she is fingerprinted and photographed. If a person is accused of drunk driving or a misdemeanor, a single fingerprint is taken.

**Preliminary Hearing** A preliminary hearing is held no later than 10 days after the arrest. During this procedure a judge must decide if there is enough evidence to send the case to trial. If there is not, the judge can dismiss, or drop, the charges against the suspect. If the charges are not dropped, the judge must decide whether to set bail. Bail is the money a suspect posts as a guarantee that he or she will return for trial.

A judge sets the bail amount, which is usually determined by the seriousness of the offense. For minor offenses, the judge may agree to release the suspect on his or her

**Holt Researcher**

**go.hrw.com**
**KEYWORD: Holt Researcher**
**FreeFind: Police**

Look up the entry on the police officer career on the Holt Researcher. Use the information in that entry to write a brief report that answers the following question: What responsibilities and duties do police officers typically have to fulfill?

**Interpreting the Visual Record**

**Booking** *Individuals suspected of serious crimes are fingerprinted for identification purposes.* **How might fingerprint records help the police identify suspects in crimes that have no witnesses?**

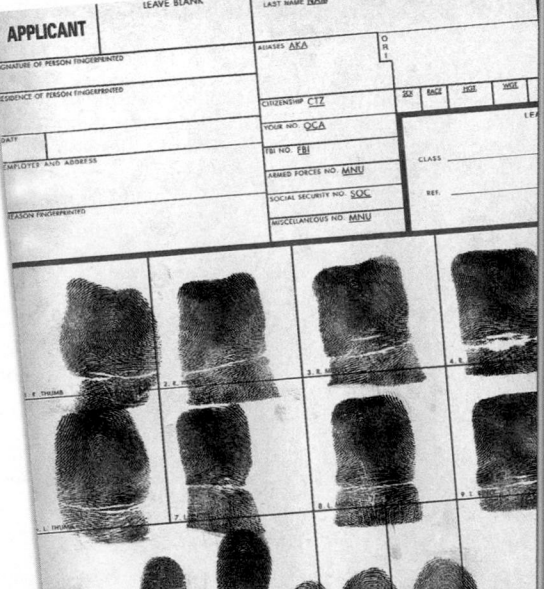

## ★ Civics Sidelight

**Policing Your Neighborhood** Efforts to deal with rising occurrences of crime have led to increased co-operation between community residents and police departments in many cities. In Seattle, Washington, for example, so-called community policing has helped lower the incidence of serious crime in many neighborhoods. Community residents and businesspeople have formed organizations, such as the South Seattle Crime Prevention Council, that work with police to tackle problems like drug dealing and violent crime in neighborhoods. Residents and businesspeople alert police to problems in their communities and help law enforcement officials set priorities in fighting crime in various neighborhoods.

**CRITICAL THINKING**

Why might community policing programs be effective in reducing crime?

**ANSWER:** Students might suggest that with community involvement there will be more people watching for criminal acts.

**Visual Record Answer**

*They allow police to determine who was at the scene of the crime.*

**LEVEL 2:** Organize students into groups. Have each group create an illustrated time line that shows the due process rights of a criminal suspect from arrest to sentencing. *(See the All Levels lesson for due process.)* Each group member should be responsible for illustrating at least one of the steps. Each step in the process should have an explanatory caption. Have a volunteer from each group present his or her group's time line to the class. **COOPERATIVE LEARNING**

**LEVEL 3:** Review with students the various steps that a suspect undergoes after he or she is arrested. Then discuss with students the details of *Gideon* v. *Wainwright*. Ask students to draw flowcharts summarizing the *Gideon* case. They should box each item and connect items with an arrow to show time order. The first item might be "Someone broke into a pool hall and stole money and food." The last item might be "Gideon was found innocent and given his freedom." Once students have completed their flowcharts, lead a class discussion about which steps in the process from arrest to sentencing were affected by the outcome of the *Gideon* case.

## Civics Sidelight

### Defending the Poor

Clarence Gideon was accused of theft but was unable to hire a lawyer to defend himself. Although he asked the court to provide counsel, the judge refused and Gideon lost his trial. While in jail he studied law books and eventually petitioned the Supreme Court to review his case. The court granted his petition and ultimately decided that Gideon's Sixth Amendment rights were violated. As a result of this landmark case, the Supreme Court ruled that an attorney must be furnished to any defendant who cannot afford to hire one. In many places around the country, judges assign attorneys from the local community or from legal aid societies to handle these cases. Since *Gideon* v. *Wainwright*, however, a growing number of state and local governments have established tax-supported public defender systems. These attorneys receive a salary for their work and handle only indigent cases. In 1970, Congress passed legislation authorizing the appointment of federal public defenders by federal courts of appeal.

#### CRITICAL THINKING

Why is it important to have the public defender system?

**ANSWER:** Students might suggest that the public defender system helps guarantee fair and equal treatment of economically disadvantaged citizens.

**own recognizance,** or without bail. If the suspect lives in the community and has a good reputation, he or she is usually released without bail. It is assumed that the suspect's community ties will ensure his or her appearance in court for the trial.

**Indictment** Next, a formal charge must be made. In some states a grand jury hears the evidence to decide whether to send the case to trial. If the grand jury finds probable cause, the suspect is indicted, or charged formally with the crime.

**Arraignment** The accused person then appears before a judge for **arraignment.** During this process the accused enters a plea of guilty or not guilty to the charge. If the person pleads guilty, no trial is necessary.

**Trial** If the accused person pleads not guilty to the charge, the case goes to trial. The **defense** represents the accused person's side of the case. The government's side of the case is presented by the **prosecution.** The defense and prosecution lawyers choose the jurors for the trial from a large group of people. Both of these lawyers have the right to question prospective jurors and reject people they believe to be prejudiced against their case.

After the jury has been selected, the prosecutor and the defense lawyer make opening statements to the jury. Each lawyer outlines the facts he or she will try to prove. First, the prosecutor presents the case against the **defendant,** or accused person. Witnesses are sworn in,

## SUPREME COURT CASE STUDY

### *Gideon* v. *Wainwright*

**Significance:** This ruling was one of several key Supreme Court decisions establishing free legal help for those who cannot otherwise afford representation in court.

**Background:** Clarence Earl Gideon was accused of robbery in Florida. Gideon could not afford a lawyer for his trial, and the judge refused to supply him with one for free. Gideon tried to defend himself and was found guilty. He eventually appealed to the U.S. Supreme Court, claiming that the lower court's denial of a court-appointed lawyer violated his Sixth and Fourteenth Amendment rights.

**Decision:** The case was decided on March 18, 1963, by a vote of 9 to 0 in favor of Gideon. The Court agreed that the Sixth Amendment (which protects a citizen's right to have a lawyer for his or her defense) applied to the states because it fell under the due process clause of the Fourteenth Amendment. Thus, the states are required to provide legal aid to those defendants in criminal cases who cannot afford to pay for legal representation.

**Why do you think legal representation is an important part of our criminal justice system?**

# TEACH OBJECTIVE 3

**LEVEL 1:** Have students draw a political cartoon identifying one of the various ways that lawbreakers can be punished. *(Those found guilty of breaking the law can be punished by one of the following sentences: imprisonment, parole, or capital punishment.)* Students should either display support for the method or disapproval for the method. Display cartoons around the classroom. **ENGLISH LANGUAGE LEARNERS**

**LEVEL 3:** Lead a class discussion about the various ways that lawbreakers can be punished. *(See the Level 1 lesson for ways.)* Then have students list the four views of the purpose of imprisonment. Ask students to write an opinion paper about the purpose of capital punishment. Finally, have students compare the four views of imprisonment with the purpose of capital punishment in their papers.

**☐ internet** connect

**TOPIC:** Mock Trial and History
**GO TO:** go.hrw.com
**KEYWORD:** SZ3 AC16

Have students access the Internet through the HRW Go site to conduct research to obtain information about the court system. Then help students set up a mock trial in class using the information that they have learned. Assign students roles such as "district attorney" and "grand jury" to make the trial more realistic.

## Interpreting the Visual Record

**Trial** *Judges often ban cameras and tape recorders from the courtroom while trials are in session. Instead, illustrators draw the courtroom scenes for news purposes.* **Why do you think judges would ban cameras or tape recorders from an ongoing trial?**

questioned by the prosecutor, and cross-examined by the defense. Next, the defense presents its case. The defendant may choose whether to testify. Under the U.S. Constitution, no defendant can be forced to testify against himself or herself.

After both sides present their evidence, each lawyer makes a closing statement that summarizes his or her arguments. The judge then tells the jurors what they can and cannot consider under the law in reaching their verdict. Finally, the jury leaves the courtroom to deliberate, or discuss, the case.

The defendant is always presumed to be innocent. It is the prosecution's job to prove that the accused person is guilty beyond a reasonable doubt. If there is reasonable doubt of guilt, the jury must **acquit** the defendant—that is, find the defendant not guilty. The jury must reach a unanimous verdict in criminal cases. This means that all jurors are in agreement. As you have learned, if the defendant believes that an error was made in the conduct of the trial, he or she may appeal the verdict.

**Sentencing** If the defendant is found guilty, the judge decides the punishment, or **sentence.** Usually the law sets a minimum (least severe) and maximum (most severe) penalty for each type of crime. In some cases the judge may suspend the sentence. This means the defendant will not have to serve the sentence. The defendant's reputation and past record greatly influence the judge's sentence.

In recent years some states have established mandatory sentences for certain crimes. That is, judges must give certain punishments for certain crimes as set by law. This trend toward mandatory sentencing reflects the growing concern that criminals are not serving long enough sentences. Critics argue that this policy prevents judges from taking into account the circumstances of each case.

✔ **Reading Check** Sequencing What are the main steps in the criminal justice process, from arrest to sentencing?

*Did You*
**KNOW?**

In the 1800s mentally ill people were often placed in prison with criminals. In 1841 reformer Dorothea Dix began a crusade to create special facilities for mentally ill individuals, eventually leading to the creation of more than 100 state mental hospitals.

## Visual Record Answer

*Students might suggest to ensure a fair trial for the accused criminal.*

## CASE STUDY ANSWER

(for page 390)
Students' answers will vary.

A criminal suspect is arrested, booked, and given a hearing. If there is sufficient evidence, the suspect is indicted and enters a plea of guilty or not guilty. Next, the suspect is tried, and if convicted, sentenced by the judge.

**HOMEWORK** Have each student create a classified advertisement for a police officer that includes a job description. Job descriptions should outline the typical duties and necessary qualifications of an officer.

# CLOSE

Invite five volunteers to form a discussion panel assuming the roles of the following individuals: a businessperson, a police officer, a judge, a gang leader, and a concerned citizen. Panel members should be prepared to suggest ways in which they might help control crime. Encourage cross-questioning within the panel as well as questions from other members of the class in the audience.

## ⭐ Constitutional Heritage

### Capital Punishment

Capital punishment was once widely practiced throughout the world. For example, in England during the 1800s death was the punishment for several offenses, including murder, treason, arson in a royal dockyard, and piracy. Following the period of Enlightenment during the 1700s and 1800s, the use of capital punishment began to decrease. By the 1970s, many European countries—including Austria, Denmark, Great Britain, Portugal, Switzerland, and Venezuela—had eliminated capital punishment.

### CRITICAL THINKING

Why might many countries have eliminated the use of capital punishment?

**ANSWER:** Students might suggest that many countries may believe that capital punishment is cruel and does not deter criminal acts well enough to justify its use.

### Visual Record Answer

*Students might suggest to provide the prisoners a means of exercise.*

**Interpreting the Visual Record**

**Prisons** *Prison facilities are expensive to build, maintain, and staff. But imprisonment is the only way to remove lawbreakers from contact with the rest of society during their sentences.* **Why do you think there is exercise equipment at this prison?**

## ⭐ Plea Bargaining

Many cases in the United States never go to trial. They are taken care of quickly by plea bargaining. In a **plea bargain** the accused person pleads guilty to a lesser offense than the original charge. The penalty is therefore lighter than if the accused were found guilty of the more serious crime in a trial.

Many people who support the use of plea bargaining believe the practice keeps the courts from becoming overloaded with cases. Without it, they charge, the number of judges and courts would have to be greatly increased. Critics argue that plea bargaining allows criminals to avoid adequate punishment. Opponents also claim that plea bargaining encourages accused persons to give up their constitutional right to a trial.

✔ **Reading Check Identifying Cause and Effect** Why are plea bargains used, and what effects do they have? Plea bargains reduce the number of cases that courts must hear. Their effects include reducing criminal sentences and reducing the need for more courts and judges.

## ⭐ Punishing Lawbreakers

People who break the law and are found guilty of their crimes must be punished. The methods used to punish lawbreakers are called **corrections.** The corrections system in the United States generally includes imprisonment, parole, and capital punishment.

**Imprisonment** While less serious crimes may be punished with fines or suspended sentences, more serious crimes are typically punished with imprisonment. People generally agree that lawbreakers should be removed from society for a period of time. Although most people believe imprisonment is a fair punishment for crime, they disagree on the purpose imprisonment serves.

Some people see the purpose of imprisonment as retribution, or revenge. They believe that society has the right to make the criminal pay for his or her crime. Other people view imprisonment as a **deterrence** to crime. They believe that the threat of a long prison term deters, or discourages, people from breaking the law.

A third view of imprisonment is that it serves as a means of **rehabilitation.** People who hold this view believe that the purpose of imprisonment is to reform criminals. Reformed, or rehabilitated, criminals can then return to society as law-abiding citizens.

Still other people view imprisonment as a means of social protection. People who are imprisoned cannot pose a threat to the lives or property of the people in the community at large.

✔ **Reading Check Summarizing** What are the different goals of imprisoning criminals? retribution, deterrence, and rehabilitation

# REVIEW AND ASSESS

Have students complete the **Section 2 Review** on page 393. Then have students complete **Daily Quiz 16.2**. As **Alternative Assessment**, you may want to use the police officer journal or due process flowchart activities in this section's lessons.

## RETEACH

Have students complete **Main Idea Activity for English Language Learners and Special-Needs Students 16.2**. Then ask each student to make a list of the key terms found in the section. Have each student write sentences that explain the significance of each term and its relation to the section material.
**ENGLISH LANGUAGE LEARNERS**

## EXTEND

Have students conduct research at the library to obtain more information about crime in other countries. Students should investigate such information as crime rates, types of punishment, and societal attitudes toward crime. Then have each student compile his or her information in an oral report that is supported by a visual guide outlining his or her research.
**BLOCK SCHEDULING**

**Parole** After serving a part of their sentences, many prisoners are eligible for **parole,** or early release. People are paroled on the condition that they obey certain rules and keep out of trouble. Parole is generally granted to prisoners who behave well and who show signs of rehabilitation. A parole board reviews each application for parole carefully. When a prisoner is paroled, he or she must report regularly to a parole officer. Parole lasts for the remaining length of the person's sentence.

In recent years prison overcrowding has forced the early release of prisoners who would otherwise have served their full sentences. Public concern about criminals committing crimes while on parole has caused some state governments to reconsider this practice. By 2000, sixteen states had eliminated parole for nearly all convicted criminals. Four others had eliminated parole for some types of violent crimes.

**Capital Punishment** The harshest punishment for crimes committed in the United States is **capital punishment,** or the death penalty. People who oppose capital punishment believe it violates the Eighth Amendment's prohibition against "cruel and unusual" punishment. Other people say the death penalty is a just punishment, particularly for a person who has committed murder. In 1976 the U.S. Supreme Court ruled that capital punishment as a penalty for murder is constitutional. However, each state passes its own capital punishment laws.

The issue of capital punishment remains controversial. Many people support the death penalty as a form of punishment for criminals. However, others question the procedures for determining how it is applied. The debate on capital punishment will continue for many years.

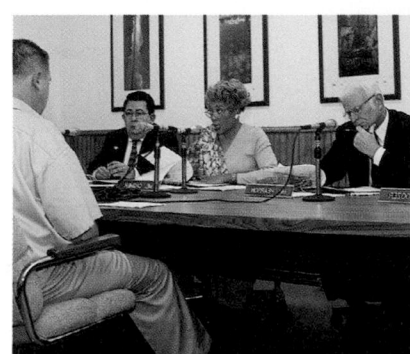

*Parole boards review a prisoner's criminal and prison records to help determine whether that person is ready to rejoin society.*

✔ **Reading Check** **Finding the Main Idea** What is the purpose of parole?
It is used both to free rehabilitated prisoners and to ease prison overcrowding.

**go.hrw.com**
**Homework Practice Online**
keyword: SZ3 HP16

# SECTION 2 Review

1. **Define** and explain:
   - criminal justice system
   - community policing
   - probable cause
   - arrest warrant
   - own recognizance
   - arraignment
   - defense
   - prosecution
   - defendant
   - acquit
   - sentence
   - plea bargain
   - corrections
   - deterrence
   - rehabilitation
   - parole
   - capital punishment

2. **Sequencing** Copy the chart below. Fill in the circles to name and briefly describe the steps in the criminal justice system from arrest to sentencing. Add more circles as needed.

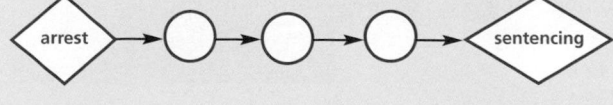

3. **Finding the Main Idea**
   a. How do people become police officers, and what are their responsibilities?
   b. How does the criminal justice system bring criminals to justice?

4. **Writing and Critical Thinking**
   **Supporting a Point of View** Write a position statement for or against parolling criminals.

   **Consider:**
   - prison overcrowding
   - the purposes of imprisonment

## Section 2 Review
### ANSWERS

**1. Define**
- criminal justice system, p. 387
- community policing, p. 388
- probable cause, p. 389
- arrest warrant, p. 389
- own recognizance, p. 390
- arraignment, p. 390
- defense, p. 390
- prosecution, p. 390
- defendant, p. 390
- acquit, p. 391
- sentence, p. 391
- plea bargain, p. 392
- corrections, p. 392
- deterrence, p. 392
- rehabilitation, p. 392
- parole, p. 393
- capital punishment, p. 393

**2.** Preliminary hearing—a judge decides if there is enough evidence to send the case to trial; Indictment—the suspect is formally charged with the crime; Arraignment—the accused enters a plea of guilty or not guilty to the charges; Trial—the court hears arguments to determine the guilt or innocence of the accused

**3. a.** to become an officer—pass intelligence, physical, and psychological exams, police academy; duties—to protect life and property, prevent crime, arrest criminals, protect rights, maintain peace, control traffic

**b.** by arresting, putting on trial, and punishing lawbreakers

**4.** Students' statements will vary but should support their opinions.

## TEACH

**ALL LEVELS:** Tell students that juvenile crime has become a common topic for writers and publishers. Have students use the *Readers' Guide to Periodical Literature* to find magazine articles about juvenile crime. Randomly assign specific years to students. Then have students tally the total number of articles for each year and report their tallies to the class. Keep track of the tallies on the chalkboard. Have students discuss any trends that can be found in the annual tallies of articles on juvenile crime.

**HOMEWORK** Have students visit their local library to conduct research on crime in their community. Have students write reports that profile the types of crime committed in their community, the frequency of those crimes, and so on. As part of their reports, ask students to include a paragraph detailing their sources, how they used each source; what types of sources they studied but did not use and why; and what resource at their library they found to be the most useful for the information that they needed.

## SKILLS ANSWERS

1. almanac

2. *Dictionary of American Biography* or an encyclopedia

3. encyclopedia

4. atlas, almanac

# Civics Skills

## WORKSHOP

### Conducting Library Research

Throughout your school career you will conduct research on many different topics. Your school library and your local public library offer a wide selection of reference books. All reference books contain facts, but the type of facts varies with the reference. Choosing the right reference book will save you time.

### How to Conduct Library Research

1. **Reacquaint yourself with encyclopedias.** Most students are familiar with encyclopedias. These reference books contain articles on a wide range of topics.

2. **Become familiar with almanacs.** A handy source of both historical and up-to-date facts is an almanac. Here you will find statistics on topics ranging from crime to presidential elections. Almanacs are updated each year and present much of their information in reference tables, graphs, and charts.

3. **Consult sources on people.** If you are looking for information on well-known people, you might go to a biographical dictionary. This reference book summarizes the key events in a person's life.

4. **Sharpen your geography skills.** To locate maps and statistics on the United States or other parts of the world, use an atlas. An atlas is a book of maps that also provides useful facts and figures, including information on population and climate.

5. **Be aware of current events.** Magazines and newspapers contain much current information on a variety of topics. Often such periodicals have an index of recent articles available.

6. **Consult the librarian.** Your most valuable resource is the librarian. This trained professional can help you find the best reference materials for your needs.

### Applying the Skill

Answer the following questions about conducting library research.

1. Where would you look to find out how many cases of arson occurred in the United States in recent years?

2. Where would you look to find Billy the Kid's real name?

3. What would be the best reference on the history of the juvenile justice system?

4. Where would you find a map of the United States with current population figures?

# SECTION 3

## OBJECTIVES

*After completing Section 3, students should be able to*

1 **Identify some of the possible causes of juvenile crime.**

2 **Analyze how the judicial system has changed the way it handles juveniles.**

3 **Explain what happens when juveniles are charged and found guilty of breaking the law.**

## 🔊 LET'S GET STARTED!

Copy the following terms and definitions onto the chalkboard: *juvenis—young person; delinquere—to offend.* As students enter the classroom, ask them the following question: Based on the Latin roots, what is a juvenile delinquent? *(Students might suggest that it is a young person who offends, or breaks, the law.)* Tell students that in Section 3 they will learn more about juveniles and the criminal justice system.

---

## SECTION 3

# Juvenile Crime

### Read to Discover

1. What are some possible causes of juvenile crime?
2. How has the judicial system changed the way it handles juveniles?
3. What happens when juveniles are charged and found guilty of breaking the law?

### Define

- juvenile
- delinquents
- probation

**WHY CIVICS MATTERS**

Community members often work together to prevent juvenile crime. Use 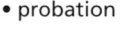 or other **current events** sources to research ways communities are trying to help young people become productive citizens. Record your findings in your journal.

## SECTION 3 RESOURCES

### REPRODUCIBLE

▶ Guided Reading Strategies 16.3

▶ Readings in Economics and Government 69: Abe Fortas's Opinion *In re Gault*

▶ Community Service Paricipation Handbook: Back Away From Crime

### TECHNOLOGY

▶ One-Stop Planner, Lesson 16.3

▶ CNN presents: American Government

▶ Homework Practice Online

### REINFORCEMENT, REVIEW, AND ASSESSMENT

▶ Section 3 Review, p. 399

▶ Daily Quiz 16.3

▶ Main Idea Activity 16.3

▶ English Audio Summary 16.3

▶ Spanish Audio Summary 16.3

## *Reading Focus*

Young people are responsible for a large percentage of the crimes committed in this country. They commit many of the crimes against property, including burglary, larceny, vandalism, arson, and automobile theft, as well as many more serious crimes. The rate of violent crime among young people has been a concern for communities around the country.

*Statistics show that young people commit many of the crimes reported to police.*

### ⭐ Defining Juvenile Crime

Every state has special laws for dealing with young offenders. The ages to which these laws apply vary from state to state. However, most states define a **juvenile** as a person under the age of 18. Some set the age as low as 16. Juveniles become **delinquents** when they are found guilty of breaking a law.

Juveniles whose parents cannot manage them or who repeatedly run away from home may be termed unruly. The laws concerning unruly behavior vary from community to community. Where such behavior is unlawful, a young person who is repeatedly unruly may be turned over to the juvenile authorities.

✔ **Reading Check** Finding the Main Idea What is juvenile delinquency? criminal activity by youth under a certain age designated by the state

## TEACH OBJECTIVE 1

**ALL LEVELS:** Have students ask people (relatives, neighbors, friends, or other students) the following question: What do you think is the primary cause of juvenile crime? (*Students might suggest poor home life, poor neighborhood conditions, gang membership, dropping out of school and unemployment, alcohol and drugs, and peer pressure.*) Have students report their findings in class and tally the results to determine which cause was cited most often. Students should discuss these results and compare their findings with the causes listed in the section. **ENGLISH LANGUAGE LEARNERS**

**LEVEL 1:** Have students list the causes of juvenile crime on the chalkboard. (*See the All Levels lesson for causes.*) Encourage

them to choose one cause and express their feelings about it in a drawing, a poem, a rap, or in some other creative way. Invite volunteers to present their projects to the class.
**ENGLISH LANGUAGE LEARNERS**

## TEACH OBJECTIVE 2

**ALL LEVELS:** To help students understand the differences between juvenile and adult courts, stage a scene from each type of court. Organize the class into two groups. One group will provide characters for juvenile court, and the other will provide characters for adult court. Set up both courts at the same time. Have judges, defendants, lawyers, and others take their proper positions in each court and identify themselves. Then lead a class discussion about how the

## ★ Civics Sidelight

**Youth and Crime** The Supreme Court ruled in a case called *In re Gault* in 1967 that juveniles have most of the same rights to due process as adults. The ruling revolved around a sentence that had been handed down by a lower court against 15-year-old Gerald Gault. Gault had been convicted of making an obscene telephone call to a female neighbor and was sentenced to nearly six years in the Arizona State Industrial School. At the time, an adult convicted of the same crime might have served 30 days in jail and paid a $50 fine. The Supreme Court ruled that the Arizona statute violated the due process rights of juveniles under the Fourteenth Amendment.

**CRITICAL THINKING**

Why might it be important for juveniles to have the same rights as adults when accused of a crime?

**ANSWER:** Students might suggest that equality and fairness are necessary to prevent abuse of rights guaranteed in the Constitution.

### Visual Record Answer

*Students' answers will vary.*

*Defacing property is a common activity of juvenile delinquents.*

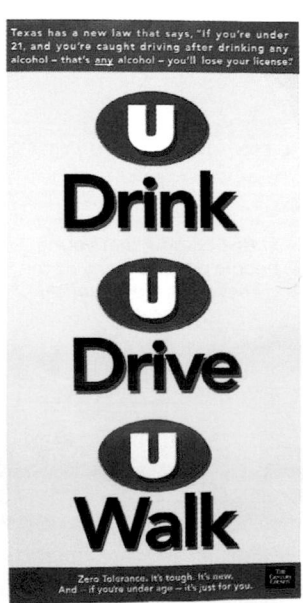

**Interpreting the Visual Record**

**Drunk driving** *To discourage drunk driving, some communities are taking away the driver's licenses of drivers under the age of 18 who are caught drinking and driving.* **What do you think of this law?**

## ★ Causes of Juvenile Crime

Why do some young people break the law or become unruly while most live law-abiding and productive lives? According to experts who have studied the problem, there is no single answer. The following are some of the main causes of juvenile crime.

**Poor Home Conditions** Many juvenile offenders come from homes in which parents take little responsibility for their children. Often one parent has permanently left or is rarely at home. Young people whose parents are alcoholics, illegal drug users, or child abusers may spend a lot of time on the streets. Without a responsible authority figure, these children may get into trouble.

**Poor Neighborhood Conditions** The poorer areas of cities frequently have higher rates of crime than other areas. People who live crowded together in poverty often feel hopeless and angry. Many young people in these areas get into trouble while seeking outlets for their frustration and unhappiness. Some young people view delinquency and crime as their only way out of poverty.

**Gang Membership** Gang members are increasingly engaging in serious crimes involving firearms and illegal drugs. The National Youth Gang Survey estimated that in 2000 there were more than 772,000 active gang members in the United States. As a result, many communities have begun to provide youth activities to help prevent juveniles from joining gangs.

**Dropping Out of School and Unemployment** Young people who drop out of school and are unemployed are often at greater risk of becoming involved in criminal activities.

**Alcohol and Drugs** Laws forbid the sale of alcoholic beverages to anyone under a certain age. They also ban the sale of habit-forming drugs to anyone who does not have a prescription from a doctor. Yet many young people use these substances and other illegal drugs. Under the influence of alcohol or drugs, they may do things that they would not do otherwise. Addicts who need money to pay for their habit often turn to crime.

**Peer Pressure** Some young people get into trouble because they are pressured by their friends to commit crimes. It takes courage to say no when friends suggest illegal acts. However, people who pressure others to break the law are not true friends.

✔ **Reading Check** Summarizing What are some of the explanations that experts offer as possible causes for juvenile crime? poor home conditions, poor neighborhood conditions, gang membership, dropping out of school, unemployment, alcohol and drugs, and peer pressure judicial system has changed the way it handles juveniles. *(Before the late 1800s juveniles at least 14 years old were held responsible for their crimes and were tried in adult courts and sentenced to prison and even death. Today there are juvenile court systems designed to handle these sensitive cases.)* **ENGLISH LANGUAGE LEARNERS , COOPERATIVE LEARNING**

**LEVEL 3:** Lead a class discussion about society's treatment of juvenile crime both before the late 1800s and today. *(See the All Levels lesson for treatment and changes.)* Then have students imagine that they are reporters interviewing a juvenile judge or lawyer in 1895. Have each student prepare a list of questions regarding juvenile treatment in the criminal justice system. Then have students write a newspaper article about the interviews.

# TEACH OBJECTIVE 3

**ALL LEVELS:** Copy the following graphic organizer onto the chalkboard, omitting the italicized answers. Have each student complete the organizer to describe what happens when juveniles are charged and found guilty of breaking the law. **ENGLISH LANGUAGE LEARNERS**

*probation* ← **Juvenile Punishment Options** → *juvenile correctional facility*

*placement in a training school* ← **Juvenile Punishment Options** → *boot camp*

## ★ Handling Juvenile Crime

Before the late 1800s, juveniles at least seven years old were held responsible for their crimes. They were tried in adult courts and sentenced to prison and even death. During the 1870s, however, reformers began working to change the way young offenders were treated. They believed that juveniles needed special understanding rather than punishment.

As a result, many communities set up juvenile court systems. Their purpose was not to punish children but to remove them from harmful environments. Reformers hoped to re-educate offenders by giving them care, discipline, supervision, and treatment.

Instead of trials, juvenile courts hold hearings, which only parents or guardians and others directly involved in the case attended. The purpose of the hearings is to determine the guilt or innocence of juveniles.

In 1967 the Supreme Court ruled in the case *In re Gault* that juvenile offenders have the same rights of due process as adults. In the ruling, Justice Abe Fortas declared,

> **Civics Voices**
>
> ❝In practically all jurisdictions, there are rights granted to adults which are withheld from juveniles. . . . Under our Constitution, the condition of being a boy [or girl] does not justify a kangaroo court [unfair trial].❞

Juveniles have the right to be informed of the charges brought against them and to be represented by a lawyer. They also have the right to question all witnesses and to refuse to testify against themselves in court. However, the Supreme Court later ruled that juveniles accused of crimes do not have the right to a jury trial.

✔ **Reading Check Comparing and Contrasting** How are juvenile court systems different from adult court systems, and how are they the same? private hearings instead of public jury trials; court systems are similar in that both court systems allow the accused specific rights

**Interpreting the Visual Record**

**Juvenile court** *The juvenile court system is intended to protect society from juvenile offenders while acting in their best interest.* **Why do you think parents, like those shown here, are asked to attend juvenile court hearings?**

**LEVEL 2:** Organize students into pairs. Have each pair develop a list of proposed punishments for offenses committed by teenagers who appear in teen courts. In short paragraphs or statements next to each punishment that they propose, pairs should explain how the punishment (or range of possible punishments) is appropriate for each offense. Then have volunteers present their list to the class. **COOPERATIVE LEARNING**

**HOMEWORK** Have students write a précis either supporting or opposing the following statement: Juveniles who commit serious crimes should be tried as adults. Students should consider the purposes of the juvenile justice system.

## CLOSE

Lead a class discussion about the four items listed under the heading Steps You Can Take on the next page. Then ask the following questions: Is this list complete? What else can teenagers do to ensure that they stay out of trouble with the law? Have students create posters on the theme of juvenile decency. Invite the principal to view the posters before displaying them in your school as part of a campaign promoting juvenile decency.

## ★ Civics Sidelight

**The Question of Boot Camp** In recent years some officials have championed military-style boot camps for juvenile offenders. Proponents believe these boot camps instill discipline and help prevent a return to crime. However, some studies have shown that boot camps do not significantly reduce the number of repeat offenders. A number of programs combine the discipline of a boot camp with counseling and training. After attending a boot camp, offenders are then enrolled in job-training programs at a detention center. They also take part in group discussions on violence prevention. Finally, after a period in a halfway house, offenders may be returned home or to another supportive environment. They are expected to attend group meetings and to work or go to school.

**CRITICAL THINKING**

Why might counseling and training be beneficial to preventing repeat juvenile offenses.

**ANSWER:** Students might suggest that counseling and training may help rehabilitate juveniles and provide them with better options than crime once they return from camp.

**Visual Record Answer**

*Students' answers will vary.*

## ★ Punishing Juvenile Offenders

Young people who are waiting for their juvenile court hearing are sometimes held in juvenile detention centers. After hearing all the evidence, the judge must decide the guilt or innocence of the juvenile offender. If the juvenile is found guilty, several outcomes are possible. If the judge finds adult supervision inadequate where the juvenile lives, the juvenile may be placed in a foster home. In serious cases the judge may have the youth sent to a juvenile corrections facility.

One type of juvenile corrections facility is a training school, where juvenile offenders may be placed for a year. Another possible outcome for the juvenile offender is probation. **Probation** is a period of time during which offenders are given an opportunity to show that they can reform. People on probation must obey strict rules, such as being home by a certain time each night and avoiding bad influences. They must also report regularly to a probation officer.

The juvenile justice system is also experimenting with the use of boot camps to rehabilitate young offenders. Like military boot camps, these rehabilitative boot camps provide a highly disciplined, structured environment. The goal of such facilities is to help young offenders gain positive values.

✔ **Reading Check Summarizing** What are some of the punishments that juvenile offenders might face? probation or placement in a training school, boot camp program, or juvenile correctional facility

## ★ Serious Crimes by Juveniles

Although the number of serious crimes committed by juveniles has dropped since the 1990s, some adults believe that juvenile offenders should be tried in adult criminal courts. In the juvenile system, a young person who commits murder may serve a short sentence in a juvenile corrections facility. Despite the good intentions of corrections officers, that juvenile may commit further crimes after release.

In most states, juveniles can also be certified to be tried in adult criminal courts. This usually happens when a youth is 14 or older and is accused of committing a felony. Young people who are found guilty of a crime in a criminal court are usually punished the way adults are punished. As more young people have been tried as adults, more have been sentenced to adult prisons. In 2001 the number of youths under 18 in adult prisons had reached 5,400—double the number from 10 years ago.

✔ **Reading Check Supporting a Point of View** Do you support or oppose trying juveniles in adult criminal courts? Explain your answer. Students might say that juveniles who commit adult crimes should be punished as adults. Or they might say that trying juveniles as adults makes rehabilitation less likely.

**Interpreting the Visual Record**

**Staying off the streets** *In some communities the government has helped establish athletic leagues to help keep young people off the streets and out of trouble. Do you think such programs are a good idea? Why or why not?*

## ★ Steps You Can Take

Most young people in the United States are good citizens who stay out of trouble and obey the law. But some young people face difficult living conditions and environments. Others lack adult role models to help them set healthy goals for themselves. Young people in these situations may not have the advice or support to help them choose their actions wisely.

Criminologists are scientists who study crime and criminal behavior. They offer the following suggestions to young people who want to avoid trouble with the law. These steps will also help you achieve the goals you set for yourself.

1. Do not use drugs. People who use drugs often end up in criminal courts and corrections facilities or jails.
2. Stay in school and get the best education possible. A good education will provide you with new opportunities and increase your chances of getting a good job.
3. Have the courage to say no when friends suggest illegal acts. Make sure that your friends and role models are a positive influence on you. Anyone can go along with the crowd, but it takes courage to stand up to one.
4. Try to live a full life, with plenty of physical activity and interesting hobbies. These can help you develop new skills. A person who is busy doing challenging things is less likely to become bored and turn to criminal activities as an outlet.

✔ **Reading Check** Finding the Main Idea How can juveniles avoid trouble with the law? by avoiding drugs and alcohol, staying in school and getting a good education, resisting peer pressure, and keeping daily life full of wholesome activities

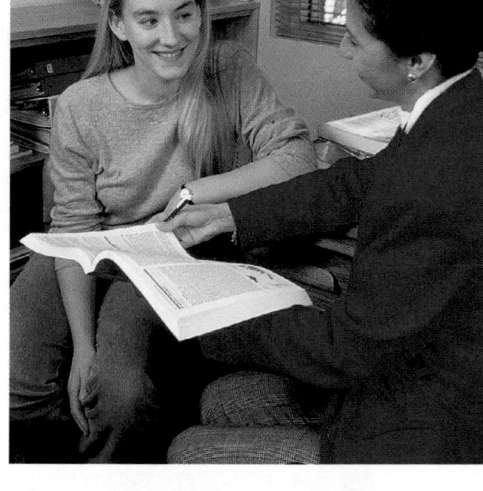

**Interpreting the Visual Record**

**Counseling** *Planning for the future and having goals to achieve are important steps toward staying out of trouble.* **What are your plans for the future?**

## SECTION 3 Review

go.hrw.com **Homework Practice Online** keyword: SZ3 HP16

1. **Define** and explain:
   • juvenile • delinquents • probation

2. **Analyzing Information** Copy the chart below. Then fill in the circles with the causes of juvenile crime. If any of the causes are related to each other, connect those circles with arrows.

3. **Finding the Main Idea**
   a. How has the treatment of juvenile offenders changed over the years?
   b. How are juvenile offenders treated and punished?

4. **Writing and Critical Thinking**
   **Supporting a Point of View** Write a letter to your state legislature describing your position on how juveniles should be treated by the judicial system.
   **Consider:**
   • the age and personal circumstances of juvenile offenders
   • the increasing number of serious offenses committed by juveniles

# Review and Assessment Resources

**REPRODUCIBLE**

▶ Chapter 16 Review, pp. 400–01

▶ Vocabulary Activity 16

▶ Chapter 16 Tutorial for Students, Parents, Mentors, and Peers

▶ Chapter 16 Test (Form A or B)

▶ Alternative Assessment Handbook

**TECHNOLOGY**

▶ Chapter 16 Test Generator (on the One-Stop Planner)

▶ Global Skill Builder CD–ROM

▶ HRW Go Site

**REINFORCEMENT, REVIEW, AND ASSESSMENT**

▶ Chapter 16 Test for English Language Learners and Special-Needs Students

## REVIEW

Have students complete the Chapter 16 Review on pages 400–01.

## ASSESS

Use one of the chapter tests to assess students' understanding of the content. For **Alternative Assessment**, see the **Alternative Assessment Handbook.**

---

3. vandalism, p. 383
4. white-collar crimes, p. 383
5. community policing, p. 388
6. sentence, p. 391
7. rehabilitation, p. 392
8. capital punishment, p. 393
9. juvenile, p. 395
10. probation, p. 398

**Understanding Main Ideas**

**1.** against persons, against property, victimless, white-collar, and organized

**2.** poverty, illegal drug use, permissive society, and urbanization

**3.** booking, hearing, indictment, arraignment, trial

**4.** imprisonment, parole, community service, or capital punishment

**5.** poor home conditions, poor neighborhood conditions, gang membership, alcohol and drug use, dropping out of school and unemployment, and peer pressure

**6.** sentence him or her to probation or placement in a training school, boot camp program, or juvenile correctional facility

**What Did You Find Out?**

**1.** crimes against persons—acts that harm or end a person's life or that threaten to do so; crimes against property—stealing or destroying someone else's property

**2.** due process, which includes the right to remain silent and to have a lawyer present during questioning, and the knowledge that anything they say can be used against them in a court

# Chapter **16** Review

## Chapter Summary

### Section 1

- Americans want and need to be protected from crime. Such protection is one of the services that governments provide for their citizens.

- Types of crime include crimes against persons, crimes against property, organized crimes, victimless crimes, and white-collar crimes.

### Section 2

- The U.S. criminal justice system operates to protect everyone, even those people who have been accused of committing criminal acts.

- Police officers are trained to deal with the public, handle emergencies, control situations that may lead to crime, and deal with criminals. They must also inform suspects of their constitutional rights.

- From the moment of arrest, all citizens suspected of crimes are entitled to due process of law.

### Section 3

- Although most of the country's young people are law-abiding citizens, juvenile crime has been a concern for communities across the country.

- Special courts and corrections facilities have been set up to deal with juvenile offenders. These courts hold private hearings, involving judges and parents or guardians, to determine what measures would be in the best interest of the offenders. However, in some states juveniles can be tried as adults for certain serious crimes.

## Define and Identify

Use the following terms in complete sentences.

1. felonies
2. burglary
3. vandalism
4. white-collar crimes
5. community policing
6. sentence
7. rehabilitation
8. capital punishment
9. juvenile
10. probation

## Understanding Main Ideas

**Section 1** *(Pages 381–86)*

1. Identify and describe specific examples of five categories of crime.
2. What are some causes of crime?

**Section 2** *(Pages 387–93)*

3. What steps does a criminal suspect go through from the time of arrest to the time of sentencing?
4. What are the punishments that a convicted criminal faces?

**Section 3** *(Pages 395–99)*

5. What are the possible causes of juvenile delinquency?
6. What may a judge do if he or she finds a juvenile guilty of a crime?

## What Did You Find Out?

1. What is the difference between a crime against a person and a crime against property?
2. What rights do all accused criminals have under the U.S. court system?
3. How are juvenile offenders treated differently than adult offenders?

## Thinking Critically

1. **Analyzing Information** People continue to discuss how to treat convicted criminals. Some people believe that prisons should focus on rehabilitating criminals and helping them rejoin society. However, others argue that prisons are intended to punish criminals and protect the rest of society. What do you think the role of prisons should be? Explain your answer.
2. **Supporting a Point of View** Should juveniles who commit serious crimes such as murder be tried in adult courts, and should those convicted of these crimes face the same punishments as adult offenders? Explain your answers.
3. **Drawing Inferences and Conclusions** Why do you think plea bargaining is controversial?

Have each student write each chapter vocabulary term on a card and put each definition or descriptive sketch of the term's meaning on another card. Have them shuffle and lay out the cards on a table to attempt to match terms with their definitions.

**ENGLISH LANGUAGE LEARNERS ,
COOPERATIVE LEARNING**

## Portfolio Extensions

**1. Interdisciplinary Connection to Math** Have students obtain information about types of crimes committed at their school last year and the various statistics used to measure crime. Then have students develop their own crime clock based on the style of the FBI *Crime Clock*. Students should categorize the crimes into major groups, then determine how frequently each crime occurs at school. *(For example, 15 lockers were burglarized last school year, which was 180 days long. If a school day is approximately*

*7 hours long, then 180 days x 7 hours per day =1260 hours of school. Divide the number of school hours by the number of crimes to determine that every 84 hours, or 3.5 days, a locker was burglarized.)*

**2. Cooperative Learning** Organize students into small groups. Have each group create a plan to organize a crime watch program in their school. Groups will need to list the current precautions the school is taking to protect the health and safety of its students and teachers. Then have groups propose what else young citizens can do to make their schools safe.

---

## Building Social Studies Skills

STANDARDIZED TEST PREP ONLINE
keyword: SZ3 STP16

### Interpreting Political Cartoons

Study the political cartoon below. Then answer the questions that follow.

"There are indications that little Tommy is being naughty. But not enough for me to authorize a wiretap."

1. Who is the judge talking to in the cartoon?
   a. a lawyer
   b. Santa Claus
   c. a police officer
   d. a plaintiff
2. A wiretap is a procedure that allows law enforcement officers to listen in on someone's phone conversations. Why do you think that a judge would be needed to authorize a wiretap? Why would a judge—such as the one in the cartoon—want to hear convincing evidence of wrongdoing before allowing a wiretap?
3. What message do you think the cartoonist was trying to convey with this cartoon?

### Analyzing Primary Sources

Read the following quotation from U.S. attorney general John Ashcroft. Then answer the following questions.

"Every newly appointed United States attorney will lead the way [toward reducing gun crimes] by establishing strategic partnerships that include five core elements. First, partnerships. The United States attorney in each judicial district will bring together all law enforcement agencies to ensure a uniform and comprehensive approach to reduce gun violence. . . . Number two, strategic planning. The strategic plans will vary from community to community, with the same goal of reducing gun violence. . . . Number three, training. . . . Number four, outreach. United States attorneys will work with existing coalitions [unions] and establish new coalitions within each community to increase awareness and participation. . . . Number five, accountability [being held responsible]. The United States attorneys will receive resources to measure the long-term impact of the programs that they implement [put in place]."

4. What are the elements outlined by Ashcroft in the gun crime reduction plan?
   a. law enforcement, communities, training
   b. partnerships, strategic planning, training, outreach, accountability
   c. partnerships, strategic planning, training, coalitions, resources
   d. reducing crime, training, participation
5. What elements do you think Ashcroft would consider important for any crime prevention plan?

of law

3. Juveniles have private hearings instead of public jury trials. The discussions and results of the hearings are kept secret. Parents and guardians, court officials, and others work together to try to do what is in the best interest of the juvenile.

### Thinking Critically

1. Students' answers will vary, but students should express an opinion on the role of prisons in the criminal justice system.

2. Students' answers will vary, but students should use sound reasoning in their responses.

3. Students' answers will vary, but some may suggest that plea bargaining results in inadequate punishment and encourages people to give up trial rights. Some students might suggest that capital punishment is controversial because it is cruel and unusual.

### Social Studies Skills

1. b

2. to ensure that legal procedures are followed correctly and to protect people's privacy

3. the need to protect citizens' right to privacy

4. b

5. Students' answers will vary, but students might suggest that law enforcement, planning, proper training, community outreach, and accountability are important elements in any crime prevention plan.

---

**Alternative Assessment**

## Building Your Portfolio

### Linking to Community
Work with your class members to complete the following activity. Locate a current local newspaper article about a person involved in a serious crime. Conduct a mock hearing or a mock trial. Assign various members of your class to play the roles of judge, attorneys, defendant, witnesses, and if necessary, jury members. Have class members research their roles so that the hearing or trial can be as realistic as possible.

**internet connect**

**Internet Activity: go.hrw.com**
keyword: SZ3 AC16

Access the Internet through the HRW Go site to research teen court in different states. Write a paper about how teen court is organized, who it benefits, and what the roles of the teen jurors, bailiffs, and attorneys are. Include a paragraph discussing whether or not you would like to participate in a teen court.

## TEACH

**LEVEL 1:** Review with students the requirements of good citizenship. Then organize students into pairs and ask each pair to create a Citizenship Map. Have pairs illustrate their maps with examples of activities that are important for good citizenship in the family, in school, and in the community. Have volunteers present their maps to the class.

**ENGLISH LANGUAGE LEARNERS , COOPERATIVE LEARNING**

**ALL LEVELS:** Point out to students that good citizenship begins at home. Then have students create good citizenship graphic organizers by drawing four concentric circles. Beginning with the innermost circle, have students label the circles *Family, School, Community,* and *Law.* Then ask each student to fill in the circles with specific examples of activities that characterize good citizenship as they relate to family, school, community, and the law. **ENGLISH LANGUAGE LEARNERS**

## APPLYING THE SKILLS

Remind students that the American legal system relies on responsible citizens who obey the law and support the officials who bring criminals to justice. Then ask students to consider how individual citizens can improve American society by obeying the law. Have students choose a simple law that they think is ignored too often. *(Students might cite laws regarding speeding, running red lights, littering, vandalism, and so on.)* Have students write letters to the editor of a local newspaper that explain why they believe that the community would be improved if citizens made an effort to obey and help enforce that specific law. Encourage students to be persuasive and to use facts to support their arguments.

# Civics Lab

## Citizen of the Year

Complete the following Civics Lab activity individually or in a group.

## Your Task

In Unit 5 you have read about the importance of good citizenship in a happy and stable society. Imagine that the United States has been invited to the "International Young Citizen of the Year" contest. You head the committee to find the student who will represent the United States. The committee needs a profile of the ideal young citizen to use as a guide in its search. Your job is to prepare that profile, which should contain written and visual materials. To prepare these materials, you will need to do the following.

## What to Do

**STEP 1** **Write** a speech titled Young Citizens Help Strengthen Their Families. In your speech, consider the factors that contribute to good citizenship in families. What obligations do young citizens have toward their families? What characteristics do all family members need to build a strong family? What challenges face the American family? How can young citizens work with their families to meet these challenges?

**STEP 2** **Observe** the actions of young people in your school for one week and write down every act of good citizenship that you see. At the end of the week, tally your results and show this information in a chart titled Young Citizens Help Strengthen Their Schools. What

### Young Citizens Help Strengthen Their Schools

| Citizenship Example | Time | Place | Alone/Group |
|---|---|---|---|
|  |  |  |  |

**LEVEL 3:** Ask students to create a survey to question their neighbors about a specific need that is not being met or a service that might be improved. Then have each student write a plan for a volunteer program that would benefit his or her neighborhood. Have students include the results of their neighborhood survey in their reports. *(For example, students might suggest creating a weekly litter patrol after learning that neighbors are upset about trash on the sidewalks.)* Invite volunteers to present their plans to the class.

**LEVEL 3:** Ask students to imagine that they have been asked by the federal government to create a brief citizenship chapter as part of a handbook for immigrants who wish to become U.S. citizens. The chapter should describe the importance of good citizenship and should explain how to be a good citizen. Ask students to include specific examples of activities that characterize good citizenship. Encourage students to provide several simple illustrations for the handbook's chapter. Invite volunteers to present their chapters to the class.

generalizations can you make from this information? Is good citizenship more likely to occur when people are alone or in groups? Do people receive praise for such acts? Do such acts encourage others to be good citizens? Answer these questions in a caption below your chart.

**STEP 3** **Conduct** a survey of students in your school. Ask these young citizens about their involvement in volunteer activities. What percentage belong to volunteer groups? What kinds of volunteer work do they do? How much time do they donate? How did they become involved in volunteer work? Create a collage that shows the types of volunteer work these young citizens perform. Below the images write a caption answering the above questions. Title your collage Young Citizens Help Strengthen Their Communities.

**STEP 4** **Create** a plan to organize a Crime Watch program in your school. Title the plan Young Citizens on the Watch. In your plan, list the precautions your school has taken or could take to protect the health and safety of its students and teachers. Consider questions such as: What can young citizens do to make their schools safer? What can young citizens do to protect their rights and the rights of others?

Keep an eye on your school

Organize your materials and present your profile to the committee (the rest of the class).

**A STEP FURTHER**

Ask students to imagine that they have each been asked to design a citizenship mural for a youth center. Encourage students to be creative in illustrating the different activities that characterize good citizenship in the family, in school, and in the community. Students should also illustrate citizens obeying the law and supporting the officials who enforce it. Remind students that since their murals are for a youth center, they should include young people in their illustrations as much as possible. Display students' murals around the classroom.

# UNIT 6

## The American Economy

## UNIT OVERVIEW

Unit 6 traces the economic development of the United States. The six chapters that make up this unit provide a comprehensive overview of the concepts and ideas essential to understanding the U.S. economic system. The unit also takes a close look at the practical everyday side of economics, including searching for a career and entering the working world.

### In Their Own Words

*"My conception of America is a land where men and women may walk in ordered freedom in the independent conduct of their occupations; where they may enjoy the advantages of wealth, not concentrated in the hands of the few but spread through the lives of all; . . . where a contented and happy people, secure in their liberties, free from poverty and fear, shall have the leisure and impulse to seek a fuller life."* –Herbert Hoover

**Using the Quotation** Have students read the quotation. Ask: Is Herbert Hoover concerned about people, places, or things in this quotation? Encourage students to list all words and phrases used to describe the people who make up Hoover's vision of America. Then have students discuss whether his is a realistic or an idealized vision.

**About the Author** Herbert Clark Hoover (1874–1964) served as the thirty-first president of the United States. Despite a well-deserved reputation as a skilled administrator and director of aid to needy people at home and abroad, President Hoover lost a 1932 bid for reelection when he was perceived as not having moved with sufficient vigor to combat the Great Depression. Hoover later led an international relief commission after World War II and commissions that recommended ways to cut waste and inefficiency in the federal government.

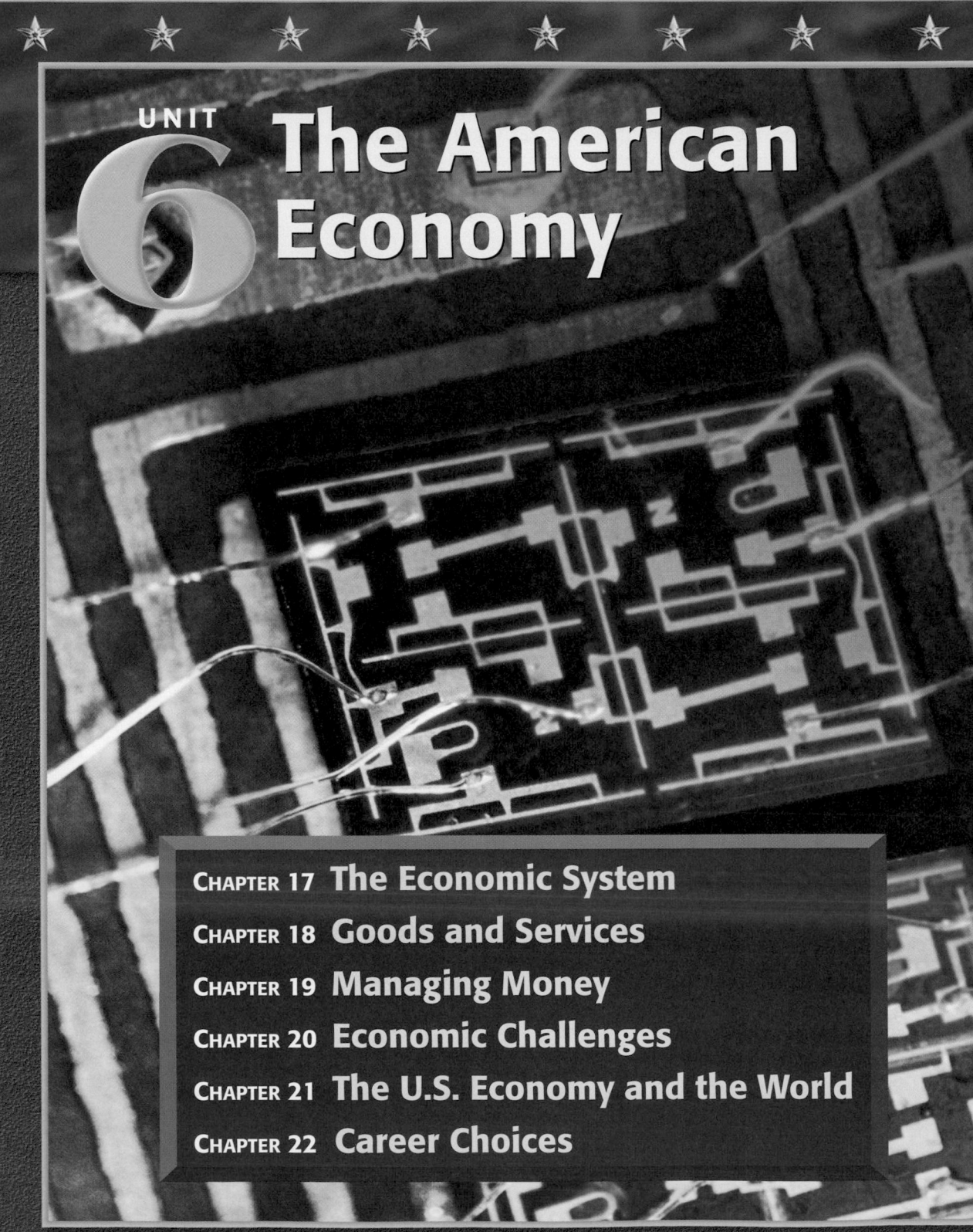

# UNIT 6 The American Economy

Ask students to consider the importance of the U.S. economy and to list examples of how the economy affects their lives. Then ask students to list how they have participated in the economy in the past. Students might list jobs that they have held or purchases that they routinely make.

Then ask students to list some careers that they might be interested in pursuing. Finally, pair students and ask pairs to discuss what economic freedoms the items on their lists have in common. Invite pairs to explain their lists and these economic freedoms to the class.

# Young Citizens

## IN ACTION

### *Foxfire* Turns Big Business

In 1966 Eliot Wigginton, a high-school teacher in northeastern Georgia, was searching for a way to inspire his language students. He also wanted them to understand their backgrounds and community. Wigginton let his students decide how they would combine English class with learning about their community's history. His students chose to publish a magazine. They named it *Foxfire,* after a local moss-like plant that glows in the dark.

Students were responsible not only for the content of the magazine but also for running the business side of the operation. These responsibilities included printing the magazine, raising money, and selling subscriptions. More than 35 years after *Foxfire* was created, the magazine has subscribers across the United States and around the world. Student writers handle all aspects of articles, from interviews to layouts. Other students run the

*A student interviews an elderly citizen to learn about local crafts.*

subscription department, filling orders and maintaining subscriber databases. The magazine has also expanded to include a series of books that has sold more than 8 million copies. The success of *Foxfire* has encouraged students in other communities across the country to start similar magazines. Program participants learn by doing, and students leave the program with a greater appreciation of their heritage. Students are also better prepared to be good citizens, consumers, and business owners.

### You Decide

1. *What might students learn about business by publishing magazines such as* Foxfire?
2. *What are some other ways students could learn about business while becoming more involved in their communities?*

## What Can We Do?

Ask students to conduct research to obtain more information about ways that they could learn about business while becoming more involved in their communities. Then organize students into groups and ask each group to develop a written proposal for a business that would help meet a local need. Groups' proposals should describe the businesses and explain how the products or services will be marketed, how many employees will be involved, and how the businesses will contribute to the community. Each proposal should also contain an estimated budget. *(Students might consider starting their own publication, opening a bicycle-repair stand, providing a grocery delivery service, and so on.)* Encourage students to design posters or other visual aids to explain and promote their business proposals. Have each group present its proposal to the class.

### YOU DECIDE ANSWERS

1. Students might learn how to market a product, how to manage workers and satisfy customers, and how to plan and stick to a budget.

2. Students' responses will vary.

| Objectives | Pacing Guide | Reproducible Resources |
|---|---|---|
| **SECTION 1:**<br>**The Economic System at Work**<br>(pp. 407–15) | ✪ Identify the freedoms found in the U.S. economy.<br>✪ Explain the laws of supply and demand.<br>✪ Describe the free-enterprise system and analyze how big business can both harm and help it. | **Regular**<br>1.5 days<br><br>**Block Scheduling**<br>.5 day<br><br>*Block Scheduling Handbook with Team Teaching Strategies, Chapter 17* | **RS** Guided Reading Strategies 17.1<br>**RS** Readings in Economics and Government 27: Woodrow Wilson's "New Freedom"<br>**RS** Readings in Economics and Government 42: Federal Trade Commission Act of 1914<br>**RS** Readings in Economics and Government 60: Principles of Economics<br>**RS** Graphic Organizer Activity: The Economic System at Work |
| **SECTION 2:**<br>**Business Organizations**<br>(pp. 416–21) | ✪ Describe the different types of business organizations.<br>✪ Explain how corporations function.<br>✪ Evaluate the difference between preferred stock and common stock. | **Regular**<br>1.5 days<br><br>**Block Scheduling**<br>.5 day<br><br>*Block Scheduling Handbook with Team Teaching Strategies, Chapter 17* | **RS** Guided Reading Strategies 17.2<br>**E** Challenge and Enrichment Worksheet 17: Calculating Business Ownership and Income |
| **SECTION 3:**<br>**Making Business Decisions**<br>(pp. 423–27) | ✪ Identify the four factors of production.<br>✪ Explain how the four factors of production are necessary to the success of business.<br>✪ Describe the ways that government regulates business. | **Regular**<br>1.5 days<br><br>**Block Scheduling**<br>.5 day<br><br>*Block Scheduling Handbook with Team Teaching Strategies, Chapter 17* | **RS** Guided Reading Strategies 17.3<br>**RS** Readings in Economics and Government 26: Theodore Roosevelt's "New Nationalism"<br>**SM** Community Service and Participation Handbook: Who Wants to Be An Entrepreneur?<br>**PS** American Civics Political Cartoon: The Power of Trusts |

## Chapter Resource Key

| | | | | | |
|---|---|---|---|---|---|
| **PS** | Primary Sources | **SM** | Skills Mastery |  | CD-ROM |
| **RS** | Reading Support | **A** | Assessment |  | Video |
| **IC** | Interdisciplinary Connections | **REV** | Review |  | Internet |
| **E** | Enrichment | **ELL** | Reinforcement and English Language Learners |  | Holt Presentation Maker Using Microsoft® PowerPoint® |
| | | | Transparencies | | |

 **One-Stop** Planner CD–ROM

See the *One-Stop Planner* for a complete list of additional resources for students and teachers.

## One-Stop Planner CD–ROM

It's easy to plan lessons, select resources, and print out materials for your students when you use the *One-Stop Planner CD–ROM with Test Generator*.

| Technology Resources | Reinforcement, Review, and Assessment |
|---|---|
| One-Stop Planner, Lesson 17.1 | REV Section 1 Review, p. 415 |
| Holt Researcher CD–ROM | A Daily Quiz 17.1 |
| Homework Practice Online | ELL Main Idea Activity 17.1 |
| | ELL English Audio Summary 17.1 |
| | ELL Spanish Audio Summary 17.1 |
| One-Stop Planner, Lesson 17.2 | REV Section 2 Review, p. 421 |
| CNN Presents: American Government | A Daily Quiz 17.2 |
| Homework Practice Online | ELL Main Idea Activity 17.2 |
| | ELL English Audio Summary 17.2 |
| | ELL Spanish Audio Summary 17.2 |
| One-Stop Planner, Lesson 17.3 | REV Section 3 Review, p. 427 |
| Transparency 21: Factors of Production | A Daily Quiz 17.3 |
| Homework Practice Online | ELL Main Idea Activity 17.3 |
| HRW Go site | ELL English Audio Summary 17.3 |
| | ELL Spanish Audio Summary 17.3 |

## internet connect

### HRW ONLINE RESOURCES
GO TO: go.hrw.com
Then type in the keyword.

**TEACHER HOME PAGE**
KEYWORD: SZ3 Teacher

**CHAPTER INTERNET ACTIVITIES**
KEYWORD: SZ3 AC17
Choose an activity to:
• create a profile of an imaginary corporation.
• create a game or quiz on the U.S. economic system and its freedoms.
• make up a business plan related to resources in your community.

**CHAPTER ENRICHMENT LINKS**
KEYWORD: SZ3 CH17

**ONLINE ASSESSMENT**
**Homework Practice**
KEYWORD: SZ3 HP17
**Rubrics**
KEYWORD: SZ3 Rubrics

**ONLINE MAPS, CHARTS, AND GRAPHS**
KEYWORD: SZ3 MCG
• Factors of Production

**HOLT PRESENTATION MAKER**
KEYWORD: SZ3 PPT17

**CONTENT UPDATES**
KEYWORD: SS Content Updates

**ONLINE READING SUPPORT**
KEYWORD: SS Strategies

**CURRENT EVENTS**
KEYWORD: S3 Current Events

## Meeting Individual Needs

### Ability Levels

**Level 1** Basic-level activities designed for all students encountering new material

**Level 2** Intermediate-level activities designed for average students

**Level 3** Challenging activities designed for honors and gifted-and-talented students

**English Language Learners** Activities that address the needs of students with Limited English Proficiency

## Chapter Review and Assessment

IC  Vocabulary Activity 17

 Global Skill Builder CD–ROM

HRW Go site

REV  Chapter 17 Tutorial for Students, Parents, Mentors, and Peers

REV  Chapter 17 Review, pp. 428–29

A  Standardized Test Practice

A  Chapter 17 Test Generator (on the One-Stop Planner)

A  Chapter 17 Test (Form A or B)

A  Alternative Assessment Handbook

A  Chapter 17 Test for English Language Learners and Special-Needs Students

## What's Your Opinion?

*To help students create their* **Themes** *Journal entries, provide the following examples of appropriate* **agree**/**disagree** *statements.*

● **Agree**  All businesses operate under the same basic organizational principles.

**Disagree**  Businesses are organized in different ways, depending upon their specific needs and products.

● **Agree**  Businesses produce products at a rate commensurate with consumer demand.

**Disagree**  Many different factors, including demand for a product, influence how much a business will produce.

● **Agree**  Successful businesses, regardless of what they produce, all need the same basic resources.

**Disagree**  The basic resources a business needs in order to be successful vary greatly from business to business.

# Internet Activity

**The Economic System**

■ **internet** connect

go. hrw .com

**TOPIC:** The U.S. Economic System
**GO TO:** go.hrw.com
**KEYWORD:** SZ3 AC17

Have students access the Internet through the HRW Go site to conduct research on the U.S. economic system. Then have each student create a game or a quiz demonstrating the characteristics of the system and the economic freedoms they have studied. Students should include an answer key if they have written quizzes. If students designed a game, they should include a full set of instructions.

**406**

---

**CHAPTER**

# 17 The Economic System

## Build on What You Know

Americans live in one of the richest countries in the world and enjoy a very high standard of living. There are many reasons for the economic success of the United States. The United States is a land of great natural resources. In addition, the U.S. government ensures the right of private enterprise. This is the right of individuals to own and operate their own businesses in pursuit of profit. And finally, the United States has developed an economic system in which people are free to make their own decisions.

**What's Your Opinion?**

 **Themes Journal**  Do you **agree** or **disagree** with the following statements? Support your point of view in your journal.

● The demand for a product is the only factor that influences how much a business will produce.

● All businesses are organized the same way.

● Successful businesses all need the same basic resources.

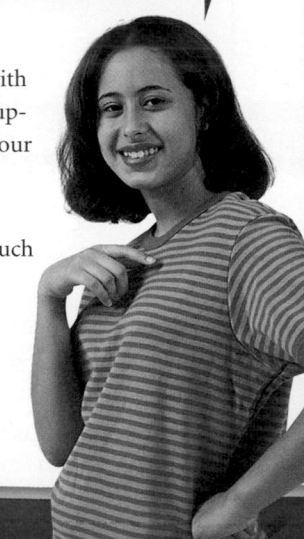

# SECTION 1

## OBJECTIVES

*After completing Section 1, students should be able to*

1. **Identify the freedoms found in the U.S. economy.**
2. **Explain the laws of supply and demand.**
3. **Describe the free-enterprise system and analyze how big business can both harm and help it.**

## LET'S GET STARTED!

As students enter the classroom, ask them to list the "businesses" and jobs they have had, from lemonade stands to paper routes and after-school jobs. Write student responses on the chalkboard and then call on volunteers to discuss the motives they had in pursuing these ventures. Ask students to describe what all of the jobs and businesses listed on the chalkboard have in common. *(Students might suggest that all involved the free choice of individuals to work and earn income at each job or business and the free choice of individuals to purchase products from those businesses.)* Tell students that in Section 1 they will learn more about the freedoms found in the U.S. economy.

# SECTION 1

## The Economic System at Work

### Read to Discover

1. What are the freedoms found in the U.S. economy?
2. What do the laws of supply and demand state?
3. What is the free-enterprise system, and how can big businesses both harm and help it?

### WHY CIVICS MATTERS

Most Americans pay close attention to the U.S. economy. Use **CNNfyi.com** or other **current events** sources to find recent news about the local or national economy. Record your findings in your journal.

### Define

- market economy
- free market
- free competition
- profit motive
- invest
- copyright
- patent
- scarcity
- law of supply
- law of demand
- capital
- capitalism
- free-enterprise system
- monopolies
- merger
- trust
- economies of scale
- conglomerate
- public utilities
- command economy
- mixed economy
- traditional economy

## SECTION 1 RESOURCES

### REPRODUCIBLE
▶ Guided Reading Strategies 17.1
▶ Graphic Organizer Activity: The Economic System at Work

### TECHNOLOGY
▶ One-Stop Planner, Lesson 17.1
▶ Holt Researcher CD–ROM
▶ Homework Practice Online

### REINFORCEMENT, REVIEW, AND ASSESSMENT
▶ Section 1 Review, p. 415
▶ Daily Quiz 17.1
▶ Main Idea Activity 17.1
▶ English Audio Summary 17.1
▶ Spanish Audio Summary 17.1

## *Reading Focus*

The U.S. government is based on certain principles of freedom. Americans enjoy free speech and freedom of religion. Eligible voters can vote in free elections. U.S. residents can do as they choose as long as they do not break the law or interfere with the freedom of others. Americans also enjoy important economic freedoms. In order to benefit from and contribute to the U.S. economy, it is important that you understand how it works.

## ★ Economic Freedoms

Because the U.S. economic system is characterized by so many freedoms, it is often called a free market economy, or simply a **market economy.** Our economic freedoms include the freedom to buy and sell what we choose when we choose as long as the products are legal. Americans also enjoy the freedom to compete, to earn a living, to earn a profit, and to own property.

**Freedom to Buy and Sell** Americans are free to buy and sell any legal product. Shoppers can search for the best quality goods and services at the lowest prices. If a price is too high, the buyers are free to look elsewhere for the product.

Producers are generally free to sell goods and services at prices they think buyers will pay. If people do not buy a product or service, the producer is free to change the price or to sell something else. The term

*American businesses and consumers are free to buy and sell any legal products.*

# TEACH OBJECTIVE 1

**LEVEL 1:** Lead a class discussion about the five freedoms of the U.S. economic system. *(The five freedoms are the freedom to buy and sell, freedom to compete, freedom to earn a living, freedom to earn a profit, and freedom to own property.)* Ask students to consider the various reasons that each of these freedoms is important to the health of the economy and the well-being of individual U.S. citizens. *(Students might indicate that "freedom to earn a profit" motivates people to start, operate, and invest in businesses.)* Then have each student create a poster representing the five economic freedoms and the importance of each freedom. Display the posters around the classroom. **ENGLISH LANGUAGE LEARNERS**

**LEVELS 1 AND 2:** Have students compile a list of items that the school needs. Ask volunteers to write items from their lists on the chalkboard. Then explain that the school has a limited budget and ask the class to discuss how the five U.S. economic freedoms help the school to acquire the items it needs within its budget. *(Students might suggest that the "freedom to buy and sell" allows the school to choose which company to purchase its supplies from, and the "freedom to compete" may lead some businesses to offer lower prices than their competitors.)*

**CHART ANSWER**
all of them

## U.S. Economic Freedoms

**Freedom to Earn Profits**

**Freedom to Own Property**

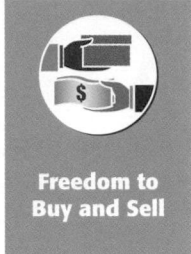

**Freedom to Buy and Sell**

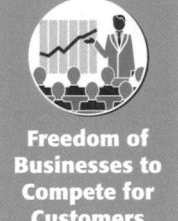

**Freedom of Businesses to Compete for Customers**

**Freedom of Workers to Compete for Jobs**

**Interpreting Charts**
*The economic system of the United States provides its citizens with several fundamental economic freedoms.* **Which of the freedoms shown here help businesses operate?**

*free market* refers to this exchange between buyers and sellers who are free to choose. The role of the government in regulating the free market is limited.

**Freedom to Compete** American businesses compete with one another for customers. Each business firm tries to persuade people to buy what it has to offer. In this system of **free competition,** buyers show which goods and services they favor every time they make a purchase. If consumers do not buy a product, producers will make something else or go out of business. Therefore, producers compete to make what they think the public will buy.

**Freedom to Earn a Living** American workers are free to seek the best jobs their training and education qualify them to perform. In addition, they may bargain with their employers for higher wages, more benefits, and better working conditions. American workers are free to leave their jobs to find better ones or to start their own businesses.

**Freedom to Earn a Profit** As you recall, profit is the income a business has left after expenses. The **profit motive,** or desire to make a profit, is essential to a free economic system. The hope of making a profit is the reason that people start and operate businesses. It is also the reason that people **invest** in, or put money into, various businesses and valuable goods.

**LEVEL 3:** Organize students into four groups. Ask two of the groups to think of businesses or products that have succeeded as a result of free competition. Ask the other two groups to think of products or businesses that have failed as a result of free competition. Ask each group to list reasons that these products and businesses succeeded or failed. Then ask each group to write a brief paragraph explaining the benefits or drawbacks of the economic freedom to compete. *(Each group should point out that the quality and price of products and services generally improve when buyers are free to choose from a variety of competing businesses.)* Ask each group to present its conclusions to the class. **COOPERATIVE LEARNING**

**LEVEL 3:** Organize students into five groups and assign one of the five economic freedoms to each group. Then ask each group to imagine that the economic freedom it has been assigned does not exist. Have each group create a chart or diagram describing the problems or limitations that the U.S. economy would experience if that specific freedom were missing. *(Students might indicate how consumers would be unable able to shop around for the best price on goods and services if they no longer had the "freedom to buy" from whomever they wanted.)* Invite each group to present its chart or diagram to the class. **COOPERATIVE LEARNING**

**Freedom to Own Property** The right to own and use property of all kinds is guaranteed in the U.S. Constitution. Americans have the right to own and use their own land, personal belongings, and other kinds of property. The free market and free competition would not be possible without such private ownership of property.

All Americans are free to do as they like with their own money. They may spend, save, or invest it. They may buy buildings, land, tools, and machines. These forms of property may be used to produce goods and services. Americans may use this property to start their own businesses and to earn profits.

Americans also have the right to protect their ideas and inventions by copyrighting what they write and by patenting their inventions. A **copyright** is the exclusive right, granted by law, to publish or sell a written, musical, or artistic work. A **patent** gives a person the exclusive right to make and sell an invention for a certain number of years.

✔ **Reading Check Summarizing** What economic freedoms do Americans enjoy? Americans have the economic freedoms to buy and sell, compete, earn a living, earn a profit, and own property.

*Many patents include diagrams illustrating the invention being submitted.*

## Resources in a Free Market

The United States, like every other country, must face a basic economic fact. People's needs and wants are greater than the resources available. In other words, there are never enough resources to meet all of our needs and wants. Depending on the circumstances, such resources can include raw materials, manufactured parts, skilled labor, or even valuable property. This problem of limited resources is called **scarcity.** Scarcity forces us to choose which needs and wants to satisfy with available resources.

Under the U.S. economic system, the free market helps determine how Americans use limited resources. To be successful, businesses must supply what buyers in the market demand. At the same time, if consumers want scarce goods, they must pay the market price.

✔ **Reading Check Finding the Main Idea** What is the basic economic fact that the people of all countries must face, and how is this issue resolved in the United States? All people must deal with scarcity. The free market determines how Americans will use their limited resources.

## Supply and Demand

You are already familiar with supply and demand. For example, you probably know that a rare baseball card costs more than a common card. The price for a rare card is higher because the demand is greater than the supply. The U.S. economy as a whole works in a similar way. People demand goods and services, and businesses supply them. The balance of supply and demand determines the prices and quantities of these goods and

**Interpreting the Visual Record**

**Demand and Investment** *High demand for oil encourages companies to invest in expensive equipment like this oil rig.* **What might companies do if the demand for oil dropped?**

### ★ Culture

**African American Patents** Before the Civil War, slaves could not receive patents on their inventions, so slaveholders often received the credit. Some historians, for example, have speculated that Jo Anderson, a slave held by Cyrus McCormick, made vital contributions to the invention of the McCormick harvester, yet Anderson received no credit for his contributions. After the war, between 1870 and 1900, African Americans received hundreds of patents. Among these were Jan Matzeliger's shoe last (1883); William Purvis's machine for making paper bags (1884); Andrew Beard's automatic railroad car coupler (1897); and Granville Woods's synchronous multiplex railway telegraph—a device invented in 1887 that allowed communications between stations and moving trains.

**ACTIVITY:** Have students conduct research to discover three other patents issued by the U.S. government between 1870 and 1900, and ask each student to write a brief description of each invention and its inventor.

**Visual Record Answer**

*Students might suggest that they could lower their prices.*

**LEVEL 1:** Have students look through newspapers and magazines to find headlines about events that illustrate the effects of supply and demand. *(Students may find headlines that read "Prices Drop As Oil Production Increases," or "Bad Orange Crop Means More Expensive Breakfast Juice.")* Ask each student to cut out these headlines, paste them onto a sheet of paper, and write a brief description of how the laws of supply and demand explain each headline. Have volunteers present their headlines to the class. **ENGLISH LANGUAGE LEARNERS**

**LEVEL 3:** Ask students to imagine that they are entrepreneurs interested in starting their own businesses. Remind students that the U.S. economic system is a capitalist system that encourages business owners to earn profits by providing consumers with goods and services. Have students write one-page business plans in which they outline the types of capital that they will need to raise in order to start their businesses. *(For example, a student who wants to open a bicycle shop will need to raise the money to purchase retail space, bicycles, tools, cycling apparel, and so on.)* Ask each student to include a paragraph about how the laws of supply and demand will benefit the new business. Have volunteers read their business plans out loud while pretending that the other members of the class are potential investors.

## Profiles

**Adam Smith** The Scottish economist Adam Smith (1723–90) wrote an influential book about the free-market system, or capitalism. In *The Wealth of Nations* (1776), Smith presented his theory of the "invisible hand" of competition that guides individuals as they make economic decisions. Merchants and other businesspeople, he wrote, will act in their own self-interest if left alone, unhindered by government regulations. Smith believed that by trying to help themselves, businesspeople actually help society by making goods and services available to everyone. Though modern capitalist states often impose many regulations on business, free enterprise is still the driving force behind their economies.

**ACTIVITY:** Ask students to conduct research on Adam Smith to learn about his other economic theories, and have each student write a report on one of Smith's ideas.

**Visual Record Answer**

*Students might suggest that it helps to ensure better quality or lower prices.*

**Interpreting the Visual Record**

**Choices** *Manufacturers must compete with each other's goods in features and price to attract consumers.* **How do you think this competition benefits consumers?**

services. The relationship between supply and demand is so predictable that economists have identified rules that it follows. These rules are the law of supply and the law of demand.

The **law of supply** states that businesses will provide more products when they can sell them at higher prices. They will provide fewer products when they must sell those goods at lower prices. The **law of demand** states that buyers will demand more products when they can buy them at lower prices. They will purchase fewer products when they must purchase them at higher prices.

The supply of products in the economy and the demand for these products balance each other. This balance provides buyers with what they need and want and provides businesses with profits. Supply and demand also affect the prices of goods and services.

For example, consider how the laws of supply and demand affect the price of DVD players. If businesses produce more than they can sell, they will either lower the price or produce fewer DVD players. In contrast, if the demand for DVD players exceeds the supply, businesses can raise their prices. They will also produce more DVD players to meet the greater demand.

✔ **Reading Check Analyzing Information** How do the laws of supply and demand affect the prices and availability of goods? More goods are available if businesses can sell them at a higher price. Consumers will buy more of a product if the price is lower.

## ★ Capitalism

**Capital** is money invested in buildings, machines, and other forms of property used to produce goods and provide services. The U.S. economic system is sometimes called **capitalism,** or the capitalist system, because it is based on private or corporate ownership of capital.

Anyone who has capital invested in a business is a capitalist. For example, the tools owned by a self-employed electrician are capital. The tools allow the electrician to earn income. Likewise, the machines that make automobile bodies are part of the capital of an automobile manufacturing company. The electrician is a capitalist on a small scale, while the automobile manufacturer is a capitalist on a large scale.

Capitalism encourages people to work and to invest so that they will do well financially and will improve their quality of life. In turn, capitalism encourages businesspeople to supply Americans with the products and services they want, at prices they are willing to pay. Businesspeople who do so usually make a profit. By encouraging work, investment, and the production of desired goods, the capitalist system works for the benefit of the American people as a whole.

✔ **Reading Check Finding the Main Idea** Based on the capitalist model, why are an individual electrician and a company that manufactures automobiles both capitalists? Both have capital invested in a business.

**HOMEWORK** Ask students to conduct research at the library about an event in which a dramatic increase or decrease in supply or demand caused an economic crisis in the United States. *(Students might research the gasoline crisis of the 1970s.)* Have each student write a one-page report incorporating his or her research.

**LEVEL 3:** Ask students to think of items that are very expensive only because they are scarce or in high demand. Point out that the value of an item is not based solely on the costs of its production and material, which are sometimes minimal, but also on the demand that consumers express for it. *(Students might suggest things such as collectibles, rare coins, trading cards, tickets to sporting events, and so on.)* Ask each student to write a letter to another student who has not studied the laws of supply and demand, explaining why one of the items on the list costs more than another item that might actually require more material or effort to manufacture. Have volunteers read their letters to the class. **ENGLISH LANGUAGE LEARNERS**

## ★ The Free-Enterprise System

American businesspeople are generally free to run their own businesses in the way they think best. They do not depend on government officials to tell them how to operate. Americans depend on their own enterprise—that is, their own ability and energy. For this reason, the U.S. economic system is sometimes called a **free-enterprise system.** The freedom to compete without unreasonable governmental interference offers enterprising businesspeople the opportunity to enjoy success and profits.

Along with this freedom to act come many risks. American business owners are free to earn profits, but they must also accept losses if they make mistakes. They may produce a new product only to find that customers do not want it. Or they may make their products inefficiently and have to charge more than people are willing to pay. Such mistakes may cause owners to lose money and to close their businesses. If their businesses fail, owners may lose all their capital. However, if there is sufficient demand for a product or service, efficiently run businesses earn profits in a free-enterprise system.

✔ **Reading Check Analyzing Information** How does a free-enterprise system help ensure that efficient businesses continue operating and inefficient businesses do not? The free-enterprise system allows open competition, so efficient businesses will earn greater profits and have greater success than the inefficient businesses they compete with.

## ★ Rise of Big Business

American businesses have always been privately owned, with business decisions made by their owners. During the early years of the country, most businesses were small and served local needs. As a result, relatively few shippers, importers, and manufacturers became wealthy. However, in the late 1800s, many big businesses developed in the United States.

These businesses benefited from the development of new technology. Machines powered first by steam and later by electricity replaced hand labor and greatly increased the amount of goods produced. Placing these machines in factories where large numbers of people were employed allowed businesses to produce large quantities of goods. Therefore, the costs of production were much lower than before.

The owners of these large factories and businesses made huge profits. However, some owners hoping to make great fortunes used business practices that would be considered unfair or illegal today.

✔ **Reading Check Summarizing** How did big business develop in the United States? During the country's early years, most businesses were small. Then in the late 1800s many big businesses began to develop and make enormous profits due to technological advances.

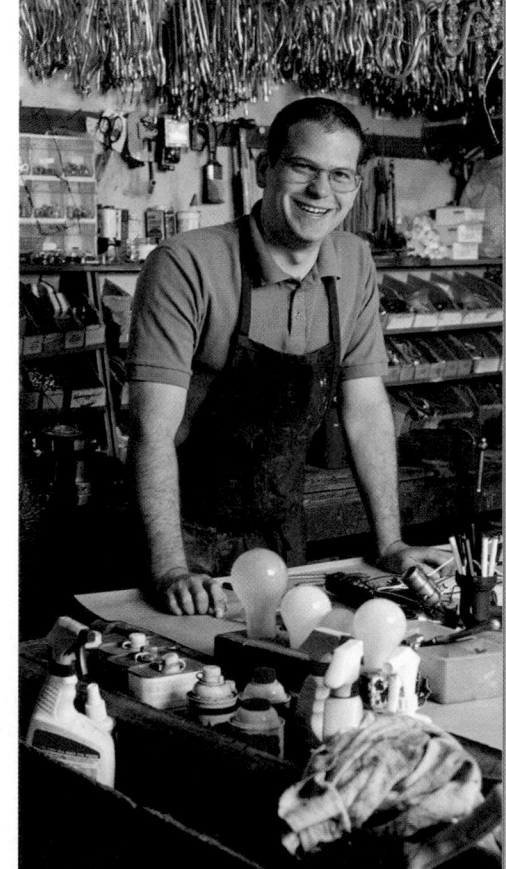

**Interpreting the Visual Record**

**Small businesses** *Small business owners must work very hard and take risks to succeed.* **Why do you think people start their own businesses?**

## ★ Economics

**Big Business** Large pharmaceutical companies are good examples of big businesses that have the considerable resources sometimes needed to develop a product—in this case, medicines. These resources include the "intellectual capital" provided by their teams of scientists to work on developing new medicines. Because these scientists are employed by the companies, patents for drugs discovered and developed are typically awarded to the companies. Some people believe that awarding these patents on drugs is problematic. Critics argue that "new" drugs actually evolve from the previous work of other scientists. They also argue that the patents permit drug companies to monopolize the market for newly discovered drugs and to reap huge profits. Pharmaceutical companies argue that the patents and the money they make on the sales of drugs are fair and necessary, considering the sometimes enormous resources they invest in developing the drugs.

**CRITICAL THINKING**

Do you think that pharmaceutical companies should be awarded patents for new drugs?

**ANSWER:** Student responses will vary.

**Visual Record Answer**

*Students might suggest to earn a better living or to pursue a dream.*

**ALL LEVELS:** Lead a class discussion about the free-enterprise system. Then copy the following graphic organizer onto the chalkboard, omitting the italicized answers. Ask students to complete the chart by listing the ways that big business can help the free-enterprise system and the ways that it can hurt free enterprise.

```
                  The Free-Enterprise System
                            │
        ┌───────────────────┴───────────────────┐
Helps the System      ┌──────────────┐      Harms the System
• Employs many people │ Big Business │ →    • monopolies
• Produces goods more └──────────────┘      • mergers
  efficiently        ←                       • trusts
                                             • unfair competition
```

**LEVELS 1 AND 2:** Remind students that big business can harm the free-enterprise system if it forms a monopoly. Ask each student to think of a monopoly that is legal, such as a public utility company. Then have students divide a sheet of paper into two columns and have them write the name of a legal monopoly at the top of the paper. Ask students to think of reasons that this monopoly is beneficial. Have students list these reasons in the first column and then ask them to list the negative effects of these monopolies in the second column. *(Students might say that a water and sewage monopoly is beneficial because one company can do the job more efficiently. However, consumers might feel powerless to get the company to improve service or lower prices since that company provides the only water service available.)*

## ★ The Democratic Process

### The Microsoft Monopoly

In May 1990 the Federal Trade Commission began an epic antitrust investigation of the Microsoft Corporation, charging that the giant software company illegally impeded competition with unfair pricing and that it had hidden codes in its operating system to prevent the use of competitors' software applications. In May 1998 the attorneys general of 20 states announced that they were suing Microsoft for violating state antitrust laws. Finally, on June 7, 2000, after a decade of complicated legal battles, a federal judge ruled that Microsoft should be divided into two smaller companies. This was the most significant antitrust decision since the breakup of Standard Oil in 1911 and AT&T in 1982. A year later a federal appeals court reversed the Microsoft decision, but the court still ruled that Microsoft had broken antitrust laws. Late in 2001 the Justice Department proposed a settlement requiring Microsoft to, among other things, allow computer manufacturers to decide which Microsoft products they load into their computers.

#### CRITICAL THINKING

Should Microsoft be divided into smaller companies, and why was this legal battle so complicated?

**ANSWER:** Students' responses will vary.

## ★ Monopolies

Unfair business practices harm a free economy. They may interfere with the free market and result in high prices for consumers.

One unfair practice used by big business owners in the late 1800s and early 1900s was the forming of **monopolies.** A company has a monopoly if it is the only firm selling a product or providing a service. If there is no competition for the product or service, the monopolist controls the price. This is particularly dangerous when the product is a necessity, such as food. People are then forced to pay the asking price in order to acquire the product or service.

A **merger** occurs when two or more companies combine to form one company. A merger may lead to the forming of a monopoly. If all the companies in an industry merge, a monopoly forms. There is no longer real competition in the industry.

Another way to create a monopoly is to form a **trust.** Under this arrangement, several companies create a board of trustees. Each company remains a separate business, but the board of trustees makes sure that the companies no longer compete with one another. If all the companies in an industry become part of the trust, a monopoly is created.

To understand how monopolies form and how they operate, consider the example of a large coffee company. It wants to lessen its competition. To do so, it might buy all of the small coffee companies. Alternatively, it might force them out of business by temporarily lowering its prices below its costs.

The large company lowering its prices would force the small coffee companies to lower their prices as well. They must be able to compete to stay in business. At first, these lower prices might seem good for consumers. Under this system, every coffee firm would be selling coffee at a loss. However, because the large company has more capital than the small companies, it can afford to lose money longer if it knows it will ultimately win. As a result, the small companies would most likely be forced to sell their businesses. They may merge with the large company or go out of business altogether.

The large company would then be a monopoly. It alone would produce all of the coffee on the market. This lack of competition would allow the company to raise the price of coffee. The only choices available to consumers would be to pay the monopoly's higher prices or to stop drinking coffee.

#### Interpreting Political Cartoons

**Monopolies** *The abuses committed by monopolies in the late 1800s led cartoonists to portray them as large bullies taking advantage of consumers.* **How are the monopolies in this cartoon showing off their power?**

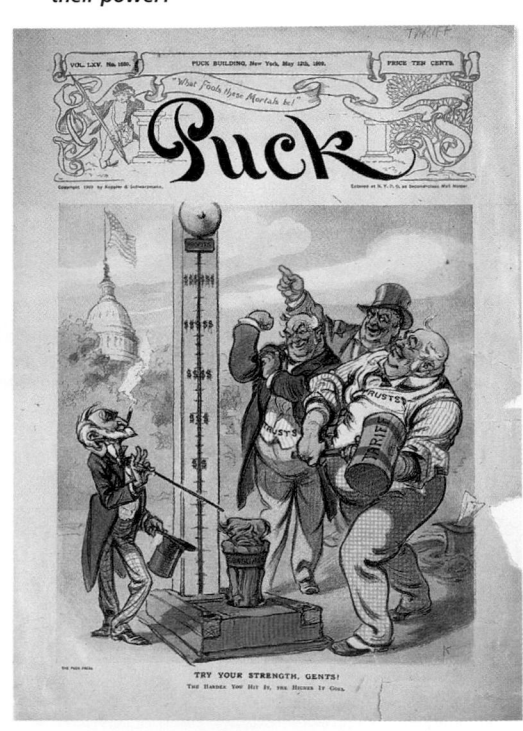

✔ **Reading Check** Drawing Inferences and Conclusions
How do monopolies harm free enterprise? By preventing competition, they negatively affect the prices that people have to pay for goods and services.

**LEVELS 2 AND 3:** Remind students that big businesses can be harmful to the free-enterprise system if they are allowed to form monopolies. Then have students consult newspapers and other periodicals to locate articles about how the U.S. government has acted as a referee in a specific business merger or acquisition. *(Some students might find, for example, articles about government intervention when a large communications company wants to purchase another television station or newspaper.)* Ask each student to create a flowchart or diagram to help illustrate the economic issues in the story to the class. Display these visual guides around the classroom.

**LEVEL 3:** Have each student research a big business that began as a small business. Ask students to identify the opportunities and desires that helped the small business grow. *(Students' answers will vary but should cite such factors as new technology, mergers, meeting consumer demand, and so on.)* Then have each student write a brief history of the big businesses he or she researched, explaining how that business has both harmed and helped the free-enterprise system. Ask volunteers to read their reports to the class.

## ⭐ Importance of Big Business

Today most large businesses in the United States face competition from other big companies and from foreign producers. Also, if a company's profits are high, other companies seeking profits are encouraged to enter the industry. Competition is then quickly restored.

Today's big businesses are essential to the economy. Many of the goods and services we need cannot be produced efficiently by small companies. For example, to produce steel, electricity, automobiles, and ships, large and very expensive equipment is needed. The term *economies of scale* describes the situation in which goods can be produced more efficiently by larger companies.

Because of economies of scale, a few companies account for most of the production and sales in some industries today. It would be beneficial to these companies to form a trust and agree on how much to produce and what to charge for their products. However, they would be abusing their size and power and there are laws to prevent such abuse.

✔ **Reading Check Analyzing Information** Why do economies of scale make large businesses important? Economies of scale allow large businesses to produce some goods and services more efficiently than small businesses.

## ⭐ Regulating Monopolies

The referee of a basketball or football game ensures that the teams observe the rules of the game. In much the same way, the federal government enforces rules to ensure that the U.S. free-enterprise system operates fairly.

To prevent monopolies and trusts from forming, Congress has passed antimonopoly and antitrust laws. For example, the Sherman Antitrust Act of 1890 was passed to prevent monopolies. It was strengthened by the Clayton Act of 1914, which forbade practices that would weaken competition. The Antitrust Division of the U.S. Justice Department and the Federal Trade Commission are responsible for enforcing these laws.

During the past several decades the number of large business combinations known as conglomerates has increased significantly. A **conglomerate** is formed by the merger of businesses that produce, supply, or sell a number of unrelated goods. For example, a single conglomerate may control communication systems, insurance companies, hotel chains, and many other types of businesses.

The government watches mergers of large companies to ensure that conglomerates do not gain too much control over an industry. If a conglomerate gains so much power that it threatens competition, the government may step in.

In some industries monopolies are legal. These legal monopolies are **public utilities,** companies that provide essential services to the

**Interpreting the Visual Record**

**Scale** *Big companies benefit from their ability to invest in expensive capital, such as the robotic equipment on this assembly line.* **What benefits does machinery like this provide for companies?**

**Holt Researcher**

**go.hrw.com**
**KEYWORD: Holt Researcher**
**Freefind: Adam Smith**
Read the biography of early philosopher and economist Adam Smith on the Holt Researcher. Then create an encyclopedia entry on Smith that answers the following question: What ideas did Smith contribute to the field of economics?

## ⭐ Economics

### Conglomerates

Conglomerates often produce a wide variety of brand-name products. Typical American conglomerates include the Sara Lee Corporation (Sara Lee, Ball Park, Hanes, L'eggs, Sanex, Kiwi, Champion); Pepsico (Pepsi, Mountain Dew, Doritos, Lay's, Cap'n Crunch, Tropicana, Quaker, Tostitos); and Philip Morris (Cool Whip, Cracker Barrel, Jell-O, Kool-Aid, Maxwell House, Oscar Mayer, Tang, Raisin Bran, Toblerone).

**ACTIVITY:** Have students choose five products that they use on a regular basis and ask them to conduct research to determine whether any of these products are owned by a conglomerate. Ask each student to create a chart identifying who owns each of the five products and if any of the companies are part of a conglomerate. Have students also list other products owned by the same conglomerate.

### Visual Record Answer

*Students might suggest the speed of assembly.*

### POLITICAL CARTOON ANSWER
(for p. 412) by taking turns at a carnival game

**LEVEL 3:** Remind students that in a free-enterprise system the government does not get involved in running the economy. Then point out that the U.S. government regulates big businesses to keep them from forming monopolies that would interfere with the free-enterprise system. Have students use an encyclopedia to conduct research about the economic system of a foreign country. Ask each student to write a report comparing the U.S. economic system to the economic system of the foreign country he or she has researched. (*Students should cite ways that the U.S. economy shares some aspects of other economies because it is a "mixed economy."*) Ask one or two volunteers to present their findings to the class.

## CLOSE

Review with students the basic economic freedoms that are a crucial part of the country's free-enterprise system. Then ask students to consider what life would be like in the United States if these economic freedoms were taken away. Have each student write a list of things that might be different. Call on volunteers to read their lists to the class.

**Interpreting the Visual Record**

**Public utilities** *Supplying the massive amounts of power needed by American homes and industries requires expensive capital investment. Power plants and power lines are the most visible parts of the power system.* **Why are utilities like electricity, natural gas, and water so important to the U.S. economy?**

public. Electric and natural gas companies are examples of public utilities. Providing such services requires very expensive capital equipment. Thus, it would be wasteful to have more than one company providing the same service in the same area. Therefore, one company is allowed to have a monopoly, but only under strict government regulation.

✔ **Reading Check** **Finding the Main Idea** How does the federal government protect the free-enterprise system? The government regulates large-business mergers to prevent monopolies.

## ⭐ Comparing Economic Systems

As you have learned, the freedom of buyers and sellers is essential to the U.S. economic system. However, the economy has grown large and complex. As a result, the federal government sometimes acts as a referee and makes economic decisions. The government makes many more economic decisions now than it did 100 years ago. Nevertheless, the U.S. economy remains a free economy.

Yet, in an economy like that of Cuba, the opposite is true. Most economic decisions are made by government officials who head planning agencies. Individuals are allowed only limited private enterprise. The Cuban government, for the most part, decides what goods and services to provide. Cuban workers are limited in the jobs they can hold.

For these reasons, Cuba's economy is called a command economy. A **command economy** is the opposite of a free economy. In a command

## REVIEW AND ASSESS

Have students complete the **Section 1 Review** on page 415. Then have students complete **Daily Quiz 17.1**. As **Alternative Assessment**, you may want to use the headlines activity or the flowchart exercise in this section's lessons.

## RETEACH

Have students complete **Main Idea Activity for English Language Learners and Special-Needs Students 17.1**. Then assign each student a subsection. Ask each student to create a diagram illustrating how his or her section describes important aspects of the U.S. economy. After students have finished their

diagrams, ask volunteers to present their guides to the class.
**ENGLISH LANGUAGE LEARNERS**

## EXTEND

Organize the class into pairs. Then have students research arguments for and against the Sherman Antitrust Act of 1890 and other trust-busting efforts of the late 1800s and early 1900s. Students should investigate the circumstances leading up to the events and identify major participants. Instruct pairs to prepare oral reports and visual guides to explain and illustrate their research for the class. **BLOCK SCHEDULING ,**

**COOPERATIVE LEARNING**

economy the government owns almost all of the capital, tools, and production equipment. The government tells the managers and workers in factories and on farms what and how much to produce. Thus, most economic decisions are made by the government, rather than by individuals as in a free market.

The U.S. economy is free, but the government still controls certain parts of the economy. For example, the government regulates businesses to make sure that working conditions are safe. Because the U.S. economic system is not an entirely free system, it can be described as a **mixed economy.**

Another type of economy is the **traditional economy.** In a traditional economy production is based primarily on customs and traditions. In traditional economies, economic roles are generally passed down from one family member to another. For example if you lived in a society with a traditional economy and one of your parents earned a living by catching fish in a nearby river, you would earn your living the same way. Note that traditional economic roles generally are passed down from father to son and from mother to daughter. Traditional economic systems still exist in parts of North America, Latin America, Asia, Australia, and Africa.

**Interpreting the Visual Record**

**Inspections** *Federal inspectors help ensure safe working conditions and safe products in many different industries.* **Why do you think the federal government takes on this responsibility?**

✔ **Reading Check Comparing and Contrasting** What are the similarities and differences between a command economy and a mixed economy? Both economic systems involve government control. However, in command economies most economic decisions are made by the government, and in a mixed economy most economic decisions are made by individuals.

## SECTION 1 / Review

**go.hrw.com Homework Practice Online**
keyword: SZ3 HP17

1. **Define** and explain:
   • market economy
   • free market
   • free competition
   • profit motive
   • invest
   • copyright
   • patent
   • scarcity
   • law of supply
   • law of demand
   • capital
   • capitalism
   • free-enterprise system
   • monopolies
   • merger
   • trust
   • economies of scale
   • conglomerate
   • public utilities
   • command economy
   • mixed economy
   • traditional economy

2. **Summarizing** Copy the graphic organizer below. Then use it to identify the five economic freedoms that Americans enjoy.

   Economic Freedoms

3. **Finding the Main Idea**
   a. What are the laws of supply and demand?
   b. Why is big business both good and bad for a free-enterprise system?

4. **Writing and Critical Thinking Contrasting** Explain how the U.S. economic system differs from the economic system in Cuba.

   **Consider:**
   • who owns capital
   • the amount of government control
   • who makes most economic decisions

**Visual Record Answer**

*Students might suggest to ensure that safety standards are met.*

## Section 1 Review
### ANSWERS

**1. Define**
• market economy, p. 407
• free market, p. 408
• free competition, p. 408
• profit motive, p. 408
• invest, p. 408
• copyright, p. 409
• patent, p. 409
• scarcity, p. 409
• law of supply, p. 410
• law of demand, p. 410
• capital, p. 410
• capitalism, p. 410
• free-enterprise system, p. 411
• monopolies, p. 412
• merger, p. 412
• trust, p. 412
• economies of scale, p. 413
• conglomerate, p. 413
• public utilities, p. 413
• command economy, p. 414
• mixed economy, p. 415
• traditional economy, p. 415

**2.** freedom to buy and sell, to compete, to earn a living, to earn a profit, to own property

**3. a.** law of supply—businesses provide more products when they can sell them at higher prices and fewer products when they must sell them at lower prices; law of demand—buyers demand more products when prices are lower and fewer products when prices are higher

**b.** good: because big business can produce many goods and services more efficiently than smaller companies; bad: if they abuse their size and power by forming trusts

**4.** Students should support their explanations.

*The Economic System* **415**

# SECTION 2

## OBJECTIVES

*After completing Section 2, students should be able to*

1 **Describe the different types of business organizations.**

2 **Explain how corporations function.**

3 **Evaluate the difference between preferred stock and common stock.**

## LET'S GET STARTED!

Write the following question on the chalkboard: *How are businesses organized?* As students enter the classroom, ask them to respond to this question. (*Students might suggest that a small business is run by its owner, who makes all the decisions, or that a large business is run by a board of directors that votes on major decisions.*) Point out that there are different types of businesses and that they are organized in different ways. Tell students that in Section 2 they will learn more about the different types of business organizations and how they function and raise money.

---

# SECTION 2

# Business Organizations

## Read to Discover

1. What are the different types of business organizations?
2. How do corporations function?
3. What is the difference between preferred stock and common stock?

### WHY CIVICS MATTERS

American history is filled with business success stories. Use **CNN fyi.com** or other **current events** sources to learn about a successful business undertaking in the United States today. Record your findings in your journal.

## Define

• sole proprietorships
• partnerships
• corporation
• stocks
• stockholders
• dividends
• preferred stock
• common stock
• nonprofit organizations

## Reading Focus

More than 120 years ago, a young clerk in a New York town used an idea to increase his store's business. He gathered several small items from the store's shelves and placed them on a counter near the entrance. He put up a sign advertising everything on the counter for five cents. Customers came into the store intending to buy only a basic need like thread or cloth. Yet they stopped at the counter for a bag of clothespins, an eggbeater, or some other item that caught their eye. But the young man's idea did not end there.

*Frank W. Woolworth founded an international chain of retail stores.*

### ★ The Creation of a Successful Business

The young man then decided to open his own store and to sell only 5-cent and 10-cent items. Unfortunately, his new store failed. He lost all the money he had saved and borrowed to start the business. Rather than give up, however, he borrowed the money he needed to buy new goods and started over. This time his business was a success.

The young man with the new idea was Frank W. Woolworth. With the profits from his successful business, he soon opened another 5-and-10-cent store, and then another and another. When he died in 1919, Woolworth had established more than 1,000 stores in the United States and Canada. He became a wealthy man because he had a good idea and the business sense to make it succeed.

# TEACH OBJECTIVE 1

**LEVEL 1:** Lead a class discussion about the different types of business organizations. *(The different types of business organiztions are sole proprietorships, partnerships, and corporations.)* Ask each student to come up with an idea for a new store or business that reflects one of these types of organizations. Remind them that a successful idea can be a simple one, such as Frank W. Woolworth's idea to sell only 5- and 10-cent items. Then ask each student to create a poster advertising the new store or business. *(Students' advertisements should include a brief explanation about what makes their store or business unique.)* Display the posters around the classroom.

**ENGLISH LANGUAGE LEARNERS**

**LEVEL 3:** Remind students that there are different types of business organizations and then ask students to imagine that they are each the sole proprietor of a business. *(See the Level 1 lesson for types of organizations.)* Then have each student write a letter to a friend, inviting that friend to become a partner in the business. Remind students that they will be giving up complete control of the business in exchange for some relief from the burden of sole ownership. *(Students' letters should explain why they want to enter into partnerships.)* Finally, call on volunteers to read their letters to the class.

## Sole Proprietorships

There are more than 23.5 million business firms in the United States today. Of these, more than 18 million are small businesses owned by one person. They include drug stores, gas stations, grocery stores, hair salons, and other businesses that serve people who live nearby. These small businesses, each owned by one person, are called **sole proprietorships.**

You probably know some of the advantages of going into business for yourself. Sole proprietors are their own bosses. They decide the hours the businesses will be open and how the businesses will operate. Because they are the owners, they take all the profits.

Yet there are disadvantages to being a sole proprietor. Owners must supply all the money needed to rent or buy buildings or office space and equipment. If they need to hire help, they must be able to pay their employees. They must also pay taxes. Most business owners are hard-working people. Although they can hire others to help them, they alone are responsible for the success or failure of their businesses.

If their businesses fail, proprietors must face the losses. While workers may lose their jobs, proprietors may have to sell their personal belongings to pay their business debts.

✔ **Reading Check Categorizing** What are the advantages and disadvantages of operating a sole proprietorship? Owners are their own bosses and take all the profits. However, they must also supply all the money needed to open and operate a business. They alone are responsible for the business's successes or failures.

## Partnerships

Each year in the United States many small businesses are started, but many small businesses also fail. Some fail because the sole proprietor lacks enough capital or the business lacks the ability to earn a good profit. For such reasons, the owner of a small business sometimes seeks another person to become a partner in the business.

**Interpreting the Visual Record**

**Local stores** *Many of the small stores found in every community are sole proprietorships.* **What types of goods does this small store sell?**

★ **Culture**

**A Business of Their Own**
Throughout U.S. history many immigrants have earned livings by running sole proprietorships. One such immigrant, a Vietnamese refugee, tells his story:

"In Vietnam, I was like your U.S. Senators. I was very respected and an important man, but when I came to your country I had to start all over again. I knew that I could not be in the government here so I asked my boys to help me think of ways that we could begin our own business here in Hawaii. It was after that when we started our lawn business and now I have nine crews working for me."

**ACTIVITY:** Ask students to conduct research to find out more about a business started by someone in their community. Then have each student write a brief essay about it.

**Visual Record Answer**

*Students should suggest convenience and snack items.*

**ALL LEVELS:** Copy the following graphic organizer onto the chalkboard, omitting the italicized answers. Ask each student to complete the organizer by filling in the five most important features of corporations. Then lead a discussion about what each of these features entails and how a corporation functions. **ENGLISH LANGUAGE LEARNERS**

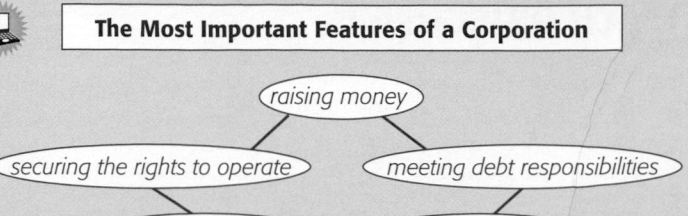

The Most Important Features of a Corporation

*raising money*

*securing the rights to operate* — *meeting debt responsibilities*

*electing directors* — *choosing executives*

---

## ★ Economics

### History and the Stock Market
Since the start of World War II in 1941, the Dow Jones Industrial Average, which analysts use to evaluate the U.S. stock market, has risen more than 7,676 percent. However, many tragedies in U.S. history have triggered sudden temporary downturns in the market. Following are a few examples of the percentage change in the stock market the day after the United States experienced a major crisis: bombing of Pearl Harbor, –3.5 percent; assassination of President Kennedy, –2.89 percent; resignation of President Nixon, –1.59 percent; terrorist attacks of September 11, 2001, –7.12 percent.

### CRITICAL THINKING
Why do historical events, such as the ones listed above, have an effect on the economy?

**ANSWER:** Students should point out that such events, though not specifically involving the economy, have an emotional or psychological effect on investors, who may choose not to invest during times of uncertainty.

### ANALYZING PRIMARY SOURCES ANSWERS
1. individualism, private property, the law of accumulation of wealth, and the law of competition

2. These laws sometimes operate unequally or unjustly.

---

## Historical Document

### ANDREW CARNEGIE'S "GOSPEL OF WEALTH"

The following excerpt is from an article written by Andrew Carnegie in 1889. Later called "The Gospel of Wealth," it explains his views on capitalism.

"Individualism, private property, and the law of accumulation [collection] of wealth, and the law of competition . . . these are the highest results of human experience, the soil in which society so far has produced the best fruit. Unequally or unjustly, perhaps, as these laws sometimes operate, and imperfect as they appear to the idealist, they are, nevertheless, . . . the best and most valuable of all that humanity has yet accomplished."

### Analyzing Primary Sources
1. What does Carnegie believe are humanity's finest accomplishments?
2. What flaws does Carnegie notice in these laws?

Each share of stock represents ownership of a fraction of the corporation.

UNITED STATES STEEL CORPORATION
GOODBODY & Co.

---

Businesses in which two or more people share the responsibilities, costs, profits, and losses are known as **partnerships.** This form of ownership gives the business a greater amount of capital and a better chance of success. In a partnership there is more than one person to provide capital, share responsibility, furnish ideas, and do the work. The partners also share the risks. If the business fails, the partners share responsibility for the debts.

Two or more persons can form a partnership. Usually the partners sign a legal agreement setting up the partnership. However, unwritten partnership agreements are legal and are recognized by the courts. There are a few large American businesses that are organized as partnerships, but most partnerships are small.

It is possible to recognize a partnership by the name of the business firm: Kim and Jackson, Contractors; Reilley, Cortés, and Clark, Attorneys. If *Inc.*— an abbreviation, or short form, of "Incorporated"—appears after the names, the business is organized as a corporation. This is the third form of business organization.

✔ **Reading Check** Finding the Main Idea Why do some businesses operate as partnerships? Partnerships can bring a greater amount of capital and business knowledge to the business, therefore giving it a better chance of success.

## ★ Corporations

Establishing a big business requires large sums of money—to buy land, build factories and offices, purchase tools and machinery, and employ workers. A big business can seldom be set up by an individual or even by a number of partners. Another form of business organization—a **corporation**—is needed. The corporation is the most common form of business organization for the country's large companies. Many of the country's smaller companies are also corporations. The corporation is a permanent organization, unlike proprietorships and partnerships, which end when their owners die.

Corporations play a vital role in the U.S. economy. How does a corporation work? How is it organized? The following are its most important features.

**Raising Money** Corporations raise money by selling **stocks,** or shares of ownership. Each share of stock represents part of the corporation. The people who buy corporate stocks are called **stockholders.**

**LEVELS 2 AND 3:** Ask students to imagine that they are all stockholders in the Classroom Corporation—the largest manufacturer of textbooks in the United States—and tell them that it is time for the annual stockholders meeting. Have the class elect a board of directors and ask the board to choose executive officers. The remaining students should assume the role of stockholders. Then ask the board and the officers to describe their duties, and ask the class to explain who among the board will be responsible for the debts of the Classroom Corporation if it fails. Have the stockholders write a list of questions for the board, and have the board write a report about the state of the company for the shareholders. *(Stockholders might ask the board about the financial health of the company, and the board might* *present ideas for future growth or improvements.)* Then have each group of students ask the other group questions during a mock stockholders meeting. **COOPERATIVE LEARNING**

**HOMEWORK** Have students write the "obituary" for an imaginary failed corporation. Tell them to describe the history of the corporation, the reasons for its failure, and the manner in which its debts were relieved. Also, ask students to include what happened to the company's stockholders, including any liabilities they have regarding the company's failure.

Suppose that a new corporation needs $1 million to set up business. The corporation has the legal right to raise this money from investors. For example, it could sell 10,000 shares of its stock at $100 a share. Each purchaser of one share of stock would then own one ten-thousandth of the company.

When profits are divided each year, each owner of a single share of stock would receive one ten-thousandth of the profits. Corporation profits paid to stockholders are called **dividends.** Some stockholders own a few shares of stock, while other stockholders own many more shares. Each stockholder receives a share of the profits in proportion to the number of stock shares he or she owns.

**Rights to Operate** Corporations receive their rights to operate from state governments. States give businesses charters, or grants, of incorporation. These charters recognize the corporation's right to conduct business, sell stock to the public, and receive the protection of state laws.

In return for these benefits, corporations must obey state regulations in regard to their organization. These regulations determine the reports corporations make public, the taxes they pay, and the way they sell their stocks.

**Elected Directors** The directors of corporations are elected by the stockholders. Every corporation is required by law to hold at least one meeting of its stockholders each year. All stockholders have the right to attend and address this meeting—even if they own only one share.

At this annual meeting, the stockholders elect a board of directors. They may also vote on changes in the corporation's business. Each share of stock entitles its owner to one vote. The board of directors, representing the stockholders, meets during the year to make decisions about the corporation.

**Choosing Executives** The board of directors chooses corporate officers, or the people who will manage the affairs of the corporation. The officers include the company's president, vice presidents, secretary, and treasurer. The president usually chooses the other major assistants. Together, these officials oversee the daily operations of the corporation.

## How a Corporation Is Organized

**Common Stockholders**
- provide capital as owners
- receive dividends from profits
- elect directors—one vote per share of common stock

**Board of Directors**
- makes corporation policies
- votes dividends on common stock
- appoints president and other officers

**Corporate Officers**
- include individuals such as the corporate president, chief executive officer, treasurer, and vice presidents of various divisions

**Department Heads**
- include leaders of departments such as advertising, finance, personnel, and sales

**Employees**
- work in all areas to contribute to the corporation's success

**Interpreting Charts** *Large companies have layers of management directing the actions of different departments.* **Who are the corporate officers?**

### Citizenship in Action

**Junior Achievement**
Many businesspeople across the United States volunteer their time and expertise to help young people learn about running businesses in the Junior Achievement program. In addition to teaching high school students how to organize and operate their own businesses, Junior Achievement provides programs that introduce elementary school students to the world of economics and business. Middle school students engage in activities designed to help them learn about the U.S. economic system, personal finance, long-term goal setting, and the importance of getting a good education. Junior Achievement also offers a dropout prevention program to teach middle school students about the economic consequences of dropping out of school. Junior Achievement activities are available to students in more than 70 countries around the world.

**ACTIVITY:** Have students find out more about Junior Achievement or other similar programs available to them in their community. Then have each student write a brief essay about the activities that are offered.

**CHART ANSWER**
include corporate president, chief executive officer, treasurer, vice presidents

**Debt Responsibility** Corporations, as you recall, are owned by the stockholders. The money received from the sale of stock becomes the corporation's capital.

But what if the business fails? In that case neither the stockholders or the corporation's executives are responsible for the corporation's debts. This is the advantage the corporation has in gathering large amounts of capital. If a corporation goes out of business, its assets (property, buildings, and other valuables) are sold. The money raised from this sale is then used to pay off the corporation's debts.

✔ **Reading Check Summarizing** How is a corporation organized? Corporations are permanent organizations that raise money through the sale of stocks. They receive the right to operate from state governments and are governed by a board of directors that is elected by the stockholders.

## Stocks and Bonds

Corporations raise money through issuing two major types of financial tools—stocks and bonds. Stocks and bonds help provide corporations with capital.

A corporation may issue two kinds of stock—preferred stock and common stock. Owners of **preferred stock** take less risk when they invest their money. As long as the company makes a profit, they are guaranteed a fixed dividend every year. The corporation must pay dividends to the preferred stockholders before paying other stockholders their dividends. Because preferred stockholders take less risk, they do not usually have a vote in the company's affairs.

Owners of **common stock** take more risk when they invest their money. They receive dividends only if the company makes good profits. There are three main advantages in owning common stock:

1. If the company's profits are high, owners of common stock may receive higher dividends than owners of preferred stock.

**Interpreting the Visual Record**

Stock market *The New York Stock Exchange is one of the biggest centers for the buying and trading of stocks in the world.* **What impression does this image give of the activity on the trading floor?**

## REVIEW AND ASSESS

Have students complete the **Section 2 Review** on page 421. Then have students complete **Daily Quiz 17.2**. As **Alternative Assessment**, you may want to use the classroom corporation or the stock and bond certificate activities in this section's lessons.

## RETEACH

Have students complete **Main Idea Activity for English Language Learners and Special-Needs Students 17.2**. Then ask students to create a series of flash cards describing the different types of business organizations. After students have finished making their cards, have them use the cards to quiz each other. **ENGLISH LANGUAGE LEARNERS**

## EXTEND

Have students conduct research to obtain representative samples of local businesses that are sole proprietorships, partnerships, and corporations, both for-profit and nonprofit. Ask students to learn how these local businesses are organized. *(Students may wish to consult the local Chamber of Commerce, or conduct brief interviews with local businesspeople.)* Then ask students to write a prospectus for investors and donors comparing the structures of each of these businesses and explaining how each business raises money. **BLOCK SCHEDULING**

2. If the company's profits are high, the market price, or selling price, of the common stock usually increases. This means stockholders can sell their shares for more than they paid for them.

3. Common-stock owners have a vote in electing the board of directors and in deciding certain company policies.

Bonds are certificates stating how much the original purchaser paid. They also declare the percentage of interest on this amount that the corporation will pay the bondholder each year. Interest, as you also know, is the percentage paid to individuals or banks for the use of their money. The company must pay the interest on its bonds before it pays dividends to stockholders. This interest must be paid whether or not the company earns any profits for the year.

✔ **Reading Check Comparing and Contrasting** What are the similarities and differences between stocks and bonds? Both are used by corporations to raise money. Stocks represent corporate ownership and provide annual dividends based on profits. Common stocks provide corporate voting rights. Bonds are loans that must be repaid regardless of profits.

## ★ Nonprofit Organizations

Some business organizations provide goods and services without seeking to earn a profit. These **nonprofit organizations** vary in size and include charities, scientific research associations, and organizations dedicated to cultural and educational programs. Among the many nonprofit organizations in the United States are the American Red Cross, the American Heart Association, the United Way, Boy Scouts, and Girl Scouts. Nonprofit organizations are not taxed by the government.

✔ **Reading Check Summarizing** What are the characteristics of a nonprofit organization? Nonprofit organizations vary in size and purpose, but they include charities, scientific research associations, and cultural and educational programs. They do not earn profits and are not taxed by the government.

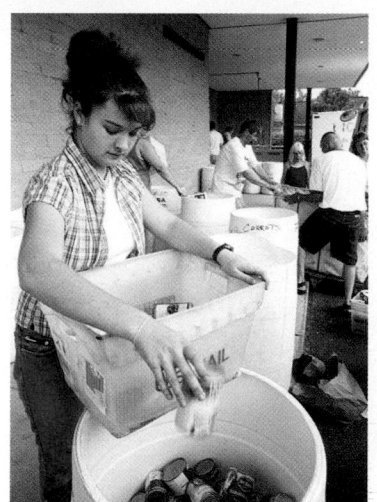

*Many charitable nonprofit organizations run food banks to provide meals to individuals and families in need.*

## SECTION 2 Review

go.hrw.com **Homework Practice Online**
keyword: SZ3 HP17

1. **Define** and explain:
   - sole proprietorships
   - partnerships
   - corporation
   - stocks
   - stockholders
   - dividends
   - preferred stock
   - common stock
   - nonprofit organizations

2. **Categorizing** Copy the chart below. Then use it to describe the four types of American businesses.

| Organization | Characteristics |
|---|---|
|  |  |
|  |  |
|  |  |
|  |  |

3. **Finding the Main Idea**
   a. How do corporations raise money, and how are the debts of a corporation paid if the corporation fails?
   b. How does preferred stock differ from common stock? Why do corporations issue bonds?

4. **Writing and Critical Thinking**
   **Decision Making** If you were to start a business of your own, would you organize it as a sole proprietorship, a partnership, a corporation, or a nonprofit organization? Explain your answer.
   **Consider:**
   - the expected size of your business
   - the risks you are willing to take
   - the purpose of your business

## Section 2 Review
### ANSWERS

**1. Define**
- sole proprietorships, p. 417
- partnership, p. 418
- corporation, p. 418
- stocks, p. 418
- stockholders, p. 418
- dividends, p. 419
- preferred stock, p. 420
- common stock, p. 420
- nonprofit organizations, p. 421

**2.** sole proprietorship: owner is own boss, does not share profits, supplies all capital, pays salaries and taxes, is responsible for failure; partnership: more than one person responsible for expenses, workload, raising capital, possible failure, profits and decision-making shared; corporation: permanent business organization owned by stockholders and run by a board of directors and corporate executives; nonprofit organizations: provide goods and services without seeking profit

**3. a.** by selling stocks, assets sold to pay debts if corporation fails

**b.** Preferred stockholders take less risk and are paid a fixed dividend every year before other stockholders are paid their dividends, but preferred stockholders usually have no vote in company affairs; owners of common stock take a greater risk and only receive dividends when the company makes a profit, but they can enjoy higher dividends and selling prices when profits are high, and they have a vote in company affairs.

**4.** Students' responses will vary.

## TEACH

**LEVEL 1:** Have each student bring in a copy of a warranty from a product that he or she or a family member has recently purchased. Point out the differences between full and limited warranties and also point out the differences in warranty periods. Ask students to read their warranties carefully and then ask them to discuss which types of products seem to have the best warranties. *(Students' answers will vary.)* Encourage students to give reasons for their responses.

**ENGLISH LANGUAGE LEARNERS**

**LEVEL 2:** Have students imagine that they have manufactured a specific product and that they must determine what type of warranty to extend to consumers. Ask each student to write a detailed warranty specifying the product, the type of warranty, and the warranty period. Remind students to determine what obligations the consumer must fulfill in order for the warranty to be valid. Students should also be prepared to discuss the disadvantages of providing too much or too little coverage in their warranties. Then encourage students to explain their warranties to the rest of the class.

### SKILLS ANSWERS

1. limited; one year for parts, 90 days for labor

2. starts on the date of purchase by original owner; owner of the product pays

3. owner must keep dealer's original bill of sale as proof of purchase and present it for service under warranty; must provide transportation to and from service center

4. accident, misuse, damage caused by improper installation, and products not purchased or used in the United States

# Civics Skills
## WORKSHOP

### Understanding Warranties

When you pay for a product, you expect it to work properly. If it does not, what should you do? Before you buy any product, make sure the business that makes the product backs it with a warranty. A warranty is a written guarantee of the condition of a product.

A warranty tells you what the manufacturer of the product will do if the product is defective. Usually, the company will promise to repair or replace the product or refund your money. However, not all companies issue warranties and those that do offer various guarantees. For all these reasons, it is important that you become familiar with warranties.

### How to Understand Warranties

1. **Distinguish between kinds of warranties.** By law, a warranty must carry one of two labels—*full* or *limited*. A full warranty promises that the company will pay the total cost of repair. A limited warranty covers only part of the expense. If the warranty is limited, you should find out what the limitations are. You may want to shop around and compare warranties to find the product with the best guarantees.

2. **Identify the warranty period.** Normally, the longer the warranty period, the better the quality of the product.

3. **Fulfill your obligations.** To take advantage of the guarantees in a warranty, you are often required to complete certain tasks. For example, you must generally provide proof of purchase when requesting warranty service. You may have further obligations as well. Find out what these responsibilities are and make sure you fulfill them.

### Applying the Skill

Study the warranty below. Then answer the questions that follow.

1. Is the warranty a full warranty or a limited warranty? How long is the warranty valid?

2. When does the warranty begin? Who pays for labor after 90 days?

3. What are the owner's obligations?

4. What does the warranty exclude?

---

**LIMITED WARRANTY**
**To Original Purchaser**
**Car Radio/Car Stereo**

- This Hi-Tech product is warranted against manufacturing defects for the following period:

| PARTS | LABOR |
|-------|-------|
| 1 YEAR | 90 DAYS |

- Hi-Tech will repair or replace at no charge, any part(s) found to be defective during the warranty period.
- This warranty period starts on the date of purchase by the original owner.
- The warranty repairs must be performed at a Hi-Tech authorized service center. A list of Hi-Tech authorized service centers can be obtained at any Hi-Tech dealer.

OBLIGATIONS OF THE ORIGINAL OWNER

- The dealer's original bill of sale must be kept as proof of purchase and must be presented to the Hi-Tech authorized service center.
- Transportation to and from the service center is the responsibility of the customer.

EXCLUSIONS OF THE WARRANTY

- This warranty does not cover accident, misuse, or damage caused by improper installation.
- This warranty is valid only on products purchased and used in the United States.

---

# SECTION 3

## OBJECTIVES

*After completing Section 3, students should be able to*

1  **Identify the four factors of production.**
2  **Explain how the four factors of production are necessary to the success of business.**
3  **Describe the ways that government regulates business.**

## LET'S GET STARTED!

As students enter the classroom, ask them to list the various factors that went into making the different articles of clothing that they are wearing. On the chalkboard, write several types of clothing worn by students. *(Examples of clothing might include sweaters, shirts, pants, shoes, and so on.)* Ask the class if there are any common factors that all of their lists share. *(Students should acknowledge that producing their clothing required natural resources, factories, labor, and management.)* Tell students that in Section 3 they will learn more about how the four factors of production are necessary to the success of business and how the government regulates business.

---

## SECTION 3

# Making Business Decisions

### Read to Discover

1. What are the four factors of production?
2. How are the four factors of production necessary to the success of business?
3. In what ways does the government regulate business?

### WHY CIVICS MATTERS

The success of businesses depends on how resources are used. Use **CNNfyi.com** or other **current events** sources to learn about how a successful business acquires and uses the resources that are necessary for the production of its product. Record your findings in your journal.

### Define

• rent
• labor
• productivity
• entrepreneurs
• gross income
• net income

## SECTION 3 RESOURCES

### REPRODUCIBLE

► Guided Reading Strategies 17.3
► Transparency 21: Factors of Production
► Community Service and Participation Handbook: Who Wants to Be An Entrepreneur?
► American Civics Political Cartoon: The Power of Trusts

### TECHNOLOGY

► One-Stop Planner, Lesson 17.3
► Homework Practice Online
► HRW Go site

### REINFORCEMENT, REVIEW, AND ASSESSMENT

► Section 3 Review, p. 427
► Daily Quiz 17.3
► Main Idea Activity 17.3
► English Audio Summary 17.3
► Spanish Audio Summary 17.3

---

## Reading Focus

You know that Americans operate businesses as individual proprietors, as members of partnerships, or as managers of corporations. The success of a business depends mainly on decisions about the use of four factors of production, or available resources. The four factors of production are natural resources, capital, labor, and entrepreneurship.

### ★ Natural Resources

Items provided by nature that can be used to produce goods and to provide services are called natural resources. Natural resources can be found on or in Earth, or in Earth's atmosphere. A natural resource is considered a factor of production only when it is scarce and some payment is necessary for its use. For example, the air you breathe on the beach is not a factor of production because it is not scarce and you do not have to pay to use it. However, if you go scuba diving, you have to pay for the bottled air in the scuba tanks.

A business also needs a place to locate a store, factory, or office. Suppose that Maria Moreno decides to start a bakery. She will need a place to conduct her business. That is, she needs land. Every business enterprise needs land. Land also provides natural resources. For example, the wheat used to make flour for Maria's bakery is considered a natural resource. The electricity that she uses to make her product is

*Bakeries require special equipment such as ovens, mixers, and baking tools.*

**LEVEL 1:** Organize students into pairs and have them consult magazines and newspapers to find pictures and advertisements that illustrate the four factors of production. *(The four factors are land, capital, labor, and management.)* Ask each pair to assemble a collage of images that includes a brief explanation of how each image represents a different factor of production. Ask volunteers to present their collages to the class. **ENGLISH LANGUAGE LEARNERS**

**LEVEL 3:** Ask students to think of a local business that manufactures a product or provides a service, and then ask students to think about how their community or region might be uniquely suited to provide one or more of the four factors of production. *(For example, students living in a community near the ocean might cite their geographical location as uniquely suited for businesses relying on shipping or fishing. Students living in a city might cite the urban environment as particularly well-suited to providing a skilled labor force.)* Have each student write a study of how one or each of the four factors of production is necessary to the success of the business they have chosen.

**HOMEWORK** Tell students to imagine that the owners of a new public building want to have an artist create a mural representing the four factors of production. Have each student design a plan for a mural using symbolic representations of land, capital, labor, and management.

## ★ Culture

**Johnson Publishing Company** While managing an insurance company's employee publication that reported news about the African American community, a young man in Chicago had an idea. Why not start a magazine, he thought, devoted to news and information about the African American community? Since that day in 1942, John Johnson has worked tirelessly to build his company into the publishing empire it is today— Johnson Publishing Company. Johnson's magazines include *Ebony, Essence,* and *Jet,* all of which are thriving. Johnson's success has continued for more than half a century. In 1972 American magazine publishers selected Johnson as publisher of the year. In 1987 *Black Enterprise* magazine named him entrepreneur of the decade. In 2000, Johnson Publishing Company reported sales of $400 million and employed 2,614 people.

**ACTIVITY:** Ask students to conduct research to learn more about a new publication started within the last five years. Have each student write a brief report about the special challenges that the new publication had to overcome in order to succeed.

**CHART ANSWER**
physical: natural resources, capital; people: labor, entrepreneurship

## Factors of Production

**Natural Resources**
• Soil and water
• Raw materials
• Other natural resources, such as forests

**Capital**
• Money
• Machinery and tools
• Factories
• Equipment

**Labor**
• Agricultural workers
• Business workers
• Industrial workers

**Entrepreneurship**
• Managers, owners, and partners who help bring together the other factors of production

**Interpreting Charts**
*Successful production relies on the presence of four key elements, or factors.* **Which factors are physical objects and which are made up of people?**

also considered a natural resource. The raw materials needed to produce goods of all kinds come from the mines, fields, and forests that help make up our country's natural resources.

The country's total supply of natural resources is limited. In some places land is so scarce that many different businesses occupy each city block. People who start businesses must decide where they want to locate or build their business.

For example, Maria must decide if she wants to own the property on which her business will be located. She can buy a piece of land with a building on it or land on which she can build. Or Maria can pay **rent** to use a building. Rent is the money a person pays to use land or other property belonging to someone else.

Rents and land prices in crowded business areas where land is scarce are higher than those in less densely populated areas. Maria must decide which location will give her the most profit. If she pays a high rent or price for land, she will be closer to customers. If she moves to the edge of town where land and rent are cheaper, customers will have to travel farther to reach her bakery. Maria must also make decisions about the quality and cost of the flour and other raw materials she will use.

✔ **Reading Check Finding the Main Idea** Why are natural resources necessary for a business enterprise? Natural resources provide the physical space for a business as well as other raw materials such as foodstuffs and wood.

*Buying or renting construction equipment is a necessary capital expense for many companies.*

## ★ Capital

Maria will also need equipment such as mixers and ovens. She may rent her equipment. If she has enough money, she may buy it. As you can see, Maria cannot start a business without money. Her decision to rent or buy equipment will depend on how much capital she has available. Capital is money used to pay for tools and other capital goods such as trucks, machines, and office equipment.

**ALL LEVELS:** Copy the following graphic organizer onto the chalkboard, omitting the italicized answers. Ask each student to complete the pie chart by listing the four factors of production. Conclude by leading a class discussion about why the four factors of production are necessary to the success of a business. **ENGLISH LANGUAGE LEARNERS**

**LEVEL 3:** Ask students to think of local businesses and have them list specific examples of how the four factors of production are necessary to the success of those businesses. Then ask students to imagine that one of the four factors is missing. Have each student write a brief essay describing, step-by-step, how the missing factor might cause the business to fail.

natural resources — capital — Factors of Production — labor — entrepreneurship

How will Maria obtain the capital she needs? Perhaps she will decide to set up her business as a sole proprietorship. To do so, she must have saved some money as capital. If she does not have enough, she may apply for a bank loan.

If the bank officials decide that Maria is a good risk, they will give her a loan. They will believe she is a good risk if she can prove that she has good ideas for a business. They must also believe that she will likely repay the loan. If Maria takes out a loan, she will have to pay interest.

Perhaps Maria will decide instead to seek one or more partners who are willing to invest in the bakery business. She also may decide to set up her business as a corporation and sell stock to raise capital. As Maria makes these decisions, she is weighing the opportunity costs and analyzing costs and benefits.

✔ **Reading Check** Analyzing Information How do people get capital for their businesses? Capital may come from saved money, bank loans, partners, or stock sales.

## Labor

All human effort used to produce goods and services is called **labor.** However, the word *labor* is often used to mean workers as opposed to owners and people who manage companies.

Workers in businesses, industries, and on farms sell their labor in exchange for money. Some workers are paid wages. Wages are payments given for work. Other workers, particularly those that manage companies or have a great deal of responsibility, are paid salaries. Salaries are fixed earnings that are paid usually on a biweekly or monthly basis.

If Maria Moreno performs her own labor, the amount of baked goods she can produce will be limited. If she hires more labor, her production will increase but she will have to pay labor costs.

The money Maria receives for selling the additional goods should be at least enough to pay her workers. If it is more than enough, she will increase her profits. If it is not enough to pay the workers, she will have to lay them off, or lower their pay. However, she might be able to find a way to increase productivity instead. **Productivity** is the amount of work produced by a worker per hour.

✔ **Reading Check** Drawing Inferences and Conclusions Why do businesses need labor, and how are they affected by productivity? Labor is necessary to produce goods and services. Businesses will make more profit with higher productivity, and less profit with lower productivity.

## Entrepreneurship

The decisions made by Maria Moreno must be made by all business owners, or **entrepreneurs.** After a business is started, entrepreneurs must make additional decisions such as how to distribute the product. They must also decide how much to charge for the product and whether to hire more people.

★★★★★★★★★★★★
**That's Interesting!**
★★★★★★★★★★★★

**Corporate Colonists** Did you know that the first European settlement in the thirteen colonies was sponsored by a corporation? A group of English investors formed the London Company to send settlers to America. The profits made by the settlers were to be distributed as dividends to shareholders.

In 1607 the company's settlers founded Jamestown, Virginia. The company owned all the colony's land. Jamestown made history, but not much money for the investors. Only when the colonists were allowed to own their own land did the settlement begin to prosper.

**Interpreting the Visual Record**

**Labor needs** *Most restaurant owners must hire workers to help with tasks such as cooking, cleaning, and serving customers.* **Why do you think restaurants have such a steady need for extra workers?**

## ★ Economics

**Big Money** The five U.S. corporations with the largest sales in 2001 were as follows: Wal-Mart Stores, $193.30 billion; Exxon-Mobil, $212.9 billion; General Motors, $177.3 billion; Ford Motor, $162.4 billion; and General Electric, $125.9 billion. The same five corporations were also the top U.S. earners during the previous year (2000): Exxon-Mobil, $210.39 billion; Wal-Mart Stores, $193.3 billion; General Motors, $184.63 billion; Ford Motor, $180.6 billion; and General Electric $129.85 billion.

**ACTIVITY:** Assign each student one of the top five companies and ask him or her to conduct research to learn more about what the company does and how it became one of the largest companies in the country. Have each student create a prospectus including a brief history of the company and a summary of its business strategy.

### Visual Record Answer

*Answers will vary, but students might suggest that people in the restaurant industry frequently change jobs.*

## TEACH OBJECTIVE 3

 **LEVEL 1:** Explain that the government has set a maximum work week of 40 hours for U.S. wage earners. Tell students that setting a maximum 40-hour work week is one way that the government gets involved in business. Organize students into small groups and have each group draw an editorial cartoon illustrating a specific role that the government plays to guarantee safe and fair business practices for consumers, workers, and business owners.

**ENGLISH LANGUAGE LEARNERS , COOPERATIVE LEARNING**

**LEVEL 3:** Ask students to think of examples of how the government regulates a specific business or industry in their local community. (*Students may cite local restaurants that must pass a* health inspection, or a local power plant that must comply with environmental safety regulations.) Ask students to write a position paper, arguing against or in favor of the specific regulations they have cited.

## CLOSE

Organize the class into two groups comprised of the managers and laborers of the Classroom Corporation. Ask each group to explain how it will be paid. Then explain that this year the company sold $1 million worth of textbooks and paid $600,000 in wages, salaries, and other costs. Ask volunteers to determine the company's gross income (*$1 million*) and net income (*$400,000*).

**COOPERATIVE LEARNING**

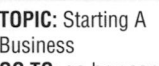
**BIOGRAPHY ANSWER**
He worked for a software company while in high school.

## BIOGRAPHY

### Bill Gates
### (1955– )

William Henry Gates III was born in Seattle, Washington. At the age of 13, Gates developed an interest in computers and programming while attending a private school. He became so successful that a local software company offered him a job while he was still a senior in high school. Gates attended Harvard University as a prelaw major, but his interest in computers led him to drop out as a junior in 1975. He and his friend Paul Allen co-founded Microsoft Corporation that same year. Microsoft became tremendously successful, first licensing the operating system MS-DOS to IBM to use on the company's new personal computers and later developing the Windows operating system. By age 31, Gates had become a billionaire. Microsoft software programs are now used by the majority of personal computers in the United States and are common throughout the world.

Gates currently serves as the chairman and chief software architect of Microsoft. In 2000 he was considered the world's richest man with an estimated worth of some $60 billion. He has donated billions of dollars to various philanthropic organizations. **How did Gates turn his early interests at school into a successful career?**

Those entrepreneurs who run businesses are called managers. The group of people who manage a single business is its management. The management's decisions determine whether the business will succeed. If management makes the wrong decisions, the business may fail. If management makes wise decisions, the business will usually prosper.

When entrepreneurs make decisions, they take risks. If businesspeople did not take risks, the average standard of living in the United States would not be so high. Thomas Edison and other businesspeople took risks that allowed Americans to be among the first people to enjoy electricity. Because Henry Ford and others took risks, Americans had the first low-priced, mass-produced cars. Bill Gates and other entrepreneurs in the computer industry have provided people with innovative computer software. They have also shaped the development of the computer and Internet industries around the world.

✔ **Reading Check Summarizing** What does management contribute to business? Management has the responsibility to make decisions that will determine the success or failure of a business.

 **Profits**

Many businesses are not successful. Businesses are willing to risk failure because they hope to produce profits. These profits depend on the businesses' income and expenses.

The total amount of money a firm receives from the sale of its goods or services is called **gross income.** Out of gross income, the firm must pay the costs of making and distributing its product.

The cost of materials and supplies used in the business must be paid. Rent must be paid. If the business owns its own land and buildings, property taxes must be paid. Machines wear out, so money must be set aside to repair machinery or replace it. If the business has borrowed money, interest must be paid. Employees must be paid. Even sole proprietors must pay themselves a salary.

If the business firm has been managed well, money will be left over after all the costs have been paid. A firm's income also depends on whether economic conditions are right. The amount left over is called **net income.** What happens to this net income? Part of it will go to pay income taxes. The rest is profit. In a corporation, profits are distributed among the stockholders as dividends.

✔ **Reading Check Analyzing Information** How are gross income, net income, and profit related? Gross income is a company's total income. Net income is gross income minus a company's operating costs. Profit is net income minus income taxes.

## ⭐ Government's Role

Although the U.S. government does not tell businesspeople what they must do, it does influence business in many ways. For example, government ensures that big corporations do not destroy competition from small businesses. The government also protects a person's rights to own private property and to buy and sell in a free market.

Many agencies of the federal government help businesses. For example, the Small Business Administration helps small businesses as they compete in the economy. The government plays many other roles in business. It helps business by providing information that managers can use in planning their production levels, sales, and costs. It sometimes provides loans and other types of assistance to businesses. The government also tries to keep the economy running smoothly.

The government protects workers' health and safety, prevents pollution of the environment, and protects buyers from dishonest practices and harmful products. The government also ensures that employers cannot discriminate against workers or job applicants.

Some people believe that the government has gone too far in doing its job as overseer. For example, tens of thousands of pages are needed to print all the business regulations issued by the federal government. Some regulations are necessary. Others are criticized for adding to the cost of doing business without providing much benefit to people. These costs can be passed on to consumers as higher prices.

Achieving the correct level of government involvement is difficult. How much regulation is needed is much debated. As a citizen in a free economy, you will help decide this issue.

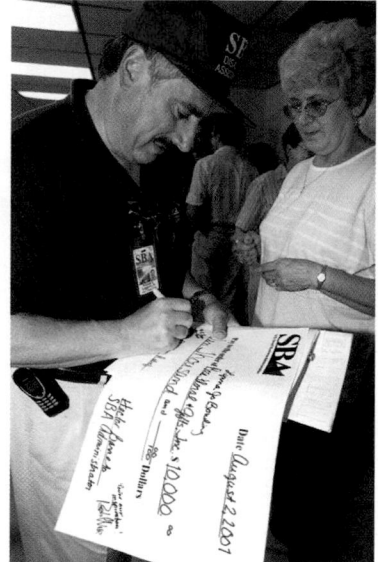

*The federal government offers several forms of financing to help people operate small businesses.*

✔ **Reading Check** Finding the Main Idea Why does the government need to regulate businesses in the United States, and how does it do so?
The government regulates businesses to preserve competition, works to protect citizens' property rights, has agencies that help businesses, and generally oversees the economy to keep it running smoothly.

## SECTION 3 Review

**go.hrw.com Homework Practice Online**
keyword: SZ3 HP17

1. **Define** and explain:
   - rent
   - labor
   - productivity
   - entrepreneurs
   - gross income
   - net income

2. **Summarizing** Copy the graphic organizer below. Then use it to identify the four factors necessary for a business to be successful.

```
[  ]   [  ]   [  ]   [  ]
 ↓      ↓      ↓      ↓
    Successful Business
```

3. **Finding the Main Idea**
   a. What is the difference between net income and gross income?
   b. What is the role of government in business?

4. **Writing and Critical Thinking**
   **Making Decisions** Imagine that you are planning to open a small business in your community. Make a list of the decisions that you must make before you can open your store.

   **Consider:**
   - what your business will sell
   - the four factors of production and how you will acquire them

---

### Section 3 Review ANSWERS

**1. Define**
- rent, p. 424
- labor, p. 425
- productivity, p. 425
- entrepreneurs, p. 425
- gross income, p. 426
- net income, p. 426

**2.** management, labor, capital, land

**3. a.** Gross income is all of the money a company receives from sales; net income is what is left over after costs have been paid.

**b.** ensure fair competition, economic freedom, worker safety; supply information; protect environment and safeguard buyers

**4.** Students' lists should determine what goods or services their businesses will provide, and they should address the factors of production.

### CHAPTER 17 REVIEW ANSWERS

**Define and Identify**
1. free market, p. 408
2. scarcity, p. 409
3. capitalism, p. 410
4. command economy, p. 414
5. sole proprietorships, p. 417
6. stockholders, p. 418
7. nonprofit organizations, p. 421
8. productivity, p. 425
9. entrepreneurs, p. 425
10. net income, p. 426

## Review and Assessment Resources

### REPRODUCIBLE
▶ Chapter 17 Review, pp. 428–29
▶ Vocabulary Activity 17
▶ Chapter 17 Tutorial for Students, Parents, Mentors, and Peers
▶ Chapter 17 Test (Form A or B)
▶ Alternative Assessment Handbook

### TECHNOLOGY
▶ Chapter 17 Test Generator (on the One-Stop Planner)
▶ Global Skill Builder CD–ROM
▶ HRW Go site

### REINFORCEMENT, REVIEW, AND ASSESSMENT
▶ Chapter 17 Test for English Language Learners and Special-Needs Students

## REVIEW
Have students complete the **Chapter 17 Review** on pages 428–29.

## ASSESS
Use one of the chapter tests to assess students' understanding of the content. For **Alternative Assessment**, see the **Alternative Assessment Handbook**.

### Understanding What You Read
**1.** freedom to buy and sell, freedom to compete, freedom to earn a living, freedom to earn a profit, freedom to own property

**2.** freedom to compete without unreasonable government interference; big business can produce things more efficiently and cheaply

**3.** raise money by selling stocks and bonds; receive rights to operate from state governments; stockholders elect a board of directors; board of directors chooses the executives; if business fails the corporation pays debt by selling its assets

**4.** preferred stocks—low risk, no voice in managing company, guaranteed fixed dividend; common stocks—high risk, voting rights in company decisions, larger dividends when profits are high

**5.** They are both ways to invest in a company.

**6.** ensures fair competition, economic freedom, worker safety; supplies information; protects environment and safeguards buyers

**7.** need place to locate the business and resources with which to produce products, capital to invest in equipment, labor to produce goods and services, and good management to run the business

## Chapter **17** Review

### Chapter Summary

#### Section 1
- The U.S. economic system is known as capitalism. It is based on a free market, free competition, private ownership of property, and the right to profit from business.
- In our mixed economy, government does not tell businesses and individuals what to do. Rather, it acts as a referee in the economic system. For example, the government acts to prevent the formation of monopolies, which limit competition.
- Other types of economic systems include command and traditional economies.

#### Section 2
- American business firms may be organized as sole proprietorships, partnerships, corporations, or nonprofit organizations.
- Corporations sell shares of stock to raise money. If the corporation makes a profit, these stock shares pay dividends to stockholders. Corporations also sell bonds to raise capital. Bonds are loans that the company must repay.
- Stockholders are not liable for the debts of a failed business. This helps encourage business investment.

#### Section 3
- All business owners must make decisions about their use of the four factors of production—natural resources, capital, labor, and entrepreneurship.
- In the U.S. economy most of these decisions are made freely by businesspeople as they seek to earn profits.
- The government plays a limited role in the economy.

### Define and Identify
Use the following terms in complete sentences.
1. free market
2. scarcity
3. capitalism
4. command economy
5. sole proprietorships
6. stockholders
7. nonprofit organizations
8. productivity
9. entrepreneurs
10. net income

### Understanding What You Read
**Section 1** *(Pages 407–15)*
1. What are the five economic freedoms that benefit Americans?
2. What is the free-enterprise system, and what roles do big businesses play in it?

**Section 2** *(Pages 416–21)*
3. What are the major characteristics of corporations, and what are their benefits?
4. What are the advantages and disadvantages of preferred stock and common stock?
5. How are stocks and corporate bonds similar and different?

**Section 3** *(Pages 423–27)*
6. What role does the government play in the U.S. economy?
7. Why must the factors of production be considered when starting a new business?

### What Did You Find Out?
1. How do the laws of supply and demand affect the prices of products?
2. What are the ways in which Americans can organize their businesses?
3. What are the four factors of production that all businesses share?

### Thinking Critically
1. **Supporting a Point of View** As you have learned, some people believe government has overregulated the economy. Do you agree or disagree with this position? What might happen if the government played no role in the economy?
2. **Drawing Inferences and Conclusions** Each year in the United States many small businesses fail to earn a profit and must close their doors. What are some of the reasons a business might fail to make a profit? Why do Americans continue to open small businesses when they know they are faced with possible failure?
3. **Finding the Main Idea** What is scarcity, and what does it force people to do?

## RETEACH

Organize students into three groups and assign each group one of the chapter's sections. Have each group create a chart explaining the main objectives in its assigned section. Then have them present their work to the class.

**ENGLISH LANGUAGE LEARNERS ,
COOPERATIVE LEARNING**

## Portfolio Extensions

**1. Interdisciplinary Connection to Art and Literature** Ask students to identify a business or corporation that regularly supports or contributes to local nonprofit arts endeavors. *(For example, students might choose a local museum, theater, or opera company that receives financial contributions from a for-profit business.)* Have each student create a poster showing how the community benefits from the cooperation of nonprofit and for-profit organizations.

**2. Cooperative Learning** Organize students into two groups. Ask one group to think of reasons that big business is important to the success of the free-enterprise system in the United States. Ask the other group to think of situations in which big business is detrimental to smaller businesses and consumers in the U.S. economy. Have each group create a poster representing the positive or negative aspects of big business and display these posters around the classroom.

---

## Building Social Studies Skills

**STANDARDIZED TEST PREP ONLINE**
go.hrw.com
keyword: SZ3 STP17

### Interpreting Graphs

Study the bar graph below. Then answer the questions that follow.

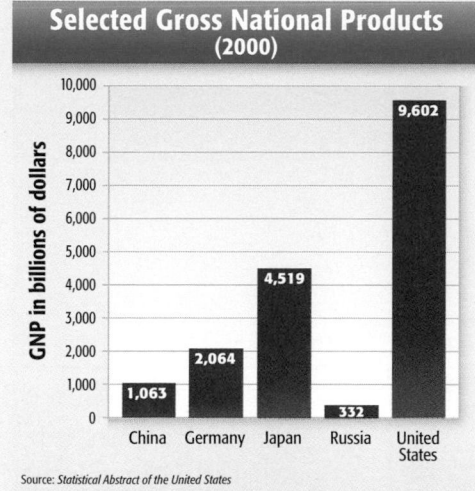

**Selected Gross National Products (2000)**

China: 1,063
Germany: 2,064
Japan: 4,519
Russia: 332
United States: 9,602

GNP in billions of dollars

Source: Statistical Abstract of the United States

1. What countries shown on the chart have the highest and lowest GNP?
   a. Japan and China
   b. The United States and Russia
   c. Japan and Russia
   d. The United States and Germany
2. What factors do you think might play a part in the gap in GNP between the United States and China and Russia?

### Analyzing Primary Sources

Read the following quotation from Lee Iacocca, former head of Chrysler Corporation. Then answer the questions that follow.

> "What I found at Chrysler were thirty-five vice presidents, each with his own turf. There was no real committee setup, no cement in the organizational chart, no system of meetings to get people talking to each other. I couldn't believe, for example, that the guy running the engineering department wasn't in constant touch with his counterpart in manufacturing. . . . Everybody worked independently. I took one look at that system and I almost threw up. That's when I knew I was in really deep trouble. . . . Nobody at Chrysler seemed to realize that you just can't run a big corporation without calling some pregame sessions to do blackboard work. Every member of the team has to understand what his job is and exactly how it fits in with every other job."

3. Which of the following statements best describes Iacocca's point of view?
   a. Chrysler benefited from the independent efforts and initiative of different departments.
   b. Chrysler needed to hire a new head of engineering.
   c. Chrysler had too many managers and they were not working hard enough.
   d. Chrysler needed much better communication and planning involving all team members.
4. Based on this quotation, can you think of two qualities that Iacocca would consider important for running a successful company? Explain your answer.

### What Did You Find Out?
1. prices rise when demand is high and price is low

2. sole proprietorship, partnership, corporation, nonprofit

3. capital, labor, natural resources, entrepreneurship

### Thinking Critically
1. Students should consider how best to ensure fair business practices and protect consumers.

2. Poor economic conditions and poor management could lead to business failure. The profit motive encourages risk-taking and entrepreneurship.

3. Scarcity is the problem of never having enough resources to meet all of your wants and needs, and it forces people to choose which wants and needs to satisfy with available resources.

### Social Studies Skills
1. b

2. Students' responses will vary.

3. d

4. Students' explanations will vary, but they should cite qualities such as communication, leadership, organization, vision, and so on.

---

### Alternative Assessment

### Building Your Portfolio

**Connecting to Community**
Complete the following activity in small groups. Identify the major concerns facing businesses in your local community today. You should interview local businesspeople, review the business section of the newspaper, and look at local business magazines. You might also contact the local chamber of commerce. Create a visual display, such as a poster, chart, or graph, profiling your community's economic concerns and activities.

**internet** connect

**Internet Activity: go.hrw.com**
keyword: SZ3 AC17

Access the Internet through the HRW Go site to research stock and stock markets. Then imagine you are a corporate officer about to issue stock to raise money for your company. Create a company profile that explains what you produce, why you are issuing the stock at this time, what kind of stock will be issued, how much each share will be, and your projections on how your stock will do in the market.

# Goods and Services

## CHAPTER RESOURCE MANAGER

| Objectives | Pacing Guide | Reproducible Resources |
|---|---|---|
| **SECTION 1:**<br>**American Production**<br>(pp. 431–36) | ★ Identify the main features of modern mass production.<br>★ Describe how the sources of power used by American factories have changed since the early years of the country.<br>★ Examine why the profit motive is an effective driver of the U.S. economic system. | **Regular**<br>1.5 days<br><br>**Block Scheduling**<br>1 day<br><br>*Block Scheduling Handbook with Team Teaching Strategies, Chapter 18* | **RS** Guided Reading Strategies 18.1<br>**RS** Readings in Economics and Government 58: *Das Capital*<br>**RS** Readings in Economics and Government 61: *The Big Money*<br>**RS** Readings in Economics and Government 71: *The Evolution of the International Economic Order*, by W. Arthur Lewis<br>**RS** Graphic Organizer Activity: From Factory to you |
| **SECTION 2:**<br>**Distributing Goods**<br>(pp. 437–42) | ★ Describe how transportation in the United States has evolved and tell why it is so important to the success of the U.S. economy.<br>★ Evaluate the benefits of mass marketing.<br>★ Identify how manufacturers, wholesalers, and retailers work together to get products to the public. | **Regular**<br>2 days<br><br>**Block Scheduling**<br>1.5 days<br><br>*Block Scheduling Handbook with Team Teaching Strategies, Chapter 18* | **RS** Guided Reading Strategies 18.2 |
| **SECTION 3:**<br>**You the Consumer**<br>(pp. 443–48) | ★ Analyze what it takes to be a wise consumer.<br>★ Determine what independent organizations and the government do to protect consumers.<br>★ Explain the factors a consumer should consider in deciding between an installment plan and a charge account. | **Regular**<br>1.5 days<br><br>**Block Scheduling**<br>1 day<br><br>*Block Scheduling Handbook with Team Teaching Strategies, Chapter 18* | **RS** Guided Reading Strategies 18.3<br>**RS** Readings in Economics and Government 64: *Price Making in a Democracy* by Edwin G. Nourse<br>**E** Creative Teaching Strategy: Editorial Page<br>**E** Challenge and Enrichment Worksheet 18: Identifying Consumers' Rights<br>**PS** American Civics Political Cartoon: Credit<br>**SM** Community Service and Participation Handbook: Where Does the Grocery Store Shop for Food? |

### Chapter Resource Key

| | | | | |
|---|---|---|---|---|
| **PS** | Primary Sources | **SM** | Skills Mastery |  CD-ROM |
| **RS** | Reading Support | **A** | Assessment |  Video |
| **IC** | Interdisciplinary Connections | **REV** | Review |  Internet |
| **E** | Enrichment | **ELL** | Reinforcement and English Language Learners | Holt Presentation Maker Using Microsoft® PowerPoint® |
| | | | Transparencies | |

 **One-Stop** Planner CD-ROM

See the *One-Stop Planner* for a complete list of additional resources for students and teachers.

## One-Stop Planner CD–ROM

It's easy to plan lessons, select resources, and print out materials for your students when you use the **One-Stop Planner CD–ROM with Test Generator**.

| Technology Resources | Reinforcement, Review, and Assessment |
|---|---|
| One-Stop Planner, Lesson 18.1 | **REV** Section 1 Review, p. 436 |
| Homework Practice Online | **A** Daily Quiz 18.1 |
| HRW Go site | **ELL** Main Idea Activity 18.1 |
| | **ELL** English Audio Summary 18.1 |
| | **ELL** Spanish Audio Summary 18.1 |
| One-Stop Planner, Lesson 18.2 | **REV** Section 2 Review, p. 442 |
| CNN Presents: American Government | **A** Daily Quiz 18.2 |
| Homework Practice Online | **ELL** Main Idea Activity 18.2 |
| | **ELL** English Audio Summary 18.2 |
| | **ELL** Spanish Audio Summary 18.2 |
| One-Stop Planner, Lesson 18.3 | **REV** Section 3 Review, p. 448 |
| Holt Researcher CD–ROM | **A** Daily Quiz 18.3 |
| Citizenship Skills Videocassette: The Critical Consumer | **ELL** Main Idea Activity 18.3 |
| Homework Practice Online | **ELL** English Audio Summary 18.3 |
| | **ELL** Spanish Audio Summary 18.3 |

## internet connect

**HRW ONLINE RESOURCES**

GO TO: go.hrw.com
Then type in the keyword.

**TEACHER HOME PAGE**
KEYWORD: SZ3 Teacher

**CHAPTER INTERNET ACTIVITIES**
KEYWORD: SZ3 AC18
Choose an activity to:
• learn how well-known products are manufactured.
• create a poster on the impact of the assembly line on daily life, culture, and society.
• create thematic graphs and charts related to the distribution of goods.

**CHAPTER ENRICHMENT LINKS**
KEYWORD: SZ3 CH18

**ONLINE ASSESSMENT**
Homework Practice
KEYWORD: SZ3 HP18
Rubrics
KEYWORD: SS Rubrics

**ONLINE MAPS, CHARTS, AND GRAPHS**
KEYWORD: SZ3 MCG
• Foundations of Modern Mass Production

**HOLT PRESENTATION MAKER**
KEYWORD: SZ3 PPT18

**CONTENT UPDATES**
KEYWORD: SS Content Updates

**ONLINE READING SUPPORT**
KEYWORD: SS Strategies

**CURRENT EVENTS**
KEYWORD: S3 Current Events

## Chapter Review and Assessment

**IC** Vocabulary Activity 18
Global Skill Builder CD–ROM
HRW Go site
**REV** Chapter 18 Tutorial for Students, Parents, Mentors, and Peers
**REV** Chapter 18 Review, pp. 450–51
**A** Standardized Test Practice
**A** Chapter 18 Test Generator (on the One-Stop Planner)
**A** Chapter 18 Test (Form A or B)
**A** Alternative Assessment Handbook
**A** Chapter 18 Test for English Language Learners and Special-Needs Students

## Meeting Individual Needs

### Ability Levels

**Level 1** Basic-level activities designed for all students encountering new material

**Level 2** Intermediate-level activities designed for average students

**Level 3** Challenging activities designed for honors and gifted-and-talented students

**English Language Learners** Activities that address the needs of students with Limited English Proficiency

Section 1    American
              Production
Section 2    Distributing Goods
Section 3    You the Consumer

## What's Your Opinion?

To help students create their **Themes** *Journal* entries, provide the following examples of appropriate **agree**/disagree *statements.*

● **Agree**   Production and distribution methods used by businesses under other economies cannot make or ship as much as those within free-enterprise economies.

**Disagree**   Each economy type has its own means of producing and distributing large amounts of goods.

● **Agree**   Factories are the ones that make the goods, therefore they are responsible for shipping them.

**Disagree**   Factories specialize in one thing: making goods.

● **Agree**   People need to acquire the skills and knowledge to become wise consumers.

**Disagree**   Some people simply do not know how to shop wisely.

## Internet Activity

**Buying Goods**

**☑ internet** connect

**TOPIC:** Distribution of Goods
**GO TO:** go.hrw.com
**KEYWORD:** SZ3 AC18

Have students access the Internet through the HRW Go site to conduct research about statistics on the ways in which goods and services are distributed, and the ways in which technology has changed traditional distribution methods such as the railroad. Then ask each student to create a thematic graph or chart that illustrates trends he or she discovered.

**CHAPTER**

# 18 Goods and Services

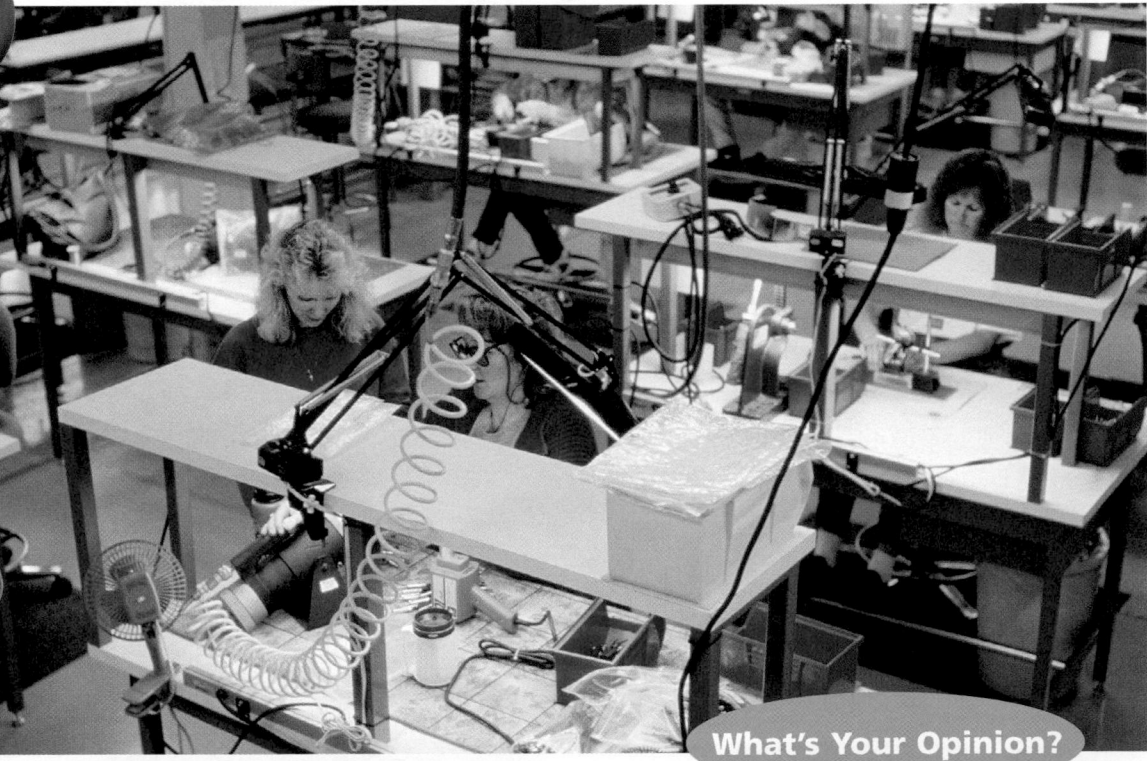

## Build on What You Know

From cereal to compact discs and sunglasses to basketballs, almost any product for sale is made somewhere in the United States. In recent years, the United States has produced more than $6 trillion worth of goods and services annually. That is more than any other country in the world. The U.S. economy has remained relatively strong for more than 200 years. How the United States makes and distributes its products has contributed to the country's economic success.

**What's Your Opinion?**

Do you **agree** or **disagree** with the following statements? Support your point of view in your journal.

- Only countries with free-enterprise economies are able to produce large quantities of goods.

- Factories are responsible for delivering products to the customer.

- Anyone can be a wise consumer.

# SECTION 1

## OBJECTIVES

*After completing Section 1, students should be able to*

1 **Identify the main features of modern mass production.**

2 **Describe how the sources of power used by American factories have changed since the early years of the country.**

3 **Examine why the profit motive is an effective driver of the U.S. economic system.**

## SECTION 1

# American Production

### Read to Discover

1. What are the main features of modern mass production?
2. How have the sources of power used by American factories changed since the early years of the country?
3. What makes the profit motive an effective driver of the U.S. economic system?

### WHY CIVICS MATTERS

The United States is a world leader in mass production. Use **CNNfyi.com** or other **current events** sources to find examples of what types of products the United States makes through mass production. Record your findings in your journal.

### Define

- gross domestic product (GDP)
- mass production
- machine tools
- interchangeable parts
- division of labor
- assembly line

## Reading Focus

In a single year the United States produced nearly 8.3 million automobiles, trucks, and buses. In 2000 it produced more than 112 million tons (102 million metric tons) of steel and more than 249 million tons (226 million metric tons) of corn. Millions of other goods are also produced in the United States each year.

*Huge grain silos such as these are used to store the crops produced by American farmers.*

### ★ Mass Production

The dollar value of all goods and services produced annually in the United States is called the **gross domestic product (GDP).** Economists use the GDP as one measure of how well the U.S. economy is performing. Other measures of economic well-being include the unemployment rate, the business failure rate, and the amount of tax revenue that American businesses and citizens produce.

Many factors make the United States capable of such an enormous output. One factor is **mass production,** or the rapid production by machine of large numbers of identical objects. Mass production requires many large, complex machines and vast amounts of power. Inventors have developed machines that can make, or help make, almost any product.

# TEACH OBJECTIVE 1

**ALL LEVELS:** Copy the following graphic organizer onto the chalkboard, omitting the italicized answers. Ask each student to complete the chart to identify the main features of modern mass production.
**ENGLISH LANGUAGE LEARNERS**

Three Main Features of Mass Production
- *machine tools*
- *standard parts*
- *division of labor*

**LEVEL 3:** Organize the class into groups and have each group choose a product (other than an automobile) that is mass-produced. Then ask them to consider how the three main features of mass production apply to that product. *(See the Level 1 lesson for features.)* Students should decide what kind of machine tools are needed, what the standard parts are, and how division of labor is used to manufacture the product. Have students present their information orally, with visual guides if helpful. **COOPERATIVE LEARNING**

**internet** connect

go.hrw.com

**TOPIC:** The Assembly Line and Mass Production
**GO TO:** go.hrw.com
**KEYWORD:** SZ3 AC18

Have students access the Internet through the HRW Go site to conduct research on the ways in which the assembly line and mechanization have impacted daily life, culture, and society. Then have each student create a poster to present his or her research. As an extension, ask students to speculate on the ways in which mechanization and mass production of goods have influenced their own lives.

*Eli Whitney invented the cotton gin and helped introduce the principle of mass production into American manufacturing.*

*Mass-production methods and interchangeable parts were commonly used to produce muskets by the time of the Civil War.*

One of the first inventors to make mass production possible was Eli Whitney. You may remember him as the inventor of the cotton gin. In 1798 Whitney signed a contract to make muskets, or guns, for the U.S. Army. He promised to manufacture and deliver 10,000 muskets in just two years.

Whitney's promise seemed impossible to keep. Up to that time guns had been made by hand, one at a time. The process took both time and skill. Whitney needed to show some government officials how he planned to make so many guns so quickly.

To prove he was serious, Whitney gave a special demonstration in Washington, D.C. From a box, Whitney took 10 gun barrels, 10 triggers, 10 stocks, and 10 locks for exploding the gunpowder. He asked the officials to choose one of each of these parts. Whitney then took the four parts and quickly put together a finished musket. To show that the parts were all alike, he continued to put together muskets until all 10 were completed. The audience was amazed at Whitney's achievement.

Eli Whitney's methods have become the basis of all mass production, from radios and sewing machines to automobiles and tractors. What are these methods?

**Machine Tools** Whitney developed **machine tools,** or machinery built to produce parts that are exactly the same. Instead of boring each gun barrel by hand, for example, Whitney made a machine that did nothing but bore identical gun barrels.

**Interchangeable Parts** Each of Whitney's machine tools made parts that were exactly alike, called **interchangeable parts.** That is, any Whitney gun barrel would fit any gun stock made by Whitney. Other parts were also interchangeable and would fit any of the guns. This interchangeability was a great advantage. If a part wore out, it could easily be replaced by a new standard, identical part.

**Division of Labor** Barrels, triggers, stocks, and locks for Whitney's guns were made by different groups of workers, each operating a separate machine. No single worker made a complete gun. The job was divided into several tasks among the various workers. In this **division of labor,** each worker was a specialist at a certain part of the job. Specialization speeded the entire process.

The use of machine tools, interchangeable parts, and the division of labor helped increase production. The early machines used by Whitney and others were small and still relatively inefficient, however. These early machines needed a better source of power.

✔ **Reading Check Categorizing** What methods of mass production did Eli Whitney develop, and what was the purpose of each method? machine tools—machinery to produce parts that are exactly the same; interchangeable parts—parts that are exactly alike; division of labor—each worker completing a specialized part of the job

# TEACH OBJECTIVE 2

**LEVELS 1 AND 2:** Lead a class discussion about how the sources of power used by American factories have changed since the early years of the country. *(Students should be aware that in the earliest years, water was the main power source. Steam power was developed in the late 1700s and was important throughout the 1800s. Gasoline and electric power became important in the late 1800s. Electricity is now the main source of power for industry.)* Then have each student write a paragraph explaining which energy source he or she thinks was most important and why. **ENGLISH LANGUAGE LEARNERS**

**LEVEL 3:** Organize the class into four groups. Assign each group one of the following sources of power: water power, steam, gas, and electrical power. Have students use their textbook for research and then have each group illustrate for the class how its assigned source of power came into use in American industry. Encourage students to explain the role their assigned source played (or still plays) in industry. Roles for students might include researcher, writer, editor, illustrator, and presenter. **COOPERATIVE LEARNING**

**HOMEWORK** Tell each student to design a billboard advertising the benefits of one of the four sources of power used by American factories.

## ★ Power Sources

For many years Americans used the force of falling water, or water-power, as the main source of power to operate their machines. Early factories, therefore, were located near streams. Dams were built to hold back water so that it could be released when necessary to turn water-wheels. As these big wheels turned, they generated power to run machines within the factory.

Steam power began to replace waterpower in the late 1700s. Scottish engineer James Watt invented a practical steam engine that made steam power possible. Steam power continued to be the leading source of industrial power during the 1800s.

In the late 1800s several new sources of power were developed. The internal combustion engine used the power released by exploding gasoline. This engine was often used to run small machines and, of course, automobiles.

The source of power that contributed most to modern mass production was electricity. In the late 1800s the work of Thomas Edison made the widespread use of electricity practical and affordable.

At first, electricity was used mainly for lighting. As time passed, it was used in many other ways. American families today use electricity to run toasters, fans, refrigerators, air conditioners, washers, dryers, vacuum cleaners, radios, and televisions. Today nearly every American factory uses electricity as its main source of power. Scientists continue to search for even better sources of power.

✔ **Reading Check Summarizing** What sources of power have Americans used over the years to run machines?
water, steam, gasoline, and electricity

**Interpreting the Visual Record**

**Early factories** *Many early American factories, such as this New England textile mill, were located near waterfalls or swiftly flowing rivers.* **Why would water be important to the functioning of such early factories?**

*Today internal combustion engines are used primarily to power vehicles such as automobiles, boats, and airplanes.*

**Interdisciplinary Connection**

▶ **Science and Technology** ◀

**Nuclear Power Use Worldwide** The major sources of electricity can vary significantly from country to country. Nuclear power, in particular, has become an important source of electricity for many industrialized countries. For example, about 75 percent of France's electricity was supplied by nuclear power plants in 2000. Nuclear power plants supplied just under 20 percent of U.S. electricity in that same year. (However, the United States is the world's largest producer of energy from nuclear power plants.)

For the world, nuclear power accounted for only about 11 percent of energy production in 1999. The largest source of energy remained petroleum. In 1999 it accounted for more than 41 percent of the world's energy.

**CRITICAL THINKING**

How might a decline in the availability of petroleum affect other energy sources?

**ANSWER:** Students might suggest that the use of other sources would increase to compensate for the loss of petroleum.

**Visual Record Answer**

*Students might suggest that it provided the power to run the mill.*

**LEVEL 1:** Organize the class into pairs and have each pair examine why the profit motive is an effective driver of the U.S. economic system. *(Students should note that it encourages people to work hard and produce more, which results in higher productivity. Additionally it drives businesspeople to remain competitive by taking risks, modernizing, and being quick to grasp new ideas.)* Then ask them to suggest how the profit motive developed as a motivator in the free-enterprise system. Call on volunteers to share their suggestions with the class.

**ENGLISH LANGUAGE LEARNERS**

**LEVEL 2:** Recall for the class why the profit motive is an effective driver of the U.S. economic system. *(See the Level 1 lesson for reasons.)* Then have students suggest other means of motivating producers and retailers to accomplish these same goals. *(Students might suggest pride in quality or the desire to help the business world run well.)* Call on volunteers to share their thoughts with the class. Have the class vote to decide which motivator they think would be best: volunteers' suggestions or the profit motive. Lead the class in a discussion about the results of the poll.

## ★ Global Perspectives

**Building on Japan's Good Ideas** Advanced mass-production methods helped give the U.S. automobile industry an advantage over foreign competitors—until Japanese companies decided to combine those methods with their own special management techniques. The result was a surge of Japanese imports into the United States by the 1980s and an embattled U.S. auto industry. Automakers in the United States began implementing the flexible work rules that have been so successful in Japan—worker teams, worker control, problem solving on the work floor where possible, sharing production information with workers, and minimizing status differences among workers. These changes continued to spread throughout the U.S. automakers' plants in the 1980s and 1990s. By the early 1990s U.S. automakers were taking advantage of improving economic conditions to post larger profits.

**ACTIVITY:** Have students use the library and other resources to conduct research about Japanese management techniques. Call on volunteers to give a demonstration of some of the techniques to the class.

## Visual Record Answer

*Students might suggest that the assembly line can be seen in the bottom left and center of the image.*

**Interpreting the Visual Record**

**Assembly line** *In the 1930s Mexican muralist Diego Rivera painted this large image of a Ford motor plant and its workers.* **Where in this image can you see an assembly line in operation?**

## ★ Modern Mass Production

One of the best ways to understand modern mass production is to visit an automobile manufacturing plant. Suppose you were to go to Detroit, Michigan, to make such a visit. What would you see?

When you first enter the factory, it may take a few minutes to get used to all the activity and noise. As you look around, you can see how Eli Whitney's methods of manufacturing are still used today.

As an engine block moves by, a team of workers begins its tasks. First, a huge machine tool bores dozens of holes into the block. As the block moves along, workers fit pistons, valves, and bolts into the holes. Each worker is highly skilled at a specialized job. The block has become an internal combustion engine. Other teams of workers fasten a carburetor, an ignition, and other parts to the engine. One automobile engine after another is made in this way, each exactly alike.

One feature of modern mass production, however, is different from Whitney's day. That feature is the **assembly line.** An assembly line uses machines and workers to move a product through stages of production until it is completed.

Back in the automobile plant, you would see a frame of a car moving along on a very large conveyor belt. The belt slowly moves many car frames at a time through the factory. As a car frame moves along the assembly line, the wheels are added to the frame. Then the engine, transmission, windshield, steering wheel, and gears are added. Seats, door panels, lights, and the dashboard are put on next. The car moves to the paint shop where it is spray painted and dried. Finally, the car is driven off the assembly line and tested.

How do the various parts arrive at the assembly line just in time to become parts of a finished automobile? At the beginning of your tour, you saw an engine being made. This engine was not on the main assembly line. It was on a side line, or feeder line. The engine's movement along the feeder line was timed. The engine was completed just as the

**LEVEL 3:** Have students write letters to fictional pen pals in some of the countries instituting free-market reforms. *(Students might select a fictional pen pal in Eastern Europe or one of the independent republics of the former Soviet Union.)* Students should explain why the profit motive is an effective driver of the U.S. economic system and should suggest why it may be equally useful for their pen pal's country. *(See the Level 1 lesson for reasons.)* The letters should relate how the profit motive encouraged the development of mass production techniques and technologies and how those innovations in turn help business increase profits. Call on volunteers to read their letters to the class.

## CLOSE

Have the class demonstrate the assembly process by producing something simple, such as a hand-held fan made with cardboard and ice cream sticks or a booklet of papers stapled together. Have an "assembly line" compete against individuals to see who can produce the most items in a given period of time.

---

feeder line met the main assembly line. In this way, feeder lines are used to assemble many parts of the car. The parts are then brought to the main assembly line exactly when and where they are needed.

Other large industries use these same methods of production. Bread from a large bakery, for example, is made in a similar way. Conveyor belts supply flour and other ingredients to large mixers and also carry loaves of bread through long ovens. The finished loaf then travels through another machine that slices and wraps it. Still another machine packs the wrapped loaves in boxes that travel on a conveyor belt to trucks for delivery to stores.

✔ **Reading Check** Finding the Main Idea What production technique revolutionized mass production, and how does it work? The assembly line revolutionized mass production. It uses machines and workers to move a product through stages of production until it is completed.

## ★ Mass Production in the World

Mass production was first developed in the United States, but it has spread to other countries around the world. Mass production is used more effectively in some countries than in others, however.

Cuba, for example, uses mass production methods, but it has not been as successful as other countries. One reason may be that in Cuba the government controls the economy. Property is not privately owned, and private enterprise is allowed only on a limited basis. The government generally decides what prices to charge and the amount of goods and services to produce. As a result, most goods like cooking oil and other foods, and even shirts and shoes, are often difficult to buy. Many Cubans buy these goods on the black market—an illegal market that the Cuban government does not regulate.

**Interpreting the Visual Record**

**Modern manufacturing** *Airplane manufacturing represents one of the most complex and large-scale production processes. Each of these jet planes costs millions of dollars and has thousands of parts that must work together properly.* **What does this image indicate about the size of an airplane production plant?**

**435**

## REVIEW AND ASSESS

Have students complete the **Section 1 Review** on page 436. Then have students complete **Daily Quiz 18.1**. As **Alternative Assessment**, you may want to use the mass-production report or pen pal letter exercises in this section's lessons.

## RETEACH

Have students complete **Main Idea Activity for English Language Learners and Special-Needs Students 18.1**. Then create a series of flash cards using the key terms listed at the beginning of this section. After they have finished their cards, have students use them to quiz a partner.

**ENGLISH LANGUAGE LEARNERS , COOPERATIVE LEARNING**

## EXTEND

Have students diagram the assembly process for the mass-produced product of their choice. Students should decide what types of workers are needed and what skills the workers must have. Encourage students to be creative, such as by developing work-saving steps in the assembly process. Remind students that advances in technology often result in revisions in a company's assembly process. Call on volunteers to present their diagram to the class for discussion. **BLOCK SCHEDULING**

### Visual Record Answer

*(for page 435)*
*Students might suggest it shows that the plants must be very large.*

### Visual Record Answer

*Students might suggest that people are seeking faster, more efficient, and less expensive ways of helping others get well.*

### Section 1 Review
### ANSWERS

**1. Define**
- gross domestic product (GDP), p. 431
- mass production, p. 431
- machine tools, p. 432
- interchangeable parts, p. 432
- division of labor, p. 432
- assembly line, p. 434

**2.** water, steam, gasoline, and electricity

**3. a.** machine tools, standard parts, and division of labor

**b.** profit motive; encourages people to work hard and produce more, which means higher productivity, and it drives businesspeople to remain competitive by taking risks, modernizing, and being quick to grasp new ideas

**4.** Students' brochures should demonstrate an understanding of the advantages, methods, and various features of mass production.

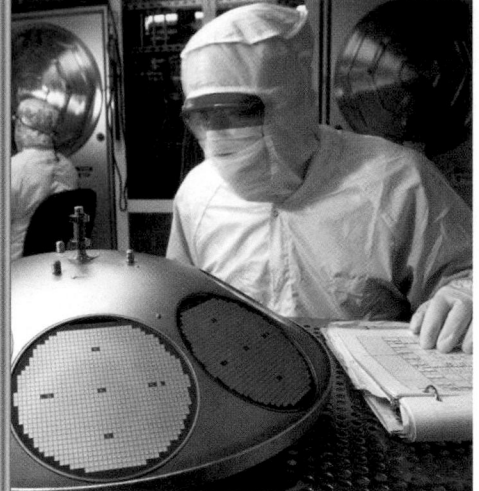

**Interpreting the Visual Record**

**Medicine** *Much of the innovation taking place in industry today involves medical research into a wide range of diseases and drug treatments.* **Why do you think there is a strong demand for medical innovations?**

A command economy like Cuba's does not have the same incentives, or motives, as a free economy. The lack of a profit motive in particular discourages people from working hard and increasing productivity. In turn, lower productivity means that there is less money available for modernizing factories.

✔ **Reading Check Identifying Points of View** Why is mass production considered to be ineffective in some countries? because the government controls the economy and there is no profit motive

### ★ Innovations

A free-market economy encourages businesspeople to take risks. When there is no incentive to make a profit by taking a risk, people may be less inclined to take risks. For example, Eli Whitney took a risk when he set about developing a new method of production to obtain a government contract.

The possibility of making a profit continues to encourage new innovations in production and marketing. When Michael Dell was in college, he was bothered by the high cost of personal computers and their lack of technical support. In 1984 Dell launched his own computer business. He used direct advertising and later the Internet to sell made-to-order computers directly to customers. This lowered his overhead and inventory costs. Dell also emphasized reliable and friendly customer service. These business methods enabled Dell to offer his customers lower prices and better service. Dell Computers is now a billion-dollar company with a widely imitated business model.

✔ **Reading Check Summarizing** How did Michael Dell change the computer industry? He created a business that built computers and sold them directly to the customer. He also lowered prices and offered better support.

---

## SECTION 1 Review

go.hrw.com **Homework Practice Online**
keyword: SZ3 HP18

**1. Define** and explain:
- gross domestic product (GDP)
- mass production
- machine tools
- interchangeable parts
- division of labor
- assembly line

**2. Sequencing** Copy the graphic organizer below. Use it to show the different power sources that have shaped manufacturing in the order they were first used.

Production

☐ → ☐ → ☐ → ☐

**3. Finding the Main Idea**
a. What three features are the basis of mass production?
b. What incentive is necessary for mass production to be effective, and why is it important?

**4. Writing and Critical Thinking**
**Summarizing** Imagine that you are an automobile manufacturer. Create an informational brochure explaining how your factory uses assembly lines to build cars and why you use mass production.

**Consider:**
- the advantages of mass production
- the methods that form the basis of mass production
- assembly lines and feeder lines

# SECTION 2

## OBJECTIVES

*After completing Section 2, students should be able to*

1 **Describe how transportation in the United States has evolved and tell why it is so important to the success of the U.S. economy.**

2 **Evaluate the benefits of mass marketing.**

3 **Identify how manufacturers, wholesalers, and retailers work together to get products to the public.**

## SECTION 2

# Distributing Goods

### Read to Discover

1. How has transportation in the United States evolved, and why is it so important to the success of the U.S. economy?
2. What are the benefits of mass marketing?
3. How do manufacturers, wholesalers, and retailers work together to get products to the public?

### Define

- distribution
- mass marketing
- self-service
- standard packaging
- one-price system
- wholesaler
- retailers
- advertising
- brand names

#### WHY CIVICS MATTERS

Transportation is a key part of selling products. Use **CNNfyi.com** or other **current events** sources to find an example of how transportation has either hurt or helped a local business. Record your findings in your journal.

## *Reading Focus*

American businesses and industries produce goods and services that supply people's needs. Production is only one part of supplying those needs, however. After goods are made, they must be delivered to the people who want them. **Distribution** is the process of moving goods from manufacturers to markets. It has two sides—transportation and marketing. Transportation moves goods, and marketing convinces people to buy those goods.

In such a vast land as the United States, transportation has always been important. Early in its history a good system of transportation was necessary to unify, or bring together, the young country. As a result, the country experienced a long period of road, canal, and railroad building. The development of a transportation system made it possible for American businesses to sell their goods throughout the country.

### ★ Railroads

The growth of railroads greatly helped American industry. Railroads helped create a single, large market for products. Long freight trains rolled from coast to coast carrying raw materials and finished products. The railroads brought new goods to every U.S. city, to most towns, and within reach of many farms. The railroads gave businesspeople a means of rapid travel and communication.

*Most trains in the United States today carry freight.*

# TEACH OBJECTIVE 1

**LEVEL 1:** Organize the class into small groups and have each group create an illustrated time line or other sequential organizer that depicts the evolution of transportation in the United States. Tell each group to add to its organizer a sentence about why transportation has been so important to the success of the U.S. economy. *(Students' organizers should show that trucks, buses, and automobiles overtook railroads as the main means of transportation by the 1970s. Transportation brings goods from producers to consumers.)* Display students' completed organizers in the classroom.

**ENGLISH LANGUAGE LEARNERS**

**LEVEL 3:** Have each student write a short expository essay that describes how transportation in the United States has evolved and that tells why this evolution has been so important to the success of the U.S. economy. *(See the Level 1 lesson for evolution and explanation.)* Ask a volunteer to read his or her essay to the class.

**HOMEWORK** Have students write a short eulogy for one of the forms of transportation that today is not as heavily relied upon by the U.S. economy. *(These forms include railroads and steamboats.)*

---

## Interdisciplinary Connection

▶ **Science** ◀

**The Erie Canal** The Erie Canal played a vital role in the growth of industry in the Midwest and in New York City in the 1800s. Opened on October 25, 1825, the 363-mile-long Erie Canal linked the Great Lakes with New York City by way of the Hudson River. Many settlers used the canal on their moves west. Their farm produce was sent back east on boats and barges pulled by horses along the canal. Those same boats and barges carried manufactured goods back to the Midwest at a tenth of the cost of shipping them overland. The state of New York paid more than $7 million to construct the Erie Canal. The canal more than paid for itself through the tolls charged for its use. The tolls ended in 1882, and the canal today is part of the New York State Barge Canal System.

### CRITICAL THINKING

Why do you think the tolls ended in 1882?

**ANSWER:** Students might suggest that the canal was already paid for, so the tolls were no longer needed.

### CASE STUDY ANSWER

by saying that the federal license took precedence over the state license

---

# SUPREME COURT CASE STUDY

## *Gibbons v. Ogden*

**Significance:** This ruling was the first to deal with the clause of the Constitution that allows Congress to regulate interstate and foreign commerce. The case was important because it reinforced both the authority of the federal government over the states and the division of powers between the federal government and the state governments.

**Background:** Steamboat operators who wanted to travel on New York waters had to obtain a state license. Thomas Gibbons had a federal license to travel along the coast, but not a state license for New York. He wanted the freedom to compete with state-licensed Aaron Ogden for steam travel between New Jersey and the New York island of Manhattan.

**Decision:** This case was decided on March 2, 1824, by a vote of 6 to 0. Chief Justice John Marshall spoke for the Court, which ruled in favor of Gibbons. The Court stated that the congressional statute (Gibbon's federal license) took priority over the state statute (Ogden's state-monopoly license). The ruling also defined commerce as more than simply the exchange of goods, broadening it to include the transportation of people and the use of new inventions (such as the steamboat).

**How did the Court's ruling reinforce the authority of the federal government over the state governments?**

---

★★★★★★★★★★★★★
### That's Interesting!
★★★★★★★★★★★★★

**Settlers Wanted** Advertising was used to settle the United States. In the late 1800s the Great Plains had few settlers. Railroad companies, extending their tracks into the region, had land they wanted to sell. They also hoped to profit from farmers who would ship freight on their lines. So the railroads started to encourage men and women to settle in the West. The railroads ran advertisements in newspapers and put up hundreds of posters. Sometimes they even offered immigrants free transportation to visit their native lands if they agreed to persuade others to return to the United States. Thousands of people responded, and many new communities grew up almost overnight.

---

Railroads were the country's chief method of transportation for nearly a century. In the mid-1900s, however, railroads found it difficult to compete with other means of transportation—trucks, buses, automobiles, and airplanes. In the 1960s and 1970s many railroads went out of business. Railroads today carry a much smaller percentage of passengers and freight than in the late 1800s.

Many of the tracks and trains in the U.S. railroad system are in poor condition. Also, U.S. trains are not as fast as more modern trains in some countries. For example, today's trains travel between New York City and Washington, D.C., at speeds of more than 100 miles (161 km) an hour. Meanwhile, trains in France travel at speeds of up to 186 miles (300 km) an hour. Germany, Japan, the United Kingdom, and other European countries also operate high-speed trains.

Railroads are still an important part of the country's transportation system, however. They carry bulk cargo, such as coal and grain. They also carry passengers and provide jobs. In an effort to support the railroads, Congress created a national rail passenger system called Amtrak in 1970. Organized with funds from the federal government, Amtrak has been the main provider of long-distance passenger trains. This system has been financially troubled, however. In 2002 a federal panel investigating Amtrak's financial problems recommended that the nation's passenger rail system be opened up to competition.

✔ **Reading Check** Comparing and Contrasting How were railroads used before the mid-1900s, and how are they used now? Railroads were the chief method of transportation. Railroads today carry fewer passengers and less freight but still carry large amounts of bulk cargo.

# TEACH OBJECTIVE 2

 **ALL LEVELS:** Copy the following graphic organizer onto the chalkboard, omitting the italicized answers. Have each student complete the organizer to evaluate the benefits of mass marketing. **ENGLISH LANGUAGE LEARNERS**

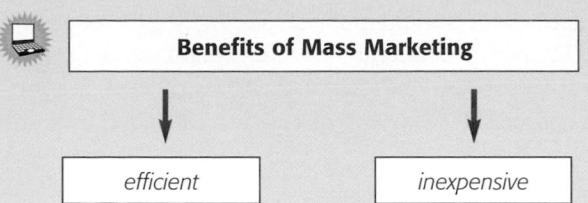

# TEACHER TO TEACHER

Michelle Bierman of Minnesota recommends the following activity:

**LEVEL 2:** Have students bring to class one example of a printed advertisement. Then have the class put all of the ads together in categories. Then ask each student to choose an ad different from the one that he or she brought and to analyze it. Students' analyses should identify the audience perspective as well as the purpose and effectiveness of the ad. Also ask students to answer these questions: Who is the intended consumer? What other ads have you seen for this same product or company?

## ★ Air Transportation

Railroads today must compete with other forms of transportation. In passenger transportation, for example, the airlines have grown rapidly. In 1950, railroads carried more than 6 percent of the passengers traveling between cities. Airlines carried 2 percent. In 2000 the airlines transported more than 19 percent of the country's passenger traffic, and the railroads had less than 1 percent. Modern research, equipment, and management methods have made airlines in the United States among the best in the world.

Airlines now carry all first-class mail between U.S. cities located over a certain distance apart. They are also important in transporting freight. Airlines can carry all kinds of freight—from small packages to large industrial machinery and automobiles—with great speed.

✔ **Reading Check Making Generalizations and Predictions** Why do you think that airlines have grown in popularity as a form of transportation? Students might say that they are faster, or they might point out that the United States has one of the best and safest airline systems in the world.

## ★ The Highway System

The automobile is the leading means of transportation in the United States. Automobiles carry about 81 percent of passengers—more than all other kinds of transportation combined. More than 131 million cars—about one vehicle for every two persons—are registered in the United States.

Rapid highway transportation depends on good roads. To speed motor traffic, the country maintains a vast highway system. The United States now has more than 3.9 million miles (6.3 million km) of roads.

Some of the country's highways are toll roads. Drivers must pay a toll, or fee, to use these roads. Other roads are freeways, which are free of charge. Together these roads form an interstate highway system that reaches every part of the United States.

Buses, cars, and trucks travel the highways at all hours. This heavy traffic on highways and roads has caused a number of problems. These problems include traffic jams, accidents, air pollution, and the heavy use of gasoline and oil.

Citizens and communities are taking steps to solve these problems. Such measures include lower speed limits, stricter automobile emission laws, smaller cars, and improved public transportation systems.

✔ **Reading Check Analyzing Information** What are some of the things that have resulted from the automobile's popularity as a form of transportation? highway system, traffic jams, accidents, air pollution, and heavy use of gasoline and oil

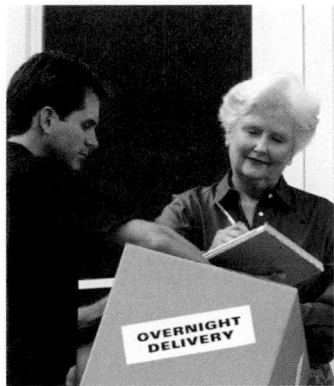

**Interpreting the Visual Record**

**Airmail** *Today businesses and individuals send many small packages by air express.* **What would be the advantages and disadvantages of shipping using the airlines?**

*Cities and towns are often located at the intersection of major interstate highways. These communities benefit from improved transportation but can also suffer from traffic.*

## ★ Civics Sidelight

**The U.S. Highway Numbering System** The U.S. highway system is vast. In its early years this factor made it complicated to drive. One method of directing travelers consisted of marking fences, telephone poles, and trees along a specific route with the same color paint. This method did not work as well in the western United States, where fences, poles, and trees often were few and far between. In addition, officials were frustrated when there were not enough colors for the many intersecting highways in some parts of the United States. The system of highway numbering we know today began in 1925. Most drivers are unaware of the significance of odd and even numbers in the interstate highway system. East-west routes carry even numbers, and north-south routes are identified by odd numbers.

**CRITICAL THINKING**

What are the benefits of a national highway numbering system?

**ANSWER:** Students might suggest that it aids navigation and communication.

**Visual Record Answer**

*Students might suggest that advantages include speed and that disadvantages include increased cost.*

**ALL LEVELS:** Prepare four placards large enough to be seen when taped to the chalkboard. Ask the class to identify the four groups involved in the production/consumption process in the United States. Write one response on each placard. (*Students should identify manufacturers, wholesalers, retailers, and consumers.*) Then call on volunteers to place the placards in the order in which products move from production to market. When the cards have been arranged in the proper order, review with the class the production/consumption cycle. (*Students should demonstrate an understanding that manufacturers make goods, that wholesalers buy large quantities at low prices, and that retailers purchase goods at wholesale prices and sell them directly to the public.*) **ENGLISH LANGUAGE LEARNERS**

**LEVEL 2:** Ask each student to draw an illustrated flowchart that shows how manufacturers, wholesalers, and retailers work together to get products to the public. (*See the Level 1 lesson for the process.*) Encourage students to write explanatory captions for each part of their flowcharts to further illustrate the specific details of the process. Display and discuss selected charts.

## ★ Economics

**A Classroom Activity Turns Big Business** You do not have to be a national corporation to create a successful product. A classroom assignment for teenagers in southeastern Georgia proved that. An English teacher at Rabun-Gap Nacooche School stumbled across a nationally successful product while looking for a way to help his students develop language arts skills and community pride. He helped the students publish *Foxfire,* a magazine about their own community. The magazine became known throughout the country due to the students' efforts. Articles from the magazine were later compiled into *The Foxfire Book,* which sold more than 3 million copies. The success of the Foxfire project encouraged students in other communities to start similar projects.

**Activity:** Have students brainstorm ideas for a magazine that would appeal to their community. Ask pairs of students to draw up proposals for such a magazine. Encourage them to incorporate the mass-marketing techniques discussed in their texts. Have students present their proposals to the class.

### Visual Record Answer

*Students might suggest that these stores need to keep their prices low to remain competitive, which means that profit comes from high volume.*

**Interpreting the Visual Record**

*Mass marketing Supermarkets are a common example of mass marketing and self-service in the United States. They count on making small but steady profits on the high volume of goods they sell.* **Why do you think supermarkets must rely on selling high volumes of goods like these to make a profit?**

### Did You KNOW?

Today canned food is a common sight on grocery store shelves. Canning was invented for the British navy in about 1810. But the modern can opener was not invented until 1873–in the United States! For many years people had to open cans with hammers and chisels.

## ★ Mass Marketing

Selling goods in large quantities is called **mass marketing.** Modern supermarkets and large department stores use this kind of large-scale selling. They also use a type of marketing called **self-service.** Self-service is an efficient and inexpensive way to sell goods because it saves time and labor.

In supermarkets, for example, customers push carts up and down the aisles, selecting items and serving themselves. When a customer has finished shopping, he or she rolls the cart to the checkout counter. A clerk rings up the purchases on a cash register or scans them with an electronic device. Some supermarkets also offer self-service checkout.

Self-service is a modern method of marketing. Prior to the use of self-service marketing, storekeepers hired clerks to sell the goods. Each clerk helped only one customer at a time. In today's self-service stores, many customers can shop at the same time, and one clerk can help many more people.

**Standard packaging** also adds to the efficiency of the self-service system. Goods come from factories already wrapped. Crackers, for example, are wrapped and sold in boxes. Sugar comes in boxes or bags of different weights. Years ago, crackers were sold from a barrel. They were weighed out for each customer. Sugar was also scooped out of a barrel. It was poured into a paper bag and weighed for each customer. Today fewer store items must be weighed or measured.

Another feature of mass marketing is the **one-price system,** in which prices are stamped or bar-coded onto products. The one-price system was first used by Wanamaker's department store in Philadelphia, Pennsylvania, more than 100 years ago. Now it is a standard practice almost everywhere.

Before the one-price system, customers often bargained with salespeople to lower the price. Imagine how much time shoppers would spend buying groceries if they had to bargain for every item. Instead, shoppers today pay the price marked on the product. However, Americans do tend to bargain for large items such as houses, boats, and automobiles.

New technology continues to provide new uses for the bar code. Grocers use the bar code to collect information about products. This allows them to keep track of how much of a particular item is being sold. Many stores are learning to communicate with their suppliers. By working more closely with suppliers, stores are able to avoid running out of popular products.

✔ **Reading Check** Summarizing What are two features of mass marketing, and why are they effective? self-service—efficient and inexpensive; one-price system—saves shoppers time

**LEVEL 3:** Organize the class into four groups. Assign each group one of the following roles: manufacturers, wholesalers, retailers, or consumers. Have each group role-play the manner in which people in their assigned role participate in the production/consumption cycle. Groups' dramatizations should clearly illustrate the process by which products move from factory to wholesaler to retailer and then to the general public. *(See the Level 1 lesson for the process.)* After each group has enacted its role, lead a class discussion about the following question: What might happen if these groups did not work together to get products to the public? **COOPERATIVE LEARNING**

## CLOSE

Ask students to consider what might happen if certain aspects of the U.S. economic system were eliminated. Aspects include the various modes of transportation, the use of shopping malls, and the various stages of the production and distribution process. *(Students might suggest that the elimination of trucks to transport goods might result in greater expense and slower time to market due to increased reliance on other methods. Others might suggest that removing wholesalers would decrease efficiency and increase cost.)* Call on volunteers to share which aspect they considered removing and to explain what they think might happen if things changed in such a way.

### ★ Shopping Malls

An outgrowth of the supermarket and department store is the shopping mall, or shopping center. These large complexes feature different types of stores, surrounded by parking areas. The center of the mall is usually a supermarket or a department store. There are often dozens of other stores and shops.

The shopping mall is an example of highly efficient marketing. Customers can drive in, park their cars, and buy almost everything they need. Many stores can afford to sell goods at lower prices because malls draw more customers than a stand-alone store might.

Many of the stores in a shopping mall are chain stores. A chain store is owned and operated by a company that has many of the same kind of store. The company may purchase its goods directly from a factory or farm, or it may have its own production centers. The chain store can offer its products at lower cost because it buys or produces those goods in large quantities.

Many other stores are independent. Some are specialty shops. They sell only certain kinds of goods, like women's or men's clothing, books, or toys and games. Some offer a particular kind of service, like video game arcades. These small independent stores can offer special services not provided by larger stores. For example, smaller stores often carry special products for which there is not a large demand. These locally owned stores contribute to the prosperity of their communities.

✔ **Reading Check Contrasting** How do specialty stores differ from chain stores? They are independently owned and offer special products or services not provided by larger stores.

### ★ Wholesalers and Retailers

Products may pass through several hands when moving from the factory to the customer. A factory often sells goods in large quantities to a **wholesaler.** This businessperson owns a large warehouse where goods are stored. The wholesaler then sells the goods to **retailers.** Retailers, or retail stores, sell the goods directly to the public.

Wholesalers are also called distributors. They perform the service of linking the factory and the retailer. In the end, of course, the customer must pay for this service. Chain stores, large department stores, and supermarkets often have their own warehouses and have no need for distributors. As a result, they can sometimes offer goods at lower prices.

The distribution and marketing of goods costs a great deal of money. Sometimes it costs as much to market a product as it did to make it. As is the case with mass production, efficiency in mass distribution reduces the prices of the items you buy.

✔ **Reading Check Finding the Main Idea** How do factories distribute their products, and how do some stores save money on distribution? Factories sell products to wholesalers, who sell the products to retailers, who then sell the goods directly to the public. Some stores have their own warehouses and therefore do not need distributors or wholesalers.

**Interpreting the Visual Record**

**Malls** *Shopping malls often attract large crowds of consumers, particularly on weekends or near holidays such as Christmas.* **Why do you think malls are effective at drawing large crowds?**

## REVIEW AND ASSESS

Have students complete the **Section 2 Review** on page 442. Then have students complete **Daily Quiz 18.2**. As **Alternative Assessment**, you may want to use the expository essay or illustrated flowchart exercises in this section's lessons.

## RETEACH

Have students complete **Main Idea Activity for English Language Learners and Special-Needs Students 18.2.** Then organize the class into pairs and have each pair create a crossword puzzle using this section's terms. Each pair should exchange its puzzle with another pair and solve the other pair's puzzle.

**ENGLISH LANGUAGE LEARNERS , COOPERATIVE LEARNING**

## EXTEND

Have students use the library and other resources to conduct research about how goods were distributed and sold in the mid-1800s. Have each student draw an illustrated map of the United States, showing how a particular product (such as wheat, minerals, or textiles, for example) moved from where it was produced or mined to various markets. Call on volunteers to explain their research and maps to the class.

**BLOCK SCHEDULING**

## Section 2 Review
### ANSWERS

**1. Define**
- distribution, p. 437
- mass marketing, p. 440
- self-service, p. 440
- standard packaging, p. 440
- one-price system, p. 440
- wholesaler, p. 441
- retailers, p. 441
- advertising, p. 442
- brand names, p. 442

**2.** Manufacturers make goods, wholesalers buy large quantities at low prices, and then retailers purchase goods at wholesale prices and sell them directly to the public.

**3. a.** Trucks, buses, and automobiles overtook railroads as the main means of transportation by the 1970s. Transportation brings goods from producers to consumers.

**b.** by providing goods to consumers in an efficient and inexpensive manner

**4.** Students' articles should explain the role of advertising in mass distribution as well as its benefits and problems.

**Interpreting the Visual Record**

Advertising awards *There are several annual awards given to advertisers for creative or successful advertising campaigns.* **What do you think helps make an advertisement interesting or informative?**

### ★ Advertising

Mass marketing of goods would not be possible without advertising. **Advertising** informs people about products and tries to persuade them to buy these products. In the competition between producers of similar products, advertising often makes the difference between the success of one product and the failure of another.

Some people believe that some forms of advertising do not accurately represent products. They also think that advertising encourages people to buy products that they do not need. Others argue that competition among mass producers, marketers, and advertisers helps keep the quality of products high and prices low.

National advertising makes it possible for producers to sell their products throughout the country. Such advertising increases people's recognition of products and their **brand names.** A brand-name product is a widely advertised and distributed product. People often buy brand-name products they have heard about most favorably or most often. By using national advertising, small producers may be able to grow into large national producers. Then they can mass produce their products for a larger market at lower costs.

Shoppers are sometimes confused by advertising, particularly when several producers claim that their product is best or most effective. However, advertising can be a useful way for a producer to inform shoppers about a new product. In the next section you will learn how to interpret the information provided and get the most for your money.

✔ **Reading Check** Analyzing Information How does mass marketing rely on advertising? Advertising informs people about products, helps increase competition, and makes it possible for producers to sell their products throughout the country.

---

## SECTION 2 Review

**go. hrw .com** Homework Practice Online
keyword: SZ3 HP18

**1. Define** and explain:
- distribution
- mass marketing
- self-service
- standard packaging
- one-price system
- wholesaler
- retailers
- advertising
- brand names

**2. Sequencing** Copy the graphic organizer below. Use it to show the order of product distribution and how a product might be transported.

[ Manufacturer makes goods. ] → [ ] → [ ] → [ Customer buys goods. ]

**3. Finding the Main Idea**
a. How has American transportation changed over time, and why does the economy depend on it?
b. How does mass marketing help the U.S. economy function?

**4. Writing and Critical Thinking**
**Identifying Points of View** Imagine that you are a newspaper reporter covering a debate on the role of advertising in the U.S. economy. Write a newspaper article outlining each argument in the debate, reporting who is debating as well as what, where, and when they are debating.

**Consider:**
- the benefits and problems of advertising
- the role of advertising in mass distribution

# SECTION 3

## OBJECTIVES

*After completing Section 3, students should be able to*

1 Analyze what it takes to be a wise consumer.
2 Determine what independent organizations and the government do to protect consumers.
3 Explain the factors a consumer should consider in deciding between an installment plan and a charge account.

## SECTION 3

# You the Consumer

### Read to Discover

1. What does it take to be a wise consumer?
2. What do independent organizations and the government do to protect consumers?
3. What should a consumer consider in deciding between an installment plan and a charge account?

### Define

- consumer
- shoplifting
- checks
- debit cards
- charge account
- credit card
- credit rating
- down payment
- balance
- installments

### WHY CIVICS MATTERS

Consumer organizations exist to protect consumers from false labeling, false advertising, and other unfair business practices. Use **CNNfyi.com** or other **current events** sources to learn how a consumer organization is working to protect consumers. Record your findings in your journal.

## Reading Focus

Each year businesses spend billions of dollars encouraging us to buy their products. They run advertisements in newspapers and magazines, on billboards, on the radio, and on television. Businesses create slogans they hope we will remember. They know that some of us will buy the product whose slogan appeals to us most. Often, however, a product's slogan has nothing to do with its quality or usefulness.

## ★ Learning Where and When to Buy

Each of us is a **consumer.** A consumer is a person who buys or uses goods and services. As consumers, we play an important part in the American free-enterprise system. However, we must also learn to be responsible shoppers.

Some shoppers are impulse buyers. Impulse buyers make purchases without thinking about a product's price or usefulness. They may make a quick decision to buy a product based on the product's slogan or television advertising. Wise shoppers spend more time thinking about what they buy.

Consumers can get the most for their limited shopping dollars in a number of ways. For example, wise food shoppers study advertisements in the newspaper to find

*Businesses create slogans hoping consumers will remember and buy their products.*

# TEACH OBJECTIVE 1

**LEVELS 1 AND 2:** Review with the class the qualities of a wise consumer. *(Students should mention that a wise consumer looks for sales, uses coupons, and is a good judge of quality and prices.)* Then provide each student with a local department store flyer or a newspaper advertising supplement. Ask students to list two items from the flyer that they think are bargains and two items that they do not think are bargains. For each item students should give a reason to support their judgment. Students' reasons should demonstrate their ability to be wise consumers: considering quality, price, and usefulness as well as making comparisons with similar products offered at other stores. **ENGLISH LANGUAGE LEARNERS**

**LEVEL 3:** Organize the class into groups and have each group design and create product advertisements for print, radio, or television. Group members should try to address the concerns of wise consumers. *(See the Level 1 lesson for these concerns.)* For example, ads may try to persuade consumers of the high value of the product. Roles for students might include writers, designers, and illustrators. Groups should present their finished advertisements to the class. Then have the class discuss how consumers can balance personal wants and needs and their household budgets, with the interests of advertisers.
**COOPERATIVE LEARNING**

## ★ Economics

**Generic Brands** More and more Americans are passing up brand-name products for generic, or "private-label," products—particularly when household budgets are tight. For years many stores have offered their own store brands at lower cost than the nationally advertised brands. Although private-label products lack the jazzy wrappers and catchy names that traditionally grab shoppers' attention, these products can cost as much as 25 percent less than comparable brand-name items. And sales of generic products are high. According to 2001 data, 25 percent of products sold in the United States are private label.

### CRITICAL THINKING

Why do you think consumers would prefer a generic brand item to a name-brand one?

**ANSWER:** Students should suggest that it would cost less.

### Visual Record Answer

*Students might say that shopping with a calculator allows the shopper to keep track of how much is being spent but that it is time consuming.*

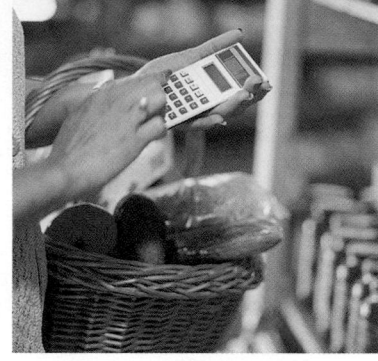

**Interpreting the Visual Record**

Careful shopping *When shopping for basic needs like groceries, some people use a calculator to help make sure they stay within their weekly budget.* **What would be the advantages and disadvantages of shopping this way?**

*Labels on meat indicate cut, fat content, and grade.*

out which stores are having special sales. Using coupons can also help shoppers save money.

By watching for sales, you can buy clothing, books, furniture, hardware, and other items at reduced prices. Some people never pay the full price for an item. They stock up when the price is low.

A low-price item is not always a bargain, however. An item is not a bargain if it is something you cannot really use or if it is poorly made.

✔ **Reading Check Summarizing** How can shoppers save money? by using coupons, buying during sales, and using good judgment when purchasing something

## ★ Judging Price and Quality

Wise shoppers must be able to judge product quality and know how they plan to use the product. They must also choose the goods and services at the best price and that best suit their own needs.

Therefore, many consumers shop only at well-known stores that guarantee the quality of every item sold or service provided. Others shop at various stores to compare products and their prices.

Many people buy an item according to its brand name because they trust certain companies. They believe that all products bearing the brand names of these companies must be of good quality. They may also have had an earlier good experience with products under the brand name. As you have learned, many large national companies sell their products under brand names for these reasons. They spend billions of dollars making consumers aware of their brand names. The best way to be sure of the quality of a product, however, is to study its labeling.

✔ **Reading Check Analyzing Information** How can shoppers judge the price and quality of products? by shopping at various stores to compare products and prices, shopping at stores that guarantee the quality of their goods, and studying labels

## ★ Studying Labels

Labels are placed on foods, clothing, and other items to protect consumers. The government requires that certain kinds of information be included on these labels to help consumers judge product quality.

There are a number of federal laws regarding labeling. The Fair Packaging and Labeling Act requires businesses to supply certain information on the packages of the goods they sell. This labeling includes manufacturer information, package contents, and the weight or quantity of the items in the package.

The Nutrition Labeling and Education Act of 1990, amended in 1994, requires food companies to label their food products. In addition to listing serving sizes, these labels identify fat, cholesterol, sodium, fiber, and nutrient totals contained in each serving. The figures are given as a percentage of a person's daily dietary allowance.

# TEACH OBJECTIVE 2

**ALL LEVELS:** Copy the following graphic organizer onto the chalkboard, omitting the italicized answers. Have students complete the organizer to determine what independent organizations and the government do to protect consumers. **ENGLISH LANGUAGE LEARNERS**

*Set and enforce regulations*

*Publish product comparisons and reports*

**How Independent Organizations and Government Help Consumers**

*Publish consumer information*

*Help consumers when treated unfairly*

**LEVELS 1 AND 2:** Have students suggest several organizations (private and government) that are available to help or protect consumers. *(Students' suggestions should include the Better Business Bureau and the Consumer Product Safety Commission.)* Then ask students to create a poster that informs the public about the services provided by such organizations as those listed by the students. *(Students' posters might suggest that they set and enforce regulations, publish product comparisons and reports, help consumers when they are treated unfairly, and publish consumer information.)* Display completed posters around the classroom.

---

In addition to weight and content information, meat packages must have instructions for the safe handling and cooking of meats. The labels must also warn consumers that improper handling or cooking of the meat may lead to illness. Even though the meat has passed government inspection, it must still have a warning label.

Many products, including milk and cheese, must include the date by which the product must be sold or used. Dating a product ensures that it will be fresh when purchased by consumers.

Some laws require unit pricing. The price tag must show price per unit of the product—per ounce or gram, for example. Larger sizes are often a better bargain because they have a lower price per unit. This is not always true, however. You must read labels carefully to get the best bargain. Otherwise, the labels are of no help to you. For example, the term *preshrunk* means little if the label does not also say how much more the clothing will shrink when washed. If the label says "Sanforized," however, you know the clothing will not shrink more than 1 percent. The term *Sanforized* is standard and means the same thing throughout the clothing industry.

✔ **Reading Check Summarizing** How do federal laws on labeling protect consumers? **They require businesses to supply certain information on the packages of the goods they sell. Other laws require unit pricing.**

## Holt Researcher
### go.hrw.com
**KEYWORD: Holt Researcher**

**Freefind:** Consumer Protection

Scan through the entries on government and private organizations that provide assistance to consumers on the Holt Researcher. Create a poster that shows several of these organizations and highlights their activities. Your poster should answer the question: What types of advice and assistance are available to consumers?

★ **Civics Sidelight**

**Understanding Labels**
Reading food product labels is important if consumers are to make wise choices. However, some labels are misleading. For example, the term *natural* on a label might lead a person to believe that all the ingredients are healthful. In reality, "natural" ingredients may include refined sugar, salt, fat, starches, fillers, and other additives that come from nature but have little or no nutritional value.

**ACTIVITY:** Ask students to find labels from a variety of similar products, such as several brands of soup. Have them compare labels and present their observations in the format of their choice. Then ask them to share their findings with the class.

---

**CHART ANSWER**
before: product comparisons and contracts; after: instructions and warranties

## Tips for Consumers

### Before you buy

- **Consider your needs.** Decide what product or service features are important to you.

- **Compare brands.** Look for product comparisons in magazines and other publications. Ask other people for their recommendations.

- **Compare stores.** Compare prices at different locations. Look for stores with good reputations.

- **Read contracts.** Make sure you understand and agree to any contract that you sign. Ask the salesperson to explain the store's return or exchange policy.

Source: U.S. Office of Consumer Affairs

### After you buy

- **Read instructions.** Learn how to properly use the product or service. Keep instructions where you can find them.

- **Read the warranty.** Understand your obligations and the manufacturer's obligations if a problem arises. Keep in mind that you may have additional warranty rights in your state. Keep all sales receipts and warranties.

- **Report and record problems.** Report any problems to the company as soon as possible. Keep a file on the problem that includes the names of individuals you speak to and the date, time, and outcome of the conversations. Keep copies of any letters you send to the company and any replies they send to you.

**Interpreting Charts** *Consumers should take steps before and after any major purchase to make sure that they are paying a fair price for a good product and that their rights are respected.* **What documents should you read before and after a purchase?**

**LEVEL 3:** Invite a representative from the local branch of the Better Business Bureau or another organization that helps consumers to talk to the class. Have students develop questions for the guest speaker, addressing the ways that such an organization helps consumers. *(See the Levels 1 and 2 lesson for these ways.)* After the interview, have students write articles about the presentation for submission to the school newspaper. Some students might choose to use the interview information to write editorials informing students that they have rights as consumers and that there are agencies that help protect them.

# TEACH OBJECTIVE 3

**ALL LEVELS:** Help students explain the factors that a consumer should consider in deciding between an installment plan and a charge account. Draw on the chalkboard two charts in which students list the advantages and disadvantages of charge accounts and installment purchases. *(Students should note the following: charge account advantages— keeps track of purchases, no need to carry cash, easier to return purchases, prior notice of sales, and established credit rating; disadvantages—unwise use, theft, and interest charges; installment account advantages—can use product while paying for it, can buy expensive items over time; disadvantages—possible repossession and increased costs.)* **ENGLISH LANGUAGE LEARNERS**

## ★ Economics

**Employee Theft** In 2001 a little more than 30 percent of inventory loss in U.S. retail stores was due to shoplifting. Employee theft was an even greater problem in 2001, however. U.S. retailers suffered 46 percent of their inventory loss at the hands of their own employees. The remaining loss was due to paperwork errors and vendor fraud. A 2001 study showed that total inventory losses cost American businesses more than $32 billion that year. In 2000, U.S. retailers lost $29 billion to inventory loss. That adds up to an increase of nearly 10 percent from the previous year.

### CRITICAL THINKING

How might inventory loss affect consumers?

**ANSWER:** Students might suggest that retailers charge more for their goods to make up for the profits lost to theft.

### BIOGRAPHY ANSWER

The labels told consumers which products were made without the labor of young children.

## BIOGRAPHY

### Florence Kelley
#### (1859–1932)

Florence Kelley was born in Philadelphia, Pennsylvania. As a young woman she attended Cornell University. After college she became active in political organizations, social reform, and the women's rights movement. She became a member of Jane Addams's settlement house in Chicago, Hull House.

One of Kelley's passionate interests was child labor reform. In 1899 she became secretary of the National Consumers' League (NCL), a position she held for the rest of her life. The league's white label certified products that were made without the use of young children as workers. Kelley helped the league expand in membership and influence across the country. Kelley summarized her approach to reform with the phrase, "investigate, educate, agitate." **How did the NCL's white-label program provide information to consumers?**

## ★ Consumer Protection Organizations

Sometimes consumers find that a product has been falsely labeled or advertised. If you believe you have been misled by an unfair business practice, you should first make a complaint to the business that sold you the product or service.

If you are still not satisfied, you should contact the local Better Business Bureau. There is a bureau in or near most communities. This organization gives advice and assistance to people who believe they have been cheated or treated unfairly by a company.

The federal government also protects consumers through such organizations as the Federal Trade Commission (FTC). The FTC has the power to bring to court any company that uses false or misleading advertising or false labeling. The Department of Agriculture inspects and grades meat, poultry, and certain other foods sold in interstate commerce. The U.S. Postal Service makes sure that businesses and individuals do not cheat the public through the mail. The Consumer Product Safety Commission (CPSC) checks products to make sure they do not cause injuries.

Most states and many cities also have consumer protection offices. They publish advice for consumers and issue warnings to businesses that violate consumer laws. The businesses are then brought to court if they continue to cheat or mislead consumers.

A number of private organizations help consumers as well. Among these is Consumers Union, which tests and rates nearly every product the public buys. Consumers Union publishes the results of its tests in magazines and special reports. An examination of these and other publications will help you compare various brands of the same product.

✔ **Reading Check** Finding the Main Idea What can consumers do if they are dissatisfied with a product or service? First, they can make a complaint to the business that sold them the product or service. If still dissatisfied, they should contact a consumer protection organization.

## ★ Problems Caused by Consumers

Consumers often accuse businesses of misleading advertising, poor service, and inferior products. However, some people cause problems for businesses. **Shoplifting,** or stealing items displayed in stores, costs businesses in the United States billions of dollars each year. Sometimes people break or damage a store owner's property. Sometimes they demand refunds for merchandise they have already used or abused. Items in motels, hotels, and restaurants are often stolen or damaged. Sometimes people fail to pay for purchases obtained on credit.

Such thefts add to the costs of doing business. Businesses pass these costs on to consumers in the form of higher prices.

✔ **Reading Check** Analyzing Information What is one way that consumers hurt other consumers? Shoplifting adds to the costs of doing business. Businesses then pass these costs on to consumers in the form of higher prices.

**LEVEL 3:** Have each student create a consumer awareness packet that explains the factors a consumer should consider in deciding between an installment plan and a charge account. *(See the All Levels lesson for factors.)* In their packets, students may address any issues that they believe are important in determining whether a person should apply for each type of account. Invite volunteers to present their packets to the class for discussion.

**HOMEWORK** Have each student refer to the factors a consumer should consider when determining whether to apply for a credit account and what type to choose. Ask them to apply the criteria to themselves and to decide if an account makes sense for them. Have them write a paragraph explaining their decision.

# CLOSE

Have students compile a list called Qualities of a Good Consumer. Ask the following question: Which of the points on your list do you think is most important? Why? Conclude by discussing the steps students should take when making a purchase, according to what they have studied in the section.

## ★ Pay Now or Later?

When you buy something, you may pay for it immediately or you may buy it using credit. What are the advantages and disadvantages of buying merchandise in these two ways?

**Paying Now** Three ways of paying up front for products are using cash, **checks,** or **debit cards.** Checks are written and signed orders to a bank to pay a sum of money from a checking account to the party named on the check. Debit cards are small cards that operate the same way that checks do—when you use the card, money is deducted from your account. Paying using one of these methods means that you will be charged the amount of your purchase within a few days at most. Thus a person may be more likely to think carefully about what they buy.

**Paying Later** Suppose you find a bargain on something you need, but you do not have the cash on hand to pay for it. Buying the item with a **charge account** or **credit card** provides you with the ability to purchase the item immediately. A charge account is a form of credit that stores grant to many of their customers. Credit cards are similar to the charge cards provided for charge accounts but are issued by banks and other lending institutions. Unlike charge cards, which can only be used at specific stores, credit cards can be used at thousands of stores and other businesses around the world.

These forms of credit allow customers to buy goods and services without paying until they receive a bill from the store or bank. People who have a record of paying their bills on time can usually open a credit account. However, if people fail to pay their bills when they are due, they become a credit risk. Their accounts may be closed and their **credit rating** may be harmed. A credit rating shows how reliable a person is at paying his or her bills. A good rating is important for buying a car or gaining a bank loan.

Charge accounts and credit cards can make shopping more convenient. They can also help you build a good credit rating. However, customers must be careful not to make foolish purchases or run up credit card debt. The interest rates that must be paid on unpaid balances can be very high, making debt harder to pay off. Some cards also have an annual fee that holders must pay just for the use of the card. If you decide to apply for a credit card, be sure that you know the fees associated with the card. Using credit cards by phone or Internet also runs the risk of having your credit card numbers used by thieves.

ETTA FORT WORTH STAR-TELEGRAM HULME N.E.A. 79

"It's a red-letter day — she took her first step, and she received her first credit card application form."

**Interpreting the Visual Record**

**Credit cards** *Some companies offer credit cards to young people with the approval of their guardians.* **Why do you think a credit card company would offer an account to a young person?**

*Most banks that issue credit cards provide customer service representatives. These people can help answer questions about accounts.*

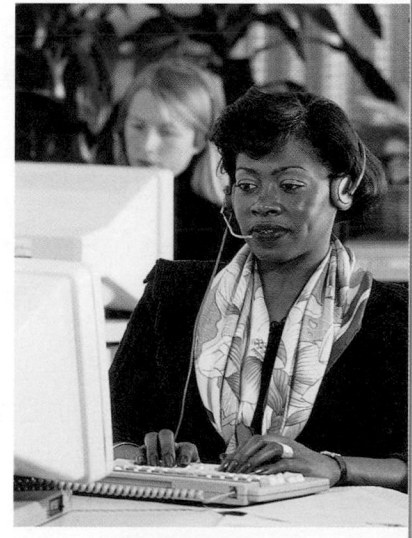

## REVIEW AND ASSESS

Have students complete the **Section 3 Review** on page 448. Then have them complete **Daily Quiz 18.3**. As **Alternative Assessment**, you may want to use the product advertisement or consumer-awareness packet exercises in this section's lessons.

## RETEACH

Have students complete **Main Idea Activity for English Language Learners and Special-Needs Students 18.3**. Then assign pairs of students one of the Read to Discover questions at the beginning of the section. Have pairs write several clues to help others arrive at the answer. **ENGLISH LANGUAGE LEARNERS** , **COOPERATIVE LEARNING**

## EXTEND

Have students use the library or other resources to obtain information about specific government laws and regulations designed to protect consumers. For example, students might research the history of the U.S. Department of Agriculture regulations regarding the handling of fresh meats and fish. Other possible topics include regulation of medicines by the Food and Drug Administration and regulations regarding children's car seats and flame-retardant children's pajamas. Have students prepare oral reports, with diagrams such as flowcharts, and present them to the class. **BLOCK SCHEDULING**

## Section 3 Review
### ANSWERS

**1. Define**
- consumer, p. 443
- shoplifting, p. 446
- checks, p. 447
- debit cards, p. 447
- charge account, p. 447
- credit card, p. 447
- credit rating, p. 447
- down payment, p. 448
- balance, p. 448
- installments, p. 448

**2.** immediate payment advantages: consumer may be more likely to think about purchases because money is taken from his or her account immediately; immediate payment disadvantages: more difficult to make large purchases without planning; credit advantages— keeps track of purchases, no need to carry cash, easier to return purchases, prior notice of sales, and established credit rating; disadvantages—unwise use, theft, and interest charges; installment account advantages—can use product while paying, can buy expensive items over time; disadvantages—possible repossession and increased costs

**3. a.** by looking out for sales, using coupons, and being a good judge of quality and prices

**b.** Students might suggest that they set and enforce regulations, publish product comparisons and reports, help consumers when treated unfairly, and publish consumer information.

**4.** Students' recommendations should display an awareness of the various ways to judge price and quality and other ways to be a wise consumer.

*Many stores that sell appliances offer installment plans to customers.*

Installment plans also allow consumers to buy goods without paying the full amount in cash when they make their purchases. In this case, the buyer uses cash to pay part of the purchase price. This money is called a **down payment.** The rest of what the buyer owes is called the **balance.** The balance is paid in equal payments, or **installments,** over a period of weeks, months, or years. An installment plan allows a buyer to use a product while paying for it.

Automobiles, houses, refrigerators, furniture, and other large items are often bought on an installment plan. The purchaser signs a written contract with the seller. The contract states how much the installment payments are and how often they must be paid. It also states that the item still belongs to the seller.

If the customer makes late or incomplete payments, the seller can repossess, or take back, the item. When this happens, the purchaser loses the item. He or she also loses the amount of money that has already been paid on the item.

Buying an item on an installment plan increases its cost. In addition to the regular price, a service charge and interest on the unpaid balance are included in the installment payments. When you buy an item under an installment plan, you may find it cheaper to take out a bank loan for a purchase. The interest and loan fees paid to the bank may be less than the service charge and interest under an installment plan. It is wise to make as large a down payment as possible. It is also wise to pay off the balance as quickly as possible to reduce the item's total cost.

✔ **Reading Check Summarizing** What are some of the alternatives to paying for an item immediately? charge accounts, credit cards, and installment plans

## SECTION 3 Review

go.hrw.com **Homework Practice Online**
keyword: SZ3 HP18

**1. Define** and explain:
- consumer
- shoplifting
- checks
- debit cards
- charge account
- credit card
- credit rating
- down payment
- balance
- installments

**2. Categorizing** Copy the chart below. Use it to show the advantages and disadvantages of paying immediately and using credit.

|  | Advantages | Disadvantages |
|---|---|---|
| Immediate payment |  |  |
| Credit payment |  |  |

**3. Finding the Main Idea**
a. How can someone become a smart shopper?
b. How do consumer groups and organizations help shoppers?

**4. Writing and Critical Thinking**
**Decision Making** A friend wants to buy a new computer and asks you for advice on choosing one. Write a list of five recommendations for your friend for finding the highest-quality product for the lowest possible price. Explain why you think those recommendations are important.

**Consider:**
- ways to judge price and quality
- how to be a wise consumer

## TEACH

**LEVEL 1:** Have students bring to class food products in jars or cans carrying the standard labels mandated by the Nutrition Labeling and Education Act of 1994. You might also bring to class meat labels with their instructions for safe handling and cooking. Have students devise questions about the information on each label and then ask them to answer each other's questions. (*Students' questions might include the following: What is the primary ingredient in your product? What percentage of the daily allowance of sodium is met in your product? And so on.*) **ENGLISH LANGUAGE LEARNERS**

## EXTEND

Invite a nutritionist or dietitian to class to clarify the terms and the percentages shown on food labels. (*Students may wish to ask your guest questions about the labels used in the Level 1 lesson.*) Suggest to the guest that he or she advise students about how to find nutritious foods. Following the visit, have students create posters encouraging elementary school students to pay attention to the nutritional value of the food they eat. Posters should include references to the information about food labels that was covered by the guest speaker. **BLOCK SCHEDULING**

# Civics Skills

## WORKSHOP

### Reading Labels

You go to the supermarket to buy, among other things, a can of beef stew. That seems simple enough. However, when you get to the aisle that has soup you see a dozen different brands of beef stew. Which brand should you buy? Reading the cans' labels will help you make this decision. As you know, product labels help and protect consumers.

### How to Read Labels

1. **Identify the ingredients.** Federal law requires companies to list the ingredients in each package of food. The ingredients must be listed in the order of their amounts. The main ingredient appears first, and the ingredient used least appears last. If there are foods you wish to avoid, such as those that contain large amounts of sugar or salt, reading the list of ingredients will help you choose the right product.

2. **Read the nutrition facts.** The federal government requires that food labels tell consumers how many servings are in the container. The labels also show the size of a serving and the number of calories and calories from fat in each serving. Labels also show the percentage of total daily allowance of fat, cholesterol, sodium, carbohydrates, and protein in a serving. You should strive to buy nutritious food.

3. **Study the other information.** Note that the label tells you that the percentages of daily values are based on a 2,000-calorie diet. Your own daily values may be higher or lower, depending on the number of calories in your diet.

4. **Be a comparison shopper.** Comparing labels for ingredients and nutritional content will help you make intelligent purchases.

### Applying the Skill

Study the food label below. Then answer the questions that follow.

1. What is the main ingredient?

2. Which ingredient is found in the smallest amount?

3. What percentage of your daily value of fat is supplied by one serving?

4. What percentage of your daily value of sodium will a single serving supply?

5. How large is one serving size? How many servings are contained in this particular can of soup?

### Beef Stew
### –SOUP–

**Nutrition Facts**

| Serv. Size 1 cup (240 mL) Servings per container about 2 | Amount/serving | % Daily Value* | Amount/serving | % Daily Value* |
|---|---|---|---|---|
| | **Total Fat** 5g | **8%** | **Total Carb.** 20g | **7%** |
| | Saturated Fat 1.5g | 8% | Dietary Fiber 5g | 20% |
| Amount per serving | **Cholesterol** 30mg | **10%** | Sugars 4g | |
| | **Sodium** 800mg | **33%** | **Protein** 13g | |
| Calories 180 Calories from Fat 45 | Vitamin A 100% • Vitamin C 2% • Calcium 2% • Iron 10% | | | |
| | *Percent Daily Values are based on a 2,000 calorie diet. Your daily values may be higher or lower depending upon your calorie needs. | | | |

INGREDIENTS: BEEF STOCK, CARROTS, POTATOES, COOKED BEEF (BEEF, WATER, SALT, SODIUM PHOSPHATE), TOMATO PUREE (WATER, TOMATO PASTE), PEAS, GREEN BEANS, POTATO STARCH. CONTAINS LESS THAN 2% OF THE FOLLOWING INGREDIENTS: WATER, WHEAT FLOUR, CORNSTARCH, VEGETABLE OIL, SALT, YEAST EXTRACT AND HYDROLYZED YEAST, WHEAT GLUTEN AND SOY PROTEIN, CARAMEL COLOR, SPICE EXTRACT, DEXTROSE.

## SKILLS ANSWERS

1. beef stock
2. dextrose
3. 8 percent
4. 33 percent
5. 1 cup; about 2

## CHAPTER 18
### REVIEW ANSWERS

**Define and Identify**

1. gross domestic product (GDP), p. 431
2. machine tools, p. 432
3. interchangeable parts, p. 432
4. division of labor, p. 432
5. self-service, p. 440
6. standard packaging, p. 440
7. one-price system, p. 440
8. brand names, p. 442
9. consumer, p. 443
10. down payment, p. 448

## Review and Assessment Resources

**REPRODUCIBLE**

▶ Chapter 18 Review, pp. 450–51

▶ Vocabulary Activity 18

▶ Chapter 18 Tutorial for Students, Parents, Mentors, and Peers

▶ Chapter 18 Test (Form A or B)

▶ Alternative Assessment Handbook

**TECHNOLOGY**

▶ Chapter 18 Test Generator (on the One-Stop Planner)

▶ Global Skill Builder CD–ROM

▶ HRW Go Site

**REINFORCEMENT, REVIEW, AND ASSESSMENT**

▶ Chapter 18 Test for English Language Learners and Special-Needs Students

## REVIEW

Have students complete the **Chapter 18 Review** on pages 450–51.

## ASSESS

Use one of the chapter tests to assess students' understanding of the content. For **Alternative Assessment**, see the **Alternative Assessment Handbook**.

---

### Understanding Main Ideas

**1.** machine tools, standard parts, and division of labor

**2.** profit motive; encourages people to work hard and produce more, which means higher productivity, and drives businesspeople to remain competitive by taking risks, modernizing, and being quick to grasp new ideas

**3.** Transportation brings goods from producers to consumers, and marketing provides information about products to consumers.

**4.** Manufacturers make goods, wholesalers buy large quantities at low prices, and then retailers purchase goods at wholesale prices and sell them directly to the public.

**5.** sales, coupons, and judgement of quality and prices

**6.** charge account and credit card advantages—keep track of purchases, no need to carry cash, easier to return purchases, prior notice of sales, and established credit rating; disadvantages—unwise use, theft, and interest charges; installment account advantages—can use product while paying for items, can buy expensive items over time; disadvantages—possible repossession and increased costs

### What Did You Find Out?

**1.** the rapid production of large numbers of identical objects using machines; profit motive of a free-enterprise system encourages risk taking and hard work, which make it successful.

---

## Chapter 18 Review

### Chapter Summary

**Section 1**

- Mass production enables the United States to produce a wide variety of products and services.

- Features of mass production include machine tools, interchangeable parts, and the division of labor.

- Assembly lines make the mass production of products possible by moving them through stages of production until they are completed.

**Section 2**

- In order to move goods from the producer to the consumer, a system of distribution is necessary.

- Transportation, a component of distribution, involves carrying products from the manufacturer to wholesalers and retailers. Goods are shipped using railroads, trucks, ships, and airplanes.

- Marketing, another component of distribution, helps sell products to customers. Advertising, self-service, the one-price system, shopping malls, and specialty shops are all parts of mass marketing.

**Section 3**

- By properly judging product price and quality, consumers can make wise purchases.

- Consumers can receive the most value for their money by consulting consumer organizations for product information and by learning when to buy items with cash, checks, debit cards, or by using credit.

---

### Define and Identify

Use the following terms in complete sentences.

1. gross domestic product (GDP)
2. machine tools
3. interchangeable parts
4. division of labor
5. self-service
6. standard packaging
7. one-price system
8. brand names
9. consumer
10. down payment

### Understanding Main Ideas

**Section 1** *(Pages 431–36)*

1. What are the three main features of mass production?
2. What incentive is a key part of mass production, and why is it important?

**Section 2** *(Pages 437–42)*

3. Why does the U.S. economy depend on the transportation and marketing of goods?
4. How are products distributed from the manufacturer to the customer?

**Section 3** *(Pages 443–48)*

5. What choices are available to help consumers make smart purchases?
6. What are the advantages and disadvantages of using charge accounts, credit cards, and installment plans?

### What Did You Find Out?

1. What is mass production, and why is it so effective in a free-enterprise economy?
2. How do businesses distribute goods?
3. Why is it beneficial to shop sensibly?

### Thinking Critically

1. **Problem Solving** The strength of the U.S. economy depends partly on the country's ability to produce millions of goods annually. What might the country do to avoid economic downturns and encourage success?

2. **Supporting a Point of View** Credit debt plagues many Americans, causing them to suffer financially. What factors do you think contribute to the widespread problem of credit card debt? What measures, if any, might help address this problem?

3. **Analyzing Information** To prevent shoplifting, many stores have installed security cameras and other devices. In your opinion, how do these efforts affect the rights of both shoppers and business owners?

## RETEACH

Ask questions to help students summarize each section of the chapter. For Section 1, ask what makes the high rate of American production possible. For Section 2, you might ask what the key elements of the distribution system for American goods are. For Section 3, you might ask what it takes to be a smart consumer. Each student should then write three paragraphs that answer the Read to Discover questions. Call on students to share their responses with the class.

**ENGLISH LANGUAGE LEARNERS**

## Portfolio Extensions

**1. Cooperative Learning** Organize the class into groups and have each group locate an article in a consumer magazine concerning the testing of a product in which the group is interested. (*Students might select computers, televisions, bicycles, CD players, and so on.*) Ask students to take notes as they examine the article. Then have them discuss the main points of the article and come to some decisions about which of the tested brands appeals to them most and why. Have them present their findings in the form of a product review and recommendation.

**2. Interdisciplinary Connection to Science** Have students conduct research using the library or other resources to identify a recent scientific invention and to learn about the safety guidelines that it was required to meet. Have them prepare an illustration of the invention and a one-page product description. Descriptions should include an explanation of the various ways that the invention meets the government safety requirements. Have students present their findings to the class.

---

## Building Social Studies Skills

STANDARDIZED TEST PREP ONLINE keyword: SZ3 STP18 go.hrw.com

### Interpreting Charts
Study the chart below. Then answer the questions that follow.

## Fundamentals of Mass Production

| Source of Power | • Operates machinery to do work faster and more cheaply than by hand |
| --- | --- |
| Machine Tools | • Used to make standard parts, which are identical to each other |
| Standard Parts | • Used to make identical products, which are easier to assemble, repair, and replace |
| Division of Labor | • Speeds process by breaking production down into many small, specialized steps |

1. What are the advantages of standard parts?
   a. They cost less to manufacture and are more durable.
   b. They are lighter and easier to assemble.
   c. They are easier to assemble, repair, and replace.
   d. They are necessary to make more complicated machines.
2. How are machine tools and standard parts related to each other?
3. When all the different fundamentals of mass production are used together, what are the manufacturing benefits?

### Analyzing Primary Sources
Read the following quotation from the Better Business Bureau on Internet shopping. Then answer the questions that follow.

❝The Better Business Bureau (BBB), along with the Federal Trade Commission (FTC), offer [Internet] shoppers the following tips. . . . Determine the company's refund and return policies before you place an order. Never give out your Internet password. . . . If the site asks you to create an account with a password, never use the same password you use for other accounts or sites. Be cautious if you're asked to supply personal information, such as your Social Security number or personal bank account information, to conduct a transaction. Personal information is rarely necessary and should raise a red flag. . . . Know your rights. The same laws that protect you when you shop by phone or mail apply when you shop in cyberspace.❞

4. Which of the following statements is accurate based on the quotation?
   a. Consumers who shop online are protected by unique laws that do not apply elsewhere.
   b. Online shopping is dangerous and a bad idea.
   c. Online shoppers are protected by the same laws that protect people shopping by phone or by mail.
   d. There are no real laws yet written that address online shopping.
5. What practices does the Better Business Bureau recommend against using when shopping online? Why do you think it suggests these measures?

---

**2.** They sell large quantities at low prices to wholesalers, who sell them to retailers, who sell directly to consumers.

**3.** It saves money and helps you avoid acquiring useless or poor-quality goods.

### Thinking Critically
**1.** Students should demonstrate an awareness of how bankruptcy and unemployment affect production as well as ways the country can maintain a strong economy.

**2.** Students should clearly state their opinions and display knowledge of wise credit use.

**3.** Students' arguments should be reasonable and well supported.

### Skills Workshop
**1.** c

**2.** Standard parts are made by machine tools.

**3.** lower costs and higher productivity

**4.** c

**5.** personal information and the same password; to protect consumers from having their information used by someone else

---

## Alternative Assessment

### Building Your Portfolio
**American Civics**

#### Linking to Community
With a group, research a consumer protection organization in your community and create a brochure explaining the services it offers. Does it register consumer complaints, evaluate products, or publish consumer information? How do consumers contact this organization? In your brochure, provide sketches or pictures of the organization's available services. Present your brochure to the class.

### internet connect

**Internet Activity: go.hrw.com**
**keyword: SZ3 AC18**

Access the Internet through the HRW Go site to go behind the scenes at the production facilities of selected companies and research how some well-known products are manufactured. Then write a newspaper or magazine article describing all the materials it takes to manufacture a product from one of the selected companies, the steps involved in production, and how the product is marketed.

# Managing Money

## CHAPTER RESOURCE MANAGER

| | Objectives | Pacing Guide | Reproducible Resources |
|---|---|---|---|
| **SECTION 1:**<br>**Money and Credit**<br>(pp. 453–58) | ★ Identify the four basic characteristics of currency.<br>★ Explain why people and businesses accept checks as payment instead of cash.<br>★ Describe how credit is important in families and in the economy as a whole. | **Regular**<br>1 day<br>**Block Scheduling**<br>.5 day<br><br>*Block Scheduling Handbook with Team Teaching Strategies, Chapter 19* | **RS** Guided Reading Strategies 19.1<br>**RS** Graphic Organizer Activity: Understanding Currency |
| **SECTION 2:**<br>**Banks and Banking**<br>(pp. 460–66) | ★ Identify the FDIC and describe how it helps depositors.<br>★ Determine what caused the savings and loan crisis in the 1980s.<br>★ Analyze how and why the Federal Reserve System regulates the amount of money in circulation. | **Regular**<br>1.5 days<br>**Block Scheduling**<br>1 day<br><br>*Block Scheduling Handbook with Team Teaching Strategies, Chapter 19* | **RS** Guided Reading Strategies 19.2<br>**RS** Readings in Economics and Government 46: Depository Institutions and Deregulation Act of 1980<br>**E** Challenge and Enrichment Worksheet 19: Locating the Federal Reserve Districts |
| **SECTION 3:**<br>**Saving and Investing**<br>(pp. 467–73) | ★ Explain why it is important to save money.<br>★ Identify some of the ways people save and invest their money.<br>★ Evaluate how saving money helps the U.S. economy. | **Regular**<br>1 day<br>**Block Scheduling**<br>.5 day<br><br>*Block Scheduling Handbook with Team Teaching Strategies, Chapter 19* | **RS** Guided Reading Strategies 19.3<br>**E** Creative Teaching Strategy: Webbing<br>**SM** Community Service and Participation Handbook: The Hidden Costs of Owning a Home |
| **SECTION 4:**<br>**Insurance against Hardship**<br>(pp. 474–81) | ★ Explain how insurance companies are able to cover the hardship costs of so many people.<br>★ Distinguish between private insurance and social insurance.<br>★ Describe why Social Security was created and why some people are concerned about its future. | **Regular**<br>1 day<br>**Block Scheduling**<br>.5 day<br><br>*Block Scheduling Handbook with Team Teaching Strategies, Chapter 19* | **RS** Guided Reading Strategies 19.4 |

## Chapter Resource Key

| | | | | | |
|---|---|---|---|---|---|
| **PS** | Primary Sources | **SM** | Skills Mastery |  | CD-ROM |
| **RS** | Reading Support | **A** | Assessment |  | Video |
| **IC** | Interdisciplinary Connections | **REV** | Review |  | Internet |
| | | **ELL** | Reinforcement and English Language Learners |  | Holt Presentation Maker Using Microsoft® PowerPoint® |
| **E** | Enrichment | | Transparencies | | |

 **One-Stop** Planner CD–ROM

**See the *One-Stop Planner* for a complete list of additional resources for students and teachers.**

## One-Stop Planner CD–ROM

It's easy to plan lessons, select resources, and print out materials for your students when you use the **One-Stop Planner CD–ROM with Test Generator**.

| Technology Resources | Reinforcement, Review, and Assessment |
|---|---|
| One-Stop Planner, Lesson 19.1<br>CNN Presents: American Government<br>Homework Practice Online | REV  Section 1 Review, p. 458<br>A  Daily Quiz 19.1<br>ELL  Main Idea Activity 19.1<br>ELL  English Audio Summary 19.1<br>ELL  Spanish Audio Summary 19.1 |
| One-Stop Planner, Lesson 19.2<br>Holt Researcher CD–ROM<br>Homework Practice Online<br>HRW Go site | REV  Section 2 Review, p. 466<br>A  Daily Quiz 19.2<br>ELL  Main Idea Activity 19.2<br>ELL  English Audio Summary 19.2<br>ELL  Spanish Audio Summary 19.2 |
| One-Stop Planner, Lesson 19.3<br>Homework Practice Online | REV  Section 3 Review, p. 473<br>A  Daily Quiz 19.3<br>ELL  Main Idea Activity 19.3<br>ELL  English Audio Summary 19.3<br>ELL  Spanish Audio Summary 19.3 |
| One-Stop Planner, Lesson 19.4<br>Homework Practice Online | REV  Section 4 Review, p. 481<br>A  Daily Quiz 19.4<br>ELL  Main Idea Activity 19.4<br>ELL  English Audio Summary 19.4<br>ELL  Spanish Audio Summary 19.4 |

## internet connect

### HRW ONLINE RESOURCES
GO TO: go.hrw.com
Then type in the keyword.

**TEACHER HOME PAGE**
KEYWORD: SZ3 Teacher

**CHAPTER INTERNET ACTIVITIES**
KEYWORD: SZ3 AC19
Choose an activity to:
• create a skit related to money, banking, and credit.
• write a biography of a historical figure in the banking industry.
• make a multimedia presentation on U.S. currency.

**CHAPTER ENRICHMENT LINKS**
KEYWORD: SZ3 CH13

**ONLINE ASSESSMENT**
Homework Practice
KEYWORD: SZ3 HP19
Rubrics
KEYWORD: SS Rubrics

**ONLINE MAPS, CHARTS, AND GRAPHS**
KEYWORD: SZ3 MCG
• Saving Keeps the Country Prosperous

**HOLT PRESENTATION MAKER**
KEYWORD: SZ3 PPT19

**CONTENT UPDATES**
KEYWORD: SS Content Updates

**ONLINE READING SUPPORT**
KEYWORD: SS Strategies

**CURRENT EVENTS**
KEYWORD: S3
Current Events

## Chapter Review and Assessment

IC  Vocabulary Activity 19
Global Skill Builder CD–ROM
HRW Go site
REV  Chapter 19 Tutorial for Students, Parents, Mentors, and Peers
REV  Chapter 19 Review, pp. 482–83
A  Standardized Test Practice
A  Chapter 19 Test Generator (on the One-Stop Planner)
A  Chapter 19 Test (Form A or B)
A  Alternative Assessment Handbook
A  Chapter 19 Test for English Language Learners and Special-Needs Students

## Meeting Individual Needs

### Ability Levels

**Level 1** Basic-level activities designed for all students encountering new material

**Level 2** Intermediate-level activities designed for average students

**Level 3** Challenging activities designed for honors and gifted-and-talented students

**English Language Learners** Activities that address the needs of students with Limited English Proficiency

# Internet Activity

## Money

**internet** connect

**TOPIC:** The U.S. Currency System
**GO TO:** go.hrw.com
**KEYWORD:** SZ3 AC19

Have students access the Internet through the HRW Go site to conduct research about U.S. currency. Then ask students to create posters or multimedia presentations to teach the class about the history of and designs on various coins and bills. Students should consider questions such as the following: Whose picture is on the $100 bill? Why was Sacagawea chosen to be on the new $1 coin? On which bill is there a picture of the White House? Are notes in some denominations no longer in circulation?

## What's Your Opinion?

To help students create their *Themes* Journal entries, provide the following examples of appropriate **agree**/**disagree** statements.

● **Agree**   People trust paper money because it has been used for transactions for many years.

**Disagree**   People are able to buy and sell things with money only because the government has assigned value to it.

● **Agree**   The banking system should be allowed to operate on its own, without any government interference.

**Disagree**   The government should regulate and oversee the banking system to protect the U.S. economy.

● **Agree**   You should not worry about saving money if you are able to obtain a loan from a bank.

**Disagree**   You should always try to save money.

# CHAPTER

# 19 Managing Money

## Build on What You Know

Suppose that you want to buy a new CD. When you have made your selection, you offer the clerk a chicken in exchange for the CD. However, the clerk refuses to accept the chicken because he or she has no need for it. You then offer the clerk several pieces of paper with the picture of President George Washington on them. Why does the clerk accept these pieces of paper? Both you and the clerk recognize the pieces of paper—a form of money—as a guaranteed standard of value in the United States.

 **Themes Journal**   Do you **agree** or **disagree** with the following statements? Support your point of view in your journal.

- People are able to buy and sell things with paper money because this practice has existed for several years.

- The federal government should not interfere with the banking system.

- If you can get a loan from a bank, you do not need to save money.

## What's Your Opinion?

# SECTION 1

## OBJECTIVES

*After completing Section 1, students should be able to*

1 **Identify the four basic characteristics of currency.**

2 **Explain why people and businesses accept checks as payment instead of cash.**

3 **Describe how credit is important in families and in the economy as a whole.**

🔊 *LET'S GET STARTED!*

As students enter the classroom, ask them to imagine that the government has removed all money from society. Have pairs of students create short stories or skits that describe what life would be like without money. *(Students should address such dilemmas as how people would obtain what they want or need and how businesses would operate.)* Call on volunteers to read their stories or present their skits to the class. Lead a class discussion about the advantages of having a uniform medium of exchange (money) for conducting business. Tell students that in Section 1 they will learn more about currency, checks, and credit as well as different types of banks and the importance of savings and insurance.

## SECTION 1

# Money and Credit

### Read to Discover

1. What are the four basic characteristics of currency?
2. Why do people and businesses accept checks as payment instead of cash?
3. How is credit important in families and in the economy as a whole?

### Define

- currency
- creditors
- short-term credit
- long-term credit
- bankruptcy

#### WHY CIVICS MATTERS

The number of credit cards issued by banks and other lending institutions has increased dramatically in the last 10 years. Use **CNNfyi.com** or other **current events** sources to research the growth of credit card use and the amount of money charged on cards in the last decade. Record your findings in your journal.

## SECTION 1 RESOURCES

### REPRODUCIBLE

▶ Guided Reading Strategies 19.1

▶ Graphic Organizer Activity: Understanding Currency

### TECHNOLOGY

▶ One-Stop Planner, Lesson 19.1

▶ CNN Presents: American Government

▶ Homework Practice Online

### REINFORCEMENT, REVIEW, AND ASSESSMENT

▶ Section 1 Review, p. 458

▶ Daily Quiz 19.1

▶ Main Idea Activity 19.1

▶ English Audio Summary 19.1

▶ Spanish Audio Summary 19.1

## *Reading Focus*

At various times and in various places, people have used many different items as money. Cows, pigs, guns, playing cards, furs, salt, olive oil, stones, knives, tobacco, copper, iron, wampum beads, shells, rings, silver, and diamonds have all been used as money.

### ⭐ Currencies

Every country in the world has a **currency**—another term for coins and paper money. All currencies share four common features:

1. Currency must be easy to carry and take up little space so people can carry it with them for everyday use.

2. Currency must be based on a system of units that are easy to multiply and divide. Figuring the number of coins and bills needed to exchange for an item should be easy to do.

3. Currency must be durable, or last a long time. It should not wear out too quickly or fall apart. People must be able to keep currency until they are ready to spend it.

4. Currency must be made in a standard form and must be guaranteed by the government of the country that issues it. In this way, citizens can be certain that their coins and bills will be accepted in exchange for goods and services.

*U.S. currency comes in a variety of denominations.*

**LEVEL 1:** Let students examine as many U.S. coins and bills as you can make available. Then have them list the four basic characteristics of currency. *(Students' lists should include the following characteristics: ease of use, simple denominations, durability, standardized design, guaranteed by the government.)* Then have the class compare and contrast the coins and bills. Ask questions such as the following: Is a quarter worth more than a dime because it might have more silver in it? *(No U.S. coin issued today has silver in it.)* Then ask: Why do you think that citizens recognize the value of coins and paper currency that have no precious materials in them?

**ENGLISH LANGUAGE LEARNERS**

**LEVELS 2 AND 3:** Organize the class into small groups and ask each group to imagine that it is a member of a special committee within the Department of the Treasury. Tell students that it is their job to redesign U.S. currency. Remind students that all currencies share four common features and tell each group to list the ways that U.S. currency already has these features. *(See the Level 1 lesson for features.)* Then ask each group to design a new and improved U.S. currency and have groups create "blueprints," or prototype samples of this currency. Finally, have each group explain the improvements of its redesigned currency to the rest of the class.

**COOPERATIVE LEARNING**

---

## ★ Economics

### The New Dollar Coin

Historically a country's coins have carried the likeness of its monarch or ruler. In the United States, a president's likeness did not appear on coins until 1909, when the Lincoln penny was minted. In 1979 a new coin without a presidential likeness was issued—the Susan B. Anthony dollar. Anthony (1820-1906) was a leader in the women's suffrage movement in the United States. Because of its similarity to the quarter, the Susan B. Anthony dollar was produced from only 1979 to 1981. However, in January 2000 the U.S. Treasury tried again with a new dollar coin. The Sacagawea dollar is gold in color, and it bears the image of the Shoshone woman who helped Meriwether Lewis and William Clark explore the West. The new dollar coin costs 3 times more to manufacture than a dollar bill, but the coins last 20 times longer. Congress's General Accounting Office has estimated that phasing out dollar bills could save taxpayers $522 million a year.

**ACTIVITY:** Ask students to conduct research on how well the Sacagawea dollar is being accepted by consumers and have students write a brief report about their findings.

### Visual Record Answer

*Some of the advantages of having a single currency might be ease of use, standard appearance, and standard denominations.*

**Interpreting the Visual Record**

**The euro** *Most members of the European Union have agreed to abandon their national currencies in favor of a shared currency called the euro.* **What might be some advantages of having a single currency for many countries?**

### Did You KNOW?

In the 1800s state banks in the United States were allowed to issue their own paper money! A national paper currency was not established until the National Banking Act of 1863. The Federal Reserve Notes familiar to us today were not introduced until 1914.

The currency used by Americans is issued, or made, by the federal government. All U.S. paper money and coins are considered legal tender. That is, the law requires that every American accept this money as payment in exchange for all goods and services.

You may recall that one of the country's weaknesses under the Articles of Confederation was the lack of a standard currency. Each state issued its own money. The different values and exchange rates for these currencies made trade more difficult. The Constitution solved this problem by granting to Congress the sole right "to coin money, [regulating] the value thereof. . . ."

In 1792 a mint, or plant where coins are made, was created in Philadelphia, Pennsylvania. This mint and another in Denver, Colorado, now make most coins for general circulation. Mints in San Francisco, California, and West Point, New York, make commemorative, or special occasion, coins.

Coins are sometimes called hard money because they are usually made of hard metal. In the United States, six coins are used: pennies, nickels, dimes, quarters, half-dollars, and the new dollar coin. For many years the value of a coin was equal to the value of the metal that it contained. A silver dollar, for example, yielded about a dollar's worth of silver when melted down. In the past, many Americans would only accept hard money. They thought it was more valuable and reliable than paper money.

Today coins make up only a small percentage of the total U.S. money supply. They no longer contain gold or silver. All coins are alloys, or mixtures, of metals. Pennies are copper-coated zinc. Nickels, dimes, quarters, and half-dollars are alloys of copper and nickel. The new dollar coin is also a mixture of copper, zinc, and other minerals.

Why do Americans accept coins that are not made of gold or silver? They accept them because they know that the coins will be accepted as legal tender, or money, when they are presented at stores, banks, or elsewhere. They also know that the government has a supply of gold and silver bullion, or bars. Most of this bullion is kept in a depository at Fort Knox, Kentucky. This and other bullion help strengthen the country's financial position.

Most of the money issued by the government today is paper money. It is printed in Washington, D.C., at the Bureau of Engraving and Printing of the Department of the Treasury. Bills are printed in denominations of $1, $2, $5, $10, $20, $50, and $100. Bills in denominations of $10, $20, $50, and $100 have been redesigned in recent years to make them more difficult to counterfeit. Bills in denominations of $500, $1,000, $5,000, and $10,000 are no longer issued, but some are still in circulation. As these bills reach the country's central bank, they are removed from circulation.

✔ **Reading Check** **Summarizing** What are the four common characteristics of all currencies? They are portable, divisible, durable, and made in a standard form.

**LEVEL 1:** Lead a class discussion about why people and businesses accept checks as payment instead of cash. (*Using checks is often more convenient than dealing with cash and the signature on a check is a promise that there is sufficient credit in an account to cover the amount of a check.*) Explain to students how a check is a written and signed order to a bank to pay a sum of money from a checking account. Then ask each student to create a flowchart explaining the process that enables consumers to make purchases and pay bills with checks instead of with cash. Invite volunteers to explain their flowcharts to the class. **ENGLISH LANGUAGE LEARNERS**

**LEVELS 2 AND 3:** Organize students into pairs. Ask pairs to imagine a scene in which a store owner who accepts only cash is waiting on a customer who insists on paying with a check or a credit card. Have each pair write a script for this scene in which students focus on the advantages and disadvantages to sellers of a cash-only policy. Students should also consider what problems or benefits, if any, that a cash-only policy might have for consumers. **COOPERATIVE LEARNING**

## ★ Checking Accounts

Very little of what is bought and sold in the United States is paid for with either coins or paper money. Americans make greater use of another kind of money, the kind represented by checks.

**Checks** Much of the total U.S. money supply is in the form of bank deposits. Bank deposits are the amounts of money in bank accounts, including checking accounts. These figures represent the amount of credit held in a personal or business account. Credit is the amount of money that the bank makes available for a person or business to use. The person or business can spend the money in a checking account at any time by writing a check. The person or business who writes the check maintains the account by depositing in it cash or checks from other persons or businesses. For example, most people deposit some portion of their paychecks into a checking account of some sort.

Checks are just pieces of paper. They are not legal tender because they are not issued and guaranteed by the federal government. However, most sellers will accept any check written by a person or business that provides proper identification and a local address.

A signature on a check is a promise that there is sufficient credit in an account to cover the amount of a check. People who knowingly write checks without having sufficient funds in their accounts may be subject to fines or criminal penalties. Even if you overdraw your account by accident, most banks and businesses will charge a fine for returned checks.

Because they use checks, many people never see most of their money. What they see instead is a column of figures the bank sends them on a monthly statement. The statement tells them how many checks they have written in the month, the amounts of the checks, and how much credit remains in their checking account. It is important for people to keep careful track of the funds in their checking account by checking their statements each month.

**Debit Cards** Many people who have checking accounts prefer to make payments with debit cards instead of writing checks. As you know, debit cards are small cards that operate the same way that checks do. When a person uses a debit card, money is then deducted from his or her account the same way it is when a check is written. Debit cards offer an increasingly popular alternative to carrying cash or a checkbook.

✔ **Reading Check** Drawing Inferences and Conclusions Why are people more likely to use a check to make a purchase than cash? Students might say that a check can be written for any amount, but paying in cash requires having the correct amount of money.

The reserves of gold stored at Fort Knox, Kentucky, help provide stability to the U.S. economy.

**Interpreting the Visual Record**

**Paying by check** *Many people use checks to make everyday purchases.* **Why is using a check for a purchase like this one convenient?**

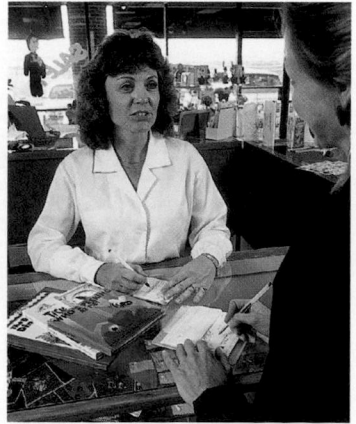

## ★ Economics

**The Smart Card** The "smart card" may be the next step toward a cashless society. Although it looks like an ordinary credit card, the smart card contains a microprocessor that can be used to store and process 80 times more information than the magnetic stripe on a regular credit card. Smart cards can store a wide range of information, such as a user's identity, bank account numbers, driver's license number, Social Security number, passport number, and so on. A smart card can be used as a credit card, or it can be used as an "electronic purse" in which monetary value is stored like cash. A consumer could load value onto the card at an Automated Teller Machine (ATM) and then this value would be subtracted as purchases are made. Some people praise the economic convenience of the smart card, but critics argue that it could threaten civil liberties if too much information is stored on it.

**CRITICAL THINKING**

What are the advantages and disadvantages of the smart card?

**ANSWER:** Students should cite the convenience as well as the ways that this technology might be misused.

**Visual Record Answer**

*Students might suggest that the woman can write a check for any sum and does not need to carry the exact amount of paper money and coins.*

**ALL LEVELS:** Copy the following graphic organizer onto the chalkboard, omitting the italicized answers. Have students complete the boxes on the flowcharts to describe how credit is good for families and the economy as a whole.

**HOMEWORK** Ask students to find out how U.S. currency has evolved over the years, and have each student create a poster showing some of the different currencies that have been in circulation in the United States during the past two centuries.

**Importance of Credit**

| In the Family | In Business | In the Economy |
|---|---|---|
| *used for emergency expenses* | *used in most sales of large amounts of goods* | *makes it possible for consumers to buy whenever there are goods to be sold, even if money supply is low* |
| *products or services needed immediately* | *allows wholesalers to buy larger quantities than they have money for* | *when production slows, banks can slow consumer spending by extending less credit and raising interest rates on loans* |
| *large purchases on short-term credit* | *wholesaler can make money to repay debt* | |
| *large purchases on long-term credit* | | |

## ★ Economics

### New Ways to Pay

Consumers have grown accustomed to using Automatic Teller Machines (ATMs) to make deposits, check account balances, make payments, and withdraw cash from their bank accounts. In 2001, 7-Eleven convenience stores tested a new Vcom kiosk that links the ATM machine to the Internet and allows consumers to cash checks, wire money, and conduct a variety of other financial transactions in a one-stop shopping format. In the future, the designers of the Vcom kiosk hope to add such services as electronic bill payment, deposit capability, event ticketing, travel directions, road maps, vehicle registration, credit reports, airline tickets, and smart cards.

**ACTIVITY:** Ask students to conduct research to find out what other venues or methods are available to consumers for conducting financial transactions, and have students prepare reports about these different options.

### Visual Record Answer

*Students might suggest that the information on a credit card statement might help users track their spending patterns and budget their money wisely.*

## ★ Charge Accounts and Credit Cards

As you know, a charge account is a method by which a store extends credit to customers. Customers receive charge cards, which allow them to buy things without paying cash at the time of purchase. The amount of the purchases is added to their charge accounts. Customers then receive a monthly bill.

The customer writes a check for all or part of the bill, keeping in mind that interest is charged on the unpaid portion. The store deposits the check in its own bank, which then sends the check to the customer's bank. The customer's bank subtracts the amount of the check from the customer's account. No currency changes hands. Banks do not actually collect from each other check by check. They use computerized systems that handle huge numbers of checks.

Credit cards are similar to charge cards but are issued by banks and other major lending institutions. Examples of credit cards include American Express®, VISA®, and MasterCard®. The customer presents the credit card when making a purchase. The store or business charges the credit card company the amount of the purchase. The credit card company then pays the store or business and charges the customer for the amount of the purchase. As with charge cards, the customer pays all or part of the credit card bill with a single check once a month. Many customers can make payments by using the Internet to transfer funds from a bank account to the credit card company. Interest charges, which often are quite high, are added to the unpaid portion of the monthly bill. Again, no currency changes hands at any point in the transaction.

✔ **Reading Check Comparing and Contrasting** How are credit and charge cards the same, and how are they different? Both allow purchases on credit, are paid monthly, and charge interest on unpaid balances. Charge cards are usually accepted only by the business that issued them, unlike credit cards.

**Interpreting the Visual Record**

Credit card statements *Each month, credit card users receive a statement listing when, where, and how much money they spent during the previous billing period.* **Why would such information be important?**

**XYZ SAVINGS BANK**

| | |
|---|---|
| Account number | 0000-0000-0000-0000 |
| Credit limit | $5,000.00 |
| Available credit | $5,000.00 |

Questions? Lost or Stolen Cards?
Call Customer Service  1-800-555-1234

Or write us at:
123 Main Street, Anytown, USA 12345-6789

Remit payment to: XYZ Savings Bank
123 Main Street
Anytown, USA 12345-6789

Statement closing date 01/10/05

| | |
|---|---|
| Previous balance | $168.00 |
| Payments | $168.00 |
| Purchases and debits | $57.24 |
| **FINANCE CHARGES** | $0.00 |
| **New balance** | $57.24 |
| **Minimum payment due** | $10.00 |
| **Payment due date** | 02/04/05 |

TO AVOID ADDITIONAL FINANCE CHARGES ON PURCHASES, PAY YOUR ENTIRE NEW BALANCE, EVEN IF YOU EXPECT TO RECEIVE A CREDIT, BY THE DUE DATE SHOWN ABOVE. MAILED PAYMENTS RECEIVED AFTER 6:00 A.M. WILL BE CREDITED THE NEXT BUSINESS DAY

**Finance Charges**
Days in Billing Period

| | | Annual Percentage Rates | | | |
|---|---|---|---|---|---|
| Average Daily Balance | $0.00 | Rates on Current Balances | Monthly Periodic Rate | ANNUAL PERCENTAGE RATE | Average Daily Balance |
| **FINANCE CHARGES** | $0.00 | Purchases | 1.042% | 12.50% | $0.00 |
| | | Cash Advances | 1.042% | 12.50% | $0.00 |

## ★ Credit in Business

Credit is used instead of currency in most sales involving large amounts of goods. A wholesale grocer may order a truckload of canned goods, for example. He or she promises to pay for this order at the end of the month or, sometimes, within 90 days. A wholesaler with good credit can take the canned goods right away.

By selling the canned goods, the wholesaler makes the money to repay the debt before it is due. Credit allows wholesalers to buy a larger quantity of goods at one time than if they had to pay for the purchase immediately. However, credit is sometimes used unwisely.

**LEVEL 3:** Ask each student to write a letter to someone who lives in an imaginary country that uses only cash to conduct all of its business. Tell students to describe in their letters how credit works, and have them explain why credit plays an important role in the family as well as in the economy as a whole. Then ask students to point out some of the problems involving a cash-only policy, and have them include advice for using credit wisely. *(Students should mention that by regulating credit, banks can help keep the economy in balance.)* Also, ask students to consider the complications that would arise in trying to conduct foreign trade on a cash-only basis. Invite volunteers to read their letters to the class.

## CLOSE

Have students divide a sheet of paper into three columns and tell them to imagine that they are going to buy the following items: (1) house, (2) toaster, (3) furnace, (4) automobile, (5) paperback book, (6) compact disc player. Ask each student to list these items in the left column. For each item, ask students to determine which type of credit (long-term or short-term) would be most appropriate to use. Have them write the answer in the middle column. Also, have them consider which purchases might be better made with cash rather than credit. Then, ask students to write the reasons for their decisions in the third column.

Suppose businesspeople use credit more often than they should. When it is time to pay their bills, they may find themselves unable to pay the entire bill. As a result, large finance charges will be added to the remaining balance. In extreme cases, their **creditors**—those people to whom they owe money—may demand payment. The businessperson might be forced to sell his or her businesses to pay the debts.

✔ **Reading Check** **Analyzing Information** How are wholesalers able to use credit to purchase large amounts of goods? Wholesalers buy large quantities of goods on credit. Then, they sell the goods and use some of the revenue to repay the debt.

### ★ Credit in the Family

If used wisely, credit can also help the average American family. For example, credit can help a family make emergency purchases, such as replacing a broken refrigerator. If the family plans to pay for an item within a few weeks or months, it needs only **short-term credit.** If the family needs more time to pay, it will pay a certain amount each month until the total has been paid. Most American families use this kind of **long-term credit** to make large purchases, such as homes, automobiles, large appliances, and furniture.

Suppose a family buys so much on credit that it cannot afford to make the payments. The stores may take back their purchases. Or the family may have to declare bankruptcy. **Bankruptcy** is a legal declaration that a person or business cannot pay debts owed. Declaring bankruptcy can hurt a family's credit rating for years. This means that it would be more difficult to obtain loans for purchasing a car, home, or other needed items. As a result, the Federal Reserve Board offers the following advice to people seeking credit:

**Civics Voices**
❝Smart consumers comparison shop for credit, whether they're looking for a mortgage, an auto loan, or a credit card. Comparison shopping . . . could save you money. . . . Find the plan that best fits your spending and repayment habits.❞

✔ **Reading Check** **Summarizing** How can credit be both helpful and harmful? helpful—allows people to pay for large purchases over a long period of time; harmful—overused, may cause those who cannot repay their debts to lose property or even be forced to declare bankruptcy

**Interpreting the Visual Record**

**Going out of business** *Most business owners must take out loans to help get their businesses running. If they are not successful, they may have to sell the business to repay these debts.* **What are some reasons that a business might not be successful?**

## REVIEW AND ASSESS

Have students complete the **Section 1 Review** on page 458. Then have students complete **Daily Quiz 19.1**. As **Alternative Assessment**, you may want to use the new currency design or credit graphic organizer activities in this section's lessons.

## RETEACH

Have students complete **Main Idea Activity for English Language Learners and Special-Needs Students 19.1**. Organize students into three groups and assign each group one of the objectives in this section. Then ask each group to create a set of flash cards to be used as a study guide for the objective that it has been assigned. After groups have finished, ask each group to use its flash cards to quiz the rest of the class.

**ENGLISH LANGUAGE LEARNERS**

## EXTEND

Have students research the availability of credit cards in today's society. Ask them to consult newspapers, magazines, radio, television, or other media to find advertisements for credit cards, and ask them to identify the special offers that banks use to attract new credit card customers. Then ask each student to write a brief argument weighing the pros and cons of having many different types of credit cards available to consumers. Have students present their arguments to the class.

**BLOCK SCHEDULING**

---

### Visual Record Answer

*(for p. 457) Students might suggest that businesses might go bankrupt due to inadequate advertising, failure to meet consumers' needs, or inability to compete with more successful businesses.*

## Section 1 Review
### ANSWERS

**1. Define**
- currency, p. 453
- creditors, p. 457
- short-term credit, p. 457
- long-term credit, p. 457
- bankruptcy, p. 457

**2.** When production is high, credit needs to be increased, making it possible for people to buy goods. When production is low, banks may extend less credit to slow consumer spending so that prices will not rise too rapidly.

**3. a.** easy to carry and take up little space, based on a system of units that are easy to multiply and divide, durable, made in standard form, and guaranteed by government

**b.** not guaranteed by government; accept as promise that sufficient funds exist to cover them

**4.** Students might point out that short-term credit is used for small purchases, and long-term credit is usually used for large purchases. Students might also say that families should not take on more debt than they are able to pay off.

---

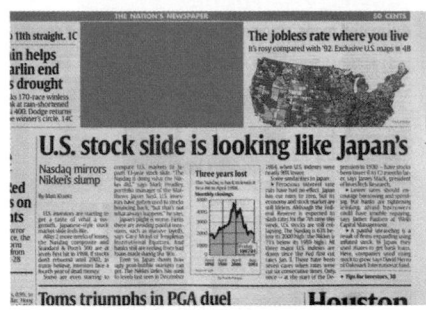

### Interpreting the Visual Record

**Financial news** *Citizens, business leaders, and government officials are all interested in the state of the country's economy.* **Why do you think topics such as inflation or the stock market are important to many Americans?**

### ★ Credit in the Economy

Credit plays several important roles in the buying and selling of goods and services in a free market. It also plays an important role in the successful operation of the U.S. economy as a whole.

In a healthy economic system, the supply of money must increase or decrease in relation to the economy's general condition. When production is high and business is doing well, there must be plenty of money available to consumers. Otherwise, the goods being produced cannot be sold. This would slow production. Slowing production could cut into profits and possibly result in layoffs of workers. Free-flowing money in the form of credit makes it possible for consumers to buy whenever there are goods to be sold.

If too much money is available when production slows, prices may rise too rapidly. That would happen because there would be more money to spend than there were goods to buy. Customers would try to outbid each other to buy the limited supply of goods. To slow consumer spending, banks may extend less credit to customers when production drops. Consumer spending tends to slow when credit is less available. Another option is for banks to raise interest rates on loans that they offer. Higher interest rates discourage people from borrowing money and can also reduce consumer spending. In this way credit helps keep the economy in balance.

The widespread use of credit is possible as a means of exchange because, by and large, most consumers are trustworthy. If buyers and sellers did not trust each other, credit would not be possible.

✔ **Reading Check Finding the Main Idea** How does credit help keep the economy in balance? When production is high, credit helps consumers purchase goods. When production is low, reduced credit can help limit consumer spending and prevent prices from being driven higher.

---

## SECTION 1 Review

**go.hrw.com Homework Practice Online**
keyword: SZ3 HP19

**1. Define** and explain:
- currency
- creditors
- short-term credit
- long-term credit
- bankruptcy

**2. Categorizing** Copy the graphic organizer below. Use it to show how credit can be used to help balance the economy.

Credit

High production → Low production

**3. Finding the Main Idea**
a. What four common features do all currencies have?
b. Why are checks not considered legal tender, and why do businesses accept them?

**4. Writing and Critical Thinking**
**Analyzing Information** Imagine that you are the editor of a financial magazine. Write an article explaining what families should consider when they buy goods on credit.

**Consider:**
- short-term credit
- long-term credit
- the benefits and dangers of credit use

# TEACH

**LEVEL 1:** Have students bring in brochures and other literature explaining various types of checking accounts offered by banks. Point out to students the proper way to fill out a check and lead students in a discussion about the advantages of using checks instead of cash to make purchases and pay bills. (*The advantages of using checks include convenience and safety, since consumers using checks do not need to carry around large amounts of cash.*) Ask students to read their brochures carefully and then ask them to discuss the advantages and disadvantages of different types of checking accounts. Encourage students to support their responses.

**ENGLISH LANGUAGE LEARNERS**

**LEVEL 2:** Have students imagine that they are bank managers who have just opened a new bank in town. Ask each student to create a newspaper advertisement encouraging new customers to open checking accounts. Students' advertisements should list the benefits of having a checking account and should describe any special advantages to opening an account with their bank. Then encourage students to present their advertisements to the rest of the class.

**SKILLS ANSWERS**

1. Doug's Sports Emporium; basketball; $51.28

2. First Cascade Bank; 111 Fifth Street, Boise, Idaho

# Civics Skills
## WORKSHOP

## Writing Checks

As you have learned, checks are a convenient way to make purchases and pay bills. Because a signed check represents money you have in your account, it is important that you follow certain procedures when you write a check.

## How to Write Checks

1. **Examine your checks.** Most checks are printed with the account owner's name and address in the upper left corner. The address listed on the checks should be a valid address where the account holder can be contacted. Near the bottom left side of the check, you will see a series of numbers. The first part of these numbers is the bank's identification number. The second part is your checking account number. Depending upon what you requested, some checks may also include your driver's license number.

2. **Date your checks.** Near the check number is a place for you to write the date.

3. **Tell the bank whom to pay.** In the middle of the left-hand side of the check are the words "Pay to the Order of" and a blank space. By filling in this blank, you indicate to your bank whom you want it to pay from your account.

4. **Write the amount of the payment.** You must write the amount of the check twice—once in figures and once in words.

5. **Sign your checks.** Signing your name on the check authorizes the bank to carry out your wishes. Banks will not accept unsigned checks.

## Applying the Skill

Study the sample check below. Then answer the following questions.

1. To whom is the check written? What did Paul buy? How much did he pay?

2. What is the name of Paul's bank? Where is his bank located?

Payee                                            Check Number

**Paul Martinez**
206 Mountain Drive
Boise, ID 83709

February 12, 2005          2838

23-32250/24

PAY TO THE ORDER OF *Doug's Sport Emporium*      $51.28

*Fifty-one and 28/100*        DOLLARS

First Cascade Bank
111 Fifth Street
Boise, Idaho 83705

FOR *Basketball*            *Paul W. Martinez*

⑆321808168⑆ ⑈029501036⑈ 2838

Your Bank    Bank identification and account numbers           Amount

# SECTION 2

## OBJECTIVES

*After completing Section 2, students should be able to*

**1** Identify the FDIC and describe how it helps depositors.

**2** Determine what caused the savings and loan crisis in the 1980s.

**3** Analyze how and why the Federal Reserve System regulates the amount of money in circulation.

## SECTION 2 RESOURCES

### REPRODUCIBLE

▶ Guided Reading Strategies 19.2

▶ Readings in Economics and Government 46: Depository Institutions and Deregulation Act of 1980

▶ Challenge and Enrichment Worksheet 19: Locating the Federal Reserve Districts

### TECHNOLOGY

▶ One-Stop Planner, Lesson 19.2

▶ Holt Researcher CD–ROM

▶ Homework Practice Online

▶ HRW Go site

### REINFORCEMENT, REVIEW, AND ASSESSMENT

▶ Section 2 Review, p. 466

▶ Daily Quiz 19.2

▶ Main Idea Activity 19.2

▶ English Audio Summary 19.2

▶ Spanish Audio Summary 19.2

## 🔊 *LET'S GET STARTED!*

Write the word *bank* on the chalkboard and as students enter the classroom, ask them to think of different services that banks provide. Invite students to come to the chalkboard and write some of the reasons that banks are important to individual consumers as well as to the overall economy. *(Students' answers should mention the usefulness of checking and savings accounts as well as the importance of being able to take out loans and mortgages.)* Tell students that in Section 2 they will learn more about banks and banking.

---

# SECTION 2

# Banks and Banking

## Read to Discover

1. What is the FDIC, and how does it help depositors?
2. What caused the savings and loan crisis in the 1980s?
3. How and why does the Federal Reserve System regulate the amount of money in circulation?

### WHY CIVICS MATTERS

Many people pay close attention to the actions of the Federal Reserve. Use **CNNfyi.com** or other **current events** sources to learn about recent economic actions that the Federal Reserve has taken. Record your findings in your journal.

## Define

- collateral
- savings and loan associations
- credit unions
- discounting
- discount rate

## Identify

- Federal Reserve System

## *Reading Focus*

Money presented problems for many people 1,000 years ago just as it does today. In fact, money was even a problem for the wealthy. Wealthy people had difficulty finding a safe place to keep their riches. Carrying it made them the target of thieves. Hiding it in their homes did not guarantee its safety either.

### ★ How Banking Began

In most communities, however, there were goldsmiths who kept their wealth heavily guarded. Because gold was so valuable, the goldsmiths kept it in strong sturdy safes.

In time, the townspeople began to bring their money to the goldsmiths for safekeeping. Before long, local goldsmiths had entered the money-keeping business, charging a small fee for the service.

Eventually, goldsmiths began providing moneylending services. Townspeople who needed money came to the goldsmiths for loans. In return for the loans, they signed a paper promising to repay the money by a certain date and to pay interest for using the money.

Borrowers guaranteed their loans by promising to give their property to the moneylender if the loans were not repaid on time. Property used to guarantee that a loan will be repaid is called **collateral.** Over time, these moneylending practices developed into the banking system we know today.

*European moneylenders were able to amass fortunes.*

# TEACH OBJECTIVE 1

**LEVEL 1:** Lead students in a discussion about how the Federal Deposit Insurance Corporation (FDIC) helps depositors. *(The FDIC is a government agency that encourages people to put their money in banks by insuring each depositor up to $100,000.)* Then ask each student to draw a diagram illustrating the purpose of the FDIC. Encourage students to create an image or symbol representing this purpose. *(For example, students might represent the FDIC as a giant safety net under a bank vault.)* Display these diagrams around the classroom. **ENGLISH LANGUAGE LEARNERS**

**LEVEL 2:** Ask students to imagine that they have met someone from a foreign country where there is no banking system. Have each student write a letter to this person, describing what a bank is, what it does, and why banks are important to consumers and the economy as a whole. Also, ask students to explain what the FDIC is and how it helps depositors. *(Students' letters will vary, but they should mention that banks provide a safe place to store money and also offer important financial services, such as making loans and extending credit. Also, students' letters should mention that depositors are insured by the FDIC for up to $100,000.)* Invite volunteers to read their letters to the class.

Most people rely on banks for their checking and savings accounts. Although depositors usually do not earn interest on regular checking accounts, they can easily access the money in these accounts. Money deposited in a checking account is called a demand deposit. That is, the bank must give depositors their money when they request, or demand, it by writing checks. Many banks also issue customers automated teller machine (ATM) cards. These cards allow them to withdraw cash from their accounts at various locations at any time of day.

Money deposited in a savings account is called a time deposit. Most banks require depositors to keep the money in their accounts for a minimum period of time. Savings accounts pay interest to depositors. The amount of interest paid depends on the type of account.

An increasingly popular type of bank account combines checking and savings—the negotiable order of withdrawal (NOW) account. With a NOW account, the customer can write checks and receive interest on the money in the account. Most banks require depositors to maintain a certain minimum balance in their NOW accounts.

✔ **Reading Check Contrasting** What is the difference between a demand deposit account and a time deposit account? demand deposit—can withdraw money on demand, usually earn no interest; time deposit—earn interest, must leave money in bank for a set time period

## ⭐ Types of Banks

A bank chartered under state laws is a state bank. One chartered under federal laws is a national bank. The type of charter determines whether the bank is supervised by state or federal officials. It also determines many of the rules that guide the bank.

There are four main types of banks in the United States—commercial banks, savings and loan associations, savings banks, and credit unions. Although the differences among these banks have blurred in recent years, some important distinctions remain.

**Commercial Banks** The most numerous banks in the United States are commercial banks, which offer a full range of services. Commercial banks offer checking, savings, and NOW accounts. They make loans to individuals and businesses. They issue credit cards and manage retirement accounts. They also have departments that help customers manage property and invest money.

Accounts in commercial banks are insured by a government agency called the Federal Deposit Insurance Corporation (FDIC). Each depositor is insured up to $100,000. This means that if for some reason a bank is unable to give its depositors their money, the FDIC will refund up to $100,000 per depositor.

Like corporations, commercial banks are owned by stockholders who buy shares in the bank. Stockholders, also called shareholders, receive cash dividends from the profits made by the bank.

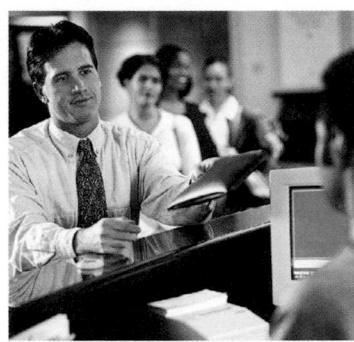

*When people deposit money into a checking account, they expect to be able to withdraw it whenever necessary.*

**Interpreting the Visual Record**

**ATMs** *ATM machines have become a very popular way for people to withdraw cash at any time.* **What is the benefit of using an ATM?**

**LEVEL 3:** Remind students that the FDIC insures depositors for up to $100,000. Then ask students to imagine that the FDIC no longer exists and that depositors' accounts are no longer insured. Ask each student to write a short story about what might happen if there were a financial crisis (such as a stock market crash) and banks were not able to give depositors any of their money. What would happen if people could no longer write checks or make withdrawals from savings accounts? *(Students' stories should discuss how this situation would not only harm individual consumers but also hurt stores and businesses.)* Invite volunteers to read their stories to the class.

**HOMEWORK** Ask students to find out how many different banks and bank branches there are in their community. Then have students identify the different types of banks. Ask each student to compile a descriptive list, and have him or her draw conclusions about what the number and types of banks indicate about the local economy.

## ★ Economics

**Making Change** The U.S. Treasury oversees the Bureau of Printing and Engraving (BPE), which produces approximately 52.5 million coins each day. Most coins are made at the Philadelphia and Denver mints, although mints at San Francisco and West Point, New York, also produce some of these coins. In addition, BPE branches in Washington, D.C., and in Fort Worth, Texas, print about 37 million bills per day, worth about $696 million. Of these bills, 45 percent are $1 bills. Ninety-five percent of the bills printed each day are made to replace worn and damaged currency. Over the years, certain denominations have been taken out of circulation by the Fed and are no longer produced by the BPE: the half-cent coin, 2-cent coin, 3-cent coin, half-dime, 20-cent coin, and various gold coins.

### CRITICAL THINKING

Why is it necessary for the Federal Reserve to remove some denominations from circulation?

**ANSWER:** Students might suggest that changing financial conditions and the changing needs of consumers determine the types of currency needed.

## Visual Record Answer

*Students might suggest that the large amounts of money and valuable items stored at banks would be an easy target for thieves if banks did not have secure vaults.*

**Interpreting the Visual Record**

**The vault** *Large banks often store money and valuable items—kept in safety deposit boxes—in highly secure vaults like this one.* **Why do you think banks find security like this necessary?**

## Holt Researcher

**go.hrw.com**
**KEYWORD: Holt Researcher**

**Freefind:** Banking and the Government

Search through the listings of executive agencies that deal with banking issues on the Holt Researcher. Then use this information to create a timeline showing when each agency was created and what its primary responsibilities are. Your timeline should describe how the federal government is involved in the U.S. banking system.

**Savings and Loan Associations** Banks known as **savings and loan associations** began in the mid-1800s to help people buy homes. They still account for a large percentage of home mortgage loans. In recent years, however, federal regulations have allowed them to expand their services. They now offer many of the services that commercial banks do. In addition to obtaining loans, customers can open checking, savings, and NOW accounts and can apply for credit cards.

In the past, almost all savings and loans were owned and operated by their depositors. Today nearly half of them are owned and operated by shareholders.

Until 1989, deposits in savings and loans were insured by the Federal Savings and Loan Insurance Corporation (FSLIC). During the 1980s, however, many of these banks were involved in risky loans, bad investments, and fraud. As a result, hundreds of savings and loans throughout the country failed. This event became known as the savings and loan crisis.

Faced with paying the costs of these failures, the FSLIC ran out of money. The government passed the FSLIC's insurance obligations on to the FDIC. It also formed the Resolution Trust Corporation (RTC) to sort out the savings and loan crisis. By August 1994 the RTC had straightened out more than 730 savings and loans. In 1999 the total cost to taxpayers was estimated at nearly $165 billion.

**Savings Banks** Savings banks began in the early 1800s to encourage savings by people who could make only very small deposits. Today these banks offer a variety of services, including home loans. Most savings banks are located in the northeastern region of the United States. As with commercial banks, deposits in savings banks are insured by the FDIC up to a maximum of $100,000 per depositor.

# TEACH OBJECTIVE 2

**ALL LEVELS:** Copy the following graphic organizer onto the chalkboard, omitting the italicized answers. Have students complete the organizer by showing the causes and effects of the savings and loan crisis in the 1980s.

**Causes**

*risky loans* →

*bad investments* → **Savings and Loan Crisis**

*fraud* →

**Effects**

*The FSLIC runs out of money.*

*The FDIC takes on FSLIC's obligations.*

*The Resolution Trust Corp. (RTC) is formed.*

*The total cost to taxpayers is nearly $165 billion.*

---

Prior to the mid-1980s most savings banks were called mutual savings banks. At that time, they passed on their profits to depositors in the form of interest. Now, however, many savings banks are owned by shareholders who receive dividends from the profits. Shareholders elect a board of directors to manage the daily operations of the bank.

**Credit Unions** Most **credit unions** are established by people who work for the same company or belong to the same organization. Credit unions are owned and operated by their members. When members make deposits, they buy interest-paying shares in the credit union. These deposits are pooled to make low-interest loans available to members. Depositors may also write checks, which are called share drafts.

Deposits in credit unions are insured by a government agency called the National Credit Union Association (NCUA). Each depositor is insured up to $100,000.

✔ **Reading Check** **Summarizing** What are the characteristics of the different kinds of banks? commercial banks—full range of financial services; savings and loan associations—specialize in home loans but offer other services; savings banks—specialize in small depositors, now expanding services; credit unions—full services but owned and operated by members

## ★ George McClain Gets a Bank Loan

What happens when a person borrows money from a bank? Consider the example of George McClain, who owns and operates a small gas station. George needs $5,000 to buy some new equipment. He visits a commercial bank to speak to a loan officer. The loan officer tells George that he probably will receive the loan. However, George must show that he is a good credit risk.

George brings in his business records, which show that his gas station makes a profit. George also points out that he owns his home and has no large business debts. This information convinces the bank that George will be able to repay the loan. The bank agrees to make the loan using George's house as collateral.

Some commercial bank loans are short-term loans that must be repaid in 30, 60, or 90 days. George receives a short-term loan of $5,000, due in 90 days. George does not receive the full $5,000 credit, however. The bank deducts a small sum in advance as the interest it is charging for the loan. It deposits the remainder as a credit in George's checking account. Deducting the interest on a loan in advance is known as **discounting.**

After he receives the loan, George buys the new equipment. He can now offer better service to his customers, which should help him

*George McClain's gas station might look something like this one. Small business owners in different fields face many similar financial challenges and responsibilities.*

★★★★★★★★★★★★
### That's Interesting!
★★★★★★★★★★★★

In 1795 the reverse half of the eagle silver dollar showed the main features of the Great Seal of the United States, on which appears the inscription *E Pluribus Unum*, meaning "One Out of Many." In 1873 the inscription was required on all coins.

**LEVEL 2:** Organize students into small groups and ask each group to imagine that it is a member of the Resolution Trust Corporation, which was formed to address the savings and loan crisis. Within groups, assign each student a specific role, such as writer, illustrator, or presenter. Then tell each group that it should create a chart or diagram explaining what caused the savings and loan crisis of the 1980s, why the RTC was formed, and what its purpose was. *(Each group will have somewhat different reports, but each should explain the causes of the savings and loan crisis.)* Ask each group to present its report to the class.

**COOPERATIVE LEARNING**

**LEVEL 3:** Ask students to pretend that they are reporters investigating how the savings and loan crisis of the 1980s affected their local community. Have each student write a front-page newspaper article describing some of the causes and consequences of the crisis. Areas of interest might include local bank failures or individuals and local businesses that were harmed by the national crisis. *(Students' articles will vary, but each article should mention risky loans, bad investments, and fraud as contributing causes. Students should also indicate that the inability of the FSLIC to bail out depositors made the situation even worse.)* Ask volunteers to read their articles to the class.

**🖳 internet** connect

**TOPIC:** The Banking System
**GO TO:** go.hrw.com
**KEYWORD:** SZ3 AC19

Have students access the Internet through the HRW Go site to research historical figures associated with the banking system in the United States. Then ask each student to choose one figure as a subject for a short biographical sketch. Ask volunteers to present their biographies to the class.

---

**BIOGRAPHY ANSWER**
Greenspan influences the national economy through his words and actions, such as raising interest rates to curb inflation during times of economic growth.

---

## BIOGRAPHY

### Alan Greenspan
#### (1926– )

Alan Greenspan was born in New York City. As a child growing up during the Great Depression, he developed an interest in mathematics and music. He studied music at the Juilliard School and played in a swing band before enrolling in New York University at the age of 19 to study economics. Upon graduating he helped start a financial consulting firm in 1954.

In the 1970s Greenspan served as chairman of the President's Council of Economic Advisers under President Gerald Ford before returning to business. President Ronald Reagan appointed Greenspan as the chairman of the Federal Reserve in 1987. Greenspan has held this office through four presidencies. As chairman, he has enormous influence over the national economy through both his actions and his words. Greenspan's knowledge of the national economy is widely respected. He has favored a tightly controlled money policy, attempting to curb inflation by raising interest rates during times of economic growth. During his time in public office, Greenspan has also served as a corporate director for many major U.S. companies and as a member or officer in many private economic organizations. **How does Greenspan influence the national economy?**

---

make more money. In turn, the equipment company uses the money it got from George and other customers to expand its business. In this way, credit circulates throughout the U.S. economy.

✔ **Reading Check Analyzing Information** How does George McClain's credit help the U.S. economy grow? When George borrows money to buy new equipment, his business helps the equipment company grow, which helps more companies grow, and so on.

## ★ Renewing the Loan

What happens when the loan is due at the end of the 90-day period? If George's business has done well, he can repay the loan. But suppose the new equipment was late in arriving, or business did not increase quite as fast as expected. George may have to go to the bank and ask that his loan be renewed, or continued. If the bank agrees, George will not have to repay the loan for another 90 days.

Usually, a bank will renew a loan to a person like George, whose credit is good. George, of course, will have to pay additional interest on the loan renewal.

Suppose, however, that bank officials think George has done a poor job managing his business with the new equipment. They may decide he is no longer a good risk and may refuse to renew the loan. George must then find some way to repay the loan at once. To save his house, which is the collateral for his loan, he may have to sell his car or other possessions. He may even have to sell his business. As you can see, a loan involves a risk for the borrower as well as the bank.

✔ **Reading Check Identifying Cause and Effect** Why might George not be able to repay his loan on time, and what might happen if he does not? If business has not increased enough, George might not have the money to repay the loan. He might have to sell his business or personal property.

## ★ Government Regulation

At one time, banks were allowed to conduct business with few rules. As a result, they sometimes loaned money without requesting enough collateral in return. In addition, they sometimes did not keep enough money in reserve.

Under these conditions, rumors might spread that the bank was shaky. Depositors would start a "run" on the bank. That is, people would panic, go to the bank, and demand their money. If too many depositors withdrew their money at once the bank would have no funds left. (Remember, banks use some of their funds to make loans.) As a result, some depositors would lose their money when the bank failed.

# TEACH OBJECTIVE 3

**LEVEL 1:** Lead students in a discussion about how and why the Federal Reserve System regulates the amount of money in circulation. *(The Federal Reserve System determines the circulation of money in the economy through its 12 branches. Money must be kept in circulation so that individuals and businesses can participate in a growing economy, but too much money in circulation can cause inflation.)* Ask each student to draw a web diagram showing the 12 Federal Reserve districts with the Fed at its center. Then have students fill in their webs with explanations or symbolic representations of the duties assigned to the Fed. **ENGLISH LANGUAGE LEARNERS**

**LEVEL 3:** Organize students into groups and ask them to imagine that it is 1913. Then tell students that they are members of a committee that must write a proposal to convince Congress of the need to establish the Federal Reserve System. Have each group consider arguments showing the need for such a system, and ask groups to think of ways to organize the Fed and its responsibilities. Then ask each group to write a report and accompany it with visual aids. **COOPERATIVE LEARNING**

## CLOSE

Have students write an editorial for a fictional banking magazine supporting or opposing banking regulation.

---

To prevent such bank failures, the federal government created a plan to regulate U.S. banking. In 1913 Congress established the **Federal Reserve System.** All national banks were required to belong to this system. State banks were permitted to join the system if they wished, and many did.

For many years the Federal Reserve had direct control over only its member banks. For example, only member banks were required to keep part of their deposits on reserve with "the Fed," as the system is called. Then in 1980 a law was passed stating that all U.S. banks must meet the Fed's requirements.

✔ **Reading Check Analyzing Information** Why did the U.S. government decide to regulate banks, and how did it do this? Worried depositors sometimes withdrew all their funds from a bank rumored to be shaky, leaving the bank with no funds. The federal government established the Federal Reserve System to regulate banking and prevent such situations.

## ★ The Federal Reserve System

The Federal Reserve System divides the United States into 12 Federal Reserve districts. A Federal Reserve bank is located in each district. Federal Reserve banks do not usually do business with individuals or business firms. Instead, they act as bankers for the federal government and for other banks.

Federal Reserve banks serve two main purposes. First, they handle the banking needs of the federal government. The secretary of the U.S. Treasury deposits government funds in these banks. The secretary writes checks on the federal government's account, just as an individual uses his or her personal checking account. The Federal Reserve banks also handle the sale of bonds issued by the government. In addition, most U.S. currency is put into circulation through the Federal Reserve System. From these banks the money spreads out into the economy for use by businesses and consumers.

Second, the 12 Federal Reserve banks provide various services to state and national banks and control the banking system. Even banks have to borrow money sometimes. A member bank can go to the Federal Reserve bank in its district and borrow money to increase its own reserve. Doing so allows the member bank to make more loans or investments. The bank must pay interest on the loans it receives from the Federal Reserve, just like individuals or businesses. The rate of interest charged to member banks by the Federal Reserve is called the **discount rate.** This rate often influences the interest rates charged by these banks to their own customers.

✔ **Reading Check Summarizing** What are the primary functions of the Federal Reserve banks? to handle the banking needs of the federal government and state and national banks

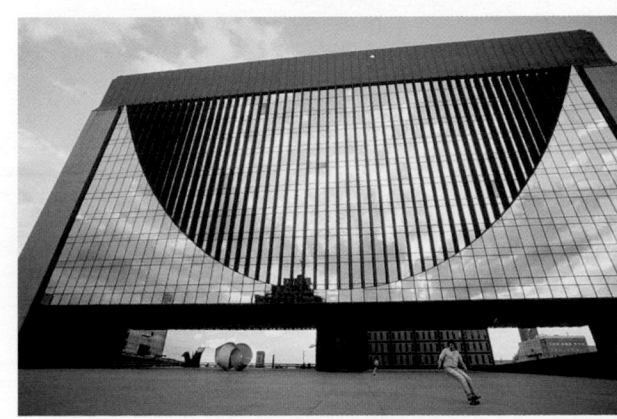

*Federal Reserve banks help provide stability for the country's banking system.*

# REVIEW AND ASSESS

Have students complete the **Section 1 Review** on page 466. Then have them complete **Daily Quiz 19.2**. As **Alternative Assessment**, you may want to use the flowchart or the web exercises in this section's lessons.

# RETEACH

Have students complete **Main Idea Activity for English Language Learners and Special-Needs Students 19.2**. Then organize students into three groups and assign each group one of the objectives in this section. Ask each group to diagram the main points of the objective that it has been assigned. After groups have finished, ask them to present their diagrams to the class, and then keep these diagrams in a file for students to use as a review. **ENGLISH LANGUAGE LEARNERS**, **COOPERATIVE LEARNING**

# EXTEND

Organize students into pairs. Then have pairs develop proposals to organize and operate a Students' Savings Bank in your school. Students should decide the operating rules of the bank, the tracking system for deposits and withdrawals, ways the safety of the deposits can be guaranteed, and rules regarding loans. The written proposals should include graphics, such as charts, that help explain the structure and policies of the bank. **BLOCK SCHEDULING**, **COOPERATIVE LEARNING**

## Section 2 Review
### ANSWERS

**1. Define**
- collateral, p. 460
- savings and loan associations, p. 462
- credit unions, p. 463
- discounting, p. 463
- discount rate, p. 465

**2. Identify**
- Federal Reserve System, p. 465

**3.** When the Fed puts more money into circulation, prices rise and the economy grows. When the Fed takes money out of circulation, banks have less money to lend and individuals have less money to spend.

**4. a.** Federal Deposit Insurance Corporation; insures depositors' accounts for up to $100,000

**b.** risky loans, bad investments, and fraud

**5.** Students' lessons will vary but should consider how the Fed provides services as the banker for the U.S. government and for other state and national banks.

**Interpreting the Visual Record**

**Federal Reserve chairman** *Alan Greenspan (at right) plays an important role in determining the policy of the Federal Reserve.* **Why would business leaders and government officials pay attention to Greenspan's actions?**

## ★ The Federal Reserve at Work

The Federal Reserve System is managed by a seven-member board of governors in Washington, D.C. Each member is appointed by the president, with the consent of the Senate, for a single 14-year term. The board of governors makes most of the major decisions for the Federal Reserve System.

Through its influence over the banking system, the Fed tries to keep the right amount of money in circulation. When the economy is growing and more goods and services are being produced, more money is needed in circulation. The additional money allows businesses and individuals to take part in a growing economy.

When the supply of money grows faster than the supply of goods, prices tend to rise. To prevent this, the Federal Reserve may try to slow the growth of the money supply or even take money out of circulation.

If the Federal Reserve wants to speed economic growth, it puts more money into circulation. It usually does this by buying U.S. government bonds from banks or individuals. These banks or people then have more money to spend or lend. This money soon enters the economy through purchases or loans. To take money out of circulation, the Federal Reserve sells government bonds back to banks or people. These individuals or banks then have less money to spend or lend.

✔ **Reading Check** **Analyzing Information** How does the Federal Reserve regulate the economy? controls how much money is in circulation, can increase the money flow to stimulate the economy or restrict the money flow to slow economic growth

---

## SECTION 2 Review

**Homework Practice Online** go.hrw.com
keyword: SZ3 HP19

**1. Define** and explain:
- collateral
- savings and loan associations
- credit unions
- discounting
- discount rate

**2. Identify** and explain:
- Federal Reserve System

**3. Summarizing** Copy the diagram below. Use it to show how the Federal Reserve keeps the right amount of money in circulation.

Fed Action → Result

To speed economic growth →

To slow economic growth →

**4. Finding the Main Idea**
a. Explain what the FDIC is and how it protects depositors.
b. What led to the savings and loan crisis that occurred during the 1980s?

**5. Writing and Critical Thinking**
**Summarizing** Imagine that you are an economics professor teaching a course to future bankers. Prepare a lesson on the purpose of the Federal Reserve banks.

**Consider:**
- services that Federal Reserve banks provide to the U.S. government
- services that Federal Reserve banks provide to state and national banks

# SECTION 3

## OBJECTIVES

*After completing Section 3, students should be able to*

1 **Explain why it is important to save money.**

2 **Identify some of the ways people save and invest their money.**

3 **Evaluate how saving money helps the U.S. economy.**

## 🔊 LET'S GET STARTED!

As students enter the classroom, organize them into three or four groups. Then ask students to think of different ways that they could save and invest their money, and ask each group to compile a list of savings and investment strategies. *(Students should consider ways of reducing personal spending through budgeting as well as ways of increasing their savings by placing money in savings accounts or other investment accounts.)* Tell students that in Section 3 they will learn more about the importance of saving money as well as the basics about saving and investing.

---

## SECTION 3

# Saving and Investing

### Read to Discover

1. Why is it important to save money?
2. What are some ways people save and invest their money?
3. How does saving money help the U.S. economy?

### Define

- certificates of deposit (CDs)
- brokers
- stock exchange
- mutual funds
- money market funds

#### WHY CIVICS MATTERS

Millions of Americans invest in companies through stock markets, such as the New York Stock Exchange or the NASDAQ. Use **CNNfyi.com** or other **current events** sources to examine the recent performance of the stock markets or the stock of a major corporation. Record your findings in your journal.

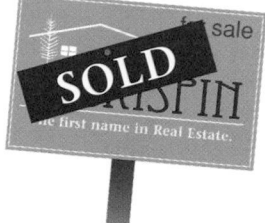

## Reading Focus

Most of us would like more money to spend. But even if we had more money, we might not have an immediate need to spend it. Fortunately, one of the features of money is that it can be stored and spent later. Most people set aside some money in case they have unexpected expenses. Keeping money by setting it aside is called saving. Saving is important for individuals, businesses, and the country.

### ★ Why People Save

Almost everyone saves or tries to save. Families set aside money for their children's education or to buy a house. They save money in case of emergencies, such as medical bills, loss of a job, or other unexpected difficulties. People save money for their retirement years. Saving is an important part of knowing how to manage money wisely.

Why do we need to save money? The credit system in the United States allows people to buy goods and services without paying cash for them at the time of purchase. However, even when using credit, the customer often has to make a large down payment in cash.

The largest purchases most people make are houses and cars. To buy a house, you must first pay a certain percentage of the total cost in cash as a down payment. Builders may advertise, "Only 10 percent down." Ten percent of the cost of an $85,000 house is still a large sum, however—$8,500. The average family has to save a long time to reach $8,500.

*Many families in the United States make saving for a college education a financial priority.*

**LEVEL 1:** Lead students in a discussion about the importance of saving money on a regular basis. Encourage students to think about the consequences of not saving money. On the chalkboard, list the benefits of saving money in one column and list the disadvantages of not saving money in another column. *(Students' responses will vary but should indicate that people who do not save money may be unable to make large purchases requiring down payments, or they may find themselves unprepared in the event of a crisis.)*

**ENGLISH LANGUAGE LEARNERS**

**LEVEL 3:** Have each student write a short poem about saving money. Some students may choose to write about how saving money is beneficial to individual consumers and good for the U.S. economy overall. Others might choose to write about the problems or consequences people might encounter if they do not save for a rainy day. Encourage students to be creative. Tell each student to target an audience, such as teenagers or young adults, in his or her poem. *(Poems will vary but each should attempt to teach a lesson about saving money.)* Call on volunteers to read their poems to the class and ask students to identify key points from each poem for a class discussion.

## ★ Economics

**Buying a House** Many people who are saving to buy a house are often concerned with being able to save enough to make the required down payment. But they might also consider how monthly house payments will affect their ability to save. For a 30-year mortgage on an $80,000 home loan at a 10 percent interest rate, the buyers will end up paying $702.06 per month (not including taxes and insurance on the home). Lenders commonly require that a monthly payment be no more than 28 percent of their monthly gross income. Thus, buyers applying for an $80,000 home loan at 10 percent interest would need a total annual income of at least $30,088.

**ACTIVITY** Ask students to conduct research to obtain more information about calculating, on average, what the down payment and monthly costs at the current interest rate would be if they were to buy a home in their community. Also, have them determine what their annual income would need to be in order to afford the mortgage payments.

## Visual Record Answer

*Students might suggest that people buy used cars because they are less expensive than new cars.*

**Interpreting the Visual Record**

**Used cars** *When shopping for used cars, buyers must be careful to choose a payment plan that fits their budget.* **Why do you think people buy used cars?**

Used-car dealers may advertise, "No money down, drive it home today!" Without a down payment, however, the monthly payments on an automobile will be higher. Also, the smaller the down payment, the greater the amount of interest charged on the loan. The extra interest will make the total cost of the car higher. Thus, saving money throughout one's lifetime is wise for everyone.

✔ **Reading Check Drawing Inferences and Conclusions** What would be the advantage of saving money for a down payment on a car even if no down payment is required? Students should say that a down payment allows people to take out a smaller loan and therefore make smaller payments.

## ★ How People Save

There are various ways to save money. You can hide your money under a mattress, put it in a cookie jar, or keep it in a piggy bank. People also buy gold, silver, jewels, paintings, sculptures, antiques, and other valuable items as a form of saving. They hope the value of these items will increase over time. If the buyer is wise or lucky, sometimes this strategy can make him or her a great deal of money. However, the value of such items can also decrease. Most Americans find that there are easier and better ways to save money.

Many Americans set aside a regular amount in a savings account each week or each month. The bank pays interest on all money deposited in a savings account. In this way, a person's money earns more money for him or her. The money can be withdrawn when it is needed.

Regular savings accounts are sometimes called passbook accounts. Some banks give depositors a small book, or passbook, in which to record their deposits and withdrawals. Regular savings accounts usually require the customer to keep only a small minimum balance. However, some banks charge a service fee if the account falls below the minimum balance or if the customer exceeds a set number of transactions within a specific time period.

**Certificates of deposit (CDs)** are issued by banks and other financial institutions. Savers invest a certain amount of money for a specified period of time. Most CDs are issued in units of $1,000 or more. The interest to be paid when the CD matures is set at the time of purchase and usually remains constant. CDs can have terms lasting weeks, months, or years. Usually, the longer the money is invested, the higher the interest paid on the CD. Investors who withdraw their money before the end of the specified term lose a percentage of the interest.

✔ **Reading Check Analyzing Information** Why might banks require a minimum balance in a savings account or a specified length of time for deposits to remain in a CD? In both cases the bank benefits by having access to the customer's money to help pay its operating costs.

**ALL LEVELS:** Copy the following graphic organizer onto the chalkboard, omitting the italicized answers. Have students complete the organizer by listing the different ways of saving and investing money. Then, have students fill in the oval at the bottom to indicate the reasons that people should save money.

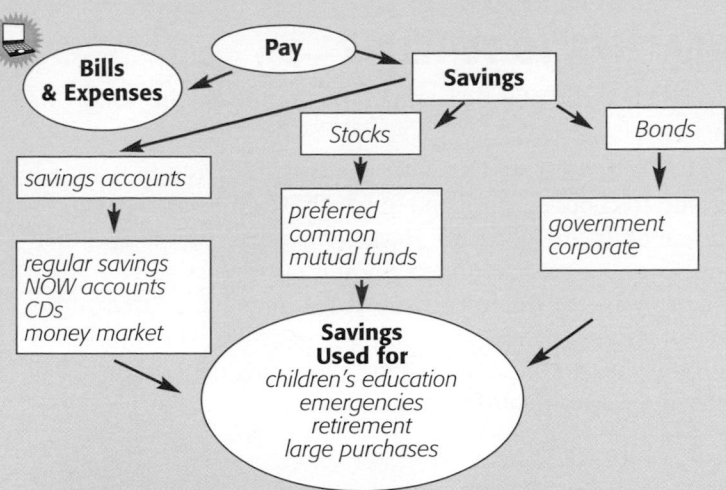

## ★ Stocks and Bonds

Another way for people to save for the future is to invest their money. Stocks and bonds are two of the most popular investments.

**Buying Bonds** You may remember that bonds are certificates of debt issued by governments and corporations to people who lend them money. When the bond reaches maturity, you get the money back plus interest it has earned.

U.S. government bonds, as well as the bonds of most states, localities, and corporations, are a relatively safe form of savings. In most cases, bondholders receive regular interest payments.

One form of bond, the U.S. savings bond, does not pay interest until it is cashed in by the bondholder. For example, a savings bond bought for $100 earns $100 in interest after an average of 12 years. The purchaser who paid $100 for a bond receives nearly $200 when he or she cashes it in. Meanwhile, the buyer's money is safe because the federal government repays its debt. However, the interest rate for savings bonds is usually not as high as it is for many other kinds of investments because there is less risk involved.

✔ **Reading Check Finding the Main Idea** What are bonds, and what is one of their advantages for investors? certificates of debt issued by governments and corporations to people who lend them money; relatively safe form of savings

**Buying Stocks** You read about common stocks and preferred stocks in Chapter 17. Business organizations known as brokerage houses buy and sell stocks for their customers. The people employed by brokerage houses are called **brokers.** Each brokerage house is a member of a stock exchange. Millions of shares of stock are bought and sold every working day at a **stock exchange.** One of the most influential stock exchanges in the world is the New York Stock Exchange in New York City.

Anyone can buy stocks by getting in touch with a brokerage house. In addition, people can easily buy and sell stocks via the Internet. However, people should know a great deal about the stock market before buying stocks. Stock prices depend on expectations of how well a company will perform in the future, making stocks a relatively risky investment.

People who buy common stocks are taking a chance. They hope their investment will earn more money than it would earn in a savings account or a bond purchase. Annual stock dividends may be higher than interest earned from a savings account or a bond. Also, if the value of a stock rises in the stock exchange, the stock can be sold at profit. However, stocks often pay small dividends or none at all. Moreover, their value on the stock market may fall.

To reduce the amount of risk in stock purchases, many people buy shares in **mutual funds.** These funds are managed by people who are

### Interpreting the Visual Record

**Bonds** *Federal bonds are backed by the full faith and credit of the national government.* **Why does the federal government issue bonds?**

### ★★★★★★★★★★★★
## That's Interesting!
### ★★★★★★★★★★★★

**Why "Wall Street"?** Did you know that the New York Stock Exchange (NYSE) began in 1792 as a group of stockbrokers meeting to trade stocks under a tree? It's true! The tree has long since vanished, but it is believed to have stood somewhere near what is now 11 Wall Street, the current location of the NYSE. By the way, Wall Street was named for the boundary stockade, or wall, that Dutch colonists built in 1653 for protection from English colonists and American Indians.

## ★ Global Perspectives

**Stock Markets around the World** If asked to name a stock exchange, many Americans would probably think of the New York Stock Exchange (NYSE). But many other countries have well-established stock exchanges as well. Investors pay particular attention to averages that indicate trends in the overall value of stocks in a particular stock exchange. Indexes in other countries include the Nikkei in Tokyo, the DAX in Frankfurt, the CAC 40 in Paris, Australia's All Ordinaries index in Sydney, and the *Financial Times* Stock Exchange 100 in London. Stock exchanges do not exist only in wealthy countries. Brazil, India, Thailand, Malaysia, Turkey, and many other countries with capitalist economic systems have what are termed "emerging markets." The People's Republic of China, a communist country with a mixed economy, also has created a stock exchange.

**ACTIVITY** Ask students to choose a foreign stock exchange and then have them conduct research to find out how the index of that stock exchange's average value is calculated. Have students write a brief report explaining what they have learned.

### Visual Record Answer

*Students should suggest that the federal government issues bonds to raise some of the money needed to pay its expenses.*

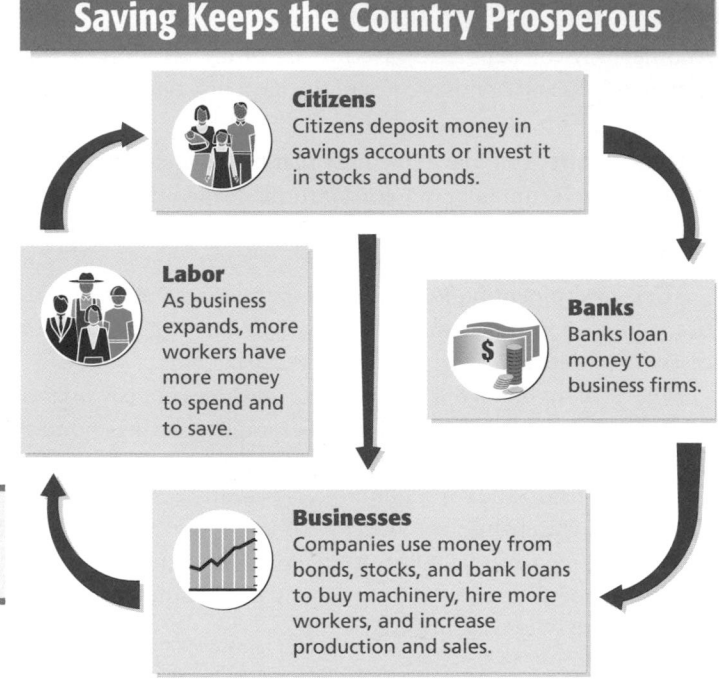

**Saving Keeps the Country Prosperous**

**Citizens** Citizens deposit money in savings accounts or invest it in stocks and bonds.

**Banks** Banks loan money to business firms.

**Businesses** Companies use money from bonds, stocks, and bank loans to buy machinery, hire more workers, and increase production and sales.

**Labor** As business expands, more workers have more money to spend and to save.

**Interpreting Charts** *Saving and investing money helps keep the economy growing.* **How do saving and investing help businesses?**

familiar with stock market conditions. Because mutual fund managers buy many different stocks, the risk in any one stock is not so great. By buying a share in a mutual fund, the purchaser owns a small piece of a large number of stocks.

Before buying shares in a mutual fund, however, consumers should research the fund. They should determine what stocks the fund holds, its performance over time, and its management. A mutual fund that is poorly managed can be risky.

**Money market funds,** like mutual funds, buy stocks that most individuals could not purchase alone. Savers can withdraw their money at any time. Money market funds do not guarantee a specified amount of interest. The rate of interest may rise or fall. Moreover, this form of saving is not insured by the government.

✔ **Reading Check Drawing Inferences and Conclusions** List some of the things that you think a person should take into consideration before investing in the stock market. A potential investor should understand the risks of the stock market and the background of the company invested in.

## ★ Savings in the Economy

What happens to the money that Americans have in savings accounts, bonds, stocks, and other forms of saving? That money is used to help expand the U.S. economy. How does saving promote such growth?

# TEACH OBJECTIVE 3

**LEVEL 1:** Lead a class discussion about how saving money helps the U.S. economy. *(The discussion should include a description of how banks use money deposited into savings accounts to make loans to growing businesses, which in turn employ more workers, who then use their pay to make purchases and investments.)* Organize students into pairs, and then ask each pair to create a poster that uses symbols to represent the different ways that the economy benefits from the savings of individual consumers. *(For example, pairs might draw a picture of a factory to show how loans funded by consumer savings help keep businesses running.)* Display the posters around the classroom. **ENGLISH LANGUAGE LEARNERS , COOPERATIVE LEARNING**

**ALL LEVELS:** Organize the class into large groups. Have groups imagine that they are board members of a bank or investment firm that is having difficulty enticing people to open savings accounts or to invest money. Ask each group to write a brief advertising campaign that encourages people to save money or make investments. *(Groups' plans will vary but should include information about offering high interest rates on savings accounts, free checking, or low fees on investment transactions.)* Invite volunteers to read their business plans to the class. **ENGLISH LANGUAGE LEARNERS , COOPERATIVE LEARNING**

---

Economic growth occurs when factories and other means of production are continually expanded. However, expanding the means of production requires capital to pay for new factories, machine tools, and other capital goods. (You read about capital in Chapter 17.) But what is the source of this capital?

It comes from savings. Suppose you have $10. You spend $5 of it and put the other $5 in a bank. The $5 you spend represents goods that you consume. That is, you spend the money on something you want. However, you do not consume the $5 you deposit in the bank, which in turn can be invested. The bank can use this money to make loans to businesspeople. In this way, savings provide capital for the continued growth of production.

✔ **Reading Check** Finding the Main Idea How does saving lead to economic growth? Banks use individuals' savings to lend money to people and businesses, who use these loans to expand their businesses.

## ★ Raising Capital

Saving and investing are not the same. Money in a piggy bank is saved, but it is not invested. Money you deposit in a savings account is both saved and invested. It is saved by you and invested by the bank. Similarly, when you buy stocks, bonds, CDs, and money market funds, you are saving and investing. All of these methods use your money to finance economic growth.

When you invest, you turn your money into capital. Instead of the money being spent on daily needs, it is used by companies to produce goods and services. The ability of American businesses to raise large amounts of capital helps keep our country prosperous. Your saving habits thus contribute to the economic well-being of the country.

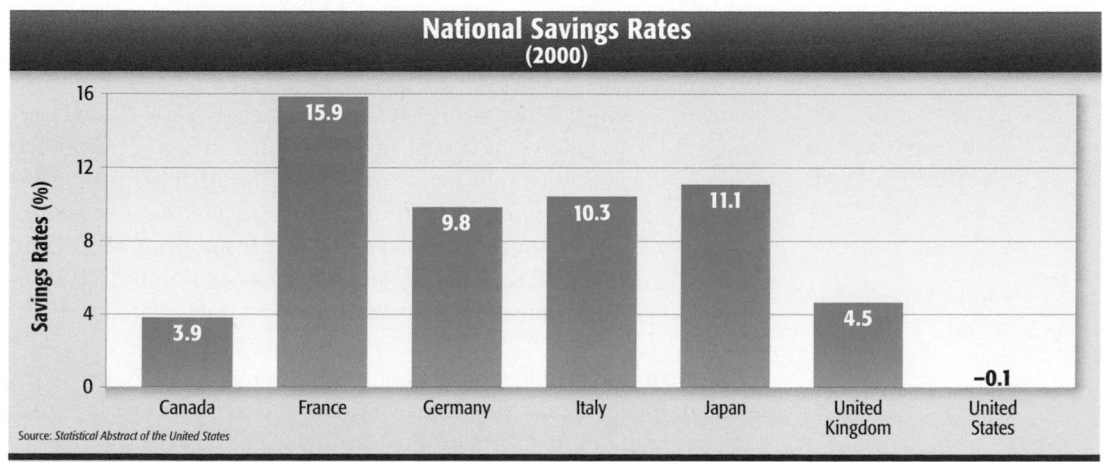

**National Savings Rates (2000)**

Savings Rates (%)

| Canada | France | Germany | Italy | Japan | United Kingdom | United States |
|--------|--------|---------|-------|-------|----------------|---------------|
| 3.9 | 15.9 | 9.8 | 10.3 | 11.1 | 4.5 | −0.1 |

Source: *Statistical Abstract of the United States*

**Interpreting Graphs** *Savings rates—the percentage of disposable income that is saved—vary widely from country to country. **What countries had savings rates greater than 10 percent in 2000?***

## Global Perspectives

**Savings and the GDP**
Countries tend to value a high rate of saving among its citizens because a high rate of saving usually means there is sufficient capital for investment. The savings rate may be thought of as the percentage of a nation's gross domestic product (GDP) that is not consumed (spent) by citizens and government. The United States is often referred to as a nation of consumers but rarely as a nation of savers. In 2001 the average American income rose 4.9 percent, and during the same period, Americans' spending also rose at 4.9 percent. But the average savings rate of Americans stayed at just 1.6 percent. Although this marked an improvement over the average savings rate of 1 percent in 2000, overall American savings in 2001 were down significantly from the average rate of 7.8 percent recorded in 1990. By the beginning of 2002, the rate at which Americans were saving had declined to 1 percent, which was equal to approximately one third of the savings rate of Japanese consumers.

**ACTIVITY** Ask students to conduct research to determine some of the reasons that Americans save less than people in other countries. Have students write a brief essay explaining what they found.

**GRAPH ANSWER**
France, Italy, and Japan

**LEVEL 3:** Ask each student to imagine that he or she is a local investment banker who has been invited to deliver a Saturday morning radio address describing the importance of saving and investing. Have students prepare brief radio addresses of two to three minutes in length. The addresses should weigh the advantages and disadvantages of different types of savings strategies. Remind students that since they will not be able to use visual aids, they need to make their oral explanations as clear as possible. Invite volunteers to read their radio addresses to the class.

## CLOSE

Begin an outline of the section by writing the major section headings on the chalkboard. Then have students complete the outline by coming to the board to list important points from each subsection under each outline heading. Use Roman numerals for major section headings and capital letters, Arabic numbers, and lowercase letters for subsequent entries. Have students copy and save the outline for use as a study guide.

**Interpreting the Visual Record**

**Operating costs** *Businesses invest much of their profit into capital to expand their companies, as in the new building being constructed here.* **What are the advantages of such investment?**

Businesses also save money to raise capital. The managers of most corporations put aside a certain portion of their companies' profits before they pay dividends to stockholders. This money is then reinvested in their business in the form of new capital. The new capital might be in the form of new machines or larger factories. It also helps businesses establish new branches or add new lines of products to what they already produce. This new capital for expansion is in addition to the money set aside for maintenance and replacement expenses.

✔ **Reading Check Contrasting** What is the difference between saving and investing, and what are some ways people invest? Saved money is not necessarily turned into capital, but invested money becomes capital. Investments include savings accounts, stocks, bonds, CDs, and money market funds.

### ★ Protecting Savings

When people deposit money in a bank, they want to know that their money will be safe. They also want to know that they will be able to get it back when they ask for it. When people buy stocks or bonds, they want to be sure they are not taking unnecessary risks.

For these reasons, the federal and state governments have passed laws to regulate the activities of those institutions that handle the savings of others. All banks must receive a state or federal charter to operate. The government charters only those banks that are properly organized and have enough capital.

After a bank is chartered, it is inspected regularly by state or federal officials. The bank's directors are responsible for ensuring that their bank obeys all banking laws. You may recall that all banks must also keep reserve funds in Federal Reserve banks.

Despite these regulations, banks sometimes fail. The officials of the bank may make unwise investments or bad loans, and the bank may be forced to close. What happens to the savings that people have deposited in a bank if the bank fails?

**Insuring Savings** Most savings are now protected by the federal government. During the 1930s many banks closed their doors because businesses of all kinds were in financial trouble. As a result, many people lost all or most of their savings. As a result, Congress took steps to protect depositors by establishing the Federal Deposit Insurance Corporation (FDIC). Similarly, the National Credit Union Association (NCUA) was formed to protect deposits in all federal and most state-chartered credit unions.

You can easily tell if your bank or credit union is an FDIC or NCUA member. It will display signs in its windows and in its advertising. Each bank or credit union insured by the FDIC or the NCUA contributes to a fund held by the federal government. If any member bank or credit union fails, depositors will be paid the amount of their deposits up to $100,000 per depositor.

**Regulating Stock Exchanges**  In the 1930s, Congress also established the Securities and Exchange Commission (SEC). This organization ensures that all offerings of stocks and bonds on the country's stock exchanges are honest.

In years past, people sometimes sold "watered-down" stock. This stock did not fully represent the value claimed for it. There were also many other types of stock fraud and deception by which dishonest people and firms cheated the American public.

The regulations of the Securities and Exchange Commission were established to stop such practices. The SEC constantly monitors the practices of the country's stock exchanges and of the brokers who buy and sell stock. This does not mean that all stocks are safe investments or that all brokers are honest. Moreover, a company can be perfectly honest, meet all the SEC's rules, and still fail.

**Regulating Savings Organizations**  As you have learned, all of the country's savings organizations come under state or federal government supervision. Banking practices are closely monitored. Savings and loan associations are also regulated by laws. Even company credit unions must allow government accountants to examine their records regularly to determine if they are operating properly. Congress has also considered new regulations for employee retirement plans. Because saving is so important to the prosperity of the United States and its citizens, it is essential that individual savings be protected.

✔ **Reading Check** Summarizing How does the government protect the savings of individuals? Banks must have charters; the FDIC and NCUA insure the deposits of individuals and businesses; the SEC monitors stock and bond transactions; and savings institutions are closely monitored by federal and state governments.

**Interpreting the Visual Record**

**The SEC** *The Securities and Exchange Commission tries to keep the operation of the country's stock exchanges fair and open to the public.* **Why do you think an agency like the SEC is necessary?**

**Visual Record Answer**

*The SEC is necessary because if people did not trust the stock market, businesses would not receive the investments they need and the economy would suffer overall.*

## Section 3 Review
### ANSWERS

**1. Define**
- certificates of deposit (CDs), p. 468
- brokers, p. 469
- stock exchange, p. 469
- mutual funds, p. 469
- money market funds, p. 470

**2.** regular savings accounts, hiding money, buying valuable items, certificates of deposit, money market funds, stocks, mutual funds, bonds

**3. a.** because large purchases sometimes require large down payments; also helps to secure one's future against unexpected expenses

**b.** Depositors' savings provide capital (through bank loans) for continued productivity.

**4.** Students' paragraphs will vary but should include the returns and risks of different investments.

---

## SECTION 3 Review

go.hrw.com **Homework Practice Online**
keyword: SZ3 HP19

**1. Define** and explain:
- certificates of deposit (CDs)
- brokers
- stock exchange
- mutual funds
- money market funds

**2. Summarizing** Copy the diagram below. Use it to show the different ways people save and invest their money.

Saving and Investing

**3. Finding the Main Idea**
a. Why is it important to save money even though the United States has an extensive system of credit?
b. How does the U.S. economy benefit when people deposit money in savings accounts, bonds, stocks, or other forms of savings?

**4. Writing and Critical Thinking**
**Decision Making** Write a paragraph telling how you would invest $1,000 and why you would choose such a form or forms of investment.

**Consider:**
- the amount of return offered by different investments
- the amount of risk you are willing to bear

# SECTION 4

## OBJECTIVES

*After completing Section 4, students should be able to*

1 **Explain how insurance companies are able to cover the hardship costs of so many people.**

2 **Determine the difference between private insurance and social insurance.**

3 **Describe why Social Security was created and why some people are concerned about its future.**

## SECTION 4

# Insurance against Hardship

### Read to Discover

1. How are insurance companies able to cover the hardship costs of so many people?
2. What is the difference between private insurance and social insurance?
3. Why was Social Security created, and why are some people concerned about its future?

| Define | Identify |
|---|---|
| • insurance | • Social Security |
| • premium | • Medicare |
| • private insurance | • Medicaid |
| • beneficiary | |
| • social insurance | |

### WHY CIVICS MATTERS

Political leaders continue to debate how the U.S government will fund Social Security as the percentage of retired Americans increases. Use **CNNfyi.com** or other **current events** sources to find a recent article about this issue. Record your findings in your journal.

## Reading Focus

Life is full of risks and uncertainties. There is the chance of illness or accident. There is the possibility of losing one's job. A fire or flood could damage one's house. There is the uncertainty of not being able to earn a living because of age or illness. The U.S. economic system includes arrangements that protect people, at least in part, against the economic impact of such risks and uncertainties. These protections are called insurance.

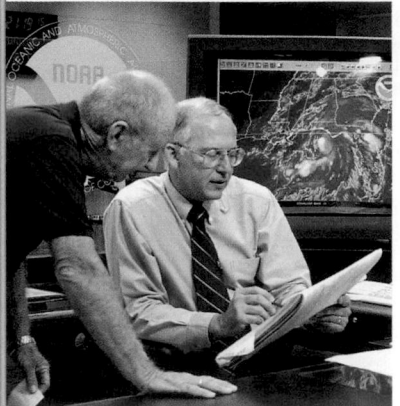

*The threat of natural disasters, such as hurricanes, is one major reason that insurance is necessary.*

### ⭐ What Is Insurance?

Suppose you figured that your losses could total $100,000 in the event of a fire, flood, or accident. Would you be willing to pay a much smaller sum—perhaps $750 each year—to make sure you did not run this risk? **Insurance** is a system of paying a small amount to avoid the risk of a large loss.

The small amount a person pays for this protection is called a **premium.** Premiums may be paid yearly or at regular times throughout the year. The contract that gives this kind of protection is an insurance policy.

✔ **Reading Check** Finding the Main Idea Why do people pay insurance premiums? For a small sum of money, people can protect themselves against the loss of a large amount of money or property.

# TEACH OBJECTIVE 1

**LEVEL 1:** Lead a class discussion about how insurance companies are able to cover the hardship costs of so many people. (*Tell students that insurance companies collect small payments from policyholders but that the company only pays large sums to those people who make claims after experiencing a hardship.*) Point out that many people who pay for insurance will never need to make a claim, so insurance companies are able to use the money paid by these people to cover the expenses of people who have accidents. Then have students write a five-sentence paragraph explaining whether they think that having insurance is a good idea. **ENGLISH LANGUAGE LEARNERS**

**LEVELS 1 AND 2:** Organize students into pairs, and ask each pair to create a pamphlet for an imaginary insurance company that offers policies for teenagers. Each pamphlet should present different types of risk faced by a typical teenager, such as losing one's homework, failing a test, getting a sports injury, or becoming ill and missing a date. Then have each pair of students place some sort of value on each risk (not necessarily a financial value) and determine what premiums (not necessarily a financial value) would be a fair price for protection against such a risk. (*Each pamphlet should offer several levels of coverage and should contain a description of a sample policy.*) Ask volunteers to try to "sell" their policies to the class. **COOPERATIVE LEARNING**

## ★ Private Insurance

**Private insurance** is voluntary insurance individuals and companies pay to cover unexpected losses. There are many different kinds of private insurance companies. Such companies write insurance policies covering almost every possible kind of economic and physical risk.

How can insurance companies take small amounts of money from people, yet pay them a large sum if a hardship occurs? The reason is simple—not everyone has a hardship. You may pay premiums on accident insurance all your life and never collect a cent because you never have an accident. However, you cannot be sure you will never have an accident, so most people buy insurance.

A large insurance company has millions of policyholders who pay their premiums regularly. Part of this money goes into a reserve fund. State laws specify how much of a reserve fund a company must maintain. The amount depends on the kind of insurance the company issues and the number of policyholders.

When someone makes an accident claim, payment in the amount specified by his or her policy is made from the reserve fund. Even with millions of policyholders, there usually are only a few thousand payments out of the reserve fund each year.

Except for money held in reserve funds, insurance companies invest the premiums they collect. The dividends, interest, and other income from the investments pay the expenses of these companies and earn profits for their shareholders.

✔ **Reading Check** **Analyzing Information** How do insurance companies stay profitable while still paying policyholders for their claims? Insurance companies set aside a fixed portion of premiums in a reserve fund to pay claims. They usually invest the rest of the money they receive.

## ★ Life Insurance

The main purpose of life insurance is to provide the policyholder's family with money in case the policyholder dies. In this way, the family is protected from financial hardship. The person named in the policy to receive the money when the policyholder dies is called the **beneficiary.**

The two kinds of life insurance are term insurance and whole-life insurance. Term insurance covers only a specified period of time. This insurance is often chosen by couples who have young children or very high bills. Because it expires at the end of the specified term, it is relatively inexpensive. However, it will allow the surviving spouse to care for the children and pay off large debts. Whole-life insurance covers the policyholder throughout his or her life, and is more expensive.

✔ **Reading Check** **Categorizing** What are the two kinds of life insurance? term insurance—covers only a specified period of time and is inexpensive; whole-life insurance—covers policyholder throughout his or her life and is more expensive

**Interpreting the Visual Record**

**Flood** *Flood insurance is common in many parts of the country. However, some people in at-risk areas go without flood insurance.* **What would be the risk of not having flood insurance during a flood such as that shown here?**

### ★ Civics Sidelight

**History of Insurance**
Insurance is not a new idea. As long ago as 3000 B.C., the merchants of Babylon (near present-day Baghdad in Iraq) insured their ships against loss at sea. Shipping at the time was quite hazardous (because of the high rates of piracy, for example), and thus interest on loans to merchants was high. If the goods were lost at sea, merchants paying these higher interest rates did not have to repay the loans. Throughout history this kind of insurance helped expand international trade, encouraging merchants to take risks that they otherwise might fear to take.

**ACTIVITY:** Ask students to conduct research into the history of insurance to learn more about early forms of insurance. Have students create time lines with illustrations showing how the insurance business has evolved over time.

### Visual Record Answer

*Students might suggest that if a family does not have flood insurance, it might not have enough money to meet the repair and replacement expenses after experiencing a bad flood.*

**ALL LEVELS:** Organize students into small groups. Then tell each group that it has been invited to design a mural for the lobby of an insurance company. Ask groups to create a plan for the mural that illustrates how insurance companies are able to cover the hardship costs of so many people. Encourage students to be creative in their use of images and symbols, and have them indicate how insurance is important to individuals and businesses. Invite volunteers to explain their murals to the class.

**COOPERATIVE LEARNING**

**LEVEL 3:** Remind students that insurance companies are able to meet the claims of a policyholder, because relatively few people actually experience hardships, compared to the number of people who pay insurance premiums. Then ask each student to consider how insurance fraud is harmful to insurance companies and other policyholders. Ask each student to write a bill proposing a law against insurance fraud and explain why the law is needed to protect insurance companies and policyholders. *(Students' bills might point out that fraudulent claims could bankrupt an insurance company and leave other policyholders without coverage.)* Invite volunteers to read their proposed laws to the class.

**HOMEWORK** Ask students to bring to class an information sheet or brochure that explains a specific type of coverage offered by an insurance company. Have them write a paragraph summarizing the information contained in their pamphlet or brochure.

**Interpreting the Visual Record**

**Medical insurance** *During their lifetime, most people will need medical care. The costs of checkups, tests, and treatments can be very high, which is a major reason that many people seek health coverage.* **Why is working for a company that provides health insurance helpful?**

## Disability Income and Health Insurance

There are many forms of insurance policies that cover policyholders if they are injured in an accident or suffer an illness. Disability income insurance, for example, provides payments to replace lost wages when a person cannot work due to total or partial disability.

Some policies cover all kinds of accidents, even breaking a leg by slipping on the soap in the bathtub. Other policies cover only accidents on common carriers—that is, on airplanes, trains, buses, and other means of public transportation. In case of death, the beneficiary receives the amount of the policy.

Health insurance includes policies that cover medical or hospital expenses. Major-medical expense insurance pays a large portion of the medical costs resulting from a serious illness or injury. Major-medical insurance premiums are higher than disability premiums because people are more likely to become ill than they are to become disabled.

Hospital expense insurance pays part of a policyholder's hospital expenses. Other insurance plans pay doctor and dentist bills and other medical expenses. Premiums for these kinds of insurance are often paid in part by policyholders and in part by their employers.

✔ **Reading Check Contrasting** What is the difference between disability income insurance and health insurance? Disability income insurance provides payments to replace lost wages when a person cannot work due to a disability. Health insurance covers major-medical and hospital expenses.

## Property and Liability Insurance

Some types of insurance protect the personal property of policyholders and also protect them against liability claims. Homeowners' insurance, for example, combines property and liability coverage. It protects people's homes and personal property from events such as fires, hurricanes, vandalism, and theft. Renters' insurance also protects individuals' property from theft or damage. The liability portion of such policies provides coverage if a visitor is accidentally injured while visiting a person's home or apartment.

The most widely purchased form of property and liability insurance is automobile insurance, which protects policyholders against financial losses due to automobile accidents. It also provides coverage if a policyholder's car is stolen, vandalized, or damaged in an accident or by an act of nature such as a tornado.

✔ **Reading Check Summarizing** Why do people buy property and liability insurance? for protection against damage to homes and personal property and to cover expenses if a visitor is accidentally injured in one's home

## TEACH OBJECTIVE 2

**LEVEL 1:** Lead students in a discussion about the difference between private insurance and social insurance. *(Private insurance is provided by companies to businesses and individuals who pay for coverage, and social insurance is provided by government programs meant to protect citizens from future hardships.)* Then ask students to consult newspapers to find several headlines for stories that are in some way related to private insurance and social insurance. Have students paste private insurance headlines on one side of a sheet of paper and social insurance headlines on the other side. Then invite volunteers to explain the headlines that they have chosen.
**ENGLISH LANGUAGE LEARNERS**

**ALL LEVELS:** Organize the class into groups and have each group create a poster that distinguishes between private insurance and social insurance. *(See the Level 1 lesson for differences.)* Each type of insurance should be defined and groups should illustrate, with explanatory captions, the different types of insurance one would find in private and social insurance. *(For example, private insurance should include life and health insurance as well as property and liability insurance. Social insurance should make reference to unemployment and disability insurance as well as public assistance programs.)* Each group member should be responsible for illustrating and explaining at least one kind of insurance. Display groups' posters around the classroom to serve as study guides.
**COOPERATIVE LEARNING**

## ★ Insurance Fraud

Although insurance companies are regulated by the states, some dishonest people and companies ignore state regulations. Sometimes it is the insurance companies themselves that are the victims of fraud. For example, dishonest doctors, dentists, pharmacists, and other health-care providers may submit claims to insurance companies for work they have not performed. They may also pad the claims with non-existent expenses.

Individuals also contribute to the high cost of insurance fraud. Some people, for example, may claim severe injuries when their injuries are actually minor or nonexistent. Others engage in insurance scams by staging false accidents.

Insurance fraud hurts everyone. Estimates suggest that such fraud drains $80 billion a year from the U.S. economy. Moreover, the costs of insurance fraud are usually passed on to the consumer. Each American family pays about $950 a year in higher insurance premiums because of insurance fraud. In an effort to crack down on insurance fraud, 15 states have adopted or strengthened insurance fraud laws.

✔ **Reading Check** Analyzing Information How does insurance fraud increase premiums? Fraudulent claims are paid out of the insurance company's reserve funds. In order to stay in business and stay profitable, the company must raise premiums to increase the funds held in reserve.

## ★ Social Insurance

The Great Depression of the 1930s caused many Americans much hardship and suffering. Many businesses and factories closed. Millions of men and women lost their jobs. Banks failed, and thousands of people lost their life savings.

In response, President Franklin D. Roosevelt recommended and Congress passed a series of laws called the New Deal. Some of the new laws brought immediate assistance to needy people. Other laws were directed at future recessions. These laws offered protection against severe economic risks and hardships.

Government programs that are meant to protect individuals from future hardship are called **social insurance.** Almost everyone can receive benefits from such laws. The Social Security Act of 1935 set up a system of social insurance called **Social Security**. It has three major parts—old-age, survivors, and disability insurance; unemployment insurance; and workers' compensation.

✔ **Reading Check** Finding the Main Idea What is the main purpose of social insurance? Social insurance is a government effort to minimize the financial effects of hardships faced by citizens.

**Interpreting Political Cartoons**

**The New Deal** *During the New Deal the federal government tried a wide variety of programs in an effort to cure the ailing national economy.* **How does this cartoon represent President Roosevelt and the New Deal?**

## ★ Economics

**The Cost of Driving** The cost of insurance—particularly automobile insurance—may vary widely from state to state. Some of the highest automobile insurance rates, for example, are in highly urbanized eastern states. Factors affecting insurance rates are traffic patterns, quality of roads and traffic, law enforcement, and costs of auto repair and medical services in an area. Since 1998, insurance premiums for automobile coverage have been declining, but this comes after several years of steep increases. Between 1989 and 1998, premiums increased nationwide by 38.9 percent, but the increases were more dramatic in some states than in others: Nebraska (81.7 percent), West Virginia (65.8 percent), and Arkansas (61.5 percent). During the same period, California experienced a 4 percent decline in auto insurance rates, because of Proposition 103, passed by voters in 1988, which increased insurance regulations.

**CRITICAL THINKING**

Is it fair that people pay different prices for the same insurance coverage, based on their geographic location?

**ANSWER:** Students' responses will vary.

**POLITICAL CARTOON ANSWER**

President Roosevelt is represented as a medical doctor, and the New Deal is represented as his medicine bag.

ALL LEVELS: Copy the following graphic organizer onto the chalkboard, omitting the italicized answers. Have students indicate the differences between private insurance and social insurance by completing the organizer with the different services or types of coverage available under each type of insurance.

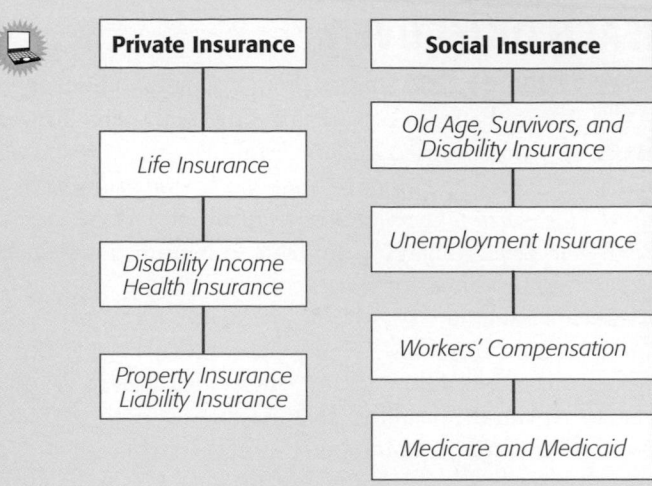

| Private Insurance | Social Insurance |
|---|---|
| Life Insurance | Old Age, Survivors, and Disability Insurance |
| Disability Income Health Insurance | Unemployment Insurance |
| Property Insurance Liability Insurance | Workers' Compensation |
| | Medicare and Medicaid |

## The ★ Democratic Process

**The New Deal** There were two parts to Roosevelt's New Deal; the first phase was intended to help the United States recover from the Great Depression, and the second phase was designed to provide social and economic plans to aid working people. Some conservative critics believed that Roosevelt's sweeping social programs turned the United States toward socialism by placing more economic responsibility in the hands of the government. Alf Landon, Roosevelt's Republican opponent in the 1936 presidential election, adopted the campaign slogan "Save the American Way of Life." Many other critics also thought the New Deal's social programs were too radical, but President Roosevelt believed they were necessary to restore Americans' faith in their democratic government.

**ACTIVITY:** Have students consult an encyclopedia to learn more about the New Deal and ask them to deliver a brief oral presentation about a specific program that was created as part of the New Deal.

### Visual Record Answer

*Your Social Security number is important because it not only identifies all of your Social Security tax contributions but is also used as an identification number on many important documents.*

### Interpreting the Visual Record

**Social Security** *All American citizens receive a Social Security number on a card such as this one. That number helps the government track their contributions and benefits.* **Why would your Social Security number be an important piece of information?**

## ★ Old-Age, Survivors, and Disability Insurance

The basic idea behind this type of insurance is simple. People pay a percentage of their salaries each month while they work to receive cash benefits later when they need them most. During the years when workers earn money, they and their employers make contributions to a fund. After workers retire, or if they become disabled and their earnings stop, they receive payments from the fund as long as they live.

If workers die before reaching retirement age, their families receive "survivors'" payments. A payment is made for each child under 18 and for the widow or widower. When children reach the age of 18, payments to them stop.

**Paying for Social Security** Monthly contributions made under the Social Security Act are paid equally by workers and by employers. The contributions actually are a tax, because they are compulsory, or required.

Today the Social Security program extends to workers in almost every industry, business, and profession. Self-employed people must also participate. They pay the entire contribution themselves.

**Receiving Social Security** The benefits paid by Social Security have gradually increased since 1935. The amount of the required contribution has also increased. The amount that workers and employers pay depends on how much money the workers earn each year. The benefits received by workers when they retire or become disabled are based on their average earnings over a long period of time. Survivors of workers who have died, retired workers, and disabled workers receive monthly checks.

Some people worry that the Social Security program will not be able to care for future generations of retired workers. Longer life expectancies and lower birthrates mean that an ever-increasing segment of the population will be made up of people of retirement age. As a result, fewer workers will be supporting a growing number of retirees. Many fear Social Security taxes will continue to rise and prefer to abolish the program. Others have recommended having a private company, rather than the government, control the funds. However, Social Security was never intended to provide the total income of retirees. It is simply a cushion against the worst hardship.

✔ **Reading Check** Making Generalizations and Predictions What could happen to the Social Security program as fewer workers support more retirees? Social Security taxes could be raised to keep benefits at the same level; benefits could be cut for all recipients.

**LEVEL 3:** Remind students about the differences between private and social insurance. *(See the Level 1 lesson for differences.)* Then ask each student to draw a political cartoon illustrating the differences between these two kinds of insurance. Encourage students to create symbols to represent the purposes of private and social insurance.

## TEACH OBJECTIVE 3

**LEVEL 1:** Lead a class discussion about the reasons that Social Security was created and why some people are concerned about its future. *(During the Great Depression many people lost their jobs and their life savings; Social Security was created to provide some relief from these hardships.)* Point out that some people are concerned about the future of Social Security because longer life expectancies and lower birthrates mean that more retirees are now being supported by fewer workers. Then ask students to draw a line down the middle of a sheet of paper. On the left side of the line have them list reasons that Social Security is still necessary. On the right side of the line, have students list alternatives to Social Security. **ENGLISH LANGUAGE LEARNERS**

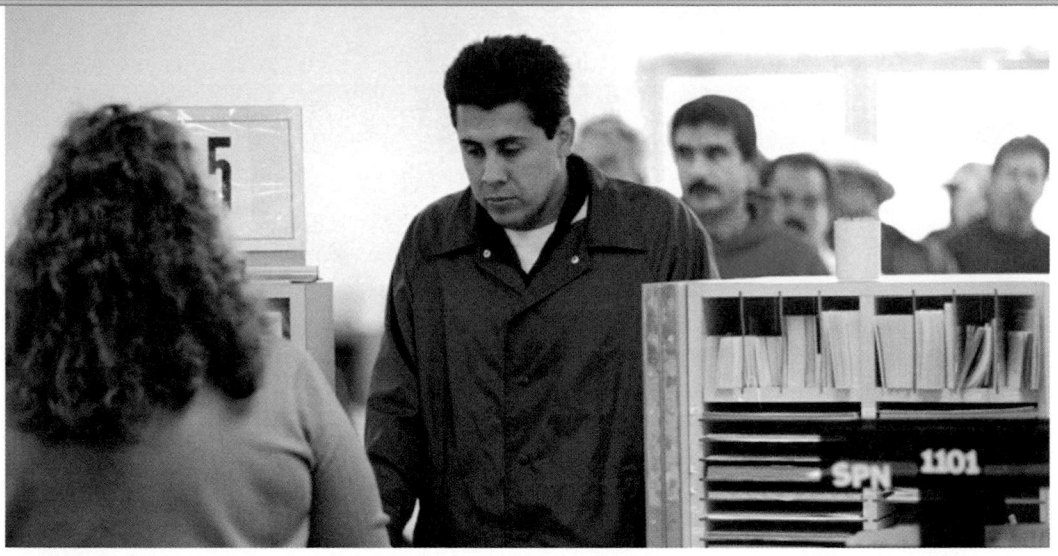

## ★ Unemployment Compensation

When the Social Security Act was passed in 1935, unemployment was a serious problem. Millions of Americans were unemployed. Most had lost their jobs because of the Great Depression. The Social Security Act contained a plan to help workers who lost their jobs due to circumstances beyond their control. This plan is called the unemployment compensation program.

To receive benefits, unemployed workers must register with a state employment office. They report periodically to the office to see if it can help them find jobs. If the job search is unsuccessful, unemployed workers receive weekly benefits based on their average earnings over a certain period of time. The amount paid varies from state to state, but most states provide benefits for up to 26 weeks. The amount received is small, but it helps families support themselves while workers look for new jobs.

The unemployment compensation program is financed by employers. Federal law requires all businesses to pay a special tax to the federal government. State governments pay unemployment compensation benefits out of the money collected by the federal government.

## ★ Workers' Compensation

The workers' compensation program helps people who have job-related injuries or who develop an illness as a result of working conditions at their jobs. The program pays the medical expenses of the workers and helps replace any lost income. Workers' compensation also pays death benefits to the survivors of workers killed while on the job. In return for these medical and death benefits, workers give up their right to sue their employers to receive compensation for their work-related injuries.

---

**Interpreting the Visual Record**

**Unemployment compensation** *Individuals who have lost their jobs may apply for unemployment compensation at the appropriate state agency. However, they must show that they are actively looking for work.* **Why do you think recipients of unemployment compensation must be looking for work?**

---

**Visual Record Answer**

*Students should suggest that unemployment compensation is intended to be a temporary relief from hardship, not a replacement for steady employment.*

**LEVEL 3:** Ask students to imagine that it is 1933 and that it is their job to draft a proposal to President Franklin D. Roosevelt recommending and outlining the Social Security program. Tell students that they should consider historical reasons for the creation of Social Security, as well as the needs that Social Security is designed to fill. *(See the Level 1 lesson.)* Then ask students if they would organize the Social Security system differently. Remind students that some people are worried that Social Security will no longer be able to meet the expenses of the growing number of retirees in the 2000s. Ask students if Social Security should be restructured to avoid these problems. *(Students' proposals will vary but should cite the specific needs that have necessitated the program, as well as ways that Social Security might be improved.)* Invite volunteers to read their proposals to the class.

## CLOSE

Tell students that a family's combined monthly payments for health, life, and automobile insurance can amount to several hundred dollars. In the event of an emergency, a family will be glad that it has insurance coverage; however, if family members remain healthy and have no accidents, the family receives nothing tangible in return for its premiums. Ask students to write an editorial in which they evaluate the system of insurance coverage as being either fair or unfair.

### Providing Health Care

Government programs and insurance currently pay more than 70 percent of all medical expenses in the United States. However, increasing costs in health-care insurance have placed a strain on American households and have left many without any health coverage at all. Throughout the 1980s and 1990s, the federal government debated several plans to help extend health coverage to more Americans. In 1993, during his first year in office, President Bill Clinton proposed a government-sponsored program to provide health insurance to most Americans. However, the expense and complexity of the program met with overwhelming opposition. The debate over how best to provide health care for all Americans continues.

### CRITICAL THINKING

Should the U.S. government provide comprehensive health-care coverage to Americans.

**ANSWER:** Students' responses will vary.

### CHART ANSWER

disability and survivor payments, retirement payments, Medicare, Medicaid, unemployment compensation benefits, workers' compensation

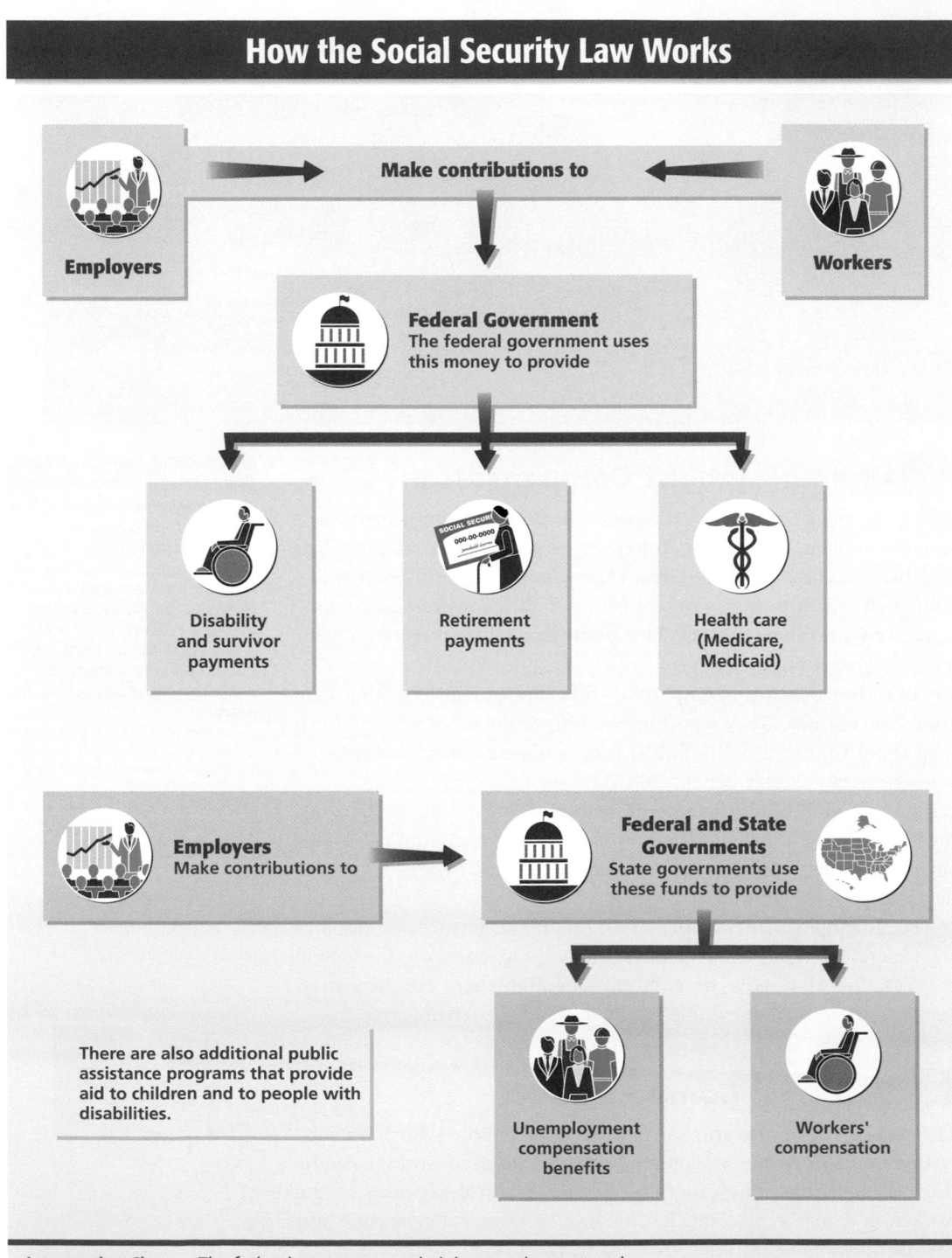

## How the Social Security Law Works

Make contributions to

**Employers**

**Workers**

**Federal Government**
The federal government uses this money to provide

**Disability and survivor payments**

**Retirement payments**

**Health care (Medicare, Medicaid)**

**Employers**
Make contributions to

**Federal and State Governments**
State governments use these funds to provide

There are also additional public assistance programs that provide aid to children and to people with disabilities.

**Unemployment compensation benefits**

**Workers' compensation**

**Interpreting Charts** *The federal government administers retirement and old-age insurance programs and sets the standards according to which states administer many other social insurance programs.* **What types of benefits are funded by contributions from employers?**

## REVIEW AND ASSESS

Have students complete the **Section 4 Review** on page 481. Then have students complete **Daily Quiz 19.4**. As **Alternative Assessment**, you may want to use the teenage insurance policy or the political cartoon activities in this section's lessons.

## RETEACH

Have students complete **Main Idea Activity for English Language Learners and Special-Needs Students 19.4**. Then assign each student one of the objectives in this section. Ask students to create a study guide for their assigned objective. After they have finished their study guides, ask volunteers to present their guides to the class. **ENGLISH LANGUAGE LEARNERS**

## EXTEND

Have students consult an encyclopedia as a reference to learn more about the history and organization of the Social Security system. Encourage students to find out how the system has changed over the years. Ask students to write a paper evaluating whether Social Security is effectively meeting the needs for which it was created, and have them recommend possible solutions to some of the problems facing the system. **BLOCK SCHEDULING**

The benefits received by workers vary by state and depend on the kind of disability the worker has and how long it lasts. The benefits also depend on the worker's weekly salary. Workers' compensation is administered by the state or by a private insurance company. In some states, administration is shared by a state agency and a private insurance company. Employers in all 50 states are required to participate in the program, and most states require employers to pay the cost.

✔ **Reading Check** Contrasting What is the difference between unemployment compensation and workers' compensation? Unemployment compensation provides income to unemployed people. Workers' compensation pays for medical expenses from work-related injuries.

### ★ Medicare and Medicaid

The federal government has programs to help poor and older citizens pay their medical expenses. In 1965 Congress passed the health insurance program called **Medicare** to help U.S. citizens who are 65 and older pay for hospital care and for some nursing home care. Medicare includes a voluntary medical insurance plan to help older citizens pay their medical bills. People with disabilities who are unable to work are also eligible for Medicare benefits. In 2003, Congress added a prescription medicine benefit to Medicare.

Congress passed the **Medicaid** health insurance program in 1965. It provides money to help states pay the medical costs of people with low incomes.

✔ **Reading Check** Contrasting What is the difference between Medicare and Medicaid? Medicare is government-sponsored health insurance for elderly people and those with disabilities who cannot work; Medicaid is government-sponsored health insurance for people with low incomes.

*As the large "baby boom" segment of the U.S. population ages, the number of U.S. citizens eligible for Medicare benefits will increase.*

## SECTION 4 Review

**go.hrw.com Homework Practice Online**
keyword: SZ3 HP19

1. **Define** and explain:
   - insurance
   - premium
   - private insurance
   - beneficiary
   - social insurance

2. **Identify** and explain:
   - Social Security
   - Medicare
   - Medicaid

3. **Summarizing** Copy the graphic organizer below. Use it to show why the U.S. government created Social Security and some of the concerns that have arisen about the program.

| Social Security | |
|---|---|
| Why Created | Concerns |
| | |
| | |
| | |

4. **Finding the Main Idea**
   a. How can insurance companies cover large risks in return for relatively small premiums?
   b. How are private insurance and social insurance different?

5. **Writing and Critical Thinking**
   **Supporting a Point of View** Do you think Social Security has encouraged Americans to become too dependent on the state and federal governments for support in times of need? Write a paragraph explaining your answer.

   **Consider:**
   - who pays for Social Security and how it is paid for
   - your future financial plans for retirement
   - the possibility that the Social Security program could fail before you retire

### Section 4 Review
### ANSWERS

1. **Define**
   - insurance, p. 474
   - premium, p. 474
   - private insurance, p. 475
   - beneficiary, p. 475
   - social insurance, p. 477

2. **Identify**
   - Social Security, p. 477
   - Medicare, p. 481
   - Medicaid, p. 481

3. to protect people against the kinds of losses experienced during the depression; growing elderly population means fewer workers will be supporting more retirees

4. a. relatively few people need to collect on their policies

   b. private—voluntary insurance purchased by individuals to cover unexpected losses social—government programs designed to protect individuals against future hardships

5. Students' responses will vary, but students should support their positions and consider the consequences of their arguments.

### REPRODUCIBLE

▶ Chapter 19 Review, pp. 482–83

▶ Vocabulary Activity 19

▶ Chapter 19 Tutorial for Students, Parents, Mentors, and Peers

▶ Chapter 19 Test (Form A or B)

▶ Alternative Assessment Handbook

### TECHNOLOGY

▶ Chapter 19 Test Generator (on the One-Stop Planner)

▶ Global Skill Builder CD–ROM

▶ HRW Go Site

### REINFORCEMENT, REVIEW, AND ASSESSMENT

▶ Chapter 19 Test for English Language Learners and Special-Needs Students

## REVIEW

Have students complete the **Chapter 19 Review** on pages 482–83.

## ASSESS

Use one of the chapter tests to assess students' understanding of the content. For **Alternative Assessment**, see the **Alternative Assessment Handbook**.

---

## CHAPTER 19
### REVIEW ANSWERS

**Define and Identify**
1. currency, p. 453
2. bankruptcy, p. 457
3. collateral, p. 460
4. credit union, p. 463
5. discounting, p. 463
6. stock exchange, p. 469
7. mutual funds, p. 469
8. insurance, p. 474
9. premium , p. 474
10. Social Security, p. 477

**Understanding Main Ideas**

1. not guaranteed by government, because written by responsible people or businesses

2. charge—accepted only by stores that issue them; credit—accepted by thousands of stores and businesses

3. risky loans, bad investments, and fraud

4. handles the banking needs of the government and other banks and regulates the amount of money in circulation

5. enables banks to make loans to businesses

6. regular savings accounts, hiding money, buying valuables, certificates of deposit (CDs), money market funds, stocks, mutual funds, bonds

7. Relatively few people need to collect on their policies.

---

# Chapter 19 Review

## Chapter Summary

### Section 1

• Very little of what is bought and sold is paid for with currency. Instead, people rely on checks, debit cards, charge accounts, and credit cards to purchase goods.

### Section 2

• Banks are safe places in which to keep money. Banks also help businesses and individuals by making loans.

• The Federal Reserve System regulates banking in the United States. It also helps regulate the use of credit and maintain the proper money supply in the economy.

### Section 3

• People can save by putting their money in savings accounts and certificates of deposit; by investing in bonds, the stock market, mutual funds, and money market accounts; and by buying precious metals, jewels, art, or other valuables.

• Saving helps the economy by providing banks with the money they need to make loans to individuals and businesses.

• The federal and state governments help protect savings and investments by regulating banks, insurance companies, and the sale of stocks and bonds.

### Section 4

• Insurance companies issue policies that seek to protect U.S. citizens from possible financial hardships.

• The federal Social Security system provides old-age, survivors, disability, and unemployment insurance, and workers' compensation. Medicare and Medicaid provide health insurance for older Americans, people with disabilities, and people with low incomes.

## Define and Identify

Use the following terms in complete sentences.
1. currency
2. bankruptcy
3. collateral
4. credit union
5. discounting
6. stock exchange
7. mutual funds
8. insurance
9. premium
10. Social Security

## Understanding Main Ideas

**Section 1** *(Pages 453–58)*
1. Why are checks not considered legal tender, and why do people accept them for payment?
2. How do charge cards differ from credit cards?

**Section 2** *(Pages 460–66)*
3. What caused the savings and loan crisis of the 1980s?
4. What are the duties of the Federal Reserve System?

**Section 3** *(Pages 467–73)*
5. How does saving money help the economy grow?
6. What options does an individual have if he or she wants to save or invest money?

**Section 4** *(Pages 474–81)*
7. What enables insurance companies to stay in business while still charging the premiums that they do?

## What Did You Find Out?

1. Why does currency have value?
2. How does the federal government regulate the banking system?
3. Why do people save money?

## Thinking Critically

1. **Drawing Inferences and Conclusions** As you know, the president appoints the Federal Reserve System's board of governors with the consent of the Senate. Why do you think that Fed board members require such high-level appointment?
2. **Supporting a Point of View** Periodically in the United States there is debate about abolishing the penny. Do you think the penny should be abolished, and how might this affect the economy?
3. **Analyzing Information** How does American money fulfill the four features of currency?

## RETEACH

Organize students into four groups and assign each group one of the chapter's sections. Have each group create a diagram explaining the main objectives in its assigned section. Then have groups present their work to the class.

**ENGLISH LANGUAGE LEARNERS ,**
**COOPERATIVE LEARNING**

## Portfolio Extensions

**1. Interdisciplinary Connection to Art and Literature** Tell students that nonprofit organizations in the arts are often required to have liability insurance before receiving financial grants from the government. Then ask students to contact a local artistic nonprofit organization to find out what types of insurance it needs and why. Have each student write a brief report to the board of directors of a nonprofit explaining what type of insurance coverage that organization needs and why.

**2. Cooperative Learning** Organize students into two groups. Ask one group to think of reasons why social insurance programs are necessary, and ask students to think of ways that these programs might be improved. Then ask the other group to think of reasons why social insurance might be detrimental to society or the economy, and ask these students to come up with solutions to the problems they have identified. Have each group present its arguments to the class.

---

## Building Social Studies Skills

go.hrw.com STANDARDIZED TEST PREP ONLINE keyword: SZ3 STP19

### Interpreting Political Cartoons

Study the political cartoon below. Then answer the questions that follow.

THE ECONOMY IS MOVING TOO FAST! RAISE THE RATES!

COULD IT BE INFLATION? RAISE THE RATES!

THE DOLLAR IS WEAK! RAISE THE RATES!!

Heller
Green Bay Press-Gazette

*The Not-So-reserved Federal Reserve Board*

1. Who do the people shown in the cartoon represent?
   a. American consumers
   b. American business leaders
   c. The directors of the Federal Reserve
   d. Members of the president's cabinet
2. What issue are the people in the cartoon reacting to?
   a. An economic slowdown
   b. Rapid growth in the economy
   c. The foreign trade deficit
   d. A change in interest rates
3. How would you describe the behavior of the people shown in the cartoon? Does it seem appropriate for them to act this way?
4. What do you think the cartoonist was trying to say about U.S. economic planning in this cartoon?

### Analyzing Primary Sources

Read the following quotation from Federal Reserve chairman Alan Greenspan. Then answer the questions that follow.

66Education is a critical issue for our country, and economic education is of particular concern to those of us at the Federal Reserve. . . . Obviously, falling into financial distress is not solely the result of lack of knowledge about finance. But in many cases such knowledge could avoid or ameliorate [reduce] the negative consequences of uninformed decisions. Thus, in considering means by which to improve the financial status of families, education can play an important role. . . . An evaluation conducted by the National Endowment for Financial Education on its high-school-based programs found that participation in financial-planning programs improved students' knowledge, behavior, and confidence with respect to personal finance, with nearly half of participants beginning to save more as a result of the program.99

5. Which of the following statements best describes Greenspan's point of view?
   a. Economic education will help everyone become rich.
   b. Economic education can help young people and families make better financial decisions.
   c. The current economy is too complicated for most people to understand.
   d. National leaders should take more time to explain their economic policies to people.
6. What were the benefits of financial-planning programs for students?

---

### What Did You Find Out?

1. guaranteed by government

2. by helping to prevent bank failures and keeping the right amount of money in circulation

3. for large purchases, children's education, emergencies, and retirement

**Thinking Critically**
1. The Fed's powers greatly influence the economy.

2. Students should use sound reasoning in their responses.

3. easy to carry and takes up little space, based on a system of units that are easy to multiply or divide, durable, made in standard form and guaranteed by government

**Social Studies Skills**
1. c

2. b

3. The people appear to be overreacting.

4. The cartoonist seems to suggest that the Fed raises interest rates unnecessarily.

5. b

6. improved students' knowledge, behavior, and confidence in issues of personal finance

---

## Alternative Assessment

### Building Your Portfolio

**Linking to Community**
Investigate the savings institutions in your community. How many banks, credit unions, and savings and loan associations are there? Where are they located? If possible, interview loan officers in each institution. What services do they offer? Present your findings in a community "banking map." Indicate the location of each institution, and write a short profile of each on the map.

**internet connect**

**Internet Activity: go.hrw.com**
keyword: SZ3 AC19

Access the Internet through the HRW Go site to research money, loans, and credit. Then create a skit to explain the importance of money, loans, and credit in terms of the national and family economies. Make sure you use correct terminology and explain the role of money, loans, and credit in your skit.

| Objectives | Pacing Guide | Reproducible Resources |
|---|---|---|
| **SECTION 1:**<br>**The Business Cycle**<br>(pp. 485–89)<br><br>★ Identify the different parts of the business cycle.<br>★ Describe the old theories of the business cycle and indicate when they existed.<br>★ Analyze how the Great Depression changed the government's role in the economy. | **Regular**<br>2 days<br><br>**Block Scheduling**<br>1.5 days<br><br>*Block Scheduling Handbook with Team Teaching Strategies, Chapter 20* | **RS** Guided Reading Strategies 20.1<br>**RS** Readings in Economics and Government 62: *Three Years Down*, by Jonathan Leonard<br>**RS** Readings in Economics and Government 63: "No Men Wanted" by Karl Monroe<br>**RS** Challenge and Enrichment Worksheet 20: Interpreting a Political Cartoon<br>**SM** Community Service Participation Handbook: Recording History<br>**RS** Graphic Organizer Activity: The Business Cycle |
| **SECTION 2:**<br>**Coping with Economic Challenges**<br>(pp. 490–95)<br><br>★ Identify the economic problems that exist and determine what causes them.<br>★ Describe how the government addresses economic problems.<br>★ Explain how citizens can work to improve the economy. | **Regular**<br>2 days<br><br>**Block Scheduling**<br>1.5 days<br><br>*Block Scheduling Handbook with Team Teaching Strategies, Chapter 20* | **RS** Guided Reading Strategies 20.2<br>**RS** Readings in Economics and Government 67: *The Affluent Society*, by John Kenneth Galbraith<br>**PS** American Civics Political Cartoon: FDR and the New Deal |
| **SECTION 3:**<br>**Labor and Management**<br>(pp. 497–505)<br><br>★ Describe the conditions that led to the rise of labor unions in the 1800s.<br>★ Identify the methods labor and employers use to negotiate with one another and describe the major labor laws that protect them.<br>★ Analyze the status of labor relations today. | **Regular**<br>2 days<br><br>**Block Scheduling**<br>1.5 days<br><br>*Block Scheduling Handbook with Team Teaching Strategies, Chapter 20* | **RS** Guided Reading Strategies 20.3<br>**RS** Readings in Economics and Government 39: Interstate Commerce Act of 1887<br>**E** Creative Teaching Strategy: Brainstorming |

## Chapter Resource Key

**PS** Primary Sources
**RS** Reading Support
**IC** Interdisciplinary Connections
**E** Enrichment

**SM** Skills Mastery
**A** Assessment
**REV** Review
**ELL** Reinforcement and English Language Learners
Transparencies

CD-ROM
Video
 Internet
 Holt Presentation Maker Using Microsoft® PowerPoint®

 **One-Stop** Planner CD-ROM

**See the *One-Stop Planner* for a complete list of additional resources for students and teachers.**

## One-Stop Planner CD–ROM

It's easy to plan lessons, select resources, and print out materials for your students when you use the **One-Stop Planner CD–ROM with Test Generator**.

| Technology Resources | Reinforcement, Review, and Assessment |
|---|---|
| One-Stop Planner, Lesson 20.1<br>Homework Practice Online | **REV** Section 1 Review, p. 489<br>**A** Daily Quiz 20.1<br>**ELL** Main Idea Activity 20.1<br>**ELL** English Audio Summary 20.1<br>**ELL** Spanish Audio Summary 20.1 |
| One-Stop Planner, Lesson 20.2<br>Holt Researcher CD–ROM<br>Homework Practice Online | **REV** Section 2 Review, p. 495<br>**A** Daily Quiz 20.2<br>**ELL** Main Idea Activity 20.2<br>**ELL** English Audio Summary 20.2<br>**ELL** Spanish Audio Summary 20.2 |
| One-Stop Planner, Lesson 20.3<br>CNN. Presents: American Government<br>Homework Practice Online<br>HRW Go site | **REV** Section 3 Review, p. 505<br>**A** Daily Quiz 20.3<br>**ELL** Main Idea Activity 20.3<br>**ELL** English Audio Summary 20.3<br>**ELL** Spanish Audio Summary 20.3 |

### ✓ internet connect

**HRW ONLINE RESOURCES**
GO TO: go.hrw.com
Then type in the keyword.

**TEACHER HOME PAGE**
KEYWORD: SZ3 Teacher

**CHAPTER INTERNET ACTIVITIES**
KEYWORD: SZ3 AC20
Choose an activity to:
- make a crossword puzzle using economic terms.
- create a vocabulary word hunt related to the business cycle.
- create a newspaper on labor unions.

**CHAPTER ENRICHMENT LINKS**
KEYWORD: SZ3 CH20

**ONLINE ASSESSMENT**
Homework Practice
KEYWORD: SZ3 HP20
Rubrics
KEYWORD: SS Rubrics

**ONLINE MAPS, CHARTS, AND GRAPHS**
KEYWORD: SZ3 MCG
- The Business Cycle

**HOLT PRESENTATION MAKER**
KEYWORD: SZ3 PPT20

**CONTENT UPDATES**
KEYWORD: SS Content Updates

**ONLINE READING SUPPORT**
KEYWORD: SS Strategies

**CURRENT EVENTS**
KEYWORD: S3 Current Events

## Meeting Individual Needs

### Ability Levels

**Level 1** Basic-level activities designed for all students encountering new material

**Level 2** Intermediate-level activities designed for average students

**Level 3** Challenging activities designed for honors and gifted-and-talented students

**English Language Learners** Activities that address the needs of students with Limited English Proficiency

## Chapter Review and Assessment

**IC** Vocabulary Activity 20
Global Skill Builder CD–ROM
HRW Go site
**REV** Chapter 20 Tutorial for Students, Parents, Mentors, and Peers
**REV** Chapter 20 Review, pp. 506–07
**A** Standardized Test Practice
**A** Chapter 20 Test Generator (Form A or B)
**A** Chapter 20 Test (on the One-Stop Planner)
**A** Alternative Assessment Handbook
**A** Chapter 20 Test for English Language Learners and Special-Needs Students

## What's Your Opinion?

To help students create their ***Themes*** *Journal entries, provide the following examples of appropriate* **agree**/**disagree** *statements.*

● **Agree**   The U.S. economy and other free-market economies follow predictable patterns.

**Disagree**   The U.S. economy has faced many unanticipated periods of expansion and contraction.

● **Agree**   The federal government allows the economy to adjust itself depending on the needs of the country.

**Disagree**   The federal government is involved in manipulating and regulating the economy.

● **Agree**   Strikes cause the greatest disruption to employers and force them to negotiate quickly.

**Disagree**   Many labor disputes can be solved through effective communication and compromise.

## Internet Activity

**Business as Usual**

▣ **internet** connect

go.hrw.com

**TOPIC:** The Business Cycle
**GO TO:** go.hrw.com
**KEYWORD:** SZ3 AC20

Have students access the Internet through the HRW Go site to conduct research about the business cycle. Then have students make up a vocabulary word game that include terms related to the business cycle.

**CHAPTER**

# 20 Economic Challenges

### Build on What You Know

Did you know that you play a role in the U.S. economy? Every time you make a purchase, deposit money in the bank, or perform work, you are contributing to the economy. Throughout most of the country's history, the economy has been strong. However, periods of slow economic growth have also occurred. These ups and downs in the economy cause problems that affect all Americans. You must do your part to work toward a healthy economy.

 **Themes Journal**

**What's Your Opinion?**

Do you **agree** or **disagree** with the following statements? Support your point of view in your journal.

- The U.S. economy always follows the same pattern.

- The federal government lets the country's economy fix its own problems.

- The most effective method for resolving labor disputes is a strike.

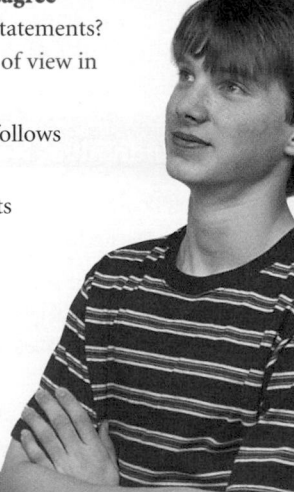

# SECTION 1

## OBJECTIVES

*After completing Section 1, students should be able to*

1 Identify the different parts of the business cycle.
2 Describe the old theories of the business cycle and indicate when they existed.
3 Analyze how the Great Depression changed the government's role in the economy.

## 🔊 LET'S GET STARTED!

As students enter the classroom, ask them to define the meaning of the word *trough*. *(Students might suggest a container from which livestock eat or the low point between waves.)* Tell students that in economics, a trough is a low point in the business cycle. Then ask students what the opposite of a trough might be. *(Students might suggest a crest or a peak.)* Then write the common definitions of *contraction (reduction in size)* and *expansion (growth, increase in size)* on the chalkboard. Tell students that in Section 1 they will learn more about the various phases of the business cycle.

## SECTION 1

# The Business Cycle

### Read to Discover

1. What are the different parts of the business cycle?
2. What are the old theories of the business cycle, and when did they exist?
3. How did the Great Depression change the government's role in the economy?

### Define

- business cycle
- expansion
- inflation
- costs of production
- peak
- contraction
- recession
- trough
- depression

### WHY CIVICS MATTERS

The performance of the U.S. economy changes with time. Use **CNNfyi.com** or other **current events** sources to learn if the economy is currently performing well or poorly. Record your findings in your journal.

## SECTION 1 RESOURCES

### REPRODUCIBLE

▶ Guided Reading Strategies 20.1
▶ Readings in Economics and Government 62: *Three Years Down*, by Jonathan Leonard
▶ Readings in Economics and Government 63: "No Men Wanted" by Karl Monroe
▶ Challenge and Enrichment Worksheet 20: Interpreting a Political Cartoon
▶ Community Service Participation Handbook: Recording History
▶ Graphic Organizer Activity: The Business Cycle

### TECHNOLOGY

▶ One-Stop Planner, Lesson 20.1
▶ Homework Practice Online

### REINFORCEMENT, REVIEW, AND ASSESSMENT

▶ Section 1 Review, p. 489
▶ Daily Quiz 20.1
▶ Main Idea Activity 20.1
▶ English Audio Summary 20.1
▶ Spanish Audio Summary 20.1

## *Reading Focus*

Although Americans enjoy a high standard of living, the economy does not always behave the way we want it to. Sometimes there is a period of prosperity, called a boom. During a boom, business is good, jobs are plentiful, and profits are high. Then business activity slows. Some companies begin to lose money, and many workers lose their jobs. The country enters a period of hard times, known as a bust.

### ★ The Business Cycle

The tendency is for the economy to go from good times to bad, then back to good times again. This process is called the **business cycle** and is quite common to free-market economies. The chart on the following page shows the various parts of the business cycle. When the economy is booming, the gross domestic product (GDP) increases. (As you recall, the GDP is the total amount of goods and services produced by the country in one year.) This period of growth is called **expansion** because the economy is expanding, or growing.

The expansion of the economy during a boom is generally good—most people have jobs and businesses are doing well. However, expansion can cause problems. One problem that often accompanies a boom is inflation. **Inflation** refers to a rise in the costs of goods and services.

> **Dow Dives 508.32 Points In Panic on Wall Street**
> **Navy blasts Iran oil site in retaliation**
> **Billions lost in trading**

*The economy is difficult to predict. In 1987 the stock market suffered a severe crash, but the economy did not collapse as it did following the crash of 1929.*

# TEACH OBJECTIVE 1

**ALL LEVELS:** Copy the following graphic organizer onto the chalkboard, omitting the italicized answers. Have students complete the chart to identify the different parts of the business cycle. **ENGLISH LANGUAGE LEARNERS**

**LEVEL 3:** Invite each student to imagine he or she is the chairperson of the Federal Reserve Board at a time when the economy is expanding. Have each student write a short statement to Congress describing this expansion, including the growth of the country's gross domestic product (GDP), what the expansion means for consumers and business, and possible hazards, such as inflation, down the road. Call on volunteers to read their statements to the class. Finally, have students discuss the different parts of the business cycle, including the relationship between inflation and expansion in the economy.

## ★ Economics

**Economic Recession Predictors** Until 2000, the last major recession to affect the U.S. economy occurred in 1991. Many economic forecasters believe that the recession of 2000 was easily predictable in light of the events leading to the recession of the early 1990s. Economic forecasters looked at several indicators and have found many similarities between the two recessions. Oil prices increased sharply in 1991 and 2000 prior to the recession. Consumer confidence (another economic indicator) also fell several points before each recession. Economic indicators provide policy makers with necessary information to adjust fiscal and monetary policies to help maintain a positive economy.

**ACTIVITY:** Have students conduct research to obtain information on the major economic indicators used to gauge the status of the economy. Ask students to predict the future trends in the economy.

## GRAPH ANSWER
it declines

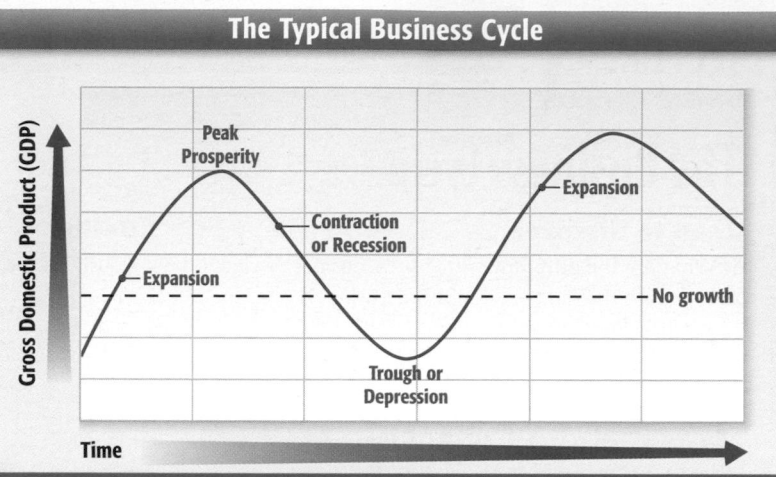

**Interpreting Graphs**
*In free-market systems periods of economic expansion are usually followed by periods of contraction.* **What happens to GDP during a recession?**

During periods of prosperity, people have money to spend, causing the demand for goods and services to increase. Prices inflate, or rise, as customers compete with each other to buy scarce products.

The costs of doing business also increase during a period of economic expansion. Increased competition forces businesses to pay higher prices for raw materials and transportation. Because jobs are more plentiful, businesses may also have to increase the wages of their workers to keep them. Wages, payments for raw materials, transportation, rent, and interest on money borrowed are the **costs of production.** When inflation makes these costs rise, business firms may have to increase the prices of their products to make a profit.

At some point, the expansion of the economy and the inflation that goes with it stop. When this happens, the business cycle has reached a **peak,** or high point.

After the economy peaks, business activity begins to slow. This economic slowdown is called a **contraction.** If the contraction becomes severe enough, a **recession** may occur. During a recession, businesses fail, more people are unemployed, and profits fall.

When the economy reaches its lowest point, it is said to be in a **trough.** When the trough is particularly low, times are very hard, and economists say the economy is in a **depression.** During a depression, unemployment is high. Unemployed people cannot buy many goods and services, so businesses suffer or close.

Usually troughs are not so low as to throw the economy into a depression. Some people lose jobs and businesses fail, but the economy bounces back and begins to grow again. Expansion begins again and the business cycle continues.

✔ **Reading Check** Sequencing List the stages of the business cycle in the correct order. expansion, peak, contraction, trough, possibly depression, renewed expansion

# TEACH OBJECTIVE 2

**ALL LEVELS:** Draw a two-column chart on the chalkboard. In the first column have volunteers list the old theories of the business cycle and indicate when these theories existed. *(Before the depression, economists believed the business cycle should be left alone. Now the government intervenes to control inflation, boost production, and end unemployment.)* Then in the second column have students explain how the events of the Great Depression went against the economic thinking of the past. Finally, have students use the chart to answer the following question: Why were old theories of the business cycle questioned after the Great Depression?
**ENGLISH LANGUAGE LEARNERS**

**LEVEL 2:** Have students create an annotated time line that displays the old theories of the business cycle and when these theories existed. *(See the All Levels lesson for theories.)* Then have students include the event or events on the time line that challenged the old theories.

# TEACH OBJECTIVE 3

**LEVEL 1:** Have each student write a journal entry about the Great Depression as if he or she were an official in the Roosevelt administration. Journal entries should analyze how the government's new role in the economy changed after the Great Depression.
**ENGLISH LANGUAGE LEARNERS**

## ★ The Great Depression

The worst depression in the country's history took place during the 1930s. This period, as you have read, is known as the Great Depression. The first sign of trouble came in October 1929, when the prices of stocks on the New York Stock Exchange fell sharply. Many banks failed, causing many people to lose their savings.

By 1932 business was producing only half as much as it had in 1929. Thousands of businesses closed. Farm prices were lower than ever before. By 1933 about one in four Americans was unemployed. Most of these people had families to support. Unable to pay their mortgages, many people lost their homes. Many Americans faced these and other severe hardships during the Great Depression.

✔ **Reading Check Summarizing** What happened during the Great Depression? In 1929 the stock market crashed, many banks failed, and people lost their savings; thousands of businesses closed, farm prices were the lowest ever, about one quarter of all workers lost jobs, and many people lost their homes.

## ★ Old Theories of the Business Cycle

Before the Great Depression of the 1930s, most economists believed the business cycle should be left alone. They maintained that it was unwise for the government to try to control inflation, boost production, or end unemployment.

These economists believed the problems that came with the business cycle would cure themselves. If prices rose too high, people would stop buying goods and services until prices fell again. Also, high prices and attractive profits would convince some people to go into business. The supply of goods and services would therefore increase, and this increase would prevent prices from rising.

**Interpreting the Visual Record**

**The Great Depression** *During the Great Depression many unemployed Americans waited for hours in bread or soup lines such as this one to receive a free meal.* **How does this image illustrate the difficulties faced during the depression?**

★★★★★★★★★★★★
**That's Interesting!**
★★★★★★★★★★★★

**Hoovervilles** How do you think the country's president reacted to the stock market crash? President Herbert Hoover did not realize how bad things were. Just a few months after the crash, he announced that the economy would soon be back on its feet. Instead, the country sank into a depression. Camps of homeless people living in makeshift shacks began to appear outside many cities. Hoover became so unpopular with hard-hit Americans that people began naming these camps Hoovervilles.

★ **Global Perspectives**

**The Great Depression**
We associate the Great Depression with the stock market crash of 1929 and the failure of U.S. banks. The Great Depression was not, however, confined to the United States or even to the capitalist countries of the West. The depression began in the industrialized countries but soon affected industrializing nations whose economies relied on the export of goods. For example, the demand for goods imported into the United States shrank dramatically because of rising unemployment and decreasing wages. Also, the United States enacted protectionist tariff laws, such as the Smoot-Hawley Tariff Act of 1930. Many countries in return hiked tariffs on their imports, thus adding to problems for U.S. businesses, which found export markets virtually closed to them.

**CRITICAL THINKING**
How might a tariff help a country during a depression?

**ANSWER:** Students might suggest that a tariff might make a foreign product more expensive than a domestic product, making it more likely that citizens will buy the domestic product.

**Visual Record Answer**

*Students might suggest that the long line indicates desperation.*

**LEVEL 3:** Organize students into two groups. Have one group develop statements supporting the government's new role in the economy after the Great Depression. Have the other group of students develop statements in protest of the government's new role. Then have the groups participate in a debate analyzing how the Great Depression changed the government's role in the economy and whether this change was beneficial to the country. **COOPERATIVE LEARNING**

**HOMEWORK** Have students create political cartoons that portray the business cycle and its effects on business and workers. Encourage students to be creative. Invite the cartoonists to present and explain their work to the class.

## CLOSE

Ask students the following question: What part of the business cycle is the economy in today? Have students establish the status of the economy according to the categories discussed in the section. Students might want to refer to articles in newspapers and other periodicals about the state of the U.S. economy. Then ask students what would be different if the economy today were in a different part of the business cycle. Have them list a few of the differences, not only regarding the national economy but also in their own lives.

**Interpreting the Visual Record**

**Public works** *During the depression the U.S. government spent millions of dollars on public works projects such as the building of dams.* **How might projects like this one help the nation during an economic slowdown?**

Many economists also thought that recessions could not last long. Workers who lost their jobs would soon be willing to accept lower wages. Businesses would then be able to hire people for lower pay. Other costs of production would also be lower than before. This situation would encourage businesses to produce more.

As businesses expanded and increased their spending, they would help other businesses. Soon new businesses would be started. The economy would improve. Salaries would be raised, and more people would be hired. People would buy more, and so on. Then came the Great Depression. The old theories did not seem to work anymore.

### Historical Document

### FDR's Inaugural Address

President Franklin D. Roosevelt's first inaugural address was broadcast on the radio. He tried to encourage struggling Americans during the depression.

"This great nation will endure as it has endured, will revive and will prosper. So, first of all, let me assert [state] my firm belief that the only thing we have to fear is fear itself. . . . Our greatest primary task is to put people to work. This is no unsolvable problem if we face it wisely and courageously. It can be accomplished in part by direct recruiting by the government itself, treating the task as we would treat the emergency of a war."

**Analyzing Primary Sources**
1. What does President Roosevelt mean by "the only thing we have to fear is fear itself"?
2. What does the president propose as a way of fighting the depression?

✔ **Reading Check** Identifying Points of View How did supporters of old theories of the business cycle view government involvement in the economy, and why did they hold these beliefs? They believed the government should not interfere in the business cycle because the problems that came with the business cycle would cure themselves.

### ★ Government Efforts

Wages were very low during the Great Depression. Rather than be without work, millions of unemployed people were willing to accept any pay, no matter how low. However, businesses were in great financial difficulty and could not afford to hire workers. Moreover, those businesses that did survive did not expand. There was no point in producing more goods when few people had enough money to buy them. To the surprise of the economists, the Great Depression did not end in a fairly short time. It lasted for more than 10 years.

Finally, many people were willing to allow the government to take steps to improve the economy. As you recall, President Franklin D. Roosevelt established a program called the New Deal. Under this program, unemployed workers were hired by the government to do work

# REVIEW AND ASSESS

Have students complete the **Section 1 Review** on page 489. Then have students complete **Daily Quiz 20.1**. As **Alternative Assessment**, you may want to use the Federal Reserve Chairperson activity or the business cycle organizer in this section's lessons.

## RETEACH

Have students complete **Main Idea Activity for English Language Learners and Special-Needs Students 20.1**. Pair students and have them write each vocabulary term on a card and put the definition or sketch of the term's meaning on another card. Ask students to shuffle the cards and to lay them face up in two vertical rows next to each other. Students should take turns matching cards labeled with terms to the appropriate definition or illustration cards.
**ENGLISH LANGUAGE LEARNERS**, **COOPERATIVE LEARNING**

## EXTEND

Have students examine books that deal with the art commissioned through the Works Progress Administration. *(Your school's art teacher may be able to help locate good sources.)* Ask students to interpret the murals in light of what they know about the Great Depression. Have students write a critique of the art and artists to determine if they believe the artists were optimistic or pessimistic about the future. **BLOCK SCHEDULING**

such as creating parks and building schools. Many young people joined the Civilian Conservation Corps. They worked on projects to restore forests and other natural resources. Homeowners and farmers were able to get loans to help pay their mortgages.

As you know from Chapter 19, the Federal Deposit Insurance Corporation (FDIC) was set up to insure bank deposits. Dishonesty and fraud in the stock market had been at least partially responsible for the Great Depression. The Securities and Exchange Commission (SEC) was established to oversee the buying and selling of stocks and bonds.

Another important part of the New Deal program was the organization of the Social Security system. This system was established to give regular payments to retired citizens and to help others in need. Unemployment compensation was created to provide workers with some money when they had lost their jobs.

Economists and historians still disagree about just what factors caused and ended the Great Depression. Many of the measures established during the Great Depression remain in effect today. However, these measures have not ended the economic challenges facing the country. Americans still disagree over the extent to which the government should intervene in the U.S. economy.

✔ **Reading Check Identifying Cause and Effect** Why did many Americans begin to support government intervention in the economy? What changes did the government make to try to improve the economy?
The Great Depression lasted much longer than people believed it would. The federal government established the New Deal, and created the FDIC and the Social Security system.

**A Most Vicious Circle**
—Costello in the Albany "News."

**Interpreting Political Cartoons**

**Public opinion** *Many Americans felt that President Hoover did not do enough to pull the country out of the depression.* **How is the public reacting to Hoover in this cartoon?**

**POLITICAL CARTOON ANSWER**
Students should suggest that they are all pointing fingers at Hoover and accusing him of not doing enough.

## Section 1 Review
### ANSWERS

**1. Define**
- business cycle, p. 485
- expansion, p. 485
- inflation, p. 485
- costs of production, p. 486
- peak, p. 486
- contraction, p. 486
- recession, p. 486
- trough, p. 486
- depression, p. 486

**2.** Federal Deposit Insurance Corporation; Securities and Exchange Commission; Civilian Conservation Corps; Social Security

**3. a.** periods of prosperous economic activity, then economic hardship, followed by good economic activity

**b.** The government became directly involved in altering the economy.

**4.** Students' paragraphs will vary but should distinguish that a depression is a period of severe recession, a recession is a severe contraction, and contraction is a period of economic slowdown.

---

# SECTION 1 Review

**go.hrw.com Homework Practice Online**
keyword: SZ3 HP20

**1. Define** and explain:
- business cycle
- expansion
- inflation
- costs of production
- peak
- contraction
- recession
- trough
- depression

**2. Categorizing** Copy the graphic organizer below. Then use it to identify the programs created by the New Deal and explain how they provided relief.

| The New Deal | |
| --- | --- |
| Problem | → Solution |
| bank problems | → |
| stock market fraud | → |
| unemployment | → |
| economic hardship | → |

**3. Finding the Main Idea**
a. What happens in the business cycle?
b. How did the government's role in the economy change during the 1930s?

**4. Writing and Critical Thinking**
**Contrasting** Write a paragraph explaining how contractions, recessions, and depressions are different.

**Consider:**
- what happens to the economy during each event
- what happens to people during each event

# SECTION 2

## OBJECTIVES

*After completing Section 2, students should be able to*

**1** Identify the economic problems that exist and determine what causes them.

**2** Describe how the government addresses economic problems.

**3** Explain how citizens can work to improve the economy.

## SECTION 2 RESOURCES

### REPRODUCIBLE

▶ Guided Reading Strategies 20.2

▶ Readings in Economics and Government 67: *The Affluent Society*, by John Kenneth Galbraith

▶ American Civics Political Cartoon: FDR and the New Deal

### TECHNOLOGY

▶ One-Stop Planner, Lesson 20.2

▶ Holt Researcher CD–ROM

▶ Homework Practice Online

### REINFORCEMENT, REVIEW, AND ASSESSMENT

▶ Section 2 Review, p. 495

▶ Daily Quiz 20.2

▶ Main Idea Activity 20.2

▶ English Audio Summary 20.2

▶ Spanish Audio Summary 20.2

## 🔔 LET'S GET STARTED!

As students enter the classroom, ask them who makes the fiscal policy in their households. *(Students might suggest one of their parents, or some may not know the definition of* fiscal policy.*)* Tell them that *fiscal policy* refers to a plan on how to spend money, and that the government is responsible for the country's fiscal policy. Finally, tell students that in Section 2 they will learn more about the monetary and fiscal policies of the United States.

---

## SECTION 2

# Coping with Economic Challenges

### Read to Discover

1. What economic problems exist, and what causes them?

2. How does the government address economic problems?

3. How can citizens work to improve the economy?

### Define

• fiscal policy
• monetary policy

#### WHY CIVICS MATTERS

People have different opinions about the degree to which government should be involved in the economy. Use **CNNfyi.com** and other **current events** sources to find out what the current administration's position is on government involvement in the economy. Record your findings in your journal.

---

## *Reading Focus*

Since the time of the Great Depression, government has expanded its role in the economy. However, maintaining a healthy economy is not easy. As you have learned, economic challenges such as inflation, unemployment, and recession often accompany the business cycle. The government must find ways to deal with these challenges while encouraging economic growth.

*During an economic recession in the 1970s, a cartoonist drew President Richard Nixon on an inflated dollar bill to criticize government policies.*

### ⭐ Causes of Economic Problems

Problems such as inflation, unemployment, and recession pose serious challenges to the economy and to individual citizens. Consider inflation, for example. When prices increase faster than wages, people cannot buy as much with their money. Rising prices thus hurt the purchasing power of the dollar and can lower the standard of living for everyone.

Unemployment is also harmful. Unemployed workers cannot pay bills or taxes. They buy fewer goods and services, which hurts American businesses. Sometimes unemployed people must seek government assistance, which costs taxpayers money.

# TEACH OBJECTIVE 1

**LEVEL 1:** Help students create a two-column chart on the chalkboard. In the first column have students write the economic problems that exist. *(Students might suggest inflation, unemployment, and recession.)* In the second column students should explain what causes these problems. *(Students might suggest too much money in circulation, banks issuing too many loans, government spending and borrowing, too little consumer saving and too much spending, and decreased productivity in the United States relative to foreign countries.)* Have each student copy the chart onto a sheet of paper for use as a review guide. **ENGLISH LANGUAGE LEARNERS**

**LEVEL 2:** Tell students of the old complaint, "A dollar just doesn't buy as much as it used to." Have students discuss why this saying is a comment about inflation. Then have students create their own sayings, perhaps in the form of rhyming couplets, that express an opinion about the causes or effects of inflation, unemployment, and recession. Encourage students to read their sayings to the class as part of a discussion about what economic problems exist and what causes them.

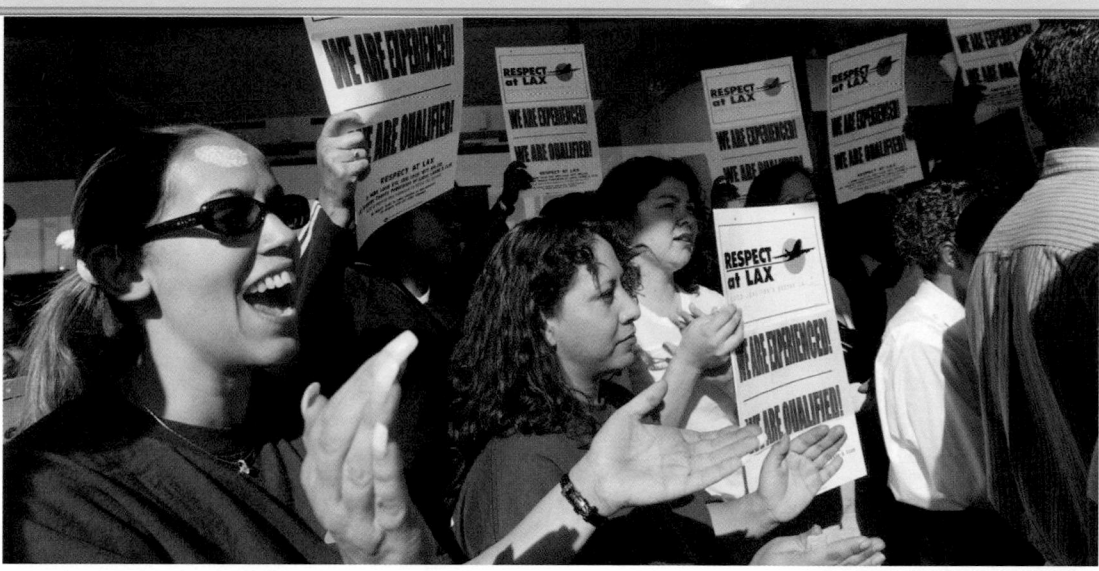

**Interpreting the Visual Record**

**Layoffs** *During periods of recession workers are often laid off, creating unemployment problems that can further hurt the economy.* **Why do you think these people are protesting layoffs? What might they hope to achieve?**

Production, spending, and consumer demand decline during periods of recession. Because businesses are producing less, they need fewer workers. As a result, unemployment increases. This unemployment contributes to a decrease in individual savings, which banks depend on. As a result, banks have less money to lend to businesses.

As you can see, inflation, unemployment, and recession pose serious challenges for the economy. What causes these economic difficulties? Economists point to many different reasons, including the money supply, government spending, and productivity.

✔ **Reading Check** **Finding the Main Idea** What are the most serious challenges to the economy? inflation, unemployment, and recession

## ★ Money and Loans

In Chapter 19 you learned how the Federal Reserve tries to control the amount of money and credit in the economy. Some economists believe that a major cause of inflation is the circulation of too much money. They argue that the Federal Reserve has put too much money into the U.S. economy. As people spend this additional money, they cause prices to rise.

Some economists blame the country's economic problems on banks for making too many loans. People and businesses who borrow money then spend that money on goods and services. Thus, loaning money has the same effect as putting more money into the economy. This process can contribute to inflation. Also, businesses that borrow and expand too rapidly may produce more goods than they can sell. These businesses must then slow their production, contributing to economic recession.

✔ **Reading Check** **Analyzing Information** How do economists believe that money supply and loans can affect the economy? An excess of either can contribute to inflation, hurting consumer spending and business production.

In the 1970s President Gerald Ford started a program called WIN, which stood for "Whip Inflation Now."

# TEACH OBJECTIVE 2

**ALL LEVELS:** Copy the following graphic organizer onto the chalkboard, omitting the italicized answers. Have students complete the organizer to describe how the government addresses economic problems.

**ENGLISH LANGUAGE LEARNERS**

 **The Government's Response to Economic Challenges**

**Changes to the fiscal policy:**
- *Reduce taxes*
- *Buy more goods and hire more people*
- *Give larger payments to unemployed, poor, and older citizens*
- *Decrease wasteful spending*

**Changes to the monetary policy:**
- *Increase money supply during a recession by reducing interest rates or by buying government bonds*
- *Raise taxes and reduce spending during a boom period*
- *Raise interest rates during a boom period*

## ★ Economics

### A Cause of Inflation

Milton Friedman, former chairperson of the Federal Reserve Board, had his own opinion about the primary cause of inflation. In an interview in 1977 he said, "There's only one place where inflation is made: that's in Washington . . . in response to pressures from the people at large. . . . The voting public . . . ask their Congressmen to enact goodies in the form of spending, but they are unhappy about having taxes raised to pay for those goodies."

### CRITICAL THINKING

What "goodies" might Friedman be referring to?

**ANSWER:** Students might suggest that the "goodies" were programs and services that required government funding.

### Visual Record Answer

*(for page 493)*
*Students might suggest that they appear to be working on computers.*

**Holt Researcher**

**go.hrw.com**
**KEYWORD:** Holt Researcher
**Freefind:** Consumer Price Index

Look up the information on the Consumer Price Index on the Holt Researcher. Use this information to create a line graph showing the index over the past 25 years. Your graph should answer the question: What has been the general trend of the Consumer Price Index in the past 25 years?

*Consumer spending affects the economy in several ways. Too much spending can contribute to inflation, while too little spending can lead to cutbacks in production.*

## ★ Government and Consumer Spending

As you know, the government spends many billions of dollars each year. Much of the money spent by the government comes from taxes paid by individuals and business firms. The government also borrows some of the money it spends.

Many people believe the government is borrowing and spending too much. Government borrowing, like bank loans to individuals, puts more money into the economy and helps raise prices. It also adds to the national debt. The increased taxes that are needed to pay this debt take money out of the hands of individuals. These individuals then find it difficult to pay the inflated prices of goods and services.

Consumers share some of the responsibility for the country's economic difficulties. Many people borrow money to buy things they cannot afford. Paying back this credit debt means that consumers can save only a small part of their income. Too little consumer saving reduces the amount of money available for business expansion. Too much spending may be partly responsible for inflation.

 **Reading Check Comparing** How can government and consumer spending affect the economy? An excess of either can lead to inflation.

## ★ Productivity

Productivity, as you recall, refers to the amount a worker produces per hour. Rising productivity usually leads to higher wages, higher profits, and lower prices. However, in recent years worker productivity in some other countries has increased faster than in the United States. Thus, foreign products can be made and sold less expensively than products made in the United States. Although this allows consumers to buy

**LEVEL 2:** Have each student imagine they are a politician and he or she is making a speech to a group of business leaders. Ask each student to write a speech that describes how the government addresses economic problems. *(Students' speeches should include monetary and fiscal policy changes that the government can undertake to address economic problems.)*

## TEACH OBJECTIVE 3

**LEVEL 1:** Have students create collages on poster-board that encourage citizens to help improve the economy. Posters should inform citizens of the various actions they can take to help improve the economy. *(Students' collages might reflect increasing savings and decreasing spending,*

*buying American-made products, or increasing worker productivity.)* Display completed posters around the classroom.
**ENGLISH LANGUAGE LEARNERS**

**LEVEL 3:** Have each student write a script for a public service announcement that advises citizens about the actions they can take to help improve the economy. *(See the Level 1 lesson for suggestions.)* Have volunteers present their announcements to the class.

less-expensive products, it hurts American businesses and can contribute to unemployment.

Many American businesses find that the only way they can increase productivity is to modernize their factories. However, modernization can cost millions of dollars. As a result, many American businesses have moved their operations to other countries where wages are low and government regulations are few. This relocation allows American businesses to reduce their costs and increase productivity. However, in the United States it has resulted in the loss of thousands of jobs.

✔ **Reading Check** Finding the Main Idea Why is productivity important? It affects how well the United States can compete economically with other countries.

### The Government's Response

The government can respond to challenges facing the U.S. economy in a number of ways. The federal government can change its **fiscal policy,** or its policy of taxing and spending, to aid the ailing economy. For example, if the economy is entering a recession the government may reduce the amount of taxes that individuals pay. Lower taxes give people new money to spend and to save. Increased spending encourages businesses to produce more, which leads to the creation of more jobs. Increased saving gives banks more money to lend to expanding businesses.

During recessions, the government may increase its own spending. It buys more goods and hires more people to work for the government. In the past, the government has employed people to build public projects, such as dams and bridges. The government may also give larger payments to the unemployed, those living in poverty, and older citizens.

The government also may respond to economic difficulties by changing its **monetary policy,** or its policy regarding money. As you have read, this policy is handled by the Federal Reserve System. The Federal Reserve, or the Fed, serves as the country's central bank. The Fed works to control the amount of money in the economy.

Imagine that the country is entering a recession. The Fed may increase the money supply by buying government bonds back from banks or lowering the interest rate that banks pay the Fed. These actions make it easier for banks to lend money to businesses. Officials believe lower interest rates will encourage businesses to expand, thus creating more jobs and income.

**Interpreting the Visual Record**

Hard at work *High productivity is important to American businesses, but it can also put pressure on individual workers.* **What type of work are these women doing?**

**GLOBAL CONNECTIONS**

### NAFTA

In 1992 President Bill Clinton signed the North American Free Trade Agreement (NAFTA). This agreement was designed to promote trade between Canada, Mexico, and the United States by lowering and eventually eliminating tariffs and customs duties. As a result, each country's markets would be open to goods and services from its neighbors. A 2001 report found that NAFTA had increased trade and investment between its member countries. Supporters argue that this growth has benefited U.S. agriculture and other areas. Opponents claim that the agreement has encouraged U.S. companies to relocate to Mexico, costing American jobs. **How does the dispute over NAFTA demonstrate the difficulties that the government faces in helping the economy?**

### ★ Economics

**Stagflation** Economic events are not entirely predictable, much less controllable. For example, in the 1970s during the presidency of Jimmy Carter, the economy was gripped by a seeming contradiction—rising inflation with stagnant output and rising unemployment. In classical economic theory, high unemployment should have put a damper on inflation. In the 1970s, however, it did not. Economists dubbed this strange set of circumstances "stagflation." Some economists have tried to explain stagflation by arguing that periods of high inflation (such as the early and mid-1970s) lead to expectations that prices will continue to increase. Such expectations then influence labor negotiations, bringing about higher wages to match expected price increases. According to this argument, the spiral of higher wages and higher prices then continues even during difficult economic times, thus producing stagflation.

**ACTIVITY:** Have students conduct research to determine if there have been other periods in the recent economy of stagflation. Ask each student to draw a time line depicting these periods.

**GLOBAL CONNECTIONS ANSWER**
Students might suggest it shows that there is always the possibility that some groups will agree and other groups will disagree with the government's intervention in the economy.

**HOMEWORK** Have each student create a list of at least 10 products in his or her home that are American-made. Then have each student list 10 products that are not American-made but are available from an American company. Finally, have students indicate in their second lists why they chose to buy foreign products instead of American products. (*Students' reasons might include that foreign products are less expensive or better in quality.*)

## CLOSE

Review the actions that the government and the Federal Reserve might take during a recession or, conversely, during an expansion period. Have each student draw diagrams to explain these actions, the reasons for the actions, and the expected results. Call on volunteers to present their diagrams to the class for discussion.

---

If the country is in a boom period, these actions may be reversed. For example, when inflation becomes too high the federal government may raise taxes and reduce its spending. The Federal Reserve may make it more difficult for banks to lend money to businesses by raising interest rates. These steps decrease the amount of money in the economy.

The United States has not yet learned to control its economy. Some people believe that it does not need to be controlled. They argue that the government should not interfere with the economy. They also believe that social welfare programs have contributed to problems such as inflation. Other people believe that the government can help the economy. These people argue that without government actions, economic difficulties would worsen. Another serious and prolonged depression might even occur.

✔ **Reading Check** Analyzing Information How might the government respond to a recession? It could lower taxes and increase spending; the Federal Reserve could increase the money supply, making it easier for banks to lend money to businesses.

## ★ Other Ways to Help the Economy

The government constantly struggles to maintain the proper balance between economic growth and inflation. However, fiscal and monetary policies do not always ensure a healthy economy. What more can be done to improve the economy?

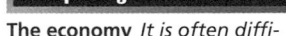

**Interpreting Political Cartoons**

**The economy** *It is often difficult for U.S. citizens to know just how their actions will affect the country's economy.* **What confusing information is the person in this cartoon being given?**

# REVIEW AND ASSESS

Have students complete the **Section 2 Review** on page 495. Then have students complete **Daily Quiz 20.2**. As **Alternative Assessment**, you may want to use the citizens helping the economy poster or the economic problems organizer in this section's lessons.

# RETEACH

Have students complete **Main Idea Activity for English Language Learners and Special-Needs Students 20.2**. Then ask each student to create a guidebook for the government. The guidebook should outline what course of action to take depending on the status of the economy. For example, the guidebook might advise the government to raise taxes and reduce spending during times of inflation. Have students consider all stages of the business cycle in their guidebooks. **ENGLISH LANGUAGE LEARNERS**

# EXTEND

Have students research past efforts to tame inflation. Some examples include wage and price controls during the Nixon administration and the "Whip Inflation Now" campaign during the Ford administration. Ask each student to investigate how successful each of these efforts was and prepare a short report that includes illustrations for the class. **BLOCK SCHEDULING**

**Reduce Government Spending** Government can reduce wasteful spending and halt unnecessary government programs. Many people believe that the government should also try to spend only the money it receives from taxes. With a balanced budget, the government would not have to borrow money and could work to reduce the national debt.

**Increase Saving** Consumers can help the economy by reducing their spending and saving more of their income. They can do this by using credit only for buying things that they really need.

**Buy American-Made Products** When consumers buy products that are made in the United States, they help American businesses prosper. This prosperity in turn helps preserve jobs for American workers and create more jobs.

**Increase Productivity** If the total amount produced each hour increases, the supply of goods increases. To help the economy, business managers could try to operate their businesses more efficiently. Workers can try to do their jobs more efficiently. If workers' productivity increases, workers may earn higher wages without contributing to inflation. Some economists suggest that to keep inflation low, wages should not increase faster than productivity increases.

The health of the U.S. economy is of vital importance to everyone. Americans must do all they can to help ensure that the United States remains a strong and prosperous country.

*Buying American-made products is one way to help keep jobs in the United States.*

✔ **Reading Check** **Summarizing** How can consumers help to improve the economy? Consumers can reduce spending and save more, buy American-made products, and increase their productivity at work.

# SECTION 2 Review

**go.hrw.com Homework Practice Online**
**keyword: SZ3 HP20**

1. **Define** and explain:
   • fiscal policy
   • monetary policy

2. **Identifying Cause and Effect** Copy the web diagram below. Then use it to list ways that citizens can improve the economy.

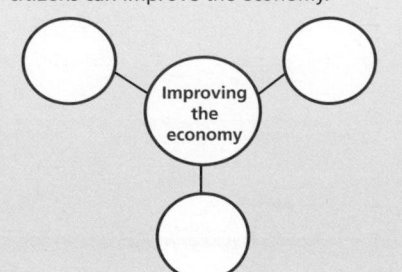

3. **Finding the Main Idea**
   a. What causes the problems that exist in the U.S. economy, and how does the federal government try to solve them?
   b. Why might the government reduce taxes during a recession? How does the Federal Reserve reduce the supply of money in circulation?

4. **Writing and Critical Thinking**
   **Supporting a Point of View** Do you think Americans should buy American-made products? Explain your answer.

   **Consider:**
   • the reasons many American businesses have moved operations to other countries
   • how this has affected American workers
   • possible price differences between imported and American-made products

## Section 2 Review
### ANSWERS

**1. Define**
• fiscal policy, p. 493
• monetary policy, p. 493

**2.** reduce spending; increase savings; buy American-made products; increase worker productivity

**3. a.** too much money in circulation; too many loans from banks; high government spending and borrowing; too little consumer saving and too much spending; decreased productivity in the United States relative to foreign countries; tries to manipulate the economy through interest rate increases and decreases, urging consumer spending, and so on

**b.** Lower taxes gives people more money to spend and save. The Fed may raise interest rates or sell bonds to decrease the money supply.

**4.** Students' answers will vary but should provide support for their points of view.

## TEACH

**ALL LEVELS:** Bring old newspapers and magazines to class. Have students look through them to find information displayed on a line graph. Have each student select a graph and determine what the subject of the graph is, what the data labels represent, and what general trend the indicator line represents. **ENGLISH LANGUAGE LEARNERS**

## SPOTLIGHT on Math

Help students distinguish between bar graphs and line graphs by asking the following questions: Which type of graph is better for comparing quantities, or amounts? Which type is better for showing changes in data, such as prices, over time? Then refer students to the Chapter 16 "Developing Civics Skills" activity (**page 394**) in which they tracked the total number of articles about juvenile crime listed each year in the *Readers' Guide to Periodical Literature*. Have students create line graphs that show the trend in the annual number of articles about juvenile crime over the period of time covered in that activity. **BLOCK SCHEDULING**

### SKILLS ANSWERS
1. 1994 and 1996
2. $1.22; $1.22
3. prices rose
4. It might help economic policy makers with decisions and economic planning.
5. The indicator line makes it easier to trace changes in price over time.

# Civics Skills
## WORKSHOP

### Reading Line Graphs
Suppose you are tired of paying more for goods and services, and you want Congress to take action to curb inflation. How might you make this point to your representatives in Congress in a simple yet dramatic way? An excellent way would be to use a line graph. As you have learned, graphs help people understand data by placing large amounts of information in easy-to-read diagrams.

### How to Read Line Graphs
1. **Determine the subject.** Read the title of the graph to determine its subject and purpose.

2. **Study the labels.** Line graphs usually have two labels. One label reads across the bottom of the graph. This label identifies the data on the horizontal axis. The other label appears beside the line that runs up and down. This label identifies the data on the vertical axis of the graph.

3. **Examine the indicator line.** The purpose of a line graph is to show changes in amounts over time. It does so with an indicator line. By following the indicator line from left to right, you are following the quantity indicated on the vertical axis through time. The period of time being studied is shown on the horizontal axis. In the line graph on this page, for example, the indicator line shows how the price of gasoline in the United States changed from 1990 to 1999.

4. **Put the data to use.** Use the graph to draw conclusions about the data. Identify any trends from the graph.

### Applying the Skill
Study the line graph below, which shows the average price of regular unleaded gasoline. Then answer the questions that follow.

1. Between what years shown on the graph did the price of gasoline increase most significantly?

2. What was the average price of a gallon of gas in 1990? What was the average price nine years later?

3. Based on this chart, what was the trend in gasoline prices in the United States between 1992 and 1996?

4. How might the information displayed on this graph affect the national economy? Explain your answer.

5. Why is a line graph better than other types of graphs for showing these kinds of data?

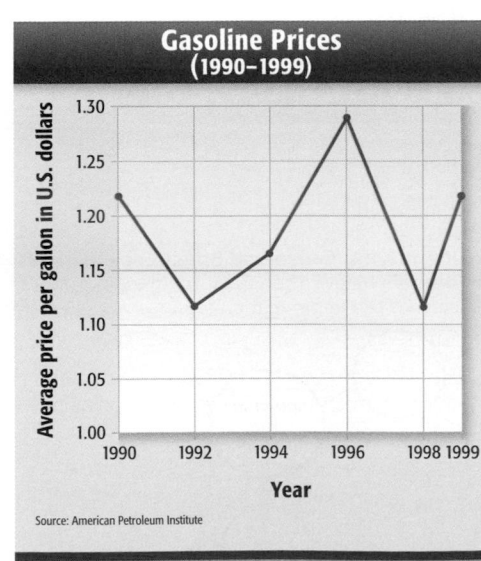

**Gasoline Prices (1990–1999)**

Average price per gallon in U.S. dollars

Year

Source: American Petroleum Institute

# SECTION 3

## OBJECTIVES

*After completing Section 3, students should be able to*

1  **Describe the conditions that led to the rise of labor unions in the 1800s.**

2  **Identify the methods labor and employers use to negotiate with one another and describe the major labor laws that protect them.**

3  **Analyze the status of labor relations today.**

## 🔊 LET'S GET STARTED!

As students enter the classroom, ask them how they settle disputes with their teachers. *(Students' answers will vary.)* Then ask students what might happen if they tried to settle a dispute by refusing to work. *(Students' might suggest that they may get into trouble for refusing to work in class.)* Tell students that refusing to work is called a strike, and that strikes are one method workers have used to make their issues or grievances known to their employers. Finally, tell students that in Section 3 they will learn more about the various methods workers and employers use to settle disputes, as well as the status of labor relations today.

---

## SECTION 3

# Labor and Management

### Read to Discover

1. What conditions led to the rise of labor unions in the 1800s?
2. What methods do labor and employers use to negotiate with one another, and what major labor laws protect them?
3. What is the status of labor relations today?

#### WHY CIVICS MATTERS

The relationship between labor and management is often a difficult one. Use **CNNfyi.com** or other **current events** sources to learn about a recent local or national conflict between labor and management. Record your findings in your journal.

### Define

- labor unions
- collective bargaining
- strike
- picketing
- job action
- blacklists
- lockouts
- closed shop
- open shop
- union shop
- agency shop
- right-to-work laws
- featherbedding
- mediation
- arbitration

## Reading Focus

One day you will join the country's working population. You may already have joined it if you have had an after-school or summer job. As a future full-time worker, you may be part of the labor force. You may be part of management—one of the owners or managers of a business. No matter what your position, you will need to understand the relationship between labor and management.

*Many early Americans were farmers who worked their own land.*

### ★ Past Working Conditions

In the early days of the United States, many Americans were self-employed. They worked for themselves on small farms or in their own workshops or stores. They sold the goods they made to neighbors and friends. Most businesses were small. They employed only a few workers, or wage earners. Wage earners often worked side by side with the owner of a business. They often knew the owner personally.

Usually if workers were dissatisfied, they could speak to the owner and ask for better wages or improved working conditions. If the owner refused, they could quit their jobs. The expansion of both industry and the country and the lack of laborsaving machinery meant there were often more jobs than workers. Because workers were in demand, employers usually treated their employees fairly and honestly.

## SECTION 3 RESOURCES

### REPRODUCIBLE

▶ Guided Reading Strategies 20.3

▶ Readings in Economics and Government 39: Interstate Commerce Act of 1887

▶ Creative Teaching Strategy: Brainstorming

### TECHNOLOGY

▶ One-Stop Planner, Lesson 20.3

▶ CNN Presents: American Government

▶ Homework Practice Online

▶ HRW Go site

### REINFORCEMENT, REVIEW, AND ASSESSMENT

▶ Section 3 Review, p. 505

▶ Daily Quiz 20.3

▶ Main Idea Activity 20.3

▶ English Audio Summary 20.3

▶ Spanish Audio Summary 20.3

**LEVEL 1:** Have each student imagine that they are a worker in the United States who has recently returned to the country after a long absence. The time is the late 1800s. Unions have become common, and fellow workers are urging them to join. Ask each student to develop a list of questions to ask the other workers that will help him or her decide whether to join a union. Students' questions should focus on the conditions that sparked the need for unions, as well as what advantages can be gained from joining a union. *(Factory managers and owners had little contact with their workers; the working day was long; wages were low; working conditions were often harsh.)* **ENGLISH LANGUAGE LEARNERS**

## TEACHER TO TEACHER

Michelle Bierman of Minnesota recommends the following activity:

**ALL LEVELS:** Have students create labor posters that represent the key issues that workers sought to address by establishing unions. *(See the Level 1 lesson for issues.)* Ask volunteers to present their posters to the class.

**ENGLISH LANGUAGE LEARNERS**

## Constitutional Heritage

### "Yellow Dog" Contracts

During the early 1900s, the U.S. Supreme Court heard several cases regarding labor issues. In *Lochner v. New York*, the Court decided that states could not limit the amount of hours employers could work their employees. In *Adair v. United States*, the Supreme Court decided on a case dealing with union membership. William Adair, a railroad employer, fired a worker for belonging to a union. This action was in direct violation of the Erdman Act of 1898, which prohibited railroads from using "yellow dog" contracts. These contracts forbade union membership. In its decision, the Court stated that the Erdman Act violated the due process clause of the Fifth Amendment, which guaranteed freedom of contract and property rights.

**ACTIVITY:** Have students research other Supreme Court cases that dealt with labor issues. Ask students to display their findings on an annotated time line.

### CASE STUDY ANSWER

Students might suggest that child labor laws and minimum-wage laws might also seem to restrict the Fourteenth Amendment.

### Visual Record Answer

*Students should suggest to avoid such abuses.*

# SUPREME COURT CASE STUDY

## Lochner v. New York

**Significance:** This decision established the Supreme Court's role in overseeing state regulations. For more than 30 years, *Lochner* was often used as a precedent in striking down state laws such as minimum-wage laws, child labor laws, and regulations placed on the banking and transportation industries.

**Background:** In 1895 the state of New York passed a labor law limiting bakers to working no more than 10 hours per day or 60 hours per week. The purpose of the law was to protect the health of bakers, who worked in hot and damp conditions and breathed in large quantities of flour dust. In 1902 Joseph Lochner, the owner of a small bakery in New York, claimed that the state law violated his Fourteenth Amendment rights by unfairly depriving him of the liberty to make contracts with employees. This case went to the Supreme Court.

**Decision:** This case was decided on April 17, 1905, by a vote of 5 to 4 in favor of Lochner. The Supreme Court judged that the Fourteenth Amendment protected the right to sell and buy labor and that any state law restricting that right was unconstitutional. The Court rejected the argument that the limited workday and workweek were necessary to protect the health of bakery workers.

**How might the Court's ruling in *Lochner* v. *New York* serve as the basis for striking down a state child labor or minimum-wage law?**

---

Between 1800 and 1850, working conditions for many wage earners changed greatly. Large factories were built that used machines to make products. Many of these factories employed hundreds of workers, including many young children.

In these new factories relations between employers and workers were different. Factory managers and owners had little or no contact with their workers. The working day was long—12 or even 16 hours. Wages were low, and working conditions were often harsh. Yet workers could do little to improve their situation. More and more settlers poured into western lands. Because of this shift, it became more difficult for dissatisfied workers to leave their jobs and start on their own. In addition, some employers hired immigrant workers who might be willing to work for lower wages.

✔ **Reading Check** Analyzing Information How did the way most Americans work change in the time between the country's beginnings through the 1850s? The majority of people went from working for themselves or in small businesses to working in large factories under harsher conditions.

### ★ Rise of Labor Unions

As American businesses continued to expand between 1850 and 1900, the number of workers also increased. American workers began to organize in groups, hoping to improve wages and working conditions. These organizations of workers became known as **labor unions.**

A number of small local labor unions had been established earlier. Local unions, however, were not always successful in dealing with

**Interpreting the Visual Record**

**Child labor** *In industries such as coal mining it was common for boys like this one to work 10 or more hours a day.* **Why do you think U.S. child labor laws now ban such situations?**

**LEVEL 2:** Have students imagine that they have just discovered a time capsule from the 1800s, prior to the rise of labor unions. The time capsule contains objects that represent the working conditions of the time period. Have students write lists of the possible items and describe how the objects might have contributed to the rise of labor unions. (*Objects might include journal entries from workers, newspaper editorials about working conditions, a time card from a factory worker showing the long hours worked, or other items to represent the working conditions.*)

# TEACH OBJECTIVE 1

 **LEVEL 1:** On the chalkboard, have students create a chart that lists the methods used by labor and employers to negotiate with each other. Charts should also include labor laws. Volunteers should supply appropriate methods used by each group under the headings *Labor Methods, Employer Methods,* and *Major Laws Protecting Labor Relations.* (*Methods might include striking, picketing, and job actions for labor, blacklists or lockouts for employers. Major laws might include the National Labor Relations Act, the Labor-Management Relations Act, and the Landrum-Griffin Act.*) Have each student copy the chart onto a sheet of paper for use as a study guide.
**ENGLISH LANGUAGE LEARNERS**

employers. Workers came to believe they needed national union organizations to be powerful enough to deal with employers as equals.

In the late 1800s and early 1900s the growing labor unions sought the right to bargain with employers. They wanted better wages, shorter hours, and improved working conditions. The unions worked hard to show employers that the best way to settle differences with workers was through **collective bargaining.**

In collective bargaining, representatives of a labor union meet with representatives of an employer to reach an agreement. The terms of the agreement are put into a written contract. This labor contract is signed by the employer and the officers of the union.

The labor contract details the agreed-upon wage rates, hours, and working conditions. The agreement is for a fixed period of time—usually one, two, or three years. When the contract nears its ending date, representatives of the union and the employer meet again and bargain for a new contract.

## ★ Methods Used by Labor

In the early years of union organization, collective bargaining often broke down. Sometimes employers refused to bargain at all. To force business owners to bargain with them, labor unions used the **strike.** In a strike, union members walk off the job if employers do not agree to labor's demands. Production stops, and the company loses money.

What prevents a company from hiring other workers when there is a strike? The strikers try to prevent the hiring of replacement workers by **picketing.** Picketing strikers walk back and forth, often carrying signs, in front of company buildings. They discourage other workers from entering and taking over their jobs. Workers who cross picket lines and enter the buildings to work are often called scabs by the strikers. Sometimes fights have broken out between strikers and strikebreakers. The law now limits the use of strikebreakers by employers.

Instead of striking, workers sometimes stay on the job but work much more slowly than usual. This union action is called a slowdown. Any kind of slowdown, or action short of a strike, is called a **job action.** For example, the union may tell its members to follow all written orders to the letter and to check and recheck their work several times. This job action slows production and costs the company money. Sometimes it gains as much for the union as a strike.

✔ **Reading Check Summarizing** Why did labor unions develop, and what methods have they used? Labor unions developed to bargain with employers for better wages, shorter hours, and improved working conditions. They have used collective bargaining, strikes, picketing, and job actions.

In 1894 a strike against the Pullman Palace Car Company ended up halting railroad traffic throughout much of the country. President Grover Cleveland responded by attaching mail cars to the trains and charging the strikers with the federal crime of interfering with the U.S. mail!

**Interpreting the Visual Record**

**Sit-down strike** *One form of strike used by union members is the sit-down strike. In this protest, strikers occupy a factory or business facility but refuse to do any work until their demands are met.* **What might be the advantages and disadvantages of this type of strike?**

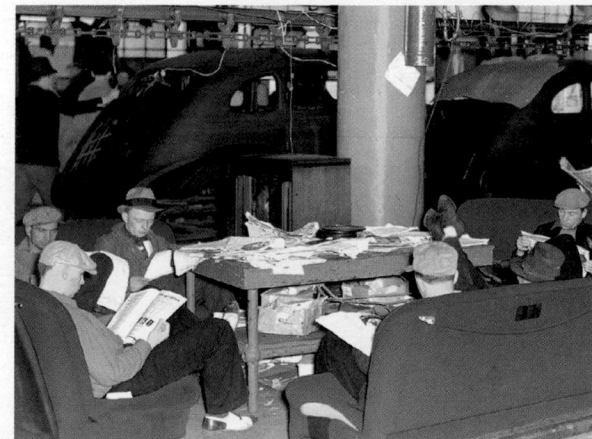

## ★ Global Perspectives

**The Boycott** The use of the boycott as a tool of social protest can be traced to Ireland in the 1800s. Charles Boycott, an English land agent, refused to comply with demands by Irish tenant farmers that he lower their high rents. To retaliate, the farmers persuaded people to refuse to do business with Boycott. This plan was so successful that Boycott and his family eventually were forced to move away from the area. Afterward, refusing to do business with someone became known as boycotting.

**ACTIVITY:** Have students conduct research to obtain information about recent or ongoing American boycotts of foreign goods. Have each student write a brief summary of why the boycott took place.

**Visual Record Answer**

*Students' responses will vary.*

**HOMEWORK** Have each student draw a flowchart to illustrate important events in the history of labor law. Each event could be boxed, with an arrow leading to the next event. Students might begin with the Wagner Act. Call on volunteers to present their flowcharts to the class.

**ALL LEVELS:** Organize students into groups. Have each group draw a political cartoon to illustrate a fictional confrontation between labor and management. Encourage groups to focus on how labor law affects the negotiations or how both sides reach a compromise. Groups should write captions for their cartoons. Remind groups that political cartoons rely on symbols to express information. Invite volunteers to present and explain their group's cartoons to the class.

**ENGLISH LANGUAGE LEARNERS , COOPERATIVE LEARNING**

## Methods Used by Employers

Most early business owners viewed union workers as troublemakers. Organizations of employers were formed to oppose the growing power of labor.

Sometimes employers hired strikebreakers to take over the jobs of workers who were on strike. Private police were sometimes hired by employers to ensure that strikers did not prevent other workers from entering the plant. A period of conflict and struggle, which sometimes turned violent, began between employers and labor.

Employers used other methods to fight the unions. They created lists containing the names of workers who were active in the labor unions. These lists were known as **blacklists.** They sent these lists to other companies and asked them not to hire anyone who was listed.

Employers also found a way to fight labor slowdowns. They closed the factory and "locked out" the workers. **Lockouts** prevented workers from earning wages. With no income, workers were soon forced to agree to return to work as usual.

✔ **Reading Check** Finding the Main Idea How have employers addressed conflicts with labor unions in the past? Employers hired new workers to replace striking workers, blacklisted workers who were active in unions, and stopped labor slowdowns with lockouts.

## Closed and Open Shops

Early labor leaders quickly realized that unions needed money to succeed. To raise money, unions began to charge their members union dues, or membership fees. This money was used by the unions to pay their officials. During strikes or lockouts, it helped feed union members and their families.

*In some shops all workers are required to be union members, while other workplaces are open to nonunion employees.*

To gather strength, the early labor unions tried to enroll every worker as a union member. It became the aim of the unions to establish a **closed shop** in every factory. In a closed shop workers cannot be hired unless they first become members of the union.

The employers opposed the closed shop. They did not want unions to have that much influence over hiring practices. They insisted on an **open shop** in every factory. In an open shop anyone can be hired. Workers do not have to be union members or have to join the union.

Much later a third type of shop was organized—the **union shop.** In a union shop an employer can hire any qualified worker, union or nonunion. However, within a short period of time, new workers must join the union to keep their jobs.

Today there is also a fourth type of shop, called the **agency shop.** In an agency shop a worker cannot be forced to join the union, but he or she must pay union dues. The unions believe workers should help pay for the protection they receive from unions. If the union fights for higher pay and better conditions, nonmembers also benefit.

Many states have passed **right-to-work laws.** In these states no one may be forced to join a union. Union members as well as nonunion members may work in the same company.

✔ **Reading Check** Contrasting How are closed shops, open shops, union shops, and agency shops different? All employees must join the union in a closed shop; in open shops, anyone can be hired; in union shops, new hires must eventually join the union; in agency shops all workers must pay union dues.

## ★ The AFL versus the CIO

Early unions were organized according to jobs or occupations. All members of the same skilled trade joined together in a craft union, or trade union. The carpenters throughout the country, the plumbers, the bakers, and so on, each had a union.

In 1886 some craft unions formed a large organization called the American Federation of Labor (AFL). Under the leadership of Samuel Gompers, the AFL grew into a powerful labor group. Each craft union in the AFL had its own officers and local branches around the country. Each union worked to improve conditions for members in its own craft. However, these craft unions joined with others in the AFL to strengthen their bargaining power.

As the country's businesses grew in size, some labor leaders pointed out that modern mass-production methods had weakened the power of craft unions in the United States. They insisted that all workers in industries such as steel and automobile industries should be members of the same union, no matter what kind of jobs they had. This kind of union is an industrial union.

Industrial unions grew rapidly during the 1930s. Industry after industry—steel, automobile, electrical equipment, rubber—was organized by labor leaders. Led by Walter Reuther and others, the industrial unions lured members away from some of the craft unions. In 1938 the industrial unions formed one large organization called the Congress of Industrial Organizations (CIO). The CIO joined together many industrial unions, welcoming unions that had African Americans, immigrants, unskilled workers, and women as members.

Workers in many industries found it difficult to choose between the CIO and the AFL. The rivalry between the two large union organizations continued for many years. An agreement was reached in 1955 when the AFL and the CIO merged to form the AFL-CIO.

Today the AFL-CIO is the largest American labor group. It has a membership of 13 million workers. Not every union belongs to this large organization, however.

✔ **Reading Check** Categorizing What different groups did the AFL and the CIO represent before they merged? Before they merged, the AFL represented skilled workers, and the CIO represented unskilled workers.

Samuel Gompers was one of the most powerful labor leaders in the United States for many years.

**Interpreting the Visual Record**

**The CIO** *For many years the AFL and the CIO were fierce rivals.* **What might be some reasons why the CIO merged with the AFL?**

502

**ALL LEVELS:** Copy the following graphic organizer onto the chalkboard, omitting the italicized answers. Have students complete the chart to analyze the status of labor relations today.

**ENGLISH LANGUAGE LEARNERS**

*Use arbitration to settle disputes*

**Labor Relations Today**

*Use collective bargaining to settle disputes*

*Use more cooperation between employers and unions*

*Use mediation to solve disputes*

**BIOGRAPHY**

## César Chávez
### (1927–1993)

César Chávez was born in Arizona, but he lived in dozens of towns as his family moved in search of farmwork. His early experiences led him to help form unions for migrant workers. Chávez viewed union work as a part of a larger fight for human rights—a goal he called La Causa, or "The Cause." His successes included the formation of the United Farm Workers and a nationally publicized hunger strike against grape growers that led to a better labor contract for farmworkers.

Chávez's patience and dedication to the cause of human rights inspired many people and won him many supporters. He helped make migrant farmworkers' rights a national issue. Before his death in 1993, Chávez insisted, "It's not me who counts, it's the movement." **How did Chávez's youth influence his goals in La Causa later in his life?**

## ★ Union Problems

Individual unions sometimes have problems with one another as well as with employers. For example, perhaps two unions want to organize the workers in the same company. In that case the unions compete to see which can get more workers to join. This competition may cause confusion on the part of the workers. They may even decide not to join either union because of the conflict.

Sometimes there are problems within a union. Many unions are called national unions because they have members in all parts of the country. However, even national unions are divided into smaller groups called local unions. Sometimes the locals disagree with the national organization's leaders. They may think the national leaders are trying to control them or are not giving them enough support.

✔ **Reading Check Analyzing Information** What problems exist among and within unions? Unions organizing in the same company compete to get workers to join. Local unions sometimes disagree with the union's leadership.

## ★ Recent Union Organization

During the 1960s the most successful attempts to organize workers took place among hospital workers and migrant farmworkers. During the 1970s the labor movement also made gains among people who worked for the government. Many federal employees, such as teachers, police, and air traffic controllers, have gone on strike, despite laws prohibiting such strikes.

In recent years, unions have not grown as rapidly as in the past. More than 120 million workers were in the workforce by 2001, but only about 16 million belonged to unions. Thus, only about 13.5 percent of all workers are union members.

The fact that the percentage of union members is small does not mean that American labor unions are weak. Many major industries are unionized. Strikes in these industries can cause serious problems for the country.

✔ **Reading Check Drawing Inferences and Conclusions** Why do you think that so few workers are union members? Answers will vary, but students may suggest that workers feel they have enough benefits without joining unions or that workers have political reasons not to join unions.

## ★ Labor Laws

Over the years, Congress has passed a number of laws dealing with the relationship between labor and management. It has done so for several reasons. One reason is that Congress wants to protect the public. When workers go on strike, the whole country may suffer. For example, a strike by coal miners might cause a coal shortage across the country. A strike by truck drivers might halt the delivery of some products.

# TEACH OBJECTIVE 3

**LEVEL 1:** Lead a class discussion on the status of labor relations today. Then have each student develop a chart that distinguishes the differences between arbitration and mediation. *(Students' charts will vary but should indicate that both methods are examples of collective bargaining. However, the decision of a mediator is not binding, whereas the decision of an arbitrator is binding to both sides.)*

**ENGLISH LANGUAGE LEARNERS**

**LEVEL 2:** Have each student develop a storyboard for a documentary about the status of labor relations today. Tell students that their storyboards should include the various scenes to be included in the movie and detail the significance of each scene. *(Students' storyboards will vary but might include scenes depicting better cooperation between employers and unions, a collective bargaining session, a mediator, and an arbitrator.)*

## Global Perspectives

**Japan's Labor Laws**
Article 23 of the UN Universal Declaration of Human Rights states: "Everyone has the right to form and to join trade unions for the protection of his interests." Many countries, such as Japan, have enacted labor laws to support this right. Japan's Trade Union Law, like the U.S. National Labor Relations Act, guarantees the right of workers to organize and encourages collective bargaining. The Japanese Constitution, which went into effect in 1947, includes provisions that directly protect trade-union activity. Among the provisions are those that affirm the right to strike; set standards for wages, hours, and working conditions; and bar the exploitation of children. Japan also established a Labor Relations Commission that helps settle disputes between labor and management.

### CRITICAL THINKING

Why were labor laws such an important issue for Japan in the late 1940s?

**ANSWER:** Students might suggest that World War II hurt Japan's economy and that, in order to rebuild its economy, the country needed a productive workforce.

Congress has passed several laws to prevent employers from using unfair practices in dealing with workers. There are also laws to make unions act fairly in their disputes with employers. Congress has tried to stop dishonest actions by some union leaders and to ensure that unions are run democratically. The following are some of the major labor laws passed by Congress.

**National Labor Relations Act** This law, usually called the Wagner Act, was passed by Congress in 1935. It guarantees the right of workers to organize and bargain collectively through representatives. The law also provides ways of settling disputes between labor unions and employers.

In addition, this act set up an independent government agency, the National Labor Relations Board (NLRB). The board judges the fairness of the activities of unions and employers toward each other. The NLRB also conducts elections within a company when a union wants to organize the workers. The workers vote to decide which union they want. They can also vote to have no union at all.

**Labor-Management Relations Act** This law, usually referred to as the Taft-Hartley Act, was passed in 1947. It served to revise the Wagner Act in several ways. The Taft-Hartley Act allows the president to order any union to delay a strike for 80 days. This can be done only if such a strike would threaten the national welfare. During this cooling-off period, a fact-finding commission may meet and recommend a settlement. At the end of the 80 days, the union may strike if no settlement is reached.

The Taft-Hartley Act also forbids the closed shop and condemns featherbedding. **Featherbedding** occurs when a union forces employers to hire more workers than are needed. In addition, the law enabled states to pass right-to-work laws.

### Interpreting the Visual Record

**Strike!** *Labor strikes, although less common than in the past, continue to take place today.* **What local union do these strikers belong to?**

### Visual Record Answer

*Students should say Local 32B-32J*

## CLOSE

Review the information about collective bargaining today. Then lead a discussion in which students identify qualities they believe an effective mediator or arbitrator should have and why. Have students answer the following question: What issues must mediators and arbitrators deal with?

---

**Landrum-Griffin Act** This law was passed in 1959 to prevent certain abuses by union officials. It prohibits convicted criminals from serving as union officials for a period of five years after being released from prison. It also forced former members of the Communist Party to wait five years before serving as a union official. In addition, the law requires unions to file reports of their finances with the secretary of labor each year. Finally, it guarantees union members the right to a secret ballot in union elections and to freedom of speech in meetings.

✔ **Reading Check Summarizing** What are the major pieces of labor legislation, and what do they provide? See the individual acts listed above and on the previous page for their names and descriptions.

## ★ Labor Relations Today

Employers and workers have struggled over the past 100 years, sometimes with government help, to work out new relationships. The attitudes of most union leaders and employers today are different from those of the past.

Modern union leaders realize that companies must make profits. If the union demands such high wages that a company goes out of business, jobs will be lost. Therefore, some modern unions cooperate with companies to run more efficient businesses.

Modern employers know that their workers must have good wages and working conditions. Some companies share a certain portion of the profits with their workers. Others allow workers to decide their work schedules or give them a voice in how the work is performed. Such actions make workers more satisfied with their jobs. They produce more goods, are absent less often, and feel more needed.

✔ **Reading Check Contrasting** How are labor relations today different from those in the past? Labor relations between workers and employers are more cooperative today.

## ★ Collective Bargaining Today

Most disputes between employers and unions are settled peacefully through collective bargaining. However, despite improved relations between labor and management, strikes occur each year. For example, in 1994 the country's major-league baseball players went on strike despite the protests of many baseball fans.

When a strike happens, both sides may suffer. Workers and companies can both lose money. Other people also are hurt by strikes. For example, during the baseball strike many small businesses located near the ballparks lost much of their business.

**Interpreting the Visual Record**

**Baseball strike** *Many fans were angered by the 1994 baseball strike. Some argued that because they earn such high salaries, baseball players should not strike for better wages or benefits.* **Do you think that professional athletes should be allowed to go on strike like other workers?**

Often a strike will not be settled until both sides agree to compromise. That is, each side gives up some of its demands. The company may agree to give a greater wage increase than it originally offered. The union may agree to drop its demand for a seven-hour day and accept an eight-hour day. Thus, both sides will be able to feel that they have won.

Unions and employers prefer to settle their differences through collective bargaining. However, if they are unable to reach an agreement, they may call for help. An expert on relations between labor and management may be asked to examine the issue and recommend a solution. This method is called **mediation.** The recommendations of the mediator are not legally binding to either the union or the employer. They are simply suggestions for a solution to the issues at hand. Sometimes another method, called **arbitration,** is used instead. In these cases the decision of the arbitrator is binding on both sides.

When collective bargaining takes place today, both sides must consider ways to increase productivity and profits. The decisions of labor and management have a powerful influence on the country's prosperity and on its future.

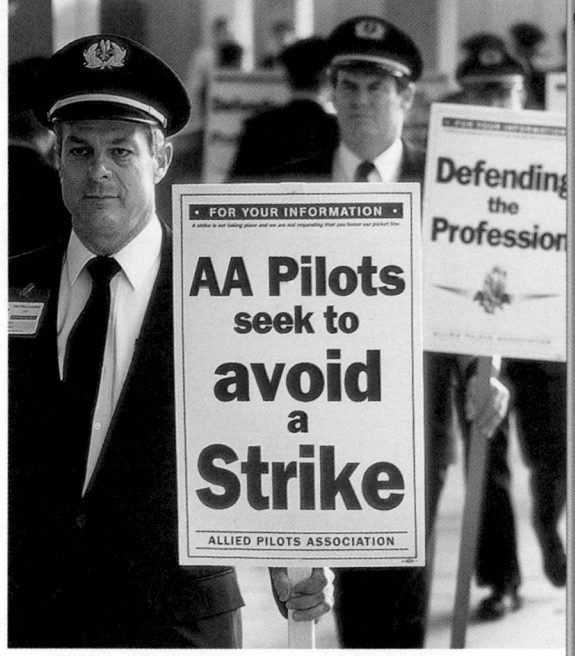

**Interpreting the Visual Record**

**Slowdown** *Strikes in some unions, such as that of the airline pilots shown here, can have a major effect on people throughout the country. **What might happen if the pilots in a major airline refused to fly?***

✔ **Reading Check** Finding the Main Idea How are most labor disputes settled today? Today both sides realize it is in their best interest to settle disputes through collective bargaining, mediation, or arbitration. However, some strikes still occur.

**Visual Record Answer**

*Students might suggest that businesses, and therefore the economy, could be affected.*

## Section 3 Review
### ANSWERS

**1. Define**
- labor unions, p. 498
- collective bargaining, p. 499
- strike, p. 499
- picketing, p. 499
- job action, p. 499
- blacklists, p. 500
- lockouts, p. 500
- closed shop, p. 500
- open shop, p. 500
- union shop, p. 500
- agency shop, p. 500
- right-to-work laws, p. 501
- featherbedding, p. 503
- mediation, p. 505
- arbitration, p. 505

**2.** Wagner Act—guarantees the right of workers to organize and bargain collectively through representatives; Taft-Hartley Act—allows the president to order any union to delay a strike for 80 days; Landrum Griffin Act—prohibits convicted criminals from serving as union officials for a period of five years after being released from prison

**3. a.** to gain strength for bargaining over wages and working conditions

**b.** labor—strikes, picketing, job actions; employers—hired new workers and private police, blacklisted activists, locked out strikers

**4.** Students' answers will vary but should address the competing interests of both groups.

## SECTION 3 Review

**go.hrw.com Homework Practice Online**
keyword: SZ3 HP20

**1. Define** and explain:
- labor unions
- collective bargaining
- strike
- picketing
- job action
- blacklists
- lockouts
- closed shop
- open shop
- union shop
- agency shop
- right-to-work laws
- featherbedding
- mediation
- arbitration

**2. Categorizing** Copy the chart below. Then use it to list the provisions of each act of labor legislation.

|  | Wagner Act | Taft-Hartley Act | Landrum-Griffin Act |
|---|---|---|---|
| Provisions |  |  |  |

**3. Finding the Main Idea**
a. Why did American workers form labor unions during the 1800s?
b. What methods do labor unions use to persuade employers to agree to union demands? What methods did employers use in the early years of labor unions to fight the unions?

**4. Writing and Critical Thinking**
**Decision Making** Imagine that you head the nurse's union in a large urban hospital. You and the other nurses are unhappy with the level of your pay. How do you think the union should address its problems with its employer?
**Consider:**
- the consequences of going on strike for both sides
- the methods unions and employers use to solve labor disputes today

## Review and Assessment Resources

**REPRODUCIBLE**
- ▶ Chapter 20 Review, pp. 506–07
- ▶ Vocabulary Activity 20
- ▶ Chapter 20 Tutorial for Students, Parents, Mentors, and Peers
- ▶ Chapter 20 Test (Form A or B)
- ▶ Alternative Assessment Handbook

**TECHNOLOGY**
- ▶ Chapter 20 Test Generator (on the One-Stop Planner)
- ▶ Global Skill Builder CD–ROM
- ▶ HRW Go site

**REINFORCEMENT, REVIEW, AND ASSESSMENT**
- ▶ Chapter 20 Test for English Language Learners and Special-Needs Students

## REVIEW

Have students complete the **Chapter 20 Review** on pages 506–07.

## ASSESS

Use one of the chapter tests to assess students' understanding of the content. For **Alternative Assessment**, see the **Alternative Assessment Handbook**.

---

## CHAPTER **20**
### REVIEW ANSWERS

**Define and Identify**
1. business cycle, p. 485
2. inflation, p. 485
3. costs of production, p. 486
4. recession, p. 486
5. fiscal policy, p. 493
6. monetary policy, p. 493
7. collective bargaining, p. 499
8. closed shop, p. 500
9. right-to-work laws, p. 501
10. arbitration, p. 505

**Understanding Main Ideas**
1. New Deal

2. It became involved in altering the economy.

3. raises or lowers interest rates and buys or sells bonds; to maintain a stable economy

4. Consumers affect the economy by reducing spending and saving money, buying American-made products to help American companies, and increasing productivity to offset inflation.

5. to gain strength for bargaining for higher wages and better working conditions

6. strikes, picketing, job actions, hiring new workers, mediation, and arbitration

---

## Chapter **20** Review

### Chapter Summary

**Section 1**
- During the business cycle the economy experiences a period of expansion. Following a peak, or high point, in economic growth, the economy slows and may enter a recession. A severe recession may become a depression.
- The hardships experienced during the Great Depression encouraged the government to become more involved in regulating the country's economy.

**Section 2**
- Problems such as inflation, unemployment, and recession pose serious challenges to the economy and to individual citizens.
- The government responds to economic problems by changing its monetary and fiscal policies.
- The economy can also be helped by reducing government spending, increasing saving, buying American-made products, and increasing productivity.

**Section 3**
- During the 1700s many Americans worked for themselves on small farms or in their own workshops or stores. In the first part of the 1800s, large factories were built that employed many workers.
- In response to long working days, low wages, and harsh working conditions, workers formed labor unions. Union members sometimes went on strike to force employers to meet their demands.
- Businesses and unions have had many conflicts over the years.
- Over the years, Congress has passed laws dealing with relations between labor and management. Today most employers and workers try to settle disputes peacefully through collective bargaining, but strikes sometimes still occur.

**AA Pilots seek to avoid a Strike**

---

### Define and Identify
Use the following terms in complete sentences.
1. business cycle
2. inflation
3. costs of production
4. recession
5. fiscal policy
6. monetary policy
7. collective bargaining
8. closed shop
9. right-to-work laws
10. arbitration

### Understanding Main Ideas
**Section 1** *(Pages 485–89)*
1. What was government's response to the Great Depression?
2. How did the government's role in the economy change during the Great Depression?

**Section 2** *(Pages 490–95)*
3. What measures does the Federal Reserve take to control the amount of money in the economy, and why does it do so?
4. How can the actions of consumers affect the economy?

**Section 3** *(Pages 497–505)*
5. What first caused workers in the United States to form labor unions?
6. What methods do unions and employers use to try to achieve their goals?

### What Did You Find Out?
1. What are the different stages of the business cycle?
2. How does the federal government try to regulate the U.S. economy?
3. Why is it important for workers and management to compromise?

### Thinking Critically
1. **Supporting a Point of View** As you have learned, some people believe that the government should not interfere in the economy. Others believe that the government must help the economy. What is your position on this issue, and why?
2. **Analyzing Information** Imagine that you are the owner of a small store. How does your knowledge of the business cycle help you run your business effectively?
3. **Contrasting** Interview a family member or a family friend who grew up during the Great Depression. How was being a teenager during the Great Depression different from being a teenager today?

## RETEACH

Organize the class into three groups and assign each group one of the sections in this chapter. Then ask each group to design a magazine cover about its assigned section. Covers should display the titles of key articles and features to be included in the magazine. **ENGLISH LANGUAGE LEARNERS** , **COOPERATIVE LEARNING**

## Portfolio Extensions

**1. Linking to Community** Have students research industries within their community that employ unionized workers. Then have each student interview a union representative to answer the following questions: How long has the union existed? Where did it start? How has it benefited the workers? What was the latest dispute between the union and the employer, and how was it resolved? Have students compile their answers into pamphlets about the particular union.

**2. Interdisciplinary Connection to Economics** Tell students to imagine that they are the owners of a mousetrap company considering a bid to be the major supplier to a national distributor. Students should determine what part of the business cycle the economy is in, whether interest rates are high or low, how strong the demand is for mousetraps, and whether workers are unionized and demanding higher wages. Have each student write a memo summarizing the market and stating whether to pursue the project.

---

## Building Social Studies Skills

go. hrw.com **STANDARDIZED TEST PREP ONLINE** keyword: SZ3 STP20

### Interpreting Graphs

Study the graph on inflation and the standard of living below. Use the information on the graph to answer the questions that follow.

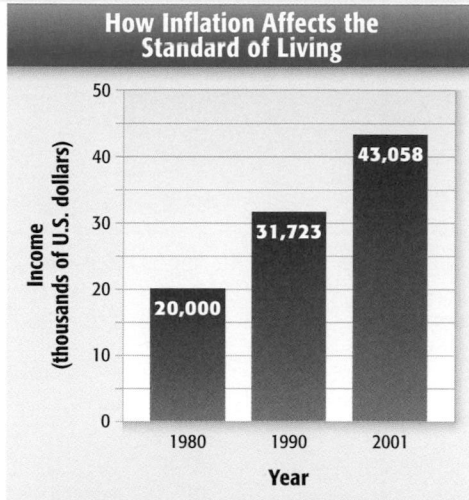

**How Inflation Affects the Standard of Living**

- 1980: 20,000
- 1990: 31,723
- 2001: 43,058

Income (thousands of U.S. dollars) / Year

A family that earned $20,000 in 1980 would need to earn significantly more money in 1990 and 2001 to maintain the same standard of living.

Source: Bureau of Labor Statistics

1. How much more money would a person need to earn in 2001 to have the same standard of living as he and she would have had in 1980?
   a. About the same
   b. About twice as much
   c. About 1.5 times as much
   d. About three times as much
2. Based on information in this chapter, why does an increase in inflation raise the cost of living?

### Analyzing Primary Sources

Read the following quotation from John J. Sweeney, president of the AFL-CIO union. Then answer the questions that follow.

"How workers fare in the global economy of the 21st Century is a critical concern to the AFL-CIO and to workers everywhere. . . . Today's unions recognize that in a relatively high wage economy, workers in the U.S.— especially those who work in industries that can easily move their production out of the country—need to be more productive and produce higher quality goods and services, and their companies need to innovate and change more rapidly if they are to succeed in today's global economy. That's why we have historically called for serious public investment in workforce development for all our nation's workers—and not just those who have been laid off. It's good for workers, good for our nation and good for companies, whose workers can contribute even more to their success."

3. Which of the following statements best describes Sweeney's point of view?
   a. American businesses should be prevented from moving production out of the country.
   b. American workers need to improve productivity and quality to protect their job security.
   c. The government should employ laid-off workers.
   d. The global economy is good for the nation and its workers.
4. What does Sweeney consider good for workers, companies, and our nation? What argument does he use to support this view?

### What Did You Find Out?

1. expansion, peak, contraction, and trough

2. changes its fiscal and monetary policies

3. allows both sides to feel that they have won something

### Thinking Critically

1. Students' answers will vary but they should use sound reasoning in the responses.

2. Students' answers will vary, but students should mention that such knowledge might help them judge the best time to expand.

3. Students' interviews will vary, but some respondents might mention that the depression caused hardships that limited opportunities for all age groups.

### Social Studies Skills

**1.** b

**2.** increases the costs of goods and services

**3.** b

**4.** public investment in workforce development; that companies can easily move their production to other nations

---

## Alternative Assessment

### Building Your Portfolio

**Cooperative Learning**
Complete the following activity in small groups. Research a current or historical labor dispute that took place in your community or state. One group will represent the workers in the dispute, and the other group will represent management. Have both sides of the dispute present their arguments in a collective-bargaining session to try to reach a compromise. One student from the group should serve as a mediator.

**internet** connect

**Internet Activity: go.hrw.com**
keyword: SZ3 AC20

Access the Internet through the HRW Go site to learn about ways you can contribute to working toward a healthy economy. Then make up a crossword puzzle and answer key using economic terms that are important for students to know.

# The U.S. Economy and the World

## CHAPTER RESOURCE MANAGER

| Objectives | Pacing Guide | Reproducible Resources |
|---|---|---|
| **SECTION 1:**<br>**Overview of the U.S. Economy**<br>(pp. 509–15)<br><br>★ Describe how goods and services flow through the U.S. economy.<br>★ Explain how the marketplace affects the price of goods.<br>★ Analyze how investments affect the economy. | **Regular**<br>2 days<br><br>**Block Scheduling**<br>1.5 days<br><br>*Block Scheduling Handbook with Team Teaching Strategies, Chapter 21* | **RS** Guided Reading Strategies 21.1<br>**PS** American Civics Political Cartoon: Markets and Prices |
| **SECTION 2:**<br>**Factors Affecting the U.S. Economy**<br>(pp. 516–21)<br><br>★ Identify the factors that influence the business cycle.<br>★ Describe the tools that economists use to predict the business cycle.<br>★ Determine how the movement and location of resources affect economic growth. | **Regular**<br>2 days<br><br>**Block Scheduling**<br>1.5 days<br><br>*Block Scheduling Handbook with Team Teaching Strategies, Chapter 21* | **RS** Guided Reading Strategies 21.2<br>**E** Creative Teaching Strategy: Open-Ended Statements |
| **SECTION 3:**<br>**Government's Role in the U.S. Economy**<br>(pp. 522–28)<br><br>★ Identify the goals of government regulation.<br>★ Examine how fiscal policy is used to influence the economy.<br>★ Analyze how the Federal Reserve uses monetary policy to influence the economy | **Regular**<br>2 days<br><br>**Block Scheduling**<br>1.5 days<br><br>*Block Scheduling Handbook with Team Teaching Strategies, Chapter 21* | **RS** Guided Reading Strategies 21.3 |
| **SECTION 4:**<br>**Living in a World Economy**<br>(pp. 529–36)<br><br>★ Explain why countries trade with one another.<br>★ Distinguish between free trade and protectionism.<br>★ Analyze the effects of international trade on jobs and consumers. | **Regular**<br>2 days<br><br>**Block Scheduling**<br>1.5 days<br><br>*Block Scheduling Handbook with Team Teaching Strategies, Chapter 21* | **RS** Guided Reading Strategies 21.4<br>**RS** Graphic Organizer Activity: Economic Systems of the World<br>**SM** Community Service and Participation Handbook: The Union Fight Over NAFTA |

### Chapter Resource Key

**PS** Primary Sources
**RS** Reading Support
**IC** Interdisciplinary Connections
**E** Enrichment

**SM** Skills Mastery
**A** Assessment
**REV** Review
**ELL** Reinforcement and English Language Learners
 Transparencies

 CD-ROM
 Video
Internet
Holt Presentation Maker Using Microsoft® PowerPoint®

 **One-Stop** Planner CD-ROM

**See the *One-Stop Planner* for a complete list of additional resources for students and teachers.**

## One-Stop Planner CD–ROM

It's easy to plan lessons, select resources, and print out materials for your students when you use the *One-Stop Planner CD–ROM with Test Generator*.

| Technology Resources | Reinforcement, Review, and Assessment |
|---|---|
| One-Stop Planner, Lesson 21.1 | REV Section 1 Review, p. 515 |
| Holt Researcher CD–ROM | A Daily Quiz 21.1 |
| Homework Practice Online | ELL Main Idea Activity 21.1 |
| HRW Go site | ELL English Audio Summary 21.1 |
| | ELL Spanish Audio Summary 21.1 |
| One-Stop Planner, Lesson 21.2 | REV Section 2 Review, p. 521 |
| Homework Practice Online | A Daily Quiz 21.2 |
| | ELL Main Idea Activity 21.2 |
| | ELL English Audio Summary 21.2 |
| | ELL Spanish Audio Summary 21.2 |
| One-Stop Planner, Lesson 21.3 | REV Section 3 Review, p. 528 |
| CNN Presents: American Government | A Daily Quiz 21.3 |
| Homework Practice Online | ELL Main Idea Activity 21.3 |
| | ELL English Audio Summary 21.3 |
| | ELL Spanish Audio Summary 21.3 |
| One-Stop Planner, Lesson 21.4 | REV Section 4 Review, p. 536 |
| Homework Practice Online | A Daily Quiz 21.4 |
| | ELL Main Idea Activity 21.4 |
| | ELL English Audio Summary 21.4 |
| | ELL Spanish Audio Summary 21.4 |

## internet connect

### HRW ONLINE RESOURCES
GO TO: go.hrw.com
Then type in the keyword.

**TEACHER HOME PAGE**
KEYWORD: SZ3 Teacher

**CHAPTER INTERNET ACTIVITIES**
KEYWORD: SZ3 AC21
Choose an activity to:
- create a poster on the Federal Reserve System.
- create graphs on leading economic indicators.
- create a brochure on the impact of NAFTA on trade and culture.

**CHAPTER ENRICHMENT LINKS**
KEYWORD: SZ3 CH21

**ONLINE ASSESSMENT**
Homework Practice
KEYWORD: SZ3 HP21
Rubrics
KEYWORD: SS Rubrics

**ONLINE MAPS, CHARTS, AND GRAPHS**
KEYWORD: SZ3 MCG
- Absolute and Comparative Advantage

**HOLT PRESENTATION MAKER**
KEYWORD: SZ3 PPT21

**CONTENT UPDATES**
KEYWORD: SS Content Updates

**ONLINE READING SUPPORT**
KEYWORD: SS Strategies

**CURRENT EVENTS**
KEYWORD: S3 Current Events

## Meeting Individual Needs

### Ability Levels

**Level 1** Basic-level activities designed for all students encountering new material

**Level 2** Intermediate-level activities designed for average students

**Level 3** Challenging activities designed for honors and gifted-and-talented students

**English Language Learners** Activities that address the needs of students with Limited English Proficiency

## Chapter Review and Assessment

| | |
|---|---|
| IC | Vocabulary Activity 21 |
| | Global Skill Builder CD–ROM |
| | HRW Go site |
| REV | Chapter 21 Tutorial for Students, Parents, Mentors, and Peers |
| REV | Chapter 21 Review, pp. 538–539 |
| A | Standardized Test Practice |
| A | Chapter 21 Test Generator (on the One-Stop Planner) |
| A | Chapter 21 Test (Form A or B) |
| A | Alternative Assessment Handbook |
| A | Chapter 21 Test for English Language Learners and Special-Needs Students |

# CHAPTER 21

## What's Your Opinion?

*To help students create their **Themes** Journal entries, provide the following examples of appropriate* **agree**/**disagree** *statements.*

● **Agree**   Consumers have to pay whatever prices are being charged for the goods they want.

**Disagree**   Consumers can refuse to pay prices that they feel are too high.

● **Agree**   The government should not interfere with the U.S. economy.

**Disagree**   Government regulations are necessary to keep the U.S. economy running smoothly.

● **Agree**   A country's economy can be harmed if its industries are not protected from foreign competition.

**Disagree**   Foreign companies should be allowed to compete freely with domestic companies.

## Internet Activity

**Analyzing Economics**

**☑ internet connect** 🖱 go.hrw.com

**TOPIC:** Leading Economic Indicators
**GO TO:** go.hrw.com
**KEYWORD:** SZ3 AC21

Have students access the Internet through the HRW Go site to conduct research about the leading economic indicators. Then have each student use the Holt Grapher to create a thematic graph or chart that shows the changes to a leading economic indicator of their choice. Students should create one graph or chart illustrating changes from month to month, and one that illustrates changes from year to year. Finally, tell students that they should include short summaries explaining what their graph or chart shows.

# CHAPTER

# 21 The U.S. Economy and the World

**What's Your Opinion?**

## Build on What You Know

You probably do not spend time thinking about how the cereal you ate for breakfast arrived on your table. You might not consider the origins of your tennis shoes, jeans, and T-shirts. However, how these things arrived in your home or school is part of the functioning of the U.S. economy. People not only in the United States but around the world make choices every day about what to make, buy, or sell. These interactions make up the global economy.

 **Themes Journal** Do you **agree** or **disagree** with the following statements? Support your point of view in your journal.

- People who buy goods cannot affect the prices they pay for those goods.

- Government should never interfere with the operation of the U.S. economy.

- A country must protect its industries from competition from foreign companies.

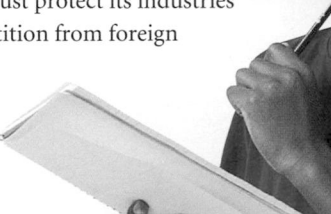

# SECTION 1

## OBJECTIVES

*After completing Section 1, students should be able to*

1 **Describe how goods and services flow through the U.S. economy.**

2 **Explain how the marketplace affects the price of goods.**

3 **Analyze how investments affect the economy.**

## 📀 LET'S GET STARTED!

As students enter the classroom, invite them to come to the chalkboard and list products that they or their families have recently purchased. Ask students to explain how companies are able to continue manufacturing these products. *(Companies make a profit from the prices that they charge for their products.)* Then ask students to describe how consumers pay for the products they purchase. *(Purchases are made using money earned from employment.)* Explain to students that the circular-flow model demonstrates how the exchanges of resources, products, and wages keeps the U.S. economy working. Tell students that in Section 1 they will learn more about the flow of goods and services and about the U.S. economy overall.

# SECTION 1

# Overview of the U.S. Economy

## Read to Discover

1. How do goods and services flow through the U.S. economy?
2. How does the marketplace affect the price of a good?
3. How do investments affect the economy?

### WHY CIVICS MATTERS

The stock market can change dramatically in response to world events. Use **CNNfyi.com** or other **current events** sources to investigate a recent issue involving the stock market in the United States. Record your findings in your journal.

## Define

- producer
- human resources
- circular-flow model
- demand
- supply
- competition
- shortage

## SECTION 1 RESOURCES

### REPRODUCIBLE

► Guided Reading Strategies 21.1

► American Civics Political Cartoon: Markets and Prices

### TECHNOLOGY

► One-Stop Planner, Lesson 21.1

► Holt Researcher CD–ROM

► Homework Practice Online

► HRW Go site

### REINFORCEMENT, REVIEW, AND ASSESSMENT

► Section 1 Review, p. 515

► Daily Quiz 21.1

► Main Idea Activity 21.1

► English Audio Summary 21.1

► Spanish Audio Summary 21.1

## *Reading Focus*

Why do people have to pay taxes? Why do some brands of jeans cost more than others? Why does your local restaurant not pay its employees $100 an hour? The study of economics can help you answer these questions. You can think of economics as the study of choices. By studying your choices and those of others, you can see how all of those choices together form an economy. You can learn how and why people exchange goods and services and how prices are set.

## ★ Types of Economic Systems

There are many different economic systems. At various points in history, these systems have been used by countries around the world. Included in these systems are the traditional economy, command economy, market economy, and mixed economy.

A traditional economy is based on customs and traditions. Goods and services are usually distributed among all members of the economy. Traditional economies include societies that depend on hunting and gathering to survive. For example, the Inuit people of Canada share their prey with one another. When a seal is killed, the meat is divided among the members of the hunting party. The hunters then share the meat with their families.

In a command economy, government officials make economic plans for the country. They decide what goods will be made and how. They

*In the Mbuti people's economy, tradition determines which tasks will be done by men, women, and children.*

# TEACH OBJECTIVE 1

 **LEVEL 1:** Lead a class discussion about how goods and services flow through the U.S. economy. *(According to the circular-flow model, employees work for businesses that produce goods and provide services. In turn, businesses pay employees, who use their wages to pay for the goods and services that they need.)* Then organize students into pairs and ask each pair to design a book jacket for a forthcoming textbook about the U.S. economy. Have students illustrate the flow of goods and services on their book jackets by using symbols, graphics, or other visual representations. Ask volunteers to explain their book jackets to the class. **ENGLISH LANGUAGE LEARNERS**, **COOPERATIVE LEARNING**

**LEVELS 2 AND 3:** Tell students that the flow of goods and services in the U.S. economy depends on the interaction of producers, consumers, laborers, who are often referred to as human resources, and government. Ask students to consider what would happen if one of part of this system failed to do its job. *(For example, if the government failed to set and enforce rigid safety standards, workers and consumers might be endangered by unsafe working conditions and dangerous products.)* Then ask each student to draw an editorial cartoon that illustrates what would happen to the flow of goods and services in the U.S. economy if this type of failure occurred. Encourage students to make use of the circular-flow model or to create a model of their own.

## BIOGRAPHY
### Adam Smith
#### (1723–1790)

Adam Smith was born in Kirkcaldy, Scotland, on June 5, 1723. He enrolled at the University of Glasgow when he was 14 years old. He later became a professor of philosophy. His important work, *An Inquiry into the Nature and Causes of the Wealth of Nations,* was published in 1776. In it, Smith argued that when the government is not involved in the economy, people make economic decisions based on self-interest. They act to fulfill their own needs and wants. Smith argued that self-interest helped the economy grow. Because many people benefit when the economy grows, individual self-interest therefore is good for society. Smith believed that government involvement limited this individual self-interest. As a result, government involvement slowed economic growth. Smith argued that the best economy is one in which the government plays little or no role. **How does the U.S. economic system reflect Smith's beliefs today?**

also decide who can own these goods. There are no pure command economies in the world today.

In a pure market economy, government plays no role at all in making economic decisions. Goods and services are exchanged without government involvement. People can make, buy, and sell whatever they please.

Most economies today are mixed economies. A mixed economy can include elements of traditional, command, and market economies. Countries with mixed economies that are closely related to the pure market model are called capitalist. The United States, which has some government involvement in the economy, is a capitalist country. Cuba, on the other hand, is closer to the command model.

✔ **Reading Check** Summarizing What are the main features of traditional, command, market, and mixed economies? See paragraphs under Types of Economic Systems.

## ★ The Free-Enterprise System

As you learned in Chapter 17, the U.S. economic system is also referred to as a free-enterprise system. Under free enterprise, individuals have the right to own private property. They can make individual choices, such as whether to draw up contracts with other individuals or groups. They can compete with others in the economy, with only limited government involvement. Finally, individuals can make economic decisions for their own benefit.

In free-enterprise economies there are two major groups that make decisions affecting the economy. The people who decide to buy goods or services are called consumers. A person or company that provides goods or services is called a **producer.**

Consumers influence producers' decisions. If consumers do not buy a product, the producer must find out why. The problem may be a high price, a defective product, or simply a lack of consumer interest. Whatever the problem, the producer must work to correct it.

As you know, producers use many resources to meet the needs of consumers. They use **human resources,** which include the labor to produce goods or services. Producers also need natural resources.

Government also plays a limited but important role in the economy. In the United States, the federal government oversees the economy as a whole and provides regulations, or guidelines, for business. You will learn more about the role of government in the economy in Section 3.

✔ **Reading Check** Evaluating What are the most important elements of a free-enterprise system? Answers will vary, but students might discuss the role of competition and limited government involvement.

**LEVEL 3:** Organize students into small groups. Then ask each group to write a brief skit that dramatizes the flow of goods and services through the U.S. economy. Remind students that the circular-flow model demonstrates how this flow takes place. *(See the Level 1 lesson for an explanation.)* Have each group include examples of the benefits of the flow of goods and services, and have them present examples of the limitations of this model. Ask each group to perform its skit for the class.
**ENGLISH LANGUAGE LEARNERS , COOPERATIVE LEARNING**

## TEACH OBJECTIVE 2

**ALL LEVELS:** Copy the following graphic organizer onto the chalkboard, omitting the italicized answers. Have students complete the organizer to show how the marketplace affects the price of goods.
**ENGLISH LANGUAGE LEARNERS**

*consumers* — *producers* — *supply*

*shortages* → **Price** ← *demand*

*surpluses* — *competition*

## ★ Circular-Flow Model

Consumers, producers, and the government interact with one another in a free-enterprise economy. These three groups exchange resources, products, and money payments. The **circular-flow model** demonstrates how these exchanges take place. It shows in a simple fashion how the U.S. economy works. (See the chart on this page.)

According to the circular-flow model, households supply resources, such as labor, to the government and to businesses. Businesses then make products for sale to households and to the government. Households and the government then pay the businesses for the products. The government produces goods and services that benefit businesses and households. It produces these goods and services by using resources such as employee labor and taxes paid by employees, households, and businesses.

Employees receive money payments, called wages or income, in exchange for the labor they provide to business and to the government. Households also receive interest, in exchange for capital that they invest. Employees and their households then act as consumers, using their income to buy goods from producers and to pay taxes to the government. The money in the economy continues to move in this circular flow among businesses, government, and households.

✔ **Reading Check Finding the Main Idea** What is the circular-flow model?
a model of how money, goods, services, and labor are exchanged in the free-enterprise system

## Circular Flow of Goods and Services

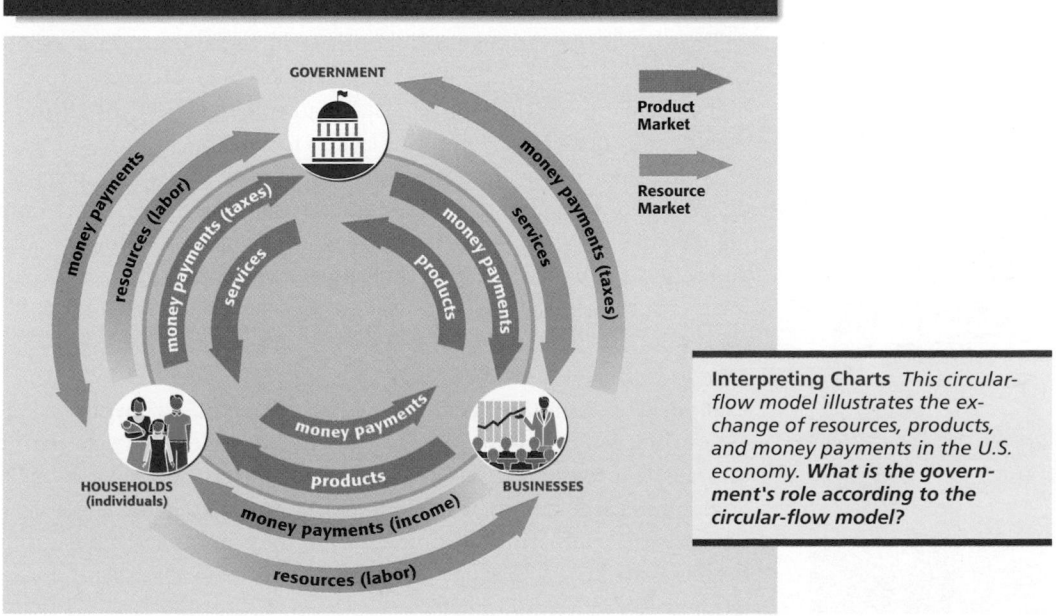

**Interpreting Charts** *This circular-flow model illustrates the exchange of resources, products, and money payments in the U.S. economy.* **What is the government's role according to the circular-flow model?**

**🖳 internet connect** go.hrw.com

**TOPIC:** NAFTA and Trade
**GO TO:** go.hrw.com
**KEYWORD:** SZ3 AC21

Have students access the Internet through the HRW Go site to conduct research about the effects of NAFTA on employment and the economy. Then ask each student to create a brochure that illustrates the impact of NAFTA on business, workers, and global culture.

**CHART ANSWER**
It is an integral part of the flow.

Hedy Thevaos of North Carolina recommends the following activity:

**ALL LEVELS:** Distribute envelopes containing equal amounts of play money to each student. Tell students that you will be hosting an auction and then display a king-size candy bar as the auction item. Explain to students how a silent auction works and announce that the bidding will commence at a particular time and end at a particular time. (You may want to limit bidding time to 5 minutes.) After the auction is over, ask the students if they think that the candy bar was auctioned at a fair price or if the price was inflated because of demand. Finally, lead a class discussion about how the marketplace affects the price of goods and how supply and demand affect product pricing. **ENGLISH LANGUAGE LEARNERS**

**LEVEL 3:** Ask students to imagine that they have been hired by an athletic shoe company to determine how much they should charge for their running shoes. Explain to students that this company only manufactures very expensive running shoes. Then remind students that the price of a product is determined by such marketplace factors as supply, demand, surpluses, shortages, and competition. Ask each student to create a business report explaining to the company how these factors will affect the range of prices that they can charge. Encourage students to propose ways that the company can boost sales through its pricing.

## ★ Economics

### Markets and Prices

Payless ShoeSource knows well the benefit of offering strong price incentives. To attract customers, Payless provides low-priced reproductions of higher-priced shoes. The shoe chain is able to keep prices low because it minimizes costs. Customers help themselves, eliminating the need for salespeople. In 2000 Payless was the number-one shoe retailer in the United States.

**ACTIVITY:** Have students conduct research to identify companies that use price incentives to attract customers. Ask students to create posters illustrating this strategy.

## ★ Global Perspectives

**The Price of Status** Supply and demand for a product are not the same in every market. For example, in the mid-1990s Levi Strauss & Co.'s 501® blue jeans sold for about $30 in the United States but for $80 or more overseas. Levi's® blue jeans had become a status symbol among Asian and European youth. Thus, overseas consumers were willing to pay more for Levi's blue jeans than were U.S. shoppers.

**CRITICAL THINKING**

Should producers be allowed to charge different prices for the same product?

**ANSWER:** Students' responses will vary.

**Tulip Mania** Tulips were brought to the Netherlands from Turkey in the 1550s and soon became very popular. People speculated on tulip prices—they bought bulbs planning to resell them at higher prices. At the height of the craze, a single bulb of a prized variety could cost the equivalent of several thousand dollars—as valuable as a ship loaded with cargo! When the tulip market crashed in 1637, many people went bankrupt.

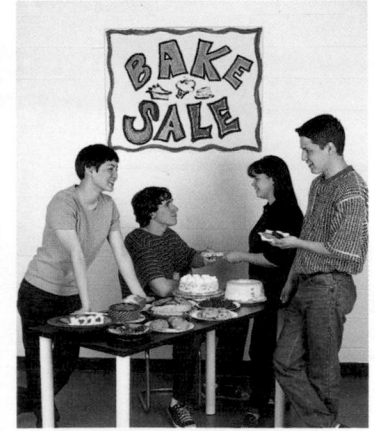

The forces of supply and demand affect every transaction between producers and consumers.

## ★ Prices and the Marketplace

Consumers and producers act in their own interests. For example, consumers will buy more pizza at low prices than at higher prices. This way they can get the most pizza for their money. Producers, however, supply more pizza when they can charge a high price. Higher prices result in higher profits for producers.

Consumers want low prices while producers prefer higher prices. What determines how much producers will charge for an item? Several factors affect the decisions producers make when searching for a price that will attract consumers and will still earn a profit.

**Supply and Demand** Supply and demand affect prices. You have wanted, or demanded, many things in your life. Everyone has. In economic terms, however, the concept of **demand** means more than simply wanting something. Demand is the amount of a good or a service that a consumer is willing to buy at various possible prices during a given time period. For example, imagine that you want to buy a new bicycle. You also have the money to pay for the bicycle. Because you want the bicycle and have the money to buy it, you have contributed to the demand for new bicycles.

The demand for a good or service is related to its price. As you read in Chapter 17, economists call this relationship the law of demand. When prices go up, demand drops. When prices go down, demand often increases. For example, suppose a typical CD player costs $100. More people are likely to buy the CD player if the price drops to $50 than if it rises to $150.

**Supply** is the quantity of goods and services that producers are willing to offer at various possible prices during a given time period. During the winter months, for example, jacket manufacturers expect a higher demand for their products. Because they expect to sell more goods, they offer a larger supply of jackets to consumers at that time.

Prices and supply are related. According to the law of supply, producers supply more goods and services when they can sell them at higher prices. When prices are lower, producers supply fewer goods and services. For example, if producers of CD players can charge $200 for their product, they will make more CD players than if they could charge only $100.

**Competition** Another factor that affects prices is competition. Free enterprise gives businesses the right to choose not only the goods and services to provide but also how and for whom to provide them. Sometimes two or more businesses make the same choice. These businesses are in **competition.** Competition is the economic rivalry among businesses selling similar products. Competition encourages producers to improve or invent products.

**TEACH OBJECTIVE 3**

**LEVEL 1:** Lead a class discussion about how investments affect the economy. *(Investments help business and government acquire capital to expand, which can lead to economic growth.)* Then organize students into pairs. Have each pair design a billboard that encourages consumers to help the economy by investing in stocks and bonds. Ask pairs to invent a slogan for their billboard and to use colorful images to catch people's attention. Display the billboard designs around the classroom and invite volunteers to explain their designs to the class. **ENGLISH LANGUAGE LEARNERS , COOPERATIVE LEARNING**

**LEVELS 1 AND 2:** Point out to students that consumers who invest in stocks and bonds not only help the economy grow, but they can also make money from their investments if corporate profits rise. Then ask each student to create a flowchart showing how this cycle of investment affects the economy as well as investors. *(Students' flowcharts might make use of symbolic representations of consumers, stocks, bonds, profits, and the economy.)* Remind students to indicate on the charts that most investments involve a level of risk. Invite volunteers to explain their flowcharts to the class.

Competition also benefits consumers because it can lower the prices of goods and services. Imagine that two stores sell exactly the same scooters. To attract consumers, one store might offer the scooters at a lower price. Thus, the competition between the two stores allows consumers to buy scooters at a lower price.

**The Effect of Competition on Output** The level of competition also affects supply. Competition tends to increase supply, and a lack of competition tends to decrease supply. Why is this so? Consider the market for home video games. When the first company produced these games, they offered few. The supply of games was low. However, demand for these games rose quickly. The company's profits encouraged dozens of businesses to enter the video game market. As a result, the supply and selection of games soon skyrocketed.

**Surpluses and Shortages** When the quantity of a good supplied is greater than the quantity demanded, a surplus is created. What happens to prices when there is a surplus? Imagine that producers decide to charge $90 for a pair of tennis shoes. At this price, the producers are willing to supply 150,000 pairs of tennis shoes. The quantity demanded at this price, however, is lower than 150,000 pairs. The producers discover that at $90, consumers are willing and able to buy only 30,000 pairs of shoes. That means that 120,000 will not be sold. There is now a surplus of 120,000 pairs. The surplus tells producers that they are charging too much for their shoes. The producers may realize that they can lower the price of the shoes and still make a profit. At the lower price, more consumers will be willing and able to purchase the shoes. The quantity demanded increases, and the surplus disappears.

A **shortage** occurs when the quantity demanded is greater than the quantity supplied. Imagine that the tennis shoe producers manufacture 30,000 pairs of tennis shoes. This time, however, they plan to sell the shoes at $30 a pair. At the price of $30, consumers are willing and able to buy 150,000 pairs of shoes. The demand for the shoes is high. That means there is a shortage of 120,000 pairs of shoes.

How do producers react to this situation? The shortage tells them that they are charging too little for the shoes. They decide to raise the price. As the price increases, the number of consumers willing and able to buy the shoes declines. The higher price decreases the quantity demanded, and the shortage disappears.

✔ **Reading Check Summarizing** How do shortages and surpluses affect prices? Shortages cause prices to rise, and surpluses cause prices to drop.

**Holt Researcher**

**go.hrw.com**
KEYWORD: Holt Researcher
Freefind: Consumer Prices

Look up the chart on prices for consumer goods on the Holt Researcher. Pick three consumer goods and take the price data shown for any 10-year period on the chart. Use this data to create a line graph showing the changing cost of each consumer good during that period.

**Interpreting the Visual Record**

**Food Shortages** *Soviet citizens stand in line to buy food in a Moscow butcher shop in 1990.* **How might food shortages affect citizens' views of their government?**

⭐ **Economics**

**Setting Prices** Many businesses use an approach called yield management, or revenue management, to set prices. With this approach, businesses raise or lower prices for the same product based on season, time of day, or type of customer. This pricing system is popular in service industries such as airlines, restaurants, and theaters. A restaurant may charge higher prices during peak hours, such as dinner time, and lower prices for the same dishes during nonpeak hours. Airlines charge higher fares during peak periods, such as holidays, and theaters may charge more for a seat on a Friday night than on a Tuesday night.

**ACTIVITY:** Ask students to conduct research to learn more about how yield management can help producers avoid surpluses and shortages. Have students create a presentation that uses charts, diagrams, or other visual aids to explain how yield management works and how it can benefit both producers and consumers.

**Visual Record Answer**

*Students might suggest that when a country experiences food shortages, citizens may become frustrated with their government.*

Organize students into groups and ask them to imagine that they have been hired by a computer manufacturer to convince consumers to buy stock in the company. Have each group prepare an advertising campaign that reminds consumers how their investments are important to the economy. *(Students' advertising campaigns might point out that consumers who invest in the computer company will be contributing to the development of new computer technologies.)* Encourage groups to create plans for television, radio, and print media as part of their campaign. Ask each group to present its advertising campaign to the class. **COOPERATIVE LEARNING**

 **HOMEWORK** Ask students to obtain examples of product advertisements for products that are expensive because they are scarce. Have students bring these advertisements to class.

## CLOSE

Organize students into groups and ask them to create pamphlets describing how investments affect the economy. Pamphlets should consider the benefits and risks of investing and should give examples of the specific effects that investing has on the economy. Assign each student a different responsibility in the group, such as illustrator, researcher, writer, and so on. Make copies of the pamphlets for all members of the class to use as study guides. **COOPERATIVE LEARNING**

---

### ★ Economics

**Investing in the Government** During World War I the U.S. government needed money. It wanted to assist Allies and to purchase military supplies and munitions. One way the government raised money was through the sale of U.S. government bonds, called Liberty Loans. Film celebrities of the time, such as Charlie Chaplin and Mary Pickford, attended public rallies across the United States to promote the sale of these bonds. The drive was successful. During the course of the war, the U.S. government raised $21 billion through the sale of defense bonds and was able to loan $10 billion to the Allies to help fund the war effort. The government also sold war bonds to raise money during World War II. Today consumers can still buy U.S. Savings Bonds to invest in the government.

#### CRITICAL THINKING

What are the advantages and disadvantages of buying U.S. Savings Bonds?

**ANSWER:** U.S. Savings Bonds are low risk investments that help the government pay its debts, but the rate of return is usually fairly low.

#### CHART ANSWER

13.50; 12.25

---

## Understanding Stock Market Reports

The annual dividend is 46 cents per share.

Trading volume of the week, in 100-share lots– thus, 19,532,000 shares were traded.

PepsiCo stock went as high as $33.62 and as low as $31.62 per share during the week.

PepsiCo closed at $31.75 per share.

PepsiCo stock price has risen 8.5% this year.

| 52 week | | | | | | Volume | Wkly | | | Change | | YTD |
| Hi | Lo | Name | Div | Yield | PE | Wkly. | Hi | Lo | Last | Fri | Wkly | %Chg |
|---|---|---|---|---|---|---|---|---|---|---|---|---|
| 16 | 7.37 | Kmart | | | 26 | 238,786 | 13.50 | 12.25 | 12.50 | -.25 | | +20.5 |
| 53.75 | 41 | McDnlds | .30 | 0.7 | 21 | 165,646 | 45.12 | 42.50 | 44.50 | -.25 | +1.25 | -1.9 |
| 35.87 | 28 | PepsiCo | .46 | 1.4 | 34 | 195,320 | 33.62 | 31.62 | 31.75 | -.12 | -1.25 | +8.5 |
| 52.87 | 26 | Reebok | .30 | 0.6 | 25 | 13,269 | 51.37 | 45.75 | 50.12 | +1.12 | +3.37 | +19.3 |

$35.87 is the highest and $28.00 is the lowest price of PepsiCo stock in the past 52 weeks, adjusted for splits.

The yield tells what percentage of each share would be returned as dividends, given the current closing price.

The price-to-earnings (PE) ratio is calculated by dividing the stock's last closing price ($31.75) by the company's earnings per share. A higher PE indicates lower earnings, and a lower PE indicates higher earnings.

PepsiCo stock dropped $.12 on Friday but dropped $1.25 per share for the week as a whole.

**Interpreting Charts**
*Stock market reports keep investors informed about their stocks' performance in the market.* **Look at the chart to determine the week's high and low price for Kmart's stock.**

---

### ★ How Your Choices Affect the Economy

In the United States you are free to spend your money on countless different items. You are free to save your money. You may also choose to invest it. Investment occurs when people exchange their money for something of value with the hope that they will earn a profit in the future.

There are many ways to invest money. People may invest in stocks. Stock represents ownership in a business. This ownership is issued in portions called shares. If you buy 100 shares of stock in a company, you own 100 pieces of that company. If the company does well, your shares will increase in value. You will receive part of the company's profits.

Investors may also purchase bonds. A bond is a certificate that a corporation issues in order to borrow money from investors. The corporation promises to repay the money and an additional sum, called interest, to the investor. Governments also issue bonds to raise money.

**Entrepreneurship** Investment also can encourage entrepreneurship, or the development of new businesses. Entrepreneurship encourages economic growth and the development of products. Money invested in new businesses is called venture capital. Venture capital helps entrepreneurs develop an idea into a new product. It can also be used to improve production facilities or to pay for product distribution.

**Business Investments** Corporations issue stocks and bonds in order to raise money. The corporation then uses this money to improve its business and to increase its profits. For example, it may hire additional employees, or it might buy additional equipment. New jobs are created, both within the company and in companies from which it buys the equipment. If corporate profits increase, investors will see the value of their stocks rise. Bondholders will be paid for loaning money to the corporation.

**Investment and Technology** Investment can bring about changes in technology. New technology is developed when companies or individuals invest money in technological research and development. As a result, these people or companies bring new products to market. Other companies can buy these new products, using money they received from their investors. These companies hope that the newly purchased technology will improve their business and increase their profits. If that happens, their investors will receive a share of the profits.

Most investments involve a level of risk. While investors hope to make a profit, there is always the chance they will lose money. The corporation in which they invested may not make a profit, causing the value of its stock to decline. Real estate prices may drop, making the land that an investor purchased worth less instead of more. However, a successful investment typically benefits not only the investor but also the economy as a whole.

*Investors can consult the Nasdaq board in New York City to check out the performance of companies in which they have invested.*

✔ **Reading Check** **Drawing Inferences and Conclusions** How might investment help the economy? Investment allows business and government to acquire capital resources to expand production, which can lead to economic growth and the development of new technologies.

## Section 1 Review
### ANSWERS

**1. Define**
- producer, p. 510
- human resources, p. 510
- circular-flow model, p. 511
- demand, p. 512
- supply, p. 512
- competition, p. 512
- shortage, p. 513

**2.** It is a circular flow with businesses creating goods, consumers buying goods, and so on.

**3. a.** It is close to being a pure market economy but does allow for some government involvement.

**b.** Investment makes it possible for businesses to acquire more human, capital, and natural resources and to use them to expand production.

**4.** Students' paragraphs should consider the role of supply and demand and how competition affects prices and output.

---

## SECTION 1 Review

**go.hrw.com Homework Practice Online**
keyword: SZ3 HP21

1. **Define** and explain:
   - producer
   - human resources
   - circular-flow model
   - demand
   - supply
   - competition
   - shortage

2. **Analyzing Information** Copy the web diagram below. Use it to describe the flow of goods and services among consumers, producers, and the government in the U.S. economy.

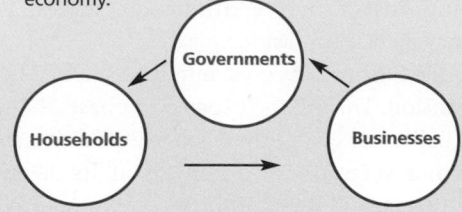

3. **Finding the Main Idea**
   a. Why is the U.S. economy considered a mixed economy?
   b. How might investment help the economy?

4. **Writing and Critical Thinking**
   **Summarizing** Write a short paragraph that explains how various factors work together to influence prices.

   **Consider:**
   - the role of supply and demand
   - how competition affects prices and output

# SECTION 2

## OBJECTIVES

*After completing Section 2, students should be able to*

1 **Identify the factors that influence the business cycle.**

2 **Describe the tools that economists use to predict the business cycle.**

3 **Determine how the movement and location of resources affect economic growth.**

## LET'S GET STARTED!

Write the words *Great Depression* on the chalkboard. As students enter the classroom, ask them what images these words bring to mind. *(Students' responses may include soup lines, unemployment, homelessness, poverty, hunger, and so on.)* Then ask students to attempt to define the word *depression* in economic terms. Write the word *depression* on the chalkboard and list definitions under it as students respond. Tell students that in Section 2 they will learn about how a depression is one part of the business cycle.

# SECTION 2

# Factors Affecting the U.S. Economy

## Read to Discover

1. What factors influence the business cycle?
2. What tools do economists use to predict the business cycle?
3. How does the movement and location of resources affect economic growth?

## Define

• leading indicators
• coincident indicators
• lagging indicators
• *maquiladoras*

### WHY CIVICS MATTERS

The U.S. economy has patterns of growth and decline. Use CNNfyi.com or other **current events** sources to investigate the current status of the U.S. economy. Record your findings in your journal.

## Reading Focus

Goods and services are constantly flowing through the U.S. economy. At times, the number of goods and services available increases. At other times, consumers have fewer choices. The number of jobs available may also vary from year to year. Many factors influence economic growth, including the business cycle, the movement of human and capital resources, and current events.

### ★ The Business Cycle

As you learned in Chapter 20, free-enterprise economies go through good times and bad times. This process is called the business cycle. The business cycle reflects the changes in economic activity. Such changes are always taking place although the length of an upturn or downturn can vary greatly. Some upturns may last only a few months or may continue for several years. Downturns, too, may be brief or last for years.

Economists divide the business cycle into four stages. The first stage is called expansion. During the expansion phase, the economy grows. Eventually, the economy reaches a peak, or a high point. In this second stage, the economy is at its strongest. Producers expand their businesses and hire new workers as they try to meet high consumer demand.

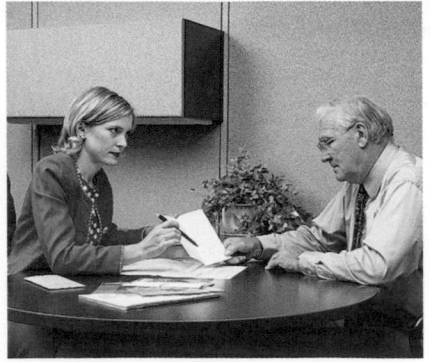

*Financial analysts try to predict the long-range performance of businesses.*

# TEACH OBJECTIVE 1

**LEVEL 1:** Lead a class discussion about the factors that influence the business cycle. *(These factors include the level of business investment, the availability of money and credit, public expectations about the future, and external factors.)* Then organize students into pairs and ask each pair to write an outline for a business magazine that is featuring an article about the business cycle. Tell students that their outlines should represent the business cycle with subheadings depicting the four stages of expansion, peak, contraction, and trough.

**ENGLISH LANGUAGE LEARNERS , COOPERATIVE LEARNING**

**LEVEL 3:** Remind students that public opinion is one of the external factors that influence the business cycle. Ask students to imagine that they are reporters for the business section of a local newspaper. Have students write a newspaper editorial that examines how a recent news report or an event has affected the business cycle. *(Students' editorials may include information about how consumer confidence has strengthened the economy, or they might examine how an event like a terrorist attack has caused a downturn in the business cycle.)* Tell students to use specific evidence to support their arguments. Invite volunteers to read their editorials to the class.

After the economy peaks, it enters a period of business slowdown. This third phase is called a contraction, or a recession. A lengthy period of contraction is called a depression. The final stage in the business cycle is the trough, when demand, production, and employment are at their lowest levels. Following the trough, the economy enters a period of recovery. The expansion phase begins once again.

✔ **Reading Check** Finding the Main Idea What are the stages of the business cycle? expansion, peak, contraction, trough

*External forces, like the price of foreign oil, can affect the business cycle.*

## ★ Influences on the Business Cycle

Many factors influence the business cycle. These factors include the level of business investment, the availability of money and credit, public expectations about the future, and external factors.

**Business Investment** As you read in Section 1, businesses invest in capital goods such as new machinery. They make these investments to increase their production of goods or services. High levels of business investment promote economic expansion in three ways.

First, by purchasing new capital goods, businesses are contributing to the demand for such goods. Rising demand encourages other companies to increase their production of goods. Economic expansion can also occur when businesses improve their efficiency by investing in new capital goods. When a business is more efficient, it can lower the cost of producing goods. It can then sell those goods at lower prices, increasing consumer demand. As you have read, growing demand encourages other companies to increase production. Third, business investment can be used for research and development. This research may lead to new technologies that increase production and that lower costs. Thus, high levels of business investment make it more likely that the economy will expand. If business investment is low, however, the economy may contract.

**Money and Credit** The availability of money and credit also affects the business cycle. Interest is the money a borrower pays to a bank or other lender in return for a loan. It plays an important role in the amount of money and credit available to individuals and businesses. Individuals and businesses generally borrow money when interest rates are low. This makes it easier and cheaper to repay the loan. When interests rates are high, borrowers must pay more money when they repay the loan. Many individuals and businesses will not borrow money when interest rates are high. This means that individuals and businesses are borrowing less for new investments. Declining investment makes it more likely that the economy will contract.

## ★ Economics

**Revolutionizing Economic Thought** British economist John Maynard Keynes published his monumental work, *The General Theory of Employment, Interest, and Money,* in 1936, in the midst of the Great Depression. This work revolutionized economic thinking and the role of government in the economy. In his book, Keynes organized the economy into the four sectors that combine to make up the gross domestic product (GDP)—consumer expenditures, investment, government expenditures, and exports and imports. Having analyzed these sectors, Keynes developed the theory that the national economy had no self-correcting mechanism to end a sustained depression. Business investment was not reliable enough to maintain high levels of employment. Thus, government needed to increase spending to offset the decline in business investment and spur economic growth so that the business cycle could move from trough to expansion.

**ACTIVITY:** Ask students to conduct research to learn more about how the U.S. government influences the business cycle and have them write a brief summary of their research.

**HOMEWORK** Ask students to look through old newspapers for headlines about current events or factors that they think might influence the business cycle. Have each student create a collage from these headlines. Finally, ask them to write brief explanations of the possible economic consequences on their collage.

# TEACH OBJECTIVE 2

**LEVEL 1:** Lead a class discussion about the tools that economists use to predict the business cycle. (*Economists use leading indicators, coincident indicators, and lagging indicators.*) Organize students into three groups and assign each group one of the three indicators. Then ask each group to invent a mascot for its type of economic indicator, and have groups create illustrations that show how this mascot represents the effects of this indicator. (*For example, students might draw an industrious ant building an anthill as the mascot for leading indicators, or students might choose a sleeping possum as a mascot for lagging indicators.*) Ask each group to explain what its mascot represents. **COOPERATIVE LEARNING**

## ★ Economics

**Forecasting the Economy** Another indicator that economists use to forecast the business cycle is *capital utilization*. A high level of capital utilization—the percentage of a nation's capital goods being used to produce goods and services—is necessary for economic growth. Unused capital goods indicate economic waste and inefficiency. On average, businesses use more of their capital goods during periods of growth and less during periods of recession. Economists can use the level of capital utilization as a coincident indicator to determine the current stage of the business cycle.

**ACTIVITY:** Ask students to conduct research to learn what other types of economic factors are used as leading, coincident, and lagging indicators by economists. Have each student present his or her findings on an illustrated chart.

*When consumers believe the economy is strong, they are inclined to spend more.*

**Public Opinion** Public expectations about the future of the economy also play a role in the business cycle. For example, if consumers believe that the economy is heading for a recession, they may limit their spending. They will save their money for the hard times they believe are coming. When consumers believe the economic future looks good, they are more willing to spend. Increased spending can promote economic growth.

The expectations of business owners can also affect the economy. If owners believe that the economy will be strong, they are more willing to borrow money and make investments. However, if they believe the economy will contract, they might decrease investment and hire fewer workers.

Changes in the global economy can also affect the business cycle in the United States. For example, during the 1970s world oil prices increased sharply. Higher prices meant that businesses had to pay more for oil, leaving less money for business investment. As a result, the economy contracted, and the United States experienced recessions during this period. When oil prices declined in the mid-1980s, businesses had to spend less money for energy. The lower costs strengthened the expansion phase of the business cycle.

War is another external factor that influences the U.S. business cycle. During wartime, the government often must spend large amounts of money. It must purchase military equipment and pay members of the armed forces. Industries expand production to meet increased demand from the government. The demand for labor also increases. As a result of these trends, the economy expands. For example, the U.S. economy expanded during World Wars I and II and the Korean and Vietnam Wars.

✔ **Reading Check** **Drawing Inferences and Conclusions** How does news about the economy affect economic growth? News affects people's opinions, which in turn can influence the growth of the economy.

## ★ Predicting the Business Cycle

Predicting changes to the business cycle is a critical job for economists. These predictions help businesses decide whether the time is right to begin new construction and to hire new employees. Government decision makers also use economic forecasts. These forecasts help them determine how much money the government should spend and how much money in taxes it can expect to receive.

Economists typically use three types of indicators, or sets of information, to study the economy. They receive their information from statistics collected by the U.S. government. They use the indicators to determine what phase the business cycle is in. The economists then use the indicators to determine if the economy will grow or contract in the future.

| | | Upturn | Downturn |
|---|---|---|---|
| **Leading Indicators** | | *increase in building permits* | *decrease in building permits* |
| **Coincident Indicators** | | *rising sales increased production* | *falling sales decreased production* |
| **Lagging Indicators** | | *appearance of new businesses* | *decline in number of businesses* |

**Leading Indicators**  To see which way the economy is headed, economists rely on **leading indicators.** These indicators, or signs, help economists make predictions about future economic growth.

One example of a leading indicator is the number of building permits issued. If more individuals and companies have applied for building permits, more buildings will probably be constructed in the near future. This means that jobs will be created in the construction industry. Construction workers will earn wages, which they will spend on goods and services. A rise in the number of building permits is a sign of future economic growth.

However, if fewer building permits are issued, construction and other related industries will not do as well. Construction companies may lay off employees. The companies will not purchase the goods necessary to build more houses and factories. A decline in the number of building permits issued reveals that the economy may not be growing or may even be contracting. Other leading indicators for the economy include stock prices and the number of business orders for consumer goods.

**Coincident Indicators**  The second group of indicators is called **coincident indicators.** These indicators show economists how the economy is doing at the present time. Coincident indicators tell economists if an upturn or downturn has begun.

For example, if people are making more money than before, the economy may have entered an upturn. If, however, personal incomes are declining, the economy may already be in a downturn. Other coincident indicators include the amount of goods being bought and the amount of goods produced.

**Lagging Indicators**  The final group of indicators is called **lagging indicators.** Lagging indicators are called "lagging" because these indicators surface well after an upturn or downturn has started. They help economists determine how long the current phase of the business cycle may last. For example, when the economy is expanding, individuals may decide to start new businesses. It will take several months, however, before they can get these businesses started. The appearance of many new businesses during an upturn is a lagging indicator. The number of new businesses and the size of these businesses help economists predict how long the upturn may last. A decline in the number of businesses during a downturn helps economists determine the severity of the downturn.

✔ **Reading Check** Summarizing How do economists determine what phase of the business cycle the economy is in? With three indicators—leading, coincident, and lagging

Consumers play an important role in the U.S. economic system. By choosing among products, they affect what producers offer and charge.

# TEACH OBJECTIVE 3

 **LEVEL 1:** Point out to students that the movement and location of resources affects economic growth. *(Companies choose locations in which it is easy to borrow money and hire workers at the lowest wages. For this reason, many U.S. companies build factories in foreign countries.)* Ask students to look at the labels in their clothing and other personal possessions to learn where these items were made. Have each student make a list of these countries. Then lead students in a discussion about why they think their possessions have been manufactured in these countries. **ENGLISH LANGUAGE LEARNERS**

**LEVEL 3:** Remind students that movement and location of resources affect economic growth. Then organize the class into two groups. Ask each student in one group to write an argument explaining the benefits of operating factories in foreign countries. Then have each student in the other group write an argument describing the disadvantages of this business practice. Have groups debate their positions. **COOPERATIVE LEARNING**

## CLOSE

Organize students into small groups and assign each group one of the four stages in the business cycle: expansion, peak, contraction, or trough. Then ask groups to imagine that they are newscasters for an all-business channel. Have members of each group prepare a newscast explaining the causes for the stage of the business cycle that they have been assigned. **COOPERATIVE LEARNING**

## ★ Human and Capital Resources

The availability of resources also plays a key role in the economy. Human and capital resources often come from different locations. The location and movement of these resources affect the U.S. economy in a number of ways. For example, imagine that you want to start a new company. You will want to choose a location in which it is easy to hire workers. Although you want the best workers for your new business, you must keep the cost of pay wages at a reasonable level. You therefore look for a place where you can find quality workers for an affordable wage.

In recent years, the desire for labor at a lower cost has led some American companies to open factories in foreign countries. Workers in some countries are willing to work for less than the common American wage. Some foreign countries want American businesses to locate there because it helps their own economies. Various countries offer additional benefits to American companies.

For example, since the 1960s Mexico has encouraged foreign businesses to set up factories called *maquiladoras.* These factories assemble parts into whole components for export. By locating factories in Mexico, U.S. companies are able to hire Mexican workers. Since these Mexican workers receive lower wages than workers in the United States do, the companies spend less money on labor costs. American computer and Internet-related companies have also begun to use foreign labor. Some American companies have set up customer-service call centers in foreign countries where labor costs are lower.

While some jobs are moving to foreign countries, many foreign workers seek employment in the United States. In 2001 alone, 1,063,732 people legally immigrated to the United States. Many came to find jobs offering higher wages than those in their home countries.

The U.S. government controls the number of immigrants by requiring them to first apply for a visa. The government gives most visas to people who already have relatives living in the United States. Those people who do not have relatives in the United States may apply for a green card. This card gives them "permanent resident" status.

Most green cards are issued to people who can perform jobs that will benefit the U.S. economy. Highly skilled workers such as doctors and computer programmers can obtain green cards fairly easily. In 2000 the U.S. government allowed 197,746 highly skilled workers to enter the United States. However, the government is less likely to grant green cards to less-skilled workers. The United States allowed only 54,469 less-skilled workers into the country in 2000.

*With improved global communication and reliance on the Internet, companies can employ staff in other countries to serve customers here in the United States.*

✔ **Reading Check Analyzing Information** In what ways does the movement of resources affect the U.S. economy? It creates opportunities for businesses to increase profit, and raises the possibility that some Americans will lose their jobs as companies move abroad and as immigrants seek work in the United States.

## ★ Current Events and the Economy

Economists and government decision makers use economic indicators to plan for needed changes to make the economy perform well. However, there are some events for which economists cannot prepare. At times, current events can affect the economy in ways no one expected.

War is one example of an event that can affect the economy. For example, entering World War II caused the U.S. economy to expand greatly. This economic growth helped end the Great Depression and led to a period of prosperity after the war.

Americans were reminded about the economic effects of war in 2001. On September 11, terrorists hijacked four planes and attacked targets in the United States. The U.S. stock markets closed soon after these attacks, which left more than 3,000 dead. Americans were shocked by the attacks. They feared that terrorism would affect not only public safety but also the economy. When the stock markets reopened on September 17, many people sold their stocks, causing the value of many stocks to plunge.

The September 11 attacks hurt several industries. Many Americans were afraid to travel by airplane, causing airlines to lose business. Many businesses reported that their sales dropped in the weeks after September 11. As a result, the unexpected tragedy of September 11 weakened the U.S. economy. As Americans began to feel more confident, economists predicted that the economy was again on the upswing.

*Current events, such as war, can have a significant effect on the economy.*

✔ **Reading Check** **Making Generalizations and Predictions** What other types of current events could affect the U.S. economy? Students' answers will vary but could include the influence of cold or hot weather on sales, natural disasters, such as hurricanes or floods, and the unexpected collapse of a major company.

## SECTION 2 Review

**go.hrw.com**
**Homework Practice Online**
keyword: SZ3 HP21

**1. Define** and explain:
- leading indicators
- coincident indicators
- lagging indicators
- *maquiladoras*

**2. Analyzing Information** Copy the graphic organizer below. Use it to explain the factors that influence the U.S. economy.

| Business Cycle | Movement of Resources | Current Events |
|---|---|---|
|  |  |  |

**3. Finding the Main Idea**
a. What tools do economists use to predict the business cycle?
b. Why have some U.S. companies opened offices or factories abroad?

**4. Writing and Critical Thinking**
**Summarizing** Write two paragraphs explaining how the tragedy of September 11 affected the U.S. economy.
**Consider:**
- the reaction of consumers
- the stock market

---

### Section 2 Review
### ANSWERS

**1. Define**
- leading indicators, p. 519
- coincident indicators, p. 519
- lagging indicators, p. 519
- *maquiladoras*, p. 520

**2.** Business cycle—the periodic upturns and downturns in the economy that consists of four stages: expansion, peak, contraction, and trough; Movement of resources—companies bring their business to areas where they can easily take out loans and hire workers at low wages; Current events—events such as war, natural disasters, or the collapse of a major company can affect the economy by increasing or decreasing consumer confidence

**3. a.** leading indicators, coincident indicators, lagging indicators

**b.** to save money because of lower labor costs in many foreign countries

**4.** Students' paragraphs should consider the government's response to the events of September 11, the reaction of consumers, and the effect on the stock market.

# SECTION 3

## OBJECTIVES

*After completing Section 3, students should be able to*

1  **Identify the goals of government regulation.**

2  **Examine how fiscal policy is used to influence the economy.**

3  **Analyze how the Federal Reserve uses monetary policy to influence the economy.**

## SECTION 3 RESOURCES

### REPRODUCIBLE

▶ Guided Reading Strategies 21.3

### TECHNOLOGY

▶ One-Stop Planner, Lesson 21.3

▶ CNN Presents: American Government

▶ Homework Practice Online

### REINFORCEMENT, REVIEW, AND ASSESSMENT

▶ Section 3 Review, p. 528

▶ Daily Quiz 21.3

▶ Main Idea Activity 21.3

▶ English Audio Summary 21.3

▶ Spanish Audio Summary 21.3

## LET'S GET STARTED!

Write this question on the chalkboard: *What do you think the economic goals of the government should be?* As students enter the classroom, ask them to think about the question and to write a list of responses. Invite students to write their lists on the chalkboard. Lead a class discussion about these responses. Tell students that in Section 3 they will learn more about the goals of government regulation and the overall role of the government in the U.S. economy.

---

## SECTION 3

# Government's Role in the U.S. Economy

### Read to Discover

1. What are the goals of government regulation?
2. How is fiscal policy used to influence the economy?
3. How does the Federal Reserve use monetary policy to influence the economy?

### Define

- infrastructure
- tax incentives
- easy-money policy
- tight-money policy
- open-market operations
- reserve requirement

#### WHY CIVICS MATTERS

The Federal Reserve can use certain tools to influence the U.S. economy. Use **CNNfyi.com** or other **current events** sources to investigate a recent decision of the Federal Reserve Bank. Record your findings in your journal.

## Reading Focus

As you read in Chapter 17, government plays several important roles in the U.S. economy. For one thing, it creates millions of jobs. In 1999 the federal, state, and local governments employed about 20.3 million people. Federal, state, and local governments also make investments by improving the country's economic **infrastructure.** The infrastructure is the network that enables producers and consumers to participate in the economy. It includes transportation systems such as roads and airports, and public facilities such as schools and universities. Governments may also loan money to small businesses, which helps the economy to grow. The government also affects the economy by collecting taxes and providing services to the people. Other important ways that the government influences the economy are through regulation, fiscal policy, and monetary policy.

### ★ Government Regulation

In the United States, all governments—federal, state, and local—regulate business. Government regulation has four main goals: to protect workers, protect consumers, limit negative effects, and encourage competition.

**Protecting Workers** Government tries to prevent businesses from taking unfair advantage of workers. Several government agencies carry

*Government investment in infrastructure helps to support the U.S. economy.*

**LEVEL 1:** Lead students in a class discussion about the four main goals of government regulation. *(These goals are to protect workers, protect consumers, limit negative effects, and encourage competition.)* Then ask each student to design a series of four postage stamps that represent the economic goals of government regulation. Encourage students to use simple but attractive designs, and to include a monetary amount on their stamps. **ENGLISH LANGUAGE LEARNERS**

**ALL LEVELS:** Copy the following graphic organizer onto the chalkboard, omitting the italicized answers. Have students complete the organizer to show the four main economic goals of government regulation. **ENGLISH LANGUAGE LEARNERS**

**Four Main Goals of Government Regulation**

*encourage competition*

*protect workers* ← **Government Regulation** → *protect consumers*

*limit negative effects*

---

out this task. For example, the Equal Employment Opportunity Commission (EEOC) protects workers from discrimination. The EEOC makes and enforces rules that prevent businesses from discriminating against people when hiring and promoting workers. It is illegal for companies to discriminate on the basis of age, sex, race, religion, or national origin.

The government also sets standards for working conditions. The Occupational Safety and Health Administration (OSHA) makes certain that employees work under safe conditions. According to government research, OSHA regulations have led to a major decline in deaths in the workplace since 1970.

**Protecting Consumers** The second goal of government regulation is to protect borrowers, consumers, depositors, and investors. For example, the Food and Drug Administration (FDA) protects people from unsafe foods and medicines. The Consumer Product Safety Commission (CPSC) makes certain that items, such as toys, are not dangerous. The federal government also insures citizens' savings and checking accounts. The Securities and Exchange Commission (SEC) protects investors from being cheated when they purchase stocks. Many state and local governments also have agencies to protect borrowers and consumers.

**Limiting Negative Effects** The third goal of government regulation is to limit the negative side effects of some economic activities. For example, negative side effects of certain industries might include pollution. The Environmental Protection Agency (EPA) creates rules to limit negative effects such as air and water pollution.

**Encouraging Competition** Encouraging competition is the final goal of government regulation. As you know, competition can benefit consumers and help the economy to grow. Government regulations make certain that companies compete fairly with one another.

✔ **Reading Check** Finding the Main Idea How does government regulate the U.S. economy? It protects consumers and workers, limits negative effects, and encourages competition.

## ★ Government Regulation of Private Property

The right to own private property is an important part of a free-enterprise system. Generally, in a free-enterprise system property owners may use their property in any way that they wish. However, government

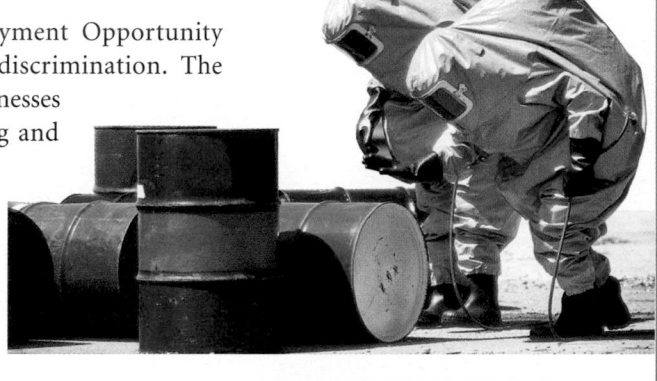

**Interpreting the Visual Record**

**Government inspections** *The EPA inspects toxic-waste sites to protect citizens from negative effects.* **What are three additional purposes for regulating business?**

---

## ★ The Democratic Process

**Equal Opportunities** The Americans with Disabilities Act, passed in 1990, protects individuals with disabilities from discrimination and guarantees them equal access to public and workplace facilities as well as equal accommodations. Before the act was three years old, more than 14,000 people had filed claims of violations of the act. Most cited that they had been unfairly dismissed from their jobs or that they did not receive reasonable accommodations.

**ACTIVITY:** Ask students to conduct research to learn more about other government regulations that protect workers. Have students list some of these regulations on a chart with a description of each.

**Visual Record Answer**

*Students should suggest protecting workers, protecting consumers, and encouraging competition.*

# TEACH OBJECTIVE 2

**ALL LEVELS:** Lead students in a class discussion about how fiscal policy is used to influence the economy. *(Fiscal policy is used to influence the economy through taxing, spending, and borrowing.)* Then organize students into pairs. Ask each pair to draw an illustrated diagram of the five main ways that the government can implement its fiscal policy. *(Students' diagrams should include taxes, tax incentives, government spending, public transfer payments, and progressive income taxes.)* Ask volunteers to explain their diagrams to the class.
**ENGLISH LANGUAGE LEARNERS , COOPERATIVE LEARNING**

## Interdisciplinary Connection

### ▶ Literature ◀

**Sinclair's Legacy** In 1906 Upton Sinclair wrote *The Jungle*, an expose of the unsanitary practices and the gruesome working conditions in the Chicago stockyards and meatpacking industry. His vivid descriptions outraged the nation and led to a public outcry for increased regulation. As a result, that same year Congress passed the Meat Inspection Act, requiring meatpackers to date their products and pass factory inspections. In addition, Congress passed the first Food and Drug Act, authorizing the government to ensure the purity and safety of foods and medicines, tasks that are now the responsibility of the Food and Drug Administration. These acts paved the way for the food and drug laws of today.

#### CRITICAL THINKING

Should the government be allowed to regulate an industry even if those regulations reduce profits and make products more expensive?

**ANSWER:** Students should weigh the benefits that such regulations often bring to workers, consumers, and the environment against the costs that the regulations may incur.

does have the power to regulate the use of property in some cases. It exercises this power in order to benefit society and the economy. For example, the government works to protect the health and safety of citizens. There are times when government regulations have to balance these concerns with the rights of property owners, however.

A main way that local governments regulate property is by controlling land use. Zoning laws are one type of land-use regulation. These laws limit certain types of economic activities to specific areas. For example, a zoning law may limit where a factory can be built. Zoning laws may allow this activity in one area while banning it in another. Because zoning laws tell property owners what they can and cannot do, they often cause disagreements.

One such disagreement took place in Georgetown, Texas, about 30 miles north of Austin. To encourage businesses to move to Georgetown, city officials passed few zoning laws. But the resulting rapid growth of the town hurt the quality of life. In response, officials passed new zoning laws limiting growth. Some residents supported these measures, but others feared that the laws would hurt economic growth.

✔ **Reading Check Summarizing** What is the purpose of zoning laws?
to dictate property use and to balance community and economic concerns

## ★ Fiscal Policy

As you learned in Chapter 20, one tool that the government uses to influence the economy is fiscal policy. Taxing, spending, and making payments are key ways in which the government implements its fiscal policy.

**Taxes** The federal government often changes tax rates to affect the nation's economy. For example, imagine that the economy seems to be entering a recession. What can the government do?

One step the government can take is to lower taxes. Lower taxes mean that people give less money to government and have more in their pockets. With more money to spend, many people buy more goods and services. Businesses sell more, and they hire new employees.

*City council meetings involving land use frequently draw large numbers of residents. Controversy is common, and council members are called on to make hard decisions.*

**LEVELS 2 AND 3:** Ask students to imagine that they have to give a speech before a local citizens group in which they explain how the government influences the economy through its fiscal policy. *(See the Level 1 lesson for influences.)* Have them write the speech that they will deliver to the citizen group. Encourage students to create a visual aid to accompany their speeches. *(Students' speeches might provide specific examples of how fiscal policy has influenced the economy in the past.)* Ask volunteers to present their speeches to the class.

**LEVEL 3:** Ask students to choose what they believe to be the most important tool in government fiscal policy. Then have each student write a newspaper editorial explaining why he or she believes that the fiscal tool he or she has chosen is the most important for influencing the economy. Tell students to include a specific example in their editorials. *(Students' editorials might also state whether the government uses a specific fiscal tool as much as it should.)* Ask volunteers to read their editorials to the class.

Suppose the concern is not a recession but inflation. Sometimes Congress raises taxes to slow down economic growth. Raising taxes takes money out of people's pockets. Because they have less to spend, they buy fewer goods and services. When demand drops, prices drop too.

Another way to promote the government's fiscal policy is through **tax incentives.** A tax incentive is a special tax reduction. One major tax incentive is the investment tax credit. This credit allows companies to lower their tax bill if they invest in new capital. By raising the investment tax credit, the federal government encourages business owners to make new investments.

**Government Spending**  To reduce unemployment, the government can increase its spending. When the government spends more, it buys more goods and services. Demand increases, and producers hire workers to meet the rising demand. The federal government can also spend less. Congress decreases spending when it wants to slow economic growth and prevent inflation. When the government spends less, it purchases fewer goods and services. Demand declines, so businesses produce less and prices do not rise too rapidly.

**Public Transfer Payments**  Another tool of fiscal policy is public transfer payments. A public transfer payment is money given by the government to a person in need. You read about many of these payments in Chapter 19.

Governments provide tax dollars to people who are not working by offering unemployment compensation. Thus, public transfer payments enable unemployed workers to receive money from the government for several weeks or months. By providing assistance to unemployed workers, governments make certain that these workers can still buy goods and services.

**Timing**  For fiscal policy to work, it must be used in the right amounts at the right time. Government decision makers use economic forecasts and predictions to decide when to use fiscal-policy tools. Sometimes these forecasts are not correct, making it difficult to decide when to use a fiscal-policy tool.

The amount of time that it takes for fiscal-policy tools to work can also be a problem. For example, the federal government may lower taxes to promote economic growth. It may take months or even years before the tax cuts make a difference in the economy. Thus, fiscal policy is used with long-term effects on the economy in mind.

**Interpreting the Visual Record**

**Tax cuts** *George W. Bush made a tax-cut proposal a central part of his campaign for the presidency in 2000.* **How does lowering taxes affect the economy?**

✔ **Reading Check** **Analyzing Information** What are the short-term and long-term effects of fiscal policy on the U.S. economy? Short-term effects are minimal because it takes time for fiscal policy to affect the economy; long-term effects include either expanding the economy or slowing its growth.

**LEVEL 1:** Lead a class discussion about how the Federal Reserve uses monetary policy to influence the economy. *(The Fed influences the economy by controlling the money supply with three tools: open-market operations, the discount rate, and the reserve requirement.)* Then organize the class into two groups. Ask the first group to list what the Fed would do with these tools under an easy-money policy. *(The Fed buys back government securities, lowers the discount rate, and lowers the reserve requirements for banks.)* Ask the second group to list what the Fed would do with these tools under a tight-money policy. *(The Fed sells government securities, raises the discount rate, and raises the reserve requirement for banks.)* Ask both groups to explain their lists to the class. **ENGLISH LANGUAGE LEARNERS , COOPERATIVE LEARNING**

**HOMEWORK** Ask students to conduct research to learn how their state or city government influences the local community. Have each student outline a specific example of local fiscal policy.

## ★ Economics

### The Protection of the Fed

Because monetary policy cannot be effective without a sound banking system, it is important for the Fed to ensure the safety and soundness of all banks. The Federal Reserve is responsible for monitoring all state and national member banks, foreign branches of U.S. banks, and U.S. branches of foreign banks. The Fed uses five criteria to assess the soundness of banks: capital, assets, management, equity, and liquidity. The Fed refers to these criteria with the acronym CAMEL.

### CRITICAL THINKING

Do you believe the Fed should have more or less responsibility in regulating the banking system? Support your answer.

**ANSWER:** Students' responses will vary.

Government spending can help to improve the economy. Too much spending or excessive tax cuts, however, can lead to a higher deficit, causing problems for the economy later on.

## ★ Monetary Policy

The federal government uses fiscal-policy tools to influence the economy. It also uses monetary policy. Like fiscal policy, monetary policy is used to promote stability. Monetary policy determines the amount of money available in the economy at any given time. By controlling the supply of money, the government can promote or slow economic growth. As you learned in Chapter 19, the Federal Reserve Bank, or "the Fed," decides monetary policy in the United States.

Before the Fed can control the amount of money available, it has to know how much money is already at work in the economy. There are many ways to measure the money supply. Some economists prefer to count only the money that is readily available. This count includes cash and coins and money in checking accounts. People can use this money to purchase goods or services right away. Other economists prefer to include money in saving accounts and in certificates of deposit (CDs). Finally, other economists also consider resources such as savings bonds in the money supply.

An **easy-money policy** increases the amount of money in the money supply. When an easy-money policy is in place, overall demand for goods and services increases. Thus, an easy-money policy encourages economic growth. The Fed usually adopts an easy-money policy to prevent the economy from contracting.

How does the Fed change the amount of money available? As you read in Chapter 19, the Fed controls the money supply by raising and lowering interest rates. When interest rates are low, individuals and businesses are more willing to borrow money. Increased borrowing means more spending, which causes the economy to expand. If the Fed wants to slow economic growth, it adopts a **tight-money policy** and raises interest rates. Higher interest rates discourage borrowing. The amount of money borrowed declines. Consumers make fewer purchases, and businesses do not expand operations. Overall demand declines, and prices do not rise quickly.

## ★ Tools of Monetary Policy

The Fed uses three monetary-policy tools to influence the economy. These tools are open-market operations, the discount rate, and the reserve requirement.

The main tool of the Fed is **open-market operations,** or the buying and selling of government securities. Government securities are bonds that the government sells to investors. Investors buy the bonds because they are guaranteed an interest payment in the future. If the Fed wants the money supply to contract, it sells government securities. The money

**LEVEL 3:** Remind students that the Fed uses monetary policy to influence the economy. Tell students to imagine that the country is in an economic depression and the Fed needs to do something to promote economic growth. Then organize students into small groups and ask each group to write a scenario about a meeting of the Federal Reserve Board. Encourage students to discuss the strategies that the Fed might use to help the economy. *(To promote growth, the Fed might buy back government securities, lower the discount rate, and/or lower the reserve requirements.)* Ask each group to perform its scenario for the class. **COOPERATIVE LEARNING**

## CLOSE

Have students consider the ways that fiscal policy and monetary policy influence the economy. Then ask each student to make a chart with two columns: *Promote Growth* and *Slow Growth.* In the first column, ask students to list the fiscal and monetary policies that would help to promote economic expansion. In the second column, have students list the fiscal and monetary policies that would help to slow economic growth. Invite volunteers to explain their charts to the class.

## Organization of the Fed

**NATIONAL LEVEL**

**BOARD OF GOVERNORS**
7 members appointed by the president of the United States

**FEDERAL OPEN MARKET COMMITTEE (FOMC)**
7 members of the Board of Governors, plus the president of the Federal Reserve Bank of New York and 4 other district bank presidents

**DISTRICT LEVEL**

**FEDERAL RESERVE BANKS**
12 Federal Reserve district banks and 25 branch offices

**LOCAL LEVEL**

**MEMBER BANKS**
Both national and state banks can be members of the Federal Reserve System.

Source: *Federal Deposit Insurance Corporation*

**Interpreting Charts**
*The Federal Reserve acts as the central bank for the United States. It is designed in a way that avoids control of the U.S. economy by a limited group of financiers.* **How does the Fed stabilize banking on a national level?**

**CHART ANSWER**
by supervising member banks, holding cash reserves, and moving money into or out of circulation

that investors use to buy the securities is withdrawn from the money supply. As a result, the money supply shrinks, and economic growth slows. If the Fed wants the economy to expand, it buys government securities back from investors. The money investors receive ends up in bank accounts, where it is once again part of the money supply. With more money available, demand increases. Producers then offer more goods and services, and the economy eventually expands.

**Discount Rate** The second tool that the Fed uses is the discount rate. The discount rate is the interest rate that the Fed charges to banks. If the Fed wants the economy to expand, it lowers the discount rate. Banks then borrow more money, which they loan to borrowers. The money supply increases, and the economy expands. If the Fed wants to slow economic growth, it raises the discount rate. Banks pass the higher

## REVIEW AND ASSESS

Have students complete the **Section 3 Review** on page 528. Then have students complete **Daily Quiz 21.3**. As **Alternative Assessment**, you may want to use the fiscal policy diagram or the Fed news brief activities in this section's lessons.

## RETEACH

Have students complete **Main Idea Activity for English Language Learners and Special-Needs Students 21.3**. Then give each student a set of four index cards. Ask each student to write a different goal of government regulation on one side of the card. (*The four goals are to protect workers, protect consumers, limit negative effects, and encourage competition.*) On the other side of the card each student should write a description of the goal and list some examples. Pair students and have them quiz each other using the index cards as flash cards.

**ENGLISH LANGUAGE LEARNERS , COOPERATIVE LEARNING**

## EXTEND

Point out to students that government regulation of business and industry has long been debated. Then ask students to conduct research to learn more about the arguments behind these debates. Have each student write a two-page position paper arguing that government regulations should be increased, decreased, or maintained as they are. Remind students to use their research to support their positions with evidence.

**BLOCK SCHEDULING**

## Section 3 Review
### ANSWERS

**1. Define**
• infrastructure, p. 522
• tax incentives, p. 525
• easy-money policy, p. 526
• tight-money policy, p. 526
• open-market operations, p. 526
• reserve requirement, p. 528

**2.** Monetary Policy: by increasing and decreasing the amount of money in circulation, the Fed can help grow or slow the economy. Fiscal Policy: the government can help the economy through spending, taxing, and borrowing. Regulation: the government protects workers and consumers, limits negative effects, and encourages competition.

**3. a.** protecting consumers and workers, limiting negative effects of economic activity, promoting competition

**b.** Federal Reserve Bank

**4.** Students should consider such issues as the goals of each policy and the tools of each policy.

*Chairman of the Federal Reserve Board Alan Greenspan and other members of the Board decide monetary policy in the United States.*

interest rate on to borrowers. With higher interest rates, fewer people can borrow money. The money supply contracts, and the economy does not grow as quickly.

**Reserve Requirement**  The third tool of monetary policy is the **reserve requirement,** the amount of money that banks must have available in their vaults or in Federal Reserve accounts. If they do not have enough money on hand, they might not be able to provide money to people who have savings and checking accounts.

If the Fed wants to expand the money supply, it lowers the reserve requirement. When the amount of money a bank has to reserve is lower, it has more money to loan. When more money is loaned, the money supply expands. Thus, the Fed lowers the reserve requirement to promote economic growth.

When the Fed wants to slow economic growth, it raises the reserve requirement. Banks must put more of their money in reserves. They then have less money to loan to customers. When the amount loaned decreases, the money supply contracts. Individuals and businesses then have less to spend. Demand for goods and services drops, and economic growth slows.

**Timing and Monetary Policy**  Timing is important to monetary policy. First, the Fed must determine the current state of the economy. Second, Fed members must decide the best way to use monetary policy at that time. Finally, it takes time for businesses and investors to adjust to changes in monetary policy. This is why the economy usually does not react instantly to the Fed's policy changes.

Monetary policy is used to slow or expand economic growth, but it takes some time to affect the economy.

✔ **Reading Check Summarizing** What are the goals of monetary policy, and how quickly does monetary policy affect the economy?

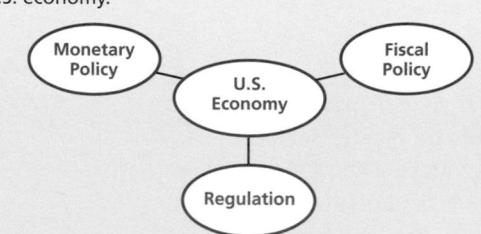

## SECTION 3 Review

**go.hrw.com**
**Homework Practice Online**
keyword: SZ3 HP21

1. **Define** and explain:
   • infrastructure
   • tax incentives
   • easy-money policy
   • tight-money policy
   • open-market operations
   • reserve requirement

2. **Analyzing Information** Copy the web diagram below to explain the ways in which government influences the U.S. economy.

```
   Monetary                    Fiscal
    Policy                     Policy
         \      U.S.         /
          \   Economy       /
                 |
             Regulation
```

3. **Finding the Main Idea**
   a. What are the goals of government regulation?
   b. What government agency conducts monetary policy in the United States?

4. **Writing and Critical Thinking**
   **Comparing and Contrasting** Compare and contrast fiscal policy and monetary policy.
   **Consider:**
   • the goals of each policy
   • the tools of each policy

# SECTION 4

## OBJECTIVES

*After completing Section 4, students should be able to*

1 **Explain why countries trade with one another.**
2 **Distinguish between free trade and protectionism.**
3 **Analyze the effects of international trade on jobs and consumers.**

## SECTION 4

# Living in a World Economy

### Read to Discover

1. Why do countries trade with one another?
2. How do free trade and protectionism differ?
3. What effects does international trade have on jobs and consumers?

#### WHY CIVICS MATTERS

The United States plays a major role in the world economy. Use **CNNfyi.com** or other **current events** sources to investigate a recent issue involving the United States and the world economy. Record your findings in your journal.

### Define

- specialize
- absolute advantage
- comparative advantage
- trade-off
- opportunity cost
- trade barrier
- imports
- import quota
- embargo
- balance of payments
- trade surplus
- trade deficit

## Reading Focus

Make a list of all the goods you use in a week, from clothing to electronic equipment to food. Then consider how many of these goods came from other countries. Your clothing may have been made in the Philippines. Your video game may have come from Japan. You may have eaten foods from Mexico, Asia, or New Zealand.

You can buy these goods because the United States trades with other countries. The history of international trade goes back thousands of years. Today it is an important part of the U.S. economy.

### ★ Interdependence of World Economies

Are you able to produce all the goods and services you need? When people and societies can fulfill their needs without outside help, they are demonstrating self-sufficiency. True self-sufficiency is rare, however.

**Specialization and Trade** Instead of being self-sufficient, people tend to **specialize**—to concentrate on producing certain kinds of goods or services. People who specialize must depend on other people for additional goods and services. For example, a farmer in Illinois is more likely to grow corn than to fish for Atlantic cod. Likewise, stockbrokers in Chicago who want goods made of cotton depend on cotton farmers who live elsewhere.

*Japanese firms captured most of the semiconductor market during the 1980s.*

# TEACH OBJECTIVE 1

**LEVEL 1:** Lead a class discussion about why countries trade with one another. *(Countries pursue trade in order to increase their wealth in terms of goods, services, or resources.)* Ask students to consider some of the benefits that they enjoy because the United States trades with other nations. Then have each student write a five-sentence paragraph explaining some of these benefits. *(Students might indicate that foreign trade makes it possible for them to buy goods from a country that specializes in a specific product.)* Invite volunteers to read their paragraphs to the class.

**ENGLISH LANGUAGE LEARNERS**

**LEVELS 2 AND 3:** Remind students that countries trade with one another to increase their wealth in terms of goods, services, or resources. Then point out that the United States has sometimes tried to take an isolationist approach with regard to its foreign policy. Ask students to consider what would happen if the United States ceased trading with foreign countries altogether as part of a strict isolationist policy. Have each student write a short story describing what a day in his or her life would be like without any foreign products. *(Students should consider both manufactured products, such as clothing and electronics, as well as natural resources, such food and fuel.)* Ask volunteers to read their stories to the class.

**Interpreting the Visual Record**

*A country decides what to produce—bananas, for example—by determining its absolute and its comparative advantage.* **How is a country's comparative advantage determined?**

Specialization makes international trade possible. Countries specialize in producing certain goods. The resources available in a country often determine the kind of goods a country produces.

**Interdependence** Relying upon other people for some goods and services is known as interdependence. Interdependence means that people and the countries they live in depend on each other for different goods and services. International trade is voluntary. Countries trade only the goods and services that they wish to trade, with the countries with which they wish to trade.

Interdependence can create problems when a good or service becomes unavailable. For example, in 1990 Iraq invaded Kuwait, a small oil-rich country. Many countries that bought oil from Kuwait feared a shortage. Without oil, their economies would weaken.

If interdependence can create problems, why do countries trade with one another? They trade in order to increase their supply of goods, services, or resources.

 **Reading Check** Finding the Main Idea Why do countries trade with one another? to obtain goods and services that they would have difficulty producing

## ★ Absolute and Comparative Advantage

How does a country choose what goods and services to produce? This question is answered by considering each country's **absolute advantage** and **comparative advantage.** A country has an absolute advantage when it can produce a good more easily than its trading partners do. For example, both Costa Rica and Panama produce coffee, cocoa, and lumber. If Costa Rica can produce each of these items at a lower cost, it has an absolute advantage over Panama.

Having an absolute advantage does not itself determine which goods a country should produce. Comparative advantage also plays a role in that decision. Economists determine comparative advantage by figuring out which product or service offers each country the greatest absolute advantage. For example, suppose that Costa Rica could produce either 25 million pounds of coffee or 5 million pounds of bananas a year. Now suppose that Panama could produce 12 million pounds of coffee or 4 million pounds of bananas a year. Which crop should each specialize in? Costa Rica would be better off producing coffee. Panama, which cannot produce as much coffee, would then be better off specializing in bananas. Costa Rica could trade coffee for bananas, while Panama could trade bananas for coffee from Costa Rica.

**LEVEL 3:** Organize students into two groups. Ask groups to consider the reasons that countries trade with one another. *(See the Level 1 lesson for reasons.)* Then ask students in the first group to write position papers that argue for the benefits of foreign trade. *(These benefits include access to inexpensive products as well as goods that are the specialty of a foreign country.)* Ask students in the second group to write position papers that point out the disadvantages of trading with other countries. *(Students might point out the danger of becoming too dependent on another country for a particular product or resource.)* Have students from each group debate each other in front of the class. **COOPERATIVE LEARNING**

# TEACH OBJECTIVE 2

**ALL LEVELS:** Lead a class discussion about the differences between free trade and protectionism. *(Free trade is international trade without any government regulation. Protectionism involves the use of protective tariffs between nations.)* Bring old newspapers to class and then ask students to study the papers to find several headlines for stories that are in some way related to free trade and protectionism. Have students paste free trade headlines on one side of a sheet of paper and have them paste protectionism headlines on the other side. Then invite volunteers to explain the headlines that they have chosen. **ENGLISH LANGUAGE LEARNERS**

When a country chooses to specialize, it is also making a **trade-off.** A trade-off is an economic sacrifice. If Costa Rica chooses to produce coffee, it cannot produce bananas. Economists use the term **opportunity cost** to explain what a trade-off means to an economy. Opportunity cost is the value of the alternative that has been sacrificed. In this case, the opportunity cost is the value of the bananas that the Costa Ricans choose not to grow.

✔ **Reading Check Drawing Inferences and Conclusions** How does a country determine which goods and services it should produce? It determines the comparative advantage in producing a certain good or service and then evaluates the trade-off made in producing that good.

## ★ Cooperation and Trade Barriers

International trade allows countries to gain wealth. For many reasons, however, countries often limit the exchange of goods across their borders. A government can establish a **trade barrier**—a limit on the exchange of goods. Governments use trade barriers to protect domestic jobs and industries from foreign competition. The major types of trade barriers are tariffs, import quotas, voluntary restrictions, and embargoes.

**Tariffs** Goods and services purchased by one country from another are called **imports.** As you learned in Chapter 12, a tax on these imports is called a tariff. There are two kinds of tariffs. Revenue tariffs are used to raise money for a government. Sometimes governments practice protectionism—the use of tariffs to restrict the number of foreign goods sold in a country. Because the foreign goods cost more, demand will be reduced. Consumers will choose the good manufactured domestically instead. The United States has used protective tariffs for much of its history.

**Import Quotas** Governments also use import quotas and voluntary trade restrictions to limit imports. An **import quota** is a law that limits the amount of a particular imported good. A voluntary trade restriction is an agreement between two countries, rather than a law. Both of these forms of regulation help domestic businesses. Because the amount of the import is limited, domestic businesses can attract more consumers because of less competition from foreign goods.

Import quotas and voluntary trade restrictions are often aimed at specific goods from specific countries. For example, in 1981 Japan agreed to voluntarily limit the number of Japanese cars sold in the United States.

*Swedish cars are just one of the many products imported by the United States from foreign nations.*

## ★ Economics

**Protecting American Steel** Following World War II, the American steel industry was booming. By the early 1980s, however, it had lost large percentages of market share to foreign steel companies. Burdened with inefficient and outdated technology, high wages, and low productivity, American steel companies could not compete. In an effort to help, the American government placed a voluntary trade restriction on steel imports. This restriction helped American steel companies earn higher profits, which they reinvested to modernize their plants and to increase efficiency. By 1992, when the voluntary trade restriction expired, American steelmakers had doubled their productivity rates and were once again a match for foreign competitors. However, supporters of free trade note that many other factors, such as the drop in the U.S. dollar in 1985, may have helped the American steel industry far more than the voluntary trade restriction.

### CRITICAL THINKING

Do tariffs contradict the philosophy of the free-market system, which allows unrestricted competition between businesses?

**ANSWER:** Students might point out that the U.S. economy is a mixed economy that permits government involvement as well as free-market competition.

There are additional barriers to trade. For example, Japan requires that all imports be tested and inspected. This process is expensive and time-consuming. Other countries require companies exporting to their country to first get special licenses before goods can be imported. These licenses can be difficult to obtain, which limits imports to such countries.

**Embargoes** An **embargo** bans trade with specific countries. Embargoes are often enacted for political rather than economic reasons. In 1985 the U.S. government placed an embargo on the sale of some military and computer goods to South Africa. It hoped to pressure South Africa into ending apartheid, a political system that oppressed black and other nonwhite South Africans. When South Africa ended apartheid, the United States lifted the embargo.

**International Cooperation** Although many countries enact trade barriers, most countries support international trade. This trade allows them to specialize by providing the opportunity to acquire goods and services not made at home from foreign countries. International trade can also make a country wealthy. As a result, countries often work together to improve trade. Some examples of trade cooperation are reciprocal trade agreements, regional trade organizations, and international trade agreements.

Reciprocal trade agreements are made between countries in an effort to reduce protective tariffs. The U.S. president has the power to reduce tariffs if other countries make a similar promise to reduce tariffs. The U.S. Congress can also grant most-favored-nation (MFN) status to other countries, which gives them lower tariff rates.

Many countries have formed regional trade organizations. These organizations reduce or eliminate trade barriers among members. Examples include the Southern Common Market (MERCOSUR) and the European Union (EU).

Countries also enter into international trade agreements. In 1947 the United States and 22 other countries signed the General Agreement on Tariffs and Trade (GATT). Over the years these countries reduced trade barriers among one another. In 1995 a new group, the World Trade Organization (WTO), replaced GATT. In 2003, 146 countries belonged to the WTO, working to reduce tariffs and eliminate quotas.

The North American Free Trade Agreement (NAFTA) was another important development for international trade. This agreement among Canada, Mexico, and the United States went into effect in 1994. The goal of NAFTA is to gradually remove all trade barriers between these three countries.

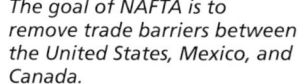
The goal of NAFTA is to remove trade barriers between the United States, Mexico, and Canada.

**LEVELS 2 AND 3:** Organize students into two groups. Then ask each group to imagine that it has been asked to deliver a speech to Congress about U.S. trade policies. Have students in the first group prepare speeches in favor of free trade. Have students in the second group prepare speeches in favor of protectionism. Remind students in both groups to give specific reasons to support their positions. Invite volunteers to read their group's speeches to the class.

**LEVEL 3:** Remind students of the differences between free trade and protectionism. *(See the All Levels lesson for differences.)* Then ask each student to draw a political cartoon illustrating these differences. Encourage students to create symbols that represent the benefits and disadvantages of each type of trade policy. *(To represent disadvantages of free trade, students' cartoons might show workers who have lost their jobs after their factory moved to another country.)* Invite volunteers to explain their cartoons to the class.

The port at Norfolk, Virginia, is an important gateway for ships taking cargo to overseas markets and those delivering goods to this country.

In recent years, more global companies have built factories in the countries in which they do business. This can help the corporation reduce shipping costs and avoid some protective tariffs and quotas.

✔ **Reading Check Evaluating** In what ways are the U.S. economy and the economies of other countries interdependent? Students should discuss the issues of specialization and offer examples of international trade and cooperation.

## ★ Free Trade versus Protectionism

The goal of NAFTA is to promote free trade between Canada, Mexico, and the United States. Free trade is international trade without any government regulation. Supporters of free trade believe that exports and imports should flow freely between countries. Not everyone supports free trade, however. Some people believe that protectionist policies are preferable. These people argue that tariffs will protect domestic industries.

**Infant Industries** Protectionists argue that "infant" industries in particular need protection from foreign competition. Infant industries are industries that are just getting started in a country and, protectionists argue, are very vulnerable to foreign competition. Many developing countries protect infant industries to promote economic growth.

Free-trade supporters believe that protection prevents infant industries from becoming efficient and competitive. They also argue that politicians are often unwilling to remove protections even if the company no longer needs protection because of potentially hurting profits.

**Job Protection** A second argument in favor of protectionism concerns jobs. Protectionists believe that reducing foreign competition creates more jobs at home by encouraging the growth of domestic industries.

Free-trade supporters reject this argument. They claim that protectionism actually costs Americans jobs. They believe that when the United States creates trade barriers, other countries will do the same. They contend that American products then lose their place in foreign

**ALL LEVELS:** Copy the graphic organizer to the right onto the chalkboard, omitting the italicized answers. Have students complete the organizer by filling in the effects that international trade can have on jobs and consumers.

**Effects of International Trade**

**Jobs**

*As demand increases, companies build new factories and hire more workers.*

*Jobs are lost when companies move to foreign countries for inexpensive labor.*

**Consumers**

*Consumers have access to goods that are scarce in their country.*

*Increased competition causes prices to decline.*

*The standard of living rises because consumers can afford more goods.*

*Consumers can enjoy more choices.*

## ★ Economics

**The Changing Job Market** Some people fear that the growing availability of inexpensive foreign labor means fewer jobs, lower wages, and a lower standard of living for U.S. workers in the future. Comparative advantage helps explain the fallacy of this reasoning. Many developing countries with lower wages and plentiful labor also have lower productivity and fewer highly skilled and educated workers. These nations tend to have a comparative advantage in less-skilled, labor-intensive industries. Highly industrialized nations tend to have a comparative advantage in knowledge-intensive, high-tech industries. Although some low-skilled manufacturing jobs in the United States are being lost to foreign labor, new knowledge-intensive, high-tech jobs are replacing these jobs. Even as productivity and skills improve in developing nations, the costs, quality, and availability of the factors of production will continue to vary by country, and within nations, by industry. Consequently, nations will continue to specialize and trade, and to see overall improvements in their standards of living as a result.

**CRITICAL THINKING**

Can high-tech jobs provide employment opportunities for all unemployed less-skilled workers?

**ANSWER:** Students might point out that not all workers who lose their less-skilled jobs will be able to train for a new high-skilled job.

## GLOBAL CONNECTIONS

### States and International Trade

The federal government negotiates trade agreements with foreign nations and sets tariff rates on imported goods. However, some states have begun their own foreign trade initiatives. For example, the Virginia Economic Development Partnership (VEDP) has a program that provides training, market information, and planning assistance to Virginia companies that want to export goods to foreign nations. As one part of the program, business students at universities within the state help companies develop export plans. The VEDP also helps organize trade shows and visits from foreign businesses interested in Virginian products. The ultimate goal of these efforts is to "enhance the quality of life and raise the standard of living for all Virginians" by promoting economic growth. **Why do you think state leaders might find it beneficial to develop such trade plans?**

markets, and American companies will lose business. As a result, they say, these companies have to lay off employees.

**Standard of Living** Protectionists claim that trade barriers help maintain high wages and a high standard of living in the United States. Without trade barriers, other countries can export goods made with less-expensive labor. Because of Americans' higher wages, American goods cost more, so consumers may buy less-expensive foreign goods. American companies then must consider lowering their workers' wages.

People who support free trade argue that U.S. businesses can produce goods cheaply. These companies rely on educated workers and capital resources to make products efficiently. The lower cost of producing goods allows employers to offer their workers high wages.

**Specialization** People who favor protectionism argue that free trade leads businesses to overspecialize. Instead of making many products, businesses instead simply specialize in a few goods not made by foreign companies. However, specialized businesses may be hard hit if world demand for their product drops.

Those who support free trade disagree. They believe that free trade allows competition that forces businesses to produce the best product possible. Competition also offers consumers the best price.

**National Security and Unfair Trade Advantages** Both protectionists and free-trade supporters agree that some industries must be protected from foreign competition. These industries must not be allowed to fail because they are important to the nation's security. In the United States, protected industries include high-tech businesses and businesses that produce energy. Protecting these industries makes the United States less dependent on foreign companies in times of crisis.

Unfair advantages between countries are another issue that divides protectionists and free-trade supporters. Protectionists argue that few foreign countries allow free trade. These countries protect their industries, and the United States should protect its industries. If the United States does not, foreign companies will have an unfair advantage. Free-trade supporters agree that some countries have an unfair advantage. However, they think that removing trade barriers is still the best way to promote economic growth and freer trade in the future.

Few governments have a trade policy that is completely protectionist or completely based on free trade. Most countries' policies are a mixture of the two. The government may protect some industries while allowing free trade in others. U.S. government officials monitor trade conditions closely so they can make any necessary changes.

✔ **Reading Check** Evaluating Why do many countries use both free-trade and protectionist policies? Students' answers will vary but should discuss issues such as national security, unfair advantage, and infant industries.

**LEVEL 3:** Remind students that international trade has benefits and disadvantages. *(International trade creates some jobs, causes others to disappear, and allows consumers access to more goods at lower prices.)* Organize students into groups and ask groups to write brief skits in which workers and consumers from different countries discuss the positive and negative effects that free trade has had on their lives. *(Students should use specific examples of benefits and disadvantages.)* Ask each group to perform its skit for the class.

## CLOSE

Tell students that although the North American Free Trade Agreement (NAFTA) has been successful in increasing trade between Canada, Mexico, and the United States, some economists estimate that 766,000 U.S. jobs have been lost to Mexico. Ask each student to write a newspaper editorial in which he or she evaluates the advantages and disadvantages of NAFTA. Encourage students to support their positions with sound reasoning and to offer possible solutions for any problems they identify. Have volunteers read their editorials to the class.

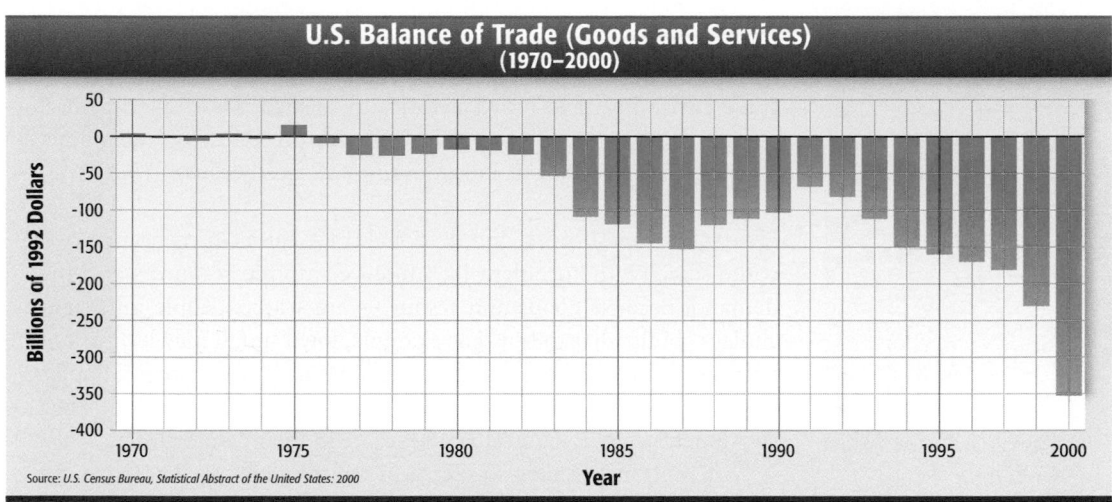

**U.S. Balance of Trade (Goods and Services)**
**(1970–2000)**

Source: U.S. Census Bureau, Statistical Abstract of the United States: 2000

**Interpreting Graphs** *Historically, the balance of trade has been the most important factor in determining the country's overall balance of payments.* **Between 1970 and 2000, in which years did the United States have a trade surplus?**

## International Trade and Global Products

How does international trade affect economies? International trade allows countries to specialize. By specializing, they can focus their efforts on producing goods and services that will bring the greatest profits. Thus, international trade allows countries to increase their wealth.

Countries must carefully watch how international trade affects their economies. The United States typically buys more than it sells. If a country buys more than it sells, it must find a way to pay for its imports.

A country's **balance of payments** is the record of all of its income and payments between consumers, businesses, and governments both at home and abroad. Trade plays an important role in determining a country's balance of payments. If a country sells more than it buys, it has a **trade surplus.** If it buys more than it sells, it has a **trade deficit.** The United States usually runs a trade deficit. For example, in 2002 the United States exported $694 billion worth of goods. Consumers in the United States, however, purchased $1.164 trillion worth of foreign goods that year. Thus, in 2002 the United States had a trade deficit of $470 billion.

**Effects on Jobs** International trade can both create jobs and reduce the number of available jobs. As a country trades, it finds new markets for its goods. Consequently, demand for its goods increases. Producers build new factories, buy more equipment, and hire new workers. Thus, international trade can contribute to economic growth that benefits workers.

International trade, however, can also affect workers in negative ways. For example, NAFTA, which allows for free trade between

⭐ **Economics**

**Dumping** Dumping refers to the practice of selling an export at a price below either its domestic price or its total production costs. Firms dump products for a number of reasons. The most frequently cited reason for dumping, however, is to undercut competitors in foreign markets, usually to gain dominant market share. Once a company has eliminated its competitors and gained control of the market, it raises its prices. Many governments have antidumping laws to protect domestic industries from unfair foreign competition. Usually these laws penalize firms caught dumping products by imposing a duty on their products.

**CRITICAL THINKING**
What might be an argument against antidumping laws?

**ANSWER:** Students might suggest that the antidumping laws keep prices higher, thus hurting both consumers and companies that buy the protected products.

**GLOBAL CONNECTIONS ANSWER**
*(for page 534)*
Students' responses will vary.

**GRAPH ANSWER**
1970, 1973, 1975

# REVIEW AND ASSESS

Have students complete the **Section 4 Review** on page 536. Then have students complete **Daily Quiz 21.4**. As **Alternative Assessment**, you may want to use the free trade vs. protectionism pamphlet or the international trade skit activities in this section's lessons.

## RETEACH

Have students complete **Main Idea Activity for English Language Learners and Special-Needs Students 21.4**. Then assign students one of the objectives in this section. Ask each student to create a study guide for the objective that he or she has been assigned. After students have finished their study guides, ask volunteers to present their guides to the class. **ENGLISH LANGUAGE LEARNERS**

## EXTEND

Have students consult an encyclopedia or other resources to learn more about the history of U.S. international trade policies. Encourage students to find out how these policies have changed over the years. Ask students to write reports analyzing the effectiveness and fairness of U.S. foreign trade policies, and have them recommend possible solutions to any problems that they identify. *(Students might want to consider issues such as trade surpluses and deficits.)* **BLOCK SCHEDULING**

---

## Section 4 Review
### ANSWERS

**1. Define**
- specialize, p. 529
- absolute advantage, p. 530
- comparative advantage, p. 530
- trade-off, p. 531
- opportunity cost, p. 531
- trade barrier, p. 531
- imports, p. 531
- import quota, p. 531
- embargo, p. 532
- balance of payments, p. 535
- trade surplus, p. 535
- trade deficit, p. 535

**2.** Students' responses will vary. Students should recognize that international trade can lead to an increase in jobs and lower prices for consumers.

**3. a.** Nations specialize to take advantage of particular resources.

**b.** Scarcity occurs when consumer demand exceeds supply, and it can cause prices to rise.

**4.** Students' stories will vary.

*Levi Strauss contracts manufacturers in numerous foreign countries.*

Canada, Mexico, and the United States, increased trade among these countries. However, many U.S. businesses took advantage of the free-trade environment to move factories to Mexico. They saw moving to Mexico as a way to increase profits by saving on labor costs. Economists estimate that 766,000 U.S. jobs moved to Mexico because of NAFTA.

**Effects on Consumers** International trade can help economies overcome scarcity, the problem of limited economic resources and high demand. Because goods and resources are scarce, people must make choices about what to buy. For example, low rainfall may lead to poor harvests and few fresh fruits and vegetables in grocery stores. Shoppers might have to buy canned or frozen foods. International trade allows consumers access to goods that are scarce in their own country.

International trade also increases competition. As a result, prices drop, and consumers can buy goods at lower prices. With the savings, they can purchase more goods or services, causing their standard of living to rise.

International trade also gives consumers more choices. If you could only buy goods made in the United States, your choices would be limited. There are some things that the United States cannot produce. For example, coffee does not grow well here. Coffee plants require a different climate. International trade allows Americans to enjoy coffee and other goods that would otherwise be unavailable.

✔ **Reading Check** Summarizing How does international trade affect the U.S. economy? creates some jobs, causes other jobs to disappear; allows consumers access to more goods; increases competition and lowers prices

## SECTION 4 Review

**1. Define** and explain:
- specialize
- absolute advantage
- comparative advantage
- trade-off
- opportunity cost
- trade barrier
- imports
- import quota
- embargo
- balance of payments
- trade surplus
- trade deficit

**2. Analyzing Information** Copy the graphic organizer below. Use it to illustrate the ways that international trade affects jobs and consumers.

**3. Finding the Main Idea**
a. Why do countries specialize in producing certain products?
b. What is scarcity, and how does it affect economies?

**4. Writing and Critical Thinking**
**Identifying Points of View** Imagine that you are a journalist writing a story on trade issues. Compare and contrast free trade and protectionism for your readers.

**Consider:**
- the benefits of each policy
- the drawbacks of each policy

## TEACH

**ALL LEVELS:** Organize the class into four groups. Have each group prepare a database composed of information compiled from each member of the group. For example, one group's database might be composed of the number of cars the family owns, the color of the family cars, the number of pets in each family, the types of pets, and so on. Have volunteers present their group's databases to the class.

**ENGLISH LANGUAGE LEARNERS** , **COOPERATIVE LEARNING**

## EXTEND

Have each student conduct research to obtain more information about his or her local economy. Then ask each student to create a database of a particular aspect of the information that he or she discovers in the research. Together with the database, have students write brief proposals outlining the subject of the database, what the database indicates, and any additional pertinent material. Ask volunteers to present their databases and proposals to the class. **BLOCK SCHEDULING**

# Civics Skills
## WORKSHOP

## Creating a Database

A database is a collection of information that is organized so that you can efficiently find the facts you need. For example, a database can be presented in the form of a chart or table. It could even be a collection of computer files that you can search to find specific information on a topic.

## How to Create a Database

By gathering and organizing the right facts, you can create your own database on a research topic. The following guidelines will help you create a database on almost any subject.

1. **Gather information.** Use the library, your textbook, or other sources to find information on the appropriate topic. Make sure that the data you collect covers the correct time period for your research. You should also record the source of your information so that you can include it in your database.

2. **Create a framework to organize the data.** Give your database a clear title. Use headings to identify the types of data it includes, such as dates, locations, or quantities.

3. **Enter the data into your framework.** Make sure the information included under each heading follows a consistent format. For example, if your heading is STATES, you should not list data that applies only to a city. If your heading is YEARS, then each date you list under that heading should include the year.

## Applying the Skill

Study the sample database below. Then answer the following questions.

1. What is the topic of the database? What information does it provide?

2. Use the library, your textbook, or other resources to find information on the U.S. economy. Use this information to create a database that clearly displays the facts and figures you have located about the economy.

### U.S. Exports and Imports in Selected Categories (1999)

| Type of Good Exported | Value in Billions of Dollars |
|---|---|
| Agricultural products | 21.96 |
| Chemicals and allied products | 66.29 |
| Clothing and related products | 8.54 |
| Crude petroleum and natural gas | 1.44 |
| Electrical machinery | 97.99 |
| Food and related products | 25.21 |
| Instruments and related products | 38.87 |
| Non-electrical machinery | 108.27 |
| Transportation equipment | 119.17 |

| Type of Good Imported | Value in Billions of Dollars |
|---|---|
| Agricultural products | 12.1 |
| Chemicals and allied products | 62.14 |
| Clothing and related products | 59.15 |
| Crude petroleum and natural gas | 42.98 |
| Electrical machinery | 163.98 |
| Food and related products | 25.48 |
| Instruments and related products | 35.06 |
| Non-electrical machinery | 126.67 |
| Transportation equipment | 182.42 |

Source: *Statistical Abstract of the United States*

### REPRODUCIBLE
▶ Chapter 21 Review, pp. 538–39
▶ Vocabulary Activity 21
▶ Chapter 21 Tutorial for Students, Parents, Mentors, and Peers
▶ Chapter 21 Test (Form A or B)
▶ Alternative Assessment Handbook

### TECHNOLOGY
▶ Chapter 21 Test Generator (on the One-Stop Planner)
▶ Global Skill Builder CD–ROM
▶ HRW Go site

### REINFORCEMENT, REVIEW, AND ASSESSMENT
▶ Chapter 21 Test for English Language Learners and Special-Needs Students

## REVIEW
Have students complete the **Chapter 21 Review** on pages 538–39.

## ASSESS
Use one of the chapter tests to assess students' understanding of the content. For **Alternative Assessment**, see the **Alternative Assessment Handbook**.

---

## CHAPTER 21
### REVIEW ANSWERS

**Define and Identify**
1. producer, p. 510
2. demand, p. 512
3. lagging indicators, p. 519
4. *maquiladoras*, p. 520
5. tax incentives, p. 525
6. tight-money policy, p. 526
7. open-market operations, p. 526
8. trade-off, p. 531
9. opportunity cost, p. 531
10. trade surplus, p. 535

**Understanding Main Ideas**
1. The circular-flow model describes the flow of goods and services among households, producers, and government in the U.S. economy.

2. Investment allows businesses to acquire more goods and services and allows for economic expansion and the development of new technology.

3. When capital and human resources are less expensive in foreign countries, U.S. corporations may choose to locate there.

4. Current events can create new and unforeseen circumstances that can cause the economy to change quickly.

5. protect workers and consumers, limit negative effects, and encourage competition

6. The Fed uses monetary policy tools to expand the economy or slow its growth as needed.

7. to raise revenue or to protect domestic industries

8. industries related to national security

---

# Chapter 21 Review

## Chapter Summary

### Section 1
- The United States has a free-enterprise economy. Goods and services are exchanged between producers, consumers, and the government.
- Prices are affected by supply, demand, surpluses, shortages, and the level of competition.

### Section 2
- The business cycle is the growth and contraction of the U.S. economy over a given period of time.
- The movement of resources affects business profits and jobs.
- The economy can change quickly because of events such as war.

### Section 3
- Government regulates the activities of businesses to prevent abuses and to promote competition.
- The federal government uses fiscal policy to influence economic growth.
- The Federal Reserve System conducts monetary policy in the United States. Monetary policy tools include open-market operations, the discount rate, and reserve requirements.

### Section 4
- International trade allows countries to specialize in the production of goods that will benefit them the most. Trade also makes countries interdependent.
- Some economists support free trade, the end of all trade barriers between countries. Other economists are protectionists who want to limit foreign competition.

## Define and Identify
Use the following terms in complete sentences.
1. producer
2. demand
3. lagging indicators
4. *maquiladoras*
5. tax incentives
6. tight-money policy
7. open-market operations
8. trade-off
9. opportunity cost
10. trade surplus

## Understanding Main Ideas
**Section 1** *(Pages 509–15)*
1. What is the circular-flow model?
2. Why is investment important in a free-enterprise system?

**Section 2** *(Pages 516–21)*
3. How does the location of capital and human resources affect the U.S. economy?
4. What role do current events play in a country's economy?

**Section 3** *(Pages 522–28)*
5. What are the goals of government regulation?
6. What is the role of the Federal Reserve System in the U.S. economy?

**Section 4** *(Pages 529–36)*
7. Why do countries have tariffs?
8. What industries do both protectionists and free-trade supporters believe must be protected from foreign competition?

## What Did You Find Out?
1. How do consumers affect the prices of goods?
2. What role does the government play in the U.S. economy?
3. Do you agree with the free-trade supporters' point of view or the protectionists' point of view regarding involvement in the economy? Why?

## Thinking Critically
1. **Contrasting** How do traditional economies differ from market economies?
2. **Evaluating** Is there a place for government regulation in the free-enterprise system? Explain your answer.
3. **Supporting a Point of View** Free trade brings many benefits to the U.S. economy. Should the United States end protectionism and eliminate trade barriers? Why?

BAKE SALE

## RETEACH

Organize students into four groups and assign each group one of the chapter's sections. Have groups create a diagram explaining the main objectives in their assigned section. Then have the groups present their work to the class.

**ENGLISH LANGUAGE LEARNERS ,**
**COOPERATIVE LEARNING**

## Portfolio Extensions

**1. Interdisciplinary Connection to Science** Ask students to conduct research to learn more about how the growth of the technology industry has affected international trade. Students might consider how some countries have become specialists in producing computer chips and software, or students might study how countries have made use of advanced technologies in communication to help expand other industries. Have each student write a news bulletin outlining and explaining the effect of technology on trade.

**2. Linking to Community** Ask each student to interview local business leaders or members of their town or city council to learn more about how U.S. fiscal policies have affected their local economy. Students should try to interview leaders with different opinions in order to get a view of both sides of the issue. Have volunteers present their interviews to the class.

---

## Building Social Studies Skills

go.hrw.com STANDARDIZED TEST PREP ONLINE keyword: SZ3 STP21

### Interpreting Graphs

Study the bar graph on average family expenses below. Then answer the questions that follow.

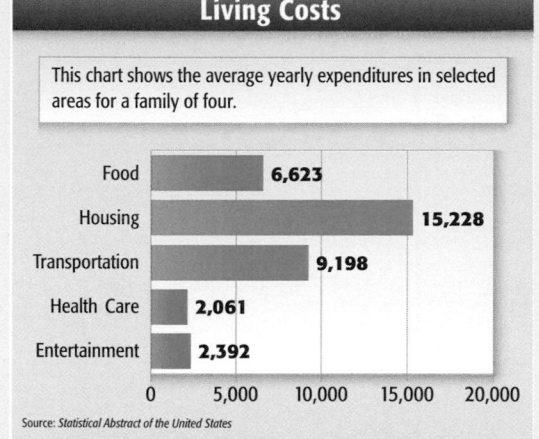

**Living Costs**

This chart shows the average yearly expenditures in selected areas for a family of four.

| | |
|---|---|
| Food | 6,623 |
| Housing | 15,228 |
| Transportation | 9,198 |
| Health Care | 2,061 |
| Entertainment | 2,392 |

0    5,000   10,000   15,000   20,000

Source: Statistical Abstract of the United States

1. About how much did the average family of four spend on food?
   a. the same as it spent on transportation
   b. more than twice as much as it spent on health care or entertainment
   c. about one quarter what it spent on housing
   d. less than it spent on any other major expense
2. What is the largest expense for a typical family of four? What is the smallest expense? What circumstances might increase that expense?
3. What do these expenses suggest about the cost of living in the United States and how families spend their money?

### Analyzing Primary Sources

Read the following quotation from U.S. Secretary of Commerce Donald Evans. Then answer the questions that follow.

❝The prospects for developments in trade in the Americas are truly remarkable. . . . Economic growth is, of course, a driving force. Tearing down barriers to trade and commerce for goods, services and capital promises a higher standard of living for all of us here at home and our neighbors abroad. But there must be more to it and there is. It's about more than wealth and physical comfort; it's about a higher quality of life. Free and open trade is an important foundation for democracy, social freedom and political stability in our hemisphere and around the world. . . . Free men and women conducting their business in free markets can pursue their economic destinies and go as far as their dreams, talents and initiative take them. Here in our country we call it the American Dream.❞

4. Which of the following best describes Evans's point of view?
   a. Free enterprise is important because it benefits Americans.
   b. Free enterprise is important because it promotes wealth and physical comfort.
   c. Free enterprise is the American dream.
   d. Free enterprise promotes a higher standard of living as well as social and political freedom.
5. What does Evans describe as the "American Dream"?
6. Do you agree or disagree with the relationship between economics and politics that Evans describes? Explain your answer.

### What Did You Find Out?

1. Consumers determine how producers set prices of the goods through the number of goods they will buy at a certain price.

2. The government establishes regulations and uses fiscal and monetary policy to influence the economy.

3. Students' answers will vary but should provide adequate explanations of their opinions.

### Thinking Critically

1. Traditional economies redistribute goods among members; market economies encourage members to work for the goods they desire.

2. Students should note that the United States is not a pure market economy, discuss the role the government plays in the U.S. economy, and then evaluate the need for government regulation.

3. Students' answers will vary but should weigh the merits of free trade against protectionism.

### Social Studies Skills

1. b

2. housing; health care—if a family member becomes ill

3. It is fairly high. Families spend money on housing and transportation.

4. a

5. free men and women going as far as their dreams and talent can take them

6. Students' answers will vary.

---

**Alternative Assessment**

## Building Your Portfolio

**Connecting to Geography**
With your group, research recent trade between Mexico and the United States. Has the level of trade grown or declined? What goods and services does the United States receive from Mexico? What goods and services does Mexico receive from the United States? Prepare a news report that shows the information you found. Present your news report to the class.

📲 **internet** connect

**Internet Activity: go.hrw.com**
keyword: SZ3 AC21

Access the Internet through the HRW Go site to research the Federal Reserve System. Then create a poster that explains the role of the Federal Reserve System in the economy and government. Include in your poster facts and statistics on recent actions by the Federal Reserve Board.

# Career Choices

## CHAPTER RESOURCE MANAGER

| | Objectives | Pacing Guide | Reproducible Resources |
|---|---|---|---|
| **SECTION 1:**<br>**The Challenge**<br>**of a Career**<br>(pp. 541–45) | ⚅ Explain why it is important for people to be able to choose their own career, and examine what influences the choices they make.<br>⚅ Determine why knowing oneself is important in making wise career choices.<br>⚅ Evaluate why people who stay in school are better served in the career world than those who drop out. | **Regular**<br>1.5 days<br>**Block Scheduling**<br>1 day<br><br>*Block Scheduling Handbook with Team Teaching Strategies, Chapter 22* | **RS** Guided Reading Strategies 22.1<br>**E** Creative Teaching Strategy: Ranking |
| **SECTION 2:**<br>**The World of**<br>**Work**<br>(pp. 546–51) | ⚅ Identify which occupations require mostly mental work, mostly physical work, or both.<br>⚅ Describe the training that workers must receive to become master craftspersons.<br>⚅ Explain what has contributed to the lowered demand for laborers and agricultural workers. | **Regular**<br>1 day<br>**Block Scheduling**<br>.5 day<br><br>*Block Scheduling Handbook with Team Teaching Strategies, Chapter 22* | **RS** Guided Reading Strategies 22.2 |
| **SECTION 3:**<br>**Unlimited**<br>**Opportunities**<br>(pp. 552–55) | ⚅ Analyze what types of qualifications are necessary for careers in government or the military.<br>⚅ Define what it means to be an "equal opportunity employer."<br>⚅ Examine why women are being encouraged to pursue careers in science and technology. | **Regular**<br>1 day<br>**Block Scheduling**<br>.5 day<br><br>*Block Scheduling Handbook with Team Teaching Strategies, Chapter 22* | **RS** Guided Reading Strategies 22.3 |
| **SECTION 4:**<br>**Learning More**<br>**about Careers**<br>(pp. 558–62) | ⚅ Determine how job seekers can find information about careers.<br>⚅ Describe how part-time jobs and hobbies play a role in choosing a career.<br>⚅ Explain why it is important to ask yourself job-related questions when thinking about your career path. | **Regular**<br>1 day<br>**Block Scheduling**<br>.5 day<br><br>*Block Scheduling Handbook with Team Teaching Strategies, Chapter 22* | **RS** Guided Reading Strategies 22.4<br>**RS** Graphic Organizer Activity: Learning About Careers |
| **SECTION 5:**<br>**Learning More**<br>**about Yourself**<br>(pp. 563–67) | ⚅ Describe why completing employment applications is an important task to practice.<br>⚅ Explain why your school history and special interests are of value to potential employers.<br>⚅ List the six skills to consider when you are trying to learn more about your abilities. | **Regular**<br>1.5 days<br>**Block Scheduling**<br>1 day<br><br>*Block Scheduling Handbook with Team Teaching Strategies, Chapter 22* | **RS** Guided Reading Strategies 22.5<br>**E** Challenge and Enrichment Worksheet 22: Making a Personal Profile<br>**SM** Community Service and Participation Handbook: Marketing Yourself |

## Chapter Resource Key

| | | | |
|---|---|---|---|
| **PS** | Primary Sources | **SM** | Skills Mastery |
| **RS** | Reading Support | **A** | Assessment |
| **IC** | Interdisciplinary Connections | **REV** | Review |
| **E** | Enrichment | **ELL** | Reinforcement and English Language Learners |

 CD-ROM
 Video
 Internet
 Holt Presentation Maker Using Microsoft® PowerPoint®
Transparencies

 **One-Stop** Planner CD–ROM

See the *One-Stop Planner* for a complete list of additional resources for students and teachers.

## One-Stop Planner CD–ROM

It's easy to plan lessons, select resources, and print out materials for your students when you use the **One-Stop Planner CD–ROM with Test Generator**.

### Technology Resources

- One-Stop Planner, Lesson 22.1
- Homework Practice Online

- One-Stop Planner, Lesson 22.2
- Homework Practice Online

- One-Stop Planner, Lesson 22.3
- Transparency 23: Job Opportunities Today and Tomorrow
- Holt Researcher CD–ROM
- Homework Practice Online

- One-Stop Planner, Lesson 22.4
- Homework Practice Online
- HRW Go site

- One-Stop Planner, Lesson 22.5
- Homework Practice Online

### Reinforcement, Review, and Assessment

| | |
|---|---|
| REV | Section 1 Review, p. 545 |
| A | Daily Quiz 22.1 |
| ELL | Main Idea Activity 22.1 |
| ELL | English Audio Summary 22.1 |
| ELL | Spanish Audio 22.1 |

| | |
|---|---|
| REV | Section 2 Review, p. 551 |
| A | Daily Quiz 22.2 |
| ELL | Main Idea Activity 22.2 |
| ELL | English Audio Summary 22.2 |
| ELL | Spanish Audio Summary 22.2 |

| | |
|---|---|
| REV | Section 3 Review, p. 555 |
| A | Daily Quiz 22.3 |
| ELL | Main Idea Activity 22.3 |
| ELL | English Audio Summary 22.3 |
| ELL | Spanish Audio Summary 22.3 |

| | |
|---|---|
| REV | Section 4 Review, p. 562 |
| A | Daily Quiz 22.4 |
| ELL | Main Idea Activity 22.4 |
| ELL | English Audio Summary 22.4 |
| ELL | Spanish Audio Summary 22.4 |

| | |
|---|---|
| REV | Section 5 Review, p. 567 |
| A | Daily Quiz 22.5 |
| ELL | Main Idea Activity 22.5 |
| ELL | English Audio Summary 22.5 |
| ELL | Spanish Audio Summary 22.5 |

## internet connect

go.hrw.com

### HRW ONLINE RESOURCES
GO TO: go.hrw.com
Then type in the keyword.

### TEACHER HOME PAGE
KEYWORD: SZ3 Teacher

### CHAPTER INTERNET ACTIVITIES
KEYWORD: SZ3 AC22
Choose an activity to:
- make a poster on your interests and aptitudes.
- write a job description for a career that interests you.
- make an oral report on job opportunities at a successful business.

### CHAPTER ENRICHMENT LINKS
KEYWORD: SZ3 CH22

### ONLINE ASSESSMENT
**Homework Practice**
KEYWORD: SZ3 HP22
**Rubrics**
KEYWORD: SS Rubrics

### ONLINE MAPS, CHARTS, AND GRAPHS
KEYWORD: SZ3 MCG
- Job Opportunities Today and Tomorrow

### HOLT PRESENTATION MAKER
KEYWORD: SZ3 PPT22

### CONTENT UPDATES
KEYWORD: SS Content Updates

### ONLINE READING SUPPORT
KEYWORD: SS Strategies

### CURRENT EVENTS
KEYWORD: S3 Current Events

## Meeting Individual Needs

### Ability Levels

**Level 1** Basic-level activities designed for all students encountering new material

**Level 2** Intermediate-level activities designed for average students

**Level 3** Challenging activities designed for honors and gifted-and-talented students

**English Language Learners** Activities that address the needs of students with Limited English Proficiency

## Chapter Review and Assessment

| | |
|---|---|
| IC | Vocabulary Activity 22 |
| | Global Skill Builder CD–ROM |
| | HRW Go site |
| REV | Chapter 22 Tutorial for Students, Parents, Mentors, and Peers |
| REV | Chapter 22 Review, pp. 568–569 |
| A | Standardized Test Practice |
| A | Chapter 22 Test Generator (on the One-Stop Planner) |
| A | Chapter 22 Test (Form A or B) |
| A | Alternative Assessment Handbook |
| A | Chapter 22 Test for English Language Learners and Special-Needs Students |

## What's Your Opinion?

To help students create their **Themes** Journal entries, provide the following examples of appropriate **agree**/**disagree** statements.

● **Agree**   Given the freedom to pursue my interests, choosing a career is easy.

**Disagree**   The competition, qualifications, and educational requirements for certain careers make choosing a career a difficult process.

● **Agree**   According to statistical data, a well-paying job requires a college education.

**Disagree**   Working as an intern can replace a college education.

● **Agree**   A good economy provides a wealth of job opportunities.

**Disagree**   A good economy does not necessarily mean that good jobs are available.

## Internet Activity

**What Do You Want To Be When You Grow Up?**

**internet connect**

**TOPIC:** Careers
**GO TO:** go.hrw.com
**KEYWORD:** SZ3 AC22

Have students access the Internet through the HRW Go site to conduct research about careers. Then ask each student to choose a career and to write a job description including information such as the nature of the work, qualifications, responsibilities, and education needed for the chosen career.

# CHAPTER 22 ★★★★★ Career Choices

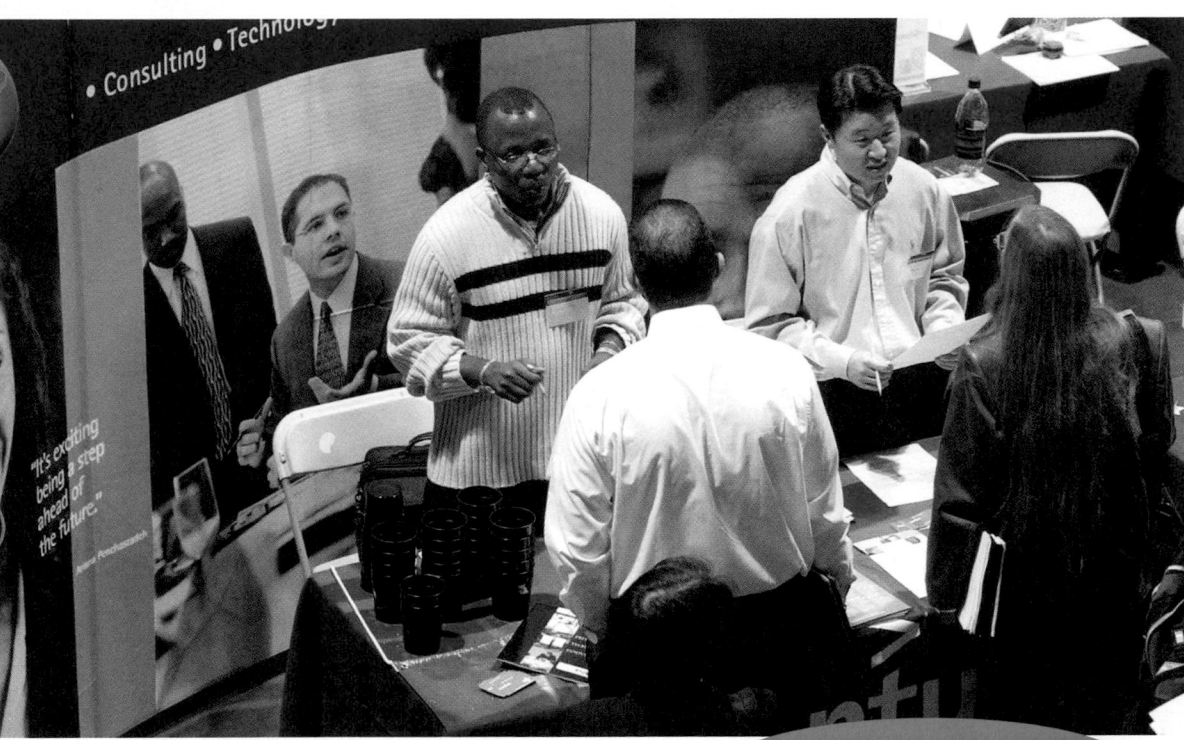

• Consulting • Technology?

"It's exciting being a step ahead of the future."

## Build on What You Know

"What do you want to be when you grow up?" You have undoubtedly been asked that question since you were a toddler. You probably have also begun to ask yourself that question recently. When the United States was founded, most Americans worked on farms. Jobs in towns and cities were limited. Today career opportunities are available in hundreds of fields. You will want to choose a career in which you can do your best. America's economic future depends on your contributions as a member of the workforce.

### What's Your Opinion?

Do you **agree** or **disagree** with the following statements? Support your point of view in your journal.

- Choosing a career is easy.
- All jobs require a college education.
- If the economy is doing well, you can find a job in any field.

# SECTION 1

## OBJECTIVES

*After completing Section 1, students should be able to*

1 **Explain why it is important for people to be able to choose their own careers and examine what influences the choices they make.**

2 **Determine why knowing oneself is important in making wise career choices.**

3 **Evaluate why people who stay in school are better served in the career world than those who drop out.**

## LET'S GET STARTED!

As students enter the classroom, ask them if they have started thinking about a career and if they have begun to plan or prepare for their future. *(Students' responses will vary.)* Discuss with students that in some countries and cultures, choices concerning marriage, education, and jobs are made for young people—either by their families or by their governments. Tell them the story of *Jonathan Livingston Seagull,* a seagull who chooses to soar and experiment with the principles of flight rather than do as all the other seagulls did. Tell them that in Section 1 they will have an opportunity to investigate how to make wise career choices.

## SECTION 1

# The Challenge of a Career

### Read to Discover

1. Why is it important for people to choose their own careers, and what influences the choices they make?
2. Why are individuals who know themselves well in a better position to make wise career choices?
3. Why are people who stay in school better served in the career world than those who drop out?

### Define
- personal values
- qualifications

#### WHY CIVICS MATTERS

Not all industries grow and hire at the same rate. Use **CNNfyi.com** or other **current events** sources to find examples of industries with high hiring and growth rates. Record your findings in your journal.

## Reading Focus

One of the most significant decisions you will make in life is choosing the kind of work you want to do. It is important to find the kind of work that best suits you and for which you are best qualified. The person who has a career that fits his or her special needs and abilities finds satisfaction in working.

### ★ Freedom to Choose a Career

U.S. citizens have the freedom to apply for whichever jobs they like. No government official tells them where, when, and how they may work. You will learn how important this freedom of choice is when you decide on a career. You will be free to pursue any kind of work that suits your interests, intelligence, and abilities.

You need not choose the same occupation as your father or mother. You are free to plan your own future and set your own goals. Young Americans are free to be as successful in their careers as their own abilities and opportunities allow.

The freedom to decide which job to take is sometimes limited by economic conditions, though. During times of high unemployment, people may have to settle

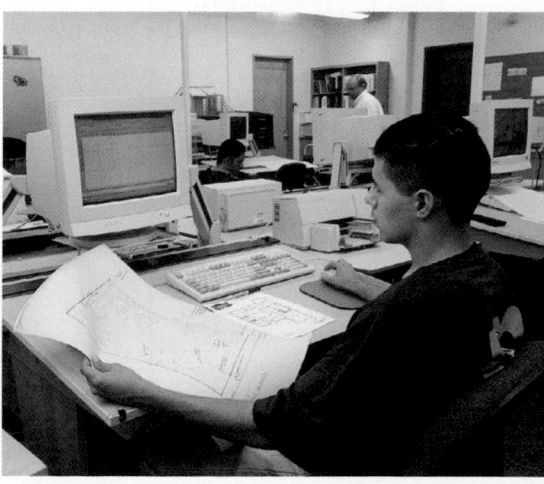

*Many jobs will continue to involve computers and technical skills, such as computer-assisted drafting.*

# TEACH OBJECTIVE 1

**ALL LEVELS:** Lead a class discussion about why it is important for people to be able to choose their own careers and what influences the choices that they make. Have students write brief descriptions of a fictional teenage character, including the person's interests, skills, and education. Then have students decide what career might best suit their characters. **ENGLISH LANGUAGE LEARNERS**

**LEVEL 2:** On individual slips of paper, write down a particular job or career. (*You might write some of the following: doctor, plumber, homemaker, stock broker, street sweeper, and so on.*) Then give each student one of the slips of paper, saying that this will be his or her profession. Then ask students to write a one-page report detailing how they feel about the career that has been chosen for them. Have each student include a paragraph about why it is important to choose your own career.

# TEACH OBJECTIVE 2

**LEVEL 1:** Explain to the class why knowing oneself is important in making wise career choices. Then organize the class into small groups. Assign each group a different purpose for seeking a career: to earn as much money as possible, to help others, to do something worthwhile, or to do something new and different. Have members of each group make a list of jobs that they believe fit their category.

**ENGLISH LANGUAGE LEARNERS , COOPERATIVE LEARNING**

for less than their first choices. Yet they are still free to succeed in the jobs they have or to change jobs when the chance comes. These freedoms do not guarantee happiness or prosperity. However, they do give Americans a chance to succeed in their chosen careers.

✔ **Reading Check Finding the Main Idea** What freedoms and limitations affect Americans' job opportunities? Americans are free to choose any job that suits their interests, intelligence, and abilities. Economic conditions such as times of high unemployment limit job choices.

 ## ★ Personal Values

How people use their freedom of choice depends on their **personal values.** People's personal values are the things they believe to be most important in their lives. Someone whose main purpose is to earn as much money as possible will seek an occupation that pays well. Someone else may consider helping others to be a more important aim and only feel happy in a service career. Such a person may become a teacher, health-care worker, or social worker. Personal values play a strong role in determining a person's career choice.

Think of the reasons people work. Doing so may help you understand why it is important to find a career that will best meet your needs. Perhaps you think that the reasons are clear—most people work to earn money for food, clothing, and shelter.

Many Americans, however, are not content to simply meet basic needs. They want more. They want new cars, compact disc players, washing machines and dryers, and many other things that are now part of the country's high standard of living. They want to be able to afford vacations and recreational activities in their free time. They want to be able to retire comfortably someday.

In addition to money, many people believe a job should offer other rewards. It should allow them to do something important. A job should also give them a chance for career advancement. Some people get into the habit of working at a particular job and are comfortable with their routine. Others want to do something new and different. These men and women seek challenging careers. They would not be happy at a routine job.

✔ **Reading Check Summarizing** What are some motivations that drive a person's career choice? desire for high income, helping others, meeting basic needs, high living standard, career advancement, challenge, and comfortable routine

**LEVELS 2 AND 3:** Remind students why knowing oneself is important in making wise career choices. Then ask students why people choose particular careers and write those reasons on the chalkboard. Have each student write a cover letter to accompany an imaginary resume to tell a prospective employer about his or her career aspirations.

## TEACH OBJECTIVE 3

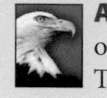 **ALL LEVELS:** Copy the following graphic organizer onto the chalkboard, omitting the italicized answers. Then have each student complete the organizer to evaluate why people who stay in school are better served in the career world than those who drop out.

**ENGLISH LANGUAGE LEARNERS**

> **Why It's Cool to Stay in School**
>
> • *Most dropouts earn low wages because they do not have the education, training, and skills needed for most occupations that provide a higher income.*
> • *Dropouts often find themselves without work.*
> • *With every year that passes, a person who does not finish high school will find it more difficult to earn a living.*
> • *Many tasks that were once done by less-skilled workers are now the work of machines.*

## ★ The Best Career for You

Before making a decision about a career, everyone should take a good, hard look at his or her own **qualifications.** Qualifications are the skills and knowledge that you have. How can you decide which career is right for you?

With your abilities, talents, interests, and skills, there are probably many different careers you can pursue. That is why it is sometimes difficult to discover which might be best. Learning about careers can help you narrow your choices to occupations that have a special appeal for you. Do not narrow your choices too soon, however. You may discover new and rewarding opportunities as you learn more about careers that interest you.

The most important step in deciding on a career is getting to know yourself. Even if you think you already know yourself well, you should still take another look. Try as honestly as possible to discover your abilities, interests, and skills. You should acknowledge your strengths and weaknesses as well.

For example, if you are afraid of speaking in front of groups, some professions require you to overcome this fear. Teachers and lawyers must address groups of people. Can you do that? Many people have. Be frank with yourself. Admit that you have weaknesses as well as strengths. Balancing career choices against your abilities and interests will increase your chances of making a wise career decision.

✔ **Reading Check** Finding the Main Idea How can you discover which career best suits you? Do not limit your options too soon. Get to know yourself and acknowledge your strengths and weaknesses.

## ★ Education Is the Key

To succeed in today's rapidly changing world, you will need the best education you can pursue. Employers want young men and women who read well, write clearly, and have learned as much as possible in school. Educated people have demonstrated that they are able to learn and can meet the challenges of new situations.

Making sure that you receive a good education benefits everyone—you, your potential employer, and your country. A good education is certainly worth all of your efforts. On average, the more years of schooling a person has, the higher his or her income. Education does not guarantee success, but it improves your chances for earning a higher income during your lifetime.

More important than money, however, is the satisfaction that comes from knowing you have made your best effort. Moreover, each person

### The Examination War in Japan

American students who work hard and achieve good grades are usually accepted into college. In Japan, however, colleges are open only to those students who can pass extremely difficult entrance examinations.

These examinations are so competitive that most students spend their entire educational lives preparing for them. To win the "examination war," as it is called, Japanese students spend an average of 20 hours a week on homework. Many also take extra classes on weekends and during vacations and hire special tutors to help them study. Students who pass the examinations and are admitted into college are virtually assured future employment in Japan's largest corporations. With such importance attached to them, the exams receive wide media attention in the country each year. **Do you think children in the United States should go through an examination system like that of Japan? Why or why not?**

**LEVEL 1:** Lead a class discussion about why people who stay in school are better served in the career world than those who drop out. Then ask each student to compose a list of careers that he or she will not be able to obtain without an education. (Students' lists may include teacher, attorney, computer programmer, electrician, office assistant, president, and so on.)

**LEVEL 2:** Lead a class discussion about why people who stay in school are better served in the career world than those who drop out. Then have students read the information contained in the side wrap on page 543. Ask students to prepare action plans that state the careers they want, that outline how they will accomplish their career goals and the time frame to reach their goals, and how remaining in school will help them in their chosen fields.

## CLOSE

Organize students into groups and assign each group the task of writing one of the following four articles: the importance of free choice, reasons for choosing certain careers, the importance of knowing oneself, and the kinds of skills and education employers want of employees. Tell groups that they will submit their articles to a fictional "Careers" magazine. When groups are finished, assemble the articles into a magazine and have groups prepare a cover and illustrations.

## ★ Civics Sidelight

**Fringe Benefits** One of the motivations for choosing a particular career may be fringe benefits. Depending on the size of the employer and the occupation, fringe benefits can range from small "packages" to lucrative benefits that may add as much as 33 percent to the value of your earnings. For example, offering workers a plan to help them to save money on medical visits, allowing employees to cash in unused vacation days, and providing company uniforms, transportation, and meals are some of the ways value is added to your earnings. Common components of a benefit package include the following: paid holidays, sick leave, personal days, vacations, insurance, and retirement. The value of fringe-benefit packages should be considered as part of the total earnings when comparing the advantages of one job to another.

### CRITICAL THINKING

Why is company-provided insurance a valuable fringe benefit?

**ANSWER:** Students might suggest that because of the high cost of medical care, an insurance package can be extremely valuable.

### Visual Record Answer

*Students might suggest that their manner of dress makes them appear more professional.*

has the potential to make unique contributions to the world. Doing less than your best shortchanges everyone.

Some students find school difficult and drop out. Some dropouts believe that quitting school and going to work will give them a head start in earning money. However, leaving school is often the worst thing to do if you are interested in earning a good income.

Although dropouts can begin to earn money sooner than students who remain in school, most dropouts earn low wages. They do not have the education, training, and skills needed for most occupations that provide a higher income.

Furthermore, dropouts often find themselves without work. With every year that passes, a person who does not finish high school will find it more difficult to earn a living. To make matters worse, many tasks that were once done by less skilled workers are now the work of machines.

✔ **Reading Check** Analyzing Information Why is education the key to success in obtaining employment? Employers want to hire educated people who can be trained to meet new challenges.

### ★ The Kinds of Workers Employers Want

Employers typically want workers who have a good general education. If special training is needed for a position, it is sometimes given on the job. When hiring a secretary, for example, an employer wants someone who types well, has computer skills, and does neat work. The employer also seeks a person who can spell accurately, follow directions, and develop new skills. When hired, the secretary is not expected to know much about the company's products. Such things can be learned on the job.

The young man or woman who does well at a job builds on information and skills learned in school. For example, a young person hired as a grocery store clerk may one day become the store manager. Such advancement is possible if he or she has a good education and is able to solve practical problems. The employer knows that the clerk can learn how to manage the store while working. Therefore, no matter what your future job, the best way to prepare is by learning everything you can in school.

**Interpreting the Visual Record**

**Applying for jobs** *Some job openings attract a large number of applicants.* **Why do you think most of the job applicants shown below are dressed formally?**

✔ **Reading Check** Analyzing Information
What skills do most employers expect workers to have, and what skills do employers provide for workers once they are hired?
Employers want workers who have a good general education. They often provide on-the-job training to new employees.

# REVIEW AND ASSESS

Have students complete the **Section 1 Review** on page 545. Then have them complete **Daily Quiz 22.1**. As **Alternative Assessment**, you may want to use the graphic organizer or newspaper article activities in this section's lessons.

## RETEACH

Have students complete the **Main Idea Activity for English Language Learners and Special-Needs Students 22.1**. Then ask each student to design a poster illustrating the necessity of an education for a particular career of his or her choice.

**ENGLISH LANGUAGE LEARNERS**

# EXTEND

Have students conduct research to obtain more information about the kinds of careers that were most common at different times throughout the country's history. Have students investigate the levels of education required for these jobs. Finally, have students prepare oral reports and illustrations that present their research to the class. **BLOCK SCHEDULING**

## ★ Beginning Your Search

You may ask, "If business is changing so rapidly, how can I know what job to prepare for?" Fortunately, you do not need to make your choice now. If you stay in school, you will have several more years in which to study the possibilities before you choose.

The first thing you can do to prepare yourself is study careers and understand the type of work each involves. Then consider the personal qualities each career requires, such as originality or mechanical ability. Once you have done this, examine your own interests and abilities. Determine how well they fit with various careers.

Gradually, you will begin to focus on one career (or perhaps several) that may best suit you. Once you have made your choice or choices, you can begin preparing for your future. The next four sections of this chapter will help you start thinking about a potential career.

*There are many careers available for you to choose from. All require hard work, a basic education, and some sort of training in order to succeed.*

✔ **Reading Check Summarizing** How can you narrow down your career choices? **Study various careers and understand the type of work each one involves. Consider the qualifications for each career. Examine your own interests and abilities to see which job they best fit.**

## SECTION 1 Review

**go.hrw.com** — Homework Practice Online
keyword: SZ3 HP22

1. **Define** and explain:
   • personal values
   • qualifications

2. **Analyzing Information** Copy the graphic organizer below. Use it to show the basic factors that shape your ability to find an appropriate career.

A Career for You

3. **Finding the Main Idea**
   a. What are the advantages of allowing individuals to choose their careers?
   b. How does education benefit job seekers, and how does lack of education disadvantage them?

4. **Writing and Critical Thinking**
   **Summarizing** You are a high-school graduate beginning your job search. Make a list of your strengths, weaknesses, interests, skills, personal values, and accomplishments. Based on the list, write a resumé summing up your accomplishments and professional goals for a job that interests you.

   **Consider:**
   • what you need to do to prepare for a job search
   • the value of getting to know yourself

## Section 1 Review ANSWERS

**1. Define**
• personal values, p. 542
• qualifications, p. 543

**2.** personal values, qualifications, interests and abilities, education

**3. a.** more likely to make wise and fulfilling career choices if people know their own abilities, interests, skills, strengths, and weaknesses

**b.** Education makes a worker more marketable, improves chances for earning higher income; dropouts must often take low paying jobs, are often unemployed, and have a lifetime of earnings that do not equal those who stay in school.

**4.** Students should make honest assessments of their strengths and weaknesses in their resumes.

# SECTION 2

## OBJECTIVES

*After completing Section 2, students should be able to*

1 **Identify which occupations require mostly mental work, mostly physical work, or both.**

2 **Describe the training that workers must receive to become master craftspersons.**

3 **Explain what has contributed to the lowered demand for laborers and agricultural workers.**

## SECTION 2 RESOURCES

### REPRODUCIBLE
▶ Guided Reading Strategies 22.2

### TECHNOLOGY
▶ One-Stop Planner, Lesson 22.2
▶ Homework Practice Online

### REINFORCEMENT, REVIEW AND ASSESSMENT
▶ Section 2 Review, p. 551
▶ Daily Quiz 22.2
▶ Main Idea Activity 22.2
▶ English Audio Summary 22.2
▶ Spanish Audio Summary 22.2

546

---

## ))) LET'S GET STARTED!

As students enter the classroom, ask them what a business license is and what occupations require a type of license. *(Students might suggest that it is a license required to operate a business.)* Generate a list of student responses. Ask students what requirements a person must meet to be allowed to teach a particular course in high school. Discuss why requirements might be different depending on the educational discipline. Tell students that in Section 2 they will focus on types of workers and occupations, on job prospects, as well as on the skills and prerequisites required for particular careers.

## SECTION 2

# The World of Work

### Read to Discover

1. Which occupations require mostly mental work, mostly physical work, or both?
2. What training must workers receive to become master craftspersons?
3. What has contributed to the lowered demand for laborers and agricultural workers?

#### WHY CIVICS MATTERS
Many types of jobs make up the workforce in the United States. Use **CNN fyi.com** or other **current events** sources to investigate the jobs most people have in your community. Record your findings in your journal.

### Define
- white-collar workers
- professionals
- technicians
- blue-collar workers
- apprenticeship
- operators
- automation
- laborers
- service industries
- agribusinesses

## Reading Focus

You may already be familiar with many of the career opportunities in your community. You have learned about jobs from your family and friends. Perhaps you have worked at part-time jobs. All these experiences have helped you learn about various fields of work. Now it is time to examine the hundreds of different occupations available to workers in the United States.

*Doctors require years of on-the-job training in medical school, in addition to a college degree.*

### ★ White-Collar Workers

**White-collar workers** make up the largest group of workers in the country today. White-collar workers are people who work in a particular profession or who perform technical, managerial, sales, or administrative support work.

**Professionals** Jobs that require many years of education and training, and in which the work tends to be mental rather than physical, are referred to as professions. Examples of **professionals** include doctors, nurses, lawyers, architects, and teachers.

In the field of science, professional workers include chemists, biologists, botanists, geologists, and many other specialists. In the business world, professionals include

**LEVEL 1:** Organize students into small groups. Assign each group a particular profession. Instruct groups to write down the level of education and the skills that they think would be necessary for someone to work in that profession. Have groups share their lists with the class. Then lead a class discussion about which occupations require mostly mental work, mostly physical work, or both. **ENGLISH LANGUAGE LEARNERS , COOPERATIVE LEARNING**

**LEVEL 1:** Invite a group of professionals to speak to your class in a roundtable discussion. Make sure students have some questions prepared beforehand that address the professionals' qualifications, the requirements and skills that are necessary for the professions of your guest speakers, as well as whether the work involves mostly mental work, mostly physical work, or both. **ENGLISH LANGUAGE LEARNERS**

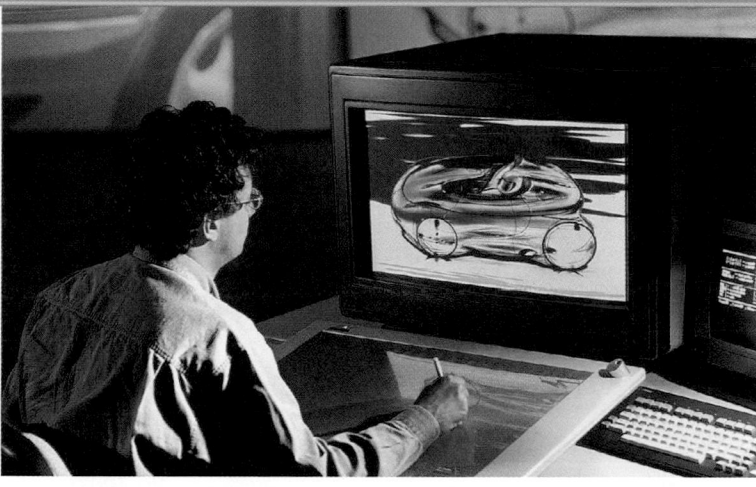

**Interpreting the Visual Record**

**Staying informed** *In many computer-related fields, professionals must continually work to stay familiar with the many changes in software and hardware technology.* **How is such ongoing training an example of lifelong learning?**

## ★ Culture

**Management Positions**

The percentage of managers, administrators, and executives who are African American rose from 4.7 percent to 6.8 percent between 1983 and 1994 and to 7.6 percent in 2000. During the same period, the percentage of Hispanics in those positions rose from 2.8 percent to 4.9 percent and to 5.4 percent, respectively. All three figures represent progress, though they lag behind the percentage of African Americans (15.6 percent) and Hispanics (13.2 percent) in the total U.S. population in 2000. Women have also made gains in management, occupying 43 percent of such jobs in 1994, up from 32.4 percent in 1983. In 2000, women held 45.3 percent of the country's executive, administrative, and managerial positions.

**ACTIVITY:** Have students conduct research to obtain more information about the management ratios of the professions of their choice. Ask each student to create a chart illustrating those ratios.

accountants, economists, computer programmers, and engineers. Among the professionals in the arts are writers, painters, conductors, composers, and entertainers.

As the economy has changed and grown, the demand for professional workers has also increased. Among today's fastest-growing career fields are those in the computer and health-care professions.

**Technicians** **Technicians** are people who perform jobs that require some specialized skill in addition to a solid, basic education. Among these skilled workers are medical laboratory technicians, medical X-ray technicians, physical therapists, and dental hygienists. Other technicians are employed in radio and television, the film industry, manufacturing, and computer industries.

A high-school education is the foundation upon which the technician builds. Some technicians learn their skills on the job. Most take special courses in colleges or in technical or vocational schools.

✔ **Reading Check Contrasting** How do the qualifications and training of professionals and technicians differ? Professional jobs require many years of education and training. Technicians require some specialized training or skill.

**Managers, Administrators, and Executives** As you know, the people in charge of large businesses and corporations are managers and administrators. They are also called executives because they execute, or carry out, the operations of a business.

American businesses are experiencing stiff competition from other countries around the world. To remain competitive in the global economy, American businesses must continue to attract experienced, well-educated, and well-trained managers and executives. Businesses build on the ideas and skills of these individuals.

The owners of American businesses know that their success depends on good management. They work hard to hire, train, and develop managers. Intelligent,

*Technicians are often needed to operate and maintain the equipment used in many different industries, such as television broadcasting.*

## Visual Record Answer

*Students might suggest that it is an example of how learning is a never-ending process.*

**LEVELS 1 AND 2:** Then lead a class discussion about which occupations require mostly mental work, mostly physical work, or both. Have each student create a chart that lists 15 different professions of his or her choosing. The chart should contain the following headings: *Mental Work, Physical Work,* and *Both.* Then have students complete the chart by placing checkmarks in the appropriate boxes. **ENGLISH LANGUAGE LEARNERS**

# TEACH OBJECTIVE 2

**ALL LEVELS:** Lead a class discussion about the training that workers receive to become master craftspersons. *(To train for a craft, the new worker usually serves as an apprentice.)* Then tell each student to make a list of at least five jobs that would require apprenticeships. Have volunteers share their lists with the class. **ENGLISH LANGUAGE LEARNERS**

**LEVEL 2:** Assign each student a particular blue-collar occupation, and have students create diagrams illustrating the training needs for their assigned occupation. Also ask students to list "soft skills" that would be necessary for their assigned occupation. (Read the side-column text about soft skills on page 550.) **ENGLISH LANGUAGE LEARNERS**

**Interpreting the Visual Record**

**Management training** *Many managers attend courses, seminars, or workshops designed to improve their planning, organizing, and interpersonal skills.* **Why do you think such classes are common?**

*Without administrative assistants, most companies would have great difficulty functioning efficiently.*

hardworking executives are needed as heads of departments, branch offices, research divisions, and special projects. Government, too, needs executives to keep the country's affairs running smoothly. In every community, there are many opportunities for people who wish to manage and run small businesses.

A person with executive ability has a good chance for success in a free economy. However, special training is needed if one is to become a successful executive. Today many top executives are college graduates who studied management in university or college business schools. Large businesses often have their own executive training programs.

Many managers and executives are self-employed, preferring to work for themselves. They take risks and hope to profit from their own efforts. Self-employed workers are often entrepreneurs—owners of small businesses. They might also be independent contractors—people who hire out their services on a project-by-project basis.

Managers and executives are not the only people who are self-employed. Many professionals, such as doctors, dentists, and lawyers, work for themselves. This is true for many writers, painters, and musicians as well.

✔ **Reading Check Analyzing Information** How do American businesses depend on managers and executives? need experienced, well-educated, and well-trained managers and executives to operate effectively.

**Administrative Support and Sales Workers** Bookkeepers, secretaries, office clerks, and word processors are examples of administrative support workers. They do much of the paperwork required to keep American businesses and industries operating smoothly. According to the Bureau of Labor Statistics, the United States will need many of these workers in the years ahead.

People who sell goods and services are sales workers. Sales workers may be clerks in retail stores or door-to-door salespeople. They also may sell to other businesses, institutions, or governments.

HOMEWORK Tell students to interview an individual in a white collar job and an individual in a blue collar job. After students have conducted their interviews, have them draw a diagram with interlocking circles to compare and contrast the two types of jobs.

## TEACH OBJECTIVE 3

**ALL LEVELS:** Copy the following graphic organizer onto the chalkboard, omitting the italicized answers. Then ask students to complete the organizer to explain what has contributed to the lowered demand for laborers and agricultural workers. **ENGLISH LANGUAGE LEARNERS**

**Lowered Demand for Laborers and Agricultural Workers**

*Automation (machine power) is replacing*

*muscle power*

Sales workers are in high demand. The skills these workers need can be learned by intelligent, hardworking individuals and do not require long periods of training. Many sales workers receive their training on the job. Other sales workers, such as real estate agents, insurance agents, and specialized sales representatives, often have college degrees. For some of these occupations, special courses and state licensing examinations are required.

✔ **Reading Check** Summarizing What duties do administrative support and sales workers perform? Administrative support workers do much of the paperwork required to keep American businesses and industries operating smoothly. Sales workers sell goods and services.

## ★ Blue-Collar Workers

Workers who perform jobs that require manual labor are known as **blue-collar workers.** They work in construction, manufacturing, mining, petroleum, steel, transportation, and many other industries. Over the past decade, the percentage of blue-collar workers in the United States has decreased.

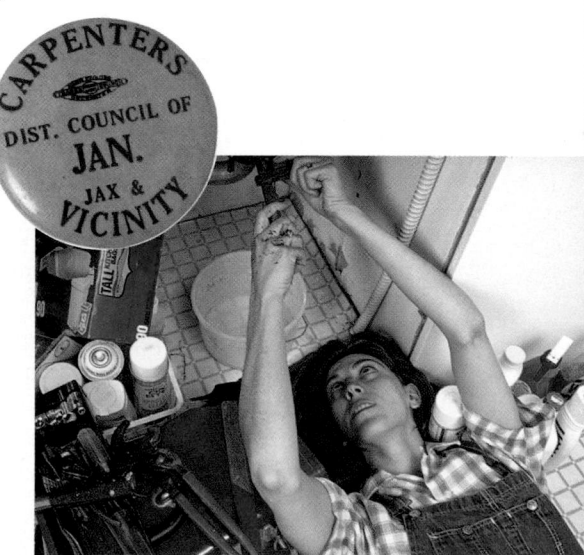

**Craftspersons** People who work in trades or handicrafts are called craftspersons. They include carpenters, electricians, machinists, bricklayers, plumbers, printers, bakers, auto mechanics, and painters. The most important requirement for workers in crafts, or trades, is manual ability. That is, they must be able to do accurate and sometimes difficult work with their hands. They must also be good at practical mathematics.

To train for a craft, the new worker usually serves an **apprenticeship,** or fixed period of on-the-job training. The length of on-the-job training varies according to the job. Some industries and labor unions reduce apprenticeship time by giving credit for job-training courses from high school or trade school.

When apprentices have learned their craft to a certain level, they receive a certificate of completion of apprenticeship. After gaining some job experience, these people can become master craftspersons and receive the highest wages in their trade.

Each craft has its own labor union that determines the number of people admitted into the craft annually. Numbers are determined by union rules, industry needs, and available trained workers. Some craftspersons, such as plumbers and electricians, must pass state examinations and receive licenses to practice their crafts.

✔ **Reading Check** Summarizing Which trades are considered crafts, and what skills and training are required for these jobs? Craftspersons include carpenters, electricians, machinists, bricklayers, plumbers, printers, bakers, auto mechanics, and painters; skills—good manual ability and math skills; training—apprenticeship.

---

★★★★★★★★★★★★
### That's Interesting!
★★★★★★★★★★★★

Labor Day, the first Monday in September, is a national tribute to workers, who have made countless contributions to the prosperity and well-being of this country. The first Labor Day was celebrated in New York City on Tuesday, September 5, 1882, after a proposal for a "workingmens" holiday was made and accepted by the Central Labor Union of New York. The Central Labor Union appointed a committee, who in turn planned a parade and a picnic. In 1884 the first Monday in September was selected as a permanent date, and the idea of a holiday to honor workers spread across the United States. On June 28, 1894, Congress made Labor Day a legal holiday.

---

### Visual Record Answer

*Students' responses will vary.*

---

**Interpreting the Visual Record**

**Working women** *In recent years women have joined many trades, such as plumbing, that were once largely restricted to men.* **What are some benefits of opening craft trades up to women workers?**

**LEVEL 1:** Ask students to explain the meaning of the term "agribusiness" (a merging of the words agriculture and business). Ask them what this merging suggests. *(Students might suggest that farming is a big business.)* Then ask students what the term "automation" means *(It is from the Greek term—self-acting.)* Have students list examples of farm equipment that have made it easier for farming to be a big business. *(Students might suggest tractors, hay balers, automatic milking machines, cotton gins, and so on.)* Discuss with students what has contributed to the lowered demand for laborers and agricultural workers. **ENGLISH LANGUAGE LEARNERS**

**LEVEL 3:** Ask each student to create a political cartoon that illustrates the lowered demand for laborers and agricultural workers. Have volunteers present their cartoons to the class.

## CLOSE

On the chalkboard draw figures representing the different kinds of careers discussed in this section. Next to each figure have volunteers write future job prospects for each of these careers on the chalkboard. Then have the class discuss why various future job prospects are better than others.

## ★ Daily Life

**Soft Skills** Other than the technical skills required to do a job, there are also other skills, known as "soft skills." "Soft skills" include basic skills, such as the ability to communicate, to compute simple math, and manage information. Communication can be verbal (answering telephones or making presentations) or nonverbal (body language and eye contact). Other "soft skills" include punctuality, personal hygiene, and appropriate attire. Employees who possess good personal/interpersonal skills have the ability to get along at work because they take initiative; display good characteristics; are cheerful and enthusiastic; are well organized; and are good leaders. Although "soft skills" are usually givens that are expected of an employee, a person who possesses good "soft skills" is more marketable and more valuable to an employer.

### CRITICAL THINKING

Do you think all "soft skills" are welcomed by every employer?

**ANSWER:** Students' responses will vary.

### Visual Record Answer

*Students might suggest that it is difficult to manage a budget or household without steady employment.*

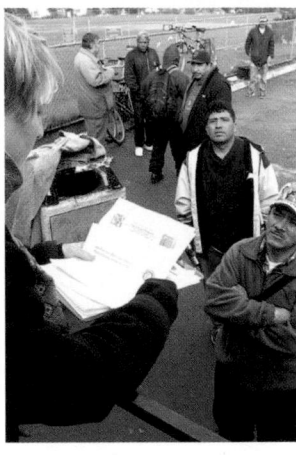

**Interpreting the Visual Record**

**Laborers** *Many laborers have little job security and must look for construction or contract work on a daily basis.* **Why would this situation be difficult?**

*Because they must work long shifts and be ready to respond to emergencies at a moment's notice, firefighters often eat together at the fire station.*

**Operators** People who operate machines or equipment in factories, mills, industrial plants, gas stations, mines, and laundries are called **operators.** Other factory workers, such as those who inspect, assemble, and package goods, are included in this group. Truck and bus drivers are also operators.

Many operators receive their training on the job. Their work usually does not require long periods of training because they often repeat the same task many times. The qualities employers look for in an operator are dependability, good health, and some manual skill. Just because a job does not require long periods of training does not mean everyone can handle it. A good truck driver gains certain skills only after many years of practice, good judgment, and good health.

Some operators face an uncertain future. The number of machine operators in American industry has declined. Factories have come to rely on **automation,** or the use of machines instead of workers to provide goods and services. This trend is likely to continue. In addition, many manufacturing plants have moved to foreign locations, where labor is less expensive. This means there are fewer jobs for operators and other people in manufacturing.

**Laborers** There are and probably always will be jobs that call for little or no training. Workers without special skills are often employed to mix cement, carry bricks, dig ditches, and handle freight. Workers who perform this type of heavy physical work are called **laborers.**

The demand for laborers will grow more slowly than the demand for other types of workers in the years ahead. Automation is increasingly replacing muscle power. More and more, machines are used to do jobs requiring heavy manual labor.

✔ **Reading Check Comparing** What training do operators and laborers receive, and what challenges do both groups of workers face? Both groups receive on-the-job training and face increasing automation of the industries they work in, as well as manufacturing plants moving to foreign locations.

## ★ Service Workers

Today one in every seven employed Americans is a service worker. Service workers provide the public with some type of needed assistance. For example, some service workers provide protection services. This group includes firefighters, police officers, correctional institution officers, and security guards. Other service workers provide health services. Among these workers are paramedics, dental and nursing assistants, and orderlies. Service workers are

## REVIEW AND ASSESS

Have students complete the **Section 2 Review** on page 551. Then have them complete **Daily Quiz 22.2**. As **Alternative Assessment**, you may want to use the roundtable discussion or the types-of-work chart exercises in this section's lessons.

## RETEACH

Have students complete **Main Idea Activity for English Language Learners and Special-Needs Students 22.2.** Then have students evaluate how this section's categorization of occupations has helped clarify the world of work for them. Call on volunteers to come to the board to list one advantage or one disadvantage of a white-collar, blue-collar, service, or agricultural career. Have students discuss what kind of work appeals to them. **ENGLISH LANGUAGE LEARNERS**

## EXTEND

Assign students a particular occupation and have them conduct research to obtain more information about the median incomes for their assigned occupations. Have each student create a bar graph illustrating the median incomes for his or her assigned occupation during the past 10 years. **BLOCK SCHEDULING**

employed by many kinds of firms. Businesses that sell services rather than products are called **service industries.** They include hospitals, security companies, hotels, restaurants, dry cleaners, laundries, barbershops, and hair salons.

Some service-industry jobs require a college education or training courses. In other industries, workers learn needed skills on the job. Today women make up around 65 percent of the workers in service occupations.

### ★ Agricultural Workers

Agricultural workers are people who operate, manage, or work on farms. The need for agricultural workers has decreased greatly during the last hundred years.

Many small family farms have been replaced by very large farms known as **agribusinesses.** Agribusinesses are owned by corporations and rely heavily on mechanized equipment. They are able to produce larger yields using fewer workers. Today many small farmers have turned to organic farming or other specialty crops.

*On large farms, machinery has automated many of the tasks once done by agricultural laborers.*

✔ **Reading Check Contrasting** How does the work performed by service workers and agricultural workers differ? Service workers provide the public with needed assistance. Agricultural workers work on, operate, or manage farms.

## SECTION 2 Review

**go.hrw.com** Homework Practice Online
keyword: SZ3 HP22

1. **Define** and explain:
   - white-collar workers
   - professionals
   - technicians
   - blue-collar workers
   - apprenticeship
   - operators
   - automation
   - laborers
   - service industries
   - agribusinesses

2. **Categorizing** Copy the table below. Use it to list occupations that require mostly mental work, mostly physical work, or both mental and physical work. Then provide examples of each type of job.

| Type of Work | Occupations | Examples of Jobs |
|---|---|---|
|  |  |  |
|  |  |  |
|  |  |  |

3. **Finding the Main Idea**
   a. What kinds of training are necessary for becoming a master craftsperson?
   b. Why are fewer people working as laborers and agricultural workers?

4. **Writing and Critical Thinking**
   **Drawing Inferences and Conclusions** Imagine you are an analyst of American business and the global economy. Write a two-paragraph article explaining why businesses need a well-educated, well-trained workforce to operate effectively and remain competitive in the global marketplace.

   **Consider:**
   - the relationships between different categories of workers
   - the relationship between workers and businesses

## Section 2 Review
### ANSWERS

1. **Define**
   - white-collar workers, p. 546
   - professionals, p. 546
   - technicians, p. 547
   - blue-collar workers, p. 549
   - apprenticeship, p. 549
   - operators, p. 550
   - automation, p. 550
   - laborers, p. 550
   - service industries, p. 551
   - agribusinesses, p. 551

2. mental, physical, both mental and physical; students' answers will vary.

3. a. on-the-job training and experience working in the craft; math is helpful

   b. Automation increasingly is replacing muscle power. Agribusinesses rely heavily on mechanized equipment and can produce larger yields with fewer workers.

4. Students might say such a workforce is more productive, creative, and innovative. Also, such a workforce is more easily trained as technology advances.

# SECTION 3

## OBJECTIVES

*After completing Section 3, students should be able to*

1 **Analyze what types of qualifications are necessary for careers in government or the military.**

2 **Define what it means to be an "equal opportunity employer."**

3 **Examine why women are being encouraged to pursue careers in science and technology.**

## 🔊 LET'S GET STARTED!

As students walk into the classroom, tell them that the term *civil* comes from a Latin word meaning "citizen." "Civil service," therefore, means "service of citizens." A civil service examination is a test used to judge jobseekers' qualifications for most federal jobs. Ask students for a term that describes those who work in such federal jobs. *(Students should suggest civil servants.)* Tell students that before civil service examinations were developed, government workers were hired on the basis of who they knew, not what they knew. Tell students that in Section 3 they will learn more about careers in government, equal opportunity employment, and careers in science and technology.

---

## SECTION 3

# Unlimited Opportunities

### Read to Discover

1. What types of qualifications are necessary for careers in government or the military?
2. What does it mean to be "an equal opportunity employer"?
3. Why are women pursuing careers in science and technology?

### Define
• equal opportunity employer

> **WHY CIVICS MATTERS**
>
> Some occupations have typically employed mostly men or mostly women but the situation is beginning to change. Use **CNNfyi.com** or other **current events** sources to show which careers traditionally held by men or women are opening up to members of the opposite sex. Record your findings in your journal.

## Reading Focus

Whether a person is a professional, technician, craftsperson, service worker, or laborer, there are opportunities for advancement. For example, young people who complete a high-school trade or technical course might start their careers as word processors, clerks, or book-keepers. By attending night school, they may qualify for better paying positions. For example, they might study accounting and learn to keep business financial records.

## ⭐ Government Jobs

The country's largest employer is the U.S. government. More than 2.7 million Americans work for the federal government, not including those men and women who serve in the armed forces. Federal employees hold a wide range of jobs.

Some workers deliver the mail, care for war veterans, or protect against counterfeiting. Others run the national parks, forecast the weather, or inspect food and medicines to make sure they are not contaminated. Many thousands of clerks, word processors, and secretaries are also needed to carry out the everyday business of the federal government.

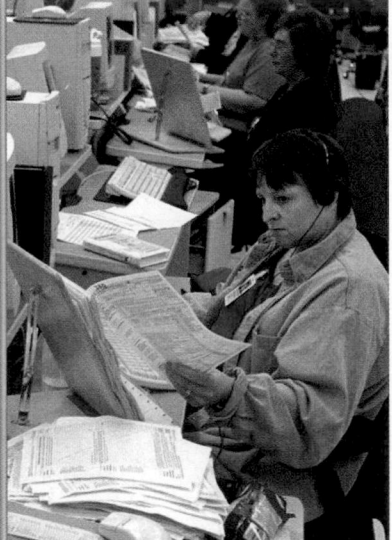

*Government agencies such as the Internal Revenue Service employ thousands of clerical workers.*

# TEACH OBJECTIVE 1

**ALL LEVELS:** Tell students that without even knowing, they have acquired many skills that will help them in a career, even a government career. Have students create newspaper want ads for various government jobs, complete with descriptions of the skills and interests required for applicants. (*Students' ads might include skills such as communication, physical endurance, manual dexterity, organization, or planning.*) Call on volunteers to present their advertisements to the class for discussion. **ENGLISH LANGUAGE LEARNERS**

**HOMEWORK** Instruct each student to research the benefits package for a particular government job and to create a fact sheet to share with the class.

# TEACH OBJECTIVE 2

**ALL LEVELS:** Review with the class the meaning of the phrase "an equal opportunity employer." Ask students what this phrase means about an employer. (*Such employers provide equal opportunities for jobs to all applicants.*) Obtain an equal opportunity statement from a local employer or government employment office and read it to the class. Have students identify specific groups of people protected from discrimination. Ask students the following question: What agency upholds fair employment standards? (*Students should suggest the Equal Employment Opportunity Commission.*) **ENGLISH LANGUAGE LEARNERS**

Applicants typically submit a resumé or an application form that includes a detailed history of their background and education. Some government agencies also require written tests for certain positions. As with any job, government agencies interview candidates and choose the best qualified for the job.

Like the federal government, state and local governments employ many different kinds of workers. The process for hiring in a state or local government agency is similar to that of the federal government. People interested in these jobs can listen to descriptions of job openings on telephone job lines. Job notices may also be posted on agency sites on the Internet. Interested people submit resumés or applications for openings and are then interviewed. Before a candidate is offered a job, he or she may be subject to an extensive background check as well.

✔ **Reading Check Summarizing** What kinds of jobs can be found with the government, and where can job seekers find notices of them? A wide range of jobs can be found through telephone job lines and agency sites on the Internet.

## ★ The Armed Forces

There are many opportunities for employment in the armed forces. A high-school diploma is required for most good jobs in the armed forces. Training in the military is available for jobs such as electronics technician, radar operator and technician, medical equipment technician, motor mechanic, and surveyor. In addition, some combat positions on aircraft and ships are open to both men and women in the armed forces.

The United States also has four officer training schools—the U.S. Army, Navy, Air Force, and Coast Guard academies. Applicants to these schools must be high-school graduates. With the exception of the Coast Guard academy, candidates must be nominated for admission. They usually obtain nominations from their district congressional representatives or from their state senators. They must also pass scholastic and physical tests.

✔ **Reading Check Finding the Main Idea** What conditions must be met to work in the military? at least a high-school diploma, also job-specific training for or acceptance into one of four officer-training schools

*Did You* **KNOW?**

Three U.S. presidents—Ulysses S. Grant, Dwight Eisenhower, and Jimmy Carter—have been graduates of the country's military academies.

**LEVELS 2 AND 3:** Tell students why women are being encouraged to pursue careers in science and technology. (*Women's struggle for equal rights has opened doors to careers previously unavailable to women.*) Tell students that one way that girls are getting a jump on careers is by participating in Take Our Daughters to Work Day, which is held each spring. On Take Our Daughters to Work Day, girls aged 9 to 15 accompany their mothers and fathers to their jobs for a firsthand glimpse of the world of work. Ask students to imagine that they have accompanied their parents to Take Our Daughters To Work Day and to write essays about their experiences.

# CLOSE

Refer students to the section title, "Unlimited Opportunities." Ask students how the title relates to increased openings for women in scientific and technical fields. Have students find further evidence in this section of expanded job opportunities. Ask a volunteer to list students' findings on the chalkboard. Then have students discuss what they must do to take advantage of the opportunities.

## ★ Economics

**Women and Data Collection** Point out to students that the increasing number of women in the workforce has caused the government to revise outdated methods of calculating unemployment rates. In January 1994 the Labor Department began basing employment statistics on new monthly household surveys that took into account the fact that many women now work outside the home. Many women had previously been falsely presumed to be homemakers rather than individuals who were searching for, but unable to find, work outside the home. The recognition that these women were not voluntarily out of the labor force caused the official unemployment rate to slightly rise after the new survey was implemented. Because of economic growth at the time, however, the official unemployment rate resumed its downward trend shortly afterward.

### CRITICAL THINKING

Why do you think so many women work outside the home?

**ANSWER:** Students might suggest that many women today are single parents, or two incomes are needed in a two-parent home, or that women simply enjoy the satisfaction of a career.

### GRAPH ANSWER

27 percent

## Job Opportunities

### Predicted Distribution of Employment by Industry, 2008*

- Professional and technical — 19%
- Executive, administrative, and managerial
- Administrative support and clerical
- Marketing and sales — 17%
- Services
- Precision production, craft, and repair
- Operators, fabricators, and laborers
- Agriculture, fishing, forestry

<3%, 11%, 11%, 11%, 13%, 16%

### Predicted Fastest-Growing Jobs (1998–2008)

1. Computer engineers
2. Computer support specialists
3. Systems analysts
4. Database administrators
5. Desktop publishing specialists
6. Paralegals and legal assistants
7. Personal care and home health aides
8. Medical assistants
9. Social and human service assistants
10. Physician assistants

\* Figures are rounded to the nearest percent.
Source: *Monthly Labor Review*

**Interpreting Graphs** *Much of the predicted job growth in the United States will take place in fields related to computers or health care.* **What percentage of U.S. jobs are predicted to involve marketing, sales, and services in 2008?**

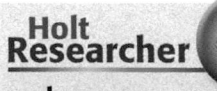

**Holt Researcher**

**go.hrw.com**
KEYWORD: Holt Researcher
Freefind: Careers

Scan through the career listings on the Holt Researcher. Pick three careers from four of the following categories: business, government, public service, or science and technology. Create a chart that compares the qualifications, salaries, and responsibilities of each career. Your chart should answer the following question: How are these careers similar and different?

## ★ Workers in Demand

The U.S. Department of Labor constantly studies jobs and job opportunities throughout the country. Each year it reports where men and women are working and what jobs they are performing. It also attempts to predict which jobs will need more workers in the coming years. The department has predicted that the health-care and computer fields in particular will need many more workers.

Of course, some kinds of workers are almost always in demand. For example, law enforcement officers and teachers are always needed. Keep in mind that the need for a particular type of worker may be greater in some parts of the country than in others. For example, some areas have more openings for manufacturing or high-tech jobs than do others.

Also remember that in all industries and fields there is a degree of turnover because of promotions, job changes, and retirements. These events almost always create job openings for new employees. The well-prepared job seeker should be ready to seize employment opportunities when they happen.

✔ **Reading Check** Analyzing Information How can employment seekers make the most of opportunities in the job world? by knowing which careers are in demand in the location of their job search, by being aware of turnover in the fields they are interested in.

## ★ Equal Employment Opportunity

In your study of career opportunities, you may have noticed the phrase "an **equal opportunity employer**" in newspaper classified advertisements. This phrase means that the employer does not discriminate against job applicants because of their sex, age, race, skin color, religion, or ethnic background.

## REVIEW AND ASSESS

Have students complete the **Section 3 Review** on page 555. Then have them complete **Daily Quiz 22.3**. As **Alternative Assessment**, you may want to use the job ad or Take Our Daughters to Work Day essay in this section's lessons.

## RETEACH

Have students complete **Main Idea Activity for English Language Learners and Special-Needs Students 22.3**. Then have students refer to the chart "Job Opportunities" and ask them to compare the growing job opportunities to the declining job opportunities. Then lead a class discussion about the reasons for the increase and decrease in certain fields. **ENGLISH LANGUAGE LEARNERS**

## EXTEND

Organize the class into small groups. Assign each group one of the following goals: to work for the U.S. government in civil service, to join the armed forces, or to enter an officer training school. Have each group design and produce a brochure that explains how to achieve its goal. Individual roles for group members might include researcher, recording secretary, writer, and illustrator. After groups have presented their projects, store the brochures in a "Career Folder" to which students can refer as needed. **BLOCK SCHEDULING , COOPERATIVE LEARNING**

---

Congress passed the Civil Rights Acts of 1964 and 1968 to help end discrimination in hiring and wage rates. These acts have created new job opportunities for women and members of minority groups. The Equal Employment Opportunity Commission, whose members are appointed by the president, upholds fair employment standards. Most states have similar commissions.

Women's struggle for equal rights has opened doors to careers previously unavailable to women. Today women are members of Congress, judges, doctors, scientists, engineers, pilots, and cab drivers. Most jobs in the military are also now open to women.

✔ **Reading Check Finding the Main Idea** What two acts passed by Congress influenced the rights of employees, and what effect did they have? The Civil Rights Acts of 1964 and 1968 helped to end discrimination in hiring and wage rates and created new job opportunities for women and members of minority groups.

### ⭐ Unemployment

As you read in Chapter 20, there are times when the U.S. economy experiences a recession or depression. During such times many people are without work. People who are working may not have been able to find jobs in their chosen fields or are working only part-time.

The young person considering possible careers should remember that there will be periods of high unemployment in the future. It is wise to have multiple interests and, if possible, to develop skills in more than one area of work.

✔ **Reading Check Summarizing** What is a recession, and how can individuals prepare themselves for it? a period when people are without work, cannot find jobs in their chosen fields, or are working only part-time; by exploring other interests and developing skills in more than one area of work, if possible

*Great strides in fighting gender discrimination have been made. Today women serve as Supreme Court justices, a job once held only by men. Here Justice Ruth Bader Ginsburg addresses a gathering of school children.*

## Section 3 Review
### ANSWERS

**1. Define**
• equal opportunity employer, p. 554

**2.** Government—take a civil service examination; Military—usually requires a high school diploma

**3. a.** The employer does not discriminate against job applicants because of sex, age, race, skin color, religion, or ethnic background.

**b.** Because women have struggled for equal rights, more doors are open to them now.

**4.** Students might suggest fields that will need more workers, how to recruit those employees, and what might happen if we do not provide the workers for the growing fields.

---

## SECTION 3 Review

**go.hrw.com Homework Practice Online**
**keyword: SZ3 HP22**

**1. Define** and explain:
• equal opportunity employer

**2. Summarizing** Copy the table below. Use it to indicate the qualifications needed to work in the civil service or in the military.

|  | Qualifications |
|---|---|
| Government |  |
| Military |  |

**3. Finding the Main Idea**
a. What is guaranteed when an employer is advertised as an "equal opportunity employer"?
b. Why is the number of women in scientific and technical areas increasing?

**4. Writing and Critical Thinking**
**Making Generalizations and Predictions** Write a speech for Congress explaining what fields will be growing in the next 10 years, and how the country can ensure that there are enough workers in these professions.

**Consider:**
• fields that will need more workers
• how to recruit more employees
• what might happen to the U.S. economy if there are not enough workers in these fields

**ALL LEVELS:** Have students use their textbooks to find additional examples of discrimination throughout U.S. history. Then ask each student to create a chart that lists in the first column the types of discrimination that have occurred throughout American history. In the second column, students should list the measures or legal acts taken to eradicate the discrimination. Ask volunteers to share their lists with the class.
**ENGLISH LANGUAGE LEARNERS**

## EXTEND

Lead a class discussion about the importance of the Civil Rights Act of 1964. Then ask students to conduct research at the library to obtain more information about the civil rights movement. Ask each student to imagine that he or she is a filmmaker and have each student write a script for a documentary about the civil rights movement that includes the importance as well as the effects of the pivotal Civil Rights Act of 1964. Ask volunteers to present their documentary scripts to the class.
**BLOCK SCHEDULING**

## Civics Sidelight

**The March** Before the passage of the Civil Rights Act of 1964, many Americans of all races and backgrounds gathered to peacefully protest discrimination. On August 28, 1963, more than 250,000 people participated in the March on Washington in support of civil rights. The demonstrators gathered near the Lincoln Memorial, where Martin Luther King, Jr. delivered his "I Have a Dream" speech. His address is remembered as one of the most powerful and effective speeches of modern times.

**ACTIVITY:** Have students conduct research about an important moment or movement during the civil rights struggle. Then ask each student to write a speech that tells and persuades others about the need for civil rights legislation.

___

**ANALYZING PRIMARY SOURCES ANSWER**
**1.** Employers cannot discriminate based on color, religion, sex, or national origin.

**2.** Students might suggest that it is meant to ensure fair hiring practices.

___

**Historical Documents**

# CIVIL RIGHTS ACT OF 1964

*The Civil Rights Act of 1964 prohibits discrimination on the basis of race, color, religion, or national origin. Under the terms of this act, discrimination is outlawed in the exercise of voting rights, and in public places, public education, and employment practices. This act supported the principles set forth in the Fourteenth and Fifteenth Amendments and helped move the country toward the goal of achieving equality for all Americans.*

## VOTING RIGHTS

No person acting under color of law shall—

in determining whether any individual is qualified under State law or laws to vote in any election, apply any standard, practice, or procedure different from the standards, practices, or procedures applied under such law or laws to other individuals within the same county, parish, or similar political subdivision who have been found by State officials to be qualified to vote. . . .

## DISCRIMINATION IN PLACES OF PUBLIC ACCOMMODATION

All persons shall be entitled to the full and equal enjoyment of the goods, services, facilities, privileges, advantages, and accommodations of any place of public accommodation, as defined in this section, without discrimination or segregation on the ground of race, color, religion, or national origin. . . .

## EQUAL EMPLOYMENT OPPORTUNITY

It shall be an unlawful employment practice for an employer—

to fail or refuse to hire or to discharge any individual, or otherwise to discriminate against any individual with respect to his compensation, terms, conditions, or privileges of employment, because of such individual's race, color, religion, sex, or national origin; or

to limit, segregate, or classify his employees in any way . . . because of such individual's race, color, religion, sex, or national origin.

**Analyzing Primary Sources**
**1.** What does this act prohibit employers from doing?
**2.** How do the provisions of this act protect your rights?

# TEACH

**ALL LEVELS:** Bring to class major newspapers from around the country, and have students compare the want ads in these newspapers with the want ads in your community's newspaper. Have the class discuss the kinds of jobs advertised in other cities. Ask students to identify required skills and qualifications listed in the want ads.

**ENGLISH LANGUAGE LEARNERS**

**LEVEL 2:** Invite students to imagine they are personnel managers for a fictitious company. Each student should develop strategies for filling a position in the firm. Have each student write a classified ad for the position, including details about the job, its requirements, and other relevant information. Invite volunteers to share their job advertisements with the class.

# Civics Skills
## WORKSHOP

## Reading Help-Wanted Ads

Choosing an occupation is one of the most important decisions you will ever make. You want to find a job that you will enjoy doing on a year-round basis for many years.

A good source of information on jobs available in your community is the classified section of your newspaper. The classified section contains help-wanted ads listing employment opportunities in your area and sometimes in other parts of the country.

Look through as many newspapers as possible. Employers may not advertise in all local papers. The Sunday editions usually contain the largest selection of help-wanted ads.

## How to Read Help-Wanted Ads

1. **Become familiar with the organization.** Most help-wanted ads follow the same general organization. They are divided into major categories such as accounting/bookkeeping, engineering, medical, office/clerical, professional, and sales. Within each of these categories, jobs are listed in rough alphabetical order. The type of job is usually listed at the top of each ad to help you spot job possibilities. Be sure to scan the entire classified section because some ads may appear in unlikely or incorrect categories.

2. **Read the ads carefully.** Note what training or experience is required. Also, study any promises made in the ad. What is the salary? Are benefits such as vacations, sick leave, and health insurance discussed? The answers to these questions will help you decide if you want to apply.

Pay special attention to ads placed by employment agencies, or businesses that charge money to fill a position. The company that has the job opening usually pays the agency's fee, but sometimes the successful applicant must pay it.

3. **Keep your options open.** Look under several of the major headings in the classified section. You may find that the type of job you are looking for is listed under more than one category.

## Applying the Skill

Read the help-wanted ad shown below. Then answer the following questions.

1. What qualifications are needed for this job?

2. Who is advertising the position?

3. Is there a fee involved?

4. If you wanted to apply for the job, how would you go about doing so?

5. What other information should you ask for about this job?

---

### RECEPTIONIST
#### Art Gallery
#### $225/fee paid

Bright, energetic, enthusiastic H.S. grad. to handle front desk and busy phones. Typing 55 w.p.m.

Neat appearance and punctuality a must. Knowledge of word processing important; knowledge of modern art useful. Excellent vacation and fringe benefits. Immediate hire.

**Winston Agency**                555-3791

An Equal Opportunity Employer

---

## SKILLS ANSWERS

1. bright, energetic, enthusiastic, high school diploma, able to handle front desk and type 55 words per minute, neat and punctual; knowledge of modern art and word processing useful

2. Winston Agency

3. $225, but will be paid by company looking for employee

4. Applicants should call the Winston Agency to set up an interview.

5. Students might mention questions regarding such things as pay, job duties, job hours, and specific benefits.

# SECTION 4

## OBJECTIVES

*After completing Section 4, students should be able to*

1 **Determine how job seekers can find information about careers.**

2 **Describe how part-time jobs and hobbies play a role in choosing a career.**

3 **Explain why it is important to ask yourself job-related questions when thinking about your career path.**

 **LET'S GET STARTED!**

Write the term *salary* on the chalkboard. As students enter the classroom, ask them to offer definitions of *salary* and then *salary range*. Tell students that the word *salary* comes from the Latin word *salarium*, which means "salt money." Ancient Roman soldiers received salt rations as part of their wages. From this practice came the saying "not worth his salt," meaning that a soldier was not earning his pay. Tell students that in Section 4 they will learn how to find information concerning careers and how to take the guesswork out of selecting a career.

## SECTION 4

# Learning More about Careers

### Read to Discover

1. How can job seekers find information about careers?
2. What roles do part-time work and hobbies play in deciding on a career?
3. What is the value of asking yourself job-related questions when thinking about your career path?

### Define

• salary range

#### WHY CIVICS MATTERS

Learning about careers can be a challenge. Use **CNNfyi.com** or other **current events** sources to research a career or occupation that interests you. Then describe a job in that field, its qualifications, responsibilities, income, and benefits. Record your findings in your journal.

## Reading Focus

You are probably discovering that you already know a great deal about careers and jobs. In other classes you have often read about the careers of well-known men and women. However, no single book—not even one on careers—can give you all the information you need about various jobs. You may have to spend time looking in many places to find the facts you need to choose a career.

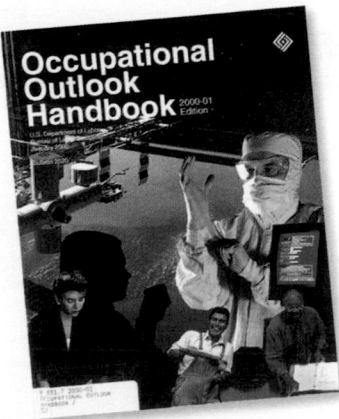

*The* Occupational Outlook Handbook *provides helpful information on career fields and their anticipated growth or decline.*

### ⭐ Reading about Careers

One of the best ways to learn about careers is to read the many books, magazines, and pamphlets available on the subject. Explore your library or a local newsstand. Your local or state employment office has a number of booklets about careers in your community. Usually, these booklets may be obtained free of charge. Because large businesses are always looking for good employees, many of them publish brochures that contain useful job information about their industry.

One of the most helpful sources of information about jobs is the U.S. Department of Labor. It publishes the *Occupational Outlook Handbook,* an important reference for job seekers. Also helpful is the *Encyclopedia of Careers and Vocational Guidance.*

Reading about career opportunities to find a career that interests you is like doing detective work. One clue leads to another. You may find

**ALL LEVELS:** Ask students to imagine that they are the person in charge of next month's Career Day, called "Searching for Career Clues." Have students create flyers advertising the presentation. Flyers should briefly list sources that job seekers can use to find information about careers. They should also include the location, date, and time of the presentation. Display the flyers around the classroom.

**ENGLISH LANGUAGE LEARNERS**

**LEVEL 2:** Ask students to choose any career that they wish. Then have them develop a "job quiz" about that career, based on the seven main job questions found in their textbook. Encourage students to share their findings so the class can assemble a careers booklet as a classroom resource.

**Interpreting the Visual Record**

**Visiting the office** *Spending a day visiting the workplace of a family member can give you insight into the daily routine of different careers.* **Why might it benefit businesses to encourage such visits?**

a clue in a novel or a biography. You may find another bit of evidence in a newspaper column or magazine article. You are acting as a detective in solving the challenge of planning your career.

As you read about jobs, of course, you must remember your own interests, needs, and abilities. You should also try to keep an open mind. You may discover a career you never thought about before.

✔ **Reading Check Summarizing** What are some of the resources that can help you find information about careers? books, magazines, and pamphlets on careers; libraries, newsstands, local or state employment offices, publications from the U.S. Department of Labor

## Watching Others at Work

You will learn a great deal about careers by taking the time to investigate job opportunities in your community. Through school-sponsored trips, you might find out about the jobs available in nearby factories, offices, and stores. Someone in your family may be able to arrange for you to visit his or her place of employment. You can also learn about jobs as you go about your daily affairs. Observe the work of bus drivers, police officers, teachers, salespeople, office workers, and others you meet each day.

You will gain more from watching people at work if you go about it in a carefully planned manner. Take notes on what you learn. Ask questions. Interview people who are working at jobs that interest you. Ask them what they like best and what they like least about their work. Talk about jobs with your family, friends, and guidance counselors. Discussing your thoughts with others will help make ideas clearer in your own mind.

✔ **Reading Check Finding the Main Idea** How can you learn the most from observing people at work? Take notes, ask questions, and interview people working at jobs that interest you. Discuss your impressions with others.

### Global Perspectives

**Women Throughout the World** Women in the United States are fortunate in that they are free to pursue any career that interests them. Although many countries around the world restrict female employment, this situation appears to be changing. In Saudi Arabia, for example, women must receive written permission from men to travel and are forbidden to drive or show their faces in public. However, the number of Saudi Arabian businesswomen registered with the Chamber of Commerce in the capital, Riyadh, has increased 500 percent in the past five years. In addition, Bangladesh now reserves 10 percent of all high-level civil service jobs for women. Even though women around the world have made some strides in the workplace, on average throughout the world, women earn 30 to 40 percent less than men for the same work.

**CRITICAL THINKING**

What can be done to help increase the opportunities for women throughout the world?

**ANSWER:** Students might suggest that the United Nations could tackle the problem by instituting economic sanctions against those countries that discriminate against women.

**Visual Record Answer**

*Students might suggest that it will better prepare tomorrow's work force.*

*Neighborhood jobs such as mowing lawns or babysitting can be a good introduction to the world of work.*

**Interpreting the Visual Record**

**Exploring options** *Talking to other students and investigating career fields together can be an interesting way to learn about possible jobs. **What sort of questions do you think these students are asking during their job search?***

## Learning by Working

Another good way to discover more about careers is to work at a job. For many students, responsibilities at home make having a job impossible. Some students, however, have enough time to work at part-time or summer jobs. You can learn from any job.

Baby-sitting, for example, may lead you to think about a future job in child care. If not, it will at least allow you to learn more about people. Baby-sitting can also teach you why being prompt, responsible, and dependable is important in any job. Being a newspaper carrier, supermarket clerk, gasoline station attendant, or movie usher are other ways you can learn about work.

Do not overlook hobbies as a means of finding out what you like to do and can do well. Some people have turned their hobbies into their life's work. Hobbies may help you determine whether you have special talents that may be useful in some jobs.

Another good way to explore your abilities is to take an active interest in school life. Try writing for the school newspaper. Manage a sports team. Serve on a class committee. Help decorate for school dances. Sell tickets for local events. These and other activities will tell you whether you enjoy writing, managing, selling, decorating, or some other skill that might be useful later in a job.

✔ **Reading Check Analyzing Information** How can part-time jobs and hobbies help you learn more about possible careers? They help you learn more about your interests and also allow you to develop skills and experience that might be helpful in future jobs.

## Questions to Ask Yourself

As you consider your future career, you can avoid some guesswork if you ask yourself the following questions. Your answers will help reveal if you are making a wise choice.

1. *What kind of work will I do in this job?* Will I be working alone or with other people? Will I be working mostly with my hands or with my mind? What skills will I need to develop to perform the job well? Does the job involve a great deal of study and careful planning, or does it involve repeating the same task?

2. *What personal qualities does the job require?* How important are neatness, promptness, dependability, and a pleasant personality in this job? Must I be able to follow directions? Will I be expected to give directions and to lead others? Does the job call for physical strength?

3. *How much education and training does the job require?* Must I be a college graduate? Is a graduate school degree necessary? Is any specialized training required? Is a period of apprenticeship needed? If so, how long does it last?

**HOMEWORK** Instruct students to interview someone whose part-time job is advantageous for him or her and someone whose part-time job creates difficulties. Have students write comparison essays concerning their findings.

## TEACH OBJECTIVE 3

**LEVELS 2 AND 3:** Explain to students why it is important to ask themselves job-related questions when thinking about possible career paths. Then have each student write a series of diary entries chronicling his or her path to deciding a career, and the ultimate career that he or she chose.

## CLOSE

Provide the class with several copies of the Occupational Outlook Handbook. Then have students study the book to learn more about the various career opportunities available to them. Then ask each student to create a "wish list" of at least 5 careers that he or she may want to pursue.

---

4. *What are the job opportunities in this field?* Are there many openings in this field now? Is this a growing field of work? Will there be more openings when I am ready to look for a job? Is this the kind of career in which I can develop my abilities and move ahead?

5. *What salary does the job pay?* Is the starting salary only the first step toward a higher income? What training must I have to receive salary increases? Will I be satisfied with the **salary range** (beginning salary, possible raises, and highest salary) that the work offers? What other benefits, such as insurance, sick pay, retirement benefits, and pleasant working conditions, are available?

6. *How do I feel about this job?* Do I believe this is a job worth doing? Will I be making a contribution to the community? Will I be happy with the kinds of people who may be working with me?

7. *Where will I have to live and work for this kind of job?* Will I have to move to another part of the country? Does the job require that I travel often? Will I have to live in a large city? Are most workers in this field employed in factories, on farms, in offices, or in their own homes?

✔ **Reading Check** Summarizing What basic information should you consider regarding a future career? qualifications, responsibilities, benefits, compensation, location, growth opportunities, and your impressions about the job

### ⭐ A Sample Job Quiz

Answering these questions is one of the best ways to find out whether the job you are considering is right for you. For example, suppose that Kim Asato, a ninth-grade student, is interested in a job as a medical laboratory technician. Answering the previous seven questions will help Kim decide if she wants that kind of career.

*Question 1:* What kind of work will I do in this job?

*Answer:* Medical technicians usually work with doctors in the laboratories of hospitals and clinics. Medical technicians perform tests that help doctors decide how to treat illnesses. They take blood tests, for example, and report the results of these tests.

*Question 2:* What personal qualities does the job require?

*Answer:* Medical technicians must be dependable, careful people who are interested in science. They must be intelligent and able to follow directions. They must also have good eyesight and be able to do precise work with their hands.

---

### BIOGRAPHY

### *Madame C.J. Walker*
**(1867–1919)**

Madame C.J. Walker was born Sarah Breedlove in Delta, Louisiana. Orphaned at a young age and later widowed, she left for St. Louis as a young woman to work washing clothes. During this time she began to experiment with hair and skin care products for African Americans. By the age of 38 she hit upon a successful skin care formula and moved to Denver to start a company.

In Denver she married Charles Walker, changed her name to Madame C.J. Walker, and began marketing what became known as the Walker System. Her products became extremely popular. She promoted them with lectures and demonstrations throughout the South and East. Walker later moved her headquarters to Indiana. She also organized her sales agents into clubs that contributed money to African American businesses and churches. She also donated money to the NAACP and various African American colleges.

At the time of her death, Walker had built a fortune of close to a million dollars and operated the largest African American–owned business in the country. "I got my start by giving myself a start," she often said. **How does Walker's career show the importance of learning by working and pursuing your personal interests?**

---

### ⭐ Economics

**Salary Comparison** There are a number of sources available to students who are interested in learning about the salaries paid for various types of jobs. Among these sources are the *American Almanac of Jobs and Salaries* (for median weekly salary) and the *Encyclopedia of Careers and Vocational Guidance* (for average annual salary). The *Statistical Abstract of the United States* is another good source of information about salaries. This book provides the median weekly salaries for the major categories of occupations. The following are the 1999 median weekly salaries for selected occupational groups, broken down by sex: professional specialty, $939 (male), $707 (female); executive, administrative, managerial, $967 (male), $652 (female); sales, $666 (male), $399 (female); mechanics and repairers, $622 (male), $592 (female); machine operators, assemblers, and inspectors, $487 (male), $340 (female).

#### CRITICAL THINKING

Why do some occupations have higher median weekly earnings than others?

**ANSWER:** Students might answer that the better-paying occupations require more educational requirements.

#### BIOGRAPHY ANSWER

Students might suggest that it shows that pursuing one's interests and dreams can translate to a satisfying career and life.

## REVIEW AND ASSESS

Have students complete the **Section 4 Review** on page 562 Then have them complete **Daily Quiz 22.4**. As **Alternative Assessment,** you may want to use the story or interview activities in this section's lessons.

## RETEACH

Have students complete **Main Idea Activity for English Language Learners and Special Needs Students 22.4.** Then have each student write a fictional interview with a person in a career that he or she wants to pursue. The interviews must be written in a script format. Have students share their interviews with the class. **ENGLISH LANGUAGE LEARNERS**

## EXTEND

Organize students into groups of three and assign each group one of the types of tests that people take to measure their skills. Have each group develop its assigned type of test. Then ask groups to exchange tests to complete them and to return texts to the original groups for evaluation. **BLOCK SCHEDULING**

---

## Section 4 Review
### ANSWERS

**1. Define**
• salary range, p. 561

**2.** reading about careers, watching others at work, learning by working, asking yourself questions, taking a sample job quiz

**3. a.** information—by reading career-related books and other publications found in libraries, newsstands, employment offices, businesses, and the U.S. Department of Labor; watch people at work; by working at part-time and summer jobs

**b.** part-time jobs—give people work experience and help teach people about the skills and interests necessary for certain jobs; hobbies—reveal special talents, interests, and abilities that may be useful in various careers

**4.** Students should create feasible, efficient plans.

*Medical technicians play an important role in hospitals and medical laboratories.*

*Question 3:* How much education and training does the job require?

*Answer:* They must have at least four years of college, including special training in a hospital to learn laboratory procedures.

*Question 4:* What are the job opportunities in this field?

*Answer:* There is a shortage of medical technicians. Well-trained workers should have no trouble getting jobs. The work can lead to a job in medical research, to a job as a laboratory supervisor, or to ownership of an independent laboratory.

*Question 5:* What salary does the job pay?

*Answer:* Nationally, the median yearly income for a college-trained medical technician is about $27,500.

*Question 6:* How do I feel about this job?

*Answer:* Medical technicians perform interesting and important work in helping the sick get well again.

*Question 7:* Where will I have to live and work for this kind of job?

*Answer:* Medical technicians work in hospitals, medical centers, private laboratories, clinics, and doctors' offices located in most communities throughout the country. They can live anywhere within commuting distance of their workplace.

This job quiz should help Kim decide whether to become a medical technician. It should also give you and the rest of your class an idea of the work a medical technician performs. You and your classmates can apply these questions to any occupations that interest you.

✔ **Reading Check Drawing Inferences and Conclusions** Why do you think the job quiz is a helpful way to approach the career search? Students might say that it helps organize the questions to ask yourself.

---

## SECTION 4 Review

**Homework Practice Online**

keyword: SZ3 HP22

**1. Define** and explain:
• salary range

**2. Summarizing** Copy the graphic organizer below. Use it to list five ways you can educate yourself about careers.

Learning about Careers

**3. Finding the Main Idea**
a. In researching possible careers, where can individuals find information?
b. What can part-time jobs and hobbies teach people exploring possible careers?

**4. Writing and Critical Thinking**
**Analyzing Information** It is time to begin exploring your career path. Create an action plan listing different ways of finding out about various fields and careers.

**Consider:**
• what types of information you will read
• the most important questions to ask yourself

# SECTION 5

## OBJECTIVES

*After completing Section 5, students should be able to*

1 **Describe why completing employment applications is an important task to practice.**

2 **Explain why your school history and special interests are of value to potential employers.**

3 **List the six skills to consider when you are trying to learn more about your abilities.**

## SECTION 5

# Learning More about Yourself

### Read to Discover

1. Why is completing employment applications an important task to practice?
2. Why are your school history and special interests of value to potential employers?
3. What are the six skills to consider when you are trying to learn more about your abilities?

### Define

- motor skills
- perceptual skills
- interpersonal skills
- aptitude tests

### WHY CIVICS MATTERS

Employers seek various qualifications in potential job candidates. Use **CNNfyi.com** or other **current events** sources to find an example of a difference and similarity in what two different employers desire in an applicant. Record your findings in your journal.

## Reading Focus

Examining your interests and skills does more than help you select a career. Once you have found a job that interests you, you must be prepared to tell a potential employer why a job interests you. You should also be able to explain why you believe you are qualified for this job. Learning about your talents and presenting them to others is an important part of getting a job.

### Preparing to Apply for a Job

When you look for your first job, you will probably have to fill out a job application. An application is a printed form on which you are asked to supply information about yourself. Your job application helps the employer decide if you are the right person for the job.

Large businesses and corporations have human resources workers whose job it is to hire or recommend new employees. Human resources workers examine job applications and interview people to determine the best-qualified applicant for an available job.

You will find it helpful to practice filling out a job application. Then when you apply for a job later, you will know what type of information you will be asked to supply.

You can practice completing job applications in several ways. Perhaps you can fill out a real application used by a local business. You

*Job applications typically ask for your educational background and former work experience.*

# TEACH OBJECTIVE 1

**LEVEL 1:** Download and print out a copy of a job application for a specific occupation and create three fictitious résumés for three different individuals. Tell students why completing employment applications is an important task to practice. Then organize students into groups of three and tell each group that it is in charge of personnel at a company and that it must choose one of the three candidates. Have groups share with the class the reasons for their selections. **ENGLISH LANGUAGE LEARNERS ,**
**COOPERATIVE LEARNING**

**LEVEL 2:** Organize the class into small groups. Have groups act as employers who wish to hire workers for entry-level jobs. Ask each group to choose the skills needed for the job and then to design a job application to use in determining the qualifications of prospective employees. Have all students "apply" for one of the jobs offered. Individual group roles might include group leader, designer, and writer. Have a representative from each group explain the reasoning used to develop his or her group's job application. **COOPERATIVE LEARNING**

## ★ Profiles

### Overcoming Obstacles

Many well-known public figures overcame obstacles to be successful. Franklin D. Roosevelt, though he had no use of his legs as a result of polio, won the U.S. presidency a record four times. Helen Keller, who lost her hearing and sight as an infant, became a popular writer. Ray Charles, blind from the age of seven, began playing piano professionally at age 15. He has won 10 Grammy Awards for his recordings. Jim Abbott, born with just one hand, grew up to be a pitcher for the California Angels and the New York Yankees baseball teams.

### CRITICAL THINKING

Ask students to relate the quote, "A hard fall results in a high bounce" to the achievements of the four individuals discussed in the text above.

**ANSWER:** Students might answer that each of the four individuals did not let obstacles prevent them from attaining success. They never gave up and their courage and perseverance led to great achievements.

### Visual Record Answer

Students might suggest that these things tell a great deal about a person.

can also prepare an outline of important facts about yourself. Many students prefer to write short autobiographies that include the chief facts about their lives.

✔ **Reading Check Summarizing** In what ways can you practice filling out work applications? Fill out a local business's job application, prepare an outline of important facts about yourself, or write a short autobiography.

## ★ What Employers Want to Know

In general, employers want the following facts about a job applicant. Therefore, you should be prepared to provide this information.

**School History** Your school record tells the employer a lot about you. List the subjects you have taken in the last two years and the grades you received. Then look at the reasons for these grades. What do grades mean? Perhaps you have high marks in English because you enjoy expressing yourself through writing. This may show that you should consider an occupation in which you can use your writing skills. In contrast, you may have poor grades in mathematics. Does this mean you should not consider a job that requires mathematical ability? Not necessarily.

Low grades in a subject are not necessarily a sign that the student cannot learn that subject. Some students who have received low marks in mathematics may be late in discovering their ability in this subject. With added effort and support, they may be able to catch up in their studies. They are then on their way to mastering math and earning higher grades.

Perhaps in listing your subjects and grades you should include a third column entitled Reasons for Grades. This column is for your personal use. It will help you judge your own abilities and interests and tell you how well you have used them.

**Health Record** Good health is an important qualification for any job. Some occupations even require that workers have special physical qualifications and pass physical examinations. Sometimes good eyesight is essential. For example, a medical technician, surgeon, or jeweler needs good eyesight. You should examine your health record and review your fitness routine.

On the other hand, having a disability should not prevent you from holding a job. There are many job opportunities for people who have a disability. The history of American business and industry, for example, contains countless stories of successful people with disabilities. Thomas Edison, inventor of the phonograph, electric light

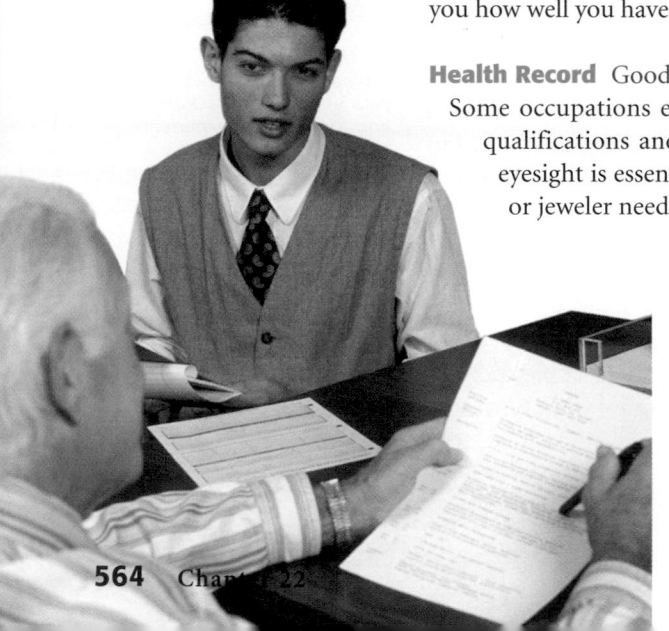

**Interpreting the Visual Record**

Job interview *Your appearance, behavior, and presentation of yourself are just as important in a job interview as your experience.* **Why do you think employers are interested in these qualities during interviews?**

**LEVEL 1:** Have students create a chart with two columns using the following headings: *What I Am Doing* and *What I Need to Do.* Ask students to fill in the first column with examples of school grades, attendance, outside activities, and special interests. Instruct students to fill in the second column with improvements they need to make to achieve the careers of their choice. Discuss with students how to set goals and how to make changes or adjustments in their current lifestyle to positively affect their future. Remind students that their school history and special interests are of value to potential employers. **ENGLISH LANGUAGE LEARNERS**

**LEVELS 1 AND 2:** Explain that job applicants often present their work histories and other relevant information such as special interests in a résumé. Obtain a sample copy of a résumé from a counselor or from a library resource to use as an example for students. Have pairs of students create ideal résumés for a teenager. Each résumé should include name, address, work history, educational achievements, activities, and special interests. Call on volunteers to lead a class discussion on why various items were included. **ENGLISH LANGUAGE LEARNERS**

**HOMEWORK** Have students create a game using the material in this section. Students may choose the format of the game, but it must be easy to teach other students to play.

---

bulb, and motion picture projector, was deaf. Yet his life was filled with outstanding achievements. Americans believe that everyone should have an equal chance to succeed. To this end, the Americans with Disabilities Act, passed by Congress in 1990, has made it illegal for employers to discriminate against people with disabilities.

**Extracurricular Activities** Make a list of your extracurricular activities. This should include hobbies, school offices you have held, sports in which you take part, school organizations to which you belong, and part-time and summer jobs. After you have completed this list, take another look at it. Does it show many different activities? What part of each activity did you like best? This review can tell you and an employer a great deal about your potential job skills.

**Special Interests** The things that interest you now may also point the way to the future. List any special interests that might help you make a career choice. Consider the subjects you like best in school. Determine whether your interests have helped you do well in these subjects. Finally, review your hobbies and your part-time jobs to find which interests they emphasize.

A future employer will know and understand you better if he or she is aware of your special interests. For example, these interests tell employers whether you prefer working alone or with others. They might also indicate if you are more of a leader or a follower. Your interests help determine your job needs as well as your career choices.

✔ **Reading Check** **Finding the Main Idea** What do employers want to know about a job applicant? *school history, why the applicant did not excel in a subject, extracurricular activities, hobbies, and interests*

## ⭐ Study Your Test Record

Tests are another means of helping you understand yourself and your abilities. Every test you take in school measures certain skills. Various tests show how well you study, how accurately you remember what you read, and how well you express yourself. Here are some of the strengths such tests seek to measure.

**Motor Skills** Certain tests are used to determine how well people can use their hands—their **motor skills.** The tests measure how fast individuals can do things with their hands. They also check for accuracy. Certain other tests determine how well people can handle and arrange small objects. Such skills are useful to a watchmaker or a worker assembling small electronic equipment, for example.

**Interpreting the Visual Record**

**Interests and hobbies** *Your hobbies and interests can sometimes help you decide on a career. For example, if you love the outdoors and are interested in studying and teaching about nature, you might enjoy being a forest ranger.* **What are some of your hobbies and interests?**

---

### ⭐ Civics Sidelight

**Vocational Interest Inventories** A vocational interest inventory is one kind of test used to measure a person's interests and experiences. An inventory asks questions about people's preferences and about the things that they enjoy doing. The questions may be indirect, so a person taking the test might not even realize what a particular item is intended to reveal. Nevertheless, the answers build a picture of an individual's interests and aptitudes. In this way, an individual can learn what kinds of occupations might be appealing and appropriate. You might want to obtain a vocational interest inventory from a school counselor or job counselor and review it with the class.

**ACTIVITY:** Administer to each student one of the many vocational interest inventories and discuss the results with the class.

**Visual Record Answer**

*Students' responses will vary.*

# TEACH OBJECTIVE 3

 **ALL LEVELS:** Copy the following graphic organizer onto the chalkboard, omitting the italicized answers. Then have each student complete the organizer to list the six skills to consider when he or she is trying to learn more about his or her abilities. **ENGLISH LANGUAGE LEARNERS**

# CLOSE

Have students write opinion columns for the school newspaper that explain how to apply for a job, what employers look for in applicants, and why it is important that students develop skills to make them attractive potential employees.

Have volunteers read their columns aloud while the rest of the class takes notes.

| Assessing Abilities |
| --- |
| 1. *Motor Skills* |
| 2. *Number Skills* |
| 3. *Perceptual Skills* |
| 4. *Special Talents* |
| 5. *Language Skills* |
| 6. *Interpersonal Skills* |

**566**

### Interpreting the Visual Record

**Special skills** *Careers such as architecture require an ability to create three-dimensional models and projections from written proposals and drawn blueprints.* **What type of skills does this task involve?**

*Many jobs require you to work closely and effectively with team members.*

**Number Skills** One of the most common tests measures a person's ability to work quickly and accurately with numbers. Such number skills are essential to bookkeepers, carpenters, and accountants. Most scientists also need to be skilled in using numbers.

**Perceptual Skills** How well can you picture things—that is, see them in your mind? To read a blueprint, for example, you must be able to picture how a building will look when finished. You must be able to visualize depth and width from a flat drawing. Such abilities are called **perceptual skills.**

✔ **Reading Check Making Generalizations and Predictions** List possible jobs that might require good motor, mathematical, or perceptual skills. Students' answers will vary.

**Language Skills** Teachers explaining an idea to students, salespersons talking to customers, and parents describing to children how to do something are all using language skills. An editor, an advertising specialist, and a company executive must be skilled in using written language. Many kinds of tests evaluate language skills.

**Special Talents** Some tests include sections that try to discover whether you have artistic and creative talent. There may also be a section that measures your ability to organize and present facts. These special talents are useful in many kinds of jobs. Publishing companies and advertising agencies, for example, need designers and writers.

**Interpersonal Skills** There are also tests to check how well you handle personal relationships or get along with others. These **interpersonal skills** are important in teaching, sales, and many other jobs that require you to interact with the public.

✔ **Reading Check Drawing Inferences and Conclusions** Why do you think some jobs might require good language and interpersonal skills? Students might say that these skills indicate an ability to communicate effectively and work well with others—skills that are necessary for many types of jobs.

## REVIEW AND ASSESS

Have students complete the **Section 5 Review** on page 567. Then have students complete **Daily Quiz 22.5**. As **Alternative Assessment**, you may want to use the résumé or assessing-abilities organizer exercises in this section's lessons.

## RETEACH

Have students complete **Main Idea Activity for English Language Learners and Special Needs Students 22.5**. Then have students design a diagram illustrating what employers want to know about a person applying for a job. Have students share their diagrams with the class. **ENGLISH LANGUAGE LEARNERS**

## EXTEND

Have each student write a brief biographical sketch of a fictional character who used his or her skills to move from one kind of job to another. For example, the person might have started out as an editor, then used her or his language skills to become an advertising specialist, and later became a publishing or marketing executive. Call on volunteers to read their biographical sketches to the class. Ask students to identify skills that are useful in a wide variety of careers. **BLOCK SCHEDULING**

**Interests and Aptitudes** Certain other tests can help you to know yourself better. These are called interest tests, or **aptitude tests**. Some schools offer aptitude tests to their students. There are also private organizations that offer aptitude tests and scoring for a fee. The tests are easy and often fun to take and reveal things about you that might otherwise be overlooked. Your teacher or counselor can explain the results of these tests.

Such tests probably will not tell you the exact job you should seek. No test can map out the future for you. What they can do is help you discover your abilities and interests, strengths and weaknesses. It is up to you to match what you have discovered about yourself with what you have learned about various career opportunities.

By now you probably have made a good start in getting to know yourself better. As you study careers, compare your opportunities with your abilities. Your present goal should be to choose a general field of work—that is, a type of work rather than a specific job. Leave the door open so that you can enter another field of work if necessary. Remember, a person's first job choice is seldom the final one.

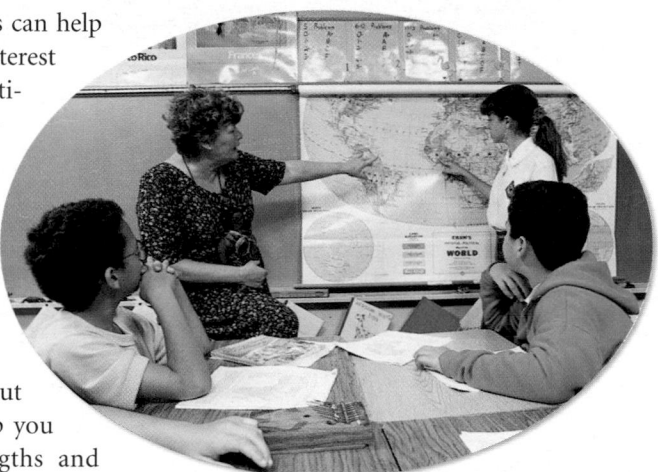

*Much of what you learn in school involves specific knowledge as well as mastering broad skills.*

✔ **Reading Check** Evaluating How do tests help measure a person's skills and talents, and why are they beneficial? They indicate strengths such as motor, language, number, perceptual, and interpersonal skills and help people understand themselves better.

---

## SECTION 5 Review

★ ★ ★

**go.hrw.com** Homework Practice Online
keyword: SZ3 HP22

1. **Define** and explain:
   - motor skills
   - perceptual skills
   - interpersonal skills
   - aptitude tests

2. **Categorizing** Copy the chart below. Use it to list the six skills to consider when you are looking for a job. Then provide possible jobs that might require each skill.

| Skill | Job Possibilities |
|-------|-------------------|
|       |                   |
|       |                   |
|       |                   |
|       |                   |
|       |                   |
|       |                   |

3. **Finding the Main Idea**
   a. Why is filling out job applications a useful exercise in preparing for employment?
   b. Why might an employer care to know about your school history and special interests?

4. **Writing and Critical Thinking**
   **Decision Making** You are ready to begin applying for jobs. However, before you can start, you want to know which jobs you are qualified for. Make an outline of various measurable skills and assess yourself honestly on each one. Identify your strengths and weaknesses and explain why you think they are such. Suggest how you can improve your level of skill in each area in which you are weak. Based on your strengths, determine which jobs you might be best qualified for.

   **Consider:**
   - the types of skills that can be tested
   - the skills specific jobs require

---

### Section 5 Review
## ANSWERS

**1. Define**
- motor skills, p. 565
- perceptual skills, p. 566
- interpersonal skills, p. 566
- aptitude tests, p. 567

**2.** motor skills—watchmaker or computer technician; number skills—accountant or carpenter; perceptual skills—architect or builder; language skills—interpreter or diplomat; special talents—professional athlete or writer; interpersonal skills—teacher or salesperson

**3. a.** to know what information is generally requested

**b.** to be able to know and understand the applicant better

**4.** Students should make an honest assessment of their skills. Those who find that they are weak in certain areas might suggest that additional study and practice would strengthen their skills in those areas.

**REPRODUCIBLE**

▶ Chapter 22 Review, pp. 568–69

▶ Vocabulary Activity 22

▶ Chapter 22 Tutorial for Students, Parents, Mentors, and Peers

▶ Chapter 22 Test (Form A or B)

▶ Alternative Assessment Handbook

**TECHNOLOGY**

▶ Chapter 22 Test Generator (on the One-Stop Planner)

▶ Global Skill Builder CD–ROM

▶ HRW Go site

**REINFORCEMENT, REVIEW, AND ASSESSMENT**

▶ Chapter 22 Test for English Language Learners and Special-Needs Students

## REVIEW

Have students complete the **Chapter 22 Review** on pages 568-69.

## ASSESS

Use one of the chapter tests to assess students' understanding of the content. For **Alternative Assessment**, see the **Alternative Assessment Handbook.**

---

## CHAPTER 22
### REVIEW ANSWERS

**Define and Identify**

1. personal values, p. 542
2. qualifications, p. 543
3. technicians, p. 547
4. blue-collar workers, p. 549
5. apprenticeship, p. 549
6. operators, p. 550
7. equal opportunity employer, p. 554
8. salary range, p. 561
9. perceptual skills, p. 566
10. aptitude tests, p. 567

**Understanding Main Ideas**

1. career often chosen on basis of personal values

2. Education creates a more marketable worker, leads to a higher income, and often results in personal satisfaction.

3. mental, physical, mental and physical, physical

4. An employer states that the organization is an equal opportunity employer.

5. by reading, by watching others at work, by learning by working, by asking questions about yourself, and by taking a sample job quiz

6. what career or job you want

7. to practice filling out a job application

8. school history—illustrates achievement; health record—illustrates physical capabilities; outside activities and special interests—illustrates potential job skills

---

# Chapter 22 Review

## Chapter Summary

### Section 1

- In order to make wise career choices, young people must know themselves well and determine which jobs best suit them.
- Education is critical to meeting the needs of a rapidly changing career world.

### Section 2

- Job opportunities in the United States can be explored by looking at four main categories of workers—white-collar, blue-collar, service, and agricultural workers.
- In considering your future career, you should familiarize yourself with a variety of career fields.

### Section 3

- In preparing for your job search, it is useful to discover which fields are growing so you know where to focus your search.
- By law, employers cannot discriminate against job applicants because of their sex, age, race, skin color, religion, or ethnic background.

### Section 4

- Before making your career choice, you can read about various jobs. You can also explore employment in your community and work at a part-time job.
- Ask yourself questions about what particular jobs involve and how they will benefit you and your future.

### Section 5

- Learning more about your strengths and weaknesses will help you decide on a career.
- Your school and health records, your interests, your activities, and your work experience will be of interest to prospective employers.

---

## Define and Identify

Use the following terms in complete sentences.

1. personal values
2. qualifications
3. technicians
4. blue-collar workers
5. apprenticeship
6. operators
7. equal opportunity employer
8. salary range
9. perceptual skills
10. aptitude tests

## Understanding Main Ideas

**Section 1** *(Pages 541–45)*

1. What is the relationship between personal values and career choice?
2. What is the importance of education in seeking a career?

**Section 2** *(Pages 546–51)*

3. What types of labor do white-collar, blue-collar, service, and agricultural workers mostly perform in their jobs?

**Section 3** *(Pages 552–55)*

4. How do job applicants know they are protected from employer discrimination?

**Section 4** *(Pages 558–62)*

5. What is the best way to learn about occupations and careers?
6. What can you learn by asking yourself questions and examining your hobbies and activities?

**Section 5** *(Pages 563–67)*

7. What is a good way to prepare for applying for jobs?
8. What information about a job applicant might be of interest to an employer, and why?

## What Did You Find Out?

1. What types of careers are there, and what levels of education and training do they require?
2. What career opportunities does the future hold?
3. How can you prepare to enter the job world?

## Thinking Critically

1. **Evaluating** Many people in the United States are self-employed. What do you think are the advantages and disadvantages of self-employment?
2. **Analyzing Information** Why is the need for agricultural workers and laborers decreasing in the United States?
3. **Supporting a Point of View** America's future depends on its workers. Do you agree with or disagree with this statement? Why?

## RETEACH

Organize students into five groups and assign each group one of the chapter's sections. Have each group create a poster or chart illustrating the main objectives in its assigned section. Then have groups present their work to the class.

**ENGLISH LANGUAGE LEARNERS ,
COOPERATIVE LEARNING**

## Portfolio Extensions

American Civics

**1. Interdisciplinary Connection to Science** Ask students to conduct research to learn more about careers in science. Instruct each student to write a one-page report outlining a career and explaining the benefits—both personal and professional—of entering that profession. Students may also choose to profile some drawbacks of choosing that career.

**2. Cooperative Learning** Organize the class into small groups. Assign each group a career and ask groups to conduct research at the library to learn more about that career. Then ask each group to create a visual display that presents information about its assigned career to be displayed at a career fair.

---

## Building Social Studies Skills

go.hrw.com **STANDARDIZED TEST PREP ONLINE** keyword: SZ3 STP22

### Interpreting Political Cartoons

Study the cartoon below. Then answer the questions that follow.

Rubes® By Leigh Rubin

Creators Syndicate, Inc.
©1992 Leigh Rubin

I'M REALLY QUITE SORRY SIR. BUT AT THIS TIME WE JUST DON'T HAVE ANY POSITIONS AVAILABLE FOR SOMEONE WITH YOUR QUALIFICATIONS.

Like so many hunter-gatherers, Thog lacked the necessary skills to compete in the high-tech job market

1. Why is the job applicant in this cartoon being rejected by the interviewer?
   a. He did not dress properly for the interview.
   b. The company is not hiring right now.
   c. He does not have the proper skills and qualifications for the job.
   d. The interviewer is being unfair.
2. Why do you think the cartoonist chose to depict the applicant in this way? How might the problem faced by the applicant apply to other job seekers?

### Analyzing Primary Sources

Read the following quotation from the Bureau of Labor Statistics job projections for 2000–2010. Then answer the questions that follow.

❝The service-producing sector will continue to be the dominant employment generator in the economy, adding 20.5 million jobs by 2010. Within the goods-producing sector, construction and durable manufacturing will contribute relatively modest employment gains. . . . Health services, business services, social services, and engineering, management, and related services . . . account for a large share of the fastest-growing industries. . . . Eight of the 10 fastest growing occupations are computer-related, commonly referred to as information technology occupations. . . . Employment in all seven education or training categories that generally require a college degree or other post secondary award is projected to grow faster than the average across all occupations.❞

3. What career areas are expected to grow only modestly in the United States between 2000 and 2010?
   a. construction and durable manufacturing
   b. engineering and manufacturing
   c. college education and training
   d. business, health, and social services
4. According to these projections, will computer skills be important in the future economy? Explain your answer.
5. What connections does the source make between education and job growth?

## What Did You Find Out?

1. white-collar: requires many years of education and training; blue-collar: requires manual labor; service workers: sometimes require education and sometimes require physical labor

2. There are opportunities for advancement in most careers but especially in the health care and computer fields.

3. by learning more about yourself and by matching skills with your potential career choices

### Thinking Critically

1. Students might mention such traits as independence and personal drive. A disadvantage might be fewer resources.

2. Students' responses will vary.

3. Students might indicate that workers are the reason for our standard of living as well as our economic and political success as a nation.

### Social Studies Skills

1. c

2. Students' responses will vary.

3. a

4. Yes; it accounts for a large share of the fastest growing industries.

5. There is a strong connection between the two.

---

### Building Your Portfolio

American Civics

#### Linking to Community

With a group, conduct interviews with people in your community who have different jobs. Ask the interviewees why they chose their particular job, how long they have held the position, and what they like and dislike about it. Write a profile about each person, organize the profiles into a booklet by work category, and present your booklet to the class.

**internet connect**

**Internet Activity: go.hrw.com**
**keyword: SZ3 AC22**

Access the Internet through the HRW Go site to research information that can help you identify your interests and abilities and guide you toward a career in an area that you might enjoy. Make a poster about your interests and a career possibility that would be well suited for you. Be creative! Use pictures from magazines, make drawings, or use cut-outs that depict your interests.

go.hrw.com

## TEACH

**LEVEL 1:** Remind students that marketing is crucial to the success of a product. Organize students into pairs, and ask pairs to think of a new product already on the market that they believe needs better advertising. Then have pairs design billboards advertising the product that they have selected. Encourage students to use attractive images and to include a slogan and an explanation of the product's key features. **ENGLISH LANGUAGE LEARNERS , COOPERATIVE LEARNING**

**ALL LEVELS:** Organize students into small groups and ask each group to imagine that it has been hired by a bicycle company to research what consumers want out of the bicycle of the future. Have each group create a detailed questionnaire that would help the company determine what most consumers already like about bicycles, what they would like to see improved in bicycle design, and what new features they would like to see added. Students' questionnaires should contain questions about subjects such as operation, appearance, and price. Then have each group use its questionnaire to interview other members of the class. Ask each group to use the information

### APPLYING THE SKILLS

Ask students to design an advertising campaign for the bicycle of the future that they researched in the first All Levels lesson. Encourage students to make use of different media, such as radio, television, and billboards. Students should also consider the marketing strategies they developed in the Civics Lab. Tell students that for each advertising campaign, they should invent a catchy name for the new bicycle and should create an illustration of what it will look like.

# Civics Lab

## Developing a New Product

Complete the following Civics Lab activity individually or in a group.

### Your Task

In Unit 6 you read about the structure and operation of the free-market economy in the United States. Imagine that you are an engineer or designer for ACME Computers. You have an idea for a new combination cell phone and digital camera. You believe that your design is much better than any existing product. In addition, you have developed a great marketing strategy for the new product.

However, you must convince the board of directors of your company that developing and marketing this cell phone/camera will be good for the company. Your presentation to the board will consist of a report accompanied by visual materials. To prepare these materials, you will need to do the following.

### What to Do

**STEP 1** **Determine** the design of your new cell phone/camera. Consider the following issues: Who will use your device? How will they use it? Where might they use it? Based on factors such as these, you need to decide what features will be most important. Will appearance, size, long range, battery life, or durability be most important to the success of your phone/camera? Once you have decided these issues, create a sketch of your phone/camera for your presentation.

**STEP 2** **Write** a company memo discussing the current economic situation and explaining why you think your project is a good idea. Your memo should answer questions such as the following: Will the project be worth the expense? How will from its questionnaire to prepare a report that describes what consumers would like to see in the bicycle of the future. Have each group present its report to the class.

**ENGLISH LANGUAGE LEARNERS , COOPERATIVE LEARNING**

**ALL LEVELS:** Have each student create a graphic organizer by drawing an arrow with the following heading: *Bringing a New Product to Market.* At the base of the arrow, have students write the word *Idea,* and at the tip of the arrow have them write the word *Market.* Then ask students to organize the following along the arrow: *Development, Advertising, Distribution, Testing, Pricing, Consumer Research, Design, Functions/Features,*

*Naming,* and *Production.* Encourage students to think of additional issues that need to be addressed during the process of bringing a new product to market.

**ENGLISH LANGUAGE LEARNERS**

**LEVEL 3:** Have students list the major characteristics of the U.S. free-market system. Then ask each student to consider which characteristic he or she thinks is the most important for successfully marketing and selling a product or service and ask students to consider which characteristic is most important for maintaining the rights of consumers. Have each student write a position paper defending his or her opinions.

the company raise the money needed to develop your device? Will there be enough consumer demand for the cell phone/camera? Include your marketing strategy.

**STEP 3** **Create** an organizational chart showing just who in the company will be responsible for each key task in developing, producing, and marketing this new product. When creating the chart, consider how you will produce and distribute your device with the greatest efficiency.

**STEP 4** **Create** an advertising poster for your cell phone/camera. This poster should include the name of your product, an interesting slogan to attract readers, and a short list of the key features your phone/camera will have.

**Project Development**

Project Coordinator
Steve Sanchez

Chief Designer
Julie Brown

Manufacturing
John Smith

Lead Engineer
Chris Walker

**STEP 5** **Make** a two-column chart with the headings *Problems* and *Solutions.* In the first column, list possible problems that might arise with the phone/camera project. These might include design or technical issues or a problem with distribution. In the second column, list the skills, talents, and experiences of your company's employees that could help solve these problems.

Organize your materials, and present your product proposal to ACME (the rest of the class).

**A STEP FURTHER**

Ask students to imagine that they serve on the board of directors of a large electronics company and must vote on whether to begin developing an expensive palm-sized television. Have each student write a brief speech that argues whether the new television will be attractive to consumers or whether the expense of developing and producing the device will outweigh consumer interest. Students' speeches should support their positions with examples from the various projects in the Civics Lab. Ask volunteers to debate their positions in front of the class.

# UNIT 7

## The United States and the World

**Chapter 23** *Foreign Policy*
**Chapter 24** *Charting a Course*

### UNIT OVERVIEW

Unit 7 stresses the obligation of citizens to be aware of world problems that affect them and the nation. Throughout the unit, students examine international situations and measures that the United States must take to ensure peace. Students are introduced to the concept of foreign policy and learn how U.S. leaders formulate that policy. The unit also focuses on past and future foreign-policy challenges of the United States.

## In Their Own Words

*"The overwhelming majority of the peoples and nations of the world today want to live in peace. They seek the removal of barriers against trade. They want to exert themselves in industry, in agriculture and in business, that they may increase their wealth through the production of wealth-producing goods rather than striving to produce military planes and bombs and machine guns and cannon for the destruction of human lives and useful property."* — Franklin D. Roosevelt

**Using the Quotation** Have students read the quotation and suggest the year or span of years in which this statement might have been made. *(Roosevelt was president from 1933 to 1945.)* Ask: Could these words have been spoken today? Discuss how the desire to achieve peace has been a goal of U.S. and world leaders for generations.

**About the Author** Franklin Delano Roosevelt (1882–1945) served as president of the United States longer than any other U.S. chief executive. Swept into office by voters seeking relief from the Great Depression, Roosevelt served from 1933 to his death in April 1945. As president, Roosevelt led the United States through almost all of World War II. His politics led to an expansion of the role of government in American economic life.

# UNIT 7 The United States and the World

CHAPTER 23 **Foreign Policy**

CHAPTER 24 **Charting a Course**

Ask students to list some issues and problems in the world that affect them and other people living in the United States. Then have students consider what steps the U.S. government should take to ensure peace between foreign nations. Also have students consider what the U.S. government should do to help the global economy. Ask students to consider what would happen if the United States decided to ignore international situations and focused only on its own domestic issues. After finishing this chapter have students compare these answers with what they have learned through reading the chapters in this unit.

# Young Citizens

## IN ACTION

### A World of Experience

High-school sophomore Laurel Geddes listened closely as a Youth for Understanding (YFU) representative spoke to her Spanish II class. As the representative talked about the adventures of studying abroad, Geddes felt inspired to apply with YFU as an international exchange student. Soon she was accepted to spend a year in Argentina, one of the many countries YFU works with.

Created in 1951, YFU was established to heal international tensions that had resulted from World War II. Since then, YFU has facilitated more than 200,000 student exchanges worldwide. The program aims to prepare youths for their roles in a changing interdependent world and to build international friendships. By living with a host family and attending school, exchange students learn about a country's art, customs, politics, religion, and trade.

Arriving two months before school started, Geddes had time to adjust to life in Rivadavia, Argentina, and to get to know her host family. At first she struggled when speaking Argentine Spanish. However, within weeks she felt more comfortable. Geddes entered a trade school as a fourth-year student—equivalent to the 11th grade in American schools—in accounting. The school year whirled by as Geddes adapted to her new classes and schedule and made new friends. At the end of the school year, the school lit a bonfire in honor of the graduating class. "Some laughed and some cried, just like the Seniors at home tend to do when they realize that their high school experience is ending," remarked Geddes. Soon after, Geddes returned to the United States, bringing a world of experience with her. "There is so much to tell about I don't know where to start!" she said.

A group of Argentine students

### You Decide

1. What does YFU hope to accomplish?
2. Why do you think it is important to learn about other countries and their people?

## What Can We Do?

Ask students to conduct research to learn more about student exchange programs and study abroad opportunities. Have students find out what opportunities are available for families to serve as hosts for foreign students wishing to study in the United States. Students might also find out how their school could begin participating in a student exchange program if it does not already do so. Encourage students to take the steps necessary to get involved in an exchange program or to get their school to participate in one.

**YOU DECIDE ANSWERS**

1. YFU hopes to prepare youths for their roles in a changing interdependent world and to build international friendships.

2. Students' responses will vary.

WE RECYCLE

# Foreign Policy

## CHAPTER RESOURCE MANAGER

| Objectives | Pacing Guide | Reproducible Resources |
|---|---|---|
| **SECTION 1:** **Conducting Foreign Relations** (pp. 575–80) | ★ Identify the purpose of foreign policy. <br> ★ Describe the president's military and diplomatic powers. <br> ★ Analyze how the powers of Congress balance the president's authority in foreign relations. | **Regular** <br> 2 days <br> **Block Scheduling** <br> 1.5 days <br> *Block Scheduling Handbook with Team Teaching Strategies, Chapter 23* | **RS** Guided Reading Strategies 23.1 <br> **PS** American Civics Political Cartoon: Multinational Corporations <br> **RS** Graphic Organizer Activity: Conducting Foreign Relations |
| **SECTION 2:** **Working for Peace** (pp. 581–86) | ★ Examine why NATO formed and describe its purpose today. <br> ★ Explain the purpose of foreign aid and identify the forms that it can take. <br> ★ Name the alliances and organizations that exist to promote international trade and economic stability, and analyze what each one does. | **Regular** <br> 2 days <br> **Block Scheduling** <br> 1.5 days <br> *Block Scheduling Handbook with Team Teaching Strategies, Chapter 23* | **RS** Guided Reading Strategies 23.2 <br> **E** Creative Teaching Strategy: Predicting Consequences |
| **SECTION 3:** **The United Nations** (pp. 588–93) | ★ Explain why the United Nations was formed, and identify its six parts. <br> ★ Determine the functions of the Economic and Social Council. <br> ★ Identify the functions of the specialized agencies of the United Nations. | **Regular** <br> 2 days <br> **Block Scheduling** <br> 1.5 days <br> *Block Scheduling Handbook with Team Teaching Strategies, Chapter 23* | **RS** Guided Reading Strategies 23.3 <br> **E** Challenge and Enrichment Worksheet 23: Identifying the Ideals of the United Nations <br> **SM** Community Service and Participation Handbook: September 11, 2001 |

## Chapter Resource Key

| | | | |
|---|---|---|---|
| **PS** Primary Sources | **SM** Skills Mastery |  CD–ROM |  **One-Stop** Planner CD–ROM |
| **RS** Reading Support | **A** Assessment |  Video | |
| **IC** Interdisciplinary Connections | **REV** Review |  Internet | See the *One-Stop Planner* for a complete list of additional resources for students and teachers. |
| **E** Enrichment | **ELL** Reinforcement and English Language Learners |  Holt Presentation Maker Using Microsoft® PowerPoint® | |
| |  Transparencies | | |

## One-Stop Planner CD–ROM

It's easy to plan lessons, select resources, and print out materials for your students when you use the **One-Stop Planner CD–ROM with Test Generator**.

| Technology Resources | Reinforcement, Review, and Assessment |
|---|---|
| One-Stop Planner, Lesson 23.1 | **REV** Section 1 Review, p. 580 |
| Holt Researcher CD–ROM | **A** Daily Quiz 23.1 |
| Citizenship Skills Videocassette Segment 7: The Citizen in Foreign Policy | **ELL** Main Idea Activity 23.1 |
| Homework Practice Online | **ELL** English Audio Summary 23.1 |
| | **ELL** Spanish Audio Summary 23.1 |
| One-Stop Planner, Lesson 23.2 | **REV** Section 2 Review, p. 586 |
| Homework Practice Online | **A** Daily Quiz 23.2 |
| HRW Go site | **ELL** Main Idea Activity 23.2 |
| | **ELL** English Audio Summary 23.2 |
| | **ELL** Spanish Audio Summary 23.2 |
| One-Stop Planner, Lesson 23.3 | **REV** Section 3 Review, p. 593 |
| Transparency 24: Organization of the United Nations | **A** Daily Quiz 23.3 |
| CNN. Presents: American Government | **ELL** Main Idea Activity 23.3 |
| Homework Practice Online | **ELL** English Audio Summary 23.3 |
| | **ELL** Spanish Audio Summary 23.3 |

## internet connect

**HRW ONLINE RESOURCES**
GO TO: go.hrw.com
Then type in the keyword.

**TEACHER HOME PAGE**
KEYWORD: SZ3 Teacher

**CHAPTER INTERNET ACTIVITIES**
KEYWORD: SZ3 AC23
Choose an activity to:
• create a pamphlet on factors leading to the decline of communism.
• prepare a newsbroadcast on the Cold War.
• make a map or chart on a formerly communist country.

**CHAPTER ENRICHMENT LINKS**
KEYWORD: SZ3 CH23

**ONLINE ASSESSMENT**
Homework Practice
KEYWORD: SZ3 HP23
Rubrics
KEYWORD: SS Rubrics

**ONLINE MAPS, CHARTS, AND GRAPHS**
KEYWORD: SZ3 MCG
• Break-up of the Soviet Union, 1991

**HOLT PRESENTATION MAKER**
KEYWORD: SZ3 PPT23

**CONTENT UPDATES**
KEYWORD: SS Content Updates

**ONLINE READING SUPPORT**
KEYWORD: SS Strategies

**CURRENT EVENTS**
KEYWORD: S3 Current Events

## Meeting Individual Needs

### Ability Levels

**Level 1** Basic-level activities designed for all students encountering new material

**Level 2** Intermediate-level activities designed for average students

**Level 3** Challenging activities designed for honors and gifted-and-talented students

**English Language Learners** Activities that address the needs of students with Limited English Proficiency

## Chapter Review and Assessment

| | |
|---|---|
| **IC** | Vocabulary Activity 23 |
| | Global Skill Builder CD–ROM |
| | HRW Go site |
| **REV** | Chapter 23 Tutorial for Students, Parents, Mentors, and Peers |
| **REV** | Chapter 23 Review, pp. 594–95 |
| **A** | Standardized Test Practice |
| **A** | Chapter 23 Test Generator (on the One-Stop Planner) |
| **A** | Chapter 23 Test (Form A or B) |
| **A** | Alternative Assessment Handbook |
| **A** | Chapter 23 Test for English Language Learners and Special-Needs Students |

Section 1    *Conducting Foreign Relations*

Section 2    *Working For Peace*

Section 3    *The United Nations*

## What's Your Opinion?

*To help students create their* **Themes** *Journal entries, provide the following examples of appropriate* **agree**/**disagree** *statements.*

● **Agree** The president is the figurehead of the country; therefore, he or she is responsible for developing policy to deal with other countries.

**Disagree** The United States creates foreign policy after much discussion among many government officials.

● **Agree** Democracy is the best method of government and should be shared worldwide.

**Disagree** The United States also provides support for countries with financial and other needs.

● **Agree** In order to accomplish global goals, a global organization is needed.

**Disagree** There are many ways to resolve conflict between foreign countries.

## Internet Activity

**Lifting the Iron Curtain**

**internet** connect

**TOPIC:** After the Cold War
**GO TO:** go.hrw.com
**KEYWORD:** SZ3 AC23

Have students access the Internet through the HRW Go site to conduct research about the economy and social issues in formerly communist countries. Then have each student create a map or chart containing information on the economy, social issues, and government of a formerly communist country.

## CHAPTER

## 23 Foreign Policy

**What's Your Opinion?**

### Build on What You Know

As improved communications and transportation draw the countries of the world closer together politically and economically, foreign policy becomes increasingly important. Have you ever traveled to a foreign land and talked to people living there? Have you made friends with schoolmates who are visiting the United States from another country? Do you have a pen pal who lives in another country? If you were able to answer yes to any of these questions, you have helped conduct U.S. foreign policy.

**Themes Journal** Do you **agree** or **disagree** with the following statements? Support your point of view in your journal.

- It is the responsibility of the president alone to determine U.S. foreign policy.
- The chief goal of U.S. foreign policy is to promote the American way of life in other countries.
- International organizations are the best way to promote peace and resolve conflicts between foreign countries.

# SECTION 1

## OBJECTIVES

*After completing Section 1, students should be able to*

1  **Identify the purpose of foreign policy.**
2  **Describe the president's military and diplomatic powers.**
3  **Analyze how the powers of Congress balance the president's authority in foreign relations.**

## SECTION 1

# Conducting Foreign Relations

### Read to Discover

1. What is the purpose of foreign policy?
2. What are the president's military and diplomatic powers?
3. How do the powers of Congress balance the president's authority in foreign relations?

### Define

- alliances
- executive agreement
- diplomatic recognition
- diplomatic corps
- couriers

#### WHY CIVICS MATTERS

The president and Congress must cooperate when deciding to send military troops into combat. Use **CNNfyi.com** or other **current events** sources to research a recent incident that required the president and Congress to decide on military action. Record your findings in your journal.

## SECTION 1 RESOURCES

### REPRODUCIBLE

▶ Guided Reading Strategies 23.1
▶ American Civics Political Cartoon: Multinational Corporations
▶ Graphic Organizer Activity: Conducting Foreign Relations

### TECHNOLOGY

▶ One-Stop Planner, Lesson 23.1
▶ Holt Researcher CD–ROM
▶ Citizenship Skills Videocassette Segment 7: The Citizen in Foreign Policy
▶ Homework Practice Online

### REINFORCEMENT, REVIEW, AND ASSESSMENT

▶ Section 1 Review, p. 580
▶ Daily Quiz 23.1
▶ Main Idea Activity 23.1
▶ English Audio Summary 23.1
▶ Spanish Audio Summary 23.1

## *Reading Focus*

The plan that a country follows for interacting with other countries is called foreign policy. The success of a country's foreign policy affects its foreign relations, or the way it interacts with other countries. In establishing its foreign policy, the United States depends on many people. Numerous government officials meet with the leaders of many other countries. In addition, the actions of American businesses and even tourists can influence foreign attitudes toward the United States.

### ⭐ Goals of U.S. Foreign Policy

The goals of U.S. foreign policy include maintaining national security, supporting democracy, promoting world peace, and providing aid to people in need. Since the 1930s, establishing open trade has become another goal of U.S. foreign policy.

Events that happen in one country can have dramatic effects in many other countries. Advances in communication and transportation have encouraged the interdependence, or mutual reliance, of the world's countries. Such interdependence means that countries must cooperate in seeking peace, freedom, and prosperity.

Forming U.S. foreign policy is a complex process. The government must strike a balance between cooperation and competition with other countries. The process requires the work of many government officials.

*The United States keeps embassies in most foreign nations to help carry out our country's foreign-policy objectives.*

**LEVEL 1:** Call on volunteers to identify the purpose of foreign policy. (*Students should note that the purpose of U.S. foreign policy is to promote peace and friendship with other nations of the world by using both humanitarian and militaristic means.*) Then have each student create a graphic organizer that shows the purpose of U.S. foreign policy. Have students classify them according to whether they are humanitarian aid or military aid. **ENGLISH LANGUAGE LEARNERS**

**LEVEL 2:** Invite each student to imagine that he or she is a U.S. ambassador to the United Nations. Tell students that they must explain the purpose of U.S. foreign policy to the UN General Assembly. (*See the Level 1 lesson for the purpose.*) Have them write out their explanations and then have volunteers present their explanations to the class. **ENGLISH LANGUAGE LEARNERS**

**LEVEL 3:** Have students look through newspapers and other periodicals to locate articles about U.S. foreign policy. Have each student summarize his or her article in a brief paragraph. Call on volunteers to read their paragraphs to the class. Then use the subjects of the articles to lead a class discussion about the purpose of foreign policy. (*See the Level 1 lesson for the purpose.*)

## The Democratic Process

### Peacemaking President

President Woodrow Wilson used his treaty-making powers extensively. In fact, he was the first president to leave American soil to do so. In a break with tradition, Wilson traveled to Europe in 1918 to meet with U.S. allies to draft a peace treaty ending World War I. Many of Wilson's advisers opposed his trip. They suggested that Wilson was putting his prestige and power on the line by becoming a mere negotiator. Wilson decided, however, that the matter was too important to trust it to anyone else.

### CRITICAL THINKING

Why do you think Wilson thought it was important to travel to Europe to make peace?

**ANSWER:** Students might suggest that because it marked the end of the first World War, the process would be a delicate matter. Therefore, Wilson might have thought his presence would help things go more quickly and smoothly.

### Visual Record Answer

*Students might suggest that foreign policy decisions are important enough to be shared with everyone.*

**Interpreting the Visual Record**

**Presidential leadership** *The president must take a leadership role in establishing and promoting America's foreign policy.* **Why is it important for the president to communicate foreign-policy plans to Congress, as shown here?**

**Did You KNOW?**

Congress passed the War Powers Act in 1973 in response to the Vietnam War. The United States had never actually declared war on North Vietnam. What started as assistance to the South Vietnamese expanded into a huge U.S. military effort under the direction of President Lyndon Johnson.

## The President's Role

President Truman once said, "I make American foreign policy." He meant that the president plays a major role in conducting U.S. foreign policy. Although assisted by State Department officials and other advisers, the president is responsible for major decisions. Article II, Section 2, of the Constitution gives the president the following powers concerning foreign relations.

**Military Powers** As commander in chief of the U.S. armed forces, the president makes recommendations to Congress about the operation of the military. The president can order troops, planes, and warships into action. For example, in 1994 President Bill Clinton sent U.S. troops to Haiti to help restore democracy in that country. However, only Congress can declare war. The War Powers Act requires U.S. troops sent abroad to be recalled within 60 to 90 days unless Congress approves the action.

**Treaty-Making Powers** As you know, treaties are written agreements between countries. They are an important part of U.S. foreign relations. With the advice and consent of the Senate, the president has the power to make three types of treaties.

Peace treaties are agreements to end wars. They spell out the terms for ending the fighting and bringing about peace. All sides in the conflict must consent to such treaties. Alliance treaties are agreements between countries to help each other for defense, economic, scientific, or other reasons. The United States has established such **alliances** with many countries of the world. Commercial treaties are solely economic agreements between two or more countries to trade with each other on favorable terms. All treaties must be approved by a two-thirds vote of the Senate.

Agreements between countries do not always require treaties. The president and the leader of a foreign government may meet and establish a mutual understanding, or **executive agreement.** The agreement

**ALL LEVELS:** Organize the class into small groups. Have each group use information from the section to create an illustrated story for elementary-age children that describes the president's military and diplomatic powers. Assign each student a role, including discussion leader, writer, editor, illustrator, and presenter. *(Students' stories should demonstrate that the president makes recommendations about the military, can send troops to trouble spots, appoints ambassadors, receives foreign ambassadors, and may grant or end diplomatic recognition.)* Ask groups to present their finished stories to the class. **ENGLISH LANGUAGE LEARNERS**

**LEVEL 3:** Invite each student to imagine that he or she is the president of the United States and is seeking a second term in office. Have students write short speeches describing how they have used their military, diplomatic, and treaty-making powers wisely. *(See the Level 1 lesson for the president's powers in these areas.)* Students might refer to actual or fictional foreign policy dilemmas facing the United States. Call on volunteers to read their speeches aloud. Then have the class discuss how each speech demonstrates the president's foreign policy powers.

**HOMEWORK** Tell students to imagine that they are members of the president's cabinet. Then have each student write a journal entry that mentions some of the military and diplomatic actions that the president has taken.

---

is announced in a joint statement to the people of the two countries. The leaders may also exchange official letters or notes in which they spell out details of their agreement. Executive agreements have been used often in recent years.

✔ **Reading Check** Analyzing Information How can the president make a formal agreement with another country without the advice and consent of the Senate? by using an executive agreement, detailed in a joint statement or official letters or notes

**Diplomatic Powers** The president, again with the approval of the Senate, appoints ambassadors to represent the United States in foreign countries. The president also receives ambassadors from other countries.

The president also has the power of **diplomatic recognition.** That is, the president may recognize, or establish official relations with, a foreign government. Sending a U.S. ambassador to that country and receiving that country's ambassador means that official recognition has taken place.

The president may refuse to recognize a government whose foreign policies are considered unfriendly or dangerous to the United States or its allies. For many years, the United States refused to recognize the Communist government of China. When recognition was granted in the 1970s, the two countries exchanged ambassadors.

Sometimes it is necessary to break off relations, or end all official dealings, with a foreign country. This action occurs only when two countries cannot settle a serious dispute.

In establishing and carrying out U.S. foreign policy, the president may call on any department of the government for assistance. The president may also hire foreign-policy experts. These experts are part of the Executive Office of the President.

✔ **Reading Check** Finding the Main Idea What are some of the president's diplomatic powers? appointing and receiving ambassadors, diplomatic recognition, refusing to recognize a country, and breaking off relations

## ★ Department of State

The Department of State is the principal organization for carrying out U.S. foreign policy as established by the president. It acts as the "eyes and ears" of the president, obtaining information on which U.S. foreign relations are based.

The secretary of state heads the Department of State and is appointed by the president. The president's appointee must be approved by the Senate. The secretary of state reports directly to the president. He or she is assisted by a large staff.

**BIOGRAPHY**

### Colin Powell

**(1937– )**

Colin Powell was born in New York City. He earned a degree in geology at City College of New York while participating in the Reserve Officers' Training Corps (ROTC) program. After graduation he joined the army as a second lieutenant. He remained in the military for 35 years, rising to the rank of four star general. In 1989 he was appointed chairperson of the Joint Chiefs of Staff. In this position he oversaw Operation Desert Storm during the Persian Gulf War.

In 1993 Powell retired from the military. He published a best-selling autobiography, *My American Journey*, and became a public speaker. Powell became chairperson of America's Promise—The Alliance for Youth, a nonprofit organization working with young Americans. In 2000 Powell's career took yet another turn when President George W. Bush nominated him as secretary of state. Powell was confirmed in 2001. His early responsibilities in his new office included coordinating U.S. foreign policy with America's campaign against global terrorism. **What experience did Colin Powell bring to his position as secretary of state?**

---

## ★ Civics Sidelight

**Spy Game** The Central Intelligence Agency was established by President Harry Truman in 1947 and was an indirect descendant of the Office of Strategic Services (OSS) in World War II. The CIA uses a wide variety of techniques to gather information, including using undercover agents, listening to foreign radio and television broadcasts, and using high-tech listening devices and spy satellites in orbit around Earth. The CIA is forbidden from spying on U.S. citizens. Nevertheless, a government commission in 1975 reported that the CIA had spied on thousands of Americans who had opposed the Vietnam War. The resulting controversy led to stricter congressional oversight of the secretive agency.

**CRITICAL THINKING**

What do you think the most important role of the CIA is today?

**ANSWER:** Students' responses will vary, but they should support their reasoning.

**BIOGRAPHY ANSWER**
35 years in the military and chairing a national organization

**ALL LEVELS:** Copy the following graphic organizer onto the chalkboard, omitting the italicized answers. Ask each student to complete the chart by explaining how the powers of Congress balance the president's authority in foreign relations. **ENGLISH LANGUAGE LEARNERS**

| Congress's Foreign-Policy Powers |
| --- |
| 1. *Approves treaties and appointments* |
| 2. *Declares war* |
| 3. *Can invoke the War Powers Act* |
| 4. *Controls finances* |

**LEVEL 3:** Have students list the powers of Congress that balance the president's authority in foreign relations. *(See the All Levels lesson for Congress's powers.)* Then ask them to rank each power in what they think is the order of importance. Then have students share their rankings. Tabulate the results on the chalkboard. Create a master list that reflects the ranking according to the students' opinions. Then call on volunteers to share their observations about the class list.
**COOPERATIVE LEARNING**

## ★ Civics Sidelight

**Embargoes** Presidents have the power to use an embargo to break off trade relations with a foreign country. They can also restore trade relations in full or in stages. In 1994 President Clinton decided to lift the 19-year-old U.S. trade embargo against the Southeast Asian country of Vietnam. His stated reasons for normalizing trade relations included the Vietnamese government's willingness to help account fully for U.S. soldiers missing in action (MIA) from the Vietnam War. In 1995 the United States formally established diplomatic relations with Vietnam.

**ACTIVITY:** Have students use the library or other resources to determine whether the United States has currently broken off relations with any countries. Ask them to research the history of the embargo as well as its likely outcome. Have students record their findings in a one-page report.

## Visual Record Answer

*Students might suggest so that each branch has an equal say.*

**Interpreting the Visual Record**
The Joint Chiefs *One of the president's most important advisory groups on foreign policy is the Joint Chiefs of Staff.* **Why do you think each branch of the military is represented on the Joint Chiefs of Staff?**

*The Central Intelligence Agency gathers information related to national defense.*

The secretary of state advises the president and supervises the activities of U.S. ambassadors, ministers, and consuls. These officials and their assistants are members of the **diplomatic corps.**

Members of the diplomatic corps work toward friendly relations with the countries in which they are stationed. They report any important events that take place in those countries to the secretary of state. Their reports may be transported by special messengers called **couriers.** Sometimes ambassadors or ministers will meet with the secretary of state or the president about a special concern.

Information from the diplomatic corps helps the president and the cabinet to set U.S. foreign policy. The economic sections of U.S. embassies also send regular reports on business and trade conditions.

✔ **Reading Check Summarizing** What are the functions of the diplomatic corps? work toward friendly relations with other countries; report to the secretary of state on important issues in foreign countries; advise the secretary of state and the president on foreign relations

## ★ Department of Defense

An important source of military information for the president is the Department of Defense. The secretary of defense advises the president on troop movements, placement of military bases, and weapons development.

The secretary of defense and the president receive advice on military matters from the Joint Chiefs of Staff. The Joint Chiefs include a chairperson, a vice chairperson, and the highest ranking military officer of the army, navy, air force, and marines.

## ★ Other Sources of Assistance

The other executive departments assist with foreign policy in various ways. The secretary of agriculture keeps the president informed of

**LEVEL 3:** Organize the class into pairs. Have pairs of students illustrate the foreign-policy powers of Congress. *(See the All Levels lesson for Congress's powers.)* The students should use newspapers, magazines, and their own drawings to create a collage (with descriptive captions) illustrating the powers of the president and Congress. Call on volunteers to present and explain their collages to the class. **COOPERATIVE LEARNING**

## CLOSE

Begin a chart on the chalkboard with *President's Role* and *Congress's Role* as headings. Call on volunteers to identify the foreign-policy powers of the president and Congress, writing the powers under the appropriate headings. Then ask the following question: How do the foreign-policy powers of Congress check those of the president? Have students copy the chart for use as a study guide.

available surplus foods that may be sent to needy countries. The secretary of the treasury handles the financial transactions relating to assistance to other countries. The secretary of health and human services supplies information essential to medical assistance for foreign lands.

Congress has also established a number of specialized agencies to help establish and carry out the country's foreign policy. The Central Intelligence Agency (CIA) is responsible for gathering information regarding national defense. The CIA also helps keep the president informed about political trends and developments in various countries.

The National Security Council (NSC) is part of the Executive Office of the President. It was created to help coordinate U.S. military and foreign policy. The NSC includes representatives from the cabinet. Meetings are also attended by representatives from the Joint Chiefs of Staff and the CIA.

Another agency that assists in foreign relations is the Agency for International Development (AID). It provides assistance to developing countries. This agency has provided billions of dollars' worth of food, fuel, medical supplies, and loans to help the world's peoples.

✔ **Reading Check** Summarizing In addition to the Departments of State and Defense, what other agencies assist with foreign policy, and what are their duties? CIA—gathers information for national defense; NSC—helps coordinate U.S. military and foreign policy; AID—provides assistance to developing countries

## ★ Congress's Role

The president leads the country in dealing with world affairs, but the president must work closely with Congress when deciding foreign-policy issues. The Senate Foreign Relations Committee and the House Committee on International Relations make foreign-policy recommendations to Congress and the president.

**Approval Powers** As you know, the Senate must approve all treaties between the United States and other countries by a two-thirds vote. What happens if the Senate refuses to approve a treaty?

*The peace conference that ended World War I included representatives from many countries.*

**Holt Researcher** go.hrw.com

**go.hrw.com**
KEYWORD: Holt Researcher
Freefind: International Organizations

Scan through the listings of international organizations on the Holt Researcher. Pick two organizations of which the United States is a member. Write a brief report that answers the following question: What responsibilities and benefits does the United States gain from membership in these organizations?

## ★ Civics Sidelight

**The World's Radio Station** Radio Free Europe/Radio Liberty is a government-funded radio service similar to the Voice of America. Authorized by the U.S. Congress, this independent service offers radio programs in 23 languages from its broadcast center in Prague, capital of the Czech Republic, to a regular audience of 25 million people across Central Europe and the former Soviet Union. Daily programming includes news broadcasts and analyses, world press reviews, reports by correspondents, and feature presentations.

Both Radio Free Europe and Radio Liberty were set up in the 1950s as alternative sources of information for people living behind the "iron curtain." The two broadcasters merged in 1976. The budgets for the radio services have been cut significantly since the end of the Cold War. The broadcasters decided in 1994 to move their operations from Munich, Germany, to Prague to reduce costs. The service has since expanded to include Internet broadcasts and Web sites in nearly 30 different languages, such as Armenian, Persian, and Uzbek.

**CRITICAL THINKING**
How does Radio Free Europe/Radio Liberty serve the people of Central Europe and the former Soviet Union?

**ANSWER:** It offers them an alternative source of news, reviews, and reports.

## REVIEW AND ASSESS

Have students complete the **Section 1 Review** on page 580. Then have students complete **Daily Quiz 23.1**. As **Alternative Assessment**, you may want to use the speech or collage exercises in this section's lessons.

## RETEACH

Have students complete **Main Idea Activity for English Language Learners and Special-Needs Students 23.1**. Then have pairs of students read aloud parts of the section to each other and then orally summarize the material they have covered. Each student should take notes on the passages read aloud

by his or her partner. **ENGLISH LANGUAGE LEARNERS , COOPERATIVE LEARNING**

## EXTEND

Have students use the library and other resources to obtain information about the foreign policy of a country of their choice. Students should use charts and diagrams to compare the structure and role of foreign policy in their selected country with those of the United States. Encourage students to address such issues as who establishes the country's foreign policy and whether the power of those persons or organizations can be checked by other parts of the government.
**BLOCK SCHEDULING**

---

## Section 1 Review
### ANSWERS

**1. Define**
- alliances, p. 576
- executive agreement, p. 576
- diplomatic recognition, p. 577
- diplomatic corps, p. 578
- couriers, p. 578

**2.** diplomatic powers—appoints ambassadors, receives foreign ambassadors, and may grant or end diplomatic recognition; military powers—makes recommendations about military and can send troops to trouble spots

**3. a.** to have a plan for dealing with other countries; the president can recommend military actions to Congress; he can construct an executive agreement with a foreign government leader; appoint ambassadors; has the power of diplomatic recognition

**b.** Congress approves treaties and appointments, has the power to declare war, can invoke the War Powers Act, and controls finances.

**4.** Students' opinions should demonstrate a sensitivity to the number of countries with which the United States interacts as well as the effect that such disclosure could have on national security.

---

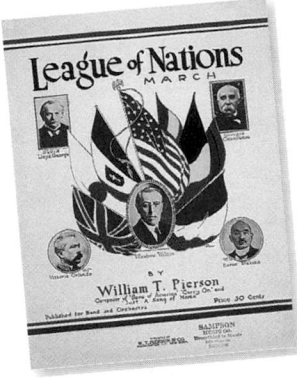

**Interpreting the Visual Record**

**The League of Nations**
*President Woodrow Wilson supported the League of Nations, but Congress did not approve the new international organization.* **How does the failure of the United States to join the League of Nations show Congress's power to shape foreign policy?**

After World War I, President Woodrow Wilson wanted the United States to join the League of Nations. A provision for joining this peacekeeping organization was included as a part of the Treaty of Versailles that ended World War I.

However, a powerful group of senators opposed U.S. membership in the League of Nations. These senators wanted the United States to stay out of European affairs and to concentrate on solving its own problems. They eventually succeeded in preventing a two-thirds majority vote of the Senate in favor of the treaty. As a result, the United States did not approve the Treaty of Versailles or join the League of Nations.

The Senate must also approve the appointment of all ambassadors by majority vote. The president's nominees for ambassadorships are almost always approved.

**The Power to Declare War**   Under the U.S. Constitution only Congress can declare war. Yet, over the years, presidents have sent troops to foreign countries without a declaration of war. In 1973 Congress passed the War Powers Act. This act limits the president's power to send troops abroad without the approval of Congress.

**Financial Powers**   As you have read, both houses of Congress must approve all expenditures of public funds. This power also allows Congress to influence foreign affairs. For example, Congress must approve all spending for national defense. The president may recommend new military spending. However, these policies cannot be carried out unless Congress votes for the necessary money.

✔ **Reading Check** Finding the Main Idea Why did Congress reject the Treaty of Versailles? Many senators opposed the involvement in European affairs that membership in the League of Nations might require. They succeeded in preventing a two-thirds majority vote in favor of the treaty.

---

## SECTION 1 Review

**go.hrw.com  Homework Practice Online**
keyword: SZ3 HP23

**1. Define** and explain:
- alliances
- executive agreement
- diplomatic recognition
- diplomatic corps
- couriers

**2. Categorizing** Copy the diagram below. Use it to identify the diplomatic and military powers of the president.

```
              President
             /         \
    Military Powers   Diplomatic Powers
     /      \           /        \
   ( )      ( )       ( )        ( )
```

**3. Finding the Main Idea**
a. What is the purpose of foreign policy, and what powers are granted to the president in that area?
b. How can Congress limit the president's activities in international affairs?

**4. Writing and Critical Thinking**
**Supporting a Point of View** Should citizens be kept informed of all foreign-policy decisions?

**Consider:**
- the number of foreign countries that the United States interacts with
- the effect that disclosing foreign-policy information could have on national security

---

# SECTION 2

## OBJECTIVES

*After completing Section 2, students should be able to*

1 **Examine why NATO formed and its purpose today.**
2 **Explain the purpose of foreign aid, and identify the forms that it can take.**
3 **Name the alliances and organizations that exist to promote international trade and economic stability, and analyze what each one does.**

### 🔔 LET'S GET STARTED!

Write the term *diplomacy* on the chalkboard. As students enter the classroom, ask them what *diplomacy* means. *(Students' responses will vary.)* Tell students that the meaning of the term *diplomacy* is "the art of dealing with foreign governments." Then call on volunteers to list on the chalkboard the purposes of diplomacy. *(Students might list preventing war, negotiating an end to conflicts, solving problems, and establishing communication between countries.)* Tell them that in Section 2 they will learn about international diplomatic organizations as well as U.S. foreign-aid programs.

## SECTION 2

# Working for Peace

### Read to Discover

1. Why did NATO form, and what is its purpose today?
2. What forms can U.S. foreign aid take?
3. What alliances and organizations exist to promote international trade and economic stability, and what does each one do?

### Define

• summit
• foreign aid
• newly industrialized countries (NICs)
• balance of trade

### WHY CIVICS MATTERS

The president frequently has summits with leaders of other countries to discuss important issues. Use **CNNfyi**.com or other **current events** sources to investigate and describe a recent summit meeting between the president and a foreign leader. Record your findings in your journal.

## SECTION 2 RESOURCES

### REPRODUCIBLE
▶ Guided Reading Strategies 23.2
▶ Creative Teaching Strategy: Predicting Consequences

### TECHNOLOGY
▶ One-Stop Planner, Lesson 23.2
▶ Homework Practice Online
▶ HRW Go site

### REINFORCEMENT, REVIEW, AND ASSESSMENT
▶ Section 2 Review, p. 586
▶ Daily Quiz 23.2
▶ Main Idea Activity 23.2
▶ English Audio Summary 23.2
▶ Spanish Audio Summary 23.2

## Reading Focus

The amount of time that government agencies and departments devote to issues of foreign policy indicates the importance of such policies. The chief goal of U.S. foreign policy is to maintain peace in the world. Government officials work in many ways to achieve this goal.

### ★ Diplomacy

The process of conducting relations between countries is called diplomacy. It is used to prevent war, negotiate an end to conflicts, solve problems, and establish communication between countries. The president is the country's chief diplomat.

To carry out this role, presidents often use personal diplomacy. They travel to other countries to meet with foreign leaders. They also consult with foreign officials in the United States. One such example of personal diplomacy is a summit. A **summit** is a meeting between the leaders of two or more countries to discuss issues that concern those countries.

Diplomacy is also carried out by other government officials. For example, State Department officials often represent the president in

*During diplomatic meetings gifts are often exchanged, such as this serving dish that Queen Elizabeth II gave to President Gerald Ford.*

**LEVEL 1:** Organize the class into groups. Have each group prepare a glossary entry. The entry should examine why NATO formed and its purpose today. Each entry should explain how one alliance differs from the other. (*Students should note that they hoped to form a united front against the threat of aggression from the Soviet Union.*) Ask a volunteer to read his or her group's glossary entry to the class.

**ENGLISH LANGUAGE LEARNERS , COOPERATIVE LEARNING**

**ALL LEVELS:** Call on a volunteer to state the reason that NATO formed and to describe its purpose today. (*See the Level 1 lesson for reason.*) Then draw on the chalkboard a two-column chart with *NATO Formation* heading one column and *NATO Today* heading the other column. Ask students to complete each column with the appropriate information. When the chart is complete, discuss the differences between the organizations. (*See the Level 1 lesson for differences.*)

**LEVEL 3:** Review the reason that NATO formed. Then ask students to write an opinion piece about the following: Are NATO's purposes today still valid? Have students support or oppose the disbanding of NATO in their assignment.

---

## ★ Civics Sidelight

**Summit Meetings** During the Cold War, Americans got used to dramatic summits between U.S. presidents and the leaders of the Soviet Union. The purposes of these meetings were to find common ground on issues of mutual concern and to reduce tensions between the superpowers. U.S. presidents and Soviet leaders met 16 times from 1961 to 1991. Five of those summits were held in the United States. U.S. presidents traveled to the Soviet Union for five summits. Six summits were held in other countries.

**ACTIVITY:** Have students use the library or other resources to conduct research about one of the summit meetings held in the United States. Ask them to write an article for a newsmagazine that summarizes their selected meetings. Remind students to provide answers to the 5W-How? questions, as a news reporter would. Also suggest that the tone of the article can be less formal than one written for a newspaper.

## Visual Record Answer

*Students might suggest language or cultural barriers.*

### ★★★★★★★★★★★★
### That's Interesting!
### ★★★★★★★★★★★★

**A Visit to Panama** Did you know that Theodore Roosevelt was the first U.S. president to leave the United States while in office? No president from George Washington to William McKinley had traveled abroad, despite all the major foreign-policy decisions and treaties that were addressed. Roosevelt himself was not even making a foreign-policy visit! He simply wanted to see the progress made on building the Panama Canal. A famous photo of his visit shows Roosevelt at the controls of a huge steam shovel. It almost looks like he is digging the canal himself.

### Interpreting the Visual Record

**Cooperation** *NATO requires U.S. troops to work in cooperation with forces from other NATO member countries.* **What types of challenges do you think might arise from the need for such cooperation?**

---

trying to settle conflicts between other countries. In recent years U.S. diplomats have traveled back and forth between different countries so often that this kind of peace seeking has become known as shuttle diplomacy.

✔ **Reading Check Summarizing** Why is diplomacy important, and what are some of the ways it is carried out? Diplomacy makes it easier to solve problems and avoid conflicts. Presidents meet with foreign leaders and foreign officials and hold summits.

## ★ Alliances

The United States has alliances with many countries, including Japan, South Korea, and the Philippines. It has also established alliances with several large groups of countries.

The United States and most countries in Latin America formed the Organization of American States (OAS) in 1948. The goal of the OAS is mutual defense and the peaceful settlement of disputes between member countries. In 1951 Australia, New Zealand, and the United States formed an alliance called ANZUS. The purpose of ANZUS is to provide mutual defense in case of attack.

Perhaps the most important security alliance of which the United States is a member is the North Atlantic Treaty Organization (NATO). NATO was formed in 1949 to establish a united front against aggression by the Soviet Union and its communist allies. Most Western European countries belong to this alliance. NATO members pledge that an attack against one member will be considered an attack on all.

The breakup of the Soviet Union and the move toward democracy in Eastern Europe has renewed interest in NATO. Three of the Soviet Union's former allies have joined the organization. NATO has also accepted 26 countries into its Partnership for Peace program. The program allows countries to join NATO in military exercises, peacekeeping operations, and other activities as preparation for future membership. However, Partnership countries are not included in NATO's mutual security guarantee.

✔ **Reading Check Drawing Inferences and Conclusions** Why might some of the Soviet Union's former allies be interested in joining NATO? Students might say that those Eastern European countries used to be protected by the Soviet Union, and now they seek the protection of NATO.

## ★ Foreign Aid

Another important part of U.S. foreign policy is foreign aid. **Foreign aid** is any government program that provides economic or military assistance to another country. The United States first gave large amounts of foreign aid during World War II. After the war's devastation the countries of Western Europe needed help. People needed food, clothing, and housing.

# TEACH OBJECTIVE 2

**ALL LEVELS:** Copy the graphic organizer to the right onto the chalkboard, omitting the italicized answers. Have each student complete the list to identify the forms that foreign aid can take. Then have students summarize the purpose of U.S. foreign aid below the organizer.

**ENGLISH LANGUAGE LEARNERS**

**LEVEL 3:** Organize the class into four groups to debate the following proposition: The United States, as one of the world's wealthiest nations, should increase the amount of money it provides in foreign aid. One group should support the statement, the second should oppose it, the third should favor more humanitarian aid, and the fourth should favor more security.

Students should offer reasoned arguments for their positions.

**COOPERATIVE LEARNING**

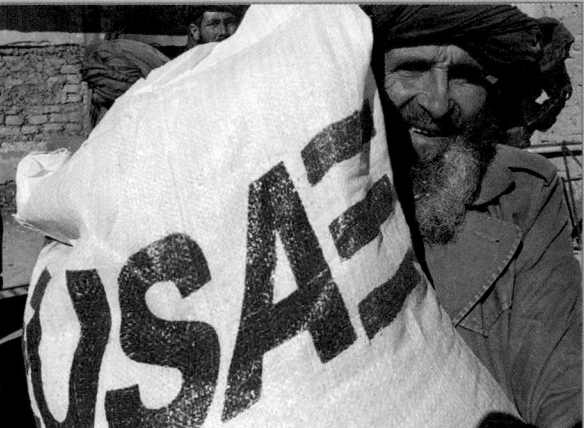

| Humanitarian | Security |
|---|---|
| *food* | *soldiers* |
| *clothes* | *arms* |
| *shelter* | *money* |
| *workers* | *information* |
| *money* | |

*The purpose of foreign aid is to provide economic or military assistance to other countries.*

In 1947 U.S. secretary of state George Marshall proposed a plan to help the war-torn countries of Europe rebuild. Many of their factories, farms, homes, and transportation systems had been all but destroyed during the war. Under the Marshall Plan, Congress granted over $13 billion in aid to these countries. By 1952 the economies of Western Europe had recovered to a remarkable degree. Marshall Plan aid, having accomplished its goal, ended.

Since World War II, the United States has given or loaned more than $515 billion in foreign aid. More than 33 percent of this U.S. foreign aid has been for military assistance. This money has helped countries throughout the world maintain their independence. U.S. economic assistance has helped countries in Africa, Asia, and Latin America become self-sufficient.

The United States also participates in humanitarian aid efforts. For example, in the early 1990s the African country of Somalia was being torn apart by civil war. Many Somali people had little or no food, and the fighting prevented relief workers from bringing help. As a result, thousands of Somalis died of starvation. In 1992 the United States joined other countries in sending troops to Somalia. This effort aimed to help relief workers bring food and supplies to the starving people. In addition, the United States sent foodstuffs.

Individual Americans provide another type of foreign aid. The Peace Corps, established by President John F. Kennedy in the early 1960s, sends volunteers to countries that request assistance. Peace Corps volunteers in fields such as teaching, engineering, agriculture, and health care work in countries throughout the world.

✔ **Reading Check Identifying Cause and Effect** Why did the United States start the Marshall Plan, and what was its result? The United States wanted to help its European allies rebuild after World War II. Within five years the economies of those countries had started to recover, and the plan ended.

## ★ Foreign Trade

As you have learned, the U.S. government must constantly struggle with various economic challenges facing the country. However, the economy at home is not the government's only economic concern. International trade worth billions of dollars links the United States with other countries. Economic events in other countries can cause serious problems for the United States. Thus, foreign trade is a central focus of U.S. foreign policy.

The United States has long held a position of strength in the global economy. However, in recent decades foreign competition and economic alliances in other parts of the world have challenged its economic position.

*Food is a common form of aid that the United States provides to other countries.*

**Interpreting the Visual Record**

**Marshall Plan** *This poster celebrates the contributions of the Marshall Plan to Europe's economic recovery.* **What is the hand in the poster holding, and what does it represent?**

## ★ Global Perspectives

**Foreign Aid** In 1992 the United States budgeted $33.5 billion in foreign aid, the highest total of any donor nation that year. Nearly a decade later, in 2001, that figure fell to about $7.5 billion. That amounts to a decrease in foreign aid by $26 billion. Figured in per-capita terms, the United States donated about $46 per U.S. citizen in 1992, and in 2001 the per capita total fell to approximately $26 per person. Nations receiving foreign aid from the United States include Afghanistan, Israel, North Korea, the Marshall Islands, the Federated States of Micronesia, and Palau.

**CRITICAL THINKING**

How does providing other nations assistance benefit the United States?

**ANSWER:** Students might suggest that the United States gains allies, secures sites for military bases, and supports democracy in developing nations.

**Visual Record Answer**

*Students might suggest that it is an apple representing prosperity.*

**ALL LEVELS:** Have each student create a three-column chart. In the first column, students should name all of the alliances and organizations that exist to promote international trade and economic stability. In the second column they should identify how each organization accomplishes that task. In the third column, they should give an example of how each group can help the United States. *(See the Level 1 lesson for names and functions.)* **ENGLISH LANGUAGE LEARNERS**

**LEVELS 1 AND 2:** Assign each student one alliance or organization that exists to promote international trade and economic stability: NAFTA, APEC, WTO, or IMF. Then have each student write a short paragraph that explains what his or her assigned group does. *(Students' paragraphs should note that NAFTA allows free trade among the United States, Canada, and Mexico; APEC brings hopes of an improved economic position for the United States in the Pacific and Asia; the WTO encourages worldwide free trade; and the IMF lends money to needy countries.)* Call on volunteers to share a paragraph about each assigned group. **ENGLISH LANGUAGE LEARNERS**

## ★ Civics Sidelight

**NAFTA Critics** Not every American favored the North American Free Trade Agreement. Many labor groups opposed NAFTA, claiming that U.S. jobs would go to Mexico. Ross Perot, the Texas billionaire who ran for president in 1992, suggested that Mexico's lack of environmental controls, low labor costs, and limited health care and retirement benefits for workers would draw U.S. industries into Mexico.

**ACTIVITY:** Have students research the economic consequences of NAFTA on Canada, Mexico, or the United States after the agreement went into effect. Then have them imagine that the agreement is about to expire. Tell students that they are to create a proposal that recommends whether their selected country should sign the renewal. Call on at least one volunteer who investigated each country to present his or her proposals to the class.

### ★★★★★★★★★★★★★
### *That's Interesting!*
### ★★★★★★★★★★★★★

As of early 2001, the United States had experienced a trade deficit with Mexico. Prior to NAFTA, it was in a trade surplus.

### Visual Record Answer

*It is a less expensive means of transport.*

*Cameras like this one are just one type of product that the United States imports from Pacific Rim countries.*

### Interpreting the Visual Record

**Cargo ships** *Many of the goods exported from and imported into the United States are carried on huge cargo ships like this one.* **Why do you think that most U.S. imports are delivered by sea rather than by air?**

The countries of the Pacific Rim, for example, compete with the United States in producing and selling goods. These countries include, among others, Australia, China, Indonesia, Japan, Malaysia, New Zealand, the Philippines, Singapore, South Korea, and Taiwan. Pacific Rim countries have the ability to produce high-quality, low-priced goods such as automobiles, computers, and electronic equipment. There is a high demand for these goods in the United States and many other countries around the world.

Japan is the economic leader in the Pacific Rim region. Yet Singapore, South Korea, and Taiwan also compete successfully in world markets. These countries, known as **newly industrialized countries (NICs),** have experienced rapid industrialization and economic growth in recent years.

The success of the Pacific Rim countries has had a significant effect on the U.S. **balance of trade.** The balance of trade is the difference in the value between a country's exports and imports over a period of time. Exports are those goods and services that the United States sells to other countries. Imports are those goods and services that the United States buys from other countries.

In recent years the United States has suffered serious trade deficits. The country spends more money buying foreign goods (imports) than it earns from selling American-made goods (exports) to other countries. Some economists believe that trade deficits and the purchase of imported goods will cause Americans to lose jobs. Others argue that a trade deficit can be a sign of a healthy economy and a high demand for products.

Economic alliances among other countries also challenge the U.S. position in the global economy. For example, the European Union (EU) was formed in 1993 when 12 Western European countries signed the Maastricht Treaty. EU countries were formerly and more loosely allied as the European Community (EC). Since its formation, the European Union has expanded. In 2004, 10 countries joined the EU, bringing the total to 25.

One of the goals of the EU is the free movement of goods, workers, and capital among member countries. The European Union recently launched a single currency, the euro, which is intended to simplify trade between member nations. If the EU is successful in its plans, member countries will share an economic relationship making the EU an extremely powerful trade group in the global economy.

✔ **Reading Check Making Generalizations and Predictions** How could the high-quality, low-priced goods of the Pacific Rim affect the U.S. trade deficit? Students might say that if Americans spend more money on these imports than foreign countries spend on our exports, our trade deficit will grow.

**LEVEL 3:** Have each student draw a political cartoon about one of the alliances or organizations that exist to promote international trade and economic stability. Tell students to incorporate the function of that entity into their cartoons. *(See the Levels 1 and 2 lesson for groups and functions.)* Encourage students to be creative and informative. Call on volunteers to share their cartoons with the class.

 **HOMEWORK** Have each student write a short paragraph describing the function of one of the alliances and organizations that exist to promote international trade and economic stability.

## CLOSE

Ask students to create an encyclopedia entry about the purposes of foreign aid and worldwide trade organizations. Then have students create an illustration to accompany their entry.

---

### ★ Meeting Global Economic Challenges

Foreign competition has led the United States to seek ways to improve its position in the global economy. For example, the United States signed the North American Free Trade Agreement (NAFTA) in 1993. This agreement allows free trade between the United States, Canada, and Mexico. By eliminating trade barriers, NAFTA members hope to open new markets, create jobs, and encourage growth in member economies.

The United States also hopes to better its economic position through its membership in the Asia-Pacific Economic Cooperation group (APEC). APEC is made up of the United States, Canada, Chile, Mexico, and 16 other countries of the Pacific Rim. Its goal is to promote cooperation among Asia-Pacific countries. In its association with APEC, the United States hopes to encourage the Pacific Rim countries, particularly Japan, to lower restrictions on U.S. exports and to expand trade in the region.

As the number of exports grew, many countries proposed the formation of an organization to set rules for international trade. In 1995, 128 countries joined together to form the World Trade Organization (WTO) to supervise international trade. By April 4, 2003, the number of WTO members had risen to 146.

The United Nations World Bank offers another way for countries to cooperate on economic issues. The International Monetary Fund (IMF), another UN agency, also lends money to countries in need. As international trade has grown, the IMF has raised the amount and number of loans it makes. The IMF has loaned money to Russia and a number of countries in Eastern Europe. This money may help these countries change from communism to free-market economies.

✔ **Reading Check Summarizing** What international agreements and organizations have been created to promote trade and economic stability? NAFTA, APEC, the WTO, and the IMF

### ★ Debating Free Trade

The WTO and NAFTA are expected to help American consumers and producers in the long run. However, not all Americans support such measures. Opponents of free trade believe that tariffs are needed to protect American industries and jobs from foreign competition. They maintain that raising the prices of foreign goods through tariffs will encourage American consumers to buy American-made goods. This approach would protect American jobs.

COME ON IN, THE WATER'S GOING TO BE FINE.

**Interpreting Political Cartoons**

**NAFTA** *The passage of NAFTA left many Americans uncertain of how the agreement would affect the U.S. economy.* **Whom does the man standing on the diving board symbolize, and how does this cartoon suggest that NAFTA will affect them?**

🖉 **internet** connect

**TOPIC:** The Cold War
**GO TO:** go.hrw.com
**KEYWORD:** SZ3 AC23

Have students access the Internet through the HRW Go site to research information on the Cold War. Then have students prepare a news report on a significant event during the Cold War period. Students should provide the historical context and background in their news reports.

**POLITICAL CARTOON ANSWER**
labor; Students might suggest that labor is being urged to accept NAFTA without any proof of its benefits.

## REVIEW AND ASSESS

Have students complete the **Section 2 Review** on page 586. Then have students complete **Daily Quiz 23.2.** As **Alternative Assessment**, you may want to use the opinion piece or the foreign-aid debate exercises in this section's lessons.

## RETEACH

Have students complete **Main Idea Activity for English Language Learners and Special-Needs Students 23.2.** Then have each student write five test questions (and the answers) about this section. Call on students and have them quiz the class with their questions. **ENGLISH LANGUAGE LEARNERS**, **COOPERATIVE LEARNING**

## EXTEND

Organize the class into groups and have each group select and research an international alliance or organization such as NATO, the United Nations, or another entity that fosters world peace. Ask students to work together to create a work of art that symbolizes their entity's role in the quest for world peace. Students may choose to make a sculpture, a painting, a collage, a song, or a poem. Then have students present their work to the rest of the class. **COOPERATIVE LEARNING**, **BLOCK SCHEDULING**

## Section 2 Review
### ANSWERS

**1. Define**
- summit, p. 581
- foreign aid, p. 582
- newly industrialized countries (NICs), p. 584
- balance of trade, p. 584

**2.** NAFTA allows free trade among the United States, Canada, and Mexico; APEC brings hopes of an improved economic position in the Pacific and in Asia for the United States; the WTO is designed to encourage free trade throughout the world; and the IMF lends money to countries in need.

**3. a.** to form a united front against the threat of aggression from the Soviet Union; to provide protection and peace for member countries

**b.** Foreign aid is any government program that provides economic or military assistance to other nations; forms include money, food, clothing, housing, workers, and volunteers.

**4.** Students' speeches should reflect a consideration of the effects of tariffs on relations with other countries and on the demand for both foreign and American products.

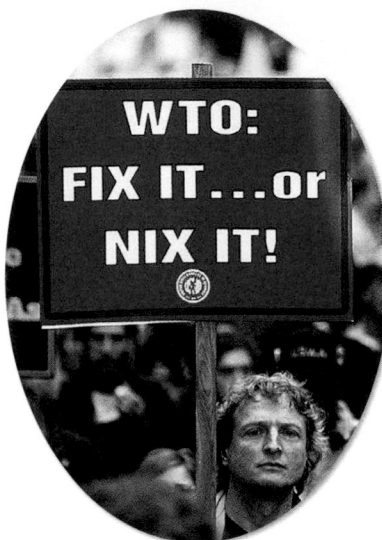

The World Trade Organization has many critics as well as supporters in the global community.

In contrast, supporters of free trade believe that opening the United States to foreign trade will help the country gain greater access to foreign markets. Greater access to foreign markets will lead to increased growth in the U.S. economy. This growth will then improve the country's position in the global economy.

✔ **Reading Check Contrasting** Why do supporters and opponents of free trade disagree on tariffs? Supporters say that reducing tariffs will open up more foreign markets to American products, leading to economic growth. Opponents believe that tariffs will encourage consumers to buy American goods.

### ★ Environmental Diplomacy

As concerns about the environment become issues of international importance, environmental policy is influencing foreign relations. The United Nations and other international organizations have served as vehicles for establishing agreements on environmental standards.

For example, in 2001 more than 160 countries met to discuss environmental policy. The main topic was the voluntary reduction of carbon dioxide and other gases held responsible for the gradual warming of Earth. (See Chapter 26 for more information about environmental issues.) However, countries have often struggled to agree on the exact terms of treaties and how they will be enforced. Negotiations for international treaties have continued. Environmental diplomacy will undoubtedly remain an important part of foreign policy.

✔ **Reading Check Contrasting** What are some of the advantages and disadvantages of international environmental agreements? They allow countries to work together to improve the environment, but it is difficult to agree on treaty terms and enforcement.

## SECTION 2 Review

Homework Practice Online
keyword: SZ3 HP23

**1. Define** and explain:
- summit
- foreign aid
- newly industrialized countries (NICs)
- balance of trade

**2. Summarizing** Copy the chart below. Use it to list the different trade alliances and organizations discussed and the purpose of each one.

| Organization | Purpose |
|---|---|
|  |  |
|  |  |
|  |  |
|  |  |

**3. Finding the Main Idea**
a. Why did NATO form, and what role does it serve today?
b. What forms does U.S. foreign aid take?

**4. Writing and Critical Thinking**
**Decision Making** Imagine that you are a member of Congress giving a speech on trade policy. Should the United States place high tariffs on imported goods?

**Consider:**
- the effect of tariffs on relations with other countries
- the effect of tariffs on the demand for both foreign and American products

## TEACH

**HOMEWORK** Ask each student to create a table like the one found in the Civics Skills Workshop. Students may create the table on any subject of their choosing, but they have to be able to show that the data is reliable by referencing their source.

## EXTEND

Organize the class into small groups. Ask each group to conduct research to obtain statistical information about the United Nations. Then have each group create a table that incorporates data outlining a financial aspect of the United Nations.

**COOPERATIVE LEARNING , BLOCK SCHEDULING**

# Civics Skills
### WORKSHOP

## Reading Tables

The United States shares the globe with nearly 200 other countries. It trades with many of these countries and has alliances, agreements, and treaties with most of them. Keeping track of the types of relationships that the United States has with so many countries can be confusing.

One effective way to clarify this information is to use a table. A table condenses a great deal of data into a format that is easy to read and understand. You will find tables in many of the library resources that you use when conducting research. You will also want to create your own tables to present data that you collect for reports and class presentations.

## How to Read Tables

1. **Determine the subject.** Read the title of the table to determine its subject and purpose.

2. **Study the headings.** Tables have several headings. Each vertical column has its own heading. There may also be headings to the left of each horizontal row. Read the headings and make sure you know to which row or column each heading refers. Also, make sure you understand the meaning of each heading before you attempt to interpret the table.

3. **Analyze the information.** To locate specific facts on a table, look down a vertical column and across a horizontal row. Where the column and row intersect, or meet, is where you will find the data you need.

4. **Put the data to use.** Use the table to draw conclusions about the data. Identify any trends and, if possible, draw conclusions about the information. You should look down each column and along each row to find trends in the data.

## Applying the Skill

Study the table below. Then answer the questions that follow.

1. What years are included in the table?

2. What is the meaning of the minus signs (–) in the "Balance" column?

3. What was the U.S. balance of trade in 1995? In 2000?

4. Do you see a trend in the value of U.S. exports included in the table? Do you see a trend in the value of goods the United States imports? Describe both trends.

5. How has the U.S. balance of trade changed during the years included in the table?

### U.S. Balance of Trade, 1995–2000
#### (In billions of dollars)

| Year | Exports | Imports | Balance |
|------|---------|---------|---------|
| 2000 | 1,065 | 1,441 | –376 |
| 1999 | 957 | 1,219 | –262 |
| 1998 | 932 | 1,099 | –167 |
| 1997 | 937 | 1,047 | –110 |
| 1996 | 851 | 959 | –108 |
| 1995 | 795 | 895 | –100 |

Source: U.S. Census Bureau

# SECTION 3

## OBJECTIVES

*After completing Section 3, students should be able to*

1 Explain why the United Nations was formed, and identify its six parts.

2 Determine the functions of the Economic and Social Council.

3 Identify the functions of the specialized agencies of the United Nations.

## SECTION 3 RESOURCES

### REPRODUCIBLE

▶ Guided Reading Strategies 23.3

▶ Transparency 24: Organization of the United Nations

▶ Challenge and Enrichment Worksheet 23: Identifying the Ideals of the United Nations

▶ Community Service and Participation Handbook: September 11, 2001

### TECHNOLOGY

▶ One-Stop Planner, Lesson 23.3

▶ CNN Presents: American Government

▶ Homework Practice Online

### REINFORCEMENT, REVIEW, AND ASSESSMENT

▶ Section 3 Review, p. 593

▶ Daily Quiz 23.3

▶ Main Idea Activity 23.3

▶ English Audio Summary 23.3

▶ Spanish Audio Summary 23.3

## 📻 LET'S GET STARTED!

Draw an empty word web on the chalkboard with the central circle containing the words *United Nations*. As students enter the classroom, ask them to fill out the web with words and phrases that relate to the international organization. *(Students might write peace, diplomats, global, conferences, foreign aid, and so on.)* Explain to students that the United Nations (UN) is an international organization whose members include many countries of the world. Tell students that in Section 3 they will learn about the United Nations, including its parts and agencies and their functions.

# SECTION 3

# The United Nations

## Read to Discover

1. Why was the United Nations formed, and what are its six parts?
2. What are the functions of the Economic and Social Council?
3. What are the functions of the specialized agencies of the United Nations?

## Identify

• United Nations
• General Assembly
• Security Council
• International Court of Justice

### WHY CIVICS MATTERS

The United Nations maintains a peacekeeping force to monitor international conflicts and settle political disputes. Use **CNNfyi.com** or other **current events** sources to research a recent United Nations peacekeeping operation. Record your findings in your journal.

The flag of the United Nations shows a map of the world as seen from the North Pole, surrounded by olive branches representing peace.

## *Reading Focus*

In 1941 President Franklin D. Roosevelt met with Prime Minister Winston Churchill of Britain to discuss the aims of the World War II Allies. The agreement that these two leaders reached was called the Atlantic Charter. The leaders agreed that all people should have the right to choose their own government and live free from fear or want. They also argued that nations should not use war to settle disputes or to gain territory. The principles established in the Atlantic Charter have continued to guide countries around the world in their search for peace.

## ⭐ Forming the United Nations

In 1945, representatives from 50 countries met to form an organization that would promote peaceful coexistence and worldwide cooperation. This organization is the **United Nations** (UN). In its charter, or constitution, countries pledge to save future generations from war. They promise to live in peace as good neighbors and agree to work toward protecting basic human rights. Today the United Nations is an international organization with 191 permanent members. The UN headquarters is located in New York City.

✔ **Reading Check** Summarizing Why was the United Nations formed in 1945? to promote peaceful coexistence and cooperation among all the countries of the world

# TEACH OBJECTIVE 1

**ALL LEVELS:** Copy the graphic organizer to the right onto the chalkboard, omitting the italicized answers. In the center of the organizer, have students explain why the United Nations was formed. Have students complete the rest of the organizer to identify its six parts.

**ENGLISH LANGUAGE LEARNERS**

**LEVEL 2:** Organize the class into pairs and have pairs create an organizational chart of the United Nations. Students can illustrate their charts by using newspapers, other periodicals, and their own drawings to depict the functions of each division. Each illustration should include a caption.

**COOPERATIVE LEARNING**

The **United Nations was formed** *to promote peaceful coexistence and cooperation among nations, maintain peace, and support human rights.*

- General Assembly
- Security Council
- Secretariat
- Economic and Social Council
- International Court of Justice
- Trusteeship Council

## ★ Organization of the United Nations

The United Nations has six main divisions, which are shown in the chart on page 590. The six divisions are described below.

**General Assembly** The body that discusses, debates, and recommends solutions to problems is called the **General Assembly**. Each member country has one vote in the General Assembly. A two-thirds majority of the Assembly is needed to decide all important issues. These issues include such matters as world peace, adding new member countries, or budgetary concerns. Other issues are decided by a simple majority vote.

The Assembly meets annually. Its sessions begin on the third Tuesday in September. If necessary, it may be called into emergency session. The Assembly elects its own president and makes its own rules of procedure.

**Security Council** The UN body that is mainly responsible for peacekeeping is the **Security Council**. It has 15 members, including 5 permanent members: China, France, Great Britain, Russia, and the United States. Ten temporary members are chosen by the General Assembly for two-year terms. Each country on the Security Council has one delegate.

All measures that come before the Security Council must receive a vote of 9 out of 15 members to pass. However, if one of the permanent members of the council votes against it, the measure is automatically defeated.

To prevent war, the Security Council may call on quarreling countries to work out a peaceful settlement. If any country refuses to negotiate or refuses the council's help in settling the dispute, the council may take action. It may call on all UN member countries to break off relations and end all trade with the offending country. In 1994, for example, North Korea refused to allow the International Atomic Energy Agency to inspect its nuclear facilities. President Bill Clinton was concerned that North Korea might be building nuclear weapons. Because of this concern, he asked the Security Council to consider imposing economic sanctions on North Korea. If diplomatic measures fail, the Security Council may recommend that UN member countries use military force against an aggressor country.

✔ **Reading Check** Contrasting How is the UN General Assembly different from the Security Council? All belong to Assembly, but only 15 members sit on Council.

**International Court of Justice** Member countries may take international legal disputes to the UN law court—the **International Court of Justice**. This court is also known as the World Court.

**Interpreting the Visual Record**

The United Nations *Outside the UN headquarters in New York City fly the flags of the many member nations.* **How are these flags symbolic of the mission of the United Nations?**

## ★ Culture

**Translating for the General Assembly** In the UN General Assembly, people of many different cultures and languages come together to make important decisions. How do they communicate? During a session, all delegates have a set of earphones available, through which they can listen to a translation of everything that is said. Speeches given on the floor are translated into six languages—Arabic, Chinese, English, French, Russian, and Spanish. The translators, sitting in a booth overlooking the General Assembly hall, hear the speaker through their own earphones and simultaneously translate the speech for the benefit of the listening UN delegates.

**CRITICAL THINKING**

What makes translation of the meetings necessary?

**ANSWER:** Students might suggest that delegates speak a variety of languages.

**Visual Record Answer**

*Students might suggest that they represent the UN's mission of bringing all of its member countries together in one place.*

**LEVEL 3:** Ask students to review the reason that the United Nations was formed and then to identify its six parts. *(See the All Levels lesson for reason and parts.)* Then have each student choose the part for which he or she would most like to work and to write a journal entry explaining a day in the life of a member of that particular division. Students' entries should refer to the role of the particular department or agency the student has chosen.

## TEACH OBJECTIVE 2

 **LEVEL 1:** As a class, discuss the functions of the Economic and Social Council. *(Students should note that it seeks to improve the lives of the world's people by conducting studies and making recommendations to the General Assembly.)* Then organize the class into an even number of groups. Assign each group one of the two ways that the Council seeks to improve lives. Have groups create a headline and several topic sentences for an article covering the key points of their assigned topic. **ENGLISH LANGUAGE LEARNERS , COOPERATIVE LEARNING**

**LEVEL 2:** Ask students to imagine that they are members of the UN Economic and Social Council. Have each student write a letter to a colleague describing the functions of the Council and the role he or she plays at the Council. *(See the Level 1 lesson for the Council's functions.)* Suggest that students include imaginary examples of their Council's functions by referring to current world issues.

**CHART ANSWER**
Secretariat

The court consists of 15 judges from various countries who are elected by the General Assembly and the Security Council. Judges serve nine-year terms, and decisions are made by majority vote. Court headquarters are located at The Hague, in the Netherlands. The court decides matters such as boundary disputes and debt payments.

**Economic and Social Council** The General Assembly elects representatives from 54 countries to serve as members of the Economic and Social Council. This council is dedicated to improving the lives of the world's people. It conducts studies in areas such as health, human rights, education, narcotics, and world population. It then makes recommendations to the General Assembly.

**Trusteeship Council** The United Nations created the Trusteeship Council to help various non-self-governing colonies at the end of World War II. These areas were called trust territories. The Trusteeship Council, which supervised the progress of trust territories, suspended operations in 1994 when the last trust territory became independent.

**Secretariat** The Secretariat manages the day-to-day activities of the United Nations and provides services to other UN divisions. Among its nearly 9,000 staff members are economists, lawyers, and translators.

**Organization of the United Nations**

General Assembly — International Court of Justice (World Court) — Security Council

Economic and Social Council — Secretariat — Trusteeship Council

Specialized Agencies
Independent organizations that report to the Economic and Social Council

**Interpreting Charts** *The members of the General Assembly and the Security Council appoint or approve the leaders of the other UN branches.* **What branch of the United Nations works with the most other branches?**

LEVEL 3: Remind the class of the functions of the UN Economic and Social Council. *(See the Level 1 lesson for functions.)* Then organize the class into small groups and present this fictional issue to the class: Oil has been discovered in Antarctica in an area no country has claimed. Some countries want to exploit this resource. Others want to preserve the Antarctic environment. Have each group represent a country in the United Nations, establish a point of view, and prepare to argue it before the council (classroom). Individual roles include researcher, discussion leader, and UN ambassador. **COOPERATIVE LEARNING**

## TEACH OBJECTIVE 3

 **LEVELS 1 AND 2:** As a class, make a list of the UN's specialized agencies. Then have students make web diagrams to identify the function of each agency. *(The World Health Organization fights worldwide disease; the Food and Agricultural Organization helps nations grow more and better food; the UN Educational, Scientific, and Cultural Organization extends educational opportunities throughout the world; the World Meteorological Organization promotes the international exchange of weather reports; the World Bank makes loans and gives economic advice to help countries improve their economies; and the International Communications Union promotes international electronic communication.)* **ENGLISH LANGUAGE LEARNERS**

The secretary-general is in charge of the Secretariat and also serves as the chief administrator of the United Nations. The secretary-general makes an annual report to the General Assembly concerning the organization's problems and achievements. He or she may also advise the Security Council on any threats to world peace.

The secretary-general, who serves a five-year term, is nominated by the Security Council and appointed by the General Assembly. All five permanent members of the Security Council must agree on the nomination, and appointment is decided by majority vote.

✔ **Reading Check** Summarizing What are the six main branches of the United Nations, and what is the purpose of each branch? General Assembly, Security Council, International Court of Justice, Economic and Social Council, Trusteeship Council, and Secretariat; see preceding text for purposes.

## ★ Specialized Agencies

Much of the work of the United Nations is carried out through its many specialized agencies. These agencies work to improve the lives of people around the world. Each agency is independent of the main UN body. The Economic and Social Council ensures that the United Nations and the specialized agencies work together. What are some of these specialized agencies, and what do they do?

**FAO** The Food and Agriculture Organization (FAO) helps countries to grow better food and increase agricultural production. For example, FAO has helped develop a special disease-resistant rice in India. FAO experts are also helping countries with reforestation, soil conservation, irrigation, and improvement of farming methods.

**UNESCO** The United Nations Educational, Scientific and Cultural Organization (UNESCO) was established to extend educational opportunities everywhere in the world. When people learn to read and write, they are better equipped to learn new skills or more efficient ways of doing things. UNESCO has sponsored programs to set up schools in less economically developed countries. In addition, it encourages people to protect and develop their cultures and ways of life.

**WMO** The World Meteorological Organization (WMO) works to promote the international exchange of weather reports. Global weather conditions are tracked by the WMO's World Weather Watch.

**World Bank** The World Bank makes loans and gives both technical and economic advice to help countries improve their economies. It is made up of three institutions that share one address—the International Bank for Reconstruction and Development (IBRD), the International Development Association (IDA), and the International Finance Corporation (IFC).

### World Health Organization

The World Health Organization (WHO) is a specialized UN branch formed in 1948 to address global public health issues. The WHO is headquartered in Geneva, Switzerland. The organization keeps member nations informed of the latest developments in medical and health research. It also sponsors research and education on disease control. These efforts include vaccination programs, health education, and improvements in sanitation. As of 1980 the efforts of the WHO had helped eliminate smallpox. The organization also helps train medical personnel and provides guidelines for national health organizations. **Why do you think fighting disease requires international cooperation to be successful?**

*The World Bank is an influential global financial institution.*

### ★ Global Perspectives

**UN Secretaries-General**
Because the appointment of UN secretaries-general must be approved by all five permanent members of the Security Council, the secretary-general usually comes from a relatively small neutral country. Following are the names and countries of origin of secretaries-general up to 2001: Trygve Lie, Norway; Dag Hammarskjöld, Sweden; U Thant, Myanmar (Burma); Kurt Waldheim, Austria; Javier Pérez de Cuellar, Peru; Boutros Boutros-Ghali, Egypt; and Kofi Annan, Ghana. Annan, who took office in 1997, has a background typical for a secretary-general. Well-educated, he was a Sloan Fellow at the Massachusetts Institute of Technology and served at the United Nations in a variety of positions for more than 30 years.

**ACTIVITY:** Ask students to conduct further research on the life of Kofi Annan. Have students incorporate their research into the format of their choice and then ask them to present their findings to the class.

### GLOBAL CONNECTIONS ANSWER
Students might suggest that it reduces costs and keeps diseases from spreading from country to country.

Heather Verdi of Connecticut recommends the following activity:

### SPOTLIGHT
#### on the United Nations

Organize students into groups. Have groups conduct research at the library to obtain more information about the specialized agencies of the United Nations. Ask each group to write an editorial explaining which agencies they view as most and least valuable. Groups' editorials should describe the events that would determine and support their views.

**COOPERATIVE LEARNING**

## CLOSE

Have students consider what the modern world would be like if there were no United Nations. Encourage each student to think of one thing that would be different. Then list students' conclusions on the chalkboard and discuss them.

---

### ★★★★★★★★★★★★ That's Interesting! ★★★★★★★★★★★★

During the 1970s UNESCO began a campaign for a "new world order." Its supporters hoped wealth would be shifted from the industrialized countries to the industrializing countries. Believing that agency had developed an anti-American bias, the U.S. government withdrew its support from UNESCO in 1984.

### Visual Record Answer

*Students might suggest that they are interacting peacefully with local citizens.*

---

**ITU** The International Telecommunication Union (ITU) works to promote international electronic communication. The ITU establishes international regulations and conducts research to improve world communication.

✔ **Reading Check Categorizing** Which specialized agencies of the United Nations relate to health and economics, and which relate to education and information? WHO and FAO—health; World Bank—economics; UNESCO—education; and ITU and WMO—information

## ★ Need for Cooperation

The United Nations provides a forum, or place, where the world's countries can express their views about problems that threaten peace. One of the four goals in the UN's charter is to "reaffirm faith in fundamental human rights, in the dignity and worth of the human person, in the equal rights of men and women and of nations large and small." The UN's Universal Declaration of Human Rights helps reinforce this view.

In its quest for peace, the organization largely depends on the cooperation of its members to settle their disputes diplomatically. This expectation of peaceful cooperation has met with great success.

Disputes between countries, however, cannot always be settled through diplomatic channels. Therefore, the United Nations has organized what is known as a peacekeeping force. Nearly 60,000 UN peacekeepers, contributed by member countries, serve in places where there is conflict or potential conflict. These peacekeepers are not authorized to use force in settling disputes. The United Nations has no permanent armed forces of its own. The main purpose of the peacekeepers is to monitor conflicts, oversee territorial agreements and cease-fires, and help stabilize political situations. UN peacekeepers are allowed to use their weapons only in self-defense.

UN peacekeepers have not always been successful. In 1993, for example, peacekeepers sent to Somalia were unable to stop the fighting between rival clans.

### Interpreting the Visual Record

**Peacekeeping** *The United States often contributes soldiers to UN peacekeeping missions.* **How does this image show that the role of peacekeepers goes beyond fighting and maintaining security?**

## REVIEW AND ASSESS

Have students complete the **Section 3 Review** on page 593. Then have them complete **Daily Quiz 23.3**. As **Alternative Assessment**, you may want to use the UN council debate or journal exercises in this section's lessons.

## RETEACH

Have students complete **Main Idea Activity for English Language Learners and Special-Needs Students 23.3**. Then have students create an outline about the United Nations, its various parts and agencies, and their functions. Encourage students to refer to the section for information.

**ENGLISH LANGUAGE LEARNERS**

## EXTEND

Have students use the library or other resources to research specific situations in history that brought action from the United Nations. Have each student prepare a report, accompanied by visual guides such as time lines and flowcharts, that explains actions taken by the United Nations and its specific agencies and divisions during the student's selected event. Call on volunteers to present their reports to the class for discussion.

**BLOCK SCHEDULING**

A lack of funding also contributes to UN peacekeeping problems. Every UN member is expected to pay a share of the organization's expenses, including peacekeeping expenses. The amount each country pays is based on its ability to pay. In 2001 nearly half of the member countries had fallen far behind in their payments. The unpaid debt now totals 3.4 billion dollars. This money could be used to expand UN peacekeeping operations around the world.

✔ **Reading Check Making Generalizations and Predictions** What might the world be like today without the United Nations? Students might say that poor countries would be even poorer, education and health advances may not have spread to developing countries, and many more conflicts would have occurred.

*The U.S. ambassador to the United Nations, John Negroponte (left), represents American interests. He appears here with UN Secretary-General Kofi Annan.*

### ⭐ Role of the United Nations

Some Americans are critical of the United Nations. They believe that the United States pays too much of the organization's operating costs. They point out that powerful nations can be outvoted in the General Assembly. They argue that the lack of a permanent UN army prevents the United Nations from ending military disputes.

In contrast, some Americans believe that the United Nations is the world's best hope for peace. They note that it has frequently succeeded in bringing quarreling countries to the conference table. These supporters do not believe the lack of a permanent UN army is a problem. They argue that U.S. leaders would not accept a force with such limited U.S. control. UN supporters claim that creating a forum where all countries can be heard encourages world peace.

✔ **Reading Check Identifying Points of View** Why do some Americans criticize the United Nations? Some Americans believe the United States pays a larger share of UN expenses than other countries but can easily be outvoted by smaller countries. They also criticize the lack of a permanent UN army.

## SECTION 3 Review

**go.hrw.com Homework Practice Online**
keyword: SZ3 HP23

1. **Identify** and explain:
   - United Nations
   - General Assembly
   - Security Council
   - International Court of Justice

2. **Categorizing** Copy the chart below. Use it to list the specialized agencies of the United Nations and the function of each one.

| Name | Function |
|------|----------|
|      |          |
|      |          |
|      |          |
|      |          |
|      |          |

3. **Finding the Main Idea**
   a. What led to the formation of the United Nations, and how is it organized?
   b. What function does the Economic and Social Council serve?

4. **Writing and Critical Thinking**
   **Supporting a Point of View** Should the United Nations establish a permanent army to enforce its decisions?

   **Consider:**
   - the sources of soldiers and money for the army
   - the authority required for the United Nations to command troops from member countries

### Section 3 Review

**ANSWERS**

1. **Define**
   - United Nations, p. 588
   - General Assembly, p. 589
   - Security Council, p. 589
   - International Court of Justice, p. 589

2. WHO: World Health Organization fights the worldwide battle against disease; FAO: Food and Agricultural Organization helps nations grow more and better food; UNESCO: UN Educational, Scientific, and Cultural Organization extends educational opportunities everywhere in the world; WMO: World Meterological Organization promotes the international exchange of weather reports; World Bank makes loans and gives economic advice to help countries improve their economies; ITU: International Telecommunication Union works to promote international electronic communication.

3. a. to promote peaceful coexistence and cooperation among nations, maintain peace, and support human rights; the General Assembly, the Security Council, the International Court of Justice, the Economic and Social Council, the Trusteeship Council, and the Secretariat

   b. to improve the lives of the world's people by conducting studies and making recommendations to the General Assembly

4. Students' responses should display an awareness of the various sources of soldiers and of money for the army as well as the authority the United Nations would require to command troops from member countries.

**CHAPTER 23**

## Review and Assessment Resources

### REPRODUCIBLE

▶ Chapter 23 Review, pp. 594–95

▶ Vocabulary Activity 23

▶ Chapter 23 Tutorial for Students, Parents, Mentors, and Peers

▶ Chapter 23 Test (Form A or B)

▶ Alternative Assessment Handbook

### TECHNOLOGY

▶ Chapter 23 Test Generator (on the One-Stop Planner)

▶ Global Skill Builder CD–ROM

▶ HRW Go site

### REINFORCEMENT, REVIEW, AND ASSESSMENT

▶ Chapter 23 Test for English Language Learners and Special-Needs Students

## REVIEW

Have students complete the **Chapter 23 Review** on pages 594–95.

## ASSESS

Use one of the chapter tests to assess students' understanding of the content. For Alternative Assessment, see the **Alternative Assessment Handbook.**

---

## CHAPTER 23
### REVIEW ANSWERS

**Define and Identify**

1. alliances, p. 576

2. diplomatic recognition, p. 577

3. diplomatic corps, p. 578

4. couriers, p. 578

5. summit, p. 581

6. foreign aid, p. 582

7. balance of trade, p. 584

8. United Nations, p. 588

9. General Assembly, p. 589

10. Security Council, p. 589

**Understanding Main Ideas**

1. to have a plan for dealing with other countries

2. to approve treaties and appointments, to declare war, to invoke the War Powers Act, and to control finances

3. to form a united front against the threat of aggression from the Soviet Union; a program designed to prepare former Soviet countries to join NATO

4. for both humanitarian and security reasons; money, arms, soldiers, food, clothing, shelter, and volunteer assistance

5. to promote peaceful coexistence and cooperation among nations, maintain peace, and support human rights; the General Assembly, the Security Council, the International Court of Justice, the Economic and Social Council, the Trusteeship Council, and the Secretariat

**594**

---

# Chapter 23 Review

## Chapter Summary

### Section 1

• The goals of U.S. foreign policy include maintaining national security, supporting democracy, promoting world peace, providing aid to people in need, and promoting open trade.

• In the area of foreign policy, the Constitution grants military powers, treaty-making powers, and diplomatic powers to the president.

• Congress votes on the amount of money needed to carry out the country's foreign policy. The Senate must approve all treaties with and appointments of U.S. representatives to foreign lands.

• Several government agencies help the president and Congress conduct foreign policy.

### Section 2

• To promote peace and stability, U.S. leaders engage in personal diplomacy with other world leaders. U.S. alliances with other countries serve mutual defense, economic, and other needs.

• U.S. foreign aid helps other countries remain independent and improve their standards of living.

• U.S. foreign trade with other countries promotes the global exchange of goods.

### Section 3

• The United Nations provides a forum in which countries may discuss serious problems and work toward solutions.

• The specialized agencies of the United Nations work to serve the needs of the people of the world.

• The future of the United Nations depends on the willingness and ability of countries to cooperate peacefully.

---

## Define and Identify

Use the following terms in complete sentences.

1. alliances
2. diplomatic recognition
3. diplomatic corps
4. couriers
5. summit
6. foreign aid
7. balance of trade
8. United Nations
9. General Assembly
10. Security Council

## Understanding Main Ideas

**Section 1** *(Pages 575–80)*

1. What is the purpose of foreign policy?

2. What foreign-policy powers does Congress have?

**Section 2** *(Pages 581–86)*

3. Why was NATO created, and what is the Partnership for Peace program?

4. Why does the United States give foreign aid to other countries, and what forms does it take?

**Section 3** *(Pages 588–93)*

5. What is the purpose of the United Nations, and what are its six divisions?

6. What are the arguments for and against a permanent UN army?

## What Did You Find Out?

1. Whose responsibility is it to design U.S. foreign policy?

2. What is the main objective of U.S. foreign policy?

3. What is the role of the United Nations in the world?

## Thinking Critically

1. **Drawing Inferences and Conclusions** Ambassadors who live in foreign countries have diplomatic immunity. This means they cannot be arrested, even if they break the law. Why do you think such a rule exists, and how might the lifting of this rule affect diplomatic relations?

2. **Supporting a Point of View** The United States faces many economic challenges, both at home and abroad. Which do you think should be the main concern of the president—the U.S. economy or the global economy? Explain your answer.

3. **Analyzing Information** While the goals of U.S. foreign policy have remained fairly constant, global challenges have changed greatly over the years. What do you think is the greatest foreign-policy challenge facing the United States today?

595

## RETEACH

Organize the class into three groups. Assign each group one of the sections taught in this chapter. Then have each group create a magazine cover illustrating and summarizing the main ideas of its section. Then ask each group to present its cover to the rest of the class. **ENGLISH LANGUAGE LEARNERS**, **COOPERATIVE LEARNING**

## Portfolio Extensions

**1. Interdisciplinary Connection to Literature** Ask each student to select a book about a recent event that involved international assistance. For example, students might select Nelson Mandela's *Long Walk to Freedom* about the South African struggle to free itself from apartheid. Students should write a report that summarizes the book's main points and describes the roles played by other countries and international organizations.

**2. Cooperative Learning** Complete the following activity in small groups. Research a humanitarian organization, such as the Peace Corps or the Red Cross, and create a mosaic that demonstrates its good works worldwide. Your mosaic should include some examples of people helping others in a manner unique to your selected organization as well as descriptions and images of its goals. Present the mosaic to the class.

---

## Building Social Studies Skills

**STANDARDIZED TEST PREP ONLINE** keyword: SZ3 STP23

### Interpreting Graphs

Study the pie graph below on U.S. foreign aid. Then answer the questions that follow.

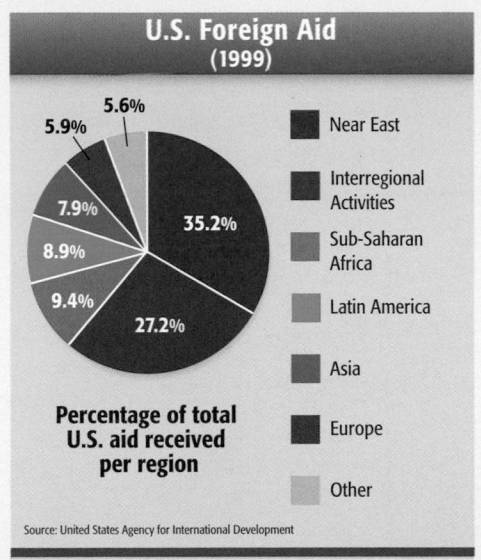

**U.S. Foreign Aid**
(1999)

- 35.2% Near East
- 27.2%
- 9.4%
- 8.9%
- 7.9% Interregional Activities
- 5.9% Sub-Saharan Africa
- 5.6% Latin America
- Asia
- Europe
- Other

Percentage of total U.S. aid received per region

Source: United States Agency for International Development

1. To which region did the third-largest percentage of U.S. foreign aid go in 1999?
   a. Sub-Saharan Africa
   b. Europe
   c. Asia
   d. Near East
2. How much U.S. aid went to Europe and Asia?
   a. About 25 percent
   b. About 15 percent
   c. About 14 percent
   d. Less than 10 percent

3. Why do you think the largest percentage of U.S. aid went to the Near East?

### Analyzing Primary Sources

Read the following quotation from Kofi Annan, the secretary-general of the United Nations. Then answer the questions that follow.

> 66 The prevention of conflict both within and between States requires, first of all, ongoing attention to possible sources of tension and prompt action to ensure that tension does not evolve into conflict. During the past year, the Secretariat, in cooperation with other branches of the United Nations system, has worked to strengthen its global watch, which is designed to detect threats to international peace and security, enabling the Security Council to carry out or to foster preventative action. Cooperation with regional organizations offers great potential. 99

4. Which of the following statements best describes Annan's point of view?
   a. Conflict between countries is inevitable.
   b. The Secretariat is responsible for ensuring that there are no new international conflicts.
   c. The best way to avoid conflict is to identify problems and address them before tensions get too high.
   d. The best response to new conflicts is immediate and powerful military action.
5. What steps does Annan say the United Nations has been taking to try to prevent future conflicts? What branch of the UN does he identify as being responsible for taking preventative action?

6. for: to provide a cooperative force to handle international issues; against: source of soldiers and arms, and difficulty managing troops from multiple nations

**What Did You Find Out?**
1. the president, the Department of State, the Department of Defense, other executive departments, and Congress

2. Students might suggest to maintain peace in the world.

3. to guide the countries of the world in their search for peace

**Thinking Critically**
1. Students might suggest that such a rule benefits diplomatic negotiations, and if the rule was lifted conflict might arise between nations.

2. Students should clearly state their opinions and display an understanding of the interdependence of the world's economy.

3. Students' answers will vary but might mention the desire to promote peaceful coexistence and worldwide cooperation.

**Skills Workshop**
1. a
2. c
3. Students' responses will vary.
4. c
5. It monitors tensions within and between countries in order to prevent conflict. the Secretariat

---

### Alternative Assessment

**Building Your Portfolio**

**Linking to Community**
Conduct library research to learn about Peace Corps volunteers from your community or state. Choose one volunteer to profile. How old was this person when he or she volunteered? Where did he or she work and for how long? Would this person recommend the experience to others? Write a profile of your chosen volunteer. You may wish to illustrate your profile with drawings or images of the country in which the volunteer served.

**internet connect**

**Internet Activity: go.hrw.com**
keyword: SZ3 AC23

Access the Internet through the HRW Go site to take a look at some of the government departments and agencies that work to maintain peace in the world. Then assume the role of a news reporter doing a piece on foreign policy for the evening news. Make a presentation or videotape about the importance of clearly defined foreign policy and how one of the departments you researched works to achieve the goal of world peace.

## CHAPTER 24

# Charting a Course

## CHAPTER RESOURCE MANAGER

| Objectives | Pacing Guide | Reproducible Resources |
|---|---|---|
| **SECTION 1:** **Development of U.S. Foreign Policy** (pp. 597–602) | ★ Explain why the United States maintained a policy of isolationism in its early years and evaluate why the policy was hard to follow. <br> ★ Analyze the effects that the War of 1812, the Monroe Doctrine, and the Good Neighbor Policy had on U.S. international relations. <br> ★ Determine what caused the United States to enter World War I and World War II. | **Regular** <br> 1.5 days <br><br> **Block Scheduling** <br> .5 day <br><br> *Block Scheduling Handbook with Team Teaching Strategies, Chapter 24* | **RS** Guided Reading Strategies 24.1 <br> **RS** Readings in Economics and Government 10: The Monroe Doctrine <br> **RS** Readings in Economics and Government 30: Franklin D. Roosevelt's "Four Freedoms" <br> **RS** Readings in Economics and Government 43: Lend-Lease Act of 1941 <br> **E** Challenge and Enrichment Worksheet 24: Measuring Opinions About Foreign Policy Goals <br> **RS** Graphic Organizer Activity: Developing Foreign Policy |
| **SECTION 2:** **The Cold War** (pp. 606–13) | ★ Identify what began the Cold War and examine the form that the early U.S. response took. <br> ★ Evaluate how the U.S. responses to the Berlin blockade and the Cuban missile crisis differed. <br> ★ Describe the events that marked the end of the Cold War. | **Regular** <br> 2 days <br><br> **Block Scheduling** <br> 1.5 days <br><br> *Block Scheduling Handbook with Team Teaching Strategies, Chapter 24* | **RS** Guided Reading Strategies 24.2 <br> **RS** Readings in Economics and Government 15: The Truman Doctrine |
| **SECTION 3:** **New Trends** (pp. 614–19) | ★ Identify the new global challenges that the United States has faced since the end of the Cold War. <br> ★ Describe how the United States was attacked on September 11, 2001, and identify the immediate suspect in the attacks. <br> ★ Examine how the U.S. government responded to the terrorist attacks. | **Regular** <br> 2 days <br><br> **Block Scheduling** <br> 1.5 days <br><br> *Block Scheduling Handbook with Team Teaching Strategies, Chapter 24* | **RS** Guided Reading Strategies 24.3 <br> **RS** Readings in Economics and Government 13: Open Door Policy in China <br> **PS** American Civics Political Cartoon: The Vietnam War <br> **E** Creative Teaching Strategy Issue Strip <br> **SM** Community Service and Participation Handbook: The First Televised War |

**Chapter Resource Key**

| | | | | | |
|---|---|---|---|---|---|
| **PS** | Primary Sources | **SM** | Skills Mastery |  | CD–ROM |
| **RS** | Reading Support | **A** | Assessment |  | Video |
| **IC** | Interdisciplinary Connections | **REV** | Review |  | Internet |
| | | **ELL** | Reinforcement and English Language Learners | 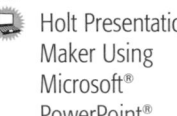 | Holt Presentation Maker Using Microsoft® PowerPoint® |
| **E** | Enrichment | | Transparencies | | |

 **One-Stop** Planner CD–ROM

See the *One-Stop Planner* for a complete list of additional resources for students and teachers.

## One-Stop Planner CD–ROM

It's easy to plan lessons, select resources, and print out materials for your students when you use the **One-Stop Planner CD–ROM with Test Generator**.

| Technology Resources | Reinforcement, Review, and Assessment |
|---|---|
| One-Stop Planner, Lesson 24.1 | **REV** Section 1 Review, p. 602 |
| Holt Researcher CD–ROM | **A** Daily Quiz 24.1 |
| CNN. Presents: American Government | **ELL** Main Idea Activity 24.1 |
| Homework Practice Online | **ELL** English Audio Summary 24.1 |
| | **ELL** Spanish Audio Summary 24.1 |
| One-Stop Planner, Lesson 24.2 | **REV** Section 2 Review, p. 613 |
| Homework Practice Online | **A** Daily Quiz 24.2 |
| | **ELL** Main Idea Activity 24.2 |
| | **ELL** English Audio Summary 24.2 |
| | **ELL** Spanish Audio Summary 24.2 |
| One-Stop Planner, Lesson 24.3 | **REV** Section 3 Review, p. 619 |
| Citizenship Skills Videocassette Segment 2: Who Has the Power? | **A** Daily Quiz 24.3 |
| Homework Practice Online | **ELL** Main Idea Activity 24.3 |
| HRW Go site | **ELL** English Audio Summary 24.3 |
| | **ELL** Spanish Audio Summary 24.3 |

### internet connect

**HRW ONLINE RESOURCES**
GO TO: go.hrw.com
Then type in the keyword.

**TEACHER HOME PAGE**
KEYWORD: SZ3 Teacher

**CHAPTER INTERNET ACTIVITIES**
KEYWORD: SZ3 AC24
Choose an activity to:
• create a pamphlet on factors leading to the decline of communism.
• prepare a news broadcast on the Cold War.
• make a map or chart on a formerly communist country.

**CHAPTER ENRICHMENT LINKS**
KEYWORD: SZ3 CH24

**ONLINE ASSESSMENT**
**Homework Practice**
KEYWORD: SZ3 HP24
**Rubrics**
KEYWORD: SS Rubrics

**ONLINE MAPS, CHARTS, AND GRAPHS**
KEYWORD: SZ3 MCG
• Break-up of the Soviet Union, 1991

**HOLT PRESENTATION MAKER**
KEYWORD: SZ3 PPT24

**CONTENT UPDATES**
KEYWORD: SS Content Updates

**ONLINE READING SUPPORT**
KEYWORD: SS Strategies

**CURRENT EVENTS**
KEYWORD: S3 Current Events

## Meeting Individual Needs

### Ability Levels

**Level 1** Basic-level activities designed for all students encountering new material

**Level 2** Intermediate-level activities designed for average students

**Level 3** Challenging activities designed for honors and gifted-and-talented students

**English Language Learners** Activities that address the needs of students with Limited English Proficiency

## Chapter Review and Assessment

| | |
|---|---|
| **IC** | Vocabulary Activity 24 |
| | Global Skill Builder CD–ROM |
| | HRW Go site |
| **REV** | Chapter 24 Tutorial for Students, Parents, Mentors, and Peers |
| **REV** | Chapter 24 Review, pp. 620–21 |
| **A** | Standardized Test Practice |
| **A** | Chapter 24 Test Generator (on the One-Stop Planner) |
| **A** | Chapter 24 Test (Form A or B) |
| **A** | Alternative Assessment Handbook |
| **A** | Chapter 24 Test for English Language Learners and Special-Needs Students |

# CHAPTER 24

Section 1    *Development of U.S. Foreign Policy*

Section 2    *The Cold War*

Section 3    *New Trends*

## Internet Activity

**Behind the Iron Curtain**

🖰 internet connect 🖰

go.hrw.com

**TOPIC:** The Cold War
**GO TO:** go.hrw.com
**KEYWORD:** SZ3 AC24

Have students access the Internet through the HRW Go site to conduct research and obtain more information about the Cold War. Then have each student prepare a news report on a significant event of the Cold War period. Students should provide the historical context and background in their news reports.

## What's Your Opinion?

📝 *To help students create their **Themes** Journal entries, provide the following examples of appropriate agree/disagree statements.*

● **Agree**   The United States needs to do more to help other countries.

**Disagree**   The United States should worry only about its own domestic problems.

● **Agree**   The only way to stop one country from taking over other countries is by using force.

**Disagree**   There are peaceful means of discouraging one country from taking over another country.

● **Agree**   The United States should deal only with foreign countries when U.S. interests are at stake.

**Disagree**   U.S. foreign policy considers the interests of other free and peaceful countries.

---

## CHAPTER

# 24 Charting a Course

**What's Your Opinion?**

## Build on What You Know

In the early years of the United States, many countries questioned whether the new country would survive. Not only did it survive, but it has become a leader in global politics. Why? Its people care about conditions both within and outside the nation. Americans understand that the world's future depends on people committed to the goal of peace. Working to achieve world peace, the United States creates foreign policies to meet changing times and new global challenges.

**Themes Journal** Do you **agree** or **disagree** with the following statements? Support your point of view in your journal.

• The United States should become more involved in world affairs.

• War is the only way to stop one country from taking over other countries.

• U.S. foreign policy promotes only the interests of the United States.

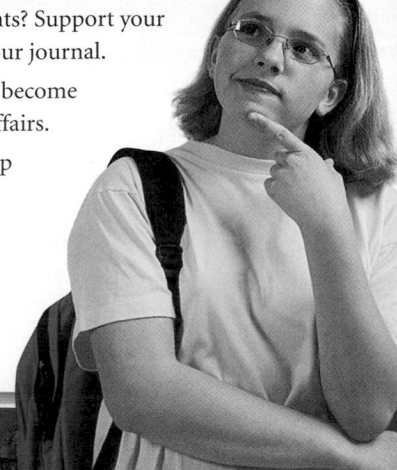

# SECTION 1

## OBJECTIVES

*After completing Section 1, students should be able to*

1 **Explain why the United States maintained a policy of isolationism in its early years and evaluate why it was hard to follow.**
2 **Analyze the effects that the War of 1812, the Monroe Doctrine, and the Good Neighbor Policy had on U.S. international relations.**
3 **Determine what caused the United States to enter World War I and World War II.**

## LET'S GET STARTED!

As students enter the classroom, invite them to list on the chalkboard some foreign problems in the news today. Ask students to locate these problems and discuss how the United States is involved in each of these issues. (*Students might talk about how the United States has served as a mediator between Israelis and Palestinians.*) Then ask students why the United States gets involved in the affairs of distant countries instead of concerning itself with domestic issues only. Tell students that in Section 1 they will learn about why the United States maintained isolationism in its early years and how U.S. foreign policy evolved.

## SECTION 1

# Development of U.S. Foreign Policy

### Read to Discover

1. Why did the United States maintain a policy of isolationism in its early years, and why was it hard to follow?
2. What effects did the War of 1812, the Monroe Doctrine, and the Good Neighbor Policy have on U.S. international relations?
3. What caused the United States to enter World War I and World War II?

### Define

- isolationism
- doctrine
- corollary
- dollar diplomacy
- neutrality

### WHY CIVICS MATTERS

U.S. officials continue to debate the degree to which the United States should be involved in the affairs of other countries. Use **CNNfyi.com** or other **current events** sources to find information about the current administration's role in foreign policy. Record your findings in your journal.

## Reading Focus

For many years U.S. foreign policy sought to avoid involvement in the affairs of other countries. This policy worked as long as the United States was somewhat isolated from the rest of the world. In time, however, transportation and communication systems improved. These developments encouraged contact and trade with other countries. As the United States became more closely tied to other countries, it became more involved in world affairs.

### ★ Isolationism

When the United States won its independence, the country was deeply in debt and struggling to build its economy. It was busy seeking solutions to many domestic problems. Most government leaders strongly believed that the United States should concentrate on its own development and growth. They felt the country should stay out of foreign politics. This belief that the United States should avoid involvement in all foreign affairs is known as **isolationism.**

At no time in U.S. history has the policy of isolationism been an easy one to follow. Even in the late 1700s President Washington found it difficult to practice this policy. To the north of the United States was the

## SECTION 1 RESOURCES

### REPRODUCIBLE

▶ Guided Reading Strategies 24.1
▶ Readings in Economics and Government 10: The Monroe Doctrine
▶ Readings in Economics and Government 30: Franklin D. Roosevelt's "Four Freedoms"
▶ Readings in Economics and Government 43: Lend-Lease Act of 1941
▶ Challenge and Enrichment Worksheet 24: Measuring Opinions About Foreign Policy Goals
▶ Graphic Organizer Activity: Developing Foreign Policy

### TECHNOLOGY

▶ One-Stop Planner, Lesson 24.1
▶ Holt Researcher CD–ROM
▶ CNN Presents: American Government
▶ Homework Practice Online

### REINFORCEMENT, REVIEW, AND ASSESSMENT

▶ Section 1 Review, p. 602
▶ Daily Quiz 24.1
▶ Main Idea Activity 24.1
▶ English Audio Summary 24.1
▶ Spanish Audio Summary 24.1

*Satellite communications are one reason isolationism is difficult in the modern world.*

**LEVEL 1:** Lead students in a discussion about why the United States maintained a policy of isolationism in its early years. (*Students might say that the United States was trying to focus on its own domestic and economic problems, but problems with the British colonies in Canada made isolationism difficult.*) Then organize students into pairs and ask each pair to draw a political cartoon illustrating how the United States isolated itself from the affairs of foreign countries at first. Also, have each pair of students present some of the difficulties of maintaining an isolationist policy. Ask volunteers to explain their cartoons to the class. **ENGLISH LANGUAGE LEARNERS , COOPERATIVE LEARNING**

**LEVELS 2 AND 3:** Ask students to imagine that they are living in the United States in 1810. Then have each student write a letter to an overseas friend explaining the reasons for the policy of international isolationism the U.S. government followed at that time. The letter should also address the problems that made isolationism a difficult policy to maintain. (*See the Level 1 lesson for reasons.*) Invite volunteers to read their letters to the class.

**HOMEWORK** Ask students to consult an encyclopedia to learn what Presidents George Washington, John Adams, and Thomas Jefferson thought about isolationism. Have each student write position statements explaining how these three presidents maintained an isolationist foreign policy.

---

 **Global Perspectives**

**Our Foreign Friend** In the years since the War of 1812, the United States and Great Britain have become strong allies. However, the relationship has also had its rocky moments. An incident during the U.S. Civil War almost led to war between the Union and Great Britain. In 1861 a Union warship stopped a British steamer near Cuba. Union sailors boarded the British vessel and removed two Confederate officials who were on their way to seek diplomatic recognition for the Confederacy. The incident enraged the British, who began to make preparations for war with the United States. Faced with the possibility of fighting two wars at the same time, President Abraham Lincoln cooled tensions by freeing the Confederate officials. Historians have pointed to the crisis as the last in which Washington and London seemed poised for war with each other.

**ACTIVITY:** Ask students to conduct research to learn more about how the alliance between the United States and Great Britain has played a role in more recent conflicts such as the Gulf War, the crisis in Kosovo, and the war against terrorism. Have each student write a report on his or her research.

**Visual Record Answer**

*Students might suggest the resolution in the men's faces.*

**Interpreting the Visual Record**

**Battle for the Great Lakes** *During the Battle of Lake Erie in the War of 1812, American commander Oliver Perry's ship was sunk. Perry ordered his crew to row him to another ship, where he led the U.S. fleet to victory.* **How does this image show the determination of Perry and his forces?**

British colony of Canada and a troubled border situation. To the south and west lay Spanish territory, which blocked U.S. expansion westward and threatened U.S. trade on the Mississippi River. When U.S. ships ventured east into the Atlantic seeking trade, British or French navy ships seized them.

✔ **Reading Check** Finding the Main Idea What foreign policy challenges did the United States face? a troubled U.S.-Canada border and Spanish territory that blocked U.S. expansion and access to the Mississippi River

## The War of 1812

Finally, in 1812 it seemed that war with Great Britain could not be avoided. Americans claimed that Britain was arming American Indians on U.S. western borders, occupying U.S. forts, and removing sailors from U.S. ships. It was time, they said, to make the British colony of Canada a part of the United States.

The War of 1812 ended in a stalemate—neither side won a clear-cut victory. However, the peace treaty that ended the war eventually led to improved relations with Great Britain. Most importantly, the War of 1812 won the United States a newly found respect among the countries of Europe. For nearly 100 years afterward, the United States was able to stay out of European conflicts and concentrate on domestic matters.

## The United States and Canada

The War of 1812 also marked a turning point in U.S. relations with British Canada. U.S. attempts to invade Canada during the war had proved unsuccessful. The United States and Canada still disagreed about who controlled the waterways along their borders. Both countries wanted to keep their navies and fishing rights on the Great Lakes.

In the spring of 1817, the two sides compromised by reaching the Rush-Bagot Agreement. Secretary of State Richard Rush negotiated this treaty. It limited naval power on the Great Lakes for both the United States and British Canada. Today the border between the two countries is the longest unfortified national border in the world. Canada is a strong U.S. ally.

✔ **Reading Check** Identifying Cause and Effect Why did the War of 1812 take place, and how did it affect U.S. relations with Canada? U.S. opposition to British actions in the West and on the high seas; ended U.S. efforts to conquer Canada and later established a peaceful U.S.-Canadian border

**ALL LEVELS:** Copy the following graphic organizer onto the chalkboard, omitting the italicized answers. Have students fill in the boxes with characteristics of U.S. international relations. **ENGLISH LANGUAGE LEARNERS**

**BEFORE**

*President Monroe worries that European powers will try to control Latin America.*

**Monroe Doctrine** ➡

**AFTER**

*United States warns that it will treat any interference in Latin America as an unfriendly act.*

*United States declares the Americas closed to future colonization.*

### U.S. Foreign Policy

**BEFORE**

*United States is threatened by British in Canada.*

*United States ships are seized by British and French.*

**War of 1812** ➡

**AFTER**

*United States earns the respect of European nations.*

*United States makes peace with England.*

*United States signs the Rush-Bagot Treaty with Canada in 1817.*

*United States is free to deal with domestic issues.*

**BEFORE**

*United States protects its investments in Latin America through dollar diplomacy.*

*United States acts as the police force of the Western Hemisphere.*

**Good Neighbor Policy** ➡

**AFTER**

*Monroe Doctrine no longer justifies U.S. interference in Latin America.*

*United States emphasizes friendly agreements between United States and Latin American countries.*

---

## The Monroe Doctrine

Most of the countries of Latin America won their independence from Spain in the early 1800s. However, President James Monroe worried that European powers might try to take control of the newly independent Latin American countries. In response, the U.S. government took a stand to prevent European countries from interfering in Latin American affairs.

In 1823 President James Monroe gave his annual message to Congress. During this speech Monroe explained the U.S. position on Latin America. He declared that the United States would consider any European interference in the affairs of any country in the Western Hemisphere an unfriendly act. Monroe also declared that the Americas were no longer open to colonization by European countries. However, he promised that the United States would not interfere in European concerns or existing European colonies in the Americas.

This policy came to be called the Monroe Doctrine. (See page 604.) A foreign-policy **doctrine** sets forth a new way of interacting with other countries. It is a statement of policy and is not necessarily an agreement with any other country. The Monroe Doctrine set the course of U.S. relations with both Latin America and Europe for many years.

✔ **Reading Check** **Evaluating** Why did President Monroe issue the Monroe Doctrine? to prevent European countries from interfering in Latin American affairs

## The United States and Latin America

At first, the countries of Latin America welcomed the support of the United States. The United States helped settle boundary disputes between Latin American countries. In later years, some European

### Interpreting the Visual Record

**Northern border** *The border between the United States and Canada is the longest unfortified border in the world. Here two bicyclists cross the border at a checkpoint.* **What are the advantages and disadvantages of having such a long undefended border?**

*President Monroe's doctrine shaped U.S. foreign policy in Latin America for many years.*

---

### ⭐ Global Perspectives

**Closing the Door** Before the Monroe Doctrine, Great Britain offered to join with the United States to keep other European countries out of Latin America. An alliance with the British would have gone against the policy of avoiding "foreign entanglements." Many officials, including former presidents and nearly all of President Monroe's advisers, favored partnership with such a powerful country. Even Monroe indicated a willingness to enter into the agreement. Ultimately, Monroe decided to reject the British offer. The reasons for Monroe's decision have been debated, though many scholars have argued that Secretary of State John Quincy Adams's strong opposition to the proposal persuaded Monroe to reject the offer. Other scholars have pointed to international and domestic political concerns as heavily influencing Monroe's decision.

**CRITICAL THINKING**

Was the Monroe Doctrine beneficial or detrimental to the development of Latin American nations?

**ANSWER:** Some students might say that it was good that the United States forbade European countries from interfering in Latin America; other students might point out that the Monroe Doctrine led to U.S. intervention in Latin America.

**Visual Record Answer**

*Students' responses will vary.*

**LEVEL 2:** Lead students in a discussion about the effects of the War of 1812, the Monroe Doctrine, and the Good Neighbor Policy on U.S. foreign relations. *(The War of 1812 earned the United States the respect of European countries, resulted in peace with England, and allowed the United States to focus on domestic issues for 100 years. The Monroe Doctrine declared that European countries should stay out of Latin American affairs. The Good Neighbor Policy emphasized friendly agreements between the United States and Latin American countries.)* Then ask each student to design a symbol representing the main effect of each event or policy. *(A student might illustrate the Monroe Doctrine by drawing a picture of an open hand preventing European warships from landing in the Americas.)* Display students' symbols around the classroom. **ENGLISH LANGUAGE LEARNERS**

# TEACH OBJECTIVE 3

 **LEVEL 1:** Lead students in a discussion about what caused the United States to enter World War I and World War II. *(The United States entered World War I because German submarines attacked U.S. merchant ships without warning. The United States entered World War II after the Japanese attacked Pearl Harbor, Hawaii.)* Then ask each student to design three postage stamps for a new series commemorating U.S. participation in these two wars. Encourage students to consider causes as well as consequences when choosing a theme for their stamps. Display the stamps around the classroom and invite volunteers to explain their stamps to the class.
**ENGLISH LANGUAGE LEARNERS**

## ⭐ Profiles

### The Rough Riders

Theodore Roosevelt's interest in Latin America stemmed in part from his participation in the Spanish-American War. A colorful figure, Roosevelt joined the First Volunteer Cavalry, known as the Rough Riders. This group included cowboys, miners, law-enforcement officials, and athletes. The Rough Riders are remembered best for their charges up Kettle Hill and San Juan Hill in a battle near Santiago, Cuba, on July 1, 1898. Roosevelt, who commanded the Rough Riders during this battle, saw many of his men killed by Spanish fire but escaped with only a minor injury.

**ACTIVITY:** Ask students to conduct research to learn more about the causes and results of the Spanish-American War. Have them draw a map that illustrates the major conflicts and events in the war.

---

### POLITICAL CARTOON ANSWER

Students might suggest that he is walking all over the sea.

---

**Interpreting Political Cartoons**

**Roosevelt and Latin America**
*President Theodore Roosevelt was known for his saying, "Walk softly but carry a big stick." In the Roosevelt Corollary, he promised that the United States would help police Latin America.* **How does this cartoon show Roosevelt treating the Caribbean Sea?**

### Holt Researcher

**go.hrw.com**
**KEYWORD:** Holt Researcher

**Freefind:** Diplomacy

Scan through the career entries on the Holt Researcher that involve foreign policy. Choose a career and create a mock resumé for an individual applying for a high-ranking position in that career. This resumé should answer the question: What qualifications and interests are important for a career in foreign affairs?

---

countries threatened to use force to collect debts owed by Latin American countries. The United States acted to prevent such interference. When Cuba rebelled against Spain in 1895, the United States declared war on Spain and defeated the Spanish fleet.

President Theodore Roosevelt strengthened the Monroe Doctrine in 1904. He announced that the United States would take on the role of policing the Western Hemisphere. If Latin American countries could not manage their own affairs, the United States would step in. This policy became known as the Roosevelt Corollary to the Monroe Doctrine. A **corollary** is a statement that follows as a natural or logical result.

After the Roosevelt Corollary, many Americans began to invest money in Latin American companies. When internal disorder threatened these investments, the United States sometimes sent troops to maintain peace. U.S. foreign policy in Latin America thus became known as **dollar diplomacy.**

✔ **Reading Check Making Generalizations and Predictions** Why do you think the United States became more involved in Latin American affairs? Students might say that the U.S. wanted to promote peace or protect its economic interests.

### ⭐ The Good Neighbor Policy

In some ways the actions of the United States in Latin America helped the countries there. However, these actions also created bad feelings. U.S. policies insulted the national pride of Latin American countries and interfered with their sovereignty, or authority to govern their own territories. Latin American leaders believed that the United States had turned from protector to oppressor. As a result, the United States took steps to improve its relations with Latin America.

In the 1930s the United States stated that the Monroe Doctrine would no longer be used to justify U.S. involvement in Latin America. In 1933 President Franklin D. Roosevelt announced the Good Neighbor Policy. This policy opposed armed intervention by the United States in Latin American affairs. It emphasized friendly agreements. In 1948, countries of the Western Hemisphere formed the Organization of American States (OAS), which you learned about in Chapter 23.

✔ **Reading Check Finding the Main Idea** What was the purpose of the Good Neighbor Policy? to improve relations between the United States and Latin America

LEVEL 3: Remind students what caused the United States to enter World War I and World War II. *(See the Level 1 lesson for causes.)* Then organize the class into two groups. Ask students in one group to write an argument for U.S. attempts to avoid getting involved in World War I and World War II. *(Students might cite U.S. isolationism and the sense that European conflicts did not involve U.S. interests.)* Then have each student in the other group write an argument for U.S. entry into World War I and World War II. Have the groups debate whether the United States should have entered these wars or remained neutral.

**CLOSE**

Organize students into groups and ask each group to create pamphlets describing the development of U.S. foreign policy through the end of World War II. Assign each student a different responsibility in the group, such as illustrator, researcher, writer, and so on. Make copies of the pamphlets so that all members of the class can have copies for use as study guides.
**COOPERATIVE LEARNING**

## ⭐ End of Isolationism

In 1914, when World War I broke out in Europe, the United States attempted to stay out of the conflict. President Woodrow Wilson announced a policy of **neutrality.** That is, the United States would not assist or favor either side. This policy was difficult to maintain, however. When German submarines sank U.S. merchant ships without warning and without regard for passenger safety, remaining neutral became impossible. In response to a war message by President Woodrow Wilson, Congress declared war on Germany in 1917.

President Wilson declared that the United States had entered the war to help "make the world safe for democracy." The victory of the United States and its allies brought hope for lasting peace. Wilson centered his hopes on a new international organization called the League of Nations. The League promised to solve disputes in a friendly fashion and to go to war only as a last resort.

As you recall, a provision for joining the League of Nations was submitted to the Senate. However, many Americans, including some powerful senators, opposed U.S. membership in the League. They feared that by joining the League, the United States would be drawn into future European conflicts. The spirit of U.S. isolationism remained

The destruction of the ocean liner Lusitania *by a German submarine shocked Americans.*

**Interpreting the Visual Record**

Trench warfare *The use of modern weapons—such as machine guns, tanks, and poison gas—turned World War I into a bloody and defensive struggle. Thousands of miles of trenches were dug for protection.* **What has happened to the forest and the landscape around this trench?**

## ⭐ Culture

**The Question of Loyalty**
When World War I broke out in Europe, many German Americans collected great amounts of money for the relief of war victims in Germany and advocated strict neutrality for the United States. However, once the United States entered the war on the side of the Allies, most German Americans stopped supporting Germany and directed their donations to the American cause. Many German Americans, among them Captain Eddie Rickenbacker and General John J. Pershing, distinguished themselves on the battlefield. However, German Americans were still sometimes mistreated by people who questioned their loyalty.

**Visual Record Answer**

*Students should suggest that the landscape has been destroyed.*

# REVIEW AND ASSESS

Have students complete the **Section 1 Review** on page 602. Then have students complete **Daily Quiz 24.1**. As **Alternative Assessment**, you may want to use the newspaper article or postage-stamp activity in this section's lessons.

## RETEACH

Have students complete **Main Idea Activity for English Language Learners and Special-Needs Students 24.1.** Then organize students into three groups and assign each group the War of 1812, the Monroe Doctrine, or the Good Neighbor Policy. Have each group create a series of headlines describing U.S. foreign policy decisions before and after its event. Then ask each group to read its headlines and to ask other students to guess whether each headline is a "before" or "after" headline. **ENGLISH LANGUAGE LEARNERS , COOPERATIVE LEARNING**

## EXTEND

Have students conduct research to learn more about how the Monroe Doctrine and the Roosevelt Corollary influenced U.S. foreign policy in Latin America. Ask each student to choose an event when the United States intervened in the affairs of a Latin American country and to write a paper explaining whether this intervention was justified. **BLOCK SCHEDULING**

**Interpreting the Visual Record**

**Pearl Harbor** *The memorial for the USS Arizona attracts many visitors to Pearl Harbor each year.* **What do you see submerged beneath the memorial?**

strong. As a result, the United States stayed out of the League of Nations.

The beginning of World War II found the United States in a neutral position once again. Congress passed a series of neutrality laws in the mid-1930s forbidding the sale of arms, or weapons, to warring countries. In 1939 the United States did agree to sell arms to foreign nations, but only on a cash-and-carry basis. That is, the arms sold had to be carried in foreign ships and paid for in cash, not on credit. However, the threat of the so-called Axis powers grew. Soon U.S. leaders agreed to lend or lease (rent) billions of dollars' worth of arms to the cash-poor Allies. The United States became the "arsenal of democracy."

The bombing of Pearl Harbor by the Japanese on December 7, 1941, completely shattered U.S. neutrality. The attack shocked the American people, who realized that isolationism in a worldwide conflict was impossible. The United States declared war on Japan. Soon afterward Germany and Italy declared war on the United States, which then recognized a state of war with those two countries.

While World War II was still being fought, plans to establish a post-war peacekeeping organization were already underway. In 1945 the United States joined with many other countries around the world to form the United Nations.

✔ **Reading Check** Identifying Points of View  Why did many Americans fear the end of isolationism? They feared the country would be drawn into European conflicts.

## Section 1 Review ANSWERS

**1. Define**
- isolationism, p. 597
- doctrine, p. 599
- corollary, p. 600
- dollar diplomacy, p. 600
- neutrality, p. 601

**2.** cause—German submarines attacked U.S. ships; effect—U.S. victory brought hopes for world peace, but spirit of U.S. isolationism remained strong, and United States did not join League of Nations; cause—United States gradually increased support for Allies, Japanese attacked Pearl Harbor; effect—United States joined with other nations to form the United Nations

**3. a.** The United States wanted to avoid foreign entanglements so that the country could develop, but hostile neighbors and foreign interference made isolationism difficult.

**b.** War of 1812—caused the United States to be viewed with greater respect, enabled it to stay out of European conflicts, and United States and Great Britain agreed to settle disputes; Monroe Doctrine—kept new Latin American nations from being conquered again by any European nation, set the tone for future relations between United States and Latin America; Good Neighbor Policy—reassured Latin American countries that United States would stay out of their affairs

**4.** Students' paragraphs will vary.

---

## SECTION 1 Review

go.
hrw
.com
**Homework Practice Online**
keyword: SZ3 HP24

**1. Define** and explain:
- isolationism
- doctrine
- corollary
- dollar diplomacy
- neutrality

**2. Identifying Cause and Effect** Copy the graphic organizer below. Use it to show why the United States entered World War I and World War II and the results of its actions.

```
Cause  →  United States enters World War I  →  Effect

Cause  →  United States enters World War II  →  Effect
```

**3. Finding the Main Idea**
a. What caused U.S. officials to pursue a policy of isolationism after independence, and what challenges did they face?
b. How did the War of 1812, the Monroe Doctrine, and the Good Neighbor Policy affect U.S. international relations?

**4. Writing and Critical Thinking**
**Identifying Points of View** You are reporting on a debate about the pros and cons of isolationism. In a three-paragraph article, describe the arguments of the debate in detail. Include examples used to support each opinion; indicate whose point of view won, and why.

**Consider:**
- early U.S. foreign policy and its results
- the role of isolationism in both world wars

## TEACH

**LEVEL 1:** Lead students in a discussion about the differences between primary and secondary sources. *(Primary sources are written by witnesses of or participants in historical events; secondary sources are usually written by authors using primary sources.)* Have students draw a chart that represents the main ideas in Washington's speech. Point out that Washington's speech is a primary source and that students' charts are secondary sources. Ask students to illustrate Washington's arguments with symbols or pictures on their charts. **ENGLISH LANGUAGE LEARNERS**

**LEVEL 3:** Remind students that primary sources provide information about events and give glimpses of the attitudes, feelings, and concerns of people who lived in the past. Ask students to imagine they are members of Congress in 1823 and have just heard President Monroe deliver the speech that became the Monroe Doctrine. Have each student write a letter to the people of the state he or she represents. Ask students to summarize Monroe's speech and critique his ideas. Ask volunteers to read their letters to the class.

# Civics Skills
## WORKSHOP

## Using Primary Sources

Primary sources of information are written by people who witnessed or participated in historical events. Primary sources differ from secondary sources. Secondary sources are usually written after an event has taken place. They are often written by an author using primary source materials.

Both primary and secondary sources provide important facts. Only primary sources, however, allow you to see events through the eyes of the people who experienced them. They not only provide information about the event, but also give you glimpses of the attitudes, feelings, and concerns of people who lived in the past.

## How to Use Primary Sources

1. **Identify the source's background.** To judge the accuracy and reliability of a primary source, you must understand who wrote the source and the conditions under which it was written. As you read, ask yourself if the author is biased in some way. Research what was happening in the world at the time the source was written. Answering these and similar questions will help you decide if the source is accurate and reliable.

2. **Read the source.** Read the source several times until you are confident you understand its meaning. Look up any words you do not know. As you read the source, be sure to identify all facts. Also note any statements that give you insight into the opinions of the author and the period in which the author lived.

3. **Draw conclusions.** Use your careful reading of the source to draw conclusions about the topic or event discussed.

## Applying the Skill

The primary source on this page is part of President George Washington's Farewell Address, written in 1796. Read the source and then answer the questions that follow.

1. Why might Washington's speech be a good source of information on early U.S. foreign policy?

2. What is the basic message of this part of the speech?

3. How does the president support his position?

*The great rule of conduct for us in regard to foreign nations is in extending our commercial relations, to have with them as little political connection as possible. So far as we have already formed engagements, let them be fulfilled with perfect good faith. Here let us stop. Europe has a set of primary interests which to us have none; or a very remote relation. . . .*

*Our detached and distant situation invites and enables us to pursue a different course. . . .*

*Why, by interweaving our destiny with that of any part of Europe, entangle our peace and prosperity in the toils of European ambition, rivalship, interest, humor or caprice?*

*It is our true policy to steer clear of permanent alliances with any portion of the foreign world.*

**SKILLS ANSWERS**

1. Washington, as the first U.S. president, was important in developing early U.S. foreign policy.

2. The United States should avoid political entanglements with foreign countries, particularly European countries.

3. Europe's interests and controversies have little relation to those of the United States; distance from Europe insulates the United States from European problems.

**LEVEL 1:** Lead a class discussion about the importance of the wording of the Monroe Doctrine. Ask students what the doctrine does not say. *(Students should suggest that it does not say that the United States will declare war on any European country that interferes in Latin America.)* Encourage students to discuss reasons that the Monroe Doctrine does not promise a specific U.S. response. *(Students might suggest that the United States was not yet as powerful as many European countries but still needed to appear forceful.)* Ask each student to illustrate a scene showing one possible way in which the United States might have responded to a European country that challenged the Monroe Doctrine. Invite volunteers to explain their illustrations to the class. **ENGLISH LANGUAGE LEARNERS**

**LEVEL 3:** Ask students to imagine that they are newspaper reporters in England at the time that President Monroe announced his doctrine. Have each student write a newspaper article describing the reaction of European governments to the U.S. declaration that the Americas are closed to colonization or interference from Europe. *(Students might indicate that foreign governments were angered or amused that the United States would presume to take such a stance.)* Ask volunteers to read their articles to the class.

**ANALYZING PRIMARY SOURCES ANSWERS**
1. that the United States would view any European country that interfered in the affairs of Latin America as unfriendly

2. The United States became a police force for Latin American countries and did not share European interests in colonization.

## Historical Documents

# THE MONROE DOCTRINE

The Monroe Doctrine is not a law passed by Congress. It is a statement of foreign policy made by President James Monroe in a State of the Union Address to Congress. The Monroe Doctrine is one of the most important documents in the country's history. It has influenced U.S. foreign policy to the present time. The Monroe Doctrine asserts the country's dedication to freedom. It warns foreign countries that the Americas—North, South, and Central—are closed to colonization.

"[It is] a principle in which the rights and interests of the United States are involved, that the American continents, by the free and independent condition which they have assumed and maintain, are henceforth not to be considered as subjects for future colonization by any European powers. . . .

We owe it, therefore, to candor and to the amicable [friendly] relations existing between the United States and those powers to declare that we should consider any attempt on their part to extend their system to any portion of this hemisphere as dangerous to our peace and safety. With the existing colonies or dependencies of any European power, we have not interfered and shall not interfere. But with the Governments who have declared their independence and maintained it, and whose independence we have, on great consideration and on just principles, acknowledged, we could not view any interposition [interference] for the purpose of oppressing them, or controlling in any other manner their destiny, by any European power in any other light than as the manifestation [evidence] of an unfriendly disposition toward the United States."

**Analyzing Primary Sources**
1. What warning did President Monroe give to the European powers in the Monroe Doctrine?
2. How do you think this warning might have affected U.S. relations with Latin American and European countries?

**LEVEL 1:** Lead students in a discussion about the four freedoms outlined in President Roosevelt's State of the Union Address. *(The four freedoms are freedom of speech and expression, freedom to worship, freedom from want, freedom from fear.)* Ask students why it was necessary for Roosevelt to enumerate these freedoms at that point in history. *(Students might mention that during World War II, these four freedoms were threatened by the spread of fascism in Europe.)* Have students consult recent newspapers and magazines to find examples of these four freedoms today. *(Students might choose examples of freedom of expression, advertisements for food and clothing, headlines about peace treaties or negotiations, and so on.)* Have each student create a collage with his or her examples and ask volunteers to explain their collages to the class.

**LEVELS 2 AND 3:** Point out to students that billboards are sometimes used to convey political messages. Then ask each student to design a billboard that promotes public awareness of the four freedoms at the heart of U.S. domestic and foreign policies and to create a slogan encouraging people to preserve these freedoms. *(Students might use drawings or a collage of images to illustrate each of the four freedoms.)* Display these billboards around the classroom.

## ANALYZING PRIMARY SOURCES ANSWERS
1. freedom of speech and expression, freedom of worship, freedom from want, freedom from fear

2. He says they apply to the world; students' responses may vary but should be supported with sound reasoning.

# FRANKLIN D. ROOSEVELT'S FOUR FREEDOMS

*President Franklin D. Roosevelt gave a State of the Union Address before Congress in January 1941. In the address Roosevelt stated four freedoms to which the United States was firmly committed. These freedoms inspired Americans during World War II and remain at the heart of the country's domestic and foreign policies.*

"I address you, the members of this new Congress, at a moment unprecedented in the history of the Union. I use the word "unprecedented," because at no previous time has American security been as seriously threatened from without [outside] as it is today. . . .

I suppose that every realist knows that the democratic way of life is at this moment being directly assailed in every part of the world—assailed either by arms or by secret spreading of poisonous propaganda by those who seek to destroy unity and promote discord in nations that are still at peace.

During sixteen long months this assault has blotted out the whole pattern of democratic life in an appalling number of independent nations, great and small. And the assailants [attackers] are still on the march, threatening other nations, great and small.

In the future days, which we seek to make secure, we look forward to a world founded upon four essential freedoms.

The first is freedom of speech and freedom of expression—everywhere in the world.

The second is freedom of every person to worship God in his own way—everywhere in the world.

The third is freedom from want—which, translated into world terms, means economic understandings which will secure to every nation healthy peacetime life for its inhabitants—everywhere in the world.

The fourth is freedom from fear—which, translated into world terms, means a world-wide reduction of armaments to such a point and in such a thorough fashion that no nation will be in a position to commit an act of physical aggression against any neighbor—anywhere in the world. That is no vision of a distant millennium. It is a definite basis for a kind of world attainable in our own time and generation. That kind of world is the very antithesis of the so-called "new order" of tyranny which the dictators seek to create with the crash of a bomb.

To that new order we oppose the greater conception—the moral order. A good society is able to face schemes of world domination and foreign revolutions alike without fear. Since the beginning of our American history we have been engaged in change, in a perpetual, peaceful revolution, a revolution which goes on steadily, quietly, adjusting itself to changing conditions without the concentration camp or the quicklime in the ditch. The world order which we seek is the cooperation of free countries, working together in a friendly, civilized society.

This nation has placed its destiny in the hands and heads and hearts of its millions of free men and women; and its faith in freedom under the guidance of God. Freedom means the supremacy of human rights everywhere. Our support goes to those who struggle to gain those rights or keep them. Our strength is in our unity of purpose.

To that high concept there can be no end save victory."

**Analyzing Primary Sources**
1. What are the four freedoms described by Roosevelt?
2. To whom does Roosevelt say these freedoms should apply? Do you agree or disagree? Explain your answer.

## OBJECTIVES

*After completing Section 2, students should be able to*

1 **Identify what began the Cold War, and examine the form that the early U.S. response took.**

2 **Evaluate how the U.S. response to the Berlin blockade and the Cuban missile crisis differed.**

3 **Describe the events that marked the end of the Cold War.**

### 🔊 LET'S GET STARTED!

As students enter the classroom, have them pass around photographs of Cold War images. *(Some images might include pictures of the Berlin airlift, the Berlin Wall, the Cuban missile crisis, Soviet military parades, and so on.)* Ask students to comment on these photographs and encourage them to point out any similarities that they see. *(Students might point out that many Cold War images show scenes of tension without actual military conflict.)* Tell students that in Section 2 they will learn more about what began the Cold War, how the U.S. response to the Berlin blockade differed from the Cuban missile crisis, and what events marked the end of the Cold War.

## SECTION 2

# The Cold War

### Read to Discover

1. What began the Cold War, and what form did the early U.S. response take?
2. How did the U.S. response to the Berlin blockade and the Cuban missile crisis differ?
3. What events marked the end of the Cold War?

### WHY CIVICS MATTERS

During its history the United States has taken steps to protect democracy throughout the world. Use **CNN fyi.com** or other **current events** sources to investigate recent U.S. actions aimed at defending democracy. Record your findings in your journal.

### Define

- communism
- satellite nations
- containment
- balance of power
- limited war
- glasnost
- perestroika
- détente

## Reading Focus

During World War II, the United States and the Soviet Union were allied in fighting Nazi Germany. Soon after the war ended, however, the two countries became rivals. The roots of the conflict lay in the two countries' very different economic systems and forms of government. The United States has always been a representative democracy, while the Soviet Union was a communist country.

### ⭐ Roots of Communism

The ideas behind modern communism come mainly from a German writer named Karl Marx. He believed that capitalists throughout the world were getting rich by treating workers unfairly. With another writer, Friedrich Engels, Marx wrote the *Communist Manifesto*.

In this book Marx and Engels proposed a new economic system called **communism.** They argued that the working class, called the proletariat, would one day take over all factories and businesses. Under communism no single group would own or control all the means of production—land, capital, and labor. Private individuals would not be permitted to own or control the means of production to make profits. Marx later expanded these ideas in a book called *Das Kapital* (from the German word meaning "capital").

*This statue is of Karl Marx, considered by many people to be the father of communism.*

## TEACH OBJECTIVE 1

 **LEVEL 1:** Lead students in a class discussion about what began the Cold War and what form the early U.S. response took. *(The Cold War began when the Soviet Union asserted its influence over Eastern Europe to establish communist satellite countries after World War II. In response, the United States and its allies began to compete with the Soviet Union and other communist countries for global power.)* Then organize students into pairs and ask each pair to design a cover for a new history book about the causes of the Cold War. Encourage students to decorate their book covers with collages of images illustrating the events that began the Cold War. Display the book covers around the classroom and invite volunteers to explain their illustrations to the class. **ENGLISH LANGUAGE LEARNERS , COOPERATIVE LEARNING**

**LEVELS 1 AND 2:** Ask students to think about the events that began the Cold War and to consider U.S. responses to these events. *(See the Level 1 lesson for some of these events.)* Then have each student draw a flowchart, using symbols or other illustrations, that links events and the U.S. responses. *(Students' charts should indicate the increasing tensions between the United States and the Soviet Union by using colors, images, and so on.)* Ask volunteers to explain their flowcharts to the class. **ENGLISH LANGUAGE LEARNERS**

According to Marx, the proletariat would also run the government. Everything from raw materials to finished products would be owned by the government in the name of the workers. In the process, capitalism would be overthrown, by force if necessary. The workers would establish a "dictatorship of the proletariat" around the world. Communism would therefore be both an economic and a political system.

✔ **Reading Check Finding the Main Idea** What is the basis of communism? proletariat ownership or control of all the means of production

## ★ Communism in the Soviet Union

In 1917 Russia became the first country to adopt a communist system. Russia then became part of the Union of Soviet Socialist Republics (USSR), or the Soviet Union. For decades, the Communist Party of the Soviet Union was all-powerful. The Soviet government made all economic decisions. It owned and managed all of the country's industries and farms. It also controlled most aspects of citizens' lives.

For years, no political party except the Communist Party was allowed to exist. The Soviet Union did not allow freedom of the press. The government forced its citizens to make the Soviet Union a modern industrial nation. By 1950 the country ranked second among the industrial powers of the world, behind only the United States. This rapid progress was an amazing feat. Such progress had a high price, however. The standard of living in the Soviet Union was much lower than that in the United States. The Soviet government concentrated its production efforts on the machinery needed for industrialization. Thus, basic consumer goods, including food, were often in short supply.

✔ **Reading Check Summarizing** What was life in the Soviet Union like? The communist government controlled most aspects of people's lives and concentrated on industrializing the country, resulting in shortages of basic consumer goods.

## ★ The Cold War Begins

The Soviet Union and the United States had been allies during World War II. This alliance was soon shattered, however. After the war, Russia used its presence in the region to interfere in the affairs of Eastern Europe. Within a few years communist governments were established in Albania, Bulgaria, Czechoslovakia, East Germany, Hungary, Romania, and Poland. The Soviet Union had turned the countries along its borders into **satellite nations** —countries that are controlled by another country.

Soviet leaders maintained that these actions were necessary to protect the Soviet Union from attack by Germany or any other Western European country. However, leaders in the United States and Western

*This early political cartoon shows an anarchist threatening American freedoms.*

**Interpreting the Visual Record**

**Soviet life** *Under communist rule, Soviet citizens often had to stand in long lines to get daily necessities such as food and fuel.* **How does this image show the disadvantages of the communist state-run economy?**

**LEVEL 3:** Organize the class into two groups. Ask both groups to think about the events that started the Cold War. Then ask each student in the first group to write an argument explaining why the United States should not enter into the Cold War. Have the second group write arguments in favor of confronting the Soviet Union in a Cold War. (*Students should support their arguments with specific reasons and might also consider the long-term consequences of entering or not entering the Cold War.*) Invite volunteers from both groups to debate their positions before the class. **COOPERATIVE LEARNING**

**LEVEL 3:** Ask students to imagine what might have happened if the events that began the Cold War had actually started a real war instead. Then ask each student to write an alternative history of the period. Encourage students to consider the weakened state of many European countries following World War II and the early U.S. response to the Communist takeover of Eastern Europe. Ask students whether a "hot" war would have been a limited engagement between the United States and the Soviet Union or a third world war. (*Students might consider various issues, such as the Soviet presence in Southwest Asia, that could have erupted in an all-out war.*) Encourage volunteers to read their alternative histories to the class.

Europe believed the Soviet Union was simply establishing Soviet-dominated communist governments.

With the satellite nations of Eastern Europe under its control, the Soviet Union tried to increase its power elsewhere. It focused on the eastern Mediterranean Sea and Southwest Asia. The United States saw this expansion of Soviet power as a serious threat to U.S. national security and to world peace.

Soon the world was caught up in the competition for global power and influence known as the Cold War. On one side of the conflict was the Soviet Union and its satellite countries. On the other side was the United States and other noncommunist countries. Both sides in the Cold War used propaganda, spying, alliances, foreign aid, and other methods to "win" the war. Issues related to the Cold War occupied most of U.S. foreign policy in the years following World War II.

✔ **Reading Check** Identifying Cause and Effect How did the Cold War begin, and how did the United States respond? After World War II, the Soviets established communist governments in Eastern Europe and tried to expand farther. Both sides used propaganda, spying, alliances, foreign aid, and other methods to "win" the war.

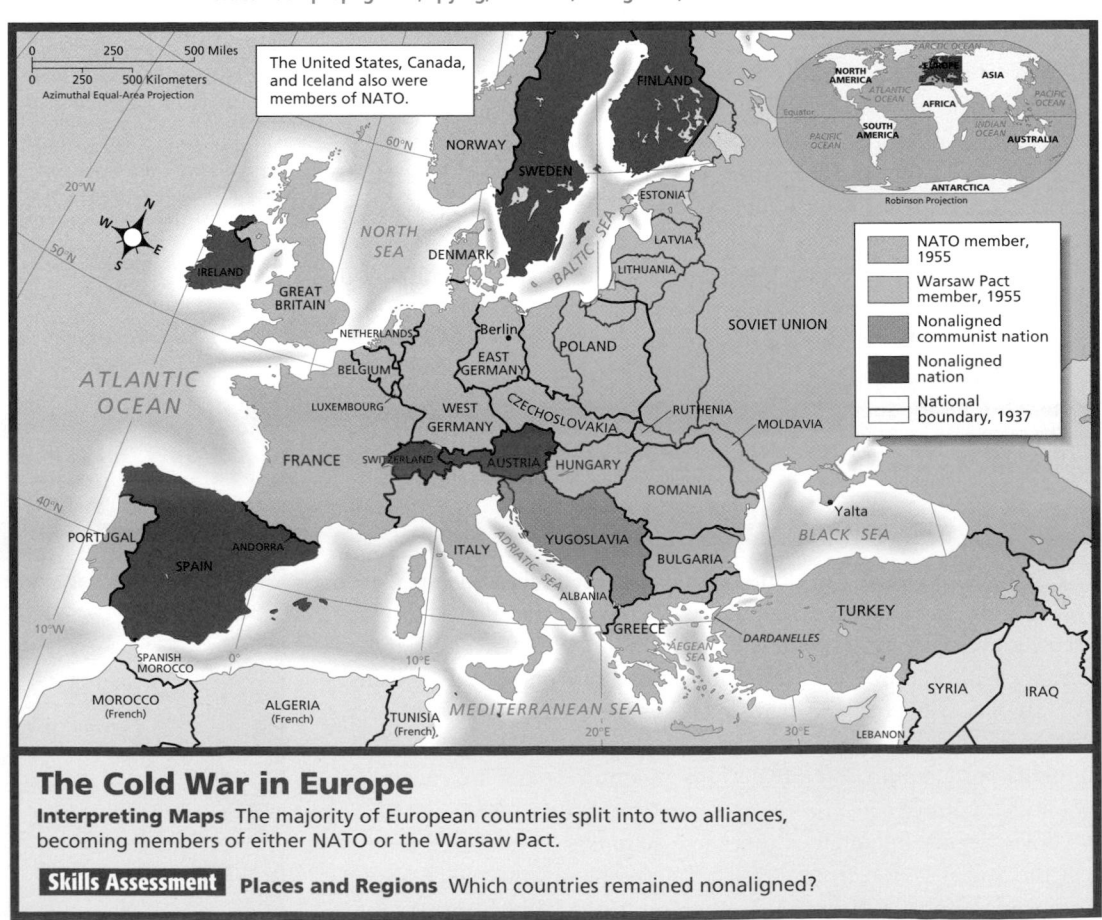

## The Cold War in Europe

**Interpreting Maps** The majority of European countries split into two alliances, becoming members of either NATO or the Warsaw Pact.

**Skills Assessment** Places and Regions Which countries remained nonaligned?

**ALL LEVELS:** Copy the following graphic organizer onto the chalkboard, omitting the italicized answers. Have students complete the columns to show how the U.S. response to the Berlin blockade differed from the Cuban missile crisis. Then have students indicate the results of each event. **ENGLISH LANGUAGE LEARNERS**

| Berlin Blockade | Cuban Missile Crisis |
|---|---|
| *United States & Great Britain begin a massive airlift of fuel, food, clothing, and other vital items.* | *United States demands immediate removal of Soviet missiles from Cuba.* |
| *Planes from the United States and Great Britain make more than 250,000 flights.* | *United States threatens military response.* |
| | *Navy and air force find and search all ships heading for Cuba.* |
| | *U.S. Army is put on alert.* |
| **Results** | **Results** |
| *Soviet Union ends blockade.* | *Soviet Union backs down and removes missiles from Cuba.* |

## The Policy of Containment

In March 1947 President Harry Truman announced that the United States would give economic aid to help countries fighting communism. This policy became known as the Truman Doctrine. Congress gave $400 million in aid to Greece and its neighbor Turkey, which helped the Greek army defeat Communist rebels.

The idea behind this policy came to be called **containment.** The purpose of containment was to prevent Soviet communism from spreading. The forces of the Soviet Union were to be "contained" within the area they had occupied up to 1947. However, U.S. policy makers expected that the Soviet Union would test the U.S. policy.

✔ **Reading Check Analyzing Information** What was the Truman Doctrine? a commitment of U.S. aid to help countries fight communism

## The Berlin Blockade

The first real test of containment came in 1948 in Berlin, Germany. At the end of World War II, Germany was divided into separate zones. The Soviet Union occupied the eastern zone. France, Great Britain, and the United States jointly occupied the western zone. The city of Berlin, located in the Soviet-occupied zone, was divided among France, Great Britain, the Soviet Union, and the United States. Each country controlled a part of the city.

In June 1948 the Soviet Union tried to force the democratic occupation troops in West Berlin to leave the city. The Soviets blockaded Berlin by closing all western land routes to the city. Residents of West Berlin were cut off from supplies such as food.

The United States and Great Britain began a massive airlift of fuel, food, clothing, and other essential items. More than 272,000 flights brought 2.3 million tons of needed supplies to West Berlin. The Soviets finally agreed to lift the blockade in 1949.

✔ **Reading Check Summarizing** What was the Soviets' plan in starting the Berlin blockade, and how did the United States respond? to take over the city; massive airlift of supplies to West Berlin

### ★★★★★★★★★★★★
### That's Interesting!
### ★★★★★★★★★★★★

**The Pumpkin Papers** Would you hide top-secret papers in a pumpkin? That's what Whittaker Chambers did. In 1948 Chambers, who had already confessed to being a Communist spy, accused former State Department official Alger Hiss of also being a traitor. Hiss denied the charges and sued Chambers for libel. Chambers then produced secret government microfilm that he said Hiss had given him years earlier. Chambers revealed that he had hidden the microfilm in a hollowed-out pumpkin on his farm. The so-called "pumpkin papers" drew even more attention to the case. Hiss was found guilty of perjury and sentenced to five years in prison.

**Interpreting the Visual Record**

**Berlin Airlift** *Day after day, in all kinds of weather, U.S. and British planes brought much-needed supplies to West Berlin. Here a group of German children wave to a supply plane.* **How does this image show the importance of the airlift effort to the people of Berlin?**

## Civics Sidelight

**Brinkmanship** One Cold War strategy espoused by President Dwight D. Eisenhower's secretary of state, John Foster Dulles, called for the United States to be willing to go to the verge, or brink, of war in order to force the enemy to back down from a confrontation. Democrat Adlai Stevenson, who opposed Eisenhower for the presidency in 1952 and 1956, called this policy "brinkmanship."

### CRITICAL THINKING

Do you think that brinkmanship is still an effective way for the United States to deal with its enemies?

**ANSWER:** Students should support their positions with examples of the successes and failures of brinkmanship.

### ★★★★★★★★★★★★
### That's Interesting!
### ★★★★★★★★★★★★

The Cold War was fought on many different fronts, including outer space. In 1957, Americans were surprised to learn that the Soviets had successfully placed the first human-made satellite, *Sputnik*, in orbit around Earth. Many historians argue that this event led to the so-called space race between the United States and the Soviet Union.

**LEVEL 3:** Ask students to think about the U.S. responses to the Berlin blockade and the Cuban missile crisis. *(See the All Levels lesson for a list of responses.)* Then have students decide whether they agree with the actions taken by the United States. Ask each student to write a position paper in which he or she defends U.S. actions or suggests actions that would have been better and explains why. *(Regardless of their positions, students' papers should consider the consequences of responses other than the ones that the United States had.)* Ask volunteers to read their position papers to the class.

**LEVEL 3:** Remind students that the Cold War began after the Soviet Union established satellite nations in Eastern Europe. Then ask students to consider whether the United States could have acted sooner to prevent the Communist Party from gaining control of Eastern Europe. Organize students into groups and ask each group to write a play about the early U.S. response to Soviet influence and the spread of communism. Encourage students to consider the difficulties facing U.S. foreign-policy makers in the early days of the Cold War. Have each group perform its play for the rest of the class. **COOPERATIVE LEARNING**

 **HOMEWORK** Ask students to imagine that it is 1962 and that the Cuban missile crisis has just begun. Then ask students to write a series of journal entries describing the day-to-day tension as the crisis unfolds.

**Cuban Missile Crisis**

After a tense standoff in October 1962 between Russian ships carrying nuclear missiles and the U.S. naval blockade, Soviet premier Nikita Khrushchev ultimately agreed to eliminate Soviet missiles from Cuba. Many Americans saw this as an outright victory for the United States. However, the resolution of the Cuban missile crisis also involved a compromise. In return for the promise that the Soviet Union would not place missiles in Cuba, President Kennedy promised Khrushchev that the United States would remove its nuclear-armed missiles from Turkey, not far from the border of the Soviet Union. On April 25, 1963, the last of the U.S. Jupiter missiles was dismantled and removed from Turkey, but the U.S. government made no public announcement.

**ACTIVITY:** Ask students to conduct research to learn more about the events of the Cuban missile crisis. Have students create a detailed time line with illustrations showing the day-by-day events of the crisis.

**POLITICAL CARTOON ANSWER**
nuclear war

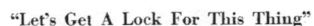

"Let's Get A Lock For This Thing"

NUCLEAR WAR

HERBLOCK

---from *Herblock: A Cartoonist's Life* (Times Books, 1998)

**Interpreting Political Cartoons**

**Cold War** *The United States and the Soviet Union competed for power around the world but avoided direct conflict with each other.* **What are President Kennedy and Premier Khrushchev struggling to contain in this cartoon?**

 *Did You* **KNOW?**

After the tense events of the Cuban missile crisis, a special "hot line" was opened between Washington, D.C., and Moscow. This hot line allowed immediate and secure communications between U.S. and Soviet leaders during the Cold War. Unlike in the movies, the hot line is not a red telephone but a satellite link.

## ★ Communism in China

After World War II, a full-scale civil war broke out in China. In 1949, Chinese Communists defeated the government led by Chiang Kai-shek. Chiang's forces fled to the island of Taiwan, off the southeastern coast of China. There they set up a government in exile, called Nationalist China, or the Republic of China. The Communists held the mainland—known as the People's Republic of China (PRC). The first head of the People's Republic of China was Mao Zedong.

The United States refused to recognize the People's Republic of China. Instead, it provided economic and military aid to Nationalist China (Taiwan). With the support of the United States and other noncommunist countries, Nationalist China was allowed to remain a member of the United Nations. In 1971, however, Nationalist China was forced out of the United Nations and replaced by the PRC.

✔ **Reading Check** Analyzing Information How did communism affect China? Communists, led by Mao Zedong, established the People's Republic of China, which the United States did not recognize. Chiang Kai-shek's Nationalist China was forced into exile in Taiwan and supported by the United States.

## ★ The Cuban Missile Crisis

After the Soviet Union tested a nuclear bomb in 1949, the world realized that the USSR and the United States both had the power to launch a nuclear attack. A **balance of power,** or situation in which countries are about equal in strength, was developing between the two countries. Each seeking to gain the upper hand, the United States and the Soviet Union continually tested each other for weaknesses.

The most dangerous of these confrontations took place on the island of Cuba. In October 1962 President John F. Kennedy was informed that the Soviet Union was building secret missile bases in Cuba. Fidel Castro had set up a communist government there in 1959. These missile bases, if finished, could threaten the United States and the entire Western Hemisphere. President Kennedy demanded that the Soviet Union remove its missiles from Cuba immediately. Kennedy declared that the United States was prepared to take whatever steps might be required, including military force.

As a first step, the U.S. government announced that it would not allow the delivery of more offensive weapons, or weapons of attack, to Cuba. The U.S. Navy and Air Force were used to seek out and search foreign ships bound for Cuba. U.S. Army troops were also put on the alert.

In part as a result of this show of U.S. military strength and determination, the Soviet Union backed down. It agreed to remove Soviet long-range missiles from Cuba and to dismantle, or take apart, the missile-launching sites.

**LEVEL 1:** On the chalkboard draw a time line that spans the years from 1945 to 1991. Then indicate some of the major events in the history of the Soviet Union. (*These events might include the spread of communism after World War II, the Berlin blockade, the Cold War, on so on.*) Invite volunteers to come to the board to fill in the time line with events that marked the close of the Cold War. Encourage students to explain the importance of the events that they write on the time line. (*Students might cite the policy of glasnost introduced in 1987, the fall of the Berlin Wall in 1990, pro-democracy elections in Eastern Europe in 1990, and the disintegration of the Soviet Union in 1991.*) **ENGLISH LANGUAGE LEARNERS**

**ALL LEVELS:** Tell students that throughout its existence, the Berlin Wall became not only a symbol of the Cold War but also an object for political expression—graffiti. Then organize students into groups and ask each group to design a graffiti mural for a monument commemorating the events that led up to the end of the Cold War. (*Students' designs might follow chronological order or might be organized as a collage of major events of the 1980s.*) Display students' murals around the classroom and ask volunteers from each group to explain their designs. **ENGLISH LANGUAGE LEARNERS** , **COOPERATIVE LEARNING**

---

From that time on, Soviet and U.S. leaders truly understood how dangerous the Cold War had become. They continued to pursue their own interests and to search for each other's weaknesses. However, they were careful to avoid situations that might develop into a third world war. Such a war would undoubtedly be a nuclear one capable of destroying much of the world.

✔ **Reading Check** Identifying Cause and Effect What caused the Cuban missile crisis, and what was the result? The Soviet Union began to build missile bases in Cuba. Soviet and U.S. leaders understood the dangers of the Cold War and were careful to avoid situations that might develop into a third world war.

## ★ The Korean War

Such caution did not keep the United States out of war. However, the wars in which the United States became involved were limited in scope. A **limited war** is fought without using a country's full power, particularly nuclear weapons.

The two wars in which the United States participated during the Cold War years took place in Asia. They both occurred in countries that had been divided into communist and noncommunist portions. The first of these two wars was fought in Korea, which juts from eastern Asia into the Pacific Ocean.

As a result of an agreement reached after World War II, Korea was divided into communist North Korea and noncommunist South Korea. In June 1950 North Korea invaded South Korea in a surprise attack. Its goal was to reunite both parts of Korea as a communist country. North Korea was equipped with Soviet weapons. Chinese troops later began helping the North Koreans.

The U.S. government called on the United Nations to halt the invasion. The UN Security Council, with the Soviet Union absent, held a special session. It voted to send military assistance to the South Koreans.

Troops from the United States and 15 other members of the United Nations helped defend South Korea. By July 1953, the conflict had reached a point where neither side could win a clear-cut victory. The two sides agreed that Korea would remain divided into communist North Korea and noncommunist South Korea. Tensions remain high between the two Korean countries.

✔ **Reading Check** Summarizing How did the Korean War end? Korea remained divided into communist North Korea and noncommunist South Korea.

## ★ The Vietnam War

Under agreements passed in 1954, several French colonies in Southeast Asia—Vietnam, Laos, and Cambodia—became independent. Vietnam, like Korea, was divided into a communist northern half and a noncommunist southern half. The agreements called for elections to be held throughout Vietnam in 1956 to reunite the country.

## BIOGRAPHY

### John Foster Dulles
#### (1888–1959)

John Foster Dulles was born in Washington, D.C. Dulles attended Princeton University and became a lawyer. During World War I and World War II, Dulles advised the government on foreign affairs.

In 1952 President Dwight D. Eisenhower appointed Dulles as secretary of state. For the next seven years, Dulles played a key role in shaping U.S. foreign policy during the Cold War. Dulles argued that the United States had to "roll back" communist expansion around the globe. He also supported the threat of nuclear attack as a political tool and sponsored U.S. covert operations that toppled governments in Iran and Guatemala.

When Dulles died in 1959, diplomats, foreign ministers, prime ministers, and kings attended the services. Although he was not always liked by his enemies or his allies, Dulles had earned their respect. **What role did Dulles play during the Cold War?**

## ★ Global Perspectives

**The Hot Line** During the Cuban missile crisis, the Soviet ambassador to Washington used a bicycle courier to carry messages for transmission to the USSR to the Western Union office. In 1963, President Kennedy proposed that the United States and the Soviet Union set up a "hotline" between their capitals. The original hotline was a direct teletype link in the Pentagon, with instantaneous translation at both ends. The hotline's main purpose was to prevent accidental war—such as a premature launch of nuclear missiles. The hotline was first used in a crisis during the Arab-Israeli Six-Day War of 1967. Soviet premier Aleksey Kosygin used the hotline to ask President Lyndon Johnson whether the U.S. was involved in Israel's attack on Egypt. Johnson and Kosygin exchanged 20 messages in an effort to prevent the conflict from escalating into a nuclear war.

**ACTIVITY:** Ask students to conduct research to find out how the United States communicates with foreign countries in times of crisis today. Have students create a detailed diagram of these lines of communication.

---

**BIOGRAPHY ANSWER**
He helped create the Eisenhower Doctrine, supported using nuclear threat as a political tool, and helped topple governments in Iran and Guatemala.

**LEVELS 2 AND 3:** Ask students to think about the events that contributed to the fall of the Soviet Union and the end of the Cold War. *(See the Level 1 lesson for a list of events.)* Then ask students what they think was the most important factor in ending the Cold War. Have each student draw a political cartoon that illustrates the factor he or she has chosen. *(Students might choose events in Europe or cite U.S. policies that brought about the Cold War's end.)* Ask volunteers to explain their cartoons to the class.

## CLOSE

Organize students into small groups and assign each group one of the following topics: the Berlin blockade, the communist takeover in China, the Cuban missile crisis, the Korean War, or the Vietnam War. Have each group prepare a "You Are There" newscast about its assigned topic. Roles for students might include narrator, reporter, scriptwriter, story illustrator, and director. *(Each group's newscast should describe important actions and the role of U.S. policy in each event.)* Have each group present its newscast to the class.

*U.S. soldiers in Vietnam often faced a concealed enemy, hostile civilians, and a harsh environment.*

### ★ Global Perspectives

**The Tet Offensive** By the end of 1967, the United States appeared to be winning the war in Vietnam. Then, on January 31, 1968, the communist forces of North Vietnam began a major offensive throughout South Vietnam, capturing many cities, including the former imperial capital. The offensive took its name from Vietnam's most important holiday, the celebration of the lunar new year. The Tet Offensive was not a military success for the North Vietnamese, and U.S. forces eventually regained control of the captured cities. However, historians point to the Tet Offensive as a turning point in the war because it was a political and psychological victory for the communist forces. In the United States, news of the Tet Offensive shocked many people and increased public opposition to the war.

**ACTIVITY:** Ask students to conduct research to learn more about how the Tet Offensive affected antiwar protests in the United States. Have students write a position paper that argues whether the opinions of the American public should have played a role in ending U.S. involvement in Vietnam.

When the elections did not take place, communist guerillas revolted. Communist forces in the south were supported by troops and supplies from North Vietnam. The North Vietnamese received military supplies from the Soviet Union and China.

U.S. officials feared that if South Vietnam fell to the Communists, other countries of Southeast Asia might also fall. This belief became known as the domino theory. But how should these new forces of communism be contained? The United States began to send economic aid and military advisers to South Vietnam.

Gradually, the United States became more deeply involved. In 1964, at the request of President Lyndon B. Johnson, Congress passed the Gulf of Tonkin Resolution. The resolution gave President Johnson the power to take all necessary actions in Vietnam. Although the resolution was not an official declaration of war, U.S. combat troops were sent into action in South Vietnam. By 1968 nearly 550,000 Americans were fighting there.

The Vietnam War spurred heated debate in the United States. Those in favor of stronger military action argued that America's honor and position of world leadership were at stake. Opponents of the war maintained that its cost in lives and money was not justified.

Finally, in January 1973 a peace agreement was announced, and the war came to an end for the United States. The war had lasted more than eight years, killed some 58,000 Americans, and wounded more than 300,000. It cost nearly $140 billion. Despite the peace agreement, fighting continued in Vietnam. In 1975 the North Vietnamese Communists launched a new offensive, and South Vietnam fell. The northern Communist government controlled all of Vietnam.

✔ **Reading Check** Analyzing Information Why did the United States become involved in the Vietnam War, and why was its involvement controversial? U.S. officials worried that if South Vietnam fell to communists, other Southeast Asian countries would, too. Americans were divided over whether the war was justified.

### ★ The End of the Cold War

The Cold War dominated global politics for more than 40 years. The United States and the Soviet Union raced to secure alliances and to build their weapons capabilities. As a result, nearly every country in the world was drawn into the Cold War. This created an uneasy balance of power between the two countries, marked by distrust and hostility.

By 1985, however, this situation seemed likely to change. In that year, Mikhail Gorbachev became leader of the Soviet Union. Faced with a failing economy, citizen unrest, and a stifling political system, Gorbachev began a series of reforms. In 1987 he introduced a policy called **glasnost,** or openness, aimed at giving the Soviet people more freedom. His policy of **perestroika,** or restructuring, sought to improve the failing Soviet economy.

## REVIEW AND ASSESS

Have students complete the **Section 2 Review** on page 613. Then have students complete **Daily Quiz 24.2.** As **Alternative Assessment**, you may want to use the flowchart or the graffiti-mural activities in this section's lessons.

## RETEACH

Have students complete **Main Idea Activity for English Language Learners and Special-Needs Students 24.2.** Organize students into groups and assign each group a different event that brought about the end of the Cold War. Ask each group to create an outline explaining the significance of its assigned event. After groups have finished, collect the outlines

and place them in a folder for the class to use as a study guide.
**ENGLISH LANGUAGE LEARNERS**

## EXTEND

Have students research the roles of the United States and the Soviet Union in other crises or events of the Cold War. Some of these crises included Arab-Israeli conflicts, independence movements in Africa, civil war in El Salvador, and the Soviet invasion of Afghanistan. Some students might want to research events that fostered cooperation, such as the 1975 Apollo-Soyuz space mission and agreements regarding nuclear weapons. Encourage students to prepare their findings in a variety of ways, including maps, illustrations, collages, or news reports.
**BLOCK SCHEDULING**

Gorbachev's reform policies also included efforts at **détente,** or a lessening of tensions, between the United States and the Soviet Union. In 1987 the two countries signed a treaty agreeing to remove their medium-range nuclear weapons from Europe.

Encouraged by Soviet reforms, citizens in a number of Eastern European countries worked to overturn their communist governments. These citizens demanded democracy and free elections. By 1990 the communist governments in six Eastern European countries fell. Germany, divided into East and West since the end of World War II, was soon reunited.

Meanwhile, the Soviet Union opened local elections to parties other than the Communist Party for the first time. In 1990, prodemocracy candidates won many of these elections. Boris Yeltsin, for example, was elected president of the Soviet Union's largest republic, Russia.

Also in 1990 a number of Soviet republics rallied for independence from the Soviet Union. Although Gorbachev tried to keep the Soviet Union intact, this proved impossible. In 1991 the Soviet Union ceased to exist. The Commonwealth of Independent States (CIS), an organization designed to help the former Soviet republics address their common problems, replaced it. With the fall of communism in Eastern Europe and the collapse of the Soviet Union, the Cold War was over.

**Interpreting the Visual Record**

**The fall of the Wall** *The Berlin Wall, built in 1961 to separate communist East Berlin from democratic West Berlin, was torn down by prodemocracy advocates in 1989.* **How was this event a symbol of the end of the Cold War?**

✔ **Reading Check Summarizing** How did the Cold War end? Gorbachev introduced economic and political reforms, Eastern European countries overturned their communist governments, the Berlin Wall was torn down, Soviet republics rallied for independence, and the Soviet Union ceased to exist.

## SECTION 2 Review

**Homework Practice Online**
keyword: SZ3 HP24

1. **Define** and explain:
   - communism
   - satellite nations
   - containment
   - balance of power
   - limited war
   - glasnost
   - perestroika
   - détente

2. **Sequencing** Copy the time line below. Use it to list some of the important events of the Cold War in their proper order.

History of Communism

3. **Finding the Main Idea**
   a. Why did the Cold War start, and how did the United States respond?
   b. How did the United States react to Soviet actions in Berlin and Cuba?

4. **Writing and Critical Thinking**
   **Problem Solving** Write a newspaper article describing the end of the Cold War.

   **Consider:**
   - Gorbachev's reforms
   - the actions of communist countries in Eastern Europe
   - the Berlin Wall

---

**Visual Record Answer**
*Students might suggest that the wall represented Soviet control.*

## Section 2 Review
### ANSWERS

**1. Define**
- communism, p. 606
- satellite nations, p. 607
- containment, p. 609
- balance of power, p. 610
- limited war, p. 611
- glasnost, p. 612
- perestroika, p. 612
- détente, p. 613

**2.** Soviet creation of satellite nations; Truman's aid to Greece and Turkey; Berlin blockade; Communist Revolution in China; Cuban missile crisis; Korean War; Vietnam War; fall of the Berlin wall; dissolution of the Soviet Union

**3. a.** The Soviet Union began spreading communism throughout Eastern Europe. The United States sent financial and military aid.

**b.** The United States airlifted supplies; U.S. Navy blockaded Cuba.

**4.** Students' articles should consider Gorbachev's reforms, the actions of communist countries in Eastern Europe, and the fall of the Berlin Wall.

# SECTION 3

## OBJECTIVES

*After completing Section 3, students should be able to*

1 **Identify the new global challenges that the United States has faced since the end of the Cold War.**

2 **Describe how the United States was attacked on September 11, 2001, and identify the immediate suspect in the attacks.**

3 **Examine how the U.S. government responded to the terrorist attacks.**

## SECTION 3 RESOURCES

### REPRODUCIBLE

▶ Guided Reading Strategies 24.3

▶ Readings in Economics and Government 13: Open Door Policy in China

▶ American Civics Political Cartoon: The Vietnam War

▶ Creative Teaching Strategy: Issue Strip

▶ Community Service Participation Handbook: the First Televised War

### TECHNOLOGY

▶ One-Stop Planner, Lesson 24.3

▶ Citizenship Skills Videocassette Segment 2: Who Has the Power?

▶ Homework Practice Online

▶ HRW Go site

### REINFORCEMENT, REVIEW, AND ASSESSMENT

▶ Section 3 Review, p. 619

▶ Daily Quiz 24.3

▶ Main Idea Activity 24.3

▶ English Audio Summary 24.3

▶ Spanish Audio Summary 24.3

**614**

## 🔊 *LET'S GET STARTED!*

Write the phrase *Global Challenges* on the chalkboard. As students enter the classroom, ask them to list challenges that the United States has faced, or might yet face, in the post–Cold War world. Encourage students to explain their ideas to the class. *(Students might cite problems in Southwest Asia, civil wars in Eastern Europe, the threat of terrorism, and so on.)* Tell students that in Section 3 they will learn more about these new global challenges as well as about the attacks of September 11, 2001, and how the U.S. government responded.

---

# SECTION 3

# New Trends

## Read to Discover

1. What new global challenges has the United States faced since the end of the Cold War?
2. How was the United States attacked on September 11, 2001, and who was the immediate suspect in the attacks?
3. How did the U.S. government respond to the terrorist attacks?

## Define

• terrorists

## Identify

• War on Drugs
• World Trade Center
• Pentagon
• Northern Alliance

---

### WHY CIVICS MATTERS

Political situations in countries around the world are constantly changing. Use **CNNfyi.com** or other **current events** sources to research a foreign country's political situation and the effect changes have had on that country. Record your findings in your journal.

---

*The fall of communism in Russia and Eastern Europe brought many changes to the region.*

## *Reading Focus*

Dramatic events occurring in many parts of the world have led governments around the world to rethink their foreign policies. New policies are emerging to deal with current events and new trends. However, the primary goal of U.S. foreign policy remains the same—to promote peace, trade, and friendship throughout the world.

The end of the Cold War changed the way the United States conducts foreign relations. In the 1990s the United States became the world's only superpower. Since then, the U.S. government has played a greater peacekeeping role in world affairs. It has also worked to strengthen democracy, promote human rights, and negotiate peace in different parts of the world.

### ⭐ Russia and Eastern Europe

Since the end of the Cold War, Russia has struggled to transition to a free-market economy. Much money is needed to modernize outdated factories and equipment, stimulate entrepreneurship, and encourage foreign investment.

In 1995 Russia joined NATO's Partnership for Peace program. Russia now joins NATO in military exercises, peacekeeping operations,

# TEACH OBJECTIVE 1

**LEVEL 1:** Lead students in a class discussion about the new global challenges that the United States has faced since the end of the Cold War. *(These challenges have included playing a greater peacekeeping role, strengthening democracy, promoting human rights, and preventing terrorism throughout the world.)* Bring current newspapers and magazines to class. Then ask students to consult newspapers and magazines to find headlines and photographs or other images that represent these challenges. Have each student cut out examples and assemble them into a collage. Then encourage volunteers to explain their collages to the class.
**ENGLISH LANGUAGE LEARNERS**

**LEVEL 1:** Tell students that the new challenges faced by the United States are not only military issues but also issues of trade and humanitarianism. *(See the Level 1 lesson for a list of these challenges.)* Organize students into pairs. Ask each pair of students to draw three political cartoons illustrating a different challenge that the United States has faced since the end of the Cold War. *(Students might illustrate new military challenges with a picture of a soldier in Kuwait, new trade agreements with a picture of a truck driving across the Mexican border, and new humanitarian challenges with a picture of medical supplies being delivered to Africa.)* Invite volunteers to explain their cartoons to the class. **ENGLISH LANGUAGE LEARNERS** ,

**COOPERATIVE LEARNING**

and other activities as preparation for possible future membership in NATO. The United States and Russia have worked to define a new relationship. At the end of 2001, President George W. Bush announced that the United States would withdraw from the Anti-Ballistic Missile Treaty that the Soviet Union and the United States had signed in 1972. Bush explained that the treaty was no longer the best way to ensure national security. However, Russian and U.S. leaders continue to communicate on global issues.

In other former communist countries, U.S. foreign policy has focused on helping governments and other groups resolve conflicts. After the collapse of the Soviet Union, ethnic divisions in parts of Eastern Europe have resulted in violence. For example, ethnic conflict and war have devastated the southeastern European region of the former Yugoslavia since the early 1990s. The United States worked to promote stability by helping the groups involved negotiate a peace agreement in Dayton, Ohio, in 1995. When new conflicts in the region arose, the United States participated in a series of NATO-led air strikes in March 1999. In June 1999 NATO and Yugoslavia reached an agreement that would end the conflict. Russia also played a role in the peace process. After the breakup of the Soviet Union, several Eastern European nations established democratic governments and became members of NATO. NATO's actions in Yugoslavia represented its first efforts as an expanded organization.

✔ **Reading Check Summarizing** Describe U.S. relations with Russia and Eastern Europe since the end of the Cold War. The United States and Russia continue to work together on global issues. In other parts of Eastern Europe, the United States has worked to promote peace.

## ★ Southwest and South Asia

Southwest Asia is particularly important to the global economy because it contains much of the world's oil. The United States has also worked to resolve conflicts in South Asia.

**Iraq** On August 2, 1990, Iraqi tanks and ground troops invaded Kuwait. Iraqi leader Saddam Hussein claimed that Kuwait belonged to Iraq. In early 1991 the United States led an international coalition in a ground and air assault on Iraq. The U.S.-allied victory in the Persian Gulf War freed Kuwait from Iraqi control. However, Hussein remained

**Interpreting the Visual Record**

**Gulf War** *During Operation Desert Storm, U.S.-led coalition forces quickly overcame Iraqi defenders. Thousands of Iraqi soldiers were captured.* **How did the Persian Gulf War affect the region?**

Some New Global Challenges

free trade

AIDS in Africa

terrorism

United States

Nuclear arms in India and Pakistan

war on drugs

conflicts between Israel and Palestinians

in power and failed to keep some of the cease-fire terms. Saddam Hussein continued to refuse UN demands for open arms inspections. In March 2003, the United States and allied forces moved into Iraq and removed Hussein from power.

**Israel** Another area that has been plagued by troubles is Israel and its surrounding Arab neighbors. A major source of conflict has been tension between Israelis and Palestinians. Palestine is a small eastern Mediterranean region that was ruled by Great Britain from World War I until the nation of Israel was created in 1948. U.S. officials have worked for years to help bring about lasting peace in the area. In September 1993 President Bill Clinton hosted the signing of a historic peace agreement between Israeli prime minister Yitzhak Rabin and Palestinian leader Yasir Arafat. The agreement set guidelines for Palestinian self-rule in occupied areas of Israel. No final agreements about the creation of a Palestinian state were reached, however. In 2003 violence again broke out between Palestinians and Israelis, leaving the future of the peace process uncertain.

✔ **Reading Check Contrasting** How have U.S. relations with Iraq and Israel differed? The United States has had continued conflict with Iraq and continues to work with Israel to resolve conflicts with Palestinians.

**India and Pakistan** India and Pakistan have fought three wars since the two countries won their independence from Great Britain in 1947. The possibility of conflict between India and Pakistan again became an issue when both countries tested nuclear arms in 1998. At first, the United States responded by imposing economic sanctions on India and Pakistan. However, recent diplomatic efforts have shifted to promoting better communication and easing tensions between the two countries.

✔ **Reading Check Finding the Main Idea** What events have shaped U.S. foreign policy toward India and Pakistan? conflicts between the two countries and the testing of nuclear arms

**China** The People's Republic of China is one of the world's few remaining communist countries. However, China has introduced many free-market reforms. Disagreements over trade practices continue, but American businesses look to expand trade with China. U.S. leaders continue to follow China's human rights record following crackdowns on government protesters in the 1980s.

✔ **Reading Check Analyzing Information** What recent reforms has the Chinese government introduced? free-market reforms

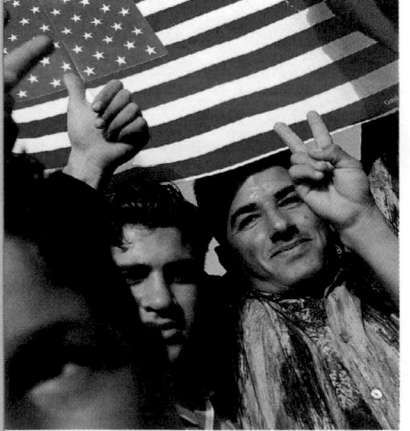

*Iraqis celebrate the liberation of Baghdad and the removal of Saddam Hussein from power.*

## ★ Africa

For decades, South Africa operated under a system of apartheid, or separation of the races. Under apartheid, white South Africans held all

**LEVELS 2 AND 3:** Ask students to imagine they must give a speech before Congress about a major global challenge facing the United States. Tell each student to write a speech urging Congress to address this challenge.

## TEACH OBJECTIVE 2

**LEVEL 1:** Lead students in a discussion about how the United States was attacked on September 11, 2001, and who the immediate suspects were. *(Terrorists hijacked four commercial jets and crashed them into the World Trade Center and the Pentagon. The fourth jet crashed in a field in Pennsylvania. The immediate suspect was Osama bin Laden.)* Then organize students into pairs. Ask each pair to draw a map of the United States, identify the locations of the attacks, and diagram the immediate U.S. response to these attacks. **ENGLISH LANGUAGE LEARNERS , COOPERATIVE LEARNING**

**LEVEL 3:** Ask each student to write a newspaper editorial explaining the significance of the events of September 11, 2001. Have students conjecture what the terrorists thought they were accomplishing, and consider how the terrorist attacks have changed the United States and the world.

**HOMEWORK** Ask students to conduct research to learn how people in their own community have reacted to or been changed by the events of September 11, 2001. Have each student write a brief poem based on this research.

---

political, social, and economic power but made up a minority of the population. The United States and other countries around the world condemned the system of apartheid. Apartheid officially ended in 1993. The country's first free elections were held in 1994. Anti-apartheid leader Nelson Mandela became the new president of South Africa.

In South Africa and other parts of sub-Saharan Africa, the spread of acquired immune deficiency syndrome (AIDS) is a major concern. All countries have battled the AIDS epidemic. However, 70 percent of the adults and 80 percent of the children diagnosed with HIV live in Africa. The U.S. government has given money toward AIDS prevention and care in Africa and other parts of the world.

✔ **Reading Check Drawing Inferences and Conclusions** Why do you think foreign-policy leaders are concerned about the AIDS epidemic? Foreign aid for problems such as epidemics is part of U.S. diplomacy.

## ⭐ Latin America and Canada

The main goal of U.S. foreign policy in Latin America today is to expand trade and open new markets. NAFTA and free-trade issues continue to shape relations between Canada, Mexico, and the United States. The United States is also interested in forming similar economic alliances with Central and South American countries. Immigration policy and border security are important issues as well.

Fighting drug trafficking has also shaped U.S. policy in Latin America. The **War on Drugs**—an organized effort to end the trade and use of illegal drugs—began in the 1970s. It has become an important part of U.S.-Latin American relations. U.S. foreign aid to some Latin American countries has sometimes been earmarked for fighting drug production and trafficking. Colombia is the world's leading supplier of cocaine and a significant source of heroin. The U.S. government has worked closely with Colombian officials to address this problem, and Congress has authorized funds to help Colombia fight drug-related problems.

Cuba is the only communist country in Latin America. The United States had put into place an embargo, or government order forbidding trade, against Cuba. However, the U.S. government now allows the donation of humanitarian supplies such as medicine, food, and clothing. It also sells medical supplies to Cuba. The U.S. government continues to work with other countries to encourage the Cuban government to adopt a more democratic form of government.

✔ **Reading Check Summarizing** What have been some key features of U.S. relations with Canada and Latin America? trade, immigration and border issues, the War on Drugs, and promoting democracy in Cuba

**Interpreting the Visual Record**

**Diplomacy** *President George W. Bush meets with Colombian president Andrés Pastrana (at left). In 1999 Pastrana created Plan Colombia, which seeks to provide Colombians with economic alternatives to the drug industry.* **Why are relations with Colombia important to the United States?**

**LEVEL 1:** Lead students in a class discussion about the U.S. response to the terrorist attacks of September 11, 2001. Then, organize the class into two groups. Ask the first group to list what the United States did domestically to respond to terrorist threats. Ask the second group to list the foreign-policy actions that the United States took. *(The first group might mention the creation of the Office of Homeland Security and the presence of soldiers from the National Guard at airports. The second group might mention NATO invoking article 5 of its original treaty and the U.S. invasion of Afghanistan.)*
**ENGLISH LANGUAGE LEARNERS , COOPERATIVE LEARNING**

**LEVEL 3:** Ask students to imagine that they have been asked to make recommendations to the Office of Homeland Security on how to protect U.S. citizens from terrorist attacks. Have each student write a proposal listing security measures that he or she thinks the United States should take to protect itself from future acts of terrorism.

## CLOSE

Have students consider the prospects for peace in the post–Cold War era. Ask them to make a chart with two columns, labeled *Conflict* and *Peace.* In the appropriate column, have students list each area of the world discussed in this section and describe its status.

## ★ Civics Sidelight

**Domestic Terrorism** Prior to September 11, 2001, the deadliest terrorist attack in the United States occurred on April 19, 1995, when a bomb inside a rented truck exploded outside the Alfred P. Murrah Federal Building in Oklahoma City, killing 169 people and injuring hundreds. The bombing was perpetrated by U.S. citizen Timothy McVeigh, who was believed to be motivated by antigovernment feelings. Ultimately, McVeigh and his accomplice, Terry Nichols, were convicted of the crime, and McVeigh received the death penalty. A third accomplice, Michael Fortier, pleaded guilty to lesser charges in exchange for his testimony. A monument to the victims has been erected on the site where the federal building once stood. The Oklahoma City bombing remains an important reminder that terrorism in the United States can have domestic origins.

**CRITICAL THINKING**

What steps can the Office of Homeland Security take to protect U.S. citizens from domestic terrorism?

**ANSWER:** Students should consider the difficulty of preserving the freedoms of U.S. citizens while maintaining security.

**Visual Record Answer**

*Students might suggest that they risked their lives to save others.*

**Interpreting the Visual Record**

**Rescue workers** *Firefighters, emergency medical teams, and other rescue workers spent weeks searching the World Trade Center site for survivors.* **How did the efforts of these workers show their dedication and heroism?**

## ★ September 11: A Changed World

On Tuesday morning, September 11, 2001, the United States experienced an event that shocked American citizens and leaders. **Terrorists** —individuals who use violence to achieve political goals—hijacked four U.S. commercial airliners. The terrorists crashed two planes into the **World Trade Center**, a business complex in New York City. The twin towers of the center collapsed as a result. The third plane hit the **Pentagon**—the headquarters of the U.S. military leadership. The fourth plane crashed in rural Pennsylvania. Thousands of people were killed in the attacks.

In a national address, President George W. Bush called the terrorist attacks an act of war. He promised that the United States would bring those responsible to justice and wage war on terrorist organizations and the national governments that supported terrorism. Bush declared,

❝We have suffered great loss. And in our grief and anger we have found our mission and our moment. Freedom and fear are at war. The advance of human freedom . . . now depends on us. . . . We will not tire, . . . . and we will not fail.❞

Bush appointed Governor Tom Ridge of Pennsylvania as head of the Office of Homeland Security, a new cabinet-level position. This office was created to coordinate the domestic national security efforts of various government agencies. Key goals included improving airport security and protecting vital systems such as transportation and power networks from attack. Political leaders such as U.S. attorney general John Ashcroft also called for expanded law-enforcement powers to combat terrorism.

A prime suspect in the attacks surfaced almost immediately—Osama bin Laden. This wealthy Saudi Arabian exile was already wanted for his suspected role in earlier terrorist attacks against U.S. forces overseas. A supporter of an extreme form of Islamic fundamentalism, bin Laden claimed that the United States had corrupted and oppressed Muslims. Bin Laden's global terrorism network is known as al Qaeda, or "the Base." Officials later produced evidence linking bin Laden to the attacks.

U.S. officials then singled out the Taliban regime of Afghanistan as a key sponsor of terrorism. Osama bin Laden was in Afghanistan when the terrorist attacks occurred. President Bush called for the Taliban to turn bin Laden over to U.S. officials or face retaliation.

## REVIEW AND ASSESS

Have students complete the **Section 3 Review** on page 619. Then have students complete **Daily Quiz 24.3**. As **Alternative Assessment**, you may want to use the political-cartoon or the newspaper-editorial activity in this section's lessons.

## RETEACH

Have students complete **Main Idea Activity for English Language Learners and Special-Needs Students 24.3**. Then give each student five index cards. Ask students to write a different global challenge that the United States has faced since the end of the Cold War on one side of each and write the U.S. response to the challenge on the other side. Pair students and have them quiz each other using the index cards as flash cards.

**ENGLISH LANGUAGE LEARNERS**, **COOPERATIVE LEARNING**

## EXTEND

Have students conduct research to contrast U.S. involvement in the Persian Gulf War with U.S. involvement in the conflict in former Yugoslavia. Remind students that the Persian Gulf War was fought after Iraq invaded Kuwait, and that the conflict in Yugoslavia was a civil war. Explain that U.S. policy makers debated the wisdom of intervention in each conflict. Ask each student to write a well-supported report that argues whether the United States was justified in getting involved in these conflicts. **BLOCK SCHEDULING**

---

### ★ Fighting Terrorism

Secretary of State Colin Powell led U.S. efforts to build an international coalition against terrorism. The leaders of countries such as Great Britain and Russia pledged their support. For the first time in its existence, NATO invoked Article 5 of its original treaty, which required members to come to the defense of an ally under attack. Even former allies of the Taliban regime supported U.S. efforts. Pakistan and Saudi Arabia were two such countries.

On October 7, 2001, the United States and Great Britain began air strikes against al Qaeda and Taliban targets in Afghanistan. The **Northern Alliance**, an Afghan group that had fought against the Taliban since the early 1990s, provided ground support. U.S. and British ground troops soon followed. As the troops advanced, they slowly drove out the Taliban and captured members of al Qaeda. On December 17, 2001, the American flag was raised at the U.S. embassy in Kabul for the first time since 1989.

Meanwhile, the international community worked with the Afghan people to help establish a new government. Hamid Karzai, an Afghan tribal chief and political leader, was sworn in as leader of the interim government on December 21. Karzai welcomed international peacekeeping forces to maintain peace and stability in Afghanistan.

Since the September 11 terrorist attacks, fighting terrorism has become a central part of U.S. foreign policy. However, the main goals of U.S. foreign policy—promoting peace, democracy, and trade—remain the same. New situations and new problems will continue to challenge U.S. policy makers.

*Tom Ridge, Director of the Department of Homeland Security, was a strong supporter of the 2003 Patriot Act, which gave additional powers to law enforcement agencies to help fight terrorism.*

✔ **Reading Check** Analyzing Information How did the United States respond to the September 11 terrorist attacks? When the Taliban did not turn over Osama bin Laden, the United States attacked Afghanistan and toppled the Taliban. Fighting terrorism has become an important part of U.S. foreign policy.

---

## SECTION 3 Review

**go.** **Homework**
**hrw** **Practice**
**.com** **Online**
keyword: SZ3 HP24

1. **Define** and explain:
   • terrorists

2. **Identify** and explain:
   • War on Drugs
   • World Trade Center
   • Pentagon
   • Northern Alliance

3. **Categorizing** Copy the chart below. Use it to list the issues that have shaped U.S. foreign policy since the end of the Cold War. Add lines as necessary.

| Country/Region | Issue |
|---|---|
|  |  |
|  |  |

4. **Finding the Main Idea**
   a. What happened on September 11, 2001?
   b. What was the U.S. response to the events of September 11?

5. **Writing and Critical Thinking**
   **Making Generalizations and Predictions**
   Imagine that you are a foreign-policy adviser to the president. Write a memo to the president explaining what foreign-policy issues will be important in the future. Be sure to explain your choices.

   **Consider:**
   • international trade
   • diseases and ethnic conflict
   • terrorism

---

---

### Section 3 Review ANSWERS

**1. Define**
• terrorists, p. 618

**2. Identify**
• War on Drugs, p. 617
• World Trade Center, p. 618
• Pentagon, p. 618
• Northern Alliance, p. 619

**3.** Russia and Eastern Europe—threat of war and transition to a free-market economy; Southwest and South Asia—resolving conflicts and maintaining access to oil; Africa—racial issues, AIDS; Latin America and Canada—maintaining trade

**4. a.** Terrorists hijacked four commercial jet airliners and crashed them into the World Trade Center and the Pentagon. A fourth plane crashed in a field in Pennsylvania.

**b.** The United States led an international coalition in military strikes against the Taliban government of Afghanistan for supporting Osama bin Laden and refusing to turn him over to the United States.

**5.** Students should consider such issues as international trade, diseases and ethnic conflict, and terrorism.

# Review and Assessment Resources

## REVIEW

Have students complete the
**Chapter 24 Review** on pages
620–21.

## ASSESS

Use one of the chapter tests to
assess students' understanding
of the content. For **Alternative
Assessment**, see the **Alternative
Assessment Handbook**.

---

## CHAPTER 24
### REVIEW ANSWERS

**Define and Identify**
1. isolationism, p. 597
2. dollar diplomacy, p. 600
3. communism, p. 606
4. containment, p. 609
5. balance of power, p. 610
6. glasnost, p. 612
7. détente, p. 613
8. War on Drugs, p. 617
9. World Trade Center, p. 618
10. Northern Alliance, p. 619

**Understanding
Main Ideas**

**1.** The United States was in debt
and needed to develop its economy and solve domestic problems; isolationism became
impractical because of tensions
with other countries.

**2.** The United States entered
World War I after U.S. ships were
attacked by German submarines;
the United States entered World
War II after the Japanese
attacked Pearl Harbor.

**3.** to stop the Soviet Union from
imposing Soviet-dominated communist governments throughout
the world

**4.** The United States and Great
Britain airlifted supplies into
Berlin during the blockade; the
U.S. Navy stopped and searched
all ships bound for Cuba during
the Cuban missile crisis.

---

# Chapter 24 Review

## Chapter Summary

### Section 1

- The foreign policy of the United States has
  transformed from one of strict isolationism
  to deep involvement in foreign affairs.

- In the 1900s the United States entered into
  two world wars, which signaled the end of
  isolationism for the United States.

### Section 2

- After World War II, a worldwide struggle
  between communist and noncommunist
  countries known as the Cold War emerged.

- Under a policy of containment, the United
  States tried to stop the spread of communism through economic and military aid to
  at-risk countries.

- In the late 1900s the Cold War ended with
  the fall of communism in Eastern Europe,
  the collapse of the Berlin Wall, and the
  breakup of the Soviet Union.

### Section 3

- The United States has revised its foreign
  policy to accommodate past and ongoing
  changes throughout the world with the
  basic goal of promoting peace, friendship,
  and trade worldwide.

- After terrorists attacked the World Trade
  Center and the Pentagon on September 11,
  2001, the U.S. government demanded that
  the Taliban turn over Osama bin Laden.
  The United States and Great Britain then
  launched a military offensive against
  Afghanistan and drove the Taliban from
  power.

## Define and Identify
Use the following terms in complete sentences.
1. isolationism          6. glasnost
2. dollar diplomacy      7. détente
3. communism             8. War on Drugs
4. containment           9. World Trade Center
5. balance of power     10. Northern Alliance

## Understanding Main Ideas
**Section 1** *(Pages 597–602)*
1. Why did many U.S. officials favor isolationism,
   and why was this policy difficult to follow?
2. What caused the United States to lose neutrality
   in the world wars?

**Section 2** *(Pages 606–13)*
3. Why did the United States pursue a policy of
   containment?
4. What was the U.S. response to the Berlin blockade and the Cuban missile crisis?

**Section 3** *(Pages 614–19)*
5. What new foreign-policy challenges have
   emerged since the Cold War ended?
6. What actions did the U.S. government take after
   the terrorist attacks on September 11, 2001?

## What Did You Find Out?
1. How did U.S. foreign policy change in the early
   years of the country?
2. What was the Cold War, and how did it influence U.S. foreign policy?
3. What recent world affairs have caused the
   United States to revise its foreign policy, and
   what types of changes have been made?

## Thinking Critically
1. **Drawing Inferences and Conclusions** Isolationism
   was not written about in the Declaration of
   Independence or the Constitution. If the founders
   of the United States were alive today, would
   they promote isolationism or U.S. involvement
   in global affairs? Support your answer.
2. **Supporting a Point of View** After the terrorist
   attacks of September 11, 2001, some people
   have called for increases in military spending to
   fight terrorism. Do you agree with this strategy?
   Explain your answer.
3. **Making Generalizations and Predictions** How
   do you think international trade and economic
   issues might affect the political situations in
   China and Cuba?

## RETEACH

Organize students into three groups and assign each group one of the chapter's sections. Then have each group create a chart explaining the main objectives in its assigned section.

**ENGLISH LANGUAGE LEARNERS ,
COOPERATIVE LEARNING**

## Portfolio Extensions

*American Civics*

**1. Interdisciplinary Connection to Art and Literature** Point out to students that Cold War tensions were felt in a variety of ways. Ask students to conduct research to find books, movies, art or music created during the Cold War. Then have students choose one artwork and examine how it reflects the anxieties and concerns of people during the Cold War era. *(For example, students might choose a film such as* The Manchurian Candidate *or a pop song such as Sting's "Russians.")* Have each student create a poster illustrating the themes in the work he or she has chosen.

**2. Cooperative Learning** Organize students into two groups. Assign one group the topic of isolationism. Assign the other group the topic of foreign intervention. Have each group create a chart presenting the positive and negative aspects of isolationism and foreign intervention. Then ask each group to present its arguments to the class.

---

## Building Social Studies Skills

**STANDARDIZED TEST PREP ONLINE** keyword: SZ3 STP24

### Interpreting Maps

Study the map below and answer the questions.

**Breakup of the Soviet Sphere**

1. Which of the following countries were former republics of the Soviet Union?
   a. Czechoslovakia, Estonia, Hungary, and Poland
   b. Bulgaria, Romania, Russia, and Serbia
   c. Belarus, Latvia, Lithuania, and Ukraine
   d. Finland, Germany, Moldavia, and Russia

2. How do you think the breakup of the Soviet sphere affected U.S. foreign policy?

### Analyzing Primary Sources

Read the following quotation from Secretary of State Colin Powell. Then answer the questions that follow.

> "NATO continues to enhance stability and security throughout the Euro-Atlantic area. Since the end of the Cold War, NATO has sought to build closer ties with Russia as a means of increasing that security. Today, the Alliance discussed ways to enhance our partnership with Russia. . . . We have made great strides since the end of the Cold War in overcoming divisions of the past and reaching out to former adversaries. But we have yet to complete our vision of a Europe whole, free and at peace. . . . NATO will continue to anchor the continent's new democracies firmly in the transatlantic community and to ensure the success of democratic institutions and the democratic transition process."

3. Which of the following is NOT a key function of NATO as described by Secretary Powell?
   a. Changing relationships with former enemies
   b. Promoting and protecting security, stability, and democracy in Europe
   c. Promoting economic cooperation between Europe and North America
   d. Building a better relationship with Russia

4. What does Secretary Powell's statement reveal about how U.S. foreign policy has changed in the past 10 years?

5. Russia and Eastern Europe— threat of war and transition to a free-market economy; Southwest and South Asia—resolving conflicts and maintaining access to oil; Africa—racial issues; Latin America and Canada— maintaining trade; fighting terrorism around the world

6. The United States created the Office of Homeland Security to improve airport security and protect vital systems from attack, expanded law enforcement to fight terrorism, identified Osama bin Laden as the organizer of the attacks, called on the Taliban to turn Osama bin Laden over to U.S. officials, attacked Afghanistan, and drove the Taliban out of power.

### What Did You Find Out?

1. became less isolationist and began intervening more in the affairs of other countries

2. the struggle for world dominance between the United States and the communist Soviet Union; led the United States to spend money and use its military to contain communism around the globe

3. the spread of terrorism and the attacks of September 11, 2001; fighting terrorism is a main goal of U.S. foreign policy

### Thinking Critically

Students should support their answers with sound reasoning and specific examples.

### Social Studies Skills

1. c

2. Students should support their answers.

3. c

4. building closer ties with Russia; promoting peace and security in Europe

---

### Alternative Assessment

**Building Your Portfolio**

*American Civics*

**Linking to Community**

Create a poster about the effects of the Cold War on your community or state. Conduct newspaper research or interviews to find out if many people were employed in defense-related industries and how the Cold War's end affected their jobs. If people feared nuclear war, how did this fear affect them? Do they still have the same fears? Title your poster and label any images.

**internet connect**

**Internet Activity: go.hrw.com
keyword: SZ3 AC24**

Access the Internet through the HRW Go site to research the causes and effects of the decline of communism in the world. Then create a pamphlet that explains the reasons for the decline of communism, the global effects, and the struggle of former communist countries to rebuild their societies.

## TEACH

**LEVEL 1:** Tell students that the U.S. Congress is not sure whether it should recognize the new nation of New Populous described in the Civics Lab. Then organize students into pairs and ask them to imagine that they have been hired by the New Populous government to run a public-relations campaign aimed at convincing the U.S. government to recognize the country. Ask each pair to design a series of bumper stickers that display slogans explaining why it would be beneficial for the United States to establish foreign relations with New Populous. **ENGLISH LANGUAGE LEARNERS**

**ALL LEVELS:** Remind students that U.S. foreign policy involves a range of strategies and programs, including financial aid. Then ask students to imagine that they are members of the U.S. Congress and that the nation of New Populous has requested financial aid to help it rebuild its capital after a terrible hurricane. Organize students into two groups, *for* and *against*, and ask students in each group to write brief arguments supporting or rejecting this request for aid. Encourage students to support their arguments with specific reasons. Then invite volunteers to debate their positions in front of the class.

**ENGLISH LANGUAGE LEARNERS , COOPERATIVE LEARNING**

## APPLYING THE SKILLS

Ask students to use the information they obtained in the Civics Lab exercise to create an effective argument for why the United Nations should encourage more nations around the world to become members. Have each student write a brief position paper, and encourage each student to cite specific reasons and examples to support his or her arguments. Ask volunteers to read their papers to the class.

# Civics Lab

## A New Nation

Complete the following Civics Lab activity individually or in a group.

## Your Task

In Unit 7 you read about some of the foreign policy issues that the United States faces. Imagine that you are a foreign policy official in the government of New Populous, the newest nation on Earth. You and your fellow officials want to apply to the United Nations for membership. Your application should include visual as well as written materials. To prepare these materials, you will need to do the following.

## What to Do

**STEP 1** **Write** a background profile of your country. Include the following information: the country's location, land area, population, capital city, form of government, and foreign policy goals. These goals may include issues such as free trade or limited trade, cooperation or competition, and so on.

**ALL LEVELS:** Have each student create a graphic organizer shaped like a wagonwheel to explain the importance of foreign policy. Tell students to place the *United States* at the center of the wheel. Then ask students to write, at the end of each spoke, a different reason for maintaining good relations with foreign countries. **ENGLISH LANGUAGE LEARNERS**

**LEVEL 3:** Remind students that sometimes the United States has difficulty maintaining good relations with foreign countries that violate civil rights, break trade agreements, and so on. Then ask each student to draw a political cartoon illustrating some of the reasons why the United States might not support the nation of New Populous as it is described in the Civics Lab.

**STEP 2** **Draw** a map of your country showing its borders, lakes, rivers, deserts, mountains, major cities, and neighboring countries. Label your map carefully so that it is easy for others to read.

**STEP 3** **Draw** a sketch of the New Populous flag. The flag's design should reflect some aspect of the history or culture of the country. Attach a small sheet explaining the reasons why the symbols or colors of the flag were chosen.

**STEP 4** **Create** a four-column chart of the alliances you hope to pursue. The first column should be titled *Allies*. It should list the country or group of countries with which New Populous hopes to ally itself. The second column should be titled *Alliance Type* and should explain the kind of alliance you are seeking. The third column should be titled *Benefits*. Here you should list the benefits that New Populous will gain from these alliances. Finally, the fourth column should be titled *Contributions*. This is where you explain the contributions that New Populous will make to the other members of the alliance.

Organize your materials, and make your presentation to the United Nations (the rest of the class).

| Alliances | | | |
|---|---|---|---|
| Allies | Alliance Type | Benefits | Contributions |
| | | | |

**A STEP FURTHER**

Ask students to imagine that they are working for a presidential candidate and that they have been asked to chart a course for New Populous's foreign policy for the next decade. Have each student prepare a press packet of information about his or her candidate's plans for foreign policy. Students' press packets should also include brief quotes or slogans that represent their candidates' positions on various foreign-policy issues. Students might also include flyers or handouts that highlight what they think are the most important foreign-policy issues facing New Populous over the next 10 years. Ask volunteers to present their press packets to the class.

**UNIT OVERVIEW**

Unit 8 explores the issues facing the United States in the coming years. Americans have already taken steps to meet some of the challenges, but more must be done. In this unit students discover how they may work to improve their communities and to secure the civil rights, health, and safety of all citizens. They also investigate the need to protect the resources of planet Earth.

## In Their Own Words

*"I think you and I must look at contemporary America, examine the communities we are a part of and activate ourselves as citizens, not just the kind of citizens that demand rights or support the demand of rights for others but citizens who call upon ourselves to act out of civic virtue. We need to rethink contemporary civic virtue all over this country, community by community, and commit ourselves to making the ideals we studied in those founding documents come closer to reality in the lives of Americans today."*—Claire L. Gaudiani

**Using the Quotation** Have students read the quotation to think about what it asks of them as citizens, now and in the future. Explain that Gaudiani wants citizens "to act out of civic virtue." Discuss possible meanings for this phrase while considering her reference to the ideals of the founding documents. Ask: What are some of these ideals?

**About the Author** Claire L. Gaudiani (1944– ) became president of Connecticut College in 1988. In addition to her numerous academic accomplishments, she has been a strong advocate of what she calls "global civic virtues." She also has been a strong advocate of volunteerism and of increased efforts to make a college education more accessible to everyone.

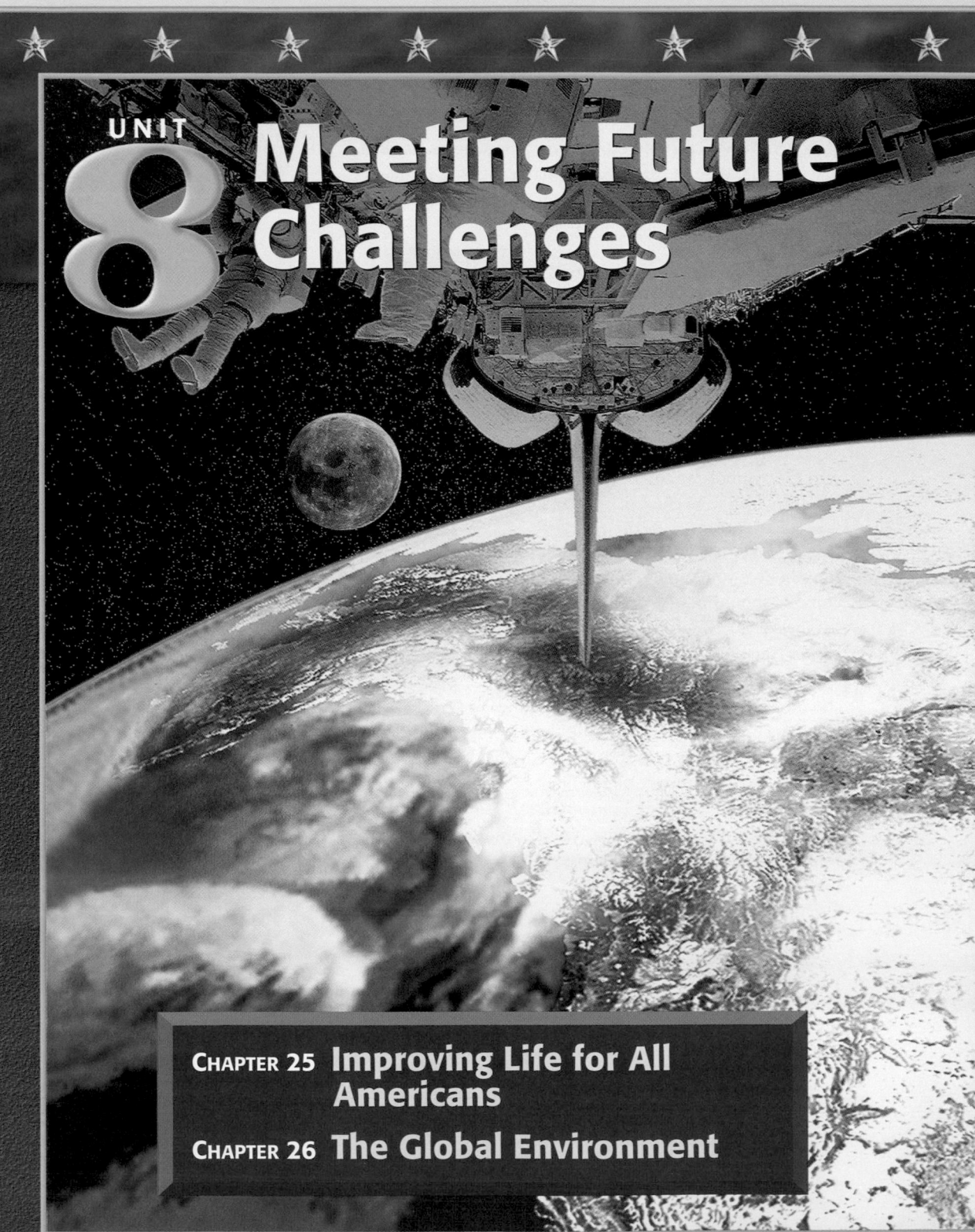

UNIT

8 Meeting Future Challenges

CHAPTER 25 **Improving Life for All Americans**

CHAPTER 26 **The Global Environment**

Ask students to list some of the major problems that they think the U.S. government and society will have to face in the future. Have them consider civil rights, health issues, safety concerns, economic concerns, and environmental issues. Then ask students to write some suggestions for how each of these issues might be addressed. After finishing this unit, have students compare their lists with what they have learned.

# Young Citizens

## IN ACTION

### Tree Musketeers

In the spring of 1987, Tara Church and 12 other Brownie troop members in California took a stand for conservation. They planted a tree to offset the use of some 15,000 paper plates at an upcoming Brownie event. The tree became known as Marcie the Marvelous Tree and marked the creation of a new environmental group—the Tree Musketeers. It was the first known nonprofit group organized and led by young people.

Church and the Tree Musketeers continued to show that young people can help protect the environment. When she was 12 years old, Church convinced the U.S. Forest Service and the Environmental Protection Agency to fund an environmental conference for young people. With the help of a team of 12 young adults, the Tree Musketeers held the first National Youth Environmental Summit in 1993. Some 600 children and adults from around the world attended the conference. Church later explained how the conference's success influenced her understanding of the environmental movement. "There is a generation of youth out there who are environmentally and socially conscious."

Church and the Tree Musketeers literally planted the seed for various programs to improve the environment. One such program was the three-year, tree-planting One In A Million Campaign. When the program concluded in November 2000, it had motivated 1 million kids to plant more than 1 million trees across the United States. The Tree Musketeers continue to bring together youths to promote environmental goals.

Here, environmentally conscious teens plant trees to improve the community.

### You Decide

1. What did the planting of Marcie the Marvelous Tree symbolize?
2. What role do young people have in shaping the world's future?

## What Can We Do?

Ask students to conduct research about volunteer youth programs available in their community that focus on improving and protecting the environment. Then have students find ways that they can get involved in improving the environment. Students might volunteer to plant trees, help to clean up a public park, attend public meetings on environmental issues, or write letters to government agencies. Encourage students to think of environmental concerns that are not being addressed in their community, and ask them to write a proposal explaining how they can start a local organization to help bring attention to these concerns.

**YOU DECIDE ANSWERS**

1. It symbolized the beginning of the Tree Musketeers, the first known nonprofit group organized by youths.

2. Students' responses will vary.

# CHAPTER 25
# Improving Life for All Americans
## CHAPTER RESOURCE MANAGER

| Objectives | Pacing Guide | Reproducible Resources |
|---|---|---|
| **SECTION 1:**<br>**Improving Communities**<br>(pp. 627–33)<br><br>⊡ Explain why people have been moving away from the central cities and how this move has affected the urban areas.<br>⊡ Describe the actions taken to reverse urban decay.<br>⊡ Analyze how the nature of homelessness has changed in recent years and why it has increased. | **Regular**<br>1 day<br><br>**Block Scheduling**<br>.5 day<br><br>*Block Scheduling Handbook with Team Teaching Strategies, Chapter 25* | **RS** Guided Reading Strategies 25.1<br>**RS** Readings in Economics and Government 33: César Chávez on Nonviolent Protest<br>**E** Challenge and Enrichment Worksheet 25: Analyzing City Growth<br>**RS** Graphic Organizer Activity: Urban Growth<br>**SM** Community Service and Participation Handbook: Helping the Homeless |
| **SECTION 2:**<br>**Ensuring Rights for All**<br>(pp. 634–41)<br><br>⊡ Identify the types of discrimination African Americans faced before the civil rights movement and determine how they protested this discrimination.<br>⊡ Explain the gains women have made in recent years to secure equal rights and evaluate why the women's movement continues.<br>⊡ Evaluate how the Americans with Disabilities Act protects civil rights. | **Regular**<br>2 days<br><br>**Block Scheduling**<br>1.5 days<br><br>*Block Scheduling Handbook with Team Teaching Strategies, Chapter 25* | **RS** Guided Reading Strategies 25.2<br>**RS** Readings in Economics and Government 14: NAACP: The Task for the Future<br>**RS** Readings in Economics and Government 16: Universal Declaration of Human Rights<br>**RS** Readings in Economics and Government 32: Martin Luther King Jr.'s "I Have a Dream"<br>**RS** Readings in Economics and Government 44: Civil Rights Act of 1964<br>**RS** Readings in Economics and Government 47: Americans with Disabilities Act of 1990 |
| **SECTION 3:**<br>**Protecting Citizens' Health and Safety**<br>(pp. 644–50)<br><br>⊡ Describe how federal, state, and local governments promote health.<br>⊡ Analyze why drug abuse and alcoholism concern all Americans.<br>⊡ Identify why AIDS is such a serious health problem and explain how the virus that causes AIDS is transmitted. | **Regular**<br>1.5 days<br><br>**Block Scheduling**<br>1 day<br><br>*Block Scheduling Handbook with Team Teaching Strategies, Chapter 25* | **RS** Guided Reading Strategies 25.3<br>**E** Creative Teaching Strategy: Unfinished Story Alternatives |

## Chapter Resource Key

| | | | | | |
|---|---|---|---|---|---|
| **PS** | Primary Sources | **SM** | Skills Mastery |  | CD–ROM |
| **RS** | Reading Support | **A** | Assessment |  | Video |
| **IC** | Interdisciplinary Connections | **REV** | Review |  | Internet |
| **E** | Enrichment | **ELL** | Reinforcement and English Language Learners |  | Holt Presentation Maker Using Microsoft® PowerPoint® |
| | | | Transparencies | | |

 **One-Stop Planner CD–ROM**

See the *One-Stop Planner* for a complete list of additional resources for students and teachers.

## One-Stop Planner CD–ROM

It's easy to plan lessons, select resources, and print out materials for your students when you use the **One-Stop Planner CD–ROM with Test Generator**.

### Technology Resources

- One-Stop Planner, Lesson 25.1
- Civics Transparency 25: How Many American Communities Grew
- Homework Practice Online

---

- One-Stop Planner, Lesson 25.2
- Holt Researcher CD–ROM
- Homework Practice Online
- HRW Go site

---

- One-Stop Planner, Lesson 25.3
- **CNN** Presents: American Government
- Homework Practice Online

### Reinforcement, Review, and Assessment

- **REV** Section 1 Review, p. 633
- **A** Daily Quiz 25.1
- **ELL** Main Idea Activity 25.1
- **ELL** English Audio Summary 25.1
- **ELL** Spanish Audio Summary 25.1

---

- **REV** Section 2 Review, p. 641
- **A** Daily Quiz 25.2
- **ELL** Main Idea Activity 25.2
- **ELL** English Audio Summary 25.2
- **ELL** Spanish Audio Summary 25.2

---

- **REV** Section 3 Review, p. 650
- **A** Daily Quiz 25.3
- **ELL** Main Idea Activity 25.3
- **ELL** English Audio Summary 25.3
- **ELL** Spanish Audio Summary 25.3

### ✓ internet connect

**HRW ONLINE RESOURCES**
GO TO: go.hrw.com
Then type in the keyword.

**TEACHER HOME PAGE**
KEYWORD: SZ3 Teacher

**CHAPTER INTERNET ACTIVITIES**
KEYWORD: SZ3 AC25
Choose an activity to:
- make a banner that promotes the health and safety of students in your school.
- prepare an oral presentation on the challenges of urban transportation.
- write a newspaper article on the Civil Rights movement.

**CHAPTER ENRICHMENT LINKS**
KEYWORD: SZ3 CH25

**ONLINE ASSESSMENT**
Homework Practice
KEYWORD: SZ3 HP25
Rubrics
KEYWORD: SS Rubrics

**ONLINE MAPS, CHARTS, AND GRAPHS**
KEYWORD: SZ3 MCG
- How U.S. Communities Grow

**HOLT PRESENTATION MAKER**
KEYWORD: SZ3 PPT25

**CONTENT UPDATES**
KEYWORD: SS Content Updates

**ONLINE READING SUPPORT**
KEYWORD: SS Strategies

**CURRENT EVENTS**
KEYWORD: S3 Current Events

### Chapter Review and Assessment

- **IC** Vocabulary Activity 25
- Global Skill Builder CD–ROM
- HRW Go site
- **REV** Chapter 25 Tutorial for Students, Parents, Mentors, and Peers
- **REV** Chapter 25 Review, pp. 652–53
- **A** Standardized Test Practice
- **A** Chapter 25 Test Generator (on the One-Stop Planner)
- **A** Chapter 25 Test (Form A or B)
- **A** Alternative Assessment Handbook
- **A** Chapter 25 Test for English Language Learners and Special-Needs Students

### Meeting Individual Needs

**Ability Levels**

**Level 1** Basic-level activities designed for all students encountering new material

**Level 2** Intermediate-level activities designed for average students

**Level 3** Challenging activities designed for honors and gifted-and-talented students

**English Language Learners** Activities that address the needs of students with Limited English Proficiency

# CHAPTER 25

**Section 1** *Improving Communities*

**Section 2** *Ensuring Rights for All*

**Section 3** *Protecting Citizens' Health and Safety*

## What's Your Opinion?

*To help students create their Themes Journal entries, provide the following examples of appropriate agree/disagree statements.*

● **Agree** Only developing countries face challenges in their cities and communities.

**Disagree** All U.S. cities and communities face challenges with growth and expansion.

● **Agree** Until all citizens are treated equally, there is a continued need to secure equal rights.

**Disagree** Equality and fairness are already the backbone of our modern society.

● **Agree** The government provides services and programs to protect and promote the health and safety of its citizens.

**Disagree** More work needs to be done by the government to ensure the safety and health of its citizens.

## Internet Activity

### The Issue of Transportation

**internet** connect

**TOPIC:** Transportation
**GO TO:** go.hrw.com
**KEYWORD:** SZ3 AC25

Have students access the Internet through the HRW Go site to conduct research about how some cities are dealing with the challenges of transportation. Then ask students to prepare and then give oral presentations on a type of transportation that would be helpful to use in their community as a means of getting to and from a major point of interest in the area.

# CHAPTER
## 25 Improving Life for All Americans

**What's Your Opinion?**

## Build on What You Know

Americans have always sought a better life for themselves and for their families. However, many communities today face serious challenges, such as overcrowding, crime, and unemployment. People are working together to solve these problems. Our communities and our country also face the challenges of ensuring rights for all citizens and protecting citizens' health and safety. The United States was founded on the ideal of equal rights and opportunities for all. We must make sure that this ideal is realized.

**Themes Journal** Do you **agree** or **disagree** with the following statements? Support your point of view in your journal.

- U.S. cities and communities face few challenges today.
- Much work still remains to be done in securing equal rights for all people.
- The government should protect the health and safety of citizens.

# SECTION 1

## OBJECTIVES

*After completing Section 1, students should be able to*

1 **Explain why people have been moving away from the central cities and how this move has affected the urban areas.**

2 **Describe the actions taken to reverse urban decay.**

3 **Analyze how the nature of homelessness has changed in recent years and why it has increased.**

## LET'S GET STARTED!

As students enter the classroom, have them answer the following questions: *What does the word* public *in* public housing project *mean? What does* mass *in* mass transit *refer to? (Students might suggest that public means government funded, and mass means a large group of people.)* Then ask students to identify examples of mass transit. *(Students might suggest buses, subways, and trains.)* Inform students that public housing and mass transit are components of communities and urban areas. Tell students that in Section 1 they will learn more about the changes and improvements to our communities.

## SECTION 1

# Improving Communities

### Read to Discover

1. Why have people been moving away from the central cities, and how has this move affected urban areas?
2. What actions have been taken to reverse urban decay?
3. How has the nature of homelessness changed in recent years?

### Define

- public housing projects
- urban-renewal programs
- homelessness
- zoning laws
- building code
- mass transit

#### WHY CIVICS MATTERS

Many people disagree about whether transportation money should be spent on more highways or developing public transit. Use **CNNfyi.com** or other **current events** sources to investigate the debate between highway and public transit supporters. Record your findings in your journal.

## SECTION 1 RESOURCES

### REPRODUCIBLE

▶ Guided Reading Strategies 25.1

▶ Readings in Economics and Government 33: César Chávez on Nonviolent Protest

▶ Challenge and Enrichment Worksheet 25: Analyzing City Growth

▶ Graphic Organizer Activity: Urban Growth

▶ Community Service and Participation Handbook: Helping the Homeless

### TECHNOLOGY

▶ One-Stop Planner, Lesson 25.1

▶ Civics Transparency 25: How Many American Communities Grew

▶ Homework Practice Online

### REINFORCEMENT, REVIEW, AND ASSESSMENT

▶ Section 1 Review, p. 633

▶ Daily Quiz 25.1

▶ Main Idea Activity 25.1

▶ English Audio Summary 25.1

▶ Spanish Audio Summary 25.1

## Reading Focus

The United States has many different kinds of communities—from small rural towns to large cities. Many of these urban areas face serious challenges, including poor housing, inefficient transportation systems, and crime. Similar problems also exist in suburbs and rural areas. They are found in communities throughout the world as well.

### ★ Urban Development

America began as a rural country with small, scattered settlements. Small communities that grew into cities usually spread over the surrounding countryside in a typical pattern. Most cities have spread outward, away from the original settlement. This trend began in the mid-1800s with the development of railroads, trolleys, and horse-car lines. New transportation allowed upper middle-class people to live outside of the city and travel in to work. With the rise of the automobile and freeways, increasing numbers of suburbs—communities built outside the city—developed.

Today cities are typically divided into two parts—the older, central part of the city and the suburbs. The older, central part of the city usually is the business center. Stores, office buildings, hotels, and convention centers are typically located in the downtown section.

*Much of colonial America was rural and rather sparsely populated.*

# TEACH OBJECTIVE 1

 **ALL LEVELS:** Organize the class into small groups. Have each group devise a growth model of your community, based on the information in this section. They might use paper, wood, or other materials to represent the various areas and well-known structures in your city or town. Students should label areas of growth from the oldest to the newest. Then have groups identify why people have been moving away from the central part of the city, and how this has affected the urban area. *(Groups should identify reasons such as cleaner air, lower crime rates, lower costs of living, and better schools or new jobs.)* **ENGLISH LANGUAGE LEARNERS , COOPERATIVE LEARNING**

**LEVEL 2:** Review with the class the reasons why people are leaving the cities. *(See the All Levels lesson for reasons.)* Then ask the class: What are the effects of this movement? Have students draw political cartoons illustrating some aspect of the move from the inner cities and the effect on the urban area caused by this migration. Call on volunteers to present their cartoons to the class.

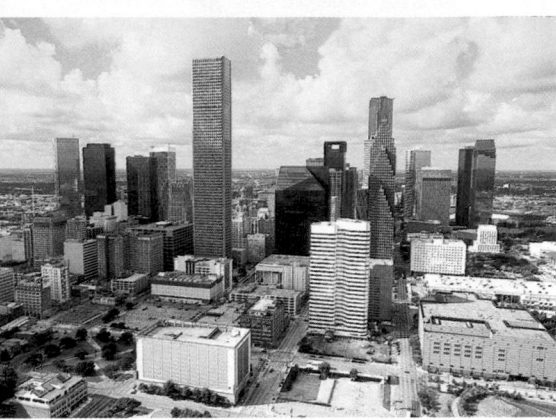

**Interpreting the Visual Record**

**Downtown** *Most major American urban areas have a downtown area of some sort in or near the city center.* **What purposes does a downtown like the one shown here serve?**

Downtown areas are also the center for banking and government. Depending on the city, there may be private homes and apartment buildings mixed in with businesses.

In many cities, apartment buildings, private homes, and neighborhood stores occupy the next circle outward from the downtown area. Past this inner circle of typically older neighborhoods is another circle of newer, suburban areas. Some suburban areas are strictly houses and parks. Residents here must travel some distance to reach stores, schools, and other community features. In other suburbs, businesses that do not need to be in the downtown center have relocated to the area for lower rents and taxes. Many of these suburban areas are like small, independent cities. These suburbs typically are made up of houses, parks, and office buildings, as well as neighborhood centers.

Some of these small cities are planned communities. In a planned community, all aspects of the city are determined before any buildings are built. Planned communities are typically a mix of open, undeveloped land, houses, limited business areas, and schools. An example of a planned community is The Woodlands, Texas, built outside of Houston. Here, residents enjoy the benefits of living in a small-town setting while still being able to commute to Houston.

Past the suburbs is the rural-urban fringe, or the area where the city meets the countryside. Farms and small towns occupy this area. The rural-urban fringe may stretch for miles beyond the downtown center. The spreading of cities into undeveloped land is known as urban sprawl. In many cases, development is so heavy that it is unclear where the city ends and where new towns begin.

During the mid- to late 1900s, the centers of American cities began losing population. Why were people leaving the cities? Some wanted fresh air and neighborhoods with yards. Many people were afraid to live in cities because of the high crime rates. Others left cities to avoid paying high rents and city taxes. Some were looking for better schools or new jobs being created in the suburbs.

This shift of people to the suburbs seriously affected U.S. cities. For the most part, those who moved were middle-income or upper-income families. Many of these people became commuters—people who travel from suburban homes to work in the city. Commuters often paid few or no taxes to city governments. Shrinking cities also received less federal aid for housing, schools, transportation, public assistance, and other services. Lower urban populations resulted in fewer voters and fewer city representatives in some state governments and in Congress.

✔ **Reading Check Summarizing** Describe the layout of a city that reflects the way it has grown and expanded outward. downtown, inner residential sector, suburbs, and rural-urban fringe

# TEACH OBJECTIVE 2

 **ALL LEVELS:** Organize the class into groups and tell each group that it is part of a city Development Commission. Groups should create a Development Action Plan designed to reverse urban decay and should propose actions that can be taken to assist the residents who live there. Each group should identify and describe the problems and the proposed actions being taken to solve the problems. Have groups use illustrations and graphics to develop a formal presentation. Finally, ask a volunteer from each group to present his or her group's plan to the class.

**ENGLISH LANGUAGE LEARNERS , COOPERATIVE LEARNING**

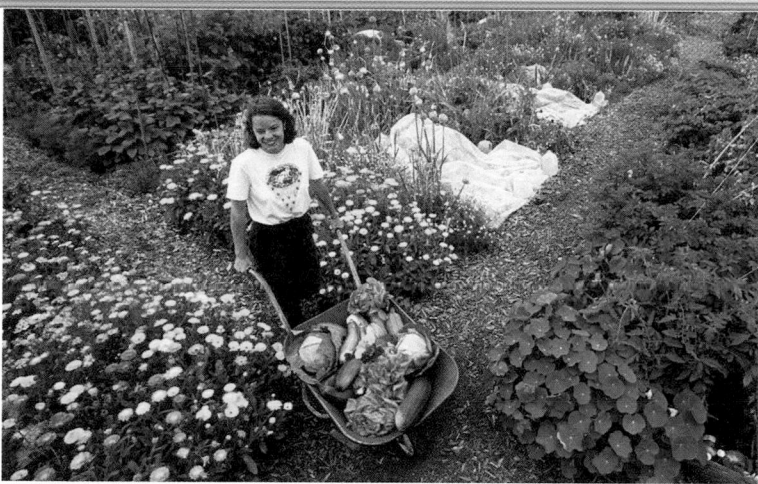

**Interpreting the Visual Record**

**Urban renewal** *One type of urban renewal effort involves the creation of neighborhood gardens in which city residents can grow flowers and vegetables.* **How might a garden like this one improve the quality of life in a city neighborhood?**

## ⭐ Urban Decay and Urban Renewal

As people moved to suburbs, the older areas of many cities became run-down. These areas faced unique challenges. Run-down areas often have more people living in poverty, higher unemployment, and higher crime rates. All the people in a city must help pay the cost for public services in these neighborhoods, which are often higher than in other parts of the city. Such services include fire and police protection as well as health and public assistance efforts.

Several different plans to improve older inner-city neighborhoods have been tried in cities throughout the country. Some communities have replaced run-down houses with **public housing projects.** These are low-rent apartment buildings built with public funds. The apartments are open primarily to families with low incomes.

Another plan to revitalize older neighborhoods calls for redeveloping, or completely rebuilding, the center of the city. Sometimes run-down buildings are torn down and replaced by a civic center. Facilities are built for business conferences, concerts, sporting events, and public exhibits. Private corporations often take part in the redevelopment project. Those people whose homes are torn down face the task of relocating. Most people are paid market value for their property or are provided alternative housing nearby.

A third plan to improve neglected neighborhoods is to restore and maintain the buildings in the area. Buildings that can be saved are repaired by their owners, who often receive financial help from the city. Buildings that cannot be repaired are replaced with new dwellings or with parks and playgrounds.

The various programs that you have just read about are called **urban-renewal programs.** These programs are usually planned and carried out by local agencies with financial support from the federal government.

Some urban renewal programs have achieved great successes. Many new schools, libraries, hospitals, and other community centers have

*New hotels and office complexes are common components of many civic center plans.*

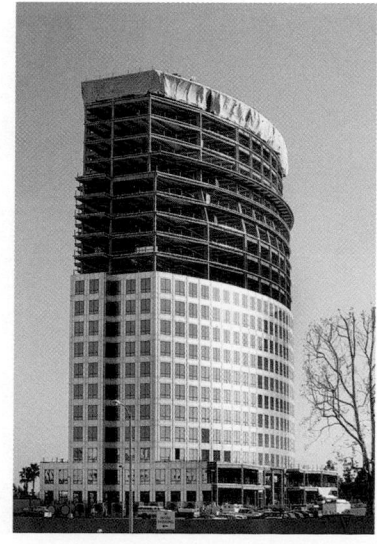

## ⭐ Civics Sidelight

**Growing Metropolis** The U.S. Census Bureau groups certain cities and nearby counties into consolidated metropolitan statistical areas (CMSA) in order to more accurately reflect the population of an urban area. A consolidated metropolitan statistical area (CMSA) combines contiguous metropolitan statistical areas. The largest CMSA in 1999 was New York–Northern New Jersey–Long Island, which also included nearby parts of Pennsylvania and Connecticut. The population of this CMSA was 20.2 million. The Los Angeles–Riverside–Orange County CMSA had a population of 16 million in 1999. Chicago–Gary–Kenosha CMSA was the third largest area with a population of 8.9 million.

**CRITICAL THINKING**
How might the population of a CMSA affect transportation?

**ANSWER:** Students might suggest that the larger the population, the more traffic and transportation problems a CMSA might have.

**Visual Record Answer**

*Students might suggest it provides a clean environment as well as a place for citizens to gather.*

**LEVEL 2:** Pair students and have pairs create an advertisement encouraging people to support urban renewal projects. The students can create print or billboard advertisements, or they might choose to create radio or television advertisements. Each advertisement should explain the advantages of supporting urban renewal projects to reverse urban decay. *(See the All Levels lesson for urban renewal projects.)* Have volunteers present their advertisements to the class. **COOPERATIVE LEARNING**

**LEVEL 3:** Have students design a layout for a Web page about urban renewal projects. Ask students to include links from their homepage to various sites that detail actions that have been used to try to reverse urban decay. *(See the All Levels lesson for urban renewal projects.)* Then ask students to expand their layouts by selecting one action used to reverse urban decay and designing the Web page for that action.

## ★ Civics Sidelight

### Rebuilding Communities

In some areas massive urban renewal programs directed by the federal government have given way to community development projects directed by local citizens. In a South Boston neighborhood, African American and Hispanic residents have joined forces to turn vacant lots into playgrounds, parks, a business center, and refurbished housing. A similar group in West Baltimore worked to secure new houses, job-training programs, school improvements, and food banks for its community. The Atlanta Project, meanwhile, has targeted 20 poor areas throughout the Georgia capital and dedicated money and programs to battle such problems as crime, teenage pregnancy, homelessness, unemployment, and drug abuse. Each area has a corporate sponsor that supplies funds and representatives to work with community leaders.

**ACTIVITY:** Have students conduct research to determine if their community or neighboring communities have undertaken urban renewal projects. Have students write brief descriptions of the project and the proposed benefits and outcome.

### Visual Record Answer

*Students might suggest because a large number of people are homeless.*

improved the lives of local residents. These improvements have also helped revive businesses in formerly run-down neighborhoods, providing jobs for many people. To encourage growth in these areas, many communities have established "enterprise zones" that offer lower taxes to businesses that move there. Unfortunately, urban renewal programs are expensive and can disrupt residents' lives by forcing them to move to make room for new development.

✔ **Reading Check Decision Making** What do you think is the best way to improve run-down neighborhoods? Explain your answer. Students' answers will vary but should reflect an understanding of urban problems and possible solutions.

## ★ Homelessness

One of the most pressing problems facing many U.S. communities is **homelessness,** or the condition of having no permanent home. An estimated 13.5 million Americans have been homeless at one time, and about 750,000 people are homeless today. Most homeless people in the United States are single men. However, in recent years a growing percentage of the homeless population has been made up of families.

Some homeless people spend nights in shelters, but these places fill quickly and are often dangerous. As a result, many homeless people sleep in bus stations, under bridges, or on benches, carrying their few possessions with them. With no permanent address and no phone number, many homeless people are unable to secure employment. Children who are homeless often find it difficult to attend school regularly.

There are many causes for homelessness. Some people become homeless when they lose their jobs. Others have low incomes that prevent them from affording rent and basic living expenses. Some people face challenges such as domestic violence, mental illness, or substance

**Interpreting the Visual Record**

**Shelters** *In many urban areas, homeless shelters such as this one do not have enough beds available to meet demand.* **Why do you think demand for a shelter like this one might be high?**

**ALL LEVELS:** Copy the following graphic organizer onto the chalkboard, omitting the italicized answers. Have students complete the organizer to analyze how the nature of homelessness has changed in recent years and why homelessness has increased. **ENGLISH LANGUAGE LEARNERS**

### Homelessness in the United States

| How it has changed | Possible causes for the increase | |
| --- | --- | --- |
| • *increased in number*<br>• *many families now homeless* | • *unemployment*<br>• *low income*<br>• *high housing costs* | • *domestic violence*<br>• *mental illness*<br>• *substance abuse* |

**LEVEL 3:** Ask students to imagine that they are homeless. Have each student write a journal entry about his or her first week on the streets and how he or she became homeless. Students should think through their circumstances before they begin writing. Encourage students to consider where they would sleep, what they would do during the day, and how they would find food to eat. Invite volunteers to read their entries to the class. Then lead a discussion about how homelessness has changed in recent years, the causes of homelessness, and why homelessness has increased. *(See the All Levels lesson for the possible changes.)*

---

abuse. When a person with any of these problems is also unemployed or working for very low wages, he or she might become homeless.

Many Americans are working to solve the problem of homelessness. Some private groups have set up shelters and programs to help homeless people. In addition, city governments are working to establish shelters and more low-cost housing. The federal government is also trying to ease the problem. In 1987 Congress passed the Homeless Assistance Act, which provided more than $1 billion in aid for homeless people during its first two years. Each year, additional aid has been authorized for the act's programs. Most of this money is used for shelters and other services that homeless Americans need.

✔ **Reading Check Identifying Cause and Effect** How has homelessness changed in recent years, and how have some people responded to the problems of homelessness? unemployment, low incomes, high housing costs, domestic violence, mental illness, substance abuse; created shelters and services, increase in government support

## ⭐ Zoning Laws

While U.S. communities try to solve existing housing problems, they must also try to prevent new problems. For example, suppose a company wants to build an oil refinery next to your house. Luckily, the company cannot build in your neighborhood because of the local **zoning laws.** Such laws regulate the kinds of buildings and businesses that may locate in a zone, or area.

Towns and cities also pass laws that builders must follow in making new structures safe and attractive. To keep track of these new buildings, local governments require builders to obtain permits before they start working. Other laws require owners to keep their buildings comfortable and in good repair. As a result, new buildings—as well as all apartment houses, office buildings, and other buildings open to the public—are inspected regularly to ensure that local regulations are followed. Such laws are part of an area's **building code.**

✔ **Reading Check Finding the Main idea** What are zoning laws, and how do they benefit most Americans? regulate the kinds of buildings and businesses that may locate in an area; maintain the quality of buildings; prevent unwanted buildings and businesses

### Interpreting Political Cartoons

**Building permits** *Building permits help ensure that people do not violate building codes or zoning laws.* **What does this cartoon suggest about the effect of building permits?**

CITY HALL PERMITS & LICENSES

MY GRANDFATHER HELPED BUILD A NATION. NOW, I NEED SIX PERMITS TO PUT UP A PORCH.

FRANK AND ERNEST

FRANK & ERNEST reprinted by permission of Bob Thaves

**Homelessness in America** According to some studies, many of the homeless in America—perhaps 25 percent—suffer from severe mental illness. In years past these people might have spent their lives in an institution. Beginning in the 1970s, however, public policy shifted toward deinstitutionalization. People with mental illnesses were moved out of hospitals and into the community. With the help of federal entitlement funds and community support programs, many benefited from and succeeded in living outside the structured environment of the institution. Others, however, did not succeed. As a result of drug abuse, failure to take medicine or follow treatment guidelines, and the inability of family and the community to cope with mental illness, many of these individuals have ended up living on the streets.

**CRITICAL THINKING**

What might a community do to help homeless individuals with mental illness?

**ANSWER:** Students might suggest offering free programs that help identify and provide medical assistance for mentally ill homeless people.

**POLITICAL CARTOON ANSWER**

Students might suggest the process has become more complicated.

## CLOSE

Invite students to imagine that they have been chosen by the government to plan the ideal community. In developing their plans, students should consider a number of questions, such as how the city would prevent homelessness and urban decay. Would people be close enough to their jobs to walk to work, or would they need other means of transportation? What types of transportation would be good for this ideal community? Why? What would they call this ideal city? Encourage students to be creative.

**Interpreting the Visual Record**

**Mass transit** *Growing traffic problems have led some urban areas to explore new rail systems as a way of easing congestion.* **Does your community have a mass transit system such as buses, light rail, or subways?**

### ★ The Transportation Tangle

Do you use mass transit in your community? **Mass transit** includes various forms of public transportation, such as subways, buses, and commuter railroads. All of these transportation systems face challenges: fewer passengers, fewer services, higher fares.

The movement of large numbers of city workers to the suburbs is one cause of the decline of mass transportation. Many suburban commuters prefer to drive their cars, even though highways leading to cities are choked with traffic. The loss of riders has caused mass transit systems to lose money. In addition, the federal government spends 75 percent of its transportation funds on highways, and only 1 percent on public transportation.

Rising operating costs can also contribute to declines in mass transit. Wages and equipment maintenance costs make up much of these operating costs. Higher operating costs often result in higher fares. Higher fares mean a further drop in the number of passengers. If the services provided are inconvenient or slow, passengers take to the highways or, if possible, walk or bicycle to work.

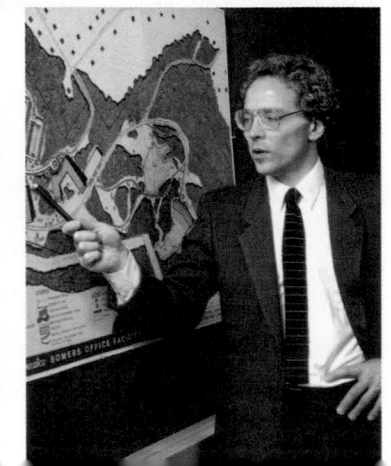

*Urban planners face many challenges when trying to determine where to build highways, rail lines, and other transportation systems.*

These factors, plus pollution and highway costs, have led some cities to modernize or build new mass transit systems. For example, Bay Area Rapid Transit (BART) began running in 1972 to link San Francisco, California, with nearby communities. A new 21-mile Hudson-Bergen light-rail transit line in northern New Jersey is under construction. An estimated 94,500 daily passengers will use the $2 billion system. Such systems are often paid for by local taxes and federal and state government funds.

Despite their problems, mass transit systems are essential to every large city. They are as vital as the highways and airlines that connect cities with the rest of the country and with the world. Their success is critical if cities and their surrounding communities are to flourish.

✔ **Reading Check** **Analyzing Information** Why has the use of mass transit declined recently? rising fares and operating expenses; preference for cars over mass transit, even on crowded roads

# REVIEW AND ASSESS

Have students complete the **Section 1 Review** on page 633. Then have students complete **Daily Quiz 25.1.** As **Alternative Assessment**, you may want to use the letter to the editor or the homelessness organizer in this section's lessons.

# RETEACH

Have students complete **Main Idea Activity for English Language Learners and Special-Needs Students 25.1.** Then have each student draw an editorial cartoon about the changes and challenges in urban areas today. Ask volunteers to present their cartoons to the class. **ENGLISH LANGUAGE LEARNERS**

# EXTEND

Have students research the issue of homeless people in foreign countries. Students should investigate the causes of homelessness, what actions have been taken to alleviate the problem in these countries, and how effective these actions have been. Then have each student report his or her results to the class. Have the class discuss whether any of the actions taken in other countries might be effective in the United States.

**BLOCK SCHEDULING**

## ★ Planning for the Future

Many counties, cities, and towns have community planning commissions that work to improve conditions. Some large groups of cities also have regional planning groups, which study the problems of an entire region. These groups are often made up of private citizens.

All planning groups employ experts to help them study the land and its uses. Among the specialists they consult are traffic engineers, economists, health experts, architects, and scientists.

One area that requires regional planning is transportation. City streets, suburban roads, and highways are part of one large transportation system. Traffic jams, air pollution, and related problems are not confined by city boundary lines. Therefore, many cities and suburbs have formed metropolitan transit authorities. These groups study regional traffic problems and work to solve them.

Similar groups are working to meet other challenges facing communities throughout the country. Among these challenges are pollution, drug abuse, overcrowding, crime, poor school systems, and unemployment. Poverty is another problem that can devastate people's lives. People who live in poverty have shorter life expectancies, are ill more often, and have fewer opportunities for education and jobs.

Solutions to problems such as these are rarely easy to find or carry out. They require money and imaginative planning. Above all, citizens must accept responsibility and do their part to make their communities better places in which to live.

**Interpreting the Visual Record**

**Healthy communities** *Creating safe and happy communities requires cooperation and effort on the part of government and citizens.* **Do you think recreational facilities like the playground shown here are important for communities? Why or why not?**

✔ **Reading Check Summarizing** What challenges do most cities and suburbs face, and how are they addressing them? the cost and provision of essential services, pollution, drug abuse, overcrowding, crime, inadequate school systems, and unemployment; planning commissions

## SECTION 1 Review

**go. hrw .com Homework Practice Online**

**keyword: SZ3 HP25**

1. **Define** and explain:
   • public housing projects
   • urban-renewal programs
   • homelessness
   • zoning laws
   • building code
   • mass transit

2. **Identifying Cause and Effect**
   Copy the chart below. Fill in the first column with reasons why people moved out of cities and fill in the second column with the effects on urban areas. Add more rows as needed.

   | Move from Cities | |
   |---|---|
   | Causes | Effects |
   | | |
   | | |
   | | |

3. **Finding the Main Idea**
   a. What actions have cities taken to improve run-down neighborhoods?
   b. How has the homeless population changed in recent years?

4. **Writing and Critical Thinking**
   **Supporting a Point of View** Imagine that you work for a metropolitan transit authority. Write a paragraph stating whether commuters from suburban areas should be encouraged or required to use mass transit.
   **Consider:**
   • the incentives that might be offered to encourage use of mass transit
   • the effects that suburban commuters have on urban transportation systems

### Visual Record Answer

*Students' answers will vary but might express that the recreational facility is important to the community.*

## Section 1 Review
### ANSWERS

**1. Define**
• public housing projects, p. 629
• urban-renewal programs, p. 629
• homelessness, p. 630
• zoning laws, p. 631
• building code, p. 631
• mass transit, p. 632

**2.** Causes of Move from Cities—to find fresh air and open spaces; for proximity to suburban jobs; to escape crime and urban life; to seek better schools; Effects on Urban Areas—shrinking cities, resulting in fewer tax dollars and less political representation as well as urban decay

**3. a.** urban-renewal programs such as replacing run-down houses with public housing projects, redeveloping the center of the city, and restoring and maintaining buildings in the area

**b.** more families have become homeless; unemployment, low income, high housing costs, domestic violence, mental illness, substance abuse have contributed to the increase

**4.** Students' answers may vary but should be supported.

# SECTION 2

## OBJECTIVES

*After completing Section 2, students should be able to*

**1** Identify the types of discrimination African Americans faced before the civil rights movement and determine how they protested this discrimination.

**2** Explain the gains women have made in recent years to secure equal rights and evaluate why the women's movement continues.

**3** Evaluate how the Americans with Disabilities Act protects civil rights.

## SECTION 2 RESOURCES

### REPRODUCIBLE

▶ Guided Reading Strategies 25.2

▶ Readings in Economics and Government 14: NAACP: The Task for the Future

▶ Readings in Economics and Government 16: Universal Declaration of Human Rights

▶ Readings in Economics and Government 32: Martin Luther King Jr.'s "I Have a Dream"

▶ Readings in Economics and Government 44: Civil Rights Act of 1964

▶ Readings in Economics and Government 47: Americans with Disabilities Act of 1990

### TECHNOLOGY

▶ One-Stop Planner, Lesson 25.2

▶ Holt Researcher CD–ROM

▶ Homework Practice Online

▶ HRW Go site

### REINFORCEMENT, REVIEW, AND ASSESSMENT

▶ Section 2 Review, p. 641

▶ Daily Quiz 25.2

▶ Main Idea Activity 25.2

▶ English Audio Summary 25.2

▶ Spanish Audio Summary 25.2

## SECTION 2

# Ensuring Rights for All

### Read to Discover

1. What types of discrimination did African Americans face before the civil rights movement, and how did they protest this discrimination?
2. What gains have women made in recent years to secure equal rights, and why does the women's movement continue?
3. How does the Americans with Disabilities Act protect civil rights?

### WHY CIVICS MATTERS

Many people are still working toward the goal of equal rights for everyone. Use **CNN fyi.com** or other **current events** sources to research a recent event involving the struggle for equal rights. Record your findings in your journal.

### Define

- minority groups
- discrimination
- ethnic groups
- civil rights movement
- boycott
- dissent
- demonstrations
- civil disobedience

## Reading Focus

The quality of life in U.S. communities is based in part on the fact that all American citizens have equal rights and opportunities. These rights, of course, are guaranteed by the U.S. Constitution. Yet, some groups of Americans have had to struggle to win their rights.

### ★ A Rich Cultural Heritage

People from all over the world have settled in the United States and contributed to its heritage. As diverse groups of people have immigrated to the United States, they brought with them many different languages, ideas, and customs. Almost every language in the world is spoken somewhere in the United States. The holidays, foods, clothing, and other customs of the many ethnic groups in American society add a richness to the lives of all Americans.

The country's many different groups are proud of their varied ethnic backgrounds. However, differences in customs and beliefs have sometimes led to misunderstandings and problems between various groups.

*The diverse American population is united by its appreciation of our country's values and opportunities.*

✔ **Reading Check** Summarizing What are the sources of the rich cultural heritage of the United States? People from many ethnic groups and countries have settled in the United States throughout history; their cultures, languages, and ideas have combined to enhance American culture.

# TEACH OBJECTIVE 1

**ALL LEVELS:** Have students use the textbook and other classroom resources to create illustrated time lines showing the history of the struggle for civil rights. Each entry on the time line should be accompanied by an explanatory caption. Call on volunteers to present and explain their time lines to the class. **ENGLISH LANGUAGE LEARNERS**

**LEVEL 1:** Invite students to imagine that they are civil rights leaders in the 1950s. Have each student write a speech identifying the types of discrimination African Americans faced at that time and how he or she can protest this discrimination. *(Students might suggest restricted voting rights; separate facilities, schools, and accommodations; and prohibition from holding certain jobs or living in certain neighborhoods as types of discrimination. Students might also suggest boycotting or organizing demonstrations as forms of protests.)* Call on volunteers to read their speeches to the class. **ENGLISH LANGUAGE LEARNERS**

## ★ Minority Groups

Some groups of people in society are referred to as **minority groups.** The word *minority* in this case does not necessarily mean that the group is outnumbered. Rather, it means that the group does not have as much political or economic power as other groups. It may also mean that the group may be separated from other groups of people in society because of its ethnic background, language, customs, or religion.

Minority groups have often experienced prejudice and discrimination. Prejudice is an opinion not based on facts but on assumptions about a person due to his or her ethnicity or membership in a group. **Discrimination** refers to unfair actions taken against people because they belong to a particular group. Prejudice and discrimination have been present throughout human history. In this country, as well, some Americans have looked at those who were different from them with fear and distrust.

For example, American Indians were often exploited by the settlers from Europe and later by the U.S. government. Some English settlers did not welcome the early Scots-Irish and German colonists. In later years some Americans feared Catholics arriving from Ireland and Germany. Still later, some people opposed the arrival of immigrants from southern and eastern Europe. Throughout this country's history, African Americans have suffered greatly as a result of prejudice and discrimination. Also, Hispanics and Asian Americans have often faced resentment and hostility.

The minority groups you have been reading about are **ethnic groups**. An ethnic group consists of people of the same race, nationality, or religion who share a common, distinctive culture and heritage. In recent years women, older Americans, and people with physical and mental disabilities have also come to be regarded as minority groups. Although not distinguished by language, race, or religion, many of these people have sometimes been denied equal rights.

✔ **Reading Check Drawing Inferences and Conclusions** Why might members of minority groups have faced discrimination? Students might say that some people are afraid of cultures that they do not understand or that some people might blame a culture or group for problems faced by the majority/country.

## ★ The Struggle for Equal Rights

The basic rights of citizenship to which all Americans are entitled are called civil rights. These rights include the right to vote, the right to equal treatment under the law, and the right to be considered for any job for which one is qualified. Civil rights also include the right to use public places and facilities.

**Interpreting the Visual Record**

**Nativists** *In the mid-1800s, anti-immigrant Americans formed a political party and sometimes rioted against immigrants.* **How does such violent prejudice harm American society?**

★ ★ ★ ★ ★ ★ ★ ★ ★ ★ ★ ★
### That's Interesting!
★ ★ ★ ★ ★ ★ ★ ★ ★ ★ ★ ★

**Birth of an Anthem** Have you heard the song "We Shall Overcome"? It includes the verse "I'll overcome some day." In the 1960s this song became an anthem of the civil rights movement. But it started out much earlier as a labor union song adopted by striking workers. It became associated with the civil rights movement when more than 500 students sang it at a sit-in in Nashville, Tennessee, in 1960. By 1965, when freedom marchers traveled to Montgomery, Alabama, the song was a symbol of the struggle against segregation and racial injustice. Black and white activists stood on the grounds of the Alabama capitol singing, "We *have* overcome."

### ★ Global Perspectives

**Roman Citizenship**
History provides many examples of conflict among ethnic groups living within the same borders. The Roman Empire, however, managed to establish unity throughout its vast territory by offering many conquered peoples a valuable reward for their loyalty: citizenship. People from lands as distant as Syria, the British Isles, and Spain could all declare, "*Civis romanus sum.*" ("I am a Roman citizen.") Citizens throughout the empire received the same rights accorded those in Rome, and they received the protection of the Roman army and the highly regarded Roman legal system. They also gained economic opportunities and access to government jobs. Although these laws surely did not eliminate all hostility among the empire's conquered peoples, some historians point to them as one reason the Roman Empire lasted as long as it did.

**CRITICAL THINKING**
Why might the Roman Empire have offered full citizenship rights to all people under its control?

**ANSWER:** Students might suggest that to offer these rights might discourage people from revolting and trying to overthrow Roman rule.

### Visual Record Answer

*It divides groups against each other instead of uniting all Americans.*

**LEVEL 2:** Organize the class into groups and have each group design the cover—or dust jacket—for an imaginary book that identifies a type of discrimination African Americans faced before the civil rights movement and explains how African Americans protested this discrimination. *(Topics might include the end of school desegregation or the extension of voting rights.)* Covers should include a catchy title, possibly an explanatory subtitle, the author's name, and art related to the theme. Display covers around the classroom. **COOPERATIVE LEARNING**

## TEACH OBJECTIVE 2

**ALL LEVELS:** Organize the class into groups and have each group write a script for a television commercial about the need to continue the women's movement. Commercials should discuss the gains made by women in recent years to secure equal rights and why the women's movement continues. Have groups present their commercials to the class. **ENGLISH LANGUAGE LEARNERS ,**
**COOPERATIVE LEARNING**

## ★ Culture

### Triumphs of the NAACP
The goal of the NAACP's founders was to end the legal abuses of African Americans. Ten years after its founding, and despite efforts in some states to make it illegal, the NAACP had almost 100,000 members across the country. The NAACP counted more than 500,000 members in 2000. Among the NAACP's triumphs have been the 1944 Supreme Court decision in *Smith v. Allwright* that political parties (specifically the Texas Democratic Party) could not prohibit African Americans from voting in primary elections, the 1954 *Brown* decision, and the passage of the 1964 Civil Rights Act. The *Smith* ruling against the so-called white primary was a major victory for African American voters.

### CRITICAL THINKING
Why might the NAACP have focused on legal abuses against African Americans?

**ANSWER:** Students might suggest that the NAACP may have realized that many laws needed to be challenged in order to ensure equal rights.

### BIOGRAPHY ANSWER
nonviolent protest, such as boycotts, demonstrations, marches, and sit-ins

## BIOGRAPHY

### Martin Luther King Jr.
**(1929–1968)**

Martin Luther King Jr. grew up in Atlanta, Georgia. He came from a family of preachers who taught him the importance of fighting for justice. After finishing college, King studied at an integrated seminary to become a minister. King also studied the writings of Mohandas Gandhi, an Indian leader who had practiced nonviolent resistance. Gandhi's ideas helped shape King's later tactics in the civil rights movement.

In 1954 King became a minister in Montgomery, Alabama. He joined the local NAACP and began his lifelong fight for civil rights. King was a key leader during the nonviolent struggle to end segregation in education, employment, and public facilities. He advocated nonviolent methods such as boycotts, demonstrations, marches, and sit-ins. As a result of his efforts, King became well-known across the country as a voice of the civil rights movement. Tragically, King was assassinated on April 4, 1968. **What form of protest did King support, and what are some examples?**

The struggle for equal rights has a long history. For more than 240 years, African Americans were forced to live as slaves. Although slavery ended after the Civil War, most African Americans were still denied their civil rights.

Some of the southern states passed laws to prevent African Americans from voting. These states also passed segregation laws. As you have read, these laws separated the races. There were separate schools, separate parks, separate drinking fountains, and other separate facilities for African Americans. African Americans could not buy homes in certain communities and could not work at certain jobs.

African Americans in the North were also denied full civil rights. In some cases, northern states passed laws that took away African Americans' civil rights. Mostly, however, the customs of the community kept African Americans separate from the rest of society. African Americans in the North had trouble finding jobs. They were also forced to live in segregated neighborhoods with inferior schools.

African Americans have worked for many years to achieve equal rights. One of the earliest groups formed to help in this struggle was the National Association for the Advancement of Colored People (NAACP), founded in 1909. The NAACP remains an active force today.

An important step toward obtaining equal rights for all Americans was made in 1954. As you learned in Chapter 7, in that year the Supreme Court made its landmark decision in the case of *Brown* v. *Board of Education of Topeka*. The Court ruled that segregation in public schools is unconstitutional.

✔ **Reading Check Finding the Main Idea** What methods did some states use to deprive African Americans of their civil rights? restricted the right to vote; African Americans forced to use separate public facilities and schools; prohibited African Americans from holding certain jobs or living in certain neighborhoods

## ★ The Civil Rights Movement

After the *Brown* decision, the struggle for equal rights grew even stronger under leaders such as Martin Luther King Jr. This struggle is known as the **civil rights movement.** Americans who supported the civil rights movement opposed laws that denied equal rights to African Americans and others.

An important test of such laws came in 1955 in Montgomery, Alabama. The South's segregation laws forced African Americans to ride in the back of public buses. African Americans also had to give their seats to white passengers when the whites-only front section was filled.

**ALL LEVELS:** Copy the following graphic organizer onto the chalkboard, omitting the italicized answers. Have students complete the organizer to identify the gains women have made in recent years to secure equal rights, and why the women's movement continues. **ENGLISH LANGUAGE LEARNERS**

**Gains Made by Women**
- *Women outnumber men in college.*
- *Women now work in jobs once reserved only for men.*

**Reasons for Continuing the Women's Rights Movement**
- *Women do not receive the same pay as men working the same job.*
- *Men outnumber women in the highest-paying jobs.*

In December 1955 Rosa Parks, an African American seamstress, was riding the bus home from work one night when the bus driver demanded that she give her seat to a white passenger. Parks refused. As a result, she was arrested and later convicted of violating the city's segregation laws. In protest, Montgomery's civil rights leaders asked African American citizens to **boycott,** or stop using, the buses. The boycott lasted for about a year and was successful. In 1956 the Supreme Court overturned Parks's conviction and ruled that segregation on buses is unconstitutional.

Americans can express their **dissent,** or disagreement, with a law in many ways. Civil rights activists used many different methods to express their dissent. In addition to staging boycotts, they wrote letters, made phone calls, and sent telegrams to their elected lawmakers. They wrote books and made speeches describing civil rights abuses. They also organized mass **demonstrations.** During a demonstration, dissenters march in public carrying signs, singing songs, and making speeches. Some Americans asked civil rights activists to be patient rather than protest. Leader Martin Luther King Jr. wrote in reply,

*Rosa Parks refused to give up her bus seat to a white passenger.*

**Civics Voices**

❝When you have to concoct [make up] an answer for a five-year-old son asking . . . 'Daddy, why do white people treat colored people so mean?' . . . then you will understand why we find it difficult to wait.❞

The right of all Americans to express their disapproval of laws through free speech or public assembly is protected by the Constitution. What can citizens do if they have used such forms of dissent without results? Is there anything more they can do to change laws they believe are wrong or unjust?

**Interpreting the Visual Record**

**The March on Washington** *During the March on Washington in 1963, more than 250,000 people gathered to listen to civil rights speeches.* **What effect do you think such a large gathering would have on other Americans?**

⭐ **Profiles**

**Mohandas Gandhi** When civil rights demonstrators practiced civil disobedience, they were following tactics devised by the great philosopher and leader Mohandas Gandhi of India. Gandhi used nonviolent resistance to lead the Indian independence movement against Great Britain. India won its independence in 1947. African Americans had long followed the struggle of Gandhi and his people in American newspapers. Also, a number of African American leaders learned directly about Gandhi's philosophy of nonviolence when they met with him in India before World War II. Gandhi was also a major influence on Martin Luther King Jr., who saw a connection between Christian teachings and Gandhi's concept of nonviolence. "Christ furnished the spirit and motivation, while Gandhi furnished the method," King said.

**CRITICAL THINKING**

Why might King and other African American leaders have decided to use Gandhi's methods of protest?

**ANSWER:** Students might suggest that the methods were successful in India, and that the tactics appealed to many leaders' religious beliefs of nonviolence.

**Visual Record Answer**

*Students might suggest it influenced them to become involved in the civil rights movement.*

LEVEL 3: Invite students to imagine that they are living in the year 2076. As part of a project commemorating 300 years of U.S. independence, students should write newspaper headlines for retrospective articles about the equal rights struggle for women during the 1900s. Students should write a descriptive headline about each gain made in the women's movement as well as headlines about rights that women continue to fight for in present time that might be secured by 2076. (*Students' headlines might include gaining the right to own property, the right to vote, increasing educational and employment opportunities, and establishing equal pay for equal work.*)

## TEACH OBJECTIVE 3

 **ALL LEVELS:** Discuss with students the various areas that are affected by the Americans with Disabilities Act and how the act protects civil rights. (*The act ensures fair and equal access to employment, transportation, accommodations in public places, and telecommunications.*) Then have students design brochures that inform businesses of changes that can be made to ensure their compliance with the ADA.
**ENGLISH LANGUAGE LEARNERS**

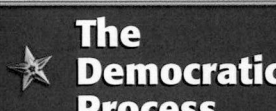
## The Democratic Process

**Protecting Rights** There are a number of organizations in the United States today that work to protect the constitutional and civil rights of U.S. citizens. The American Civil Liberties Union (ACLU), for example, is dedicated to defending civil rights and constitutional freedoms. The ACLU has been a strong supporter of school integration, the rights of the accused, free speech, and strict separation of church and state. Yet, providing constitutional and civil rights for citizens means that the rights of unpopular groups must also be protected. Acknowledging this fact, the ACLU in 1978 defended the right of the American Nazi party to march in Skokie, Illinois, and to display Nazi symbols during its march. The march proceeded despite a massive outcry from the Skokie community, which has a large Jewish population.

### CRITICAL THINKING

Why might the ACLU have decided to support the Nazi Party's right to march?

**ANSWER:** Students might suggest that all citizens should share the same rights, even if their beliefs may upset or anger other citizens.

### Visual Record Answer

*Students might suggest it shows a commitment to equality and fairness for all citizens.*

638

**Interpreting the Visual Record**

**Progress** *Today it is illegal to segregate public facilities such as movie theaters.* **How does desegregation in public facilities reflect changes in American society?**

During the civil rights movement and at other times in the past, some Americans have shown their dissent by intentionally disobeying laws they believed to be wrong. This practice is called **civil disobedience.** Civil rights supporters who disobeyed laws knew they could be arrested as a result of their actions. They hoped their willingness to lose their freedom would make other people work to have the laws changed. Such activists generally use civil disobedience only when other tactics fail.

✔ **Reading Check Summarizing** What were some of the ways that participants in the civil rights movement protested discrimination?
Montgomery bus boycott, books, speeches, demonstrations, civil disobedience

## ★ Progress in Civil Rights

The civil rights movement has had a great effect on the country. In response to demands for equal rights, Congress passed several civil rights laws. These civil rights laws established the following principles to guarantee the rights of all Americans:

- Discrimination in public schools must not be allowed.
- The right to work or belong to a union shall not be denied because of race or color.
- Any business open to the public, such as a restaurant or theater, shall be open equally to all people.
- Public places of amusement, such as parks and swimming pools, shall be open to all people.
- Discrimination in access to housing must not be allowed.

The voting rights of minority groups were further strengthened by various voting rights acts and by the Twenty-fourth Amendment to the Constitution. This amendment, ratified in 1964, prohibits the use of poll taxes or other taxes as a requirement for voting.

✔ **Reading Check Identifying Cause and Effect** What caused Congress to pass civil rights laws, and what were the effects of these laws? Civil rights protests prompted Congress to pass laws protecting the right to vote and to have equal access to schools, housing, employment, and amusements.

## Holt Researcher

**go.hrw.com**
**KEYWORD: Holt Researcher**
**Freefind:** Civil Rights Groups

Scan through the entries on civil rights organizations on the Holt Researcher. Choose two or more of these groups and create a table that describes their creation, goals, and activities. Your table should answer the question: What civil rights organizations are active today and what are their goals?

HOMEWORK Have students compose song lyrics protesting discrimination in America. Students can write songs about racial discrimination, gender discrimination, or discrimination against people with disabilities. Have students present their song lyrics to the class.

**LEVEL 2:** Have students imagine that they have been away from the United States for 15 years and that they missed the passage of the Americans with Disabilities Act. Have each student write a paragraph describing all of the changes that have taken place to meet the requirements of the ADA. (*Students might suggest changes such as ramp access to buildings and public transportation, closed captioning on television programs, and changes in hiring practices for employment.*)

## ★ Extending Equal Rights

In recent years the progress made by African Americans has encouraged other minority groups to work to end discrimination. These groups include Hispanics, American Indians, women, older citizens, and Americans with disabilities.

**Hispanics** Hispanics form the largest and fastest-growing minority group in the United States. Hispanics include people whose origins can be traced to Mexico, Puerto Rico, Cuba, and other parts of Central and South America. Like African Americans, Hispanics have suffered discrimination in many areas of life.

Hispanics have become increasingly united in their struggle for civil rights. They now hold almost 6,000 elected and appointed offices in the United States. In addition, two Hispanics, Mel Martinez and Alberto Gonzalez, have held high-level positions in the federal government. Martinez has served as the secretary of housing and urban development, and Gonzalez was White House general counsel.

**American Indians** American Indians make up one of the country's smallest minority groups. For most of the country's history, the federal government considered American Indians to be conquered peoples with their own separate governments. As a result, they were long denied many of their civil rights. For example, most American Indians could not vote until 1924, when they were granted U.S. citizenship.

Inspired by the civil rights movement, American Indians formed their own movement using protests, court cases, and lobbying efforts to secure their civil rights. Increased awareness of American Indian culture led to the founding in 1989 of a museum of American Indian history in Washington, D.C., as part of the Smithsonian Institution.

**Women** From the earliest period in the country's history, women have not had the same rights as men. For many years, married women could not even own property. They could not vote until the Nineteenth Amendment was approved by the states in 1920. They also did not enjoy the same educational and career opportunities as men.

In recent years, women's efforts to secure equal rights have brought many changes. For example, women now outnumber men on college campuses. In addition, women now work in occupations that once were closed to them, including medicine, law, and engineering. Only a few positions in the military are still open to men only. However, men still greatly outnumber women in the highest-paying jobs. Also, women do not always receive the same pay as men working in the same jobs. The movement for women's rights continues today.

*World War II veteran Hector P. Garcia founded the American GI Forum in 1948 to help defend the rights of Mexican Americans.*

**Interpreting the Visual Record**

Cultural education *At the Museum of the American Indian, visitors can gain new knowledge about and insight into American Indian cultures.* **How does exposure to various cultures benefit U.S. citizens?**

### ★ Profiles

**Eugene Connor** In his attempt to stop the Birmingham demonstrators from exercising their constitutional rights, Public Safety Commissioner Eugene "Bull" Connor added fuel to the growing civil rights movement. His use of fire hoses and dogs against the demonstrators was so outrageous that newspapers across the nation gave the story front-page coverage, adding support for federal civil rights legislation.

**CRITICAL THINKING**

How might the actions of Connor have helped the civil rights movement?

**ANSWER:** Students might suggest that Connor's actions angered many and swayed support toward the civil rights movement.

**Visual Record Answer**

*Students might suggest it allows citizens to become aware of different cultures and helps people become more sensitive to cultural differences.*

**LEVEL 3:** Ask students to evaluate areas around their community that do not meet the standards established under the Americans with Disabilities Act. *(See the All Levels lesson for areas that are affected by the act.)* Have students keep a list of how these areas violate the act. Then have each student write a script for a public service announcement describing the need to change these areas to make them accessible to citizens with disabilities.

## CLOSE

Invite students to imagine that they are the authors of a constitution for a newly independent country. Students should consider how the constitution will guarantee equal rights to all citizens of the country. Have each student write the section, article, or amendment that meets that goal. Students should review the U.S. Constitution and the Voting Rights Act before beginning their writing assignment. Invite volunteers to present their finished products to the class.

**internet connect** go.hrw.com

**TOPIC:** Civil Rights For All
**GO TO:** go.hrw.com
**KEYWORD:** SZ3 AC25

Have students access the Internet through the HRW Go site to research information about how some groups of Americans have struggled to win their rights as citizens. Then ask each student to write a newspaper article about one of these groups and how these Americans won their rights.

**CASE STUDY ANSWER**
It stated that gender discrimination violated the equal protection clause of the Fourteenth Amendment.

## SUPREME COURT CASE STUDY

### Reed v. Reed

**Significance:** This ruling was the first in a century of Fourteenth Amendment decisions to declare that gender discrimination violated the equal protection clause. The precedent established by this case was later used to strike down other statutes that discriminated against women.

**Background:** Cecil and Sally Reed were separated. When their son died without a will, the law gave preference to Cecil to be appointed as the administrator of the son's estate. Sally sued Cecil for the right to administer the estate, challenging the gender preference in the law.

**Decision:** This case was decided on November 22, 1971, by a vote of 7 to 0. Chief Justice Warren Burger spoke for the unanimous Supreme Court. Although the Court had upheld laws based on gender preference in the past, it reversed its position in this case. The Court declared that gender discrimination violated the equal protection clause of the Fourteenth Amendment and therefore could not be the basis for a law.

**Why do you think this ruling inspired other cases regarding gender discrimination?**

**Older Citizens** As you know, the U.S. population is growing older. Today about 35 million Americans are age 65 and over. As the number of older citizens has increased, so have concerns for their rights.

Older Americans, like other minority groups, have faced discrimination. This discrimination is based on the prejudiced views of younger people that older Americans are unproductive. This prejudice has cost the country a great deal. Older citizens, with their wealth of experience, can make many valuable contributions to society.

In recent years, older citizens have used strong lobbying efforts to make their concerns known to legislators. In addition, groups such as the American Association of Retired Persons (AARP) and the Gray Panthers work on behalf of older Americans.

*Today an increasing number of women hold important leadership positions in business and politics.*

**Americans with Disabilities** The approximately 52.5 million Americans with disabilities have faced discrimination in areas such as housing, employment, and transportation. In 1990 disabled rights activists won their most important victory with the passage of the Americans with Disabilities Act (ADA). The ADA addresses four main areas: employment, transportation, public accommodations, and telecommunications.

In employment, for example, the ADA makes it illegal to discriminate against people with disabilities on job applications and when making decisions about hiring, advancement, and salary and benefits. In the area of transportation, the ADA requires that all new public buses and trains provide easy access to people with disabilities.

# REVIEW AND ASSESS

Have students complete the **Section 2 Review** on page 641. Then have students complete **Daily Quiz 25.2**. As **Alternative Assessment**, you may want to use the television commercial or ADA brochure in this section's lessons.

## RETEACH

Have students complete **Main Idea Activity for English Language Learners and Special-Needs Students 25.2**. Then have each student create a crossword puzzle using the terms from this section. Have students exchange and complete each other's puzzles. Compile the puzzles into a notebook to be used as study guides. **ENGLISH LANGUAGE LEARNERS , COOPERATIVE LEARNING**

## EXTEND

Have students conduct research to obtain more information about a leader in the struggle to secure equal rights. Students may select a civil rights leader, a women's rights leader, or any other appropriate historical figure. Ask each student to develop an annotated time line of his or her chosen leader's role in securing equal rights. Then have students illustrate their time lines with images that reflect the various actions displayed on the time line. **BLOCK SCHEDULING**

The ADA has required public accommodations to meet the needs of Americans with disabilities. This requirement means that businesses such as hotels and restaurants have had to install ramps, widen doors, and make other needed changes to provide access to people with disabilities. In telecommunications, the ADA requires that people with hearing and speech impairments have round-the-clock access to appropriate telephone services.

✔ **Reading Check** **Summarizing** What are some of the successes that minority groups have had while working toward equal rights?
See preceding paragraphs for information on groups.

### ⭐ Protecting Citizens' Rights

Much has been accomplished while moving toward the goal of equal rights for all Americans. Women, minorities, and disabled individuals enjoy greater equality and opportunity today than in the past. However, many groups throughout the country continue to work toward achieving full civil rights and opportunities.

The United States was founded and made free through the efforts and contributions of the many groups that live here. As our country moves into the twenty-first century, the American population is increasing in its diversity. Its many different groups continue to help the United States prosper. It is up to all of us as responsible citizens to uphold the laws that guarantee the rights of all Americans.

✔ **Reading Check** **Analyzing Information** Who bears responsibility for securing and guaranteeing equal rights for all Americans? all citizens

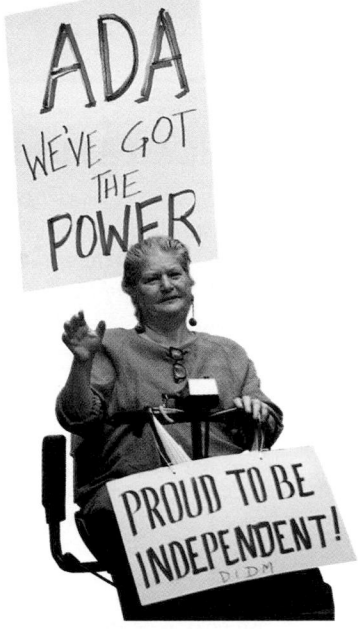

**Interpreting the Visual Record**

**The ADA** *The Americans with Disabilities Act provided greater access to public facilities to disabled individuals.* **How does this woman's sign indicate the value of the ADA for disabled Americans?**

## SECTION 2 Review

**go.hrw.com** **Homework Practice Online**
keyword: SZ3 HP25

1. **Define** and explain:
   - minority groups
   - discrimination
   - ethnic groups
   - civil rights movement
   - boycott
   - dissent
   - demonstrations
   - civil disobedience

2. **Categorizing** Copy the chart below. Use it to show the rights that different minority groups have won.

| Group | Right |
|---|---|
| African Americans | |
| Hispanics | |
| American Indians | |
| Women | |
| Older Americans | |
| Persons with disabilities | |

3. **Finding the Main Idea**
   a. How were African Americans discriminated against prior to the civil rights movement, and how did they show their dissent?
   b. What types of discrimination does the Americans with Disabilities Act prohibit?

4. **Writing and Critical Thinking**
   **Evaluating** Write a paragraph explaining why people use different types of dissent to protest government policies.
   **Consider:**
   - the effectiveness of different types of dissent
   - the consequences people face for dissenting

**Visual Record Answer**

*Students might suggest it shows that disabled individuals were eager for the independence that the ADA provides.*

## Section 2 Review
### ANSWERS

**1. Define**
- minority groups, p. 635
- discrimination, p. 635
- ethnic groups, p. 635
- civil rights movement, p. 636
- boycott, p. 637
- dissent, p. 637
- demonstrations, p. 637
- civil disobedience, p. 638

**2.** African Americans—ended public school discrimination, gained the right to work or belong to a union, access to public places, ended housing discrimination; Hispanics—secured hundreds of elected and appointed government positions; American Indians—used protests, court cases, and a new history museum to expand awareness; Women—opened the doors to many professions that were historically closed to them; Older Americans—created lobbying groups to work on their behalf; Persons with disabilities—gained equal rights through the ADA

**3. a.** denied the right to vote; forced to use separate public accommodations, prohibited from holding certain jobs or living in certain neighborhoods and so on; Montgomery bus boycott, speeches, demonstrations, civil disobedience

**b.** employment, transportation, public accommodations, and telecommunications

**4.** Students' answers will vary.

**ALL LEVELS:** Ask students to imagine that they are members of a women's rights organization that has been seeking support, but has encountered an uninformed public. Have students create posters promoting awareness of the organization and the women's rights movement. Encourage students to include specific issues that are addressed by women's groups. Ask volunteers to explain their posters to the class.
**ENGLISH LANGUAGE LEARNERS**

**LEVEL 3:** Lead a class discussion about how the women's rights movement has changed society. Ask each student to write a letter to a person interested in fighting for women's rights about one of the following leaders of the women's rights movement: Elizabeth Cady Stanton, Lucy Stone, or Susan B. Anthony. Have students describe the individual's efforts to achieve equality between men and women.

## ★ Profiles

### Stanton and Anthony

Elizabeth Cady Stanton and Susan B. Anthony formed a close friendship and became an excellent team for leading the women's rights movement. Stanton gave Anthony encouragement and moral support, and Anthony kept Stanton—who was raising seven children—up to date on developments in the movement. As a single woman, Anthony sometimes became frustrated with Stanton's family duties. "Those of you who have the talent to do honor to poor womanhood," Anthony wrote to Stanton, "have all given yourselves over to baby-making."

#### CRITICAL THINKING

What might be the advantages of close friends leading a movement together?

**ANSWER:** Students might suggest that the friendship might provide flexibility, understanding, and the contribution of everyone's strengths.

#### ANALYZING PRIMARY SOURCES ANSWERS

1. The language and style of the document closely resemble the Declaration of Independence.

2. Students' answers will vary, but some might suggest that some, but not all, of the treatments demanded have been granted.

## SENECA FALLS DECLARATION OF SENTIMENTS

The first women's rights convention in the United States met in 1848 at Seneca Falls, New York. The delegates adopted a series of resolutions stating their belief in the equality of men and women. Their declaration appeals to the principles of freedom and equality set forth in the Declaration of Independence.

"When, in the course of human events, it becomes necessary for one portion of the family of man to assume among the peoples of the earth a position different from that which they have hitherto occupied, but one to which the laws of nature and of nature's God entitle them, a decent respect to the opinions of mankind requires that they should declare the causes that impel them to such a course.

We hold these truths to be self-evident: that all men and women are created equal; that they are endowed by their Creator with certain inalienable rights; that among these are life, liberty, and the pursuit of happiness; that to secure these rights governments are instituted, deriving their just powers from the consent of the governed. . . .

The history of mankind is a history of repeated injuries and usurpations [seizures] on the part of man toward woman, having in direct object the establishment of an absolute tyranny [unjust rule] over her. To prove this, let facts be submitted to a candid [fair] world.

He has never permitted her to exercise her inalienable right to . . . [the vote]. . . .

He has taken from her all right in property, even to the wages she earns. . . .

He has monopolized nearly all the profitable employments, and from those she is permitted to follow, she receives but a scanty remuneration [payment]. He closes to her all the avenues to wealth and distinction. . . .

He has denied her the facilities for obtaining a thorough education, all colleges being closed against her. . . .

He has endeavored, in every way that he could, to destroy her confidence in her own powers, to lessen her self-respect, and to make her willing to lead a dependent and abject [hopeless] life.

*Resolved,* That all laws which prevent woman from occupying such a station in society as her conscience shall dictate, or which place her in a position inferior to that of man, are contrary to the great precept [example] of nature, and therefore, of no force or authority.

*Elizabeth Cady Stanton*

*Resolved,* That woman is man's equal—was intended to be so by the Creator, and the highest good of the race demands that she should be recognized as such. . . .

*Resolved,* That it is the duty of the women of this country to secure to themselves their sacred right to the elective franchise [the vote]. . . ."

**Analyzing Primary Sources**
1. What parts of this document echo the language of the Declaration of Independence?
2. Do you think that women today receive the treatment demanded in the Declaration of Sentiments? Explain your answer.

**LEVEL 2:** Discuss with the class the changes in the civil rights movement of the late 1960s. Have students write dialogues for an imaginary discussion between Martin Luther King Jr. and someone interested in joining the civil rights movement. Dialogues should discuss the purpose and goals of the movement and describe some of the protest methods.

## EXTEND

Organize the class into groups. Then have students work together to find out more about Martin Luther King Jr. and his ideas about peaceful protest. Students may wish to locate quotations from King's speeches or books and give a reading for the class. Other students might wish to provide a biographical sketch of King for the class to discuss. **BLOCK SCHEDULING** , **COOPERATIVE LEARNING**

# MARTIN LUTHER KING JR.'S "I HAVE A DREAM"

*I*n 1963 civil rights leader Martin Luther King Jr. addressed more than 250,000 Americans at the civil rights rally known as the March on Washington. His speech, made to the huge crowd assembled before the Lincoln Memorial, sets forth his dream of a country where all Americans are truly equal and free.

"I say to you today, my friends, that in spite of the difficulties and frustrations of the moment I still have a dream. It is a dream deeply rooted in the American Dream.

I have a dream that one day this nation will rise up and live out the true meaning of its creed: 'We hold these truths to be self-evident: that all men are created equal. . . .'

I have a dream that my four little children will one day live in a nation where they will not be judged by the color of their skin but by the content of their character. . . .

I have a dream today . . . .

This is our hope. This is the faith with which I return to the South. With this faith we will be able to cut out of the mountain of despair a stone of hope. With this faith we will be able to change the jangling discords of our nation into a beautiful symphony of brotherhood. With this faith we will be able to work together, to pray together, to struggle together, to go to jail together, to stand up for freedom together, knowing that we will be free some day.

This will be the day when all of God's children will be able to sing with new meaning 'My country 'tis of thee, sweet land of liberty, of thee I sing. Land where my fathers died, land of the pilgrim's pride, from every mountainside, let freedom ring.' And if America is to be a great nation, this must become true. . . . From every mountainside, let freedom ring.

When we let freedom ring, when we let it ring from every village and every hamlet, from every state and every city, we will be able to speed up that day when all of God's children, black people and white people, Jews, Protestants, and Catholics, will be able to join hands and sing in the words of the old Negro spiritual, 'Free at last! Free at last, thank God almighty we are free at last!'"

**Analyzing Primary Sources**
1. What does King dream will happen someday in America?
2. What document and songs does King make reference to in his speech? Why do you think he chooses these references?

The sidebar text:

Each speaker at the March on Washington was allowed only seven minutes to address the crowd. Martin Luther King Jr. worked all night on his speech. However, when he spoke the following day, he departed from his prepared text. It is said that during the speech, singer Mahalia Jackson called out, "Tell them about the dream, Martin." At this point, King abandoned the written speech and launched into telling of his dream of a better America. The "I Have a Dream" speech inspired many Americans to join the civil rights struggle.

**ANALYZING PRIMARY SOURCES ANSWERS**

1. that one day all men will be treated equally, people will not be judged based on their race, but rather on their character

2. the Declaration of Independence, "My Country 'Tis of Thee," "Free at Last"; to show his patriotism and his desire for equal treatment for all people

# SECTION 3

## OBJECTIVES

*After completing Section 3, students should be able to*

1 Describe how federal, state, and local governments promote health.

2 Analyze why drug abuse and alcoholism concern all Americans.

3 Identify why AIDS is such a serious health problem and explain how the virus that causes AIDS is transmitted.

## SECTION 3 RESOURCES

### REPRODUCIBLE

► Guided Reading Strategies 25.3

► Creative Teaching Strategy: Unfinished Story Alternatives

### TECHNOLOGY

► One-Stop Planner, Lesson 25.3

► CNN Presents: American Government

► Homework Practice Online

### REINFORCEMENT, REVIEW, AND ASSESSMENT

► Section 3 Review, p. 650

► Daily Quiz 25.3

► Main Idea Activity 25.3

► English Audio Summary 25.3

► Spanish Audio Summary 25.3

## ⏰ LET'S GET STARTED!

As students enter the classroom, ask them what the phrase *Just Say No* refers to. *(Students might suggest that it refers to refusing to use illegal drugs.)* Tell students that the slogan "Just Say No" was part of a government campaign against drug abuse. Then tell students that not only are illegal drugs a major health concern but alcoholism and certain diseases, such as AIDS, are also of great concern. Tell students that in Section 3 they will learn more about the government's role in promoting health and safety.

## SECTION 3

# Protecting Citizens' Health and Safety

### Read to Discover

1. How do federal, state, and local governments promote health?
2. Why do drug abuse and alcoholism concern all Americans?
3. Why is AIDS considered such a serious health problem, and how is the virus that causes AIDS transmitted?

### Define

• drug abuse
• addicts
• alcoholism

### WHY CIVICS MATTERS

Communities must work together to fight drug and alcohol abuse. Use **CNNfyi.com** or other **current events** sources to learn about efforts to fight substance abuse in your state or community. Record your findings in your journal.

## Reading Focus

Being healthy means more than not being sick. The World Health Organization of the United Nations defines health as "a state of complete physical, mental, and social well-being and not merely the absence of disease or infirmity." Many people also refer to this state of well-being as "wellness." Everyone has the responsibility to look after his or her own wellness. The lack of wellness in individuals can affect an entire community. Thus, the welfare of our communities and the country depends on the wellness of *all* citizens. For this and other reasons, the health and safety of Americans are of concern to the government. How does the government promote wellness?

### ★ The Role of Government

The federal government has many divisions that promote the health of the American people. For example, the Department of Health and Human Services spends billions of dollars each year on health programs. It advises state and local governments and distributes federal funds to local health programs.

One of the department's most important agencies is the U.S. Public Health Service. It conducts medical research on treatments of ailments such as cancer and heart disease. In addition, it works with

*The federal government created the food pyramid to help educate U.S. citizens about proper nutrition.*

# TEACH OBJECTIVE 1

**LEVEL 1:** Pair students and have pairs create charts that list the roles of federal, state, and local governments in promoting health. *(The roles are providing funds for programs, conducting research, preventing the spread of diseases, ensuring that health laws are followed, providing information to the public, and offering free or low cost health care.)* Students should list information about each level of government under the appropriate headings. Have students make a copy of the chart so that both students can use it as a study guide.
**ENGLISH LANGUAGE LEARNERS**

**LEVEL 2:** Have each student create posters about protecting citizens' health and safety. The posters should be targeted at elementary-level schoolchildren and should illustrate ways that federal, state, and local governments promote health and safety. *(See the Level 1 lesson for the ways governments promote health and safety.)* Posters should also emphasize what schoolchildren can do to protect themselves and should contain a slogan and illustrations that will appeal to young people.

foreign governments to prevent the spread of disease, and it maintains the world's largest medical library. The Public Health Service directs many other health-related agencies. These include the Centers for Disease Control and Prevention (CDC) and the National Institutes of Health.

In recent years, health care has become an issue of major concern in the country. An aging population; rising doctor, prescription drug, and hospital fees; and rising insurance premiums have caused health care costs to skyrocket. The government continues to look for ways to ensure that all Americans have access to health insurance, including the approximately 40 million people who are now uninsured.

Each state has a department of public health. Its function is to see that health laws are carried out in every part of the state. This department has broad powers covering every city, town, village, and rural community.

State public health departments work with local health boards during outbreaks of contagious diseases, such as measles or the flu. They provide laboratory services to diagnose diseases and provide medicines and vaccines for disease prevention. State public health departments regularly publish useful information for the general public. These agencies also inspect all public buildings, factories, and other workplaces to determine if they are safe and have satisfactory air quality and clean conditions. Also under the supervision of these departments are state water systems and the disposal of garbage and sewage.

Nearly every U.S. city and town has a local health department to enforce proper rules of sanitation and cleanliness. These local departments also help to prevent and cure disease.

Many communities have local hospitals that are supported in part by local funds. Some communities also provide public clinics that offer free or low-cost medical care.

✔ **Reading Check Categorizing** List some of the public health departments and agencies as well as their responsibilities. An example of federal agencies is the U.S. Public Health Service. There are also state and local agencies that enforce health regulations, perform inspections, and operate clinics.

**Interpreting the Visual Record**

**Food safety inspection** *One of a health inspector's jobs is to ensure that meat is stored at the proper temperature.* **What might happen if government officials did not perform health inspections?**

**Interpreting the Visual Record**

**Medical care** *Many local governments provide funding for some sort of hospital or clinic to meet the basic health care needs of their residents.* **Why do you think governments help support such efforts?**

**ALL LEVELS:** Copy the following graphic organizer onto the chalkboard, omitting the italicized answers. Have students complete the organizer to analyze why drug abuse and alcoholism concern all Americans.

**ENGLISH LANGUAGE LEARNERS**

| Drug and Alcohol Abuse in America | |
| --- | --- |
| **Concerns Regarding Drug Abuse** | **Concerns Regarding Alcohol Abuse** |
| 1. *habit-forming*<br>2. *harmful to health*<br>3. *drug users might resort to crime to get drugs* | 1. *deaths and injuries from alcohol-related accidents*<br>2. *physical illness caused by alcohol abuse*<br>3. *criminal activity by people under the influence of alcohol*<br>4. *mental and emotional strain on families and relationships* |

## Civics Sidelight

**Drug Abuse** The 2000 National Household Survey on Drug Abuse revealed that 14 million Americans age 12 and older had used an illegal drug in the month preceding the survey. While slightly higher than the figure for 1999 (13.8 million), the 2000 figure was far below the 25.3 million drug users reported in 1979. Since that date, there has generally been a steady decline in the use of illegal drugs, particularly among so-called casual users. In discussing the report, government officials said the remaining drug users were chronic, long-term users who were more difficult to help.

### CRITICAL THINKING

Why might the number of drug users have decreased in recent years?

**ANSWER:** Students might suggest that greater public awareness and education programs have helped reduce the numbers of drug users.

### Visual Record Answer

*Students might suggest it provides support and an outlet for expressing problems that may have contributed to their dependency.*

**Interpreting the Visual Record**

**Counseling and therapy** *Many people—young and old—who have drug or alcohol dependencies find help breaking their addiction by participating in counseling sessions.* **Why do you think talking to other people can help individuals overcome drug and alcohol dependencies?**

## Drugs and Drug Abuse

Widespread use of legal and illegal drugs is a major issue for people concerned with health and safety in U.S. communities. We live in a society in which drugs are a part of everyday life for many people. The medicine chest in the average American home usually contains several kinds of drugs. Drugs are prescribed by physicians for the treatment of disease. Drugs are also used for self-medication. When taken as directed, they benefit people. However, some people take drugs for recreation. Using drugs in this way is called **drug abuse.**

Most of the drugs used by drug abusers are habit-forming and can cause life-threatening health problems. Drug abuse also impairs personal judgment, often putting the drug user and others at risk. Continued use of drugs causes the users to become **addicts,** or people who feel the compulsive need to do something. Addicts must have the drug or they suffer headaches and pains in the stomach, muscles, and bones. As their drug dependence grows, they often need stronger and stronger doses of the drug to reach the effect they desire.

The quality of drugs sold illegally by drug dealers is not regulated. Drug users may buy drugs that are too strong or mixed with something harmful. These inconsistencies can lead to life-threatening overdoses.

Much of the crime in the United States is related to the sale, possession, and purchase of illegal drugs. Some addicts turn to crime to get money for drugs.

Many people believe that drug addiction is an illness. Both public and private hospitals have programs for treating and rehabilitating addicts. Private groups also run special centers where addicts may live while being treated. However, recovering from drug addiction is a difficult process. The best way to treat drug abuse and drug addiction is to prevent it. Therefore, public health officials offer many prevention programs to educate students, school officials, and parents.

✔ **Reading Check** Analyzing Information Why is drug abuse a problem, and what can communities do to fight drug abuse? Some drugs are habit-forming and bad for your health. Drug users might resort to crime to get drugs. Communities provide drug prevention programs to educate people.

**LEVEL 2:** Provide students with a copy of the Surgeon General's warnings that are found on cigarette packages. Then pair students and have each pair develop similar warnings about drug and alcohol use as a part of an overall campaign to combat drug abuse and alcoholism. *(Students might suggest that drug abuse is harmful, habit-forming, and might cause drug users to resort to crime to get drugs. Students might also suggest that many deaths and injuries as well as physical illness, criminal activity, and emotional strain can result from alcohol abuse.)* Call on volunteers to present their alcohol and drug warnings to the class. Then lead a discussion on why the issues of drug abuse and alcoholism concern all Americans.

**COOPERATIVE LEARNING**

**HOMEWORK** Have each student research and prepare a report about one of the following diseases: smallpox, tuberculosis, polio, bubonic plague, typhus, yellow fever, or cholera. Students should determine the causes of the disease, how the government has fought it, and the status of the disease in the world today.

## ★ Alcohol and Alcohol Abuse

Many people do not think of drinking alcohol as a problem, but too much alcohol can be harmful to your health. In fact, alcohol is a drug, and, like many drugs, it is habit-forming. More than 12 million Americans are problem drinkers, or alcoholics. They suffer from **alcoholism**—the continued excessive use of alcohol.

The costs of alcohol abuse to the country are tremendous. Alcohol is a factor in nearly half of all fatal automobile accidents. In addition, thousands of people die each year from physical illnesses caused by drinking too much alcohol. People who drink too much may strain family relationships and have trouble keeping jobs. Also, many crimes are committed by people who have been drinking alcohol.

It is important to remember that alcohol, like other drugs, can be dangerous to your health and well-being. The best way to avoid the dangers of alcohol is to not use it.

✔ **Reading Check Summarizing** What effects does alcohol abuse have on health? deaths and injuries from alcohol-related automobile accidents; physical illnesses caused by alcohol abuse; criminal activity by people under the influence of alcohol; emotional strain on families and relationships

## ★ Smoking

Since the 1950s scientists have studied the lives and health of people who smoke. These scientists have reported that smokers are much more likely than nonsmokers to have lung cancer, respiratory ailments, and heart disease. So powerful was the evidence that in 1969 Congress banned cigarette advertisements from television. A federal law also requires all cigarette packages and all cigarette advertisements to display warnings about the dangers of smoking.

In 1993 a report issued by the Environmental Protection Agency concluded that environmental tobacco smoke, or secondhand smoke, poses a health risk to nonsmokers. This report has fueled a mounting drive across the country to ban smoking in public places, including workplaces. In 1994 the Department of Defense announced a ban on smoking in workplaces at U.S. military sites around the world. In addition, smoking now is banned on domestic airline flights in the United States. Many public universities have also banned smoking in campus buildings.

In recent years, states filed lawsuits against the tobacco industry to recover billions of Medicaid dollars spent on tobacco-related illnesses. A total of 46 states received $21.3 billion dollars in settlements with tobacco companies. The remaining four states have settled separately with the companies.

✔ **Reading Check Making Generalizations and Predictions** What might be the effect of a nationwide ban on smoking in public places? Students might say that the health of nonsmokers may improve since they would not be exposed to secondhand smoke and that more people might quit smoking because the ban would make smoking too inconvenient.

**Interpreting the Visual Record**

**Testing** *This individual is taking a blood-alcohol-level test using a breath analyzer similar to that used by police officers to determine if people are legally drunk.* **What are some of the dangers associated with alcohol abuse?**

*In recent years smoking has been banned in an increasing number of public places.*

# TEACH OBJECTIVE 3

**ALL LEVELS:** Organize the class into groups and have each group create pamphlets designed to provide high-school students with information about AIDS. The pamphlets should include a brief history of the disease, why AIDS is a serious health problem, projections for the future, and information about how the virus that causes AIDS is transmitted. *(AIDS is fatal and has become an epidemic. It is easily transmitted through sexual contact, or through the use of needles that have been used by people who carry the virus.)* Invite the principal to review the pamphlets to decide if any are appropriate for distribution throughout your school.

**ENGLISH LANGUAGE LEARNERS , COOPERATIVE LEARNING**

**LEVEL 2:** Have students create public service announcements designed to inform citizens about why AIDS is a serious health problem and to explain how the virus is transmitted. *(See the All Levels lesson for answers.)* Ask volunteers to present their announcements to the class.

## Global Perspectives

### A Worldwide Epidemic

The number of AIDS cases and HIV infections worldwide continues to increase rapidly. By 2001, nearly 40 million people were living with HIV or AIDS according to the World Health Organization (WHO). All parts of the world have been affected by the pandemic. The WHO estimated that by the end of 2001, over 28 million of the cases of adults and children living with HIV/AIDS occurred in Africa. About 940,000 had occurred in North America and another 1.8 million in the Caribbean and South America. Health officials were increasingly concerned about the rapid spread of HIV in Asia, particularly in South and Southeast Asia.

**CRITICAL THINKING**

Why might Africa and Asia have such high rates of HIV and AIDS?

**ANSWER:** Students might suggest that countries on these continents may not have the resources to educate citizens about the risks of the disease and may not have the ability to effectively combat its spread.

**TABLE ANSWER**
1988–1992

**Visual Record Answer**

*Students might suggest that it shows the devastation of the disease.*

### Reported Cases of AIDS in the United States

| Years | Reported Cases | Deaths |
|---|---|---|
| 1981–1987 | 50,280 | 47,993 |
| 1988–1992 | 202,520 | 181,212 |
| 1993–1995 | 257,262 | 159,048 |
| 1996–2002 | 345,173 | 92,121 |

Source: Centers for Disease Control and Prevention

**Interpreting Tables** *The AIDS epidemic has claimed thousands of lives, and many Americans are currently infected.* **During what period shown on the table above was the number of deaths attributed to AIDS the highest?**

**Interpreting the Visual Record**

**AIDS quilt** *The AIDS quilt is a memorial to those who have died of AIDS.* **How might the quilt help educate the public about the AIDS epidemic?**

## ★ AIDS

In 1981 the Centers for Disease Control and Prevention began recording cases of a new deadly disease in the United States. This disease is acquired immune deficiency syndrome (AIDS). In just a few years, the disease turned into an epidemic, or a disease affecting large numbers of people. By the late 1980s the U.S. surgeon general had identified AIDS as the country's most serious health problem.

AIDS is caused by the human immunodeficiency virus (HIV). HIV destroys a body's immune system, leaving it unable to fight infection and illness. As a result, people with AIDS are more likely to suffer from diseases such as cancer and pneumonia. Although the federal government and other organizations have spent millions of dollars on AIDS research, there is still no cure for this deadly disease.

People who contract AIDS may not show any signs of illness for many years. The AIDS virus is transmitted through blood and some other body fluids. Most people who contract AIDS are infected with the virus through sexual contact or by using needles that were used by people who carry the virus. Pregnant women with AIDS can pass it on to their unborn children. Before 1985, recipients of blood transfusions sometimes contracted the virus by receiving infected blood. Today, the country's blood supply is checked carefully to prevent such infections.

Researchers originally identified homosexual and bisexual men as the group in the U.S. population most likely to contract AIDS. Another group at high risk was users of intravenous drugs (drugs injected with a needle). In recent years, AIDS appears to be spreading most rapidly among heterosexuals, including women. The World Health Organization estimates that millions of people worldwide are infected with HIV.

✔ **Reading Check** Finding the Main Idea Why is AIDS considered such a major health risk? It is fatal, incurable, and easily transmitted through sexual contact or through the use of needles that were used by people who carry the virus.

648

**LEVEL 3:** Have students prepare statements and questions for a panel discussion about the AIDS epidemic in America. Students should be able to identify why AIDS is the country's most serious health problem and how the virus that causes AIDS is transmitted. *(See the All Levels lesson to identify why AIDS is a serious health problem and how the virus is transmitted.)* Organize the class into small groups and have each group participate in the discussions. **COOPERATIVE LEARNING**

## CLOSE

Lead a class discussion about the government's role in protecting Americans and also citizens' responsibilities to protect themselves and others. Have students create a chart of the problems discussed in the section, including problems concerning health, substance abuse, and accidents. For each problem, students should suggest what preventive actions citizens and the federal, state, and local governments may reasonably be expected to take.

## ★ Accidents

Every American wants to live in a community in which it is safe to live, work, and play. Each year, however, millions of Americans are injured in accidents. About 18 million of these people are disabled for at least one day after the accident. More than 90,000 Americans die in accidents each year, and accidents cost hundreds of billions of dollars annually in medical care, wage loss, property damage, and other costs.

What kinds of accidents cause so much suffering? Automobile accidents, falls, poisoning, and suffocation are among the leading categories of accidents in the United States. Many of these accidents take place at home or on the job. The rest occur on highways, in schools, in parks, and in other public places.

**Safety on the Highway** Most of the country's serious accidents take place on streets and highways. Nearly 6 million people are injured in the United States each year in accidents involving motor vehicles. About 42,000 people are killed in these automobile accidents.

Nearly half of these deaths involve alcohol. That is, drinking and driving contribute in some way to more than 15,500 deaths each year. In recent years, local and state governments have responded to the growing public outcry over drinking and driving by passing stricter drunk-driving laws.

One of the main causes of automobile accidents is speeding. For this reason, law enforcement officials devote much time and energy to catching people who exceed the speed limit. In many states, a driver with a certain number of speeding tickets can lose his or her driver's license.

Government officials also promote safety on the highway by encouraging the use of seat belts. Many state governments now have laws that require everyone to wear a seat belt. Experts estimate that thousands of lives could be saved each year if everyone wore a seat belt. All state

**Interpreting the Visual Record**

**Highway safety** *Many of the thousands of traffic fatalities that occur each year are alcohol-related.* **Do you think displays such as this wrecked van are an effective way to warn people about the dangers of drunk driving?**

*Did You* **KNOW?**

The number of traffic fatalities in 2000 was more than twice the number of reported murders. The Department of Transportation reported 37,049 traffic accident fatalities in 2000 while the FBI reported 15,517 murders.

## REVIEW AND ASSESS

Have students complete the **Section 3 Review** on page 650. Then have students complete **Daily Quiz 25.3**. As **Alternative Assessment**, you may want to use the drug abuse and alcoholism organizer or the AIDS brochure activity in this section's lessons.

## RETEACH

Have students complete **Main Idea Activity for English Language Learners and Special-Needs Students 25.3**. Then ask each student to prepare a quiz consisting of 10 questions pertaining to the information in the section. Then have students take each other's quizzes. When they are done, have the quiz makers grade the quizzes. **ENGLISH LANGUAGE LEARNERS**

## EXTEND

Have students conduct research at the library about the history of the U.S. Public Health Service. Students should investigate how and when the service was begun, as well as the histories of the agencies the service directs. Have each student compile his or her information in a short written report that includes graphics such as a time line. Invite volunteers to present their reports to the class.

---

## Section 3 Review
### ANSWERS

**1. Define**
- drug abuse, p. 646
- addicts, p. 646
- alcoholism, p. 647

**2.** Federal—funds health programs and state and local health initiatives, offers health services through the U.S. Public Health Service, works with other governments to prevent disease, and offers other services through the FDA and National Institutes of Health; State—enforces health regulations, manages disease outbreaks, inspects restaurants and other public facilities, and provides services through clinics and hospitals; Local—enforces health regulations, manages disease outbreaks, and provides services through clinics and hospitals

**3. a.** It is fatal, incurable, and easily transmitted through sexual contact, or through the use of needles that were used by people who carry the virus.

**b.** Some drugs are habit-forming and bad for your health, and drug users might resort to crime to get drugs; deaths and injuries from alcohol-related automobile accidents; physical illnesses caused by alcohol abuse; criminal activity by people under the influence of alcohol; mental and emotional strain on families and relationships all cause concern for citizens

**4.** Students' speeches will vary but should discuss current health issues in the United States.

---

*Fire drills are a common fire safety method used at schools and businesses across the country.*

governments have passed child restraint laws, which require that children riding in cars be placed in specially designed child seats or harnesses.

These government measures save lives. The responsibility for highway safety still rests with individual citizens, however. Americans must act with care on the country's roadways.

**Fire Safety** Nearly 2 million fires occur in the United States each year. These fires cause the deaths of more than 4,000 people annually and cost more than $11 billion in property damage.

What causes all of these fires? Most are caused either by carelessness or by defective equipment. Thus, most fires that occur in the United States could be prevented. In fact, the best way to fight a fire is to prevent it from happening. Every citizen has the responsibility to follow commonsense rules of fire prevention in the home, at school, at work, in the community, and while outdoors. One of the best ways to avoid the hazards of fire is to install smoke detectors in homes and other buildings. A smoke detector is a small device that sounds an alarm when it detects smoke. This early warning can help people in a home or other building escape safely. Most U.S. communities require that smoke detectors be installed in newly constructed homes and office buildings.

**Protecting Your Safety** Safety is a life-and-death matter. Fortunately, many health problems, accidents, and fires can be prevented. The key is education. All Americans have the responsibility to learn and follow the commonsense rules of safety. As citizens learn to protect their own health and safety, the country becomes safer for everyone.

✔ **Reading Check Summarizing** What government actions protect citizens from highway accidents and fire? enforcing speeding and other traffic laws; encouraging people to wear seat belts; requiring child safety seats; requiring smoke detectors in new residences and buildings

---

## SECTION 3 Review

go.hrw.com **Homework Practice Online**
keyword: SZ3 HP25

**1. Define** and explain:
- drug abuse • addicts • alcoholism

**2. Summarizing** Copy the web diagram below. Then use it to show some of the actions taken by federal, state, and local governments to promote and protect public health.

State Government — Public Health — Federal Government — Local Government

**3. Finding the Main Idea**
a. What makes AIDS such a serious health problem, and how is the virus that causes AIDS transmitted?
b. Why is drug and alcohol abuse considered to be a threat to the public health?

**4. Writing and Critical Thinking**
**Problem Solving** Write a speech called "Wellness in the Year 2010," which you will deliver to your class.

**Consider:**
- current health issues facing the country
- ideas for addressing these issues

---

## TEACH

 **LEVEL 1:** Bring copies of newspapers to class. Suggest to students that one of the best ways to compare points of view about local issues is to read the newspaper every day. Tell them that issues evolve over time. Local leaders on both sides of a debate consider the facts as the facts emerge and draw conclusions from them. Those conclusions often appear in newspaper articles. If students follow the issues closely, they will be able to sort out the arguments on both sides, distinguish fact from opinion, and arrive at their own conclusions about issues. Have students identify an important local issue. Then ask students to follow the issue by reading a newspaper to help them identify the various points of view regarding the issue. Have students chart the issue and describe how viewpoints on the issue have changed over time as new facts arise.

**ENGLISH LANGUAGE LEARNERS**

**HOMEWORK** Have students research a local issue by reading about it in back issues of your community newspaper at the library. Then have students create charts that describe the points of view on both sides of the issue and how each side argued its point. Students should note how the issue was settled.

# Civics Skills
## WORKSHOP

## Comparing Points of View

As a citizen, you are free to make choices and take stands on issues. During your lifetime, you will face hundreds of questions such as the following: Whom should I vote for? Which proposals should I support?

Different people will have different answers to these questions. Comparing points of view on an issue will enable you to make a well-informed decision.

## How to Compare Points of View

1. **Identify the issue.** Before you can compare points of view, you must understand the issue. Often it helps to put the issue in the form of a question. For example the issue of who should be elected governor might be phrased in this way: "Who should be governor of the state?"

2. **List each side's arguments.** Listing the arguments side-by-side on a piece of paper will help you compare each side's argument on a point-by-point basis.

3. **Examine the evidence.** Just because someone gives a reason for a position does not mean the position is a valid one. Evaluate the evidence and facts behind each position to determine its validity.

4. **Distinguish between facts and opinions.** When comparing points of view, focus on the relevant facts, not the opinions expressed by the writer or speaker.

## Applying the Skill

Compare the points of view below. Then answer the questions that follow.

1. What issue is being discussed?

2. What arguments does each person use to support his or her view? What evidence does each person offer?

3. State your own point of view on the issue under consideration.

### VALERIE'S POINT OF VIEW

There is nothing more important than saving lives on American highways. An important step toward improving auto safety is to require automakers to install side-curtain air bags in all new cars. Frontal air bags may not protect passengers from a side collision. Studies show that side air bags can provide better protection from head injuries in such accidents. The federal government estimates that such air bags could save hundreds of lives each year. A significant number of people could be saved using this technology. The sooner the government acts, the sooner more American lives will be saved.

### LUIS'S POINT OF VIEW

Side-curtain air bags are expensive and will add hundreds of dollars to the price of new cars. Consumers should have the choice of whether they feel the added safety is worth the extra cost. The federal government has also warned that some types of side air bags may actually *cause* injuries when they inflate. These accidents can happen if young children are not properly seated in the back of a car. The cost and risk of side air bags are things American consumers should have a choice about. For these reasons the government should not require that side air bags be installed in all new cars.

## SKILLS ANSWERS

1. auto safety and side-curtain air bags

2. Valerie—frontal air bags do not offer enough protection and side-curtain air bags would save hundreds of lives; Luis—side-curtain air bags are expensive and consumers should have a choice, some side air bags may cause injuries

3. Students' answers may vary.

**REPRODUCIBLE**

▶ Chapter 25 Review, pp. 652–53

▶ Vocabulary Activity 25

▶ Chapter 25 Tutorial for Students, Parents, Mentors, and Peers

▶ Chapter 25 Test (Form A or B)

▶ Alternative Assessment Handbook

**TECHNOLOGY**

▶ Chapter 25 Test Generator (on the One-Stop Planner)

▶ Global Skill Builder CD–ROM

▶ HRW Go Site

**REINFORCEMENT, REVIEW, AND ASSESSMENT**

▶ Chapter 25 Test for English Language Learners and Special-Needs Students

## REVIEW

Have students complete the **Chapter 25 Review** on pages 652–53.

## ASSESS

Use one of the chapter tests to assess students' understanding of the content. For **Alternative Assessment**, see the **Alternative Assessment Handbook**.

---

## CHAPTER **25**

### REVIEW ANSWERS

**Define and Identify**
1. urban-renewal programs, p. 629
2. homelessness, p. 630
3. mass transit, p. 632
4. minority groups, p. 635
5. discrimination, p. 635
6. civil rights movement, p. 636
7. boycott, p. 637
8. dissent, p. 637
9. civil disobedience, p. 638
10. drug abuse, p. 646

**Understanding Main Ideas**

1. to find fresh air and open spaces, for proximity to suburban jobs, to escape crime and urban life, to seek better schools; resulting in fewer tax dollars and less political representation and urban decay

2. by instituting urban-renewal programs

3. write letters, make telephone calls, march, demonstrate, boycott, and use civil disobedience

4. by making it illegal to discriminate in employment, transportation, public accommodations, and telecommunications

5. have a variety of departments that conduct research, distribute information, enforce health laws, check purity of food and water, set up health centers, perform other health-related activities

6. It is fatal, incurable, and easily transmitted through sexual contact, or through the use of needles that were used by people who carry the virus.

---

## Chapter **25** Review

### Chapter Summary

#### Section 1

- Early in the country's history, settlements were small and scattered across the countryside. Many of these small communities grew into cities.

- With new developments in transportation, Americans began leaving large cities for smaller towns and suburbs.

- Many city centers have deteriorated, some areas have been neglected, and mass transportation has declined. As the populations of small towns and suburbs have grown, these areas have developed similar problems.

- Many communities across the country are working hard to improve conditions through urban-renewal programs.

#### Section 2

- The United States is home to many minority groups. These groups have enriched American society.

- Unfortunately, many groups have faced prejudice and discrimination. They continue to work to achieve their full civil rights.

#### Section 3

- The wellness of people in our communities is important, as it affects the health of these communities and of the country as a whole.

- Learning about drug- and alcohol-abuse prevention is one of the many ways that people can safeguard their and others' health and safety.

---

### Define and Identify
Use the following terms in complete sentences.

1. urban-renewal programs
2. homelessness
3. mass transit
4. minority groups
5. discrimination
6. civil rights movement
7. boycott
8. dissent
9. civil disobedience
10. drug abuse

### Understanding Main Ideas

**Section 1** *(Pages 627–33)*
1. Why have some people moved from the cities to the suburbs, and what has been the result?
2. How have cities acted to revitalize run-down neighborhoods?

**Section 2** *(Pages 634–41)*
3. What types of dissent are most commonly used to protest against the government?
4. How does the Americans with Disabilities Act protect the civil rights of individuals with disabilities?

**Section 3** *(Pages 644–50)*
5. What are some of the ways that local, state, and federal governments try to improve public health?
6. Why is AIDS considered one of the country's most serious health problems, and how is the virus that causes AIDS transmitted?

### What Did You Find Out?
1. What are some of the challenges facing U.S. cities and communities today?
2. What advances have been made in recent years toward securing equal rights for all people?
3. What functions does the government perform related to public health?

### Thinking Critically
1. **Problem Solving** You have recently been elected mayor of a large city. What actions will you take to improve older neighborhoods in your city?
2. **Supporting a Point of View** Explain how prejudice and discrimination are contrary to the ideals on which the United States is based—freedom, justice, and democracy.
3. **Analyzing Information** What types of risks to health and well-being do young Americans commonly face today? How might you encourage other young people to avoid these health threats and to concentrate on positive actions?

## RETEACH

Organize the class into pairs. Have pairs work together to outline the chapter. Section heads should be designated by Roman numerals. Subheads should be designated by capital letters. Information under each subhead should be designated by Arabic numbers. Make copies of the outlines so both students will have one for use as a study guide. **ENGLISH LANGUAGE LEARNERS, COOPERATIVE LEARNING**

## Portfolio Extensions

*American Civics*

**1. Interdisciplinary Connection to Physical Education** Have students conduct interviews with the physical education teachers at their school to determine what accommodations have been made to ensure that students with disabilities have access to physical education classes. Have students write a research paper to determine what physical education classes are available to disabled students and what changes have been made to facilities to ensure compliance with the Americans with Disabilities Act.

**2. Cooperative Learning** Organize students into small groups. Then have groups conduct research to determine what effect the drive for equal rights has had on their school over time. Then ask groups to write a proposal to the school administration listing further methods that the school can use to ensure equal educational opportunities for all students.

---

## Building Social Studies Skills

go.hrw.com
**STANDARDIZED TEST PREP ONLINE**
keyword: SZ3 STP25

### Interpreting Maps

Study the map of African American voter registration during the 1960s below. Then answer the questions that follow.

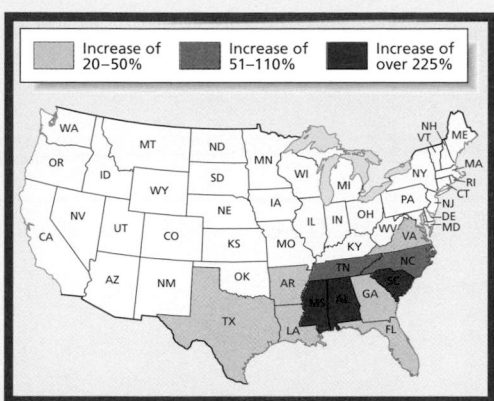

| Increase of 20–50% | Increase of 51–110% | Increase of over 225% |

## African American Voter Registration, 1965

1. Which states show the greatest increases in voter registration?
   a. Arkansas, Florida, Georgia, Louisiana, Texas, and Virginia
   b. Alabama, Mississippi, and South Carolina
   c. Tennessee and North Carolina
   d. The states all show the same increase in African American voter registration.
2. Which states show the smallest increase in voter registration? What do you think might account for the differences in voter registration?

### Analyzing Primary Sources

Read the following letter written by Martin Luther King Jr. during his imprisonment in a Birmingham jail. Then answer the questions that follow.

"We know through painful experience that freedom is never voluntarily given by the oppressor; it must be demanded by the oppressed. . . . For years now I have heard the word 'Wait!' It rings in the ear of every Negro with a piercing familiarity. This 'Wait' has almost always meant 'Never.' It has been a tranquilizing [drug], relieving the emotional stress for a moment. . . . We must come to see with the distinguished jurists [judges] of yesterday that 'justice too long delayed is justice denied.' We have waited for more than 340 years for our constitutional and God-given rights. The nations of Asia and Africa are moving with jetlike speed toward the goal of political independence, and we still creep at horse-and-buggy pace toward the gaining of a cup of coffee at a lunch counter."

3. Which of the following statements best describes King's point of view?
   a. People should wait for the right time to demand their civil rights.
   b. If people are patient, civil rights reform will be granted to them.
   c. People must demand their rights and be willing to struggle for them rather than wait.
   d. Real civil rights reform is not possible.
4. What did King mean by the phrase, "justice too long delayed is justice denied"? Do you agree or disagree with this statement? Explain your answer.

### What Did You Find Out?

1. urban decay, homelessness, increased growth and overcrowding, transportation problems

2. Students' answers will vary but should display an understanding of the many advancements made in securing equal rights.

3. have a variety of departments that conduct research, distribute information, enforce health laws, check purity of food and water, set up health centers, perform other health-related activities

### Thinking Critically

1. Students' answers will vary but should provide workable solutions.

2. Students' answers will vary but should demonstrate an understanding that these U.S. ideals apply to all Americans.

3. drug and alcohol abuse, AIDS; Students' responses will vary.

### Social Studies Skills

1. b

2. Arkansas, Georgia, Florida, Louisiana, Texas, Virginia; Students' responses will vary.

3. c

4. Students' answers will vary.

---

### Alternative Assessment

*American Civics*

## Building Your Portfolio

### Linking to Community

Research and report on homelessness in your community. Approximately how many people in your community are without homes? What organizations exist to help the homeless in your community? How is your local government helping to solve the problem? How can individuals contribute to these efforts? You may wish to create charts or other visuals to illustrate the information you collect.

**internet** connect

**Internet Activity: go.hrw.com**
keyword: SZ3 AC25

Access the Internet through the HRW Go site to research information on how you and the government work together to guard your safety and that of others in your community. Present your research on a banner to hang at your school that promotes the health and safety of people at your school and in your community.

go.hrw.com

# The Global Environment
## CHAPTER RESOURCE MANAGER

| Objectives | Pacing Guide | Reproducible Resources |
|---|---|---|
| **SECTION 1:**<br>**Understanding Ecology**<br>(pp. 655–61)<br><br>★ Identify the role that all living things have in an ecosystem and describe how this balance has been disturbed.<br>★ Explain why some people think that overpopulation might harm the planet.<br>★ Describe what farmers are doing to care for the soil. | **Regular**<br>1.5 days<br><br>**Block Scheduling**<br>1 day<br><br>*Block Scheduling Handbook with Team Teaching Strategies, Chapter 26* | **RS** Guided Reading Strategies 26.1<br>**E** Creative Teaching Stratedy: Dialogue Debate |
| **SECTION 2:**<br>**Pollution**<br>(pp. 662–68)<br><br>★ Explain what makes pollution a worldwide problem.<br>★ Identify the results of air pollution and describe how these occurrences can be harmful to the environment.<br>★ Explain how water and ground pollution threaten the environment. | **Regular**<br>1.5 days<br><br>**Block Scheduling**<br>1 day<br><br>*Block Scheduling Handbook with Team Teaching Strategies, Chapter 26* | **RS** Guided Reading Strategies 26.2<br>**E** Challenge and Enrichment Worksheet 26: Interpreting a Cartoon on Pollution |
| **SECTION 3:**<br>**Energy Resources**<br>(pp. 670–76)<br><br>★ Distinguish between renewable and nonrenewable resources.<br>★ Identify some alternative forms of energy and explain why they are being explored.<br>★ Analyze the debate between development and conservation. | **Regular**<br>2 days<br><br>**Block Scheduling**<br>1.5 days<br><br>*Block Scheduling Handbook with Team Teaching Strategies, Chapter 26* | **RS** Guided Reading Strategies 26.3 |
| **SECTION 4:**<br>**Our Future on Earth**<br>(pp. 677–81)<br><br>★ Describe what the federal government did to preserve the environment before the 1950s.<br>★ Evaluate how the Clean Air and Water Acts help the environment.<br>★ Determine what the Environmental Protection Agency does. | **Regular**<br>1.5 days<br><br>**Block Scheduling**<br>1 day<br><br>*Block Scheduling Handbook with Team Teaching Strategies, Chapter 26* | **RS** Guided Reading Strategies 26.4<br>**RS** Readings in Economics and Government 35: Albert Gore Jr.'s, "Global Environmental Crisis"<br>**RS** Readings in Economics and Government 68: *Silent Spring* by Rachel Carson<br>**SM** Community Service and Participation Handbook: Recycling and You<br>**RS** Graphic Organizer Activity: Our Future on Earth |

## Chapter Resource Key

| | | | |
|---|---|---|---|
| **PS** | Primary Sources | **SM** | Skills Mastery |
| **RS** | Reading Support | **A** | Assessment |
| **IC** | Interdisciplinary Connections | **REV** | Review |
| | | **ELL** | Reinforcement and English Language Learners |
| **E** | Enrichment | | Transparencies |

 CD-ROM

 Video

 Internet

Holt Presentation Maker Using Microsoft® PowerPoint®

 **One-Stop** Planner CD–ROM

**See the *One-Stop Planner* for a complete list of additional resources for students and teachers.**

## One-Stop Planner CD-ROM

It's easy to plan lessons, select resources, and print out materials for your students when you use the **One-Stop Planner CD-ROM with Test Generator**.

| Technology Resources | Reinforcement, Review, and Assessment |
|---|---|
| One-Stop Planner, Lesson 26.1<br>CNN Presents: American Government<br>Homework Practice Online | REV Section 1 Review, p. 661<br>A Daily Quiz 26.1<br>ELL Main Idea Activity 26.1<br>ELL English Audio Summary 26.1<br>ELL Spanish Audio Summary 26.1 |
| One-Stop Planner, Lesson 26.2<br>Homework Practice Online<br>HRW Go site | REV Section 2 Review, p. 668<br>A Daily Quiz 26.2<br>ELL Main Idea Activity 26.2<br>ELL English Audio Summary 26.2<br>ELL Spanish Audio Summary 26.2 |
| One-Stop Planner, Lesson 26.3<br>Holt Researcher CD-ROM<br>Homework Practice Online | REV Section 3 Review, p. 676<br>A Daily Quiz 26.3<br>ELL Main Idea Activity 26.3<br>ELL English Audio Summary 26.3<br>ELL Spanish Audio Summary 26.3 |
| One-Stop Planner, Lesson 26.4<br>Homework Practice Online | REV Section 4 Review, p. 681<br>A Daily Quiz 26.4<br>ELL Main Idea Activity 26.4<br>ELL English Audio Summary 26.4<br>ELL Spanish Audio Summary 26.4 |

### internet connect

**HRW ONLINE RESOURCES**
GO TO: go.hrw.com
Then type in the keyword.

**TEACHER HOME PAGE**
KEYWORD: SZ3 Teacher

**CHAPTER INTERNET ACTIVITIES**
KEYWORD: SZ3 AC26
Choose an activity to:
• create a banner explaining the ways you and the government can protect the environment.
• make a collage related to ecology.
• make a list of the types and sources of pollution.

**CHAPTER ENRICHMENT LINKS**
KEYWORD: SZ3 CH26

**ONLINE ASSESSMENT**
**Homework Practice**
KEYWORD: SZ3 HP26
**Rubrics**
KEYWORD: SS Rubrics

**ONLINE MAPS, CHARTS, AND GRAPHS**
KEYWORD: SZ3 MCG
• Acid Rain

**HOLT PRESENTATION MAKER**
KEYWORD: SZ3 PPT26

**CONTENT UPDATES**
KEYWORD: SS Content Updates

**ONLINE READING SUPPORT**
KEYWORD: SS Strategies

**CURRENT EVENTS**
KEYWORD: S3 Current Events

### Meeting Individual Needs

**Ability Levels**

**Level 1** Basic-level activities designed for all students encountering new material

**Level 2** Intermediate-level activities designed for average students

**Level 3** Challenging activities designed for honors and gifted-and-talented students

**English Language Learners** Activities that address the needs of students with Limited English Proficiency

### Chapter Review and Assessment

IC Vocabulary Activity 26
Global Skill Builder CD-ROM
HRW Go site
REV Chapter 26 Tutorial for Students, Parents, Mentors, and Peers
REV Chapter 26 Review, pp. 682–83
A Standardized Test Practice
A Chapter 26 Test Generator (on the One-Stop Planner)
A Chapter 26 Test (Form A or B)
A Alternative Assessment Handbook
A Chapter 26 Test for English Language Learners and Special-Needs Students

# CHAPTER 26

Section 1  Understanding Ecology

Section 2  Pollution

Section 3  Energy Resources

Section 4  Our Future on Earth

## What's Your Opinion?

 *To help students create their* **Themes** *Journal entries, provide the following examples of appropriate* **agree**/**disagree** *statements.*

● **Agree**   There is nothing we can do to control pollution.

**Disagree**   We can do many things to help alleviate pollution.

● **Agree**   Protecting the environment occasionally has some drawbacks.

**Disagree**   Protecting the environment benefits everyone.

● **Agree**   The government should not play a role in protecting the environment.

**Disagree**   Taking care of Earth is everyone's responsibility, including the government's.

# Internet Activity

**Ecology**

**■ internet** connect ≣

**TOPIC:** Ecology
**GO TO:** go.hrw.com
**KEYWORD:** SZ3 AC26

Have students access the Internet through the HRW Go site to research information about ecology. Then have students create collages that depict their understanding of ecology and how living things relate to each other and the environment.

## CHAPTER

# 26 The Global Environment

## What's Your Opinion?

## Build on What You Know

December 1968: U.S. astronaut James Lovell, halfway to the Moon, looked out the window of his spacecraft. He saw Earth partly shadowed and partly streaked with beautiful shades of blue, brown, green, and white. To Lovell, Earth seemed much like a craft that we ride through space and rely on for the necessities of life. These necessities include air, water, food, and raw materials. Today we know that these precious resources cannot be taken for granted and must be protected.

 **Themes Journal**  Do you **agree** or **disagree** with the following statements? Support your point of view in your journal.

● We cannot control pollution.

● There are drawbacks to protecting the environment.

● Individuals, not the government, are responsible for taking care of Earth.

# SECTION 1

## OBJECTIVES

*After completing Section 1, students should be able to*

1. Identify the role that all living things have in an ecosystem and describe how this balance has been disturbed.

2. Explain why some people think that overpopulation might harm the planet.

3. Describe what farmers are doing to care for the soil.

## SECTION 1

# Understanding Ecology

### Read to Discover

1. What role do all living things play in an ecosystem, and how has this balance been disturbed?
2. Why do some people think that overpopulation might harm the planet?
3. What are farmers doing to care for the soil?

### Define

- ecology
- ecosystem
- erosion
- desertification
- fertilizers
- pesticides
- organic farming

#### WHY CIVICS MATTERS

Over the years the environment has changed drastically because of human activity. Use **CNN fyi.com** or other **current events** sources to research how people have affected the environment. Record your findings in your journal.

## *Reading Focus*

The world around us is our environment. It is made up of layers of air, land, and water, which covers about three fourths of Earth's surface. We depend on our environment for everything we need to live.

So what happens when the environment changes? Each day new buildings and highways are built. Jet planes streak through the skies. These changes can be helpful, but they can also create serious problems.

### ★ What Is Ecology?

All living things depend on each other for survival. The study of living things in relation to each other and to their environment is called **ecology.** The entire Earth can be considered one large ecological unit. However, ecologists usually study Earth by dividing it into a number of ecosystems. An **ecosystem** is a community of interdependent living things existing in balance with their physical environment. Typical examples of ecosystems are deserts, forests, and ponds.

All living things within an ecosystem play a vital role in maintaining the stability of the system. For example, human beings and animals depend on green plants to produce the oxygen they breathe. Plants take carbon dioxide out of the air. They then break it down

*Scientists view Earth's surface from space.*

# TEACH OBJECTIVE 1

**LEVEL 1:** Lead a class discussion about the interdependence of all living things in the ecosystem. Then draw a web diagram on the chalkboard with the Earth in the center. Ask students to group some of the elements that comprise the many different ecosystems of Earth. *(Students might indicate that the oceans contain fish, algae, plants, whales and so on. At another part of the web, students might indicate that some deserts contain cacti, birds, snakes, and rodents.)* Then point out that these elements are interdependent and ask students to specify how the balance of these ecosystems has been disturbed. *(Students might observe that pollution has affected life in the oceans, which in turn affects humans dependent on drinking water and seafood. Students might also point out how development has destroyed forests and farmland in some areas.)*
**ENGLISH LANGUAGE LEARNERS**

**LEVEL 1:** Lead a class discussion about the interdependence of all living things in an ecosystem and then describe how the balance of Earth's ecosystem has been upset. *(See the Level 1 lesson for examples.)* Organize students into pairs and ask each pair to create a collage using images and headlines from newspapers and magazines. On one side of the collage, ask students to paste examples illustrating interdependence within an ecosystem. On the other side of the collage, have students paste examples of different practices that have upset the balance of ecosystems. Have each pair present its collage to the class.
**ENGLISH LANGUAGE LEARNERS , COOPERATIVE LEARNING**

## ★ Civics Sidelight

### Ecosystem Pyramid

Ecologists use the image of a pyramid to characterize the way that food, or energy, is transferred through an ecosystem from species to species. All energy for sustaining life on Earth comes from sunlight. At the bottom of the pyramid, plants convert sunlight into chemical energy. Plants also convert carbon dioxide and water into sugar, which is stored in the plant. This stored energy is transferred to the insects and animals that eat these plants. In turn, these animals become food for other animals higher up the pyramid. At each stage of energy transfer, ecologists point out that large amounts of energy are lost. The pyramid is an appropriate image for this process because at each level larger resources are required to support a smaller number and mass of organisms.

#### CRITICAL THINKING

What other symbols and shapes can be used to explain the interdependence of an ecosystem?

**ANSWER:** Students might mention the food chain, a web, a circle, and so on.

#### Visual Record Answer

*Students might suggest that offshore oil drilling, pollution, and tourism are some human activities that might pose a threat to coral reefs.*

The bald eagle was declared an endangered species to keep it from becoming extinct.

**Interpreting the Visual Record**

**A delicate ecosystem** *Ocean coral reefs, which depend on living coral, are among the world's most beautiful and fragile ecosystems.* **What types of human activity do you think might pose a threat to coral reefs?**

into carbon and oxygen. The plants use the carbon to make their own food. The pure oxygen, which plants cannot use, is released back into the atmosphere. Human beings and animals breathe in this oxygen, which they need to live. They breathe out carbon dioxide, and the cycle begins again. Without green plants and the oxygen they supply, no animal or human being can live.

The living things within an ecosystem depend on each other in other ways as well. For example, bacteria feed on fallen leaves, causing the leaves to decay. This decaying matter enriches the soil so that plants and trees can continue to grow. The plants in turn supply food for insects, birds, other animals, and more bacteria.

Likewise, tiny marine animals called plankton live in marshes and wetlands and provide food for shrimp, oysters, and minnows. These in turn become food for larger fish. Human beings, dolphins, seals, bears, and many other animals then depend on these fish for food.

As these examples show, all living things in an ecosystem are dependent on one another. If one type of living thing decreases in number, many living things will suffer. For example, reducing the amount of forests in the world also decreases the wild bird population living in the forests. Without enough birds to eat them, insects will multiply quickly. Increased numbers of insects will do more damage to the food crops on which they feed. As a result, people who depend on the crops for a living (farmers) and for food (consumers) will suffer.

Similarly, reducing the amount of undeveloped areas of a country also decreases the number of eagles, coyotes, mountain lions, and other predators. These animals need large areas of wilderness to thrive. Without these natural enemies, other animals such as mice and deer will increase quickly. With too many plant-eating animals not enough plants will decay to enrich the soil and hold moisture. Later there will be fewer plants, and the plant eaters, too, will suffer.

**LEVEL 2:** Organize students into small groups and have each group create a flowchart that illustrates the balance of nature in an ecosystem. *(See the Level 1 lesson.)* Ask groups to use captions to explain the consequences to the ecosystem if one of the species in the balance of nature becomes extinct. Then have students indicate what human activities have upset the balance of the ecosystem. **COOPERATIVE LEARNING**

**LEVEL 3:** Remind students that all living things play a role in the ecosystem. Then ask students to write editorials for the school newspaper in which they describe how the balance of the ecosystem in their region has been upset. Have students cite specific examples and give reasons why it is important that a balance in nature be maintained.

## TEACHER TO TEACHER

Heather Verdi of Connecticut recommends the following activity:

**HOMEWORK** Have students go to the grocery store to compare prices of regular produce compared to organic produce. Ask students to note the difference—which items are more expensive? Then have students ask the produce manager from where both types of items are shipped. When students return to class, compile information in a class chart complete with illustrations. As a further activity, you might conduct an in-class taste test. Ask students if there is a difference in taste between the two types of produce.

As you can see, all living things depend on the delicate balance of nature within their environments. People sometimes do not realize they are part of this balance. Many do not understand that their activities can have harmful side effects that upset the balance of nature. Because changes in the environment can have far-reaching effects, we must all learn that our actions have consequences.

✔ **Reading Check Finding the Main Idea** What is an ecosystem, and how can it be altered? a community of interdependent living things existing in balance with their physical environment; by decreasing the number of one type of living thing in the system

### ⭐ America's Early Environment

The North American continent is a land of great natural wealth and beauty. This part of the world has plenty of sunshine and a good supply of rain in most places. Before the continent was heavily settled, trees grew thick and tall in the forests. The plains were covered with wild grasses. The river valleys were fertile and green. Many kinds of wild animals roamed the wilderness.

The great forests provided protection and food for many kinds of animals. Other animals, such as the great herds of American bison (buffalo), grazed on the open plains. Various species of birds, insects, and mammals lived in balance.

Human beings were also part of the balance of nature. North America's first inhabitants—Native Americans—hunted animals for food. Animals hides were used for clothing and shelter. Early Native American peoples usually killed only what they needed and did not hunt for sport.

✔ **Reading Check Summarizing** What was the environment of North America like before it was heavily settled? covered with thick forests, and fertile land and was home to a diverse wild animal population

### ⭐ The Effect of Settlement

North America's natural wealth amazed the early European settlers. In Europe most of the land had been farmed for hundreds of years. There were few forests and few wild animals left in many countries. Thus, the fertile land, forests, and wildlife of North America seemed unlimited to the European settlers.

America's forests were so thick with growth that early settlers had to clear the land of trees to grow crops. They used some of the wood to build their houses and furniture. They burned some timber for heat or

**Interpreting the Visual Record**

**Forests** *When European colonists first arrived in the United States, they found huge forests.* **How are forests like this one valuable as both a resource and a source of recreation?**

*The Great Plains of the United States were once home to herds of millions of buffalo.*

### ⭐ Culture

**Who Owns the Land?**
European claims to American Indian land were a foreign concept to American Indians, who believed people could not "own" land. American Indians believed they were part of the ecosystem that existed on the land. In 1806 Chief Tecumseh of the Shawnee protested against the notion that anyone could own the land. The land, he said, "was never divided, but belonged to all. No tribe has the right to sell, even to each other, much less to strangers. Sell a country! Why not sell the air, the great sea, as well as the earth?"

**CRITICAL THINKING**
Do human beings ever really own the land?

**ANSWER:** Students' answers may vary, but they should consider the meaning and responsibility of "ownership" and should support their positions with well-reasoned arguments.

**Visual Record Answer**

*Students might suggest that as a resource forests provide lumber for construction. As a source of recreation, forests provide places to hike and camp.*

**657**

# TEACH OBJECTIVE 2

**LEVEL 1:** Lead a class discussion about how some people think that overpopulation might harm the planet. Then organize students into pairs and ask pairs to draw time lines showing how the world population has increased over time. Have each pair represent this increase with symbols above the line. Then ask each pair to illustrate the consequences of this growth below the line. (*Students should show that the global population has been doubling steadily since 1850, and students should also illustrate how natural resources such as drinking water, wood, and oil are being consumed at an increasing rate.*) Invite pairs to present their timelines to the class.

**ENGLISH LANGUAGE LEARNERS , COOPERATIVE LEARNING**

**LEVELS 2 AND 3:** Tell students to imagine that they are museum curators living in the future. At that time, Earth's natural resources have been exhausted by human beings as a result of overpopulation. Then ask students to design displays for a natural history museum showcasing resources and ecosystems that have vanished from Earth. Encourage students to think specifically about the types of resources that might no longer exist. (*Students might include such "artifacts" as certain trees, animals, clean drinking water, or an entire ecosystem such as the rainforest.*) Invite volunteers to explain their displays to the class.

## ★ Global Perspectives

### Disappearing Forests

American settlers turned forestland into cropland by cutting down and burning trees. Today settlers in the tropical forests of developing countries carry on these practices as their nations' economies grow. Many scientists, however, now warn that deforestation can cause losses of entire species of plants and animals and lead to erosion and other harmful environmental effects. Deforestation during the 1980s was particularly severe in Brazil, Indonesia, Malaysia, Zaire, and Colombia. Governments in these countries are working to implement plans designed to sustain development in the forests while protecting the regions from widespread deforestation.

**ACTIVITY:** Ask students to conduct research to learn what other countries are doing to preserve their forests and maintain balanced ecosystems. Have each student write a report about his or her findings.

### ★★★★★★★★★★★
**That's Interesting!**
### ★★★★★★★★★★★

The Shaanxi province in China has made it illegal to produce, use, or sell disposable wooden chopsticks. The Chinese news agency Xinhua reports that each year 25 million trees are cut down in China in order to make 45 billion pairs of the disposable chopsticks.

*Hunters known as mountain men trapped and killed thousands of animals—such as beavers—to supply the European demand for furs.*

**Interpreting the Visual Record**

**Ideal farm** *Many settlers viewed their actions as a way of civilizing the wilderness by creating farms and ranches. This painting shows the ideal view of an early American farm as a symbol of peace and prosperity.* **What aspects of this painting show changes to the natural environment?**

THE RESIDENCE OF DAVID TWINING 1787.

shipped it to Europe as lumber. The tallest and straightest trees were used to make the masts of great sailing ships.

As the number of settlers in America increased and the demand for wood grew, more forests were cut down. No new trees were planted in their place. As settlers wanted more wood, they got it from forests farther west.

As settlers destroyed the forests they destroyed more than just trees—they damaged the forest ecosystem. As the trees disappeared, so did much of the wildlife that depended on them for food and shelter. Many other wild animals were killed by settlers, not only for food but also for their furs or for sport.

Beavers were trapped because beaver hats were popular in Europe. Whole herds of buffalo were shot for hides or for sport, and their meat was often left to rot. Other animals were shot as pests because they attacked livestock or ate crops. These species included foxes, bears, mountain lions, owls, hawks, and eagles. Some species became extinct or were almost destroyed.

Farming also affected the environment. The land cleared for farming was very fertile at first. This rich soil produced large crops of cotton, oats, tobacco, vegetables, and wheat. However, when the farmers planted a crop and harvested it, nothing was left to decay and fertilize the soil. As the land was farmed year after year, the nutrients in the soil were used up and never replaced. Near the end of the 1700s, farmers began practicing crop rotation—planting different crops on the land each year. Crop rotation helped keep the soil from wearing out. In the mid-1800s, farmers also began using fertilizer to add nutrients to the soil.

In the West cattle ranchers and sheepherders had a major effect on the land. Their huge herds ate all the grasses and plants on the prairies. When the plants died, the soil blew away. Much good grassland was ruined in this way. People moved to new land where it was available.

✔ **Reading Check** Finding the Main Idea
How did early settlers change the environment of North America? through building, hunting, farming, and ranching

## ★ Modern Agriculture

By the early 1900s it became apparent that there was not an endless supply of fertile land. When the southwestern United States went through a long drought in the 1930s, no grass was left to hold the soil down. Huge amounts of soil were blown away by

# TEACH OBJECTIVE 3

**ALL LEVELS:** Copy the following graphic organizer onto the chalkboard, omitting the italicized answers. Have students complete the boxes with problems and solutions to show how some farmers are working to preserve and restore ecosystems that have been damaged by many years of farming.

| Farmers Helping the Environment | |
|---|---|
| **Problem** | **Solution** |
| *nutrients in soil depleted* | *fertilizer, crop rotation* |
| *soil erosion* | *grow trees or grass, practice contour farming, plant cover crops* |
| *pesticides dangerous to animals, plants, and humans* | *organic farming* |

Alexandre Hogue, *Drouth Stricken Area*, 1936, Oil on canvas, Dallas Museum of Art, Dallas Art Association purchase, 1945.6

the wind. Soon the region became known as the Dust Bowl. One woman from Kansas recalled the following:

**Civics Voices**

❝ The door and windows were all shut tightly, yet those tiny particles seemed to seep through the very walls. It [dust] got into cupboards and clothes closets; our faces were as dirty as if we had rolled in the dirt. ❞

In the 1980s Congress established a program encouraging farmers to plant trees or grass instead of crops. These practices were designed to prevent **erosion,** or the wearing away of land by water and wind.

Farmers in many parts of the world use methods such as contour farming and terracing to care for the soil. Contour farming involves plowing and planting across the slope of the land to prevent the soil from being washed away. With terracing farmers create flat spaces on the slopes to prevent water erosion. Many farmers also use soil preservation techniques that were developed in the 1800s. For example, some farmers plant cover crops such as clover because their roots hold the soil in place. They also continue the practice of crop rotation.

Despite such agricultural techniques, however, some of the world's available farmland is lost each year. In industrialized countries such as the United States, farmland is mainly being lost to the spread of urban areas. Other countries are losing their soil to a process called **desertification.** This process occurs when years of overgrazing and removal of plants harm the soil and once-fertile areas become deserts.

✔ **Reading Check** Analyzing Information What has been done to protect the farmlands in the United States? development and use of soil conversion techniques

---

**Interpreting the Visual Record**

**Dust Bowl** *During the 1930s a combination of drought and soil erosion turned thousands of acres in the Southwest into a barren Dust Bowl.* **How has the farm in this painting been affected by the drought?**

---

★ **Culture**

**Old Methods/Modern Uses** Some of the agricultural methods that work so well today have a long history in the Americas. For example, the Inca of South America mastered the art of terrace farming well before the arrival of Europeans in the 1400s. The Inca lived and farmed on the slopes of the Andes, where fertile soil was at a minimum. They could not afford to have the soil wash away down the hillside, so they constructed elaborate terraces, with stone walls to hold the soil in place. Like farmers today, the Inca built irrigation canals and drainage channels. They also practiced crop rotation, alternating their plantings of maize, potatoes, beans, and other crops from year to year.

**ACTIVITY:** Ask students to conduct research to learn more about agricultural methods practiced by past civilizations. Have students create charts or diagrams to explain these methods.

---

**Visual Record Answer**

*Students might suggest that because of the drought, crops have died, animals are starving and thirsty, and the farmer can no longer afford to make necessary repairs on the property.*

---

**Visual Record Answer**

*(for page 658)*
*Students might suggest the building of houses or farming.*

*The Global Environment* **659**

**659**

**LEVEL 3:** Remind students that some farmers have found a way to increase crop yields and control pests without using chemicals. Then ask each student to imagine that he or she is an organic farmer. Have students write letters giving advice to another farmer who is considering adopting organic farming methods. Ask students to describe the benefits and challenges of organic farming. Encourage students to be persuasive in their letters. *(Students might mention the benefits to the environment and the improved quality and healthfulness of organically produced food. Also students might mention the expense of making the transition to organic farming.)* Invite volunteers to read their letters to the class.

## CLOSE

Have pairs of students create brochures that could be used to educate the public about the interdependence of ecosystems. Brochures should describe ways in which ecosystems and the balance of nature are threatened, such as through irresponsible economic development, overuse of pesticides, and overpopulation. Encourage students to include in their brochures some suggestions for how ecosystems can be protected. Call on volunteers to present their brochures to the class for discussion.

## Global Perspectives

**Agricultural Disaster in the U.S.S.R.** Agricultural planning in the former Soviet Union led to an ecological disaster in the early 1990s. In order to irrigate farmland, planners had diverted water from two rivers that flowed into the Aral Sea—formerly the fourth largest inland body of water in the world. As a result of the diversion of water, the Aral Sea shrank to less than half of its size by the early 1990s. As the water receded, salt and mineral content in the sea rose, killing the fish that inhabited the sea. Port cities were left high and dry. The local climate became harsher, with greater extremes of heat and cold. In addition, fertilizer residues mixed with parched soil to produce a toxic dust that the wind spread throughout the area. Incidences of anemia and infant mortality rose, and life expectancy fell. In 1994 several former Soviet republics agreed to set up a committee and a fund to try to save the Aral Sea.

**ACTIVITY:** Ask students to conduct research to learn what has happened to the Aral Sea since 1994 and have students write a brief essay about what they discover.

**BIOGRAPHY ANSWER**
Carson's books sparked a nationwide debate over pesticides and their effect on the environment.

### BIOGRAPHY
## Rachel Carson
### (1907–1964)

Rachel Carson was born in Springdale, Pennsylvania. After graduating from Johns Hopkins University, Carson went to work as a biologist for the U.S. Bureau of Fisheries. She conducted research and wrote articles promoting the country's wildlife resources.

Carson's 1951 book, *The Sea Around Us,* was on the U.S. nonfiction best-seller list for a year and a half. It won the National Book Award. Her 1962 publication of *Silent Spring,* however, is what Carson is best known for. In this book Carson painted a gloomy picture of a world destroyed by the overuse of pesticides, particularly DDT. The book sparked a nationwide debate over the use of pesticides.

As a spokesperson for environmental protection, Carson helped to pass a law requiring warning labels on all chemical products. Although Carson died in 1964, her efforts had a lasting effect on the environmental movement. **How did Carson influence Americans' views of the environment?**

## Fertilizers and Pesticides

To help grow more food on less land, many farmers around the world use chemical fertilizers and pesticides. **Fertilizers** are plant foods that make crops grow faster and bigger. The most important fertilizers are nitrates, which contain nitrogen. Nitrates can be spread over farmland to soak in with the next rain. Crops fertilized with nitrates produce bigger yields.

**Pesticides** are chemicals that kill insect pests and weeds. Many insects attack crops, ruining entire harvests. Weeds also lower crop production. The use of chemical pesticides has dramatically reduced crop losses to insects and weeds.

Although the thousands of pesticides used around the world increase crop production, they also pose potential health and environmental hazards. For example, in 1972 the United States severely restricted the use of the pesticide DDT, first introduced in 1939. Scientists found that several species of birds were dying out because DDT weakened the shells of their eggs. However, DDT is still used in many parts of the world. Some scientists believe it may be responsible for higher rates of death and disease among people in these areas.

Pesticides have other potential negative effects. They kill insects that are beneficial to plants, such as ladybugs and honeybees. Moreover, many damaging insects build a tolerance to pesticides over time, requiring new and stronger chemicals to defeat them. Pesticides also leak into the surrounding soil and water, where they can stay active for many years. Many of the long-term effects of pesticides on humans, animals, and the environment are still undetermined.

Because of potential problems caused by pesticide use, some people practice **organic farming,** or farming without using artificial substances. Using natural substances, beneficial insects, and special farming methods, farmers can increase crop yields and control pests without using chemicals. However, farmers who shift to organic farming face financial costs when making this transition. Only a small percentage of American crops are grown on organic farms.

✔ **Reading Check Contrasting** How are the uses for fertilizers and pesticides different? *fertilizers—plant food; pesticides—kill insects and weeds*

## Overpopulation

The population of the world has been increasing at an astonishing rate. It took more than 1 million years for the human population to reach 1 billion. The population had reached this point by the year 1850. By 1930 this figure had doubled to 2 billion. By 1975 the world's population had doubled again. Today the population of the world has grown beyond 6 billion. If the present rate of growth continues, the world's

# REVIEW AND ASSESS

Have students complete the **Section 1 Review** on page 661. Then have students complete **Daily Quiz 26.1**. As **Alternative Assessment**, you may want to use the overpopulation time line or the organic farming letter exercises in this section's lessons.

# RETEACH

Have students complete **Main Idea Activity for English Language Learners and Special-Needs Students 26.1**. Then organize students into two groups. Ask the first group to create an outline showing what happens when the balance of an ecosystem is upset. Have the second group outline some ways that ecosystems can be protected in order to restore the balance of nature. **ENGLISH LANGUAGE LEARNERS**

# EXTEND

Have students conduct research to learn more about how various governments around the world, as well as the United Nations, have acted to end overuse of pesticides (such as in Indonesia), to slow deforestation (such as in Brazil), or to save endangered species (such as with the tiger preserves in India). Ask students to focus on a specific program through which a nation has successfully helped the ecosystem. Have each student prepare a presentation on the program he or she has chosen. **BLOCK SCHEDULING**

population will reach nearly 8 billion by the year 2025.

Such rapid population growth strains the world's resources. Growing numbers of people need more food, for example. In many of the world's poorer countries, food production cannot keep up with population growth. Even with aid from wealthier countries, millions of people die from hunger-related causes each year.

Overpopulation strains other natural resources as well. Growing numbers of people use more minerals, water, energy, and timber. It is estimated that millions of acres of Earth's tropical rain forest are lost each year. These forests are home to thousands of species of plants and animals. They also generate large amounts of oxygen.

Growing numbers of people also produce more waste. Increased amounts of waste can harm the environment and upset the balance of nature. Controlling population growth so that future generations can have a healthier environment is a challenge facing the entire global community.

✔ **Reading Check** **Analyzing Information** How has the world's rate of population growth been changing, and why is the current rate of growth a concern? increasing steadily in the past 100 years; results in overpopulation, which can strain the planet's resources

*The tremendous growth of the global population has put an increasing strain on the world's resources.*

## Section 1 Review
### ANSWERS

**1. Define**
- ecology, p. 655
- ecosystem, p. 655
- erosion, p. 659
- desertification, p. 659
- fertilizers, p. 660
- pesticides, p. 660
- organic farming, p. 660

**2.** ecosystem—trees, plants, bacteria, birds, fish, animals, human beings; human changes—trees cut down for lumber, fields cleared for farming, soil depleted of nutrients, animals hunted for food and hides

**3. a.** by straining the natural resources, such as food, minerals, water, energy, and timber and by producing more waste

**b.** crop rotation, planting cover crops, contour farming

**4.** Students' paragraphs might consider the environmental effects of pesticide use, the effects of chemical fertilizers on crop growth, and the costs of switching to organic farming.

# SECTION 1 Review

**Homework Practice Online**
keyword: SZ3 HP26

1. **Define** and explain:
   - ecology
   - ecosystem
   - erosion
   - desertification
   - fertilizers
   - pesticides
   - organic farming

2. **Summarizing** Copy the graphic organizer to the right. Use it to show how all living things are a part of the ecosystem and how this balance has changed.

ecosystem — human changes

3. **Finding the Main Idea**
   a. How might overpopulation harm the environment?
   b. List some of the things that farmers do to protect soil.

4. **Writing and Critical Thinking**
   **Drawing Inferences and Conclusions** Some farmers prefer to grow food organically rather than to use chemical fertilizers or pesticides. In a three-paragraph essay, explain why farmers might choose organic farming over other farming methods. Describe the advantages and disadvantages of organic farming.

   **Consider:**
   - the environmental effects of pesticide use
   - the effects of chemical fertilizers on crop growth
   - the costs of switching to organic farming

# SECTION 2

## OBJECTIVES

*After completing Section 2, students should be able to*

1. **Explain what makes pollution a worldwide problem.**
2. **Identify the results of air pollution, and describe how these occurrences can be harmful to the environment.**
3. **Explain how water and ground pollution threaten the environment.**

## SECTION 2 RESOURCES

### REPRODUCIBLE

- ▶ Guided Reading Strategies 26.2
- ▶ Challenge and Enrichment Worksheet 26: Interpreting a Cartoon on Pollution

### TECHNOLOGY

- ▶ One-Stop Planner, Lesson 26.2
- ▶ Homework Practice Online
- ▶ HRW Go site

### REINFORCEMENT, REVIEW, AND ASSESSMENT

- ▶ Section 2 Review, p. 668
- ▶ Daily Quiz 26.2
- ▶ Main Idea Activity 26.2
- ▶ English Audio Summary 26.2
- ▶ Spanish Audio Summary 26.2

---

### LET'S GET STARTED!

Write the word *pollution* on the chalkboard. As students enter the classroom, ask them to think of different types and sources of pollution. Invite volunteers to come to the chalkboard to list these examples. *(Students might cite car exhaust, factory emissions, landfills, and so on.)* Tell students that in Section 2 they will learn more about the different types of pollution and what makes pollution a worldwide issue.

## SECTION 2

# Pollution

### Read to Discover

1. What makes pollution a worldwide problem?
2. What are the results of air pollution, and how can these occurrences be harmful to the environment?
3. What types of water and ground pollution threaten the environment?

### Define

- pollution
- renewable resource
- smog
- greenhouse effect
- ozone layer
- acid rain
- hydrologic cycle
- landfills
- recycling

#### WHY CIVICS MATTERS

Government officials continue to debate what environmental policy the country should have. Use CNNfyi.com or other **current events** sources to learn what environmental issues policy makers are discussing today. Record your findings in your journal.

## Reading Focus

Our natural resources are precious. Unfortunately, many people have taken the air, land, and water around them for granted. They have polluted the environment.

### ★ A Global Concern

**Pollution** results when any part of the environment becomes contaminated, or unfit for use. Pollution can destroy plants and animals and can upset the balance of nature. Among the countless living creatures affected are the ones who cause pollution—human beings.

During the 1950s and 1960s many Americans became concerned about the possible dangers posed by pollution. They believed that pollution was causing health problems and killing vegetation and wildlife in many American communities. In response to public concerns about pollution, Congress passed a series of laws to protect the environment.

However, in the 1980s a nuclear accident made it clear that environmental protection was an international issue. In 1986 an explosion at the Chernobyl nuclear power plant in the former Soviet Union, killed at least 31 plant workers. More than 135,000 people living near the plant were evacuated. To add to the devastation, the explosion scattered radioactive material over wide areas of the Soviet Union and Europe. Many people were contaminated by radiation, and much plant life died.

*Pollution generated in one area can easily spread by air or water to other regions.*

**LEVEL 1:** Lead a class discussion about what makes pollution a worldwide problem. *(It is a worldwide problem because pollution in the air, water, and soil, crosses the political boundaries of nations.)* Then ask students to look through newspapers and magazines to find headlines and articles about pollution in other parts of the world. Have each student create a collage from these headlines and articles. *(Students might find articles about air pollution, acid rain, oil spills, contaminated water supplies, industrial accidents, and so on.)* Invite volunteers to present their collages to the class. **ENGLISH LANGUAGE LEARNERS**

**LEVEL 2:** Remind students that pollution is a global problem. Organize students into small groups. Then ask each group to imagine that it is an advertising agency. The agency has been hired to create a campaign to increase public awareness of the global problems of pollution. Encourage students to design advertisements for different media such as billboards, newspapers, magazines, radio, television, and so on. Have each group present its ad campaigns to the class. **COOPERATIVE LEARNING**

**LEVEL 3:** Discuss with students how political boundaries do not prevent the spread of airborne and waterborne pollutants. Then ask each student to draw a political cartoon illustrating how pollution is a global problem. Have students emphasize the need for countries to work together to reduce pollution.

The Chernobyl accident made it frighteningly clear that environmental pollution cannot be contained within national borders. Pollution in one country can affect neighboring countries and the world environment. It can harm the air we breathe and the water we need for life. It can devastate the land we live on. Pollution is a problem of global concern.

✔ **Reading Check** Finding the Main Idea How did the Chernobyl accident show that pollution was a global concern? The explosion scattered radioactive material beyond the borders of the Soviet Union.

## ★ Air Pollution

The air we breathe is a mixture of nitrogen, oxygen, carbon dioxide, and small amounts of other gases. It is a **renewable resource** and can therefore be replaced. Dirt and harmful gases released by furnaces, factories, and automobiles cause air pollution. Natural occurrences such as volcanic eruptions can pollute the air. For example, when Mount Pinatubo erupted in the Philippines, it released 2 cubic miles of ash into the air. Under normal conditions, natural processes clean the air of pollution. However, in recent years this air pollution has become so great that nature cannot easily get rid of it.

The air over many of the world's cities is filled with **smog**—a combination of smoke, gases, and fog. Smog burns the eyes and lungs. High levels of smog can be harmful to human health. For example, a 1995 study found that people living in the U.S. cities with high levels of air pollution are more likely to die at younger ages than people living in the country's cleanest cities.

Air pollution has caused other problems as well. Over the last hundred years the level of carbon dioxide and other gases released into the atmosphere has risen dramatically. At the same time, millions of acres of forests, whose trees absorb carbon dioxide, have been destroyed. Some scientists believe the resulting high level of carbon dioxide causes

---

**Interpreting the Visual Record**

**Chernobyl** *Thousands of people evacuated the city of Chernobyl after the nuclear reactor accident. They abandoned everything, as the photo of this carnival shows.* **Why would people have felt it necessary to leave the city?**

---

*High levels of smog can cloak a city in a brown fog-like haze.*

---

**internet** connect

**TOPIC:** Pollution
**GO TO:** go.hrw.com
**KEYWORD:** SZ3 AC26

Have students access the Internet through the HRW Go site to research information about pollution. Then have each student make an annotated list of the different types of pollution, the sources from which the pollution comes, and the ways to prevent pollution in the environment.

---

**Visual Record Answer**

*Students might suggest that radiation can linger in the soil and water for many years, and it can be deadly to plants, animals, and humans.*

**ALL LEVELS:** Copy the graphic organizer to the right onto the chalkboard, omitting the italicized answers. Have students complete the "atmosphere" with some examples of different causes of air pollution as well as some of the effects that air pollution has on the atmosphere.

## ENGLISH LANGUAGE LEARNERS

**HOMEWORK** Have students find out what types of health hazards air pollution poses for human beings and ask them to create a pamphlet educating people about the dangers of air pollution.

**Causes and Effects of Air Pollution**

Ozone layer

Atmosphere

**CAUSES** *burning gas, oil, and coal; dirt; natural occurrences; chlorofluorocarbons (CFCs)*

Earth

**EFFECTS** *global warming greenhouse effect acid rain*

## ★ Citizenship in Action

### Making a Difference

Young people throughout the nation are becoming involved in environmental issues and are working to bring about change. In 1990, for example, a ninth-grade student in Maine found out that hundreds of thousands of dolphins were dying each year after being caught in the nets used by tuna companies. This student and 75 others wrote to the tuna company officials and asked them to find a way to stop the needless deaths of the dolphins. Shortly thereafter, the nation's three leading tuna companies acknowledged the public concern about the dolphins and pledged to keep them safe from tuna nets. Students in California drafted state legislation that now requires state buildings in California to use water-saving plants in their landscaping.

**ACTIVITY:** Ask students to think about ways that they can become involved in environmental issues affecting their community, either by addressing an overlooked problem or by participating in an existing program. Have students write a brief description of what they plan to do.

## Visual Record Answer

*Students might suggest that these areas provide recreational opportunities as well as the opportunity for scientists to study animal species in their natural habitat.*

*This computer-enhanced image shows the hole in Earth's ozone layer over Antarctica.*

**Interpreting the Visual Record**

**Vulnerable forest** *Northern forests and lakeside areas such as this one are particularly vulnerable to the effects of acid rain.* **What value do you think an area like the one shown here has to society?**

Earth's atmosphere to absorb more of the Sun's heat. For millions of years Earth's atmosphere has naturally absorbed the Sun's rays and has maintained a temperature that made the planet habitable for life. However, some scientists believe that increased amounts of carbon dioxide in Earth's atmosphere cause Earth's temperature to rise—a process called the **greenhouse effect.**

Many people are concerned with the greenhouse effect because it may lead to global warming, a general increase in Earth's temperature. This warming effect could have devastating results for the environment. It could change global climates and weather patterns and possibly even destroy ecosystems. The issue of global warming is still controversial. Much of the research on global warming is based on computer models that simulate Earth's environment. Some scientists have argued that Earth's atmosphere is too complicated to accurately model in a computer simulation.

Another problem posed by air pollution is a thinning of Earth's ozone layer. The **ozone layer** is a thin layer in Earth's upper atmosphere that shields the planet from the Sun's ultraviolet rays. Scientists have discovered that chemicals called chlorofluorocarbons (CFCs) damage the ozone layer. In the past CFCs have been used in items such as refrigerators, air conditioners, and aerosol spray cans. Many countries have banned the use of CFCs in new products. By 1993 the amount of CFC emissions had dropped dramatically.

The greatest damage to the ozone layer thus far has been above Antarctica. However, some scientists suspect that other areas of the ozone layer are thinning as well. The damaged ozone layer allows more ultraviolet radiation to reach Earth. As a result, these scientists anticipate increased cases of skin cancer and eye disease in humans. They also expect increased environmental damage.

Air pollution has also led to acid rain. **Acid rain** occurs when pollution from burning gas, oil, and coal mixes with water vapor. This acid then combines with snow or rain and falls to Earth. Acid rain increases the levels of acid in soil, lakes, and streams, making them less able to support life. Gradually, trees die and lakes and streams become unfit for fish and plant life.

✔ **Reading Check Identifying Cause and Effect** What causes pollution, and what is the result? furnaces, factories, and automobiles; smog, possibly the greenhouse effect, thinning ozone layer, and acid rain

## ⭐ The Water Supply

Water, like air, is essential to all life on the planet. Protecting ourselves and the planet requires us to protect the water supply.

All freshwater comes from clouds—as rain, snow, or other forms of precipitation. It sinks into the soil, follows underground routes, and forms underground pools. The excess water runs into rivers, lakes, and oceans. Eventually, it evaporates into the atmosphere to fall again as precipitation. This process is called the **hydrologic cycle.**

Underground water reserves are a key part of this cycle. Underground water nourishes plants and helps supply water to people and animals. When trees, plants, and grasses cover Earth's soil, a good supply of underground water is more likely to be maintained. The roots of trees and other plants help keep the soil moist by slowing the flow of water. Trees and plants release moisture into the atmosphere as part of the hydrologic cycle.

When trees and plants are removed, rain tends to rush down slopes instead of sinking slowly into the ground. This change has happened in many parts of the United States. The level of water under the ground—the water table—is slowly sinking. As a result, the country's supply of usable freshwater is decreasing in some areas. This decrease is also occurring in countries whose rapidly growing populations are placing great demands on the water supply. Intensive agriculture in dry regions can also deplete the water table.

Along with the quantity of available water, the quality of Earth's water is a matter of international concern. Increasingly the world's water supply, freshwater and saltwater, is being polluted. This pollution poses hazards not only for human beings but also for thousands of marine species of animal and plant life.

✔ **Reading Check Finding the Main Idea** Why is it important to protect Earth's water supply? Water is the basis for all life, and we need to maintain water quality and underground water reserve levels.

## ⭐ Water Pollution

Anything in the water that makes the water harmful or less useful to living things is a pollutant. Water pollution can be classified into five general types—chemical pollutants, sewage, thermal pollution, silt, and crud.

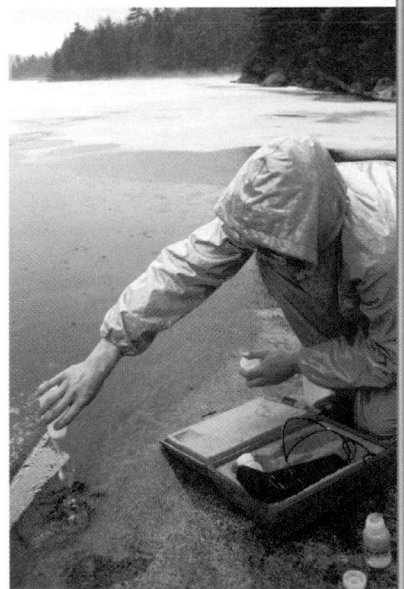

**Interpreting the Visual Record**

**Water testing** *Testing water supplies for pollutants is an important way of protecting public health.* **Why is having a safe water supply important?**

# TEACH OBJECTIVE 3

**LEVEL 1:** Discuss with students how water and ground pollution threaten the environment. *(Pollution from one area or country can affect the entire global environment.)* Organize students into small groups and ask each group to draw a poster illustrating the maintenance of clean water and land. Display the posters around the classroom.
**ENGLISH LANGUAGE LEARNERS , COOPERATIVE LEARNING**

**LEVEL 2:** Organize students into pairs and ask them to consider how water and ground pollution threaten the environment. Then ask each pair to draw a diagram illustrating the process and importance of the hydrologic cycle. *(The hydrologic cycle is the process by which fresh water falls from clouds, sinks into the soil, runs into rivers, lakes, and oceans, and evaporates into the atmosphere to fall again as precipitation.)* Have students also show what happens when this cycle is contaminated by pollutants or interrupted by the widespread removal of trees and plants. *(Students might illustrate that when large numbers of trees are removed, there is no longer a root system to slow the flow of water underground or to keep the ground moist and fertile.)* Invite pairs to explain their diagrams to the rest of the class.
**COOPERATIVE LEARNING**

**Visual Record Answer**

*Students might suggest that cleanup efforts are important for the environment because oil from a spill can work its way throughout the ecosystem where it can harm living things.*

**Interpreting the Visual Record**

**Cleanup** *Cleaning up oil spills is difficult and time-consuming work. Here volunteers try to remove oil residue from a beach following a spill.* **Why are such cleanup efforts important for the environment?**

Chemical pollutants come mainly from industrial plants. In fact, industry—factories, mills, and mines—accounts for more than half of all water pollution. Pesticides and artificial fertilizers used in agriculture also are major sources of chemical water pollution.

Other forms of chemical pollution also exist. For example, many washing detergents contain substances called phosphates, which make detergents act more quickly. However, phosphates also pollute water.

Sewage comes mainly from cities, towns, and other communities that dump raw waste, including human waste, into lakes, rivers, and streams. Water contaminated by untreated sewage is extremely dangerous to human beings. The diseases of cholera, typhoid, amebic dysentery, and hepatitis are transmitted in human waste. In addition, this polluted water eventually makes its way to the sea. There it can contaminate the water and kill fish and other marine life.

Thermal pollution occurs when industries use cold water from streams or lakes to cool their products. They then pump the warmer water back into the streams or lakes. For example, steel plants and nuclear power plants pump heated water into streams. The temperature of the water, raised in this manner, may kill fish and other marine life.

In addition, algae, or tiny water plants, may grow in the warmer water and begin to smell. Algae draw large amounts of oxygen from the water as they die and rot, depriving other marine life of oxygen. In this way thermal pollution upsets the balance of nature that helps renew Earth's water.

Silt is very fine soil or mud that results from water washing into streams. Silt comes mainly from sloping land that does not have enough trees or other plants to hold soil in place. Silt pollution is often caused by improper mining and agricultural practices, road building, and moving soil. In some bodies of water even small amounts of silt can interfere with the reproduction of water insects. Fish depend on these insects for food and will die without them.

Although sometimes a slang word, *crud* can also refer to trash, such as old tires, bottles, and other used items. Such items become crud when people discard them into lakes, rivers, forests, or other ecosystems. Crud poses many hazards to living things. For example, aquatic birds can drown when they become entangled in the plastic rings used to hold aluminum cans together. Marine animals can eat pieces of plastic and other trash that injure or eventually kill them.

✔ **Reading Check** **Categorizing** List and describe the different forms of water pollution. chemical—comes mainly from industrial plants; sewage—raw waste, contains diseases and extremely dangerous to people and animals; thermal—warm water pumped into cool streams or lakes; silt—soil or mud that has washed into streams; crud—trash

## SPOTLIGHT on Pollution

Ask students to imagine that they are living in a future world where all the trees have been cut down and most plants have died. Ask each student to write a short story about what would happen to the water supply in a world without trees and plants. Encourage students to use their imaginations to think about what human beings would have to do to get clean drinkable water. *(Students' stories will vary, but they should mention that without plants and trees Earth's water supply would be in jeopardy.)* Invite volunteers to read their short stories to the class. **BLOCK SCHEDULING**

## CLOSE

Ask students to imagine that they are delegates to another Earth Summit, similar to the one held in Rio de Janeiro in 1992. Have each student draw up a proposed international treaty on pollution that builds on the agreements made at the first Earth Summit. A preamble to the treaty should state the reasons that such a treaty is necessary. *(The treaty should include goals and ways for countries to meet those goals. Students might also make use of charts, diagrams, illustrations, or maps.)* Call on volunteers to present their treaties to the class. Then have the class discuss the ways that all nations can come together to meet those goals.

## ★ Ground Pollution

Global population growth and the increased production of certain goods have resulted in overwhelming amounts of garbage for many cities. This ground pollution is a matter of urgent global concern.

For example, the inhabitants of Tokyo, Japan, produce 12,600 tons of garbage each day. Some of this garbage is burned, and some is turned into items that can be used. However, most of it ends up in dump sites. Tokyo is running out of room for these dump sites and has built artificial islands in Tokyo Bay to hold the garbage. These islands have threatened both its fishing and shipping industries.

In the United States most garbage is deposited in landfills. **Landfills** are huge pits dug in the ground in order to store large amounts of garbage. The garbage is supposed to decompose in the same way that leaves decay on the forest floor. Unfortunately, recent discoveries show that garbage does not decompose as rapidly as people once thought. Some materials can take decades to decompose.

Moreover, landfills leak toxic materials into the surrounding soil and groundwater. People do not want to live near a landfill. Thus, as existing landfills fill up, locating places to dig new ones becomes more difficult.

✔ **Reading Check** **Analyzing Information** Why can ground pollution be difficult to control? amounts increasing rapidly, limited places to store it, and decomposition slow

## ★ Responding to Pollution

The problems of environmental pollution have no political boundaries. Polluted air and water from one country may drift into the air and water of other countries. Thus, pollution from one country can affect the global environment, and providing solutions to these problems calls for international cooperation. Acknowledging this fact, delegates from 178 countries met in 1992 for the United Nations Conference on Environment and Development. This effort is often referred to as the Earth Summit.

At the 1992 Earth Summit, held in Rio de Janeiro, Brazil, the participants signed treaties and other agreements to reduce global warming, preserve forests, limit ocean pollution, and protect the world's animal, plant, and microbe species. However, a great deal of time, money, and effort will be required to put these agreements into effect. Some people worry that countries

**Interpreting the Visual Record**

**Trash** *Americans produce enormous amounts of trash. This garbage fills landfills and garbage barges across the country.* **What might be some benefits of reducing the amount of trash we produce?**

*These children are posing in front of an environmental mural at the Earth Summit in Rio de Janeiro.*

### ★ Global Perspectives

**Irrigating the Land** Providing clean freshwater for the expanding world population promises to be an important issue in years to come. About 97 percent of Earth's water is salty. Only 3 percent is fresh, and two thirds of that is in frozen regions. Many people in the United States take fresh water for granted. Americans use about 1,300 gallons of water a day per person, which is three times the average usage rate in Europe and many times the rate of industrializing nations. Most freshwater is used for agriculture. Innovative irrigation methods in the United States and elsewhere have helped reduce water use. In Israel, for example, a "drip irrigation" program uses computers and sensing monitors to make sure plants receive just the right amount of water that they need to thrive.

**ACTIVITY:** Ask students to conduct research to learn more about the different types of irrigation techniques being used by farmers in the United States and in foreign countries. Have each student create a chart or diagram illustrating how these irrigation techniques help to conserve water used in agriculture.

### Visual Record Answer

*Students might suggest that producing less trash would reduce our need for landfills.*

## REVIEW AND ASSESS

Have students complete the **Section 2 Review** on page 668. Then have students complete **Daily Quiz 26.2.** As **Alternative Assessment,** you may want to use the global pollution advertising or the hydrologic cycle activities in this section's lessons.

## RETEACH

Have students complete **Main Idea Activity for English Language Learners and Special-Needs Students 26.2.** Then organize students into two groups. Ask each student in the first group to write a short poem describing how air pollution is harmful to the ecosystem. Have each student in the second group write a short poem describing how trees and plants affect Earth's water supply. **ENGLISH LANGUAGE LEARNERS , COOPERATIVE LEARNING**

## EXTEND

Have students conduct research to learn more about the steps that local industries or local government agencies are taking to protect and improve air and water quality. Encourage students to contact a local government office for information, or have students interview a public-relations representative at a local business. Ask students to write a brief report based on what they discover. *(Students might describe government regulations that protect local water supplies, or they might show how local businesses are complying with such regulations.)* **BLOCK SCHEDULING**

## Section 2 Review
### ANSWERS

**1. Define**
- pollution, p. 662
- renewable resource, p. 663
- smog, p. 663
- greenhouse effect, p. 664
- ozone layer, p. 664
- acid rain, p. 664
- hydrologic cycle, p. 665
- landfills, p. 667
- recycling, p. 668

**2.** chemicals, industries, contaminated water; sewage, raw waste dumping, disease and contaminated water; thermal, repumped water, destroys ecosystem

**3. a.** because pollution is not confined to a country's borders

**b.** gases / automobiles, factories / smog that burns eyes and lungs; chlorofluorocarbons (CFCs) / refrigerators, aerosol spray cans / thins the ozone layer; acid rain / burning gas, oil, coal / makes soil, lakes, and streams less capable of supporting life

**4.** Students' speeches might consider the effects of air, water, and ground pollution and might also suggest alternative forms of waste reduction.

### Visual Record Answer

*Students might suggest that recycling helps reduce waste.*

**Interpreting the Visual Record**

**Recycling** *At this recycling center plastic bottles are compressed so that they can be stored and treated more easily.* **Why is recycling products like plastic a beneficial activity?**

will not carry out the agreements. Still, the Earth Summit stands out as the largest international effort to deal with global environmental problems.

Individuals, too, are taking steps to help protect the environment. Many communities have started recycling programs. **Recycling** is the process of turning waste into something that can be used again. For example, aluminum cans can be melted and used to make new cans. Recycling reduces the amount of trash that ends up in landfills.

Individuals can also help the environment by reducing the amount of disposable goods, water, and energy that they use. Some people have begun bringing cloth bags to grocery stores. This way they do not have to use the stores' paper or plastic bags. People can also recycle many of the items that they typically use and discard.

For example, plastic forks and spoons can be washed and reused. Some people walk and ride bicycles whenever possible instead of driving. Even something as simple as turning the water off while you brush your teeth helps save water. Switching off the light when you leave a room reduces the amount of electricity you use.

Everyone in the world depends on the environment for life. Earth's future as a home for all living things depends on how well we all cooperate to prevent pollution.

✔ **Reading Check Summarizing** What are some of the ways that individuals can protect the environment? by reducing the amount of disposable goods, water, and energy they use

---

## SECTION 2 Review

**go. hrw .com Homework Practice Online**

**keyword: SZ3 HP26**

**1. Define** and explain:
- pollution
- renewable resource
- smog
- greenhouse effect
- ozone layer
- acid rain
- hydrologic cycle
- landfills
- recycling

**2. Identifying Cause and Effect** Copy the table below. Use it to list the different kinds of water pollution and their effects on the environment.

| Pollutant | Cause | Effect |
|-----------|-------|--------|
|  |  |  |
|  |  |  |
|  |  |  |
|  |  |  |

**3. Finding the Main Idea**
a. Why do some people believe that pollution is a global problem?
b. What are some causes of air pollution, and how do they affect the environment?

**4. Writing and Critical Thinking**
**Problem Solving** You are an activist promoting the protection of the environment. Write a speech describing current dangers to the environment. Then explain some ways that communities and individuals can help conserve the environment.

**Consider:**
- air, water, and ground pollution
- alternative forms of waste reduction

## TEACH

**LEVEL 1:** Ask students to bring in maps that highlight the geographical features of their state. Organize students into pairs and ask pairs to familiarize themselves with their maps. Then lead a class discussion in which pairs use their maps to identify significant features of their state's landscape, whether natural or human-made. *(For example, students might point out mountainous regions, open plains, waterways, reservoirs, state parks, nature preserves, urban areas, and so on.)* Ask students to discuss how human beings have altered the natural features of the map.

**ENGLISH LANGUAGE LEARNERS** , **COOPERATIVE LEARNING**

**LEVEL 3:** Ask students to conduct research at the library to determine how industry, agriculture, and development have changed the natural landscape of the United States. Then ask each student to draw a map of the United States that illustrates these changes. *(Students might use different colors or draw small symbols on their maps to indicate changes in the ecosystem.)* Display these maps around the classroom.

# Civics Skills
## WORKSHOP

### Reading Maps

Maps are flat diagrams of all or part of Earth's surface. Like charts and graphs, they are excellent ways to organize large amounts of data.

### How to Read Maps

1. **Determine the subject.** Reading the title of the map will alert you to the kind of information you can learn from the map. Note the area shown on the map.

2. **Study the legend.** Examine the legend, or key, to learn the meanings of the map's symbols and colors.

3. **Use the scale and the compass rose.** The scale of a map tells you how distances on the map compare with the actual distances on Earth's surface. The compass rose on a map indicates direction and orientation.

4. **Study the labels.** The names of important geographic features and key terms often appear on the map.

5. **Put the data to use.** Taking all of the map's information into account, draw conclusions about what the map shows.

### Applying the Skill

Study the map of hazardous waste sites in the United States below. Then answer the questions that follow.

1. How many states have between 0 and 20 hazardous waste sites? Which states have the highest number of sites?

2. What is the approximate distance between the southern tips of Florida and Texas?

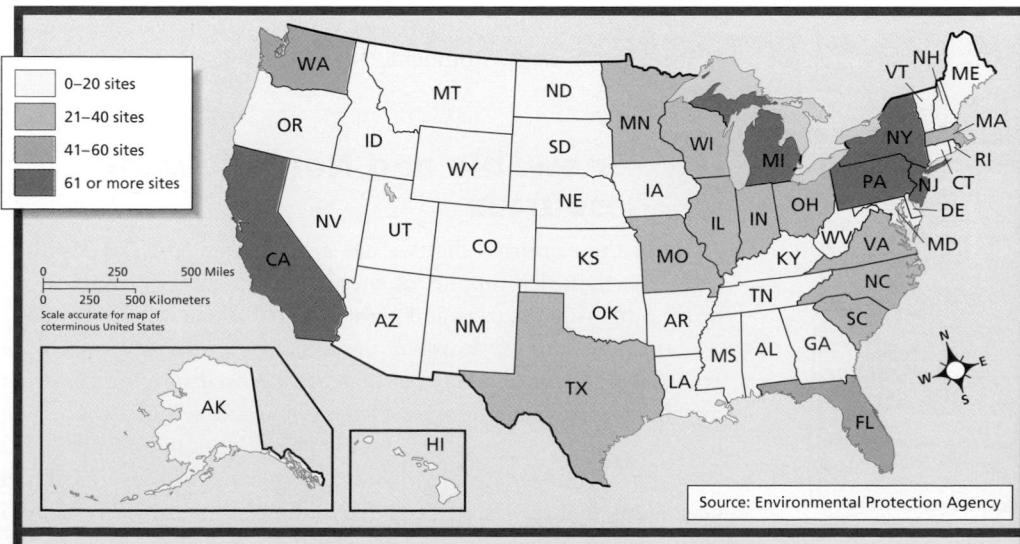

**U.S. Superfund Hazardous Waste Sites, 2001**

Legend:
- 0–20 sites
- 21–40 sites
- 41–60 sites
- 61 or more sites

0   250   500 Miles
0   250   500 Kilometers
Scale accurate for map of coterminous United States

Source: Environmental Protection Agency

# SECTION 3

## OBJECTIVES

*After completing Section 3, students should be able to*

1 **Distinguish between renewable and nonrenewable resources.**

2 **Identify some alternative forms of energy and explain why they are being explored.**

3 **Analyze the debate between development and conservation.**

## SECTION 3 RESOURCES

### REPRODUCIBLE
▶ Guided Reading Strategies 26.3

### TECHNOLOGY
▶ One-Stop Planner, Lesson 26.3
▶ Holt Researcher CD–ROM
▶ Homework Practice Online

### REINFORCEMENT, REVIEW, AND ASSESSMENT
▶ Section 3 Review, p. 676
▶ Daily Quiz 26.3
▶ Main Idea Activity 26.3
▶ English Audio Summary 26.3
▶ Spanish Audio Summary 26.3

## 📢 *LET'S GET STARTED!*

As students enter the classroom, ask them to imagine how their lives would be affected if Earth's supply of oil, coal, and gas suddenly ran out. Ask volunteers to describe to the class some of the things that they would no longer be able to do. *(Students might indicate that it might be difficult to get electricity for appliances and lighting. Heating and cooling their homes might also become difficult.)* Then ask students to discuss whether there are other sources of energy that people might use today in the place of oil, coal, and gas. Tell students that in Section 3 they will learn more about renewable and nonrenewable resources, alternative energy, and the debate between development and conservation.

# SECTION 3

# Energy Resources

### Read to Discover

1. What are renewable and nonrenewable resources?
2. What are some alternative forms of energy, and why are they being explored?
3. What is the debate between development and conservation?

### Define
- nonrenewable resources
- fossil fuels
- conservation
- strip mining
- biomass

### WHY CIVICS MATTERS
The use of nuclear energy is a controversial topic. Use **CNNfyi.com** or other **current events** sources to investigate the debate surrounding nuclear energy usage and the views that some people hold. Record your findings in your journal.

## *Reading Focus*

The people of the world depend on energy resources to run their factories and to provide heat and light for their homes. They need energy to drive their automobiles and to cook their food. The forms of energy that we use and the ways we acquire that energy can have significant effects on the environment.

### ★ Renewable and Nonrenewable Resources

Some of the resources that we use are renewable. Every day the Sun bathes Earth in rich supplies of energy. The resources that are sustained by the Sun—such as trees and plants—are also renewable.

Some resources, however, are nonrenewable. **Nonrenewable resources** are those resources that can be used only once. Minerals, metals, and ores are examples of nonrenewable resources. The world's deposits of these resources cannot increase. They can only decrease.

Earth's nonrenewable resources also include **fossil fuels**—petroleum, natural gas, and coal. Fossil fuels were formed over millions of years from the fossilized remains of plants and animals.

As the world continues to industrialize and increase in population, greater demands are placed on its nonrenewable energy sources.

*The gasoline used in cars is produced from a nonrenewable resource.*

**LEVEL 1:** Bring a variety of magazines to class. Lead a class discussion about the difference between renewable and nonrenewable resources. *(The difference is that renewable resources can be sustained, but nonrenewable resources can be used only once.)* Organize students into pairs and ask pairs to look through the magazines to find pictures of renewable and nonrenewable resources. Then ask each pair to draw a line down the middle of a sheet of posterboard and create a collage with pictures of renewable resources on one side, nonrenewable resources on the other. *(Students might include advertisements showing people using fossil fuels, or they might cut out pictures of* the ocean, the Sun, and so on to represent renewable sources of energy.) Display students' collages around the classroom. **ENGLISH LANGUAGE LEARNERS , COOPERATIVE LEARNING**

**LEVEL 2:** Ask each student to design a T-shirt that shows the differences between renewable and nonrenewable resources. The front of the shirt should show a renewable resource, and the back should feature a nonrenewable source. *(See the Level 1 lesson for definitions.)* Encourage students to make their designs stylish and ask them to consider creating a slogan to emphasize their design. *(Students might draw a tree on the front of their shirt, and a picture of an oil well on the back.)* Ask volunteers to show their T-shirt designs to the class.

---

Although improvements in technology can stretch the world's supply of nonrenewable resources, these resources will eventually run out. Dealing with shortages of nonrenewable energy resources and seeking new sources of energy are issues that should concern all the world's people.

## ★ Petroleum

Petroleum, or oil as it is commonly called, lies deep beneath Earth's surface in great pools. These pools formed from microscopic plants and animals that lived millions of years ago. These organisms were covered with mud, rocks, and water, and after centuries of decay and pressure from Earth, petroleum formed.

Pumped to the surface and refined, petroleum furnishes the fuel that heats many homes and the gasoline that powers automobiles. Petroleum also provides the lubricating oil to grease the wheels of industry. It is also the basis of a wide variety of byproducts, such as plastics, pesticides, and many chemicals.

Today the world's largest reserves of petroleum are found in Saudi Arabia and the countries of the Persian Gulf. The largest oil reserves in the United States are found in Alaska, Louisiana, and Texas.

The use of petroleum as an energy source is not without problems. Burning oil to heat homes and gasoline to power automobiles contributes to air pollution and possibly to global warming. The millions of tons of plastic produced from petroleum each year end up in dump sites and landfills. Plastic and other petroleum products take a very long time to decompose.

In addition, the world's supply of oil is limited. Some experts believe that the world's existing oil reserves will run out sometime in the next century. Of course, discovery of new oil deposits could extend the supply. Dependence on oil as an energy source is increasing worldwide. Thus, it is difficult to estimate how long existing and new deposits might last.

### Holt Researcher
**go.hrw.com**

**go.hrw.com**
**KEYWORD: Holt Researcher**
**Freefind: Energy Policy**

Scan through the Holt Researcher to find U.S. federal agencies responsible for managing or monitoring an aspect of energy production or use in the United States. Choose one of these organizations and create a poster that describes its function. Your poster should answer the question: What role does this federal agency play in energy regulation?

### Interpreting the Visual Record

**Oil field** *When a major reserve of oil is discovered, dozens of oil wells like these may be drilled to pump the fossil fuel from underground.* **What does this image suggest about the expense of drilling for and pumping oil?**

### Visual Record Answer

*Students might suggest that drilling for and pumping oil is an expensive and difficult process.*

**ALL LEVELS:** Copy the following graphic organizer onto the chalkboard, omitting the italicized answers. Have students complete the boxes with examples of alternative energy sources and the reasons that those sources are being explored. **ENGLISH LANGUAGE LEARNERS**

**Alternative Forms of Energy**

| Energy Sources | → | Reasons for Exploring |
|---|---|---|
| *solar energy* | → | *limited fossil fuels, cannot be used up, clean and efficient* |
| *geothermal energy* | → | *limited fossil fuels, relies on water and underground heat* |
| *hydroelectric energy* | → | *limited fossil fuels, pollution-free source of electricity* |
| *biomass* | → | *limited fossil fuels, makes use of garbage and other waste products* |

## Citizenship in Action

### Grassroots Environmentalism

Although the Environmental Protection Agency plays a central role in regulating pollution and conserving natural resources, many U.S. citizens are also involved in protecting the environment. People often donate time, expertise, and money to organizations dedicated to conservationism. One well-known environmental group is the Sierra Club, founded in California in 1892 by Scottish American John Muir. With more than 630,000 members, the Sierra Club focuses on the preservation and expansion of the world's parks, wildlife, and wilderness areas. The Sierra Club also lobbies Congress for stronger anti-pollution and environmental protection laws. Other well-known environmentalist organizations include the Nature Conservancy, the World Wildlife Fund, and the Wilderness Society.

**ACTIVITY:** Ask students to conduct research to learn more about the activities of a national conservationist organization and to write a brief report.

### Visual Record Answer

*Students might suggest that undetected natural gas leaks can pose a health hazard and may lead to explosions.*

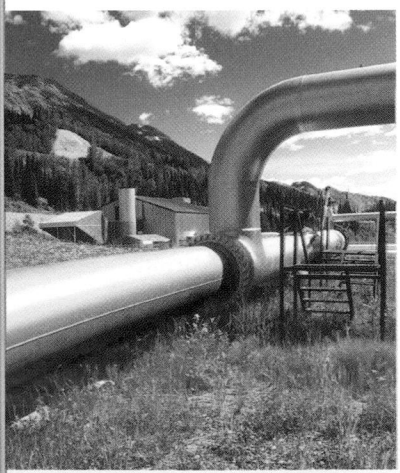

**Interpreting the Visual Record**

**Gas pipeline** *Natural gas is usually distributed to homes and businesses through pressurized pipelines. An odor is added to the invisible gas so that leaks may be detected more easily.* **Why do you think it is important to detect natural gas leaks?**

One way to stretch available oil resources is through conservation. **Conservation** refers to the safeguarding of natural resources by using them wisely. Using smaller cars, for example, helps save oil. Smaller cars travel more miles or kilometers per gallon of gas than larger cars. Likewise, many industries have installed new machinery that requires less energy to run, thus conserving oil.

Home owners can also do their part to help conserve oil. Lowering home temperatures, insulating attics and walls, and installing storm windows and doors are ways to conserve heating oil. People can also reduce their reliance on petroleum-based products such as plastic, and they can recycle what plastic they do use.

✔ **Reading Check Finding the Main Idea** What are the uses of petroleum, and why is conservation of petroleum needed? heats homes, powers automobiles, lubricates machinery, forms basis of products such as plastics, pesticides, and many chemicals; to extend the limited oil supply

## ★ Natural Gas

Natural gas, another fossil fuel, is usually found with petroleum. At one time, natural gas was burned off as it came out of an oil well. However, this clean-burning fuel has found favor with industry and home owners. Its use around the world as an energy source is growing rapidly.

Most of the energy contained in natural gas is used to generate steam for electricity and steam engines. It is also used to heat buildings and for cooking. Today the world's largest reserves of natural gas are found in Russia and in the countries of the Persian Gulf region.

Natural gas is the cleanest-burning fossil fuel because it is naturally refined during its formation beneath Earth's surface. As a result, natural gas does not release harmful pollutants or by-products when it burns. Because it is a clean-burning energy source, worldwide demand for natural gas has increased greatly in recent years. At their present rate of consumption, natural gas reserves may only last slightly longer than petroleum reserves.

In addition, natural gas is usually shipped great distances through overland pipelines. These pipelines often require large areas of land and can interfere with the migration patterns of wildlife.

✔ **Reading Check Summarizing** What are the benefits and drawbacks of using natural gas? benefits—clean-burning; drawbacks—limited in quantity, pipelines interfere with wildlife migration patterns

## ★ Coal

Coal is a fossil fuel that developed over millions of years from plant debris that accumulated in ancient swamps and bogs. The partially decomposing debris formed layers of peat, which became buried below marine sediments. The weight of the marine sediments compressed the peat and formed coal.

Coal is an important source of energy. Much of the heat energy from coal is used to produce electricity or operate steam engines. Coal is also used in the manufacture of steel. It is the source of many chemical products, such as plastics, paints, and synthetic rubber. Many countries of Asia and Europe use coal to heat homes and other buildings. Today the largest reserves of coal are found in China, Europe, Russia, and the United States.

Although coal is the most plentiful fossil fuel available, it is also a nonrenewable resource. Experts believe that available coal reserves might last another 200 years. However, coal is difficult to remove from the ground. Coal mines sometimes cave in and can release dangerous gases. Miners working underground to remove coal are prone to accidents and to diseases such as black lung.

Some deposits of coal lie near Earth's surface and can be reached by removing the top layers of soil—a process called **strip mining.** However, the practice of strip mining is harmful to the environment. It often leaves large pits and ugly scars in the land. Without trees or plants to hold the soil in place, it washes down the hills and valleys into streams. It pollutes the water with silt and sometimes clogs waterways.

In addition, the burning of coal can result in air pollution and acid rain. Many of the world's large coal-burning power plants have installed scrubbers and filters to control the level of pollutants emitted. However, such devices are costly. Techniques also exist to turn coal into a cleaner-burning liquid or gas, but these techniques are extremely expensive as well.

*Underground coal mining is a complicated and often dangerous activity requiring extensive tunnels.*

✔ **Reading Check** **Analyzing Information** How is coal a valuable form of energy, and how does it contribute to pollution? It provides heat, is used to manufacture steel, and is a source of many chemical products; mining leads to pollution of water with silt; burning coal pollutes air and leads to acid rain.

**Interpreting the Visual Record**

**Strip mining** *Strip mining avoids some of the risks of underground coal mining, but it is very damaging to the environment.* **How does this image reveal some of the effects of strip mining on the local environment?**

## TEACH OBJECTIVE 3

![eagle icon] **LEVELS 1 AND 2:** Organize the class into two groups. Tell the members of one group that they are conservationists and tell the members of the other group that they are developers. Then lead the two groups in a debate and encourage both groups to cite specific examples to support their positions. (*Students in one group might cite the need to develop land to provide housing while students in the other group might cite the need to conserve the land to keep the air and water clean.*) After a period of time, tell the groups to switch sides and then continue the debate. **ENGLISH LANGUAGE LEARNERS**

**LEVELS 2 AND 3:** Lead a class discussion about the debate between development and conservation. (*See the Levels 1 and 2 lesson.*) Then tell students to imagine that they have been assigned the task of redesigning their community so that it meets the needs of its citizens while also conserving the land and natural resources. Have each student create a map illustrating the plan for this community. (*Students' maps might include hydroelectric power plants and land reserved for parks and wildlife preservation.*) Ask volunteers to explain their plans to the class.

## ★ Civics Sidelight

**An Alternative to Nuclear Fission** Although it is still in its experimental stages, some scientists believe that the nuclear fusion reactor will be able to meet the world's future energy needs while avoiding the current problems of the fission reactors. At present, fission reactors create energy by splitting the nuclei of uranium atoms. By contrast, in a fusion reactor energy is created not by splitting atoms, but by combining or fusing them. The primary obstacle to the development of the fusion reactor is the containment of the plasma fuel, which must be heated to millions of degrees in order for fusion to occur. Scientists hope to one day produce a working fusion reactor because of the many advantages of nuclear fusion over nuclear fission. For example, current fission reactors produce large amounts of energy, but they also produce radioactive waste that is difficult and dangerous to store. A nuclear fusion reactor, however, would produce less hazardous waste. Fusion reactors would also be less expensive to operate since the main fuel for fission is deuterium, a hydrogen isotope that is obtained from water.

**ACTIVITY:** Ask students to conduct research to learn more about nuclear fusion and scientists' efforts to develop a working fusion reactor. Have students draw a diagram showing the differences between fission and fusion reactors.

*The safe use of nuclear power requires sophisticated equipment and highly trained engineers.*

### ★★★★★★★★★★★
### *That's Interesting!*
### ★★★★★★★★★★★

**Cold Fusion?** Can nuclear power be generated in a glass beaker using heavy water and some rare elements? That's what researchers Stanley Pons and Martin Fleischmann claimed they had done in 1989. Pons and Fleischmann said that they had observed a phenomenon called "cold fusion" taking place. All that was required was a special type of water called deuterium and the elements palladium and platinum. At first their claims caused a sensation. People imagined all the uses for a new, inexpensive, clean source of power. But then other groups of researchers challenged and disproved the researchers' results. Today most scientists believe that cold fusion was a hoax or a mistake. However, some researchers continue to examine the phenomenon, hoping to achieve a breakthrough that will change our ideas about nuclear physics.

## ★ Nuclear Energy

Some people believe nuclear energy is the answer to the world's growing shortages of fossil fuels. Nuclear reactors run on a small amount of radioactive uranium and produce large amounts of energy efficiently. However, much controversy surrounds the use of nuclear energy.

For example, in 1979 an accident occurred at the nuclear-powered electric plant at Three Mile Island in Middletown, Pennsylvania. Because of a series of human and mechanical errors, the radioactive core of the nuclear reactor started to overheat. This overheating caused some radioactive gas to escape into the air. Days passed before there was no longer a danger of an explosion at the plant.

The Chernobyl nuclear power plant in Ukraine was not so lucky. As you have read, a major explosion occurred there in 1986. The radioactive material released by the explosion was detected as far away as Canada and Japan. Human beings, plants, and animals were contaminated by the radiation. There have been higher rates of thyroid cancer among people who lived near the plant at the time of the accident. In addition, there have been higher numbers of genetic mutations in children born to these people.

The use of nuclear energy also brings with it the problem of how to dispose of nuclear waste. The wastes from nuclear plants remain radioactive and hazardous for thousands of years. One method for disposing of nuclear waste is to bury it in underground sealed containers. However, this form of disposal is controversial. Even sealed containers may leak because nuclear waste causes the containers to corrode. Furthermore, transporting nuclear waste to storage facilities increases the risk of accidents.

Because of the problems and hazards associated with nuclear energy, many people question its use. Some countries, including Sweden and Germany, are phasing out their existing nuclear plants. Other countries are reluctant to build new nuclear power plants within their boundaries.

✔ **Reading Check** Identifying Points of View What different opinions do people have about nuclear energy? answer to shortage of fossil fuels; too dangerous to use

## ★ Alternative Sources of Energy

Growing shortages of fossil fuels and the dangers of nuclear energy have brought new attention to alternative sources of energy. It is anticipated that these alternative energy sources will lessen the world's reliance on nonrenewable resources.

**LEVEL 3:** Ask each student to draw a political cartoon illustrating the debate between development and conservation. *(See the Levels 1 and 2 lesson for debate.)* Ask students to consider the consequences that would result if people were to continue developing the land without giving any thought to conservation. *(Students' cartoons might show a picture of the Grand Canyon with skyscrapers lining both sides and so on.)* Display these cartoons around the classroom.

## CLOSE

Ask students to imagine that the governor of their state has appointed them to create a comprehensive plan for helping the state become more environmentally friendly over the course of the next decade. Then have each student create an outline showing how the state could decrease its dependence on nonrenewable energy sources by taking advantage of alternative forms of energy. Also, ask students to take into consideration how their state might conserve its land while meeting the needs of its population. *(Students' outlines might also include a map or diagram explaining how the plan could be implemented.)* Invite volunteers to explain their outlines to the class.

One of the most promising sources of energy is energy from the Sun, or solar energy. The Sun gives off an enormous amount of energy. Solar energy is produced by capturing the Sun's energy and converting it into heat and electricity. Solar energy is a clean and efficient form of energy for specially constructed homes and offices.

Another alternative source of energy is geothermal energy, or underground heat. This energy is generated whenever water comes in contact with hot underground rocks and turns to steam. The steam, released through hot springs and geysers, can be captured and used to generate electricity. Countries throughout the world, including Iceland, Italy, Japan, New Zealand, and the United States, have developed geothermal power plants.

Hydroelectric energy is produced by storing water behind large dams. When the water is released, it spins special engines producing pollution-free electricity. Hydroelectric plants now contribute to energy production in countries such as Canada, Norway, Russia, and the United States.

Some countries are using the power of the wind to generate energy. In fact, windmills are one of the world's oldest devices for producing power. Today's windmills provide a cheap and clean source of energy. Yet, wind energy is practical only in areas that have strong steady winds.

Also being considered as a possible source of alternative energy is **biomass.** Biomass consists of wood and waste products (garbage, yard trimmings, and so on) that can be burned or used to make fuel. Biomass is a commonly used household fuel in many of the world's poorer countries. Burning biomass does produce some degree of air pollution. However, researchers are testing new ways to turn biomass into efficient, convenient, and clean-burning fuel products.

These alternative energy sources rely mainly on the world's renewable resources, such as Sun, water, and wind. To meet the ever-increasing global demand for energy, these alternative sources and others must be studied, improved, and used.

✔ **Reading Check Contrasting** What are some advantages and disadvantages to using alternative forms of energy? rely on the world's renewable resources, efficient, and often clean; limited by geography

*Researchers are developing less-expensive and more-efficient types of solar panels to generate electricity for homes and offices.*

**Interpreting the Visual Record**

**Wind power** *In some regions of the United States, such as parts of California, windmill "farms" generate large amounts of electric power.* **Based on this picture, why do you think these windmill sites are sometimes called farms?**

**Marketing and the Environment** Many businesses now advertise "environmentally friendly" products. But what exactly does this mean? The Federal Trade Commission (FTC) discourages the use of the phrase "environmentally friendly" because the term is still not clearly defined, and it is often misused by marketers and misunderstood by consumers. Environmental friendliness is based on two factors: biodegradability and ecotoxicity. Biodegradability is the ability of a substance to be decomposed by microbes and safely absorbed into the ecosystem. Ecotoxicity is the degree to which a substance is poisonous or harmful to the ecosystem. To be environmentally friendly, a product must have good biodegradability and low ecotoxicity. However, there is no uniform standard by which to measure these factors, and it is difficult to compare products.

**CRITICAL THINKING**

How can you determine whether a product is friendly or unfriendly to the environment before purchasing it?

**ANSWER:** Almost all products affect the environment, but consumers can read labels to look for toxic substances or to learn whether or not a product can be recycled.

**Visual Record Answer**

*Students might suggest that the windmills are arranged in rows, just like crops on a farm.*

Have students complete the **Section 3 Review** on page 676. Then have students complete **Daily Quiz 26.3**. As **Alternative Assessment**, you may want to use the resources pamphlet or the political cartoon exercises in this section's lessons.

## RETEACH

Have students complete **Main Idea Activity for English Language Learners and Special-Needs Students 26.3**. Then organize students into three groups and assign each group an objective from this section. Ask each group to create an outline of its section. **ENGLISH LANGUAGE LEARNERS ,**
**COOPERATIVE LEARNING**

## EXTEND

Have students conduct research to learn more about how the debate between conservation and development has affected their community or state. Students should consider developments that have disturbed the ecosystem, as well as actions taken to conserve the environment. Where possible, students should find examples of how both developers and conservationists have met their goals through compromise. Ask each student to write a brief presentation for a television news segment about the debate between development and conservation. **BLOCK SCHEDULING**

---

**Visual Record Answer**

*Students should suggest that they are protesting the pollutants affecting beaches.*

## Section 3 Review
### ANSWERS

**1. Define**
• nonrenewable resources, p. 670
• fossil fuels, p. 670
• conservation, p. 672
• strip mining, p. 673
• biomass, p. 675

**2.** renewable—solar power, trees and plants, hydroelectric power; nonrenewable—petroleum, natural gas, coal

**3. a.** Alternative energy sources such as solar power, geothermal energy, hydroelectric energy, wind, and biomass are being studied because these sources are renewable and, in most cases, cleaner and more efficient than burning fossil fuels.

**b.** Leaders will have to balance the need for development and the improvements in technology, science, and so on with the serious concerns about preserving the quality of our environment.

**4.** Students' reports should consider the benefits and limitations of alternative energy sources, and they should consider as well the controversy surrounding development.

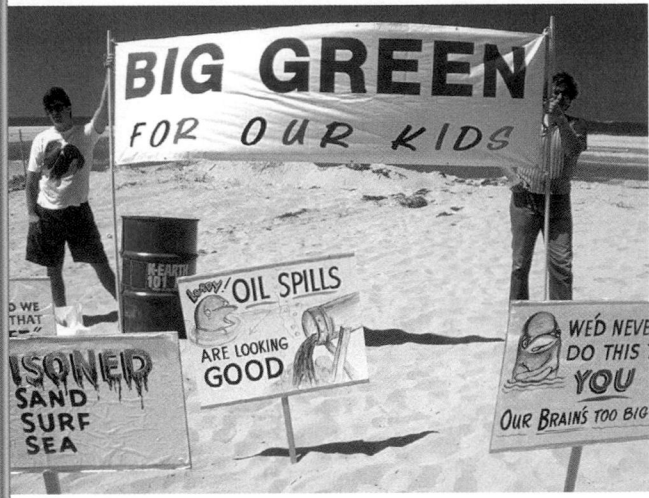

**Interpreting the Visual Record**

**Protecting the future** *A major concern of many conservationists is that the environment inherited by future generations will be badly damaged unless we protect it now.* **What are these people protesting?**

## ★ Development and Conservation

Each time an area is developed, delicate ecosystems may be upset. Development, of course, is necessary for the growth and well-being of countries. However, people in many countries today are determined to halt the environmental harm that has been common in the past.

Some people worry about the high costs of keeping the environment clean. They argue that new safeguards and equipment make it too costly to build new plants or to begin new development. To supply the resources we need, many believe we must continue to use natural resources as we always have. They believe it may even be necessary to relax some of the environmental health standards set in recent years.

In contrast, other people argue that whatever harms the land, sea, and air also harms people and all other living things. They say that people need to be more cautious about ensuring that Earth remains a healthy and livable place. Balancing the needs of development and conservation will be a challenge for leaders in the coming years.

✔ **Reading Check Supporting a Point of View** What is your opinion about balancing the needs of development with those of conservation? Explain your answer. *Answers will vary but should be clear and logical.*

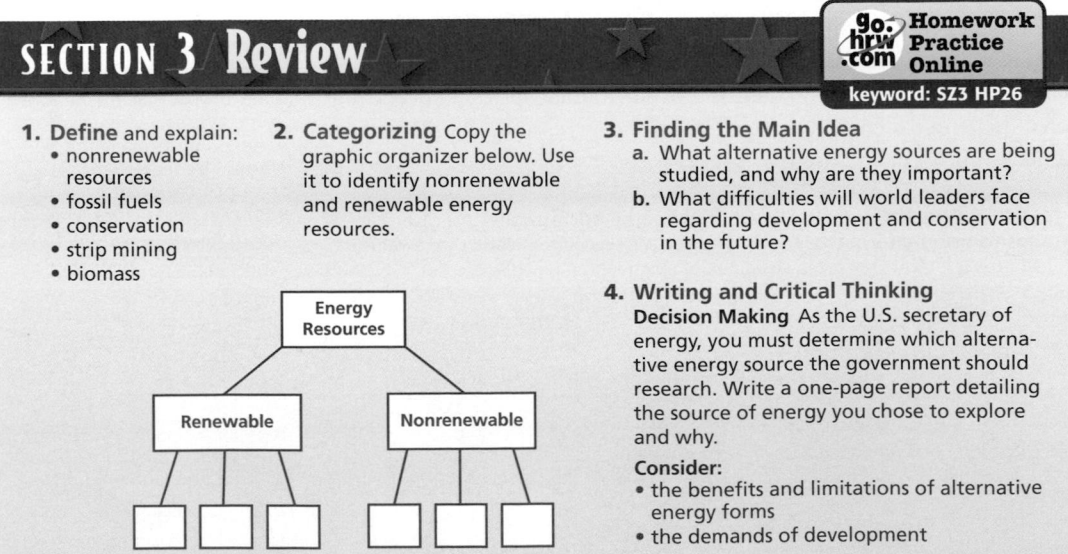

**SECTION 3 Review**

**go.hrw.com**
**Homework Practice Online**
**keyword: SZ3 HP26**

**1. Define** and explain:
• nonrenewable resources
• fossil fuels
• conservation
• strip mining
• biomass

**2. Categorizing** Copy the graphic organizer below. Use it to identify nonrenewable and renewable energy resources.

Energy Resources
→ Renewable
→ Nonrenewable

**3. Finding the Main Idea**
a. What alternative energy sources are being studied, and why are they important?
b. What difficulties will world leaders face regarding development and conservation in the future?

**4. Writing and Critical Thinking**
**Decision Making** As the U.S. secretary of energy, you must determine which alternative energy source the government should research. Write a one-page report detailing the source of energy you chose to explore and why.

**Consider:**
• the benefits and limitations of alternative energy forms
• the demands of development

# SECTION 4

## OBJECTIVES

*After completing Section 4, students should be able to*

1 **Describe what the federal government did to preserve the environment before the 1950s.**

2 **Evaluate how the Clean Air and Water Acts help the environment.**

3 **Determine what the Environmental Protection Agency does.**

## 🔊 LET'S GET STARTED!

As students enter the classroom, ask them to read the excerpt from *Silent Spring* by Rachel Carson that can be found in Readings in Economics and Government. Then ask students to think of ways that people, businesses, and the government work to protect the environment. Ask volunteers to come to the chalkboard to list some of those ways. *(Students might cite the creation of the national parks system, government regulations of air and water pollution, laws protecting endangered species, local conservation efforts, and so on.)* Tell students that in Section 4 they will learn more about what we can do to protect our environmental future.

## SECTION 4

# Our Future on Earth

### Read to Discover

1. Before the 1950s, what did the federal government do to preserve the environment?
2. How do the Clean Air and Water Acts help the environment?
3. What does the Environmental Protection Agency do?

### Identify

• Endangered Species Acts
• Environmental Protection Agency
• Earth Day

#### WHY CIVICS MATTERS

Federal, state, and local governments all work to protect the environment. Use **CNNfyi.com** or other **current events** sources to find out what environmental issues the government is currently working to resolve. Record your findings in your journal.

## *Reading Focus*

The United States has long been interested in conservation and the environment. For example, in 1872 the U.S. government set aside a portion of northwestern Wyoming as a national park. The land was to remain in its natural state, to be enjoyed by all. Yellowstone National Park was the first national park in the world and an important effort in preserving natural resources. However, caring for the planet also requires the ongoing efforts of government and citizens alike.

### ★ Early Conservation Efforts

The National Park Service is only one of many agencies that help preserve the natural resources of the United States. The U.S. Department of Agriculture (USDA) Forest Service was established to supervise vast areas of forest land and to help conserve their timber. Later, laws limited the amount of minerals that could be taken from the ground each year. Laws passed to govern grazing practices helped limit the destruction of grasslands. The USDA encouraged and helped farmers use soil conservation methods.

In 1908 President Theodore Roosevelt called a conference of U.S. governors to consider how best to conserve the land and its resources. Under President Franklin D. Roosevelt, a program encouraging farmers to grow soil-conserving crops was established.

*National parks allow people to enjoy the natural resources of the United States.*

**LEVEL 1:** Lead a class discussion about what the federal government did to protect the environment before the 1950s. Point out that during this period, little was done to limit waste and pollution. Ask students to draw posters illustrating the main types of environmental programs sponsored by the government prior to 1950. *(Students might represent the establishment of national parks, the building of dams, the preservation of forests, and so on.)* Display students' posters around the classroom. **ENGLISH LANGUAGE LEARNERS**

**LEVELS 2 AND 3:** Organize students into groups. Then ask each group to write a one-act play that dramatizes the efforts of the U.S. government to protect the environment before the 1950s. In order to place these efforts in a historical context, have students make references in their plays to significant events of the period. *(Students might mention the establishment of Yellowstone National Park or the efforts of Presidents Theodore Roosevelt or Franklin Roosevelt.)*
**COOPERATIVE LEARNING**

 **HOMEWORK** Ask students to find examples of pre-1950s programs or measures to protect the environment that are still of benefit today. Then ask students to create a pamphlet that describes this ongoing effort.

## Global Perspectives

**The National Park System** The United States established the world's first national park in 1872. Since then, most other countries have also set aside land for national parks. These parks, which number in the hundreds, showcase not only great natural scenery but also beautiful or rare animals and plants, as the following limited selection shows. Finders Chase in Australia is home to kangaroos, anteaters, koalas, and emus. Amazônia in Brazil is 3,838 square miles of plains and rain forest. Banff in Canada contains mountain goats and bighorn sheep. Fuji-Hakone-Izu in Japan is the site of Mount Fuji volcano. Serengeti in Tanzania is a vast, open grassland where lions, antelope, and zebras roam. Victoria Falls in Zimbabwe boasts a spectacular 400-foot waterfall that is more than a mile (1.6 km) wide.

**ACTIVITY:** Ask each student to conduct research about a national park in a different country. Then have students write a brief tour-guide description of the parks they have researched.

### Visual Record Answer

*Developers cannot build homes or businesses on land where there is no water, but diverting water with dams can deprive other ecosystems of the water they need to thrive.*

**Interpreting the Visual Record**

**Dams** *Huge dam projects provide power and irrigation but can also harm the surrounding ecosystems. How do such projects demonstrate the difficulty of balancing development and conservation?*

established National Park Service, limited grazing and mining, encouraged soil conservation, and worked with state governments

However, other government programs of the 1900s created environmental problems. For example, dams were built to irrigate farmland, control floods, and provide hydroelectric power. These dams also caused severe changes to local ecosystems.

By the 1950s large numbers of citizens were concerned about environmental problems, including waste and pollution. They called for new laws to address these problems.

✔ **Reading Check** Finding the Main Idea What were some of the ways that the federal government worked to protect the environment in the late 1800s and early 1900s?

 ## The Federal Government and Conservation

The U.S. Congress has passed a number of laws aimed at reducing pollution and restoring the environment. The following are some of the most significant of these acts.

**The National Environmental Policy Act** This act, passed in 1969, is sometimes called the Environmental Bill of Rights. It set up the Council on Environmental Quality to advise the president on environmental issues. The council was also to oversee the country's pollution controls. As a result of advice from this body, stricter laws were passed regulating pesticides, oil spills, and ocean dumping. The 1969 act also requires every federal agency to draft and publish an environmental impact statement. This document must describe the expected effects on the environment of any project to be undertaken with federal money.

**Clean Air Acts** The first Clean Air Act was passed in 1963 and has been amended several times, most recently in 1990. The Clean Air Acts provide funds for research and set standards to be met by all industries and buildings. These acts make it possible for the government to reduce certain forms of air pollution.

**Water Pollution Control Acts** As early as 1899, Congress passed a law making it a crime to dump refuse into any navigable waterway. However, this law was not strictly enforced until the mid-1900s. Then the law was strengthened by the Water Quality Act of 1965. This law sets standards of water quality for the interstate waters of the United States.

**LEVEL 1:** Lead the class in a discussion about the Clean Air and Water Acts. Then organize students into pairs, and ask pairs to create bumper stickers advertising the benefits of the Clean Air and Water Acts. *(For example, students' bumper stickers might read "The Clean Air Act Lets Us All Breathe Easier," or "The Water Quality Act Keeps America Healthy," and so on.)* Display students' bumper stickers around the classroom. **ENGLISH LANGUAGE LEARNERS , COOPERATIVE LEARNING**

**LEVELS 2 AND 3:** Organize students into pairs. Then ask pairs to imagine that they have been invited to explain the provisions of the Clean Air and Water Acts at a local community meeting. Ask pairs to create a presentation that makes use of a written report, visual aids, and handouts to describe the specific provisions of each act. *(Pairs' might also include a brief description of the causes and effects of each piece of legislation.)* Invite volunteers to deliver their presentations to the class. **COOPERATIVE LEARNING**

Laws further regulating water pollution were passed by Congress in 1965, 1966, and 1970. Under these acts the federal government has helped many communities build their own sewage treatment plants. In 1972 a law was passed to limit the discharge of wastes into lake or river waters.

**Other Acts of Congress** Americans have also become aware of the problems of using and disposing of chemicals. These substances, some of which are toxic, pollute the land, water, and air. To protect citizens' health, Congress passed the Resource Conservation and Recovery Act in 1976. It enables the government to regulate the transportation and storage of dangerous chemicals. Environmentalists are urging Congress to provide aid to farmers who practice conservation and reduce their reliance on chemical fertilizers and pesticides.

Americans have also pressed Congress to preserve the beauty of the land and to protect wildlife. The Wild and Scenic Rivers Act and the Wilderness Act designated areas of land to be kept in their natural state.

In the United States alone hundreds of plant and animal species are threatened with extinction. These species, such as the brown pelican and the woodland caribou, are protected from harm under the **Endangered Species Acts.** Such laws have helped some species increase in population. For example, in 1995 the American bald eagle was reclassified as "threatened," rather than as the more serious "endangered." However, many species remain near extinction.

The United States is also concerned with saving wildlife in other parts of the world. Federal laws forbid the importation of the feathers, skins, and other parts of many endangered animals from other countries.

✔ **Reading Check Summarizing** List and describe some of the legislation that Congress has passed to protect the environment. See subheadings and highlighted terms above for names and descriptions of key laws.

## ★ The Environmental Protection Agency

Many federal bureaus that deal with pollution and other environmental issues have been organized under an independent government agency. This agency is called the **Environmental Protection Agency** (EPA). The EPA includes several offices responsible for controlling and monitoring water and air pollution. Other divisions oversee the management of solid wastes and radiation. In addition, the EPA deals with pesticide problems and performs studies of ecosystems. The head of the EPA reports directly to the president.

✔ **Reading Check Summarizing** What makes up the Environmental Protection Agency, and what is the purpose of the EPA? federal bureaus that deal with pollution and other environmental issues; to control and monitor water and air pollution

### GLOBAL CONNECTIONS

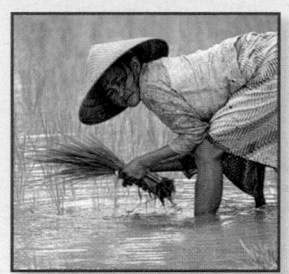

### Pest Management in Indonesia

Many U.S. farmers are looking for ways to reduce their reliance on chemical pesticides. Farmers on Java, an island in Indonesia, have found success with a system called Integrated Pest Management (IPM). The Food and Agriculture Organization (FAO) of the United Nations helped start the program.

For years Indonesian farmers used pesticides heavily. At first, crop yields rose, but after a few years farmers faced many problems. Pesticides were posing health and environmental hazards. In addition, the pesticides were killing helpful insects while harmful insects became resistant.

Under the IPM system, Indonesian farmers now use pesticides only when absolutely necessary and only in small amounts. They observe the number of beneficial and harmful insects on their crops to determine if pesticides are needed. They also plan crops carefully to avoid providing a constant source of food to the harmful insects. In these ways the harmful pests can be controlled without endangering people and the environment. **How has the IPM system helped Indonesian farmers?**

### ★ Civics Sidelight

**The Endangered Symbol of America** The removal of the American bald eagle from the endangered species list was made possible by the cooperation of government agencies, environmentalists, and the agricultural industry. Some estimates have put the number of bald eagles at the time of European settlement in North America at between 25,000 and 75,000. Researchers identified only 417 breeding pairs of the birds in the 48 contiguous states in 1963. Not quite 30 years later, researchers estimated that about 15,000 bald eagles existed in those states in 1992. The key to this victory was the banning of the insecticide DDT in 1972 by the Environmental Protection Agency—10 years after Rachel Carson's 1962 publication of *Silent Spring,* which called attention to the plight of the national bird and other birds of the United States.

**ACTIVITY:** Ask students to conduct research to learn more about which animal populations have been saved through environmental programs, and which animals remain on the endangered species list. Have students present their findings on charts.

**GLOBAL CONNECTIONS ANSWER**
The IPM system helps Indonesian farmers control pests without endangering people and the environment.

## TEACH OBJECTIVE 3

**ALL LEVELS:** Copy the following graphic organizer onto the chalkboard, omitting the italicized answers. Have students complete the boxes with descriptions of the problems that the Environmental Protection Agency monitors as well as the duties the EPA fulfills.

**LEVEL 3:** Ask each student to write a press release stating the purposes and duties of the EPA.

## CLOSE

Organize students into groups and have each group create a chart showing the duties and responsibilities of the Environmental Protection Agency. **COOPERATIVE LEARNING**

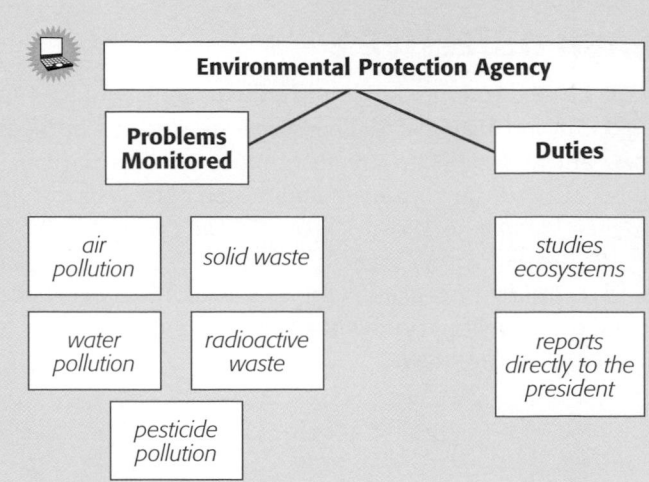

**Environmental Protection Agency**

**Problems Monitored**
- *air pollution*
- *solid waste*
- *water pollution*
- *radioactive waste*
- *pesticide pollution*

**Duties**
- *studies ecosystems*
- *reports directly to the president*

## Did You KNOW?

The first Earth Day celebration was the largest organized political demonstration in history. About 20 million Americans participated in Earth Day activities ranging from neighborhood cleanups to massive demonstrations.

**Interpreting the Visual Record**

**Earth Day** *Americans continue to celebrate Earth Day along with many other people around the world.* **What do you think the large blue object at the left of the photo represents?**

### ★ State and Local Activities

Every state government and most local governments in the country have laws regulating the environmental quality of their communities. These laws range from provisions for the preservation of natural resources to local laws governing the disposal of trash.

Some states have taken great steps forward by studying certain ecosystems and starting programs to preserve or restore their ecological balance. For example, Oregon has made its entire Pacific shoreline public property. It also has a program to preserve the state's natural beauty. Thirty-one U.S. states now require that environmental education be a part of their public school curricula.

Local governments act to preserve the environment as well. Many communities regulate the amount of pollution released by factories. More cities are starting recycling programs. These and similar actions are largely the result of growing citizen concern about the environment.

✔ **Reading Check** Analyzing Information Why do state and local governments act to safeguard the environment? growing citizen concern about the environment

### ★ Earth Day

One example of citizen involvement is **Earth Day,** which is designated for April 22 each year. Earth Day is an unofficial holiday dedicated to caring for Earth. The first Earth Day was held on April 22, 1970. Events included cleanups, demonstrations, and workshops that provided environmental tips. Earth Day showed that millions of Americans were concerned about current and future threats to the environment. The government responded with a number of laws to protect the environment.

Today more than 140 countries around the world take part in annual Earth Day celebrations. The people who participate in these celebrations have made caring for the planet a significant part of their lives.

✔ **Reading Check** Finding the Main Idea What has been the effect of Earth Day? moved the government to pass laws protecting the environment and raised awareness that the planet needs care and protection

## REVIEW AND ASSESS

Have students complete the **Section 4 Review** on page 681. Then have students complete **Daily Quiz 26.4**. As **Alternative Assessment**, you may want to use the bumper sticker or press release activities in this section's lessons.

## RETEACH

Have students complete **Main Idea Activity for English Language Learners and Special-Needs Students 26.4**. Then organize students into two groups. Ask one group to create a poster explaining what the federal government and the Environmental Protection Agency do to help the environment. Ask the second group to create a poster illustrating what individual citizens can do to protect the environment. After the groups have finished, display their posters around the classroom as study aids. **ENGLISH LANGUAGE LEARNERS**, **COOPERATIVE LEARNING**

## EXTEND

Ask students to conduct research to learn more about how they can get involved in local organizations that help protect and preserve the environment. Have each student design a Web site displaying what these organizations do, what they have accomplished, and what opportunities for involvement they offer. **BLOCK SCHEDULING**

---

## ★ Your Role in Conservation

Federal, state, and local laws cannot guarantee that the environment will be protected. Nor can private environmental organizations do the job alone. Only through the cooperation and actions of citizens can the environment be preserved for the enjoyment of future generations.

Here are some steps you can take to help conserve resources:

1. Prevent waste of all kinds in your home and school.
2. With your class, take part in a conservation project, such as planting trees, cleaning up streams, or picking up litter.
3. Take an interest in the natural resources in your community.
4. Participate in recycling projects. Reduce your reliance on disposable goods, and reuse items as many times as possible.
5. Beware of the danger of fire when in a forest or wooded area.
6. Do not destroy wildlife or damage public resources.
7. Obey laws against open burning, littering, polluting, and other actions that damage the environment.
8. Stay informed about the ecological issues in your area. Make your opinions known by writing to your government representatives.
9. Make it a point to appreciate the beauty of the natural world.
10. Think about what you can do to make the world a healthy place for people to live.

**Interpreting the Visual Record**

**Foundation for the future** *These young volunteers are planting trees in their community.* **How do actions like this help the environment and the community?**

✔ **Reading Check** Analyzing Information  Why do citizens have a direct responsibility to preserve the planet? because laws and private agencies alone cannot guarantee the protection of the planet

---

## SECTION 4 Review

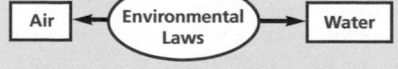
**go.hrw.com** **Homework Practice Online**
keyword: SZ3 HP26

1. **Identify** and explain:
   • Endangered Species Acts
   • Environmental Protection Agency
   • Earth Day

2. **Summarizing** Copy the graphic organizer below. Use it to show the ways that environmental laws protect the air and water.

```
   Air  ←  Environmental  →  Water
              Laws
```

3. **Finding the Main Idea**
   a. What conservation efforts were made before the 1950s?
   b. What responsibilities does the Environmental Protection Agency have?

4. **Writing and Critical Thinking**
   **Problem Solving**  You are an organizer for the next Earth Day celebration. Write a two-paragraph proposal indicating what you think are the top three environmental issues that should be addressed. Also discuss the problems associated with these issues and how they should be resolved.

   **Consider:**
   • the purpose of Earth Day
   • the goals of various environmental protection acts

---

## Section 4 Review
### ANSWERS

**1. Identify**
• Endangered Species Acts, p. 679
• Environmental Protection Agency, p. 679
• Earth Day, p. 680

**2.** Air—provide funds for research, set standards for industry and buildings, require automobile manufacturers to reduce auto emissions; Water—enforce existing laws, set standards for U.S. interstate and coastal waters, help local communities build sewage treatment plants, limit the discharge of wastes into the waters

**3. a.** National Parks Service and National Forest Service established limitations on the amount of oil and minerals that could be taken from the ground each year, managed grazing practices to preserve grasslands, promoted soil conservation, and built dams for irrigation and flood control.

**b.** includes several offices responsible for monitoring water and air pollution, overseeing management of solid wastes and radiation; deals with pesticide problems; performs studies of the ecosystem

**4.** Students' proposals should consider the purpose of Earth Day and the goals of various environmental protection acts.

## Review and Assessment Resources

**REPRODUCIBLE**
▶ Chapter 26 Review, p. 682–83
▶ Vocabulary Activity 26
▶ Chapter 26 Tutorial for Students, Parents, Mentors, and Peers
▶ Chapter 26 Test (Form A or B)
▶ Alternative Assessment Handbook

**TECHNOLOGY**
▶ Chapter 26 Test Generator (on the One-Stop Planner)
▶ Global Skill Builder CD–ROM
▶ HRW Go site

**REINFORCEMENT, REVIEW, AND ASSESSMENT**
▶ Chapter 26 Test for English Language Learners and Special-Needs Students

### REVIEW
Have students complete the **Chapter 24 Review** on pages 682–83.

### ASSESS
Use one of the chapter tests to assess students' understanding of the content. For **Alternative Assessment**, see the **Alternative Assessment Handbook**.

---

## CHAPTER 26
### REVIEW ANSWERS

**Define and Identify**
1. ecology, p. 655
2. ecosystem, p. 655
3. renewable resource, p. 663
4. greenhouse effect, p. 664
5. hydrologic cycle, p. 665
6. landfills, p. 667
7. fossil fuels, p. 670
8. conservation, p. 672
9. Endangered Species Acts, p. 679
10. Earth Day, p. 680

**Understanding Main Ideas**
1. All living things depend on each other for maintaining stability and balance.

2. strain resources such as food, minerals, water, energy, timber; more waste produced

3. Pollution is not contained within national borders.

4. smog, chlorofluorocarbons, acid rain, radiation

5. fossil fuels are limited; solar energy, geothermal energy, hydroelectric power, wind, biomass

6. Development is necessary for the growth and well-being of nations, but whatever harms the land, sea, and air harms human beings and all living things.

7. created parks; National Forest Service efforts to conserve timber; limited grazing and extraction of oil and minerals; promoted soil conservation; built dams for irrigation and flood control

---

# Chapter 26 Review

## Chapter Summary

### Section 1
- The balance of nature is delicate and can be easily upset by even the smallest environmental changes.
- Urban growth, farming, and overpopulation can affect the environment and ecosystems in harmful ways.

### Section 2
- Air, water, and ground pollution present some of the most serious dangers currently facing Earth.
- Many countries have agreed to cooperate to reduce pollution, and individuals are taking steps to protect the environment as well.

### Section 3
- Conservation has been one response to global shortages of energy, particularly fossil fuels.
- The most widely used fossil fuels are oil, natural gas, and coal.
- Alternative forms of energy, such as solar, wind, hydroelectric, and biomass power, are being explored as possible ways to decrease reliance on nonrenewable resources.

### Section 4
- To help protect the environment, the United States has passed laws to ensure that natural resources are used wisely.
- Individual citizens also have a responsibility to conserve and care for the planet.

---

## Define and Identify
Use the following terms in complete sentences.
1. ecology
2. ecosystem
3. renewable resource
4. greenhouse effect
5. hydrologic cycle
6. landfills
7. fossil fuels
8. conservation
9. Endangered Species Acts
10. Earth Day

## Understanding Main Ideas

**Section 1** *(Pages 655–61)*
1. What roles do living things play in an ecosystem?
2. What damage can overpopulation cause the environment?

**Section 2** *(Pages 662–68)*
3. What has the world learned about pollution?
4. What types of pollution pose the biggest threats to the environment?

**Section 3** *(Pages 670–76)*
5. Why are renewable energy sources being researched, and what are they?
6. What arguments surround the issues of development and conservation?

**Section 4** *(Pages 677–81)*
7. How did the United States try to protect the environment in the first half of the 1900s?
8. How does the Environmental Protection Agency work to protect the environment?

## What Did You Find Out?
1. What does pollution contaminate, and how can it be reduced?
2. What are some of the concerns about environmental regulation and its effects on development?
3. How can governments, organizations, and individuals safeguard the environment?

## Thinking Critically
1. **Supporting a Point of View** Conservationists say that environmental regulations are needed to protect natural resources. Some businesses claim that following these laws is too expensive. What is your view on this situation? Explain your answer.
2. **Evaluating** What are some of the advantages and disadvantages of organic farming for farmers and consumers?
3. **Analyzing Information** What affects the amount of waste we produce, and how can we better control our waste production?

# RETEACH

Organize students into four groups and assign each group one of the chapter's sections. Then have each group create an outline explaining the main objectives in its assigned section.

**ENGLISH LANGUAGE LEARNERS ,**
**COOPERATIVE LEARNING**

## Portfolio Extensions

**1. Interdisciplinary Connection to Science** Point out to students that new technologies in the areas of energy, recycling, and hazardous waste disposal may possibly make environmental protection easier and more efficient. Ask students to conduct research to learn more about some of these new technologies. Then have each student choose one example to create a poster illustrating how this new technology might help to protect the environment.

**2. Cooperative Learning** Remind students that the settling of America upset the balance of the ecosystem. Then organize students into committees and ask each committee to imagine that the EPA has assigned it the task of writing a plan for restoring and protecting the ecosystem in its local region. Encourage students to think of creative yet practical ways that local businesses and individual people could work together to clean up and preserve the local ecosystem. Ask each group to present its plan to the class.

---

## Building Social Studies Skills

### Interpreting Political Cartoons

Study the political cartoon below, which illustrates the effect of rising oil prices. Then use the cartoon to help you answer the questions that follow.

1. What is about to happen in the cartoon?
   a. The U.S. economy is about to grow at a faster rate than oil prices.
   b. Rising oil prices are about to collide with and seriously hurt the U.S. economy.
   c. Rising oil prices are about to cause train fares to rise, and many Americans will be forced to find new forms of transportation.
   d. As a result of an economic downturn, government leaders will encourage Americans to use fuels other than oil.
2. What does this cartoon suggest about the relationship between the supply and cost of energy and the national economy? Do you agree or disagree with this idea? Explain your answer.

### Analyzing Primary Sources

Read the following quotation from a speech by Secretary of the Interior Gale Norton. Then answer the questions that follow.

> "Our shared mission is both simple and noble. We must explore ways to better capture the sun's light, the sky's winds, the land's bounty, and the earth's heat to provide energy security for America's families. . . . There is a lot at stake. Renewable energy, including hydropower, supplies 9 percent of America's energy. Renewable energy production is growing faster than other forms of energy. Renewable energy diversifies our energy portfolio. . . . Yes, we can be proud of our accomplishments. But if our work was perfect, we would not need this conference. The truth is we have work to do. . . . We must also ask tough questions. In our free market society, what economic factors have prevented renewable energy from gaining greater market share?"

3. Which of the following statements best expresses Norton's point of view?
   a. The United States has made as much progress as possible in developing renewable energy.
   b. Renewable energy is not important because it supplies only 9 percent of our current needs.
   c. Renewable energy can be a great benefit to American businesses.
   d. Renewable energy is an important resource that needs to be further developed.
4. What question does Secretary Norton ask in her speech? Based on what you have read in this chapter, what do you think the possible answers to this question might be?

---

8. controls water and air pollution, oversees management of solid wastes and radiation, deals with pesticide problems, studies ecosystems

**What Did You Find Out?**

1. contaminates the air, soil, and water; by monitoring what gets put into the environment

2. Some people are concerned that environmental regulations make it too expensive to build new developments.

3. Governments can regulate and monitor pollution. Organizations can lobby for laws and work to restore and preserve ecosystems. Individual people can get involved in protecting the environment in their own communities by promoting conservation laws, and so on.

**Thinking Critically**

1. Students should provide specific examples of possible solutions.

2. Students should support their positions with well-reasoned arguments.

3. Students should base their answers on current conditions and available waste disposal technologies.

**Social Studies Skills**

1. b

2. Students' answers will vary, but they should acknowledge that the supply and price of oil have a significant effect on the U.S. economy.

3. d

4. What has prevented renewable energy from gaining a greater market share? Students should support their answers with specific examples from this chapter.

---

### Alternative Assessment

#### Building Your Portfolio

**Linking to Community**
Create a list of things that teenagers can do to help protect your community's environment. Ask members of your community for their suggestions. Research what your community does to preserve the environment and what you can do to help. Use your materials to make a pamphlet titled Protecting the Environment of (your community's name).

**internet connect**

**Internet Activity: go.hrw.com**
keyword: SZ3 AC26

Access the Internet through the HRW Go site to learn about ways that you can protect the environment. Then make a sign out of recycled materials (paper grocery sacks, construction paper scraps, old cardboard or poster board, school papers, etc.) that promotes taking care of the environment. Hang your sign up at school or in the community.

## TEACH

 **LEVEL 1:** Organize students into pairs and ask each pair to consider the changes that will take place in American society by 2010. Ask each pair to draw a poster representing its school in the future. Students' posters should also illustrate what skills the typical student will need to learn in school in order to be a good citizen in the year 2010.

**ENGLISH LANGUAGE LEARNERS , COOPERATIVE LEARNING**

**ALL LEVELS:** Organize students into pairs. Ask each pair to design a Web page explaining the organization of its local school system. Remind students that the Web page should make use of graphics and illustrations to present information. Have students include a brief description of the responsibilities of the various administrative offices. Encourage students to include links to other educational sites on their Web page.

**ENGLISH LANGUAGE LEARNERS**

## APPLYING THE SKILLS

Organize students into small groups. Ask each group to write a brief skit describing what its school board should do to prepare for 2010 based on the proposal in the Civics Lab. Students' skits should depict a day in the life of a teacher and a student at their school in 2010. Each skit should discuss a major issue in the future, such as the economy, the job market, the environment, and so on. Also encourage students to pay attention to small details such as what the student might be wearing and what types of supplies he or she might be using. Have each group perform its skit for the class.

# Civics Lab

## Operation 2010

**Complete the following Civics Lab activity individually or in a group.**

## Your Task

In Unit 8 you read about the future challenges facing the United States, including the extension of equal rights to all Americans and environmental issues. Imagine that the members of your local school board have asked you to draft a proposal that will help your school prepare for the challenges of the future.

Specifically, the board wants to create a long-term plan that will meet upcoming challenges through the year 2010. To plan for future challenges, however, the school board must know what challenges have arisen in the past and how they were handled. Your proposal for Operation 2010 will need to include written and visual materials. To prepare these materials, you will need to do the following.

## What to Do

**STEP 1** **Prepare** a map of your local community, identifying your school's location and its surrounding area. Also mark the location of any nearby schools.

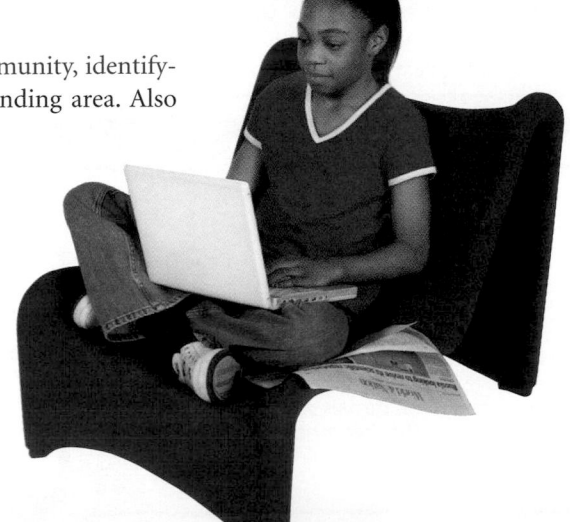

**ALL LEVELS:** Have each student create a graphic organizer by drawing a web diagram and placing the name of his or her school in the middle. Then have students fill in the rest of the web diagram by listing the many responsibilities and objectives that their school fulfills. Encourage students to include programs offered by their school as well as important issues that affect how the school is run. **ENGLISH LANGUAGE LEARNERS**

**LEVEL 3:** Ask students to use the information they researched in the Civics Lab to consider what would happen if their school board were to take no action to prepare for the future. What student needs would be overlooked, and how would society in general be affected? Ask each student to write a short story describing what life would be like if the school system in 2010 did not do enough to prepare students to enter the world.

**STEP 2** **Create** a graph showing how the population of your school has changed over time.

**STEP 3** **Research** the challenges that your school has faced in previous years. Prepare a report that answers questions such as the following: Has the school had a sharp increase or decrease in the number of students? Has the school run into difficulties involving the need for repairs or new school supplies? Have school budgets or school performance been a concern?

**STEP 4** **Create** a diagram with several circles labeled *Key Skills.* Each circle should list a skill that you think is important for finding a job and being a good citizen. Examples might include Writing, Mathematics, or U.S. History. Around each circle, list the classes offered at your school that you think help teach that skill. Are these classes available to all students? If you think there are classes not currently offered that should be added to your diagram, list these on the side.

**STEP 5** **Create** one or more posters of your school that show some of the ways that students and faculty at your school could help or are helping the environment. These include measures such as energy conservation, cleaning up litter, planting trees, or recycling. Include some practical suggestions on how these environmental steps could be taken if they are not being taken already.

Organize your materials, and make your presentation to the school board (the rest of the class).

**A STEP FURTHER**

Ask students to imagine that they are members of the school board in 2010 and that their school's environmental reforms have helped to improve the local environment. Then have each student write an article for a local newspaper explaining how the school's environmental initiative produced these improvements. Students' articles should also offer suggestions for how other schools might adopt their school's environmental policies. Students' articles should draw examples from the Civics Lab. Ask volunteers to read their articles to the class.

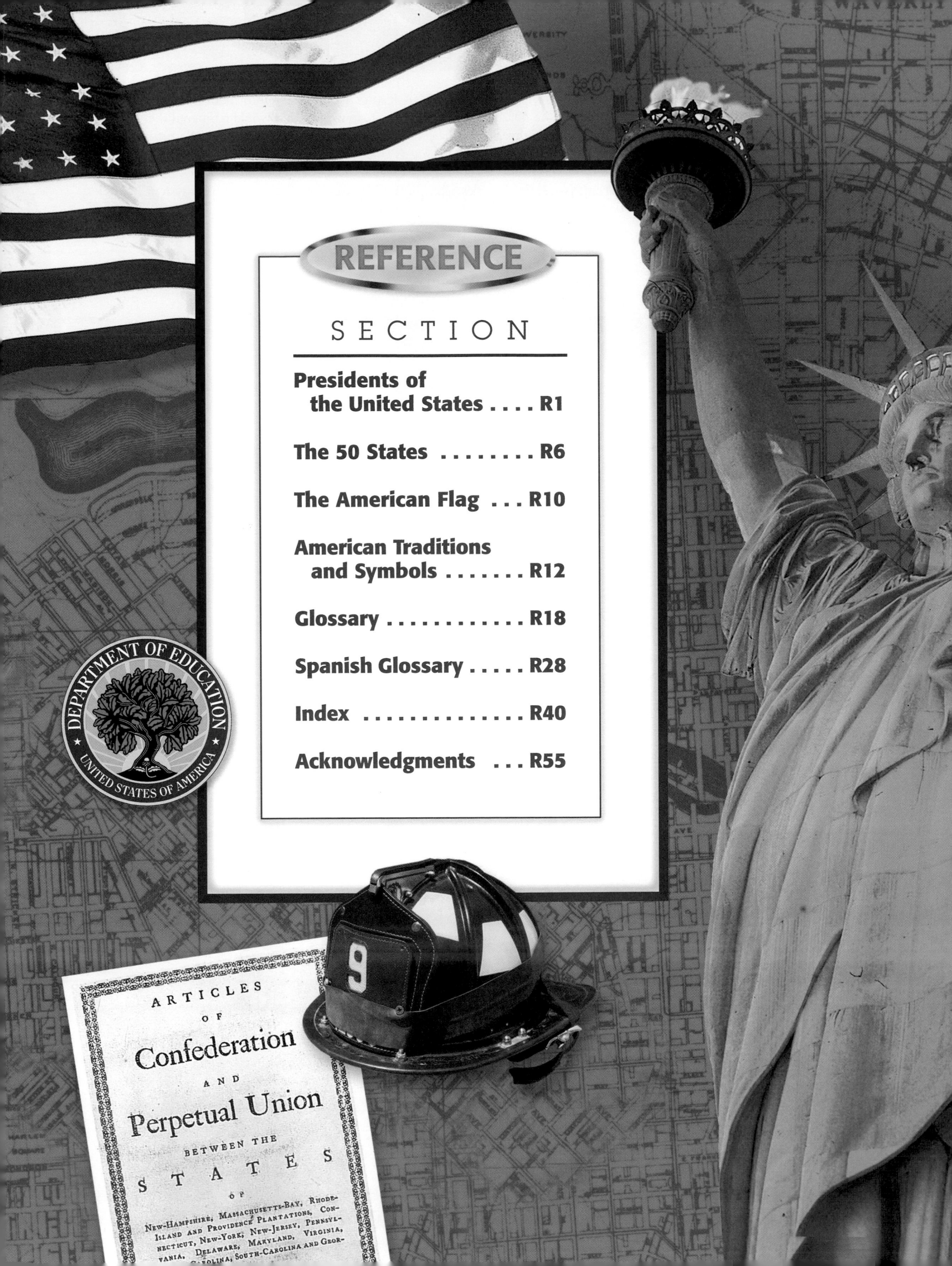

# REFERENCE

## SECTION

DEPARTMENT OF EDUCATION · UNITED STATES OF AMERICA

ARTICLES

OF

Confederation

AND

Perpetual Union

BETWEEN THE

STATES

OF

NEW-HAMPSHIRE, MASSACHUSETTS-BAY, RHODE-ISLAND AND PROVIDENCE PLANTATIONS, CONNECTICUT, NEW-YORK, NEW-JERSEY, PENNSYLVANIA, DELAWARE, MARYLAND, VIRGINIA, CAROLINA, SOUTH-CAROLINA AND GEOR-

# Presidents of the United States

## The Official Portraits

**1 GEORGE WASHINGTON**
Born: 1732    Died: 1799
Years in Office: 1789–97
Political Party: None
Home State: Virginia
Vice President: John Adams

**2 JOHN ADAMS**
Born: 1735    Died: 1826
Years in Office: 1797–1801
Political Party: Federalist
Home State: Massachusetts
Vice President: Thomas Jefferson

**3 THOMAS JEFFERSON**
Born: 1743    Died: 1826
Years in Office: 1801–09
Political Party: Republican*
Home State: Virginia
Vice Presidents: Aaron Burr,
  George Clinton

**4 JAMES MADISON**
Born: 1751    Died: 1836
Years in Office: 1809–17
Political Party: Republican
Home State: Virginia
Vice Presidents: George Clinton,
  Elbridge Gerry

**5 JAMES MONROE**
Born: 1758    Died: 1831
Years in Office: 1817–25
Political Party: Republican
Home State: Virginia
Vice President: Daniel D. Tompkins

**6 JOHN QUINCY ADAMS**
Born: 1767    Died: 1848
Years in Office: 1825–29
Political Party: Republican
Home State: Massachusetts
Vice President: John C. Calhoun

**7 ANDREW JACKSON**
Born: 1767    Died: 1845
Years in Office: 1829–37
Political Party: Democratic
Home State: Tennessee
Vice Presidents: John C. Calhoun,
  Martin Van Buren

* The Republican Party of the third through sixth presidents is not the party of Abraham Lincoln, which was founded in 1854.

**8 MARTIN VAN BUREN**
Born: 1782   Died: 1862
Years in Office: 1837–41
Political Party: Democratic
Home State: New York
Vice President: Richard M. Johnson

**9 WILLIAM HENRY HARRISON**
Born: 1773   Died: 1841
Years in Office: 1841
Political Party: Whig
Home State: Ohio
Vice President: John Tyler

**10 JOHN TYLER**
Born: 1790   Died: 1862
Years in Office: 1841–45
Political Party: Whig
Home State: Virginia
Vice President: None

**11 JAMES K. POLK**
Born: 1795   Died: 1849
Years in Office: 1845–49
Political Party: Democratic
Home State: Tennessee
Vice President: George M. Dallas

**12 ZACHARY TAYLOR**
Born: 1784   Died: 1850
Years in Office: 1849–50
Political Party: Whig
Home State: Louisiana
Vice President: Millard Fillmore

**13 MILLARD FILLMORE**
Born: 1800   Died: 1874
Years in Office: 1850–53
Political Party: Whig
Home State: New York
Vice President: None

**14 FRANKLIN PIERCE**
Born: 1804   Died: 1869
Years in Office: 1853–57
Political Party: Democratic
Home State: New Hampshire
Vice President: William R. King

**15 JAMES BUCHANAN**
Born: 1791   Died: 1868
Years in Office: 1857–61
Political Party: Democratic
Home State: Pennsylvania
Vice President: John C. Breckinridge

**16 ABRAHAM LINCOLN**
Born: 1809   Died: 1865
Years in Office: 1861–65
Political Party: Republican
Home State: Illinois
Vice Presidents: Hannibal Hamlin,
Andrew Johnson

**17  ANDREW JOHNSON**
**Born:** 1808    **Died:** 1875
**Years in Office:** 1865–69
**Political Party:** Republican
**Home State:** Tennessee
**Vice President:** None

**18  ULYSSES S. GRANT**
**Born:** 1822    **Died:** 1885
**Years in Office:** 1869–77
**Political Party:** Republican
**Home State:** Illinois
**Vice Presidents:** Schuyler Colfax,
  Henry Wilson

**19  RUTHERFORD B. HAYES**
**Born:** 1822    **Died:** 1893
**Years in Office:** 1877–81
**Political Party:** Republican
**Home State:** Ohio
**Vice President:** William A. Wheeler

**20  JAMES A. GARFIELD**
**Born:** 1831    **Died:** 1881
**Years in Office:** 1881
**Political Party:** Republican
**Home State:** Ohio
**Vice President:** Chester A. Arthur

**21  CHESTER A. ARTHUR**
**Born:** 1829    **Died:** 1886
**Years in Office:** 1881–85
**Political Party:** Republican
**Home State:** New York
**Vice President:** None

**22  GROVER CLEVELAND**
**Born:** 1837    **Died:** 1908
**Years in Office:** 1885–89
**Political Party:** Democratic
**Home State:** New York
**Vice President:** Thomas A. Hendricks

**23  BENJAMIN HARRISON**
**Born:** 1833    **Died:** 1901
**Years in Office:** 1889–93
**Political Party:** Republican
**Home State:** Indiana
**Vice President:** Levi P. Morton

**24  GROVER CLEVELAND**
**Born:** 1837    **Died:** 1908
**Years in Office:** 1893–97
**Political Party:** Democratic
**Home State:** New York
**Vice President:** Adlai E. Stevenson

**25  WILLIAM MCKINLEY**
**Born:** 1843    **Died:** 1901
**Years in Office:** 1897–1901
**Political Party:** Republican
**Home State:** Ohio
**Vice Presidents:** Garret A. Hobart,
  Theodore Roosevelt

**26   THEODORE ROOSEVELT**
**Born:** 1858     **Died:** 1919
**Years in Office:** 1901–09
**Political Party:** Republican
**Home State:** New York
**Vice President:** Charles W. Fairbanks

**27   WILLIAM HOWARD TAFT**
**Born:** 1857     **Died:** 1930
**Years in Office:** 1909–13
**Political Party:** Republican
**Home State:** Ohio
**Vice President:** James S. Sherman

**28   WOODROW WILSON**
**Born:** 1856     **Died:** 1924
**Years in Office:** 1913–21
**Political Party:** Democratic
**Home State:** New Jersey
**Vice President:** Thomas R. Marshall

**29   WARREN G. HARDING**
**Born:** 1865     **Died:** 1923
**Years in Office:** 1921–23
**Political Party:** Republican
**Home State:** Ohio
**Vice President:** Calvin Coolidge

**30   CALVIN COOLIDGE**
**Born:** 1872     **Died:** 1933
**Years in Office:** 1923–29
**Political Party:** Republican
**Home State:** Massachusetts
**Vice President:** Charles G. Dawes

**31   HERBERT HOOVER**
**Born:** 1874     **Died:** 1964
**Years in Office:** 1929–33
**Political Party:** Republican
**Home State:** California
**Vice President:** Charles Curtis

**32   FRANKLIN D. ROOSEVELT**
**Born:** 1882     **Died:** 1945
**Years in Office:** 1933–45
**Political Party:** Democratic
**Home State:** New York
**Vice Presidents:** John Nance Garner,
Henry Wallace,  Harry S Truman

**33   HARRY S TRUMAN**
**Born:** 1884     **Died:** 1972
**Years in Office:** 1945–53
**Political Party:** Democratic
**Home State:** Missouri
**Vice President:** Alben W. Barkley

**34   DWIGHT D. EISENHOWER**
**Born:** 1890     **Died:** 1969
**Years in Office:** 1953–61
**Political Party:** Republican
**Home State:** Kansas
**Vice President:** Richard M. Nixon

**35  JOHN F. KENNEDY**
**Born:** 1917    **Died:** 1963
**Years in Office:** 1961–63
**Political Party:** Democratic
**Home State:** Massachusetts
**Vice President:** Lyndon B. Johnson

**36  LYNDON B. JOHNSON**
**Born:** 1908    **Died:** 1973
**Years in Office:** 1963–69
**Political Party:** Democratic
**Home State:** Texas
**Vice President:** Hubert H. Humphrey

**37  RICHARD M. NIXON**
**Born:** 1913    **Died:** 1994
**Years in Office:** 1969–74
**Political Party:** Republican
**Home State:** California
**Vice Presidents:** Spiro T. Agnew,
    Gerald R. Ford

**38  GERALD R. FORD**
**Born:** 1913
**Years in Office:** 1974–77
**Political Party:** Republican
**Home State:** Michigan
**Vice President:** Nelson A. Rockefeller

**39  JIMMY CARTER**
**Born:** 1924
**Years in Office:** 1977–81
**Political Party:** Democratic
**Home State:** Georgia
**Vice President:** Walter F. Mondale

**40  RONALD REAGAN**
**Born:** 1911
**Years in Office:** 1981–89
**Political Party:** Republican
**Home State:** California
**Vice President:** George Bush

**41  GEORGE BUSH**
**Born:** 1924
**Years in Office:** 1989–93
**Political Party:** Republican
**Home State:** Texas
**Vice President:** J. Danforth Quayle

**42  BILL CLINTON**
**Born:** 1946
**Years in Office:** 1993–2001
**Political Party:** Democratic
**Home State:** Arkansas
**Vice President:** Albert Gore Jr.

**43  GEORGE W. BUSH**
**Born:** 1946
**Years in Office:** 2001–
**Political Party:** Republican
**Home State:** Texas
**Vice President:** Richard B. Cheney

# The 50 States

The name of each state is followed in parentheses by a number indicating the order in which it was admitted to the Union. For the original 13 states, this is the order in which each state approved the Constitution. Population figures are based on the 2000 U.S. Census.

### Alabama (22)
Admitted to Union: 1819
Capital: Montgomery
Population: 4,447,100

### Alaska (49)
Admitted to Union: 1959
Capital: Juneau
Population: 626,932

### Arizona (48)
Admitted to Union: 1912
Capital:  Phoenix
Population: 5,130,632

### Arkansas (25)
Admitted to Union: 1836
Capital: Little Rock
Population: 2,673,400

### California (31)
Admitted to Union: 1850
Capital: Sacramento
Population: 33,871,648

### Colorado (38)
Admitted to Union: 1876
Capital: Denver
Population: 4,301,261

### Connecticut (5)
Admitted to Union: 1788
Capital: Hartford
Population: 3,405,565

### Delaware (1)
Admitted to Union: 1787
Capital: Dover
Population: 783,600

### Florida (27)
Admitted to Union: 1845
Capital: Tallahassee
Population: 15,982,378

### Georgia (4)
Admitted to Union: 1788
Capital: Atlanta
Population: 8,186,453

### Hawaii (50)
Admitted to Union: 1959
Capital: Honolulu
Population: 1,211,537

### Idaho (43)
Admitted to Union: 1890
Capital: Boise
Population: 1,293,953

**Illinois** (21)
Admitted to Union: 1818
Capital: Springfield
Population: 12,419,293

**Indiana** (19)
Admitted to Union: 1816
Capital: Indianapolis
Population: 6,080,485

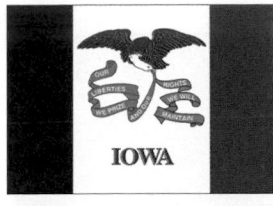

**Iowa** (29)
Admitted to Union: 1846
Capital: Des Moines
Population: 2,926,324

**Kansas** (34)
Admitted to Union: 1861
Capital: Topeka
Population: 2,688,418

**Kentucky** (15)
Admitted to Union: 1792
Capital: Frankfort
Population: 4,041,769

**Louisiana** (18)
Admitted to Union: 1812
Capital: Baton Rouge
Population: 4,468,976

**Maine** (23)
Admitted to Union: 1820
Capital: Augusta
Population: 1,274,923

**Maryland** (7)
Admitted to Union: 1788
Capital: Annapolis
Population: 5,296,486

**Massachusetts** (6)
Admitted to Union: 1788
Capital: Boston
Population: 6,349,097

**Michigan** (26)
Admitted to Union: 1837
Capital: Lansing
Population: 9,938,444

**Minnesota** (32)
Admitted to Union: 1858
Capital: St. Paul
Population: 4,919,479

**Mississippi** (20)
Admitted to Union: 1817
Capital: Jackson
Population: 2,844,658

**Missouri** (24)
Admitted to Union: 1821
Capital: Jefferson City
Population: 5,595,211

**Montana** (41)
Admitted to Union: 1889
Capital: Helena
Population: 902,195

**Nebraska** (37)
Admitted to Union: 1867
Capital: Lincoln
Population: 1,711,263

**Nevada** (36)
Admitted to Union: 1864
Capital: Carson City
Population: 1,998,257

**New Hampshire** (9)
Admitted to Union: 1788
Capital: Concord
Population: 1,235,786

**New Jersey** (3)
Admitted to Union: 1787
Capital: Trenton
Population: 8,414,350

**New Mexico** (47)
Admitted to Union:  1912
Capital: Santa Fe
Population: 1,819,046

**New York** (11)
Admitted to Union: 1788
Capital: Albany
Population: 18,976,457

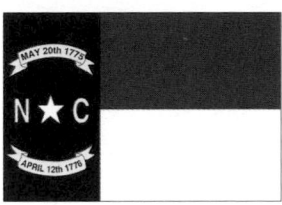

**North Carolina** (12)
Admitted to Union: 1789
Capital: Raleigh
Population: 8,049,313

**North Dakota** (39)
Admitted to Union: 1889
Capital: Bismarck
Population: 642,200

**Ohio** (17)
Admitted to Union: 1803
Capital: Columbus
Population: 11,353,140

**Oklahoma** (46)
Admitted to Union: 1907
Capital: Oklahoma City
Population: 3,450,654

**Oregon** (33)
Admitted to Union: 1859
Capital: Salem
Population: 3,421,399

**Pennsylvania** (2)
Admitted to Union: 1787
Capital: Harrisburg
Population: 12,281,054

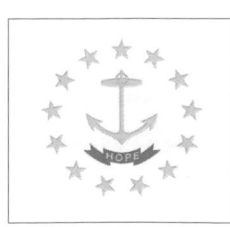

**Rhode Island** (13)
Admitted to Union: 1790
Capital: Providence
Population: 1,048,319

**South Carolina** (8)
Admitted to Union: 1788
Capital: Columbia
Population: 4,012,012

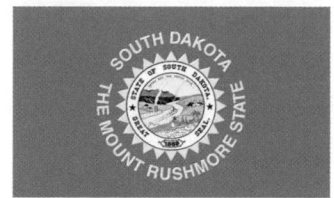

**South Dakota** (40)
Admitted to Union: 1889
Capital: Pierre
Population: 754,844

**Tennessee** (16)
Admitted to Union: 1796
Capital: Nashville
Population: 5,689,283

**Texas** (28)
Admitted to Union: 1845
Capital: Austin
Population: 20,851,820

**Utah** (45)
Admitted to Union: 1896
Capital: Salt Lake City
Population: 2,233,169

**Vermont** (14)
Admitted to Union: 1791
Capital: Montpelier
Population: 608,827

**Virginia** (10)
Admitted to Union: 1788
Capital: Richmond
Population: 7,078,515

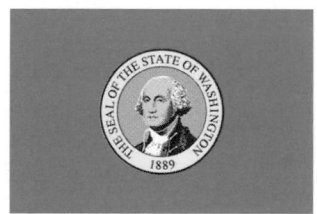

**Washington** (42)
Admitted to Union: 1889
Capital: Olympia
Population: 5,894,121

**West Virginia** (35)
Admitted to Union: 1863
Capital: Charleston
Population: 1,808,344

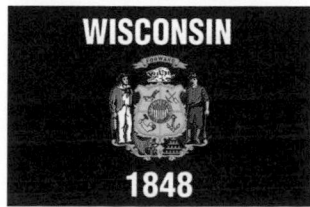

**Wisconsin** (30)
Admitted to Union: 1848
Capital: Madison
Population: 5,363,675

**Wyoming** (44)
Admitted to Union: 1890
Capital: Cheyenne
Population: 493,782

# The American Flag

The American flag is a symbol of the nation. It is recognized instantly, whether as a big banner waving in the wind or a tiny emblem worn on a lapel. The flag is so important that it is a major theme of the national anthem, "The Star-Spangled Banner." One of the most popular names for the flag is the Stars and Stripes. It is also known as Old Glory.

## THE MEANING OF THE FLAG

The American flag has 13 stripes—7 red and 6 white. In the upper-left corner of the flag is the union—50 white five-pointed stars against a blue background.

The 13 stripes stand for the original 13 American states, and the 50 stars represent the states of the nation today. According to the U.S. Department of State, the colors of the flag also are symbolic:

Red stands for courage.

White symbolizes purity.

Blue is the color of vigilance, perseverance, and justice.

## DISPLAYING THE FLAG

It is customary not to display the American flag in bad weather. It is also customary for the flag to be displayed outdoors only from sunrise to sunset, except on certain occasions. In a few special places, however, the flag is always flown day and night. When flown at night, the flag should be illuminated.

Near a speaker's platform, the flag should occupy the place of honor at the speaker's right. When carried in a parade with other flags, the American flag should be on the marching right or in front at the center. When flying with the flags of the 50 states, the national flag must be at the center and the highest point. In a group of national flags, all should be of equal size and all should be flown from staffs, or flagpoles, of equal height.

The flag should never touch the ground or the floor. It should not be marked with any insignia, pictures, or words. Nor should it be used in any disrespectful way—as an advertising decoration, for instance. The flag should never be dipped to honor any person or thing.

## SALUTING THE FLAG

The United States, like other countries, has a flag code, or rules for displaying and honoring the flag. For example, all those present should stand at attention facing the flag and salute it when it is being raised or lowered or when it is carried past them in a parade or procession. A man wearing a hat should take it off and hold it with his right hand over his heart. All women and hatless men should stand with their right hands over their hearts to show respect. The flag should also receive these honors during the playing of the national anthem and the reciting of the Pledge of Allegiance.

## THE PLEDGE OF ALLEGIANCE

The Pledge of Allegiance was written in 1892 by Massachusetts magazine (*Youth's Companion*) editor Francis Bellamy. (Congress added the words "under God" in 1954.)

**I pledge allegiance to the flag of the United States of America and to the republic for which it stands, one nation under God, indivisible, with liberty and justice for all.**

Civilians should say the Pledge of Allegiance with their right hands over their hearts. People in the armed forces give the military salute. By saying the Pledge of Allegiance, we promise loyalty ("pledge allegiance") to the United States and its ideals.

## "THE STAR-SPANGLED BANNER"

"The Star-Spangled Banner" is the national anthem of the United States. It was written by Francis Scott Key during the War of 1812. While being detained by the British aboard a ship on September 13–14, 1814, Key watched the British bombardment of Fort McHenry at Baltimore. The attack lasted 25 hours. The smoke was so thick that Key could not tell who had won. When the air cleared, Key saw the American flag that was still flying over the fort. "The Star-Spangled Banner" is sung to music written by British composer John Stafford Smith. In 1931 Congress designated "The Star-Spangled Banner" as the national anthem.

Sheet music to the national anthem

### I

Oh, say, can you see, by the dawn's early light,
What so proudly we hailed at the twilight's last gleaming,
Whose broad stripes and bright stars through the perilous fight,
O'er the ramparts we watched were so gallantly streaming?
And the rockets' red glare, the bombs bursting in air,
Gave proof through the night that our flag was still there.
Oh, say, does that star-spangled banner yet wave
O'er the land of the free, and the home of the brave?

### II

On the shore, dimly seen through the mists of the deep,
Where the foe's haughty host in dread silence reposes,
What is that which the breeze, o'er the towering steep,
As it fitfully blows, half conceals, half discloses?
Now it catches the gleam of the morning's first beam,
In full glory reflected, now shines on the stream.
'Tis the star-spangled banner; oh, long may it wave
O'er the land of the free, and the home of the brave!

### III

And where is that band who so vauntingly swore
That the havoc of war and the battle's confusion
A home and a country should leave us no more?
Their blood has washed out their foul footsteps' pollution.
No refuge could save the hireling and slave
From the terror of flight, or the gloom of the grave:
And the star-spangled banner in triumph doth wave
O'er the land of the free, and the home of the brave!

### IV

Oh! thus be it ever when freemen shall stand
Between their loved homes and the war's desolation!
Blest with victory and peace, may the heaven-rescued land
Praise the Power that hath made and preserved us a nation!
Then conquer we must, for our cause it is just,
And this be our motto: "In God is our trust!"
And the star-spangled banner in triumph shall wave,
O'er the land of the free, and the home of the brave!

## "AMERICA, THE BEAUTIFUL"

One of the most beloved songs celebrating our nation is "America, the Beautiful." Katharine Lee Bates first wrote the lyrics to the song in 1893 after visiting Colorado. The version of the song we know today is set to music by Samuel A. Ward. The first and last stanzas of "America, the Beautiful" are shown below.

O beautiful for spacious skies,
For amber waves of grain,
For purple mountain majesties
Above the fruited plain!
America! America!
God shed his grace on thee
And crown thy good with brotherhood
From sea to shining sea!
• • • • • • • • • • • • • • • • • • • • • • • • • • •

O beautiful for patriot dream
That sees beyond the years
Thine alabaster cities gleam
Undimmed by human tears!
America! America!
God shed his grace on thee
And crown thy good with brotherhood
From sea to shining sea!

# American
## TRADITIONS AND SYMBOLS

### ★ AMERICAN TRADITIONS

Holidays are special occasions usually marked by celebrations and vacations from school and work. Religious holidays are celebrated by people of various faiths. For example, Christians celebrate Christmas (marking the birth of Jesus), and Jews celebrate Rosh Hashanah (marking the beginning of the Jewish New Year). On legal holidays, banks, schools, and most government and business offices are closed.

National holidays usually commemorate, or remind people of, a special event in a country's past. Strictly speaking, the United States has no official national holidays. It is up to the states, not the federal government, to determine which days will be celebrated. However, the federal government influences the states by designating the days to be observed in Washington, D.C., and by all federal employees. Along with New Year's Day (January 1) and Christmas (December 25), the following eight federal holidays are observed throughout the United States.

### Martin Luther King Jr.'s Birthday
*(third Monday in January)*
An act of Congress established the birthday of Martin Luther King Jr. as the newest federal holiday. King helped begin the civil rights movement in the 1950s, working to end discrimination against African Americans. He led many peaceful protest marches and demonstrations in cities across the United States. Largely because of King's efforts, Congress passed the Civil Rights Act of 1964.

King's brilliant career was cut short when he was assassinated on April 4, 1968. After King's death, many people called for a national holiday to recognize his efforts. The holiday became official in 1986.

### Presidents' Day *(third Monday in February)*
In 1971 President Richard Nixon created Presidents' Day to honor all past presidents. He combined the dates of George Washington's birthday and Abraham Lincoln's birthday to determine the date—the third Monday in February.

Washington was born on February 11 according to the calendar in use in 1732, the year of his birth. However, according to the modern calendar, his birthday is February 22. Abraham Lincoln was born on February 12, 1809.

*Presidents' Day honors all past presidents.*

### Memorial Day (last Monday in May)

Originally, Memorial Day honored the soldiers who died in the Civil War. Today the holiday honors all Americans who died in all the wars in which the United States has fought. Many Americans also mark Memorial Day as a day to honor loved ones who have died. Memorial Day, sometimes called Decoration Day, was first celebrated on May 30 instead of the last Monday in May. Some states celebrate the holiday on the traditional day.

### Independence Day (July 4)

Fireworks, parades, and picnics mark this holiday, regarded as the birthday of the country. It commemorates the day in 1776 when the Continental Congress adopted the Declaration of Independence.

John Adams, one of the leaders in the struggle for American independence, believed it would be a significant day. "I am apt to believe that it will be celebrated by succeeding generations as the great anniversary festival," he said. Time has proved Adams to be right about Independence Day celebrations.

*Memorial Day honors all Americans who died in all wars fought by the United States.*

### Labor Day (first Monday in September)

Union leader Peter J. McGuire first suggested a holiday to honor working people across the country. The first Labor Day parade was held in New York City in 1882. Labor Day has been celebrated as a federal holiday since 1894.

Labor Day is marked with parades and speeches honoring workers. It also has come to mean the end of summer. It is often celebrated with a last day at the beach, a picnic or cookout, or community festivities.

### Columbus Day (second Monday in October)

Christopher Columbus first reached the Americas on October 12, 1492. The first Columbus Day was celebrated in New York City, New York, in 1792—the 300th anniversary of Columbus's voyage. Today Columbus Day is observed on the second Monday in October. Parades and special banquets mark this holiday. Columbus Day has been a legal federal holiday in the United States since 1971. However, some states have chosen to eliminate this holiday from their official calendars. Instead, they have designated a holiday honoring American Indians.

*Independence Day is celebrated with fireworks, parades, and picnics.*

American Traditions and Symbols   **R13**

### Veterans Day *(November 11)*

This holiday is unusual because it is also a special day in many European nations. Formerly called Armistice Day, it originally marked the armistice, or truce, that ended World War I on November 11, 1918.

In 1954 the United States changed the observance of this holiday to honor all people who have served in the U.S. armed forces. Some communities hold military parades on Veterans Day. Reenactments of famous battles are also occasionally held. Special services are held at the Tomb of the Unknown Soldier in Arlington National Cemetery which is near Washington, D.C.

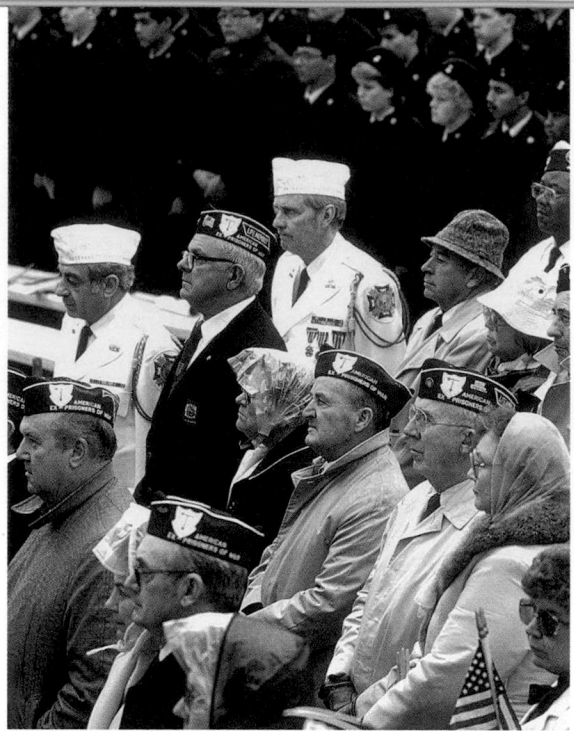

*Veterans Day services*

### Thanksgiving Day

*(fourth Thursday in November)*

For hundreds of years, people have held autumn festivals to give thanks for a good harvest. The American celebration of Thanksgiving began with the Pilgrims in Plymouth colony. They observed the first Thanksgiving in 1621 to mark the end of their first difficult year in America. Their celebration lasted three days. During that time the Pilgrims feasted on good food with their American Indian friends, who had helped them survive.

Thereafter, many communities observed a day of thanksgiving at various times in the fall. Finally, in 1863, President Abraham Lincoln declared that the day should be celebrated nationally. Thanksgiving Day is, above all, a time for family togetherness, commitment, and celebration.

*Below is a reenactment of the first Thanksgiving, held in Plymouth colony in 1621.*

*The Statue of Liberty was a gift from the people of France to the United States.*

## ⭐ AMERICAN SYMBOLS

### The Statue of Liberty

At the entrance to New York Harbor stands one of the best-known symbols of the United States—the Statue of Liberty. The official name of this colossal figure is *Liberty Enlightening the World.* Slightly more than 151 feet (46 m) tall, it is the largest statue ever made.

The statue was a gift from the people of France to the United States. It was presented as a symbol of friendship and in honor of the 100th anniversary of American independence. It was designed by Frédéric-Auguste Bartholdi and constructed by Alexandre-Gustave Eiffel.

The Statue of Liberty was built in Paris, taken apart, and then shipped to the United States in 214 crates. It was reassembled on a pedestal built with money raised by the American people. President Grover Cleveland dedicated the statue in 1886.

The statue depicts a woman dressed in long flowing robes and wearing a crown with seven spikes. At her feet are the broken chains of tyranny. Her right arm holds a torch high in the air. In her left hand is a law book with the date of the Declaration of Independence—July 4, 1776.

Until the attacks on the United States on September 11, 2001, visitors could climb the stairs to the statue's crown, which provides a beautiful view of New York Harbor. However, the attacks closed the statue to the public indefinitely.

The Statue of Liberty has long been a symbol of freedom for millions of immigrants to the United States. "The New Colossus," a poem by Emma Lazarus to welcome immigrants, was inscribed on a tablet in the pedestal in 1903. It ends with the following lines:

> Give me your tired, your poor,
> Your huddled masses yearning to
>     breathe free,
> The wretched refuse of your teeming shore.
> Send these, the homeless, tempest-tost
>     to me,
> I lift my lamp beside the golden door!

Over the years, rust and corrosion from weather and pollution have damaged the Statue of Liberty. By the early 1980s the statue was badly in need of repair. In 1982 President Ronald Reagan formed a special commission of private citizens to oversee the statue's restoration. The project was funded by millions of dollars in private donations. Special rededication ceremonies took place in July 1986.

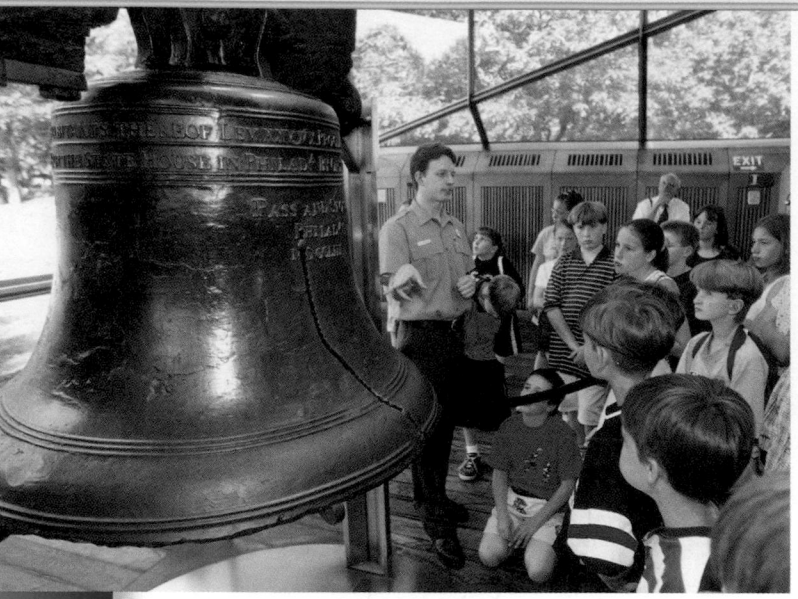

*The Liberty Bell has long been a symbol of American freedom.*

### The Liberty Bell

The Liberty Bell has been a symbol of American freedom ever since it rang on July 8, 1776. It announced the adoption of the Declaration of Independence. This giant bronze bell was made in England in 1752 for the State House (now Independence Hall) in Philadelphia, Pennsylvania. The bell's inscription—"Proclaim Liberty throughout all the land unto all the inhabitants thereof "—is from the Bible.

The Liberty Bell cracked soon after its arrival in Philadelphia and had to be recast. It rang at every event of national importance until 1835. In that year it cracked again while tolling after the death of John Marshall, chief justice of the Supreme Court. In 1846 the bell was severely damaged while ringing in honor of George Washington's birthday. It was never tolled again.

The bell was on display in Independence Hall until 1976. In celebration of the country's 200th anniversary, the bell was moved to its own building.

### The Great Seal of the United States

Government officials often use seals, or engraved stamps,

as guarantees that documents are authentic. The Great Seal of the United States was adopted by the new country in 1782. Today it is kept in the Department of State. It is used only on certain important kinds of documents, such as treaties. Only the face of the seal is used to seal official documents. However, both sides of the seal appear on the back of the $1 bill.

The face of the seal shows an American bald eagle with raised wings. On its breast is a shield with 13 alternate red and white stripes representing the original states. In the eagle's right claw is an olive branch with 13 leaves and 13 olives. In its left claw are 13 arrows. These symbols indicate the country's wish to live in peace, but also its ability to wage war.

In the eagle's beak is a ribbon with the words *E Pluribus Unum.* This Latin phrase means "from many, one." In other words, the many U.S. states form one united nation. Above the eagle's head are 13 stars surrounded by rays of light breaking through a cloud.

The reverse side of the Great Seal shows a pyramid made up of 13 layers of stone representing the new country. The base of the pyramid has a date shown in Roman numerals—MDCCLXXVI (1776)—the year of the signing of the Declaration of Independence. The pyramid is guarded by an eye surrounded by rays of light. Above are the Latin words *Annuit Coeptis,* meaning "He [God] has favored our undertaking." Below is the phrase *Novus Ordo Seclorum,* which means "a new order of the ages."

*The Great Seal of the United States*

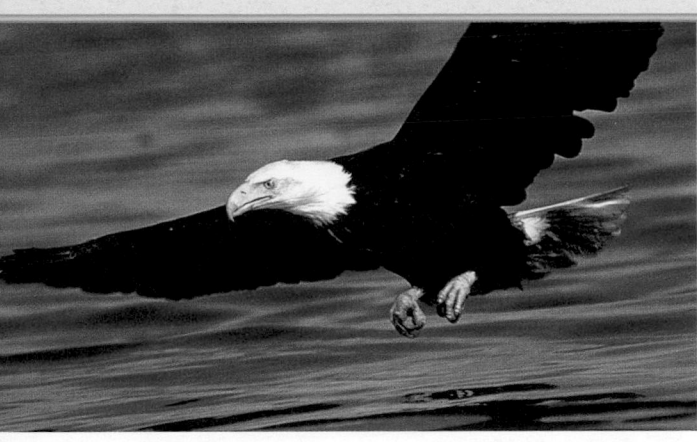

### The Bald Eagle

The bald eagle, which appears on the Great Seal, is the official emblem of the United States. This bird is not actually bald, but sometimes appears to be so because its head and neck are pure white. The eagle has symbolized official power since the days of ancient Egyptian civilizations.

The bald eagle was chosen as the national bird of the United States in 1782. However, the choice was not unanimous. Benjamin Franklin preferred a native bird, the turkey, but he was overruled.

### Uncle Sam

The figure of Uncle Sam is an American symbol as widely recognized as the American flag. He has symbolized the United States since the War of 1812.

One legend has it that during that war, a storage facility in Troy, New York, stamped the initials "U.S." on barrels of salted meat for American soldiers. The "U.S." stood for United States. However, workers jokingly

*The figure of Uncle Sam is an American symbol as widely recognized as the American flag.*

claimed that the initials really stood for "Uncle Sam" (Samuel) Wilson, who managed the storage facility. The idea of equating Uncle Sam with the United States spread rapidly. After all, Great Britain, the country's opponent in the War of 1812, already had a personal symbol of its own. That was the figure of an English farmer, John Bull.

Uncle Sam as we know him today was first drawn in the 1860s by the American cartoonist Thomas Nast. The symbol of Uncle Sam usually has long hair and a white beard. His pants have red and white stripes, and his stovepipe hat is decorated with stars and stripes. He wears a cutaway coat.

### The Donkey and the Elephant

Two well-known symbols—the donkey and the elephant—represent the major political parties in the United States. They were first drawn as symbols of the Democratic Party and the Republican Party by American cartoonist Thomas Nast.

The donkey was used for the first time as a political symbol by Andrew Jackson. His opponents in the 1828 presidential election had called him a "jackass." Later, Nast used the donkey in his cartoons to stand for the Democratic Party. The donkey soon became recognized as the symbol of the Democratic Party.

The elephant as a symbol of the Republican Party first appeared in a cartoon by Nast in *Harper's Weekly* in 1874. He used the elephant to represent the Republican vote. It soon came to stand for the Republican Party.

# Glossary

This Glossary contains terms you need to understand as you read your textbook. After each key term there is a brief definition or explanation of the meaning of the term as it is used in your textbook. The page number refers to the page on which the term is introduced in the textbook.

## Phonetic Respelling and Pronunciation Guide

Many of the key terms in this textbook have been respelled to help you pronounce them. The letter combinations used in the respelling throughout the narrative are explained in the following phonetic respelling and pronunciation guide. The guide is adapted from *Webster's Tenth New College Dictionary*, *Merriam-Webster's New Geographical Dictionary*, and *Merriam-Webster's New Biographical Dictionary*.

| MARK | AS IN | RESPELLING | EXAMPLE |
|---|---|---|---|
| a | alphabet | a | *AL-fuh-bet |
| ā | Asia | ay | AY-zhuh |
| ä | cart, top | ah | KAHRT, TAHP |
| e | let, ten | e | LET, TEN |
| ē | even, leaf | ee | EE-vuhn, LEEF |
| i | it, tip, British | i | IT, TIP, BRIT-ish |
| ī | site, buy, Ohio | y | SYT, BY, oh-HY-oh |
|  | iris | eye | EYE-ris |
| k | card | k | KAHRD |
| ō | over, rainbow | oh | OH-vuhr, RAYN-boh |
| ú | book, wood | ooh | BOOHK, WOOHD |
| ò | all, orchid | aw | AWL, AWR-kid |
| òi | foil, coin | oy | FOYL, KOYN |
| aú | out | ow | OWT |
| ə | cup, butter | uh | KUHP, BUHT-uhr |
| ü | rule, food | oo | ROOL, FOOD |
| yü | few | yoo | FYOO |
| zh | vision | zh | VIZH-uhn |

*A syllable printed in small capital letters receives heavier emphasis than the other syllable(s) in a word.

**absolute advantage** Situation that exists when a country can produce a good better than its trading partners can. 530

**absolute monarchs** Kings or queens with absolute, or total, power. 25

**acid rain** Acid formed when pollution from burning gas, oil, and coal mixes with water vapor in the air. 664

**acquit** To find a defendant not guilty. 391

**act** A law. 132

**addicts** People who feel the compulsive need to do something. 646

**administrative laws** Laws made by government agencies. 171

**adopt** To legally establish a child as one's own. 331

**advertising** The use of the mass media by businesses to inform people about products and to persuade them to buy these products. 442

**agency shop** A business in which workers cannot be forced to join a union but must pay union dues. 500

**aggravated assault** A physical injury done intentionally to another person. 382

**agribusinesses** Large farms that are owned by corporations and that rely heavily on mechanized equipment. 551

**alcoholism** A disease in which a person is addicted to alcohol. 647

**aliens** People who live in a nation but are not citizens of that nation. 10

**alliances** Agreements in which two or more countries commit to helping each other for defense, economic, scientific, or other reasons. 576

**ambassadors** The highest-ranking officials representing a government in a foreign country. 155

**amendment** A written change to the Constitution. 83

**Antifederalists** Opponents of the Constitution who urged its rejection. 45

**appeal** The right of a convicted person to ask a higher court to review his or her case. 173

**appellate jurisdiction** The authority of some courts to review decisions made by lower courts. 175

**apportioned** To be distributed, as in the seats in the House of Representatives. 114

**apprenticeship** A fixed period of on-the-job training. 549

**appropriation bill** A bill approving the spending of extra public money. 132

**aptitude tests** Tests that help people determine their interests and talents. 567

**arbitration** A method of settling differences between labor unions and employers in which a third party's decision must be accepted by both sides. 505

**arraignment** Process during which an accused person appears before a court to enter a plea of guilty or not guilty. 390

**arrest warrant** An authorization by a court to make an arrest. 389

**arson** The destruction of property by setting fire to it. 383

**assembly line** A system in which workers and machines perform specialized jobs that move a product through the stages of production. 434

**attorney general** The chief legal officer of the nation or of a state. 155

**audit** An examination by an accountant of a government's or business's income and expenditures. 315

**authoritarian** Controlled by rulers that answer only to themselves. 26

**automation** The use of machines instead of workers to provide goods and services. 550

**bail** Money or property an accused person gives a court to hold as a guarantee that he or she will appear for trial. 94

**balance** The remainder owed on a bill or a loan. 448

**balanced budget** A budget in which revenue equals expenditures. 313

**balance of payments** The record of all the income a country earns from other nations and all its spending with other nations. 535

**balance of power** A situation in which countries or groups of countries have equal levels of strength. 610

**balance of trade** The difference in value between a country's imports and exports. 584

**bankruptcy** A legal declaration that a person or business cannot pay his or her or its debts. 457

**beneficiary** The person named in an insurance policy to receive the amount of the policy when the policyholder dies. 475

**bicameral** Consisting of two houses, as in a lawmaking body. 41

**bills** Proposed laws being considered by a lawmaking body. 121

**bill of attainder** A law sentencing a person to jail without a trial. 130

**Bill of Rights** The first 10 amendments to the Constitution, which set forth basic rights guaranteed to all Americans. 89

**biomass** Wood or waste products that can be burned or used to make fuel. 675

**birthrate** The annual number of live births per 1,000 members of a population. 15

**blacklists** Methods once used by employers in which companies create and share lists of workers active in labor unions and refuse to hire those workers. 500

**blended families** Families in which one or both partners brings children from a previous marriage into the new marriage. 326

**block grants** Federal funds given to state and local governments for broad purposes. 244

**blue-collar workers** People who perform jobs requiring manual labor. 549

**bond** A certificate of debt issued by governments and corporations to persons from whom they have borrowed money. 303

**boycott** To stop buying or using a good or service. 637

**brand names** Widely advertised products usually distributed over a large area. 442

**brief** A written statement explaining the main points of one side's argument in a court case. 185

**brokers** Brokerage house employees who buy and sell stock. 469

**budget** A plan of income and spending. 153

**building code** A set of local laws that regulate the construction and repair of buildings in a community. 631

**bureaucracy** The many departments and agencies at all levels of government. 165

**burglary** The forcible or illegal entry into a home or other property with the intent to steal. 382

**business cycle** Economic patterns in which a free-market economy goes through periods of prosperity and depression. 485

**cabinet** The leaders of the executive departments, who also act as advisers to the president. 84

**candidates** People who run for election to public office. 254

**capital** Money invested in business; also, property and equipment used to produce goods or services. 410

**capitalism** An economic system based on private ownership of the means of production. 410

**capital punishment** The death penalty. 393

**caucuses** Meetings of party leaders to determine party policy or to choose the party's candidates for public office. 120

**censure** The formal disapproval of the actions of a member of Congress by the other members. 118

**census** An official count of the number of people in a country. 14

**certificates of deposit (CDs)** Investments in which an amount of money invested for a specified period of time earns a guaranteed rate of interest. 468

**charge account** A form of credit that stores grant to customers to buy goods now and pay for them later. 447

**charters** Basic plans of government granted by state legislatures to local governments. 223

**checks** Written and signed orders to a bank to pay a sum of money from a checking account to the person or business named on the check. 447

**checks and balances** A system in which the powers of government are balanced among different branches so that each branch can check, or limit, the power of the other branches. 79

**child abuse** The mental, physical, or sexual mistreatment of a child. 331

**circuit** The judicial district covered by a court of appeals. 177

**circular-flow model** An economic model which displays how households, businesses, and the government interact in the U.S. economy. 511

**citizen** A legal member of a country. 3

**city** The largest type of municipality. 234

**city council** The lawmaking body of a city. 235

**civics** The study of what it means to be a U.S. citizen. 3

**civil cases** Court cases involving disputes over money or property between individuals or businesses. 215

**civil disobedience** The intentional breaking of a law to show dissent. 638

**civilian** A nonmilitary person. 157

**civil rights** The rights guaranteed to all U.S. citizens. 96

**civil rights movement** The struggle for equal rights for all Americans. 636

**closed primary** A primary election in which only voters who are members of the party can vote for the party's candidates. 266

**closed shop** A business in which only union members can be hired. 500

**cloture** A limit on the debate of a bill in the Senate. 137

**coalition** An agreement between two or more political parties to work together to run a government. 256

**coincident indicators** Economic signs that help economists determine how the economy is doing at the present time. 519

**collateral** Property used to guarantee that a loan will be repaid. **460**

**collective bargaining** A process in which representatives of a labor union and an employer work to reach an agreement about wages and working conditions. **499**

**colleges** Four-year institutions of higher learning. **345**

**command economy** An economic system in which the government controls a country's economy. **414**

**commission** A local government body that has both legislative and executive powers. **238**

**committees** Small groups in Congress formed to consider bills. **121**

**common law** Customary law that develops from judges' decisions and is followed in situations not covered by statutory law. **170**

**common stock** Shares in a corporation that do not earn a fixed dividend but give shareholders a voice in managing the company. **420**

**communication** The passing along of ideas, information, and beliefs from one person to another. **369**

**communism** An economic system based on the theories of Marx and Engels in which the means of production are owned by government and the government decides what will be produced. **606**

**community colleges** Two-year colleges that typically offer low tuition, training in specialized fields, and preparation for advanced study. **344**

**community policing** A system in which police officers and citizens are encouraged to work together to prevent crime in a community. **388**

**commutation** The act of making a convicted person's sentence less severe. **151**

**comparative advantage** Method of determining which products or services offer a nation the greatest absolute advantage. **530**

**competition** The economic rivalry among businesses selling products. **512**

**complaint** A lawsuit. **216**

**compromise** An agreement in which each side gives up part of its demands. **44**

**compulsory** Required by law. **374**

**concealed propaganda** Propaganda presented as fact and whose source is kept secret. **281**

**concurrent powers** Powers shared by the federal government and the states. **75**

**concurring opinion** A statement written by a Supreme Court justice who agrees with the majority's decision but for different reasons. **185**

**conditioning** Learning that is the result of experience involving the motor nerves. **354**

**confederation** A loose association of states. **32**

**conference committees** Temporary congressional committees made up of senators and representatives who try to reach an agreement on different versions of a bill. **123**

**conglomerate** A large company formed by the merger of businesses that produce, supply, or sell a number of unrelated goods and services. **413**

**conservation** Safeguarding of natural resources through wise use. **672**

**constables** Officers who enforce township laws. **232**

**constituents** People represented by members of a lawmaking body. **131**

**constitution** A written plan of government. **28**

**constitutional law** Law based on the Constitution and Supreme Court decisions. **171**

**consul** An official who works to promote U.S. commercial interests in a foreign country. **156**

**consulate** The office of a consul. **156**

**consumer** A person who buys or uses products and services. **443**

**containment** The U.S. foreign policy of preventing the spread of communism. **609**

**contraction** A period in a business cycle during which the economy is slowing. **486**

**copyright** An exclusive right, granted by law, to publish or sell a written, musical, or art work for a certain number of years. **409**

**corollary** A statement that follows as a natural or logical result. **600**

**corporation** A business organization chartered by a state government and given power to conduct business, sell stock, and receive protection of state laws. **418**

**corrections** Methods used to punish lawbreakers. **392**

**costs of production** Business costs, such as wages, payments for raw materials, transportation, rent, and interest on borrowed money. **486**

**council members at large** Members of a local council who are elected by all the voters of a community. **235**

**counterfeiting** The making or distributing of fake money. **156**

**counties** Subdivisions of state government formed to carry out state laws, collect taxes, and supervise elections. **225**

**county clerk** The official who keeps county records. **227**

**county seat** The town or city in which a county government is located. **225**

**couriers** Special government messengers. **578**

**court-martial** A trial of a person in the armed services accused of breaking military law. **179**

**courts of appeals** Federal courts that review decisions appealed from district courts. **177**

**creativity** The ability to find new ways of thinking and doing things. **356**

**credit card** A form of credit issued by banks and other major lending institutions and accepted by most businesses worldwide. **447**

**creditors** People who are owed money. **457**

**credit rating** A report that shows how reliable a customer is at paying his or her bills. **447**

**credit unions** Banks that are owned by their members to create a pool of money for low-interest loans. **463**

**crime** Any act that breaks the law and for which a punishment has been established. **381**

**criminal** A person who commits any type of crime. **381**

**criminal cases** Court cases in which a person is accused of breaking a criminal law. **215**

**criminal justice system** The system of police, courts, and corrections used to bring criminals to justice. **387**

**critical thinking** A type of thinking one does to reach decisions and solve problems. **356**

**cross-examine** To question an opponent's witness in court. **173**

**crossroads** A location where two roads meet. **363**

**currency** Coins and paper money. **453**

**death rate** The annual number of deaths per 1,000 members of a population. **15**

**debit cards** Small cards that operate the way that checks do, deducting money directly from a bank account. **447**

**deductions** Expenses taxpayers are allowed to subtract in figuring their taxable income. **304**

**defendant** A person accused of a crime in a court case. **390**

**defense** An accused person's side in a court case. **390**

**deficit** The amount by which expenditures exceed income. **313**

**delayed marriage** The tendency to marry at older ages. **326**

**delegates** Representatives. **40**

**delegated powers** Powers given to the federal government by the Constitution. **74**

**delinquents** Juveniles who break the law. **395**

**demand** The amount of a good or service that a consumer is willing to buy at various prices during a time period. **512**

**democracy** A form of government in which the people of a country either rule directly or through elected representatives. **26**

**demonstrations** Gatherings in which people express dissent by marching, carrying signs, singing songs, and making speeches. **637**

**deport** To force a person such as an illegal alien to leave a country. **11**

**depression** A sharp decline in a country's business activity, during which many workers lose their jobs and many businesses close down. **486**

**desertification** The loss of soil, due to overgrazing and removal of trees and plants, that results in once fertile areas becoming deserts. **659**

**détente** A lessening of tensions. **613**

**deterrence** Discouraging people from certain behavior by the threat of punishment. **392**

**dictatorship** A form of government in which all power is in the hands of one person or a small group of people. **26**

**diplomacy** The art of dealing with foreign governments. **149**

**diplomatic corps** The ambassadors and other representatives of a nation serving in foreign countries. **578**

**diplomatic notes** Written communications between diplomats. **150**

**diplomatic recognition** The power of the president to decide whether to establish official relations with a foreign government. **577**

**direct democracy** A form of government in which all the people meet together at one place to make laws and decide what actions to take. **26**

**discounting** The practice of deducting interest on a loan before money is given to the borrower. **463**

**discount rate** The rate of interest charged by Federal Reserve banks on loans to member banks. **465**

**discrimination** Unfair actions taken against people because they belong to a particular group. **635**

**dissent** Disagreement, as with a law. **637**

**dissenting opinion** A statement written by a Supreme Court justice who disagrees with the majority's decision. **185**

**distribution** The process of moving goods from manufacturers to the people who want them. **437**

**district attorney** The official who represents the state government in county trials. **227**

**district courts** Lower federal courts that have original jurisdiction in most cases involving federal laws. **175**

**dividends** Profits paid to corporate stockholders. **419**

**division of labor** A system in which each worker performs a specialized portion of a total job. **432**

**divorce** A legal ending of a marriage. **331**

**docket** A calendar of cases to be heard by a court. **184**

**doctrine** A statement that sets forth a new government policy with respect to other countries. **599**

**dollar diplomacy** The practice of sending U.S. troops to other countries to protect U.S. investments. **600**

**double jeopardy** Being tried a second time for the same crime. **93**

**down payment** An initial cash payment on an installment loan or on an item bought under an installment plan. **448**

**draft** A policy requiring men to serve in the military. **102**

**drug abuse** The use of drugs for recreation. **646**

**due process of law** The fair application of the law to one's case. **93**

**Earth Day** Unofficial holiday on April 22 each year dedicated to caring for Earth. **680**

**easy-money policy** An economic policy that increases the amount of money in the money supply. **526**

**ecology** The study of living things in relation to each other and to their environment. **655**

**economies of scale** A situation in which goods can be produced more efficiently and cheaply by larger companies. **413**

**ecosystem** A community of interdependent living things existing in balance with their physical environment. **655**

**elastic clause** Article 1, Section 8, of the Constitution; known also as the "necessary and proper" clause that allows Congress to extend its delegated powers. **127**

**electors** People elected by the voters in a presidential election as members of the electoral college. **274**

**electoral college** The group of electors that casts the official votes that elect the president and vice president. **274**

**electoral votes** The votes cast by the electoral college for president and vice president. **274**

**embargo** Measure that bans imports from specific countries. **532**

**embassy** The official residence of an ambassador in a foreign country. **155**

**embezzlement** Taking money that has been entrusted to one's care for one's own use. **383**

**eminent domain** The power of the government to take private property for public use. **94**

**Endangered Species Acts** Laws designed to protect threatened species. **679**

**entrepreneurs** Business owners. **425**

**Environmental Protection Agency** Independent government agency that deals with pollution and other environmental issues. **679**

**equal opportunity employer** An employer who does not discriminate against job applicants because of their sex, age, race, skin color, religion, or ethnic background. **554**

**erosion** The wearing away of land by water and wind. **659**

**estate tax** A tax on all the wealth left by a person who has died. **307**

**ethnic group** A group of people of the same race, nationality, or religion who share a common and distinctive culture and heritage. **635**

**excise taxes** Federal taxes collected on certain luxury items produced and sold in the United States. **306**

**executive agreement** A mutual understanding between the president of the United States and the leader of a foreign government. **576**

**executive branch** The branch of government that carries out the laws. **78**

**executive departments** Departments in the executive branch of the federal government. **154**

**executive orders** Orders issued by the head of the executive branch to set up methods of enforcing laws. **211**

**exemptions** Amounts of money taxpayers are allowed to subtract from taxable income for themselves and for dependents. **304**

**expansion** A period in a business cycle during which the economy is growing. **485**

**experience** Direct observation or participation in events. **354**

***ex post facto* law** A law that applies to an action that took place before the law was passed. **130**

**expulsion** The removal of a person from an institution, such as Congress, for serious misconduct. **118**

**extracurricular activities** Activities that students participate in outside of the classroom. **353**

**extradition** A legal process for returning criminals to the place from which they fled. **201**

**family law** The legal regulation of marriage, divorce, and the duties of parents and children. **329**

**favorite sons or daughters** Men or women, popular in their home state, who are nominated for president by their state's delegates on the first ballot at the national nominating convention. **272**

**featherbedding** A practice once used by unions to force employers to hire more workers than are needed. **503**

**federalism** A system of government in which the powers of government are divided between the national government, which governs the whole country, and the state governments, which govern the people of each state. **43**

**Federalists** Supporters of the Constitution who urged its adoption. **45**

**Federal Reserve System** The U.S. banking system that handles the banking needs of the federal government and regulates the money supply. **465**

**fees** Small government charges for a service or license. **302**

**felonies** Serious crimes, such as homicide and kidnapping. **381**

**fertilizers** Plant foods that make crops grow faster and bigger. **660**

**filibuster** A method of delaying action on a bill in the Senate by making long speeches. **137**

**fine** Money paid as a penalty for breaking certain laws. **302**

**fiscal policy** A government's policy of taxation and spending. **493**

**fixed expenses** Expenses that occur regularly. **337**

**floor leader** A political party leader in Congress who works for the passage of bills the party favors. **120**

**forcible rape** The sexual violation of a person by force and against the person's will. **382**

**foreign aid** A government program that provides economic and military assistance to other countries. **582**

**foreign policy** A country's plan for dealing with other countries of the world. **149**

**fossil fuels** Nonrenewable resources (petroleum, natural gas, or coal) that formed over millions of years from the fossilized remains of plants and animals. **670**

**foster homes** Homes of people who are unrelated to a child but who agree to act as the child's caregivers. **331**

**franking privilege** The right of members of Congress to mail official letters free of charge. **117**

**fraud** Cheating someone out of their money or property. **383**

**free competition** A system in which business owners compete among themselves for customers. **408**

**free-enterprise system** An economic system in which people are free to operate their businesses as they see fit, with little government interference. **411**

**free market** An economic system in which buyers and sellers are free to exchange goods and services as they choose. **408**

**full faith and credit clause** The provision in the Constitution ensuring that each state will accept the decisions of civil courts in other states. **201**

**General Assembly** The body within the United Nations that discusses, debates, and recommends solutions to problems. **589**

**general election** An election in which the voters elect their leaders. **266**

**general trial courts** Courts that handle major criminal and civil cases. **217**

**gerrymandering** The process of drawing congressional district lines to favor a political party. **114**

**gift tax** A tax on items received as gifts that are worth more than $10,000. **307**

**glasnost** A policy of openness begun by Mikhail Gorbachev that aimed to give more freedom to the people of the Soviet Union. **612**

**government** Organizations, institutions, and individuals that exercise political authority on behalf of a group of people. **3**

**governor** The chief executive of a state government. **210**

**graduate school** An institution of higher learning that offers advanced degrees. **345**

**grand jury** A group that hears evidence in a criminal case and decides whether there is enough evidence to bring the accused person to trial. **93**

**grand larceny** The theft of goods worth more than a certain amount. **382**

**grants-in-aid** Federal funds given to state and local governments for specific projects. **244**

**grassroots** Originating, as in political support, from many individuals rather than from national parties and large organizations. **266**

**greenhouse effect** The trapping of the Sun's heat by high levels of carbon dioxide in the atmosphere, resulting in the possible long-term raising of temperatures on Earth. **664**

**gross domestic product (GDP)** The value of all goods and services produced in a country each year. **431**

**gross income** The total amount of money a company receives from the sale of its goods and services. **426**

**guardian** A person appointed by a state court to look after an individual who is not an adult or who is unable to care for himself or herself. **331**

**habit** An action performed automatically. **355**

**homelessness** The situation of being without a place to live. **630**

**home rule** The power of a city to write its own municipal charter and to manage its own affairs. **234**

**homicide** The killing of one person by another person. **381**

**human resources** The labor needed to produce goods or services. **510**

**human rights** The basic rights to which all people are entitled as human beings. **31**

**hung jury** A jury that cannot reach a verdict. **173**

**hydrologic cycle** The process in which water circulates through Earth's environment. **665**

**immigrants** People who come to a country to settle as permanent residents. **8**

**immunity** Legal protection. **117**

**impeachment** A formal charge brought against a government official. **128**

**implied powers** Powers not specifically granted to Congress by the Constitution that are suggested to be necessary to carry out the powers delegated to Congress under the Constitution. **128**

**import quota** A law that limits the amount or number of a certain import. **531**

**imports** Goods or services bought from another country. **531**

**income taxes** Taxes on the income that individuals and companies earn. **304**

**independent agencies** Agencies in the executive branch of the federal government formed by Congress to help enforce laws and regulations not covered by the executive departments. **163**

**independent voters** Voters who are not members of a political party. **265**

**indict** To formally accuse a person of a crime. **93**

**inflation** A rise in the costs of goods and services. **485**

**infrastructure** The network that enables consumers to participate in the economy. **522**

**inheritance tax** A tax on money and property received from an estate. **307**

initiative A process by which citizens of a state may propose a law by collecting signatures on a petition. **208**

insight A process by which people unconsciously take what they know about a subject and apply it to a problem or question in order to find an answer. **356**

installments Payments made on a balance owed. **448**

insurance A system of protection in which people pay small sums periodically to avoid the risk of a large loss. **474**

interchangeable parts Parts that are exactly alike. **432**

interest Payment for the use of loaned money. **300**

interest groups Organizations of people with common interests who try to influence government policies and decisions. **287**

International Court of Justice The international legal court of the United Nations, also known as the World Court. **589**

interpersonal skills Skills involving an individual's ability to interact with others. **566**

invest To put money into businesses or valuable articles in hopes of making a profit. **408**

isolationism A policy of avoiding involvement in foreign affairs. **597**

item veto The power of the head of the executive branch to reject one part of a bill but approve the rest of it. **207**

job action Any kind of slowdown or action short of a strike. **499**

Joint Chiefs of Staff The group made up of the highest-ranking officers from the Army, Navy, and Air Force that advises the president on military affairs. **157**

joint committees Committees made up of members of both houses of Congress to deal with matters of mutual concern. **122**

judicial branch The branch of government that interprets the laws and punishes lawbreakers. **78**

judicial review The power of the U.S. Supreme Court to determine if a law passed by Congress or a presidential action is in accord with the Constitution. **183**

jurisdiction The authority to interpret and administer the law; also, the range of that authority. **174**

jurors Members of a trial jury who judge evidence and determine the verdict in a court case. **173**

jury duty Serving on a jury. **173**

justice of the peace A judge who presides over a state justice court, usually in rural areas and small towns, and who tries misdemeanors and civil cases involving small sums. **216**

juvenile In most states, a person under the age of 18. **395**

labor Human effort used to make goods and services. **425**

laborers People who perform unskilled or heavy physical labor. **550**

labor unions Organizations of workers formed to bargain for higher wages and improved working conditions and to protect workers' rights. **498**

lagging indicators Economic signs that help economists determine how long the current economic situation will last. **519**

landfills Huge pits dug to store garbage. **667**

larceny The theft of property without the use of force or violence. **382**

law of demand An economic rule that states that buyers will demand more products when they can buy them at lower prices and fewer products when they must buy them at higher prices. **410**

law of supply An economic rule that states that businesses will provide more products when they can sell them at higher prices and fewer products when they must sell them at lower prices. **410**

laws Rules of conduct enforced by government. **28**

leading indicators Economic signs that help economists make predictions about future economic growth. **519**

legislative branch The lawmaking branch of government. **77**

legislature A lawmaking body of government. **44**

libel Written falsehoods that damage another person's reputation. **91**

lieutenant governor The official who succeeds the governor if the governor dies, resigns, or is removed from office. **213**

limited government A system in which government powers are carefully spelled out to prevent government from becoming too powerful. **75**

limited war A war fought without using a country's full power, particularly nuclear weapons. **611**

lobby An interest group. **287**

lobbyist A person paid to represent an interest group's viewpoint. **287**

lockouts Methods once used by employers to fight labor slowdowns by locking workers out, thus preventing them from earning wages. **500**

long-term credit An advance of money to be repaid in installments over a long period of time. **457**

machine tools Machinery built to produce identical parts. **432**

magistrate judges Officials who hear cases against accused persons and decide whether those cases should be brought before a grand jury. **176**

mainstreaming The practice of placing students with special needs in regular schools and classes. **346**

majority party The political party that has more members in Congress or in a state legislature. **120**

majority rule A system in which the decision of more than half the people is accepted by all. **73**

*maquiladoras* Factories established by foreign businesses in Mexico. **520**

market economy An economic system in which individuals are free to compete, to earn a living, to earn a profit, and to own property. **407**

marshal An official in each federal district court who makes arrests, delivers subpoenas, keeps order in courtrooms, and carries out court orders. **176**

mass marketing The process of selling goods in large quantities. **440**

mass media Forms of communication that transmit information to large numbers of people. **280**

mass production The rapid production by machine of large numbers of identical objects. **431**

mass transit Public transportation, including buses, subways, and commuter railroads. **632**

mayor The chief executive of a city government. **235**

mediation A method of settling disputes between labor unions and employers through the use of a third party who offers a nonbinding solution. **505**

Medicaid A federal program that helps the states pay the medical costs of low-income people. **481**

Medicare A federal program of health insurance for people age 65 and over. **481**

megalopolis A continuous, giant urban area that includes many cities. **368**

merger A combination of two or more companies into one company. **412**

metropolitan areas Large cities and their suburbs. **17**

migration The movement of people from region to region. **18**

ministers Officials sent to a small country to represent the U.S. government. **155**

**minority groups** Groups set apart from other groups of people in society because of ethnic background, language, customs, or religion. **635**

**minority party** The political party that has fewer members in Congress or in a state legislature. **120**

**misdemeanors** Less serious crimes, such as traffic violations or disorderly conduct. **381**

**mixed economy** An economic system that combines elements of free and command economies. **415**

**monetary policy** A government's policy of regulating the amount of money in the economy. **493**

**money market funds** Investments that are similar to a mutual fund but do not guarantee a specified amount of interest and are not insured by the government. **470**

**monopolies** Companies that control all production of a good or service. **412**

**motivation** An internal drive that stirs people and directs their behavior. **355**

**motor skills** How well people can perform tasks with their hands. **565**

**multiparty system** A political system in which many political parties play a role in government. **256**

**municipal courts** Courts in a large city that handle minor civil and criminal cases. **217**

**municipalities** Local governmental units that are incorporated by the state and have a large degree of self-government. **223**

**mutual funds** Investments that reduce risk to shareholders by investing in many different stocks. **469**

**national debt** The total amount of money owed by the U.S. government plus the interest that must be paid on this borrowed money. **300**

**native-born citizen** A person who has citizenship based on birth in the United States or its territories. **10**

**naturalization** A legal process by which aliens become citizens. **12**

**net income** The money a company has left over after all its costs have been paid. **426**

**neutrality** A policy of not favoring one side or the other in a conflict. **601**

**newly industrialized countries (NICs)** Nations experiencing rapid industrialization and economic growth. **584**

**no-fault divorce** A divorce in which a couple states the marriage has problems that cannot be resolved. **331**

**nominate** To select candidates to run for public office. **254**

**nonprofit organizations** Business organizations that provide goods and services without seeking to earn a profit. **421**

**nonrenewable resources** Natural wealth that can be used only once. **670**

**Northern Alliance** A rebel group in Afghanistan that opposed the Taliban regime. **619**

**one-party system** A political system in which a single political party controls the government and all other parties are banned. **258**

**one-price system** A system in which the price is stamped or bar-coded on a product. **440**

**open-market operations** The buying and selling of government securities. **526**

**open primary** A primary election in which voters may vote for the candidates of any party. **266**

**open shop** A business that employs both union and nonunion workers. **500**

**operators** People who operate machinery, who inspect, assemble, and pack goods in a factory, or who drive a truck, bus, or automobile. **550**

**opinion** A written statement by the U.S. Supreme Court explaining its reasoning behind a decision. **185**

**opportunity cost** The value of an alternative good or service that a company or country has chosen not to produce in order to specialize in something else. **531**

**ordinances** Regulations that govern a local governmental unit. **224**

**organic farming** Farming without the use of artificial substances. **660**

**original jurisdiction** The authority of a court to be the first court to hold trials in certain kinds of cases. **175**

**own recognizance** The legal responsibility for one's own behavior, as in an arrested suspect being released without bail. **390**

**ozone layer** A thin layer in Earth's upper atmosphere that shields the planet from the Sun's ultraviolet rays. **664**

**pardon** An official act by the president or by a governor forgiving a person convicted of a crime and freeing that person from serving out his or her sentence. **151**

**Parliament** The lawmaking body of British government. **41**

**parole** An early release from prison granted under certain conditions. **393**

**partnerships** Business organizations in which two or more persons share responsibilities, costs, profits, and losses. **418**

**party platform** A written statement outlining a political party's views on issues and describing the programs it proposes. **271**

**party whip** The assistant to the floor leader in each house of Congress who tries to persuade party members to vote for bills the party supports. **120**

**passports** Formal documents that allow U.S. citizens to travel abroad. **156**

**patent** An exclusive right given to a person to make and sell an invention for a certain number of years. **409**

**patronage** A system in which government jobs are given to people recommended by political party leaders and officeholders. **214**

**peak** A high point in a business cycle. **486**

**penal code** A set of criminal laws. **215**

**Pentagon** The headquarters of the U.S. military leadership. **618**

**perceptual skills** Skills involving an individual's ability to visualize objects in their mind. **566**

**perestroika** A policy by which Mikhail Gorbachev sought to restructure and improve the economy of the Soviet Union. **612**

**personal property** Possessions such as money, stocks, jewelry, and cars. **306**

**personal values** Things that people believe are most important in their lives. **542**

**pesticides** Chemicals that kill insect pests and weeds. **660**

**petition** A formal request. **92**

**petit jury** A trial jury of between 6 and 12 persons. **173**

**petty larceny** The theft of goods worth less than a certain amount. **382**

**picketing** Marching in front of one's workplace, often with signs urging others not to work for the company or buy its goods and services. **499**

**plaintiff** The person or company filing the complaint in a civil lawsuit. **216**

**plea bargain** An agreement between the prosecutor and the defense in which an accused person pleads guilty to a reduced charge. **392**

**pocket veto** A means by which the president can reject a bill, when Congress is not in session, by not signing it. **139**

political action committees (PACs) The political arms of an interest group that collect voluntary contributions from members to fund political candidates and parties the interest group favors. 294

political party An organization of citizens who have similar views on issues and who work to put their ideas into effect through government action. 253

poll A survey taken to measure public opinion. 284

polling place A place where citizens go to vote. 261

poll tax A special tax that had to be paid in order to vote. 99

pollution Contaminants of land, air, or water. 662

popular sovereignty Government by consent of the governed. 71

popular vote The votes cast by citizens in a presidential election. 274

Preamble The beginning of the U.S. Constitution, which describes its purposes. 71

precedent An earlier court decision that guides judges' decisions in later cases. 170

precincts Local voting districts in a county, city, or ward. 261

preferred stock Shares in a corporation that earn a fixed dividend but do not give shareholders a voice in managing the company. 420

prejudice An opinion not based on careful and reasonable investigation of the facts. 358

premium A payment made for insurance protection. 474

presidential primaries Primary elections in which voters in a state select the presidential candidate they wish their delegates to support at the party's national nominating convention. 270

presidential succession The order in which the office of president is to be filled if it becomes vacant. 146

president *pro tempore* The official who presides over the Senate in the vice president's absence. 121

primary election An election in which the voters of various parties choose candidates to run for office in a general election. 266

private insurance Insurance individuals and companies voluntarily pay to cover unexpected losses. 475

probable cause The reason for an arrest, based on the knowledge of a crime and the available evidence. 389

probation A period of time during which a person guilty of an offense does not go to prison but instead must follow certain rules and report to a probation officer. 398

producer A person or company who provides a good or service that satisfies consumers' needs. 510

productivity The amount of work produced by a worker in an hour. 425

professionals People whose jobs require many years of education and training and who perform mostly mental, rather than physical, work. 546

profit The income a business has left after paying its expenses. 305

profit motive The desire to make money from a business or investment. 408

progressive tax A tax that takes a larger percentage of income from high-income groups than from low-income groups. 305

propaganda Ideas used to influence people's thinking or behavior. 281

property tax A local or state tax collected on real property or personal property. 306

proposition A proposed law resulting from a petition. 208

prosecution The government's side in a criminal case. 390

public housing projects Apartment complexes for low-income families that are built with public funds and that charge low rents. 629

public interest groups Groups seeking to promote the interests of the general public rather than just one part of it. 288

public opinion The total of the opinions held concerning a particular issue. 279

public utilities Legal monopolies that provide essential services to the public. 413

qualifications The skills and knowledge possessed by an individual. 543

quorum The minimum number of members who must be present before a legislative body can conduct business. 136

quotas Set numbers, such as for immigrants who may enter a country in a year. 10

ratification Approval by a formal vote. 45

real property Land and buildings. 306

recall A process by which voters may remove an elected official from office. 208

recession A severe contraction in a business cycle. 486

recreation Relaxation or amusement. 370

recycling The process of turning waste into something that can be used again. 668

referendum A method of referring a bill to the voters for approval before the bill can become law. 208

refugees People who flee persecution in their homeland to seek safety in another nation. 10

regressive tax A tax that takes a larger percentage of income from low-income groups than from high-income groups. 306

regulatory commissions Independent agencies created by Congress that can make rules concerning certain activities and bring violators to court. 164

rehabilitation Reforming criminals and returning them to society as law-abiding citizens. 392

remand To return an appealed case to a lower court for a new trial. 184

remarriages Marriages in which one or both of the partners has been married before. 326

renewable resource Natural wealth that can be replaced. 663

rent A payment for the use of land or other property belonging to another person. 424

repealed Canceled. 83

representative democracy A form of government in which the people elect representatives to carry on the work of government for them. 26

reprieve A postponement in the carrying out of a prison sentence. 151

republic A form of government in which the people elect representatives to carry on the work of government for them. 26

reserved powers Powers set aside by the Constitution for the states or for the people. 75

reserve requirement The amount of money that banks must have on hand. 528

retailers Businesspeople who sell goods directly to the public. 441

revealed propaganda Propaganda that openly attempts to influence people. 282

revenue Income. 301

right-to-work laws Laws passed by certain states that forbid closed shops and make union membership voluntary. 501

robbery A theft accompanied by the threat of force. 382

roll-call vote A vote in Congress in which a record is made of how each member votes. 136

runoff An election in which voters choose between the two leading candidates in a primary to determine the party's candidate in the general election. 266

rural areas Regions of farms and small towns. 17

**salary range** The lowest to highest earnings for a particular job. **561**

**sales tax** A state or city tax on items or services sold to the public. **306**

**satellite nations** Countries that are controlled by other countries. **607**

**savings and loan associations** Banks originally established to help people buy homes. **462**

**scarcity** The problem of limited resources. **409**

**search warrant** A legal document granted by a judge that permits police to enter and search a place where there is reason to believe evidence of a crime will be found. **93**

**secretary** An official who heads an executive department in the federal government. **155**

**secret ballots** Method of voting in which a voter marks a ballot in secret. **267**

**Security Council** The United Nations body mainly responsible for peacekeeping. It has 15 members, including 5 permanent members and 10 temporary members who serve on a rotating basis. **589**

**segregated** Separated on the basis of race. **186**

**select committees** Temporary House or Senate committees appointed to deal with issues not handled by standing committees. **122**

**self-incrimination** Testifying against oneself. **93**

**self-service** A type of marketing in which customers serve themselves. **440**

**seniority system** The custom of giving leadership of committees to members of Congress with the most years of service. **123**

**sentence** A punishment given to a person convicted of a crime. **391**

**separation of church and state** The division between religion and government. **90**

**service industries** Businesses that sell services rather than products. **551**

**sessions** Meetings of Congress. **119**

**sheriff** The chief law-enforcement official in some county governments. **227**

**shoplifting** Stealing items displayed in a store. **446**

**shortage** When demand exceeds supply. **513**

**short-term credit** An advance of money to be repaid within a short period of time. **457**

**single-parent families** Families with only one parent, typically formed through divorce, widowhood, adoption by single people, and births to single women. **328**

**slander** Spoken false statements that damage another person's reputation. **90**

**small claims courts** State courts that hear civil cases involving small amounts of money. **217**

**smog** A combination of smoke, gases, and fog in the air. **663**

**social insurance** Government programs that are meant to protect individuals from future hardship and that individuals and businesses are required to pay for by state and federal laws. **477**

**Social Security** A system of government insurance that provides benefits for retired people, people with disabilities, unemployed people, and people with job-related injuries or illnesses. **477**

**Social Security tax** A kind of income tax that is used mainly to provide income to retired people and people with disabilities. **305**

**sole proprietorships** business organizations owned by one person. **417**

**sovereignty** A government's absolute power or authority. **32**

**Speaker** The presiding officer of the House of Representatives. **120**

**special district** A unit of local government set up to provide a specific service. **232**

**specialize** To become good at producing certain kinds of goods. **529**

**split ticket** A ballot on which a person votes for the candidates of more than one political party. **268**

**standard packaging** The practice of wrapping and weighing goods before they reach customers. **440**

**standing committees** Permanent House or Senate committees that consider bills in a certain area. **122**

**State of the Union Address** A yearly report by the president to Congress describing the nation's condition and recommending programs and policies. **147**

**statutory laws** Laws passed by lawmaking bodies. **170**

**stocks** Shares of ownership in a corporation. **418**

**stock exchange** A market where stocks are bought and sold. **469**

**stockholders** People who own corporate stock. **418**

**straight ticket** A ballot on which a person votes for all the candidates of one political party. **268**

**strike** A situation in which workers walk off the job and refuse to work until labor issues are settled. **499**

**strip mining** The practice of stripping away the top layer of soil to remove the minerals underneath. **673**

**subcommittees** Divisions of standing congressional committees that deal with specific issues in the area handled by their primary committees. **122**

**subpoenas** Official court orders that require a person to appear in court. **176**

**suburbs** Residential communities near a large city. **17**

**suffrage** The right to vote. **97**

**summit** A meeting among the leaders of two or more nations. **581**

**Sunbelt** A U.S. region made up of states in the South and West. **18**

**supply** The quantity of goods and services that producers offer during a given period. **512**

**surplus** An amount by which income exceeds expenditures. **313**

**tariff** A tax on products imported from other countries. **308**

**taxable income** The amount of income, less deductions, on which individuals and businesses must pay taxes. **305**

**tax incentives** Special tax breaks for businesses to encourage investment. **525**

**technicians** Skilled workers who handle complex instruments or machinery. **547**

**term limits** Laws that limit the number of terms elected officials can serve. **115**

**territorial courts** Federal courts that administer justice to people living in U.S. territories. **179**

**territory** An area that is governed by a country and is eligible to become a state. **199**

**terrorists** Individuals who use violence to achieve political goals. **618**

**testimony** Evidence given in court by a witness. **173**

**third parties** Minor political parties in a two-party system. **256**

**tight-money policy** Economic policy that involves raising interest rates to decrease the amount of money borrowed and reduce inflation. **526**

**totalitarian** Form of government that has total control over the lives of the people. **26**

**town** A unit of local government, usually larger than a village and smaller than a city. **228**

**town meeting** A form of government in which all citizens meet regularly to discuss town issues. **229**

**townships** Units of local government that maintain local roads and rural schools within counties. **231**

trade barrier A government action that limits the exchange of goods. 531

trade deficit Situation in which a nation buys more goods than it sells. 535

trade-off An economic sacrifice. 531

trade surplus Situation in which a nation buys fewer goods than it sells. 535

traditional economy An economy in which production is based on customs and traditions and economic roles are typically passed down from one generation to the next. 415

treason An act that betrays and endangers one's country. 128

treaties Written agreements between nations. 150

trough A low point in a business cycle. 486

trust A form of business organization in which several companies create a board of trustees that ensures the companies no longer compete with one another. 412

two-income families Families in which both partners work. 327

two-party system A political system with two strong political parties. 255

unconstitutional In conflict with the Constitution of the United States. 183

unicameral Consisting of one house, as in a lawmaking body. 205

union See labor unions

union shop A business in which a nonunion worker may be hired but must join a union within a certain period of time. 500

unitary system System of government in which the national government possesses all legal power. 43

United Nations An international organization that promotes peaceful coexistence and global cooperation. 588

university An institution of higher learning that includes one or more colleges as well as graduate programs. 345

urban areas Cities or large towns. 17

urban-renewal programs Programs to recover run-down areas of cities. 629

vandalism The willful destruction of property. 383

verdict A decision of a jury. 173

veto A refusal by the president or a governor to sign a bill. 79

victimless crimes Crimes in which there is no victim whose rights are invaded by another person. 383

village A unit of local government, usually smaller than a town. 228

visas Documents that allow people from one country to visit another country. 156

volunteers People who work without pay to help others. 293

wards Election districts within a city or county. 235

War on Drugs Organized effort to end the trade and use of illegal drugs. 617

warrant An order to pay out government funds. 213

white-collar crimes Crimes committed by people in the course of their work. 383

white-collar workers People in a profession or who perform technical, managerial, sales, or administrative support work. 546

wholesaler A businessperson who buys goods from manufacturers and sells to retailers. 441

World Trade Center A business complex in New York City that was destroyed by terrorist attack on September 11, 2001. 618

writ of *habeas corpus* A court order requiring that an accused person be brought to court to determine if there is enough evidence to hold the person for trial. 130

zoning laws Local laws that regulate the kinds of buildings that may be constructed in a certain area. 631

# Glossary/Glosario

**This Glossary contains terms you need to understand as you read your textbook. After each key term there is a brief definition or explanation of the meaning of the term as it is used in your textbook. The page number refers to the page on which the term is introduced in the textbook.**

**absolute advantage/ventaja absoluta** Situación que se produce cuando un país genera mejores bienes que sus socios comerciales. 530

**absolute monarchs/monarcas absolutos** Reyes o reinas con poder absoluto. 25

**acid rain/lluvia ácida** Ácido que se forma cuando los gases producidos con la combustión de petróleo, gas y carbón se combinan con el vapor de agua del aire. 664

**acquit/exonerar** Hallar que un acusado no es culpable. 391

**act/ley** Legislación. 132

**addicts/adictos** Esclavos de un hábito, como el uso de drogas. 646

**administrative laws/leyes administrativas** Leyes creadas por los departamentos de un gobierno. 171

**adopt/adoptar** Crear un vínculo legal para que un niño ajeno se convierta en hijo de una persona. 331

**advertising/anunciar** Uso de los medios masivos por parte de las empresas para mostrar a las personas sus productos y persuadirlos de que los compren. 442

**agency shop/tienda de agencias** Empresa cuyos trabajadores no están obligados a pertenecer a un sindicato, pero sí a pagar las cuotas de uno. 500

**aggravated assault/asalto con agravante** Daño físico hecho de manera intencional a otra persona. 382

**agribusinesses/agrocomercio** Granjas propiedad de grandes empresas cuya producción se basa en el uso intensivo de maquinaria agrícola mecanizada. 551

**alcoholism/alcoholismo** Enfermedad que produce una dependencia de las bebidas alcohólicas. 647

**aliens/extranjeros** Personas que viven en un país sin ser ciudadanos del mismo. 10

**alliances/alianzas** Acuerdos entre dos o más países para ayudarse en materia de defensa, desarrollo económico o científico, etcétera. 576

**ambassadors/embajadores** Los funcionarios de más alto rango que representan a un gobierno ante otra nación. 155

**amendment/enmienda** Cambio por escrito hecho a una constitución. 83

**Antifederalists/Antifederalistas** Oponentes de la constitución que en 1787 exigieron que ésta fuera rechazada. 45

**appeal/apelar** Derecho de una persona acusada de un delito para que su caso sea revisado por una corte de mayor jerarquía. 173

**appellate jurisdiction/jurisdicción de apelación** Autoridad de algunas cortes para revisar las decisiones tomadas en cortes de menor jerarquía. 175

**apportioned/asignación** Distribución, como los puestos en la Cámara de representantes. 114

**apprenticeship/aprendizaje** Periodo de aprendizaje de un oficio. 549

**appropriation bill/carta de apropiación** Ley que aprueba un incremento del gasto público por parte de un gobierno. 132

**aptitude tests/pruebas de aptitud** Pruebas que ayudan a las personas a medir sus intereses y habilidades. 567

**arbitration/arbitraje** Método de resolución de diferencias en el que un tercero toma una decisión que debe ser aceptada por las dos partes de un conflicto. 505

**arraignment/arreglo** Proceso en el que una persona acusada de un delito debe presentarse ante la corte y declararse culpable o inocente. 390

**arrest warrant/orden de aprehensión** Autorización que una corte da para arrestar a una persona. 389

**arson/incendio provocado** Incendio intencional de una propiedad para ocasionar su destrucción. 383

**assembly line/cadena de montaje** Sistema en el que un gupo de trabajadores realizan operaciones individuales para armar un producto que se desplaza sobre una banda transportadora. 434

**attorney general/ministro de justicia** Representante legal de una nación o estado. 155

**audit/auditar** Examen fiscal que se hace a los registros de gastos e ingresos de las empresas privadas y del gobierno. 315

**authoritarian/autoritario** Gobierno cuyos líderes sólo responden a sus propias demandas. 26

**automation/automatización** Uso de máquinas en lugar de humanos en la fabricación de bienes o en la producción de servicios. 550

**bail/fianza** Dinero que una persona acusada de un delito proporciona a una corte para garantizar que se presentará al juicio correspondiente. 94

**balance/saldo** Dinero que falta por pagar de una deuda o préstamo. 448

**balanced budget/presupuesto equilibrado** Programa económico en el que los gastos son iguales a los ingresos. 313

**balance of payments/balanza de pagos** Registro del dinero que un país obtiene de otras naciones y el dinero que gasta en el extranjero. 535

**balance of power/equilibrio de poder** Situación que se genera cuando cada país de un grupo tiene la misma fuerza. 610

**balance of trade/balanza comercial** Diferencia de valor entre importaciones y exportaciones de un país. 584

**bankruptcy/bancarrota** Declaración legal que hace una persona o empresa cuando no puede pagar sus deudas. 457

**beneficiary/beneficiario** Persona que recibe la cantidad especificada en un seguro cuando el poseedar de la póliza muere. 475

**bicameral/bicameral** Sistema político que consta de dos cámaras como cuerpos legisladores. 41

**bills/proyectos de ley** Leyes planteadas a una legislatura. 121

**bill of attainder/carta de proscripción** Ley que sentencia a una persona a prisión sin derecho a juicio. 130

**Bill of Rights/Carta de derechos** Primeras 10 enmiendas hechas a la Constitución para garantizar los derechos básicos de los ciudadanos estadounidenses. 89

**biomass/biomasa** Madera o productos de desecho que pueden usarse como combustible. 675

**birthrate/tasa de natalidad** Número de nacimientos anuales por cada 1,000 habitantes en una región. 15

**blacklists/listas negras** Método usado por los empresarios para registrar a los trabajadores inscritos en sindicatos para que ninguna empresa los contratara. 500

**blended families/familias combinadas** Familias en las que uno o ambos integrantes de la pareja llevan a la nueva relación hijos procreados en matrimonios anteriores. 326

**block grants/garantías de bloque** Fondos federales otorgados a los gobiernos estatales y locales para cumplir sus objetivos. 244

**blue-collar workers/trabajadores de cuello azul** Personas que realizan labores manuales en las empresas. 549

**bond/bono** Certificado de deuda emitido por gobiernos y corporaciones para las personas que les han prestado dinero. 303

**boycott/boicot** Rechazo de compra o uso de ciertos bienes y servicios. 637

**brand names/marcas** Nombre que usan las empresas en la publicidad comercial para anunciar sus productos. 442

**brief/resumen legal** Escrito que explica los puntos principales de un caso ante la corte. 185

**brokers/corredores de bolsa** Empleados del mercado accionario dedicados a la compra y venta de acciones. 469

**budget/presupuesto** Plan de ingresos y egresos. 153

**building code/código de construcción** Conjunto de leyes que regulan la construcción y reparación de los edificios de una comunidad. 631

**bureaucracy/burocracia** Conjunto de departamentos y agencias en todos los niveles de un gobierno. 165

**burglary/robo** Ingreso fozado a una propiedad privada con la intención de extraer objetos de la misma en forma ilegal. 382

**business cycle/ciclo comercial** Tendencia de avance y retroceso del mercado libre según las circunstancias. 485

**cabinet/gabinete** Líderes de los departamentos del gobierno federal que actúan como consejeros del presidente. 84

**candidates/candidatos** Personas que compiten por los cargos públicos. 254

**capital/capital** Dinero, propiedad y equipo invertido en un negocio de producción de bienes y servicios. 410

**capitalism/capitalismo** Sistema económico basado en la propiedad privada de los medios de producción. 410

**capital punishment/pena capital** Castigo de muerte. 393

**caucuses/juntas** Reuniones en que los líderes de los partidos nombran a sus candidatos a los cargos públicos. 120

**censure/censura** Desaprobación formal de las acciones del congreso por parte de sus integrantes. 118

**census/censo** Conteo oficial de los habitantes de una nación. 14

**certificates of deposit (CDs)/certificados de depósito** Inversiones hechas en un periodo específico que ofrecen ganancias con una tasa garantizada de interés. 468

**charge account/cuenta de crédito** Forma de crédito que ofrece a los consumidores la posibilidad de pagar sus compras cierto tiempo después de hacerlas. 447

**charters/cartas constitucionales** Planes de gobierno proporcionado por las legislaturas estatales a las autoridades locales. 223

**checks/cheques** Órdenes escritas y firmadas con las que un banco paga una suma determinada a la persona cuyo nombre se escribió en el cheque. 447

**checks and balances/revisión y balance** Sistema mediante el cual los poderes de un gobierno revisan y limitan el poder de sus contrapartes. 79

**child abuse/abuso de menores** Maltrato físico, sexual o mental de algún menor. 331

**circuit/circuito** Distrito judicial que abarca una corte de apelaciones. 177

**circular-flow model/modelo de flujo circular** Modelo económico que muestra la interacción de las empresas, los comercios y el gobierno en la economía de Estados Unidos. 511

**citizen/ciudadano** Persona que forma parte de una nación. 3

**city/ciudad** El tipo más grande de municipalidad. 234

**city council/consejo ciudadano** Cuerpo legislador de una ciudad. 235

**civics/civismo** Estudio de las acciones de un ciudadano. 3

**civil cases/casos civiles** Casos en los que que se resuelven disputas económicas o de propiedad entre individuos o comercios. 215

**civil disobedience/desobediencia civil** Rompimiento intencional de una ley para mostrar desacuerdo con la misma. 638

**civilian/civil** Persona que no pertenece a un cuerpo militar. 157

**civil rights/derechos civiles** Garantías de todos los ciudadanos de Estados Unidos. 96

**civil rights movement/movimiento de derechos civiles** Lucha por la igualdad de derechos para todos los estadounidenses. 636

**closed primary/primarias cerradas** Elecciones en las que sólo participan votantes registrados en un partido para elegir a sus candidatos para cargos públicos. 500

**closed shop/taller agremiado** Empresa que sólo contrata a las personas registradas en un sindicato. 266

**cloture/límitación de debate** Tiempo máximo permitido para un debate en el senado. 137

**coalition/coalición** Acuerdo entre dos o más partidos políticos para trabajar juntos en la administración de un país. 256

**coincident indicators/indicadores coincidentes** Señales económicas usadas por los economistas para determinar el desarrollo de la economía. 519

**collateral/colateral** Propiedad usada para garantizar el pago de un préstamo. 460

**collective bargaining/contrato colectivo** Reunión de los representantes de un sindicato laboral y un empleador para llegar a un acuerdo en salarios y condiciones de trabajo. 499

**colleges/colegios** Instituciones de educación a nivel superior que ofrecen carreras de cuatro años de duración. 345

**command economy/economía de mando** Sistema en que el gobierno controla la economía de una nación. 414

**crossroads/encrucijada** Punto de encuentro de dos caminos. 363

**currency/circulante** Conjunto de monedas y billetes. 453

**death rate/tasa de mortalidad** Número de muertes anuales por cada 1,000 habitantes de una región. 15

**debit cards/tarjetas de débito** Tarjetas que operan como los cheques al tomar dinero directamente de una cuenta de banco. 447

**deductions/deducciones** Gastos que los contribuyentes pueden restar del total de impuestos que deben pagar. 304

**defendant/acusado** Persona presentada en un juicio como la parte que ha cometido un crimen. 390

**defense/defensa** Parte que protege los derechos del acusado en un juicio legal. 390

**deficit/déficit** Cantidad en la que los gastos superan a los ingresos. 313

**delayed marriage/matrimonio postergado** Tendencia a contraer matrimonio a edad avanzada. 326

**delegates/delegados** Representantes. 40

**delegated powers/poderes delegados** Poderes otorgados por la constitución al gobierno federal. 74

**delinquents/delincuentes** Jóvenes que rompen la ley. 395

**demand/demanda** Cantidad de un producto o servicio que un consumidor está dispuesto a comprar en un periodo determinado. 512

**democracy/democracia** Forma de gobierno en la que un pueblo se rige de manera directa o mediante un grupo de representantes electos. 26

**demonstrations/manifestaciones** Reuniones en las que un grupo de personas expresa su inconformidad mediante marchas, letreros de protesta, canciones y discursos. 637

**deport/deportar** Obligar a una persona a abandonar un país, como en el caso de los extranjeros ilegales. 11

**depression/depresión** Importante reducción de las actividades comerciales de una nación en la que los trabajadores pierden sus empleos y las empresas se ven obligadas a cerrar. 486

**desertification/desertificación** Pérdida del suelo debida al abuso de las tierras de pastoreo y la tala de árboles en la que regiones que algún día fueron verdes se convierten en desiertos. 659

**détente/detente** Reducción de tensiones entre naciones. 613

**deterrence/disuación** Castigos que desalientan a las peronas que intentan violar las leyes. 392

**dictatorship/dictadura** Forma de gobierno en la que todo el poder está en manos de una persona o pequeño grupo. 26

**diplomacy/diplomacia** Arte de negociar con los gobiernos extranjeros. 149

**diplomatic corps/cuerpos diplomáticos** Embajadores y representantes de una nación en otros países. 578

**diplomatic notes/notas diplomáticas** Comunicación escrita entre los líderes de los gobiernos. 150

**diplomatic recognition/reconocimiento diplomático** Poder del presidente para decidir si debe o no establecer relaciones diplomáticas con un país específico. 577

**direct democracy/democracia directa** Forma de gobierno en la que los habitantes de un país se reúnen para crear leyes y decisiones legales. 26

**discounting/descuento** Reducción de los intereses de un préstamo antes de la entrega del mismo. 463

**discount rate/tasa de descuento** Tasa de interés aprobada por la Reserva Federal y aplicada por los bancos afiliados a la misma. 465

**discrimination/discriminación** Acciones injustas en contra de los integrantes de un grupo en particular. 635

**dissent/disentir** No estar de acuerdo (con una ley, por ejemplo). 637

**dissenting opinion/disentimiento** Declaración en la que la Suprema Corte de Justicia expresa su desacuerdo con una decisión mayoritaria. 185

**distribution/distribución** Proceso de transporte de bienes de las fabricas a los centros de consumo. 437

**district attorney/fiscal del distrito** Funcionario que representa al gobierno estatal en los juicios de los condados. 227

**district courts/tribunal del distrito** Tribunales federales de menor jerarquía que pueden intervenir en la mayoría de los jucios relacionados con las leyes federales. 175

**dividends/dividendos** Ganancias que reciben los accionistas de una empresa. 419

**division of labor/división laboral** Sistema en el que cada trabajador realiza parte de una labor conjunta. 432

**divorce/divorcio** Terminación legal de un matrimonio. 331

**docket/sumario de procedimientos** Calendario de casos de un tribunal de justicia. 184

**doctrine/doctrina** Declaración de una nueva política de gobierno en relación con otras naciones. 599

**dollar diplomacy/diplomacia del dólar** Envío de tropas estadounidenses a otros países con la finalidad de proteger los intereses de Estados Unidos en esos lugares. 600

**double jeopardy/doble riesgo** Ley que no permite juzgar a alguien dos veces por el mismo crimen. 93

**down payment/enganche** Primero de una serie de pagos en una compra de pagos diferidos. 448

**draft/reclutamiento** Política que requiere a los ciudadanos hombres a servir en las fuerzasmilitares. 102

**drug abuse/abuso de drogas** Uso de drogas como escape o fuente de nuevas sensaciones. 646

**due process of law/proceso legal** Derecho de las personas a recibir un trato legal justo. 93

**Earth Day/Día de la Tierra** Celebración no oficial, los días 22 de abril de cada año, dedicada al cuidado de la Tierra. 680

**easy-money policy/política de dinero fácil** Política económica que incrementa la emisión de circulante. 526

**ecology/ecología** Estudio de los seres vivos, la relación que tienen unos con otros y el ambiente en que se desarrollan. 655

**economies of scale/economía de escala** Situación que permite a las grandes empresas elaborar productos de manera más eficaz y económica. 413

**ecosystem/ecosistema** Comunidad de seres interdependientes que se desarrollan en equlibrio con su entorno natural. 655

**elastic clause/cláusula elástica** Artículo 1, Sección 8 de la Constitución, también conocida como cláusula "propia y necesaria" que permite al Congreso ampliar sus poderes delegados. 127

**electors/electores** Personas elegidas como votantes del Colegio electoral en las elecciones presidenciales. 274

**electoral college/colegio electoral** Personas elegidas por el colegio electoral como votantes oficiales en la elección de presidente y vicepresidente. 274

**electoral votes/voto electoral** Votos del colegio electoral en la elección de presidente y vicepresidente. 274

**embargo/embargo** Ley que prohíbe la importación de productos de ciertos países. 532

**embassy/embajada** Residencia oficial de un embajador en otro país. 155

**embezzlement/peculado** Uso del dinero ajeno en fines propios. 383

**eminent domain/dominio supremo** Poder del gobierno para ocupar propiedad privada para uso público. 94

**Endangered Species Acts/Leyes sobre Especies en Peligro de Extinción** Leyes creadas para proteger a las especies amenazadas. 679

**entrepreneurs/empresarios** Individuos que emprenden un negocio por cuenta propia. 425

**Environmental Protection Agency/Agencia de Protección al Medio Ambiente** Agencia independiente de gobierno para los problemas relacionados con la contaminación y el medio ambiente. 679

**equal opportunity employer/empleo de iguales oportunidades** Empleo que no discrimina a los trabajadores por su género, edad, raza, color de piel, religión o formación cultural. 554

**erosion/erosión** Desgaste de la tierra ocasionado por el agua y el viento. 659

**estate tax/impuesto sucesorio** Impuesto aplicado a los bienes que deja una persona fallecida. 307

**ethnic group/grupo étnico** Personas de la misma raza, nacionalidad o religión que comparten una cultura o herencia tradicional. 635

**excise taxes/impuestos al consumo** Impuestos federales aplicados a ciertos artículos de lujo fabricados y vendidos en Estados Unidos. 306

**executive agreement/acuerdo ejecutivo** Acuerdo mutuo entre el presidente de Estados Unidos y el líder de otra nación. 576

**executive branch/Poder Ejecutivo** Rama del gobierno que aplica las leyes. 78

**executive departments/departamentos ejecutivos** Departamentos del poder ejecutivo del gobierno federal. 154

**executive orders/mandatos ejecutivos** Órdenes emitidas por el jefe del poder ejecutivo para crear métodos de aplicación de las leyes. 211

**exemptions/exenciones** Parte del ingreso de un contribuyente que éste puede tomar para uso personal y de sus dependientes sin pagar impuestos. 485

**expansion/expansión** Periodo de crecimiento económico en un ciclo comercial. 304

**experience/experiencia** Observación o participación directa en los sucesos. 354

**exports/exportaciones** Bienes y servicios vendidos a otros países. 584

**ex post facto law/ley ex post facto** Ley que se aplica a una acción cometida antes de la aprobación de la misma. 130

**expulsion/expulsión** Remoción de un integrante del Congreso por conducta inapropiada. 118

**extracurricular activities/actividades extracurriculares** Actividades que realizan los estudiantes fuera del salón de clases. 353

**extradition/extradición** Proceso legal de devolución de un criminal al lugar donde cometió la falta. 201

**family law/ley familiar** Regulación legal del matrimonio, el divorcio y los derechos de los padres e hijos. 329

**favorite sons or daughters/hijos predilectos** Hombres o mujeres populares en su estado, que son nominados por sus delegados para las elecciones presidenciales en la primera votación de sus convenciones nacionales. 272

**featherbedding/imposición** Práctica usada alguna vez por los sindicatos para obligar a las empresas a contratar más trabajadores de los necesarios. 503

**federalism/federalismo** Sistema en el que los poderes del gobierno se dividen entre el gobierno federal, que rige a la nación, y los gobiernos estatales, que rigen las localidades. 43

**Federalists/Federalistas** Personas que apoyaban la Constitución y pedían su adopción en 1787. 45

**Federal Reserve System/Sistema de la Reserva Federal** Sistema bancario estadounidense que regula las necesidades monetarias del gobierno federal y la emisión de circulante. 465

**fees/derechos** Pequeños cobros del gobierno por la prestación de servicios o la emisión de permisos. 302

**felonies/delitos mayores** Crímenes serios como robo, secuestro y asesinato. 381

**fertilizers/fertilizantes** Productos que hacen que las plantas crezcan más rápido y alcancen mayor tamaño. 660

**filibuster/filibustería** Método que retrasa la aprobación de propuestas en el senado mediante la presentación de discursos muy largos. 137

**fine/multa** Dinero que una persona paga como sanción cuando rompe ciertas leyes. 302

**fiscal policy/política fiscal** Plan de gastos y recaudación fiscal del gobierno. 493

**fixed expenses/gastos fijos** Egresos que se presentan de manera regular. 337

**floor leader/líder parlamentario** Líder de un partido político en el Congreso que sólo apoya las propuestas que favorecen a sus intereses. 120

**forcible rape/violación forzada** Abuso sexual de una persona por la fuerza y en contra de su voluntad. 382

**foreign aid/ayuda externa** Programas del gobierno que ofrece ayuda económica y militar a otras naciones. 582

**foreign policy/política exterior** Plan de una nación para establecer relaciones con otros países. 149

**fossil fuels/combustibles fósiles** Recursos no renovables (petróleo, gas natural y carbón) que se formaron a lo largo de millones de años con los restos de plantas y animales. 670

**foster homes/hogares adoptivos** Hogares que aceptan a niños que no son sus hijos para hacer el papel de sus padres. 331

**franking privilege/privilegio de franqueo** Derecho de los integrantes del Congreso a enviar documentos oficiales por correo sin pagar el porte de los mismos. 117

**fraud/fraude** Engaño económico sobre el dinero o las propiedades de otras personas. 383

free competition/libre competencia Sistema en el que los dueños de los comercios compiten entre sí por la clientela. **408**

free-enterprise system/sistema de libre empresa Sistema económico en el que las personas son libres de operar un negocio sin mayores restricciones del gobierno. **411**

free market/mercado libre Sistema económico en el que compradores y vendedores tienen la libertad de intercambiar los bienes y servicios que prefieran. **408**

full faith and credit clause/cláusula de fe y crédito Parte de la Constitución que establece que cada estado debe respetar las decisiones de los tribunales de otros estados. **201**

General Assembly/Asamblea General Cuerpo legal estadounidense que plantea, debate y recomienda soluciones a diversos problemas. **589**

general election/elección general Elección en la que los votantes eligen a sus líderes. **266**

general trial courts/tribunales generales de juzgado Tribunales que resuelven los casos penales y civiles más importantes. **217**

gerrymandering/tergiversación Creación de medidas congresistas que favorecen a cierto partido político. **114**

gift tax/impuesto sobre donaciones Impuesto aplicado a los bienes con valor superior a 10 mil dólares que son recibidos como obsequios. **307**

glasnost/glasnost Política de apertura creada por Mikhail Gorbachev para dar mayor libertad a los habitantes de la Unión Soviética. **612**

government/gobierno Organizaciones, instituciones e individuos que ejercen autoridad a nombre de un grupo de personas. **3**

governor/gobernador Jefe ejecutivo de un gobierno estatal. **210**

graduate school/escuela de graduados Institución de aprendizaje superior que ofrece cursos avanzados de estudio. **345**

grand jury/gran jurado Grupo que considera las evidencias de un caso criminal y decide si son suficientes para iniciar un juicio en contra del acusado. **93**

grand larceny/robo mayor Robo de bienes con un valor superior a una cantidad específica. **382**

grants-in-aid/garantías de ayuda Fondos federales otorgados a los gobiernos estatales y locales para desarrollar proyectos específicos. **244**

grassroots/populismo Apoyo (político, por ejemplo) de muchos individuos, en lugar de partidos nacionales y grandes organizaciones. **266**

greenhouse effect/efecto invernadero Situación que se produce cuando el aumento de la cantidad de bióxido de carbono en la atmósfera atrapa el calor del Sol, lo cual genera un aumento de la temperatura de la Tierra. **664**

gross domestic product (GDP)/producto interno bruto (PIB) Valor de todos los bienes y servicios producidos en un país durante un año. **431**

gross income/ingresos brutos Suma total de dinero que recibe una empresa por la venta de los bienes y servicios que produce. **426**

guardian/guardián Persona asignada por un tribunal para cuidar a un individuo que no es un adulto y que no puede cuidarse a sí mismo. **331**

habit/hábito Acción realizada de manera automática. **355**

homelessness/indigentes Personas que no poseen un lugar donde vivir. **630**

home rule/poder local Poder de una ciudad para crear leyes municipales y administrar sus propios asuntos. **234**

homicide/homicidio Asesinato de una persona. **381**

human resources/recursos humanos Conjunto de personas que producen bienes y servicios. **510**

human rights/derechos humanos Derechos básicos de las personas. **31**

hung jury/jurado colgado Jurado que no logra llegar a un veredicto. **173**

hydrologic cycle/ciclo hidrológico Recorrido del agua en su ambiente natural. **665**

immigrants/inmigrantes Personas que llegan a otra nación para convertirse en residentes de la misma. **8**

immunity/inmunidad Protección legal. **117**

impeachment/imputación Cargo oficial realizado en contra de un funcionario del gobierno. **128**

implied powers/poderes implícitos Poderes que no son otorgados al Congreso por la Constitución, pero que complementan los poderes que se le otorgan de manera oficial. **128**

import quota/cuota de importación Límite máximo de importaciones. **531**

imports/importaciones Bienes o servicios adquiridos en otro país. **531**

income taxes/impuesto sobre la renta Impuesto a los ingresos que obtienen los individuos y las empresas. **304**

independent agencies/agencias independientes Agencias del poder ejecutivo federal creadas por el Congreso para supervisar la aplicación de las leyes no contempladas en los departamentos ejecutivos. **163**

independent voters/votantes independientes Votantes que no pertenecen a ningún partido político. **265**

indict/denuncia Acusación formal de una persona que ha cometido un crimen. **93**

inflation/inflación Aumento del costo de los bienes y servicios. **485**

infrastructure/infraestructura Red que permite a los consumidores participar en la economía. **522**

inheritance tax/impuesto heredado Impuesto aplicado al dinero y propiedades provenientes de un estado. **307**

initiative/iniciativa Proceso que permite a los ciudadanos de una población hacer propuestas de ley mediante la recopilación de firmas de apoyo a la misma. **208**

insight/discernimiento Proceso inconsciente en el que las personas usan lo que saben sobre un tema para encontrar la solución de un problema. **356**

installments/pagos parciales Serie de pagos que completan el costo total de un artículo. **448**

insurance/seguro Sistema de protección en el que se pagan pequeñas cantidades periódicas para evitar pagar una gran suma en caso de una pérdida total. **474** interchangeable parts/piezas intercambiables Máquinas que usan el mismo mecanismo de funcionamiento. **432**

interdependence/interdependencia Apoyo mutuo. **575**

interest/interés Pago por el uso de una suma de dinero prestada. **300**

interest groups/grupos de interés Organizaciones con intereses comunes que influyen en las decisiones de los gobiernos. **287**

International Court of Justice/Tribunal Internacional de Justicia Tribunal de asesoría legal de Estados Unidos al mundo, también conocido como Tribunal Mundial. **589**

interpersonal skills/destrezas interpersonales Capacidad necesaria para relacionarse con otras personas. **566**

invest/inversión Dinero gastado en el desarrollo de comercios o artículos para obtener ganancias económicas. **408**

isolationism/aislacionismo Política que rechaza la participacion del país propio en los asuntos de otras naciones. **597**

item veto/veto parcial Capacidad del jefe del poder ejecutivo para rechazar parte de una propuesta. **207**

job action/paro parcial Reducción del proceso laboral, sin llegar a la huelga. **499**

Joint Chiefs of Staff/jefes de equipo Grupo formado por los funcionarios de mayor nivel en el ejército, la armada y la fuerza aérea para brindar asesoría al presidente sobre temas militares. **157**

joint committees/comités unidos Comités formados por integrantes de ambas cámaras del Congreso para analizar temas comunes. **122**

judicial branch/Poder Judicial Rama del gobierno que interpreta las leyes y castiga a quienes las violan. **78**

judicial review/revisión judicial Capacidad de la Suprema Corte de Justicia estadounidense para determinar si una ley aprobada por el Congreso o una acción presidencial se adapta a las normas de la Constitución. **183**

jurisdiction/jurisdicción Capacidad y rango de autoridad para interpretar y aplicar la ley. **174**

jurors/jurado Personas que juzgan la evidencia y determinan el veredicto en un juicio. **173**

jury duty/deber de jurado Participación en un jurado. **173**

justices/jueces Integrantes de la Suprema Corte de Justicia. **182**

justice of the peace/juez de paz Persona que preside un tribunal de justicia estatal, por lo general en zonas rurales y pequeñas poblaciones, con la finalidad de resolver quejas civiles y conflictos monetarios menores. **216**

juvenile/jóvenes En la mayoría de los estados, personas menores de 18 años. **395**

labor/trabajo Esfuerzo humano usado en la producción de bienes y servicios. **425**

laborers/obreros Personas que realizan tareas no especializadas o que requieren de arduo esfuerzo físico. **550**

labor unions/sindicatos laborales Organizaciones creadas para mejorar las condiciones de trabajo, derechos y salarios de los trabajadores. **498**

lagging indicators/indicadores de retraso Señales económicas que permiten determinar la duración potencial de las condiciones actuales de la economía. **519**

landfills/rellenos sanitarios Grandes hoyos excavados en el suelo para almacenar desechos. **667**

larceny/hurto Robo de propiedades sin uso de la fuerza física o violencia. **382**

law of demand/ley de la demanda Regla económica que explica que los consumidores compran más productos cuando los precios son bajos y menos productos cuando los precios son altos. **410**

law of supply/ley de la oferta Regla económica que explica que los negocios surtirán más productos cuando pueden venderlos a precios altos y menos productos cuando tengan que venderlos a precios bajos. **410**

laws/leyes Reglas de conducta aplicadas por el gobierno. **28**

leading indicators/indicadores de punta Señales económicas que permiten predecir el desarrollo de la economía en el futuro. **519**

legislative branch/Poder Legislativo Rama legisladora del gobierno. **77**

legislature/legislatura Organismo que crea las leyes de un gobierno. **44**

libel/libelo Escritos falsos que dañan la reputación de una persona. **91**

lieutenant governor/gobernador teniente Funcionario que reemplaza al gobernador en caso de que éste fallezca, renuncie o sea removido de su cargo. **213**

limited government/gobierno limitado Sistema de gobierno cuyos poderes son controlados en forma meticulosa para evitar que desarrollen poder en exceso. **75**

limited war/guerra limitada Guerra que no se realiza a su máxima capacidad, en especial la nuclear. **611**

lobby/cámara de cabildeo Grupo de interés. **287**

lobbyist/cabildero Persona que recibe un pago por representar los intereses de un grupo particular. **287**

lockouts/cierre forzoso Métodos usados por los empleadores para combatir los ataques de los sindicatos mediante el bloqueo de salarios de los trabajadores. **500**

long-term credit/crédito a largo plazo Suma de dinero que se obtiene en préstamo y se liquida en pagos parciales. **457**

machine tools/maquinaria Máquinas usadas para fabricar piezas idénticas. **432**

magistrate judges/jueces magistrados Funcionarios que escuchan casos de personas acusadas y deciden si éstos deben ser resueltos por un gran jurado. **176**

mainstreaming/corriente principal Colocación de estudiantes con necesidades especiales en escuelas y clases regulares. **346**

majority party/partido mayoritario El partido político con más integrantes en el Congreso o legislatura estatal. **120**

majority rule/gobierno mayoritario Sistema en el que las únicas decisiones aceptadas son aquellas aprobadas por más de la mitad de la población. **73**

*maquiladoras/maquiladoras* Fábricas establecidas en México por empresas extranjeras. **520**

market economy/economía de mercado Sistema conómico en el que los individuos son libres de elegir cualquier oficio o método de obtención de ganancias y de poseer propiedades. **407**

**marshal/jefe de policía** Funcionario de un distrito federal que cuenta con autoridad para realizar arrestos, mantener el orden y aplicar órdenes judiciales. **176**

**mass marketing/mercadeo masivo** Venta de productos en grandes cantidades. **440**

**mass media/medios masivos** Formas de comunicación que transmiten información a grandes cantidades de personas. **280**

**mass production/producción en masa** Fabricación rápida de grandes cantidades de productos idénticos mediante el uso de máquinas. **431**

**mass transit/tránsito en masa** Sistemas de transporte público, incluidos autobuses, ferrocarriles subterráneos y otros trenes. **632**

**mayor/alcalde** Jefe del poder ejecutivo de un gobierno local. **235**

**mediation/mediación** Método de resolución de disputas entre sindicatos y empleadores en el que un tercer partido ofrece soluciones factibles para ambas partes. **505**

**Medicaid/Medicaid** Programa federal de asistencia médica para personas de escasos recursos. **481**

**Medicare/Medicare** Programa federal de asistencia médica para personas de 65 años o más. **481**

**megalopolis/megalópolis** Gran zona urbana que abarca varias ciudades. **368**

**merger/fusión** Combinación de dos o más compañías en una sola empresa. **412**

**metropolitan areas/zonas metropolitanas** Grandes ciudades y sus alrededores. **17**

**migration/migración** Movimiento de personas de una ciudad a otra. **18**

**ministers/ministros** Representantes del gobierno enviados a naciones pequeñas. **155**

**minority groups/grupos minoritarios** Grupos que no ocupan puestos de poder y son relegados de la sociedad por su origen étnico, idioma, costumbres o religión. **635**

**minority party/partido minoritario** Partido político con menos integrantes en el Congreso o en una legislatura estatal. **120**

**misdemeanors/delito menor** Penas legales menores como violaciones de tránsito o alteraciones del orden público. **381**

**mixed economy/economía mixta** Sistema económico que combina elementos de la economía libre y la economía de orden. **415**

**monetary policy/política monetaria** Política usada por el gobierno para regular el flujo de dinero en su economía. **493**

**money market funds/fondos de mercado** Inversiones parecidas a los fondos de inversión. **470**

**monopolies/monopolios** Compañías que controlan la producción total de ciertos bienes o servicios. **412**

**motivation/motivación** Sentimiento que anima y dirige la conducta de las personas. **355**

**motor skills/destrezas motrices** Habilidad de las personas para realizar labores con las manos. **565**

**multiparty system/sistema multipartidista** Sistema político en el que varios partidos políticos participan en el gobierno. **256**

**municipal courts/tribunales municipales** Tribunales establecidos en las grandes ciudades que resuelven casos civiles y penales menores. **217**

**municipalities/municipalidades** Unidades locales de gobierno incorporadas a los estados, pero que cuentan con suficiente autonomía. **223**

**mutual funds/fondos de inversión** Inversiones que reducen el riesgo de pérdida de los accionistas al realizarse en diferentes medios accionarios. **469**

**national debt/deuda nacional** Cantidad total de dinero que debe el gobierno de Estados Unidos, más los intereses correspondientes. **300**

**native-born citizen/ciudadano nativo estadounidense** Ciudadano nacido en Estados Unidos. **10**

**naturalization/naturalización** Proceso legal que convierte a un extranjero en ciudadano estadounidense. **12**

**net income/ingresos netos** Ganancias de una compañía después de pagar todos sus gastos. **426**

**neutrality/neutralidad** Política que no favorece a ninguna de las partes de un conflicto. **601**

**newly industrialized countries (NICs)/países recién industrializados** Naciones que experimentan un rápido crecimiento en sus industrias y economías. **584**

**no-fault divorce/divorcio necesario** Divorcio solicitado debido a la existencia de problemas que no tienen solución. **331**

**nominate/nominar** Elección de candidatos para cargos públicos. **254**

**nonprofit organizations/organizaciones no lucrativas** Instituciones que ofrecen bienes y servicios sin esperar una remuneración económica. **421**

**nonrenewable resources/recursos no renovables** Materiales de la tierra que no pueden reemplazarse cuando se agotan. **670**

**Northern Alliance/Alianza del Norte** Grupo rebelde formado en Afganistán que se opone al régimen Talibán. **619**

**one-party system/sistema unipartidista** Sistema político en el que un solo partido político controla el gobierno y prohíbe el desarrollo de otros partidos. **258**

**one-price system/sistema de precio fijo** Sistema en el que el precio de los productos es impreso o grabado con un código de barras en el empaque. **440**

**open-market operations/operaciones de mercado abierto** Compra y venta de bonos del gobierno. **526**

**open primary/primarias abiertas** Elección primaria en la que los votantes pueden optar por cualquier partido. **266**

**open shop/talleres no agremiados** Comercio que da empleo a trabajadores sindicalizados y no sindicalizados por igual. **500**

**operators/operadores** Personas que operan maquinaria, inspeccionan, ensamblan o empacan productos en una fábrica o conducen un camión, autobús o automóvil. **550**

**opinion/opinión** Declaración escrita de la Suprema Corte de Justicia en la que explica las razones en las que basa una decisión. **185**

**opportunity cost/costo de oportunidad** Valor de un bien o servicio alternativo que una compañía o país ha decidido no producir para especializarse en algo más. **531**

**ordinances/ordenanzas** Regulaciones que rigen las unidades locales de gobierno. **224**

**organic farming/agricultura orgánica** Técnicas agrícolas en las que no se usa ningún tipo de sustancia artificial. **660**

**original jurisdiction/jurisdicción original** Autoridad de una corte para ser la primera en resolver cierto tipo de casos. **175**

**own recognizance/reconocimiento propio** Responsabilidad legal de la conducta de alguien, como en la liberación de un sospechoso sin el pago de una fianza. **390**

**ozone layer/capa de ozono** Delgada capa de la atmósfera superior que protege a la Tierra de los rayos ultravioleta del sol. **664**

**pardon/perdón** Acción oficial que cancela el castigo de una personad acusada de un crimen y le otorga su libertad. **151**

**Parliament/Parlamento** Cuerpo legislador del gobierno británico. **41**

**parole/libertad bajo palabra** Liberación anticipada de una persona encarcelada, con ciertas condiciones. **393**

**partnerships/sociedades** Organizaciones comerciales en las que dos o más personas comparten responsabilidades, costos, ganancias y pérdidas. **418**

**party platform/plataforma partidista** Declaración escrita del punto de vista de un partido político sobre temas y programas que propone. **271**

**party whip/capataz de partido** Asistente del jefe de piso en cada cámara del Congreso cuya función es convencer a los integrantes de su partido de apoyar las propuestas que les favorezcan. **120**

**passports/pasaportes** Documentos legales que permiten a los ciudadanos estadounidenses viajar libremente a otros países. **156**

**patent/patente** Derecho exclusivo otorgado a una persona para producir y vender un invento durante un periodo determinado. **409**

**patronage/patronazgo** Sistema en el que los empleos del gobierno son ofrecidos a personas recomendadas por los líderes políticos y los funcionarios públicos. **214**

**peak/pico** El punto más alto de un ciclo comercial. **486**

**penal code/código penal** Compendio de leyes penales. **215**

**Pentagon/Pentágono** Cuartel general de las fuerzas armadas de Estados Unidos. **618**

**perceptual skills/destrezas perceptuales** Habilidades relacionadas con la capacidad de visualización de una persona. **566**

**perestroika/perestroika** Política creada por Mikhail Gorbachev para restaurar y mejorar la economía de la Unión Soviética. **612**

**personal property/propiedad personal** Posesiones en forma de dinero, acciones, joyería y automóviles. **306**

**personal values/valores personales** Los elementos más importantes en la vida de las personas. **542**

**pesticides/pesticidas** Productos químicos usados para acabar con los insectos y hierbas que destruyen los cultivos. **660**

**petition/petición** Solicitud formal. **92**

**petit jury/pequeño jurado** Jurado integrado por 6 a 12 personas. **173**

**petty larceny/robo menor** Robo cuyo valor no supera una cantidad determinada **382**

**picketing/piquete de huelga** Marcha de protesta realizada frente al lugar de trabajo con carteles que piden a otros no trabajar para esa compañía ni comprar los bienes o servicios que produce. **499**

**plaintiff/plenitivo** Persona o compañía que llena una forma de demanda civil. **216**

**plea bargain/alegato** Acuerdo entre la parte acusadora y la defensa, creado con la finalidad de que el acusado se declare culpable y enfrente cargos menores. **392**

**pocket veto/veto indirecto** Capacidad del presidente para rechazar una propuesta con sólo negarse a firmarla aunque el Congreso no esté en sesiones. **139**

**political action committees (PACs)/comités de acción política** Divisiones de un grupo de interés que reúnen aportaciones voluntarias de sus intregrantes para patrocinar a los candidatos y partidos de su preferencia. **294**

**political party/partido político** Organización de ciudadanos con puntos de vista similares que trabajan en conjunto para cumplir sus objetivos mediante acciones del gobierno. **253**

**poll/sondeo** Encuesta realizada para conocer la opinión pública. **284**

**polling place/sitio de la encuesta** Lugar al que los ciudadanos acuden a votar. **261**

**poll tax/impuesto de encuesta** Impuesto especial que debía pagarse para tener derecho al voto. **99**

**pollution/contaminación** Conjunto de partículas que ensucian la tierra, el aire y el agua. **662**

**popular sovereignty/soberanía popular** Sistema de gobierno que actúa con consentimiento de los gobernados. **71**

**popular vote/voto popular** Votos de los ciudadanos en las elecciones presidenciales. **274**

**Preamble/preámbulo** Texto inicial de la Constitución de Estados Unidos en el que se describe el propósito de la misma. **71**

**precedent/precedente** Decisión previa de un tribunal que sirve de base para tomar futuras decisiones. **170**

**precincts/precintos** Distritos locales de votación en condados, ciudades o municipios. **261**

**preferred stock/acciones de preferencia** Acciones de una compañía que generan dividendos fijos, pero que no dan voz a sus poseedores en la administración de la compañía. **420**

**prejudice/prejuicio** Opinión que no se basa en un análisis cuidadoso y una investigación adecuada de los hechos. **358**

**premium/prima** Pago realizado para recibir protección de una compañía de seguros. **474**

**presidential primaries/primarias presidenciales** Elecciones primarias en las que los votantes de los estados pueden elegir al candidato que desean que sus delegados apoyen en la convención nacional de nominaciones. **270**

**presidential succession/sucesión presidencial** Orden en que el puesto de presidente de la nación debe ocuparse si se encuentra vacante. **146**

**president *pro tempore*/presidente interino** Funcionario que preside el senado en ausencia del vicepresidente. **121**

**primary election/elecciones primarias** Elección en la que votantes de diferentes partidos eligen a los candidatos que competirán en las elecciones generales. **266**

**private insurance/seguro privado** Seguros que individuos y compañías adquieren de manera voluntaria para cubrir pérdidas inesperadas. **475**

**probable cause/causa probable** Razón de un arresto, basada en el conocimiento del crimen y las evidencias disponibles. **389**

**probation/libertad condicional** Periodo en el que una persona declarada culpable de un delito no es enviada a prisión, sino que debe seguir ciertas reglas y presentarse de manera regular ante un funcionario de la corte. **398**

**producer/productor** Persona o compañía que proporciona un bien o servicio que satisface ciertas necesidades de los consumidores. **510**

**secretary/secretario** Funcionario que administra un departamento del Poder Ejecutivo federal. **155**

**secret ballots/boletas secretas** Método de votación en el que las personas marcan en secreto una opción en una boleta. **267**

**Security Council/Consejo de Seguridad** Organismo creado por la Organizacíon de las Naciones Unidas para mantener la paz. Cuenta con 15 naciones integrantes, 5 de ellas permanentes y 10 temporales que siguen un proceso de rotación. **589**

**segregated/segregado** Separado por su origen racial. **186**

**select committees/comités selectos** Comités temporales del Senado o la Cámara de representantes que resuelven asuntos no incluidos en la agenda de los comités regulares. **122**

**self-incrimination/autoincriminación** Testificar en contra de sí mismo. **93**

**self-service/autoservicio** Mercado en el que los clientes toman por sí mismos los productos que desean comprar. **440**

**seniority system/sistema de jerarquía** Costumbre de nombrar como líderes de los comités del Congreso a los funcionarios con más años de servicio. **123**

**sentence/sentencia** Castigo que se da a una persona acusada de un crimen. **391**

**separation of church and state/separación de la iglesia y el estado** División entre la religión y el gobierno. **90**

**service industries/industrias de servicio** Comercios que venden servicios en lugar de productos. **551**

**sessions/sesiones** Reuniones del Congreso. **119**

**sheriff/alguacil** Oficial encargado de aplicar la ley en los condados. **227**

**shoplifting/robo de tiendas** Robo de objetos exhibidos en los aparadores de las tiendas. **446**

**shortage/escasez** Ocurre cuando la demanda es mayor que la oferta. **513**

**short-term credit/crédito a corto plazo** Préstamo económico que debe pagarse en poco tiempo. **457**

**single-parent families/familias sin padre o madre** Familias que sólo cuentan con padre o madre, por lo general a causa de divorcio, viudez, adopción de madre o padre soltero, o hijos nacidos de madres solteras. **328**

**slander/calumnia** Declaraciones falsas que dañan la reputación de otra persona. **90**

**small claims courts/cortes de demandas menores** Cortes estatales que atienden casos civiles menores y conflictos de pequeñas cantidades de dinero. **217**

**smog/smog** Combinación de humo, gases y niebla en el aire. **663**

**social insurance/seguro social** Programa del gobierno que protege a los ciudadanos de situaciones adversas a futuro mediante el pago de una cuota estatal y federal constante. **477**

**Social Security/Seguridad Social** Programa de gobierno que ofrece beneficios a personas de edad avanzada, con discapacidad, desempleadas y con lesiones o enfermedades ocasionadas por su oficio. **477**

**Social Security tax/impuesto de Seguridad Social** Impuesto usado principalmente para proporcionar ingresos a personas retiradas o con discapacidades. **305**

**sole proprietorships/propiedades de un dueño** Comercios que son propiedad de una sola persona. **417**

**sovereignty/soberanía** Poder o autoridad absoluta de un gobierno. **32**

**Speaker/portavoz** Funcionario que preside la Cámara de representantes. **120**

**special district/distrito especial** Unidad local de gobierno creada para proporcionar servicios específicos. **232**

**specialize/especialización** Aumento de la capacidad de producción de un tipo específico de bienes. **529**

**split ticket/boleto dividido** Boleta en que una persona puede votar por los candidatos de más de un partido político. **268**

**standard packaging/empaquetar** Envolver los productos antes de enviarlos a los centros de consumo. **440**

**standing committees/comités de apoyo** Comités permanentes del Senado o la Cámara de representantes creados para considerar las propuestas de un área específica. **122**

**State of the Union Address/informe presidencial** Documento presentado cada año por el presidente de la nación para informar al Congreso las condiciones del país y sugerir programas y medidas de mejoramiento. **147**

**statutory laws/leyes de estatutos** Leyes aprobadas por el Congreso y los cuerpos legisladores estatales o locales. **170**

**stocks/acciones** Acciones de propiedad de una corporación. **418**

**stock exchange/mercado de acciones** Sistema de compra y venta de acciones empresariales. **469**

**stockholders/accionistas** Personas que poseeen acciones corporativas. **418**

**straight ticket/boleto directo** Boleta en la que las personas votan por todos los candidatos de un partido político. **268**

**strike/huelga** Paro de labores realizado por los trabajadores de una empresa hasta que sus peticiones sobre temas laborales son atendidas. **499**

**strip mining/minería a cielo abierto** Proceso en que se remueve el suelo superficial para extraer los minerales de ese estrato. **673**

**subcommittees/subcomités** Divisiones de los comités del Congreso que analizan temas específicos en un área sujeta a los comités primarios. **122**

**subpoenas/citatorios** Órdenes oficiales de la corte que demandan la presencia de una persona ante un tribunal. **176**

**suburbs/suburbios** Comunidades residenciales ubicadas en los alrededores de las grandes ciudades. **17**

**suffrage/sufragio** Derecho al voto. **97**

**summit/reunión cumbre** Reunión entre los líderes de dos o más naciones. **581**

**Sunbelt/Franja del Sol** Región estadounidense formada por los estados del sur y del oeste. **18**

**supply/oferta** Cantidad de productos y servicios que los productores ofrecen en un periodo determinado. **512**

**surplus/excedente** Cantidad en la que los ingresos superan a los gastos. **313**

**tariff/arancel** Impuesto que se aplica a los productos importados de otras naciones. **308**

**taxable income/impuesto sobre la renta** Ingreso total, menos deducciones, sobre el que cada individuo o empresa debe pagar un impuesto. **305**

**tax incentives/incentivos ficales** Reducción especial de impuestos para las empresas que fomentan la inversión. **525**

**technicians/técnicos** Obreros especializados que operan complicadas piezas de maquinaria. **547**

**term limits/límite de término** Leyes que limitan los periodos que un funcionario público puede servir en un cargo público. **115**

**territorial courts/cortes territoriales** Cortes federales que administran la impartición de justicia para los ciudadanos de Estados Unidos. **179**

**territory/territorio** Zona que puede convertirse en estado. **199**

**terrorists/terroristas** Individuos que usan la violencia para lograr objetivos políticos. **618**

**testimony/testimonio** Evidencias presentadas por un testigo ante la corte. **173**

**third parties/partidos de terceros** Partidos políticos menores que participan en un sistema bipartidista. **256**

**tight-money policy/política de recorte monetario** Política económica de alza de las tasas de interés que desalienta a quienes piden préstamos y reduce la inflación. **526**

**totalitarian/totalitario** Forma de gobierno que posee control absoluto sobre una nación. **26**

**town/poblado** Unidad local de gobierno que suele ser más grande que una aldea, pero más pequeña que una ciudad. **228**

**town meeting/ayuntamiento** Forma de gobierno en que los ciudadanos se reúnen de manera regular para analizar temas comunes. **229**

**townships/municipios** Unidades locales de gobierno que administran los caminos y escuelas entre condados. **231**

**trade barrier/barrera comercial** Acción del gobierno que limita el intercambio comercial. **531**

**trade deficit/déficit comercial** Situación que se produce cuando un país compra más bienes de los que vende. **535**

**trade-off/intercambio negativo** Sacrificio económico. **531**

**trade surplus/excedente comercial** Situación que se produce cuando un país compra menos bienes de los que vende. **535**

**traditional economy/economía tradicional** Economía cuya producción se basa en las costumbres y tradiciones o papeles económicos heredados de una generación a otra. **415**

**treason/traición** Acción contraria a lo debido que pone en riesgo a una nación. **128**

**treaties/tratados** Acuerdos escritos entre naciones. **150**

**trough/caída** Punto bajo en un ciclo comercial. **486**

**trust/trust** Organización formada por varias compañías mediante un sistema comercial tan fuerte que las demás empresas no pueden competir con éste. **412**

**two-income families/familias de dos ingresos** Familias en las que la dos cabezas contribuyen al gasto familiar. **327**

**two-party system/sistema bipartidista** Sistema político en el que predominan dos partidos políticos. **255**

**unconstitutional/anticonstitucional** Acción que entra en conflicto con la Constitución de Estados Unidos. **183**

**unicameral/unicameral** Sistema de un solo cuerpo legislador. **203**

**union/sindicato.** *Véase* **sindicatos laborales**

**union shop/taller sindical** Empresa que contrata trabajadores no sindicalizados con la condición de que se afilien a un sindicato en un periodo determinado. **500**

**unitary system/sistema unitario** Sistema de gobierno en que el gobierno federal posee poder total sobre la nación. **43**

**United Nations/Organización de las Naciones Unidas** Organización internacional que promueve la paz y la cooperación global. **588**

**university/universidad** Institución de aprendizaje superior que agrupa carreras profesionales y programas de educación avanzada. **345**

**urban areas/zonas urbanas** Ciudades o poblados muy grandes. **17**

**urban renewal programs/programas de renovación urbana** Programas de recuperación de diversas zonas de las ciudades. **629**

**vandalism/vandalismo** Destrucción intrencional de propiedades privadas. **383**

**verdict/veredicto** Decisión de un jurado. **173**

**veto/veto** Rechazo de una propuesta legal por parte del presidente de una nación. **79**

**victimless crimes/crímenes sin saldo** Delitos en los que no se registran víctimas. **383**

**village/aldea** Unidad local de gobierno, por lo general de menor tamaño que un poblado. **228**

**visas/visas** Documentos que permiten a los habitantes de un país visitar otras naciones. **156**

**volunteers/voluntarios** Personas que trabajan sin un salario para ayudar a otras. **293**

**wards/barrios** Distritos electorales de una ciudad o condado. **235**

**War on Drugs/guerra contra las drogas** Esfuerzo organizado para acabar con el comercio y consumo de drogas. **617**

**warrant/garantía** Orden de pago de fondos del gobierno. **213**

**white-collar crimes/criminales de cuello blanco** Personas que cometen acciones ilegales en su trabajo. **383**

**white-collar workers/trabajadores de cuello blanco** Profesionistas que laboran en áreas técnicas, de administración, de ventas o de apoyo. **546**

**wholesaler/mayorista** Comerciante que compra grandes cantidades de productos y los vende a comerciantes minoristas. **441**

**World Trade Center/World Trade Center** Complejo comercial localizado en Nueva York que fuera destruido por un ataque terrorista el 11 de septiembre del 2001. **618**

**writ of** *habeas corpus***/auto de comparecencia** Orden de la corte que demanda la presencia de una persona acusada de un crimen para determinar si existen suficientes evidencias para iniciar un juicio. **130**

**zoning laws/leyes de zonificación** Leyes locales que regulan el tipo de edificios que pueden construirse en una zona determinada. **631**

# Index

child care, *p19*, *p327*
child labor, 498, *p498*
Children's Defense Fund, 331
children's rights, 331
Chile, 585
China. *See* People's Republic of China
chlorofluorocarbons (CFCs), 664
Christians, 143
Churchill, Winston, 588
CIA. *See* Central Intelligence Agency
cigarettes, 647
circuit, (def.) 177
circuit courts, 217
circular-flow model, (def.), 511
cities, *p234*, (def.) 234, *g236*; attractions of, 368; city government, 234–39. *See also* communities; local governments; urban areas
citizens, (def.) 3, 6, 10, 29, 132; diversity of, *p10*; responsibilities of, 5
citizenship, 3–4, 10, 11, *p12*, *p13*, *g103*, 380, 635; active, 350; and African Americans, 97; and communities, 362–77; duties of, 100–02; families and, 335; good, 6, 335, 377; ideals of American, 4; naturalization and, 12; responsibilities of, 5, 100, *g103*, 102–04
city, (def.) 234
City College of New York, 577
city council, (def.) 235, *g236*
city manager, *g236*, 239
civic center, 629
civics, (def.) 3; importance of, 7
civil cases, (def.) 215, *p216*
civil disobedience, (def.) 638
civilian, (def.) 157
Civilian Conservation Corps, 489
civil rights, (def.) 96, 97, 188, 635–41, 643
Civil Rights Act of 1964, 555, 556
Civil Rights Act of 1968, 555
civil rights movement, (def.) 636, 636; progress of, 638
Civil War, 9, 96, 97, 99, 636
Clay, Henry, *p114*
Clean Air Acts, 678
clear-and-present-danger rule, 90, 91
Cleveland, Ohio, 311
climate, 365
Clinton, Bill, 11, 128, 129, *p139*, 257, 288, 314, 493, 576, 589, 616; as a candidate for president, *p257*
closed primary, (def.) 266
closed shop, (def.) 500
cloture, (def.) 137
coal, 672, *p673*
coalition, (def.) 256
Coast Guard, 160, 553
Coast Guard Academy, U.S., 157
coincident indicators, (def.) 519
coins. *See* currency
cold fusion, 674
Cold War, 606–13; *m608;* end of, 612–14
collateral, (def.) 460
collective bargaining, (def.) 499, 504–05

College of New Jersey, 41
College of William and Mary, 75
colleges, 19, (def.) 345; enrollment, *g343*. *See also* schools; individual colleges
Colombia, 617
colonial America, *p627*
colonies. *See* American colonies
colonists, *p8*, 37
Colorado: African American voter registration in, *m653*; congressional representation of, *m115*; date of admission into the Union, *m200*; electoral votes in, *m274*; pollution in, *m669*; population growth rate of, 18; taxes in, *m317*
Colorado Springs, Colorado, 157
Columbus, Christopher, 8
command economy, (def.) 414
commander in chief, 57, 148
Commerce, Department of, *g158,* 159; promoting industry, *p159*
commercial banks, 461
commission, (def.) 238
commission government, *g236*, 238
Commission on Civil Rights, U.S., 163
Committee of the Whole, 136
committees, (def.) 121, 121–24, 133, *g141*; bills in, 135; chairperson of, 123; congressional, *p122*; membership on, 123
common law, (def.) 170
common stocks, (def.) 420, 469
Commonwealth of Independent States (CIS), 613
communications, 281, (def.) 369–70, 592; access to, 641; satellite, *p597*
communism, 258, 585, (def.) 606, 606, 607, 611; fall of, 613; in China, 610
Communist Manifesto, 606
Communist Party, 504
communities, 104, 362–77, *g370*, *g379*, 627; citizens serving, 374, 377; community action, 295; community groups, *p295*; community service, 371–72; improving, 375–77; kinds of, 363–368; planned, 628; planning commission, 633; problems with, 633; purposes of, 369–70, *g370*; rural, 366–67; volunteers in, *p4*, 376–77; voting locations in, *p291*. *See also* cities; local governments
community colleges, (def.) 344
community planning commission, 633
community policing, (def.) 388
commutation, (def.) 151
commuting, *p17*, 628
comparative advantage, (def.) 530
competition, (def.) 512–13, 523; economic, 584; international, 575
complaint, (def.) 216
compromise, (def.) 44, 505
Compromise of 1850, *p114*
comptroller, 311
compulsory, (def.) 374
computer crimes, 384
computers, 436; and elections, 273
concealed propaganda, (def.) 281

concurrent powers, *g73*, (def.) 75, 199
concurring opinion, (def.) 185
conditioning, (def.) 354
Confederacy, 96
confederation, (def.) 32
conference committees, (def.) 123
Conference of Mayors, U.S., 244
conglomerate, (def.) 413
Congress (U.S.), 41, 44, 51, 57, 59, *g69*, 77, 79, 112–24 *p116*, *g117*, 126–139, *g127*; budgetary powers of, 313; committees of, 121–124; elections, 51, 65, 114; and ethnic minority members, 116; impeachment power of, 128; implied powers of, 127; leaders of, 120–21; and lobbyists, 288–89; limits of, 130; organization of, 120; other roles of, 131; powers granted to, 126; qualifications of, 116; role in foreign policy, 579–80; rules of conduct of, 118; salaries of, 53, 117; salaries of senators and representatives in, 53; special powers of, 129; staffs of, 124; terms and sessions of, 119; two houses of, 113; and women, 116. *See also* House of Representatives; legislative branch; Senate
Congress of Industrial Organizations (CIO), 501
congressional districts, 114
Congressional Record, 134
Connecticut, 39, 60, 225; African American voter registration in, *m653*; congressional representation of, *m115*; date of admission into the Union, *m200*; electoral votes in, *m274*; pollution in, *m669*; taxes in, *m317*
consanguinity, 38
conservation, 659, (def.) 672, 676; early efforts in, 677; federal government and, 678; individuals role in, 681; oil, 672
constables, (def.) 232
constituents, (def.) 131, 295
constitution, (def.) 28
Constitution (U.S.), 40, 41, 43, 46, 50–69, 70–84, 82, *p82*, 115, 120, 126, 130, 142, 145, 147, 171, 180, 183, 202, 241, 264, 576; amendment process, 59, 83, *g83;* amendments to, 61–69, 89–99; *g83;* Article I, 51–55, 113; Article II, 56–58, 78; Article III, 58, 174; Article IV, 58–59; Article V, 59; Article VI, 60; Article VII, 60; Articles of Confederation and, 43, *g43*; Bill of Attainder in, 55; Bill of Rights, 61–62, 89–95, *g94*; census in, 51; Commander in Chief in, 57; congressional salary in, 53; courts in, 174; Elastic Clause in, 54; *ex post facto* law in, 55; executive branch in, 56–58; flexibility of, 82–84, 186; framers of, 40–43, *p70*, 71, 76, 89; goals of, 72; House of Representatives in, 51; ideals of, 34–36; impeachment in, 52; judicial branch in, 58; legislative branch in, 51–55; naturalization and, 13; Preamble, 50; presidential appointments in, 57; presidential elections in, 56; presidential salary in, 57;

federal system, 74, 197
Federal Trade Commission (FTC), 413, 446
fees, (def.) 302
felonies, (def.) 381
Ferraro, Geraldine, 144, 273
fertilizers, (def.) 660, 679
Fifteenth Amendment, 64, 97
Fifth Amendment, 61, 93–94
filibuster, (def.) 137, p137
finance charges, 456
fine, (def.) 302
fire department, p27, 28, p151, 234, 244, p244, 371
fire safety, 650
First Amendment, 61, 89–92, p90
First Congress, 119
fiscal policies, (def.) 493, 494, 524–25
Fish and Wildlife Service, U.S., 159
fixed expenses, (def.) 337
Fleischmann, Martin, 674
floor leader, (def.) 120
Florida: African American voter registration in, m653; congressional representation of, m115; date of admission into the Union, m200; election 2000 in, 292, 293; electoral votes in, m274; pollution in, m669; settlement of, 9; taxes in, m317
flowcharts, 85, g85
Food and Agriculture Organization (FAO), 591
Food and Nutrition Service, 159
food stamps, 159
forcible rape, (def.) 382
Ford, Gerald, 146, p146, 464
foreign aid, (def.) 582, g595
foreign mercenaries, 38
foreign policy, (def.) 149, 150, g150, 575–83, 597–602, 604, 605, 607–19; changes triggered by September 11, 619; development of, 597
foreign trade, 583
Forest Service, 159
forests, p657, 658
Fort Knox, Kentucky, 454, p455
fossil fuels, (def.) 670, 672
foster homes, (def.) 331
Fourteenth Amendment, 63–64, 97, 186–87, 206, 390, 498, 640
Fourth Amendment, 61, 93–94, p93
France, 41, 180, 438, 589, 598, 609, 611; immigrants from, 9
franking privilege, (def.) 117, 118
Franklin, Benjamin, 39, 41, 44, 60, p199; as writer of Pennsylvania law, p228
fraud, (def.) 383
free competition, (def.) 408
freedoms, 130, g408; economic, 407; Four Freedoms, 605; of assembly, 61, p92, 92, g94; of petition, 61, 92; of press, 61, 91, g94; of religion, 61, 81, 89, g94, 407; of speech, 61, 90, 91, g94, 407, 504; Virginia Statute of Religious Freedom, 81. See also rights
free elections, 613

free-enterprise system, (def.) 411, 510
free market, (def.) 408, 409
free-market economies, 436, 485, 585
free trade, 533, 575, (def.) 585–86, 617; debate of, 585
Frist, William, 121
full faith and credit clause, (def.) 201

Galveston, Texas, 238
Gandhi, Mohandas, 636
gangs, 396
Gates, Bill, p426; biography of, 426
gender discrimination, 640
General Accounting Office, 315
General Agreement on Tariffs and Trade, (GATT) 532
General Assembly, (def.) 589
general election, (def.) 266, 267
General Services Administration, 164
general trial courts, (def.) 217
Geneva, Switzerland, 591
George III (England), 30, 33, 37
Georgetown University, 11
Georgia, 39, 60; African American voter registration in, m653; congressional representation of, m115; date of admission into the Union, m200; electoral votes in, m274; pollution in, m669; taxes in, m317
geothermal energy, 675
Germany, 258, 438, 601, 602, 606, 613, 674; minority groups from, 635; immigrants from, 9
gerrymandering, (def.) 114
Gettysburg, Pennsylvania, 9
Gettysburg Address, 9, 97
Gibbons, Thomas, 438
Gibbons v. Ogden, 438
Gideon v. Wainwright, 390
gift tax, (def.) 307
Ginsberg, Ruth Bader, p178, 182
Girl Scouts, 421
Giuliani, Rudolph, p237
glasnost, (def.) 612
glittering generalities, 283
global economy, 584
global warming, 586, 664
Goals 2000 Educate America Act, 346
goldsmiths, 460
Gompers, Samuel, p501
Gonzalez, Alberto, 639
Good Neighbor Policy, 600
Gorbachev, Mikhail, 612, 613
Gore, Al, 270, 273, 275, 292; as presidential candidate, p252, p259, p279
government bonds, 466
governments, (def.) 3, g247, g312; borrowing, 303; by the people, 5; city, 234–39; commission, 238; competition between, 245; cooperation between, 242–44; cooperation in, 241; cost of, 299; county, 225–26; early, 229; federal

system, 197; foundations of, 24, 520–28; ideals of American, 31; intervention in economy, 489–53; jobs, p163; jobs in, 552–53; local, 200, 224–47, 372; paying for, 298–315; purpose of, 26; regulations of, 127, 165, 414, 464, 473; revenues, 314; role in business, 427; services provided by, 27–28; spending of, 131, 311, 492, 493, 495, 525; totalitarian, 258; tribal, 159; types of, 25–26. See also federal government; local governments; states
governor, (def.) 210, 211, g212; powers and duties of, 211, 212; qualifications of, 210; salaries of, 210; term of, 210
graduate school, (def.) 345
grand jury, 61, (def.) 93, 172
grand larceny, (def.) 382
Grant, Ulysses S., 553
grants-in-aid, (def.) 244
grasslands, 658, 677
grassroots, (def.) 266
Gray Panthers, 640
Great Britain, 30, 37, 41, 93, 589, 598, 609, 616; and September 11, 619
Great Compromise, 44
Great Depression, 367, 477, 479, 487. See also depression
Great Lakes, 598
Great Plains, p657, 658
Greece, 608, 609
greenhouse effect, (def.) 664
Greenspan, Alan, p464; biography of, 464, p528
gross domestic product (GDP), (def.) 431, 485, 486
gross income, (def.) 426
gross national product (GNP), g429
ground pollution, 667
groundwater, 667
Guam, 114, 179, 199
guardian, (def.) 331
guerrillas, 612
Gulf of Tonkin Resolution, 612
gun control, 92, p139

habit, (def.) 355
Hague, The, 590
Hamilton, Alexander, 41, 45, 60, 254; as cabinet member, p84
Hancock, John, 39
Handgun Violence Prevention Act, p139
Harvard University, 426
Hawaii, 114, 120, 199, 213, 273, 602; African American voter registration in, m653; congressional representation of, m115; date of admission into the Union, m200; electoral votes in, m274; pollution in, m669; senate of, 120; taxes in, m317
Head Start programs, 224

For permission to reprint copyrighted material, grateful acknowledgment is made to the following sources:

**The American Red Cross National Headquarters:** From "Volunteering in 2001" by Charlotte J. Lunsford delivered before The 1988 National Volunteer Conference, San Francisco, CA, June 21, 1988. Copyright © 1988 by The American Red Cross.

**Claire L. Gaudiani:** From "Developing Global Civic Virtues" by Claire L. Gaudiani delivered to Phi Beta Kappa, University of Connecticut, Storrs, CT, May 1, 1993. Copyright © 1993 by Claire L. Gaudiani.

**Little, Brown and Company, (Inc.):** From *Epic of America* by James Truslow Adams. Copyright 1931, 1933 by James Truslow Adams; copyright renewed © 1959 by James Truslow Adams.

# Acknowledgments

For permission to reproduce copyrighted material, grateful acknowledgment is made to the following sources:

**American Legion Nevada Boys' State:** From "What Boys' State and the American Legion have done for me" by Ben Johnson from *Nevada Boys' State* Web site, accessed March 12, 2002, at www.nevadaboysstate.org/stories/bjohnson.html. Copyright © 2002 by Nevada Boys' State.

**Bantam Books, a division of Random House, Inc. www.randomhouse.com:** From *Iacocca: An Autobiography* by Lee Iacocca with William Novak. Copyright © 1984 by Lee Iacocca.

**Council of Better Business Bureaus, Inc., 4200 Wilson Blvd., Arlington, VA 22203:** From "Cybershopping–What You Need to Know" from *Better Business Bureau* Web site, accessed March 11, 2002, at www.bbb.org/library/cybershop.asp. Copyright © 2002 by the Council of Better Business Bureaus.

**The Gallup Organization, Inc.:** Opinion poll, "How much of the time do you think you can trust government…" from the Gallup Poll News Service, October 2001. Copyright © 2001 by The Gallup Organization, Inc.

**The Heirs to the Estate of Martin Luther King, Jr., c/o Writers House, Inc. as agent for the proprietor, New York, NY:** From "I Have a Dream" by Martin Luther King, Jr. Copyright © 1963 by Martin Luther King, Jr.; copyright renewed © 1991 by Coretta Scott King. From "Letter from Birmingham City Jail" by Martin Luther King, Jr. from *Why We Can't Wait* by Martin Luther King, Jr. Copyright © 1963 by Martin Luther King, Jr., copyright renewed © 1993 by Coretta Scott King.

**National Civic League:** From "Reinvigorating Democratic Values: Challenge and Necessity," by Henry G. Cisneros and John Parr from *National Civic Review,* September/October 1990. Copyright © 1990 by National Civic League Press, Denver, CO.

**National Education Association:** From "All in the Family: Educating Our Children in Post-September 11 America" by Bob Chase from NEA Web site, accessed March 11, 2002, at www.nea.org/nr/sp011116.html. Copyright © 2001 by the National Education Association.

## Sources Cited:

From "City Government" from *Know Your City: A Guide to Alexandria.* Prepared by The Alexandria Office of Citizen Assistance and The League of Women Voters of Alexandria, Virginia, 2000.

From "The Way We Wish We Were: Defining the Family Crisis" from *The Way We Never Were* by Stephanie Coontz. Published by HarperCollins Publishers, New York, 1992.

Quote by a Garden City, Kansas woman from *Kansas City Times,* March, 1935.

## Photography Credits

Abbreviated as follows: (t) top, (b) bottom, (l) left, (r) right, (c) center.
Cover Photo: (flag) ©Joseph Sohm; ChromoSohm Inc./Corbis: (crowd) AP/Photo/Ed Reinke

Title Page: (flag) ©Joseph Sohm; ChromoSohm Inc./Corbis: (crowd) AP/Photo/Ed Reinke

Ii, (flag) ©Joseph Sohm; ChromoSohm Inc./Corbis: (crowd) AP/Photo/Ed Reinke ; Iv (b), Chuck Pefley/Stock, Boston Inc./PictureQuest; v(tc), ©2001 Jay Mallin; v(tl),REUTERS/Kevin Lamarque; v(br),Dennis Cook/AP/Wide World Photos; v(tr), HRW Photo Research Library; vi Paula Lerner/Woodfin Camp & Associates; vii(t), Reuters NewMedia Inc./CORBIS; vii(bl), Sam Dudgeon/HRW; viii AP/Wide World Photos; ix(bl), Rich La Salle/PictureQuest; ix(tr), Detail, Mural: Detroit Industry, South Wall, by Diego M. Rivera, Gift of Edsel B. Ford, The Detroit Institute of Arts; x(tl),Jean Miele/CORBIS; x(br),Rob Crandall/Stock Connection/PictureQuest; xi(b), © Pallava Bagla/CORBIS; xii Tim Boyle/Getty Images; xvii(cr), Victoria Smith/HRW; xvii(tr), Sam Dudgeon/HRW; xvii(cl),David Muench/CORBIS; xviii(c), Senate Historical Society; xvii(tr), Sandy Schaeffer; xvii(tl),Araldo de Luca/CORBIS; xx Michael Newman/PhotoEdit; 2 Wally McNamee/CORBIS; 2(tc), David Austen/Stock, Boston Inc./PictureQuest; 3(tr), Sam Dudgeon/HRW; 3(br),The Image Bank/Getty Images; 4 AP/Wide World Photos; 5 Tom & DeeAnn McCarthy/Corbis Stock Market; 6 Bob Daemrich/Stock, Bosto Inc./PictureQuest; 7 AP/Wide World Photos; 8(cl),The Granger Collection, New York; 8(tr), Andre Jenny/Focus Group/PictureQuest ; 10(all),Sam Dudgeon/HRW; 11 Rick Friedman/Black Star Publishing/PictureQuest; 12(bl), ©2001 Jay Mallin; 12(b), Chuck Pefley/Stock, Boston Inc./PictureQuest;13 AP/Wide World Photos;14(cl,cr),Spencer Grant/PhotoEdit; 15 Spencer Grant/PhotoEdit; 16 Library of Congress, Detroit Publishing Co. Photo Collection; 17 Gunnar Kullenberg/Stock Connection/PictureQuest; 18 Buddy Mays/CORBIS; 19 Jonathan Nourok/PhotoEdit; 20 Kevin Fleming/CORBIS; 21 Courtesy Turner Learning / Cable Network News; 24 Nebraska State Historical Society; 25(cr), Independence National Historical Park Collection; 25(br),HRW Photo Research Library; 26 AFP/CORBIS; 27 Michael S. Yamashita/CORBIS; 28(tr), Stone/Getty Images; 28(bl), Aaron Haupt/Stock Boston; 29 Bob Daemrich/Stock Boston; 30(bl), The Granger Collection, New York; 30(candle), Stock Editions/HRW Photo Research Library; 30(tr), The Granger Collection, New York; 31 Archive Photos; 32 SuperStock; 33 Rare Books and Manuscripts Division, The New York Public Library, Astor, Lenox and Tilden Foundations; 34 North Wind Picture Archives; 35(tr), Courtesy of the Massachusetts Historical Society; 35(cr), The Granger Collection, New York; 36(bl), Larry Lee/CORBIS; 40(bl), The Granger Collection, New York; 40(cr), Sam Dudgeon/HRW; 41 The Granger Collection, New York; 42 Bob Krist/CORBIS; 44 The Granger Collection, New York; 45 The Granger Collection, New York; 46 Courtesy of the John Carter Brown Library at Brown University; 47 Library Company of Philadelphia; 50 Independence National Historical Park Collection; 71 The Granger Collection, New York; 72 Bob Krist/CORBIS; 75 Courtesy, Supreme Court of the United States, The Supreme Court Historical Society; 76 The Granger Collection, New York; 77(br),Sygma/CORBIS; 77(cr), Cosmo Condina/Getty Images; 79(tr), ©2001 Jay Mallin; 79 (pen), Sam Dudgeon/HRW; 80 The Granger Collection, New

York; 81(cr), H. Armstrong Roberts; 81(t), State Capitol, Commonwealth of Virginia, Courtesy Library of Virginia, image altered.; 82(cr), The Granger Collection, New York; 82(bl), Alex Wong/Getty Images; 84 Bettmann/CORBIS; 86(bl), HRW Photo Research Library; 86(bl), HRW Photo Research Library; 87 from THE HERBLOCK GALLERY (Simon & Schuster, 1968); 88(t), Andy Sacks/Getty Images/Stone; 89 Independence National Historical Park Collection; 90 Rich Pedroncelli/AP/Wide World Photos; 91(cr), Victoria Smith/HRW; 92 Dennis Cook/AP/Wide World Photos; 93 Bob Daemmrich Photo, Inc.; 95 Jim Cole/AP/Wide World Photos; 96(cl,tr),Library of Congress; 97 The Granger Collection, New York; 100(cl),Mary Kate Denny-Bim/PhotoEdit; 100(tr), Victoria Smith/HRW; 102(b), Mary Schroeder/AP/Wide World Photos; 104 Myrleen Cate/Index Stock Imagery/PictureQuest; 110 Ron Watts/CORBIS; 112(t), David Muench/CORBIS; 113(br),Victoria Smith/HRW; 113(tr), Sam Dudgeon/HRW; 114 The Granger Collection, New York; 116(t), Sandy Schaeffer; 116(bl), Senate Historical Society; 118(tl),Sam Dudgeon/HRW; 119 Bettmann/CORBIS; 120 Courtesy Senator Daniel Inouye; 121 © Reuters NewMedia Inc./CORBIS; 122 Rob Crandall/Stock Connection/PictureQuest; 123 Grin and Bear It, Courtesy Field Enterprises, Inc.; 124 Paul Conklin/PhotoEdit; 125 Copyright 1975 by Herblock in The Washington Post; 126(bl), AFP/CORBIS; 126(cr), HRW Photo by Victoria Smith; 128 Bettmann/CORBIS; 129(b), AP/Wide World Photos; 129(tr), Bettmann/CORBIS; 131 REUTERS/Kevin Lamarque; 131 REUTERS/Larry Downing/NewsCom; 132(tr), Newsmakers/NewsCom; 132(bl), Angela Rowlings/AP/Wide World Photos; 134 Bettmann/CORBIS; 135 Isaac Menashe/AI WIRE/NewsCom; 136 National Cable Satellite Corporation; 137 Bettmann/CORBIS; 139 AP/Wide World Photos; 142(t), Dallas and John Heaton/CORBIS; 143(br),Reuters NewMedia, Inc./CORBIS; 143(tr), Burstein Collection/CORBIS; 144 CORBIS; 145 REUTERS/Kevin Lamarque/TimePix; 146 Bettmann/CORBIS; 147(tr), HRW Photo Research Library; 147(br),Wally McNamee/CORBIS; 148 REUTERS/Hyungwon Kang/TimePix; 151 © Anja Niedringhaus/Pool/Reuters NewMedia Inc./CORBIS; 153 Tomas Muscionico/Contact Press Images; 154 AFP/CORBIS;155 Mark Wilson/Newsmakers/Getty Images; 156(tl),Image Copyright ©2003 PhotoDisc, Inc./HRW; 156(b), AP/Wide World Photos; 157 David&Peter Turnley/CORBIS; 159 Richard Nowitz/Phototake/PictureQuest; 160 CORBIS/Fotografia, Inc.; 161 Galen Rowell/CORBIS; 163(br),Paul Conklin/PhotoEdit; 163(tr), Wally McNamee/CORBIS; 164 AFP/CORBIS; 165 Grin and Bear It, Courtesy Field Enterprises, Inc.; 167, Stock Montage, Inc.; 168(t), Joseph Sohm/ChromoSohm Inc/CORBIS; 169 H. Armstrong Roberts; 170 Sam Dudgeon/HRW;171 AFP/CORBIS; 172 Bob Daemmrich/Stock Boston; 173 David R. Frazier Photolibrary; 174, Stapko/Collection of the Supreme Court of the United States; 175 Michael Dwyer/Stock Boston; 176 Mike Wintroath/AP/Wide World Photos; 178 Collection, The Supreme Court Historical Society; 179 Bettmann/CORBIS; 182 Ernest Ludwig Ipsen/Collection of the Supreme Court of the United States; 183 North Wind Picture Archives; 185 Franklin McMahon/CORBIS; 186 The Granger Collection, New York; 187(bl), AP/Wide World Photos; 187(br),Carl Iwasaki/TIMEPIX; 188 Collection, The Supreme Court of the United States, Courtesy The Supreme Court Historical Society; 189 Franklin D. Roosevelt Presidential Library; 190 H. Armstrong Roberts; 191 Franklin D. Roosevelt Presidential Library; 198(t), Tom Bean/CORBIS; 199(cr), HRW Photo Research Library; 199(tr), Sam Dudgeon/HRW;199(tr), Sam Dudgeon/HRW; 201(br), The Granger Collection, New York; 203 AP/Wide World Photos; 204 Geoffrey Biddle/TimePix; 205(br),Tom Pantages Photography; 205 HRW Photo Research Library; 208(b), Jim McKnight/AP/Wide World Photos; 209 Karen Tam/AP/Wide World Photos; 210 Bettmann/CORBIS; 211(br),HRW Art by Jason Wilson; 212(bl), David Stover/Stock South/PictureQuest; 212 HRW Photo Research Library; 213 AP/Wide World Photos; 215 AP/Wide World Photos; 216 Alan Diaz/AP/Wide World Photos; 217(br),Victoria Smith/HRW; 217 Image Copyright ©2003 PhotoDisc, Inc.; 218(t), Bob Daemmrich Photos; 218(cl),David R. Frazier Photolibrary; 218(cl),© Mikael Karlsson; 219 Cindy Karp/Black Star/TimePix ; 222(t), David R. Frazier Photolibrary; 223(br), David R. Frazier Photolibrary; 224 David &Peter Turnley/CORBIS; 225(t), Buddy Mays/CORBIS; 227 Michael S. Yamashita/CORBIS; 228(bl), Hulton Archive/Getty Images; 228(tr), Eric Newrath/Stock Boston; 229(t), Colonial Williamsburg Foundation; 230(t), Paula Lerner/Woodfin Camp & Associates; 230(cl),Jane Dixon; 232 David R. Frazier Photolibrary; 233 Lee Snider/CORBIS; 234(bl), SuperStock; 234(tr), Richard Levine; 235(b), Charles Gupton/Stock Boston; 237 AP/Wide World Photos; 238(t), David R. Frazier Photolibrary; 238(tl),David R. Frazier Photolibrary; 241(br),David R. Frazier Photolibrary; 241(tr), David R. Frazier Photolibrary; 242(t), Maryland Historical Society, Baltimore, Maryland; 243(tr), Pete Seaward/Getty Images/Stone; 243(br),AFP/CORBIS; 244 Ecoscene/CORBIS; 245 Mark Richards/PhotoEdit; 252(t), AFP/CORBIS; 252(br),Sam Dudgeon/HRW; 253(tr), Victoria Smith/HRW; 253(br),The Granger Collection, New York; 253(tr), Victoria Smith/HRW; 256 National Portrait Gallery, Smithsonian Institute, Gift of the Swedish Colonial Society through Mrs. William Hacker/Art Resource, NY; 257 Dirck Halstead; 258 Richard Bickel/CORBIS; 259 NewsCom; 259 NewsCom; 260 Bob Daemmrich Photo, Inc.; 261 AP/Wide World Photos; 262 AP/Wide World Photos; 263 Naples Cartoon Research; 264 Tony Freeman/PhotoEdit; 265(tr), Susan Sterner/AP/Wide World Photos; 265(cr), HRW Photo Research Library; 266 AP/Wide World Photos; 268 Reuters NewMedia Inc/CORBIS; 270(bl), Reuters NewMedia Inc/CORBIS; 270(tr), Underwood & Underwood/CORBIS; 271 Chris Hondros/Newsmakers/Getty/NewsCom; 272 Lisa Quinones/stockphoto; 273(tr), AP/Wide World Photos; 273(cr), AP/Wide World Photos; 278(t), David Young-Wolff/PhotoEdit; 278(br), Sam Dudgeon/HRW; 279(br),AFP/CORBIS; 279(tr), HRW Photo Research Library; 280 Anthony Bolante/REUTERS/TimePix; 281(br), Sam Dudgeon/HRW; 281(tr), Raoul Minsart/CORBIS; 282 Joe Mitchell/UPI/NewsCom; 284 Bettmann/CORBIS; 285 Bob Daemrich/Stock Boston; 287(br),Lauren McFalls/AP/Wide World Photos; 287(tr), AP/Wide World Photos; 288 William Philpott/NewsCom; 290 PictureQuest; 291(br),Joseph Sohm; ChromoSohm Inc/CORBIS; 291(tr), Sam Dudgeon/HRW; 293(t), Reuters NewMedia Inc./CORBIS; 293(tr), Sam Dudgeon/HRW; 294(tl),Michael Newman/PhotoEdit; 294(bl), AP/Wide World Photos; 295 Joseph

Sohm; ChromoSohm Inc/CORBIS; 297 Gary Brookings, 1988, Richmond Times-Dispatch; 298(t), Sam Dudgeon/HRW; 298(br),Sam Dudgeon/HRW; 299(br),Michael Newman/PhotoEdit; 299(tr), Doug Wilson/CORBIS; 299 Courtesy of Karl Hubenthal, Los Angeles Herald-Examiner.; 301 Larry Kolvoord Photography; 302(b), Brian Yarvin ©1990/The Image Works; 302(cl),Robert Feltes, Simply License Plates; 302(cd),Robert Feltes, Simply License Plates; 303 Sam Dudgeon/HRW; 304 Walter Hodges/CORBIS; 305 Sam Dudgeon/HRW; 306 Tina Fineberg/AP/Wide World Photos; 307 Kevin Fleming/CORBIS; 308 AP/Wide World Photos; 310(tr), Sam Dudgeon/HRW; 310(bl), Bob Rowan; Progressive Image/CORBIS; 311 Bettmann/CORBIS; 313 Etta Hume reprinted by permission of Newspaper Enterprise Association, Inc.; 322(t), Warren Morgan/CORBIS; 322(br),Sam Dudgeon/HRW; 323(br),The Granger Collection, New York; 323(tr), Library of Congress; 325 HRW Photo Research Library; 326 Bevil Knapp/TimePix; 327 Paul Conklin/PhotoEdit/PictureQuest; 328 Frank Siteman/Index Stock Imagery/PictureQuest; 329(tr), (PhotoDisc) - Digital Image copyright (c) 2003; 329(br),Scott Vallance/VIP Photographic Associates; 330(t), Kevin Horan/Getty Images/Stone; 330(bl), AP/Wide World Photos; 331 AP/Wide World Photos; 332 AP/Wide World Photos; 334(tr), Scott Vallance/VIP Photographic Associates; 334(bl), Greg Nikas/CORBIS; 335 Michael Newman/PhotoEdit; 336 The Image Works; 337 Vic Thomasson, Rex Instock/Stock Connection/PictureQuest; 340(t), Scott Vallance/VIP Photographic Associates; 340(br),Sam Dudgeon/HRW; 341(tr), Scott Vallance/VIP Photographic Associates; 341(br),Department of Education; 342 Greg Mathieson/TimePix; 344 Michael Newman/PhotoEdit; 345 Peter Armenia Photography; 348 David Young Wolff/PhotoEdit; 349(tr), Sam Dudgeon/HRW; 349(br),Mary Kate Denny/PhotoEdit; 350 Michelle D. Bridwell/PhotoEdit; 351 Cleve Bryant/PhotoEdit; 352(tl),Tom McCarthy/PhotoEdit; 352(bl), Michael Newman/PhotoEdit; 353 Chris Anderson/Aurora/PictureQuest; 354 (diploma), Scott Vallance/VIP Photographic Associates; 354(tr), HRW Photo Research Library; 354(bl), Michael Newman/PhotoEdit; 355 Michael Newman/PhotoEdit; 356 Michael Newman/PhotoEdit; 357 Michelle D. Bridwell/PhotoEdit; 358 Tony Freeman/PhotoEdit; 361 Bruce Beattie; 362(t), H. Armstrong Roberts; 362(br),Sam Dudgeon/HRW; 363(tr), Bob Poynter/AP/Wide World Photos; 363(br),Bettmann/CORBIS; 364 The Granger Collection, New York; 365 Grant Heilman Photography; 366 Tom and Pat Valenti/Getty Images/Stone; 367 Image Copyright © 2001 PhotoDisc, Inc./HRW; 368 Angelo Hornak/CORBIS; 369(tr), Scott Vallance/VIP Photographic Associates; 369(br),Michael Newman/PhotoEdit; 371 John Gillis/AP/Wide World Photos; 372 Mitch Wojnarowicz/AP/Wide World Photos; 373 Jeff Greenberg/PhotoEdit; 374(tr), Sam Dudgeon/HRW; 374(bl), Scott Vallance/VIP Photographic Associates; 375 Clay Jackson/AP/Wide World Photos; 376 Lloyd Ostendorf Collection; 377 David Young-Wolff/PhotoEdit; 378 Mitch Wojnarowicz/AP/Wide World Photos; 380(t), CORBIS; 380(br),Sam Dudgeon/HRW; 381© 2001 Mikael Karlsson; 382(tl), Jane Dixon; 382(bl), George Widman/AP/Wide World Photos; 383 David & Peter Turnley/CORBIS; 384 AP/Wide World Photos; 386 Bob Daemmrich Photo, Inc.; 387 Bob Daemmrich Photo, Inc.; 388 J.B. Boykin/PhotoEdit; 389 Randy Faris/CORBIS; 391 Peter Cowie/AP/Wide World Photos; 392(cl),© 2001 Mikael Karlsson; 392(bl), Scott Anger/AP/Wide World Photos; 393 © Mikael Karlsson; 394 Dennis Degnan/CORBIS; 395(tr), © 2001 Mikael Karlsson; 395(br),Michael S. Wirtz/NewsCom; 396(tl), Jay Nubile/The Image Works; 396(bl), The Century Council; 397 Richard Hutchings/PhotoEdit; 398 Bob Galbraith/AP/Wide World Photos; 399 Michelle D. Bridwell/PhotoEdit; 401 ©Arnie Levin from The Cartoon Bank. All rights reserved.; 406(t), Scott T. Smith/CORBIS; 406(br),Sam Dudgeon/HRW; 407 Carl & Ann Purcell/CORBIS; 409(br),CORBIS; 409(tr), Bettmann/CORBIS; 410 Bill Aron/PhotoEdit; 411 Image Copyright ©1997-99 PhotoDisc, Inc./HRW; 412 Culver Pictures, Inc.; 413 Mark Joseph/Getty Images/Stone; 414 Jonathan Blair/CORBIS; 415 Rich Frishman/Getty Images/Stone; 416(tr), Victoria Smith/HRW; 416(bl), The Granger Collection, New York; 417 Joel Page/AP/Wide World Photos; 418 Sam Dudgeon/HRW; 420 Premium Stock/CORBIS; 421 Brent Hood/AP/Wide World Photos; 423(br),Ralph Talmount/Aurora; 424 Tim Roske/AP/Wide World Photos; 425 John S. Stewart/AP/Wide World Photos; 426 Jim Lake/CORBIS; 427 Bob Bird/AP/Wide World Photos; 430(t), Bob Rowan; Progressive Image/CORBIS; 430(br),Sam Dudgeon/HRW; 431(tr), Kim Neilsen/Smithsonian Institute, Washington, DC/PRC Archive; 431(br),Mark Gibson Photography; 432 The Granger Collection, New York; 432(bl), Bettmann/CORBIS; 433(t), Bettmann/CORBIS; 433(br),Benelux Press/Getty Images/FPG International; 434(t), Detail, Mural: Detroit Industry, South Wall, by Diego M. Rivera, Gift of Edsel B. Ford, The Detroit Institute of Arts; 435 Ed Kashi/Aurora; 436 Rich La Salle/PictureQuest; 437(cr), Joe Sohm/Chromosohm/PictureQuest; 437(br),George D. Lepp/CORBIS; 439(tr), ©Inc. Janeart/Getty Images/The Image Bank; 439(br),Scott Vallance/VIP Photographic Associates; 440 Mark Gibson Photography; 441 Nik Wheeler/CORBIS; 442 Courtesy Brett Elliott; 443(tr), Sam Dudgeon/HRW; 444(bl), Sam Dudgeon/HRW; 446 CORBIS; 447(tr), Etta Hulme; 447(br),Frank Siteman/The Picture Cube; 448 Bob Daemmrich/Stock Boston, Inc./PictureQuest; 452(t), Greg Plachta/Picturesque/PictureQuest; 452(br),Sam Dudgeon/HRW; 453(tr), Lawrence Migdale; 453(br),HRW Photo Research Library; 454 HRW Photo Research Library; 455 SuperStock; 455(br), Bob Daemmrich Photo, Inc.; 457(t), Mark Gibson Photography; 458 Courtesy USA Today, published by Gannett Co., Inc.; 460(tr), Araldo de Luca/CORBIS; 460(bl), Archivo Iconografico, S.A./CORBIS; 461(tr), (PhotoDisc) Digital Image ©2003; 461(br),Bob Daemmrich Photo, Inc.; 462 Lake County Museum/CORBIS; 463 Morton Beebe/CORBIS; 464 Reuters NewMedia Inc/CORBIS; 465 Raymond Gehman/CORBIS; 466 Jamal A. Wilson/AFP/CORBIS; 467(br),Bob Daemmrich Photo, Inc.; 468 Mark Gibson Photography; 469 Treasury Department/AP/Wide World Photos; 472 Mark Gibson Photography; 473 Joe Marquette/AP/Wide World Photos; 474(tr), HRW Photo Research Library; 474(bl), AP/Wide World Photos; 475 Stephen Morton/AP/Wide World Photos; 476 Mark Gibson Photography; 477 The Granger Collection, New York; 478 Dale Atkins/AP/Wide World Photos; 479 Denis Poroy/AP/Wide World Photos; 481 Mark Gibson Photography; 483, Heller, Green Bay Press-Gazette; 484(t), Jim Pickerell/Stock Connection/PictureQuest; 484(br),Sam Dudgeon/HRW; 485(br),Sam Dudgeon/HRW; 485, HRW Photo Research Library; 487 Bettmann/CORBIS; 488 Department of the Interior, National Park Service, 1937. National Museum of American Art, Washington, DC/Art Resource, NY; 489 Brown Brothers; 490(tr), Michael J. Okonlewski/Getty Images; 490(bl), Archive Photos/Getty Images; 491 David McNew/NewsCom; 491(br),Bettmann/CORBIS; 492 Lynn Goldsmith/CORBIS; 493 Annie Griffiths Belt/CORBIS; 494 TOLES copyright 1991 The Buffalo News. Reprinted with permission of Universal Press Syndicate. All Rights Reserved.; 495 Sam Dudgeon/HRW;497 John Deere and Co.; 498 Bettmann/CORBIS;

499 Library of Congress/PRC Archive; 500 Leslie Renken/AP/Wide World Photos; 501(cr), Bettmann/CORBIS; 501(br), Sam Dudgeon/HRW; 502 Archive Photos; 503 Marty Lederhandler/AP/Wide World Photos; 504 Robert Maass/CORBIS; 505 Shelly Katz/Getty Images; 508(t), Peter Van Steen/HRW; 508(br),Sam Dudgeon/HRW; 509(cr), Sam Dudgeon/HRW; 509(br),Nick Robinson/Panos Pictures; 510 Peter Van Steen/HRW; 510 Bettmann/CORBIS; 513 Filip Horvat/SABA ; 515 Jean Miele/Corbis Stock Market; 516(cr), Brian Atkinson/Getty Images/Stone; 516(bl), Peter Van Steen/HRW; 517 Los Angeles Times Syndicate; 518 Peter Van Steen/HRW; 519 Peter Van Steen/HRW; 520 CORBIS; 521 Najlan Feanny/SABA ; 522(bl), Bryan F. Peterson/Corbis Stock Market; 523 Jeffrey D. Smith/Woodfin Camp & Associates; 524 Stephen J. Carrera/AP/Wide World Photos; 525 AFP/CORBIS; 526 Morin reprinted by King Features Syndicate, Inc.; 528 AP/Wide World Photos; 529 Karen Kasmauski/Woodfin Camp & Associates; 530 David Ball/Corbis Stock Market; 532 David McNew/Getty Images; 533 Tim Wright/CORBIS; 540(t), AP/Wide World Photos; 540(br),Sam Dudgeon/HRW; 541(tr), HRW Photo Research Library; 541(br),Bob Daemmrich Photo, Inc.; 542 Bob Daemmrich Photo, Inc.; 544 Tony Freeman/PhotoEdit; 545 Randy Piland/AP/Wide World Photos; 546 R.W. Jones/CORBIS; 547(tl), Michael Rosenfeld/Getty Images/Stone; 547(br),Joseph Sohm; ChromoSohm Inc/CORBIS; 548(t), Rob Crandall/Stock Connection/PictureQuest; 548(bl), Spencer Grant/PhotoEdit; 549(cr), Michael Newman/PhotoEdit; 549(cl),Sam Dudgeon/HRW; 550(tl),George Nikitin/AP/Wide World Photos; 550(bl), Richard Hutchings/PhotoEdit; 551 Ed Lallo/Index Stock Imagery/PictureQuest; 552(tr), HRW Photo; 552(bl), David Kohl/AP/Wide World Photos; 553 Jim Hollander/TimePix; 555 Paul S. Conklin; 556 Bettmann/CORBIS; 558(cr), Sam Dudgeon/HRW; 558(bl), Spencer Grant/PhotoEdit; 559 Joe Wilssens/AP/Wide World Photos; 560(tl),Michelle Bridwell/HRW; 560(bl), Michael Newman/PhotoEdit; 561 PRC Archive; 562 Robert Brenner/PhotoEdit; 563(br),Felicia Martinez/PhotoEdit; 563(cr), HRW Photo Research Library; 563(cr), HRW Photo Research Library; 563(cr), HRW Photo Research Library; 564 Dana White/PhotoEdit; 565 Bob Rowan/CORBIS; 566(t), Michael Tweed/AP/Wide World Photos; 566(bl), Spencer Grant/PhotoEdit; 567 Will Hart/PhotoEdit; 574(t), Getty Images; 574(br),Sam Dudgeon/HRW; 575(tr), Bettmann/CORBIS; 575(br),Ric Ergenbright/CORBIS; 576 Kenneth Lambert/AP/Wide World Photos; 577 Getty Images; 578(tr), Gary Cameron/Reuters/TimePix; 578(bl), Bettmann/CORBIS; 579 Trustees of the Imperial War Museum, London; 581(tr), Sam Dudgeon/HRW; 581(br),Courtesy Gerald R. Ford Library; 582 Visar Kryeziu/AP/Wide World Photos; 583(tr), B.K. Bangash/AP/Wide World Photos; 583(br),Library of Congress/CORBIS; 584(tl),Sam Dudgeon/HRW; 584(bl), Kevin Bartram/AP/Wide World Photos; 586 Newsmakers/Getty Images; 588(tr), HRW Photo Research Library; 588(bl), ©1995 Knight-Ridder Tribune, Inc./NewsCom; 589 Joseph Sohm; ChromoSohm Inc/CORBIS; 591 Newsmakers/Getty Images; 592 David Guttenfelder/AP/Wide World Photos; 593 Marty Lederhandler/AP/Wide World Photos; 596(t), Erik Campos/NewsCom; 596(br),Sam Dudgeon/HRW; 597(tr), CORBIS; 597(br),Chris Dorst/AP/Wide World Photos; 598 The Granger Collection, New York; 599(t), Michael S. Yamashita/CORBIS; 599(br), Bettmann/CORBIS; 600 The Granger Collection, New York; 601(tr), Detroit News; 601(b), Culver Pictures, Inc.; 602 Dana Edmunds/Pacific Stock; 604 Bettmann/CORBIS; 605 HRW Photo Research Library; 606(tr), Leif Skoogfors/CORBIS; 606(bl), Ric Ergenbright/CORBIS; 607(tr), The Granger Collection, New York; 607(br),Igor Gavrilov/TimePix; 608 UPI/Bettmann/CORBIS; 611 Noel Clark/stock-photo; 612 Larry Burrows/TimePix; 613 AP/Wide World Photos; 614(bl), Deborah Harse/Peter Arnold, Inc.; 615(b), AP/Wide World Photos; 615(t),Getty/NewsCom; 616 © Lynsey Addario/CORBIS; 617 Larry Downing/TimePix; 618 AP/Wide World Photos; 619 © AFP/CORBIS; 626(t), Mark L. Stephenson/CORBIS; 626(br),Sam Dudgeon/HRW; 627(cr), Michael Newman/PhotoEdit; 627(br),Darrell Gulin/CORBIS; 628 Bob Daemmrich Photo, Inc.; 629(tl),Joel W. Rogers/CORBIS; 629(br),Tony Freeman/PhotoEdit; 630 Bob Rowan/CORBIS; 631 FRANK & ERNEST reprinted by permission of Bob Thaves; 632(tr), SuperStock; 632(bl), Elena Rooraid/PhotoEdit; 633 Vincent Pugliese/AP/Wide World Photos; 634(tr), HRW Photo Research Library; 634(bl), Mark Richards/PhotoEdit; 635 The Granger Collection, New York; 636 Bettmann/CORBIS; 637(tr), Don Cravens/TimePix; 637(b), Bettmann/CORBIS; 638(tr), Spencer Grant/PhotoEdit; 638(tc), HRW Photo Research Library; 639(br),© 2001 Jay Mallin; 640 Peter Cosgrove/AP/Wide World Photos; 641 Richard Levine ; 644(tr), HRW Photo Research Library; 644(bl), U.S. Department of Agriculture/U.S. Department of Health and Human Services; 645(tr), Mark Richards/PhotoEdit; 645(bl), Michael Newman/PhotoEdit; 646 Michael Newman/PhotoEdit; 647(tr), Bob Daemmrich Photo, Inc.; 647(br), Sam Dudgeon/HRW; 649 David Young-Wolff/PhotoEdit; 650 Tony Freeman/PhotoEdit; 654(t), SuperStock; 654(br),Sam Dudgeon/HRW; 655(tr), Chuck Place; 655(br), HRW Photo Research Library; 656(t), Gray Hardel/CORBIS; 656(bl), Liaison; 657(cr), Gary Braasch/CORBIS; 657(br),Darrell Gulin/CORBIS; 658(tl),The Granger Collection, New York; 658(bl), Abby Aldrich Rockefeller Folk Art Museum; 659 Dallas Museum of Art; 661 David Guttenfelder/AP/Wide World Photos; 662(tr), HRW Photo Research Library; 662(bl), Charles O'Rear/CORBIS; 663(t), Caroline Penn/CORBIS; 663(br),Nik Wheeler/CORBIS; 664(b), Bob Rowan/CORBIS; 665 Ted Spiegel/CORBIS; 666 Joseph Sohm; ChromoSohm Inc/CORBIS; 667(tr), Liaison/Getty Images; 667(br),Woodfin Camp & Associates; 668 Jose Azel/AURORA; 670(tr), Bill Gallery/Stock Boston, Inc./PictureQuest; 670(bl), Peter Van Steen; 671 Bill Ross/CORBIS; 672 Gunter Marx Photography/CORBIS; 673(tr), Spencer Platt/Getty Images; 673(b), Beth Wald/AURORA; 674 Sean Gallup/Newmakers; 675(tr), Tim Boyle/Getty Images; 675(b), CORBIS Images/HRW; 676 Joseph Sohm;ChromoSohm Inc./CORBIS; 677(tr), HRW Photo Research Library; 677(br),Bettmann/CORBIS; 678 Peter Essick/AURORA; 680 Todd Gipstein/CORBIS; 681 AFP/CORBIS; R12(tr), Bettmann/CORBIS; R12(c), Bettmann/CORBIS; R13(tr), AFP/CORBIS; R13(bl), Joseph Sohm; Visions of America/CORBIS; R13 (flag), Philip James Corwin/CORBIS; R14(tr), Joseph Sohm; ChromoSohm Inc./CORBIS; R14(b), Bettmann/CORBIS; R15(t), Joseph Sohm; ChromoSohm Inc./CORBIS; R15(b),Bettmann/CORBIS; R16(tl),Bob Krist/CORBIS; R16(bc), HRW Photo Research Library; R17(bl), National Archives/HRW Photo Research Library; R17(br),HRW Photo Research Library; R17(c), Bettmann/CORBIS; R17(tl),Liaison.

**Illustration Credits**
Organizational charts, flowcharts, graphs, and icons created by NETS. Maps created by MapQuest.com. All other illustrations created by Holt, Rinehart and Winston.